written and researched by

J.D. Dickey, Nick Edwards,
Paul Whitfield, and Mark Ellwood

with additional contributions by
Jeff Cranmer

ROUGH GUIDES

NEW YORK · LONDON · DELHI

www.roughguides.com

Contents

Exploring the outdoors color section following p.216

West Coast sounds color section following p.408

Epicurean California color section following p.696

◄◄ Joshua Tree National Park ◄ Rafters on the Merced River, Yosemite

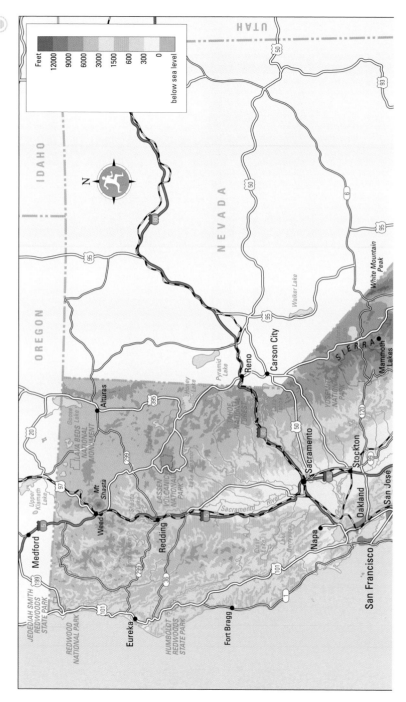

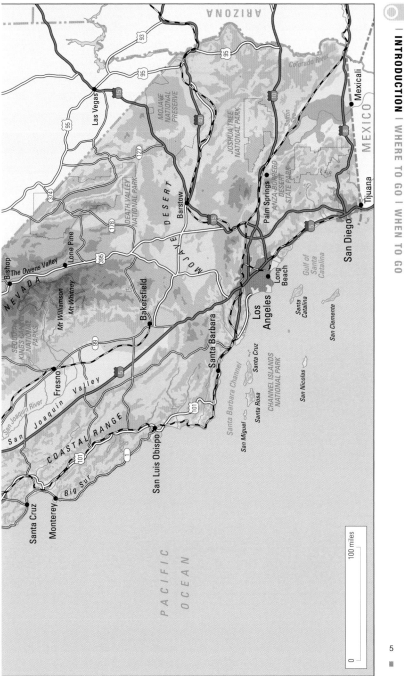

Introduction to
California

Perhaps no region of the world has been as idealized as California, and few, if any, actually manage to live up to the hype to the same degree. Justly celebrated for its sun, sand, surf, and sea, the state offers much more: towering mountain ranges, glitzy big cities, deep primeval forests, and charming historic hamlets.

As with the rest of America, California doesn't dwell too much on the past, and, in some ways, represents the ultimate "now" society: urban life is lived in the fast lane, conspicuous consumption is often paramount, and, in some circles, having the right hairstyle, wardrobe, tan, and income is everything. Once you get out of the cities, though, the environment changes dramatically, giving way to dense groves of ancient trees, primitive rock carvings left by Native Americans, and the eerie ghost towns of the Gold Rush. A land of superlatives, California really is full of the oldest, the tallest, the largest, and the most spectacular – all of which go far beyond local bravura.

It's important to bear in mind that the supposed "superficiality" of California is just one side of the coin, created in equal measure by outsiders and Californians themselves – by San Franciscans contemptuous of LA's position as entertainment, theme park, and beach culture capital of America, and by Angelenos with a disregard for San Francisco as an outpost of snooty yuppies with pretensions to hipster, and hippy, culture. While there may be plenty of such elements in both towns, the full range of peoples, cultures, and communities of California cannot easily

be reduced to any one stereotype – there's simply too much going on here.

Politically, California is probably America's most polarized state, home to right-wing bastions like Orange County and San Diego and some of US history's most reactionary figures – Ronald Reagan and Richard Nixon come to mind – yet also a principal source of America's most dynamic left-wing movements: environmentalism, women's lib, and gay and immigrant rights. Some of the fiercest protests of the 1960s took root here, and in many ways this is still the heart of liberal America, as California continues to set the standard for the rest of the country (if not

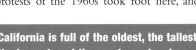

California is full of the oldest, the tallest, the largest, and the most spectacular

the world) regarding progressive action and social tolerance. The region is economically crucial as well: California's film and music industries dominate the cash-flush entertainment field; financial services, real estate, and even technology (despite the dot-com crash in the early 2000s) continue to be fundamental economic bulwarks; and all manner of politicians drop in to fatten their bankrolls with high-flying political fundraisers.

Fact file

- California is known as the **"Golden State,"** a nickname that derives from the Gold Rush days of the 1840s and 1850s and is perpetuated by the golden poppy, or *Eschscholtzia californica*, which appears all over California each spring and is the state flower.

- California raised the flags of Spain, England, Mexico, and the short-lived Bear Republic before it was admitted to the Union on September 9, 1850 as the **thirty-first state**.

- Each year, California becomes home to more **immigrants** than any other state, with most settlers hailing from Latin America and Asia, though a smattering come from Europe, Russia, and the Middle East. Almost a third of all immigrants to the US settle here.

- The **third largest state** in the US (after Alaska and Texas), California boasts an almost 700-mile coast along the Pacific and around 25,000 square miles of desert.

- Based on agriculture and the electronic, aerospace, film, and tourism industries, the state's **economy** is the strongest in the US. Indeed, if it were a country, California's economy would rank as **seventh largest** in the world.

Where to go

Almost twice the size of Great Britain, California covers nearly 160,000 square miles: keep in mind that distances between the main destinations can be huge, and naturally you won't be able to see everything on one trip. Even a comprehensive vacation may only just scratch the surface.

In an area so varied, it's hard to pick out specific highlights, and much will depend on the kind of vacation you're looking for. You may well start off in **Los Angeles**, far and away the biggest and most stimulating California city: a maddening collection of freeways and beaches, seedy suburbs and high-gloss neighborhoods, and extreme lifestyles. From here you can head south to **San Diego**, with its broad, welcoming beaches and a handy position close to the Mexican border, or inland to the California **deserts**, notably **Death Valley** – as its name suggests, a barren, inhospitable landscape of volcanic craters and windswept sand dunes that in summer becomes the hottest place on earth. An alternative is to make the steady journey up the **Central Coast**, a gorgeous run following the shoreline north of LA through some of the

The birth of Tinseltown

The town of **Hollywood** was given its name by real estate magnate H.J. Whitley in 1886, and became the headquarters of the early American film industry a quarter-century later. Southern California was not, however, the original site for the early nickelodeon biz or any other economies built

▲ Warner Bros. Studios, Burbank

around primitive motion pictures. Initially, New York was the dominant location for the production of movies – a term coined in 1908 – with Thomas Edison's Motion Picture Patents Company (MPPC) monopolizing the production and distribution of film. Chafing under Edison's control, numerous independent producers tried to escape his grasp by migrating to the West Coast in the second decade of the twentieth century, drawn by Southern California's variety of landscapes, frequent sun, low taxes, cheap labor, and sheer distance from New York. Federal court action put an end to the MPPC's control in 1915, but by that time California's hold over the motion picture industry in America (and later the world) was set.

state's most dramatic scenery, and taking in some of its liveliest small towns, particularly Santa Barbara and Santa Cruz.

The Central Coast marks the transition from Southern to Northern California – a break that's more than just geographical. **San Francisco**, California's other defining metropolis, is quite different from LA: the coast's oldest, most European-styled city, it's set compactly over a series of steep hills, with wooden Victorian houses tumbling down to water on both sides. From here you have access to some of the state's most extraordinary scenery, not least in the national parks to the east, especially **Yosemite**, where

▲ Black bear cub, Klamath National Forest

powerful waterfalls cascade into a sheer glacial valley that's been immortalized by Ansel Adams – and countless others – in search of the definitive landscape photograph. Yosemite is the highlight of the Sierra Nevada Mountains; south from it are the vast national parks of **Sequoia** and **Kings Canyon**, and north an interesting mix of quaint towns like Nevada City and resorts such as Lake Tahoe.

North of San Francisco, the population thins and the physical look changes yet again. The climate is wetter up here, the valleys that much greener and flanked by a jagged coastline shadowed by mighty **redwoods**, the tallest trees in the world. Though many visitors choose to venture no further than

California missions

▲ Carmel Mission

Among the oldest European settlements in California, the state's 21 **missions** were supposedly established by the Spanish in the late eighteenth century in a burst of religious zeal aimed at Christianizing the local heathens. In truth, each mission was accompanied by a pueblo, or secular settlement, and, most importantly, a presidio, or military fortress. Masterminded by Franciscan Father **Junípero Serra**, the entire network ran largely along what was known as the Camino Real, or Royal Road, from San Diego to Solano, just north of San Francisco, ensuring that every mission was one day's ride or hard walk from the next. This proximity enabled easy commerce and communication along the chain.

The missions flourished for more than a hundred years, converting and killing thousands of locals through a combination of forced evangelism and smallpox. Eventually, when the missions were secularized under Mexican rule in 1834, much of the land was given not to the indigenous peoples, but to the Spanish-speaking Californio ranchers. The missions' checkered reputation lasted at least until the later Victorian era, when sentimentalist writer **Helen Hunt Jackson** gave them an idyllic gloss in her bestselling potboiler *Ramona* – a hugely influential book responsible for the current image of missions as charming outposts of quiet spirituality and quaintly austere architecture.

The largest and most populous settlement was San Luis Rey de Francia (p.232) – its huge lavandería, or washing area, is now an impressive sunken garden – while arguably the most famous is San Juan Capistrano (p.148), which welcomes migrating swallows every March. Visitors will find the most evocative, if not necessarily authentic, sense of early settler life at the restorations at San Antonio de Padua (p.445) and La Purísima (p.429).

The interior is as different from the stereotype of California as you could imagine

the **Wine Country** and the Russian River Valley on weekend forays from the city, it's well worth taking time out to explore the state's northernmost regions, which are split distinctly in two. The coastline is simultaneously rugged and serene, guarded by towering redwoods; the interior, meanwhile, dominated by majestic **Mount Shasta**, is a volcano-scarred wilderness that's as different from the stereotype of California as you could imagine.

When to go

California's climate is as varied as its landscape: in **Southern California**, for one, count on endless days of sunshine from May to October, and warm, dry nights – though LA's notorious **smog** is at its worst when temperatures are highest, in August and September.

Along the **coast**, mornings can be hazily overcast, especially in May and June, though you'll still get a suntan – or sunburn – under gray skies. In

11

On shaky ground

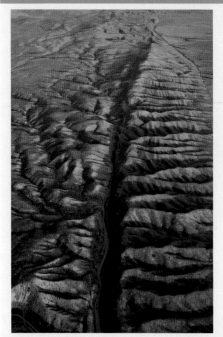

▲ San Andreas Fault

With an estimated 500,000 tremors detected annually in the state, California is a seismic time bomb, bisected by the most famous faultline in the world, the **San Andreas**, which runs loosely from San Francisco to Los Angeles and marks the junction of the Pacific and North American tectonic plates. Given its fearsome reputation, though, it's not the most active fault at the moment – that honor goes to one of its connected faults, known as the **Hayward**.

Despite the 1906 **San Francisco earthquake**'s notoriety, it wasn't actually the quake itself that leveled the city, but a careless homeowner cooking breakfast on a gas stove at the time; the ensuing fire raged for four days, razed 28,000 buildings, and left at least 3000 dead. Since then, there have been several significant temblors, most recently in 1989, when San Francisco again shook during the **Loma Prieta**, named after its epicenter close to Santa Cruz and responsible for the horrifying collapse of a double-decker freeway, and in 1994, when the **Northridge** quake tore through the north side of LA, rupturing freeways and flattening an apartment building.

Of course, everyone's waiting for the so-called **Big One**, a massive earthquake that, it's feared, could wipe out Los Angeles or San Francisco. Speculation has intensified recently, since experts have pegged the interval between major ruptures in the southern reaches of the San Andreas at 140 years: the last such quake was Fort Tejon in 1857.

winter temperatures drop somewhat, but, more importantly, weeks of rain can cause massive mudslides that wipe out roads and hillside homes. Inland, the **deserts** are warm in winter and unbearably hot (120°F is not unusual) in summer; desert nights can be freezing in winter, when it can even snow. For serious white stuff, head to the **mountains**, where hiking trails at the higher elevations are covered with snow from November to June: skiers can take advantage of well-groomed slopes among the Sierra Nevada Mountains and around Lake Tahoe.

The coast of **Northern California** is wetter and cooler than the south, its summers tempered by sea breezes and fog, and its winters mild but damp. **San Francisco**, because of its exposed position at the tip of a peninsula, can be chilly all year, with summer fog often rolling in and chasing off what may have started off as a pleasant day. Head across the bay to Oakland, though, and you'll be back in the sun.

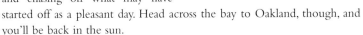

Average temperatures and rainfall

	Jan	Apr	Jul	Oct
Death Valley				
max/min (°F)	66/39	89/62	115/86	92/61
max/min (°C)	19/4	32/17	46/30	33/16
rain (inches/mm)	0.4/10	0.1/3	0.0/0	0.1/3
Eureka				
max/min (°F)	55/41	57/44	63/53	61/48
max/min (°C)	13/5	14/7	17/12	16/9
rain (inches/mm)	5.9/150	2.9/74	0.2/5	2.4/61
Lake Tahoe				
max/min (°F)	41/15	53/26	79/40	62/26
max/min (°C)	5/-9	12/-3	26/4	17/-3
rain (inches/mm)	6.9/175	2.5/64	0.5/13	2.2/56
Los Angeles				
max/min (°F)	68/48	73/54	84/65	79/60
max/min (°C)	20/9	23/12	29/18	26/16
rain (inches/mm)	3.3/84	0.8/20	0.0/0	0.4/10
San Diego				
max/min (°F)	66/50	69/56	76/66	74/61
max/min (°C)	19/10	21/13	24/19	23/16
rain (inches/mm)	2.3/58	0.8/20	0.0/0	0.4/10
San Francisco				
max/min (°F)	56/43	64/48	71/55	70/52
max/min (°C)	13/6	17/9	22/13	21/11
rain (inches/mm)	4.5/114	1.2/31	0.0/0	1.0/25

things not to miss

It's not possible to see everything that California has to offer in one trip – and we don't suggest you try. What follows is a selective taste of the state's highlights, from its bustling beaches to its deserted Gold Rush outposts. They're arranged in five color-coded categories to help you find the very best to see, do, and experience. All highlights have a page reference to take you straight into the guide, where you can find out more.

01 **Tufa towers of Mono Lake** Page 334 • See the fluffy, sandcastle-like tufa spires that have frothed up from below the surface of this fast-shrinking body of water.

02 Mexican food Page **42** •
Duck into a roadside taqueria or burrito joint to enjoy one of the state's signature cuisines.

04 Sequoia National Park
Page **369** • If you've never been too impressed by plants, prepare yourself for a revelation: the trees for which this park is named are some of the world's biggest – and oldest – living things.

03 Balboa Park Page **203** •
San Diego's staggering collection of museums, lush greenery, and evocative Spanish Colonial buildings provides a wealth of opportunities for exploration.

05 Berkeley's bookstores
Page **573** • The radical town holds a wide range of first- and secondhand bookstores, which make for an excellent day's browsing.

06 La Jolla Page **215** • A glittering oceanside enclave where the San Diego elite reside in period revival mansions and where day-trippers come for the striking scenery, beachside coves, and quality museums.

07 Cholla Cactus Garden Page **273** • One of the high points of any trip to Joshua Tree National Park is this cactus garden, part of a circular hike that takes in the unique "jumping" cholla.

08 The Third Street Promenade Page **126** • Sooner or later, all visitors to LA make their way to this Santa Monica pedestrian mall for its eccentric performers, swinging nightlife, and fine dining options.

09 Gay Pride parade Page **553** • In late June, the Gay Pride parade takes over the streets of San Francisco's Castro district in exuberant fashion.

10 **Red Rock Canyon petroglyphs** Page **324** • Once used as a backdrop in Spielberg's Jurassic Park, the canyon's rock formations present a panoply of aboriginal carvings.

11 **The Mojave National Preserve** Page **290** • The Mojave Desert can be shocking in its extremes and should not go unappreciated – some of the imposing sand dunes of the preserve, in the desert's eastern portion, rise as high as 4000ft above sea level.

12 **Riding a cable car** Page **500** • No visit to San Francisco is complete without a ride on one of the city's cable cars, the best means of scaling the city's hills and enjoying the views.

13 Hearst Castle Page **441** • Of all California's lavish dreams, none quite rivals William Randolph Hearst's monument to himself, which boasts a Mudejar cathedral facade and a private cinema.

14 Klamath Basin National Wildlife Refuge Page **756** • Each year, travelers from the avian world rest up in the gigantic sanctuary of the Klamath Basin before resuming their journeys along the Pacific Flyway.

15 **Hiking Mount Whitney** Page **314** • Climb the tallest mountain in the continental US, which sits right on the edge of Sequoia National Park.

16 **La Purísima Mission** Page **429** • Just east of Lompoc, La Purísima reveals a faithful glimpse of late eighteenth-century mission life.

17 **Cruising the Sunset Strip** Page **120** • The Sunset Strip has long been a choice LA hangout, jammed with groovy bars and clubs, swanky hotels, and towering billboards selling all manner of vices.

18 **Surfing** Page **131** & **594** • From the gargantuan waves at Mavericks to the hot-dogging longboard heaven of Malibu, California's consummate pastime can be enjoyed year-round on beaches all along its coast.

19 **Golden Gate Park** Page **530** • A long strip of green stretching from San Francisco's Haight-Ashbury neighborhood to the Pacific Ocean, this urban oasis is packed with museums, gardens, live music, and countless other diversions.

20 **The Chinese Theatre** Page **107** • A cherished relic of the 1920s, LA's Chinese Theatre recalls the glory years of Hollywood cinema, both with its Art Deco interior and the celebrity hand- and footprints pressed into the pavement outside.

21 Skiing and snowboarding at Lake Tahoe
Page **653** • Hit the renowned slopes around lovely Lake Tahoe, home to unbeatable downhill skiing and snowboarding.

22 Disney Hall Page **93** •
Although Frank Gehry's architectural marvel was designed in 1987, sixteen years passed before it was finally built, and today this inspired, sculptural creation serves as the monumental home of the LA Philharmonic.

23 Ride the Coast Starlight
Page **33** • While most visitors take to the highways, the best way to see the hundred-mile-long coast between Santa Barbara and San Luis Obispo is by rail.

24 Big Sur Page **449** • Bask in the secluded beauty of Big Sur's approximately ninety miles of rocky cliffs and crashing waves along the Pacific.

25 Whale watching Page **609** • Springtime is your best chance of seeing gray whales during their annual migration in the Pacific.

26 Yosemite Valley Page **396** • There's much stunning geology up and down the state, but nothing surpasses Yosemite Valley, where El Capitan and Half Dome are just two of the awe-inspiring monoliths that await you.

27 **Santa Monica Mountains** Page **130** • The verdant canyons and rocky crags of this range of low mountains, bordering the northern edge of Los Angeles, provide an escape from the pressures of the city.

28 **Redwood National Park**
Page **722** • The tallest trees in the world – some close to 400ft high – preside over this dramatic national park, home to Roosevelt elk, black bears, and serene hiking trails.

29 **Rafting on the Kern River** Page **349** • The Kern River offers some of the most thrilling whitewater rafting anywhere in the States.

30 **Wind farms** Page **283** •
California wind farms like Tehachapi – home to over 5000 windmills and turbines – represent some of the world's most powerful sources of renewable energy and are spectacles unto themselves.

31 **Bodie Ghost Town** Page **337** • Well past its 1880s gold-mining heyday, when it was the second largest town in the state, Bodie is now an intriguing time capsule of some 150 atmospheric wooden buildings.

32 **Salvation Mountain** Page **274** • This only-in-California creation is a kaleidoscopic mound of concrete, hay bales, and vast quantities of paint, peppered liberally with Biblical quotes.

Basics

Basics

Getting there

The second largest state in the continental US, California presents an easy target for both domestic and international visitors. All the main airlines operate daily scheduled flights to San Francisco and Los Angeles from all over the world, and the state is easily accessible by road or rail throughout the year.

Generally, the most expensive time to fly is **high season**, roughly between June and August and around Christmas. April–May and September–October are considerably less pricey, and the rest of the year is considered low season and is cheaper still.

Flights from the US and Canada

Most domestic flights are likely to take you to one of the following international airports: **Los Angeles** (airport code LAX), **San Francisco** (SFO), **Oakland** (OAK), **San Jose** (SJO), or **San Diego** (SAN). Some flights, however, use smaller airports in the vicinity of those metropolitan areas and you can also fly direct to one of the minor cities such as Sacramento, Redding, or Reno (in Nevada) for the Lake Tahoe region.

Flying is the best but usually the most expensive way to travel within North America. Published round-trip prices during the midweek in summer on the major airlines start at around $350 from New York and other eastern seaboard cities, $270 from Midwest cities, and $500 from Toronto and Montréal, although regular airline **promotions and savers** can substantially reduce that price at slack times. What makes more difference than your choice of carrier are the conditions governing the ticket – whether it's fully refundable, the time and day, and, most importantly, the **time of year** you travel. Least expensive of all is a non-summer-season midweek flight, booked and paid for at least three weeks in advance. Keep in mind too that one-way tickets are sometimes more expensive than round-trip tickets.

In addition to the big-name scheduled airlines, a few lesser-known carriers run no-frills flights, which can prove to be very good value, especially if you have a flexible schedule and can put up with a few delays; try **JetBlue** or Frontier Airlines, for example, who can often get you across the country and back for well under $200.

Flights from the UK and Ireland

Although you can fly to the US from many airports in the region, the only **nonstop flights** from Britain to California are from London, most of which land in Los Angeles (LA). The nonstop **flight time** is around eleven hours from London to San Francisco or LA. Flights are often advertised as "direct" because they keep the same flight number but actually land elsewhere first. The first place the plane lands is your point of entry into the US, which means you'll have to collect your bags and go through customs and immigration formalities there, even if you're continuing on to California on the same plane. Many other routings involve a change of aircraft.

Britain remains one of the best places in Europe to obtain flight **bargains**, though fares vary widely according to season, availability, and the current level of inter-airline competition. Be sure to shop around carefully for the best offers by cross-checking the prices quoted by travel agents and websites with the travel ads in the weekend papers and other publications. Prices definitely rocket if you do not stay over a Saturday night.

Aer Lingus operates the only **nonstop flight** to Los Angeles from Dublin five times a week. The cheapest flights from Ireland – if you're under 26 or a student – are available from USIT (see p.52). Student-only return **fares** directly to San Francisco or Los Angeles range from €450 to €850,

Fly less – stay longer! Travel and climate change

Climate change is the single biggest issue facing our planet. It is caused by a build-up in the atmosphere of carbon dioxide and other greenhouse gases, which are emitted by many sources – including planes. Already, flights account for around three to four percent of human-induced global warming: that figure may sound small, but it is rising year on year and threatens to counteract the progress made by reducing greenhouse emissions in other areas.

Rough Guides regard travel, overall, as a global benefit, and feel strongly that the advantages to developing economies are important, as are the opportunities for greater contact and awareness among peoples. But we all have a responsibility to limit our personal "carbon footprint." That means giving thought to how often we fly and what we can do to redress the harm that our trips create.

Flying and climate change

Pretty much every form of motorized travel generates CO_2, but planes are particularly bad offenders, releasing large volumes of greenhouse gases at altitudes where their impact is far more harmful. Flying also allows us to travel much further than we would contemplate doing by road or rail, so the emissions attributable to each passenger become truly shocking. For example, one person taking a return flight between Europe and California produces the equivalent impact of 2.5 tonnes of CO_2 – similar to the yearly output of the average UK car.

Less harmful planes may evolve but it will be decades before they replace the current fleet – which could be too late for avoiding climate chaos. In the meantime, there are limited options for concerned travelers: to reduce the amount we travel by air (take fewer trips, stay longer!), to avoid night flights (when plane contrails trap heat from Earth but can't reflect sunlight back to space), and to make the trips we do take "climate neutral" via a carbon offset scheme.

Carbon offset schemes

Offset schemes run by **climatecare.org**, **carbonneutral.com**, and others allow you to "neutralize" the greenhouse gases that you are responsible for releasing. Their websites have simple calculators that let you work out the impact of any flight. Once that's done, you can pay to fund projects that will reduce future carbon emissions by an equivalent amount (such as the distribution of low-energy light bulbs and cooking stoves in developing countries). Please take the time to visit our website and make your trip climate neutral.

Ⓦwww.roughguides.com/climatechange

depending on the time of year; nonstudents can expect to pay €550 to €1000. Flights via London may cost less, but you pay slightly more tax.

"Open-jaw" tickets can be a good idea, allowing you to fly into LA, for example, and back from San Francisco for little or no extra charge; fares are calculated by halving the return fares to each destination and adding the two figures together. This makes a convenient option for those who want a **fly-drive** deal, which gives cut-rate (and sometimes free) car rental when you buy an air ticket.

Many airlines also offer **air passes**, which allow foreign travelers to fly between a given

One word of **warning**: it's not a good idea to buy a **one-way** ticket to the States. Not only are they rarely good value compared to a round-trip ticket, but US immigration officials usually take them as a sign that you aren't planning to go home and may refuse you entry. With increased airport checks, you are unlikely to be allowed even to board your flight to begin with.

Sample airfares from Britain

The prices given below (in £ sterling) are a general indication of the minimum transatlantic round-trip **airfares, including taxes**, you are likely to find at the given periods; youth discount fares and special deals may be cheaper. Each airline decides the exact dates of its seasons. Prices are for departures from London to LA or San Francisco.

low	Nov–March (except Christmas)	340
shoulder	April, May, Sept, Oct	450
high	June–Aug, Christmas	700

number of US cities for one discounted price.

Packages – fly-drive, flight-accommodation deals, and guided tours – can work out cheaper than arranging the same trip yourself, especially for a short-term stay. The obvious drawbacks are the loss of flexibility and the fact that most schemes use hotels in the midrange bracket, but there is a wide variety of options available. Travel agents have plenty of brochures and information about the various combinations.

Flights from Australia, New Zealand, and South Africa

If you are coming from Australia or New Zealand, there's very little price difference between airlines and no shortage of flights, either via the Pacific or Asia, to Los Angeles and San Francisco. Most flights crossing the Pacific are nonstop, with twelve to fourteen hours' travel time between Auckland/Sydney and LA, though some include stopovers in Honolulu and a number of the South Pacific islands. If you go via Asia (a slightly more roundabout route that can work out a little cheaper), you'll usually have to spend a night, or the best part of a day, in the airline's home city.

Traveling from **Australia**, fares to LA and San Francisco from eastern cities cost the same, while from Perth they're about Aus$400 more. Flights from Sydney or Melbourne to LA and San Francisco range between Aus$1800 and Aus$2200, depending on the season, with airline specials and student fares sometimes reducing that to around Aus$1500. Seat availability on most international flights out

of Australia and New Zealand is limited, so it's best to book at least several weeks ahead.

From **New Zealand**, most flights are out of Auckland; add about NZ$200 for Christchurch and Wellington departures. Seasonal prices vary between around NZ$1950 and NZ$2400, again with occasional special deals and student fares reducing those figures significantly.

Travel to California is not particularly cheap from **South Africa**; prices are about the same out of Cape Town or Johannesburg but several hundred rand more from Durban and other smaller cities. Fares start at around R10000, including all taxes, and rise as high as R14000 at peak times, which are roughly the same as those from Australia. Direct flights with US or South African carriers invariably involve a refueling stop somewhere in the Atlantic like Cape Verde, though a more roundabout route with one of the national airlines from further north in Africa can be cheaper.

Round-the-world tickets

No matter what continent you are starting from, if you intend to take in California as part of a world trip, a round-the-world (**RTW**) ticket offers the greatest flexibility and can work out far more economically than booking separate flights. The most US-oriented are the seventeen airlines making up the "Star Alliance" network; for more details, visit ⓦwww.staralliance.com or call individual carriers (see p.30). The Star Alliance deals offer three to fifteen stopovers worldwide, with a total trip length from ten days to a year. Another option is the "One World Alliance" (including Qantas, American, and British Airways; ⓦ www.oneworld.com), which bases its rates on travel to and within the six populated continents, allowing three to six possible stopovers in each. Even cheaper are fares with the Escapade group (including Virgin, Singapore Air, and Air New Zealand; ⓦ www.thegreatescapade.com), though routing possibilities are somewhat more limited.

RTW tickets from London are the best value and can start at £1000 depending on mileage and number of stops. Expect to pay from around Aus$3000 from Australia, NZ$3300 from New Zealand, and R16000 from South Africa.

Trains

If you are willing to pay for extra creature comforts and have the time and inclination to take in some of the rest of the US on your way to California, then an Amtrak **train** may be just the ticket. The most spectacular train journey of all has to be the **California Zephyr**, which runs all the way from Chicago to San Francisco (53hr; departs 2pm daily) and comes into its own during the exquisitely scenic ride through the Rockies west of Denver, followed by the mighty Sierra Nevada, as it traces the route of the first transcontinental railroad. It actually terminates in Emeryville, where you change onto a bus for the ride into San Francisco. Two other useful services are the **Texas Eagle**, which also starts in Chicago and travels through chunks of the Midwest and Southwest before eventually arriving in Los Angeles, and the **Coast Starlight** (see p.33), which covers all of the West Coast between Seattle and Los Angeles.

Amtrak **fares** can be more expensive than flying, though **off-peak discounts** and special deals, advertised on Amtrak's website (see p.32), can make the train an economical and aesthetic choice; visit ⓦ www.amtrak.com, where international travelers can reap further savings with **rail passes** (see box, p.34). If you want to travel in a bit more comfort, costs rise quickly – **sleeping compartments**, which include meals, small toilets, and showers, start at around $150 per night for one or two people.

Buses

Bus travel is the most tedious and time-consuming way to get to California but can save you a lot of money if you don't mind the discomfort. **Greyhound** is the sole long-distance operator and has an extensive network of destinations in California.

The best reason to go Greyhound is if you're planning to visit a number of other places en route; Greyhound's **Discovery Pass** is good for unlimited travel within a certain time, and is explained in the box on p.34.

An alternative, in every sense, is the San Francisco-based **Green Tortoise** bus company; see p.34 for details.

Airlines, agents, and operators

Online booking

ⓦ www.expedia.co.uk (in UK),
ⓦ www.expedia.com (in US),
ⓦ www.expedia.ca (in Canada),
ⓦ www.expedia.co.za (in South Africa)
ⓦ www.lastminute.com (in UK)
ⓦ www.opodo.co.uk (in UK)
ⓦ www.orbitz.com (in US)
ⓦ www.travelocity.co.uk (in UK),
ⓦ www.travelocity.com (in US),
ⓦ www.travelocity.ca (in Canada)
ⓦ www.zuji.com.au (in Australia),
ⓦ www.zuji.co.nz (in New Zealand)

Airlines in North America

Air Canada ☏ 1-888/247-2262, ⓦ www .aircanada.com
Air France US ☏ 1-800/237-2747, ⓦ www .airfrance.com, Canada
☏ 1-800/667-2747, ⓦ www.airfrance.ca
Alaska Airlines ☏ 1-800/252-7522, ⓦ www .alaska-air.com
American Airlines ☏ 1-800/433-7300, ⓦ www .aa.com
Continental ☏ 1-800/523-3273, ⓦ www .continental.com
Delta Airlines ☏ 1-800/221-1212, ⓦ www.delta .com
Frontier Airlines ☏ 1-800/432-1359, ⓦ www .flyfrontier.com
Hawaiian Airlines ☏ 1-800/367-5320, ⓦ www .hawaiianair.com
JetBlue ☏ 1-800/538-2583, ⓦ www.jetblue.com

Northwest/KLM ☎1-800/225-2525, ⓦwww
.nwa.com, ⓦwww.klm.com
Southwest ☎1-800/435-9792, ⓦwww
.southwest.com
United Airlines ☎1-800/864-8331, ⓦwww
.united.com
US Airways ☎1-800/428-4322, ⓦwww.usair
.com
Virgin Atlantic Airways ☎1-800/821-5438,
ⓦwww.virginatlantic.com

Airlines in the UK and Ireland

Aer Lingus UK ☎0800/587 2324, Ireland
☎0818/365 000, ⓦwww.aerlingus.com
Air Canada UK ☎0871/220 1111, Ireland
☎01/679 3958, ⓦwww.aircanada.com
American Airlines UK ☎0845/778 9789, Ireland
☎01/602 0550, ⓦwww.aa.com
British Airways UK ☎0870/850 9850, Ireland
☎1890/626 747, ⓦwww.ba.com
Continental UK ☎0845/607 6760, Ireland
☎1890/925 252, ⓦwww.continental.com
Delta Airlines UK ☎0845/600 0950, Ireland
☎1850/882 031, ⓦwww.delta.com
Northwest/KLM UK ☎0870/507 4074, ⓦwww
.nwa.com, ⓦwww.klm.com
United Airlines UK ☎0845/844 4777, ⓦwww
.united.co.uk
US Airways UK ☎0845/600 3300, Ireland
☎1890/925 065, ⓦwww.usair.com
Virgin Atlantic Airways UK ☎0870/380 2007,
ⓦwww.virginatlantic.com

Airlines in Australia, New Zealand, and South Africa

Air New Zealand Australia ☎132 476, ⓦwww
.airnz.com.au; New Zealand ☎800/737 000,
ⓦwww.airnz.co.nz
Air Pacific Australia ☎1800/230 150, New
Zealand ☎800/800 178, ⓦwww.airpacific.com
Air Tahiti Nui Australia ☎02/9244 2899, New
Zealand ☎09/308 3360, ⓦwww.airtahitinui.com
Cathay Pacific Australia ☎131 747, New Zealand
☎09/379 0861, South Africa ☎11/700 8900,
ⓦwww.cathaypacific.com
China Airlines Australia ☎02/9244 2121, New
Zealand ☎09/308 3364, ⓦwww.chinaairlines.com
Continental Airlines Australia ☎02/9244 2242,
New Zealand ☎09/308 3350, ⓦwww.continental
.com
Delta Air Lines Australia ☎1300/302 849, New
Zealand ☎09/977 2232, South Africa ☎011/482
4582, ⓦwww.delta.com
EgyptAir South Africa ☎011/880 4126, ⓦwww
.egyptair.com

JAL (Japan Airlines) Australia ☎2/9272
1111, New Zealand ☎09/379 9906, South Africa
☎011/214 2560, ⓦwww.jal.com
Kenya Airways South Africa ☎011/881 9795,
ⓦwww.kenya-airways.com
Korean Air Australia ☎02/9262 6000, New
Zealand ☎09/914 2000, ⓦwww.koreanair.com
Qantas Australia ☎131 313, New Zealand
☎9/357 8900, South Africa ☎011/441 8550,
ⓦwww.qantas.com
Singapore Airlines Australia ☎131 011, New
Zealand ☎800/808 909, South Africa ☎011/880
8560, ⓦwww.singaporeair.com
United Airlines Australia ☎131 777, New Zealand
☎9/379 3800, ⓦwww.unitedairlines.com.au
Virgin Atlantic Airways Australia ☎1300/727
340, South Africa ☎11/340 3400, ⓦwww
.virgin-atlantic.com

Travel specialists and tour operators in the US

Abercrombie & Kent ☎1-800/323-7308,
ⓦwww.abercrombiekent.com. Well-tailored but
rather upmarket tours.
Adventure Center ☎1-800/228-8747, ⓦwww
.adventurecenter.com. Hiking and "soft adventure"
specialists.
Backroads ☎1-800/462-2848, ⓦwww
.backroads.com. Cycling, hiking, and multisport tours.
Mountain Travel Sobek ☎1-888/687-6235,
ⓦwww.mtsobek.com. Conducts hiking, kayaking,
and rafting tours.
REI Adventures ☎1-800/622-2236, ⓦwww
.rei.com/travel. Climbing, cycling, hiking, cruising,
paddling, and multisport tours.
STA Travel ☎1-800/781-4040, ⓦwww.statravel
.com. Nationwide student agency that also does good
deals for older travelers.

Travel specialists and tour operators in the UK and Ireland

American Holidays Northern Ireland ☎028/9023
8762, Republic of Ireland ☎1/673 3840, ⓦwww
.american-holidays.com. All sorts of package tours to
the US, including California, from Ireland.
Bon Voyage UK ☎0800/316 3012, ⓦwww
.bon-voyage.co.uk. Flight-plus-accommodation deals
in San Francisco, Los Angeles, Palm Springs, and
Las Vegas.
Bridge the World UK ☎0870/443 2399, ⓦwww
.bridgetheworld.com. Good all-around agency that
specializes in USA travel.
Contiki Travel UK ☎020/8290 6777, ⓦwww
.contiki.co.uk. West Coast coach tours aimed at
18–35-year-olds willing to party.

Flight Centre UK ☎0870/890 8099, ✆www .flightcentre.co.uk. Near-ubiquitous high-street agency frequently offering some of the lowest fares around.

Holiday America UK ☎01424/224 400. Flight-plus-accommodation and fly-drive combinations.

Kuoni UK ☎1306/747 002, ✆www.kuoni.co.uk. Flight-plus-accommodation-plus-car deals featuring Los Angeles, San Francisco, and San Diego. Special deals for families.

North South Travel UK ☎01245/608 291, ✆www.northsouthtravel.co.uk. Nonprofit agency offering friendly and efficient service.

STA Travel UK ☎0870/160 0599, ✆www .statravel.co.uk. A major player in student, youth, and budget travel with branches in or near many universities.

Trailfinders UK ☎020/7938 3939, ✆www .trailfinders.com; Ireland ☎1/677 7888, ✆www .trailfinders.ie. Well-established travel specialists, particularly adept at organizing RTW tickets.

TrekAmerica UK ☎01295/256 777, ✆www .trekamerica.com. Touring adventure holidays, usually small groups in well-equipped 4WD vans.

USIT Northern Ireland ☎028/9032 7111, ✆www .usitnow.com; Republic of Ireland ☎0818/200 020, ✆www.usit.ie. Ireland's premier student travel center, which can also find good nonstudent deals.

Virgin Holidays UK ☎0870/220 2788, ✆www .virginholidays.co.uk. Packages to a wide range of California destinations.

Travel specialists and tour operators in Australia, New Zealand, and South Africa

Canada & America Travel Specialists Australia ☎02/9922 4600, ✆www.canada-americatravel .com.au. North American specialists offering everything from flights and hotels to travel passes and adventure sports.

Flight Centre Australia ☎133 133, ✆www .flightcentre.com.au; New Zealand ☎800/243 544, ✆www.flightcentre.co.nz; South Africa ☎0860/400 727, ✆www.flightcentre.co.za. Near-ubiquitous

high-street agency frequently offering some of the lowest fares around.

Journeys Worldwide Australia ☎07/3221 4788, ✆www.journeysworldwide.com.au. All US travel arrangements available.

Peregrine Adventures Australia ☎03/9663 8611, ✆www.peregrine.net.au. With offices in Brisbane, Sydney, Adelaide, and Perth, Peregrine offers active small-group holidays, from short walking and camping tours to longer overland trips through California.

STA Travel Australia ☎1300/733 035, ✆www .statravel.com.au; New Zealand ☎508/782 872, ✆www.statravel.co.nz. A major player in student, youth, and budget travel with branches in many universities.

Sydney International Travel Centre Australia ☎02/9250 9320, ✆www.sydneytravel.com.au. Individually tailored holidays, Disneyland passes, flights, and bus and rail tours.

Trailfinders Australia ☎02/9247 7666, ✆www .trailfinders.com.au. Knowledgeable staff skilled at turning up odd itineraries and good prices.

Travel.com.au Australia ☎02/9249 5444, ✆www.travel.com.au; New Zealand ☎800/788 336, ✆www.travel.co.nz. Youth-oriented center with an efficient travel agency offering good fares, a travel bookshop, and Internet café.

USA Travel Australia ☎02/9250 9320, ✆www .usatravel.au. Good deals on flights, accommodation, city stays, car rental, and trip packages.

Train

Amtrak ☎1-800/872-7245, ✆www.amtrak.com. Call or click for schedules, fares, and reservations. Don't call individual stations.

Bus

Greyhound ☎1-800/231-2222, ✆www .greyhound.com, ✆www.disoverypass.com. Fares, schedules, reservations, and information on the Discovery Pass (see p.34).

Getting around

Although distances can be great, getting around California is seldom much of a problem. Certainly, things are always easier if you have a car, but between the major cities there are good bus links and a reasonable train service. The only regions where travel is more difficult using public transportation are the isolated rural areas, though even here, by adroit forward planning, you can often get to the main points of interest on local buses and charter services, details of which are in the relevant sections of this guide.

By plane

A **plane** is obviously the quickest way of getting around California, and much less expensive than you may think. Airlines with a strong route structure in the state include Alaska, American, Delta, Northwest, Southwest, and United. At **off-peak times** (see p.27), flights between Los Angeles and San Francisco can cost as little as $50 one-way (less than the train fare), though they may require booking 21 days in advance. If you're flying between other cities, such as Sacramento and San Jose or Santa Barbara and San Diego, bear in mind that a stopover at LAX or SFO may be necessary, even if it means flying twice the distance.

By train

Unlike elsewhere in the US, California is well covered by the Amtrak **rail** network, thanks to the number of Amtrak Thruway buses that bring passengers from the many rail-less parts of the state to the trains. Traveling by train is more expensive than Greyhound — for example, $70 one way between Los Angeles and San Francisco (by way of Oakland) — but most major cities are connected and the carriages rarely crowded, though delays can be frequent since Amtrak shares rail lines with commercial freight carriers.

Probably the prettiest route is the **Coast Starlight**, which runs between Seattle and Los Angeles and passes some of the most attractive scenery in the state, from an evening trip around Mount Shasta to coastal whale watching between San Luis Obispo and Santa Barbara. Shorter in-state routes include the **Pacific Surfliner**, which connects San Diego to San Luis Obispo,

Capitol Corridor, from Sacramento to San Jose, and the less appealing **San Joaquins**, connecting Oakland to Bakersfield across the San Joaquin Valley.

If California is part of wider travels, it may be economic to buy one of Amtrak's rail passes (see box, p.34).

By bus

If you're traveling on your own and making a lot of stops, **buses** are the cheapest way to get around. The main long-distance service is **Greyhound**, which links all major cities and many smaller towns. Out in the country, buses are fairly scarce, sometimes appearing only once a day; as a result, you'll need to plot your route with care. But along the main highways, buses run around the clock to a fairly full timetable, stopping only for meal breaks (almost always fast-food dives) and driver changeovers.

It used to be that any sizeable community had a Greyhound station; now in some places, the post office or a gas station doubles as the bus stop and ticket office, and in many others the bus service has been canceled altogether. Note that advance reservations, either in person at the station or on the toll-free number, are useful for getting cheaper tickets but do not guarantee a seat, so it's still wise to arrive in good time and join the **line** at busy stations.

Fares average 10¢ a mile, which can add up quickly; for example, $44 one way from Los Angeles to San Francisco. Though long-distance travel by bus is inefficient, it's the best deal if you plan to visit a lot of places, and Greyhound's **Discovery Pass** (see box, p.34) can work out to be good value. To plan your

Rail and bus passes

Amtrak Rail Passes

Travelers have a choice of several **Rail Passes** that cover California, which can be useful if you're on an extended tour of the state and have plenty of time to explore your destinations.

	15-day (June to Aug)	15-day (Sept to May)	30-day (mid-May to Oct)	30-day (Nov to mid-May)
North America	–	–	$999	$709
USA – West	$369	$329	$459	$359

The **North America Rail Pass** is available to all travelers, issued in conjunction with Canada's VIA Rail and valid for 30 consecutive days of travel up to one year from the date of purchase; you may travel up to four times, one way, over any given route segment and must travel at least once between the US and Canada. The pass is valid for coach (second-class) travel, but can be upgraded for an additional charge. The **USA Rail Pass** covers different segments of the US (in this case, the West) and is available only to foreign travelers. **Rail 2 Rail** offers free travel on Amtrak trains for riders of LA's Metrorail and San Diego's Coaster systems (see p.78 and 190), for linking between stations. The **California** pass ($159) is available to all, covering any seven days of travel in a 21-day window for in-state routes such as Capitols, Coast Starlight, Pacific Surfliner, and San Joaquins. Many trains fill quickly, so it's worth making reservations.

Greyhound Discovery Passes

Foreign visitors and US and Canadian nationals can all buy a **Greyhound Discovery Pass**, offering unlimited travel within a set time limit: you can order online at ⓦwww .discoverypass.com. A seven-day pass costs $283, fifteen days for $415, thirty days for $522, and the longest, a sixty-day pass, is $645. The company website has a list of international vendors if you don't want to purchase online. The first time you use your pass, the ticket clerk will date it (which becomes the commencement date of the pass), and you will receive a ticket that allows you to board the bus. Repeat this procedure for every subsequent journey. Greyhound's nationwide toll-free **information service** (ⓣ1-800/231-2222) can give you routes and times, plus phone numbers and addresses of local terminals, and help you make reservations.

route, pick up the free route-by-route time-tables from larger stations, or consult Greyhound's website.

Bear in mind that fair distances can be covered for very little money – if also very slowly – using **local buses**, which connect neighboring districts. It's possible, for example, to travel from San Diego to Los Angeles for around $6, but it'll take all day and at least three changes of bus to do it. And of course, there's always the hippyish **Green Tortoise** (ⓣ1-800/867-8647, ⓦwww .greentortoise.com), which offers seasonal trips to sights like the redwoods, Yosemite, Mono Lake, and Joshua Tree National Monument (most multiday trips $150–500), and more practically runs every Sunday from mid-June to mid-October between San Francisco and LA on the **Hostel Hopper** route ($39).

By car

Unless you're going from one end of the state to the other, driving is by far the best way to get around California. Los Angeles, for example, sprawls for so many miles in all directions that your hotel may be fifteen or twenty miles from the sights you came to see. Away from the cities, points of interest are much harder to reach without your own transportation; most national and state parks are only served by infrequent public transportation as far as the main visitor center, if that much. What's more, if you are planning on doing a fair amount of camping, renting a car can save you money by

City-to-city distances (in miles)

	Los Angeles	Sacramento	San Diego	San Francisco
Bakersfield	115	272	231	297
Eureka	694	314	800	272
Los Angeles	-	387	116	412
Monterey	335	185	451	116
Palm Springs	111	498	139	523
Redding	551	164	667	223
Sacramento	387	-	503	87
San Diego	116	503	-	528
San Francisco	412	87	528	-
San Jose	367	114	483	45
Santa Barbara	95	406	211	337

allowing access to less expensive, out-of-the-way campgrounds.

Drivers under 25 years old who wish to rent a car may encounter problems, and will probably get lumbered with a higher than normal insurance premium – and if you're not 21, it's unlikely you'll be permitted to rent at all. Car rental companies will also expect you to have a **credit card**. The likeliest tactic for getting a good deal is to phone the major firms' toll-free numbers and ask for their best rate – most will try to beat the offers of their competitors, so it's worth haggling. See p.37 for a directory of car rental agencies.

In general, the lowest **rates** are available at the airport branches – $150 is roughly the floor on price for a week's rental. Always be sure to get free unlimited mileage and be aware that leaving the car in a different city than the one in which you rent it will incur a **drop-off charge** that can be $200 or more. However, many companies do not charge drop-off fees within California itself, so check before you book if you plan a one-way drive. If you are planning to venture outside California, inquire if there are any limitations; some companies don't allow travel beyond Reno or into Mexico, while others simply ramp up their insurance charges.

Alternatively, various **local companies** rent out vehicles that are new – and not so new (as does the national Rent-A-Wreck company; see p.37 for details). They are certainly cheaper than the big chains if you just want to spin around a city for a day, but you have to drop them back where you picked them up, and free mileage is seldom included, so they can work out more costly for long-distance travel. Addresses and phone numbers are listed in the *Yellow Pages*.

When you rent a car, read the small print carefully for details on the **Collision Damage Waiver (CDW)** – sometimes called a Liability Damage Waiver (LDW) or a Physical Damage Waiver (PDW) – a form of insurance which usually isn't included in the initial rental charge. Americans who have their own car insurance policy may already be covered (check before you leave home), but foreign visitors should definitely consider taking this option. It specifically covers the car that you are driving, as you are in any case insured for damage to other vehicles. At $15 a day,

Road conditions

The California Department of Transportation (CalTrans) operates a toll-free **24-hour information line** (℡1-800/427-7623) giving up-to-the-minute details of road conditions throughout the state. Simply input the number of the road ("5" for I-5, "299" for Hwy-299, etc) and a recorded voice will tell you about any relevant weather conditions, delays, detours, snow closures, and so on. From out of state, or without a touch-tone phone, road information is also available on ℡916/445-1534. You can also check online at ⓦwww.dot.ca.gov.

it can add a third to the daily rental fee, but without it you're liable for every scratch to the car – even those that aren't your fault. Smaller companies may offer low-cost CDW that still leaves you liable for, say, the first $500 of any claim. Before stumping up for their optional Personal Accident Coverage (or similar), consult your travel insurance policy, which may cover you for a certain amount of rental vehicle excess, eliminating the need for this extra cost.

Alternately, your **credit card company** may cover your rental when you use its card for the transaction; however, policies can vary widely, depending on the company, and there may be strict limitations on the liability coverage offered, with collision coverage even less common. If you do a lot of traveling in rental cars, great-value yearlong policies for multiple rentals (around $200 per year including CDW) can be found at ⓦwww.insurance4carhire.com.

Driving for foreign visitors

Most visitors can **drive** in the US on their own driver's license if they've also obtained an International Driving Permit from their home country. The most important differences between driving in the US and in other countries is the need in the US to **drive on the right**. Once you have rented a vehicle, you'll find that **petrol** (US "gasoline") is fairly cheap, though California is one of the more expensive states for it; a self-serve US gallon (3.8 liters) of **unleaded** costs $3 or more, depending on the location of the gas station. In California, most gas stations are self-service and you always have to prepay; full-service pumps, where available, often charge upwards of 30¢ extra per gallon.

There are several **types of roads**. The best for covering long distances quickly are the wide, straight, and fast interstate highways, usually at least six-lane motorways and always prefixed by "I" (eg I-5). Even-numbered interstates usually run east–west and those with odd numbers north–south. Drivers **change lanes** frequently; in California, you are also permitted to stay in the fast lane while being overtaken on the inside, although common courtesy dictates that slower drivers stay to the right. A grade down, and broadly similar to British dual carriageways and main roads, are the **state highways** (eg Hwy-1) and the **US highways** (eg US-395). In rural areas, you'll also find much smaller county or rural roads; their number is preceded by a letter denoting their county or area.

The maximum **speed limit** in California is 70mph, with lower signposted limits – usually around 35–55mph – in urban areas, and 20mph near schools when children are present. If given a ticket for **speeding**, your case will come to court and the size of the fine will be at the discretion of the judge; $200 is a rough estimate. If the **police** do flag you down, don't get out of the car, make any sudden moves, or reach into the glove compartment, as the cops may think you have a gun. Simply sit still with your hands on the wheel; when questioned, be polite and don't attempt to make jokes.

As for other possible violations, US law requires that any **alcohol** be carried unopened in the boot (US "trunk") of the car, and **driving under the influence (DUI)** is a very serious offense (see p.57). At intersections, one rule is crucially different from many other countries: you can turn right on a red light (having first come to a halt) if there is no traffic approaching from the left, unless there is a "no turn on red" sign; otherwise red means stop. Stopping is also compulsory, in both directions, when you come upon a school bus disgorging passengers with its lights flashing, and not doing so is regarded as a serious infraction. Blinking red lights should be treated as a stop sign (as should devices at an intersection where stoplights are temporarily disabled), and blinking yellow lights indicate that you should cross the intersection with caution, but do not need to come to a complete stop. And at any intersection with more than one **stop sign**, cars proceed in the order in which they arrived; if two vehicles arrive simultaneously, the one on the right has right of way. Two other rules to be aware of: it is illegal to park within ten feet of a fire hydrant anywhere in the US; in California, you have to **curb your wheels** when parking on a hill.

One variation on renting is a **driveaway**. Companies operate in most major cities, and are paid to find drivers to take a customer's car from one place to another. The company will normally pay for your insurance and your first tank of gas; after that, you'll be expected to drive along the most direct route and to average a set number of miles a day. Many driveaway companies are keen to use foreign travelers, so if you can convince them you are a safe bet they'll take something like a $300 deposit, which you get back after delivering the car in good condition. It makes obvious sense to get in touch in advance, to spare yourself a week's wait for a car to turn up. Look under "Automobile transporters and driveaway companies" in the *Yellow Pages* and phone around for the latest offers, or check through the database on ⓦ www.movecars.com for a list of companies.

Car rental companies

Advantage ⓣ 1-800/777-5500, ⓦ www.arac .com
Alamo ⓣ 1-800/462-5266, ⓦ www.alamo.com
Avis ⓣ 1-800/230-4898, ⓦ www.avis.com
Budget ⓣ 1-800/527-0700, ⓦ www.budget.com
Dollar ⓣ 1-800/800-3665, ⓦ www.dollar.com
Enterprise ⓣ 1-800/261-7331, ⓦ www .enterprise.com
Hertz ⓣ 1-800/654-3131, ⓦ www.hertz.com
National ⓣ 1-800/227-7368, ⓦ www.nationalcar .com
Payless ⓣ 1-800/729-5377, ⓦ www .paylesscarrental.com
Rent-A-Wreck ⓣ 1-800/944-7501, ⓦ www .rentawreck.com
Thrifty ⓣ 1-800/847-4389, ⓦ www.thrifty.com

Cycling

In general, **cycling** is a cheap and healthy method of getting around all the big **cities**, though hilly San Francisco will test your legs. Even Los Angeles has its appeal, mostly along the beach and in the mountains. Some cities have cycle lanes and local buses equipped to carry bikes, strapped to the outside. In **rural areas**, certainly, there's much scenic and largely level land, especially around Sacramento and the Wine Country.

Bikes can be **rented** for $20–30 a day, and $120–150 a week from most bike stores; local visitor centers will have details. Apart from the coastal fog, which tends to clear by midday, you'll encounter few **weather** problems (except perhaps sunburn), but remember that the further north you go, the lower the temperatures and the more frequent the rains become.

For **long-distance cycling**, a route avoiding the interstates – on which cycling is illegal – is essential, and it's also wise to cycle **north to south**, as the wind blows this way in the summer and can make all the difference between a pleasant trip and a journey full of acute leg aches. Be particularly careful if you're planning to cycle along Hwy-1 on the Central Coast since, besides heavy traffic, it has tight curves, dangerous precipices, and is prone to fog.

If you're camping as well as cycling, look out for **hiker/biker campgrounds** (around $3–5 per person per night), which are free of cars and RVs, dotted across California's state parks and beaches. Many of them were set up in 1976 as part of the **Pacific Coast Bicentennial Bike Route** (which no longer includes the "Bicentennial" in its title), running 1825 miles from the Mexican border to Vancouver, Canada. Sites are allotted on a first-come, first-served basis, and all offer water and toilet facilities but seldom showers. For more information, call ⓣ 1-800/444-7275 or check with Hostelling International – USA (details on p.40), the Adventure Cycling Association (ⓣ 1-800/755-2453, ⓦ www.adv-cycling.org), or the Sierra Club (see box, p.50).

Hitchhiking

The usual advice given to **hitchhikers** is that they should use their common sense; in fact, common sense should tell anyone that hitchhiking in the US is a **bad idea**. We do not recommend it, though it is practiced commonly enough by hikers seeking access to Sierra trailheads and in certain parts of Northern California. In Southern California, standing anywhere near a highway is an invitation for a quick death.

Accommodation

Accommodation standards in California – as in the rest of the US – are high, and costs inevitably form a significant proportion of the expenses for any trip to the state. You can pare costs down by sleeping in dormitory-style hostels, though outside the main cities these are rare. Groups of two and up will find it only a little more expensive to stay in the plentiful motels and hotels, many of which will increase the rate only slightly for a third or fourth adult, reducing costs considerably. By contrast, the solo traveler will have a hard time of it: "singles" are usually double rooms at an only slightly reduced rate.

However, with the exception of the budget interstate motels, there's rarely such a thing as a set rate for a room, most applying **seasonal** and often **weekend** rates. A basic motel in a seaside or mountain resort may double its prices according to the season, while a big-city hotel which charges $200 per room during the week will often slash its tariff at the weekend when all the business types have gone home.

Since cheap accommodation in the cities, on the popular sections of the coast, and

Accommodation price codes

Throughout this book, **accommodation** has been price-coded according to the cost, excluding tax, of the **least expensive double room** in high season; we have given individual prices for hostel beds and campgrounds plus a price code if double rooms are also available.

In **resort areas** you can expect places to jump into the next highest category on Friday and Saturday nights, and almost all lodging (except state- and federally run campgrounds) is subject to additional local hotel taxes, which are generally around ten percent but may soar to twenty percent.

❶ **up to $45** The cheapest motels in unfashionable small towns and desert areas. Also cabins at some campgrounds.

❷ **$45–60** No-frills motel rooms – with bathroom, TV, phone, coffeemaker, and perhaps a pool – in an unpopular location.

❸ **$60–80** You'll get a fairly high-standard chain motel or even decent hotel in desert and country areas, but in resorts and cities you can expect only a basic motel.

❹ **$80–100** Midrange chain hotels (with fitness room, hot tub, and on-site restaurant) in cheaper parts of the state, and well-appointed motels (perhaps with hot tub and laundry) in more poplar areas. The least expensive country B&Bs start in this category.

❺ **$100–140** & ❻ **$140–180** Expect to stay in good-quality hotels and comfortable B&Bs everywhere except in the most expensive resort areas and cities, where standards will be lower. At the upper end you're getting into real luxury, with antique-furnished rooms, substantial breakfast, and lavish attention to detail.

❼ **$180–240** & ❽ **$240–300** Top-line city hotels with concierge and a range of bars and restaurants, or an exclusive resort where privacy and pampering take priority. Expect extraordinary accommodation and outstanding service.

❾ **$300+** All you might expect from a Code 8 place but in unique locations such as a historic landmark – *The Ahwahnee* in Yosemite Valley, for example.

close to the major national parks is snapped up fast, **book ahead** whenever possible. **Reservations** are only held until 5 or 6pm unless you've told them you'll be arriving late.

Wherever you stay, you'll be expected to **pay in advance**, at least for the first night and perhaps for further nights too, particularly if it's **high season** – generally summer, but most likely winter in desert and ski areas – and the hotel expects to be busy. Payment can be in cash or travelers' checks, though it's more common to give your credit card number and sign for everything when you leave.

Hotels and motels

Hotels (❸–❼) and motels (❶–❺) are essentially the same thing, although motels tend to congregate along the main approach roads to cities, around beaches, and by the main road junctions in country areas. Highrise hotels predominate along the popular sections of the coast and are sometimes the only accommodation in city centers.

In general, there's a uniform standard of comfort everywhere, with all rooms featuring one or more double or queen beds, plus bathroom, cable TV, phone, refrigerator, a coffeemaker, and maybe a microwave. The budget places will be pretty basic and possibly run down, but an extra $10–15 will get you more space, modern fittings, and better facilities, such as a swimming pool. Most hotels (and the better motels) provide a **complimentary breakfast**. Sometimes this will be no more than a cup of coffee and a soggy Danish pastry, but it can also be a sit-down affair likely to comprise fruit, cereals, muffins, and toast. In the pricier places, you may also be offered made-to-order omelets.

Enormous roadside signs make finding cheap hotels and motels pretty simple, and you'll soon become familiar with the numerous **chains**, such as *Econolodge*, *Days Inn*, and *Motel 6*. For mid-priced options try *Best Western*, *Howard Johnson*, *Travelodge*, and *Ramada*, though if you can afford to pay this much there's normally somewhere with more character to stay. When it's worth blowing a hunk of cash on somewhere really atmospheric we've said as much in the guide. Bear in mind that the

most upscale establishments have all manner of services which may appear to be free but for which you'll be expected to **tip** in a style commensurate with the hotel's status – ie big.

Discounts and reservations

During **off-peak periods**, many motels and hotels struggle to fill their rooms, and it's worth **haggling** to get a few dollars off the asking price. Staying in the same place for more than one night will bring further reductions, and motels in particular offer worthwhile discounts (usually ten percent) for seniors and members of various organizations, particularly the American Automobile Association (AAA). Members of sister motoring associations in other countries may also be entitled to such discounts. Additionally, pick up the many **discount coupons** which fill tourist information offices and look out for the free *Traveler Discount Guide*. Read the small print, though – what appears to be an amazingly cheap room rate sometimes turns out to be a per-room charge for two people sharing, and limited to midweek.

Bed and breakfasts

Staying at a **bed and breakfast** (❹–❽) in California is a luxury. Typically, the bed-and-breakfast inns, as they're usually known, are restored buildings and grand houses in the smaller cities and more rural areas, although the big cities also have a few, especially San Francisco. Even the larger establishments tend to have no more than ten rooms, often without TV and phone but with plentiful flowers, stuffed cushions, and a sometimes-contrived homely atmosphere. Others may just be a couple of furnished rooms in someone's home, or an entire apartment where you won't even see your host. Victorian and Romantic are dominant themes; while selecting the best in that vein, we've also gone out of our way to find those that don't conform.

While always including a huge and wholesome **breakfast** (five courses is not unheard of), prices vary greatly: anything from $80 to $300 depending on location and season. Most fall between $100 and $150 per night for a double, a little more for a whole apartment. Bear in mind, too, that they are frequently booked well in advance, and even if they're not full, the cheaper rooms that determine our price code may be already taken.

As well as the B&Bs listed in the guide, there are hundreds more throughout the state, many of them listed on various **accommodation websites** such as California B&B Travel (Ⓦwww.bbtravel.com), the California Association of B&B Inns (Ⓦwww.cabbi.com), and B&B Inns of North America (Ⓦwww.inntravels.com).

Hostels

At an average of $20 per night per person (though $23–26 in San Francisco and at Santa Monica in LA), **hostels** (❶–❷) are clearly the cheapest accommodation option in California other than camping. There are two main kinds of hostel-type accommodation in the US: the internationally affiliated Hostelling International – USA hostels, and a growing number of independent hostels variously aligned with assorted umbrella organizations.

Altogether California has around twenty **Hostelling International – USA** hostels ("HI" in accommodation reviews; Ⓦwww.hiusa.org), mostly in major cities and close to popular hiking areas, including national and state parks. Most urban hostels have 24-hour access, while rural ones may have a curfew and limited daytime hours.

Dormitory bed rates at HI hostels range from $17 to $26 for members. Membership is international, though people typically join in their home country (see opposite for contacts), which will cost the equivalent of $20–30 annually. Nonmembers pay an additional $3 per night for the first six nights at an HI hostel, at which point membership is granted – a cheaper option than joining up front.

HI hostels don't allow sleeping bags, though they provide sheets as a matter of course. Few hostels provide meals, but most have **cooking** facilities. Alcohol and smoking are banned.

Particularly if you're traveling in high season, it's advisable to make **reservations**, either by contacting the hostel directly or

booking online at least 48 hours in advance. There's also the IBN booking service (Ⓦwww.hihostels.com), which helps you book certain big-city and gateway hostels through your home organization. San Diego, LA, and San Francisco hostels can be booked this way.

Independent hostels now number around fifty and are concentrated in the big cities. They're usually a little less expensive than their HI counterparts, and have fewer rules, but the quality is not as consistent; some can be quite poor, while others are absolutely wonderful. In popular areas, especially LA, San Francisco, and San Diego, they compete fiercely for your business with airport and train station pickups, free breakfasts, and free bike hire. There is often no curfew and, at some, a party atmosphere is encouraged at barbecues and keg parties. Their independent status may be due to a failure to measure up to the HI's (fairly rigid) criteria, yet often it's simply because the owners prefer not to be tied down by HI regulations.

Keep in mind that hostels are often shoestring organizations, prone to changing address or closing down altogether. Similarly, new ones appear each year; check the noticeboards of other hostels for news or consult hostel websites, particularly Ⓦwww.hostels.com.

Youth hostel contacts

Australia YHA Australia ☎02/9565 1699, Ⓦwww.yha.com.au
Canada ☎1-800/663-5777, Ⓦwww.hihostels.ca
England and Wales ☎0870/770 8868, Ⓦwww.yha.org.uk
New Zealand New Zealand Youth Hostels Association ☎800/278 299 or 03/379 9970, Ⓦwww.yha.co.nz
Northern Ireland ☎028/9032 4733, Ⓦwww.hini.org.uk
Republic of Ireland ☎01/830 4555, Ⓦwww.anoige.ie
Scotland ☎01786/891 400, Ⓦwww.syha.org.uk
USA ☎301/495-1240, Ⓦwww.hiusa.org

Campgrounds

California **campgrounds** range from the primitive – a flat piece of ground that may or may not have a pit toilet and water tap – to others that are more like open-air hotels, with shops, restaurants, and washing facilities. In major cities, campgrounds tend to be inconveniently sited on the outskirts, if they exist at all.

When camping in national and state **parks**, as well as **national forests**, you can typically expect a large site with picnic table and fire pit, designed to accommodate up to two vehicles and six people. It is usually a short walk to an outhouse and drinking water. Note that sites fill up quickly and it's worth reserving well in advance (see the list on opposite for contact numbers). **Vacancies** often exist in the grounds outside the parks – where the facilities are usually marginally better – and by contrast, some of the more basic campgrounds in isolated areas will often be empty whatever time of year you're there.

Naturally enough, **prices** vary accordingly, ranging from nothing for the most basic plots, up to $30 a night for something

comparatively luxurious, and more like $30–40 if you want to hook your RV up to electricity, water, sewage, and cable TV. For comprehensive listings of these check out ⓦwww.californiacampgrounds.org and Kampgrounds of America (ⓦwww.koa.com). Often rural campgrounds have no one in attendance (though a ranger may stop by), and if there's any charge at all you'll need to pay by posting the money in the slot provided; save your small bills.

Look out too for **hiker/biker** or **walk-in** campgrounds, which, at $3–5 per person per night, are much cheaper than most sites but only available if you are traveling under your own steam.

Camping reservation contacts

National Forests and National Parks Reserve through ☏1-877/444-6777 or 518/885-3639, ⓦwww.recreation.gov
State Parks California State Parks Reservations ☏1-800/444-7275, ⓦwww.reserveamerica.com

Eating and drinking

It's not too much of an exaggeration to say that in California – its cities, at least – you can eat whatever you want, whenever you want. On every main street, a mass of restaurants, fast-food places, and coffee shops try to outdo one another with bargains and special offers. Be warned, though, that in rural areas you might go for days finding little more than diners and cheap Mexican joints.

California's cornucopia stems largely from its being one of the most agriculturally rich parts of the country. Junk food is as common as anywhere else in the US, but the state also produces its own range of high-quality produce, often organic. You'll rarely find anything that's not fresh, be it a bagel or a spinach-in-Mornay-sauce croissant, and even fast food won't necessarily be rubbish.

California is also one of the most **health-conscious** states in the country, and the supermarket shelves are chock-full of products which, if not fat-free, are low-fat, low-sodium, low-carb, zero-transfat,

caffeine-free, and dairy-free. The same ethic runs through the menus of most restaurants, though you needn't worry about going hungry: portions are universally huge, and what you don't eat can always be "boxed up" for later consumption.

Breakfasts

For the price, on average $5–9, breakfast is the best-value and most filling meal of the day. Go to a diner, café, or coffee shop, all of which serve breakfast until at least 11am, with some diners serving them all day.

The breakfasts themselves are pretty much what you'd find all over the country. **Eggs** are served in a variety of styles, usually with some form of **meat** – ham, bacon, or sausages – and generally accompanied by toast or a muffin. **Waffles**, **pancakes**, or **French toast** are typically consumed swamped in butter with lashings of sickly-sweet "maple" syrup, though you may be offered **fruit**: maybe apple, banana, orange, pineapple, or strawberry.

Lunch and snacks

Between 11am and 3pm you should look for the excellent-value **lunchtime set menus** on offer – Chinese, Indian, and Thai restaurants frequently have help-yourself buffets for $7–10, and many Japanese restaurants give you a chance to eat sushi much more cheaply ($8–12) than usual. Most Mexican restaurants are exceptionally well priced all the time: you can get a good-sized lunch for $5–8. In Northern California, watch out for seafood restaurants selling **fish'n'chips**: the fish is breaded and then fried, and the chips are chunky chipped potatoes rather than the matchstick French fries you normally find. A plateful is about $8. Look as well for **clam chowder**, a thick, creamy shellfish soup commonly served for $5–6, sometimes using a hollowed-out sourdough cottage loaf as a bowl ($6–8).

As you'd expect, there's also **pizza** ($12–15 for a basic two-person pie) available from chains like *Pizza Hut*, *Round Table*, and *Shakey's*, or local, more personalized restaurants. If you can't face hot food, delis usually serve a broad range of salads from about $5, ready-cooked meals for $6–8, and a range of **sandwiches** which can be meals in themselves: huge French rolls filled with a custom-built combination of meat, cheese, and vegetables. **Bagels** are also everywhere, filled with anything you fancy. **Street stands** sell hot dogs, burgers, tacos, or a slice of pizza for around $3, and most shopping malls have ethnic fast-food stalls, often pricier than their equivalent outside, but usually edible and filling. Be a little wary of the grottier **Mexican fast-food** stands if you're buying meat, although they're generally filling, cheap, and more authentic than the Tex-Mex outlets. There are chains,

too, like *El Pollo Loco*, *Del Taco*, and *Taco Bell*, which sell swift tacos and burritos from $1 up. And of course the burger chains are as ubiquitous here as anywhere in the US: best to seek out the few *In-n-Out* burger chain franchises if possible, all made to order and as delicious as you'll find.

Restaurants

Even if it often seems swamped by the more fashionable regional and ethnic cuisines, traditional **American cooking** – juicy burgers, steaks, fries, and salads (invariably served before the main dish) – is found all over California. Cheapest of the food chains is the California-wide *Denny's*, although you'll rarely need to spend more than $12 for a solid blowout anywhere.

By contrast, though, it's **California cuisine**, geared towards health and aesthetics, that's raved about by foodies on the West Coast – and rightly so. Restaurants serving California cuisine build their reputation by word of mouth; if you can, ask a local enthusiast for recommendations, or simply follow our suggestions, especially in Berkeley, the recognized birthplace of California cuisine.

Although technically ethnic, **Mexican** food is so common that it often seems like (and, historically, often is) an indigenous cuisine, especially in Southern California. What's more, day or night, it's the cheapest type of food to eat: even a full dinner with a beer or margarita will only be over $15 at the more upmarket establishments. Californian Mexican food is generally different from what you'll find in Mexico, making more use of fresh vegetables and fruit, but the essentials are the same: lots of rice and pinto beans, often served refried (ie boiled, mashed, and fried), with variations on the **tortilla**, a thin maize or flour-dough pancake. You can eat it as an accompaniment to your main dish; wrapped around the food and eaten by hand (a **burrito**); filled and folded (a **taco**); rolled, filled, and baked (an **enchilada**); or fried flat and topped with a stack of food (a **tostada**). One of the few options for vegetarians in this meat-oriented cuisine is the **chile relleno**, a mild, green pepper stuffed with cheese, dipped in egg batter, and fried. Veggie burritos, filled with beans, rice, lettuce, avocado, cheese, and sour cream are another prevalent option for those averse to meat.

Other ethnic cuisines are plentiful, too. **Chinese** food is everywhere, and during lunchtime can often be as cheap as Mexican. Ditto **Indian**, which has flooded the state in the last few years. Seldom expensive, it can often be exceedingly cheap if you go for the buffet lunches and dinners, often around $10. **Thai**, **Korean**, **Vietnamese**, and **Indonesian** food is also available and generally fairly cheap. Moving upscale, you find **Italian**, which can be pricey once you explore specialist Italian regional cooking, and **French**, which is seldom cheap and rarely found outside the larger cities.

Drinking

In freeway-dominated Los Angeles, the traditional neighborhood bar is as rare as the traditional neighborhood. There are exceptions, but LA bars tend to be either extremely pretentious or extremely seedy, neither good for long bouts of social drinking. On the other hand, San Francisco is the consummate boozing town, still with a strong contingent of old-fashioned, get-drunk bars that are fun to spend an evening in, even if you don't plan to get legless. Elsewhere in the state you'll find the normal array of spots in which to imbibe.

To buy and consume alcohol in California, you need to be 21, and bars almost always have someone at the door **checking ID**: you'll probably need to be into your thirties before getting waved through automatically. Alcohol can be bought and consumed any time between 6am and 2am, seven days a week in bars, nightclubs, and many restaurants. Some **restaurants** only have a beer and wine license, and many allow you to bring your own bottled wine, where the corkage fee will be $10–15. You can buy beer, wine, or spirits more cheaply and easily in supermarkets, many delis, and, of course, liquor stores.

American **beers** fall into two distinct categories: wonderful and tasteless. The latter are found everywhere: light, fizzy brands such as Budweiser, Miller, Schlitz, and so on. The alternative is a fabulous range of **microbrewed beers**, the product of a wave of backyard and in-house operations that swelled in the late 1980s. Head for one of the brewpubs (many are listed in the guide), and you'll find handcrafted beers such as crisp pilsners, wheat beers, and stouts on tap, at prices only marginally above those of the national brews. Bottled microbrews, like Chico's hoppy Sierra Nevada Pale Ale and the full-bodied, San Francisco-brewed Anchor Steam Beer, are sold throughout the state, while Red Tail Ale is found throughout Northern California. Expect to fork out $5 for a glass of draught beer, about the same for a bottle of imported beer.

California is justly known around the country and indeed the world as a wine-producing powerhouse. You can learn a lot about California wine by taking a **winery tour** at one (or several) of the state's boutique vintners, most including free tastings (although some charge $4–5 for a full glass or two). Alternatively, the visitor centers in popular wine-producing areas can provide informative regional directories. The best lesson of all, of course, is simply to buy the stuff. It's fairly inexpensive: a decent glass of wine in a bar or restaurant costs $6–8, a bottle $20–30 (perhaps more in LA and San Francisco). Buying from a supermarket is better still – a tolerable bottle can be purchased for as little as $7.

Cocktails are extremely popular, especially during **happy hours** (usually any time between 5pm and 7pm), when drinks may have a couple of dollars knocked off and there may be some finger food thrown in. Varieties are innumerable, sometimes specific to a single bar or cocktail lounge, and they cost $4–15, though typically around $7.

Increasingly an alternative to drinking dens, **coffee shops** play a vibrant part in California's social scene, and are havens of high-quality coffee far removed from the stuff served in diners and convenience stores. In larger towns and cities, cafés will boast of the quality of the roast, and offer a full array of espressos, cappuccinos, lattes, and the like, served straight, iced, organic, or flavored with syrups. Herbal teas and light snacks are often also on the menu.

The media

Like the rest of the country, California has a welter of media for an English-speaking (and, increasingly, Spanish-speaking) public. The quality and level of parochialism varies but you'll never be short of a paper to read, radio channel to tune in to, or TV station to watch.

Newspapers

Every major urban center in California has its own newspaper, from the politically obsessed *Sacramento Bee* to the Hollywood hype of the *Los Angeles Times*. You'll also be able to pick up *USA Today*, the moderate if rather toothless national daily, while such East Coast stalwarts as the *New York Times*, the *Washington Post*, and the *Wall Street Journal* should be available in most towns, with a slight price premium.

As in any North American town, the best place to turn for **entertainment listings** – not to mention an irreverent take on local government and politics – is one of the many freesheets available on most street corners. Since nightlife venues, clubs, and bars open and close so rapidly, they're the best source of up-to-date listings available. We've noted local titles in relevant towns throughout the text; note that many have online editions, too, so you can check them out before you travel.

Radio

Listening to the radio – and how its mix of stations changes during your travels – is often one of the smartest ways to gauge the character of the local area. And as the land of the roadtrip, it's not surprising that California is well served by diverse radio stations. It's best to skip most specialty stations on the AM frequency – although AM chat shows, with their often angry, confrontational callers and hosts can be hilarious and illuminating, if not in the intended sense. On FM, you'll find the usual mix of rock, Latin, and R&B; stations are too numerous to list, although pop-rock stations KLLC (97.3 FM, known as "Alice") in San Francisco and KROQ (106.7 FM) in Los Angeles are especially well known. Expect commercials interrupted by an occasional tune during drive time (6–9am and 4–7pm); also note that many stations have an astonishingly limited playlist – songs in heavy rotation will often be played half a dozen times a day – thanks to monopolies held by corporate behemoths such as Clear Channel. You could also tune in to satellite radio, which comes with most rental cars these days. You'll have fewer advertisements to suffer through, but often less local character to enjoy as well.

In Southern California especially, you'll also frequently come across **Mexican stations** (some local, others broadcasting from over the border), which can be enjoyable even for non-Spanish speakers.

If you're struggling to find satisfying local news, a safe harbor is **National Public Radio (NPR)**, the listener-funded talk station with a refreshingly sober take on news and chat (FM frequencies vary). To check for local frequencies for the World Service log on to the BBC (ⓦ www.bbc.co.uk/worldservice), Radio Canada (ⓦ www.rcinet.ca), or the Voice of America (ⓦ www.voa.gov).

Television

In California, you'll have access to all the usual stations: from major networks like ABC, CBS, and NBC to smaller netlets like the WB and UPN. Expect talk shows in the morning, soaps in the afternoon, and marquee-name comedies and dramas during primetime. If that's all too maddeningly commercial-heavy, there's always PBS, the rather earnest, ad-free station, which fills its schedule with news, documentaries, and imported period dramas. The precise channel numbers vary from area to area.

There's a wider choice on **cable**, including CNN for news and pop culture on MTV, as well as educational channels such as Discovery, the History Channel, and NGEO (National Geographic); well-regarded **premium channels** like HBO and Showtime are often available on hotel TV systems, showing original series and block-buster movies.

Festivals and public holidays

Someone, somewhere is always celebrating something in California, although apart from national holidays, few festivities are shared throughout the entire state. Instead, there is a disparate multitude of local events: art and craft shows, county fairs, ethnic celebrations, music festivals, rodeos, sandcastle-building competitions, and many others of every hue and shade.

Among California's major annual events are the **gay and lesbian freedom** parades held in June in LA and, particularly, San Francisco (see pp.159 & 553, respectively); the **Academy Awards** in LA in late February (see p.158); and the world-class **Monterey Jazz Festival** in September (see p.468). In addition, California tourist offices can provide full lists, or you can just phone the visitor center in a particular region ahead of your arrival and ask what's coming up.

The biggest and most all-American of the national festivals and holidays is **Independence Day** on the fourth of July, when Americans commemorate the signing of the Declaration of Independence in 1776 by getting drunk, saluting the flag, and taking part in fireworks displays, marches, and more. **Halloween** (October 31) lacks any such patriotic overtones and is not a public holiday despite being one of the most popular yearly flings. Traditionally, kids run around the streets banging on doors and collecting pieces of candy, but in bigger cities Halloween has grown into a massive gay celebration: in West Hollywood in LA and San Francisco's Castro district, the night is marked by mass cross-dressing, huge block parties, and general licentiousness. More sedate is **Thanksgiving Day**, on the last Thursday in November. The third big event of the year is essentially a domestic affair, when relatives return to the familial nest to stuff themselves with roast turkey, and (supposedly) fondly recall the first harvest of the pilgrims in Massachusetts. **Christmas Day** is another family occasion and is celebrated much as it is in other countries – preceded, of course, by commercial overkill.

Opening hours

No matter how carefully you've planned your trip to California, you may find the gates of that must-see park or museum closed if you don't check in advance about the various public holidays taking place throughout the year, which may shut down certain businesses altogether and otherwise throw a wrench into your well-laid plans. Beyond this, regular opening hours are more predictable, and though listed for each attraction in the guide, most operate according to the same general schedule.

As a general rule, most **museums** are open Tuesday through Saturday (occasionally Sunday, too) from 10am until 5 or 6pm, with somewhat shorter hours on the weekends. Many museums will also stay open late one evening a week – usually Thursday, when ticket prices are sometimes reduced. Government **offices**, including post offices, are open during regular business hours, typically 8 or 9am until 5pm, Monday through Friday (though some post offices are open Saturday morning until the early afternoon). Most stores are open daily from 10am until 5 or 6pm, while specialty stores can be more erratic, usually opening and closing later in the day, from noon to 2pm until 8 or 9pm, and remaining shuttered for two days of the week. **Malls** tend to be open from 10am until 7 or 8pm daily, though individual stores may close before the mall does.

While some diners stay open 24 hours, the more typical **restaurants** open daily around 11am or noon for lunch and close at 9 to 10pm. Places that serve breakfast usually open early, between 6 to 8am, serve lunch later, and close in the early or mid-afternoon. Dance and live music **clubs** often won't open until 9 or 10pm, and many will serve liquor until 2am and then either close for the night or stay open until dawn without serving booze. **Bars** that close at 2am may reopen as early as 6am to grab bleary-eyed regulars in need of a liquid breakfast.

On the national **public holidays** listed on below, banks, government offices, and many museums are liable to be closed all day. Small stores, as well as some restaurants and clubs, are usually closed as well,

but shopping malls, supermarkets, and department and chain stores increasingly remain open, regardless of the holiday. Most parks, beaches, and cemeteries stay open during holidays, too. Some tourist attractions, information centers, motels, and campground are only open during the traditional **tourist season**, from Memorial Day to Labor Day, though California's benign weather extends that considerably, and the desert areas have their peak season through the winter.

National holidays

New Year's Day Jan 1
Martin Luther King's Birthday observed third Mon in Jan
Presidents' Day third Mon in Feb
Memorial Day last Mon in May
Independence Day July 4
Labor Day first Mon in Sept
Columbus Day second Mon in Oct
Veterans' Day Nov 11
Thanksgiving fourth Thurs in Nov
Christmas Dec 25

Sports and outdoor pursuits

Nowhere in the country do the various forms of athletic activity and competition have a higher profile than in California. The big cities generally have at least one team in each of the major professional sports – football, baseball, and basketball – and support teams in soccer, volleyball, ice hockey, wrestling, and even roller derby.

For foreign visitors, American sports can appear something of a mystery; one unusual feature is that in all the major sports the divisions are fixed, apart from the occasional expansion, so there is no fear of relegation to lower leagues. Another puzzle is the passion for **intercollegiate sports** – college and university teams, competing against one another in the Pacific-10 Conference, usually with an enthusiasm fueled by passionate local rivalries. In Los Angeles, USC and UCLA have an intense and high-

powered sporting enmity, with fans on each side as vociferous as any European soccer crowd, and in the San Francisco Bay Area, the rivalry between UC Berkeley and Stanford is akin to that of Britain's Oxford and Cambridge.

And in California, where being physically fit and adventurous often appears to be a condition of state citizenship, the locals are passionate about their **outdoor pursuits**; the most popular include surfing, cycling, and skiing. When and where to enjoy any of California's most popular outdoor activities are detailed in the relevant chapters of the text, along with listings of guides and facilities.

Football

Professional football in America attracts the most obsessive and devoted fans of any sport, during its short season from September until the **Super Bowl** at the end of January.

The game lasts for four fifteen-minute quarters, with a fifteen-minute break at half-time. But since time is only counted when play is in progress, matches can take at least three hours to complete, mainly due to interruptions for TV advertising.

Teams and tickets

All major teams play in the National Football League (**NFL**; ⓦwww.nfl.com), the sport's governing body, which divides the teams into two conferences of equal stature, the National Football Conference (**NFC**) and the American Football Conference (**AFC**). In turn, each conference is split into four divisions, North, East, South, and West. For the end-of-season playoffs, the best team in each of the eight divisions, plus two wildcards from each conference, fight it out for the title.

The California teams are the **Oakland Raiders**, who have promised much but delivered little since being the last California team to reach the Super Bowl in 2003; the **San Diego Chargers**, who performed best of the three in 2006–7; and the **San Francisco 49ers**, who have recently been letting down the team's history of five Super Bowl wins (a record shared with the Dallas Cowboys and Pittsburgh Steelers).

Tickets usually cost at least $60 for professional games and can be very hard to come by, while college games can be as low as $10 and are more readily available – check at the respective campuses covered in the text.

Booking tickets

Oakland Raiders ☏1-800/724-3377, ⓦwww .raiders.com
San Diego Chargers ☏1-877/242-7437, ⓦwww.chargers.com

San Francisco 49ers ☏1-800/746-0764, ⓦwww.sf49ers.com

Baseball

Baseball is often called "America's pastime," though its continuing steroids scandals have somewhat tarnished its old-time image. Despite this, the sport's stars continue to earn a lot of publicity, not to mention money.

Games are played – 162 each in the regular season – all over the US almost every day from April to September, with the division and league championship playoffs, followed by the **World Series** (the best-of-seven match-up between the American and National League champions), lasting through October.

Teams and tickets

All major league (ⓦwww.mlb.com) baseball teams play in either the **National League** or the **American League**, each of equal stature and split into three divisions, East, Central, and West. For the end-of-season playoffs and the World Series, the best team in each of the six divisions plus a second-place wildcard from each league fight it out for the title. The 2002 Giants v Angels World Series was unique in being the first time both leagues' wildcards had reached the final stage but since then no California outfit has reached the showpiece event.

California's other major-league clubs are the **Oakland Athletics (A's)**, **Los Angeles Dodgers**, and **San Diego Padres**. There are also numerous minor-league clubs, known as farm teams because they supply the top clubs with talent. Tickets for games cost $10–70 per seat, and are generally available on the day of the game.

Booking tickets

Anaheim Angels ☏1-888/796-4256, ⓦwww .angelsbaseball.com
Los Angeles Dodgers ☏1-866/363-4377, ⓦwww.dodgers.com
Oakland Athletics ☏1-877/493-2255, ⓦwww .oaklandathletics.com
San Diego Padres ☏1-877/374-2784, ⓦwww .padres.com
San Francisco Giants ☏1-877/483-4849, ⓦwww.sfgiants.com

Basketball

Basketball is one of the few professional sports that is also actually played by many ordinary Americans, since all you need is a ball and a hoop. The men's professional game is governed by the National Basketball Association (**NBA**; ⓦ www.nba.com), which oversees a season running from November until the playoffs in June. Games last for an exhausting 48 minutes of actual playing time, around two hours total.

The women's professional game is run by the **WNBA**; the season goes through the summer.

Teams and tickets

California's professional men's basketball teams consist of the **Los Angeles Lakers**, the **Golden State Warriors** (who play in Oakland), the **Sacramento Kings**, and the **Los Angeles Clippers**. After winning the first three championships of the millennium, the historically most successful Lakers have gradually declined, while the Warriors made an unexpected run to the second round of the playoffs in 2007. LA's **UCLA** once dominated the college game, winning national championships throughout the 1960s; they emerged to win again in 1995. **USC**, **UC Berkeley**, and **Stanford** also field perpetually competitive intercollegiate teams, the last being the predominant force in the Pac-10 athletic conference in recent years.

Local **women's basketball teams** (ⓦ www.wnba.com) are in LA and Sacramento; tickets (beginning at about $10) are much more reasonable than the $50-plus for a decent seat at the men's game.

Tickets for NBA teams

Golden State Warriors ☎ 1-888/479-4667, ⓦ www.nba.com/warriors
Los Angeles Clippers ☎ 1-888/895-8662, ⓦ www.nba.com/clippers
Los Angeles Lakers ☎ 1-800/462-2849, ⓦ www.nba.com/lakers
Sacramento Kings ☎ 916/928-3650, ⓦ www.nba.com/kings

Tickets for WNBA teams

Los Angeles Sparks ☎ 310/330-2434, ⓦ www.wnba.com/sparks

Sacramento Monarchs ☎ 916/419-9622, ⓦ www.wnba.com/monarchs

Ice hockey

Despite California's sun-and-sand reputation, **ice hockey** enjoys considerable popularity in the state, although most of the players are imported from more traditionally hockey-centric regions in Canada, Eastern Europe, and Scandinavia. The domestic title is the **Stanley Cup**, contested by the playoff winners of the two **NHL** (National Hockey League; ⓦ www.nhl.com) conferences (Eastern and Western).

The season runs from October to June and, amazingly for such a fast and physical sport, each team plays several times a week.

Teams and tickets

California boasts three NHL teams which manage to draw considerable crowds. The **San Jose Sharks** sell out nearly every game and regularly reach the playoffs, and the **Anaheim Mighty Ducks** came from nowhere to reach the Stanley Cup final in 2003 and win it in 2007, comprehensively thumping the Ottawa Senators. The **Los Angeles Kings** complete the trio. Tickets start at about $25.

Booking tickets

Anaheim Mighty Ducks ☎ 1-877/945-3946, ⓦ www.mightyducks.com
Los Angeles Kings ☎ 1-888/546-4752, ⓦ www.lakings.com
San Jose Sharks ☎ 1-800/755-5050, ⓦ www.sj-sharks.com

Soccer

In the main, the traditional American sports rule, but **soccer** has been gaining some ground, especially as a participation sport for youngsters of both sexes. At the professional level, the successful US bid to host the 1994 World Cup led to the establishment of **Major League Soccer** (MLS; ⓦ www.mlsnet.com) in 1996, where twelve teams are divided into two conferences. The game continues to get injections of exposure, most recently with the signing of world-famous English star David Beckham by the Los Angeles Galaxy in 2007.

Teams and tickets

The **Los Angeles Galaxy** and Carson-based **Chivas USA**, a recent replacement for the defunct San Jose Clash, both play in the Western Conference of the MLS. The Galaxy have had some success in recent seasons, winning the MLS Cup in 2002 and 2005. The season runs through the summer and tickets cost $15–50.

Booking tickets

Chivas USA ☎1-877/244-8271, ⓦchivas.usa .mlsnet.com/t120
Los Angeles Galaxy ☎1-877/342-5299, ⓦwww .lagalaxy.com

Outdoor pursuits

Surfing is probably the best-known California pastime, immortalized in the songs of the Beach Boys and Frankie Avalon. The California coast up to a little north of San Francisco, especially the southern half, is dotted with excellent surfing beaches. Some of the finest places to catch a wave, with or without a board, are at Tourmaline Beach near San Diego, Huntington Beach and Malibu in Los Angeles, along the coast north of Santa Barbara, and at Santa Cruz – where there's a small but worthy surfing museum. **Windsurfing** is more commonly practiced on lakes and protected inland lagoons, as the ocean is usually too rough, and again there are plenty of places to hire a board or get lessons.

Cycling is an extremely popular outdoor activity, with California home to some highly competitive, world-class road races, particularly around Wine Country. The heavy-duty, all-terrain **mountain bike** was invented here, designed to tackle the slopes of Mount Tamalpais in Marin County. Weekend enthusiasts now put their knobby tires to use on the countless trails that weave throughout California's beautiful backcountry. Special mountain-bike parks, most operating in summer only, exploit the groomed, snow-free runs of the Sierra ski bowls of Lake Tahoe and Mammoth. In such places, and throughout California, you can rent bikes for $25–50 a day; see p.37 for more on general cycling.

Skiing and **snowboarding** are also wildly popular, with downhill resorts all over eastern California – where, believe it or not, it snows heavily most winters. In fact, the Sierra Nevada Mountains offer some of the best skiing in the US, particularly around Lake Tahoe (see p.653), where the 1960 Winter Olympics were held. You can rent equipment for about $30–40 a day, plus another $40 to $70 a day for lift tickets. A cheaper option is **cross-country skiing**, or ski-touring. A number of backcountry ski lodges in the Sierra Nevada offer a range of rustic accommodation, equipment rental, and lessons, from as little as $20 a day for skis, boots, and poles, up to about $200 for an all-inclusive weekend tour.

During the summer months, when the snows have melted and laid bare the crags of California's peaks, there is also a thriving **mountaineering** community, especially around Mount Shasta in the far north and in parts of the High Sierras. If you are not very experienced and do not have your own equipment, you can hire just about anything you might possibly need and get expert advice, lessons, or a guided expedition from numerous businesses that specialize in these areas.

California also has some of the world's best **rafting** rivers, most of which cascade off the western side of the Sierra Nevada. The majority are highly seasonal, normally rafted from mid-April to the end of June. Rivers and rapids are classed according to a grading system, ranging from a Class I, which is painstakingly easy, to a Class VI, which is literally dicing with death. Trips can be as short as a couple of hours, taking in the best a river has to offer (or just the most accessible section), or extend up to several days, allowing more time to hike up side canyons, swim, or just laze about on the bank. You might typically expect to pay around $100 for a four- to six-hour trip, going up to $160–200 a day for longer outings, including food and camping equipment rental. **Kayaking** is another popular water-based activity, both on the many rivers and, increasingly, in the ocean. Equipment rental starts at around $20 per hour, and can exceed $65 for longer, guided day-trips.

Other outdoor activities include both fresh and saltwater **fishing** – it's usually easier if you have your own gear but it can be rented in some places – and **horseback riding**.

Prices vary more widely than for other activities, ranging from $40 to $100 for rides that might not differ all that much in length, so it's a good idea to seek out the best deals in the places you will be visiting.

Finally, California offers virtually unlimited **hiking** opportunities, from coastal trails through dense forest paths to some stunning mountain ranges that are bound to test your stamina. All you need, of course, is stout footwear and to be prepared for the possibility of some drastic changes in the weather. Serious backcountry hiking is covered in the following section.

Backcountry camping and hiking

California's landscape is an enormously compelling reason to visit the state, with some of the most fabulous backcountry and wilderness areas in the US, coated by dense forests and capped by great mountains. While there are huge areas reachable only on foot, the excellent road system makes much of it easily accessible, aided by well-equipped and beautiful campgrounds right where you need them. Unfortunately, it isn't all as wild as it once was, and the more popular areas can get pretty crowded.

The US's protected backcountry areas fall into a number of potentially confusing categories. Most numerous are California **state parks** (Ⓦ www.parks.ca.gov), which include beaches, historic parks, and recreational areas, not necessarily in rural areas. Typically you pay for parking rather than entry, with daily fees usually $4–14, but you are unlikely to save money by buying the **"Golden Poppy" Annual Day-Use Pass** ($90) available online and at most parks.

In California, the San Francisco-based **Sierra Club** (Ⓣ 415/977-5500, Ⓦ www.sierraclub.org) offers a range of backcountry hikes into otherwise barely accessible parts of the High Sierra wilderness, with food and guide provided. The tours are mostly in the summer, and are heavily subscribed, making it essential to book at least three months in advance: check the website for availability and to make reservations. You can expect to pay at least $700 for seven days and will also have to pay $39 to join the club.

National parks – such as Yosemite, Death Valley, and Joshua Tree – generally charge entry fees of $15–20 per car (valid seven days). These are supplemented by the smaller **national monuments** (free to $5), like Devils Postpile, with just one major feature. If you plan on visiting a few of these, invest in the **America the Beautiful Annual Pass** ($80 from any national park entrance), which grants both driver and passengers (or if cycling or hiking, the holder's immediate family) twelve months' access to all the federally run parks and monuments, historic sites, recreation areas, and wildlife refuges across the country.

California's eighteen **national forests** cover twenty percent of the state's surface area. Most of them border the national parks and are less tightly regulated. The federal government also operates **national recreation areas**, often huge hydro dams where you can jet ski or windsurf free of the necessarily restrictive laws of the national parks. Campgrounds and equipment-rental outlets are always abundant. Excellent free **ranger programs** – guided walks, video presentations, and campfire talks – are held throughout the year.

All the above forms of protected land can contain **wilderness areas**, which aim to protect natural resources in their most native state. In practice, this means there's no commercial activity at all; buildings, motorized vehicles, and bicycles are not permitted, nor are firearms or pets. Overnight camping is allowed, but **wilderness permits** (usually free) must be obtained from the land management agency responsible. In California, Lava Beds, Lassen, Death Valley, Sequoia and Kings Canyon, Joshua Tree, Pinnacles, Point Reyes, and Yosemite all have large wilderness areas – 94 percent of Yosemite, for example – with only the regions near roads, visitor centers, and buildings designated as less stringently regulated "front country."

Backcountry camping

When **camping rough**, check that fires are permitted before you start one; in times of high fire danger, campfire permits (available free from park rangers) may be necessary even for cooking stoves. Stoves are preferable to local materials, since in some places firewood is scarce, although you may be allowed to use deadwood. No open fires are allowed in wilderness areas, where you should also try to camp on previously used sites. Where there are no toilets, **bury human waste** at least four inches into the ground and a hundred feet from the nearest water supply and camp. Always **pack out what you pack in** (or more if you come across some inconsiderate soul's litter), and avoid the old advice to burn rubbish; wildfires have been started in this way. A growing problem is giardia, a water-borne protozoan causing an intestinal disease, symptoms of which are chronic diarrhea, abdominal cramps, fatigue, and loss of weight. To avoid catching it, **never drink** directly from rivers and streams, no matter how clear and inviting they may look (you never know what unspeakable acts people – or animals – further upstream have performed in them). **Water** should be boiled for at least five minutes, or cleansed with an iodine-based purifier (such as Potable Aqua) or a giardia-rated filter, available from camping and sports shops.

Finally, don't use **soaps or detergents** (even special ecological or biodegradable soaps) anywhere near lakes and streams; people using water purifiers or filters downstream won't thank you at all. Instead carry water at least a hundred feet (preferably two hundred) from the water's edge before washing.

For more information on camping logistics, see p.40.

Camping equipment

Choose your tent wisely. Many Sierra sites are on rock with only a thin covering of soil, so driving pegs in can be a problem; freestanding dome-style tents are therefore preferable. Go for one with a large area of mosquito netting and a removable flysheet: tents designed for harsh European winters can get horribly sweaty once the California sun rises. In fact, traveling in summer you may seldom use a flysheet, as it rarely rains and little dew settles in the night.

Most developed campgrounds are equipped with fire rings with some form of grill for cooking, but many people prefer a **Coleman stove**, powered by white gas (a kind of super-clean gasoline). Both stoves and white gas (also used for MSR backcountry stoves) are widely available in camping stores. Other camping stoves are less common. Equipment using butane and propane – Camping Gaz and, to a lesser extent, EPI gas, Scorpion, and Optimus – is on the rise, though outside of major camping areas you'll be pushed to find supplies: stock up when you can. If you need methylated spirits for your Trangia, go to a hardware store and ask for denatured alcohol.

Be warned that **airlines** have a complete ban on transporting fuel and gas canisters, and are now extremely touchy about transporting stoves. Liquid fuel bottles and fuel pumps for MSR and similar stoves (even if empty, washed out, and virtually odorless) are routinely confiscated at check-in, so fly-in visitors are better bringing a gas burner and buying canisters once they arrive.

Hiking

No special permits are required for **day-hikes**. Simply front up at the trailhead of your choice with the appropriate gear – map, raincoat, comfortable boots, etc – and head

You'll probably meet many kinds of **wildlife** and come upon unexpected **hazards** on your travels through the wilderness, but only a few are likely to cause problems. With due care, many potential difficulties can be avoided. For more on California wildlife in general, see p.778 of Contexts.

Acute Mountain Sickness With much of the High Sierra above ten thousand feet, altitude sickness is always a possibility. Only those planning to bag one of the 14,000-foot peaks are likely to have to contend with much more than a slight headache, but it pays to be on the alert and to **acclimatize** slowly. Try to limit your exertions for the first day or so, drink plenty of fluids, eat little and often, and note any nausea, headaches, or double vision. If you experience any of these symptoms, the only solution is to descend until they ease, then ascend more gradually.

Bears Other than in a national park, you're highly unlikely to encounter a bear. Even there, it's rare to stumble across one in the wilderness, and if you do it will be a black bear – the last California grizzly was shot in 1922. To reduce the likelihood of an unwanted encounter, make noise as you walk. If you see a bear before it detects you (they've got fairly poor eyesight but an acute sense of smell), give it a wide berth; but if a bear visits your camp, scare it off by yelling and banging pots and pans. Basically, the bear isn't interested in you but in your food, and you should do everything you safely can to prevent them from getting it – bears who successfully raid campsites can become dependent on human food. Bears within state and national parks are protected, but if they spend too much time around people the park rangers are, depressingly, left with no option but to shoot them. Campgrounds in areas where bears are common come equipped with steel **bear lockers**, which you are obliged to use for storing food when not preparing or eating it. In the backcountry, you are strongly advised to store food within a hard plastic **bear-resistant food canister**. These can be purchased ($75) or rented (usually $5 per trip) from camp stores in Yosemite and Sequoia and Kings Canyon national parks. The alternatives are far inferior. Hanging food in a tree is a disaster, as Sierra bears simply chew through the supporting rope. The recommended variation is the counterbalance method (where food is balanced over a high tree branch in two equally weighted sacks on the opposite ends of a rope), but your chances of finding a suitable tree after a long day's hike are slim. Finally, never feed a bear or get between a mother and her cubs. Cubs are cute; irate mothers are not.

Cacti Most cacti present few problems, but you should keep an eye out for the eight-foot **cholla** (pronounced "choy-uh"), or jumping cholla as some are called, because of the way segments seem to jump off and attach themselves to you if you brush past. Don't use your hands to get them off – you'll just spear all your fingers. Instead, use a stick or comb to flick off the largest piece and remove the remaining spines with tweezers. The large pancake pads of prickly pear cactus are also worth avoiding: in addition to the larger spines, they have thousands of tiny, hair-like stickers that are almost impossible to remove. You should expect a day of painful irritation before they begin to wear away. For more on the delights of desert flora and fauna, see p.784 in Contexts.

Campground critters Ground squirrels, chipmunks, and raccoons are usually just a nuisance, though they tend to carry diseases and you should avoid contact. Only the **alpine marmot** is a real pest, as it likes to chew through radiator hoses and car electrics to reach a warm engine on a cold night. Before setting off in the morning from high-country trailheads, check under the hood for gnawed components; otherwise you might find yourself with a seized engine and a cooked or, at best, terrified marmot as a passenger. Boots and rucksacks also can fall prey to marmot scrutiny.

Drowning Fast-flowing meltwater rivers are the single biggest cause of death in Sequoia and Kings Canyon and are a danger elsewhere in the Sierra Nevada. The riverbanks are strewn with large, slippery boulders – keep well clear unless you are specifically there for river activities.

Mosquitoes Common around water, these insects are more pesky than dangerous. Cover up around dusk and carry insect repellent or candles scented with citronella to keep them at bay.

Mountain lions Also known as cougars, panthers, and pumas, these magnificent beasts are being hard hit by increasing urban expansion into former habitats (from deserts to coastal and subalpine forests). Sightings are rare, but to reduce the already small chance of an unwanted encounter, avoid walking by yourself, especially after dark, when lions tend to hunt. Make noise as you walk, wield a stick, and keep children close to you. If you encounter one, **don't run**. Instead, face the lion and make yourself appear larger by raising your arms or holding your coat above you, and it will probably back away. If not, throw rocks and sticks in its vicinity. If it attacks, fight back. Its normal prey doesn't do this and it will probably flee.

Poison oak This is one thing that isn't going to come and get you, though you may come up against it. Recognized by its shiny configuration of three dark-green-veined leaves (turning red or yellow in the fall) that secrete an oily juice, this twiggy shrub or climbing vine is found in open woods or along stream banks throughout much of California. It's highly **allergenic**, so avoid touching it. If you do, washing with strong soap usually helps, though you are better off applying an oil-removal product such as Tecnu as soon after contact as possible. In extreme cases, see a doctor.

Rattlesnakes In the desert areas and drier foothills up to around 6000ft you may come across rattlesnakes, which seldom attack unless provoked: do not tease or try to handle them. When it's hot, snakes lurk in shaded areas under bushes and around wood debris, old mining shafts, and piles of rocks. When it's cooler, they sun themselves out in the open, but they won't be expecting you and, if disturbed, may attack. When hiking, you'll be far better served by **strong boots** and long trousers than sport sandals and shorts. Not only do they offer some protection in case of attack, but firm footfalls send vibrations through the ground, giving ample warning of your approach. Walk heavily and you're unlikely to see anything you don't want to.

Rattlesnake **bites** are rarely fatal, but you might suffer severe tissue damage. If bitten, forget any misconceptions you may harbor about sucking the poison out – it doesn't work and even tends to hasten the spread of venom. The best way of inhibiting the diffusion is to wrap the whole limb firmly, but not in a tourniquet, then contact a ranger or doctor as soon as possible. Do all you can to keep calm – a slower pulse rate limits the spread of the venom. Keep in mind that even if a snake does bite you, about fifty percent of the time it's a dry – or non-venomous – strike: snakes don't want to waste their venom on something too large to eat.

Scorpions They're generally non-aggressive, but they are extremely venomous and easily disturbed.

Tarantulas These spiders are not at all dangerous. A leg span of up to seven inches means they're pretty easy to spot, but if you're unlucky and get bitten, don't panic – cleansing with antiseptic is usually sufficient treatment once you've gotten over the initial pain.

Ticks When hiking in the foothills you should periodically check your clothes for ticks – pesky, bloodsucking, burrowing insects that are known to carry Lyme disease. If you have been bitten, and especially if you get flu-like symptoms, get advice from a park ranger.

off into the wilderness. **Overnight trips** usually require **wilderness permits** (see p.51), which operate on a quota system in popular areas in peak periods. If there's a specific hike you want to take, obtain your permit well ahead of time (at least two weeks, more for popular hikes). Before completing the form for your permit, be sure to ask a park ranger for weather conditions

and general information about the hike you're undertaking.

Hikes covered in the guide are given with length and estimated walking time for a healthy, but not especially fit, adult. **State parks** have graded trails designed for people who drive to the corner store, so anyone used to walking and with a moderate degree of fitness will find their ratings conservative.

Shopping

Not surprisingly, the richest state in the land of rampant consumerism is something of a shopper's paradise and, especially in the two major metropolises, you'll be able to find just about anything your heart may desire. That said, California cannot really boast a wealth of intrinsically Californian souvenirs to take home, beyond the obvious mini Golden Gate Bridges and ironic LA snowglobes found in the tackier tourist shops. Details of specific shopping locations are given throughout the guide but here is a general indication of what you are likely to come across.

The mall

Visitors to California, especially on their first visit to the US, cannot fail to be impressed by the ubiquitousness of the ultimate American shopping venue, the mall. Whether these are of the **"strip mall"** variety, strung out along major arteries on the edges of most towns, or showpiece complexes in desirable neighborhoods, they unabashedly glorify commercialism and consist mostly of well-known multinational chains. The summit of consumer excess is Rodeo Drive in Beverly Hills, where the Hollywood stars go to shop. Many chic designers have flagship boutiques on the strip, and menswear merchant Bijan, at no. 420, claims to be the most expensive shop in the world, with the average customer dropping $100,000 at one visit.

Arts and crafts

California is home to many **artists** and their paintings, sculptures, and other creations can easily be found, both in big city galleries

and in smaller communities with a reputation for creativity, such as Mendocino. Being original artworks, these will set you back a fair penny, maybe even thousands of bucks, depending on how established the artist is. Quaint gift shops selling attractive items from all over the world also abound and are a good source of souvenirs and presents, even if they are not specifically local. Some places like the Gold Country towns do offer more indigenous goods, as do the few Indian reservations.

Books and music

There is a strong intellectual tradition in the state, which shows in its manifold quality **bookshops**. The most famous browsing territory is around UC Berkeley, but all the large cities and quite a few small towns offer lots of reading material. Likewise, the state that spawned psychedelia and other musical trends is rich in music shops, both for listening material and quality instruments. The three branches of Amoeba Records in

Clothing and shoe sizes

Women's dresses and skirts

American	4	6	8	10	12	14	16	18	
British	8	10	12	14	16	18	20	22	
Continental	38	40	42	44	46	48	50	52	

Women's blouses and sweaters

American	6	8	10	12	14	16	18	
British	30	32	34	36	38	40	42	
Continental	40	42	44	46	48	50	52	

Women's shoes

American	5	6	7	8	9	10	11	
British	3	4	5	6	7	8	9	
Continental	36	37	38	39	40	41	42	

Men's suits

American	34	36	38	40	42	44	46	48	
British	34	36	38	40	42	44	46	48	
Continental	44	46	48	50	52	54	56	58	

Men's shirts

American	14	15	15.5	16	16.5	17	17.5	18	
British	14	15	15.5	16	16.5	17	17.5	18	
Continental	36	38	39	41	42	43	44	45	

Men's shoes

American	7	7.5	8	8.5	9.5	10	10.5	11	11.5
British	6	7	7.5	8	9	9.5	10	11	12
Continental	39	40	41	42	43	44	44	45	46

Berkeley, San Francisco, and LA are among the biggest and best in the world. Areas strong on books and music also tend to inspire related alternative shopping possibilities, with anti-establishment and political T-shirts, posters, and so on readily available.

Farmers' markets, food, and drink

One fine tradition that has survived since more rustic times is the "farmers' market," examples of which pop up regularly in the metropolitan areas, as well as in the state's smaller towns. It can come as a pleasant surprise to stumble on a street full of stalls selling fresh country fare in the middle of Downtown Oakland, for example. Most concentrate solely on consumable goods, but the larger ones may have a few gift stalls as well.

California's famous **wineries** are not only great for tastings (see pp.681–692) – you can also take away a couple of bottles for a special occasion or even get a case shipped abroad, though complicated laws mean not all companies are allowed to do so. If you've come by road from within the US, you can, of course, do the hauling yourself. Meanwhile, other seasonal and specialty **produce** proliferates in certain locales, such as olives in Corning and artichokes in Moss Landing.

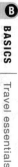

Travel essentials

Costs

Despite the relatively weak US dollar, the United States remains a fairly expensive place to travel and, with its large urban population, California is one of the pricier states. It is true that car rental, gas, clothes, and consumer goods are usually somewhat cheaper than in Western Europe and Australasia, but the benefit is often less than it seems once you've factored in the additional sales tax or added the cost of rental-car insurance. Eating and drinking seem a bargain (and fast-food joints are), but in more upscale establishments you'll be adding close to 25 percent to your expected total to cover taxes and tips. It soon mounts up.

For museums and similar attractions, the prices we quote are generally for adults; you can assume that **children** (typically aged from 5 to 12 or 14) get in for half-price. Generally youth and **student cards** are of little benefit; take it if you have one, but don't make any special effort to get one.

Daily costs vary enormously, and the following estimates are per person for two people traveling together. If you are on a tight budget, using public transportation, camping or staying in hostels, and cooking most of your own meals, you could scrape by on $40 a day. A couple renting a car, staying in budget motels, and eating out a fair bit are looking at more like $80–100 per person. Step up to comfortable B&Bs, nicer restaurants, and a few whale watching trips and shows, and you can easily find yourself spending $200 a day.

Remember that a **sales tax** is added to virtually everything you buy except for groceries and prescription drugs; it is seldom included in the quoted price. The base rate is 7.25 percent, but some counties exact an additional tax of half to one percent. In addition, a bed tax is sometimes levied, so hotel rooms usually cost 10–12 percent more than the quoted price.

Tipping adds a further 15–17 percent to the bill in restaurants and elsewhere (see p.57).

Crime and personal safety

Though California isn't trouble-free, you're unlikely to have any run-ins if you stick to the tourist-friendly confines of the major cities, or most rural areas. The lawless reputation of Los Angeles is far in excess of the truth; at night, though, a few areas – notably Compton, Inglewood, and East LA – are off-limits. San Francisco, too, has its pockets of **crime** and decay, especially around the South of Market area. But by being careful, planning ahead, and taking care of your possessions, you should be able to avoid any problems.

Mugging and theft

If you're unlucky enough to get mugged, just hand over your money; resistance is generally not a good idea. After the crime occurs, immediately report it to the police at ☎911 so you can later attempt to recover your loss from an insurance provider – unlikely, but worth a try. One prime spot to be mugged is at an ATM outside the tourist areas, where you may be told to make the maximum withdrawal and hand it over. Needless to say, you should treat ATM use with the strictest caution and not worry about looking paranoid.

Also, keep a record of the numbers of your **travelers' checks** separately from the actual checks; if you lose them, ring the issuing company. They'll ask you for the check numbers, the place you bought them, when and how you lost them, and whether it's been reported to the police. All being well, you should get the missing checks reissued within a couple of days.

If your **passport** is stolen (or if you lose it), call your country's consulate (see list on p.59) and pick up or have sent to you an application form, which you must submit with a notarized photocopy of your ID and a reissuing fee, often at least $30.

Car crime and safety

Though crimes committed against tourists driving rental cars are rare, you should still exercise common sense. Keep doors locked and hide valuables out of sight, either in the trunk or the glove compartment, and leave any valuables you don't need for your journey back in your hotel safe. If your car breaks down at night while on a major street, activate the emergency flashers to signal a police officer for assistance. During the day, find the nearest phone book and call for a tow truck. Should you be forced to stop your car on a freeway, pull over to the right shoulder – never the left – and activate your flashers. Wait for assistance either in your vehicle, while strapped in by a seatbelt, or on a safe embankment nearby.

Breaking the law

Aside from speeding or parking violations, one of the most common ways visitors accidentally break the law is through jaywalking, or crossing the road against red lights or away from intersections. Fines can be stiff, and the police will most assuredly not take sympathy on you if you mumble that you "didn't think it was illegal."

Alcohol laws provide another source of irritation to visitors, particularly as the law prohibits drinking liquor, wine, or beer in most public spaces like parks and beaches, and, most frustrating of all to European tourists, alcohol is officially off-limits to anyone under 21. Some try to get around this with a phony driver's license, even though getting caught with a **fake ID** will put you in jeopardy particularly if you're from out of the country. Driving under the influence, or **drunk driving**, is aggressively punished throughout the state, with loss of license, fines, and potential jail time for those caught breaking the law with a police-enforced "Breathalyzer" test. The current limit is a blood-alcohol level of .08, or three drinks within a single hour for a 150-pound person.

The same is true for misdemeanor **marijuana possession**, which some locals chance for amounts under an ounce, and which may get foreign visitors thrown out of the country – or into jail for larger amounts or for any other narcotics. Other infringements include **insulting a police officer** (ie arguing with one) and **riding a bicycle at night** without proper lights and reflectors.

Culture and etiquette

In the national consciousness, California exists as a kind of **liberal enclave** where leftist, neo-hippy ethics, gay culture, and minority rights hold sway. In some areas – particularly San Francisco – this is largely true, but elsewhere it is far from the case. Some areas can seem as reactionary as anywhere else in the US and guns, pickup trucks, and redneck values are as prevalent as global perception would have you believe (the Governator is, of course, a Republican).

In addition to these general observations, there are also a few practical points that warrant a mention. For starters, some form of **picture ID** should be carried at all times. A driver's license will probably do the trick, though having a passport as well should diffuse any suspicion.

One point of eternal discussion is **tipping**. Many workers in service industries get paid very little and rely on tips to bolster their income. Unless you've had abominable service (in which case you should tell the management), you really shouldn't leave a bar or restaurant without leaving a tip of at least **fifteen percent**, and about the same should be added to taxi fares. A hotel porter deserves roughly $1 for each bag carried to your room; a coatcheck clerk should receive the same per coat. When paying by credit card you're expected to add the tip to the total bill before filling in the amount and signing.

Smoking is a much frowned-upon activity in California, which has banned it in all indoor public places, including bars and restaurants. In fact, you can spend weeks in the state barely ever smelling cigarette smoke. Nevertheless, cigarettes are sold in virtually any food shop, drugstore, or bar, and also from the occasional vending machine. Of course, **drugs** are illegal but widespread.

Electricity

The US operates on 110V at 60Hz and uses two-pronged plugs with the flat prongs parallel. Foreign devices will need both a plug adapter and a transformer, though laptops and phone chargers usually automatically detect and cope with the different voltage and frequency.

Entry requirements

Keeping up with the constant changes to **US entry requirements** since 9/11 can sometimes feel like a hopeless task. At least once a year the American government announces new, often harsher, restrictions on foreign entry into the country, adding considerably to the red tape involved in visiting it. Nonetheless, there are several **basic rules** that apply to these requirements, which are detailed (and should be frequently checked for updates) on the US State Department website (⊛ travel.state.gov).

Under the **Visa Waiver Program (VWP)**, if you're a citizen of the UK, Ireland, Australia, New Zealand, most western European states, or other selected countries like Singapore, Japan, and Brunei (27 in all), and visiting the US for less than ninety days, at a minimum you'll need an onward or return ticket, a visa waiver form, and a Machine Readable Passport (MRP). MRPs issued before October 2005 are acceptable to use on their own; those issued from October 2005 to October 2006 must include a digital photograph of the passport holder; and those issued after October 2006 require a high-tech security chip built into the passport. It is up to the various countries covered by the Visa Waiver Program to provide such passports to their citizens; for more information, inquire at American embassies or consulates.

The **I-94W Nonimmigrant Visa Waiver Arrival/Departure Form** will be provided either by your travel agency or embassy or when you board the plane, and must be presented to Immigration on arrival. The same form covers entry across the US borders with Canada and Mexico (for non-Canadian and non-Mexican citizens). If you're in the Visa Waiver Program and intend to work, study, or stay in the country for more than ninety days, you must apply for a **regular visa** through your local US embassy or consulate. You will not be admitted under the VWP if you've ever been arrested (not just convicted), have a criminal record, or have been previously deported from or refused entry to the US. Under no circumstances are visitors who have been admitted under the Visa Waiver Program allowed to extend their stays beyond ninety days. Doing so will bar you from future use of the program.

Canadian citizens, who have not always needed a passport to get into the US, should have their passports on them when entering the country. If you're planning to stay for more than ninety days you'll need a **visa**, which can be applied for by mail through the US embassy or nearest US consulate. If you cross the US border by car, be prepared for Customs officials to search your vehicle. Remember, too, that without the proper paperwork, Canadians are barred from working in the US.

Citizens of **all other countries** should contact their local US embassy or consulate for details of current entry requirements, as they are often required to have both a valid passport and a nonimmigrant visitor's visa. To obtain such a visa, complete the application form available through your local American embassy or consulate and send it with the appropriate fee, two photographs, and a passport. Beyond this, you can expect **additional hassles** to get a visa, including one or more in-depth interviews, supplemental applications for students and "high-risk" travelers, and long delays in processing time. Visas are not issued to convicted criminals, those with ties to radical political groups, and visitors from countries identified by the State Department as being "state sponsors of terrorism" (eg North Korea, Iran, etc). Complications also arise if you are HIV positive or have TB, hepatitis, or other communicable diseases, or have previously been denied entry to the US for any reason. Furthermore, the US government now electronically fingerprints most visitors and applies spot background checks looking for evidence of past criminal or terrorist ties.

For further information or to get a **visa extension** before your time is up, contact the nearest US Citizenship and Immigration Service office, whose address will be at the front of the phone book under the Federal Government Offices listings, or call ☎1-800/877-3676. You can also contact the

National Customer Service Center at ☎1-800/375-5283. Immigration officials will assume that you're working in the US illegally, and it's up to you to prove otherwise. If you can, bring along an upstanding American citizen to vouch for you, and be prepared for potentially hostile questioning.

US embassies and consulates abroad

Australia

Embassy Canberra: 21 Moonah Place, Yarralumla ACT 2600 ☎02/6214 5600, ⓦcanberra.usembassy.gov
Consulates Melbourne: 553 St Kilda Rd, VIC 3004 ☎03/9526 5900
Perth: 16 St George's Terrace, 13th Floor, WA 6000 ☎08/9202 1224
Sydney: MLC Centre, Level 10, 19–29 Martin Place, NSW 2000 ☎02/9373 9200

Canada

Embassy Ottawa: 490 Sussex Drive, ON K1N 1G8 ☎613/238-5331, ⓦcanada.usembassy.gov
Consulates Calgary: 615 Macleod Trail SE, Room 1000, AB T2G 4T8 ☎403/266-8962
Halifax: Wharf Tower II, 1969 Upper Water St, Suite 904, NS B3J 3R7 ☎902/429-2480
Montréal: 1155 St Alexandre St, QC H3B 1Z1 ☎514/398-9695, ⓦmontreal.usconsulate.gov
Québec City: 2 Place Terrasse Dufferin, QC G1R 4T9 ☎418/692-2095, ⓦquebec.usconsulate.gov
Toronto: 360 University Ave, ON M5G 1S4 ☎416/595-1700, ⓦtoronto.usconsulate.gov
Vancouver: 1095 W Pender St, 21st Floor, BC V6E 2M6 ☎604/685-4311, ⓦvancouver.usconsulate.gov
Winnipeg: 201 Portage Ave, Suite 860, MB R3B 3K6 ☎204/940-1800, ⓦwww.usconsulatewinnipeg.ca

Ireland

Embassy Dublin: 42 Elgin Rd, Ballsbridge 4 ☎01/668 8777, ⓦdublin.usembassy.gov

New Zealand

Embassy Wellington: 29 Fitzherbert Terrace, Thorndon ☎04/462 6000, ⓦnewzealand.usembassy.gov
Consulate Auckland: 3rd Floor, Citibank Building, 23 Customs St ☎09/303 2724

South Africa

Embassy Pretoria: 877 Pretorius St 0083 ☎12/431 4000, Ⓕ12/342 2299, ⓦusembassy.state.gov/pretoria

UK

Embassy London: 24 Grosvenor Square, W1A 1AE ☎020/7499 9000, visa hotline ☎09042/450 100, ⓦlondon.usembassy.gov
Consulates Belfast: Danesfort House, 223 Stranmillis Road, Belfast BT9 5GR ☎028/9038 6100
Edinburgh: 3 Regent Terrace, EH7 5BW ☎0131/556 8315

Consulates in California

Australia

Los Angeles 2049 Century Park E, 19th Floor, CA 90067 ☎310/229-4800, ⓦwww.dfat.gov.au/missions
San Francisco 575 Market St, Suite 1800, CA 94105-2815 ☎415/536-1970

Canada

Los Angeles 550 S Hope St, 9th Floor, CA 90071-2627 ☎213/346-2700, Ⓕ213/620-8827, ⓦwww.dfait-maeci.gc.ca
San Diego 402 W Broadway, 4th Floor, CA 92101 ☎619/615-4287, Ⓕ619/615-4286
San Francisco 580 California St, 14th Floor, CA 94104 ☎415/834-3180, Ⓕ415/834-3189

South Africa

Los Angeles 6300 Wilshire Blvd, Suite 600, CA 90048 ☎323/651-0902, Ⓕ323/651-5969, ⓦwww.link2southafrica.com

UK

Los Angeles 11766 Wilshire Blvd, Suite 1200, CA 90025 ☎310/481-0031, Ⓕ481-2960, ⓦwww.britainusa.com/la
San Francisco 1 Sansome St, Suite 850, CA 94101 ☎415/617-1300, Ⓕ415/434-2018, ⓦwww.britainusa.com/sf

Gay and lesbian travelers

California's easy-going attitude is evident in its vibrant gay and lesbian scene. The heart of gay California (and, arguably, of gay America) is San Francisco, which has been almost synonymous with gay life since World War II, when suspected homosexuals, purged by the military at their point of embarkation, stayed put rather than going home to face stigma and shame. This, and the advent of gay liberation in the early 1970s, nurtured a community with powerful political and social connections.

San Francisco's gay, lesbian, bisexual, and transgender scene is easy to find, but there are also strong communities in Los Angeles, centered in **West Hollywood**, **Palm Springs**, and **Santa Cruz**, which has become something of a lesbian enclave in recent years. Be aware, though, that outside major urban centers and particularly in the deserts of interior California, attitudes may be more conservative and openness about your sexuality may provoke uneasiness in locals.

Health

Foreign travelers should be comforted that if you have a serious accident while you're in California, emergency services will get to you sooner and charge you later. For emergencies, dial toll-free ☏911 from any phone. If you have medical or dental problems that don't require an ambulance, most hospitals will have a walk-in emergency room: for your nearest hospital or dental office, check with your hotel or dial information at ☏411.

Should you need to see a **doctor**, lists can be found in the *Yellow Pages* under "Clinics" or "Physicians and Surgeons." Be aware that even consultations are costly, usually around $75–100 each visit, which is payable in advance. Keep receipts for any part of your medical treatment, including prescriptions, so that you can claim against your insurance once you're home.

For minor ailments, stop by a local **pharmacy**, many of which are open 24 hours. Foreign visitors should note that many medicines available over the counter at home – codeine-based painkillers, for one – are **prescription-only** in the US. Bring additional supplies if you're particularly brand-loyal.

By far the most common tourist illness in California is **sunburn**: south of Santa Barbara and in the state's interior, the summer sun can be fierce, so plenty of protective sunscreen (SPF 15 and above) is a must. Surfers and swimmers should also watch for strong currents and **undertows** at some beaches: we've noted in the text where the water can be especially treacherous. Note that despite the media's frenzied circling around stories of man-eating **sharks**, it's still a blip on beach safety compared with sunburn and swimming difficulties.

Insurance

Even though EU healthcare privileges apply in America, UK residents would do well to take out an insurance policy before traveling to cover against theft, loss, and illness or injury.

A typical **travel insurance policy** usually provides cover for the loss of baggage, tickets, and – up to a certain limit – cash or checks, as well as cancellation or curtailment of your journey. Most of them exclude so-called dangerous sports unless an extra premium is paid: in America, this can mean scuba diving, whitewater rafting, windsurfing, and trekking, though probably not kayaking or jeep safaris. If you take medical coverage, ascertain whether benefits will be paid as treatment proceeds or only after return home, and if there is a 24-hour medical emergency number. When securing **baggage cover**, make sure that the per-article limit – typically under £500 – will cover your most valuable possession. If you need to make a claim, you should keep receipts for medicines and medical treatment, and in the event you have anything stolen, you must obtain an official theft report from the police.

Rough Guides has teamed up with Columbus Direct to offer you travel insurance that can be tailored to suit your needs. Products include a low-cost **backpacker** option for long stays; a **short break** option for city getaways; a typical **holiday package** option; and others. There are also annual **multitrip** policies for those who travel regularly. Different sports and activities (trekking, skiing, etc) can usually be covered if required. See our website (☏www .roughguides.com/insurance) for eligibility and purchasing options. Alternatively, UK residents should call ☏0870/033 9988, Australians ☏1300/669 999, and New Zealanders ☏0800/55 99 11. All other nationalities should call ☏+44 870/890 2843.

For information on rental car insurance, see p.35.

Internet

The spread of **wireless hotspots** all over the state means anyone traveling with a WiFi–enabled laptop or PDA should have no trouble getting connected, often at blisteringly fast speeds at no cost. At some cafés (notably the ubiquitous *Starbucks*) you'll need to use your credit card to sign up for a service, though many other cafés have unsecured access or will give you the password when you buy a coffee or muffin. Many libraries have free WiFi, as do lots of motels and even restaurants.

If you need to borrow a computer to log on, the best bets are **public libraries**, which almost invariably have **free Internet access**, usually available for an hour a day – just ask at the front desk. You may have to wait for an opening, or sign up for a later slot. Espresso **cafés** are another good bet. You'll sometimes find a couple of computers in the corner for which there'll be a small charge, though these are becoming increasingly rare as places have taken out their machines when they've installed a WiFi network. You'll also come across dedicated **cyber cafés** with a dozen or more machines usually charged at around $5 an hour. Many motels, hotels, and hostels also offer Internet access with a machine or two in the lobby, but again, WiFi is taking over.

If you are traveling with a **laptop** and want to get connected, visit ⓦwww.kropla.com, which gives details of how to plug your laptop in when abroad, phone country codes around the world, and information about electrical systems in different countries.

Laundry

The larger hotels provide a laundry service at a price. Cheaper motels and hostels may have self-service laundry facilities, but in general you'll be doing your laundry at a laundromat. Found all over the place, they're usually open fairly long hours and have a powder-dispensing machine and another to provide change. A typical wash and dry might cost $4–6.

Mail

Post offices are usually open Monday through Friday from 9am to 5pm and Saturday from 9am to the early afternoon, and there are blue **mailboxes** on many street corners. **Ordinary mail** within the US costs 41¢ for letters weighing up to an ounce; addresses must include the zip code, which can be found at ⓦwww.usps.com. The return address should be written in the upper left corner of the envelope.

Airmail from California to Europe generally takes about a week. Letters weighing up to an ounce (a couple of sheets) cost 84¢, and postcards cost 75¢ (63¢ to Canada and 55¢ to Mexico).

Letters can be sent c/o **General Delivery** (what's known elsewhere as poste restante) to the one relevant post office in each city, but must include the zip code and will only be held for thirty days before being returned to sender – so make sure there's a return address on the envelope. If you're receiving mail at someone else's address, it should include "c/o" and the regular occupant's name, or it may be returned.

Rules on sending **parcels** are very rigid: packages must be sealed according to the instructions given at the start of the *Yellow Pages*. To send anything out of the country, you'll need a green **customs declaration form**, available from the post office. Postal rates for airmailing a parcel weighing up to 1lb to Europe, Australia, and New Zealand are $14–18.

Maps

Rough Guides produce an excellent double-sided, rip-proof Map of California ($10), which has all the sights and most useful campgrounds marked. With that, the maps in this book, and free maps supplied by local tourist offices, you can't go far wrong.

Rand McNally produces a good low-cost foldout map of the state ($4.95) and its Road Atlas ($10), covering the whole country plus Mexico and Canada, is a worthwhile investment if you're traveling further afield. For **driving or cycling** through rural areas, the *Atlas & Gazetteer: Northern California* and *Atlas & Gazetteer: Southern California* ($19.95 each; published by DeLorme, ⓦwww.delorme.com) are valuable companions, with detailed city plans, marked campground, and reams of national park and forest information.

The **American Automobile Association** (ⓦwww.aaa-calif.com) has offices in most large cities and provides excellent free maps and travel assistance to its members, and members of affiliated organizations elsewhere.

Hikers should visit ranger stations in parks and wilderness areas, which all sell good-quality local topographic maps for around $6–10. Camping stores generally have a good selection, too. The *National Geographic/Trails Illustrated* topographic maps ($8–10) are particularly good and cover such destinations as Sequoia and Kings Canyon, Yosemite, Death Valley, and Joshua Tree national parks and Santa Monica Mountains National Recreation Area.

Money

US banknotes (typically $1, $5, $10, $20, $50, and $100) are all the same color and size so be sure to check what you are handing over; anyone frequently dealing with money usually states the denomination of the bill they have just received. Revamped $10 and $20 bills have a faint orange tinge intended to foil counterfeiters. The dollar is made up of 100 cents with coins of 1 cent (known as a penny, and regarded as worthless), 5 cents (a nickel), 10 cents (a dime), and 25 cents (a quarter). Quarters are very useful for buses, vending machines, parking meters, and telephones, so always carry plenty.

If you don't already have a **credit card**, you should think seriously about getting one before you set off. For many services, it's simply taken for granted that you'll be paying with plastic. When renting a car (or even a bike) or checking into a hotel, you may well be asked to show a credit card to establish your creditworthiness – even if you intend to settle the bill in cash. **Visa**, **MasterCard**, **Diners Club**, **American Express**, and **Discover** are the most widely used. When paying with a credit card, you'll sometimes be required to show supporting photo ID, so be sure to carry your driver's license or passport.

It is worth carrying a second major credit card as a backup, but you may feel more comfortable with a wad of **US dollar**

Current exchange rates

Australian dollar = 83¢
British pound = $2
Canadian dollar = 90¢
Euro = $1.36
New Zealand dollar = 74¢
South African rand = 14¢

travelers' checks, which will be replaced if lost or stolen. You should have no problem using the better-known checks, such as American Express and Visa, in the same way as cash in shops, restaurants, and gas stations. Be sure to have plenty of the $10 and $20 denominations for everyday transactions, and don't be put off by "no checks" signs, which only refer to personal checks.

With credit cards, cash cards, and travelers' checks, you may never need to visit **banks**, which are generally open from 9am until 5pm Monday to Thursday and 9am to 6pm on Friday, and sometimes on Saturday morning. Some banks in major towns will change major **foreign currency**, but it is far better to buy US dollars before you arrive. Credit card **cash advances** and debit card withdrawals are easy at abundant **ATMs**, though there is sometimes a transaction fee of $2–3.

Phones

Despite downsizing in this time of ubiquitous mobiles, **public phones** are generally plentiful: local calls mostly cost 50¢, and any number prefixed by 1-800/, 1-888/, 1-877/, or 1-866/ is free (as well as from landlines, though cell phones will incur normal charges). Some numbers covered by the same area code are considered so far apart that calls between them count as non-local ("zone calls") and cost much more. Pricier still are long-distance calls (ie to a different area code and always preceded by a 1), for which you'll need plenty of change. Rates are much cheaper using **phone cards** – typically in denominations of $5, $10, and $20 – bought from general stores and some hostels. There are many brands, some quoting long-distance rates as low as 5¢ a minute, but beware of the 50¢ connection fee only mentioned in the fine print. Making telephone calls from **hotel rooms** is usually more expensive than from a payphone, though many hotels offer free local calls from rooms – ask when you check in.

One of the most convenient ways of phoning home from California is via a **telephone charge card** from your phone company back home. Calls made from most hotel, public, and private phones will be charged to your account. Since most major charge cards are free to obtain, it's certainly worth getting one at least for emergencies;

but bear in mind that rates aren't necessarily cheaper than calling from a public phone.

Of course, almost everyone has a **mobile phone** ("cell phone" in US parlance), and with excellent reception in all but the remotest areas, taking your phone to California makes a lot of sense. Ask your provider to confirm that your phone will work on US frequencies (most do these days) and get it set up for international use. **Roaming** calling rates can be pretty high and if you're planning to make a lot of calls it may work out cheaper to **buy a phone** in California, though the lower cost is counterbalanced by the need to tell all your friends your new phone number. Basic, new phones can be picked up for as little as $30; it is probably most convenient to go for a pre pay service, which you can top up as you go.

All providers have good **coverage** in the more populated areas, but if you are spending a lot of time in the national parks and deserts, go with one of the companies with the widest networks, such as Verizon (ⓦwww .verizonwireless.com) or AT&T (ⓦwww.att .com). Note that in the US you are charged for both sending and receiving calls.

Calling home from California

Australia 00 + 61 + city code
Canada 1 + area code
New Zealand 00 + 64 + city code
UK and Northern Ireland 00 + 44 + city code
Republic of Ireland 00 + 353 + city code
South Africa 00+ 27 + city code

Useful numbers

Emergencies ☏911; ask for the appropriate emergency service: fire, police, or ambulance.
Directory information ☏411
Directory inquiries for toll-free numbers ☏1-800/555-1212
Long-distance directory information ☏1- (area code)/555-1212
International operator ☏00

Photography

With fabulous scenery and great light much of the time, California is a photographer's paradise. Bring plenty of digital memory or be prepared to periodically visit photo shops and burn your images onto CD. As ever, try to shoot in the early morning and late afternoon when the lower-angled light casts deeper shadows and gives greater depth to your shots. Wildlife is also more active at these times.

It is never a good idea to take photos of **military installations** and the like, and with the current heightened security, airports and some government buildings may be considered sensitive.

Senior travelers

Seniors are defined broadly in the US as anyone older than 55 to 65 years of age. Those traveling can regularly find discounts of anywhere from ten to fifty percent at movie theaters, museums, hotels, restaurants, performing arts venues, and the occasional shop. On Amtrak, they can get a 15% discount on most regular fares, and 10% off the purchase of a North America Rail Pass. On Greyhound the discount is smaller, in the range of five to ten percent. If heading to a national park, don't miss the America the Beautiful Senior Pass, which, when bought at a park for a mere $10, provides a lifetime of free entry to federally operated recreation sites, as well as half-priced discounts on concessions such as boat launches and camping. In California, low-income seniors can apply for a Golden Bear Pass ($5; ⓦwww.parks.ca.gov), which allows complimentary parking at all state-operated facilities, though it doesn't cover boating fees, camping, and the like.

Time

California runs on Pacific Standard Time (PST), which is eight hours behind GMT, and jumps forward an hour in summer (the second Sunday in March to the first Sunday in November). During most of this eight-month daylight saving period, when it is noon Monday in California it is 3pm in New York, 8pm in London, 5am Tuesday in Sydney, and 7am Tuesday in Auckland.

Tourist information

California's official tourism website (ⓦwww .visitcalifornia.com) is a reasonable starting point for advance information. Much of the same material is available in its free tourism information packet, which can be ordered online, by calling ☎1-800/472-2543, or by contacting California Tourism, P.O. Box 1499, Sacramento, CA 95812-1499 (☎1-800/862-2543).

Visitor centers go under a variety of names, but they all provide detailed information about the local area. Typically they're open Monday through Friday 9am–5pm and Saturday 9am–1pm, except in summer, when they may be open seven days a week from 8am or 9am until 6pm or later. In smaller rural towns many offices will close for the winter from about mid-September to mid-May. In the US, visitor centers are often known as the "Convention and Visitors Bureaus" (CVB), while in small towns many operate under the auspices of the **Chamber of Commerce**, which promotes local business interests. You'll also find small visitor centers in the state's airports, where there's usually a free phone system connecting to leading hotels.

Park visitor centers should be your first destination in any national or state park. Staff are usually outdoors experts, and can offer invaluable advice on trails, current conditions, and the full range of outfitting or adventure specialists. These are also the places to go to obtain national park permits and, where applicable, permits for fishing or backcountry camping.

Travelers with disabilities

The US is quick to accommodate travelers with mobility problems or other physical disabilities. All public buildings have to be wheelchair accessible and provide suitable toilet facilities, almost all street corners have dropped curbs, public telephones are specially equipped for hearing-aid users, and most public transport systems have such facilities as subways with elevators and buses that "kneel" to let riders board. Even movie theaters have been forced by courts to allow people in wheelchairs to have a reasonable, unimpeded view of the screen.

Easy Access to National Parks, by Wendy Roth and Michael Tompane, is a Sierra Club publication that explores every national park from the point of view of people with disabilities, senior citizens, and families with children, and *Disabled Outdoors* is a quarterly magazine specializing in facilities for disabled travelers who wish to get into the outdoors.

The major hotel and motel chains are your best bet for accessible **accommodation**. At the higher end of the scale, *Embassy Suites* has been working to comply with new standards of access that meet or, in some cases, exceed the requirements of the Americans with Disabilities Act (ADA), by building new facilities, retrofitting older hotels, and providing special training to all employees. To a somewhat lesser degree, the same is true of *Hyatt Hotels* and the other big chains such as *Hilton*, *Best Western*, and *Radisson*.

Getting to and from California

Major car rental firms can provide vehicles with hand controls for drivers with leg or spinal disabilities, though these are typically available only on the pricier models. Parking regulations for disabled motorists are now uniform: license plates for the disabled must carry a three-inch-square international access symbol, and a placard bearing this symbol must be hung from the car's rearview mirror.

American **air carriers** must by law accommodate customers with disabilities, and some even allow attendants of those with serious conditions to accompany them for a reduced fare. Almost every **Amtrak train** includes one or more cars with accommodation for disabled passengers, along with wheelchair assistance at train platforms, adapted on-board seating, free travel for guide dogs, and discounts on fares, all with 24 hours' advance notice. Passengers with hearing impairment can get information by calling ☎1-800/523-6590 (TDD) or checking out ⊛www.amtrak.com.

By contrast, traveling by **Greyhound** and **Amtrak Thruway** bus connections is often problematic. Buses are not equipped with platforms for wheelchairs, though intercity carriers are required by law to provide assistance with boarding, and disabled passengers may be able to get priority seating. Call Greyhound's ADA customer assistance line for more information (☎1-800/752-4841, ⊛www.greyhound.com).

Information

The **California Office of Tourism** (ⓦwww .gocalif.ca.gov) has lists of handicapped facilities at places of accommodation and attractions. **National organizations** facilitating travel for people with disabilities include SATH, the Society for the Advancement of Travelers with Handicaps (☏212/447-7284, ⓦwww.sath.org), a nonprofit travel-industry grouping made up of travel agents, tour operators, and hotel and airline management; contact them in advance so they can notify the appropriate members. **Mobility International USA** (☏541/343-1284, ⓦwww.miusa .org) answers transportation queries and operates an exchange program for people with disabilities. **Access-Able** (☏303/232-2979, ⓦwww.access-able.com) is an information service that assists travelers with disabilities by putting them in contact with other people with similar conditions.

The great outdoors

Blind or disabled citizens or permanent residents of the US can obtain the **America the Beautiful Access Pass**, a free lifetime entrance pass to those federally operated parks, monuments, historic sites, recreation areas, and wildlife refuges that charge entrance fees. It also provides a fifty percent discount on fees charged for facilities such as camping, boat launching, and parking. The pass is available from the National Park Service (ⓦwww.nps.gov/fees_passes.htm) and must be picked up in person from the areas described. The **Disabled Discount Pass** ($3.50; ⓦwww.parks.ca.gov) offers half-priced concessions such as parking and camping at state-run parks, beaches, and historic sites.

Traveling with children

There's plenty to occupy kids in California, from Disneyland to the miles of beachfront, so you're unlikely to encounter major problems when traveling as a family. Hotels and motels will usually allow kids under a certain age (often 14) to stay free in the same room as their parents; most will add extra cots at nominal charges.

Restaurants often try hard to lure parents in with their kids. Most of the national chains offer high chairs and a special menu, packed with huge, excellent-value (if not necessarily healthy) meals like mini-burgers and macaroni and cheese. Most large cities have natural history museums or aquariums, and quite a few have hands-on children's museums. Virtually all **museums** and tourist attractions offer reduced rates for kids. Contact the California Office of Tourism (☏1-800/862-2543, ⓦgocalif.ca.gov) for excellent, free brochures that can answer most questions.

Getting around

Children under 2 fly free on domestic routes, and usually for ten percent of the adult fare on international flights – though that doesn't necessarily mean they get a seat. Kids aged from 2 to 12 may be entitled to half-price tickets, though recent airline-industry economic troubles have reduced perks like these in some measure.

Traveling **by bus** (see p.33) may be the cheapest way to go, but it's also the most uncomfortable for kids. Babies and toddlers can travel (on your lap) for free, whereas children aged 2 to 4 are charged ten to fifty percent of the adult fare (depending on the distance), as are any toddlers who take up a seat. Children 5–12 are charged about sixty percent of the standard fare.

Even if you discount the romance of the rails, **train travel** is the best option for long journeys – not only does everyone get to enjoy the scenery, but you can get up and walk around, relieving pent-up energy. Most cross-country trains have sleeping compartments, which may be quite expensive but are a great adventure. Children's discounts are slightly better than for bus or plane travel, with babies and toddlers riding free and kids from 2 to 15 receiving half-priced fares.

Most families choose to travel **by car**, but if you're hoping to enjoy a driving holiday with your kids, it's essential to plan ahead. Don't set unrealistic targets, pack plenty of sensible snacks and drinks, plan to stop (don't make your kids make you stop) every couple of hours, arrive at your destination well before sunset, and avoid traveling through big cities during rush hour. Note that when **renting a car** the company is legally obliged to provide free car seats for kids.

Women travelers

A woman traveling alone is certainly not the attention-grabbing spectacle in California that she might be elsewhere in the world (or even elsewhere in the US), and you're unlikely to come across much harassment. Don't hitchhike and avoid traveling at night by public transportation if possible. On Greyhound buses, follow the example of other women traveling alone and sit as near to the front – and the driver – as possible.

California **cities**, especially San Francisco, can feel surprisingly safe, and **muggings** are an uncommon occurrence. But as with anywhere, particular care has to be taken **at night**, and a modicum of common sense can often avert disasters. Walking through unlit, empty streets is never a good idea, and you should take cabs wherever possible. The advice that women who look confident tend not to encounter trouble is, like all home truths, grounded in fact but not written in stone; those who stand around looking lost and a bit scared are prime targets, but nobody is immune. Going into **bars** and **clubs** alone should pose no problems, especially in San Francisco and LA, where there's generally a pretty healthy attitude towards women who choose to do so. But **small towns** in rural areas are not blessed with the same liberal attitudes toward lone women travelers.

Should disaster strike, all major towns have some kind of **rape counseling** service available; if not, the local sheriff's office will make adequate arrangements for you to get help and counseling, and, if necessary, to get you home.

The **National Organization for Women** (⊛ www.now.org) is a women's issues group whose lobbying has done much to affect positive social legislation. NOW branches, listed in local phone directories and on their website, can provide referrals for specific concerns, such as rape crisis centers and counseling services, feminist bookshops, and lesbian bars. Specific women's contacts are listed where applicable in the city sections of the guide.

Guide

Guide

1

Los Angeles

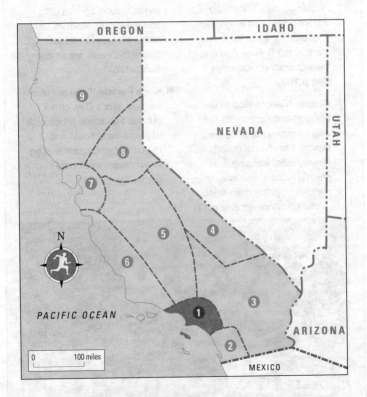

CHAPTER 1 # Highlights

* **Disney Hall** A marvelous piece of sculptural art masquerading as a (spectacular) concert hall, which has been described as resembling anything from broken eggshells to origami. See p.93

* **Musso and Frank Grill** This classically dark and moody watering hole has long been a favorite hangout for movie stars of the Golden Age and today's brattier celebrities. See p.106

* **Golden Triangle/Rodeo Drive** For high-end consumers (and avid window-shoppers), this compact section of downtown Beverly Hills, featuring jewelry, fashion, and beauty merchants, is the main reason to visit Los Angeles. See p.121

* **Getty Center** A colossal, modernist arts center, the Getty is stuffed with treasures of the Old World and does much to help the city shake off its reputation as a culture-free zone. See p.123

* **Pacific Coast Highway** This sinewy stretch of Highway 1 winds around coastal cliffs and legendary beaches from Santa Monica to Malibu, where the views are stunning. See p.125

* **Rose Parade** If you are here on New Year's Day, check out this Pasadena procession of grand floral floats and marching bands, culminating in a momentous football game. See p.158

▲ Mickey and Minnie at Disneyland

Los Angeles

LOS ANGELES spreads across its great desert basin in an eye-popping array of fast-food joints, palm trees, movie studios, and swimming pools. Bordered by snowcapped mountains and the Pacific Ocean, it's stitched together by an intricate network of freeways crossing a thousand square miles of architectural, social, and cultural anarchy. It's an extremely visual city, colorful and brash in myriad ways – a maddening patchwork like nowhere else on earth – and is made up of dozens of constituent cities, each with a character all its own.

The entertainment industry has been hyping the place ever since filmmakers arrived in the 1910s, attracted by a climate that allowed them to film outdoors year-round, plenty of open land on which to build elaborate sets, nearby landscapes varied enough to form an imaginary backdrop to just about anywhere in the world, and of course, the ever popular lures of cheap labor and low taxes. Since then, the money and glitz of Hollywood have enticed countless thousands of would-be actors, writers, designers, and other budding artistes and celebrities to cast their lot in this hard-edged glamour town, their triumphs and failures becoming intrinsic to the city's towering myths. So, too, has the threat of sudden disaster: floods, fires, and earthquakes are facts of life here, and the coexistence of both extremes – spectacle and tragedy – lends a perilous, unhinged personality to the city.

Some history

Originally settled by Chumash and Tongva peoples about a thousand years before the arrival of Spanish settlers in 1781, Los Angeles was named for the Spanish phrase for "**Our Lady Queen of the Angels**." Not surprisingly, it later became a link in Junípero Serra's lengthy chain of 21 Franciscan missions (see p.10), as well as a staging ground for Spanish military expeditions. In 1821, Mexico gained control of California, and the entire terrain was subdivided into huge **ranchos** under the control of politically powerful land bosses, only to be swallowed up again during the Mexican-American War in 1847 by the US, which did everything it could to eradicate the society and government created by Spain and Mexico.

Up until the Civil War, LA was a multicultural burg of white American immigrants, poor Chinese laborers, and wealthy Mexican ranchers, with a population of less than fifty thousand. It wasn't until the completion of the **transcontinental railroad** in the 1870s that the city really began to grow, doubling in population every ten years, with hundreds of thousands coming to live in what was billed as a Mediterranean-styled paradise for clean living and healthy air (ironic, considering today's omnipresent brown haze). Ranches were broken up into innumerable suburban lots, and scores of new towns, like San

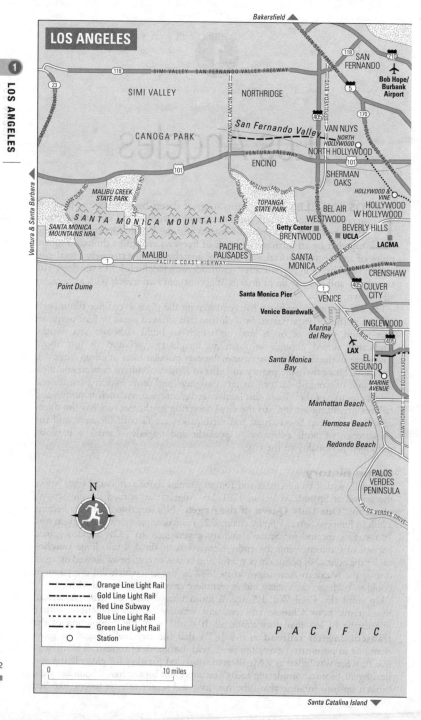

LOS ANGELES

Bakersfield ▲

118 SAN FERNANDO

Bob Hope/
Burbank
Airport

210

5

SIMI VALLEY · SAN FERNANDO VALLEY FREEWAY
118

23

SIMI VALLEY NORTHRIDGE

170

CANOGA PARK San Fernando Valley VAN NUYS

NORTH
HOLLYWOOD

101 Ventura Freeway NORTH HOLLYWOOD 101

ENCINO SHERMAN
OAKS

MULHOLLAND DRIVE

MALIBU CREEK
STATE PARK TOPANGA
STATE PARK HOLLYWOOD &
VINE

HOLLYWOOD

SANTA MONICA MOUNTAINS BEL AIR W HOLLYWOOD
WESTWOOD

SANTA MONICA
MOUNTAINS NRA Getty Center ■ BEVERLY HILLS
BRENTWOOD ■ UCLA ■ LACMA

MALIBU PACIFIC
PALISADES SANTA
MONICA SANTA MONICA FREEWAY

1 PACIFIC COAST HIGHWAY CRENSHAW
405 CULVER
CITY

Point Dume Santa Monica Pier 1 VENICE

Venice Boardwalk INGLEWOOD

Marina
del Rey LAX
405

Santa Monica
Bay EL
SEGUNDO

MARINE
AVENUE

Manhattan Beach

Hermosa Beach

Redondo Beach

PALOS
VERDES
PENINSULA

PALOS VERDES DRIVE

N

P A C I F I C

- - - - Orange Line Light Rail
-·-·-· Gold Line Light Rail
·········· Red Line Subway
· · · · · Blue Line Light Rail
-·-·- Green Line Light Rail
○ Station

0   10 miles

Ventura & Santa Barbara ◀

Santa Catalina Island ▼

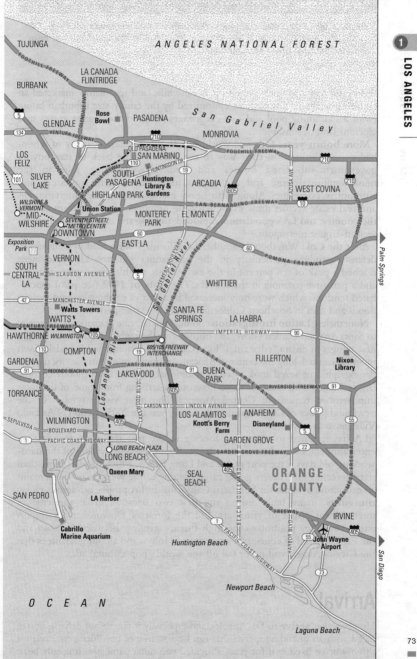

TUJUNGA

BURBANK

FOOTHILL FREEWAY

LA CAÑADA
FLINTRIDGE

ANGELES NATIONAL FOREST

GLENDALE

Rose
Bowl

PASADENA

San Gabriel Valley

134

VENTURA FREEWAY

210

MONROVIA

LOS
FELIZ

2

OLD PASADENA
SAN MARINO

FOOTHILL FREEWAY

210

SILVER
LAKE

101

110

SOUTH
PASADENA

HUNTINGDON DR

19

ARCADIA

WEST COVINA

WILSHIRE &
VERMONT
MID-
WILSHIRE

PASADENA FREEWAY

HIGHLAND PARK

Huntington
Library &
Gardens

AZUSA AVE

605

FOOTHILL FREEWAY

10

GOLDEN STATE FREEWAY

Union Station

SAN BERNARDINO FREEWAY

SEVENTH STREET/
METRO CENTER
DOWNTOWN

MONTEREY
PARK

EL MONTE

Exposition
Park

60

EAST LA

SOUTH
CENTRAL
LA

VERNON

60

POMONA FREEWAY

SLAUSON AVENUE

5

ROSEMEAD BOULEVARD

San Gabriel River

SAN GABRIEL RIVER FREEWAY

WHITTIER

42

MANCHESTER AVENUE

WATTS
Watts Towers

SANTA FE
SPRINGS

LA HABRA

90

HAWTHORNE WILMINGTON

CENTURY FREEWAY

105

SANTA ANA FREEWAY

IMPERIAL HIGHWAY

GARDENA

110

COMPTON

605/105 FREEWAY
INTERCHANGE

19

FULLERTON

Nixon
Library

91

REDONDO BEACH HWY

LAKEWOOD

ARTESIA FREEWAY

91

BUENA
PARK

605

RIVERSIDE FREEWAY

91

TORRANCE

SAN DIEGO FREEWAY

Los Angeles River

CARSON ST

LINCOLN AVENUE

57

55

SEPULVEDA

LAKEWOOD BLVD

LOS ALAMITOS
Knott's Berry
Farm

ANAHEIM
Disneyland

5

WILMINGTON

BOULEVARD

405

GARDEN GROVE

1

PACIFIC COAST HIGHWAY

LONG BEACH PLAZA
LONG BEACH

GARDEN GROVE FREEWAY

22

SEAL
BEACH

ORANGE
COUNTY

Queen Mary

405

BEACH BOULEVARD

SAN PEDRO

LA Harbor

SAN DIEGO FREEWAY

HARBOR BLVD

COSTA MESA FREEWAY

IRVINE

Cabrillo
Marine Aquarium

1

PACIFIC COAST HIGHWAY

Huntington Beach

55

John Wayne
Airport

405

OCEAN

73

Newport Beach

Laguna Beach

▶ Palm Springs

▶ San Diego

LA area codes

Because the Los Angeles metro region has eleven telephone **area codes** – ☏213, ☏310, ☏323, ☏562, ☏626, ☏661, ☏714, ☏805, ☏818, ☏909, and ☏949 – we have included the code before each number.

Pedro and Santa Monica, sprang up. Meanwhile, land speculators marketed an enduring image of Los Angeles, epitomized by the family-size suburban house (with a swimming pool and two-car garage) set amid the orange groves in a glorious land of sunshine.

More **boom years** followed World War II, when veterans, many of whom had passed through on their way to the Pacific, came back to stay, buying government-subsidized houses and finding well-paying jobs in the mushrooming defense and aeronautics industries or with oil, steel, and automotive companies. Along with heavy manufacturing, the entertainment and real estate sectors drew ever-increasing numbers of people from around the country, and LA's population exploded, turning the city into the nation's second-largest metropolis.

After the Cold War, though, Southern California was hit hard by cutbacks in defense spending, particularly in the aeronautics industry. Unemployment reached a peak of ten percent in the early 1990s, resulting in a spike in crime and a pervasive paranoia in the suburbs. The **riots of 1992** (see p.96) exacerbated tensions, which were only increased by a pair of earthquakes and various floods and fires in Southern California during the same period.

Nonetheless, **Latino immigration** continued to increase dramatically, especially to Santa Ana and Garden Grove, and once-entrenched white suburbanites sought new refuges in distant "edge cities" like Rancho Cucamonga and Palmdale. Even in South Central, long the center of African-American culture in the city, massive demographic upheaval took place as traditional black neighborhoods become largely Latino, with many of those newcomers arriving from some of the most impoverished regions of Central America. The most visible symbol of the newfound power of LA's Hispanic community was the 2005 election of Antonio Villaraigosa as mayor.

LA has regained its economic footing in the past ten years, focusing on entertainment and real estate once more. About the only symbol of the hardworking old days is the port of LA and Long Beach, which handles more than sixty percent of the ocean-going cargo coming to the West Coast and remains an economic dynamo for Southern California. In LA proper, numerous glossy **museums**, many built during the past two decades, make the city an international center of visual art, and the forest of Downtown skyscrapers attests to its key position as the high-finance gateway between America and the Far East. And of course, the presence of Hollywood all but guarantees that the City of Angels will never fall off the world's pop-cultural atlas.

Arrival

However you **arrive** in Los Angeles, and especially if you're not driving, you're faced with an unending sprawl that can be a source of bewilderment even for those who've lived in it for years. Provided you don't panic, this ungainly beast of a city can be managed and even navigated, if not necessarily tamed.

By plane

All international and most domestic **flights** use Los Angeles International Airport (**LAX**) sixteen miles southwest of Downtown LA (T310/646-5252, Wwww.los-angeles-lax.com). **Shuttle bus A** is for intra-airport connections (carrier-to-carrier), while buses B and C serve their respective parking lots round the clock, with parking lot C being the place to board city buses (the citywide MTA and individual lines to Santa Monica, Culver City, and Torrance) – see p.79 for more details. You could also take the direct-routed **LAX Flyaway** service, which uses buses in freeway carpool lanes to provide minimally traffic-impeded public transit. The three destinations in town are Union Station, the UCLA campus in Westwood (at parking structure 32 on Kinross Avenue), or the private Van Nuys Airport. Heading to the airport, buses leave from these points every thirty minutes around the clock, except at Westwood, where the service runs from 5am to 1am ($4 one way; information at T1-866/435-9529).

Another way into town is to ride a town car such as **LAX Chequer Shuttle** (T310/670-1731, Wwww.laxchequer.com) or minibuses like **SuperShuttle** (T1-800/258-3826, Wwww.supershuttle.com) and **Prime Time Shuttle** (T1-800/733-8267, Wwww.primetimeshuttle.com), which run to Downtown, Hollywood, West LA, and Santa Monica, as well as Long Beach and Disneyland. They'll have signs on their windshields advertising their general destination. Fares depend on the destination, but are generally around $15–20 for minibuses and $30 for town cars, plus tip for both. The shuttles run around the clock from outside the baggage reclaim areas, and you should never have to wait more than fifteen or twenty minutes; pay the fare when you board.

Taxis charge at least $35 to West LA or Hollywood, around $100 to Disney-land, and a flat $42 to Downtown; a $2.50 surcharge applies for all trips starting from LAX (all airport trips are a minimum of $17.50). For more information check out Wwww.taxicabsla.org. Using the **Metro** system to get to your desti-nation from LAX is difficult. The nearest light-rail train, the **Green Line**, stops miles from the airport, and the overall journey involves three time-consuming transfers (very difficult with luggage) before you even arrive in Downtown Los Angeles. If you'd like to try anyway, shuttle service leaves from the lower level of the terminal to access the Metro stop at Aviation Station.

If you're arriving from elsewhere in the US or from Mexico, you can land at one of the **smaller airports** in the LA area – Burbank, Long Beach, Ontario, or Orange County's John Wayne Airport in Costa Mesa. These are similarly well served by car rental firms; if you want to use public transportation, phone the MTA Regional Information Network on arrival (Mon–Fri 6am–7pm, Sat 8am–6pm; T1-800/266-6883, Wwww.mta.net), and tell them where you are and where you want to go.

By train

Arriving in LA by **train**, you'll be greeted with the expansive Mission Revival architecture of Union Station, on the north side of Downtown at 800 N Alameda St (T213/624-01710), from which you can reach Metrorail and Metrolink lines and also access the nearby Gateway Transit Center, which offers connections to bus lines. Amtrak trains also stop at outlying stations in the LA area; for all listings, call Amtrak (T1-800/872-7245, Wwww.amtrak.com).

By bus

The main **Greyhound** bus terminal, at 1716 E 7th St (T213/629-8401, Wwww.greyhound.com), is in a seedy section of Downtown – though access is restricted to ticket holders and it's safe enough inside. Check the website for other metropolitan stops and locations. Only the Downtown terminal is open around the clock; at all others, only toilets and left-luggage lockers are open 24 hours.

By car

The main routes by **car** into Los Angeles are the interstate highways, all of which pass through Downtown. From the east, I-10, the San Bernardino Freeway, and I-210, the Foothill Freeway, head in through the eastern suburbs from Phoenix, Arizona; from the north and south, I-5 connects LA with Sacramento and San Diego. Of the non-interstate routes into the city, US-101, the scenic route from San Francisco, cuts across the San Fernando Valley and Hollywood into Downtown; Hwy-1, or the Pacific Coast Highway (PCH), follows the coast of California and takes surface streets through Santa Monica, the South Bay, and Orange County; and US-60, the Pomona Freeway, parallels I-10 through the eastern suburbs – though a bit slower, it provides a less hair-raising interchange when it reaches Downtown.

Information

For free maps, accommodation suggestions, and general information, the Convention and Visitors Bureau (CVB) operates two **visitor centers**: Downtown; other LA areas have their own bureaus. See the box below for contact information.

All centers offer free **maps** of their areas, but if you're in LA for a while, you may want to invest in the thick, comprehensive *2007 Thomas Guide LA County Street Guide & Directory* ($19.95), the city's definitive road atlas, used by tourists and locals alike to navigate the bewildering maze of LA streets. There are also *Thomas Guides* for most neighboring counties if you're venturing further afield.

Visitor centers in and around LA

Downtown: 685 S Figueroa Street (Mon–Fri 9am–5pm; ☎213/689-8822, ⓦwww.lacvb.com) and at the Hollywood & Highland mall, 6801 Hollywood Boulevard (Mon–Sat 10am–10pm, Sun 10am–7pm; ☎323/467-6412)

Beverly Hills: 239 S Beverly Drive (Mon–Fri 8.30am–5pm; ☎1-800/345-2210, ⓦwww.beverlyhillscvb.com)

Long Beach: 1 World Trade Center, 3rd Floor (Mon–Fri 9am–5pm; ☎1-800/452-7829, ⓦwww.visitlongbeach.com)

Orange County: near Disneyland at 640 W Katella Avenue (daily 8am–8pm; ☎714/991-INFO, ⓦwww.anaheim411.com or www.anaheimoc.org)

Pasadena: 171 S Los Robles Avenue (Mon–Fri 8am–5pm, Sat 10am–4pm; ☎626/795-9311, ⓦwww.pasadenacal.com)

Santa Monica: 1400 Ocean Avenue (daily 10am–4pm, summer 9am–5pm; ☎310/393-7593, ⓦwww.santamonica.com) and in the Santa Monica Place mall, Colorado Boulevard at Third Street (daily 9am–6pm; ☎1-800/544-5319)

West Hollywood: in the Pacific Design Center, 8687 Melrose Avenue #M38 (Mon–Fri 9am–5pm; ☎310/289-2525, ⓦwww.visitwesthollywood.com)

Newspapers and magazines

LA has just one **daily newspaper** of national consequence: the *Los Angeles Times* (ⓦ www.latimes.com), available from street-corner racks all over Southern California. The Sunday edition is huge, and its "Calendar" section contains the most complete listings of what's on where, as well as reviews and arts and entertainment listings. Alternately, the *LA Daily News* (ⓦ www.dailynews.com) is more focused on local concerns. Of the city's many **free papers**, the fullest and most useful are the *LA Weekly* (ⓦ www.laweekly.com) and *Orange County Weekly* (ⓦ www.ocweekly.com), featuring news, reviews, and listings with an alternative bent. Numerous small local papers covering individual neighborhoods, musical scenes, and political activism are available all over the city, especially at cafés, record stores, and bookshops. If all else fails, the glib and touristy *Where LA* public-relations magazine can be found for free inside many hotel rooms.

To get a sense of how style-conscious LA sees itself, pick up a copy of the monthly *Los Angeles* magazine (ⓦ www.lamag.com), packed with gossipy news and celeb profiles, as well as reviews of the city's trendiest restaurants and clubs. There are also dozens of less glossy, more erratically published 'zines focusing on LA's diverse gay and lesbian culture and nightclubs.

City transportation

However you're **getting around** LA, you should allow plenty of time to reach your destination. The confusing entanglements of freeways and the gridlock common during rush hours (or any hours) can make car trips lengthy slogs – and the fact that most local buses stop on every other corner hardly makes bus travel a speedy option.

Driving and car rental

Not surprisingly, the best way to get around LA is to **drive**. Despite the traffic being bumper-to-bumper much of the day, the **freeways** are the only way to cover long distances with any efficiency. The system, however, can be confusing, especially since each stretch can have two or three names (often derived from their eventual destination, however far away) as well as a number. Out of an unbelievable four-level interchange known as "The Stack," four major freeways fan out from Downtown: the Hollywood Freeway (US-101) heads northwest through Hollywood into the San Fernando Valley; the Santa Monica Freeway (I-10) connects the northern edge of South Central LA with Santa Monica; the Harbor Freeway (I-110) runs south to San Pedro (heading northeast it's called the Pasadena Freeway); and the Santa Ana Freeway (I-5) passes Disneyland and continues to Orange County and San Diego. **Other area freeways** include the San Diego Freeway (I-405), following the coast through West LA and the South Bay (but not actually reaching San Diego); the Ventura Freeway (Hwy-134), linking Burbank, Glendale, and Pasadena to US-101 in the San Fernando Valley; the Long Beach Freeway (I-710), a truck-heavy route connecting East LA and Long Beach; the Foothill Freeway (I-210), skirting the suburbs at the base of the San Gabriel Mountains; and the San Gabriel River Freeway (I-605), linking those suburbs with Long Beach. For **shorter journeys**, especially between Hollywood and West LA, the wide avenues and boulevards are a better – and sometimes the only – option.

All the major **car rental** companies have branches in the city (check the *Yellow Pages* for the nearest office or call one of the numbers listed on p.37), and most have their main office close to LAX, linked to each terminal by a free shuttle bus.

Parking is a particular problem Downtown, along Melrose Avenue's trendy Westside shopping zone, on central Hollywood Boulevard, in downtown Beverly Hills, and in Westwood. Anywhere else is less troublesome, but watch out for restrictions – some lampposts boast as many as four placards listing do's and don'ts.

Public transportation

The bulk of LA's public transportation is operated by the LA County Metropolitan Transit Authority (**MTA** or **"Metro"**). Its massive **Gateway Transit Center**, east of Union Station on Chavez Avenue at Vignes Street, serves many thousands of daily commuters traveling by Metrorail, Metrolink, Amtrak, and the regional bus systems. The Center comprises **Patsaouras Transit Plaza**, where you can hop on a bus; the glass-domed **East Portal**, where you can connect to a train; and the 26-story **Gateway Tower**, where you can find an MTA customer service office (Mon–Fri 6am–6.30pm; ☎1-800/266-6883, ⓦ www.mta.net) on the ground floor. Another prominent customer service office is at 5301 Wilshire Boulevard, Mid-Wilshire (Mon–Fri 9am–5pm).

Metrorail and Metrolink

LA's **Metrorail** subway and light-rail system encompasses five major lines, though extensions are planned in coming years. The **Orange Line** crosses the San Fernando Valley and links Canoga Park with North Hollywood, where it connects to the northern terminus for the underground **Red Line**, heading south under the Hollywood Hills to connect Central Hollywood and Downtown (stopping at the Gateway Transit Center, as do all Downtown routes). Of more use to residents than tourists, the **Green Line** runs between industrial El Segundo (where you can pick up an LAX shuttle at Aviation Station; see p.75) and colorless Norwalk in South LA. The **Blue Line** leaves Downtown and heads overland through South Central to Long Beach, while the more appealing **Gold Line**, another light-rail route, connects Downtown with northeast LA, Highland Park, and Old Pasadena, before ending at drab Sierra Madre; another section of the Gold Line, to East LA, is due to open in late 2009. **Fares** are $1.25 one way, with day passes available for $3. Trains run daily from 5am to 12.30am, at five- to six-minute intervals during peak hours and every ten to fifteen minutes at other times. No smoking, eating, or drinking is allowed while on board.

As one rail alternative, **Metrolink** commuter trains ply primarily suburban-to-Downtown routes on weekdays, which can be useful if you find yourself in any such far-flung districts, among them places in Orange, Ventura, Riverside, and San Bernardino counties. Although casual visitors may find the service useful mainly for reaching the outlying corners of the San Fernando Valley, the system does reach as far as Oceanside in San Diego County, where you can connect to that region's Coaster commuter rail (see p.190) and avoid the freeways altogether. One-way fares range from $4.75 to $12.50, depending on when you're traveling (most routes run during daily business hours, often to LA in the morning and back to the suburbs in the evening) and how far you're going. For information on specific routes and schedules, call ☎1-800/371-5465 or visit ⓦ www.metrolinktrains.com.

Buses

Car-less Angelenos not lucky enough to live near a train route have to settle for **buses**. Although initially bewildering, the MTA network is really quite simple: the main routes run east–west (eg between Downtown and the coast) and north–south (eg between Downtown and the South Bay). With a bit of planning you should have few real problems – though always allow plenty of time.

Free brochures are available from MTA offices, as are diagrams and timetables for individual bus routes and regional bus maps showing larger sections of the metropolis. Buses on the major arteries between Downtown and the coast run roughly every fifteen minutes between 5am and 2am; other routes, and the **all-night services** along the major thoroughfares, are less frequent, usually

MTA bus routes

MTA **buses** fall into the route categories shown below. Whatever bus you're on, if traveling alone, especially at night, sit up front near the driver.

#1–99 – local routes to and from Downtown
#100–299 – local routes between other areas
#300–399 – limited-stop routes (usually rush hours only)
#400–499 – express routes to and from Downtown
#500–599 – express routes between other areas
#600–699 – special service routes (for sports events and the like)
#700–799 – Metro Rapid service

Major LA bus services
Metro routes unless otherwise stated.

From LAX parking lot C to:
Beverly Hills Santa Monica line #3 or Culver City line #6 to Metro #720
Culver City Culver City line #6
Downtown #42, #439
Hollywood Santa Monica line #3 to Metro #4 or #304
Long Beach #232
Santa Monica Santa Monica line #3
Watts Towers #117
West Hollywood Santa Monica line #3 to Metro #4 or #304

From Downtown along:
Beverly Blvd #14, #714
Hollywood Blvd #2, #4, #10, #11, #14, or #714, then connect at La Brea Ave onto #212 or #312 north
Melrose Ave #10, #11
Olympic Blvd #28, #328
Santa Monica Blvd #4, #304
Sunset Blvd #2, #302
Venice Blvd #33, #333
Wilshire Blvd #20, #21, #720

From Downtown to:
Beverly Hills #14, #20, #21, #714, #720
Burbank Studios #96
Exposition Park #81, #381
Forest Lawn Cemetery, Glendale #90, #91
Getty Center #2 or #302, then transfer at Brentwood to #761
Hermosa Beach/Redondo Beach #130, then transfer to #444
Hollywood #2, #302
Huntington Library #79
Long Beach #60, #360
Orange County, Knott's Berry Farm, Disneyland #460
Rancho Palos Verdes #444
San Pedro #445, #446, #447
Santa Monica #4, #20, #304, #720
Venice #33, #333

every thirty minutes or hourly. At night, be careful not to get stranded Downtown waiting for connecting buses.

The standard **one-way fare** is $1.25, except for night routes (9pm–5am), when the cost is only 75¢; **express buses** (a limited commuter service) and any others using a freeway are usually $1.75–2.25. Put the correct money (coins or bills) into the slot when getting on. If you're staying a while, you can save some money with a **weekly** or **monthly pass**, which cost $14 and $52, respectively, and also give reductions at selected shops and travel agents. If you're staying about two weeks, consider a semi-monthly pass, sold for $27. Finally, "EZ Transit" passes give you the option of traveling on MTA and DASH buses, as well as Metrorail trains, for a flat $58 per month.

Metro Rapid routes run throughout the region, offering modified bus service (along special #700 lines) with special red-colored identification, waiting kiosks with enhanced displays, and technology to reduce waiting times at red lights. There are also the mini **DASH** buses, which operate through the LA Department of Transportation, or LADOT (☎808-2273 for area codes 213, 310, 323, and 818; ⓦwww.ladottransit.com), with a flat fare of 25¢ for broad coverage throughout Downtown and limited routes elsewhere in the city. The LADOT also operates quick, limited-stop routes called **commuter express**, though these cost a bit more (90¢–$3.10) depending on distance.

Other **local bus services** include those for Orange County (OCTD; ☎714/636-7433, ⓦwww.octa.net), Long Beach (LBTD; ☎562/591-2301,

---

Guided tours of LA

One quick and easy way to see LA is on a **guided tour**. The mainstream tours carry large busloads around the major tourist sights; specialist tours usually carry smaller groups and are often a better, quirkier option; and media studio tours are covered on day-trips by most of the mainstream operators, though again you'll save money by turning up on your own.

Mainstream tours

By far the most popular of the mainstream tours is the half-day "stars' homes" jaunt. Usually including the Farmers' Market, Sunset Strip, Rodeo Drive, the Hollywood Bowl, and, of course, the "stars' homes," these tours are typically the most visible, and the area around the Chinese Theatre is thick with tourists lining up for tickets. Other programs include tours around the Westside at night, to the beach areas, the *Queen Mary*, day-long excursions to Disneyland, and shopping trips to Tijuana.

Costs are $30–95 per person, with some simple hour-long trips around Hollywood for around $20. You can make reservations at – and be picked up from – most hotels. Otherwise contact one of the following booking offices:

Hollywood Fantasy Tours ☎323/469-8184, ⓦwww.hollywoodfantasytours.com.

LA Tours ☎323/460-6490, ⓦwww.latours.net.

Red Line Tours ☎323/402-1074, ⓦwww.redlinetours.com.

Starline Tours ☎1-800/959-3131, ⓦwww.starlinetours.com.

VIP Tours ☎310/641-8114, ⓦwww.viptoursandcharters.com.

Specialist tours

The specialist tours listed are also generally $30 or more per person.

Architecture Tours LA ☎323/464-7868, ⓦwww.architecturetoursla.com. Driving tours of the master buildings of the LA region, with packages focusing on Hollywood, West LA, Pasadena, and Downtown. Cost varies depending on itinerary.

Ⓦ www.lbtransit.org), Culver City (Ⓣ 310/253-6500, Ⓦ www.culvercity.org /depts_bus.html), and Santa Monica (Ⓣ 310/451-5444, Ⓦ www.bigbluebus .com), which is the best option for reaching the Getty Center (see p.123).

Taxis

You can find **taxis** at most terminals and major hotels. Among the more reliable companies are Independent Cab Co (Ⓣ 1-800/521-8294), Checker Cab (Ⓣ 1-800/300-5007), Yellow Cab (Ⓣ 1-800/200-1085), and United Independent Taxi (Ⓣ 1-800/411-0303). Fares, which are set by the city, start at $2.65 plus $2.45 for each mile (or 44¢ per minute of waiting time), with a $2.50 surcharge if you're picked up at LAX. The driver won't know every street in LA but will know the major ones; ask for the nearest junction and give directions from there. If you encounter problems, call Ⓣ 1-800/501-0999, or visit Ⓦ www.taxicabsla.org.

Cycling

Cycling in LA may sound perverse, but in some areas it can be one of the better ways of getting around. There is an excellent **beach bike path** between Santa Monica and Redondo Beach, and another from Long Beach to Newport Beach, as well as many equally enjoyable inland routes, notably around Griffith Park and the grand mansions of Pasadena. For maps and information, contact

Architours Ⓣ 323/294-5821, Ⓦ www.architours.com. Walking, driving, and custom tours of the art and architecture highlights of the city. Multiday trips also available. Prices vary according to itinerary.

Neon Cruises Ⓣ 213/489-9918, Ⓦ www.neonmona.org. Popular, three-hour evening tours of LA's best remaining neon art, once a month on Saturdays (June–Oct), organized by the Museum of Neon Art. You may need to book months in advance. $45.

SPARC tours: the Murals of LA 685 Venice Blvd, Venice Ⓣ 310/822-9560, Ⓦ www .sparcmurals.org. Enlightening tour of the "mural capital of the world." Along with being an excellent art center, SPARC conducts two-hour mural tours ($400), personalized to your interests and sometimes including discussions with the artists.

To Fly LA 16303 Waterman Drive, Van Nuys Ⓣ 877/863-5952, Ⓦ www.toflyla.com. Tours by helicopter of some of the more prominent visual sights in the region, such as movie studios, skyscrapers, and the Hollywood sign, for $225–395, with dinner packages available.

Studio tours

For some insight into how a film or TV show is made, or just to admire the special effects, there are guided studio tours at Warner Brothers ($35; Ⓦ www.burbank .com/warner_bros_tour.shtml), NBC ($7.50; Ⓣ 818/840-3537), Sony ($25; Ⓣ 323/520-8687), Paramount ($35; Ⓦ www.paramount.com/studio), and Universal ($53, plus $7 parking; Ⓦ www.universalstudioshollywood.com), all near Burbank except for Sony, in Culver City, and Paramount, in Hollywood. If you want to be part of the **audience** in a TV show, Hollywood Boulevard, just outside the Chinese Theatre, is the spot to be: TV company reps regularly appear handing out free tickets, and they'll bus you to the studio and back. All you have to do once there is be willing to laugh and clap on cue.

▲ Bikers on Venice Boardwalk

AAA, 2601 S Figueroa Street (Mon–Fri 9am–5pm; ☎213/741-3686, ⓦwww
.aaa-calif.com), or the LA office of the state's Department of Transportation,
known as CalTrans, 100 S Main Street (Mon–Fri 8am–5pm; ☎213/897-3656,
ⓦwww.dot.ca.gov).

Walking and hiking

Although some people are surprised to find sidewalks in LA, let alone
pedestrians, **walking** is in fact the best way to see much of Downtown and
districts like central Hollywood, Pasadena, Beverly Hills, Santa Monica, and
Venice. You can structure your stroll by taking a **guided walking tour**, the
best of which are organized by the Los Angeles Conservancy (☎213/623-
2489, ⓦwww.laconservancy.org), whose treks around Downtown are full of
Art Deco movie palaces, once-opulent financial monuments, and architectural
gems. You can enjoy guided **hikes** through the wilds of the Santa Monica
Mountains and Hollywood Hills free of charge every weekend with a variety
of organizations and bureaus, including the Sierra Club (☎213/387-4287,
ⓦwww.angeles.sierraclub.org), the State Parks Department (☎818/880-0350,
ⓦwww.parks.ca.gov), and the Santa Monica Mountains National Recreation
Area (☎805/370-2301, ⓦwww.nps.gov/samo).

Accommodation

Since LA has 100,000-plus rooms, finding **accommodation** is easy, and,
whether you seek basic budget motels or world-class resorts, the city has
something for everyone. **Motels** and the bottom-end hotels start at about $40
for a double, but many are situated in seedy or out-of-the-way areas. **Bed and
breakfasts** are still uncommon in central LA, and tend to be quite expensive,
often fully booked, and sited in out-of-the-way places. For those on a tight

budget, a handful of **hostels** are dotted all over the city, many in good locations, though at some stays are limited to a few nights. Surprisingly, there are a few campgrounds on the edge of the metropolitan area – along the beach north of Malibu and in the San Gabriel Mountains, for example – but you'll need a car to get to them.

LA is so big that if you want to see it all without constantly having to cross huge expanses, it makes sense to divide your stay between several **districts**. Downtown has both chic hotels and basic dives; Hollywood has similar options, with roadside motels providing cheap and adequate rooms; more salubrious West LA, Santa Monica, Venice, and Malibu are predominantly mid-to-upper-range territory, with the odd hostel here and there. It's only worth staying in Orange County, thirty miles southeast of Downtown, if you're aiming for Disneyland or are traveling along the coast.

Hotels are listed here by **neighborhood**, with specific options for gay and lesbian travelers on p.177. In case you're arriving on a late flight, or leaving on an early one, we've also included a few places near the airport: cheap hotels near LAX are blandly similar and generally around $50–75, but most have complimentary transportation to and from the terminals.

Airport hotels

Comfort Inn & Suites 4922 W Century Blvd ☎310/671-7213, ⓦwww.comfortinn.com. Modern facility near Inglewood with Internet access, in-room fridges, complimentary breakfast, and airport transportation. ⑤

Days Inn 901 W Manchester Blvd ☎310/649-0800, ⓦwww.daysinn.com. Modern hotel with clean rooms, Internet access, and an outdoor pool by the 405 freeway. Offers free parking and free LAX shuttle. ③

Travelodge LAX 5547 W Century Blvd ☎310/649-4000, ⓦwww.travelodge.com. Reliable chain motel with continental breakfast, gym, pool, and airport shuttle. ④

Downtown and around

See the map on p.89 for hotel locations.

Downtown LA Standard 550 S Flower St ☎213/892-8080, ⓦwww.standardhotel.com. The downtown branch of LA's self-consciously trendy chain features sleek furnishings and quirky decor, but is best for its rooftop bar. Although billed as a "business hotel," the party scene is pretty much constant. Avoid the posey, depressing West Hollywood branch. ⑥

Hilton Checkers 535 S Grand ☎1-800/445-8667, ⓦwww.hiltoncheckers.com. Modern appointments in historic 1920s architecture, and nicely furnished rooms, gym, rooftop deck with pool and spa, and swank *Checkers* restaurant. ⑦

Los Angeles Athletic Club 431 W 7th St ☎213/625-2211, ⓦwww.laac.com. While still home to an exclusive club, the top three floors make up a hotel with 72 nicely furnished rooms

and nine expensive suites; a real plus is free use of the club's track, pool, exercise equipment, and handball and basketball courts, plus a whirlpool and sauna. ⑦

🏃 **Millennium Biltmore** 506 S Grand Ave ☎1-800/245-8673, ⓦwww.thebiltmore .com. Neoclassical 1923 architecture combined with modern luxury, with a health club modeled on a Roman bathhouse, cherub and angel decor, and a view overlooking Pershing Square. ⑥

Omni Los Angeles 251 S Olive St at 4th St ☎213/617-3300, ⓦwww.omnilosangeles.com. Fancy Bunker Hill hotel with plush rooms with Internet access, swimming pool, and weight room. Adjacent to MOCA and the Music Center. ⑥

Westin Bonaventure 404 S Figueroa St ☎213/624-1000, ⓦwww.westin.com. Modernist luxury hotel with five glass towers that resemble cocktail shakers, a six-story atrium with a "lake," and elegantly remodeled, cone-shaped rooms. A breathtaking exterior elevator ride ascends to a rotating cocktail lounge. ⑥

Hollywood

See the map on p.103 for hotel locations.

Dunes Sunset 5625 Sunset Blvd ☎323/467-5171. On the dingy eastern side of Hollywood, but far enough away from the weirdness of Hollywood Blvd to feel safe; adequate motel rooms with high-speed Internet and good access to major sights. ③

Holiday Inn Hollywood 2005 N Highland Ave ☎323/876-8600, ⓦwww.holiday-inn.com. Chain hotel with prime location three blocks from the center of the action, with pool, spa, gym, and Internet access. ⑥

Hollywood Metropolitan 5825 Sunset Blvd ☎1-800/962-5800, ⓦwww.metropolitanhotel .com. Sleek high-rise in central Hollywood. Good value for the area, with serviceable rooms with mini-fridges and disabled access. ➏

Hollywood Roosevelt 7000 Hollywood Blvd, between Highland and La Brea ☎323/466-7000, ⓦwww.hollywoodroosevelt.com. The first hotel built for the movie greats in 1927. The place reeks of atmosphere, with recently renovated boutique rooms, cabanas, and suites, plus a Jacuzzi, fitness room, and swimming pool. ➐

Orchid Suites 1753 Orchid Ave ☎1-800/537-3052, ⓦwww.orchidsuites.com. Roomy, if spartan, suites with cable TV, kitchenette, laundry room, and heated pool. Very close to the most popular parts of Hollywood and adjacent to the massive Hollywood & Highland mall; fairly basic, but good value. ➎

Renaissance Hollywood 1755 N Highland Blvd ☎323/856-1200, ⓦwww.renaissancehollywood .com. The centerpiece of the Hollywood & Highland mall, with arty, boutique-style rooms and suites and prime location in the heart of Tinseltown. The upscale chain lodging in the center of the district guarantees you'll pay top dollar for a room. ➑

Saharan Motor Hotel 7212 Sunset Blvd ☎323/874-6700, ⓦwww.saharanmotel.com. The cheapest decent digs you'll find in Hollywood, a simple roadside motel with fairly clean rooms and central location. ➌

West LA and Beverly Hills

See the map on pp.114–115 for hotel locations.

Avalon 9400 W Olympic Blvd ☎310/277-5221, ⓦwww.avalonbeverlyhills.com. A hipster-oriented hotel with cozy rooms and modern furnishings, along with in-room CD players and fax machines and a fitness club. The poolside bar is where the young elite go to pose. ➐

Bel Air 701 Stone Canyon Rd ☎1-800/648-1097, ⓦwww.hotelbelair.com. The nicest hotel in LA bar none – and the only business in Bel Air – in a lushly overgrown canyon above Beverly Hills. Go for a beautiful brunch by Swan Lake if you can't afford the rooms. ➒

Beverly Hills Hotel 9641 Sunset Blvd ☎1-800/283-8885, ⓦwww.beverlyhillshotel.com. The classic Hollywood resort, with a bold color scheme and Mission-style design, and surrounded by its own exotic gardens. Features in-room marbled bathrooms, VCRs, Jacuzzis, and other such luxuries, and the famed *Polo Lounge* restaurant. ➒

Beverly Hilton 9876 Wilshire Blvd ☎1-800/922-5432, ⓦwww.hilton.com. High-end hotel with in-room plasma TVs, boutique decor, and many rooms

with balconies. Also has one of the few remaining *Trader Vic's* bars. ➐

Beverly Laurel 8018 Beverly Blvd ☎323/651-2441. The hotel coffee shop, *Swingers*, attracts the most attention here, primarily as a hangout for locals and inquisitive tourists. No-frills accommodation, with basic and clean rooms, and a good location. ➍

Beverly Terrace 469 N Doheny Drive ☎310/274-8141, ⓦwww.hotelbeverlyterrace.com. Good, clean accommodation with complimentary breakfast, a few boutique touches, and some balconies. Central location on the border between Beverly Hills and West Hollywood, making it one of the area's better deals. ➏

Chateau Marmont 8221 Sunset Blvd ☎323/656-1010, ⓦwww.chateaumarmont.com. Iconic Norman Revival hotel, which resembles a dark castle or Hollywood fortress and has hosted all manner of celebrities. A bit worn these days, though, despite the glamour. Come for the history, but don't expect any kind of deal; rooms start at $350. ➒

Culver Hotel 9400 Culver Blvd ☎310/838-7963, ⓦwww.culverhotel.com. A lovely, restored landmark, once the offices of town founder Harry Culver and hotel of the midget cast during filming of *The Wizard of Oz*, today featuring old-fashioned decor, marble floors and iron railings in the lobby, and cozy rooms with good views of the city. ➎

Grafton 8462 Sunset Blvd ☎323/654-6470, ⓦwww.graftononsunset.com. Mid-level boutique hotel with attractive furnishings and CD and DVD players, plus a pool, fitness center, and complimentary shuttle to nearby malls and businesses. ➐

Hilgard House 927 Hilgard Ave ☎310/208-3945, ⓦwww.hilgardhouse.com. Ignore the higher-priced *W Hotel* across the street and stay at this pleasant, friendly spot with clean, tasteful rooms and an excellent location for UCLA. Some higher-end units come with Jacuzzis and kitchens. ➏

Le Montrose 900 Hammond St ☎310/855-1115, ⓦwww.lemontrose.com. West Hollywood hotel with Art Nouveau stylings, featuring rooftop tennis courts, pool, and Jacuzzi. Most rooms are suites with full amenities. ➑

Maison 140 140 S Lasky Drive ☎310/281-4000, ⓦwww.maison140.com. High-profile entry for swank hipsters, boasting rooms with CD and DVD players, Internet access, and nice appointments, plus salon, bar, fitness room, and complimentary breakfast. ➐

Santa Monica, Venice, and Malibu

See the map on p.127 for most hotel locations.

Bayside 2001 Ocean Ave, Santa Monica ☎310/396-6000, ⊛www.baysidehotel.com. Just a block from Santa Monica's beach and Main Street. Bland exterior, but generally comfortable rooms – the higher-priced units with ocean views, fridges, Internet access, and kitchenettes. ⑤

Carmel 201 Broadway, Santa Monica ☎1-800/445-8695, ⊛www.hotelcarmel.com. Drab and only functional, but these are the cheapest adequate rooms in the immediate area, with the ocean two blocks away and the Third Street Promenade a block in the other direction. ⑥

Casa Malibu Inn 22752 Pacific Coast Hwy ☎310/456-2219. Located opposite Carbon Beach and featuring superb, well-appointed rooms – facing a courtyard garden or right on the beach – with great modern design and some rooms with fireplace, Jacuzzi, and balcony. ⑤

Channel Road Inn 219 W Channel Rd, Pacific Palisades ☎310/459-1920, ⊛www.channelroadinn .com. B&B rooms in a romantic getaway nestled in lower Santa Monica Canyon (northwest of the city of Santa Monica), with ocean views, a hot tub, and free bike rental. Enjoy complimentary grapes and champagne in the sumptuous rooms, each priced according to its view. Rooms ⑦, suites ⑨

Inn at Venice Beach 327 Washington Blvd ☎1-800/828-0688, ⊛www.innatvenicebeach .com. A good, basic choice for visiting Venice Beach (a block away) and the canals, with simple, tasteful rooms featuring fridges and balconies. ⑦

Loew's Santa Monica Beach 1700 Ocean Ave, Santa Monica ☎310/458-6700, ⊛www.loewshotels .com. One of Santa Monica's chicest hotels, a deluxe edifice overlooking the ocean and Santa Monica Pier. The rooms can be a bit cramped and overpriced ($349), though they come with boutique furnishings and high-speed Internet access. ⑨

Malibu Shores Motel 23033 Pacific Coast Hwy ☎310/456-6559. Best for its location across from Surfrider Beach, this basic, no-frills spot is a cheap and decent place to lay your head with a minimum of hassle. ⑤

Shutters on the Beach 1 Pico Blvd at Appian Way, Santa Monica ☎1-800/334-9000, ⊛www .shuttersonthebeach.com. The seafront home to the stars, a white-shuttered luxury resort south of the pier. Amenities include hot tubs (with shuttered screens), pool, spa, sundeck, ground-floor shopping, and ocean views, all for the low price of $450. ⑨

Venice Beach House 15 30th Ave, Venice ☎310/823-1966, ⊛www.venicebeachhouse.com. A quaint bed-and-breakfast in a 1915 Craftsman house, with nine comfortable rooms and suites finished with lush period appointments and named

for famous guests – Charlie Chaplin, Abbot Kinney, etc – and, true to the name, right next to the beach. ⑥

Viceroy 1819 Ocean Ave, Santa Monica ☎310/451-8711, ⊛www.viceroysantamonica .com. Luxury item with great bay views and nicely appointed rooms with CD players, on-site pool, and lounge. Rooms start at $315 and reach $500. ⑨

The South Bay and Harbor Area

Beach House at Hermosa 1300 Strand, Hermosa Beach ☎310/374-3001, ⊛www.beach-house .com. The height of luxury in the South Bay, offering two-room suites with fireplaces, wet bars, balconies, hot tubs, stereos, and refrigerators, with many rooms overlooking the ocean. On the beachside concourse of the Strand. ⑧

Portofino Hotel and Yacht Club 260 Portofino Way, Redondo Beach ☎310/379-8481, ⊛www .hotelportofino.com. Elegant suite-hotel by the ocean. The best choices are the well-furnished, comfortable two-room suites with hot tubs and nice vistas, which look out over the elite playground of King Harbor. ⑧–⑨

Westin Long Beach 333 E Ocean Blvd, Long Beach ☎562/436-3000, ⊛www.westin.com. A solid bet for bayside luxury at affordable prices (cheaper when booked online), right by the convention center, with a spa, fitness center, and pool. ⑦

The San Gabriel and San Fernando valleys

Artists' Inn 1038 Magnolia St, South Pasadena ☎1-888/799-5668, ⊛www.artistsinns.com. Themed B&B with ten rooms and suites (some with spas) honoring famous painters and styles. Best of all is the Italian Suite, with an antique tub and sun porch. Located just two blocks from a Gold Line Metro stop. ⑤

Graciela Burbank 322 N Pass Ave ☎818/842-8887, ⊛www.thegraciela.com. Ultra-modern boutique accommodations. Many rooms have fridges, DVD and CD players, and high-speed Internet access. Also with on-site pool, gym, sauna, and rooftop sundeck with Jacuzzi. ⑦

Ritz-Carlton Huntington 1401 S Knoll Ave, Pasadena ☎626/568-3900, ⊛www.ritzcarlton .com. Utterly luxurious landmark 1906 hotel on an imposing hilltop. Palatial grounds, ponds and court-yards, three restaurants, expansive rear lawn, and terrific San Gabriel Valley views. The elegant rooms are a bit on the small side (though they start at $379). For even bigger bucks, inquire about the private bungalows. ⑨

Safari Inn 1911 W Olive St, Burbank
☎818/845-8586, ⊛www.safariburbank
.com. A classic mid-century motel, renovated but
still loaded with Pop-architecture touches (Tiki and
Googie styles). Features a pool, fitness room,
Burbank airport shuttle, and in-room fridges, with
some suites also available. ❺

Disneyland and around

Courtyard by Marriott 7621 Beach Blvd, Buena
Park ☎714/670-6600, ⊛www.courtyard.com
/snabp. The best bet for visiting Knott's Berry Farm,
and a good choice for its business-oriented
accommodations, with in-room fridges and Internet
access, plus free parking, pool, spa, bar, and
restaurant. ❺

Desert Palms 631 W Katella Ave, Anaheim ☎1-
888/788-0466, ⊛www.desertpalmshotel.com.
Rooms and suites with fridges, microwaves, high-
speed Internet access, and continental breakfast –
and suites also with kitchenettes. Conventions in
town make prices jump, but the hotel usually offers
good amenities at agreeable rates. ❻

Disneyland Hotel 1150 W Cerritos Ave, Anaheim
☎714/956-6400, ⊛www.disneyland.disney.go
.com. A thousand cookie-cutter rooms in a huge,
monolithic pile – but still, an irresistible stop for
many. Also with pools, faux beach, and interior
shopping. The Disneyland monorail stops outside,
though park admission is separate. One of three
similar Disney hotels. Basic rooms begin at $225,
one-bedroom suites at $500. ❼–❾

Park Place Inn 1544 S Harbor Blvd, Anaheim
☎714/776-4800, ⊛www.parkplaceinnandminisuites
.com. Best Western chain hotel across from Disneyland, with the customary clean rooms with fridges
and microwaves, plus pool, sauna, Jacuzzi, and
continental breakfast. ❺

Pavilions 1176 W Katella Ave, Anaheim
☎714/776-0140, ⊛www.pavilionshotel.com.
Convenient chain hotel offering basic rooms with
fridges and microwaves, as well as a pool, spa,
sauna, and shuttle to Disneyland. ❹

The Orange County Coast

Hilton Waterfront Beach Resort 21100 Pacific
Coast Hwy, Huntington Beach ☎714/960-7873,
⊛www.waterfrontbeachresort.hilton.com. A
towering high-rise with nicely furnished rooms and
the added attractions of private balconies, serpentine pool, spa, and rentals of everything from
surfboards to rollerblades; rooms have views of
gardens or ocean. ❼

Ritz-Carlton Laguna Niguel Pacific Coast Hwy at
1 Ritz-Carlton Drive ☎949/240-2000, ⊛www
.ritzcarlton.com/resorts/laguna_niguel. A stunning
Ritz-Carlton, this one perhaps the best in town for
its oceanside beauty (on the cliffs overlooking the
sea around Dana Point) and rooms and suites
chock full of luxury. The high-end amenities –
swank decor, pool, spa, racquet club, etc – are
everything you'd expect if paying $525 a night. ❾

Seacliff Laguna Inn 1661 S Coast Hwy, Laguna
Beach ☎1-866/732-1400, ⊛www.seaclifflaguna
.com. Renovated motel with close ocean access,
heated pool, and complimentary breakfast. Rates
start at $95, but jump if you want a room with a
sea view or a balcony ($145–240, depending on
the season). ❹–❼

Surf and Sand Resort 1555 S Coast Hwy,
Laguna Beach ☎1-888/869-7969, ⊛www
.surfandsandresort.com. Among the best of the
coast's hotels, with terrific oceanside views, easy
beach access, and luxurious rooms and suites with
many features, including balconies. Rates begin at
$500. ❾

Hostels

Some hostels add on booking fees of $3–4 per night; these are included in the
costs below.

Banana Bungalow 5920 Hollywood Blvd
☎1-888/977-5077, ⊛www.bananabungalow
.com. Large, popular hostel, now in a smart new
location just east of the heart of Hollywood, with
airport-shuttle reimbursement, high-speed
Internet, city tours to Venice Beach and theme
parks, chic decor in spots, and movie, billiards,
and "chill" lounges. Hiking and walking tours,
BBQs, and other activities. Dorms $20, private
doubles from $65.

HI–Anaheim/Fullerton 1700 N Harbor Blvd at Brea,
Fullerton ☎714/738-3721, ⊛www.hihostels.com.

Convenient and comfortable, five miles north of
Disneyland on the site of a former dairy farm. The
hostel's excellent facilities include a grass volleyball
court, golf driving range, and picnic area. There are
only twenty dorm beds, so reservations are a must.
OCTA bus #43 stops outside. $25.

HI–LA/Santa Monica 1436 2nd St at Broadway,
Santa Monica ☎310/393-9913, ⊛www
.hilosangeles.org. A few blocks from the beach and
pier, the building was LA's Town Hall from 1887 to
1889, and retains its historic charm, with a
pleasant inner courtyard, Internet café, movie room

LA area campgrounds

Reserve America (☎1-800/444-7275, ⓦwww.reserveamerica.com) processes reservations at many of the **campgrounds** listed below and can look for an alternative if your chosen site is full. It charges $7 per reservation per night up to a maximum of eight people per site, including one vehicle.

Bolsa Chica Campground ☎714/846-3460. Facing the ocean in Huntington Beach, also near a thousand-acre wildlife sanctuary and birders' paradise, with fishing opportunities as well. $34–44 for campers with a self-contained vehicle. No tent camping.

Chilao Recreation Area On Hwy-2, 26 miles north of I-10 ☎818/899-1900, ⓦwww .fs.fed.us/r5/angeles. The only campground in the San Gabriel Mountains reachable by car, though there are others accessible on foot. For details contact the Angeles National Forest Ranger Station at 701 N Santa Anita Ave, Arcadia (☎626/574-5200). $12, with $5 vehicle pass; open April to mid-Nov. Bears are active in the area.

Crystal Cove State Beach 8471 Pacific Coast Hwy, north of Laguna Beach ☎1-800/444-7275. Two thousand acres of woods and nearly four miles of coastline (rich with tide pools) make this tent-camping park a good, and affordable, choice for all manner of hiking, horseback riding, snorkeling, scuba diving, and surfing. $11–15. Also with beach cottages ($31–41), which are often reserved many months in advance.

Dockweiler Beach County Park 8255 Vista del Mar ☎1-800/950-7275, ⓦwww .beaches.co.la.ca.us. On a noisy coastal strip, almost at the western end of the LAX runways. Mainly for RVs. A popular urban beach, which can get a little dicey on weekends. $28–32.

Doheny State Beach Campground 25300 Dana Point Harbor Drive ☎1-800/444-7275. Often packed with families, especially on weekends. Located at the southern end of Orange County, not far from Dana Point Harbor. $25, add $10 for beachfront sites.

Leo Carrillo State Park Northern Malibu ☎1-800/444-7275. Pronounced "ca-REE-oh," near one of LA's best surfing beaches, 25 miles northwest of Santa Monica on the Pacific Coast Hwy. $25.

Malibu Creek State Park 1925 Las Virgenes Rd, in the Santa Monica Mountains ☎1-800/444-7275. A rustic campground in a park which can become crowded at times. Sixty sites in the shade of huge oak trees, almost all with fire pits, solar-heated showers, and flush toilets. One-time filming location for TV show *M*A*S*H*. $25.

San Clemente State Beach Campground 3030 Avenida del Presidente, two miles south of San Clemente ☎1-800/444-7275. A prime spot for hiking, diving, and surfing, around an area that was once home to Richard Nixon's "Western White House." $25, add $9 for beachfront sites.

– and 260 beds ($32–34). Reservations essential in summer; open 24hr.

HI–LA/South Bay 3601 S Gaffey St #613, San Pedro ☎310/831-8109, ⓦwww.hihostels.com. Sixty beds in old US Army barracks, with a panoramic view of the Pacific Ocean. Ideal for seeing San Pedro, Palos Verdes, and the Harbor Area. Dorms $26; private rooms from $48. MTA bus #446 passes by, but it's a two-hour journey from Downtown. During Oct–May only open to groups of 20 or more.

Hollywood International Hostel 6820 Hollywood Blvd ☎1-800/750-6561, ⓦwww.hollywoodhostels .com. Centrally located, with game room,

gymnasium, patio garden, kitchen, and laundry. Offers tours of Hollywood, theme parks, Las Vegas, and Tijuana. Dorms $17, private rooms from $40.

Orange Drive Manor 1764 N Orange Drive, Hollywood ☎323/850-0350, ⓦwww.orangedrive hostel.com. Centrally located hostel (right behind the Chinese Theatre), offering tours to film studios, theme parks, and homes of the stars. Members $25, others $29, private rooms $55–69.

Orbit Hotel 7950 Melrose Ave, West Hollywood ☎1-877/672-4887, ⓦwww .orbithotel.com. Retro-1960s hotel and hostel with sleek Day-Glo furnishings and ultra-hip modern decor, offering complimentary breakfast, movie screening room, patio, café, private baths in all rooms, and shuttle tours. The area, while central to the Melrose District, can get dicey at night. Dorms $22, private rooms $69–99.

USA Hostels – Hollywood 1624 Schrader Ave ☎1-800/524-6783, ⓦwww.usahostels.com. A block south of the center of Hollywood Blvd, near major attractions, and with a game room, private

baths, main bar, Internet access, and garden patio, as well as airport and train shuttles. Shared rooms $23–27, private doubles $72.

Venice Beach Cotel 25 Windward Ave, Venice ☎310/399-7649, ⓦwww.venicebeachcotel.com. Located in a historic beachside building near Muscle Beach, this colonnaded hostel (or "cotel") has dorm rooms for $22–26 and private rooms from $53.

Downtown LA

Nowhere else do the social, economic, and ethnic divisions of LA clash quite as loudly and visibly as in the square mile (surrounded by the 10, 110, and 101 freeways) that makes up **DOWNTOWN LA**. In the space of a few short blocks, adobe buildings and Mexican market stalls give way to Japanese shopping plazas and avant-garde art galleries. Each part of Downtown has its own history, cultural institutions, and architecture. Much of it can be seen on foot, starting with LA's historic and governmental heart at the **Civic Center**, crossing into the brasher, corporate-tower-dominated **Bunker Hill**, continuing past the street vendors, swap meets, and movie theaters of **Broadway**, and finally, checking out the lively **Garment District**.

Downtown can easily be seen in a day, and if your feet get tired you can hop aboard the **DASH** buses that run every five to ten minutes through key areas, costing only 25¢. Parking in lots can be expensive; street parking is a good alternative, except on Bunker Hill, where the meters cost at least $2 per hour. Downtown is the hub of the MTA networks and easily accessible by public transportation, especially around the grand colossus of Union Station.

El Pueblo de Los Angeles and Chinatown

Just across US-101 from the current seat of local government at the Civic Center, you can get a glimpse of LA's early frontier days at **El Pueblo de Los Angeles**, 845 N Alameda Street (daily 9am–5pm; free; ☎213/628-2381 or 628-3562, ⓦwww.ci.la.ca.us/elp). The site of the original late eighteenth-century Spanish settlement of Los Angeles, its few remaining early buildings evoke a strong sense of LA's Hispanic origins – the rest is filled in with period replicas and a few modern buildings with kitschy Spanish Colonial facades. Las Angelitas, a docent group, offers regular free tours of this and Olvera Street (Wed–Sat 10am, 11am & noon; ☎213/628-1274, ⓦwww.lasangelitas.org); there are also tour brochures available at the plaza's central information desk at 130 Paseo de la Plaza or in the Sepulveda House. The church here, **La Placita**, 535 N Main Street (daily 6.30am–8pm; ☎213/629-3101, ⓦwww.laplacita.org), is the city's oldest and has long served as a sanctuary for Central American refugees (who are perpetually at the center of one of the city's most potent political issues). If you'd like to take part in one of the church **masses**, they occur three or four times daily, with twelve Eucharist services on Sunday. The early nineteenth-century **Avila Adobe**, 10 Olvera Street, is touted as the oldest structure in Los Angeles (from 1847), although it was almost entirely rebuilt out of reinforced concrete following the 1971 Sylmar earthquake. Inside are two museums (daily 9am–5pm, winter 10am–4pm; free) covering the rise and restoration of the pueblo and a sanitized history of LA's unquenchable demands

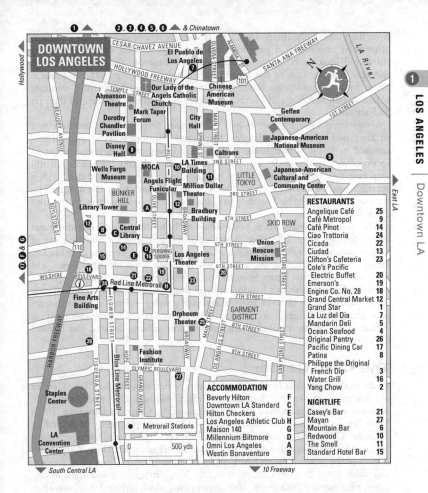

DOWNTOWN LOS ANGELES

Hollywood

CESAR CHAVEZ AVENUE

HOLLYWOOD FREEWAY

TEMPLE STREET

Ahmanson Theatre

Mark Taper Forum

Dorothy Chandler Pavilion

Disney Hall ❽

Wells Fargo Museum

MOCA ❿

Angels Flight Funicular

Library Tower

BUNKER HILL

Central Library

Our Lady of the Angels Catholic Church

El Pueblo de Los Angeles

OLVERA STREET

ALAMEDA ST.

SANTA ANA FREEWAY

LA River

Chinese American Museum ❼

Geffen Contemporary

Japanese-American National Museum ❾

City Hall

MAIN STREET

SPRING STREET

1ST STREET

Caltrans

LA Times Building ⓫

Million Dollar Theater

LITTLE TOKYO

Japanese-American Cultural and Community Center

2ND STREET

3RD STREET

East LA

Bradbury Building

SKID ROW

Union Rescue Mission

4TH STREET

5TH STREET

SAN PEDRO STREET

PERSHING SQUARE

Los Angeles Theater

6TH STREET

110

WILSHIRE BOULEVARD

Red Line Metrorail

Fine Arts Building

FLOWER STREET

7TH STREET

GARMENT DISTRICT

Orpheum Theater

8TH STREET

BROADWAY

LOS ANGELES STREET

MAIN STREET

SAN PEDRO STREET

Fashion Institute

HOPE STREET

GRAND AVENUE

OLYMPIC BOULEVARD

9TH STREET

Blue Line Metrorail

Staples Center

FIGUEROA STREET

LA Convention Center

Metrorail Stations

0   500 yds

South Central LA

10 Freeway

RESTAURANTS

Angelique Café	25
Café Metropol	9
Café Pinot	14
Ciao Trattoria	24
Cicada	22
Ciudad	13
Clifton's Cafeteria	23
Cole's Pacific Electric Buffet	20
Emerson's	19
Engine Co. No. 28	18
Grand Central Market	12
Grand Star	1
La Luz del Dia	7
Mandarin Deli	5
Ocean Seafood	4
Original Pantry	26
Pacific Dining Car	17
Patina	8
Philippe the Original French Dip	3
Water Grill	16
Yang Chow	2

NIGHTLIFE

Casey's Bar	21
Mayan	27
Mountain Bar	6
Redwood	10
The Smell	11
Standard Hotel Bar	15

ACCOMMODATION

Beverly Hilton	F
Downtown LA Standard	C
Hilton Checkers	E
Los Angeles Athletic Club	H
Maison 140	G
Millennium Biltmore	D
Omni Los Angeles	A
Westin Bonaventure	B

for a water supply. Across the street, the **Sepulveda House**, 125 Paseo de la Plaza (Mon–Sat 10am–3pm; free; ☎213/628-1274), is a quaint 1887 Eastlake structure that used to provide space for stores and a boardinghouse. Nowadays, it presents rooms highlighting different periods in Mexican-American cultural history, shows an informative film on the history of LA, and acts as the park's visitor center.

Along with its Mexican heritage, the pueblo also features the remnants of Chinese, Italian, and even French settlements. Of particular note, the **Chinese American Museum**, 425 N Los Angeles Street (Tues–Sun 10am–3pm; $5; ☎213/485-8567, ⓦwww.camla.org), details the local history of Chinese settlement, society, and culture. Artifacts from the nineteenth and twentieth centuries, such as revealing letters, photos, and documents, are displayed along with a smattering of contemporary art and a re-created Chinese herb shop circa 1900. Also worth a look is the city's first **firehouse** (Tues–Sun 10am–3pm; free) – later a boardinghouse and saloon – which has a small but intriguing roomful of fire-fighting gear and dates back to 1884. **Olvera Street**, which runs north from the plaza (daily 10am–7pm; free; ⓦ www.olvera-street.com), is a curious attempt at restoration, a pseudo-Mexican village market comprising about thirty old-looking buildings. Taken over for numerous festivals throughout the year, like the Day of the Dead on November 2 (see p.161), the street is at its best on such communal occasions, and regularly features strolling mariachi bands, Aztec and Mexican-themed processions, and various dancers and artisans.

Across from Olvera Street at 800 N Alameda Street, **Union Station** is a striking mix of monumental Art Deco and Mission Revival architecture, finished in 1939. Although the building is no longer the evocative point of locomotive arrival and departure it once was, Amtrak and commuter rail still stop here (see Basics, p.33), and the structure itself is in fine condition, with a spacious vaulted lobby, heavy wooden benches, and intact Art Deco signs. The station famously doubled as the dark, smoky police headquarters in the film *Blade Runner*.

What is now **Chinatown** was established by 1938 along North Broadway and North Spring Street following its residents' abrupt transplant from the site of Union Station. It's not the bustling affair you'll find in a number of other US cities, unless it's Chinese New Year, when there's a parade of dragons and firework celebrations. Apart from the many good restaurants here (see p.157), official culture consists of a handful of small shopping malls, where you can pick up an assortment of lanterns, teapots, and jade jewelry – aimed more at tourists than residents. (To get a truer sense of contemporary Chinese culture, visit Alhambra or Monterey Park, both lively ethnic suburbs located just beyond LA's eastern boundary.)

The Civic Center

South of the Santa Ana Freeway from Olvera Street, most of the **Civic Center** is a collection of plodding bureaucratic office buildings. One exception is the strangely futuristic glass walls and steel panels of the **Caltrans Building**, 100 S Main Street, an ultra-modern office for state freeway planners that helped its designer, Thom Mayne, win the 2005 Pritzker Prize, architecture's highest honor. More traditional, a block north, is LA's famous Art Deco **City Hall**, known to the world through LAPD badges seen in TV shows ever since *Dragnet*, and until 1960 the city's tallest structure. You can get a good look at the cityscape from its 28th-story 360° observation deck (Mon–Fri 10am–4pm; free), but for a more in-depth view of the building and its architecture, the LA Conservancy offers monthly tours (first Sat of month 11am; 1hr 45min; $5; ☏213/623-CITY, ⓦ www.laconservancy.org).

On the south side of the Civic Center plaza, the **Los Angeles Times**, 202 W 1st Street, provides free tours (tour hours vary; by reservation only at ☏213/237-5757, ⓦ www.latimes.com) of its facility, offering a glimpse of how the West Coast's biggest newspaper is put together.

Little Tokyo and around

East of the Civic Center, the colorful shopping precinct of **Little Tokyo** is centered around the Japanese American Cultural and Community Center, 244 S San Pedro Street (☏213/628-2725, ⓦ www.jaccc.org), whose **Doizaki Gallery** (Tues–Fri noon–5pm, Sat & Sun 11am–4pm; free) shows traditional and contemporary Japanese drawing and calligraphy, along with costumes, sculptures, and other associated art forms. The center also includes the **Japan America Theater** (box office Mon–Sat noon–5pm; ☏213/680-3700), which

▲ Los Angeles City Hall

regularly hosts Kabuki theater and more contemporary performances. Located between the two and easy to miss, the stunning **James Irvine Garden** (daily 9am–5pm; free), with a 170-foot stream running along its sloping hillside, was carved out of a flat lot to become the "garden of the clear stream," and makes the site seem a world away from the outside expanse of asphalt and concrete. At 369 E First Street, the **Japanese-American National Museum** (Tues–Sun 11am–5pm, Thurs until 8pm; $8; ☎213/625-0414, Ⓦwww.janm.org) houses exhibits on everything from origami to traditional furniture and folk craftwork to the internment of Japanese-Americans during World War II.

Near the museum is the **Geffen Contemporary**, 152 N Central Avenue (same hours, prices as the Museum of Contemporary Art, to which a ticket also entitles same-day entrance; see below) – an exhibition space in a converted police garage, designed by local maverick Frank Gehry. An alternative exhibition space to its more mainstream sibling, the Geffen presents huge installation pieces, architecture retrospectives, and other big shows with a voracious need for space.

Bunker Hill

Until a century ago the area south of the Civic Center, **BUNKER HILL**, was LA's most elegant neighborhood, its elaborate Victorian mansions and houses connected by funicular railroad to the growing business district down below on Spring Street. These structures were all wiped out by 1960s urban renewal and replaced with a forest of glossy high-rises, which, if viewed from the window of a passing airplane, almost give Downtown the look of a real urban center.

When it's in operation, the **Angels Flight** funicular is a bright and colorful memory of a long-departed era. These inclined train cars were removed in 1969 but restored in 1996. The short section of railroad leads up from the corner of Hill and Fourth streets to the top of Bunker Hill. The funicular was closed in 2001 after the death of a passenger in an accident, but recently began operating again. At the top rise the austerely modern office blocks of the **Financial District**, whose fifty-story towers have shops and restaurants at their base – neon-lit shopping malls intended to provide a synthetic street life for the brokers and traders, and about as dreary as you might expect. One of the few notable structures is the **Gas Company Tower**, 555 W Fifth Street, a metallic blue building whose crown symbolizes a natural-gas flame on its side.

The Museum of Contemporary Art

Based at the California Plaza, a billion-dollar complex of offices and luxury condos, the **Museum of Contemporary Art (MOCA)**, 250 S Grand Avenue (Mon & Fri 11am–5pm, Thurs 11am–8pm, Sat & Sun 11am–6pm; $8, students $5, free Thurs; ☏213/626-6222, ⓦwww.moca.org), has become the leading institution for contemporary art in Southern California. Designed by showman architect Arata Isozaki, its playful exterior offers an array of geometric red shapes recognizable from the occasional TV commercials filmed here.

Much of the gallery is used for temporary exhibitions and the bulk of the **permanent collection** is mid-twentieth-century American, particularly from the Abstract Expressionist period, including work by Franz Kline and Mark Rothko. You'll also find plenty of Pop Art, in Robert Rauschenberg's urban junk, Claes Oldenburg's papier-mâché representations of hamburgers and gaudy fast foods, and Andy Warhol's print-ad black telephone. Aside from more recent highlights like Alexis Smith's quirky collages, Charles Ray's Amazon-sized mannequins, and Martin Puryear's anthropomorphic wooden sculptures, the museum is also strong on **photography**, exhibiting Diane Arbus, Larry Clark, Robert Frank, Lee Friedlander, John Pfahl, and Gerry Winograd, as well as a few choice, and thoroughly disturbing, images by Cindy Sherman.

The theater on the lower floor of MOCA hosts some bizarre multimedia shows and performances, as well as the more standard lectures and seminars. The best time to visit the museum is during an evening concert in summer, when entry is free, and jazz and classical concerts are played outdoors under the red pyramids. At other times, a ticket to MOCA also entitles you to same-day entrance to downtown's Geffen Contemporary (see p.91), and to the branch at the Pacific Design Center (see p.119) out in West Hollywood.

Disney Hall and Our Lady of the Angels

Just north of the museum, around the stodgy music and theater establishments of the Music Center, 135 Grand Ave, **Disney Hall**, First Street at Grand Avenue, is LA's finest jewel of modern architecture, a Frank Gehry-designed, 2300-seat acoustic showpiece whose titanium exterior resembles something akin to colossal broken eggshells, or stylized habits worn by nuns, or various other images depending on your view. The LA Philharmonic (ⓦwdch .laphil.com) is based here, and with the Hall's rich, warm acoustics and features such as a colossal, intricate pipe organ, it may be the best place to hear music in the city, perhaps in all of California. Hours and days vary for **tours**, which run between 10am and 2pm and cost $12–15 for an hour-long visit (information at ☎213/972-7211 or 323/850-2000).

One long block north of Disney Hall stands LA's other modernist colossus, the $200-million **Our Lady of the Angels** Catholic church, 555 W Temple Street (Mon–Fri 6.30am–6pm, Sat 9am–6pm, Sun 7am–6pm; ☎213/680-5200, ⓦwww.olacathedral.org). The church, the centerpiece of the local archdiocese, is a truly massive structure in its own right – eleven concrete stories tall and capable of holding three thousand people. The interior is the highlight, featuring tapestries of saints, giant bronze doors, ultra-thin alabaster screens for diffusing light, a grand marble altar, and $30 million worth of art and furnishings.

South of MOCA

South of MOCA, the **Wells Fargo History Museum**, 333 Grand Avenue (Mon–Fri 9am–5pm; free; ☎213/253-7166, ⓦwww.wellsfargohistory.com), sits at the base of the Wells Fargo Center, and is one of nine such museums in the US. It tells the history of Wells Fargo & Co, the bank of Gold Rush California and current international giant, and displays among other things a two-pound nugget of gold and a simulated stagecoach journey from St Louis to San Francisco.

A block away, the shining glass tubes of the **Westin Bonaventure Hotel**, 404 S Figueroa Street (see p.83), have become one of the city's most unusual landmarks since the late 1970s. The structure is built with a flurry of ramps, elevators, concrete columns, and catwalks in a soaring atrium. Make sure to ride in the glass elevators that run up through the atrium and climb the outside walls, giving views over much of Downtown and beyond.

A short distance away, the **Richard J. Riordan Central Library**, 630 W Fifth Street (Mon–Thurs 10am–8pm, Fri & Sat 10am–6pm, Sun 1–5pm; ☎213/228-7000, ⓦwww.lapl.org/central), was built in 1926 but was renamed for LA's billionaire mayor of the 1990s; its striking, angular lines set the tone for many LA buildings, most obviously City Hall. Across Fifth Street, the **Library Tower** is the tallest office building west of Chicago. Now owned by US Bank (which has named the tower after itself, with little public effect), the cylindrical tower is open to tours run through operators such as Red Line Tours (see p.78), and features Lawrence Halprin's huge **Bunker Hill Steps** at its base, supposedly modeled after the Spanish Steps in Rome.

Broadway and around

Downtown's north–south axis of **Broadway** once formed the core of Los Angeles's most fashionable shopping and entertainment district, brimming with movie palaces and department stores. Today it's a bustling Hispanic community, whose vendors operate out of hundred-year-old buildings, the salsa music and street culture making for one of the city's most electric environments. You get a taste of the area amid the pickled pigs' feet, sheep's brains and other delicacies inside the indoor **Grand Central Market** (daily 9am–6pm; ☎213/624-2378, Ⓦwww.grandcentralsquare.com), on Broadway between Third and Fourth. Across the street, the **Bradbury Building** (lobby open Mon–Sat 9am–5pm; free) has a magnificent sunlit atrium surrounded by wrought-iron balconies, open-cage elevators set around a narrow court, and elaborate staircases at either end; scenes from both *Blade Runner* and *Citizen Kane* were filmed here. Tourists are only permitted in the lobby, but it's worth a look for the great view up. (Los Angeles Conservancy tours often begin here; see p.82 for more information.)

Broadway was first known for its **Theater District**. Although Hollywood has some of LA's most famous grand moviehouses, those Downtown also constitute one of the last remaining urban pockets of classic cinema architecture in the country. Several structures are especially noteworthy: next to the Grand Central Market, the opulent 1918 **Million Dollar Theater**, 307 S Broadway, its whimsical terracotta facade mixing buffalo heads with bald eagles in typical Hollywood Spanish Baroque style, was originally built by theater magnate Sid Grauman, who went on to build the Egyptian and Chinese theaters in Hollywood; though closed, there's always talk of refurbishing it someday. The **Los Angeles Theater**, 615 S Broadway, is considered the best movie palace in the city and one of the finest in the country. Its plush lobby behind the triumphal arch facade is lined by marble columns supporting an intricate mosaic ceiling, while the 1800-seat auditorium is enveloped by trompe l'oeil murals and lighting effects. It's no longer open to the public for regular screenings, but a June program called Last Remaining Seats draws huge crowds to this and the nearby **Orpheum Theatre**, 842 S Broadway, to watch revivals of classic Hollywood films (tickets $20 per film, often with live entertainment; call ☎213/623-CITY or visit Ⓦwww.laconservancy.org for details).

A few other architectural gems stand out within a few blocks of Broadway. The **Millennium Biltmore Hotel** (see p.83) stands over the west side of Pershing Square two blocks west of Broadway, its three brick towers rising from a Renaissance Revival arcade along Olive Street and its grand old lobby (the original main entrance) offering an intricately painted Spanish-beamed ceiling. A block south, the Art Deco **Oviatt Building**, 617 S Olive Street, features elevators with hand-carved oak paneling designed and executed by Parisian craftsman René Lalique. Also striking is the intricate 1928 design of the building's exterior, especially its grand sign and looming clock above. Finally, three more blocks west, the **Fine Arts Building**, 811 W Seventh Street (Mon–Fri 8.30am–5pm; free; ☎310/286-2989), is notable for its grand entry arch featuring gargoyles and griffins, intricate Romanesque Revival styling, and an eye-catching lobby where you'll find medieval-flavored carvings and the occasional art exhibit presented under dramatic lighting.

In the vicinity

A block **east** of Broadway, **Spring Street**, between Fourth and Seventh streets, was once the axis of the city's commerce and banking in the early twentieth century, but was abandoned in the 1980s. In the last decade, however, it has re-emerged as a center for upmarket loft housing. Behind these Neoclassical facades you can find a handful of interesting nightclubs, galleries, and theaters, though one impediment to the neighborhood's revival is its closeness to **Skid Row**, just a few blocks east, supposedly the largest concentration of homeless people in the US.

Further south near Grand Hope Park, the **Fashion Institute of Design and Merchandising**, 919 S Grand Avenue (Tues–Sat 10am–4pm; free; ☎1-800/624-1200, Ⓦwww.fashionmuseum.org), features items drawn from its collection of ten thousand pieces of costume and apparel – French gowns, Russian jewels, quirky shoes, and so on. The main draw is the "**Art of Motion Picture Costume Design**" show that runs from February to April – roughly Oscar time – displaying colorful outfits that may include anything from Liz Taylor's Cleopatra garb to Austin Powers' retro-Sixties gear. The other major attraction in the area is the welter of commercial activity in the **Garment District**, bounded by Los Angeles and San Pedro streets and Seventh and Ninth avenues, where you can pick up decent fabric for as little as $2 per yard.

Around Downtown

The area **around Downtown** is united by little more than freeways and large distances separating the major points of interest, though there's quite a bit worth seeing, either on the perimeter of Downtown or beginning nearby and continuing for many miles south or west. The districts immediately northwest of Downtown, **Angelino Heights** and **Echo Park**, are where the upper crust of LA society lived luxuriously in the late nineteenth and early twentieth centuries in stylish Victorian houses (now either preserved or decrepit), though the drabness surrounding them evidences the blight that later befell the area. Directly south of Downtown, the long succession of low-rent housing developments is interrupted only by the nearly walled-off **USC campus**, with a smattering of sights, and neighboring **Exposition Park**, with acres of gardens and several excellent museums. Beyond here, the vast urban bleakness of **South Central LA** has a few isolated spots of interest; it's generally a place to visit with caution or with someone who knows the area, though it's safe enough in daytime around the main drags. More appealing is colorful **East LA**, the largest Mexican-immigrant enclave outside Mexico, a buzzing district of markets, shops, and street-corner music. Things are less hectic northeast of Downtown, where, on the way to Pasadena, amid the preserved homes of **Highland Park**, the **Southwest Museum** holds a fine and comprehensive collection of Native American artifacts.

Angelino Heights and Echo Park

LA's first suburb, **Angelino Heights**, just northwest of Downtown off US-101, was laid out in the flush of a property boom at the end of the 1880s on a pleasant hilltop. Though the boom soon went bust, around a dozen of the elaborate houses that were built here, especially along **Carroll Avenue**, have survived and been restored – their wraparound verandas, turrets, and pediments set appealingly against the Downtown skyline. The best of the lot is the **Sessions House**, no. 1330, a Queen Anne masterpiece with Moorish detail, decorative glass, and a circular "moon window." On the first Saturday of the month, you can take a two-and-a-half-hour tour of the neighborhood with the LA Conservancy (10am; $10; reserve at ☎213/623-CITY, ⊛www.laconservancy.org), and visit the interiors of two of these classic homes as well.

At the foot of the hill, to the west of Angelino Heights, **Echo Park** is a small oasis of palm trees and lotus blossoms set around a lake. In the large white **Angelus Temple** on the northern side of the lake, the evangelist **Aimee Semple McPherson** used to preach sermons to five thousand people in the 1920s, with thousands more listening in on the radio. In Roman Polanski's film *Chinatown* detective Jake Gittes follows the town water boss to a clandestine meeting here, spying on him in a rowboat – the kind which you can still rent (along with paddleboats; typically $10 per hour) from vendors along Echo Park Avenue, running along the eastern edge of the lake. In 2008 Echo Park began to be drained and its wetlands restored to something resembling their original state.

Wilshire Boulevard and around

Wilshire Boulevard leaves Downtown between Sixth and Seventh streets as the main route across 25 miles of Los Angeles to Santa Monica's beachside Palisades Park. The large plot of land west of the Westlake district, **MacArthur Park**, has a Red Line Metrorail connection, scattered patches of green, and a seemingly idyllic lake – though drug-dealing is still a popular activity and the park should be strictly avoided after dark. Nearby, at 403 S Bonnie Brae Street, the **Grier–Musser Museum** (Wed–Sat noon–4pm; $6; ⊕213/413-1814) –

Cops, riots, and scandals

Los Angeles has had a long-standing reputation as having one of the most brutal police forces in the nation – the **LAPD** – whose paramilitary tactics were developed under 1950s super-cop William Parker and allowed to flourish under later chiefs, most notoriously the 1980s' champion of reaction, **Daryl Gates**. The methods of Gates during those economic boom years presented a frightening spectacle: the department's very own tank bashing down the walls of alleged drug suspects, its helicopter gunships patrolling the skies over South Central LA, and its chief himself proudly arguing, in front of Congress, that casual drug users should be taken out and shot. The unexpected acquittal in 1992 of five white Los Angeles police officers, charged with using excessive force after they were videotaped kicking and beating black motorist **Rodney King**, could almost have been calculated to provoke a **violent backlash** in LA's poverty-stricken ghettos. What few predicted, however, was the sheer scale of the response to the verdict, which was partly – and ironically – fueled by the almost total lack of a police presence during the first evening's bloodshed. The violence and anger far surpassed the Watts Riots of 1965, beginning in South Central LA with motorists being pulled from their cars and attacked, and quickly escalating into a chaos of arson and shooting that spread across the city from Long Beach to Hollywood. Before long, the arsonists around town gave way to looters, who became the focus of the national media's attention, openly stealing stereos, appliances, and even diapers from large and small retail stores. Ultimately, it took the imposition of a four-day dusk-to-dawn curfew, and the presence on LA's streets of several thousand well-armed US National Guard troops, to restore calm – whereupon the full extent of the rioting became apparent. The riots, the second-worst urban violence in US history, left 58 dead, nearly 2000 injured, and caused an estimated $1 billion worth of damage. A second federal trial, on charges that the officers violated Mr King's civil rights, resulted in prison sentences for two of the officers.

In 2000, the LAPD's gung-ho militaristic culture was once again on display in the **Rampart police scandal**, this time in the form of elite CRASH units sent to investigate drug-related crimes around the MacArthur Park and Temple-Beaudry barrios. Accused by ex-cop-turned-informant Rafael Perez of all manner of vigilante actions – from framing suspects for drug arrests to beating innocent civilians to shooting suspects in cold blood – most of the alleged perpetrators in blue walked away from the charges. Since then, even though New York's trailblazing former police chief **William Bratton** has been brought in to turn things around, little has changed. Gang violence is again on an upswing, this time with many more Latino suspects than before (given the groundswell of immigration), and a tepid, indifferent response from LA bureaucrats and power brokers, who can tolerate blood flowing freely in the ghetto as long as it doesn't reach into surrounding, more well-heeled districts.

the one functional museum of some note in the area – provides a glimpse of the luxurious furnishings and stylish architecture of the nineteenth century, overflowing in six rooms with all manner of Victorian bric-a-brac and precious decor.

Half a mile west of MacArthur Park, the **Bullocks Wilshire** department store, 3050 Wilshire Boulevard, is a stunning monument to 1920s Los Angeles and the most complete and unaltered example of Zigzag Art Deco architecture in the city. Built in 1929, in what was then a beanfield in the suburbs, Bullocks was the first department store in LA built outside Downtown and the first with its main entrance at the back of the structure, adjacent to the parking lot. Transportation was the spirit of the time, and throughout the building, triumphant murals and mosaics of planes and ocean liners celebrate what was then the modern world. The building is now the law library of adjacent **Southwestern University**; to inquire about visiting during special events, visit Ⓦ www.swlaw.edu/campus/building.

Wilshire Boulevard continues west into the so-called "Miracle Mile", while two blocks south of Wilshire, between Vermont and Western, **Koreatown** is home to the largest concentration of Koreans outside Korea and five times bigger than Chinatown and Little Tokyo combined. In reality, the comparison is unfair, for Koreatown is an active residential and commercial district, not just a tourist sight, and boasts as many bars, theaters, community groups, banks, and shopping complexes as it does restaurants. To check out the community's art and culture, the **Korean Cultural Center**, in the Miracle Mile at 5505 Wilshire Boulevard (Mon–Fri 9am–5pm; free; ℡323/936-7141, Ⓦ www.kccla.org), is an excellent place to begin. Along with a museum displaying photographs, antiques, and craftwork from Korea and the local immigrant community, the center features an art gallery with rotating exhibitions of fine art, folk work, and applied crafts, and puts on periodic theatrical and performance arts.

The USC campus

The **USC Campus** (University of Southern California), a few miles south of Downtown along Figueroa Street, is an enclave of wealth in one of the city's poorer neighborhoods, South Central LA. USC, or the "University of Spoiled Children," is one of the most expensive universities in the country, its undergraduates thought of as more likely to have rich parents than fertile brains. Though sizeable, the campus is reasonably easy to get around. You might find it easiest to take the free fifty-minute **walking tour** (leaving on the hour Mon–Fri 10am–3pm; by reservation at ℡213/740-6605, Ⓦ www.usc.edu). Without a guide, a good place to start is in the **Doheny Library** (hours vary; often Mon–Thurs 8am–10pm, Fri 8am–5pm, Sat 9am–5pm, Sun 1–10pm; ℡213/740-2924), an inviting 1932 Romanesque Revival structure where you can pick up a campus map and investigate a large stock of overseas newspapers and magazines. Another good place for general information is the **Student Union** building, across the quadrangle from the library.

Of things to see, USC's art collection is housed in the **Fisher Gallery**, 823 Exposition Boulevard (Tues–Sat noon–5pm; free; ℡213/740-4561, Ⓦ www .fishergallery.org), focusing on a wide range of art, from international and multicultural to avant-garde and contemporary. Elsewhere are smaller shows of students' creative efforts, and in the **Verle Annis Architecture Gallery** in the USC School of Architecture, 850 W 37th Street (Mon–Fri 10am–6pm, Sat noon–5pm; free; ℡213/740-2723) you can see retrospective shows featuring the models, blueprints, and sketches of internationally famous architects. The **Helen Lindhurst Fine Arts Gallery**, room 103 in the same complex (Mon–Fri 9am–4pm; free; ☎213/740-2787), focuses on contemporary and experimental works from student and regional artists. Finally, the campus is also home to the notable **School of Cinematic Arts**, where you'll find little reason to linger for more than a few minutes to see the big Hollywood names on the brick and concrete buildings.

Between USC and Exposition Park, sports fans may want to stop at the **Coliseum**, 3939 S Figueroa Street. The site of the 1932 and 1984 Olympic Games hosts home games for the dominant USC football team, one of the top squads in the country, which allows them to charge a minimum of $75–87 per game for nosebleed seats (☎213/740-GOSC, ⓦusctrojans.cstv.com). Otherwise, the imposing grand arch on the facade and muscular, headless commemorative statues create enough interest to make the place worth a look.

Exposition Park

Across Exposition Boulevard from the USC campus, **Exposition Park** incorporates lush landscaped gardens and a number of good, or at least adequate, museums off Figueroa Street at 700 State Drive. One of the highlights, the **California Science Center** (daily 10am–5pm; free, parking $6; ☎213/744-7400, ⓦwww.californiasciencecenter.org), is a multimillion-dollar showcase for scientific education with scores of working models and thousands of pressable buttons. The museum's displays include a walk-in periscope, imitation earthquake, and demonstrative wind tunnel, and three of the museum's attractions – a "high-wire" bicycle, motion simulator, and rock-climbing wall – cost $7 jointly. In the same complex, an **IMAX Theater** ($8, kids $4.75; information at ☎213/744-2015) plays a range of kid-oriented documentaries on a gigantic curved screen. Nearby, the **Air and Space Gallery** (same admission with Center) is marked by a sleek jet stuck to its facade and offers a series of satellites and telescopes, a slew of airplanes and rockets, and the menacing presence of an LAPD helicopter "air ship" – to complement their constant drone in the skies above.

To the south, head for the stimulating **California African-American Museum**, 600 State Drive (Tues–Sat 10am–5pm, Sun 11am–5pm; free, parking $6; ☎213/744-7432, ⓦwww.caamuseum.org), which has diverse temporary exhibitions on the history and culture of black people in the Americas, as well as a good range of painting and sculpture from local and national artists. Not far away, the **Natural History Museum of Los Angeles County**, 900 Exposition Boulevard (Mon–Fri 9.30am–5pm, Sat & Sun 10am–5pm; $9; ☎213/763-3466, ⓦwww.nhm.org), is the home of the park's biggest collection, as well as its most striking building – an explosion of Spanish Revival architecture with echoing domes, travertine columns, and a marble floor. Foremost among the exhibits is a tremendous stock of dinosaur bones and fossils, and some individually imposing skeletons (usually casts) including the crested duckbilled dinosaur, the skull of a Tyrannosaurus Rex, and the astonishing frame of a Diatryma – a huge prehistoric bird incapable of flight. Exhibits on rare sharks, the combustible native plant chaparral, and a spellbinding insect zoo – centered on a sizeable ant farm – add to the appeal. In the fascinating pre-Columbian Hall are Maya pyramid murals and the complete contents of a reconstructed Mexican tomb. Topping the whole place off is the gem collection, several breathtaking roomfuls of crystals, and an enticing display of three hundred pounds of gold, safely protected from your prying fingers. On a sunny day, spare some time for walking through Exposition Park's **Rose Garden, 701 State Drive** (mid-Mar to Dec daily 9am–dusk; free; ⊤213/765-5397). The flowers are at their most fragrant in April and May, when the bulk of the visitors come by to admire the 16,000 rose bushes and the overall prettiness of their setting.

South Central LA

Lacking the scenic splendor of the coast, the glamour of West LA, and the history of Downtown, **SOUTH CENTRAL LA** comprises such notable neighborhoods as **Watts**, **Compton**, and **Inglewood**, but hardly ranks on the tourist circuit – especially since it burst onto the world's TV screens as the focal point of the April 1992 **riots** (see box, p.96). A big, roughly circular chunk reaching from the southern edge of Downtown to the northern fringe of the Harbor Area, most LA visitors go out of their way to avoid the district, but there are a handful of sights that may be worth your while during daylight hours.

The Watts Towers

The district of **Watts**, on the eastern side of South Central, achieved notoriety as the scene of the six-day **Watts Riots** of August 1965. Despite the district's violent and troubled history, there is one valid reason to come here, to see the internationally famous, Gaudí-esque **Watts Towers**, 1765 E 107th Street (30-minute tours Fri 11am–3pm, Sat 10.30am–3pm, Sun 12.30–3pm; $7; ⊤213/847-4646), one of Southern California's most important visual landmarks. Constructed from iron, stainless steel, old bedsteads, and cement, and decorated with fragments of bottles and around 70,000 crushed seashells, these striking pieces of street art were built by Simon Rodia, who had no artistic training but labored over the towers' construction from 1921 to 1954,

refusing offers of help and unable to explain either their meaning or why he was building them. Once finished, he left the area, refused to talk about the towers, and faded into obscurity. One especially good time to come is during a late-September weekend that hosts the Saturday Day of the Drums Festival and Sunday Watts Towers Jazz Festival, both signature events in the city, which take place at the adjoining **Cultural Crescent Amphitheater**; call the Watts Tower Arts Center, 1727 E 107th Street (⊤213/847-4646, ⓦ www.wattstowers.org), for details and program listings.

Compton and Inglewood

Between Watts and the Harbor Area, only a few districts are of passing interest. Despite its fame as the home of many of LA's

▲ Natural History Museum of Los Angeles

rappers – NWA, for example, sang venomously of its ills on their album *Straight Outta Compton* – not to mention of tennis phenoms Serena and Venus Williams, **Compton** is not a place where strangers should attempt to sniff out the local music or sports scenes. History buffs secure in their cars, however, might enjoy a stop for the free conducted tours at the **Dominguez Ranch Adobe**, 18127 S Alameda Street (Sun & Wed 1, 2 & 3pm; ☎310/603-0088), a restored mission that chronicles the social ascent of its founder, Juan José Dominguez – one of the soldiers who left Mexico with Padre Junípero Serra's expedition to found the California missions – whose long military service was acknowledged in 1782 by the granting of 75,000 acres of land (long since subdivided into tiny modern parcels). As the importance of the area grew, so did the influence of Dominguez's descendants, who became powerful in local politics. The six main rooms of the 1826 adobe are on display with their original furnishings, or at least replicas of them, and are well worth a look for anyone intrigued by the pre-American period in California.

Closer to LAX, on the other side of the Harbor Freeway, **Inglewood**, unenticing in itself, is home to the **Hollywood Park Racetrack** (☎310/419-1500, ⓦwww.hollywoodpark.com), a landscaped track with lagoons and tropical vegetation. Nearer to the 405 freeway, two gems of Pop architecture are worth a look: **Randy's Donuts**, 805 Manchester Boulevard (☎310/645-4707, ⓦwww.randysdonuts.com), an iconic fast-food drive-though operation that's famed for its giant rooftop donut, and **Pann's**, a mile north at La Tijera and Centinela boulevards (☎310/337-2860, ⓦwww.panns.com), one of the last true Googie coffee shops around, with a pitched roof, big neon sign, exotic plants, and wealth of primary colors. If you have a taste for more historic architecture, make sure to check out the **Centinela Adobe**, just south of *Pann's* at 7636 Midfield Avenue (Wed & Sun 2–4pm; free; ☎310/649-6272), an 1834 structure whose earthen bricks were made at the site, and which is loaded with period antiques and Victorian furnishings.

West Adams

The charming but faded **West Adams** neighborhood, along Adams Boulevard from Crenshaw Boulevard to Hoover Street, was one of LA's few racially mixed neighborhoods in the early part of the twentieth century. It was also one of the spots where movie stars tended to live, known in the Twenties and Thirties as "**Sugar Hill**" and full of notable celebrities such as movie-musical director Busby Berkeley and silent-film heavyweights Fatty Arbuckle and Theda Bara. Many of the grand houses and mansions have since become religious institutions. Berkeley's estate, the 1910 **Guasti Villa**, 3500 W Adams Boulevard, is a graceful Renaissance Revival creation that might fit nicely in Italy but is now home to a New Age spiritual institute. Nearby, the **Lindsay House**, no. 3424, a terracotta curiosity with a heavy stone facade and unique tilework (the first owner was a tile manufacturer), has become the Our Lady of Bright Mount, a Polish Catholic church (☎323/734-5249). And the **Walker House**, no. 3300 (☎323/733-6260), a mishmash of Craftsman bulk and Tudor half-timbering with a Mission-style tile roof, has turned into a Korean Seventh-Day Adventist church.

The finest building in the area is the French Renaissance **William Clark Memorial Library**, 2520 Cimarron Street (Mon–Fri 9am–4.45pm; free; tours Mon–Fri 10am–2pm by reservation only, at ☎323/735-7605, ⓦwww.humnet .ucla.edu/humnet/clarklib), with its elegant symmetry, yellow-brick walls, formal gardens, and grand entrance hall. As millionaire heir to a copper fortune, founder of the LA Philharmonic, and a US Senator from Montana, Clark amassed this great collection before donating it to UCLA, which continues to oversee it as a non-circulating library. Besides rare volumes by Pope, Fielding, Dryden, Swift, and Milton, plus a huge set of letters and manuscripts by Oscar Wilde, the library includes four Shakespeare folios, a group of works by Chaucer, and copies of key documents in American history pertaining to the Louisiana Purchase and the like. Four annual **exhibitions** of selected works from the collection typically take place.

East LA

Of the many Hispanic neighborhoods all over LA, one of the longest standing is **East LA**, beginning two miles east of Downtown. There was a Mexican population here long before white settlers came, and from the late nineteenth century onward millions more arrived, coming chiefly to work on the land. As the white inhabitants moved west towards the coast, the Mexicans stayed, creating a vast Spanish-speaking community that's one of the most historic in the country.

Other than the lively markets, street life, and murals, however, there are few specific "sights" in East LA. The best plan is just to turn up on a Saturday afternoon – the liveliest part of the week – and stroll along **Cesar Chavez Avenue**, formerly Brooklyn Avenue, going eastward from Indiana Street, checking out the wild pet shops, with free-roaming parrots and cases of boa constrictors, and **botanicas shops**, which cater to practitioners of Santería – a religion that is equal parts voodoo and Catholicism. Browse amid the shark's teeth, dried devilfish, and plastic statuettes of Catholic saints, and buy magical herbs, ointments, or candles after consulting the shopkeeper and explaining (in Spanish) what ails you. Only slightly less exotic fare can be found in **El Mercado de Los Angeles**, 3425 E First Street (daily 10am–8pm; ☏323/268-3451), an indoor market somewhat similar to Olvera Street (see p.89) but much more authentic. Outdoor murals depict a Maya god and warrior, as well as actor Edward James Olmos, and an indoor warren of vendor stalls sells *botanicas*, clothing, Latin American food, and arts-and-crafts pieces; the top floor, where the restaurants are located, is the most rhythmic, with mariachi bands playing well after midnight every day.

Guadalupe, the Mexican image of the Virgin Mary, appears in mural art all over East LA, nowhere better than at the junction of Mednik and Cesar Chavez avenues. Lined with blue tile, it now forms an unofficial shrine where worshipers place fresh flowers and candles.

Non-Hispanic visitors are comparatively thin on the ground in East LA, but you are unlikely to meet any hostility on the streets during the day – though you should steer clear of the rough and male-dominated bars, and avoid the whole area after dark.

Highland Park

Two miles north of Downtown, **Highland Park** has a number of exuberantly detailed Victorian houses brought together from around the city to form **Heritage Square**. This fenced-off ten-acre park at 3800 Homer Street (Fri–Sun noon–5pm, tours on the hour Sat & Sun noon–3pm; $10; ☏323/225-2700, ⓦ www.heritagesquare.org) uncomfortably sites a railway station next to an octagonal house next to a Methodist church, and although the buildings are interesting enough, the park's freeway-adjacent home is a less-than-ideal spot to escape into a Victorian world of buggies and gingerbread.

Just beyond the next freeway exit, at 200 E Avenue 43, the **Lummis House** (Fri–Sun noon–4pm; free; ☏323/222-0546, ⓦ www.socalhistory.org) is the well-preserved home of **Charles F. Lummis**, a publicist who was at the heart of LA's nineteenth-century boom. An early champion of civil rights for Native Americans, and one who worked to save and preserve many of the missions, Lummis built his home as a cultural center where the literati of the day would meet to discuss poetry and the art and architecture of the Southwest. He built it in an ad hoc mixture of Mission and Medieval styles, naming it *El Alisal* after the many large sycamore trees that shade the gardens, and constructing the thick walls out of rounded granite boulders taken from the nearby riverbed and the beams over the living room from old telephone poles. The solid wooden front doors are similarly built to last, reinforced with iron and weighing tons, while the plaster-and-tile interior features rustic, hand-cut timber ceilings and homemade furniture, all a fitting reflection of its rugged owner, one of the few individuals to reach LA by walking – from Cincinnati.

The Southwest Museum of the American Indian

The **Southwest Museum of the American Indian** (☎ 323/221-2164, ⓦ www.southwestmuseum.org), which rises castle-like below Mount Washington, was Charles F. Lummis's most enduring achievement, as it's one of the state's best museums for Native American art and artifacts. Half a mile north of the Lummis House (with its own Gold Line light-rail stop), the museum is the oldest in Los Angeles, founded in 1907. Its name is a bit deceptive – there are displays of tribal artifacts from all over North America, with exhibits of pre-Columbian pottery, coastal Chumash rock art, and a full-sized Plains Indian Cheyenne tepee. Its traveling exhibitions, educational programs, and theatrical events have made it an international center for indigenous American cultures. However, while this facility will continue as a cultural center, the museum collection is in the process of relocating, ongoing through 2009 or beyond, so inquire at the website for the latest details.

Hollywood

Ever since movies and their stars became international symbols of the good life, **HOLLYWOOD** has been a magnet to millions of tourists on celebrity-seeking pilgrimages and an equal number of hopefuls drawn by the prospect of riches and glory.

In reality, Hollywood was more a center of corruption and scandal than the city of dreams the studio-made legend suggests. Successful Hollywood residents actually spent little time here – leaving as soon as they could afford to for the privacy of the hills or coast. Even by the 1930s Hollywood had developed into a gritty district rife with prostitution and petty thievery, and subsequent decades only accelerated the decline. Although the area continues to be a secondary center for the film business, with abundant technical service companies like prop shops and equipment suppliers, all the big film companies (other than Paramount) relocated long ago to places like Burbank, leaving Hollywood to urban blight, drug dealing, and seedy adult bookstores. Things have brightened up in the past few years, however, with public and private capital financing the construction of new tourist plazas and shopping malls – places which, with their focus on the golden age of moviemaking, try to take the tarnish off the Hollywood myth once more.

Approaching from Downtown via Sunset Boulevard, **East Hollywood** offers the first taste of the district, an assortment of cheap housing and low-rent

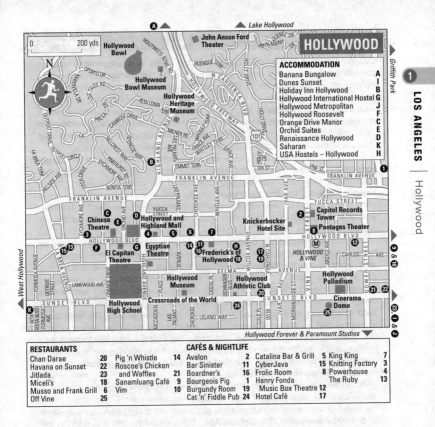

HOLLYWOOD

ACCOMMODATION

Banana Bungalow	A
Dunes Sunset	B
Holiday Inn Hollywood	G
Hollywood International Hostel	J
Hollywood Metropolitan	F
Hollywood Roosevelt	C
Orange Drive Manor	E
Orchid Suites	D
Renaissance Hollywood	K
Saharan	H
USA Hostels – Hollywood	I

RESTAURANTS

Chan Darae	20	Pig 'n Whistle	14
Havana on Sunset	22	Roscoe's Chicken	
Jitlada	23	and Waffles	21
Miceli's	18	Sanamluang Café	9
Musso and Frank Grill	6	Vim	10
Off Vine	25		

CAFÉS & NIGHTLIFE

Avalon	2	Catalina Bar & Grill	5
Bar Sinister	11	CyberJava	15
Boardner's	16	Frolic Room	8
Bourgeois Pig	9	Henry Fonda	
Burgundy Room	19	Music Box Theatre	12
Cat 'n' Fiddle Pub	24	Hotel Café	17

King King	7
Knitting Factory	3
Powerhouse	4
The Ruby	13

businesses with a few interesting sights scattered here and there, among them **Los Feliz**, which has become a trendy place to live and socialize, with a number of eye-catching modernist homes glittering above in the hills. Further west, **Central Hollywood** is the signature part of the area, a compact zone loaded with movie history and swamped by an eccentric street mix of social derelicts and starstruck tourists along the legendary stretch of Hollywood Boulevard. Protecting Hollywood from the outside world, the slopes of the Santa Monica Mountains contain **Griffith Park** – several thousand acres of nature offering rugged hiking trails and busy sports and picnic grounds, which form a scenic northern edge to the area. Beyond the park to the west, the **Hollywood Hills** hold exclusive homes perched on snaking driveways that are the most tangible reminders of the wealth generated in the city – and the brand-name celebrities that have sprung from it.

East Hollywood: Silver Lake and Los Feliz

Off the radar screen of most visitors, **EAST HOLLYWOOD** finds its focus near the eastern intersection of Hollywood and Sunset boulevards, a hardscrabble stretch that represents the "real" LA with its blend of working-class Latinos, bohemian artists and musicians of all stripes, and assorted punks and prostitutes. Even here, the perimeter neighborhoods bordering the hills are highly sought

A history of Hollywood

Strangely enough, Hollywood started life in the 1880s as a **temperance colony**, created to be a sober, God-fearing alternative to raunchy Downtown LA, eight miles away by rough country road. In 1911 residents were forced, in return for a regular water supply, to become an LA suburb. The film industry, then gathering momentum on the East Coast, needed a place with cheap labor, guaranteed sunshine, and a diverse assortment of natural backdrops to enable pictures to be made quickly, and most importantly, a distant spot to dodge Thomas Edison's patent trust, which tried to restrict filmmaking nationwide. Southern California, with its climate, scenery, and isolation, was the perfect spot. A few offices affiliated with Eastern film companies appeared Downtown in 1906 and the first true studios opened in nearby Silver Lake, but independent hopefuls soon discovered the cheaper rents on offer in Hollywood. Soon, the first **Hollywood studio** opened in 1911, and within three years the place was packed with filmmakers – many of them, like **Cecil B. DeMille**, who shared his barn-converted office space with a horse, destined to be the big names of the future.

The industry expanded fast, bringing riches and fame – with momentum provided by the overnight success of DeMille's *The Squaw Man*, filmed inside the former barn itself, which is now the **Hollywood Heritage Museum**, 2100 N Highland Boulevard (Sat & Sun 11am–4pm; $5; ☎323/874-4005, ⓦ www.hollywoodheritage.org), exhibiting interesting antiques and treasures from the silent era. Yet moviemaking was far from being a financially secure business, and it wasn't until the release of D.W. Griffith's **The Birth of a Nation** in 1914 that the power of film was demonstrated. The film's racist account of the Civil War and Reconstruction caused riots outside cinemas and months of critical debate in the newspapers, and for the first time drew the middle classes to moviehouses – despite the exorbitant $2 ticket price. It was also the movie which first perfected the narrative style and production techniques that gradually became standard in classic Hollywood cinema.

Modern Hollywood took shape from the 1920s on, when film production grew more specialized, the **"star system"** was perfected, and many small companies either went bust or were incorporated into one of the handful of bigger studios that came to dominate filmmaking. The **Golden Age** of the studio system peaked from the 1930s through the late 1940s, when a Supreme Court ruling put an end to studio monopolies owning their own exhibitors and theaters. Despite lean years from the later 1950s until the 1970s, and the onslaught of competition from television, Hollywood slowly rebounded until, in the modern era, the studios have become simple adjuncts to global media empires. Whatever the structure of the business, the film industry's enduring success is in making slick, unchallenging movies that sell – from Rhett Butler romancing Scarlett O'Hara to Yoda dueling with a light saber.

after, the streets around Beachwood Avenue have evolved into popular places to live and hang out, and upscale Mediterranean-style homes clutter the hillside.

Four blocks north of Sunset, **Silver Lake** was once home to some of Hollywood's first studios, since converted into restaurants and galleries, or at least warehouses and storage units. Walt Disney opened his first studio at 2719 Hyperion Avenue in 1926 (now a parking lot), and the Keystone Kops were dreamed up in Mack Sennett's studio at 1712 Glendale Boulevard (now a storage facility), when the zone was known as **Edendale**, and where just a single sound studio now remains. Otherwise there are no official "sights" in Silver Lake, except for a collection of interesting modernist houses in the hills designed by the likes of Richard Neutra and R.M. Schindler and highlighted by John Lautner's **Silvertop**, 2138 Micheltorena Street (best viewed from 2100 Redcliff Drive), an eye-grabbing marvel with projecting roofs and balconies, wraparound glass windows, and sweeping concrete curves. Architecture buffs can take an in-depth look at these and other top-notch works through Architecture Tours LA (daily 9.30am & 1.30pm; $75 per person; reserve at ℡323/464-7868, ⓦwww.architecturetoursla.com).

The district is also known for its gay bars, quirky dance clubs, and leftist bookstores that represent a hint of what central Hollywood looked like before the redevelopment dollars began to flow. The full effect is on display during the **Sunset Junction Street Fair** in August (℡323/661-7771, ⓦwww.sunsetjunction.org), a social carnival known for its loud music, ethnic food, and vintage clothing stalls, which draw everyone from aging hippies with their families to pierced and tattooed youth looking for a little raucous amusement.

Nearby **Los Feliz** is the home of the **American Film Institute** campus, Los Feliz Boulevard at Western Avenue, whose **Louis B. Mayer Library** (Mon, Tues & Thurs 9am–5pm, Wed 9am–7pm, Sat 10am–4pm; free; ℡323/856-7654, ⓦwww.afi.com) is a non-circulating research facility with 14,000 books, 5000 scripts, and all manner of archives on classic and contemporary movies, with special collections devoted to Martin Scorsese, Sergei Eisenstein, and many others. Further south, the **Hollyhock House**, on a small hill close to the junction of Vermont Avenue at 4800 Hollywood Boulevard (Wed–Sun tours at the bottom of the hour 12.30–3.30pm; $7; ℡323/662-8139, ⓦwww.hollyhockhouse.net), was the first of architect Frank Lloyd Wright's contributions to LA and was largely supervised by his student, Rudolf Schindler, later one of LA's pre-eminent architects. Covered with Maya motifs and stylized, geometric renderings of the hollyhock flower, the house, completed in 1921, is an intriguingly obsessive dwelling, whose original furniture (now replaced by detailed reconstructions) continued the conceptual flow. The house and the surrounding land now make up the **Barnsdall Art Park**, featuring a number of galleries devoted to the work of regional artists, and making for a pleasant stop while you're waiting for the Hollyhock tour to begin.

Another Wright building, the 1924 **Ennis House**, looms over Los Feliz at 2655 Glendower Avenue. One of four of his local structures to feature "textile" concrete block, its ominous, pre-Columbian appearance has added atmosphere to more than thirty film and TV productions, from Vincent Price's *The House on Haunted Hill* to David Lynch's *Twin Peaks* to Ridley Scott's *Blade Runner*. The house has been undergoing much-needed restoration, so call or email to inquire about tours (℡323/660-0607, ⓦwww.ennishouse.org). Further into the hills, Richard Neutra's **Lovell House**, 4616 Dundee Drive, is a set of sleek, white rectangles and broad window bands that looks quite contemporary for a 1929 building, making it one of LA's landmarks of early modernism. More garish is the **Sowden House**, 5121 Franklin Avenue, a pink box with concrete jaws designed by Frank Lloyd Wright's son Lloyd. It's not open for tours, though it and other homes in the area can be viewed (at least from the outside) on a trip sponsored by Architecture Tours LA (see p.80).

Central Hollywood

The few short blocks of **CENTRAL HOLLYWOOD** contain the densest concentration of celebrity glamour and film mythology in the world, and a pervasive nostalgia that makes the area deeply appealing in a way no measure of commercialism can diminish. The decline that blighted the area from the early 1960s is slowly receding in the face of prolonged efforts by local authorities, which have included repaving Hollywood Boulevard with a special glass-laden tarmac that sparkles in the streetlights and inviting all manner of new malls to take root here. Nevertheless the place still gets hairy after dark away from the main tourist zones, when petty thieves go hunting for the odd purse or wallet. The contrasting qualities of freshly polished nostalgia, corporate hype, and deep-set seediness also make Hollywood one of LA's most diverse areas – and one of its best spots for funky bar-hopping and nightclubbing, with a range of affordable options.

Along Hollywood Boulevard

HOLLYWOOD BOULEVARD is, of course, the axis of all the accumulated movie lore, and if you follow it west, the first notable sight is the junction of **Hollywood and Vine**, where, during the early studio era (1910s–20s), the rumor spread that any budding star had only to parade around this junction to be spotted by big-name film producers or directors (the major studios were all concentrated nearby), who nursed coffees behind the windows of neighboring restaurants. In fact, while many real stars did pass by, it was only briefly on their way to and from work, and the crossing did nothing but earn an inflated reputation. For a commemoration of the era, you'll have to proceed underground to the local **Red Line** subway stop, which is decorated with all sorts of film-related geegaws and memorabilia.

Much of the pavement along this stretch of Hollywood Boulevard is marked by the brass nameplates of the **Walk of Fame** (officially beginning at Hollywood and Vine). The laying of the plates began in 1960, instigated by the local chamber of commerce, which set about honoring the big names in radio, television, movies, music, and theater to boost tourism. Local newspapers announce induction ceremonies for such worthies, and selected stars have to part with several thousand dollars for the privilege of being included: among them are Marlon Brando (1717 Vine St), Marlene Dietrich (6400 Hollywood Blvd), Michael Jackson (6927 Hollywood Blvd), Elvis Presley (6777 Hollywood Blvd), and Ronald Reagan (6374 Hollywood Blvd).

Other Hollywood icons can be found just off the Walk: at 1750 N Vine Street, for one, the **Capitol Records Tower** resembles a stack of 45rpm records and served as the music company's headquarters until it was sold to a developer in 2006. Nearby, at 6233 Hollywood Boulevard, the **Pantages Theater** (T 323/468-1770) has one of the city's greatest interiors, a melange of Baroque styling that sees mainly touring stage productions. Next door, the **Frolic Room** is an old-time watering hole (see p.165) that has appeared in countless movies, notable for its dynamic neon sign and interior mural of the stars drawn by the cartoonist Al Hirschfeld. Also in the vicinity, the bulky **Knickerbocker Hotel**, 1714 Ivar Avenue, now a retirement center, was where the widow of legendary escapologist Harry Houdini conducted a rooftop seance in an attempt to assist her late spouse in his greatest escape of all. During the 1930s and 1940s, the hotel had a reputation for rooming some of Hollywood's more unstable characters, and a number of lesser names jumped from its high windows; in the 1950s the likes of Elvis Presley and Jerry Lee Lewis stayed here. Further south on Ivar, between Sunset and Hollywood boulevards, the popular **Hollywood Farmers Market** (Sun 8am–1pm; T 323/463-3171, W www .farmernet.com) has been doling out agrarian goodies for more than a decade, its hundred vendors selling their wares to locals and tourists alike.

Back on Hollywood Boulevard, the **Musso and Frank Grill**, no. 6667 (see p.155), is a 1919 restaurant that has been a fixture since the days of silent cinema, where writers, actors, and studio bosses would meet (and still do, occasionally) to slap backs, cut deals, and drink potent lunches. A block away, the **Egyptian Theatre**, 6712 Hollywood Boulevard, was the site of the very first Hollywood premiere (*Robin Hood*, an epic swashbuckler starring Douglas Fairbanks Sr) in 1922. Financed by impresario Sid Grauman, the Egyptian was a glorious fantasy in its heyday, modestly seeking to re-create the Temple of Thebes, with usherettes dressed as Cleopatra. It has since been lovingly restored by the American Cinematheque film foundation, and now plays an assortment of classics, documentaries, avant-garde flicks, and foreign films to small but appreciative crowds (typical ticket $10). Tourists are encouraged to check out a short documentary, presented hourly, chronicling the rise of Hollywood as America's movie capital (usually Sat & Sun 11.40am; $7; ☎ 323/466-3456, ⓦ www.egyptiantheatre.com). Alternatively, you can get the grand tour of the theater itself in hour-long, in-depth visits to sights like the backstage dressing rooms and projection booth, usually presented twice monthly in the middle of the month (10.30am only; $10; ☎ 323/461-2020 ext. 3). Much less appealing, the eastern corners of the Hollywood and Highland intersection feature a handful of overpriced tourist traps – wax museum, oddities gallery, world-record exhibit – that are worthwhile only for the easily amused.

West of the Egyptian, the **Hollywood & Highland** complex (☎ 323/467-6412, ⓦ www.hollywoodandhighland.com), on the northwest side of the eponymous intersection, was the spur to much recent development, its chain retailers making central Hollywood safe again for corporate America and its specially designed **Kodak Theatre** annually hosting the Oscars. Still, despite its eye-catching Pop architecture – a replica of the Babylonian set from the 1916 D.W. Griffith spectacular *Intolerance*, with super-sized columns, elephant statues, and colossal archway – it's still no better than your average suburban mall and won't distract anyone but the most ardent shoppers for more than an hour.

One site that the mall has swallowed up is the **Chinese Theatre**, 6925 Hollywood Boulevard (☎ 323/464-8111, ⓦ www.manntheatres.com/chinese), which has been expanded into a multiplex and its main auditorium restored to its gloriously kitschy origins. This was another of Sid Grauman's showpieces from the early days of the movie biz, an odd version of a classical Asian temple, replete with dubious Chinese motifs and upturned dragon-tail flanks, and the lobby's Art Deco splendor and the grand chinoiserie of the auditorium make for interesting viewing. For $5 you can take in a tour of a theater, complete with a look at VIP seating, a lounge, and balconies for the glitterati who attend premieres of big-budget spectaculars. Afterward, on the street outside the

---

Hollywood impressions at the Chinese Theatre

Opened in 1927 as a lavish setting for premieres of swanky new productions, the **Chinese Theatre** was for many decades *the* spot for movie first nights, and the public crowded behind the rope barriers in the thousands to watch the movie aristocrats arriving for the screenings. The main draw, of course, has always been the assortment of **cement handprints** and **footprints** embedded in the theater's forecourt. The idea came about when actress Norma Talmadge accidentally – though some say it was a deliberate publicity stunt – trod in wet cement while visiting the construction site with owner Sid Grauman, who had established a reputation for creating garish movie palaces with gloriously vulgar designs based on exotic themes. The first formally to leave their marks were Mary Pickford and Douglas Fairbanks Sr, who ceremoniously dipped their digits when arriving for the opening of **King of Kings**, and the practice continues today. It's certainly fun to work out the actual dimensions of your favorite film stars, and to discover if your hands are smaller than Julie Andrews' or your feet are bigger than Rock Hudson's.

The Hollywood sign

The **Hollywood sign** began life on the slopes of Mount Lee in 1923 as little more than a billboard for the **Hollywoodland** development and originally contained its full name; however, in 1949 when a storm knocked down the "H" and damaged the rest of the sign, the "land" part was removed and the rest became the familiar symbol of the area and of the entertainment industry. Unfortunately, the current incarnation has literally lost its radiance: it once featured 4000 light bulbs that beamed the district's name as far away as LA Harbor, but a lack of maintenance and an abundance of thievery put an end to that practice.

The sign has also gained a reputation as a suicide spot, ever since would-be movie star Peg Entwistle terminated her career and life here in 1932, aged 24 – no mean feat, with the sign being as difficult to reach then as it is now. Less fatal mischief has been practiced by students of nearby Caltech, who on one occasion renamed the sign for their school. More unsavory acts of sign desecration have also occurred, and because of this history, there's no public road to the sign (Beachwood Drive comes nearest, but ends at a closed gate) and you'll incur minor cuts and bruises while scrambling to get anywhere near. In any case, infrared cameras and radar-activated zoom lenses have been installed to catch graffiti writers, and innocent tourists who can't resist a close look are also liable for a steep fine. For a much simpler look, you can check out the sign from your computer by visiting Ⓦwww.hollywoodsign.org.

▲ The Hollywood sign

theater, hop aboard a tour for a look at the "homes of the stars" (see p.80), or linger with hundreds of other sightseers amid the celebrity impersonators, low-rent magicians, and assorted oddballs vying for your amusement and money.

Similarly, the **El Capitan Theater**, no. 6834, is a colorful 1926 movie palace, with Baroque and Moorish details and a wild South Seas-themed interior of sculpted angels and garlands, plus grotesque sculptures of strange faces and creatures. Twice restored in recent years, the theater also has one of LA's great marquees, a multicolored profusion of flashing bulbs and neon tubes, and now hosts Disney movies as well as the TV talk show of frat-guy humorist Jimmy Kimmel (TV tickets at ☏866/546-6984, movie tickets at Ⓦwww.elcapitantickets .com). A few doors down, the **Hollywood Roosevelt**, 7000 Hollywood Boulevard, was movieland's first luxury hotel (see p.84). Opened in the same year as the Chinese Theatre, it fast became the meeting place of top actors and screenwriters, its *Cinegrill* restaurant feeding and watering the likes of W.C. Fields, Ernest Hemingway, and F. Scott Fitzgerald, and has since been sumptuously restored into one of the more elegant redoubts of old Tinseltown.

Just south of Hollywood Boulevard, the **Hollywood Museum**, 1660 Highland Boulevard (Thurs–Sun 10am–5pm; $15; ⓦ www.thehollywoodmuseum.com), exhibits on its four levels the fashion, art design, props, and special effects taken from a broad swath of movie history, including the latest Hollywood spectaculars. However, even though it's located in America's film capital, the museum pales in comparison to the much more comprehensive and informative Museum of Television and Radio in Beverly Hills (see p.121).

Along Sunset Boulevard

Paralleling Hollywood Boulevard to the south is another famous stretch nearly as steeped in movie legend, **Sunset Boulevard**, which sports both contemporary decay and countless sites for Tinseltown nostalgia. At no. 6360, the huge, white **Cinerama Dome** was built in 1963 to exhibit giant three-projector films on a curved screen and is now part of a larger retail complex of theaters, shops, and eateries called ArcLight (ⓣ 323/464-1478, ⓦ www .arclightcinemas.com). Luckily, you can still see (single-projector) block-busters in the dome on a large, curved screen – as fun and engaging a cinematic experience as any in LA – and occasionally even view such three-projector flicks as *This is Cinerama!* Nearby, the Spanish Revival-style building at 6525 Sunset Boulevard was, from the 1920s until the 1950s, known as the **Hollywood Athletic Club**. Another of Hollywood's legendary watering holes, the likes of Charlie Chaplin, Clark Gable, and Tarzan himself (Johnny Weismuller) lounged beside its Olympic-sized pool, while Johns Barrymore and Wayne held olympic drinking parties in the apartment levels above, with the Duke himself prone to chucking billiard balls at passing automobiles below. Now the club opens only for special parties and events.

The grouping of business offices at **Crossroads of the World**, 6672 Sunset Blvd, isn't much to look at these days, but when finished in 1936, it was one of LA's major tourist attractions and one of the very first local malls. The central plaza supposedly resembles a ship, surrounded by shops designed with Tudor, French, Italian, and Spanish motifs – the idea being that the shops are the ports into which the shopper would sail. Finally, nearby are the grand gates of **Paramount Studios**, south entrance at 5555 Melrose Avenue (2-hour tours Mon–Fri 10am & 2pm; $35; by reservation at ⓣ 323/956-1777, ⓦ www .paramount.com/studio), though the original entrance – which Gloria Swanson rode through in *Sunset Boulevard* – is now inaccessible. The tour isn't quite up to the standard of Universal's theme-park madness or Warner Brothers' close-up visit, but if you want to poke around soundstages and a mildly interesting backlot (and have plenty of cash to spare), it may be worth it. Further on down Sunset, the **Guitar Center**, 7425 Sunset Boulevard (ⓣ 323/874-1060, ⓦ www .rockwalk.com), a musical-instrument store, features handprints of your favorite guitar gods embedded in the manner of the movie stars' at the Chinese Theatre, in this case with performers from AC/DC to ZZ Top.

Hollywood Forever

Not surprisingly for a town obsessed with marketing and PR, even the cemeteries are renamed to draw the crowds. Thus the former Hollywood Memorial Park has been reincarnated as **Hollywood Forever**, a few blocks below Sunset at 6000 Santa Monica Boulevard (daily dawn–dusk; free; ⓣ 323/469-1181, ⓦ www.hollywoodforever.com), though the graves have luckily been kept in the same places. Overlooked by the famous water tower of neighboring Paramount Studios, the cemetery displays myriad tombs of dead celebrities, most notably in its southeastern corner, where a cathedral mausoleum includes, at no. 1205, the resting place of **Rudolph Valentino**. In 1926, 10,000 people packed the cemetery when the celebrated screen lover died aged just 31, and to this day on each anniversary of his passing (23 August), at least one "Lady in Black" will likely be found mourning – a tradition that started as a publicity stunt in 1931 and has continued ever since.

Fittingly, outside the mausoleum, the most pompous grave belongs to **Douglas Fairbanks Sr**, who, with his wife Mary Pickford (herself buried at Forest Lawn Glendale), did much to introduce nouveau-riche snobbery to Hollywood. Even in death Fairbanks keeps a snooty distance from the pack, his ostentatious memorial (complete with pond) only reachable by a shrub-lined path from the mausoleum. More visually appealing, on the south side of Fairbanks' memorial lake stands the appropriately black bust of **Johnny Ramone**, erected in 2004 following his death and showing the seminal punk pioneer rocking out with dark, mop-top intensity. Further west, **Mel Blanc**, "the man of a thousand voices" – among them Bugs Bunny, Porky Pig, Tweety Pie, and Sylvester – has an epitaph that simply reads "That's All, Folks."

Griffith Park

Built on land donated by Gilded Age mining millionaire Griffith J. Griffith, vast **GRIFFITH PARK**, between Hollywood and the San Fernando Valley (daily 5am–10.30pm, mountain roads close at dusk; free; ⊤323/913-4688), offers gentle greenery and rugged mountain slopes, a welcome respite from the chaos of LA. Above the landscaped flat sections, where the crowds assemble to picnic, play sports, or visit the fixed attractions, the hillsides are rough and wild, marked only by foot and bridle paths, leading into desolate but unspoiled terrain that gives great views over the LA basin and out towards the ocean. The only thing marring the landscape is the occasional presence of **wildfires**, the most recent of which, in May 2007, laid a fair swath of devastation to part of the park, burning out well-loved spots like Dante's View and narrowly missing the most popular sites. Be alert if you arrive at the height of summer.

There are four **main entrances** to Griffith Park. Western Canyon Road, north of Los Feliz Boulevard, enters the park through the **Ferndell** – as the name suggests, a lush glade of ferns, from which numerous trails run deeper into the park – and continues up to the **Griffith Observatory**, 2800 E Observatory Road (Tues–Fri noon–10pm, Sat & Sun 10am–10pm; free; ⊤213/473-0800, ⓦwww.griffithobservatory.org), familiar from its use as a backdrop in *Rebel Without a Cause* and numerous low-budget sci-fi flicks such as *The Amazing Colossal Man*. This astronomical icon, one of the city's most enjoyable spots, now presents an array of high-tech exhibits for young and old alike – highlighted by the twelve-inch Zeiss refracting telescope, the trio of solar telescopes for viewing sunspots and solar storms, and other assorted, smaller telescopes set up on selected evenings for inspecting the firmament at your own pace. A full range of modern exhibits covers the history of astronomy and human observation, including a camera obscura, and a 150-foot timeline of the universe provides the lowdown on cosmological history and explains wormholes, black holes, and other out-of-this-world notions. For planetarium shows you'll need to reserve a space at the observatory and pay $7 for tickets. There's so much at the facility – which has quickly become a contender for

Hiking in Griffith Park

The steeper parts of Griffith Park, which blend into the foothills of the Santa Monica Mountains, offer a variety of hiking trails. You can get maps from the **ranger station**, at 4400 Crystal Springs Road (daily during daylight hours; ☎323/913-4688), which is also the starting point for guided hikes and atmospheric evening walks, held whenever there's a full moon. Nearby, at 4730 Crystal Springs Drive, is a bike-rental location (summer Fri–Sun 2–8pm, rest of year Sat & Sun noon–dusk; ☎323/653-4099). The rangers have driving maps that detail the best vantage points for views over the whole of LA, not least from the highest place in the park – the summit of Mount Hollywood.

the nation's top observatory and museum – that reservations for visiting are required and parking disallowed; to visit, call ☎1-888/695-0888 and prepare to pick up the shuttle ($8 per person) at the Hollywood & Highland mall, LA Zoo parking lot, or Greek Theatre.

Descending from the observatory on Vermont Canyon Road (effectively the continuation of Western Canyon Road) brings you to a small **bird sanctuary** set within a modest-sized wooded canyon. Across the road is the **Greek Theatre** (☎323/665-5857, ⓦwww.greektheatrela.com), an open-air amphitheater that seats nearly five thousand beneath its quasi-Greek columns – though if you're not going in for a show (the Greek is a venue for big-name rock, jazz, and country music concerts during the summer), you'll see just the bland exterior.

The **northern end** of the park, over the hills in the San Fernando Valley, is best reached directly by car from the Golden State Freeway, although you can take the park roads (or explore the labyrinth of hiking trails) that climb the park's hilly core past some of its wildlife lurking in the brush. Caged animals, meanwhile, are plentiful in the **LA Zoo**, 5333 Zoo Drive (daily 10am–5pm; $10, kids $5; ⓦwww.lazoo.org), one of the biggest zoos in the country and home to more than 1600 creatures, divided by continent and in pens representing various parts of the world. Despite the zoological inventory and layout, it's still not terribly impressive, especially in comparison to its San Diego counterpart (see p.207). Even less intriguing is the nostalgic **Travel Town Museum**, 5200 Zoo Drive (Mon–Fri 10am–4pm, Sat & Sun 10am–5pm; free; ⓦwww.traveltown.org), touted as a transportation museum but more a dumping ground for old trains and fire trucks. Bounding Griffith Park's northwest rim, **Forest Lawn Hollywood Hills**, 6300 Forest Lawn Drive (daily 8am–5pm; ☎1-800/204-3131, ⓦwww.forestlawn.com), is a cemetery of the stars that, while not quite as awe-inspiringly vulgar as its Glendale counterpart, is no less pretentious, with showy grave-markers and fancy memorials to such esteemed figures as Buster Keaton, Marvin Gaye, Charles Laughton, Liberace, and Jack Webb.

Museum of the American West

Sharing a parking lot with the zoo, the **Museum of the American West**, near the junction of the Ventura and Golden State freeways at 4700 Western Heritage Way (Tues–Sun 10am–5pm; $9, students $5; ☎323/667-2000, ⓦwww.museumoftheamericanwest.org), was founded by Gene Autry, the "singing cowboy" who cut more than six hundred discs beginning in 1929, starred in blockbuster Hollywood Westerns during the 1930s and 1940s, became even more of a household name through his TV show in the 1950s, and died in 1999 after a very lengthy career. Autry fans hoping for a shrine to the man who penned the immortal *That Silver-Haired Daddy of Mine* are in for a surprise, however. The **collection** – from buckskin jackets and branding irons to Frederic Remington's sculptures of early twentieth-century Western life and the truth about the shootout at the OK Corral – is a serious and credible attempt to explore the mindset and culture of those who colonized the West. The museum includes engaging sections on native peoples, European exploration, nineteenth-century pioneers, the Wild West, Asian immigrants, and, of course, Hollywood's versions of all of the above.

The Hollywood Hills

Apart from offering the chance to see the endlessly flat expanse of the LA basin, the views from the **HOLLYWOOD HILLS** feature perhaps the oddest and most opulent selection of properties to be found anywhere. Around these canyons and slopes, which run from Hollywood itself into Benedict Canyon above Beverly Hills, mansions are so commonplace that only the half-dozen fully blown castles really stand out.

Mulholland Drive, named after LA's most renowned hydro-engineer, runs along the crest, passing some of the most famous sites: Rudolph Valentino's extravagant **Falcon Lair** (1436 Bella Drive), Errol Flynn's **Mulholland House** (7740 Mulholland Drive), and the former home of actress Sharon Tate (10066 Cielo Drive) – and studio of Trent Reznor of Nine Inch Nails – where some of the Manson family killings took place. If you're more interested in peeking at the homes of today's stars, check out one of the many tours designed expressly for celebrity gazing (see p.80), or look up a master list on the Internet (Ⓦwww.seeing-stars.com is a good place to start). Doubtless the most bizarre sight is the **Chemosphere**, 776 Torreyson Drive, a giant UFO house hovering above the canyon on a long pedestal, designed by quirky architect John Lautner and now home to irreverent publisher Benedikt Taschen, who sometimes throws outrageous parties in its alien confines.

Other architectural treats can be found with sufficient effort as well, notably the stunning **Case Study House #21**, 9038 Wonderland Park Avenue, Pierre Koenig's hillside glass-and-steel box, part of the influential Case Study Program that tried to bring modernism to the middle class in the Forties and Fifties. Unfortunately, most of the area's other houses are hidden away, and there's no real way to explore in depth without your own car, a copy of the latest *Thomas Guide* map and, if possible, a detailed guide to LA architecture.

Lake Hollywood

Hemmed in among the hills between Griffith Park and the Hollywood Freeway, **Lake Hollywood** is a small piece of open country in the heart of the city. The clear, calm waters, actually a reservoir intended for drought relief, are surrounded by clumps of pines in which squirrels, lizards, and a few scurrying skunks and coyotes easily outnumber humans. You can't get too near the water, as metal fences protect it from the public, but the footpaths that encircle it are pleasant for a stroll, especially for a glimpse of the stone bears' heads that decorate the reservoir's curving front wall.

You can only reach the lake by car. Although opening and closing times vary widely throughout the year, the lake **access road** is generally open from 6.30am until 6.30pm. To get to it, go north on Cahuenga Boulevard past Franklin Avenue and turn right onto Dix Street, left into Holly Drive and climb to Deep Dell Place; from there it's a sharp left on Weidlake Drive. Follow the winding little street to the main gate.

The Hollywood Bowl

Near the Hollywood Freeway at 2301 N Highland Avenue, the **Hollywood Bowl** is an open-air auditorium that opened in 1921 and has since become something of an icon for outdoor bandshells. The Beatles played here in the mid-1960s, but the Bowl's principal function is as the occasional summer home of the Los Angeles Philharmonic, which gives evening concerts from July to September (☎323/850-2000, ⊛www.hollywoodbowl.org). These events are less highbrow than you might imagine, many of them featuring spirited crowd-pleasers like *Victory at Sea* and the *1812 Overture*, as well as selections of smooth jazz, film music, and other inoffensive fare. More about the Bowl's history can be gleaned from the video inside the **Hollywood Bowl Museum** near the entrance (July to mid-Sept Tues–Sat 10am to showtime, Sun 4pm to showtime; mid-Sept to June Tues–Sat 10am–5pm; free; ☎323/850-2000). It's not an essential stop by any means, but is worth a visit if you have any affection for the grand old concrete structure. With a collection of musical instruments from around the world, the museum also features recordings of notable symphonic moments in the Bowl's history and architectural drawings by Lloyd Wright, Frank's son (more famous for his Wayfarer's Chapel, p.133, and spooky Sowden House, p.105), who contributed a design for one of the Bowl's many shells. The fifth and newest of these dates from the summer of 2004.

West LA

What is loosely called the Westside of Los Angeles begins immediately beyond Hollywood in **WEST LA** – which contains some of the city's most expensive, and exclusive, neighborhoods. Bordered by the Santa Monica Mountains to the north and the Santa Monica Freeway to the south, and Hollywood and the beach cities to the respective east and west, the swath of West LA best embodies the stylish images that the city projects to the outside world.

One of the best reasons to come to West LA is the impressive collection of the **LA County Museum of Art (LACMA)**, on the eastern perimeter of the **Fairfax District**, forming the centerpiece of the resurgent cultural zone touted as the **Museum Mile** (sitting at the west end of the classic 1930s auto strip known as the Miracle Mile). West of Fairfax Avenue and north of Beverly Boulevard, **West Hollywood** is known for its art and design, loaded with posey restaurants and boutiques, and is surprisingly low-slung except for a giant design center at its core. **Beverly Hills**, a little farther west, is less friendly but more affluent: you may need an expense account to buy a sandwich but it's a matchless place to indulge in window-shopping on the way to the more roundly appealing **Westwood**. The main activity in this low-rise, Spanish Revival, pedestrianized area has always been movies – seeing them rather than making them. The original Art Deco palaces still retain most of their original glory, and are a hop from the **UCLA Campus**, home to a number of galleries and museums, with a lively student atmosphere. The **Sepulveda Pass** forms the western edge of West LA and leads the visitor to the essential **Getty Center** and the **Skirball Cultural Center**, both positioned high above the basin's turmoil.

Fairfax Avenue and the Miracle Mile

Between Santa Monica and Wilshire boulevards, **Fairfax Avenue** is still the backbone of the city's Jewish culture. Apart from temples, yeshivas, kosher

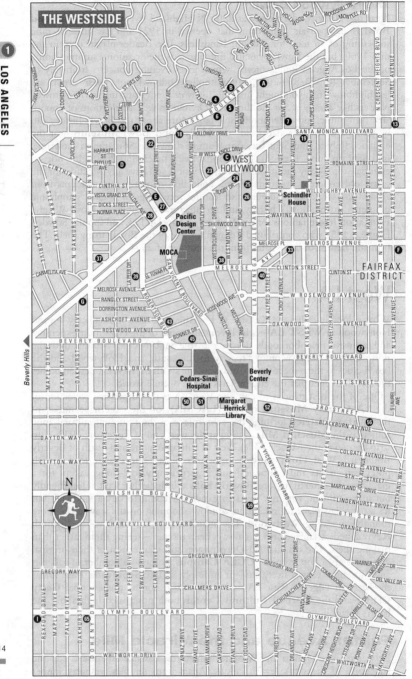

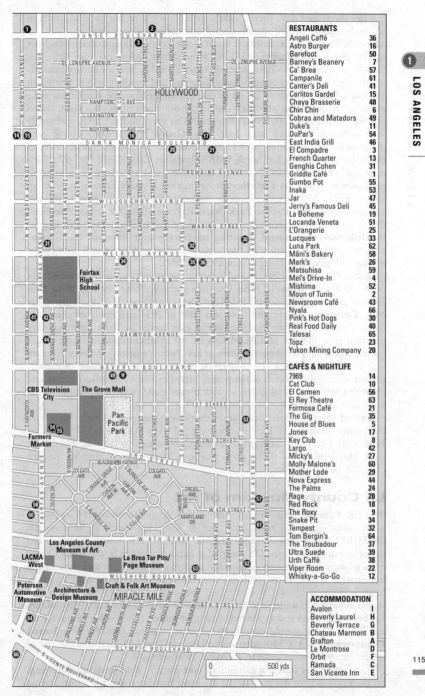

butcher shops, and delis, there's little actually to see here, but by local standards it's a refreshingly vibrant neighborhood, and easily explored on foot.

From Wilshire, Fairfax continues north to the long-standing wooden structures of the **Farmers' Market**, 6333 W Third Street (Mon–Fri 9am–9pm, Sat 9am–8pm, Sun 10am–7pm; free; ℡323/933-9211, ⓦwww.farmersmarketla .com), a rabbit warren of restaurants, bakeries, and produce stands. Started in 1934 as a little agricultural co-op during the Depression, the market has since expanded to the point where it's a social phenomenon in its own right, always buzzing with tourists and locals who come to meet and eat, and increasingly shop – the recent mall next door, **The Grove** (℡323/900-8080, ⓦwww .thegrovela.com), is a three-level, $100 million colossus that offers branches of all the major chain stores. Just north, **CBS Television City** (℡818/295-2700) is a thoroughly contemporary, sprawling black cube – and something of an architectural eyesore – but also a worthwhile destination if you're in town to sit in an audience for a sitcom, game show, or the network's *Late Late Show*. To the east on Third Street, **Pan Pacific Park** (Mon–Fri 9am–10pm, Sat & Sun 9am–6pm; ℡323/939-0263) has sports facilities and a jogging path, but is most affecting for its **Holocaust Memorial**, featuring six black-granite columns (each representing a million Jews killed by the Nazis) inscribed with the events taking place in that dark period in Europe from 1933 to 1945.

Back at the corner of Fairfax and Wilshire, the premier property development of the 1930s, the **Miracle Mile**, stretched along Wilshire eastward to La Brea Avenue and is still lined with faded Art Deco monuments. At this corner, the **May Company** department store was built in 1934 and has been compared to an oversized, golden perfume bottle ever since; its main contemporary function is as the site of **LACMA West**, an exhibition annex to the larger museum down the road (same details as LACMA, see below). When this annex isn't showing big-ticket blockbusters, it presents a good selection of experimental work, historic and contemporary pieces by Native American artists, and children's art in a special gallery – with pieces made to be jumped on, played with, and laughed at.

Most of the old department stores that once lined the Miracle Mile have long since closed, but look out for the **El Rey Theater**, 5515 Wilshire Boulevard, a thriving concert venue (see p.169) with a yellow-and-red design, sleek king's head, and flashy neon marquee, unmistakable amid its modern concrete-box neighbors.

LA County Museum of Art

The **LA County Museum of Art**, 5905 Wilshire Boulevard (Mon, Tues & Thurs noon–8pm, Fri noon–9pm, Sat & Sun 11am–8pm; $9, students $5; ℡323/857-6000, ⓦwww.lacma.org), is one of the least-known of the important museums in the US, dwarfed in national prestige by the Getty Center even though its collection is considerably broader and is, in fact, one of the largest west of the Mississippi. Since its creation in 1965, the museum's homely beige-and-green blocks have attracted the scorn of architecture critics and served as plodding, uninspired places to house a range of world art. The museum has been renovated and expanded, making it more of the proper venue for art exhibition that it should have been all along, and in 2008 the new **Broad Contemporary Art Museum** opens between LACMA West and the rest of the facility, with other galleries substantially refurbished.

Most big-budget traveling exhibitions take place in the **Hammer Building**, on the north side of the site, leaving the other two large structures to showcase selections from the permanent collection. Across the courtyard, the **Modern and Contemporary Art Building** presents prominent pieces of twentieth-century art, including works by Picasso, Magritte, and Abstract Expressionists like Mark Rothko and Franz Kline. Less celebrated, but just as appealing, is Mariko Mori's hypnotic video presentation *Miko No Inori*, in which the platinum-blonde artist stares at the viewer with ice-blue eyes, manipulating a glowing orb to a hushed and haunting soundtrack; Bill Viola's *Slowly Turning Narrative*, a huge, rotating projection screen displaying discordant images; and Ed Kienholz's *Back Seat Dodge '38*, looking just as perverse as it did in the 1960s when it caused political outrage. (Note that some of these pieces are relocating to the Broad building.)

Just west, the **Ahmanson Building's** central attractions are undoubtedly the **European art rooms**, which begin with a good overview of Greek and Roman art and continue into the medieval era with religious sculptures and ecclesiastical ornamentation, notably a series of stone carvings of the Passion cycle. The Renaissance and Mannerist eras are represented by compelling works such as Paolo Veronese's *Two Allegories of Navigation*, great Mannerist figures filling the frame from an imposing low angle, El Greco's *The Apostle Saint Andrew*, an uncommonly reserved portrait, and Titian's *Portrait of Giacomo Dolfin*, a carefully tinted study by the great colorist. Northern European painters are well represented by Hans Holbein's small, resplendent *Portrait of a Young Woman with White Coif*, a number of Frans Hals' pictures of cheerful burghers, and Rembrandt's probing *Portrait of Marten Looten*.

Alongside many excellent collections of Southeast Asian sculpture and Middle Eastern decorative arts in the Ahmanson Building, the **Fearing Collection** consists of funeral masks and sculpted guardian figures from the ancient civilizations of pre-Columbian Mexico. Where the museum really excels, however, is in its specializations, notably the prints and drawings in the **Rifkind Center for German Expressionist Studies** (in the Bing Center; by appointment only), which includes a library of magazines and tracts from Weimar Germany, and the **Pavilion for Japanese Art**. The pavilion was created by iconoclastic architect Bruce Goff to re-create the effects of traditional shoji screens, filtering varying levels and qualities of light through to the interior. Displays include painted screens and scrolls, ceramics, and lacquerware, viewable on a ramp spiraling down to a small, ground-floor waterfall that trickles pleasantly amid the near-silence of the gallery. Across from the Pavilion, the **Leo S. Bing Theatre** in the **Bing Center** presents a regular series of film programs that focus on classic Hollywood, art-house, and foreign favorites, for about the cost of a regular movie ($9; ℡323/857-6010).

Other Museum Mile attractions

Just east of LACMA, the **La Brea Tar Pits**, a large pool of smelly tar ("la brea" in Spanish), are one of LA's most familiar natural formations. Tens of thousands of years ago during the last Ice Age, primeval creatures from tapirs to mastodons tried to drink from the thin layer of water covering the tar in the pits, only to become stuck fast and preserved for modern science. Millions of bones belonging to the animals (and one set of human bones) have been found here, with some of them reconstructed in the **George C. Page Discovery Center** (daily 9.30am–5pm, Sat & Sun from 10am; $7, students $4.50; ℡323/934-7243, ⓦwww.tarpits.org). Here you can spot the skeletons of your favorite extinct creatures, from giant ground sloths to menacing saber-toothed tigers – in fact, it was a petroleum geologist, William Orcutt, who found the modern world's first such skull here in 1916. Tar still seeps from the ground, but most of the sticky goo oozes behind chain-link fences.

South of LACMA, across from LACMA West at 6060 Wilshire Boulevard, the **Petersen Automotive Museum** (Tues–Sun 10am–6pm; $10, parking $6; ☎323/930-2277, ⓦwww.petersen.org) offers three floors loaded with all kinds of vehicles, with periodic exhibits on topics like the golden age of custom cars in the 1950s and 1960s and "million-dollar" vehicles like the 1919 Bentley and 1961 Ferrari. The ground floor features an asphalt path that takes you on a journey through the city's vehicular past, from crude early twentieth-century flivvers and early hot rods that raced on dangerous wooden tracks, to a classic 1930s gas station, post–World War II gas guzzlers, and so on.

For another dose of art on the strip, check out the **Architecture + Design Museum**, 5900 Wilshire Boulevard (Mon–Sat 10am–6pm, Sun 11am–5pm; $5; ⓦwww.aplusd.org), which puts on rotating exhibits of the latest trends in art, photography, and architecture, with most of the famous international names represented. The last significant museum on the Museum Mile is the **Craft and Folk Art Museum**, 5814 Wilshire Boulevard (Tues, Wed & Fri 11am–5pm,

A trip to Culver City

South of West LA and east of Venice, **Culver City** was one of the towns that helped give rise to the American movie industry in the 1910s. Much of this tradition is still visible at the gates of the old Triangle Pictures, 10202 Washington Boulevard, the early studio of film pioneer and producer **Thomas Ince**, a major figure in the industry until he was mysteriously killed on William Randolph Hearst's yacht. Triangle became MGM by the 1920s, which in turn was swallowed up by Sony. Unfortunately, most of the glorious backlot was torn down, so if you go on a tour of the facility (Mon–Fri 9.30am, 10.30am, 1.30pm & 2.30pm; $25; ☎323/520-8687) you'll have to be content with sauntering through massive, often empty soundstages and sets for such TV shows as *Jeopardy!* Fans of *Gone With the Wind*, however, may recognize Ince's other former complex, now the **Culver Studios**, at 9336 Washington Boulevard – predictably, this Colonial Revival "mansion" is no more than a facade.

While you're in the area, take a look at the **Hayden Tract**, LA's premier showplace for modern, deconstructivist architecture, lying near Hayden Avenue and National Boulevard and featuring the stunning work of avant-garde master builder **Eric Owen Moss**. A few of his more striking works include Pittard Sullivan, 3535 Hayden Avenue, a giant gray box with massive wooden ribs; 8522 National, featuring a jangled-up facade with a white staircase leading to nowhere; the huge Samitaur, 3457 S La Cienega Boulevard, huge, gray, warehouse-like offices with gnarled, jagged points and a truly freakish sense of geometry; and the Beehive, 8520 National Blvd, a bulbous take on the concept of the (business) hive, with curving bands, a rooftop stairway, and grassy landscaping so undulating it looks ready to twist the knee of the unwary.

If movie history and weird architecture aren't enough for you, top off your trip with a visit to the always bizarre **Museum of Jurassic Technology**, 9341 Venice Boulevard (Thurs 2–8pm, Fri–Sun noon–6pm; $5; ⓦwww.mjt.org). As much an art museum as a science center, it features a great range of oddities from the pseudo-scientific to the paranormal to the just plain creepy. Several regularly rotating exhibits include a trailer-park art display, showing various junk collections next to tiny models of RVs and mobile homes about to be swallowed up by the earth; depictions of folk superstitions, with a memorable image of dead mice on toast used as a cure for bedwetting; written and oral narratives of crank scientists and researchers, many of whom have reputedly disappeared under strange circumstances or gone mad; a strange re-creation of a Baroque-era museum run by a Jesuit scholar; and a series of unearthly insects, like an Amazonian bug that kills its prey through the use of a giant head-spike.

Thurs 11am–7pm, Sat & Sun noon–6pm; $5; ☏323/937-4230, ⓦwww.cafam .org), which has a small selection of handmade objects – rugs, pottery, clothing, and more. The limited gallery space also hosts a few rotating exhibitions, including vintage circus posters, ceramic folk art, and highly detailed Japanese paper arts-and-crafts.

West Hollywood

Between Fairfax Avenue and Beverly Hills, **WEST HOLLYWOOD** is synonymous with social tolerance and upmarket trendiness, established as an autonomous city in 1983 to represent the interests of gays, pensioners, and renters. **Santa Monica Boulevard** is the district's main drag, with flashy dance clubs and designer clothing stores, while the eastern end of the boulevard has become home to a large and growing contingent of Russian expats, many of whom don't mesh too well with the libertine scene around them.

Melrose Avenue, LA's trendiest shopping street, runs parallel to Santa Monica Boulevard four blocks south. In its heyday, Melrose was an eccentric world of its own, but since the 1990s a crush of designer boutiques, salons, and restaurants has been gaining ground at the expense of the older, quirkier tenants, diluting the strip's funky allure and making it more of a touristy, homogenized place. The west end of Melrose is a rather snooty precinct, with furniture shops and art galleries spread out around the hulking, bright-blue glassy pile of the **Pacific Design Center** (Mon–Fri 9.30am–5pm; ☏310/657-0800, ⓦwww .thepacificdesigncenter.com), a design marketplace at 8687 Melrose Avenue near San Vicente Boulevard, known as the "Blue Whale" for the way it dwarfs its low-rise neighbors, along with its counterpart, a geometric emerald monolith known as the "Green Giant." The center also features a Westside branch of the **Museum of Contemporary Art** (Tues–Fri 11am–5pm, Thurs closes 8pm, Sat & Sun 11am–6pm; free; ☏310/289-5223, ⓦwww.moca.org/museum/moca _pdc.php), focusing on architecture and industrial and graphic design with a sleek, modern bent, and often participating in exhibitions with the Downtown MOCA and Geffen Contemporary (see pp.91 and 92).

The stylistic extremes of Melrose Avenue are also reflected in the area's domestic architecture. The 1922 **Schindler House**, 835 N Kings Road (Wed–Sun 11am–6pm; $7), was for years the blueprint of California Modernist architecture, designed by master architect R.M. Schindler with sliding canvas panels meant to be removed in summer, exposed roof rafters, and open-plan rooms facing onto outdoor terraces. Now functioning as the **MAK Center for Art and Architecture**, the house plays host to a range of avant-garde music, art, film, and design exhibitions (☏323/651-1510, ⓦwww.makcenter.com). Four blocks west of the Schindler House, **La Cienega Boulevard** divides West Hollywood roughly down the middle, separating the chic trendies on the Hollywood side from the establishment couturiers on the Beverly Hills border. La Cienega ("the swamp" in Spanish) holds a mixture of LA's best and priciest restaurants and art galleries, and passes the huge **Beverly Center** shopping mall at 8500 Beverly Boulevard (☏310/854-0071, ⓦwww.beverlycenter.com) – a looming fortress of brown plaster that is nonetheless the city's main consumer icon, and teenager central on the weekends.

Further south, on the Beverly Hills border at 333 S La Cienega, the Academy of Motion Picture Arts and Sciences' **Margaret Herrick Library** (Mon, Thurs & Fri 10am–6pm, Tues 10am–8pm; ☏310/247-3000, ⓦwww.oscars.org/mhl) is a non-circulating research library that holds a hoard of film memorabilia and scripts inside a Moorish-style building that was once a water-treatment plant.

Sunset Strip

Above West Hollywood, the roughly two-mile-long conglomeration of restaurants, plush hotels, and nightclubs on Sunset Boulevard has long been known as the **Sunset Strip**. These establishments first began to appear during the early 1920s, along what was then a dusty dirt road serving as the main route between the Hollywood movie studios and the West LA "homes of the stars." With the rise of TV, the Strip declined, only reviving in the 1960s when a scene developed around the landmark *Whisky-a-Go-Go* club, which featured seminal rock bands such as Love and Buffalo Springfield, as well as the manic theatrics of Jim Morrison and The Doors. Since then, the striptease clubs and "head shops" have been phased out, and this fashionable area now rivals Beverly Hills for entertainment-industry executives per square foot. Some tourists come to the strip just to see the enormous **billboards**: fantastic commercial murals animated with eye-catching gimmicks, movie ads with names like Bruce Willis in gargantuan letters, and self-promotions for only-in-LA characters like the busty blonde "Angelyne," who can often be seen looming over Tinseltown in all her Day-Glo splendor.

Greta Garbo was only one of many stars to visit the huge Norman castle that is the **Chateau Marmont** hotel, towering over the east end of Sunset Strip at no. 8221. Built in 1927 as luxury apartments, this stodgy block of white concrete has long been a Hollywood favorite for its elegant private suites and bungalows (see p.84). Across the street, the **House of Blues**, no. 8430, is a corrugated tin shack, with imported dirt from the Deep South, that is one of the area's chief tourist attractions. However, it pales in comparison with the more authentic scenes found around the **Whisky-a-Go-Go**, no. 8901, and the **Roxy**, no. 9009, both of which still offer shows from some of the loudest and angriest rock and punk bands. Other spots, like the **Viper Room**, no. 8852, and the **Sunset Hyatt**, no. 8401, have also established their own sordid histories – Johnny Depp's trendy lair for rockers is the spot where River Phoenix OD'd, and the upscale hotel was the staging ground for the lurid antics of The Who and Led Zeppelin – who took to racing motorcycles down its hallways.

Beverly Hills

Probably the most famous small city in the world, **Beverly Hills** has, through its relentless PR machine, made itself internationally synonymous with free-spending wealth and untrammelled luxury, if not necessarily good taste. Visitors are

▲ Shoppers on Rodeo Drive, Beverly Hills

expected to gaze at the designer boutiques of Rodeo Drive, pressing their noses against the glass, perhaps spotting a fading glamour queen strolling along with her chihuahua. Whatever you do, don't try to make off with any of the merchandise: Beverly Hills has more police per capita than anywhere else in the US.

The town divides into two distinct halves, separated by Santa Monica Boulevard. To the south is the flashy **Golden Triangle** business district, which fills the wedge between Santa Monica and Wilshire boulevards. **Rodeo Drive** cuts through the triangle in a two-block-long, concentrated showcase of the most expensive names in international fashion. It's a dauntingly stylish area, each boutique trying to outshine the rest: none as yet charges for admission, though some require an invitation. Avoid the tourist trap of **Two Rodeo** at Wilshire, a faux European shopping alley that is the height of pretentious kitsch, its phony cobblestoned street really hiding a parking lot below. For a complete overview of the shopping scene, including Rodeo Drive and beyond, take a trip on the **Beverly Hills Trolley** (Sat 11am–4pm on the hour; $5; ☏310/285-2438), which offers tourists a forty-minute glimpse of the town's highlights, departing hourly from the corner of Rodeo Drive and Dayton Way. Even more appealing is the **Museum of Television and Radio**, 465 N Beverly Drive (Wed–Sun noon–5pm; $10 donation, kids $5; ⓦ www.mtr.org), which features a collection of more than 120,000 TV and radio programs and presents rotating exhibits on such subjects as political image-making in an age of high-tech propaganda, famous advertising characters from the twentieth century, and the best of radio and TV sitcoms, dramas, and thrillers.

Above Santa Monica Boulevard is the upmarket part of residential Beverly Hills, its gently curving drives converging on the florid pink-plaster **Beverly Hills Hotel**, on Sunset Boulevard at Rodeo Drive (see p.84). Built in 1913 to attract wealthy settlers to what was then a town of just five hundred people, the hotel's social cachet makes its *Polo Lounge* a prime spot for movie execs to power-lunch. In the verdant canyons and foothills above Sunset, a number of palatial estates lie hidden away behind landscaped security gates. **Benedict Canyon Drive** climbs up from the hotel near many of them, including, at 1040 Angelo Drive, Harold Lloyd's **Green Acres**, where the actor lived for forty years. With its secret passageways and large private screening room, the home survives intact, though the grounds, which contained a waterfall and a nine-hole golf course, have since been broken up into smaller lots. One of the few estates in the area that is open to the public is the wooded **Virginia Robinson Gardens**, 1008 Elden Way (tours Tues–Fri 10am & 1pm; $10, students $5; by appointment only at ☏310/276-5367), which holds six acres of over a thousand plant varieties, including some impressive Australian king palm trees.

The grounds of the biggest house in Beverly Hills, **Greystone Mansion**, are now maintained as a public park by the city, and the 50,000-square-foot manor was once the property of oil titan Edward Doheny. Although the house itself is rarely open (except for political fundraisers and filming music videos), you can visit the sixteen-acre **Greystone Park** (daily 10am–5pm; free) at 905 Loma Vista Drive, admire the mansion's limestone facade and intricately designed chimneys, then stroll through the sixteen-acre park, with its koi-filled ponds and expansive views of the LA sprawl.

Century City

The bland high-rise boxes of **Century City**, just west of Beverly Hills, were erected during the 1960s on what was the backlot of the 20th Century-Fox film studio. The district's main focus, as is so often the case in LA, is a large shopping mall, the **Century City Shopping Center**, 10250 Santa Monica Boulevard (☏310/277-3898, ⓦ www.westfield.com/centurycity), loaded with upscale boutiques and department stores and one of the better moviehouses for current films. To the southwest, the still-functional **20th Century-Fox** studios is strictly off-limits and doesn't offer tours.

Less frivolously, just east of Century City below Beverly Hills, an inauspicious white building at 9786 W Pico Boulevard houses the **Simon Wiesenthal Center for Holocaust Studies**. The US headquarters of the organization devoted to tracking down ex-Nazis, the center has an extensive library of Holocaust-related documents, photographs, and accounts – but the main draw for visitors is the affecting **Beit HaShoa Museum of Tolerance** (April–Oct Mon–Thurs 11am–6.30pm, Fri 11am–5pm, Sun 11am–7.30pm; Nov–March Fri closes 3pm; $10, students $7; ⓦwww.wiesenthal.com/mot), an extraordinary interactive resource center and one of the most technologically advanced institutions of its kind. Among many other exhibits, it leads the visitor through re-enactments outlining the rise of Nazism to a harrowing conclusion in a replica gas chamber.

Westwood and UCLA

Just west of Beverly Hills, on the north side of Wilshire Boulevard, **WESTWOOD** is one of LA's more user-friendly neighborhoods, a grouping of low-slung Spanish Revival buildings that went up in the late 1920s under the name **Westwood Village**, along with the nearby campus of the nascent University of California, Los Angeles (UCLA), which had moved from East Hollywood. It's an area that's easily explored on foot and one very much shaped by the proximity of the university. Because of its ease for pedestrians, the neighborhood has limited parking; for minimum frustration, find a cheap parking lot and dump your vehicle there for a few hours while you explore. Otherwise you'll be constantly feeding a meter or risking a sizeable parking ticket.

Broxton Avenue, Westwood's main drag, has plenty of record stores, vintage clothiers, and diners. It's also a big movie-going district, with thirty or so cinema screens within a quarter-mile radius. Much of the original Spanish design has survived the intervening years of less imaginative construction, though the ordinary businesses of the old days have been replaced by fancy boutiques and designer novelty shops. The spire at the end of the street, at 961 Broxton Avenue, belongs to the Art Deco-styled 1931 **Fox Village** theater (ⓣ310/248-6266), which, together with the neon-signed **Bruin** across the street (ⓣ310/208-8998), is sometimes used by movie studios for sneak previews of films to gauge audience reaction.

Inside one of the towers on the corner with Westwood Boulevard, art lovers shouldn't miss a trip to the **UCLA Hammer Museum**, 10899 Wilshire Boulevard (Tues–Sat 11am–7pm, Thurs closes 9pm, Sun 11am–5pm; $5, kids free, Thurs free to all; ⓣ310/443-7000, ⓦwww.hammer.ucla.edu). The minor Rembrandts and Rubenses may be less than stunning, but make sure to seek out the impressive early-American works of Gilbert Stuart, Thomas Eakins, and John Singer Sargent, and a range of insightful, sometimes risk-taking, modern and avant-garde temporary exhibitions. Across Wilshire from the museum, at the end of the driveway behind the tiny Avco movie theater at 1218 Glendon Avenue, you'll find Hammer's speckled marble tomb sharing the tiny cemetery of **Westwood Village Memorial Park** (ⓣ310/474-1579) with the likes of movie stars Peter Lorre, Burt Lancaster, and Dean Martin, jazz drummer Buddy Rich, and, to the left of the entrance in the far northeast corner, Marilyn Monroe, who rests under a lipstick-covered plaque. You can also see some of these stars on the radiant mural inside the **Crest Theater**,

1262 Westwood Boulevard (℡310/474-7866), notable as well for its brash neon marquee advertising the best moviehouse outside the Village.

The UCLA campus

The **UCLA Campus** is the dominant feature in Westwood, a group of lovely Romanesque Revival buildings spread across well-landscaped grounds. It's worth a wander if you've time to kill, particularly for a couple of good exhibition spaces. Before embarking on your exploration, pick up a **map** from various information kiosks scattered around campus. Of things to see, the **Powell Library** (Mon–Thurs 7.30am–11pm, Fri 7.30am–6pm, Sat 9am–5pm, Sun 1–10pm; ⓦwww.library.ucla.edu) has a spellbinding interior with lovely Romanesque arches, columns, and stairwell, and an array of medieval ornament to complement its ecclesiastical feel. The highlight is the dome above the **reading room**, where Renaissance printers' marks are inscribed, among them icons representing such pioneers as Johann Fust and William Caxton. (Ask at the reference desk for a guide to the art and architecture of the library.) At the northern end of campus, the large **Franklin D. Murphy Sculpture Garden** (always open; free) has seventy works by such major names as Jean Arp, Henry Moore, Henri Matisse, and Jacques Lipchitz, as well as other notable works including Rodin's *Walking Man*, a stark nude composed of only a torso and legs; Gaston Lachaise's Amazonian *Standing Woman*, a proud, if grotesque, 1932 sculpture; and George Tsutakawa's *OBOS-69*, an odd example of fountain art resembling abstracted TV sets. Free garden tours are available by reservation at ℡310/443-7040.

Just to the east, UCLA's **film school** is less industry-dominated than its counterpart at USC, and has produced filmmakers like Francis Ford Coppola, Alison Anders, and Alex Cox; it also has one of the most extensive collections of old films and TV programs in the world, examples of which are shown to the public in the James Bridges Theater (tickets usually $10). Check the bulletin board in the lobby, phone ℡310/206-FILM, or visit ⓦwww.cinema.ucla.edu for the current schedule. Also worth a look is the nearby **Fowler Museum of Cultural History**, Bruin Walk at Westwood Plaza (Wed–Sun noon–5pm, Thurs closes 8pm; free; ⓦwww.fowler.ucla.edu), which offers an immense range of multicultural art – including ceramics, religious icons, paintings, and musical instruments. The museum's highlights include a worldwide selection of native masks, more than ten thousand textile pieces from different cultures, and an extensive collection of African and Polynesian art and various folk designs. For a more contemplative experience, travel just north of campus to UCLA's **Hannah Carter Japanese Garden**, 10619 Bellagio Road (Tues, Wed & Fri 10am–3pm; free; by appointment only at ℡310/794-0320 or ⓦwww.japanesegarden.ucla .edu), an idyllic spot featuring magnolias, Japanese maples, and traditional structures and river rocks brought directly from Japan. Adding to the calming Zen feel are a pagoda, a teahouse, quaint bridges, and assorted gold and stone Buddhas.

The Sepulveda Pass: The Getty Center and Skirball Museum

The gap through the Santa Monica Mountains known as the **Sepulveda Pass** is best known for the 405 freeway that cuts through it. Starting at Sunset Boulevard just northwest of UCLA, the pass divides several of LA's most exclusive residential zones. The most famous, to the east, is **Bel Air**, a hillside community that boasts a particularly fine hotel, the *Bel Air* (see p.84).

Further northwest, Getty Center Drive leads up to the monumental **Getty Center** (Tues–Thurs & Sun 10am–6pm, Fri & Sat 10am–9pm; free, parking $8; ℡310/440-7300, ⓦwww.getty.edu), a gleaming complex that towers over the city as oil baron J. Paul Getty once towered over his competitors. If you're arriving by bus, you'll need to take MTA line #761 from UCLA after taking line #2 or #302 from Downtown.

Designed by arch-modernist **Richard Meier**, the center was built for about $1 billion and was a decade in the making, constructed from classical travertine. Although the Getty Foundation plunked down a ten-figure sum for the Center, it still has billions in reserve and must, by law, spend hundreds of millions each year from its endowment. Thus, it plays an elephantine role on the international art scene and can freely outbid its competitors for anything it wants.

Getty started building his massive collection in the 1930s, storing much of it in his house until the Getty Museum opened in 1974 on a bluff overlooking the Pacific Ocean. That site has now reopened as the **Getty Villa**, a showcase for the foundation's antiquities (see p.130). As the main museum's collection is, not surprisingly, determined by the enthusiasms of Getty himself, there's a formidable array of ornate furniture and **decorative arts**, with clocks, chandeliers, tapestries, and gilt-edged commodes, designed for the French nobility from the reign of Louis XIV, filling several overwhelmingly opulent rooms. Getty was much less interested in **painting** – although he did scoop up a very fine stash from the Renaissance and Baroque periods, including works by Rembrandt, Rubens, and La Tour – but a large collection has been amassed since his death, featuring all the heavy hitters from the thirteenth century to the present: drawings by Raphael and Bernini, paintings from the Dutch Golden Age, and a handful of French Impressionists, to name just a few. The museum's biggest catch is probably Van Gogh's *Irises*, which was snatched up for a still undisclosed sum. Also fascinating is the museum's excellent collection of medieval **illuminated manuscripts**, depicting Biblical scenes such as the Passion cycle as well as notable saints. Exquisitely drawn letters introduce chapters from Scripture and maintain their radiance to this day, especially when lit from behind in a dark, dramatic gallery.

Elsewhere in the museum, there's an extensive and highly absorbing collection of **photographs** by Man Ray, Laszlo Moholy-Nagy, and other notables, along with a respectable assortment of **sculpture** from the seventeenth to the nineteenth centuries. The museum also boasts a wide collection of **drawings**. Among the best are Albrecht Dürer's meticulous *Study of the Good Thief*, a portrait of the crucified criminal who was converted on the cross; his *Stag Beetle*, precise enough to look as if the bug were crawling on the page itself; Giovanni Piranesi's dramatic image of a ruined, but still monumental, *Ancient Port*; and William Blake's bizarre watercolor of *Satan Exalting over Eve*, an expressionless devil hovering over his prone captive.

From the museum, continue up the Sepulveda Pass until you come to the **Skirball Cultural Center**, 2701 N Sepulveda Boulevard (Tues–Sat noon–5pm, Sun 11am–5pm; $10, students $7; ☏310/440-4500, ⓦ www.skirball.org), which devotes its attention to the history, beliefs, and rituals of Judaism. Concentrating on the more mystical elements of the faith, the fairly absorbing center hosts a range of exhibitions and lectures designed to illuminate the American Jewish experience. It also features a wide collection of artifacts, everything from an early copy of the Declaration of Independence to a replica of a Holy Ark (a cabinet for Torah scrolls) from a German synagogue.

Santa Monica Bay

Set along a twenty-mile white-sand beach and home to some of LA's finest stores, restaurants, and galleries, the small communities that line the **Santa**

Monica Bay have little of the smog or searing heat that can make the rest of the metropolis unbearable. The entire area is well served by public transit and near enough to the airport, plus there's a wide array of accommodation, making it a good base for seeing the rest of LA.

Santa Monica, lined by palm-tree-shaded bluffs above the Pacific Ocean, is the oldest, biggest, and best known of the towns. Once a wild beachfront playground and memorable location for many scenes from the underworld stories of Raymond Chandler, it's a self-consciously healthy and liberal community that has attracted a large expatriate British contingent. Directly south, Venice's beachfront boardwalk brings together a lively mixture of street performers, roller skaters, and casual voyeurs, while its remaining network of canals gives a hint of what the place looked like a hundred years ago.

North from Santa Monica along the Pacific Coast Highway, Pacific Palisades is a gathering of hugely expensive houses clinging to the lower foothills of the nearby mountains, though there's really not much to see beyond Will Rogers State Park, holding the home and museum of one of the legends of the American West, and the spectacular Getty Villa, a treasure house of antiquities in the form of a Roman hillside villa. A few miles farther along the coastal road, Topanga Canyon offers more hiking; though its reputation as a haven of back-to-nature hippydom is gone, it still holds a surprisingly wild set of trails leading into the deep, wooded canyons and sculptured rock outcrops of the Santa Monica Mountains. Malibu, at the top of the bay, twenty miles from Santa Monica and the northern and westernmost edge of the LA region, is studded with beach-colony houses owned by those who are famous enough to need privacy and rich enough to afford it, despite the constant threat of hillside wildfires. However, you don't have to be a millionaire to enjoy its fine surfing beaches, or the birds, seals, and whales that seasonally migrate offshore.

Santa Monica

For a lot of Westsiders not rolling in dough, SANTA MONICA represents the impossible dream – a low-slung, tolerant beachside burg with a relaxed air and easy access to the rest of the city. Of course, many of its upper-crust homes may be just as expensive as those found in Beverly Hills or West LA, but what it lacks in affordability it makes up for in humility. Friendly and unpretentious, Santa Monica is a great spot to visit, a compact, accessible bastion of oceanside charm.

Lying across Centinela Avenue from West LA, Santa Monica splits into three distinct portions. The town itself, holding a fair chunk of Santa Monica's history and its day-to-day business, is mostly inland but is more interesting closer to the coastal bluffs. Just to the west there's the pier and beach, while Main Street, running south from close to the pier towards Venice, is a style-conscious quarter, with designer restaurants and fancy shops. You can easily travel between these areas on the Tide Shuttle (every 15min; Sun–Thurs noon–8pm, Fri & Sat noon–10pm; 25¢; ☎310/451-5444), ponying up a mere quarter to hit many of the town's shopping highlights.

The Town

Santa Monica reaches nearly three miles inland, but most of its attractions lie within a few blocks of the beach. Make your first stop the Visitor Information Office, 1400 Ocean Avenue (daily 10am–4pm, summer 9am–5pm; ☎310/393-7593, ⓦ www.santamonica.com), in a kiosk just south of Santa Monica Boulevard in Palisades Park, the famous, cypress-tree-lined strip that runs along the top of the bluffs and makes for striking views of the surf below. The visitor center's handy free map shows the layout of the town and the routes of the Santa Monica Big Blue Bus transit system, a useful Westside complement to the MTA network (☎310/451-5444, ⓦwww.bigbluebus.com). There's another visitor center in the nearby mall (see below), but this one's a bit more central.

Two blocks east of Ocean Avenue, between Wilshire and Broadway, the **Third Street Promenade** is a pedestrian stretch long popular with buskers, musicians, and itinerant evangelists. It's fun simply to hang out in the cafés, bars, and nightclubs, play a game of pool, or browse through the many mainstream and oddball boutiques – though chain retailers have basically conquered the strip and drained it of much of its former off-kilter energy. Still, it's especially busy on weekends, when huge numbers of tourists and locals jostle for space with sidewalk poets, swinging jazz bands, and street lunatics, under the watchful eyes of water-spewing dinosaur sculptures draped in ivy. Anchored at its southern end is the expensive **Santa Monica Place**, a white stucco mall that's among architect Frank Gehry's least inspired work.

Santa Monica has a number of fine **galleries** selling works by emerging local and international artists. Near the intersection of 26th Street and Cloverfield Boulevard, **Bergamot Station**, the city's aesthetic hub at 2525 Michigan Avenue, is a collection of former tramcar sheds housing around thirty small art galleries (most open Tues–Fri 10am–6pm; free). Many of LA's latest generation of artists have shown here, and the highlight is, of course, the **Santa Monica Museum of Art**, in Building G-1 (Tues–Sat 11am–6pm; $5; ☎310/586-6488, ⓦwww.smmoa.org). This is a good space to see some of the most engaging and curious work on the local scene, in temporary exhibitions ranging from simple paintings to complex, space-demanding installations and career-spanning retrospectives of California art pioneers. Among the regular galleries, don't miss the **Gallery of Functional Art**, Building E-3 (free; ☎310/829-6990, ⓦwww.galleryoffunctionalart.com), which offers an array of mechanical gizmos and eccentric furniture like cubist lamps and neon-lit chairs. If you want to check out more art, the **18th Street Arts Complex**, further inland at 1639 18th Street (☎310/453-3711, ⓦwww.18thstreet.org), is a hip and modern center for various types of art, much of it experimental. The performance space **Highways**, 1651 18th Street (☎310/315-1459, ⓦwww.highwaysperformance.org), is one such example in the complex, showcasing edgy political and gender-based work.

Elsewhere inland, it's less easy to stumble upon Santa Monica's worthwhile sights. On the northern border, **San Vicente Boulevard**'s grassy tree-lined strip is a joggers' freeway, while south of San Vicente, the flashy eateries and boutiques of **Montana Avenue** are better for spotting B-list stars than for finding any bargains. Fans of big-name architect Frank Gehry will no doubt want to check out one of the first structures that made his reputation, the artist's own **Gehry House**, 22nd Street at Washington Avenue (not open to the public), a deconstructivist fantasy with random structural ideas thrown together and bundled up with concrete walls and metal fencing.

Santa Monica Pier and around

Jutting out into the bay at the foot of Colorado Avenue, the **Santa Monica Pier** (☎310/458-8900, ⓦwww.santamonicapier.org) is a great example of an old-fashioned, festive beach-town hub, with a giant helter-skelter and a restored 1922 wooden **carousel** (March–Sept Mon–Thurs 11am–5pm, Fri–Sun 11am–7pm; Oct–March Thurs–Mon only; 50¢ a ride), with more than forty colorful hand-carved horses, featured in the 1973 movie *The Sting*. Although

VENICE & SANTA MONICA

ACCOMMODATION

Bayside	F
Carmel	B
HI-LA/Santa Monica	A
Inn at Venice Beach	H
Loew's Santa Monica Beach	C
Shutters on the Beach	E
Venice Beach Cotel	G
Venice Beach House	I
Viceroy	D

RESTAURANTS		
Abbot's Pizza Company	29	
Babalu	2	
Border Grill	4	
Café 50s	25	
Chaya Venice	23	
Chinois on Main	15	
Drago	6	
Figtree's Café	24	
Flower of Siam	14	
Gaucho Grill	7	
Hal's	27	
Joe's	26	
Mariasol	11	
Michael's	3	
Norm's	10	
Uncle Darrow's	28	
Wildflour Pizza	17	

CAFÉS & NIGHTLIFE		
Circle Bar	21	
Finn McCool's	16	
Harvelle's	9	
Hinano Café	30	
Library Alehouse	19	
Mor	22	
Novel Café	20	
Rick's Tavern	18	
Rusty's Surf Ranch	12	
Temple Bar	5	
Urth Caffé	13	
Ye Olde King's Head	8	
Zanzibar	1	

the familiar thrill rides of **Pacific Park** (June–Aug daily 11am–11pm, Sat & Sun closes at 12am, rest of year hours vary; $17, kids $9; ☎310/260-8744, ⓦwww.pacpark.com) may catch your eye, featuring a rollercoaster and various other amusements, it's still a rather overpriced attempt to lure back the suburban families – you're better off saving your money for a real theme park. Better yet, visit the **Santa Monica Pier Aquarium**, below the pier at 1600 Ocean Front Walk (Tues–Fri 2–6pm, Sat & Sun 12.30–6pm; $5, kids free; ☎310/393-6149, ⓦwww.healthebay.org/smpa), where you can find out about marine biology and touch sea anemones and starfish.

Just south of the pier, Santa Monica has its own miniature version of Venice's Muscle Beach: a workout area loaded with rings, bars, and other athletic equipment designed for would-be bodybuilders and fitness fans. The adjacent **International Chess Park** is a fancy name for a serviceable collection of chessboards that attracts a range of players from rank amateurs to slumming pros. Finally, a **bike path** begins at the pier and heads twenty miles south, a stretch that ranks as one of the area's top choices for cycling.

Main Street

Five minutes' walk from the pier, **Main Street** is an enticing collection of boutiques, bars, and restaurants that forms one of the most popular shopping strips on the Westside. Beyond shopping, eating, and drinking, though, there's not much to do or see. One of the few actual sights, the **California Heritage Museum**, 2612 Main Street (Wed–Sun 11am–4pm; $5; ☎310/392-8537, ⓦwww.californiaheritagemuseum.org), hosts temporary displays on Californian cultural topics like old-time amusement parks, and permanent exhibits on regional pottery, furniture, and decorative arts. There are also several noteworthy buildings on and around Main Street, including the angular gray volumes and strange geometry of Frank Gehry's **Edgemar** shopping development, no. 2415, a deliberately awkward construction whose chain-link fencing and sheet-metal design bring to mind an abstract sculpture.

Venice

Immediately south of Santa Monica, connected by Main Street, **VENICE** was laid out in the marshlands of Ballona Creek in 1905 by developer **Abbot Kinney** as a romantic replica of the northern Italian city. Intended to attract artists to sample its pseudo-European air, this twenty-mile network of canals, lined by sham palazzos and waterfront homes, never really caught on, although a later remodel into a low-grade version of Coney Island postponed its demise for a few decades. These days, a few evocative shards of the original plan survive, and the bohemian atmosphere has since worked to draw in the artistic community Kinney was targeting. Main Street, for instance, is home to the offices of advertising firm **TBWA/Chiat/Day**, just south of Rose Street and marked by Claes Oldenburg's huge pair of binoculars at the entrance to the Frank Gehry-designed offices. Just to the north, the frightening **Ballerina Clown**, a gargantuan sculpture by Jonathan Borofsky, looms over a nearby intersection, its stubbly clown head and lithe body making for an unforgettably disturbing combination. A strong alternative arts scene centers around the **Beyond Baroque Literary Arts Center and Bookshop** in the old City Hall at 681 Venice Boulevard ($7 per event; ☎310/822-3006, ⓦwww.beyondbaroque.org), which holds readings and workshops of poetry, prose, and drama, while next door, SPARC offers pricey tours (see p.81) of some of the more remarkable murals around LA.

Windward Avenue is the district's main artery, running from the beach into what was the Grand Circle of the canal system – now paved over – and the original Romanesque arcade, around the intersection with Pacific Avenue, is alive with health-food shops, used-record stores, and rollerblade rental stands. Here and there colorful and portentous giant **murals** depict everything from a shirtless Jim Morrison (1811 Ocean Front Walk) to Botticelli's Venus on rollerskates (Windward at Speedway Avenue). The remaining **canals** are just a few blocks south, where the original quaint little bridges survive. It's a great place to walk around, though if you're in a car and wish to avoid the tiny, maze-like streets between the canals, the only way to see the area is by heading north on Dell Avenue

▲ Venice Boardwalk

between Washington and Venice boulevards. Also a short distance inland, much of **Abbot Kinney Boulevard** is a fine stretch for hanging out, sipping a latte, deciphering modern art, and having a bite in a smart eatery.

Still, it's **Venice Beach** that draws most people to the town, and nowhere else does LA parade itself quite so openly, colorfully, and aggressively as it does along the **Venice Boardwalk**, a wide pathway also known as Ocean Front Walk. Year-round at weekends and every day in summer it's packed with jugglers, fire-eaters, Hare Krishnas, rasta guitar players and, of course, teeming masses of tourists. West of Windward is **Muscle Beach**, a legendary weight-lifting center where serious hunks of muscle pump serious iron, and high-flying gymnasts swing on the adjacent rings and bars. If you'd like to check the place out yourself, contact the Venice Beach Recreation Center, 1800 Ocean Front Walk, for more information (☎310/399-2775, ⓦwww.laparks.org /venice), or if you're a real weightlifting enthusiast, visit in July when the Bench Press Championships are held here, one of many such competitions taking place during the year. There are **rental shacks** along the beach for picking up skates, surfboards, or bikes, and plenty of merchants selling Day-Glo tube tops and wraparound sunglasses – if you really want to fit in with the locals, or at least the tourists.

Incidentally, be warned that Venice Beach at night can be a dangerous place, and walking on the beach after dark is illegal in many stretches.

Pacific Palisades and Will Rogers State Historic Park

The district of **Pacific Palisades**, rising on the bluffs two miles north of Santa Monica Pier, is slowly but very surely falling away into the bay, most noticeably on the point above the Pacific Coast Highway – otherwise known as "PCH." With each winter's rains, a little more of the bluffs gets washed away in mud slides, blocking traffic on PCH and gradually shrinking the backyards of the cliff-top homes. Although there are few places of interest among the suburban ranch houses, a handful of the most influential buildings of postwar LA were constructed here. The **Eames House**, for example, at 203 Chautauqua Street, was fashioned out of prefabricated industrial parts in 1947 as part of the Case Study Program. Only the grounds and exterior are viewable (Mon–Fri 10am–4pm, Sat 10am–3pm; free; by appointment at ☎310/459-9663, ⊛www.eamesfoundation.org).

A mile east along Sunset Boulevard is **Will Rogers State Historic Park** (summer daily 8am–dusk; rest of year daily 8am–6pm; free; ☎310/454-8212), the home and ranch of the Depression-era cowboy philosopher and journalist **Will Rogers**. At the time he was one of America's most popular figures, renowned for saying that he "never met a man he didn't like." The overgrown ranch-style house serves as an informal **museum** (tours Tues–Sun 11am, 1pm & 2pm; free), filled with cowboy gear and Native American art. Though the house has been renovated recently, the state is still working on restoring the grounds to something resembling their appearance in Rogers' time. The surrounding 200-acre park has miles of foot and bridle paths, including **polo grounds** where matches take place during the spring and summer (April–Oct Sat 2–5pm, Sun 10am–1pm; free).

The Getty Villa

Just west of Sunset Boulevard's intersection with PCH, the **Getty Villa,** 17985 PCH (Thurs–Mon 10am–5pm; free, parking $8 or take Metro Bus #534; by reservation at ☎310/440-7300, ⊛www.getty.edu), reopened in 2006 after extensive renovation and serves as the Getty Foundation's spectacular showcase for its wide array of Greek and Roman antiquities. If classical art is your forte, this should be your one essential stop in Southern California. Modeled after a Roman country house buried by Mount Vesuvius in 79 AD, the villa is set among its own fetching gardens. Highlights include the *Getty Kouros*, a rigidly posed figure of a boy that conservators openly state could be a later forgery, a *Cult Statue of Aphrodite* from the Golden Age of Greece (fifth century BC), with flowing robe and voluptuous limestone figure, and a Hellenistic *Statue of a Victorious Youth*, wearing only an olive wreath, that was carefully restored after having been recovered from the sea floor. Athenian vases are also well represented, many of them the red-ground variety, as are ancient kylikes, or drinking vessels, and ceremonial amphorae, or vases given as prizes in athletic contests. Not to be missed is a wondrous Roman skyphos, a fragile-looking blue vase decorated with white cameos of Bacchus and his friends, properly preparing for a bacchanalia.

Topanga Canyon and the Santa Monica Mountains

Surprisingly for LA, **Topanga Canyon** provides an excellent natural refuge. With hillsides covered in golden poppies and wildflowers, 150,000 acres of these mountains and the adjacent seashore have been protected as the **Santa Monica Mountains National Recreation Area**. Park rangers offer free guided hikes throughout the mountains most weekends (☎818/597-9192), and there are self-guided trails through the canyon's Topanga State Park, off

Old Topanga Canyon Road at the crest of the mountains, with spectacular views over the Pacific. To find out more, contact the visitor center in neighboring Thousand Oaks, 401 W Hillcrest Drive (daily 9am–5pm; ℡805/370-2301, ⓦwww.nps.gov/samo).

The nearby community of **Topanga** was, in the 1960s, a well-known proving ground for West Coast rock music, when Neil Young, the Byrds, and other artists moved here and held all-night jam sessions in the sycamore groves along Topanga Creek. Few real bohemians are left, however, and most of the upscale residents just affect an enlightened, pseudo-hippy New Age style. Before leaving the area, don't miss **Red Rock Canyon**, off Old Topanga Canyon Road via Red Rock Road (ⓦwww.smmc.ca.gov or www.lamountains.com), a stunning red-banded sandstone gorge and state park whose colorful rock formations, surrounding gardens, and riparian wildlife give you a good reason to leave your car behind and go exploring.

Malibu and around

Everyone has heard of **MALIBU**, and while its upscale Hollywood image is not so very far from the truth, you might not think so on arrival. The succession of ramshackle surf shops and fast-food stands scattered along both sides of PCH around the graceful Malibu Pier don't exactly reek of money, but the secluded estates just inland are as valuable as any in the entire country.

Facing south by the pier, **Surfrider Beach** is a major surfing nexus, first gaining traction when the sport was brought over from Hawaii and mastered by Southern California pioneers. The waves are best in late summer, when storms off Mexico cause them to reach upwards of eight feet – not huge for serious pros, but big enough for you. Just beyond is **Malibu Lagoon State Park** (daily 8am–dusk; ℡818/880-0350), a nature reserve and bird refuge; birding walks around the lagoon are offered some weekends. Nearby is the **Adamson House**, 23200 PCH (grounds 8am–sunset, house Wed–Sat 11am–3pm; $5; ℡310/456-8432, ⓦwww.adamsonhouse.org), a stunning, historic Spanish Colonial–style home featuring opulent decor and colorful tilework.

Much of **Malibu Creek State Park** (daily dawn–dusk; ℡818/880-0367), at the crest of Malibu Canyon Road along Mulholland Drive, used to belong to 20th Century-Fox studios, which filmed many Tarzan pictures here and used the chaparral-covered hillsides to simulate South Korea for the TV show *M*A*S*H*. The 4000-acre park includes a large lake, some waterfalls, and nearly fifteen miles of hiking trails, making it crowded on summer weekends but fairly accessible and pleasant the rest of the time (for camping, see box, p.87). The **Paramount Ranch**, near Mulholland Drive at 2813 Cornell Road (daily 8am–5pm), is another old studio backlot, with a phony railroad crossing, cemetery, and Western movie set used for, among other things, the interminable TV drama *Dr Quinn, Medicine Woman*. Finally, **Ramirez Canyon Park**, north of Point Dume and PCH at 5750 Ramirez Canyon Road (by reservation only at ℡310/589-2850, ⓦwww.lamountains.com), is set around a 22-acre complex of houses and gardens that Barbra Streisand donated to the state in 1993. Amid extensive flower, herb, and fruit gardens, you can get a glimpse into her former residences, highlighted by the "Deco House," with its red-and-black colors, geometric decor, and stainless-steel panels.

The beaches

Five miles up the coast from Malibu Pier, **Zuma Beach** (most beaches below daily 7am–10pm) is the largest of the LA County beaches, easily connected to the San Fernando Valley by Kanan Dume Road. Adjacent **Point Dume State Beach**, below the bluffs, is more relaxed, and the rocks here are also a good place to look out for seals and migrating gray whales in winter, as the point above – best accessed by car or a longish path – juts out into the Pacific at the northern lip of Santa Monica Bay. **El Matador State Beach**, about 25 miles up the coast from Santa Monica, is about as close as you can get to the private-beach seclusion enjoyed by the stars, thanks to its northern location and an easily missable turn off PCH. Another five miles along the highway, where Mulholland Drive reaches the ocean, **Leo Carrillo** ("ca-REE-oh") **State Park** marks the northwestern border of LA County. The mile-long sandy beach is divided by Sequit Point, a small bluff that has underwater caves and a tunnel you can pass through at low tide, and is also one of LA's best campgrounds (see p.87). Five miles farther on, at **Point Mugu State Park**, there are some good walks through mountain canyons, and campground right on the beach.

The South Bay and LA Harbor

South of Venice, the charmless high-rise condos of Marina del Rey and the faded resort town of Playa del Rey offer little to interest visitors. Heading south of LAX, however, is an eight-mile strip of beach towns – **Manhattan Beach**, **Hermosa Beach**, and **Redondo Beach**, collectively known as the **SOUTH BAY** – which are quieter, smaller, and more suburban than the Westside beach communities.

Visible all along this stretch of the coast, the large green peninsula of **Palos Verdes** is an upmarket residential area, while the rough-hewn working town of **San Pedro** is sited on the LA Harbor, which with its municipal LA and Long Beach sections is the busiest cargo port in the world outside of China and Singapore, and still growing. On the other side of the harbor, **Long Beach** is best known as the resting place of the *Queen Mary* – even though it's also the region's second-largest city, with nearly half a million people – while inland are a pair of historically interesting sites in otherwise bland **Wilmington**. Perhaps the most enticing place in the area is **Santa Catalina Island**, twenty miles offshore and easily reached by ferry. It's almost completely conserved wilderness, with many unique forms of plant and animal life and just one main town, **Avalon**.

Manhattan, Hermosa, and Redondo Beaches

Along the South Bay cities' shared beach boardwalk, known as **The Strand** (which ends at Redondo Beach), the joggers and roller skaters are more likely to be locals than tourists. Each city has at least one municipal pier and a beckoning strip of white sand, with most oceanside locations equipped for surfing and beach volleyball – world-class events for both sports are regularly held here, and a two-week international surf festival occurs each August.

The most northerly city, **Manhattan Beach**, is a likable place with a healthy, well-to-do air, home mainly to white-collar workers whose middle-class stucco homes tumble towards the beach. These days, Manhattan Beach's pier is used mainly for strolling, but is also the site of the accurately named **Roundhouse**, sitting at the end, which encloses a fine **aquarium** (Mon–Fri 3pm–dusk, Sat & Sun 10am–dusk; $2; ℡310/379-8117, Ⓦwww .roundhouseaquarium.org), a mildly interesting spot where you can look at crabs, eels, lobsters, squid, and – in their own "touch tank" – tide-pool creatures like anemones and sea stars.

To the south, **Hermosa Beach**, across Longfellow Avenue, has a lingering bohemian feel of the Sixties and Seventies in certain spots, and features a lively beachside strip, most energetic near the foot of the pier on 12th Street. Packed with restaurants and clubs, the area has long been a major hangout for revelers of all stripes. A good time to come is during the **Fiesta Hermosa** (ⓦwww .fiestahermosa.com), a three-day event held over Memorial Day and Labor Day that's good for fun music (including surf rock), tasty food, and displays of regional arts and crafts.

Despite some decent strips of sand and fine views of Palos Verdes' stunning greenery, **Redondo Beach**, south of Hermosa, is much less inviting than its relaxed neighbor. Condos and hotels line the beachfront, and the yacht-lined King's Harbor is off limits to curious visitors.

Palos Verdes

A great green hump marking LA's southwest corner, **Palos Verdes** is a rich enclave holding a number of gated communities, but can be enjoyable for the bluffs and coves along its protected coastline. One of these, **Abalone Cove**, 5970 Palos Verdes Drive S (Mon–Fri noon–4pm, Sat & Sun 9am–4pm; free, parking $5; ⓣ310/377-1222), boasts rock and tide pools and offshore kelp beds with rock scallops, sea urchins, and, of course, abalone. While you're in the area, don't miss **Wayfarer's Chapel**, 5755 Palos Verdes Drive S (daily 8am–5pm; ⓣ310/377-7919, ⓦwww.wayfarerschapel.org), designed by Frank Lloyd Wright's son as a tribute to the eighteenth-century Swedish scientist and mystic Emanuel Swedenborg. It's now LA's ultimate spot for weddings, the redwood grove around the chapel symbolically growing and weaving itself into the glass-framed structure. A few miles farther on, just before the end of Palos Verdes Drive, **Point Fermin Park** is a small tip of land poking into the ocean at LA's southernmost point. The squat wooden **lighthouse** here (tours usually on the hour Tues–Sun 1–4pm; donation; ⓣ310/241-0684) is an 1874 Eastlake structure with a cupola that once contained a 6600-candlepower light which beamed 22 miles out to sea, and a whale watching station lets you read up on the winter migrations. Below the bluff, the excellent **Cabrillo Marine Aquarium**, 3720 Stephen White Drive (Tues–Fri noon–5pm, Sat & Sun 10am–5pm; $5, parking $1/hr; ⓣ310/548-7562, ⓦwww.cabrilloaq.org), displays a diverse collection of marine life that has been imaginatively and instructively assembled: everything from predator snails, octopi, and jellyfish to larger displays on otters, seals, and whales.

About ten miles inland on the peninsula and not really close to anything else worth seeing, the curious **South Coast Botanic Garden**, 26300 Crenshaw Boulevard (daily 9am–5pm; $7; ⓣ310/544-1948, ⓦwww.southcoastbotanic garden.org), was once the site of a huge landfill stuffed with 3.5 tons of trash, but has since been covered over and turned into a charming array of themed gardens filled with cacti, ferns, bromeliads, several types of palm trees, and even a small French-style garden. The only hint of its former life is its undulating terrain, evidence of the refuse slowly shifting below the surface.

San Pedro

Three miles north of the Cabrillo Aquarium, the scruffy harbor district of **San Pedro** was a small fishing community until the late nineteenth century, when the construction of the LA Harbor nearby brought a huge influx of labor, much of it from Portugal, Greece, and Yugoslavia. Many of these immigrants, and their descendants, never left the place, lending a striking ethnic mix to the town. A good chunk of the district's nautical history is revealed in the **Maritime Museum**, on the harbor's edge at the foot of Sixth Street (Tues–Sat 10am–5pm, Sun noon–5pm; $3; ☏310/548-7618, ⓦwww.lamaritimemuseum.org), housed in a grand structure that was the Municipal Ferry Building from World War II up to the early 1960s. These days, the old ferry tower is a storehouse for art and artifacts from the glory days of San Pedro's fishing and whaling industries, among other collections, and focuses on everything from old-fashioned clipper-ship voyages to contemporary diving expeditions. Farther north, the **SS Lane Victory**, in Berth 94 off Swinford Street (daily 9am–3pm; $3; ☏310/519-9545, ⓦwww.lanevictory.org), is a huge, ten-thousand-ton cargo ship that was built in the shipyard in 1945 and operated in Korea and Vietnam. A tour will take you through its many cramped spaces, including the engine and radio rooms, crew quarters, galley, and bridge.

Four blocks west of the Maritime Museum, old downtown San Pedro is centered around the restored, opulent **Warner Grand Theater**, 478 W Sixth Street (☏310/548-7672, ⓦwww.warnergrand.org), a terrific 1931 Zigzag Moderne moviehouse and performing arts center with dark geometric details, grand columns, and sunburst motifs, a style that almost looks pre-Columbian. Nearby, the **San Pedro Red Car Trolley** (Fri–Mon 10am–6pm; $1) is a collection of three classic 1908 Pacific Electric Red Cars (two replicas, one restored) brought back to life as a tourist route linking most of the city's major attractions. Although it's accessible from the trolley, don't bother with the banal **Ports o' Call Village** – a dismal batch of wooden and corrugated-iron huts supposedly capturing the flavor of seaports around the world.

Wilmington

Between San Pedro and Long Beach soar two tall road bridges, giving aerial views of huge facilities thick with oil wells and docks. Just inland, the community of **Wilmington** is the site of the Greek Revival **Banning House**, 401 E Main Street (guided tours at the bottom of the hour Tues–Thurs 12.30–2.30pm, Sat & Sun 12.30–3.30pm; $5; ☏310/548-7777, ⓦwww.banningmuseum.org), the opulent Victorian home of mid-nineteenth-century entrepreneur Phineas Banning, who, through his promotion of the rail link between the harbor and central LA, became known as "the father of Los Angeles transportation" – back when the local transit system was one of the best in the world. While you're in the area, make sure to visit the **Drum Barracks and Civil War Museum**, 1052 Banning Boulevard (hourly tours Tues–Thurs 10am–1pm, Sat & Sun 11.30am–2.30pm; $3; ☏310/548-7509, ⓦwww.drumbarracks.org), the Civil War–era federal staging point for attacks in the Southwest against Confederates and, later, Indians. The sole remaining building houses a collection of military antiques and memorabilia, such as a 34-star US flag and assorted guns, muskets, and weaponry, including an early prototype of a machine gun.

Long Beach

Combined with San Pedro, **LONG BEACH** is home to one of the largest ports in the world – making it the point of entry for the majority of goods shipped (and then trucked) to the Western US. It's fairly upmarket near the water, with office buildings, a convention center, hotels, a shopping mall, and some of the best-preserved circa-1900 buildings on the coast. Inland from downtown, however, it's a different story – grim, uninviting housing developments on the perimeter of South Central LA. Most of the town's highlights can be accessed aboard the **Village Tour d'Art** shuttle (daily 10am–7pm; free; ☎562/591-2301, ⓦwww.lbtransit.com).

Running from Magnolia Avenue to Alamitos Boulevard and Ocean Boulevard to Tenth Street, downtown Long Beach offers a wide array of boutiques, antique dealers, and bookstores, many of them around a three-block strip known as **The Promenade**, lined with touristy restaurants and stores that can get busy on weekend nights. Two blocks west of the Promenade, at the terminus of the Blue Line light railway to Downtown LA, **Pine Avenue** has some of the city's best architecture. To the south, Shoreline Village is a waterfront entertainment belt that used to feature carnival rides and a carousel until the 1940s, but is now mostly a ragtag collection of shops and restaurants. One sight worth a stop is the intriguing, though pricey, **Aquarium of the Pacific** (daily 9am–6pm; $21, kids $12; ☎562/590-3100, ⓦwww.aquariumofpacific.org), which exhibits the aquatic flora and fauna of three distinct climates and regions from around the world, including the Southern Pacific, Northern Pacific, and tropical zones.

A mile east, the **Long Beach Museum of Art**, 2300 Ocean Boulevard (Tues–Sun 11am–5pm; $7; ☎562/439-2119, ⓦwww.lbma.org), is home to local art and tasteful displays of early-modernist furniture and sculpture. Several blocks north of the ocean, the **Museum of Latin American Art**, 628 Alamitos Avenue (Tues–Fri 11.30am–7pm, Sat 11am–7pm, Sun 11am–6pm; $5; ☎562/437-1689, ⓦwww.molaa.com), is LA's only major museum devoted solely to Latino art. Showcasing artists from Mexico to South America, the collection includes big names like Diego Rivera and José Orozco, as well as newcomers working within contexts that range from social criticism to magical realism.

Between November and March, more than fifteen thousand whales cruise the "**Whale Freeway**" past Long Beach on their annual migration to and from winter breeding and berthing grounds in Baja California. Harbor Breeze, at Rainbow Harbor next to the Aquarium of the Pacific (☎562/432-4900, ⓦwww.longbeachcruises.com), operates good two-hour whale watching trips for $20 per adult, $10 per child.

The Queen Mary

Long Beach's most famous attraction is, of course, the mighty ocean liner **Queen Mary** (daily 10am–6pm; $23 guided tours, kids $12; ⓦwww.queenmary.com), acquired by the local authorities with the specific aim of bolstering tourism – which it has succeeded in doing, well beyond expectations. Now a luxury hotel, the ship's exhibits suggest that all who sailed on the vessel – the flagship of the Cunard Line from the 1930s until the 1960s – enjoyed the extravagantly furnished lounges and luxurious cabins, all carefully restored and kept sparkling. But a glance at the spartan third-class cabins reveals something of the real story: the tough conditions experienced by the impoverished migrants who left Europe hoping to start a new life in the US. You can add to the basic tour from a range of special visits themed around ghosts, spycraft, scavenger hunts, and more, boosting the admission up to $30. One of the more peculiar sights alongside the ship is a Foxtrot-class **submarine** (tours $11) that was until 1994 used in the service of the Soviet, and then Russian, navy, carrying a payload of 22 nuclear weapons and powered by clunky diesel engines.

Santa Catalina Island

The enticing island of **Santa Catalina**, twenty miles offshore from Long Beach, is mostly preserved wilderness, but does have substantial charm and offers a nice break from the metropolis. Indeed, with cars largely forbidden, the two thousand islanders walk, ride bikes, or drive golf carts. **Ferry** trips run several times daily from Long Beach, and cost $50–60 round trip. Operators include Catalina Explorer (ᐳ1-877/432-6276, ⓦwww.catalinaferry.com), Catalina Express (ᐳ1-800/481-3470, ⓦwww.catalinaexpress.com), and, from Newport Beach, Catalina Flyer (ᐳ949/673-5245, ⓦwww.catalina-flyer.com).

The island's one town, **Avalon**, narrowly escaped devastation in the May 2007 wildfires, which did damage the more rural parts of the island. The town can be fully explored on foot in an hour, with maps issued by the Chamber of Commerce at the foot of the ferry pier (ᐳ310/510-1520, ⓦwww.catalinachamber.com). Begin at the sumptuous Art Deco **Avalon Casino**, 1 Casino Way, a 1920s structure that still shows movies and features mermaid murals, gold-leaf ceiling motifs, an Art Deco ballroom, and a small **museum** (daily 10am–4pm, Jan–March closed Thurs; $4; ⓦwww.catalinamuseum.com) displaying Native American artifacts from Catalina's past and explaining Hollywood's use of the island as a film location. Roughly three miles southwest of Avalon, the **Wrigley Memorial and Botanical Garden**, 1400 Avalon Canyon Road (daily 8am–5pm; $5; ᐳ310/510-2595), displays all manner of endemic flora and fauna on forty acres. **Santa Catalina Island Company** (ᐳ1-800/626-1496, ⓦwww.visitcatalinaisland.com) offers tours of the Avalon Casino ($16), bus trips through the outback ($69–99), and harbor cruises and glass-bottom-boat rides ($16–36), while **Catalina Adventure Tours** provides slightly cheaper versions of the same ($15–63; ᐳ310/510-2888, ⓦwww.catalinaadventuretours.com); check both companies to see if schedules or routes have changed, especially after any recent island fires.

The most interesting **hotel** is the *Zane Grey Pueblo*, 199 Chimes Tower Road (ᐳ310/510-0966, ⓦwww.zanegreypueblohotel.com; ⑥), which has sixteen rooms overlooking the bay or mountains, with an enticing off-season (Nov–April) weekday rate of $65. If you really have a bundle to spend, the *Inn on Mt Ada*, 398 Wrigley Road (ᐳ310/510-2030, ⓦwww.innonmtada.com; ⑨, from $390), is the final word in Catalina luxury. The only budget option is **camping**: Hermit Gulch is the closest site to Avalon and the busiest. Four other sites in Catalina's interior – Blackjack, Little Harbor, Parsons Landing, and Two Harbors (all $12 per person, kids $6) – are much more distant, but also roomier. Book at ᐳ310/510-8368 or ⓦwww.scico.com/camping.

The San Gabriel and San Fernando valleys

Running north of central LA, beyond the crest of the hills, lie two long, expansive valleys that start close to one another a few miles north of Downtown and span outwards in opposite directions – east to the deserts around Palm Springs, west to Ventura on the Central Coast.

To the east, the **SAN GABRIEL VALLEY** was settled by farmers and cattle ranchers who set up small towns on the lands of the eighteenth-century Mission San Gabriel, foothill communities which grew into prime resort towns, luring many here around the turn of the last century. **Pasadena**, the largest of the modest cities, holds many elegant period houses, as well as the fine

Earthquake Central: The San Fernando Valley

The devastating 6.7-magnitude **earthquake** that shook LA on the morning of January 17, 1994 was one of the biggest disasters in US history. Fifty-five people were killed, two hundred more suffered critical injuries, and the economic cost was estimated at $8 billion. One can only guess how much higher these totals would have been had the quake hit during the day, when the many collapsed stores would have been crowded with shoppers and the freeways full of commuters. The quake, with its epicenter in the San Fernando Valley community of **Northridge**, eclipsed LA's previous worst earthquake in modern times, the 6.6-magnitude temblor of February 1971, which had its epicenter in Sylmar – also in the Valley.

In the unlikely event a sizeable earthquake strikes when you're in LA, protect yourself under something sturdy, such as a heavy table or a doorframe, and well away from windows or anything made of glass. In theory, all the city's new buildings are "quake-safe," though as the 1994 quake recedes in memory, the retrofitting of older buildings seems to diminish in perceived importance. So when the inevitable "Big One" – a quake in the 8-plus-range – arrives, no one knows exactly what will be left standing.

Norton Simon Museum and the **Old Pasadena** outdoor shopping mall, featuring dining, moviegoing, and other cultural activities in stylish old buildings. Above Pasadena, the southern slopes of the San Gabriel Mountains are great spots for hiking and rough camping, though you'll nearly always need a car to get to the trailheads. South of Pasadena, WASP-ish **San Marino** is dominated by the **Huntington Library and Gardens**, a stash of art and literature ringed by botanical gardens that in itself is worth a trip to the valley.

North of Downtown LA and spreading west, the **SAN FERNANDO VALLEY** is, to most Angelenos, simply "the Valley": a sprawl of tract homes, mini-malls, fast-food drive-ins, and auto-parts stores that has more of a middle-American feel than anywhere else in LA. For most people, the main reason to come out here is to drop in on the tourable movie studios in **Burbank** and **Universal City**. Elsewhere, **Forest Lawn Cemetery** is a prime example of graveyard kitsch that's hard to imagine anywhere except in LA, and ultra-conservative **Simi Valley** is the home of the **Ronald Reagan Presidential Library** (daily 10am–5pm; $7; ☎1-800/410-8354, ⓦwww.reaganlibrary.com /pma), containing the memorial site and papers pertaining to the eight-year reign of the Gipper.

Pasadena

In the 1880s, wealthy East Coast tourists who came to California looking for the good life found it in **PASADENA**, ten miles north of LA and connected via the I-10 (Pasadena) Freeway. Luxury hotels went up and a funicular railway cut into the nearby San Gabriel Mountains, leading to a resort and observatory on the mile-high crest. Many of the early, well-heeled visitors stayed, building the rustically sprawling houses that remain. A century later the downtown area underwent a major renovation, with modern shopping centers slipped in behind 1920s facades, but the historic parts of town have not been forgotten. Maps and booklets detailing self-guided tours of city architecture and history are available from the **Pasadena Visitors Bureau**, 171 S Los Robles Avenue (Mon–Fri 8am–5pm, Sat 10am–4pm; ☎626/795-9311, ⓦwww.pasadenacal .com). The town's most notable attraction, the New Year's Day **Tournament of Roses**, began in 1890 to celebrate and publicize the mild Southern

California winters, and now attracts more than a million visitors every year to watch its marching bands and elaborate flower-emblazoned floats (see box, p.158). Also fascinating is the **Tournament House**, 391 S Orange Grove Boulevard (tours Feb–Aug Thurs 2–4pm; free; ☎626/449-4100), a pink 1914 Renaissance Revival mansion that's well worth a look for its grand manor and surrounding gardens – containing up to 1500 types of roses.

Between Fair Oaks and Euclid avenues along Colorado Boulevard, the historic shopping precinct of **Old Pasadena** draws visitors for its fine restaurants, galleries, and theaters, and is accessible by light-rail connection on the Metro Gold Line (see p.78). Downtown Pasadena's most prominent architectural work and its municipal centerpiece, **Pasadena City Hall**, 100 N Garfield Avenue (Mon–Fri 9am–5pm; ☎626/744-7073), recently underwent an extensive renovation; it's one of several city buildings in Mediterranean Revival styles, in this case Spanish Baroque, with a large, tiled dome and imperious facade with grand arches and columns. The local preservation society, **Pasadena Heritage**, offers periodic tours of this and other city landmarks (first Sat of month at 9am; $10; reserve at ☎626/441-6333, ⊛www.pasadenaheritage.org).

Just to the east of City Hall, a replica Chinese Imperial palace houses the **Pacific Asia Museum**, 46 N Los Robles Avenue (Wed–Sun 10am–6pm; $7; ☎626/449-2742, ⊛www.pacificasiamuseum.org), which has a wide range of objects from Japan, China, and Thailand, including ceramics, hand-woven garments and finely detailed scrolls. One particular highlight is the Courtyard Garden, with koi fish, marble statues, and trees native to the Far East. Just around the corner, at 490 E Union Street, the three-story **Pasadena Museum of California Art** (Wed–Sun noon–5pm; $6; ☎626/568-3665, ⊛www.pmcaonline.org) focuses on the many aspects of the state's art world since it became part of the Union in 1850, in all kinds of media from painting to digital.

The Norton Simon Museum

Although somewhat unfamiliar to outsiders, the **Norton Simon Museum**, 411 W Colorado Boulevard (Wed–Mon noon–6pm, Fri until 9pm; $8; students free; ☎626/449-6840, ⊛www.nortonsimon.org), merits at least an afternoon for wandering through its spacious galleries. The core of the massive collection is **Western European painting**, and though much of it is rotated, most of the major pieces are on view constantly. Highlights include Dutch paintings of the seventeenth century – notably Rembrandt's vivacious *Titus, Portrait of a Boy* and Frans Hals' quietly aggressive *Portrait of a Man* – and Italian Renaissance work from Botticelli, Raphael, Giorgione, Bellini, and others. There's also a good sprinkling of French Impressionists and post-Impressionists: Monet's *Mouth of the Seine at Honfleur*, Manet's *Ragpicker*, and a Degas capturing the extended yawn of a washerwoman in *The Ironers*, plus works by Cézanne, Gauguin, and Van Gogh.

Unlike the Getty Museum, the Norton Simon also boasts a solid collection of modernist greats, from Georges Braque and Pablo Picasso to Roy Lichtenstein and Andy Warhol. As a counterpoint to the Western art, the museum has a fine collection of **Asian art**, including many highly polished Buddhist and Hindu figures, some inlaid with precious stones, and many drawings and prints – the highlight being Hiroshige's masterful series of colored woodblock prints, showing nature in quiet, dusky hues.

Arroyo Seco

The residential pocket northwest of the junction of the 134 and 210 freeways, known as **Arroyo Seco**, or "dry riverbed" in Spanish, features some of LA's best architecture. Orange Grove Boulevard leads you into the neighborhood from central Pasadena and takes you to the **Pasadena Historical Society**, 470 W Walnut Street at Orange Grove Boulevard (Wed–Sun noon–5pm; $5, kids free; ☎626/577-1660, ⓦwww.pasadenahistory.org), which has fine displays on Pasadena's history and tasteful surrounding gardens, but is most interesting for the on-site **Feynes Mansion** (tours Wed–Fri 1pm, Sat & Sun 1.30 & 3pm; $4). Decorated with its original 1905 furnishings and paintings, this elegant Beaux Arts mansion was once the home of the Finnish Consulate. But it's the **Gamble House**, nearby at 4 Westmoreland Place (60-minute tours on the hour Thurs–Sun noon–3pm; $10, kids free; reserve at ☎626/793-3333 ext. 13, ⓦwww .gamblehouse.org), which really brings people out here. Built in 1908, this Craftsman masterpiece combines elements from Swiss chalets and Japanese temples in a romantic, sprawling shingled house. The area around the Gamble House is filled with at least eight other houses by the two brothers (the firm of Greene & Greene) who designed it, including Charles Greene's own house at 368 Arroyo Terrace (closed to the public).

Almost incongruously, the 104,000-seat **Rose Bowl** is just to the north, out of use for most of the year but home to a very popular **flea market** (second Sun of month; $7, reserve tickets at ☎323/560-7469) and, in the autumn, the place where the UCLA football team plays its home games (☎626/577-3101, ⓦwww.uclabruins.com).

Into the foothills
On the other side of the Foothill Freeway (I-210), **Descanso Gardens**, 1418 Descanso Drive (daily 9am–5pm; $7, kids $2; ☎818/949-4200, ⓦwww .descansogardens.org), in the nearby city of La Cañada Flintridge, concentrates all the plants you might see in the mountains into 155 acres of landscaped park, especially brilliant in the spring when all the camellias, tulips, lilies, and daffodils are in bloom. From La Cañada, the winding **Angeles Crest Highway** (Hwy-2) heads up into the mountains above Pasadena, an area once dotted with resort hotels and wilderness camps. The highway leads up to Mount Wilson, high enough to be the major siting spot for TV broadcast antennae, and with a small **museum** (daily 10am–4pm; donation; ☎404/651-2932, ⓦwww.mtwilson.edu) near the 100-inch telescope of the 1904 Mount Wilson Observatory.

The Huntington Library and Gardens
South of Pasadena, **San Marino** is a dull, upper-crust suburb with little of interest beyond the **Huntington Library, Art Collections and Botanical Gardens**, off Huntington Drive at 1151 Oxford Road (Tues–Fri noon–4.30pm, Sat & Sun 10.30am–4.30pm; $15, kids $6; ☎626/405-2100, ⓦwww.huntington.org), based on the collections of Henry Huntington, who owned and operated the Southern Pacific Railroad. In the nineteenth century he held a virtual monopoly on transportation in California, later moving to the manor he had built in San Marino and devoting himself full-time to buying rare books and manuscripts.

You can pick up a self-guided walking tour of each of the three main sections from the bookstore and information desk in the covered pavilion. The **Library**, right off the main entrance, has a two-story exhibition hall containing rare manuscripts and books, among them a Gutenberg Bible, a folio edition of Shakespeare's plays, and the **Ellesmere Chaucer**, a circa-1410 illuminated manuscript of *The Canterbury Tales*. Displays around the walls trace the history of printing and of the English language from medieval manuscripts to a

King James Bible, from Milton's *Paradise Lost* and Blake's *Songs of Innocence and Experience* to first editions of Swift, Dickens, Woolf, and Joyce.

The recently renovated **Huntington Gallery**, a grand mansion done out in Louis XIV carpets and later French tapestries, has works by Van Dyck and Constable and the stars of the whole collection – Gainsborough's *Blue Boy* and Reynolds' *Mrs Siddons as the Tragic Muse*. More striking, perhaps, are Turner's *Grand Canal, Venice*, awash in hazy sunlight and gondolas, and Blake's *Satan Comes to the Gates of Hell*, which is quite the portrait of Old Nick, in this case battling Death with spears.

Nearby, the **Scott Gallery for American Art** displays paintings by Edward Hopper and Mary Cassatt and a range of Wild West drawings and sculpture, though for all the art and literature, it's the grounds that make the Huntington really special. The acres of beautiful themed **gardens** surrounding the buildings include a Zen Rock Garden, complete with authentically constructed Buddhist temple and teahouse, and a "Desert Garden" with the world's largest collection of desert plants, including twelve acres of cacti in an artful setting. While strolling through these assorted wonders, you might also call in on Huntington and his wife, buried in a neo-Palladian **mausoleum** at the northwest corner of the estate.

Along Foothill Boulevard

Parallel to the Foothill Freeway, **Foothill Boulevard** was once best known as part of Route 66, and nowadays leads to the town of **Arcadia**, whose **LA County Arboretum**, 301 N Baldwin Avenue (daily 9am–4.30pm; $5; ☎626/821-3222, Ⓦwww.arboretum.org), contains many impressive gardens and waterfalls, flocks of peacocks, and, of course, a great assortment of trees arranged according to their native continents. The fanciful white Victorian manor along a palm-treed lagoon was famously used in the 1970s TV show *Fantasy Island*.

Southwest of Arcadia in small **San Gabriel** stands the valley's original settlement, the church and grounds of **Mission San Gabriel Arcangel**, 428 S Mission Drive (daily 9am–4pm; $5; ☎626/457-3035, Ⓦwww .sangabrielmission.org). The mission was established here in 1771 by Junípero Serra and the current building finished in 1812. Despite decades of damage by earthquakes and the elements, the church and grounds have been repaired and reopened, their old winery, cistern, kitchens, gardens, and antique-filled rooms giving some sense of mission-era life.

Forest Lawn Cemetery

Jumping many miles west, to the opposite side of the San Gabriel Valley, **Glendale** is best known for its branch of **Forest Lawn Cemetery**, 1712 S Glendale Avenue (daily 8am–5pm; free; ☎1-800/204-3131, Ⓦwww.forestlawn .com), its pompous landscaping and pious artworks attracting celebrities by the dozen. It's best to climb the hill and see the cemetery in reverse from the **Forest Lawn Museum**, whose hodgepodge of historical bric-a-brac includes coins from ancient Rome, Viking relics, medieval armor, and a mysterious sculpted Easter Island figure – the only one on view in the US. Next door to the museum, the **Resurrection and Crucifixion Hall** houses the biggest piece of Western religious art in the world: *The Crucifixion* by Jan Styka – an oil painting nearly 200ft tall and 50ft wide – though you're only allowed to see it during the ceremonial unveiling every hour on the hour.

From the museum, the terrace gardens lead down past sculpted replicas of the greats of classical European art, and on to the **Freedom Mausoleum**, home to a handful of the cemetery's better-known graves. Just outside the mausoleum's doors, Errol Flynn lies in an unspectacular plot, rumored to have been buried with six bottles of whiskey at his side, while nearby is the grave of Walt Disney, who wasn't frozen, as urban legend would have it. Inside the mausoleum itself you'll find Clara Bow, Nat King Cole, Jeanette MacDonald, and Alan Ladd, all close to each other on the first floor. To the left, heading back down the hill, the **Great Mausoleum** is notable for the tombs of Clark Gable and Jean Harlow.

The Burbank studios

On the eastern edge of the San Fernando Valley, dull **Burbank** is the place where many movie studios relocated from Hollywood long ago. Although you can't get into Disney, **Warner Brothers**, Warner Boulevard at Hollywood Way, does offer worthwhile "insider" tours of its sizeable facilities and active backlot (Mon–Fri 8.30am–4pm; $42; T818/972-TOUR, Wwww2.warnerbros.com /vipstudiotour). **NBC**, 3000 W Alameda Street (Mon–Fri 9am–4pm; $8; T818/840-3537), allows 75-minute tours of the largest production facility in the US, and gives you the chance to be in the audience for the taping of a TV program (phone ahead for free tickets) such as Jay Leno's *Tonight Show*.

The largest of the backlots belongs to **Universal Studios**, whose high-priced four-hour tours (hours vary, often summer daily 8am–10pm; rest of year daily 10am–6pm; $61, kids $51; T818/508-9600, Wwww.universalstudioshollywood .com) are more like a trip around an amusement park, with high-tech rides, stuntman shows, and "evening spectaculars" based on current movies. The theme rides are inspired by the studio's more popular films, including *Back to the Future* (a jerky trip on a motion simulator), *Jurassic Park* (close encounters with prehistoric plastic), *Terminator 2* (a 3-D movie with robot stuntmen), and *Shrek 4-D* (another motion simulator, plus another 3-D movie). You never actually get to see any actual filming, though.

North of the Valley and beyond

At the north end of the Valley, the San Diego, Golden State, and Foothill freeways join together at I-5. Just east of the junction, **Mission San Fernando Rey de España**, 15151 San Fernando Mission Boulevard (daily 9am–4.30pm; $5; T818/361-0186), had to be completely rebuilt following the 1971 Sylmar earthquake. Nowadays there's a good collection of historic pottery, furniture, and saddles, and a replica of an old-time blacksmith's shop. Up the road in nearby Sylmar, the wondrous **San Sylmar**, 15180 Bledsoe Street (Tues–Sat 9am–4.30pm; tours by reservation Thurs–Sat 10am &

North Hollywood

The **North Hollywood Arts District** (Wwww.nohoartsdistrict.com), located around Magnolia Boulevard between Burbank and the western San Fernando Valley, and accessible by a nearby Metro Red Line station, was named "NoHo" by county bureaucrats as a play on New York's SoHo. While the district has nothing on Manhattan, it's still a lively enough spot that's well worth a trip if you're in the area, with twenty live theaters and plenty of coffee shops, galleries, bookstores, restaurants, and odd little boutiques to attract your interest. This despite the fact that the district has almost nothing to do with the more rambunctious Hollywood, except in name.

1.30pm; free; ☎818/367-2251, ⓦwww.nethercuttcollection.org), is one of LA's most interesting museums, a storehouse for Wurlitzer organs, antique player-pianos, cosmetic paraphernalia, Tiffany stained glass, and classic French furniture, but most notably the **Nethercutt Collection**, a stunning showroom loaded with the finest array of automobiles imaginable – with classic Packards, Mercedes, Bugattis, and especially Duesenbergs.

Just north of the freeway junction in the town of **Santa Clarita**, the **William S. Hart Ranch and Museum**, 24151 San Fernando Road (Wed–Fri 10am–1pm, Sat & Sun 11am–4pm; summer Wed–Sun 11am–4pm; free; ☎661/254-4584, ⓦwww.hartmuseum.org), holds a fine assemblage of Western history, featuring native artworks, Remington sculptures, displays of spurs, guns, and lariats, Tinseltown costumes, and authentic cowhand clothing, all housed in a Spanish Colonial mansion on a surrounding 265-acre ranch once owned by the silent-era cowboy actor. Continuing north, Hwy-14 splits off east to the Mojave Desert, while I-5 heads on past Valencia to **Magic Mountain**, 26101 Magic Mountain Parkway (hours vary, often summer daily 10am–10pm; rest of year Sat & Sun 10am–8pm; $60, kids $30, $15 parking; ⓦwww.sixflags.com /magicmountain), which has some of the wildest rollercoasters and rides in the world – a hundred times more thrilling than anything at Disneyland. The adjacent water park, **Hurricane Harbor** (same hours; $30, kids $21, or $70 for both parks; ⓦwww.sixflags.com/hurricaneharborla), is another fun choice, providing plenty of aquatic fun if you don't mind getting splashed by throngs of giddy pre-adolescents.

Inland Orange County

Although **ORANGE COUNTY** has long been emblematic of insular white suburbia, the reality is becoming a bit different. Especially in the inland part of the region, Hispanics and Asians increasingly populate cities like Anaheim, Garden Grove, Santa Ana, and Westminster, and certain sections of the county even have a tolerant, sometimes progressive, bent – a far cry from the days when the area was the vote-rich stomping ground for Ronald Reagan and Richard Nixon.

For most visitors, however, Orange County means **Disneyland**; even though it only exists on roughly one square mile of land, it continues to dominate the **Anaheim** area. Elsewhere, the thrill rides at **Knott's Berry Farm** go some way to restoring antique notions of what amusement parks used to be like; the **Crystal Cathedral** is an imposing reminder of the potency of the evangelical movement; and the **Richard Nixon Library and Birthplace** is a good spot to find out about the illustrious life and career of Tricky Dick.

Disneyland

In the early 1950s, illustrator and filmmaker **Walt Disney** conceived a theme park where his internationally famous cartoon characters – Mickey Mouse, Donald Duck, Goofy, and the rest – would come to life, animated quite literally, and his fabulously successful company would rake in even more money. **DISNEYLAND**, 1313 Harbor Boulevard (hours vary, usually summer daily 8am–1am; rest of year Mon–Fri 10am–6pm, Sat 9am–midnight, Sun 9am–10pm; $63, $53 kids, parking $11; ☎714/781-4565, ⓦwww.disneyland .com), is still world-renowned as one of the defining hallmarks of American culture, a theme-park phenomenon with the emphasis strongly on family fun. Thus while visitors have been known to cruise around Disneyland on LSD, it is not a good idea; the authorities take a dim view of anything remotely antisocial, and anyone acting out of order will be thrown out. In any case, the place is surreal enough without the need for mind-expanding drugs.

Practicalities

Disneyland is about 45 minutes by **car** from Downtown LA on the Santa Ana Freeway (I-5). By **train** from Downtown, it's a thirty-minute journey to Fullerton, from where OCTD buses will drop you at Disneyland or Knott's Berry Farm. By **bus**, MTA #460 from Downtown takes about ninety minutes, and Greyhound takes 45 minutes to get to Anaheim, from where it's an easy walk to the park.

As for **accommodation**, most people try to visit Disneyland just for the day and spend the night somewhere else. If you must stay, we've listed some reasonable options on p.86. If you don't want to eat the fast food available in the park, the listings for the area (see p.152) suggest some of the more palatable options.

The main park

Not including the new California Adventure annex (see p.144), the Disneyland admission price includes all the rides, although during peak periods you might have to wait in line for hours – lines are shortest when the park opens, so choose a few top rides and get to them very early. From the front gates, **Main Street** leads through a scaled-down, camped-up replica of a bucolic Midwestern town, filled with souvenir shops and diners, toward **Sleeping Beauty's Castle**, a pseudo-Rhineland palace at the heart of the park that isn't much more than a giant, walk-through prop. **New Orleans Square**, nearby, contains the two best rides in the park: the Pirates of the Caribbean, a boat trip through underground caverns, singing along with drunken pirates, and the Haunted Mansion, a riotous "doom buggy" tour in the company of the house spooks. In **Adventureland**, the antiquated Jungle Cruise offers "tour guides" making crude puns about the fake animatronic beasts creaking amid the scenery, and Tarzan's Treehouse is little more than a movie tie-in with ramps and catwalks circling around the trees. Much more appealing is the nearby **Indiana Jones Adventure**, a giddy journey down skull-encrusted corridors in which you face fireballs, burning rubble, venomous snakes, and, inevitably, a rolling-boulder finale.

Less fun are the contiguous areas of **Critter Country** and **Frontierland**, the smallest and most "all-American" section of the park. The main attraction, Big Thunder Mountain Railroad, is a drab, slow-moving coaster, while Splash Mountain at least has the added thrill of getting drenched by a log-flume ride, and Tom Sawyer Island offers an elaborate playground with treehouses, caves, and pirate-themed scavenger hunts. Continuing counterclockwise around the park, **Fantasyland** shows off the cleverest, but also the most sentimental, aspects of the Disney imagination: Peter Pan, a fairytale flight over London, and It's a Small World, a tour of the world's continents in which animated dolls warble the same cloying song over and over. Tots who just can't get enough saccharine can wander into **Toontown**, thick with slow-moving bumper cars and other kiddie amusements.

Fantasyland mercifully gives way to **Tomorrowland**, Disney's vision of the future, where the Space Mountain rollercoaster zips through the pitch-blackness of outer space, and R2D2 pilots a runaway space cruiser through

George Lucas's Star Tours galaxy. This fun zone has been updated somewhat in recent years, with new rides like the Jules Verne–inspired Astro Orbiter, the Finding Nemo-themed Submarine Voyage, and Innoventions, a fun opportunity to look at, and play with, the latest special effects.

The California Adventure

Opened in 2002, the **California Adventure** is technically a separate park but is connected to the main one in architecture and style – although it's much less popular and of middling interest to most visitors. Aside from its slightly more exciting rollercoasters and better food, the California Adventure is really just another "land" to visit, albeit a much more expensive one – you'll have to shell out another $63 or plunk down $83 for a two-day pass that covers both.

The lack of visitors is telling: it's hard to justify spending the money when most of Disneyland's classic, and memorable, attractions are on the other side of the park. That said, there are a handful of highlights if you're looking to visit both areas. **Grizzly River Run** is a fun giant-inner-tube ride, splashing around through various plunges and "caverns"; **Soarin' Over California** is a fairly exciting trip on an experimental aircraft that buzzes you through hairpin turns and steep dives; the **Twilight Zone Tower of Terror** is a chilling 13-story plunge; and the **Electrical Parade** is the classic parade of brightly lit floats and vehicles, relocated from the main park, that takes place nightly at 8.45pm.

Knott's Berry Farm

If you're a bit fazed by the excesses of Disneyland, you might prefer the more down-to-earth **Knott's Berry Farm**, four miles northwest, off the Santa Ana Freeway at 8039 Beach Boulevard (hours vary, usually summer Sun–Thurs 9am–11pm, Fri & Sat 9am–midnight; rest of year Mon–Fri 10am–6pm, Sat 10am–10pm, Sun 10am–7pm; $44, kids $19; ⓦwww.knotts.com), whose rollercoasters are far more exciting than anything at its rival. Although there are ostensibly six themed lands here, you should spend most or all of your time in just half of them: **Fiesta Village**, home to the Jaguar, a high-flying coaster that spins you around the park concourse; **Ghost Town**, with fun wooden coasters and log flumes; and the **Boardwalk**, which is all about heart-thumping thrill rides. Knott's also has its own adjacent water park, **Soak City USA** (June–Sept only, hours vary but generally daily 10am–5pm or 6pm; $28, $17 for children or adult entry after 3pm), offering 22 drenching rides of various heights and speeds.

Around Disneyland

To the south of Disneyland, the giant **Crystal Cathedral**, just off the Santa Ana Freeway on Chapman Avenue (tours Mon–Sat 9am–3.30pm; free; ☎714/971-4013, ⓦwww.crystalcathedral.org), is a famous Philip Johnson design of tubular space-frames and plate-glass walls that forms part of the vision of evangelist Robert Schuller. A more worthwhile attraction, perhaps, lies in the nearby, unappealing burg of **Santa Ana**, where the splendid **Bowers Museum of Cultural Art**, 2002 N Main Street (Tues–Sun 10am–4pm; $19; ☎714/567-3600, ⓦwww.bowers.org), features anthropological treasures from early Asian, African, Native American, and pre-Columbian civilizations. Showcasing artifacts as diverse as ceramic Maya icons, hand crafted baskets from native Californians, and Chinese funerary sculpture, the museum is an essential stop for anyone interested in civilizations outside the West.

North of Disneyland, bland **Fullerton** is the site of the **Muckenthaler Cultural Center**, 1201 W Malvern Avenue (Wed–Sun noon–4pm; free; ⓦ www .muckenthaler.org), located in an attractive 1924 Renaissance Revival mansion and hosting a wide range of international multicultural art, with Native American art and textiles, African craftwork and jewelry, and contemporary Korean ceramics being only a few of the highlights. In May, an annual display of "automotive art" presents numerous, colorful car-related illustrations and designs.

The Richard Nixon Library and Birthplace

In freeway-caged **Yorba Linda**, about eight miles northeast of Disneyland, the **Richard Nixon Library and Birthplace**, 18001 Yorba Linda Boulevard (Mon–Sat 10am–5pm, Sun 11am–5pm; $10; Ⓣ 714/993-5075, ⓦ www .nixonfoundation.org), is an unrelentingly hagiographic library and museum that features oversized gifts from world leaders, amusing campaign memorabilia, and a collection of obsequious letters written by and to Nixon. The high points are a miniature, seventy-foot-long replica of the White House – looking strangely like an imperial dollhouse – the gallery of ten statues of world leaders from the Nixon era, from Khrushchev to deGaulle, and the re-creation of the **Lincoln Sitting Room** of the White House, replicated in architecture and decor.

It's in the constantly running archive radio and TV recordings that the distinctive Nixon persona really shines through, from his notorious Checkers Speech to his disastrous debates with John F. Kennedy. Throughout the museum, Nixon's face leers down in Orwellian fashion, but only inside the **Presidential Auditorium** (at the end of the corridor packed with notes attesting to the former president's innocence in the Watergate scandal) do you get the chance to ask him a preprogrammed question – though "I am not a crook" is never one of the answers.

The Orange County Coast

On the **ORANGE COUNTY COAST**, a string of towns from the edge of the LA Harbor Area to the borders of San Diego County 35 miles south, swanky condos line the sands and the ambience is easy-going, affluent, and conservative or libertarian depending on the area. As the names of the main towns suggest – **Huntington Beach**, **Newport Beach**, and **Laguna Beach** – there's no real reason beyond sea and sand to go here. The other place that merits a stop is just inland at **San Juan Capistrano**, site of the best kept of all the California missions. Further on, there's little to see before you reach adjoining San Diego County, but the campground at **San Clemente** provides the only cheap accommodation along the southern part of the coast (see p.87).

The fastest way to **travel** from LA to San Diego skips the coast by passing through Orange County on the inland San Diego Freeway, the 405. The coastal cities, though, are linked by the more appealing **Pacific Coast Highway** (PCH), part of Hwy-1, which you can pick up from Long Beach (or from the end of Beach Boulevard in Anaheim), though it's often busy in the summer. OCTD bus #1 rumbles along PCH regularly during the day, though Greyhound largely avoids this part of Orange County. Amtrak's Pacific Surfliner route connects Downtown LA (or Disneyland) to San Juan Capistrano and San Clemente, though you can travel all the way along the coast from LA to San

Diego using local buses for about $6 – but you should allow a full day for the journey. A slightly pricier but more worthwhile transit option is the Metrolink commuter train line (see p.78), which not only connects Downtown LA with Orange County down to San Clemente, but continues on to Oceanside in San Diego County, from where you can pick up that region's Coaster and connect to Downtown San Diego.

Huntington Beach

Huntington Beach is a compact town composed of engaging single-story cafés and beach stores grouped around the foot of a long pier, off PCH at Main Street – also the place where the **Surfers Walk of Fame** commemorates the sport's towering figures. Otherwise the beach is the sole focus: it was here that California surfing began, imported from Hawaii in 1907. You can check out the **International Surfing Museum**, 411 Olive Avenue (Oct–May Thurs–Mon noon–5pm; June–Sept open daily; $3; ☎714/960-3483, ⓦwww.surfingmuseum.org), which features exhibits on such legendary figures as Corky Carroll and Duke Kahanamoku, historic posters from various world surfing contests, and an array of traditional, contemporary, and far-out boards, including one shaped like a Swiss Army Knife. If all this appeals to you, see the full glory of the sport at the various **surfing competitions** held throughout the summer (ⓦwww.hbsurfseries.com).

Several miles north, nature lovers won't want to miss the **Bolsa Chica State Ecological Reserve**, PCH at Warner Avenue, a sizeable wetland preserve. Taking a one-and-one-half-mile loop tour will get you acquainted with some of the current avian residents of this salt marsh, including a fair number of herons, egrets, and grebes, and even a few peregrine falcons and endangered snowy plovers. Self-tours are free, and guided tours are available on the first Saturday of the month (9am & 10.30am; $1; groups by reservation at ☎714/840-1575, ⓦwww.amigosdebolsachica.org).

Newport Beach and Corona Del Mar

Ten miles south of Huntington, **Newport Beach**, with its nine yacht clubs and ten thousand yachts, is upmarket even by Orange County standards. Although there are hardly any conventional "sights" in town, the place to hang out is on the thin **Balboa Peninsula**, along which runs the three-mile-long strand. The most youthful and boisterous section is about halfway along, around **Newport Pier** at the end of 20th Street. North of here, beachfront homes restrict access, but to the south, around the **Balboa Pier**, is a tourist-friendly zone with a marina from which you can escape to Santa Catalina Island (see p.136). Away from the peninsula, Newport Beach is home to the **Orange County Museum of Art**, 850 San Clemente Drive (Tues–Sun 11am–5pm, Thurs until 8pm; $10, free Thurs; ☎949/759-1122, ⓦwww.ocma.net), a surprisingly good institution that stages engaging exhibitions of contemporary work.

A few miles along PCH from Newport, **Corona Del Mar** is worth a short stop for the **Sherman Library and Gardens**, 2647 East PCH (daily 10.30am–4pm; $3; ☎949/675-5458, ⓦwww.slgardens.org), devoted to the horticulture of the Southwest and raising many vivid blooms in its botanical gardens, including cacti, orchids, roses, and an array of different herbs. Between here and Laguna Beach lies an unspoiled three-mile-long coastline, protected as **Crystal Cove State Park** – perfect to explore on foot, far from the crowds, and offering good beachside accommodation (see p.87).

▲ Kitesurfer near Newport Beach

Laguna Beach

Six miles south of Crystal Cove, nestled among the crags around a small sandy strip, **Laguna Beach** has a relaxed and tolerant feel among its inhabitants, who range from millionaires to middle-class gays and lesbians, and offers a flourishing arts scene in the many streetside galleries. PCH passes right through the center of town, a few steps from the small main **beach**. From the beach's north side, an elevated wooden walkway twists around the coastline above a conserved ecological area with tide pools. One of the few conventional attractions is the excellent **Laguna Art Museum**, 307 Cliff Drive (daily 11am–5pm; $10; ☎949/494-8971, ⓦwww.lagunaartmuseum.org), which holds fine exhibitions drawn from its stock of Southern California art from the 1900s to the present.

Laguna Beach festivals

Laguna hosts a number of large summer **art festivals** over six weeks in July and August. The best known is the **Pageant of the Masters**, in which participants pose in front of a painted backdrop to portray a famous work of art. It's surprisingly impressive and takes a great deal of preparation – something reflected in the prices: $20–100 for shows that sell out months in advance. You may, however, be able to pick up cancellations on the night (shows begin at 8.30pm; ☎1-800/487-3378, ⓦwww.foapom.com). The pageant is combined with the **Festival of the Arts** (daily 10am–11.30pm; $7; contact information as above), held at the same venue and featuring the work of 150 local artists.

The excitement of both festivals waned in the 1960s, when a group of hippies created the alternative **Sawdust Festival**, 935 Laguna Canyon Road (July & Aug, 10am–10pm; $7, season pass $13; ☎949/494-3030, ⓦwww.sawdustartfestival.org), in which local artists set up makeshift studios to demonstrate their skills. It is now just as established, but easier to get into than the other two.

About two and a half miles inland from downtown Laguna Beach is a sight not to be missed by lovers of sea life: the **Pacific Marine Mammal Center**, 20612 Laguna Canyon Road (daily 10am–4pm; free; ⊕949/494-3050, ⊛www .pacificmmc.org), a rehabilitation center that lets you watch as underweight, injured, or otherwise threatened seals and sea lions are nursed back to health.

Dana Point

From South Laguna, it's possible to see **Dana Point**, a town and promontory jutting into the ocean about four miles south. It was named after sailor and author Richard Henry Dana Jr, whose *Two Years Before the Mast* described how cattle hides were flung over these cliffs to trading ships waiting below, and did much to romanticize the California coast while still viewing it with a wary eye. He ended his voyaging career here in 1830, and there's a statue of him and a replica of his vessel, *The Pilgrim*, at the edge of the harbor on the grounds of the **Ocean Institute**, 24200 Dana Point Harbor Drive (Sat & Sun 10am–4.30pm; $6; ⊕949/496-2274, ⊛www.ocean-institute.org). Marine-biology cruises are offered here as well as public visits, during which you can view oceanic wildlife, from lobsters to anemones, in glass-enclosed tanks.

San Juan Capistrano

Further south, and three miles inland along the I-5 freeway, most of the small town of **San Juan Capistrano** is built in a Spanish Colonial style derived from **Mission San Juan Capistrano**, Ortega Highway at Camino Capistrano in the center of town (daily 8.30am–5pm; $7; ⊕949/234-1300, ⊛www.missionsjc.com), a short walk from the Amtrak stop. The seventh of California's missions, founded by Junípero Serra in 1776, the mission was within three years so well populated that it outgrew the original chapel. Soon after, the **Great Stone Church** was erected, the ruins of which are the first thing you see as you walk in. The huge structure had seven domes and a bell tower, but was destroyed by an earthquake soon after its 1812 completion. The mission **chapel** is small and narrow, decorated with Indian drawings and Spanish artifacts, set off by a sixteenth-century altar from Barcelona. In a side room, the tiny chapel of **St Pereguin** is kept warm by the heat from the dozens of candles lit by miracle-seeking pilgrims who arrive here from all over the US and Mexico. Other restored buildings include the kitchen, smelter, and workshops used for dyeing, weaving, and candlemaking.

The city is further noted for its **swallows**, popularly thought to return here from their winter migration on March 19. They sometimes do arrive on this day, but are much more likely to show up as soon as the weather is warm enough, and when there are enough insects on the ground to provide a decent homecoming banquet.

San Clemente

Five miles south of San Juan Capistrano down I-5, **San Clemente** is a pretty little town, its streets contoured around the hills, lending it an almost Mediter-ranean air. Because of its proximity to one of the largest military bases in the state, **Camp Pendleton**, it's a popular weekend retreat for military personnel. It's also home to some of Orange County's better surfing beaches, especially toward the south end of town, and has a reasonable campground, too (see p.87). It's here, around the city's southern tip, that San Clemente had a brief glimmer of fame when President Richard Nixon convened his **Western White House** here from 1969 to 1974, regularly meeting with cronies and political allies. The

25-acre estate is located off of Avenida del Presidente and is visible from the beach – though off-limits if you want a closer look.

Eating

Whatever you want to eat and however much you want to spend, LA's **restaurants** leave you spoiled for choice. **Cheap food** is, of course, plentiful here, ranging from historic diners to street-corner coffee shops to trusty burger shacks. Almost as common and just as cheap, **Mexican food** is the closest thing you'll get to an indigenous LA cuisine. The options are almost endless for quick and cheap meals, and include free grub available for the price of a drink at **happy hours**. Many of the city's **higher-end restaurants** serve superb food in consciously cultivated surroundings, driving up their prices on the back of a good review, and typically specializing in French, Italian, Japanese, or **California cuisine** – the latter the signature style of top-notch LA eating since the 1980s, blending French-styled cuisine with fresh local ingredients in an eclectic, harmonious brew.

Delis, diners, and stands

Affordable food is everywhere in LA, at its best in the many small and stylish **delis** and **diners** that serve soups, omelets, sandwiches, and burgers; it's easy to eat this way constantly and never have to spend much more than $8 for a full meal. There are, of course, the franchise fast-food joints on every street, though the local **hamburger** and **taco stands** (many open 24hr) are always much better – some of them, such as *Pann's* near Inglewood, catering to fans of old-fashioned Formica diners, with their neon signs, boomerang roofs, and classic steak-and-eggs breakfasts.

Downtown and around

Clifton's Cafeteria 648 S Broadway ☏213/627-1673. Classic 1930s cafeteria with much bizarre decor: redwood trees, waterfall, and mini-chapel. The food is traditional meat-and-potatoes American, and cheap, too. Open until midnight.

Cole's Pacific Electric Buffet 118 E 6th St ☏213/622-4090. This place has been here a very long time – since 1908, making this LA's oldest extant restaurant. The decor and food haven't changed much since then, either, and the rich, hearty French dip sandwiches are still loaded with steak, pastrami, or brisket – a dish invented at this very spot.

Emerson's 606 S Olive St ☏213/623-3006, 862 S Los Angeles St ☏213/623-8807. Solid breakfast-and-lunch spot with some of the city's best cheap sandwiches, with the *croque monsieur* and chicken-salad baguette among the highlights. Sip espresso and munch on a regular salad, too, or sample the clam chowder or jambalaya, for less than $10 each.

Grand Central Market 317 S Broadway ☏213/624-9496. Selling plenty of tacos, deli sandwiches, and Chinese food, plus a few more exotic items, like pigs' ears and lamb sweetbreads. A fun, cheap place to eat.

Langer's Deli 704 S Alvarado St ☏213/483-8050. Offers more than twenty ways of eating what is easily LA's best pastrami sandwich. Open daylight hours only in a dicey spot; curbside pickup available.

LA restaurants

▲ Pink's Hot Dogs, Hollywood

Original Pantry 877 S Figueroa St ☎213/972-9279. There's always a queue for the hearty portions of meaty American cooking – chops and steaks, mostly – in this diner owned by former mayor Dick Riordan. Breakfast is the best option (available 24hr).

Philippe the Original French Dip 1001 N Alameda St ☎213/628-3781. 1908 sawdust café that serves up the eponymous sandwich with turkey, ham, lamb, pork, or beef – an amazingly good and filling treat for less than $6.

Hollywood

DuPar's 6333 W 3rd St ☎323/933-8446. A long-standing LA institution, located in the Farmers' Market, which draws a whole host of old-timers for its tasty hotcakes and heavy-duty cheeseburgers. Make sure to sample a piece of pie – they come in a full range of bright colors and flavors.

Fred 62 1854 N Vermont Ave, Los Feliz ☎323/667-0062. Designed like something out of the 1950s, this diner offers stylish, affordable California-cuisine twists on familiar staples like salads, burgers, and fries, and a tempting array of pancakes and omelets.

Mel's Drive-In 8585 Sunset Blvd ☎310/854-7200. Calorie-packing milkshakes, fries, and, of course, burgers make this 24-hour diner an essential stop if you've got the late-night munchies.

Pink's Hot Dogs 709 N La Brea Ave ☎323/931-4223. The quintessence of chili dogs. Depending on your taste, these monster hot dogs – topped with anything from bacon and chili cheese to pastrami

and Swiss cheese – are lifesavers or gut bombs. Open 'til 2am, or 3am weekends.

Roscoe's House of Chicken and Waffles 1514 N Gower St ☎323/466-7453. This diner attracts all sorts for its fried chicken, greens, and thick waffles. One of five area locations.

Tommy's 2575 Beverly Blvd ☎213/389-9060. One of the prime LA spots for big, greasy, tasty burgers and scrumptious fries – and, many would say, the best. Located right off the 101 freeway in a somewhat grim section of East Hollywood. 24hr.

West LA and Beverly Hills

The Apple Pan 10801 W Pico Blvd ☎310/475-3585. Grab a spot at the counter and enjoy freshly baked apple pie and nicely greasy hamburgers. An old-time joint that opened just after World War II. Weekdays open 'til midnight, weekends 'til 1am.

Barney's Beanery 8447 Santa Monica Blvd ☎323/654-2287. Hundreds of bottled beers and hot dogs, hamburgers, and bowls of chili served in a hip, grungy environment. Angelenos can be divided up by those who love or hate the place – everyone knows it.

Canter's Deli 419 N Fairfax Ave ☎323/651-2030. Huge sandwiches and excellent kosher soups served by waitresses in pink uniforms and running shoes. Open 24hr. Live music nightly in *Canter's* adjoining "Kibitz Room" 'til 1.40am.

Duke's 8909 Sunset Blvd ☎310/652-3100. A favorite haunt of visiting rock stars (the *Roxy* and *Whisky-a-Go-Go* clubs are up the street), this breakfast diner attracts a motley crew of night owls and bleary-eyed locals. Closes weekends at 3pm.

Jerry's Famous Deli 8701 Beverly Blvd ☎310/289-1811. Unavoidable are the many *Jerry's* locations in LA, and this one like the others has a sizeable deli menu, and it's open 24hr. Occasionally, celebrities stop in to nosh.

John o' Groats 10516 W Pico Blvd ☎310/204-0692. Excellent breakfasts and lunches (mostly staples like bacon and eggs, oatmeal, and waffles), but come at an off hour; the morning crowd can cause a headache. Prices aren't cheap, either.

Nate 'n' Al's 414 N Beverly Drive ☎310/274-0101. The best-known, and perhaps best, deli in Beverly Hills, popular with movie people and one of the few reasonable places in the vicinity. Get there early (opens daily 7am) to grab a booth.

Oki Dog 5056 W Pico Blvd ☎323/938-4369. An essential LA stop for all lovers of "red hots," in this case wieners wrapped in tortillas and stuffed with all manner of gooey, super-caloric ingredients – from pastrami to cheese to chili.

Topz 8593 Santa Monica Blvd ☎310/659-8843. A local chain of fast-food joints that focuses, somehow, on the healthier side of eating burgers, hot dogs, and French fries, with lo-cal cooking oils and lean meats on the culinary agenda.

Santa Monica, Venice, and Malibu

Benito's Taco Shop 11614 Santa Monica Blvd ☎310/442-9924. Tacos rolled up in a flour tortilla and served with beef, pork, or fish, and for just a few bucks. Most combos are around $5, making this a good spot to gulp and run. One in a chain of four 24-hour diners.

Café 50s 838 Lincoln Blvd, Venice ☎310/399-1955. Grubby little diner that's nonetheless kept going for years because of its savory eats – pancakes, French toast, milkshakes – and rock'n'roll jukebox.

Café Montana 1534 Montana Ave, Santa Monica ☎310/829-3990. The eclectic menu is highlighted by solid soups, excellent salads, and hearty grilled fish. Breakfast is the main attraction.

Norm's 1601 Lincoln Blvd, Santa Monica ☎310/450-0074. One of the last remaining classic diners, this local chain has 16 other LA branches and serves breakfasts and lunches for around $7. Great Googie architecture and open 24hr, too.

Rae's Diner 2901 Pico Blvd, Santa Monica ☎310/828-7937. Solid 1950s diner with heavy comfort food. Its turquoise-blue facade and interior have been seen in many films, notably *True Romance*.

LAX and the South Bay and Harbor Area

East Coast Bagels 5753 E PCH, Long Beach ☎562/985-0933. Located in a mini-mall, but with an excellent, wide selection of bagels, ranging from New York staples to California hybrids like the jalapeño-cheddar bagel stuffed with cream cheese.

Johnny Reb's 4663 N Long Beach Blvd, Long Beach ☎562/423-7327. The waft of BBQ ribs, catfish, and hush puppies alone may draw you to this prime Southern spot, where the portions are large and the price is cheap.

Pann's 6710 La Tijera Blvd, Inglewood ☎310/337-2860. One of the all-time great Googie diners, where you can't go wrong with the classic burgers or biscuits and gravy.

Pier Bakery 100 Fisherman's Wharf #M, Redondo Beach ☎310/376-9582. A small but satisfying menu with jalapeño-cheese bread, churros, and cinnamon rolls. Probably the best food in this touristy area.

24-hour eats

These places satisfy hunger at all hours. For full restaurant reviews, see the appropriate sections.

Benito's Taco Shop 11614 Santa Monica Blvd, Santa Monica ☎310/442-9924 – p.151

Canter's Deli 419 N Fairfax Ave, West LA ☎323/651-2030 – p.150

Fred 62 1854 N Vermont Ave, Los Feliz ☎323/667-0062 – p.150

Jerry's Famous Deli 8701 Beverly Blvd, West LA ☎310/289-1811 – p.151

Mel's Drive-In 8585 Sunset Blvd ☎310/854-7200 – p.150

Norm's 1601 Lincoln Blvd, Santa Monica ☎310/450-0074 – p.151

Original Pantry 877 S Figueroa St, Downtown ☎213/972-9279 – p.150

Pacific Dining Car 1310 W 6th St, Downtown ☎213/483-6000 – p.154

Tommy's 2575 Beverly Blvd, Hollywood ☎213/389-9060 – p.150

Randy's Donuts 805 W Manchester Ave, Inglewood ☎310/645-4707. This Pop Art fixture is hard to miss, thanks to the colossal donut sitting on the roof. Excellent for its piping hot treats, which you can pick up at the drive-through on your way to or from LAX.

The San Gabriel and San Fernando valleys

Art's Deli 12224 Ventura Blvd, Studio City ☎818/762-1221. Longtime deli favorite, with a good range of hefty, scrumptious sandwiches and soups like the good ol' chicken-noodle.

Bob's Big Boy 4211 W Riverside Drive, Burbank ☎818/843-9334. The classic chain diner, fronted by the plump burger lad, and a veritable Pop-architecture classic, saved from demolition through the efforts of preservationists. Open 'til midnight.

Dr Hogly-Wogly's Tyler Texas Bar-B-Q 8136 Sepulveda Blvd, Van Nuys ☎818/780-6701. Long lines for some of the best chicken, sausages, ribs, and beans in LA, despite the long drive to the middle of nowhere.

Fair Oaks Pharmacy and Soda Fountain 1526 Mission St, South Pasadena ☎626/799-1414. Restored soda fountain with many old-time drinks like lime rickeys, root beer floats, milkshakes, and egg creams – a historic 1915 highlight along the former Route 66.

Porto's Bakery 315 N Brand Blvd, Glendale ☎818/956-5996. Top-notch café serving Cuban flaky pastries and sandwiches, rum-soaked cheesecakes, muffins, Danishes, croissants, torts, tarts, and cappuccino.

Wolfe Burgers 46 N Lake Ave, Pasadena ☎626/792-7292. Knockout gyros, chili, tamales, and burgers – a long-standing Valley favorite.

Disneyland and around

Angelo's 511 S State College Blvd, Anaheim ☎714/533-1401. Straight out of *Happy Days*, a drive-in complete with roller-skating car-hops, neon signs, vintage cars, and, incidentally, good burgers.

Heroes 125 W Santa Fe Ave, Fullerton ☎714/738-4356. The place to come if you're starving after hitting the theme parks, a spot to knock back one of the 100 beers available or chow down on items like hamburgers, chili, ribs, or meatloaf.

Mimi's Café 1400 S Harbor Blvd, Anaheim ☎714/956-2223. Huge servings, low prices, and solid breakfasts and lunches. Part of a sizeable chain in Los Angeles and Orange counties, and popular in both.

Mrs Knott's Chicken Dinner Restaurant Just outside Knott's Berry Farm at 8039 Beach Blvd, Buena Park ☎714/220-5080. Serving cheap and tasty meals for over 65 years. People flocked here for delicious fried-chicken dinners long before Disneyland was around, and they still do; there's also a mean boysenberry pie.

Orange County Coast

The Cottage 308 N Coast Hwy, Laguna Beach ☎949/494-3023. Hungry beachgoers can choose from filling American breakfasts, or else affordable seafood, pasta, and chicken dishes at lunch and dinner.

Crab Cooker 2200 Newport Blvd, Newport Beach ☎949/673-0100. The hefty plates of crab legs, clams and steaming bowls of chowder make the long lines here a bit more bearable.

Jack Shrimp 2400 W Coast Hwy, Newport Beach ☎949/650-5577. One in a chain of Cajun dinner establishments in various spots along the Orange County Coast, with an appealing assortment of spicy seafood and fairly authentic Louisiana staples.

Ruby's 1 Balboa Pier, Newport Beach ☎949/675-RUBY. The first and finest of the retro-streamline 1940s diners in this chain – in a great location at the end of Newport's popular pier. Mostly offers the standard burgers, fries, and soda fare.

Zinc Café 344 Ocean Ave, Laguna Beach ☎949/494-2791. A popular breakfast spot offering simple soup-and-salad meals and other vegetarian fare, with some tasty desserts. Good for a day on the sands.

Mexican and Latin American

LA's **Mexican** restaurants offer some of the city's best – and most plentiful – foodstuffs, serving tasty and filling meals for as little as $5. Those in East LA are some of the finest, though you can find a good selection of both authentic and Americanized fare all over the city. **Caribbean** food is less visible but, when sought out, can be quite rewarding, especially in its Cuban incarnation. The cuisine of the rest of **Latin America** includes a mix of flavors and spices from Central American countries like Honduras and Nicaragua, a tasty blend of local seafood and native Peruvian cuisine (aka "Peruvian seafood"), or the hot, garlicky platters of Argentine beef that have found aficionados throughout the Westside.

Downtown and around

Ciro's 705 N Evergreen Ave, East LA ☎ 323/267-8637. A split-level cave of a dining room, serving enormous platters of shrimp and *mole* specials. The garlic shrimp and *flautas* are the main draw, and they also offer takeout.

El Cholo 1121 S Western Ave ☎ 323/734-2773. One of LA's first big Mexican restaurants and still one of the best – offering a solid array of staples like enchiladas and tamales, with some vegetarian options – despite the wait to get in during peak hours.

El Taurino 2306 W 11th St ☎ 213/738-0961. Tacos, burritos and especially tostadas are the draw at this popular and authentic eatery – where the green and red salsas burn all the way down.

La Luz del Dia 107 Paseo de la Plaza ☎ 213/628-7495. Authentic Mexican eatery on Olvera St that's worth seeking out for its fiery burritos, enchiladas, and stews, served in sizeable enough portions to make you sweat with a smile.

Luminarias 3500 W Ramona Blvd, Monterey Park ☎ 323/268-4177. Dance to salsa and merengue between bites of seafood-heavy Mexican food. The Spanish name refers to honorary candles in brown paper bags. Also see p.171.

Hollywood

Casa Carnitas 4067 Beverly Blvd, south of Hollywood ☎ 323/667-9953. Tasty Mexican food from the Yucatán: the dishes are inspired by Cuban and Caribbean cooking – lots of fine seafood, too.

Cha Cha Cha 656 N Virgil Ave ☎ 323/664-7723. Offering scrumptious paella, black-pepper shrimp, jerk chicken, and other Caribbean treats. Also at 7953 Santa Monica Blvd, West Hollywood ☎ 323/848-7700.

El Compadre 7408 W Sunset Blvd ☎ 323/874-7924. With potent margaritas, live mariachi bands, and cheap Mexican standards, this is a gourmand's delight. One of several locations, most in more distant parts of the metropolis.

El Floridita 1253 N Vine St ☎ 323/871-8612. Despite the uninspiring strip-mall facade, a lively Cuban restaurant where the dance floor swings on the weekends. The menu features solid standards like plantains, croquetas, and yucca, all affordably priced.

Havana on Sunset 5825 Sunset Blvd ☎ 323/464-1800. Like the name says, everything is Cuban at this festive eatery, from the lively music to the rich, authentic meals of soups, seafood, and garlic-heavy entrées.

Mario's Peruvian Seafood Restaurant 5786 Melrose Ave ☎ 323/466-4181. Delicious and authentic Peruvian fare: supremely tender squid and rich and flavorful mussels, among many other good choices.

Mexico City 2121 N Hillhurst Ave ☎ 323/661-7227. Spinach enchiladas, chicken *mole*, and other semi-authentic versions of Mexican standards at this reliable choice.

Xiomara 6101 Melrose Ave ☎ 323/461-0601. An upscale eatery serving tasty Cuban and Latin American meals, with the accent on beef, pork, and fish entrees and a nice range of stews and colorful sauces.

West LA

Carlitos Gardel 7963 Melrose Ave ☎ 323/655-0891. Seriously rich and tasty Argentine cuisine – ie, heavy on the beef and spices, with sausages and garlic adding to the kick.

La Salsa 10800 W Pico Blvd ☎ 310/234-8338. The place to come for fresh, delicious, soft tacos and burritos, on the lower end of the price scale. One of many Westside branches.

Monte Alban 11927 Santa Monica Blvd ☎ 310/444-7736. Forget the tacky mini-mall setting and focus on the fine, affordable selection of *mole* sauces and Mexican staples that make any trip here worthwhile.

Versailles 10319 Venice Blvd ☎ 310/558-3168. Busy and noisy authentic Cuban restaurant with excellent fried plantains, paella, and black beans and rice. Also nearby at 1415 S La Cienega Blvd (☎ 310/289-0392).

Zabumba 10717 Venice Blvd, Culver City ☎ 310/841-6525. A Brazilian favorite for its bossa nova music, Latin American–inflected pizzas, tasty seafood, and convivial atmosphere.

Santa Monica, Venice, and Malibu

Babalu 1002 Montana Ave, Santa Monica ☎ 310/395-2500. The pumpkin pancakes at this pan-ethnic, Caribbean-influenced restaurant are delightful, as are the sweet potato tamales and fried plantains. Service can be erratic, especially at peak times.

Border Grill 1445 4th St, Santa Monica ☎ 310/451-1655. Good place to sup on shrimp, pork, plantains, and other Latin American-flavored fixings, with excellent desserts, too.

Gaucho Grill 1251 Third Street Promenade, Santa Monica ☎ 310/394-4966. One in a fine local chain

of Argentine beef-houses, where the steaks come rich and garlicky and the spices can bowl you over.
Mariasol 401 Santa Monica Pier, Santa Monica ☏310/917-5050. Cervezas with a view, hidden away at the end of the pier, with good, straightforward Mexican staples. On weekend afternoons, the small rooftop deck affords a sweeping panorama from Malibu to Venice.
Marix Tex-Mex Playa 118 Entrada Drive, Pacific Palisades ☏310/459-8596. Flavorful fajitas and big margaritas in this rowdy beachfront cantina.

The South Bay and Harbor Area

By Brazil 1615 Cabrillo Ave, Torrance ☏310/787-7520. Hearty and affordable Brazilian fare, mostly grilled chicken and beef dishes; worth a visit to inland Torrance for a taste.
El Pollo Inka 1100 PCH, Hermosa Beach ☏310/372-1433. Good Peruvian-style chicken, catfish, and hot and spicy soups to make your mouth water.

Taco Beach 211 Pine Ave, Long Beach ☏562/983-1337. As you might guess, fish tacos are the main draw here, though the rest of the eatery's south-of-the-border fare is also quite serviceable.

The San Gabriel and San Fernando valleys

Don Cuco's 3911 W Riverside Drive, Burbank ☏818/842-1123. Good food, mainly familiar Mexican staples, as well as solid fish, seafood and margaritas. One of several in a Valley chain.
El Tepeyac 800 S Palm Ave, Alhambra ☏626/281-3366. Huge, luscious burritos and hot salsa bring true lovers of Mexican food out to this rather removed section of the San Gabriel Valley.
Izalco 10729 Burbank Blvd, North Hollywood ☏818/760-0396. Salvadoran cuisine presented with grace and style, from plantains and pork ribs to corn cakes and pupusas.

American and California cuisine

American cuisine – with its steaks, ribs, baked potatoes, and salads – has a low profile in faddish LA, although it's available almost everywhere and may not even cost more than $15 for a comparative blow out. More prominent – and more expensive, at upwards of $20 per entrée – is **California cuisine**, based on fresh local ingredients, more likely grilled than fried, and stylishly presented with a nod to nouvelle **French** cuisine.

Downtown and around

Angelique Café 840 S Spring St ☏213/623-8698. A marvelous Continental eatery in the middle of the Garment District, where you can sit on the quaint patio and dine on well-crafted pastries for breakfast or savory sandwiches, rich casseroles, and fine salads for lunch.
Café Metropol 923 E Third St ☏213/613-1537. The area may still be industrial, but this artsy eatery is worth a visit for its hearty sandwiches, salads, pizza, and pasta.
Café Pinot 700 W 5th St ☏213/239-6500. Located next to the LA Public Library, this elegant restaurant offers a touch of French cooking for its nouvelle California cuisine.
Engine Co. No. 28 644 S Figueroa St ☏213/624-6996. Expensive, all-American grilled steaks and seafood, served in a renovated 1912 fire station. Great French fries and an excellent wine list round out this classic local eatery.
Pacific Dining Car 1310 W 6th St ☏213/483-6000. Would-be English supper club, here since 1921, located inside an old railroad carriage where the Downtown elite

used to cut secret deals. Open 24hr for very expensive and delicious steaks. Breakfast is the best value.
Patina 141 S Grand Ave ☏213/972-3331. Fancy, ultra-swank Disney Hall branch of one of LA's top eateries, where you can devour pheasant, pork loin medallions, and other rotating items on the menu, if you're prepared to drop a wad of cash.
Taylor's 3361 W Eighth St ☏213/382-8449. Good old-fashioned American meat in a darkly lit, old-school steakhouse ambience, priced a bit more reasonably – though still expensive – than at similar Westside spots.
Water Grill 544 S Grand Ave ☏213/891-0900. One of the top-priced, top-notch spots for munching on California cuisine in LA, or anywhere, with the focus on seafood, prepared in all manner of colorful and ever-changing ways.

Hollywood

Griddle Café 7916 Sunset Blvd ☏323/874-0377. The postmodern Hollywood version of a diner, where the pancakes, chili, and omelets come with various outlandish, but often tasty, toppings, and the real point is to be seen by slumming producers and casting directors.

🏃 **Musso and Frank Grill** 6667 Hollywood Blvd ☏ 323/467-7788. A 1919 classic, loaded with authentic Hollywood atmosphere and history in a dark-paneled dining room. The drinks (see p.165) are better than the pricey, mostly upscale diner food. Also see p.106.

Off Vine 6263 Leland Way ☏ 323/962-1900. Dine on eclectic Cal cuisine – pecan chicken, duck sausage, and steak with Roquefort Cabernet sauce – in a renovated but still funky Craftsman bungalow.

Pig 'n Whistle 6714 Hollywood Blvd ☏ 323/463-1473. Historic 1927 eatery refurbished as a swank Cal-cuisine restaurant, with the emphasis on all things porcine, from ribs to pork roast to bacon. Although much of the old spirit and decor are the same, the prices are not: no diner has food this pricey.

vermont 1714 N Vermont Ave ☏ 323/661-6163. One of the better Cal-cuisine eateries in the area. The entrées are predictable enough – roasted chicken, crab cakes, ravioli, etc – but the culinary presentation is effective and, on occasion, inspired.

West LA and Beverly Hills

Barefoot 8722 W 3rd St ☏ 310/276-6223. Good pasta, pizza, and seafood between Beverly Hills and the Beverly Center. Considering the prime location, very affordable.

Cut 9500 Wilshire Blvd, Beverly Hills ☏ 310/276-8500. Since this Wolfgang Puck steakhouse was designed by Richard Meier, it looks like the Getty Center cafeteria – nonetheless, if you like (and can afford) $50 steaks, Kobe short ribs, and Maine lobsters, this is the place.

The Gumbo Pot 6333 W 3rd St in the Farmers' Market ☏ 323/933-0358. Delicious, dirt-cheap Cajun food in a busy setting; try the gumbo yaya (chicken, shrimp, and sausage) or the fruit-and-potato salad.

Jar 8225 Beverly Blvd ☏ 323/655-6566. A steakhouse that features all the usual red-meat fare with an inspired Cal-cuisine flair, throwing in different spices and exotic flavors to create an unusual, yet strangely traditional, result.

L'Orangerie 903 N La Cienega Blvd, West Hollywood ☏ 310/652-9770. Super-upscale nouvelle California-style French cuisine; if you can't afford around $50 per entrée, enjoy the view from the bar.

La Boheme 8400 Santa Monica Blvd, West Hollywood ☏ 323/848-2360. The dark, somewhat spooky decor is matched by the indulgent melange

of Cal-cuisine flavors enlivening the pasta, risotto, and steak entrées.

Lucques 8474 Melrose Ave ☏ 323/655-6277. Expensive but tasty eatery that doles out fine food for the culinary elite. Veal cheeks, wild mushroom lasagna, and the "devil's chicken" are but a few of the items that helped the place win a 2006 James Beard award.

Luna Park 672 S La Brea Ave ☏ 323/934-2110. Reliable Cal-cuisine spot that serves up smart versions of diner items like burgers, mac'n'cheese, and grilled sandwiches for lunch, and chic seafood, steak, and pasta for dinner.

McCormick and Schmick's 206 N Rodeo Drive, Beverly Hills ☏ 310/859-0434. Swank seafood joint for business types known for a great weekend dinner special; part of an esteemed national chain.

Spago 176 N Cañon Drive, Beverly Hills ☏ 310/385-0880. Flagship restaurant that helped nationalize Cal cuisine (in a different location), and still good for supping on Wolfgang Puck's latest concoctions, among them designer pizzas.

Santa Monica, Venice, and Malibu

Hal's 1349 Abbot Kinney Blvd, Venice ☏ 310/396-3105. Popular restaurant along a hip shopping zone in Venice, with a range of well-done American standards, including marinated steaks, turkey burgers, and salmon dishes.

Joe's 1023 Abbot Kinney Blvd, Venice ☏ 310/399-5811. One of the less heralded of LA's better eateries, offering appealing California-cuisine dishes using staples like crispy chicken, pork, and salmon.

Michael's 1147 3rd St, Santa Monica ☏ 310/451-0843. Long-standing favorite for California cuisine, and one of the restaurants that invented it, served here amid modern art. This venerable establishment always attracts the crowds for its steaks, pasta, and fowl – reservations are essential.

Saddle Peak Lodge 419 Cold Canyon Rd, Calabasas ☏ 818/222-3888. On the San Fernando Valley side of the Santa Monica Mountains, this is elite LA's nod to rustic hunting lodges, where exquisite California cuisine is presented below mounted game heads, and you can elegantly devour anything from venison to boar to antelope.

Uncle Darrow's 2560 S Lincoln Blvd, Venice ☏ 310/306-4862. A bit south of the main beach action, but worth a stop if you like savory catfish, gumbos, and other down-home Cajun and Creole cooking.

Italian, Spanish, and Greek

LA has a good number of eateries specializing in regional **Italian** cooking, and the phenomenon of **designer pizza** features toppings such as duck, shiitake mushrooms, and other exotic ingredients. It doesn't come cheap, of course. A pasta dish in the above-average Italian restaurant can cost upwards of $15–20, and the least-elaborate designer pizza will set you back $10. **Spanish** food and tapas bars have also become popular, and pricey. In contrast, if you want **Greek** food, you'll have to look hard – restaurants are good but uncommon.

Downtown and around

Ciao Trattoria 815 W 7th St ☎213/624-2244. Housed in a striking Romanesque building, full of lovely historic-revival decor, a good choice for upscale, Northern Italian dining. Somewhat pricey, but not as bad as you might think.

Cicada 617 S Olive St ☎213/488-9488. Lodged in the stunning Art Deco Oviatt Building, this Northern Italian restaurant offers fine pasta, fish and steak entrées.

Ciudad 445 S Figueroa St ☎213/486-5171. Ceviche and paella are some of the highlights of this colorful Mexican-influenced Spanish spot, where the live Latin music competes with the delicious food for your attention.

Papa Cristo's 2771 W Pico Blvd ☎323/737-2970. Consider venturing to a grim neighborhood near the 10 freeway to sample the authentic delights at this Greek joint, where you can munch on delicious gyros and spanakopita or have a hefty meal of lamb chops or roast chicken without spending more than $10.

Hollywood

Angeli Caffè 7274 Melrose Ave ☎323/936-9086. Refreshingly simple pizzas – baked in a wood-burning oven – make this a worthwhile stop, as do its tasty frittatas and croquettes.

Miceli's 1646 N Las Palmas Ave ☎323/466-3438. Hefty, old-style pizzas that come laden with gooey cheese and plenty of tomato sauce. It's hardly nouvelle cuisine, but you'll be too busy scarfing it down to notice.

Palermo 1858 N Vermont Ave ☎323/663-1178. As old as Hollywood, and with as many devoted fans, who flock here for the rich Southern Italian pizzas, cheesy decor, and gallons of cheapish red wine.

West LA

Ca' Brea 346 S La Brea Ave ☎323/938-2863. One of LA's best-known, and best, choices for Italian cuisine, and especially good for osso buco and risotto. Getting in is difficult, so reserve ahead and expect to pay a bundle.

Campanile 624 S La Brea Ave ☎323/938-1447. Incredible but very expensive Northern Italian food – if you can't afford a dinner, try the dessert or the best bread in Los Angeles at the adjacent La Brea Bakery.

Cobras and Matadors 7615 Beverly Blvd ☎323/932-6178. A fine tapas restaurant just down the street from Pan Pacific Park, where you can sample all your favorite Castilian delights in a hushed, dramatic setting.

Delphi 1383 Westwood Blvd ☎310/478-2900. The place to come in West LA for authentic Greek cooking, from flavorful *dolmas* and tabouli to the hearty pitas and *souvlaki* – an unpretentious joint that offers plenty of food for a reasonable price.

Locanda Veneta 8638 W 3rd St ☎310/274-1893. Scrumptious ravioli, risotto, veal, and carpaccio – you can't go wrong at one of LA's culinary joys. But be prepared to wait.

Santa Monica, Venice, and Malibu

Abbot's Pizza Company 1407 Abbot Kinney Blvd, Venice ☎310/396-7334. Named after the old-time founder of the district, this home of the bagel-crust pizza allows your choice of seeds, tangy citrus sauce, or shiitake and wild mushroom sauce.

Drago 2628 Wilshire Blvd, Santa Monica ☎310/828-1585. One of the better of LA's super-chic Italian eateries, offering meat and pasta dishes with eclectic ingredients and sauces.

Valentino 3115 Pico Blvd, Santa Monica ☎310/829-4313. Some call this the best Italian cuisine in the US, served up in classy surroundings with great flair. For a hefty sum, you can be the judge.

Wildflour Pizza 2807 Main St, Santa Monica ☎310/392-3300. Serving up a great thin-crust pizza, this cozy little spot often draws the crowds on the Main Street shopping strip.

The South Bay and Harbor Area

Alegria Cocina Latina 115 Pine Ave, Long Beach ☎562/436-3388. Tapas, gazpacho, and a variety of *platos principales* served with sangría on the patio, and to the beat of live flamenco on weekends. Good location near the harbor in Downtown Long Beach.

L'Opera 101 Pine Ave ☎ 562/491-0066. Very swank Italian dining – mixed with a fair bit of California-cuisine style – in a historic old building near the center of Long Beach's Downtown activity.

Mangiamo 128 Manhattan Beach Blvd, Manhattan Beach ☎ 310/318-3434. Like the name says, "Let's eat!" Fairly pricey but worth it for the specialist Northern Italian seafood – and near the beach, too.

The San Gabriel and San Fernando valleys

Café Santorini 64–70 W Union St, Pasadena ☎ 626/564-4200. A fine mix of Greek and Italian food – capellini, *souvlaki*, and risotto, among other treats. Located in a relaxed plaza and offering some patio dining.

La Luna Negra 44 W Green St, Pasadena ☎ 626/844-4331. An affordable spot for mouth-watering tapas, including classic croquetas, paellas, and spicy seafood dishes, with regular Latin music and dancing.

Panzanella 14928 Ventura Blvd, Sherman Oaks ☎ 818/784-4400. Some of the best Italian cuisine in LA, taking foodways from central Italy and adding a dash of California creativity, while staying true to the simple, delicious character of traditional pasta, rice, and beef dishes.

Japanese, Chinese, and other Asian cuisine

LA has many fine **sushi** bars and **dim sum** restaurants, favored by foreign visitors and fast-lane yuppies alike, where you can easily eat your way through more than $30. Lower-priced outlets tend to be Downtown, where you can get a fair-sized meal for around $15. There are also a good number of excellent **Thai, Vietnamese**, and **Korean** eateries – for which you can expect to pay around $15 per meal, or around $50 or more for top-notch Korean spots.

Downtown and around

Dong Il Jang 3455 W 8th St ☎ 213/383-5757. Cozy little Korean restaurant where the meat is cooked at your table and the food is consistently good, especially the grilled chicken, seafood pancakes, and BBQ beef. Tempura dishes and a sushi bar are an added draw.

Grand Star 934 Sun Mun Way, Chinatown ☎ 213/626-2285. While the traditional Chinese soups and meat dishes here are flavorful and authentic, the real appeal is the lively video-karaoke scene.

Mandarin Deli 727 N Broadway #109 ☎ 213/623-6054. Very delectable and cheap noodles, pork, and fish dumplings, and other hearty staples in the middle of Broadway's riot of activity.

Ocean Seafood 750 N Hill St ☎ 213/687-3088. Busy Cantonese restaurant serving inexpensive and excellent food – dim sum, crab, shrimp, and duck are among the standout choices.

Pho 2000 215 N Western Ave ☎ 323/461-5845. One of several Koreatown restaurants specializing in hot, spicy bowls of the Vietnamese soup *pho*: cheap, authentic and succulent, drawing a loyal crowd of regulars.

Yang Chow 819 N Broadway, Chinatown ☎ 213/625-0811. Solid Chinese restaurant, where you can't go wrong with the Szechuan beef or any shrimp dish.

Hollywood

Chan Darae 1511 N Cahuenga Blvd ☎ 323/464-8585. Terrific Thai food, and the locals know it, with a full range of scrumptious staples such as *tom yum* soup and pad thai.

Jitlada 5233 Sunset Blvd ☎ 323/667-9809. In a dreary mini-mall, but the spicy chicken, squid, and seafood curries more than make up for the setting. Affordable prices, too.

Sanamluang Café 5176 Hollywood Blvd ☎ 323/660-8006. You can't beat the cheap, excellent, and plentiful noodles at this nearly-all-night Thai eatery.

Shibucho 3114 Beverly Blvd ☎ 213/387-8498. Seriously tasty, locally popular sushi bar just south of Silver Lake. The squid and eel are quite fine, along with the famed *toro*, an expensive but delicious tuna delicacy.

Singapore's Banana Leaf 6333 W Third St, in the Farmers' Market ☎ 323/933-4627. A fine little hole in the wall where you can sample Malaysian cuisine at its spiciest and most savory, with nice curry soups, satay, and tandoori dishes.

Vim 5132 Hollywood Blvd ☎ 323/662-1017. Authentic Thai and Chinese food at low prices. Especially good are the seafood soup and that old favorite, pad thai.

January

1 Japanese New Year. Art displays, ethnic cuisine, and cultural exhibits at this annual Little Tokyo festival, centered around the Japanese American Cultural and Community Center (℡213/628-2725, ⓦwww.jaccc.org).

1 Tournament of Roses in Pasadena. A parade of floral floats and marching bands along a five-mile stretch of Colorado Boulevard. Coincides with the annual Rose Bowl football game (℡626/795-9311 or 449-4100, ⓦwww.tournamentofroses.com).

mid Golden Globe Awards. The annual run-up to the Oscars, attracting ever-increasing attention. Tourists are encouraged to watch the stars arrive, and gape accordingly (℡310/657-1731, ⓦwww.hfpa.org).

mid Martin Luther King Parade and Celebration. The civil rights hero is honored with activities at King Park, Baldwin Hills, and Crenshaw, and many other city locations (℡323/290-4100, ⓦwww.sclclosangeles.org).

February

early to mid Chinese New Year. Three days of dragon-float street parades, tasty food, and various cultural programs, based in Chinatown, Monterey Park, and Alhambra (℡213/617-0396, ⓦwww.lachinesechamber.org).

mid Bob Marley Reggae Festival. A two-day event that exalts the reggae god with food, music, and plenty of spirit. At the Long Beach Convention and Entertainment Center (℡310/515-3322, ⓦwww.bobmarleydayfestival.com).

mid Mardi Gras. Floats, parades, costumes, and lots of singing and dancing at this Latin fun-fest, with traditional ceremonies on Olvera Street downtown (℡213/625-7074) and colorful antics in West Hollywood (℡310/289-2525).

mid Queen Mary Scottish Festival. All the haggis you can stand at this two-day Long Beach celebration, along with highland dancing and bagpipes (℡562/499-1650, ⓦwww.queenmary.com).

end The Academy Awards. Presented at the Kodak Theatre in the Hollywood & Highland mall (see p.107). Bleacher seats are available to watch the stars arrive (℡310/247-3000, ⓦwww.oscars.org).

March

early LA City Marathon. All over the streets around town you can cheer on the runners – or sign up to participate yourself (℡310/444-5544, ⓦwww.lamarathon.com).

mid St Patrick's Day. Parade along Colorado Boulevard in Old Town Pasadena, and another in Hermosa Beach (℡310/376-0951, ⓦwww.stpatricksday.org). No parade but freely flowing green beer in the "Irish" bars along Fairfax Avenue.

mid Spring Festival of Flowers. An explosion of floral color is displayed at Descanso Gardens with different types of tulips, lilies, and daffodils, among others (℡818/949-4200, ⓦwww.descansogardens.org).

April

early The Blessing of the Animals. A long-established ceremony, Mexican in origin. Locals arrive in Olvera Street to have their pets blessed, then watch the attendant parade (℡213/625-5045, ⓦwww.olvera-street.com/html/fiestas.html).

weekend nearest 13 Songkran Festival/Thai New Year. The Wat Thai Temple in North Hollywood is the focus for this cultural celebration, with spicy food and authentic music, and plenty of monks (℡818/997-9657, ⓦwww.watthaiusa.org).

mid Long Beach Grand Prix. Scores of locals come out to watch the Indy cars race around Shoreline Drive (℡562/981-2600, ⓦwww.longbeachgp.com).

mid to late California Poppy Festival. North of LA, Lancaster's huge poppy reserve of 1800 acres draws big crowds to see its eye-blinding, fiery orange colors that appear every spring. The festival presents foodstuffs, folk art, and crafts to go with the blooms (℡661/723-6075, ⓦwww.poppyfestival.com).

late Cowboy Poetry and Music Festival. Plenty of folk music from the Old West and accompanying cowboy poems are the highlights of this three-day Santa Clarita celebration, just north of LA (℡661/286-4021, ⓦwww.cowboyfestival.org).

late Fiesta Broadway. Lively music from Hispanic pop singers and tasty Mexican food are the highlights of this street fair along Broadway Downtown (℡310/914-0015, ⓦwww.fiestabroadway.la).

May

5 Cinco de Mayo. Spirited parade along Olvera Street, and several blocks Downtown are blocked off for Latino music performances. There are also celebrations in most LA parks (℡213/628-1274, ⓦwww.olvera-street.com/html/fiestas.html).

mid NoHo Theater and Arts Festival. The San Fernando Valley district of North Hollywood presents a cavalcade of music, food, poetry, theater, and dance (℡310/537-4240, ⓦwww.nohoartsdistrict.com/festival).

mid Venice Art Walk. A great chance to peer into the private art studios in town, where you can see the work of both big-name local artists and lesser-known up-and-comers – though it will cost you $50 (℡310/392-9255).

late Strawberry Festival. Garden Grove in Orange County is the setting for this huge, old-fashioned display of carnival rides, games, parades, and other festivities – all in honor of the humble strawberry (℡714/638-0981, ⓦwww.strawberryfestival.org).

late UCLA Jazz & Reggae Festival. Spirited music, food, and activities take place on the campus (℡310/825-9912, ⓦwww.jazzreggaefest.com).

June

all Last Remaining Seats. A great film festival that draws huge crowds to the grand Los Angeles and Orpheum movie palaces (see p.175) to watch revivals of classic Hollywood films, often with live entertainment (℡213/623-2489, ⓦwww.laconservancy.org).

mid LA Film Festival. Ten-day event screening notable independent and art-house films across West LA at a variety of venues (℡1-866/345-6337, ⓦwww.lafilmfest.com).

mid Playboy Jazz Festival. Renowned event held at the Hollywood Bowl, with a lineup of traditional and non-traditional musicians and groups (tickets ℡213/480-3232, ⓦwww.playboy.com/arts-entertainment/features/jazzfest2007).

mid to late Irish Fair and Music Festival. Sizeable music, food, and cultural celebration held in the Orange County town of Irvine (℡949/489-1172, ⓦwww.irishfair.org).

late Bayou Festival. Heaps of Creole food, wild parades, and plenty of high-spirited Cajun and Zydeco music at this colorful Long Beach event (℡562/427-3713, ⓦwww.longbeachfestival.com).

late Gay Pride Celebration. Parade on Santa Monica Blvd in West Hollywood. Carnival atmosphere, hundreds of vendors, and an all-male drag football cheerleading team (℡323/969-8302, ⓦwww.lapride.org).

July

4 Independence Day. The *Queen Mary* in Long Beach hosts a particularly large fireworks display, as well as colorful entertainment. Fireworks displays in many

LA's festivals (Contd.)

places in LA (Ⓣ562/435-3511 in Long Beach, or Ⓣ323/848-6530 for West Hollywood's Plummer Park).

first weekend after 4 Lotus Festival. An Echo Park celebration with dragon boats, ethnic food, pan-Pacific music, and, of course, the resplendent lotus blooms around the lake (Ⓣ213/485-1310, Ⓦwww.laparks.org/grifmet/lotus.htm).

early July to late Aug Pageant of the Masters. Laguna Beach's signature street festival, which not only features the standard displays of food, arts, and dancing, but also living presentations of classic paintings (see box, p.147; Ⓣ949/494-1145, Ⓦwww.foapom.com).

mid South Bay Greek Festival. Three days of food and music at St Katherine Greek Orthodox Church in Redondo Beach, with arts and crafts displays and energetic dancing adding to the festivities (Ⓣ310/540-2434, Ⓦwww.sbgreekfestival.com).

late Central Avenue Jazz Festival. Celebration of both jazz and blues by big names and lesser-known performers, held in front of the historic *Dunbar Hotel* in South Central (Ⓣ323/234-7882, Ⓦwww.centralavenuejazzfestival.com).

late Festival of the Chariots. Another strange and unique LA phenomenon: giant decorated floats parade down Venice Boardwalk to the sound of lively music and the smell of ethnic food (Ⓣ310/836-2676, Ⓦwww.festivalofchariots.com).

August

early International Surf Festival. Tournament and celebration in the South Bay that provides for an exciting three-day spectacle, which also includes volleyball, fishing, and sand-castle design (Ⓣ310/305-9546, Ⓦwww.surffestival.org).

mid Long Beach Jazz Festival. At the Rainbow Lagoon park in downtown Long Beach, relax and enjoy famous and local performers (Ⓣ562/424-0013, Ⓦwww.longbeachjazzfestival.com).

mid Sunset Junction Street Fair. A spirited neighborhood party – always one of LA's most enjoyable fetes – along Sunset Boulevard in Silver Lake, with live music, ethnic food, and a carnivalesque atmosphere (Ⓣ323/661-7771, Ⓦwww.sunsetjunction.org).

mid to late Nisei Week in Little Tokyo. A celebration of Japanese America, with martial arts demonstrations, karaoke, Japanese brush painting, beauty pageant, baby shows, and performances (Ⓣ213/687-7193, Ⓦwww.niseiweek.org).

mid-Aug to early Sept African Marketplace and Cultural Faire. Hundreds of arts and crafts booths and many different entertainers make up this annual celebration at Rancho Cienega Park in South Central LA. (Ⓣ323/293-1612, Ⓦwww.africanmarketplace.org).

September

early LA's birthday. A civic ceremony and assorted street entertainment around El Pueblo de Los Angeles to mark the founding of the original pueblo in 1781 (Ⓣ213/625-5045, Ⓦwww.olvera-street.com/html/fiestas.html).

early Long Beach Blues Festival. Hear the region's and the country's top blues performers at this annual event at Cal State University at Long Beach (Ⓣ562/985-5566, Ⓦwww.kkjz.org/events).

early to late LA County Fair. In Pomona, in the San Gabriel Valley. The biggest county fair in the US, with livestock shows, pie-eating contests, rodeos, and carnival rides (Ⓣ909/623-3111, Ⓦwww.fairplex.com).

late Watts Towers Day of the Drum/Jazz Festival. Two days of free music – a wealth of African, Asian, Cuban, and Brazilian drumming – with the towers as the striking backdrop. Taking place the same weekend, at the same place, the Jazz Festival is the most long-standing such event in LA (☎213/485-1795, ⓦwww.wattstowers.org).

late through Oct Oktoberfest. Venture into Alpine Village, in the South Bay suburb of Torrance, to revel in Teutonic culture: hearty German food, music, and dancing abound (☎310/327-4384, ⓦwww.alpinevillage.net). Also a spirited event in the Orange County town of Huntington Beach (☎714/895-8020, ⓦwww.oldworld.ws).

October

first three weekends Catalina Island Jazz Trax. A huge lineup of major and rising stars in jazz perform in the historic surroundings of this island's beautiful Art Deco Avalon ballroom (☎1-866/872-9849, ⓦwww.jazztrax.com).

early Detour Festival. Symbolizing the revitalizing of Downtown LA, this recently inaugurated music fest features some of the top names in indie rock for an affordable price ($36; ⓦwww.laweekly.com/detour).

early Eagle Rock Music Festival. This funky district, due north of Downtown LA near Glendale, hosts a freewheeling festival of food, crafts and an eclectic assortment of independent music (☎323/226-1617, ⓦwww.myspace.com/eaglerockmusicfestival).

mid Los Angeles Bach Festival. Revel in the Baroque master's music at the First Congregational Church, just north of Lafayette Park in Westlake (☎213/385-1345, ⓦwww.fccla.org).

31 Halloween. A wild parade in West Hollywood, with all manner of bizarre and splashy outfits and characters on display (☎310/289-2525). Or you can opt for the Halloween-themed events on the Queen Mary (☎562/435-3511).

November

2 Dia de los Muertos. The "Day of the Dead," celebrated authentically throughout East LA and more blandly for tourists on Olvera Street. Mexican traditions, such as picnicking on the family burial spot and making skeleton puppets, are morbidly upheld (☎213/625-5045, ⓦwww.olvera-street.com/html/fiestas.html).

Sunday before Thanksgiving Doo-dah Parade. Quintessential LA event that began as a spoof of the Tournament of Roses parade, with a cast of absurdly costumed characters marching through Pasadena (☎626/205-4029, ⓦwww.pasadenadoodahparade.info).

late Griffith Park Light Festival. Tremendous spectacle along Crystal Springs Road in the park, with tunnels of light, thematic displays, and representations of familiar LA sights like the Hollywood sign. A hugely popular draw (☎323/913-4688 ext. 9).

December

1 Hollywood Christmas Parade. The first and best of the many Yuletide events, with a cavalcade of mind-boggling floats, marching bands, and famous and quasi-famous names from film and TV (☎323/469-2337).

1 Belmont Shore Christmas Parade. East Long Beach is the setting for holiday floats and marching bands (☎562/434-3066).

early Holiday Boat Parade. Marina del Rey is the site for this annual, ocean-going display of brightly lit watercraft, supposedly the largest boat parade in the West (☎310/670-7130, ⓦwww.mdrboatparade.org). Another big display takes place along Shoreline Village in Long Beach (☎562/435-4093).

West LA

Chaya Brasserie 8741 Alden Drive ☏310/859-8833. Pan-Asian bistro with moderate-to-expensive prices for fancy, French-influenced presentations of noodle, curry, and fish dishes. Worth a splurge if you like your Asian fare with LA trendiness.

Genghis Cohen 740 N Fairfax Ave ☏323/653-0640. Familiar Chinese dishes with a Yiddish touch: the menu abounds with culinary puns. The Szechuan beef, dumplings, and kung pao chicken are quite good.

Matsuhisa 129 N La Cienega Blvd ☏310/659-9639. The biggest name in town for sushi, charging the highest prices for sea urchin, eel, black cod, and more. Essential if you're a raw-fish aficionado with a wad of cash.

Mishima 8474 W 3rd St ☏323/782-0181. Great miso soup, soft-shell crab salad, and udon and soba noodles, at very affordable prices at this popular Westside eatery.

Mori Sushi 11500 W Pico Blvd ☏323/479-3939. A quietly stylish spot that resists trendiness, but still offers up some of the city's finest sushi, almost always delicious and always fresh and not farmed.

Talesai 9198 Olympic Blvd, Beverly Hills ☏310/271-9345. Excellent curried seafood, corn cakes, and Cal-cuisine-leaning noodle dishes served to knowing gourmets in a drab strip mall.

Santa Monica, Venice, and Malibu

Chaya Venice 110 Navy St, Venice ☏310/396-1179. Elegant mix of Japanese and Mediterranean foods in an arty sushi bar, with a suitably snazzy clientele.

Chinois on Main 2709 Main St, Santa Monica ☏310/392-9025. Expensive Wolfgang Puck restaurant, skillfully mixing nouvelle French and Chinese cuisine with dash for a ravenous yuppie crowd.

Flower of Siam 2553 Lincoln Blvd, Venice ☏310/827-0050. Some swear by this spicy but succulent, authentic Thai food, guaranteed to set your tastebuds on fire and your eyes watering.

The Sushi House 12013 W Pico Blvd, Santa Monica ☏310/479-1507. A fine, small sushi bar with limited seating. Try the "Superman," a rainbow-colored roll of salmon, yellowtail, whitefish, and avocado, among other good choices.

The San Gabriel and San Fernando valleys

Ocean Star 145 N Atlantic Blvd, Monterey Park ☏626/308-2128. One of the prime names in a city bursting with excellent Chinese diners, in this case specializing in dim sum, with the fried shrimp, dumplings, and salty chicken among the highlights. Very popular, too.

Saladang 363 S Fair Oaks Ave, Pasadena ☏626/793-8123. Don't miss out on the pad thai, curry, and salmon at this chic spot, or the spicy noodles that would pass muster anywhere. The restaurant's annex, *Saladang Song*, offers even spicier Thai concoctions.

Shiro 1505 Mission St, South Pasadena ☏626/799-4774. One of LA's few top-notch restaurants in South Pasadena, perhaps the only one. Seafood – particularly the grilled catfish and smoked salmon – is best here, prepared in an assortment of rich, tangy flavors.

Sushi Nozawa 11288 Ventura Blvd, Studio City ☏818/508-7017. Traditional, pricey sushi dishes served to trendy, masochistic regulars, who don't mind being berated by the famously imperious chef: if you sit at the bar, he will decide what you'll eat. Period.

Indian, Sri Lankan, and Middle Eastern

Indian and **Sri Lankan** food is fairly popular in LA – with menus embracing a mix of traditional and uniquely Californian dishes. **Middle Eastern** places in LA encompass a good range of Levantine cookery, but tend toward the traditional. Most of the Indian and Middle Eastern restaurants in Hollywood or West LA fall into a fairly midrange price bracket – around $15 for a full meal, less for a vegetarian Indian dish.

Hollywood

East India Grill 345 N La Brea Ave ☏323/936-8844. Southern Indian cuisine given the California treatment: impressive specialties include tomato-chili chicken wings, lamb stir fry, mango ribs, and adventurous "parmesan naan."

Electric Lotus 4656 Franklin Ave ☏323/953-0040. While somewhat cramped and located in a mini-mall, a fine choice for traditional staples – pakora, vindaloo, curries, stuffed naan, etc – with DJs and private booths creating a clubby atmosphere.

Moun of Tunis 7445 Sunset Blvd ☏323/874-3333. Mouthwatering Tunisian fare presented in huge, multi-course meals, heavy on the spices and rich on the exotic flavors – plus regular belly-dancing.

Zankou Chicken 5065 Sunset Blvd ⓣ 323/665-7845. The top Middle Eastern value in town (and part of a citywide chain), with delicious garlicky chicken cooked on a rotisserie and made into a delicious sandwich, plus all the traditional salads – tabouli, hummus, and more.

West LA

Bombay Café 12021 Pico Blvd ⓣ 310/473-3388. One of LA's finest Indian restaurants, with terrific traditional and nouveau offerings and a helpful, friendly staff.
Koutoubia 2116 Westwood Blvd ⓣ 310/475-0729. Good Moroccan lamb, couscous, lentil soup, and seafood, in a comfortable environment enlivened by belly-dancing.
Magic Carpet 8566 W Pico Blvd ⓣ 310/652-8507. Unexpected treats like fried pancakes and more traditional falafel – both in generous portions – bring loyal crowds to this excellent Yemeni restaurant.
Nyala 1076 S Fairfax Ave ⓣ 323/936-5918. One of several Ethiopian favorites along Fairfax, serving

staples like doro wat (marinated chicken) and kitfo (chopped beef with butter and cheese) with the delightfully spongy injera bread.
Shamshiry Grill 1712 Westwood Blvd ⓣ 310/474-1410. Top Iranian restaurant in the area, offering scrumptious kebabs, pilafs, savory rice cakes, and exotic sauces.

The San Gabriel and San Fernando valleys

Burger Continental 535 S Lake Ave, Pasadena ⓣ 626/792-6634. Although it sounds like a fast-food joint, this is actually one of the valley's better Middle Eastern restaurants, where you can get mounds of chicken and lamb kebabs for affordable prices.
Carousel 304 N Brand Ave, Glendale ⓣ 818/246-7775. A Lebanese charmer in downtown Glendale, chock-full of Levantine cultural artifacts and deliciously authentic food, from roasted chicken and quail to several different kinds of kebabs.

Vegetarian and wholefood

As you might expect, LA has many **wholefood** and **vegetarian** restaurants, most of them on the consciousness-raised Westside. Some veggie places can be a good value, but watch out for the ones that flaunt themselves as a New Age experience – these can be three times as much. Otherwise, for a picnic try the area's **farmers' markets**, loaded with organic produce and advertised in the press.

West LA

Inaka Natural Foods 131 S La Brea Ave ⓣ 323/936-9353. Located in the trendy La Brea district and featuring vegetarian and macrobiotic food, including some tasty soups, with a Japanese theme.
Mäni's Bakery 519 S Fairfax Ave ⓣ 323/938-8800. An array of veggie treats – from sugarless brownies to meatless sandwiches – for breakfast or lunch are the draw at this coffeehouse and bakery.
Newsroom Café 120 N Robertson Blvd ⓣ 310/652-4444. A prime spot to eat veggie burgers and drink wheatgrass "shooters." Especially popular for lunching; also offers magazine racks (thus the name) and Internet terminals.
Real Food Daily 414 N La Cienega Blvd ⓣ 310/289-9910. Tempeh burgers, hemp bread,

and various soups and salads draw a good crowd at this vegan restaurant, which also operates a branch at 514 Santa Monica Blvd, Santa Monica (ⓣ 310/451-7544).

Santa Monica, Venice, and Malibu

Figtree's Café 429 Ocean Front Walk, Venice ⓣ 310/392-4937. Tasty veggie food and grilled fresh fish on a sunny patio just off the Boardwalk. Health-conscious yuppies come in droves for breakfast.
Inn of the Seventh Ray 128 Old Topanga Rd, Topanga Canyon ⓣ 310/455-1311. The ultimate New Age restaurant in a supremely New Age area, serving vegetarian and other wholefood meals in a relatively secluded environment. Excellent desserts, too.

Bars, cafés, and clubs

Nightlife in LA can be among the best and most frenetic in the country, with options for serious drinking, partying, and debauchery available throughout the metropolis. Weekend nights are the busiest at the various bars and clubs, but during the week things are often cheaper. Where they exist, most cover charges range widely, depending on the night and the establishment (often $5–20). Except at all-ages, alcohol-free clubs, the minimum age is 21, and it's normal for ID to be checked, so bring your passport or other photo ID. For listings, check out the *LA Times'* "Calendar" section or the *LA Weekly*.

You can find **cafés** throughout LA, too, from artsy holes-in-the-wall to sanitized yuppie magnets. Well-trafficked areas like Melrose Avenue, West Hollywood, and Santa Monica are loaded with spots to grab a caffeinated jolt, as well as tea, food, and even alcohol in some cases. A few of the better ones may also offer more sublime amusements like music, poetry, or truly eye-popping decor.

Bars

As you'd expect, LA's **bars** reflect their locality: a clash of artists and financial whiz kids Downtown; serious hedonists and leather-clad rockers in Hollywood; movie-star wannabes and self-proclaimed producers in West LA; a mix of tourists and locals in Santa Monica; and the more oddball selection in Venice. A few hard-bitten bars are open the legal maximum hours (from 6am until 2am daily), though the busiest hours are between 9pm and midnight. During **happy hour**, usually from 5 to 7pm, drinks are cheap and sometimes half-price.

Downtown and around

Barragan's 1538 W Sunset Blvd ☎213/250-4256. Actually a Mexican restaurant with serviceable food, but producing one of the stronger margaritas in LA. Be alert for the dicey neighborhood, though.

Casey's Bar 613 S Grand Ave ☎213/629-2353. Old-time Irish pub with white floors and dark wood-paneled walls, and friendly, rousing ambience, making it something of a local institution.

HMS Bounty 3357 Wilshire Blvd ☎213/385-7275. An authentic dive experience. Advertising "Food and Grog," a grungy bar that's a hotspot for hipsters and grizzled old-timers – they come for the dark ambience, cheap and potent drinks, and kitschy nautical motifs.

Mountain Bar 475 Gin Ling Way ☎213/625-7500. Since it's hidden in a nook in Chinatown, this bar is hard to find off Bamboo Lane, but if you want a colorful environment loaded with Asian decor to knock back your well drinks and cocktails, this is the spot.

Mr T's Bowl 5621 N Figueroa Ave, Highland Park ☎323/960-5693. Former bowling alley whose inspired dumpiness draws a regular crowd of hipsters and local characters. Cheap prices, karaoke, and rockin' live shows add to the allure.

Redwood 316 W 2nd St ☎213/617-2867. Not overly flashy or eventful, but a solid Downtown choice for serious boozing and cheap all-American grub since 1943, attracting a mix of imbibers for its dark and cozy setting and affordable drinks.

Standard Hotel Bar 550 S Flower St ☎213/892-8080. The poseur pinnacle in Downtown LA, a rooftop, alcohol-fueled playpen where the silk-shirted-black-leather-pant crowd goes to hang in red metallic "pods" with waterbeds and sprawl out on an Astroturf lawn, amid modern corporate towers looming overhead.

Hollywood

Akbar 4356 Sunset Blvd ☎323/665-6810. A curious blend of patrons – manual laborers and bohemians, gays and straights, old-timers and newbies – frequent this cozy, unpretentious watering hole. Also presents occasional dance events.

Boardner's 1652 N Cherokee Ave ☎323/462-9621. Formerly one of Hollywood's premier dive bars, now remade into more yuppie-friendly digs to reflect this more sanitized and gentrified stretch of Tinseltown. Have a cosmo if you're exhausted from mall-hopping.

Burgundy Room 1621 Cahuenga Blvd ☎323/465-7530. A classic place to get down and dirty with the old Hollywood dive-bar vibe, with tight confines, gloomy lighting, stiff drinks, a growling crowd of regulars, decent DJs, and a rocking jukebox.

Cat 'n' Fiddle Pub 6530 Sunset Blvd ☎323/468-3800. A boisterous but comfortable pub with darts, British food, English beers on tap, and live jazz on Sun nights. Also see p.171.

Dresden Room 1760 N Vermont Ave ⊕ 323/665-4298. One of the neighborhood's classic bars, perhaps best known for its nightly entertainment (except Sun), in which the husband-and-wife lounge act of Marty and Elayne has for 25 years been taking requests from the crowd of old-timers and goateed hipsters.

Formosa Café 7156 Santa Monica Blvd ⊕ 323/850-9050. Started in 1925 as a watering hole for Charlie Chaplin's adjacent United Artists studios, this creaky old spot is still alive with the ghosts of Bogie and Marilyn. Imbibe in the potent spirits, but stay away from the insipid food.

Frolic Room 6245 Hollywood Blvd ⊕ 323/462-5890. Classic LA bar decorated with Hirschfeld cartoons of celebrities and offering affordable drinks and a dark, authentic old-time ambience. Right by the Pantages Theater.

Good Luck Bar 1514 Hillhurst Ave ⊕ 323/666-3524. A hip Los Feliz retro-dive, this hangout is popular for its cheesy Chinese decor and drinks straight from the heyday of *Trader Vic's*. Located near the intersection of Sunset and Hollywood blvds.

Jones 7205 Santa Monica Blvd ⊕ 323/850-1726. Groovy, youthful scene with a colorful atmosphere and decent American cuisine, though the main draw is the head-spinning drinks named after rock stars.

Lucy's El Adobe Café 5536 Melrose Ave ⊕ 323/462-9421. Something of a celebrity hotspot in the 1970s for figures such as (then-Governor, now-Attorney General) Jerry Brown, this Mexican restaurant serves only adequate food, but the house specialty is worth a try: lethal green margaritas.

Musso and Frank Grill 6667 Hollywood Blvd ⊕ 323/467-7788. If you haven't had a drink in this landmark bar (located in the center of the district), you haven't been to Hollywood. It also serves pricey diner food. Also see p.155.

The Powerhouse 1714 N Highland Ave ⊕ 323/463-9438. Enjoyable, long-standing rockers' watering hole just off Hollywood Blvd; few people get here much before midnight.

Smog Cutter 864 N Virgil Ave ⊕ 323/667-9832. Dive bar that attracts a mix of boozers and smirking Gen-Xers. Don't miss the karaoke scene, which, like the liquor, can be pleasantly mind-numbing.

Tiki Ti 4427 W Sunset Blvd ⊕ 323/669-9381. Grass-skirted cocktail bar straight out of *Hawaii-Five-0*, which for decades has been packed with kitschy pseudo-Polynesian decor and no more than a handful of patrons – it's pretty cozy inside.

West LA

Barney's Beanery 8447 Santa Monica Blvd ⊕ 310/654-2287. Well-worn poolroom/bar, stocking hundreds of beers, with a solid, rock'n'roll-hedonist history. It also serves all-American, rib-stuffing food; see p.150.

El Carmen 8138 W 3rd St ⊕ 323/852-1552. Faux dive-bar with a south-of-the-border theme pushed to the extreme, with black-velvet pictures of Mexican wrestlers, steer horns, stuffed snakes, and much tongue-in-cheek grunge, as well as signature margaritas.

Liquid Kitty 11780 Pico Blvd ⊕ 310/473-3707. As its quirky name might suggest, this primo neighborhood bar is aimed solidly at the hipster contingent, with a fine selection of cocktails and nightly lounge and dance music to set the mood.

Molly Malone's Irish Pub 575 S Fairfax Ave ⊕ 323/935-1577. Self-consciously authentic Irish bar, from the food (corned-beef sandwiches, burgers, and other belly-fillers) to the music – mostly grinding rock and Celtic folk – to the shamrocks in the foaming Guinness.

Red Rock 8782 Sunset Blvd ⊕ 310/854-0710. Energetic watering hole with a wide array of drafts on tap and a similarly broad assortment of customers, everyone from bleary-eyed club kids to slumming preppies.

Snake Pit 7529 Melrose Ave ⊕ 323/653-2011. One of the better bars along the Melrose shopping strip, small and not too showy, with a mix of jaded locals and inquisitive tourists who come to slurp down tropical concoctions and other drinks.

Tom Bergin's 840 S Fairfax Ave ⊕ 323/936-7151. Old-time drinking joint from 1936, a great place for Irish coffee (supposedly invented here), and less rough-and-ready than *Molly Malone's* down the road. You can spot the regulars from the pictures on the walls.

Trader Vic's 9876 Wilshire Blvd, Beverly Hills ⊕ 310/276-6345. Long-standing favorite for Tiki style and Polynesian-themed cocktails, a great old spot with a broad mix of customers, and a place where you can finally get that Zombie or Blue Hawaiian mixed just as you like it.

Santa Monica, Venice, and Malibu

Circle Bar 2926 Main St, Santa Monica ⊕ 310/392-4898. Old-fashioned dive bar that mainly draws a crowd of high-fiving dudes. If you get plastered on the pricey drinks, Venice is well within staggering distance.

Encounter 209 World Way, at LAX ⊕ 310/215-5151. A strange bar that lurks in the upper reaches of the boomerang concrete "Theme Building" in the

LAX parking lot. Believe it or not, it's worth a visit to sample the potent, if pricey, Day-Glo drinks and watch the jets land.

Finn McCool's 2700 Main St, Santa Monica ⊤310/452-1734. Despite the dubious name, a worthwhile Irish pub with a savory selection of Emerald Isle brews and neo-Celtic artwork, plus hefty platters of traditional food that require a pint of Guinness to consume properly.

Hinano Café 15 Washington Blvd, Venice ⊤310/822-3902. Low-attitude chill bar by the beach – a good place to drink without too many tourists breathing down your neck, with pool tables, good and cheap burgers, shambling decor, and a crowd of mostly locals.

Library Alehouse 2911 Main St, Santa Monica ⊤310/314-4855. Presenting the choicest brews from West Coast microbreweries and beyond, this is a good spot to select from a nice range of well-known and obscure labels while munching on a decent selection of food.

Rick's Tavern 2907 Main St, Santa Monica ⊤310/392-2772. Dark and boisterous neighborhood joint off the Main Street shopping strip, with sports on TV and boisterous regulars on the bar stools.

Ye Olde King's Head 116 Santa Monica Blvd, Santa Monica ⊤310/451-1402. British-heavy joint with jukebox, dartboards, and signed photos of all your favorite rock dinosaurs; don't miss the steak-and-kidney pie, afternoon tea, or the fish and chips.

The San Gabriel and San Fernando valleys

Amazon 14649 Ventura Blvd, Sherman Oaks ⊤818/986-7502. A small wonderland of kitsch where you can knock back *Trader Vic's*-style tropical concoctions amid pseudo-South American and Polynesian decor: waterfalls, ferns, and so on.

Clear 11916 Ventura Blvd, Studio City ⊤818/980-4811. An attempt to draw Westsiders up to the Valley: a chic lounge with the requisite minimal-but-swanky decor, overpriced cocktails, and preening crowd of beautiful types. Worth a visit to see the Valley at its maximum pose.

Clearman's North Woods 7247 N Rosemead Blvd, San Gabriel ⊤626/286-3579. A kitsch-lover's delight with fake snow on the outside and moose heads on the walls inside; a great place for devouring steaks while throwing peanut shells on the floor.

The Colorado 2640 E Colorado Blvd ⊤626/449-3485. A bright spot along a bleak Pasadena stretch. Salty bartenders, cheap drinks, and a couple of pool tables amid a decor based around hunting.

Ireland's 32 13721 Burbank Blvd, Van Nuys ⊤818/785-5200. One of San Fernando Valley's better spots for quaffing Irish drafts, powering down traditional stews and chops, and soaking in a fair amount of Emerald Island decor, shamrocks and all.

The Sapphire 11938 Ventura Blvd, Studio City ⊤818/506-0777. About as enticing as Valley watering holes get if you don't like your bars divey – in this case the mod furnishings, comfortable couches, inventive drinks, and (reasonably) laid-back clientele make for an appealing, toasty vibe.

Cafés

Cafés in LA don't quite carry the same cultural cachet as they do in the Pacific Northwest or San Francisco, but they are good spots for socializing, whiling away the hours, and in some cases accessing the Internet. And the people you see conspicuously writing on their laptops are less likely to be budding novelists than would-be screenwriters plotting bloody action flicks over soy-milk lattes.

Abbot's Habit 1401 Abbot Kinney Blvd, Venice ⊤310/399-1171. Prototypical coffeehouse for Venice – rich, tasty coffee and homemade snacks and desserts, assorted artwork on the walls, occasional music and spoken-word events, and a friendly neighborhood vibe.

Bourgeois Pig 5931 Franklin Ave, Hollywood ⊤323/962-6366. Self-consciously hip environment and overpriced cappuccinos – you really pay for the artsy atmosphere, but the agreeable java and colorful people-watching might make it worthwhile.

Cacao Coffee 11609 Santa Monica Blvd, West LA ⊤310/473-7283. Fun and friendly joint with all kinds of kitsch and retro-Tiki bric-a-brac for decor, and good snacks and coffee served to an amenable crowd of regulars.

Cobalt Café 22047 Sherman Way, Canoga Park ⊤818/348-3789. Grungy but hip coffeehouse in the Valley, with coffee, food, and live music – along with poetry readings.

Coffee Table 2930 Rowena Ave, Silver Lake ⊤323/644-8111. Casual, unpretentious space with affordable coffees and relaxed surroundings. Good for its breakfasts, too.

CyberJava 7080 Hollywood Blvd, Hollywood ☎ 323/466-5600, ⓦ www.cyberjava.com. Located near the corner of La Brea Ave, this spot offers DSL Internet access while selling web surfers the usual range of smoothies, java drinks, and assorted sweets.

King's Road Espresso House 8361 Beverly Blvd, West Hollywood ☎ 323/655-9044. Sidewalk café in the center of a busy shopping strip, with good breakfasts and lunches. Popular with the hipster crowd as well as a few interloping tourists.

🏃 Nova Express 426 N Fairfax Ave, West LA ☎ 323/658-7533. Designed with retro-futuristic sci-fi decor, with weird colors and lighting, and additional curiosities like lava lamps and alien lounge and dance music most nights. Other than the design, coffee and pizza are the main draws. Open weekdays 'til 2am, weekends 'til 4am.

The Novel Café 212 Pier Ave, Santa Monica ☎ 310/396-8566. Used books and high-backed wooden chairs set the tone; good coffees, teas, and pastries, though with many self-consciously studious patrons. Located near the Venice border. Also at 1101 Gayley Ave, Westwood ☎ 310/208-6410.

Stir Crazy 6917 Melrose Ave ☎ 323/934-4656. Cozy haunt that provides a glimpse of what this stretch of Melrose used to be like before the chain retailers moved in – with mellow attitudes, decent java, and Western-themed decor.

Urth Caffè 8565 Melrose Ave ☎ 310/659-0628. Customers at this high-priced tea-and-java vendor tend toward navel-gazing and celebrity-watching, but the coffees here are certainly tasty enough, and the atmosphere is pleasant and fairly well-scrubbed. Also at 267 S Beverly Drive, Beverly Hills (☎ 310/205-9311), and 2327 Main St, Santa Monica (☎ 310/314-7040).

Clubs

The **clubs** of LA are among the best and wildest in the country. Ranging from posey hangouts to industrial noise cellars, city clubs offer a huge range of choices. The more image-conscious joints are like singles bars, with everybody claiming to be a rock musician or a movie producer. Some of the hottest clubs are usually the most transient, especially those catering to the house, ambient, techno, or hip-hop scenes, disappearing within a few months of being branded by the media as an "essential stop" for club-hoppers. As a result, you should always check the *LA Weekly* before setting out.

Most of the top clubs are either in Hollywood or West Hollywood. Beverly Hills is a lifeless yuppie desert; Downtown is home to a handful of itinerant clubs operating above and below board; Santa Monica has a smattering of compelling spots; and the San Fernando Valley's more rough-and-ready scene is usually confined to the weekends. For gay and lesbian clubs and discos, see p.177.

Downtown and around

Jewel's Catch One 4067 W Pico Blvd ☎ 323/734-8849. Sweaty barn catering to a mixed crowd of gays and straights and covering two wild dance floors. A longtime favorite for many club-hoppers of all sorts. Especially busy Fri–Mon, though located in the middle of nowhere.

🏃 Little Temple 4519 Santa Monica Blvd ☎ 323/660-4540. This Silver Lake scene is themed around moody Asian decor, and with the mood lighting, tasty beverages like the coconut martini, and an expressive, shmoozy clientele, it draws the smarter club-hoppers around town.

Mayan 1038 S Hill St ☎ 213/746-4674. Formerly a groovy pre-Columbian-styled movie palace, now hosting Latin rhythms and nonstop disco, salsa and house tunes on three floors.

Hollywood

Arena 6655 Santa Monica Blvd ☎ 323/462-0714. Work up a sweat to funk, hip-hop, Latin, and house sounds on a massive dance floor inside a former ice factory. Gay-friendly scene, playing host to ever-changing club nights.

Avalon 1735 N Vine St ☎ 323/462-3000. Major dance club spinning old-school faves, along with the usual techno and house, with the occasional big-name DJ dropping in. Prices are among the most expensive in town.

Bar Sinister 1652 N Cherokee ☎ 323/462-1934. A collection of sprightly dance beats most nights of the week, then memorably spooky Goth music and anemic-looking vampire types on Sat ($10 if in costume). Connected to *Boardner's* bar (see p.164).

The Derby 4500 Los Feliz Blvd ☎ 323/663-8979. Restored supper club in east side of Hollywood

What's on and tickets

The best sources of **information** are the LA Weekly and the "Calendar" section of the LA Times. You can buy seats for concerts or sports events from **Ticketmaster** (Ⓣ213/480-3232 or 714/740-2000, Ⓦwww.ticketmaster.com). A quick way through the maze of LA's **theaters** is to phone the **LA Stage Alliance** (Ⓣ213/614-0556, Ⓦwww.lastagealliance.com) and ask for the availability of discount tickets for a given show, under its LA Stage Tix program.

with gorgeous high wooden ceilings and round bar that was one of the originators of the retro-swing craze. Now plays all sorts of indie tunes, mostly Wed & Fri.

Dragonfly 6510 Santa Monica Blvd Ⓣ323/466-6111. Unusual decor, two large dance rooms, and a mix of house and disco club nights and live music.

King King 6555 Hollywood Blvd Ⓣ323/960-5765. A solid Hollywood bet for live dance music, with house, funk, rap, and retro-pop all on the DJ docket.

The Ruby 7070 Hollywood Blvd Ⓣ323/467-7070. A wide range of feverish dance nights Thurs–Sun, everything from retro-kitsch to grinding industrial to perky house and garage.

Tempest 7323 Santa Monica Blvd Ⓣ323/850-5115. After 10pm on the weekends, the eclectic grooves start to spin here, from retro-funk and disco to Britpop, drawing a mixed, energetic gay and straight crowd.

Three Clubs 1123 N Vine St Ⓣ323/462-6441. Dark, perennially trendy bar and club where the usual crowd of hipsters drops in for retro, rock, and funk music, and gets pleasingly plastered. Colorless exterior and lack of good signage makes the joint even hipper.

West LA

7969 7969 Santa Monica Blvd Ⓣ323/654-0280. Classic WeHo dance club – a landmark for its frenetic assortment of gay-themed (but straight-friendly) shows, from go-go girls to male strippers to drag queens. One of LA's most colorful spots for dancing and grinding.

Backstage Café 9433 Brighton Way, Beverly Hills Ⓣ310/777-0252. Epitomizing nightlife on the Westside, a Cal-cuisine bar and restaurant where the nice decor and well-made cocktails are offset by pretension, high prices, and a corporate feel.

Carbon 9300 Venice Blvd Ⓣ310/558-9302. Though hardly located near anywhere you'd want to be, a

good spot for eclectic nightly DJs, whose turntables glow with Latin, retro, jungle, drum & bass, hip-hop, soul, and rock beats, depending on the night.

Ultra Suede 661 N Robertson Blvd, West Hollywood Ⓣ310/659-4551. The spot for superior retro-dancing, heavy on 1970s disco and Eighties technopop, with a mixed gay and straight crowd.

Santa Monica

Mor 2941 Main St Ⓣ310/396-6678. Nightly selections of techno, trance, house, and soul, mixing it up for groovy club nights most evenings in this hip, moody lounge.

Temple Bar 1026 Wilshire Blvd Ⓣ310/392-1077. Popular Latin club, with doses of world beat thrown in as well, and all manner of electronica. A fun, engaging scene.

Zanzibar 1301 5th St Ⓣ310/451-2221. DJs spinning sounds with a house, hip-hop, and soul bent, but also with a bit of funk and bossa nova thrown in on selected nights.

The San Gabriel and San Fernando valleys

Bigfoot Lodge 3172 Los Feliz Blvd Ⓣ323/662-9227. On the far side of East Hollywood in dreary Atwater, but a prime draw for its nightly DJs, who set feet to stomping with retro-rock and punk tunes, with glam, goth, thrash, and rockabilly sounds thrown in as well.

CIA 11334 Burbank Blvd, North Hollywood Ⓣ818/506-6353. A truly odd venue where art and music collide, with curious visual installations (often based on circus clowns and freak shows) and sounds from punk to avant-garde.

Coda 5248 Van Nuys Blvd, Sherman Oaks Ⓣ818/783-7518. Fairly hip for the Valley, and not as posey as you might think, drawing locals for its blend of rap, pop, and electronica.

Live music

LA has an overwhelming choice of **live music** venues. Since the nihilistic punk bands of thirty years ago drew the city away from its spaced-out cocaine-cowboy image, LA's **rock** and **pop music** scene has been second to none. The old **punk** scene has been revitalized with up-and-coming bands, and heavy metal can be found here and there. The influence and popularity of **hip-hop** is also prevalent, whether mixed in dance music by Westside DJs or in its more authentic form in the inner city (best avoided by out-of-towners). Surprisingly, **country music** is fairly common, and the valleys are hotbeds of bluegrass and swing. There's also **jazz**, best in the few genuinely authentic downbeat dives, while Latin **salsa** music can be found in a few Westside clubs.

There are always plenty of big names on tour, from major artists to independents, and an enormous number of venues. Most venues open at 8 or 9pm; headline bands are usually onstage between 11pm and 1am. Cover ranges widely from $5 to $75. You'll need to be 21 and will likely be asked for ID. As ever, *LA Weekly* is the best source of **listings**.

Major performance venues

Cerritos Center for the Performing Arts 12700 Center Court Drive ☎1-800/300-4345, ⊛www .cerritoscenter.com. North of Long Beach, a top draw for mainstream country, gospel, classical, pop, and jazz acts – usually nothing too quirky or adventurous.

Gibson Amphitheatre 100 Universal City Plaza ☎818/622-4440, ⊛www.hob.com/venues/concerts/universal. A big but acoustically excellent auditorium with regular rock, pop, and Latin shows. Located on the Universal Studios lot.

Greek Theatre 2700 N Vermont Ave, Griffith Park ☎323/665-1927, ⊛www.greektheatrela.com. Outdoor, summer-only venue (May–Oct) hosting mainstream rock and pop acts and seating for five thousand. Parking can be a mess, so come early.

Grove of Anaheim 2200 E Katella Ave ☎714/712-2700, ⊛www.thegroveofanaheim.com. Orange County concert space aimed at showcasing old-time performers and mid-level entertainers in soul, country, pop, rock, and jazz.

Hollywood Palladium 6215 Sunset Blvd, Hollywood ☎323/962-7600, ⊛www.hollywoodpalladium.com. Once a big-band dance hall, with an authentic 1940s interior, now a home to all manner of hard rock, punk, and rap outfits. Remodeled in 2007.

Kodak Theatre 6801 Hollywood Blvd, Hollywood ☎323/308-6300, ⊛www.kodaktheatre.com. Part of the colossal Hollywood & Highland mall, a media-ready theater partly designed to host the Oscars, as well as major and minor pop acts.

Staples Center 865 S Figueroa St, Downtown ☎213/742-7340, ⊛www.staplescenter.com. Big, glassy sports arena (home to the LA Lakers and Clippers) that's also a good showcase for Top 40 rock and pop acts.

Wiltern Theater 3790 Wilshire Blvd, Mid-Wilshire ☎323/388-1400, ⊛www.wiltern.com. A striking blue Zigzag Art Deco movie palace, renovated and converted into a top performing space for standard pop acts as well as edgy alternative groups.

Rock and pop

The Cat Club 8911 Sunset Blvd, West Hollywood ☎310/657-0888. Hard, meaty jams every night of the week, with the focus on rock, punk, and rockabilly, often courtesy of lip-snarling cover bands.

The Echo 1822 Sunset Blvd ☎213/413-8200. Like the name says, an Echo Park club with scrappy indie-rock bands playing in a dark, intense little hole for a crowd of serious hipsters. A good place to catch what's bubbling up in the underground music scene.

El Rey Theater 5515 Wilshire Blvd, Mid-Wilshire ☎323/936-4790. Although not as famous as its Sunset Strip counterparts, this rock and alternative venue is possibly the best spot to see explosive new bands and still-engaging oldsters.

Gabah 4658 Melrose Ave, Hollywood ☎323/664-8913. Eclectic spot serving up a mix of reggae, funk, dub, and rock, with a mix of club and live-music nights. The dicey neighborhood leaves much to be desired; always let the valet take charge of your car.

The Gig 7302 Melrose Ave ☎323/936-4440. Central Melrose hotspot for hard rocking and fist-shaking, with a regular lineup of spirited groups and a good group of spirits, too.

Henry Fonda Music Box Theatre 6126 Hollywood Blvd ☎323/464-0808. A charming, renovated old theater that began life in 1926 and still hosts theatrical productions, but more typically alternative rock and dance acts.

Key Club 9039 Sunset Blvd ☎310/274-5800. A hotspot in the most lively section of the strip, attracting a young, hip group for its regular concerts in the rock, punk, and metal vein, with occasional lighter fare as well.

Largo 432 N Fairfax Ave, West LA
☎ 323/852-1073. Cozy cabaret with some unusual live acts, though mostly jazz, rock, and pop, often of the acoustic variety, with some comedy as well.

The Lighthouse 30 Pier Ave, Hermosa Beach ☎ 310/376-9833. Adjacent to the beach, this old-time favorite offers rock, jazz, and reggae as well as karaoke and occasional comedy.

The Roxy 9009 Sunset Blvd, West LA ☎ 310/276-2222. Among the top showcases for the music industry's new signings, intimate and with a great sound system, on the western – but still frenetic – end of the strip.

The Smell 247 S Main St, Downtown ☎ 213/625-4325. A funky space with groovy art grunge, including strange decor, frenetic rock and punk music, and a grim location.

Spaceland 1717 Silver Lake Blvd, Silver Lake ☎ 323/661-4380. Doesn't have the national rep of places like the *Roxy* and *Whisky*, but you're unlikely to find a better spot in LA to catch up-and-coming rockers and other acts, including punk and alternative musicians.

The Troubadour 9081 Santa Monica Blvd, West Hollywood ☎ 310/276-6168. An old 1960s mainstay that's been through a lot of incarnations in its fifty years. Used to be known for folk and country rock, then metal, now for various flavours of indie rock.

The Viper Room 8852 Sunset Blvd, West Hollywood ☎ 310/358-1880. Great live acts, a famous owner, and a headline-hitting past. Expect almost any musician to show up onstage.

▲ Whisky-a-Go-Go, West Hollywood

Whisky-a-Go-Go 8901 Sunset Blvd, West Hollywood ☎ 310/652-4202. Legendary spot in the 1960s, and still important for LA's rising music stars. Mainly hard rock, though you might catch an alternative act now and then.

Country and folk

Boulevard Music 4136 Sepulveda Blvd, Culver City ☎ 310/398-2583. This unglamorous music store manages to host some fairly interesting folk acts on weekends, from roots country to delta blues, with international groups adding even more to the eclectic mix.

Cowboy Palace Saloon 21635 Devonshire St, Chatsworth ☎ 818/341-0166. Worth a trip to this distant corner of the San Fernando Valley for plenty of down-home helpings of tub-thumping country-and-western concerts and Sunday BBQ fixin's.

CTMS Center 16953 Ventura Blvd, Encino ☎ 818/817-7756, ⓦ www.ctmsfolkmusic.org. The home base for the California Traditional Music Society, which throughout the year puts on perfor-mances of ancient and modern folk music, offering education, monthly jam sessions (open to the public), and occasional concerts.

Hotel Café 1623 N Cahuenga Blvd, Hollywood ☎ 323/461-2040. Comfortable, intimate spot for acoustic acts and earnest singer-songsmiths.

McCabe's 3101 W Pico Blvd, Santa Monica ☎ 310/828-4497. LA's premier acoustic-guitar shop; long the scene of some excellent and unusual folk and country shows, with the occasional alternative act thrown in as well.

Rusty's Surf Ranch 256 Santa Monica Pier ☎ 310/393-7437. Offers not only surf music – and displays of old-time long boards – but also rock, pop, folk, and even karaoke. Always a popular spot for tourists, near the end of the pier.

Viva Fresh Cantina 900 Riverside Drive, Burbank ☎ 818/845-2425. A Mexican restaurant on the far side of Griffith Park, where you can hear some of LA's most engaging country, bluegrass, and honky-tonk artists performing nightly.

Jazz and blues

Babe & Ricky's Inn 4339 Leimert Blvd, South Central ☎ 323/295-9112. Long a top spot for blues on Central Ave, this premier music hall continues to attract quality, nationally known acts at its Leimert Park location.

The Baked Potato 3787 Cahuenga Blvd W, North Hollywood ☎ 818/980-1615. A small but near-legendary contemporary jazz spot, where many reputations have been forged.

Catalina Bar & Grill 6725 Hollywood Blvd, Hollywood ☎ 323/466-2210. A jazz institution with plenty of style and atmosphere, filling, pricey meals, and potent drinks.

Cat 'n' Fiddle Pub 6530 Sunset Blvd, Hollywood ☏ 323/468-3800. An English-style pub with jazz on Sun from 7 until 11pm; no cover. Also see p.164.

Cozy's Bar & Grill 14048 Ventura Blvd, Sherman Oaks ☏ 818/986-6000. Listen to blues on the weekend, or periodically during the week, at this restaurant and lounge that also features karaoke, funk, and soul performances.

Fais Do-Do 5257 W Adams Blvd ☏ 323/954-8080. Though it often hosts DJ nights of the dance, funk, and rap variety, this spot, between Downtown and Culver City, also presents concerts from regional reggae, jazz, and R&B acts.

Harvelle's 1432 4th St, Santa Monica ☏ 310/395-1676. A stellar blues joint near the Third Street Promenade, for more than seven decades offering different performers nightly and a little funk, R&B, and burlesque thrown in as well.

House of Blues 8430 Sunset Blvd, West Hollywood ☏ 323/848-5100. Over-commercialized mock sugar shack, with good but pricey live acts. Very popular with tourists as it's the flagship of a national chain. Cover can reach $40 or more.

Jax 339 N Brand Blvd, Glendale ☏ 818/500-1604. A combination restaurant and performing stage where you can take in a good assortment of jazz sounds, from traditional to contemporary.

Jazz Bakery 3233 Helms Ave, Culver City ☏ 310/271-9039. More performance space than club, where these best local musicians play alongside big-name visitors. In an actual former bakery building.

Knitting Factory 7021 Hollywood Blvd ☏ 323/463-0204. West Coast branch of New York's landmark club, housed in a mini-mall and featuring a wide range of highly eclectic interpretation, much of it experimental or avant-garde.

Spazio 14755 Ventura Blvd, 2nd Floor, Sherman Oaks ☏ 818/728-8400. Swank Italian eatery that's one of the bigger-name spots for mainstream jazz, hosting regular nightly performances.

Vibrato Grill and Jazz 2930 Beverly Glen Circle, West LA ☏ 310/474-9400. You're not going to find anything too challenging at this Bel Air club, but for traditional and smooth jazz sounds, it might fit the bill.

Salsa

El Floridita 1253 N Vine St, Hollywood ☏ 323/871-8612. Decent Mexican and Cuban food complements a fine lineup of Cuban and salsa artists, who play on weekends and jam on other nights.

Luminarias 3500 Ramona Blvd, Monterey Park, East LA ☏ 323/268-4177. Hilltop restaurant (see p.153) with regular live salsa and mariachi music reckoned to be as good as its Mexican food.

Mama Juana's 3707 Cahuenga Blvd West, Studio City ☏ 818/505-8636. Spanish/Mexican restaurant that also serves up nightly helpings of live salsa, merengue, and other Latin-flavored tunes. Also salsa lessons on weekends before the shows begin.

Zabumba 10717 Venice Blvd, Culver City ☏ 310/841-6525. In a colorful building amid drab surroundings, this venue is more bossa nova Brazilian than straight salsa, but it's still great, and very lively.

Performing arts and film

While it's true that LA's range of **performing arts** offerings was at one time quite limited, confined to art-house cinemas and a handful of mainstream theaters, since then the city has firmly established itself in the field thanks to a renewed push from old-money and corporate interests.

LA boasts a world-class conductor and orchestra for **classical music**, along with less-familiar entities like chamber-music groups, and the fields of **opera** and **dance** are represented by several fine companies. **Theater** is always a growth industry here, with more than a thousand shows annually, plenty of actors to draw from, and a burgeoning audience for both mainstream and fringe productions. **Comedy** is a big draw, too, and it comes as no surprise that this is one of the prime entertainment options that first-time visitors seek out. Not surprisingly, though, it's **film** that is still the chief cultural staple of the region, and there is no shortage of excellent theaters in which to catch a flick.

Classical music, opera, and dance

LA has a good number of outlets for **classical music** and **opera**. The Los Angeles Philharmonic and LA Opera are the major names in the city, and perform regularly, while smaller groups appear more sporadically. Watch the press, especially the *LA Times*, for details, and expect to pay from $10 to $120 for most concerts, more for really big names. **Dance** in Los Angeles has its annual big event with the **Dance Kaleidoscope**, held over two weeks in July. Otherwise, check for performances at the **universities**, where many important names in dance have residencies.

Major venues

Disney Hall 1st St at Grand Ave, Downtown ☎ 323/850-2000, ⒲ wdch.laphil.org. LA's most renowned cultural attraction (along with the Getty Center), which hosts the LA Philharmonic in a striking Frank Gehry design (see p.93).

The Dorothy Chandler Pavilion In the Music Center, 135 N Grand Ave, Downtown ☎ 213/972-7211 or 972-7460, ⒲ www.musiccenter.org. Long-standing warhorse of the arts community, used by LA Opera and other top names.

The Hollywood Bowl 2301 N Highland Ave, Hollywood ☎ 323/850-2000, ⒲ www.hollywoodbowl .org. A famed bandshell (see p.113) that hosts the LA Philharmonic and open-air concerts, usually of the pop variety, during the summer.

Japan America Theater 244 S San Pedro St, Little Tokyo ☎ 213/680-3700, ⒲ www.jaccc.org. Dance and performance works drawn from Japan and the Far East.

John Anson Ford Theater 2850 Cahuenga Blvd, Hollywood ☎ 323/461-3673, ⒲ www .fordamphitheater.org. An open-air venue that has eclectic productions by local classical and operatic groups as well as sporadic pop and rock concerts.

Orange County Performing Arts Center 600 Town Center Drive, Costa Mesa ☎ 714/556-ARTS, ⒲ www.ocpac.org. Orange County home of the Pacific Symphony Orchestra and Opera Pacific, as well as touring big names in pop and jazz.

Pasadena Dance Theatre 1985 Locust St, Pasadena ☎ 626/683-3459, ⒲ www .pasadenadance.org. One of the San Gabriel Valley's most prominent dance venues, hosting diverse groups throughout the year.

Royce Hall On the UCLA campus, Westwood ☎ 310/825-2101, ⒲ www.uclalive.org. Classical concerts, often involving big names, occur at this splendid historic-revival structure throughout the college year (Sept–June).

The Shrine Auditorium 665 W Jefferson, South Central LA ☎ 213/749-5123 or 748-5116, ⒲ www .shrinela.com. Huge 1926 Moorish curiosity that hosts touring pop acts, choral gospel groups, and countless award shows.

Thornton School of Music On the USC campus, South Central ☎ 213/740-6935, ⒲ www.usc.edu /music. A fine array of large and small venues, from 90–1200 seats, for sonatas, concertos, and other works (usually Sept–May), with most tickets less than $20.

UCLA Center for the Performing Arts On the UCLA campus, Westwood ☎ 310/825-2101, ⒲ www.uclalive.org. Coordinates a wide range of touring companies in music, theatre, and dance (Sept–June).

Groups and institutions

Da Camera Society Rotating venues ☎ 213/477-2929, ⒲ www.dacamera.org. This organization's "Chamber Music in Historic Sites" provides a great opportunity to hear chamber works in stunning settings, from grand churches to private homes, including Doheny Mansion near USC. Ticket prices vary depending on the venue.

LA Opera At the Music Center, 135 N Grand Ave, Downtown ☎ 213/972-8001, ⒲ www.laopera.com. Stages productions between September and June, from epic *opera seria* to lighter operettas. The mainstream heavyweight in town.

Long Beach Opera At the Carpenter Center, 6200 Atherton St ☎ 562/439-2580, ⒲ www .longbeachopera.org. Despite being eight years older than the LA Opera, this alternative company presents the freshest and edgiest work in town, from lesser-known pieces by Monteverdi to craggy newer works by local composers and librettists.

Los Angeles Chamber Orchestra Rotating venues ☎ 213/622-7001 ext. 215, ⒲ www.laco .org. Appearing at venues such as UCLA's Royce Hall, Glendale's Alex Theatre, and Culver City's Jazz Bakery, the orchestra presents a range of chamber works, not all canonical, from different eras.

Los Angeles Master Chorale At Disney Hall and rotating venues, 135 N Grand Ave, Downtown ☎ 213/972-2782, ⒲ www.lamc.org. Classic canonical works, along with newer commissions and experimental pieces, are showcased by this choral institution.

Los Angeles Philharmonic At Disney Hall, 1st St and Grand Ave, Downtown ☎323/850-2000, ⓦwww.laphil.org. The one big name in the city performs regularly during the year, and conductor Esa-Pekka Salonen always provides a diverse, challenging program.

Opera Pacific Orange County Performing Arts Center, 600 Town Center Drive, Costa Mesa ☎1-800/346-7372, ⓦwww.operapacific.org. Performs mostly mainstream grand opera and operettas.

Pacific Symphony Orchestra Orange County Performing Arts Center, 600 Town Center Drive, Costa Mesa ☎714/755-5788, ⓦwww .pacificsymphony.org. Orchestra that draws big crowds for its excellent, stylish performances of mostly canonical works.

Pasadena Symphony 300 E Green St ☎626/793-7172, ⓦwww.pasadenasymphony.org. Veering between the standard repertoire and more contemporary pieces, this esteemed symphony plays at the stately Pasadena Civic Auditorium, a 1932 Renaissance Revival gem.

Southwest Chamber Music Rotating venues, ☎1-800/726-7147, ⓦwww.swmusic.org. A nationally recognized troupe that offers a wide range of music, from medieval to modern (Oct–May). Venues include the Norton Simon Museum and the Huntington Library.

Comedy

LA has a wide range of **comedy** clubs. While rising stars and beginners can be spotted on the "underground" open-mike scene, most of the famous comics, both stand-up and improv, appear at the more established clubs in Hollywood, West LA, or the valleys. These venues usually have a bar (and a two-drink minimum) and put on two shows per evening, generally starting at 8pm and 10.30pm – the later one being more popular. The better-known places are open nightly, but are often solidly booked on weekends.

Acme Comedy Theater 135 N La Brea Ave, Hollywood ☎323/525-0202, ⓦwww.acmecomedy .com. A fancy venue with sketch and improv comedy, as well as variety shows and theme-comedy performances. $10–16.

Bang Improv Theater 457 N Fairfax Ave, Hollywood ☎323/653-6886, ⓦwww.bangstudio .com. One-person shows and long-form improvisation are the specialties at this small theater/comedy club, with the popular shows running on weekends. $10.

Comedy & Magic Club 1018 Hermosa Ave, Hermosa Beach ☎310/372-1193, ⓦwww .comedyandmagicclub.info. Notable South Bay comedy space where Jay Leno sometimes tests material. Tickets can run up to $30, depending on the performer.

The Comedy Store 8433 W Sunset Blvd, West LA ☎323/656-6225, ⓦwww.thecomedystore.com. LA's premier comedy showcase and popular enough to be spread over three rooms – which means there's usually space, even at weekends. Run by Pauly Shore's mom. Most shows $15–20.

Empty Stage 2372 Veteran Ave, West LA ☎310/470-3560, ⓦwww.emptystage.com. Sometimes funny, sometimes irritating sketch comedy that draws upon long improvisational routines. Cast mainly with up-and-comers of varying hilarity. $10–15.

Groundlings Theater 7307 Melrose Ave, West LA ☎323/934-4747, ⓦwww.groundlings.com. Pioneering venue where only the gifted survive, with furious improv events and high-wire comedy acts that can inspire greatness, or groans. $10–20.

Ha Ha Café 5010 Lankershim Blvd, North Hollywood ☎818/508-4995, ⓦwww.hahacafe .com. Amateur and a few professional comedians face off for your amusement nightly at this combination comedy club and café space around the NoHo Arts District. $15.

The Ice House 24 N Mentor Ave, Pasadena ☎626/577-1894. The comedy mainstay of the Valley, very established and fairly safe; often amusing, with plenty of old warhorses and the occasional big name. $15–20.

The Improv 8162 Melrose Ave, West LA ☎323/651-2583. Long-standing brick-walled joint that spawned a national chain. Still known for hosting some of the best acts working in both stand-up and improv. One of LA's top comedy spots – so book ahead. $10–20.

Improv Olympic West 6366 Hollywood Blvd ☎323/962-7560, ⓦwww.iowest.com. A spot for those who like their improv drawn out and elaborate, with comedy routines more like short theater pieces than a set of wacky one-liners. $5–10.

LA Connection 13442 Ventura Blvd, Sherman Oaks ☎818/710-1320. Cozy space for sketch comedy, improv, group antics, and individual jokesters. Often memorable. $7–12.

The Laugh Factory 8001 Sunset Blvd, West Hollywood ☎ 323/656-1336, ⓦ www.laughfactory .com. Stand-ups of varying reputations, with the odd big name and regular ensemble shows. $18–30.

Second City Studio Theater 6560 Hollywood Blvd, Hollywood ☎ 323/464-8542, ⓦ www.secondcity.com. Groundbreaking comedy troupe with numerous branches, in LA hosting nightly improv and sketch comedy sometimes built around lengthy routines and theme performances. Mostly up-and-comers. $5–15.

Theater

From huge Broadway shows to small avant-garde productions, LA has a very active **theater** scene. While the bigger venues host a predictable array of retread musicals and classics with an all-star cast of celebrities, more than a hundred small theaters with fewer than a hundred seats can be found around the city, enabling a vast network of fringe writers, actors, and directors to showcase their talent. **Tickets** are less expensive than you might expect: a big show will cost you at least $40 (matinees are cheaper), and smaller shows around $10 to $30. Always book ahead (see box, p.168).

Fringe theaters

The Complex 6476 Santa Monica Blvd, Hollywood ☎ 323/465-0383, ⓦ www .complexhollywood.com. A group of alternative companies revolving around a group of five small theaters, where you're likely to see any number of dynamic productions.

Highways 1651 18th St, Santa Monica ☎ 310/315-1459, ⓦ www.highwaysperformance .org. Located in the 18th Street Arts Complex, an adventurous performance space that offers a range of topical drama and politically charged produc- tions, with a strong bent toward the angry, polemical, and subversive.

Hudson Theaters 6539 Santa Monica Blvd, Hollywood ☎ 323/856-4252 (each theatre has different contacts), ⓦ www.hudsontheatre.com. Socially conscious "message" plays alternate with more satiric, comedic works at this venue for upcoming actors. Complex consists of four stages, each with less than a hundred seats, plus a coffeehouse.

Open Fist Theatre 1625 N La Brea Ave, Hollywood ☎ 323/882-6912, ⓦ www.openfist.org. As you might expect from the name, biting and edgy works are often the focus at this small theater company, employing a limited cast of spirited unknowns.

Powerhouse Theater 3116 Second St, Santa Monica ☎ 310/396-3680, ⓦ www .powerhousetheatre.com. Cozy venue not far from Venice, worth visiting for the adventurous and risk- taking experimental shows.

Stages Theater Center 1540 N McCadden Place, Hollywood ☎ 323/465-1010, ⓦ www .stagestheatrecenter.com. With three stages offering twenty to one hundred seats, an excellent place to catch a wide range of comedies and dramas, including restagings of canonical works and contemporary productions as well.

Theatre West 3333 Cahuenga Blvd West, Hollywood ☎ 323/851-7977, ⓦ www.theatrewest .org. A classic venue that's always a good spot to see inventive, sometimes odd, productions with a troupe of excellent young up-and-comers.

Theatricum Botanicum 1419 N Topanga Canyon Blvd, Topanga Canyon ☎ 310/455-3723, ⓦ www .theatricum.com. Terrific spot in the Santa Monica Mountains showing a range of classic (often Shakespearean) and modern plays amid an idyllic outdoor setting.

Major theaters

Actors Gang Theater 9070 Venice Blvd, Culver City ☎ 310/838-4264, ⓦ www .theactorsgang.com. A cross between a major and an alternative theater; having fewer than a hundred seats keeps it cozy, though it does host the odd spectacular production that features semi-famous names from film or TV.

Ahmanson Theatre At the Music Center, 135 N Grand Ave, Downtown ☎ 213/628-2772, ⓦ www .taperahmanson.com. A two-thousand-seat theater hosting colossal traveling shows from Broadway. If you've seen a major production advertised on TV and on the sides of buses, it's probably playing here.

Alex Theatre 216 N Brand Blvd, Glendale ☎ 818/243-7700, ⓦ www.alextheatre.org. Glori- ously restored movie palace bedecked with green- and-yellow decor and neon spire, hosting a fine range of musical theater, dance, comedy, and film.

Geffen Playhouse 10886 Le Conte Ave, Westwood ☎ 310/208-5454. A five-hundred seat, quaint

Spanish Revival building that often hosts one-person shows. There's a decided Hollywood connection, evident in the crowd-pleasing nature of many of the productions.

Mark Taper Forum 135 N Grand Ave, Downtown ☏213/628-2772, ⊛www.taperahmanson.com. Mainstream theater in the three-quarter round, with a mix of classic and contemporary works. Located in the Music Center complex.

Pantages Theater 6233 Hollywood Blvd, Hollywood ☏323/468-1770, ⊛www.nederlander.com/wc. Quite the stunner: an exquisite, atmospheric Art Deco theater in the heart of historic Hollywood, hosting major touring Broadway productions.

Pasadena Playhouse 39 S El Molino Ave, Pasadena ☏626/792-8672 or 356-7529. A grand old space that provides enjoyable mainstream entertainment. Actors are often a mix of youthful professionals and aging TV and movie stars.

South Coast Repertory 655 Town Center Drive, Costa Mesa ☏714/708-5555. ⊛www.scr.org. Orange County's major entry for theater, with well-executed performances of the classics on the main stage, and edgier works by new writers on the smaller second stage.

Film

Major feature **films** are often released in LA months (or years) before they play anywhere else, and a huge number of cinemas show both the new releases and the classics – with fewer screens showing independent and foreign movies. Depending on where you go and what you see, a ticket will be from $7 to $10, with much higher costs for special events such as the Last Remaining Seats Festival ($20).

Classic moviehouses

Bruin 948 Broxton Ave, Westwood ☏310/208-8998. Dashing 1930s moviehouse that's a city landmark for its wraparound marquee and sleek Moderne styling.

Chinese 6925 Hollywood Blvd, Hollywood ☏323/464-8111. With its forecourt thick with tourists and wild chinoiserie design, this Hollywood icon shows relentlessly mainstream films, but is still worthy of all the postcard images (see p.107).

Cinerama Dome 6360 Sunset Blvd, Hollywood ☏323/464-1478. This white hemisphere has the biggest screen in California, a giant curved panel with slight distortion at the corners. Now part of a larger complex of theaters and shops called ArcLight (see p.109).

Egyptian 6712 Hollywood Blvd, Hollywood ☏323/466-3456. Has showings of revival, experi-mental, and art films, and has been lovingly restored as a kitschy masterpiece of the Egyptian Revival – all grand columns, winged scarabs, and mythological gods (see p.106).

El Capitan 6834 Hollywood Blvd, Hollywood ☏323/467-7674. Whether or not you enjoy the typically kiddie-oriented fare offered here – thanks to its Disney ownership – the twice-restored splendor of this classic Hollywood movie palace is bound to impress.

Fine Arts 8556 Wilshire Blvd, Beverly Hills ☏310/652-1330. Proof that modern moviehouses don't necessarily have to be ugly concrete boxes. The simple exterior and lobby give way to a grandly opulent 1936 theater showing a mix of mainstream and art-house films.

Los Angeles 615 S Broadway, Downtown. Boasting an exquisite French Second Empire lobby, with triumphal arches lined by marble columns supporting an intricate mosaic ceiling and trompe l'oeil murals. One of the best moviehouses in the country, though only open to the public during the Last Remaining Seats film festival in June (tickets $20; see p.94).

Orpheum 842 S Broadway, Downtown ☏213/239-0939. A spellbinding mix of French Renaissance and Baroque decor, with a pipe organ, brazen chandeliers, ornamental grotesques, nude nymphs, and grand arches in gold leaf. Visible during the Last Remaining Seats festival (tickets $20; see p.94), but also for periodic performance arts events.

Rialto 1023 Fair Oaks Ave, South Pasadena ☏626/388-2122. A 1925 movie palace and historic landmark that also served as a theatrical stage and vaudeville locale, with Moorish organ screens, Egyptian columns, winged harpies, and a central Medusa head.

Village 961 Broxton Ave, Westwood ☏310/248-6266. One of the best places to watch a movie in LA, with a giant screen, fine seats, and good balcony views, and a frequent spot for Hollywood premieres. The marvelous 1931 exterior features a white spire on top.

Warner Grand 478 W 6th St, San Pedro ☏310/548-7672. Restored 1931 Zigzag Moderne masterpiece with dark geometric details, great columns, and sunburst motifs – a style that almost looks pre-Columbian. Now a repertory cinema and performance hall.

Art houses and revival cinemas

Aero 1328 Montana Ave, Santa Monica ☎310/466-3456. American Cinematheque presents classic and art-house movies in this fine old venue from 1940 (often the same fare playing at the organization's Egyptian). The movies are eclectic and well programmed.

Bing At the LA County Art Museum, 5905 Wilshire Blvd, Mid-Wilshire ☎323/857-6010. Offers engaging retrospectives of famed actors and directors, as well as full-priced evening programs of classic, independent, foreign, art-house, and revival cinema.

Los Feliz 1822 N Vermont Ave, Hollywood ☎323/664-2169. Three small screens showing international and low-budget American independent fare.

New Beverly Cinema 7165 Beverly Blvd, Mid-Wilshire ☎323/938-4038. Worthwhile for its excellent art films and revival screenings, with some imaginative double bills.

Nuart 11272 Santa Monica Blvd, West LA ☎310/281-8223. Shows rarely seen classics, documentaries, and edgy foreign-language films, and is the main option for independent filmmakers testing their work. Sometimes offers brief Dec previews of Oscar contenders.

Old Town Music Hall 140 Richmond St, El Segundo ☎310/322-2592. An old-fashioned spot to see historic movies, with accompanying organ or piano music on some nights; tickets $20.

Silent Movie 611 N Fairfax Ave, Mid-Wilshire ☎323/655-2520. Offers an enjoyable mix of silent comedies and adventure flicks – Douglas Fairbanks swashbucklers and the like – along with darker fare like Fritz Lang's *Metropolis* and the occasional talkie.

Sunset 5 8000 Sunset Blvd, West Hollywood ☎323/848-3500. This art-house complex sits on the second floor of the Sunset Plaza outdoor mall and shows a good assortment of edgy independent flicks.

Vista 4473 Sunset Drive, Hollywood ☎323/660-6639. A nicely renovated moviehouse with very eclectic offerings – from mindless action flicks to micro-budgeted indie productions – located near the intersection of Sunset and Hollywood boulevards.

Gay and lesbian LA

Although nowhere near as big as that of San Francisco, LA's **gay and lesbian scene** is almost as well established. The best-known area is the city of **West Hollywood**, which is synonymous with the (affluent, white) gay lifestyle, where Santa Monica Boulevard east of Doheny Drive has many chic restaurants, shops, and bars. **Silver Lake**, especially along Hyperion and Sunset boulevards, has much more of a vibrant ethnic and working-class mix. Surprisingly, perhaps, even Orange County has its pockets of gay and lesbian culture, centered mainly around the upscale confines of **Laguna Beach** and its trendy restaurants and bars.

Gay couples will find themselves readily accepted at just about any LA **hotel**, but there are a few that cater especially to gay travelers and can also be useful sources of information on the local scene. This is also true of a number of **restaurants** and various **bars** and **clubs**.

Resources

AIDS Project Los Angeles 611 S Kingsley Drive, Hollywood ☎213/201-1600, ⊛www.apla.org. Has office-based programs and services and sponsors fundraisers throughout the year, including a well-attended annual six-mile walkathon.

A Different Light 8853 Santa Monica Blvd, West Hollywood ☎310/854-6601, ⊛www.adlbooks.com. The city's best-known gay and lesbian bookshop, with art shows, readings, music events, and comfortable chairs for lounging.

LA Gay and Lesbian Center 1625 N Schrader Blvd, Hollywood ☎323/993-7400, ⊛www.laglc.org. Counseling, health-testing, and information. Publishes two informative monthly newsletters as well.

One Institute and Archives 909 W Adams Blvd, South Central LA ☎213/741-0094, ⊛www.onearchives.org. The world's biggest library of rare books and magazines, literature, artworks, and related information on gay and lesbian culture, social issues, and politics.

Hotels

Coral Sands 1730 N Western Ave, Hollywood ☎323/467-5141, ⊛www.coralsands-la.com. Cruisy spot exclusively geared towards gay men. All rooms face the inner courtyard pool. Also with on-site sauna, Jacuzzi, and gym. ❹

Holloway Motel 8465 Santa Monica Blvd, West Hollywood ☎323/654-2454, ⊛www .hollowaymotel.com. Typical clean roadside motel, if rather dreary looking. Comes with fridges and complimentary breakfast. Add $50+ during holidays like Halloween and Gay Pride. ❹

Hollywood Metropolitan 5825 Sunset Blvd ☎323/962-5800, ⊛www.metropolitanhotel.com. Central hotel with a mix of small, comfortable rooms with mini-fridges and larger suites; features the *Havana on Sunset* restaurant (see p.153). ❺

Ramada 8585 Santa Monica Blvd, West Hollywood ☎310/652-6400, ⊛www.ramadaweho.com. A modern place with clean and comfortable rooms with high-speed Net access, plus pool and gym, in the center of the community. ❻

San Vicente Inn 854 N San Vicente Blvd, West Hollywood ☎310/854-6915, ⊛www.gayresort .com. Small and comfortable bed and breakfast located just north of Santa Monica Boulevard, with pool, spa, and sauna. Add $50 for private bath. ❺

Restaurants

Champagne French Bakery 8917 Santa Monica Blvd, West Hollywood ☎310/657-4051. Convenient bakery and coffee shop with serviceable pastries and baked treats in a central location – good for breakfast or lunch on the main drag. One of several LA locations.

Fat Fish 616 N Robertson Blvd, West Hollywood ☎310/659-3882. Enjoyable and upscale pan-Asian and Cal-cuisine restaurant with inventive cocktails and good sushi.

French Quarter 7985 Santa Monica Blvd, West Hollywood ☎310/654-0898. Inside the *French Market Place*, a New Orleans-themed restaurant that's more of a draw for its convivial atmosphere than its inauthentic cuisine.

Marix Tex-Mex Playa 118 Entrada Drive, Pacific Palisades ☎310/459-8596. Flavorful fajitas and big margaritas in this rowdy beachfront cantina, which attracts mixed crowds. An even livelier branch at 1108 N Flores St, West Hollywood ☎323/656-8800.

Mark's 861 N La Cienega Blvd, West Hollywood ☎310/652-5252. High-end establishment serving California cuisine, with good crab cakes, osso buco, and lamb chops.

Yukon Mining Company 7328 Santa Monica Blvd ☎323/851-8833. Colorful 24-hour diner where you're likely to see an odd mix of drag queens, Russians, and pensioners.

Bars and clubs

7969 7969 Santa Monica Blvd, West Hollywood ☎323/654-0280. Legendary club hosting high-energy dance tunes, frenetic DJs, and colorful theme-party nights (also see p.168).

Akbar 4356 Sunset Blvd ☎323/665-6810. A mellow and unpretentious Silver Lake watering hole that draws a diverse, bohemian crowd, including a loyal coterie of gay visitors.

Arena 6655 Santa Monica Blvd, Hollywood ☎323/462-0714. Many clubs under one roof, large dance floors throbbing to funk, house, and hi-NRG grooves, and sometimes with live bands and mind-blowing drag shows (also see p.167).

Boom Boom Room 1401 S Coast Hwy, Laguna Beach ☎949/494-7588. The pulse-pounding name says it all: house and disco tunes spun by local DJs on weekends, male strip shows, and all kinds of other performances and spectacles.

Jewel's Catch One 4067 W Pico Blvd, Mid-Wilshire ☎323/734-8849. Sweaty barn catering to a mixed crowd – gay and straight, male and female – all on two wild dance floors.

Micky's 8857 Santa Monica Blvd ☎310/657-1176. Lively, pulsating scene with a full range of club nights, including the usual retro-Seventies and Eighties dance-pop, thundering house and hip-hop beats, and drag shows.

Mother Lode 8944 Santa Monica Blvd ☎310/659-9700. Strong drinks, wild dancing to house and garage music, and periodic drag antics make this one of the more colorful and frenetic of WeHo's clubs.

The Palms 8572 Santa Monica Blvd, West Hollywood ☎310/652-6188. Mostly house and dance nights at West Hollywood's most established lesbian bar, which increasingly caters to a mixed crowd.

Rage 8911 Santa Monica Blvd, West Hollywood ☎310/652-7055. Very flashy gay men's club and neighborhood favorite, playing the latest house to a long-established crowd. Nightly cover can reach $10.

Shopping

Shopping in LA is an art – besides the run-of-the-mill chain retailers you'll find anywhere, there are big **department stores** and mega-sized **malls** where most of the hardcore shopping goes on, and of course **Rodeo Drive**, two blocks of the world's most exclusive shopping. The trendiest boutiques line **Melrose Avenue**, between La Brea and Fairfax avenues, **Old Town Pasadena** boasts a few more upmarket chains, and the few blocks above Prospect on Vermont Avenue in **Los Feliz** are home to some of the underground's groovier shops.

LA also has a good assortment of **bookshops** and **record stores**, whether you're in search of a cozy secondhand shop or a behemoth with all the new releases, plus a café to boot. There's an equally diverse array of **food stores**, from delis and supermarkets to exquisite cake stores and gourmet markets.

Department stores and malls

Each of LA's neighborhoods has a collection of ordinary **stores** and **mini-malls**. A step up from these in price and quality are **department stores**, which are often included within massive **malls** and resemble self-contained city suburbs, around which Angelenos do the bulk of their serious buying.

Beverly Center 8500 Beverly Blvd, West Hollywood ☏ 310/854-0070. Seven acres of boutiques, Macy's and Bloomingdale's, and a multiplex cinema, all in one complex that resembles a giant brown concrete bunker – built over a parking garage.

Century City Marketplace 10250 Santa Monica Blvd, Century City ☏ 310/553-5300. An outdoor mall with one hundred upscale shops and one of the better food courts around. The place to come to see stars do their shopping, and a spot to catch a first-run movie in excellent surroundings at the AMC Century 15 Theaters.

Del Amo Fashion Square Hawthorne Blvd at Carson St, Torrance ☏ 310/542-8525. The South Bay's own super-mall, one of the country's largest, with five major anchor stores and a wealth of mid-level retailers and shoppers.

The Grove 6301 W 3rd St, Mid-Wilshire ☏ 323/900-8080. A giant, open-air mega-structure by the Farmers' Market; has all the usual chain retailers and restaurants, movie theaters, and a more stylish design than the typical "dumb-box" construction found elsewhere.

Hollywood & Highland At the same intersection in Hollywood ☏ 323/960-2331. Colossal mega-mall with a design inspired by an ancient film set, but offering the same old corporate boutiques and trendy shops, and a cineplex connected to the Chinese Theatre.

Paseo Colorado E Colorado Blvd at S Los Robles Ave, Pasadena ☏ 626/795-8891. Two levels of (mostly chain) stores with street-front entrances, an open-air design that invites strolling, and several levels of condos built over the retailers.

Santa Monica Place Broadway at 2nd St, Santa Monica ☏ 310/394-5451. Sunny, skylit mall with three tiers of shops and an outdated postmodern-pastel decor. The chain-link-walled parking garage is of minor note as an early Frank Gehry design experiment.

South Coast Plaza 3333 Bristol St, north of 405 freeway, Costa Mesa ☏ 714/435-2000. Orange County's main super-mall, with nearly three hundred shops, five anchor stores, plus a good mix of retailers. You're sure to get a good workout from navigating the place.

Third Street Promenade Between Broadway and Wilshire Blvd, Santa Monica. Major outdoor mall, packed on weekend evenings with mobs scurrying about to get to bookstores, boutiques, restaurants, and cinemas, amid throngs of itinerant musicians, homeless folks, street preachers, and ivy-covered dinosaur fountains.

Westside Pavilion Pico Blvd at Westwood Blvd, West LA ☏ 310/474-6255. Postmodern shopping complex with two different wings branching out from Westwood Blvd – the most central mall to West LA.

Food and drink

Since eating out in LA is so common, you may never have to shop for **food** at all. But if you're preparing a picnic or want to indulge in a spot of home cooking, there are plenty of places to stock up. **Delis**, many open round the clock, are found in many areas; **supermarkets** are almost as common, some open 24 hours, or at least until 10pm; and there are also **ethnic groceries** and more expensive **gourmet markets**.

Bakeries and desserts

Diamond Bakery 335 N Fairfax Ave, West LA ℡323/655-0534. In the heart of the Fairfax District, this great old Jewish bakery provides a good number of traditional favorites, including, babka, challah, mandelbrot, and rugelach, and a legendary pumpernickel bread.

🎿 **Fosselman's** 1824 W Main St, Alhambra ℡626/282-6533. Reason alone to visit this San Gabriel Valley town: what many Angelenos regard as the area's best ice cream, a long-standing (70+ years) seller of creamy concoctions, highlighted by the macadamia crunch and burgundy cherry.

Gourmet Cobbler Factory 33 N Catalina Ave, Pasadena ℡626/795-1005. Bakery selling a nice range of scrumptious, fruity cobblers in a wide range of prices, depending on how huge you want them. Occupies a prime spot near Old Pasadena.

Hansen's Cakes 193 S Beverly Drive, Beverly Hills ℡310/273-3759. Local institution with a collection of resplendently decorated, and very tasty, cakes.

La Brea Bakery 624 S La Brea Ave, West LA ℡323/939-6813. Perhaps LA's best bakery, selling everything from cheap sourdough rolls to thick, heavy breads made with olives, cherries, and cheese. Connected to the equally appealing *Campanile* restaurant (see p.156).

Mousse Fantasy/Beard Papa's 2130 Sawtelle Blvd #110, West LA ℡310/479-6665. Pair of combined patisseries featuring a range of tasty tarts and pastries, highlighted by the éclairs, cream puffs, and various mousses and cakes.

Viktor Benes Continental Pastries 8330 Santa Monica Blvd, West Hollywood ℡310/654-5543. The place to go for freshly baked bread, coffee cakes, Danish pastries, and various chocolate-oriented treats, and appreciative local fans know it. Fifteen other area locations as well.

Delis and groceries

Alpine Village 833 W Torrance Blvd, Torrance ℡310/327-4384. Though quite a hike, and in a rather drab South Bay area, this place has all the bratwurst and schnitzel you'll ever need, and plays host to one of LA's more spirited Oktoberfest celebrations.

Bay Cities Italian Deli 1517 Lincoln Blvd, Santa Monica ℡310/395-8279. A gigantic store with piles of fresh pasta, spices, meats, sauces, many French and Middle Eastern imports, and some terrific lunchtime sandwiches.

Bharat Bazaar 11510 Washington Blvd, Culver City ℡310/398-6766. One of several excellent Indian grocers around this stretch of Culver City, providing some savory samosas and all the goods for making your own curries and vindalo.

🎿 **The Cheese Store** 419 N Beverly Drive, Beverly Hills ℡310/278-2855. More than four hundred types of cheese from all over the world, including every kind produced in the US, with many of them suspended invitingly over your head. Typically high prices to match.

Claro's Italian Market 1003 E Valley Blvd, San Gabriel ℡626/288-2026. A compact but well-stocked haven of Italian wines, chocolate, crackers, and cheeses, with a deli and bakery.

Olson's Deli 5560 Pico Blvd, Mid-Wilshire ℡323/938-0742. Herring, meatballs, and assorted sausages at this Swedish grocer, one of the few Scandinavian food retailers in LA and definitely worth a try.

Porto's Bakery 315 N Brand Blvd, Glendale ℡818/956-5996. In a town that used to be a major home of Cuban immigrants, this great throwback to the old days offers tasty baked goods and desserts, along with flaky Cuban pastries, cheesecakes soaked in rum, muffins, Danishes, croissants, and tortes.

Say Cheese 2800 Hyperion Ave, Silver Lake ℡323/665-0545. A distinctive array of French and other international cheeses, priced moderately to steeply. The delicious sandwiches may be your best bet.

Books

LA is home to a great variety of **bookshops**, from big-name chain dealers to some good **general-interest** booksellers, selling a smaller but more well-considered selection of titles. The city also has a wide range of **specialist** and **secondhand bookshops**, which will help you find that obscure physics text or gardening tome you're looking for, and may reward several hours' browsing along the miles of dusty shelves.

New books

Bodhi Tree 8585 Melrose Ave, West Hollywood ⊕310/659-1733. Ultra-trendy Westside book retailer in a chic part of Melrose, with a range of New Age, occult, and psychobabble titles, with plenty of information on the healing power of crystals, pyramids, and the like.

Book Soup 8818 W Sunset Blvd, West Hollywood ⊕310/659-3110. Great selection, right on Sunset Strip. Narrow, winding aisles stuffed pell-mell with books, strong in entertainment, travel, and photography. Celebs are sometimes known to come in, attempting to look studious.

A Different Light 8853 Santa Monica Blvd, West Hollywood ⊕310/854-6601. The city's best-known gay and lesbian bookstore, with monthly art shows, readings, and musical events. Also see p.176.

Dutton's 11975 San Vicente Blvd, Brentwood ⊕310/476-6263. One of the better general-interest stores in town, an ungainly complex built around a central courtyard. Its aisles tend to be cluttered, but it's a fine store; just try to visit during the less-crowded weekdays.

Hennessey and Ingalls 214 Wilshire Blvd, Santa Monica ⊕310/458-9074. An impressive range of art and architecture books makes this bookstore the best in LA in its field, though many of the volumes are quite expensive.

Larry Edmunds Book Shop 6644 Hollywood Blvd ⊕323/463-3273. Many stacks of books, a large number of them out of print, are offered on every aspect of film and theater, with movie stills and posters. Located at the center of tourist-oriented Hollywood.

Norton Simon Museum Bookstore 411 W Colorado Blvd, Pasadena ⊕626/449-6840. One of LA's better museum bookstores, with a superb stock of material – often with sizeable volumes on artists in the museum's collection.

Samuel French Theatre & Film Bookshop 7623 Sunset Blvd, West Hollywood ⊕323/876-0570. LA's broadest selection of theater books is found in this local institution, along with a good collection of movie and media-related titles.

Taschen 354 N Beverly Drive, Beverly Hills ⊕310/274-4300. Fun, edifying, and weird titles that focus on everything from Renaissance art to Americana kitsch to fetish photography. Cheap volumes on both familiar and obscure subjects.

Vroman's 695 E Colorado Blvd, Pasadena ⊕626/449-5320. One of the San Gabriel Valley's major retailers, offering a good selection with a café. Although there are no real bargains, other, smaller used bookstores can be found within a few blocks.

Secondhand books

Acres of Books 240 Long Beach Blvd, Long Beach ⊕562/437-6980. Worth a trip down the Blue Line Metrorail just to wallow in LA's largest, and most disorganized, secondhand collection. You may not be able to find the exact title you're looking for, but chances are you'll stumble across something good.

Atlantis Book Shop 145 N San Fernando Blvd, Burbank ⊕818/845-6467. History, fiction, and politics are some of the specialties, and even more so the paranormal, extraterrestrial, and mythological.

Book Alley 611 E Colorado Blvd, Pasadena ⊕626/683-8083. A handsome bookshop with used volumes on a variety of subjects, with many of the books quite affordable.

Brand Book Shop 231 N Brand Blvd, Glendale ⊕818/507-5943. Valley used-bookseller with a broad range of liberal-arts titles and particular strengths in entertainment, history, and politics. Located in the pulsing heart of downtown Glendale.

Cliff's Books 630 E Colorado Blvd, Pasadena ⊕626/449-9541. With many narrow aisles of tomes on a wide assortment of subjects, this longstanding used-bookseller has a greater selection than some of its neighbors, though the prices are known to be a bit higher.

Cosmopolitan Book Shop 7017 Melrose Ave ⊕323/938-7119. The cozier Westside equivalent to Acres of Books, a dealer loaded with thousands of titles stacked high on oversized cases, on a variety of subjects but especially strong on film and media.

Wilshire Books 3018 Wilshire Blvd, Santa Monica ⊕310/828-3115. The best used-bookstore in LA for its size, which is quite small and cramped. Still, a solid collection of art, politics, religion, music, science, and other books, all well-organized.

Music

As elsewhere, many **record stores** have closed in LA in recent years due to competition from the Internet. While CDs are the dominant format, vinyl fans will be happy to find LPs here and there, thanks in equal parts to diehard collectors and the constant need for "scratching" by club DJs. The selection below leans toward LA's more one-of-a-kind record stores, though chain lovers will inevitably be drawn to the Virgin Megastore, 8000 Sunset Blvd (⊕323/650-8666), on the Sunset Strip.

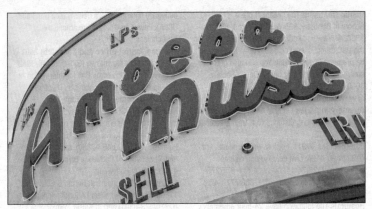

▲ Amoeba Music record store

Amoeba Music 6400 W Sunset Blvd, Hollywood ☎323/245-6400. A vast selection of titles – supposedly numbering around half a million – on CD, tape, and vinyl, which you can freely hear at listening carrels throughout the store. Also presents occasional in-store live music.

Backside Records 139 N San Fernando Rd, Burbank ☎818/559-7573. Though very much geared toward the vinyl-minded, this two-level, DJ-oriented store stocks both LPs and CDs with a broad range of electronica, plus some jazz, rap, and soul.

Counterpoint 5911 Franklin Ave, Hollywood ☎323/957-7965. Offers a terrific smorgasbord of used vinyl, CDs, movies on cassette and DVD, books, and even antique 78 records. Also connected to its own underground art gallery.

Fingerprints 4612 E Second St, Long Beach ☎562/433-4996. Fine indie outfit in the South Bay, offering alternative-leaning CD and vinyl, plus in-store performances from local rockers.

Penny Lane 1661 E Colorado Blvd, Pasadena ☎626/535-0949. New and used records at reasonable prices. Often crowded, this local chain features listening stations and has a good number of LPs as well. Also at 569 S Lake Ave, Pasadena (☎626/568-9999).

Record Surplus 11609 W Pico Blvd, West LA ☎310/478-4217. Massive LP collection of surf music, ancient rock'n'roll, Sixties soundtracks, and unintentionally hilarious spoken-word recordings. Prices are excellent, with many CDs and cassettes offered for low prices.

Rockaway Records 2395 Glendale Blvd, Silver Lake ☎323/664-3232. Great place to come for both used CDs and LPs, as well as DVDs. Also offers old magazines, posters, and memorabilia. Located just east of the Silver Lake reservoir.

Vinyl Fetish 1614 Cahuenga Blvd, Hollywood ☎323/957-2290. Besides the punk and post-punk sounds, a good place to discover what's new on the LA music scene.

Listings

AAA of Southern California 2601 S Figueroa St, South Central LA ☎213/741-3686, ⓦwww .aaa-calif.com. For maps, guides, and other auto information.

Airport information Bob Hope/Burbank ☎818/840-8840, ⓦwww.bobhopeairport.com; John Wayne/Orange County ☎949/252-5006, ⓦwww.ocair.com; LAX ☎310/646-5252, ⓦwww.los-angeles-lax.com; Long Beach ☎562/570-2600, ⓦwww.longbeach.gov/airport; Ontario ☎909/937-2700, ⓦwww.lawa.org.

Beach information Weather conditions for the northern beaches around Malibu ☎310/457-9701, ⓦwww.watchthewater.org, central around Santa Monica ☎310/578-0478, and southern around the South Bay ☎310/379-8471.

Coast Guard Search and Rescue ☎562/980-4444. **Currency exchange** Outside of banking hours, exchange offices are scattered inconveniently throughout town. Most reliable are those at LAX; hours vary by terminal (often daily until 11pm; ☎310/649-2801).

Dental treatment The cheapest place is USC School of Dentistry, 925 W 34th St (☏ 1-888/872-3368, ⓦ www.usc.edu/hsc/dental/patient_care), on the USC Campus, costing $50–200+. Turn up and be prepared to wait all day. You can also get emergency treatment at the LA Dental Society, 3660 Wilshire Blvd #1152 (☏ 213/380-7669, ⓦ www.ladental.com).

Directory inquiries Local ☏ 411 (this is a free call at pay phones); long distance ☏ 1, then area code, then 555-1212.

Emergencies ☏ 911. For less urgent needs: fire ☏ 323/890-4194; civil defense and disaster services ☏ 213/974-1120; police ☏ 1-877/275-5273; poison control center ☏ 1-800/777-6476; food poisoning reports ☏ 213/240-7821.

Hospitals The following have 24-hour emergency departments: Cedars-Sinai Medical Center, 8700 Beverly Blvd, Beverly Hills (☏ 310/423-3277, ⓦ www.csmc.edu); Good Samaritan Hospital, 1225 Wilshire Blvd, Downtown (☏ 213/977-2121, ⓦ www.goodsam.org); UCLA Medical Center, 10833 Le Conte Ave, Westwood (☏ 310/825-9111, ⓦ www.healthcare.ucla.edu).

Internet Available from cyber-oriented coffee shops (see p.166), the *Newsroom Café* (p.163), many city libraries, and sit-down terminals near flight gates at LAX. Outside of libraries, expect to pay around 10–30¢ per minute to browse the Web.

Libraries Downtown's Central Library is the city's finest (see p.93), with branches throughout LA. Other cities also have good main libraries, notably Beverly Hills, 444 N Rexford Drive (☏ 310/288-2244, ⓦ www.bhpl.org), and Santa Monica, 601 Santa Monica Blvd (☏ 310/458-8600, ⓦ www.smpl.org). Specialist libraries are quite common, too, such as the Margaret Herrick Library (p.119) for film-related materials, and the One Institute (see box, p.176) for gay and lesbian publications. For collegiate libraries, USC's Doheny (see p.97) and UCLA's Powell (see p.123) are among the best choices.

Mexican Tourist Office and Consulate 2401 W 6th St, 5th floor, Downtown (☏ 1-800/446-3942, ⓦ www.visitmexico.com). Call for information or pick up a tourist card – necessary if you're crossing the border. Mon–Fri 7am–1pm.

Newspapers USC and UCLA have libraries with overseas newspapers. European papers are on sale at Universal News Agency, 1655 N Las Palmas Ave (☏ 323/467-3850), and World Book and News, 1652 N Cahuenga Blvd (☏ 323/465-4352), both in Hollywood.

Pharmacies Late hours at Horton & Converse, 11600 Wilshire Blvd, West LA (until midnight; ☏ 310/478-0801) and at Kaiser Permanente's West LA hospital, 6041 Cadillac Ave (24hr; ☏ 323/857-2151).

Post office The main Downtown post office is at 900 N Alameda St (☏ 213/617-4404), north of Union Station. Zip Code is 90012; hours are Mon–Fri 8am–5.30pm, Sat 8am–4pm.

Smog LA's air quality can often be very poor and, especially in the valleys in late summer, sometimes dangerous. An air-quality index is published daily in the *LA Times*; if the air is really bad, warnings are issued on TV, radio, and in newspapers. For more information contact the South Coast Air Quality Management District (☏ 1-800/288-7664, ⓦ www.aqmd.gov).

Taxes LA sales tax is 8.25 percent; hotel tax variable, generally around 14 percent.

Traffic Check radio news channels for updates on which freeways are suffering from congestion; if a highway section is particularly immobile, a "SigAlert" will be issued, meaning "avoid at all costs." Radio stations emphasizing traffic reports include KNX 1070 AM; also try ⓦ www.sigalert.com on the Internet.

Travel details

Amtrak trains

Los Angeles to: Anaheim (12 daily; 40min); Fullerton (for Disneyland; 8 daily; 35min); Las Vegas (3 daily; 5hr 50min, bus connection); Oceanside (9 daily; 1hr 50min); Oxnard (6 daily; 1hr 35min); Palm Springs (2 daily; 2hr 35min); Sacramento (1 daily; 14hr); San Bernardino (1 daily; 1hr 45min); San Diego (9 daily; 2hr 50min); San Francisco (3 daily; 9–12hr, with bus connection); San Juan Capistrano (9 daily; 1hr 20min); Santa Barbara (6 daily; 2hr 35min); Tucson (2 daily; 10hr); Ventura (5 daily; 1hr 50min).

Greyhound buses

Los Angeles to: Bakersfield (13 daily; 2hr 45min); Las Vegas (15 daily; 6–8hr); Palm Springs (4 daily; 2–3hr); Phoenix (8 daily; 7–9hr); Sacramento (8 daily; 7–10hr); San Diego (16 daily; 2hr 30min–3hr); San Francisco (14 daily; 8–13hr); Santa Barbara (6 daily; 2–3hr); Santa Cruz (6 daily; 9hr); Tijuana, Mexico (16 daily; 3hr 30min–4hr 30min); Tucson (7 daily; 10–13hr).

2

San Diego and
around

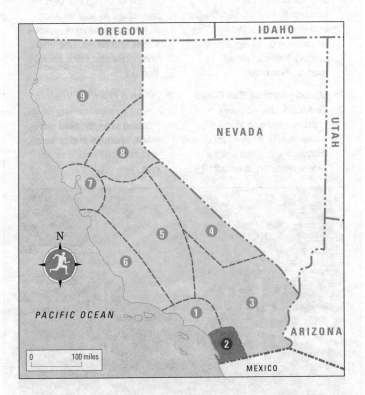

CHAPTER 2 # Highlights

✻ **Balboa Park** The museum centerpiece of San Diego, a 1400-acre green space loaded with history, science, and art, and crowned with the city's popular zoo. See p.203

✻ **Old Town State Historic Park** Stroll among these twenty-five preserved structures from mid-nineteenth-century San Diego, and take in the adjacent re-creation of an eighteenth-century Mexican street market. See p.208

✻ **Mission Basilica San Diego de Alcalá** This complex features medieval stalls, a museum with Native American craftworks, and the state's oldest cemetery. See p.210

✻ **Mission Beach** The most free-spirited and hedonistic of the city's surfing beaches, with acres of bronzed flesh and bikini babes, chaotic bars, and even carnival rides. See p.214

✻ **La Jolla** One of Southern California's swankiest beach towns, offering cozy digs for relaxation, as well as a top-notch art museum, evocative sands and coves, and many fine hotels and restaurants. See p.215

✻ **Julian** A charming Western town that's compelling for its fetching scenery, gold mine relics, antiques and galleries, and especially good apple pies. See p.236

▲ The Botanical Building, Balboa Park

2

San Diego and around

Lacking much of the urban chaos, social vitality, and pop-cultural energy of its neighboring megalopolis to the north, **San Diego** and its surrounding county represent the acceptable, conservative veneer of Southern California. Surpassed long ago by Los Angeles in the race to become the region's essential city, San Diego was for some time considered an insignificant blot between LA and Mexico, home only to right-wing pensioners and cloistered suburbanites. Although that stereotype still has a large measure of truth, San Diego also boasts considerable charm, its gracefully curving bay, appealing oceanside vistas, clutch of fine museums, and big-name tourist attractions rivaling anything in LA and making for an excellent weekend, or week, of travel in the California sun.

Outside San Diego County's eponymous urban center, you can find a host of compelling destinations. The **North County** includes small, enticing coastal communities from the northern edge of San Diego itself to the Camp Pendleton marine base, as well as the vineyards and avocado groves that reach east into wilder mountain country. Beyond the tiny and insular beach towns, several deep forests and state parks are ideal for exploring via hiking trails and obscure backroads.

As most media-watchers know, countless Mexicans stream into Southern California, above and below official radar. Many are hotel and restaurant workers, but first- and especially second-generation immigrants are gradually becoming integrated into less menial levels of the workforce. However, unlike in LA, where Latino newcomers are flexing their political muscle, those of San Diego County are largely ghettoized, still viewed by the blinkered white gentry as welfare-cheating detriments to society, rather than essential boosters of the local economy. Not surprisingly, then, the first stop for many migrants isn't the more convenient San Diego, but its urban big brother another two hours north.

San Bernardino (30 miles)

SAN DIEGO & AROUND

Los Angeles (45 miles)

Borrego Springs (5 miles)

Arizona (90 miles)

CLEVELAND NATIONAL FOREST

Mission San Antonio De Pala

PALOMAR MOUNTAIN STATE PARK AND OBSERVATORY

ANZA-BORREGO DESERT

CAMP PENDLETON MARINE BASE

Mission San Luis Rey

GUAJOME COUNTY PARK

Lawrence Welk Resort

Mission Santa Ysabel

VOLCAN MOUNTAIN PRESERVE

Oceanside

Carlsbad

Legoland

San Pasqual Battlefield

Santa Ysabel

South Carlsbad Beach

Leucadia

Escondido

SAN DIEGO WILD ANIMAL PARK

Julian

San Elijo Beach

Encinitas

Rancho Santa Fe

Ramona

California Wolf Center

Solana Beach

Del Mar

CUYAMACA RANCHO STATE PARK

TORREY PINES STATE PRESERVE

PACIFIC OCEAN

Blacks Beach

LA JOLLA

CLEVELAND

PACIFIC BEACH

MISSION BEACH

NATIONAL

OCEAN BEACH

OLD TOWN

FOREST

POINT LOMA

DOWNTOWN

Balboa Park

San Diego

N

CORONADO

IMPERIAL BEACH

BORDER FIELD STATE PARK

San Ysidro

0   15 miles

Tijuana   MEXICO

San Diego

Baking in the sun, its humidity tempered by ocean breezes, **SAN DIEGO** is an ideal holiday resort for hordes of tourists, most of whom arrive for its terrific beaches, major attractions like the San Diego Zoo and SeaWorld, and excellent museums in Balboa Park. More enterprising visitors may also wish to explore the city's historic Downtown, namely the Gaslamp District, whose style of preservation varies from architecturally animated to high-gloss corporate to thick historic kitsch.

The traditional image of San Diegans as conformist, affluent, and Republican is true to a large extent – San Diego has as much in common with Salt Lake City or Phoenix as it does with Los Angeles or San Francisco. However, there are also a few unexpected undercurrents, from the emergence and tolerance of a vibrant, upscale gay scene in Hillcrest to increasing numbers of liberal students and professionals. The presence of three **college campuses** – SDSU, UCSD, and USD – has also helped the city lose some of its rigid and reactionary character. Still, while the city's once-notorious smugness and orthodoxy has diminished, its insular civic character remains – the town is notorious as having one of the most corrupt political cultures in the nation, and ongoing scandals involving bribes, municipal kickbacks, and all manner of secret wheeling-and-dealing do little to help this image.

Obviously, the political culture is much less interesting to tourists than the sparkling weather, and travelers will hardly notice this darker side while enjoying the long white beaches, sunny weather, and bronzed bodies – giving rise to the city's nickname, "Sandy Ego." Paradoxically, though, for such a sunny place throughout the year, San Diego is susceptible to extended periods of overcast skies and light rain when you'd least expect it – the so-called "June Gloom" that's caused by a climatic anomaly and leaves visitors scratching their heads as they trudge through damp beach sands.

Some history

The first European to land on California soil, Portuguese adventurer and Spanish agent Juan Rodríguez Cabrillo, put ashore at Point Loma, ten miles from today's Downtown San Diego, in 1542. White settlement didn't begin until two centuries later, however, with the building in 1769 of a Catholic mission – the first in California – and a military garrison on a site overlooking San Diego Bay. Later conflict between land-holding *Californios* and the fresh waves of settlers from the East led to America's capture of San Diego in 1847, in the midst of the Mexican-American War. However, the city missed out on the new mail route to the West and was plagued by a series of droughts through the 1860s, causing many bankruptcies and economic problems. Although the transcontinental Santa Fe Railroad link was short-lived – repeated flooding forced the terminus to be moved north to Los Angeles, depriving San Diego of direct rail service to the East – its establishment resulted in an economic boom through the 1880s. In 1915 came the first of two international expositions in Balboa Park, which were to establish San Diego's nationwide reputation.

In part because of its lack of direct railway access to the East Coast, the city has long been overshadowed by Los Angeles in trade and economic significance, though it has used its strategic seaside location to become a military stronghold. During World War II, the US Navy took advantage of the city's sheltered bays and made San Diego its Pacific Command Center – a function it retains, as the military continues to dominate the local economy.

However, it is San Diego's reputation as an ocean-oriented "resort city" that provides much of its modern relevance (at least to those not in uniform). Although it has a formidable population of more than a million people, making it the seventh-largest city in the US, for most tourists it's synonymous only with getting tanned, yachting around the bay, surfing a killer break, and hanging out at the zoo – all worthwhile pursuits to be sure, but intrepid visitors will find much more here if staying longer than just a few days.

Arrival and information

Motorists will find it simple to reach the city center from any of three interstate **highways**: I-5, the main artery from Los Angeles and the rest of California, follows the coast and the northern parts of the central city, hits Downtown (with I-805 as a bypass that skirts it), and heads on to Mexico; from the east, I-8 runs by Old Town before terminating in Ocean Beach; and I-15, coming from inland San Diego County and Arizona, cuts through the city's northern and eastern suburbs. **Parking lots** are scattered around Downtown, and there's plenty of metered parking – free overnight, but not allowed on evenings reserved for street cleaning.

All forms of **public transportation** drop you in or near the heart of Downtown San Diego. Amtrak **trains** on the Pacific Surfliner route from LA use the Santa Fe Railroad Depot, close to the western end of Broadway at 1050 Kettner Boulevard (℡ 1-800/872-7245), while the Greyhound **bus** terminal is six blocks east at Broadway and First Avenue (℡ 619/239-6737). Lindbergh Field **airport** (aka San Diego International; ℡ 619/400-2400, 🌐 www.san.org) is only two miles from Downtown, and is connected to it by buses #923 ($1.75) and #992 ($2.25); the services start at 5am and finish around 11pm to midnight. Given the short distance, **taxis** to Downtown aren't expensive ($10 one way), and some hotels offer guests a free **airport limo** service; alternatively, **ground-transit services** such as EZ Ride (℡ 1-800/777-0585, 🌐 www.ezrideshuttle .com) and XPress Shuttle (℡ 1-800/900-RIDE, 🌐 www.xpressshuttle.com) offer transportation downtown in a shuttle bus for $8–10 one way. The main **car rental** firms all have desks at the airport (see p.37).

A good first stop in the city is the **International Visitor Information Center**, near the bay at 1040 W Broadway (daily 9am–4pm, summer until 5pm; ℡ 619/236-1212, 🌐 www.seeyouinsandiego.com), which has maps, visitor's guides, and other publications covering the arts and local museums; another outlet is located in La Jolla at 7966 Herschel Avenue (℡ 619/236-1212). The HI-AYH office, inside the hostel foyer at 521 Market Street (24hr; ℡ 619/525-1531, 🌐 www.hihostels.com), is another good resource. For eating and entertainment information, the free, weekly *San Diego Reader* (🌐 www.sdreader.com) can be found in many shops, bars, and clubs; the entertainment section of the *San Diego Union-Tribune* (🌐 entertainment.signonsandiego.com) is also useful.

City transportation

Despite its size, **getting around** San Diego without a car is slow but not too difficult, whether you use buses, the light-rail-like San Diego Trolley, or a rented bike. Traveling can be harder at night, with most transit routes closing down around 11pm or midnight. The transportation system won't break anyone's budget, especially with longer-term tickets and passes reducing costs over a few days or weeks. **Taxis** are also an affordable option: the average fare is anywhere from $5 for a jaunt around Downtown, to $10 for Coronado, to $20 or so to get up to the more northerly beaches (Ocean, Mission, or Pacific).

Buses

The overarching **bus** system within San Diego County is called the Metropolitan Transit System (MTS), of which there are three major units. By far the most prominent is San Diego Transit Corporation, or SDTC (℡ 1-800/266-6883, 🌐 www.sdcommute.com), which offers typical one-way fares of $1.75 and $2.25, $2.50–4.00 for more distant routes, and $5–10 for the most lengthy journeys into rural terrain; the exact fare is required when boarding (dollar bills are accepted). Transfers are often free, but those made onto express buses or between transit systems (bus to trolley, bus to Coaster, etc) will require the price

Reduced-rate tickets and passes

If you intend to use public transportation a lot, buy the **Day Tripper** transit pass, which lasts from one to four consecutive days ($5, $9, $12, and $15, respectively) and is valid on any San Diego Transit bus, as well as the trolley. If you're around for a few weeks and plan to use buses regularly, get a **Monthly Pass**, giving unlimited rides throughout one calendar month for $60 (kids under 18 for $30), or the half-price, two-week version which goes on sale midway through each month (pass information at ☏1-800/266-6883, ⊛ www.sdcommute.com).

of the higher fare. Service is reliable and frequent, particularly Downtown, which is known on route maps and timetables as "Center City." If you're headed anywhere in the North County, the major operator is North County Transit District (fares $2; ☏1-800/266-6883, ⊛ www.gonctd.com).

If you have any queries about San Diego's local buses, call the **Transit Store**, at First and Broadway (Mon–Fri 9am–5pm; ☏619/234-1060), for detailed timetables, the free *Regional Transit Guide*, and information on the Day Tripper Transit Pass and monthly passes. If you know your point of departure and destination, you can get automated bus information by phoning ☏619/685-4900.

The trolley

Complementing county bus lines is the **San Diego Trolley**, often called the "Tijuana Trolley" because it travels sixteen miles from the Santa Fe Railroad Depot (departures from C Street) to the US–Mexico border in San Ysidro – a 45-minute trip. Fares are $1.25–3.00, depending on how long you stay on, and Day Tripper packages are also available (see above). One-way tickets should be bought from the machines at trolley stops, which also offer round-trip tickets. Of the two routes, the **Blue Line** is the more visitor-oriented, starting in the north with Qualcomm Stadium and Mission San Diego and continuing through to Old Downtown and Downtown San Diego, then turning south to Mexico. From the transfer station at Imperial and 12th, the trolley's **Orange Line** usefully loops around Downtown, but offers little else of interest to visitors, darting out toward the eastern suburbs. The newer **Green Line** also reaches these suburbs, starting at Old Town, but is really only useful for visitors if you're headed to Mission San Diego or Qualcomm Stadium. Trolleys leave

Useful San Diego bus routes

The following buses connect **Downtown San Diego** with the surrounding area:
Balboa Park #1, #3, #3A, #7, #7A, #7B, #120

Coronado #901, #904

East San Diego #1, #7, #7A, #7B, #10, #13, #15, #955, #965

Hillcrest #1, #3, #10, #11, #83, #120

Imperial Beach #901, #933, #934

La Jolla #30

Mission Beach #8, #9

Ocean Beach #35, #923

Old Town #8, #9, #10, #14, #28A, #28B, #35, #44, #105

Pacific Beach #8, #9, #27, #30

Point Loma peninsula #28A, #28B

Old Town Trolley Tour

Not to be confused with the San Diego Trolley, the **Old Town Trolley Tour** is a two-hour narrated trip around San Diego's most popular spots, including Downtown, Balboa Park, the San Diego Zoo, Old Town, and Coronado, aboard an open-sided motor-driven carriage. A single ticket (available daily 9am–4pm, summer until 5pm; $30, kids $15) lasts all day and you can board and reboard the trolley at any of its stops. If you're short of time, the tour is a simple way to cover a lot of ground quickly. Leaflets detailing the various routes are found in hotel lobbies and at tourist information offices (☏619/298-8687, ⊛www.historictours.com/sandiego).

every fifteen minutes during the day (starting around 5am); the last service back from San Ysidro leaves at 1am, so an evening of south-of-the-border revelry and a return to San Diego the same night is quite possible.

The Coaster

North San Diego County is linked to Downtown via a simple commuter light-rail system called **The Coaster**, which includes eight stops from Oceanside through Carlsbad, Encinitas, Solana Beach, Sorrento Valley, and Old Town, ending up at the Santa Fe Railroad Depot. On weekday mornings, six trains run southbound, with the same number returning northbound for the late-afternoon and early-evening commute, while four trains make the trip on Saturdays. Fares range from $4 to $5.50 one way, $2 to $2.75 for seniors, and $115 to $154 for a monthly pass (☏1-800/262-7837, ⊛www.gonctd.com). The Coaster also provides a good alternative way of reaching Los Angeles, with transfers at Oceanside onto the Metrolink commuter rail system (see p.78), linking San Diego County all the way to Downtown LA and even up to Oxnard in Ventura County.

Cycling

San Diego is a fine city for **cycling**, with many miles of bike paths as well as some agreeable park and coastal rides. **Rental shops** are easy to find, especially around bike-friendly areas, and some outlets also rent skateboards, rollerblades, and surfboards (prices for all start around $5–8 per hour, $15–20 per day; $25–35 per day for surfboards). Reliable shops include Bicycle Barn, 746 Emerald Street, Pacific Beach (☏858/581-3665), and Cheap Rentals, 3689 Mission Boulevard, Mission Beach (☏858/488-9070, ⊛www.cheap-rentals.com). You can carry bikes on the San Diego Bay ferry for an extra 50¢, and on several city bus routes for no added charge. Board at any bus stop displaying a bike sign and tack your machine securely to the back of the bus. The Transit Store (☏619/234-1060, ⊛www.sdcommute.com) provides information on bicycle commuting, and distributes free passes that allow you to take your bike on the trolley. You can also order a regional bike map in advance of your trip from RideLink (☏1-800/266-6883, ⊛www.ridelink.org).

Accommodation

Accommodation is readily available in San Diego, with abundant hotels and motels, and a decent selection of hostels and B&Bs. However, there are just a few inconveniently located **campgrounds** in the area.

Downtown offers the best base if you're without a car, featuring two hostels and a batch of affordable hotels in renovated classic buildings – along with a few chic **boutique hotels**. Prices are more expensive at beach **motels** and hotels – and nearly stratospheric at the bigger-name golf-and-tennis resorts – though Ocean Beach and Pacific Beach have **hostels**, too. Another group of motels can be found around Old Town (useful if you're driving or just staying for a night while seeing the area), and some of the cheapest motels line the roads into the city.

Bed and breakfasts are a popular option, especially in Hillcrest. Contact the Downtown visitor center (see p.188) for more information on some of the local options, or get in touch with the Bed & Breakfast Guild of San Diego (℡1-800/619-7666, Ⓦwww.bandbguildsandiego.org).

If you're arriving in summer, when prices increase and availability is limited, it's wise to **book in advance**. The International Visitor Information Center (see p.188) has accommodation leaflets (many with discount vouchers) and will phone hotels, motels, or hostels on your behalf at no charge.

Gay travelers are unlikely to encounter hostility in San Diego, and several hotels and bed and breakfasts are particularly noted for their friendliness (see p.227 for more information).

Downtown

See the map on p.200 for locations.

Bristol 1055 First Ave ℡619/232-6141, Ⓦwww.thebristolsandiego.com. Centrally located boutique hotel with stylish modern decor and tasteful amenities. With in-room CD players and high-speed Internet access, it's worth a visit, especially considering the area. ❼

Comfort Inn 600 G St at Seventh Ave ℡619/238-4100, Ⓦwww.comfortinn.com. Fairly unexciting but serviceable chain hotel in the Gaslamp District, with cable TV, microwaves, Internet access, and fridges in each room. ❼ A cheaper branch, with similar amenities, is at 719 Ash St (℡619/232-2525; ❺).

Courtyard San Diego 530 Broadway ℡619/446-3000, Ⓦwww.marriott.com. Stunning historic renovation of a 1920s Renaissance Revival bank, now home to upscale guestrooms and suites, and loaded with beautiful period detail in the lobby and even a conference room in an old-time bank vault. ❼

Horton Grand 311 Island Ave at Third Ave ℡1-800/542-1886, Ⓦwww.hortongrand.com. Classy amalgam of two 120-year-old hotels, with fireplaces in most of the 132 antique-flavored rooms (some with balconies), on-site restaurant, piano bar, and Saturday-afternoon high tea from 2.30 to 5pm. ❻

La Pensione 606 W Date St at India St ℡619/236-8000, Ⓦwww.lapensionehotel.com. Great-value small hotel in a quiet area within walking distance of the core of the city center. The rooms, around a central court, are small but tastefully decorated and equipped with fridges, and there's an on-site laundry and two restaurants. ❹

Manchester Grand Hyatt One Market Place at Harbor Dr ℡619/232-1234, Ⓦwww.manchestergrand.hyatt.com. The most prominent hotel along the waterfront (and among the biggest in the state), a pair of gleaming white slabs of luxury with all the top-notch amenities: pool, spas, health club, several restaurants and lounges, and rooms with expansive views of the bay. Also ground zero for conventioneers. ❻

Omni San Diego 675 L St ℡619/231-6664, Ⓦwww.omnihotels.com. Sleek modern high-rise in the Gaslamp District and linked to Petco Park by skybridge; rooms come with Internet access and good city or bay views, and some with flatscreen TVs and DVD players. Also an on-site gym, pool and spa, and several fine restaurants. ❽

Solamar 435 6th Ave ℡619/531-8740, Ⓦwww.hotelsolamar.com. Very tasteful and modern boutique hotel central to the Gaslamp District, whose rooms have Internet access, flatscreen TVs and CD and DVD players, and which also offers spa and gym facilities and in-room yoga accessories. Suites with soaking and jetted tubs add to the hip appeal. ❽

🏃 **The U.S. Grant** 326 Broadway between Third and Fourth avenues ℡1-800/237-5029, Ⓦwww.usgrant.net. Across from Horton Plaza, Downtown's poshest address since 1910, with grand Neoclassical design, chandeliers, marble floors, and cozy but comfortable guestrooms ($300) with Internet access and more capacious suites. The elegant ballrooms and swank conference rooms are also worth a peek. ❾

Westgate 1055 Second Ave ℡1-800/522-1564, Ⓦwww.westgatehotel.com. Centrally sited hotel

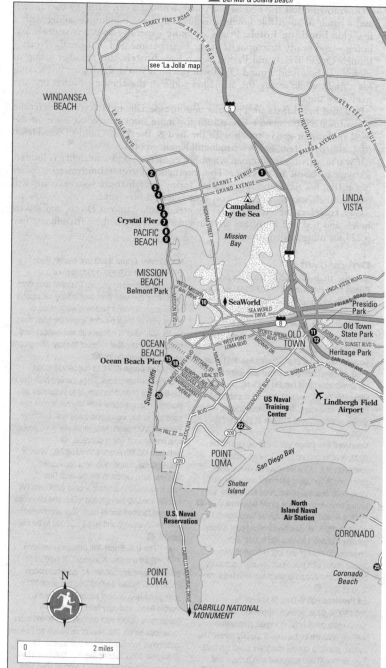

▲ Del Mar & Solana Beach

TORREY PINES ROAD

ARDATH ROAD

see 'La Jolla' map

WINDANSEA
BEACH

LA JOLLA BLVD

CLAIREMONT DRIVE

GENESEE AVENUE

BALBOA AVENUE

GARNET AVENUE ①
GRAND AVENUE

LINDA
VISTA

②
③
④
⑤
⑥
⑦ Crystal Pier
⑧
⑨

INGRAHAM STREET

Campland
by the Sea

Mission
Bay

PACIFIC
BEACH

MISSION
BEACH
Belmont Park

WEST MISSION
BAY DRIVE

MISSION BLVD

⑩

SeaWorld

SEA WORLD
DRIVE

LINDA VISTA ROAD

FRIARS ROAD

Presidio
Park

SPORTS ARENA BLVD

WEST POINT
LOMA BLVD

MIDWAY DR

Old Town
State Park

OLD
TOWN

⑪
⑫ JUAN ST

SUNSET BLVD

Heritage Park

SAN DIEGO AVE

OCEAN
BEACH
Ocean Beach Pier

Sunset Cliffs

⑮ ⑱
W. VOLTAIRE ST

NEWPORT AVE
UDAL ST

SUNSET CLIFFS BLVD

NARRAGANSETT
AVENUE

CATALINA
BLVD

VOLTAIRE ST

BARNETT AVE

PACIFIC HIGHWAY

US Naval
Training
Center

✈ Lindbergh Field
Airport

⑳

HILL ST

(209)

�22
(209)

POINT
LOMA

San Diego Bay

Shelter
Island

North
Island Naval
Air Station

U.S. Naval
Reservation

CABRILLO MEMORIAL DRIVE

CORONADO

POINT
LOMA

Coronado
Beach

⑤

CABRILLO NATIONAL
MONUMENT

N

0   2 miles

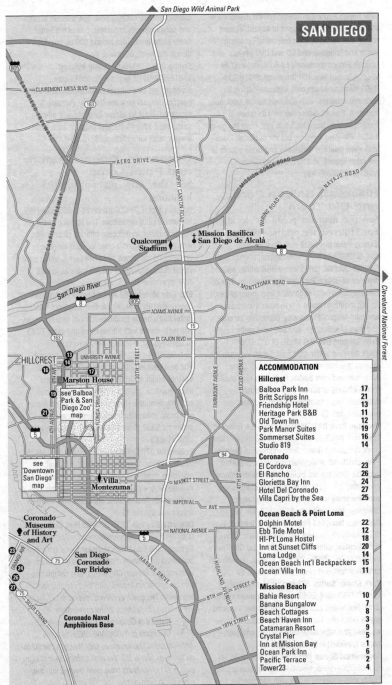

San Diego Wild Animal Park

SAN DIEGO

CLAIREMONT MESA BLVD

SAN DIEGO FREEWAY

AERO DRIVE

MURPHY CANYON ROAD

MISSION GORGE ROAD

WARING ROAD

NAVAJO ROAD

Qualcomm Stadium

† Mission Basilica San Diego de Alcalá

San Diego River

MONTEZUMA ROAD

ADAMS AVENUE

EL CAJON BLVD

Cleveland National Forest

HILLCREST

University Avenue

6TH AVE

4TH AVE

Marston House

see 'Balboa Park & San Diego Zoo' map

see 'Downtown San Diego' map

30TH STREET

FLORIDA DRIVE

FAIRMOUNT AVENUE

EUCLID AVENUE

47TH ST

Villa Montezuma

MARKET STREET

IMPERIAL AVE

NATIONAL AVENUE

Coronado Museum of History and Art

San Diego-Coronado Bay Bridge

HARBOR DRIVE

HIGHLAND AVENUE

8TH AVENUE STREET

18TH STREET

SILVER STRAND

ORANGE AVE

Coronado Naval Amphibious Base

Imperial Beach

ACCOMMODATION

Hillcrest
Balboa Park Inn	17
Britt Scripps Inn	21
Friendship Hotel	13
Heritage Park B&B	11
Old Town Inn	12
Park Manor Suites	19
Sommerset Suites	16
Studio 819	14

Coronado
El Cordova	23
El Rancho	26
Glorietta Bay Inn	24
Hotel Del Coronado	27
Villa Capri by the Sea	25

Ocean Beach & Point Loma
Dolphin Motel	22
Ebb Tide Motel	12
HI-Pt Loma Hostel	18
Inn at Sunset Cliffs	20
Loma Lodge	14
Ocean Beach Int'l Backpackers	15
Ocean Villa Inn	11

Mission Beach
Bahia Resort	10
Banana Bungalow	7
Beach Cottages	8
Beach Haven Inn	3
Catamaran Resort	9
Crystal Pier	5
Inn at Mission Bay	1
Ocean Park Inn	2
Pacific Terrace	6
Tower23	4

near Horton Plaza with classic French overtones in the lobby (almost to the point of kitsch), elegant rooms that variously offer balconies, European decor and antiques, and CD and DVD players, and upscale French restaurant *Le Fontainebleau*. ❼

Westin Broadway 400 Broadway ☎619/239-4500, ⊛www.westin.com. Upscale lodging for business travelers, with spacious rooms, pool, spa, and gym. Visually distinctive with its green-lit towers, looking like a high-rise relic from the go-go 1980s. ❼ Also a nearby branch at Horton Plaza with even swankier amenities and close access to the retail spaces, at 910 Broadway Circle (☎619/239-2200; ❽).

Hillcrest, Balboa Park, and Old Town

See the map on p.203 for locations. For Hillcrest, see pp.192–193.

Balboa Park Inn 3402 Park Blvd, Hillcrest ☎1-800/938-8181, ⊛www.balboaparkinn.com. Spanish Colonial, gay-oriented B&B within walking distance of Balboa Park and the museums. The 26 themed suites (with oceanside, Impressionist, and Tarzan motifs, to name a few) have microwaves and mini-fridges. Prices vary, depending on size and level of kitsch. ❺, add $40 for a suite.

Britt Scripps Inn 406 Maple St ☎1-888/881-1991, ⊛www.brittscripps.com. Smart Victorian inn located in a marvelously restored 1887 Queen Anne mansion near Balboa Park, with nine plush rooms offering antiques, wireless Internet, flatscreen TVs, and some modern boutique amenities, too. ❽

Heritage Park B&B 2470 Heritage Park Row, Old Town ☎1-800/995-2470, ⊛www.heritageparkinn .com. A restored Queen Anne mansion in Heritage Park, chock-full of Victorian trappings. Breakfast and afternoon tea are included. The twelve rooms and suites are in the usual lace-and-chintz style, with one small unit going for $140 per night. Otherwise most units are $170–180. ❻

Old Town Inn 4444 Pacific Hwy, Old Town ☎1-800/643-3025, ⊛www.oldtown-inn.com. Convenient location within a few strides of the Old Town's liveliest areas, offering Internet access, complimentary breakfast, and clean, simple rooms. ❸

Park Manor Suites 525 Spruce St, near Balboa Park ☎1-800/874-2649, ⊛www.parkmanorsuites .com. Renovated apartment complex that's around eighty years old. The tasteful hotel suites feature kitchens and nice, large sitting areas, and continental breakfast is included. ❻

Sommerset Suites 606 Washington St, Hillcrest ☎1-800/962-9665, ⊛www.sommersetsuites.com. Eighty well-equipped suites with kitchenettes and

Internet access, offering pool, spa, Internet access, and complimentary breakfast. One of the better deals in the area. Save around $30 by booking during the week, otherwise ❼.

Studio 819 819 University Ave, Hillcrest ☎619/542-0819, ⊛www.studio819.com. Standard but safe budget accommodation in the heart of Hillcrest near the freeway. Primarily a residential hotel for longer-term stays, it offers microwave, kitchenette, and fridge in each room. Weekly rates for as little as $378. ❸

Coronado, Ocean Beach, and Point Loma

See the map on pp.192–193 for locations.

Dolphin Motel 2912 Garrison St ☎866/353-7897, ⊛www.dolphin-motel.com. The epitome of the roadside motel, in this case offering clean rooms with queen beds and a good location roughly between Ocean Beach and Point Loma, within easy reach of the airport. Off-reason rates as low as $50, otherwise ❸.

Ebb Tide Motel 5082 W Point Loma Blvd, Ocean Beach ☎619/224-9339. Modest-sized, pet-friendly motel that's handy for the beach and features clean, adequate rooms with kitchenettes and cable TV. ❸

El Cordova 1351 Orange Ave, Coronado ☎1-800/229-2032, ⊛www.elcordovahotel.com. The best deal in Coronado, comprising Spanish Colonial buildings from 1902 arranged around lovely gardens. There's a pool, and many rooms have kitchenettes. Huge price spread, from cheap and basic units without a/c to grandly elegant suites for $839. Save $40 on basic rooms in winter, otherwise ❻.

El Rancho 370 Orange Ave, Coronado ☎619/435-2251, ⊛www.elranchocoronado.com. Small, attractive motel with pleasant but ultra-basic decor, making for one of the cheapest deals on this side of the water. Rooms come equipped with microwaves and fridges. ❸

Glorietta Bay Inn 1630 Glorietta Blvd, Coronado ☎619/435-3101, ⊛www.gloriettabayinn.com. Striking 1908 Edwardian mansion that's since been converted into swank modern rooms and suites, all with Internet access, CD players, and complimentary breakfast, and some with kitchenettes and balconies. The place drips with period detail, from the antique chandeliers to the grand piano. ❼

🏃 **Hotel del Coronado** 1500 Orange Ave, Coronado ☎1-800/468-3533, ⊛www .hoteldel.com. The luxurious spot that put Coronado on the map and is still the area's major tourist sight (see p.211) – millions have been poured into the complex in renovations, and the striking rooms and suites, expansive bay views, and old-fashioned Victorian charm from 1888 still give the place much appeal. ❽

Inn at Sunset Cliffs 1370 Sunset Cliffs Blvd, Point Loma ☎1-866/786-2543, ⊛www .innatsunsetcliffs.com. Perched on a precipice above the ocean, this property has a range of units, from its entry-level suites with poolside access or kitchens to its more elaborate digs with Jacuzzi tubs, luxury decor, and stunning oceanside views. From ❻

Loma Lodge 3202 Rosecrans St, Ocean Beach ☎1-800/266-0511, ⊛www.lomalodge.com. Among the best values in the area, a decent motel with an agreeable pool and complimentary breakfast; good for exploring the peninsula, but not close to the beach. ❹

Ocean Villa Inn 5142 W Point Loma Blvd, Ocean Beach ☎1-800/759-0012. Handy for visiting the sands, and a main draw for canine-lovers, since the place is pet-friendly and next to Dog Beach; the ocean-view rooms feature kitchenettes, fridges, and microwaves, and some have patios or balconies; there's also a pool. ❺

Villa Capri by the Sea 1417 Orange Ave, Coronado ☎1-800/231-3954, ⊛www .villacapribythesea.com. Old-style motel-like accommodation that has more going for it than you might expect at first glance. Offers fourteen suites with kitchenette, Internet access, VCR, and a homely feel in a classic 1950s structure with some modern style inside. Pool and central location by the beach are other big pluses. ❻

Mission Beach and Pacific Beach

See the map on pp.192–193 for locations.

Bahia Resort 998 W Mission Bay Drive, Mission Beach ☎1-800/576-4229, ⊛www.bahiahotel.com. Prime beachside accommodation with expansive ocean views, watersport rentals, pool, and Jacuzzi. Options range from cozy but pleasant rooms in a palm-garden setting to pricier bayside suites. Off-season ❻, summer ❼

Beach Cottages 4255 Ocean Blvd, Mission Beach ☎858/483-7440, ⊛www.beachcottages.com. Beside the beach, three blocks south of the pier, this relaxing spot offers a wide range of accommo-dation. Most units have kitchenettes, all have fridges. Prices vary by season: motel ❹–❺, studios ❻–❼, cottages and apartments ❼–❽.

Beach Haven Inn 4740 Mission Blvd, Pacific Beach ☎1-800/831-6323, ⊛www.beachhaveninn .com. Clean and tidy motel accommodation with comfortable, tastefully decorated rooms around a heated pool; continental breakfast included. One of

the nicest places to unwind at the beach, and plenty cheap to boot. Off-season ❸ but can double in summer.

Catamaran Resort 3999 Mission Blvd, Pacific Beach ☎1-800/422-8386, ⊛www .catamaranresort.com. A range of upscale units, from entry-level garden-view rooms to swank bayside suites; rooms come with Internet access, and many with prime seaward views. There's also an on-site restaurant, bar, water sports, spa, Jacuzzi, and volleyball courts. ❼

Crystal Pier 4500 Ocean Blvd, Pacific Beach ☎1-800/748-5894, ⊛www.crystalpier.com. Quaint, deluxe cottages built in the 1920s and situated right on the pier. All units are suites with private decks and most have kitchenettes. Can get pricey, but you stay literally on the water. ❼

Inn at Mission Bay 4545 Mission Bay Drive ☎858/483-4222, ⊛www.innatmissionbay.com. If you're headed to SeaWorld (3 miles away), you'll need to save your money for the sky-high tickets – and with that in mind, this is a good, economical choice whose clean motel rooms have Internet access, fridges, and microwaves, plus access to a heated pool and continental breakfast. Save $25 by booking midweek. ❹

Ocean Park Inn 710 Grand Ave, Pacific Beach ☎1-800/316-4140, ⊛www.oceanparkinn.com. Another solid beachfront choice, offering Internet access, microwaves, fridges, and complimentary breakfast, plus a pool and spa. Nothing too flashy for the price, but the central location on the boardwalk is a good draw. Summer ❼, though rates can drop by $70 in the low season.

Pacific Terrace 610 Diamond St, Pacific Beach ☎858/581-3500, ⊛www.pacificterrace.com. Entrancing, chic accommodation on the beach, with rooms ($419) offering kitchenettes, fridges, Internet access, and sea-facing balconies, and suites with the full range of swanky amenities. ❾

Tower23 723 Felspar St, Pacific Beach ☎1-866/869-3723, ⊛www.tower23hotel.com. Named after a lifeguard tower, this is among the most chic of all boutique hotels, offering rooms ($389) with flatscreen TVs, Internet access, and designer furnishings, and even more stylish suites that variously come with balconies, cabanas, and whirlpool tubs. Summer ❾, off-season ❽

La Jolla

See the map on p.216 for locations.

Bed & Breakfast Inn at La Jolla 7753 Draper Ave ☎1-800/582-2466, ⊛www.innlajolla.com. Designed in 1913 by early modernist Irving Gill, a collection of fifteen themed rooms – topped by the $459-a-night Irving Gill Penthouse, inexplicably decorated in Victoriana – with tranquil gardens, great service, and nice proximity to the beach and art museum. ❼

Empress 7766 Fay Ave ☎858/454-3001. ⓦwww .empress-hotel.com. A range of rooms and suites at this centrally located property, where the larger units also have jetted tubs and there's on-site Internet access, continental breakfast, gym, spa, and sauna. ❼

Grande Colonial 910 Prospect St ☎1-888/530-5766, ⓦwww.thegrandecolonial.com. A 1920s landmark in the heart of La Jolla and a short walk from the cove. Vaguely Victorian decor in cozy but elegant rooms with boutique furnishings and a handful of larger suites, and excellent package deals – especially in winter. ❼

Hotel Parisi 1111 Prospect St ☎1-858/454-1511, ⓦwww.hotelparisi.com. Top-shelf boutique hotel with a New Age twist, offering *feng shui* design and rooms ($305) with balconies, designer furnishings, spas, CD and DVD players, and some ocean views. If all this luxury still doesn't relax you, there's a full complement of aromatherapy, acupuncture, meditation, and other "wellness" services to properly align your chakras. ❾

La Jolla Cove Suites 1155 Coast Blvd ☎1-888/525-6552, ⓦwww.lajollacove.com. Kitchen-equipped rooms and suites right by the sea – some of the rooms have sprawling oceanfront balconies. Also with on-site Jacuzzi, pool, and complimentary breakfast. Basic studio units go for around $200, but for anything spacious you'll need to drop at least $100 more. ❼

La Jolla Inn 1110 Prospect St ☎1-888/855-7829, ⓦwww.lajollainn.com. Charming European-style lodge, well priced for the area, with ocean views (for a few dollars more), fridges, balconies, Internet access, complimentary breakfast, and afternoon tea on the sundeck. The inn offers studios as well. ❼

🏃 **La Valencia** 1132 Prospect St ☎1-800/451-0772, ⓦwww.lavalencia.com. Radiant pink favorite of Hollywood celebs in the

1920s. Today only a slightly less glamorous spot, but no less plush, with capacious rooms (starting at $275), suites ($600 and up), and elaborate villas ($1500). All boast beautiful decor, nice amenities, and good sea or garden views, plus an on-site pool, spa, and fitness center. ❽

Hostels

Banana Bungalow 707 Reed Ave, Pacific Beach ☎1-800/546-7835, ⓦwww.bananabungalow.com. Although the rooms are small and drab, the beachside location, volleyball, BBQ cookouts, and lively atmosphere make it worthwhile. Free breakfasts, Internet access, parties, and a communal kitchen are included. Six-person dorms $20–25 by season; private rooms $65–105. Take bus #30 with a five-minute walk to arrive.

HI-Point Loma Hostel 3790 Udall St, Ocean Beach ☎619/223-4778, ⓦwww.sandiegohostels .org. Well-run and friendly, though without the party atmosphere prevailing in other hostels. Located a few miles from the beach and six miles from Downtown (via bus #923), the hostel features a large kitchen, free breakfast, a patio, and weekly bonfires. Eight-bed (or smaller) dorms $17–22, private rooms for three or more $42–48.

HI-San Diego Downtown Hostel 521 Market St at Fifth, Downtown ☎619/525-1531, ⓦwww. sandiegohostels.org. Centrally located, especially good for the Gaslamp District and Horton Plaza. HI members pay $19–24 for a dorm bed, nonmembers $22–27; private doubles cost $50–57. Free wireless Internet access, free breakfast, garden, library, and trips to Tijuana. No curfew.

USA Hostels – San Diego 726 Fifth Ave between F and G streets, Downtown ☎1-800/438-8622, ⓦwww.usahostels.com/sandiego/s-index.html. Well-placed hostel on the edge of the Gaslamp District. Six to eight beds per room with sheets for $20–25 by season; private rooms $42–57. Free breakfast, cheap Internet access, and organized tours to Tijuana make this one of the best city hostels.

Campgrounds

Of the city's half-dozen **campgrounds**, only two accept tents. The best-placed of these is *Campland on the Bay*, 2211 Pacific Beach Drive (☎1-800/422-9386, ⓦwww.campland.com), where a basic site starts at $39–59, though larger, more elaborate sites stuffed with more amenities can run at $150–250. *Campland* boasts a number of pools and hot tubs, as well as a marina, activity rentals, and a general store; it is linked to Downtown by bus #30. For a more serene alternative, San Elijo State Beach, Route 21 south of Cardiff-by-the-Sea, offers fishing, hiking, swimming, and wireless Internet, and campsites run from $11 to $25. Call ☎760/753-5091 for information or ☎1-800/444-7275 for reservations, or go to ⓦwww.reserveamerica.com.

The City

Like most other major cities in California, San Diego is set along a wide, curving bayfront, its climate among the most agreeable in the country and its atmosphere friendly and relaxed. Much more staid than Los Angeles, its hedonism is on display mainly at the beaches, and there's a conservative air throughout. It shares with LA many of the same extremes of rich and poor, which are analogous to oceanside and inland, respectively, with most of the prime time tourist draws on or within a few miles of the water.

San Diego divides into several easily defined sections, the most prominent of which is **Downtown**, where anonymous high-rise bank buildings and hotel complexes cluster around the epicenter of the Horton Plaza mall. These stand beside older, often renovated structures from San Diego's earlier boom days, notably in the **Gaslamp District**, home to a number of worthwhile cafés and bars, making it the focus of the weekend party scene. A few miles northeast, the well-maintained oasis of **Balboa Park** contains many of the city's major museums and the ever-popular San Diego Zoo, and is perfectly suited for strolls and picnics through acres of carefully tended gardens and natural greenery, set amid splendid Spanish Revival buildings from the 1920s. Just northwest of Downtown, **Old Town** is a somewhat isolated enclave where the first white settlement developed near the site of the original San Diego Mission, an area now featuring an array of modern shops and theme restaurants intended to evoke the style of Old Mexico; it's easily accessible via a convenient trolley stop, and makes for at least a half-day of wandering if you're so inclined. Other districts near Downtown don't have any official "sights," but can be interesting as well. The most prominent of these is **Hillcrest**, whose eclectic mix of yuppies, gays, bohemians, and artists makes it one of the city's best areas for dining and nightlife.

If you're mainly interested in pure relaxation, simple beach-bumming, or a golf-and-tennis weekend, the **seaside towns** are the obvious first choice; each of them, from **Ocean Beach** to **Pacific Beach** to **Mission Beach**, has its own style and social scene, but all feature the same beckoning sands and waves that are perfect for volleyball, surfing, and other sports throughout the year. Finally, the aquatic diversions of the **SeaWorld** theme park, within easy reach of Downtown, are good for a half-day trip – or longer if you really want to get your money's worth from the steep admission price.

Downtown San Diego

Loosely bordered by the curve of San Diego Bay and the I-5 freeway, **DOWNTOWN** is, for those not headed straight to the beach, the inevitable nexus of San Diego and the best place to start a tour of the city. Kick-started in the late 1970s, various preservation and restoration projects have improved many of the area's older buildings, resulting in several pockets of stylishly renovated turn-of-the-century architecture, while the corporate towers left over from the boomtown Eighties and Nineties showcase the city's bustling trade with the Pacific Rim and the inflated real-estate market. Although Downtown is largely safe by day, at night it can be unwelcoming, with much of it becoming a high-rise dead zone. Unless you're with a local, then, or someone who knows their way around, after-dark activities are best confined to the popular and well-policed Gaslamp District.

Along Broadway

BROADWAY slices through the center of Downtown and is most lively between Fourth and Fifth avenues, where the pedestrian traffic is a mix of shoppers, sailors, yuppies, the homeless, and tourists. Although this is hardly the free-spirited strip of LA's Broadway (much less New York's), there are still a few points of interest here and there. From the west, if you roll into town by train or trolley, you'll be dropped off at the tall Spanish Colonial archways of the **Santa Fe Railroad Depot** (Ⓦwww.sdrm.org/sfd.html), which were built to welcome visitors to the 1915 Panama-California International Exposition in Balboa Park. With the bayfront just to the west, the depot's old historic-revival architecture provides a dramatic contrast to the postmodern contours of the neighboring **American Plaza**, a high-rise complex left over from the finance-fueled boom of the late twentieth century. The plaza still has a certain chic, if dated, appeal, and around it the construction continues apace these days, though most of the eye-catching structures are the hotel tower blocks that have risen in the last few years. The plaza encompasses a central terminal of the San Diego Trolley, as well as the Downtown branch of the **Museum of Contemporary Art**, or MCA San Diego, 1001 Kettner Boulevard (Mon, Tues, & Sat 11am–6pm, Thurs & Fri 11am–9pm; $10; Ⓣ858/454-3541, Ⓦwww.mcasd.org), which is the essential first stop for art in Southern California outside of LA. Its permanent collection focuses on American works, Pop Art, and the indigenous art of Mexico, and also offers the usual mainline retrospectives of Abstract Expressionism, Minimalism, Conceptual Art, and various other vices of modern art. But its temporary shows are the real appeal, often involving irreverent imagery drawn from the intersection of pop-culture surrealism, ethnic subcultures, and regional socioeconomic problems. The complex recently expanded to include property across the street in the former baggage building of the Santa Fe Depot, whose elegant spaces have been preserved (if slightly altered) as the **Jacobs Building** – now showcasing oversized sculpture such as Richard Serra's rusted, tilted walls and various installation and multimedia pieces that would be too huge to display elsewhere. Adjacent to the Jacobs Building is the new metal, concrete, and glass box of the **Copley Building**, which also presents contemporary and twentieth-century art in rotating exhibitions. The museum also has a La Jolla branch; see p.215.

Further east, many visitors linger around the fountains on the square outside **Horton Plaza**, between First and Fourth avenues south of Broadway (hours vary, often Mon–Fri 10am–9pm, Sat 10am–8pm, Sun 11am–7pm; Ⓣ619/239-8180, Ⓦwww.westfield.com/hortonplaza), a giant mall of some 140 stores and San Diego's de facto city center. Planned in 1977 and completed in 1985, Horton Plaza's quick success caused local real estate prices to soar and condo development to surge, and gave shopping-mall developer **Jon Jerde** the green light to stamp his neon-bedecked, pop-art-flavored design on malls across the country – most prominently at LA's Universal CityWalk and Minnesota's formidable Mall of America. For better or worse, the complex's whimsical, colorful postmodern style is inevitably a colossal tourist draw, and though there's nothing on the shopping front you won't find in every other American mall, the 21-foot-tall **Jessop Clock**, on level one, is the one inescapable highlight, an intriguing antique from the California State Fair of 1907. If the mall is the primary reason you came to San Diego, make a weekend of it by staying at the swank *Westin* hotel within the complex (see p.194).

On the eastern edge of the mall, the striking **Balboa Theatre**, 850 Fourth Avenue (Ⓦwww.thebalboa.org), is one of the city's marvelous old moviehouses and a gem of historic restoration, built in an appealing Spanish Revival style in 1924 and finally restored in late 2007 to present a range of theater, film, dance, and music events.

Further along, Broadway is rather uninviting until you reach a handful of the secondhand bookstores, such as **Wahrenbrock's Book House**, 726 Broadway

(Mon–Sat 9.30am–5.30pm; ☎619/232-0132), supposedly the oldest and largest in the city, and the **Central Library**, 820 E Street (Mon & Wed noon–8pm, Tues & Thurs–Sat 9.30am–5.30pm, Sun 1–5pm; ☎619/236-5800, ⓦwww .sandiego.gov/public-library), which has regular book sales on the weekend and an extensive reference section where you can pore over California magazines and newspapers. The functional site serves its purpose, though a flashy new downtown library will eventually open on the block bordered by Park Boulevard, 11th Avenue, and J and K streets. Tucked away on the third floor, the **Wangenheim Room** (Mon–Sat 1.30–4.30pm; ☎619/236-5834 ext. 6) holds the fascinating collection of early twentieth-century patrician Julius Wangen- heim. Among its many treasures are Babylonian cuneiform tablets, palm-leaf books from India, silk scrolls from China, and many more global curios documenting the history of the written word.

If you have plenty of time to explore, another interesting diversion is the **Firehouse Museum**, six blocks north of Broadway at 1572 Columbia Street (Wed–Fri 10am–2pm, Sat & Sun 10am–4pm; donation; ☎619/232-3473, ⓦwww.thesdfirehousemuseum.org), which is situated in San Diego's oldest firehouse and displays firefighting equipment, paraphernalia, and uniforms, as well as archaic hand pumps, cranks and sirens, and photographs recalling some of San Diego's most horrific conflagrations and the horses and firefighters who had to battle them. The museum is located in the **Little Italy** district (ⓦwww .littleitalysd.com), one of the city's historic ethnic neighborhoods, which today is mostly worth visiting for its restaurants and occasional festivals. These include the annual Art Walk in late April (☎619/615-1090, ⓦwww.artwalkinfo.com), the late-May Sicilian Festival (☎619/469-2206, ⓦwww.sicilianfesta.com), and mid-October Festa – the latter two, not surprisingly, featuring the spicy, delicious food of the Old World.

The Gaslamp District

South of Broadway, the **GASLAMP DISTRICT** occupies a sixteen-block area running south to K Street, bordered by Fourth and Seventh avenues. The core of San Diego when it was still a frontier town, the district – known then as **Stingaree** after a stingray found in San Diego Bay – was rife with prostitution, opium dens, and street violence, a chaotic scene that played out beneath the wrought-iron balconies and Victorian gingerbread of the nineteenth-century piles lining the street. The area predictably decayed until its revitalization in the late 1970s under an intensive urban-renewal campaign, after which it started to mutate into the heavily tourist-oriented zone it is today.

What remaining flophouses and dive bars there are make a dramatic contrast with the nearby yuppie-centric cafés, antique stores, and art galleries – all under the glow of ersatz "gaslamps" powered by electricity. The focus of San Diego nightlife, especially on the weekend, there are a number of worthwhile restau- rants, bars, and clubs here to keep you occupied and well lubricated, and the district's relatively high police profile is designed to keep the area clean and safe, and to keep the tourists coming. This flow of visitors has been ensured by the construction of **Petco Park**, Seventh Avenue at Harbor Drive (ⓦsandiego .padres.mlb.com), which draws plenty of Padres baseball fans but has more limited options for parking and is colloquially known as "The Litter Box." If you've come to play spectator, make an early trip on the Blue Line trolley (which passes alongside) – mass transit around game time resembles a rail- bound journey into deepest tourist hell.

Beyond the ballpark, the Gaslamp District is intriguing to explore, not least for the scores of late nineteenth-century buildings – rich with period detail and

ACCOMMODATION

Bristol **C**	Manchester Grand Hyatt **L**
Comfort Inn Gaslamp **I**	Omni San Diego **N**
Courtyard San Diego **B**	Solamar **M**
HI-San Diego Downtown	USA Hostel – San Diego **H**
Hostel	The U.S. Grant **E**
Horton Grand **J**	Westgate **D**
La Pensione **K**	Westin Broadway **F**
	Westin Horton Plaza **G**
A	

DOWNTOWN SAN DIEGO

0   200 yds

N

RESTAURANTS

Alambres	22	Croce's	18
Anthony's Fish Grotto	4	de' Medici	14
Bandar	15	Dobson's	12
Bella Luna	24	Filippi's Pizza Grotto	2
Café 222	32	Grand Central Café	9
Caffè Italia	1	Indigo Grill	21
Candelas	34	Olé Madrid	21
The Cheese Shop	26	Rei Do Gado	11
Chive	28	Sammy's Woodfired	
Confidential	17	Pizza	19
		Taka	31

CAFÉS & NIGHTLIFE

4th and B	5	Karl Strauss Brewery	6
Altitude Sky Bar	36	Martini Ranch	16
Bitter End	25	On Broadway	7
Café Lulu	20	Onyx Room	13
Café Sevilla	23	Spreckels Theatre	10
Coffeehouse	23	Upstart Crow	33
Dizzy's	35	
Dublin Square	30	
Henry's Pub	27	
House of Blues	8	

styles from Eastlake to Queen Anne, with some Spanish Colonial and Baroque Revival touches as well – in various stages of renovation. Few are better than the grandiose **Louis Bank of Commerce**, 835 Fifth Avenue, an eye-popping Victorian confection from 1888 that's almost too busy for its own good, replete with carved wooden and terracotta bay windows, a sheet-metal frieze across the front, and a pair of squat, colorful little towers on top. In its early years it was variously home to an ice cream parlor, a brothel, and an oyster bar run by Wyatt Earp. This classic building is best examined – and the area's general history gleaned – during the two-hour **walking tour** (Sat 11am; $10, includes admission to the William Heath Davis House; ☎619/233-4692, ⓦwww .gaslampquarter.org/tours) that begins from the small cobbled square at Fourth and Island avenues, covering the exploits of the gunslinger Earp, the more colorful of the town's Victorian-era whores, and other assorted miscreants who made "Stingaree" the notorious, dynamic town it once was.

The square is within the grounds of the **William Heath Davis House**, 410 Island Avenue (Tues–Sat 9am–6pm, Sun 9am–3pm; $5; ☎619/233-4692), whose owner founded modern San Diego and built his saltbox-styled home here in 1850, believing that a waterfront location would stimulate growth (the fledgling city had previously been located a few miles inland and to the north – the site of Old Town San Diego; see p.208). Although Davis was initially wrong and had to leave the city in short order, eventually dying penniless, the more influential Alonzo Horton (namesake of the city's signature mall) did manage to fulfill some of his goals for waterfront growth in later years. Copious with photographs, each room of the house commemorates a different period with its decor, and should be fascinating to anyone with an interest in Southern California history.

Even without the walking tour, there are a few other evocative sights in the area, including the **Horton Grand Hotel** (see p.191), opposite the William Heath Davis House, created in the mid-1980s by cobbling together two older hotels, the **Grand Horton** and the **Brooklyn Kahle Saddlery** – where Wyatt Earp lived for seven years in the early twentieth century. Dating back to the 1880s, the hotels were carefully dismantled and moved about four blocks from their original sites. In the lobby of the *Horton Grand*, the small **Chinese Museum**, 404 Third Avenue (Tues–Sat 10.30am–4pm, Sun noon–4pm; free; ☎619/338-9888, ⓦwww.sdchm.org), is a reminder of the once-thriving Chinatown area, where railroad laborers and their families lived, and offers a series of artifacts, from household items to small sculptures to paintings and calligraphy, that give some sense of life in the era. The museum also hosts monthly walking tours of Asian American history in the district (second Sat 11am; $2; same contact as museum), covering eight blocks and a couple dozen sights of interest.

Villa Montezuma

A half-mile east of the Gaslamp District, at 1925 K Street, the site of **Villa Montezuma** (☎619/239-2211, ⓦwww.villamontezuma.org) is doubtless one of the more unusual entries on the National Register of Historic Places. Ignored by most visitors to San Diego, possibly due to its location, the villa is a florid show of Victoriana, with a rich variety of onion domes and all manner of loopy eccentricities. Known to some as the "haunted house," it was built for **Jesse Shepard** – English-born but noted in the US as a composer, pianist, author, and all-round aesthete – and financed by a group of culturally aspiring San Diegans in 1887. The glorious stock of furniture remains, as do many ornaments and oddments and the dramatic stained-glass windows. It's a place that well reflects Shepard's introspective nature and interest in spiritualism – he claimed that his musical gifts were a result of his "channeling" the spirits of great composers of the past – all of which must have been entirely out of step with brash San Diego through the boom years, or even today. Note that the Villa was temporarily closed in 2007 for renovation, so call or check the website for updates about its reopening.

The bayfront

The streets south of the Gaslamp District are now occupied by expensive condos and the **San Diego Convention Center**, a $165-million complex with a sail-like roof resembling the yachts in the nearby marina. Continuing north along San Diego's curving, enjoyable **bayfront**, the pathway of the **Embarcadero** runs a mile or so along the bay, curling around to the western end of Downtown; along this stretch, the expansive green lawn of **Embarcadero Marina Park South** provides some summertime amusement in its mainstream concerts (see p.224). Although the route is favored by strollers, joggers, and kite-flyers, some tourists get no farther than **Seaport Village** (daily 10am–9pm; ☎619/235-4014, ⓦwww.spvillage.com), a predictable array of trinket shops, mid-level boutiques, and diners, though nothing worth detaining you more than a half-hour. Beyond this, if you can't get enough of the US military on your TV set at home, clamber aboard for a tour of the **USS Midway**, 910 N Harbor Drive (daily 10am–5pm; last admission 4pm; $15, kids $8; ☎619/544-9600, ⓦwww .midway.org), which is permanently docked here to show off its formidable collection of naval hardware and weapons to the public. Although touring the innards of an old-time aircraft carrier may not be for everyone – and can induce claustrophobia in spots – for those with a taste for naval combat from World War II to the first Gulf War (the life cycle of the ship), the experience is a memorable one, enhanced by the presence of flight simulators and a handful of old-time planes parked at the site. Other, more vintage, ships can be visited further north at the **Maritime Museum**, 1492 Harbor Drive (daily 9am–9pm, winter closes 8pm; $12; ☎619/234-9153, ⓦwww.sdmaritime.com), highlighted by the 1863 **Star of India**, the world's oldest iron sailing ship still afloat, which began its career hauling cargo and then working-class immigrants. Other interesting vessels include the **Californian,** a modern replica of an 1847 cutter that served as a federal lawboat patrolling the Pacific during the Gold Rush; the **HMS Surprise**, a replica of an eighteenth-century, 24-gun frigate, built for the film *Master and Commander*; and a creaky Soviet diesel submarine, the **B-39**, which was only decommissioned in the 1990s, well into the nuclear-sub era. On the *Pilot*, a 1914 commercial pilot boat, you can take a half-hour cruise on the bay for an extra $3 on top of museum admission. Keep in mind that since most of these craft are seaworthy, some may be cruising around elsewhere when you come to visit; call ahead to make sure the boat you seek will be on view.

▲ The Star of India, Maritime Museum

Finally, architecture enthusiasts may enjoy the nearby **San Diego County Administration Center**, 1600 Pacific Highway (Mon–Fri 8am–5pm; free; ☏858/694-3900), one of the more distinctive public buildings in California: a rich mix of Spanish Colonial and Beaux Arts styles, decorated with gold and azure tiles. From Harbor Drive you can walk right through the building's foyer to its main entrance, on the way viewing the eye-catching granite *Guardian of Water* statue and three interior murals painted during the Depression.

Balboa Park and the San Diego Zoo

A healthy walk away, northeast of downtown, the 1400 sumptuous acres of **BALBOA PARK** feature one of the largest collections of museums in the US, marked by a verdant landscape of trees, gardens, promenades, and Spanish Colonial buildings – and of course, the ever-popular **San Diego Zoo**. A desolate stretch of cacti and scrubland until 1898, the park began to take shape when one Kate Sessions began cultivating nurseries and planting trees in lieu of rent. The first buildings were erected for the 1915 Panama-California International Exposition, held to celebrate the opening of the Canal, and

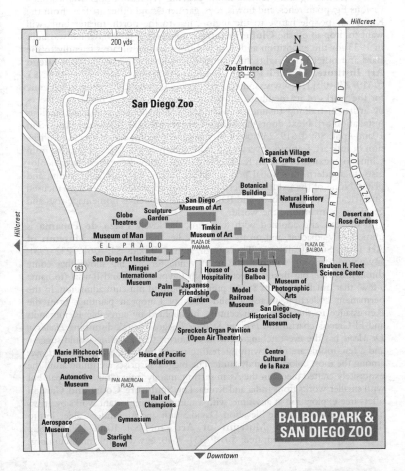

memories of its success lingered well into the Depression, until in 1935 another building program occurred for the California-Pacific International Exposition. Five years later the park was in such sparkling condition that Orson Welles decided to film close-up shots here of Charles Foster Kane's monumental Xanadu enclave for the film *Citizen Kane* (especially prominent in the "News on the March" segment near the beginning of the movie), and today the park's allure hasn't diminished much, making it one of the essential stops on any trip to Southern California.

Along El Prado

Most of the major museums flank **EL PRADO**, the park's pedestrian-oriented east-west axis, which encompasses the charming Plaza de Panama at the heart of the park, and is best explored from the west via Laurel Street and the Cabrillo Bridge. From this direction, the first institution you'll come to will be the handsome neo-Baroque folly of the **Museum of Man** (daily 10am–4.30pm; $8; ☎619/239-2001, ⊛www.museumofman.org), which veers from the banal to the engaging to the bizarre, including demonstrations of tortilla-making and Mexican loom weaving, replicas of huge Maya stones, various Egyptian relics, and bowls, toys, garments, and other artifacts from the Kumeyaay people native to the region. Just to the north, theater buffs will want to drop in on the **Globe Theatre** complex (see p.226), which was built in 1935 for the exposition and now features a trio of theatres friendly to the Bard and other playwrights. Just across El Prado to the east, the **San Diego Art Institute, 1439 El Prado** (Tues–Sat 10am–4pm, Sun noon–4pm; $3; ☎619/236-0011, ⊛www.sandiego-art.org), is a sporadically interesting venue for the works of its members, showcasing everything from pedestrian pieces by artists-in-training to unexpectedly fascinating mixed-media and curious installation art. Next door, the **Mingei International Museum** (Tues–Sun 10am–4pm; $6; ☎619/239-0003, ⊛www.mingei.org) has a rotating collection of folk art, featuring everything from international styles of jewelry from China to Mexico, to golden Kazakh artifacts recently discovered by archeologists, to modern, functional pop sculpture in the form of vases, mugs, and plates. None of the exhibits is permanent, though previous ones have focused on African, pre-Columbian, and Romanian art, as well as homemade toys and garments from around the world.

To the east and adorned with fountains, the lovely **Plaza de Panama** is immediately adjacent, and on its north side lies the **San Diego Museum of Art** (Tues–Sun 10am–6pm, Thurs until 9pm; $10, kids $4; ☎619/232-7931, ⊛www.sdmart.org), which is the main venue for any big shows that come through town – big-ticket collections from Egypt, China, and Russia (to name a few) that usually charge a $5–10 premium beyond museum admission. In the permanent collection, there's a solid stock of European paintings from the Renaissance to the nineteenth century, highlighted by agreeable Rembrandts and El Greco's charismatic *Penitent St Peter*. Diego Rivera's disturbing *Hands of Dr Moore* has the eye-catching element of horror that its name would suggest, and a few rooms are filled with interesting modern works, Stuart Davis' *Terrace* among the most colorful and dynamic. The biggest surprises are found amid the exquisitely crafted pieces in the Asian section, mainly from China and Japan but with smaller works from India and Korea. The **Sculpture Court and Garden** offers free exploration at any time, with a number of important works by artists like Henry Moore, Louise Nevelson, David Smith, and Alexander Calder. Just to the east, the **Timken Museum of Art** (Tues–Sat 10am–4.30pm, Sun 1.30–4.30pm; Sept closed; free; ☎619/531-9640, ⊛www.timkenmuseum.org)

stands out for its squat, drab modern design. Most of the works – from the early Renaissance to the Impressionist era – are fairly minor. Still, portraits by Hals, David, van Dyck, and Rubens stand out, as does Rembrandt's moving incarnation of *St Bartholomew*, while Veronese's *Madonna and Child with St Elizabeth* is the highlight of the small Italian collection. Albert Bierstadt's *Cho-Looke, the Yosemite Fall*, is appropriately monumental, as is Thomas Moran's evocative *Opus 24: Rome from the Campagna, Sunset*. More appealing for many will be the museum's stirring collection of Russian religious icons, showcasing the imposing wood-paneled *Last Judgment*, arranged in a strict, five-story hierarchy like a business office for the afterlife.

North of the Timken Museum, the wood-ribbed **Botanical Building** (Fri–Wed 10am–4pm; free) dates back over ninety years to the 1915 Exposition and features some two-thousand regional and tropical plants – making for a nice break from all the museums, along with the other seven themed gardens scattered throughout the park. On the south side of the Timken, the Spanish Baroque-flavored **House of Hospitality** hosts the visitor center (daily 9.30am–4.30pm; see box, p.206), while just to the east, **Casa de Balboa** is home to three museums. The **Museum of Photographic Arts** (Tues–Sun 10am–5pm, Thurs until 9pm; $6; ☎619/238-7559, ⓦwww.mopa.org) offers a fine permanent collection dating back to the daguerreotype and includes the work of Matthew Brady, Alfred Stieglitz, Paul Strand, and other big names, as well as compelling temporary exhibitions with wide topical reach. Virtually next door, the **San Diego Historical Society Museum** (daily 10am–5pm; $5; ☎619/232-6203, ⓦwww.sandiegohistory.org) charts the booms that have elevated San Diego from scrubland into the seventh largest city in the US within 150 years, focusing on topics such as the city's use as a Hollywood backlot and the architectural and historical background of Balboa Park. The **Model Railroad Museum** (Tues–Fri 11am–4pm, Sat & Sun 11am–5pm; $6; ☎619/696-0199, ⓦwww.sdmodelrailroadm.com), the biggest of its kind in the world, displays tiny, elaborately conceived replicas of cityscapes, deserts, and mountains, as well as the industrious little trains that chug their way through them. Aficionados of miniature railways might also enjoy the park's pint-sized **antique railroad** that takes you on a half-hour trip around the grounds on open-air "rail cars" (mid-June to Aug daily 11am–6.30pm, rest of year Sat & Sun 11am–4.30pm; $2; ☎619/239-0512).

Continuing east, near the Park Boulevard end of El Prado, the **Reuben H. Fleet Science Center** (Mon–Thurs 9.30am–5pm, Fri 9.30am–9pm, Sat 9.30am–8pm, Sun 9.30am–6pm; Science Center $7, Science Center and theater or simulator $11.75, all three $15.75; ☎619/238-1233, ⓦwww.rhfleet.org) presents an assortment of child-oriented exhibits of varying interest, loaded with flashy buttons, high-tech gizmos, and wacky sounds and goofy effects, and focusing on the glitzier, more rudimentary aspects of contemporary science, as well as the expected IMAX theatre and motion simulator. More impressive and appealing, though, is the **Natural History Museum**, on the north side of El Prado at its eastern end (daily 10am–5pm; $9; ☎619/232-3821, ⓦwww.sdnhm.org), which features a great collection of fossils, a curious array of stuffed creatures, hands-on displays of minerals, and entertaining exhibits on dinosaurs and crocodiles. The more scholarly topics – on subjects such as the controversial links between birds and late-period, chicken-sized dinos – are interspersed with crowd-pleasing exhibits on chocolate, T-Rexes, and other kid-friendly topics. A short walk behind the Natural History building, the **Spanish Village Arts and Crafts Center** (daily 11am–4pm; free; ☎619/233-9050, ⓦwww.spanishvillageart.com) dates from the California

Pacific 1935 Expo and features some three hundred craftspeople displaying their work in forty different studios and galleries, where you can watch them practice their skills at painting, sculpture, photography, pottery, and glass-working. If you continue north from here you'll find yourself at the gates of the San Diego Zoo (see opposite).

Pan American Plaza and around

The attractions arrayed along El Prado are by far the highlights of the park, and only if you have a significant amount of time (or are a car, airplane, or sports enthusiast) should you venture south, in the direction of **Pan American Plaza**. At the outset, the **Palm Canyon**, two acres holding some 450 palms, and the **Japanese Friendship Garden**, with the familiar bonsai, koi, and Zen garden, are pleasantly appealing, if not particularly essential, but the **Spreckels Organ Pavilion** (free Sunday concerts 2–3pm; ☎619/702-8138, ⓦ www.serve.com /sosorgan) is definitely worth a look as the home of one of the world's largest pipe organs, with no fewer than 4500 pipes. If you miss one of the concerts, you may be able to hear the house organist practicing through the closed metal grate. Continuing on to the north end of the plaza, the cottages of the **House of Pacific Relations** (Sun noon–4pm; free; ☎619/234-0739, ⓦ www.sdhpr .org) comprise an international collection of kitsch that evokes a cut-rate version of Epcot Center – enjoy the proffered tea, coffee, and cakes, but don't expect any real multicultural education, though the occasional events featuring folk music and dance can be diverting enough. More compelling are the **Marie Hitchcock Puppet Theater** (Wed–Fri shows at 10am & 11.30am, Sat & Sun at 11am, 1pm & 2.30pm; $5, kids $3; ☎619/544-9203, ⓦ www .balboaparkpuppets.com), in the nearby Pacific Palisades building, with lively and festive productions involving fairy tales, ventriloquists, and other kid-oriented elements, and the **Automotive Museum** (daily 10am–5pm; $8, kids $4; ☎619/231-2886, ⓦ www.sdautomuseum.org), offering a host of classic cars and motorcycles, from old-time Model Ts and fancy Rolls Royces to more obscure models like the 1912 Flying Merkle cycle and the 1948 Tucker Torpedo – one of only fifty left.

At the southern end of Pan American Plaza, the cylindrical **Aerospace Museum** (daily 10am–4.30pm; $12; ☎619/234-8291, ⓦ www.aerospacemuseum .org) showcases a worthwhile history of aviation, loaded with 69 planes like the Spitfire, Hellcat, and the mysterious spy plane Blackbird. There's also a replica of the *Spirit of St Louis* in the entrance hall. Heading back north, on the west side of the Plaza is the **Starlight Bowl** (tickets at ☎619/544-7827, ⓦwww .starlighttheatre.org), a long-standing performance space for local operettas and musicals, while the **Hall of Champions** (daily 10am–4.30pm; $8; ☎619/234-2544, ⓦwww.sdhoc.com) is a sports museum stuffed with memorabilia from baseball to skateboarding, mainly of interest if you have a thing for old jerseys, helmets, and trading cards.

Visiting all the museums in Balboa Park could well leave you too jaded even to notice the unassuming round building on the edge of the area, beside Park Boulevard. This, the **Centro Cultural de la Raza** (Thurs–Sun noon–4.30pm; free; ☎619/235-6135, ⓦwww.centroraza.com), mounts thoughtful temporary exhibits on Native American and Hispanic life in an atmosphere altogether less stuffy than the showpiece museums of the park, focusing on murals, folk art, literature, dance, and theater.

The San Diego Zoo

The **San Diego Zoo** (daily: mid-June to early Sept 9am–8pm; early Sept to mid-June 9am–4pm; one-day ticket $23, kids $15.50; two-day ticket $39, kids $27; ☎619/231-1515, ⓦwww.sandiegozoo.org), immediately north of the main museums in Balboa Park, is one of the city's biggest and best-known attractions, possibly the premier zoo in the country. As zoos go, it undoubtedly deserves its reputation, with more than four thousand animals from eight hundred different species, as well as some pioneering techniques for keeping them in captivity: animals are restrained in "psychological cages," with moats or ridges rather than bars. It's an enormous place, and you can easily spend a full day here, soaking in the major sections devoted to the likes of chimps and gorillas, sun and polar bears, lizards and lions, flamingos and pelicans, and habitats such as the rainforest. There's also a children's zoo in the park, with walk-through birdcages and an animal nursery. Take a bus tour early on to get a general idea of the layout, or survey the scene on the vertiginous **Skyfari** overhead tramway. Bear in mind, though, that many of the creatures get sleepy in the midday heat and retire behind bushes to take a nap. Moreover, the giant **pandas** Bai Yun and Shi Shi and four others spend a lot of time sleeping or being prodded by biologists in the park's Giant Panda Research Station, where the creatures are on loan from China.

Regular **admission** only covers entry to the main zoo and the children's zoo; to add a 35-minute bus tour and a round-trip ticket on Skyfari, you'll need the $33 Deluxe Ticket Package. A $59 ticket (kids $39) also admits you to the San Diego Wild Animal Park (near Escondido; see p.236) within a five-day period. Finally, truly motivated tourists will enjoy all of the above, as well as admission to SeaWorld (see p.213), for the rather staggering sum of $107 (kids $97).

Hillcrest

North of Downtown and on the northwest edge of Balboa Park, **Hillcrest** is a lively and artsy area, thanks to the wealthy liberals who've moved into the district in recent decades and the general sprucing-up of the place – predictably followed by skyrocketing rents that have driven lower-income bohemians out. Altogether, it feels rather more disconnected from the culture of San Diego in a way that, say, Haight-Ashbury in San Francisco or West Hollywood in LA do not. Perhaps its most familiar local characteristic is as the center of the city's **gay community**, with a handful of gay-oriented hotels (see p.227) and some colorful street life around University and Fifth, where the district's signature sign is prominently displayed. Easily reached from Downtown on buses #1, #3, #10, and #11, Hillcrest also has a cache of interesting cafés and restaurants (see p.219), decent book and music shops, and an appealing collection of Victorian homes. Among these, and the only conventional "attraction" in the area, is the **Marston House**, 3525 Seventh Avenue (Fri–Sun tours on the hour 11am–3pm; $5; ℡619/298-3142), a 1905 Craftsman charmer whose rustic Arts and Crafts design little resembles the later modernist work of its co-architect Irving Gill. Nonetheless, it has a warmly elegant late-Victorian feel, and is well worth a look for anyone with a flair for houses of the era.

Old Town

Old Town State Historic Park, or just **OLD TOWN**, commemorates San Diego from the 1820s through the 1870s. Featuring 25 structures, some of them original **adobe dwellings**, the district's period atmosphere is only diminished by the inevitable souvenir shops. In 1769, Spanish settlers chose what's now **Presidio Hill** as the site of the first of California's missions. After their military service, as the soldiers began to leave the mission and the presidio, or fortress, they settled at the foot of the hill. This settlement was the birthplace of San Diego, later to be administered by Mexican officials and afterwards by migrants from the eastern US. The area was preserved in 1968 and is still a good place to get a sense of the city's Hispanic roots away from its modern high-rises; thus, it's also somewhat out in the middle of nowhere, isolated from anything else worthwhile in town. Luckily, buses #8, #9, #10, and #14 and the Blue Line trolley from Downtown make the place conveniently accessible; by car, take I-5 and exit on Old Town Avenue, following the signs. Alternatively, from I-8 turn off onto Taylor Street and left onto Juan Street; signs should prevent any confusion.

The old buildings themselves are generally open 10am to 5pm and free (exceptions are noted below), but most things in the park that aren't historical – the shops and restaurants – open around 10am and close at 9 or 10pm. The best time to be around is during the afternoon, when you can enter the more interesting adobe structures with an excellent **free walking tour**, leaving at 11am and 2pm from outside the Seeley Stables, just off the central plaza. You can get details on this, and check out a scale model of Old Town circa 1872, at the **visitor center** (daily 10am–5pm; ℡619/220-5422, Ⓦwww.sandiegohistory.org or Ⓦwww.oldtownsandiego.org), located inside the **Robinson–Rose House**, where you can also pick up a fine walking-tour book.

Exploring Old Town

A number of the historic structures in the park are well preserved and display many of their original furnishings. One of the more significant structures is the **Casa de Estudillo** on Mason Street, built by the commander of the presidio, José Maria de Estudillo, in 1827. The chapel in this most elaborate of the original adobes served as the setting for the wedding in Helen Hunt Jackson's overblown, though highly influential, romance about early California, *Ramona*. When the house was bought in 1910 by sugar baron J.D. Spreckels, he advertised it as "Ramona's Marriage Place." Next door, the **Casa de Bandini** was the home of the politician and writer Juan Bandini and acted as the social center of San Diego during the mid-nineteenth century. After the United States took control of California, the house became the **Cosmopolitan Hotel**, considered among the finest in the state, its many elegant period appointments still visible in the dining room; the site later became a grocery and a pickle cannery before its current incarnation as a Mexican restaurant. Of somewhat less appeal are the **San Diego Union Building**, showing the 1868 print room and editor's office that helped produce a four-page weekly, where the city's newspaper began in 1868, and the **Seeley Stables**, the reconstruction of a stable and barns for an 1880s stage line to LA, which houses various carriages and buggies left over from the era. The **Wells Fargo History Museum** (℡619/238-3929, Ⓦwww.wellsfargohistory.com/museums_sd.htm), one in the bank's national chain of Wild West museums, showcases some old telegraphs, an overland coach, and assorted coins, maps, and assay supplies – housed in the former Colorado House, an 1851 hotel and saloon that retains its pokey Western charm.

An idealized re-creation of an eighteenth-century Mexican street market, **Bazaar del Mundo**, 4133 Taylor Street (Sun & Mon 10am–5.30pm, Tues–Sat 10am–9pm; ℡619/296-3161, Ⓦwww.bazaardelmundo.com), abuts the state park. Though rife with tacky gift shops, it's enjoyable enough on a Sunday afternoon, when there's free music and folk dancing in its tree-shaded courtyard. It's also a fair place to **eat**: stands serve fresh tortillas, and the two sit-down Mexican restaurants are decent enough if you can grab an outside seat.

Just beyond the park gates at 2476 San Diego Avenue, the **Thomas Whaley Museum** (summer daily 10am–10pm; rest of year Mon & Tues 10am–5pm, Thurs–Sun 10am–10pm; $6; ℡619/297-7511, Ⓦwww.whaleyhouse.org) was the first brick building in California and the home of Thomas Whaley, a New York entrepreneur drawn by the Gold Rush. It displays furniture and photos from his time, as well as a reconstruction of a courtroom from 1869, when the building housed the county courthouse. Oddly enough, the place has been officially stamped by the US Department of Commerce as haunted, possibly by one of the occupants of the neighboring **El Campo Santo Cemetery**. Once the site of public executions (Antonio Garra, leader of an 1851 uprising by the San Luis Rey Indians, was forced to dig his own grave here before he was killed), it contains tombs that read like a Who's Who of late nineteenth-century San Diego, though the cemetery (Spanish for "holy field") is most renowned for being haunted by the ghost of "Yankee Jim" Robinson, hanged in 1852 by a kangaroo court for the "capital crime" of stealing a rowboat. More crime is on display around the corner at the **Sheriffs Museum** (Tues–Sat 10am–4pm; free; ℡619/260-1850), which starts its timeline in the early-American period and continues to the present day, showing the way in which county law enforcers have acted to control street crime with guns, batons, and helicopters, and the response of criminals with guns, knives, and brass knuckles.

Just north on Juan Street, **Heritage Park** is where several Victorian buildings have been gathered from around the city and preserved, instead of summarily destroyed in a manic burst of urban renewal. They're now mostly shops and offices, and include the agreeable ecumenical grouping of an 1889 **Temple Beth Israel** and the contemporaneous **Christian House** – now a bed and breakfast (the *Heritage Park B&B*; see p.194) – and a few cottages and Victorian structures that were once home to the town sheriff, the doctor, and a cousin of General Sherman. The view of the harbor from the park is worth the climb, as is the walk along Conde Street, which lets you peer into the atmospheric, sculpture-filled interior of the **Old Adobe Chapel**, dating from the 1850s, used as a place of worship until 1917 and restored twenty years later.

Presidio Hill and Mission Basilica San Diego

The Spanish Colonial building that now sits atop **Presidio Hill** is only a 1929 approximation of the original 1769 mission – moved in 1774 – but contains the intriguing **Junípero Serra Museum**, 2727 Presidio Drive (Mon–Fri 11am–3pm, Sat & Sun 10am–4.30pm; $5; ℡619/297-3258), which holds Spanish furniture dating back to the sixteenth century, along with weapons, diaries, and documents pertaining to the leading Catholic missionary of California. The museum additionally lionizes the yeoman struggles of a few devoted historians to preserve the area's Spanish past in the face of dollar-hungry developers. The **Mormon Battalion Memorial Visitor Center**, nearby at 2510 Juan Street (daily 9am–9pm; free; ℡619/298-3317), presents artifacts, paintings, and multimedia about the 500-troop, 2000-mile saga of the Mormon Battalion March during the Mexican-American War – the longest US military infantry march in history, slogging more than halfway across the continent from Council Bluffs, Iowa, to San Diego.

Outside the Serra Museum, the striking **Serra Cross** serves as a modern marker on the site of the original 1769 mission. To find the later site of the mission, you'll need to travel six miles north to 10818 San Diego Mission Road, where the **Mission Basilica San Diego de Alcalá** (daily 9am–4.45pm; donation; ℡619/283-7319, ⓦwww.missionsandiego.com) was relocated in 1774 to be closer to a water source and fertile soil and further from conflict with Native Americans – which still didn't prevent Padre Luis Jayme, California's first Christian martyr, from being clubbed to death a year later. Though most of the mission site was fully reconstructed in 1931, the church dates from 1813 and still hosts a working parish, offering confession, weddings, baptisms, and daily masses (tours available Mon & Thurs 12.30–2.30pm; by reservation at ℡858/565-9077). Walk through the dark and echoey church – the fourteenth-century stalls and altar were imported from Spain – to the **garden**, where two small crosses mark the graves of Native American neophytes, making this California's oldest cemetery. A small **museum** holds a collection of Native American craft objects and historical articles from the mission, including the crucifix held by Junípero Serra at his death in 1834. Despite claims that his missionary campaign was one of kidnapping, forced baptisms, and virtual native slavery, Serra was summarily beatified in 1998 during a Vatican ceremony.

To arrive here from Downtown, take the Orange Line light rail and transfer to bus #13, or take bus #14A from Old Town.

The beaches

For many visitors, San Diego's renowned **beaches** are reason enough to visit. If you're after seclusion and any sense of privacy, you've come to the wrong place, but the beaches do live up to their reputation for top-notch sunbathing, surfing, and swimming, and if you have any other aim beyond heat, water, and sport, you'll probably be disappointed – unless, of course, you're here for SeaWorld.

Directly southwest of Downtown across San Diego Bay, **Coronado** is a plush, well-heeled settlement, best known as the site of a large naval base and a famous resort hotel. Just beyond, and much less upscale, **Imperial Beach**'s chief draw is simply the peace of its sands, and, if you have an equestrian bent, its nearby horseback riding trails.

Across the bay to the north, the rugged **Point Loma Peninsula** marks the entrance to San Diego Bay, with oceanside trees along its spine and a craggy shoreline often dotted by easily explored tide pools – though offering little opportunity for sunbathing. **Ocean Beach**, further north at the end of the I-8 freeway, was once known to be freewheeling, though is now tempered by tourists and well-heeled residents. These days, some of Ocean Beach's former vitality has migrated to **Mission Beach**, eight miles northwest of Downtown, and the adjoining, and slightly more salubrious, **Pacific Beach** – "PB" – linked by an exuberant beachside walkway. Both towns make up a peninsula that provides the western edge of **Mission Bay**, known best as the site of the colossal tourist draw of **SeaWorld**, several miles inland. To see the area at its most chic and upscale, travel a few miles further north up the coast to **La Jolla**, whose coastline of caves and coves is matched by short, clean streets lined with coffee bars, art galleries, and a stylish art museum.

Coronado

Across San Diego Bay from Downtown, the bulbous isthmus of **CORONADO** is a well-scrubbed resort community with a **naval air station** at its western end, one of the reasons you're apt to see so many sailors and soldiers in town. Although Coronado has an interesting, vaguely New England air, with an assortment of cozy "saltbox" houses, the town is of limited interest, save for a historic hotel and the long, thin beach – a natural breakwater for the bay – that runs south. Although you could trek way down to the base of the peninsula, a much simpler way to get here is on the **San Diego Bay ferry** (daily 9am–9pm; $3 each way, $3.50 with bikes; ☎619/234-1111, ⓦwww.sdhe.com), which leaves Broadway Pier on the hour, returning on the half-hour. Tickets are available on the pier at **San Diego Harbor Excursion**, 1050 N Harbor Drive, which offers many other cruises for a range of budgets. From the ferry landing on First Street, shuttle bus #904 (half-hourly 10am–6pm; $1) runs the mile up Coronado's main street, Orange Avenue, to the *Hotel del Coronado*; alternatively, use bus #901 from Downtown. By road, you cross the **Coronado Bridge**, its struts decorated with enormous murals depicting Hispanic life, best seen from the park under the bridge in the district of Barrio Logan.

The town of Coronado grew up around the **Hotel del Coronado**, 1500 Orange Avenue (see p.194), a Victorian whirl of turrets and towers erected as a health resort in 1888. Using Chinese laborers who worked round-the-clock shifts, the hotel was built to appeal to well-heeled enthusiasts of healthy living, as well as rich hypochondriacs. If you're in the neighborhood, the place is certainly worth a look. Through the lobby and courtyard, a small basement **museum** (free) details the history of the "Del," including its most notable moment, when Edward VIII (then Prince of Wales) met Coronado housewife Wallis Warfield Simpson here in 1920, which eventually led to their marriage and his abdication of the British throne. Also not to be missed is the tablecloth signed by Marilyn Monroe and the rest of the cast who filmed Billy Wilder's *Some Like It Hot* here in 1958, when it doubled as a ritzy Miami Beach resort. Outside are the sands upon which Monroe memorably flirted with Tony Curtis as he pretended to be a yachting playboy with a Cary Grant accent. A bit less memorably, the hotel was the site of the 1980 cult film *The Stuntman*, starring Peter O'Toole. A guided, hour-long **historical** tour (Fri–Sun 2pm; $15) takes in many of these highlights as it wends its way around the hotel, beginning in the lobby.

You can also explore Coronado's past at the **Coronado Museum of History and Art**, 1100 Orange Avenue (Mon–Fri 9am–5pm, Sat & Sun 10am–5pm; $5; ☎619/435-7242, ⓦwww.coronadohistory.org), which offers displays chronicling the town's early pioneers and first naval aviators, as well as its history of yachting, architecture, and ferries. For a look at the historical and architectural importance of the various buildings in town, the museum offers hour-long **tours** (Wed 2pm & Fri 10.30am; $10). Next to the museum, the **Coronado Visitor Center** (Mon–Fri 9am–5pm, Sat & Sun 10am–5pm;

☎619/437-8788, ⓦwww.coronadovisitorcenter.com) provides much useful information on the area.

Silver Strand State Beach and around

Heading south from the *Hotel del Coronado* (bus #901), follow Silver Strand Boulevard to find plenty of good spots to stretch out and relax, foremost among them **SILVER STRAND STATE BEACH** (daily 8am–dusk; ☎619/435-5184), where you can rollerblade or bike in a pleasant atmosphere. There are camping facilities, but for RVs only. At the end of Silver Strand Boulevard, less engaging **Imperial Beach** is a full half-hour south of Downtown San Diego, nearly at the Mexican border. It does, however, have an enjoyable and fairly quiet beach, as well as the **US Open Sandcastle Competition** (10am–3pm; free; ⓦwww.usopensandcastle.com), one of the nation's largest such events in late July, where you're apt to see anything from sea monsters and fairytale figures to sandy skyscrapers and the face of Elvis – at least until the next high tide. Nearby **Border Field State Park** (daily 9.30am–5pm; ☎619/575-3613) was named for the place where surveyors from the US and Mexico agreed on an international boundary after their war in 1848; it's also compelling for its **Tijuana River estuary**, a brackish marsh that's home to pelicans, teal, and migrating waterfowl. You can access the beach from here, take in a ride along a horse trail, or enjoy a weekend tour of the natural beauty.

To return directly to San Diego from Imperial Beach, take bus #934 to the Blue Line trolley and head north through dreary Chula Vista and National City.

Ocean Beach

Ruled by the Hell's Angels in the 1960s, **OCEAN BEACH**, six miles northwest of Downtown via bus #35 or #923, is a fun and relaxed beachtown that big-moneyed interests have been trying to develop for decades, with limited success. While the single-story adobe dwellings that were home to several generations of Portuguese fishing families as recently as the 1980s have virtually disappeared, the odor of over-development has otherwise been kept at bay (at least in the downtown area). Indeed, the quaint, old-time streets and shops near the coast have preserved some of their ramshackle appeal and funky character. The two big hangouts include the main drag of **Newport Street**, where backpackers slack around at snack bars, surf and skate rental shops, and some of the best secondhand music stores around, and **Voltaire Street**, which, true to its name, has a good range of independent-minded local businesses. There is often good surf, and the beach itself can be quite fun – especially on weekends, when the local party scene gets cranking. Ocean Beach has one of the state's longest **piers**, at 2000ft, meant mainly for fishing and strolling. Where Voltaire Street meets the waves, you can visit Ocean Beach's other major attraction, **Dog Beach**, the only sand-strip in the area where pooches are allowed to frolic without leashes – great for canines, if not necessarily for small children. South of the pier rise the dramatic **Sunset Cliffs**, a prime spot for twilight vistas, though notoriously unstable – more than a few people have tumbled over the edge following an afternoon of excess on the beach.

Point Loma

South of Ocean Beach, the hilly green peninsula of **POINT LOMA** is mostly owned by the US Navy, which keeps it attractive, unspoiled, and largely inaccessible. To get here from Downtown, take bus #28A or #28B. After a long, tedious ride to the point's southern extremity, you reach **Cabrillo National Monument** (daily 9am–5pm; seven-day pass $5 per vehicle, $3 per pedestrian or cyclist; ☎619/557-5450, ⓦwww.nps.gov/cabr), the spot where captain Juan Rodríguez Cabrillo and his crew became the first Europeans to land in California in 1542, though they quickly reboarded their vessel and sailed off. In the American era, the site was recognized for its military value, and various abandoned gun emplacements and fortifications now dot the landscape, left over from the first half of the twentieth century; more military information, photos, and relics are available in the creaky old **radio station** building.

The monument's startling vistas, across to Downtown and along the coast to Mexico, easily repay the journey here. After enjoying the view, you can discover the marine life in the many tide pools around the shoreline, reached on a clearly marked **nature walk** beginning near the monument. Also nearby, the visitor center has information on the history and wildlife of the point, and lies near the **Old Point Loma Lighthouse**, whose historical tours lead you past replica Victoriana and equipment from the 1880s. As it was, the structure's main purpose was ultimately unfulfilled: soon after it was built, it was discovered that its beacon would be obscured by fog, and another lighthouse was erected at a lower elevation.

On the southwest-facing cliffs of the lighthouse, a sheltered viewing station with telescopes makes it easy to see the November-to-March **whale migration**, when scores of gray whales pass by on their journey between the Arctic Ocean and their breeding waters off Baja California.

Mission Bay and SeaWorld

Heading northwest from Downtown toward the coast (or along Sunset Cliffs Boulevard from Ocean Bay), you pass through a drab, cheerless zone – frequented by sailors for its strip clubs and by tourists for its cheap hotels – before reaching **MISSION BAY**, whose mud flats quickly become landscaped lagoons and grassy flatlands crowded with watersports fanatics; especially nice is a long, circuitous walking and biking concourse that covers much of the shoreline. The other source of Mission Bay's popularity is, of course, the formidable amusement park **SEAWORLD** (hours vary, often mid-June to Labor Day 9am–dusk; rest of year 10am–dusk; $57, children $47, parking $10; ☎1-800/257-4268, ⓦwww .seaworld.com), the San Diego branch of an entertainment colossus that stretches from California to Texas to Florida, which you can reach by taking SeaWorld Drive off I-5 or bus #9 from Downtown. Although the entrance fee is very steep, SeaWorld is San Diego's most popular attraction for its undeniable kid-friendly appeal. But for adults, experiencing the local sea life by whale watching and snorkeling may be much more rewarding, and a lot cheaper. The park's entry price demands that you allow a full day to make it worthwhile; for $107 (kids $77) you can also get admission to the San Diego Zoo (see p.207).

Highly regimented, SeaWorld has numerous exhibits and events, including the killer-whale shows that make up "Believe – the Shamu Show" (where you shouldn't sit in the first fourteen rows unless you're prepared to be soaked by belly flops from a high-flying orca) and "Shamu Rocks!," an unfortunate pairing of orcas with flashing lights and rock music; "Forbidden Reef," stocked with moray eels and stingrays; "Wild Arctic," populated by walruses, beluga whales, and polar bears; and "Shark Encounter," where sharks circle menacingly around visitors walking through a submerged viewing tunnel. Some of the park's other attractions, however, have devolved into the sort of standard-issue theme-park fare that includes the likes of giant-inner-tube rides, motion simulators, sky trams, and splashy rollercoasters, though if you've come here for this sort of diversion, you're better off just sticking to Disneyland.

Mission Beach and Pacific Beach

The biggest-name public beaches in San Diego are **MISSION BEACH**, the peninsula that separates Mission Bay from the ocean, and its northern extension, **PACIFIC BEACH**. If you aren't up for bronzing on the sands, you can always nurse a beer at one of the many beachfront bars while observing the toasty sands overrun with scantily clad babes and surfboard-clutching dudes. Or you could rollerblade or bike down **Ocean Front Walk**, the concrete boardwalk running the length of both beaches, and the fastest way to travel when summer traffic is bumper-to-bumper on Mission Boulevard.

After much effort, city authorities have mostly succeeded in curbing the hedonism and drunken debauchery long associated with this classic slice of Southern California beachlife, including approving the revitalization of the once-derelict **Belmont Park**, near the southern end of Ocean Front Walk at 3146 Mission Boulevard (hours vary, often Mon–Thurs 11am–8pm, Fri–Sun 11am–10pm; rides $2–6; ☎858/228-9283, ⊕www.belmontpark.com). Although there are twelve official rides, the two main attractions, both from 1925, are the **Giant Dipper** rollercoaster, one of the few of its era still around, and the **Plunge**, once the largest saltwater plunge in the world, and the setting for famous celluloid swimmers Johnny Weismuller and Esther Williams. The newest draw, **Flowrider**, is a simulated-wave pool that allows you to get a vague sense of what surfing and wakeboarding are like without having to venture into the ocean; you'll pay $25 for the privilege. Beyond the main draws, the park offers an assortment of lesser carnival thrills, trinket stores, a pricey fitness center, and countless seaside snack joints.

By following Mission Boulevard north, you cross from the spirited amusements of Mission Beach into the more sedate Pacific Beach, where expensive oceanside

▲ Pacific Beach boardwalk

homes with tidy lawns suggest haute-bourgeois refinement, though there's still plenty to enjoy and the vibe is friendly and unpretentious. A serviceable beach around Crystal Pier is a decent spot for a suntan (and has a decent hotel to boot; see p.195), while **Garnet Avenue**, running inland from the pier, is lined by funky eating joints and nightspots. For many, though, Pacific Beach is synonymous with **surfing**, as one of the prime strips of coastline in the area specifically marked for it. Indeed, a mile north of the pier, **Tourmaline Surfing Park**, La Jolla Boulevard at Tourmaline Street (☎619/221-8900), or "Turmo," is regularly pounded by heavy waves and is reserved exclusively for the sport, as well as for windsurfing – no swimmers are allowed. If you don't have a board, a good alternative is a few miles north, **Windansea Beach**, a favorite surfing hotspot that's also fine for swimming and hiking alongside the oceanside rocks and reefs. You can also drink alcohol openly on the shore of Pacific Beach from noon to 8pm, enjoying the setting sun with the aid of beer or wine (though glass containers aren't allowed).

La Jolla and around

"A nice place – for old people and their parents," wrote Raymond Chandler of **LA JOLLA** (pronounced "la hoya") in the 1950s, though that didn't stop him from moving here (his former house is at 6005 Camino de la Costa) and setting much of his final novel *Playback* in the town, renaming it "Esmeralda." Since Philip Marlowe concluded his last case, La Jolla has been infused with scads of new money, and its opulence is now less stuffy and more welcoming than before. The main section, around Prospect Street and Girard Avenue, has spotless sidewalks flanked by crisply trimmed grass, and the many upscale art galleries sit alongside chic cafés and swanky boutiques.

Although it's fairly expensive, La Jolla is worth a visit at least once to savor the town's sense of elegance, which includes the ornate pink **La Valencia Hotel**, 1132 Prospect Street, frequented by Hollywood's elite in the Thirties and Forties (see p.196). On a quieter section of the same thoroughfare, the La Jolla site of the **Museum of Contemporary Art**, 700 Prospect Street (daily 11am–5pm, Thurs until 7pm; $10, free third Tues of month; ⓦwww.mcasandiego.org), has a huge, rotating stock of works from 1955 onwards. Minimalism, Pop Art, and regional California work are in evidence, bolstered by a strong range of temporary shows involving installations, sculpture, and numerous Latin American exhibitions – ultimately a collection of work no less daring or fascinating than that presented by the museum's Downtown counterpart. There is also a Garden Gallery with outdoor sculptural pieces, along with fabulous views of the Pacific surf crashing against the rocks below the building's huge windows. Curiously, the museum building was once the home of **Ellen Scripps**, a local philanthropist who injected her seemingly endless wealth into La Jolla through the first half of the twentieth century. She commissioned early-modernist architect Irving Gill (who built several distinctive buildings in La Jolla and San Diego, including the Marston House; see p.208) to design her house, and today the Scripps name is still almost everywhere, notably in the small, neat, and tasteful **Ellen Scripps Browning Park**, on the seaward side of the museum. Where the park meets the coast is the start of **La Jolla Cove** (daily 9am–dusk), a craggy and beautiful expanse featuring the Underwater Park Ecological Reserve, whose clear waters make it perfect for snorkelling or scuba diving, though you should keep your hands off the officially protected aquatic flora and fauna no matter how enticing it looks. One problem, however, is access: parking spaces can be notoriously difficult to find in the high season.

Architecture fans inspired by the work of Gill will not want to miss a chance to tour the local citadel of high modernism, the **Salk Institute for Biological Studies**, 10010 N Torrey Pines Road (guided tours Mon & Wed–Fri at noon; by reservation at ☎858/453-4100 ext. 1287, ⓦwww.salk.edu), not only a respected institution for molecular biology and genetics, but also a considerably influential design by American architect Louis I. Kahn. A collection of spartan concrete blocks and walls, the complex features stark vistas that look out over the Pacific Ocean and a strange, austere serenity that's both welcome and unexpected. Although the site should be avoided by fans of, say, Horton Plaza mall, it nonetheless will appeal to anyone with a taste for Le Corbusier or any icon of the mid-twentieth-century International Style.

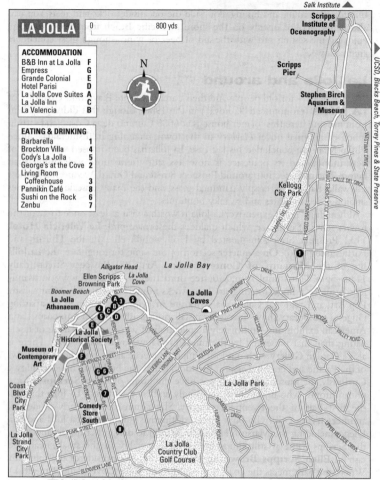

LA JOLLA

0   800 yds

ACCOMMODATION
B&B Inn at La Jolla   F
Empress   G
Grande Colonial   E
Hotel Parisi   D
La Jolla Cove Suites   A
La Jolla Inn   C
La Valencia   B

EATING & DRINKING
Barbarella   1
Brockton Villa   4
Cody's La Jolla   5
George's at the Cove   2
Living Room
 Coffeehouse   3
Pannikin Café   8
Sushi on the Rock   6
Zenbu   7

N

Scripps
Pier

Stephen Birch
Aquarium &
Museum

Kellogg
City Park

La Jolla Bay

Alligator Head
Ellen Scripps
Browning Park
La Jolla
Cove

Boomer Beach

La Jolla
Athanaeum

La Jolla
Caves

La Jolla
Historical Society

Museum of
Contemporary
Art

Coast
Blvd
City
Park

La Jolla Park

Comedy
Store
South

La Jolla
Strand
City
Park

La Jolla
Country Club
Golf Course

▼ Pacific Beach & San Diego

To find out more about the local heritage and various attractions in town,
drop by the La Jolla Historical Society, 7846 Eads Avenue (Tues & Thurs
noon–4pm; ☎858/459-5335, ⓦwww.lajolla.org/hist_soc), which can suggest
some of the better old houses, hidden coves, and relevant sites to visit. Information on similar attractions is available at the town's visitor center, 7966 Herschel
Avenue (summer daily 10am–7pm, Sun until 6pm; otherwise hours vary, often
Sun 10am–4pm, Mon–Thurs 11am–4pm, Fri 11am–5pm, Sat 10am–6pm;
☎619/236-1212, ⓦwww.seeyouinsandiego.com).

North along the coast

North of La Jolla Cove, upmarket residential neighborhoods stretch from the
cliff tops to the main route, Torrey Pines Road. Following this thoroughfare and
then La Jolla Shores Drive, which soon branches left, several uneventful miles
precede the **Stephen Birch Aquarium and Museum** (daily 9am–5pm; $11,

Exploring the
outdoors

The
outdoors
is one of
California's
treasures, and the
state's fabulous parks
and preserves come
thick with superlatives.
Sequoia National Park
holds the largest trees in the
world, Death Valley contains
the lowest point in the Western
Hemisphere, and both are rivaled
by the extraordinary domes and
spires of Yosemite. This array of
astonishing landscapes makes a
matchless backdrop for outdoor
activities – hiking in summer,
skiing in winter, surfing all year,
and rock climbing whenever the
fancy takes you. And don't forget
camping, mountain biking, and
enjoying an impressive range of
flowers and wildlife.

▲ Mammoth Mountain

Hitting the slopes

From November to June there's almost always somewhere to **ski** or **snowboard** in California. Some even claim to have skied every month of the year, but for that you'd have to trudge up to the Sierra crest, and then you'd only squeeze in a few icy turns.

Most people head for the main resorts. The closest major field to LA is **Mammoth Mountain** in the Owens Valley, a gargantuan and growing area that always seems to be installing new tows and gondolas. With 3000 vertical feet of skiing nicely balanced among beginner, intermediate, and advanced slopes (plus terrain parks and halfpipes), you'll not be disappointed. If you're based in the San Francisco Bay Area it's more convenient to head to the cluster of resorts around **Lake Tahoe** – Heavenly, Homewood, Squaw Valley, and others all deliver the goods.

Climbing and bouldering

Rock climbers travel the world to test themselves against the granite walls of Yosemite Valley, such an icon of the sport that no climber feels their life is complete without a visit. Some come with quite modest ambitions, but for many the dream is to climb the 3000-foot face of **El Capitan**, an imposing monolith that guards the entrance to the valley. Even the easiest routes take most mortals four days (with nights spent sleeping on a kind of camp bed lashed to the face), though some superhuman climbers have managed it in just a few hours.

When the mountains are snowbound, climbers head for the deserts, particularly **Joshua Tree National Park**, where glorious routes thread their way up rough monzogranite boulders. After a day in the warm spring sun, there's great camaraderie at the *Hidden Valley* campground (see p.270), where everyone gathers for a few beers as the calls of coyotes break the cold night air.

▶ Climber in Yosemite Valley

Not all California skiing is downhill. With mile after mile of accessible, snow-covered high country, **cross-country skiing** and **snowshoeing** are affordable and hugely pleasurable ways to spend time in the mountains. With your own gear you can go just about anywhere in the Sierra Nevada, but for novices, **Badger Pass** in Yosemite National Park is a great place to start (see box, p.389).

▲ Cross-country skiing in the Sierra backcountry

Riding the waves

It's hard to think of California without conjuring up images of bronzed bodies poised atop Pacific breakers, an alluring vision and in many cases a realistic one. With mild temperatures through most of the year and literally hundreds of surf breaks from San Diego to Santa Cruz and beyond, a surfer's choices are endless.

In recent years the publicity machine has focused on big-wave surfing, much of it pioneered at **Mavericks**, a reef break off Half Moon Bay south of San Francisco, where winter swells frequently bring beautifully barrelling twenty-footers (see p.594). Only regularly surfed since the early 1990s, it quickly became an institution and has since attracted tow-in surfers who use jet skis to build enough speed to catch the occasional fifty-foot monster.

If that's not your scene (and it isn't many people's scene) there are masses of other breaks to go at. Some, like **Malibu**, just north of LA, **Rincon**, up towards Santa Barbara, and Santa Cruz's **Steamer Lane**, are hugely popular and known around the world from surfing magazines and DVDs. Others are secrets, preciously guarded by the local community, though perhaps only a couple of headlands over from the well-known beaches.

▼ Surfers at Mavericks Beach

Excellent hikes

California may be one of the more urbanized states in the union, but its national parks, national forests, and state parks offer boundless opportunities for **hiking**.

▶▶ **Golden Canyon to Zabriskie Point** Sample the badlands of Death Valley on this five-mile hike that finishes at one of the finest viewpoints around. Best avoided during the heat of high summer. p.309

▶▶ **John Muir Trail** This 211-mile hike from Yosemite Valley to the summit of 14,497-foot Mount Whitney is the pinnacle of Sierra hiking. Most people take about three weeks, sometimes spread over two or three vacations. p.314

▶▶ **Lost Coast Trail** Wonderful 24-mile coastal trail well away from civilization and with great camping. p.714

▶▶ **Mount Shasta** For much of the year you'll need crampons and an ice axe to tackle this 14,000-foot volcano. An exhausting but rewarding undertaking. p.748

▶▶ **Pacific Crest Trail** For the ultimate challenge, and the widest cross-section of desert and lowland landscapes, consider this mammoth, 2650-mile journey from Mexico into Canada, most of it passing through California. p.381

◀ Hikers in Yosemite

kids $7.50; ☎858/534-3474, ⓦwww.aquarium.ucsd.edu), part of the Scripps Institute of Oceanography, which provides entertaining close-up views of captive marine life and informative displays on ecology. The highlights include the Hall of Fishes, a huge, 70,000-gallon tank with a thick kelp forest home to countless sea creatures, and the somewhat smaller Shark Reef, displaying a nice range of the fearsome creatures, including a few pint-sized versions. Altogether, the museum is a much more edifying experience than anything at SeaWorld, and a lot cheaper, too.

On a hillside setting above the museum and also reached from Torrey Pines Road, the **University of California, San Diego (UCSD)** campus mainly merits a visit for its specially commissioned artworks scattered about the 1200-acre grounds. These pieces constitute the **Stuart Collection of Sculpture** (☎858/534-2117, ⓦwww.stuartcollection.ucsd.edu), including works by Bruce Nauman, Robert Irwin, William Wegman, Nam June Paik, and Jenny Holzer. The first acquisition, from 1983, is still among the best: Niki de Saint Phalle's **Sun God**, a chunky, colorful bird whose outstretched wings welcome visitors to the parking lot opposite Peterson Hall, and which acts as the university's unofficial icon, routinely decorated in garish outfits during key events or holidays. To find the other sculptures, pick up a leaflet from the office in the Visual Arts Building or one of the campus's two visitor information booths. Without a car, you can reach the campus on bus #30 from Downtown, which terminates its route a few miles away at the University Town Center shopping mall.

As it leaves campus, La Jolla Shores Drive meets North Torrey Pines Road. A mile north of the junction, Torrey Pines Scenic Drive, branching left, provides the only access (via a steep path) to **Torrey Pines City Beach Park** – almost always called **Blacks Beach** – the region's premier (unofficially) clothing-optional beach and one of the top surfing beaches in Southern California, known for its huge barreling waves during big swells. The beach lies within the southern part of the **Torrey Pines State Preserve** (daily 8am–sunset; parking $8; ☎858/755-2063, ⓦwww.torreypine.org), best entered a few miles further north, which protects the country's rarest species of pine, the Torrey Pine – one of two surviving stands. Thanks to salty conditions and stiff ocean breezes, the pines contort their ten-foot frames into a variety of tortured, twisted shapes that can be viewed at close quarters from the **Guy Fleming Trail**, a two-thirds-mile loop starting near the beachside parking lot. The small **museum and interpretive center** (May–Oct daily 9am–5pm; Nov–April 10am–5pm; free) will tell you all about pines, especially if your visit coincides with a guided nature tour (Sat & Sun 10am & 2pm). The shorter and less scenic **beach trail** leads from the center down to Flat Rock and a popular beach, great for sunbathing and picnics, though there is no picnicking allowed on the cliffs above the beach. Continuing beyond the preserve will lead you into the North County town of Del Mar (see p.229).

Eating

San Diego typically offers good **food** at reasonable prices, everything from old-time coffee shops to stylish ethnic restaurants. Although its range of culinary fare isn't quite as wide as LA's, San Diego still has a number of solid staples, as well as places to drop a wad if you're feeling extravagant. Mexican food is much in evidence, especially in **Old Town**, while the **Gaslamp District** has the greatest concentration of tourist-friendly restaurants and bars, which are especially crazy on weekend nights and heavy on the all-American food like ribs, burgers, and such. Ascendant **Little Italy**, on the northern fringes of Downtown, mainly appeals for its handful of decent restaurants, but is still too small to challenge the bohemian allure of **Hillcrest**, the most attractive area to simply hang out and chow down.

Downtown and Little Italy

See the map on p.200 for locations.

Alambres 756 5th Ave ☎619/233-2838. Affordable Mexican food in a casual atmosphere, popular with the Gaslamp crowd for its cheap, hefty burritos and its eponymous Alambres, fat tortillas stuffed to order.

Anthony's Fish Grotto 1360 Harbor Drive ☎619/232-5103. Fish'n'chips and other fish-related favourites, from oysters to lobster tail, are the draw at this long-standing bayside haunt. One of several area locations.

Bandar 825 4th Ave ☎619/238-0101. Tasty Persian cuisine that tempts the palate with staples like lamb kebabs and stuffed grape leaves, as well as more inventive items like black cherry rice. Located near Horton Plaza.

Bella Luna 748 5th Ave ☎619/239-3222. A romantic, moon-themed bistro with an artsy feel, serving up mid-priced dishes from different regions of Italy, with hefty servings of pasta and calamari.

Café 222 222 Island Ave at 2nd Ave ☎619/236-9902. Hip café serving some of the city's best breakfasts and lunches, with excellent pancakes, French toast, and pumpkin waffles, and inventive twists on traditional sandwiches and burgers (including vegetarian) at reasonable prices.

Caffè Italia 1704 India St, Little Italy ☎619/234-6767. Sandwiches, salads, coffee, and great desserts, including solid gelato, served in a sleek modern interior or out on the sidewalk.

Candelas 416 3rd Ave ☎619/702-4455. A Gaslamp District restaurant offering swank, pricey Mexican fare with inventive combinations of seafood and meat dishes with a California-cuisine influence – try the halibut, Serrano ham, or any dessert.

The Cheese Shop 627 4th Ave ☎619/232-2303. Scrumptious deli sandwiches stuffed with different savory meats, from lamb to salami to pork loin, with the roast beef a solid pick as well as the old favorite grilled-cheese.

Chive 558 4th Ave ☎619/232-4483. Chic and innovative are the buzzwords at this trendy eclectic joint. The prices can be steep, but worth it for the winter truffle risotto and crab mac'n'cheese, as well as staples like ravioli and dumplings.

Confidential 901 4th Ave ☎619/696-8888. Solid Gaslamp choice for tapas in a trendy modern environment; the small plates come in a range of (usually pricey) choices, from glazed pork ribs to Indian lamb burgers to "deconstructed" pizza. Essential for adventurous, upscale eaters.

Croce's 802 5th Ave ☎619/233-4355. Pricey but excellent range of pastas, desserts, risotto, steaks, and salads in the Gaslamp District. Also with nightly jazz; see p.224.

de' Medici 815 5th Ave ☎619/702-7228. Upscale Italian fare that draws plenty of suits for the Old World style; the food is scrumptious, with the oysters Rockefeller, langostino lobster, crab legs, and saltimbocca rounding out a solid menu.

Dobson's 956 Broadway Circle ☎619/231-6771. An upscale restaurant in an old two-tier building, loaded with business types in power ties. The cuisine leans toward Continental, including everything from crab hash and oyster salad to flatiron steak and rack of lamb.

Filippi's Pizza Grotto 1747 India St, Little Italy ☎619/232-5094. Thick, chewy pizzas and pasta dishes, including a solid lasagna, served in a small room at the back of an Italian grocery. No-nonsense atmosphere and a good spot for devouring old, no-nonsense favorites.

Grand Central Café 500 Broadway ☎619/234-2233. Loaded with train decor, this cozy café serves inexpensive, gut-busting fare like hefty omelets, pork chops and eggs, and *chilaquiles* – tortillas with eggs, beans, and cheese.

Indigo Grill 1536 India St, Little Italy ☎619/234-6802. Among the most upscale of Little Italy's restaurants, this one appeals for its California cuisine experiments like blueberry rack of lamb, duck nachos, jalapeno papardelle, and fried pumpkin bread – though the dinner entrées can be expensive.

Olé Madrid 755 5th Ave ☎619/557-0146. Enjoyable, mid-priced Spanish restaurant with a wide range of tapas – anything from crab cakes to portobello mushrooms – and some solid paella and pasta choices. Also a nightclub scene – see p.223.

Rei Do Gado 939 4th Ave ☎619/702-8464. Barbecue Brazilian-style, delivered in a grand buffet atmosphere, where you pick what you want from an array of meat skewers – piping hot and ready to stuff your gut.

Sammy's Woodfired Pizza 770 4th Ave ☎619/230-8888. Affordable California cuisine: pasta, salads, and seafood are the staples, but the eclectic pizzas, calzones, tapas, and "messy sundaes" are the real reasons to come. One in a local chain of eateries, so the food isn't overwhelmingly delicious, but it is worth a try, and good value.

Taka 555 5th Ave ☎619/338-0555. Good sushi and hot and cold appetizers – as well as sashimi and noodles – in a modern atmosphere with a fair mix of hipsters and families.

Hillcrest

Celadon 3671 Fifth Ave ☎619/269-9209. Quality Thai eats at this solid, affordable favorite with a mix of staples and unique inventions – from spicy chili rice and Thai barbecue chicken to savory "jungle" curry and red duck curry.

City Delicatessen 535 University Ave ☎619/295-2747. Huge deli menu – liver, brisket, and cabbage rolls make appearances – with belt-loosening portions to match and late hours. One of the better choices in a city not known for its delis.

Crest Café 425 Robinson Ave ☎619/295-2510. Solid, tasty American fare presented on the cheap. The salads, burgers, and pancakes will make your stomach happy, as will the delicious home-made desserts. The salmon scramble, meatloaf, and flatiron chimichurri steak are also worth a try.

El Cuervo Taco Shop 110 W Washington St ☎619/295-9713. Long-standing cheap and tasty Mexican joint that can hit the spot after a day at Balboa Park – featuring good carne asada, burritos, shrimp *diablo*, and more exotic offerings like beef-tongue tacos.

Ichiban 1449 University Ave ☎619/299-7203. Altogether scrumptious Japanese cuisine, featuring a range of good rolls, bento boxes, soups, and sushi in an unpretentious and popular restaurant. The combination platters are well-priced, and the sushi's half-priced during happy hour. Cash only.

Pizza Nova 3955 5th Ave ☎619/296-6682. Trendy California-style pizzas with a range of savory toppings. Good, palatable fare draws a sizeable contingent of locals and tourists. Also in Solana Beach, 945 Lomas Santa Fe Drive (☎858/259-0666), and Point Loma, 5050 N Harbor Drive (☎619/226-0268).

Taste of Thai 527 University Ave ☎619/291-7525. Terrific Thai staples – spicy noodles,

marinated shrimp, curry dishes, and pad thai – for reasonable prices in the center of Hillcrest; expect a wait on weekends.

Old Town

Berta's 3928 Twiggs St ☎619/295-2343. A far cry from a conventional south-of-the-border restaurant, offering well-priced, authentic cooking from all over Latin America, with savory offerings like chimichurri steak, paella, and other unexpected dishes, and a range of hot and spicy cocktails to help you knock it back.

Café Coyote 2461 San Diego Ave ☎619/291-4695. Reliable choice for a predictable array of Mexican food, and especially good for its fresh tortillas, enchiladas, quesadillas, and of course, the strong margaritas. A bit touristy, but a first stop for many Old Town gourmands.

Casa de Bandini 2660 Calhoun St ☎619/297-8211. The crowds come in thick, ravenous packs to sample this restaurant's delicious combo plates, potent margaritas, and appealing (or annoying) mariachi musicians. Chow down on tostadas, Aztec soup, and shrimp olé salad on the festive patio.

Casa Guadalajara 4105 Taylor St ☎619/295-5111. Serviceable Mexican fare that includes a wide range of savory choices, such as grilled chicken and *mole* enchiladas. Moderately priced and open late on weekends.

Jack and Giulio's 2391 San Diego Ave ☎619/294-2074. Although not too many diners come to this part of town seeking Italian food, this comfy, affordable spot fits the bill for those who do. Take in the lasagna or gnocchi, or pay a little more for top-notch scampi and veal.

La Piñata 2836 Juan St ☎619/297-1631. Affordable Mexican food with hefty portions of old-fashioned, fattening fare: steak-stuffed "fajita-dillas" as well as the formidable "Piñata Supreme" and *camarones rancheros*. Pitchers of margaritas will give you a powerful jolt to go with your combo plates.

Old Town Mexican Café 2489 San Diego Ave ☎619/297-4330. Lively and informal Mexican diner where the crowds expect to queue up before dining on ribs, *chile colorado*, and Aztec steak; only at breakfast are you unlikely to have to wait for a table.

Coronado

Chez Loma 1132 Loma Ave ☎619/435-0661. Aromatic and delicious selection of French cuisine, especially strong on old-line favorites, though with nouvelle influences too. Good for its rack of lamb, sea scallops, black mussels, onion soup and, of course, filet mignon.

Costa Azul 1031 Orange Ave ☎619/435-3525. A popular choice for Mexican eats, with a range of mid-priced staples from shrimp *diablo* to lobster burritos and even swordfish tacos. One of the better Mexican choices for this area.

Miguel's Cocina 1351 Orange Ave ☎619/437-4237. Savory fish tacos, burritos, huevos rancheros, margaritas, and a full range of other solid items make this Mexican eatery worth seeking out.

🏃 **Peohe's** 1201 1st St ☎619/437-4474. One of Coronado's top choices for fine dining, a restaurant whose supreme bayside views of downtown are matched only by its pricey but delicious bourbon pork chops, lobster tail, Pacific fire shrimp, and assorted steaks.

Primavera 932 Orange Ave ☎619/435-0454. Swank and scrumptious Italian cuisine that's among the best in town – *carpaccio*, pasta, and risotto for those a little lighter in the wallets, steak and lamb chops for the big spenders.

Tartine 1106 1st St ☎619/435-4323. Compelling French bistro that has a range of delicious sandwiches with prosciutto, gorgonzola, eggplant, and more, along with soups, salads, and entrées like duck, mussels and flatiron steak. Good desserts and breakfasts, too – and all for affordable prices.

Ocean Beach and Point Loma

Humphrey's by the Bay 2241 Shelter Island Drive, Point Loma ☎619/224-3577. Eclectic California cuisine, heavy on inventive seafood platters – anything from crab cakes to ahi tuna sticks to seafood risotto – but especially good for eye-catching bayside views, groovy weekend live music, and DJs.

Livingston's Chicken Kitchen 5026 Newport Ave, Ocean Beach ☎619/224-8088. Simply put, a top spot to get your gut stuffed on cheap and scrumptious burritos, rotisserie chicken, tostadas, and other filling treats – none costing more than a few bucks.

Old Venice 2910 Canon Ave, Point Loma ☎619/222-5888. Upscale, romantic atmosphere at this moderately priced café and bar. Great for pizza, pasta, seafood, and salads – no real surprises here, just hearty Italian favorites.

🏃 **Point Loma Seafoods** 2805 Emerson St ☎619/223-1109. Fast, inexpensive counter serving up San Diego's freshest fish in a basket, along with mean crabcake and scallop sandwiches that make the locals cheer. Justly popular joint is

packed on weekends; don't even try to find an adjacent parking spot.

Ranchos Cocina 1830-H Sunset Cliffs Blvd, Ocean Beach ☎619/226-7619. A healthy, affordable joint with well-made staples like enchiladas, burritos, and quesadillas – many combining Tex-Mex, Spanish, and even Aztec elements. Try the seafood and veggie specials.

South Beach Bar and Grill 5059 Newport Ave #104, Ocean Beach ☎619/226-4577. A relaxed and friendly place known for its excellent fish tacos, including versions with mahi mahi, shark, and oysters, plus seafood tostadas, steamed mussels, and other oceanic dishes.

Theo's 4953 Newport Ave, Ocean Beach ☎619/225-9404. Hearty subs and pizza at cheap prices. A popular choice with the locals. Also in a good Pacific Beach location at 967 Garnet Ave (☎858/273-6300).

The Venetian 3663 Voltaire St, Ocean Beach ☎619/223-8197. Excellently priced pizzas and pasta, mostly Italian staples with big portions and affordable prices.

Mission Beach and Pacific Beach

The Eggery 4150 Mission Blvd, Mission Beach ☎858/274-3122. A coffee shop with imagination, serving breakfast – omelets, eggs benedict, pancakes, and other favorites – for decent prices. Be prepared to wait on weekends.

The Fishery 5040 Cass St, Pacific Beach ☎858/272-9985. Good range of seafood for varying prices at this straightforward fishhouse, where you can get your fill of oysters, jumbo lump crabcake, and mussel linguini, as well as halibut, cod, or shrimp'n'chips.

JRDN 723 Felspar St, Pacific Beach ☎858/270-5736. With its trendy name pronounced "Jordan," this is swanky beachside dining for the young and beautiful, which despite its trendy overtones is pretty good for its sushi bar, cocktails, and entrées like pan-seared scallops, Sonoma rabbit, squab, bacon-wrapped quail, and full range of steaks – all for steep prices.

Kono's 704 Garnet Ave, Pacific Beach ☎858/483-1669. A dependable choice for breakfast or lunch on the boardwalk, with inexpensive, sizeable portions of eggs, potatoes, toast, and sandwiches, and especially plump burgers and burritos. Beware the long line of hungry surfers. Adjacent to Crystal Pier.

Luigi's 3210 Mission Blvd, Mission Beach ☎858/488-2818. Sup on cheap and enormous pizzas while you take part in the rowdy beachside atmosphere, screaming at one of the sports games on competing TV sets.

Sportsmen's Seafood 1617 Quivira Rd, Mission Beach ☎619/224-3551. For the serious fish-lover, a combo diner/market where the catch of the day is laid out before your eyes. A no-frills environment with cheap and delicious fare – the shrimp cocktails, squid steak, tuna burgers, fish'n'chips, crab or lobster platters, and fish tacos are all worth a try.

World Famous 711 Pacific Beach Drive, Pacific Beach ☎858/272-3100. Lobster bisque and lobster tacos, firepot chicken, calamari sandwiches, mahi mahi tortas, and crab and shrimp enchiladas make this place a perennially popular, affordable lunchtime spot, which also has solid breakfasts and decent pasta- and steak-oriented dinners.

Zanzibar 976 Garnet Ave, Pacific Beach ☎858/272-4762. A great place to chill out, especially on the back patio, with inexpensive snacks, pizzas, sandwiches, smoothies, coffees, and desserts. As a major plus, breakfast is served all day. Open late on weekends.

La Jolla

Barbarella 2171 Avenida de la Playa ☎858/454-7373. Eclectic Italian eatery that serves up a hearty menu of pizza and pasta, risotto and seafood, and even burgers and fries. Justifiably popular with the swells as well as the proles.

Brockton Villa 1235 Coast Blvd ☎858/454-7393. Superior American and California cuisine, featuring a nice range of rotating entrees, typically seafood, rack of lamb, stews, and pasta – plus nice views of the cove. Also features good choices for breakfast like gingerbread pancakes and lobster and crab benedict.

Cody's La Jolla 8030 Girard Ave ☎858/459-0040. Innovative California cuisine: especially notable are the bouillabaise, lingcod, duck breast, and scrumptious burgers – with dinner entrées about twice as expensive as the affordable lunch dishes. Sit on the patio and catch a glimpse of La Jolla Cove.

George's at the Cove 1250 Prospect St ☎858/454-4244. A long-standing local favorite recently remodeled and split into two sections – the chic but affordable Ocean Terrace, with predictably nice views and savory salmon, steak, pasta, and seafood dishes, and the much pricier California Modern, aimed at the Cal-cuisine crowd for its osso buco, oyster chowder, and grilled squab.

Lorna's Italian Kitchen 3945 Governor Dr ☎858/452-0661. A reliable choice for its handcrafted Old World fare, from gnocchi and tortelloni to filet of sole, mussel soup, shrimp primavera, and other scrumptious, mid-priced selections. Located in a strip mall.

Sushi on the Rock 7734-A Girard Ave ☎858/456-1138. Tempting array of sushi combination plates and rolls, many of them quite colourful, affordable, and experimental – anything from a fiery "911 Roll" to the fearsome-sounding "Monkey Balls" – throwing in different pan-Asian flavors and styles to test your taste buds.

Zenbu 7660 Fay Ave ☎858/454-4540. Another hip, swanky sushi bar in this upscale town, where you can enjoy delicious salmon rolls, sashimi, and swordfish steak – as well as rolls like the "Jackie Chan," with crab and cucumber, and "Wind-N-Sea," an odd combination of eel, avocado, and banana.

Bars, cafés, and clubs

San Diego has a respectable range of appealing **bars** that can be found throughout much of the city, with the Gaslamp District being a good place to get dressed up for cocktails or for pure sports-bar swilling, while the beach communities offer a more rowdy atmosphere, abetted by plenty of beer and loud music. As with its lively bars, Pacific Beach boasts the best selection of the city's **cafés**, which, aside from the usual espresso drinks and pastries, may also offer Internet access and quirky artwork. Decent **clubs**, though, are a bit harder to find – Hillcrest is notable for its gay-oriented spots (see p.227), while other clubs can be found mainly in the Gaslamp, catering to the silk shirt and leather pants crowd.

Bars

The Alibi 1403 University Ave, Hillcrest ☎619/295-0881. The place to hit when you just want to get ripped – a classic dive bar with potent drinks, pool tables, occasional live acts, and a grungy but cozy decor for your hedonistic adventures.

Altitude Skybar 660 K St, at *Marriott Gaslamp Hotel* ☎619/696-0234. For obvious reasons, tourists are just about the only people drinking at this hotel rooftop bar, but if you enjoy watching a baseball game with a good view, knocking back pricey drinks, and lounging on the plush furniture with other out-of-towners, this can be an agreeable choice.

Callahan's 8111 Mira Mesa Blvd ⊕858/578-7892. Located north of Downtown and east of the beach, in the middle of mini-mall nowhere, but worth the trip for its excellent combination of Irish food and style, and microbrewed faves like blueberry wheat beer and a "Nameless Nutbrown." Open until 1am weekends.

Coronado Brewing Company 170 Orange Ave ⊕619/437-4452. Not as frenetic, quirky, or irreverent as some of the other microbreweries around town, but a solid choice if you want basic pasta, seafood, and burgers served with handcrafted brews like an Islandweizen, Mermaid's Red Ale, and Idiot IPA.

Dublin Square 554 4th Ave, Downtown ⊕619/239-5818. Get your fill of leek soup, shepherd's pie, and lamb-shank stew as you quaff Irish beer and spirits at this Emerald Isle-styled pub. Even the breakfast steak is marinated in Guinness, and the chocolate cake is given a whiskey boost.

Karl Strauss Brewery & Grill 1157 Columbia St at B, Downtown ⊕619/234-2739. Reasonable selection of ales and lagers – from the Windansea Wheat to the Red Trolley Ale – brewed here on the premises, and an adequate array of bar food. Part of a local chain.

Kensington Club 4079 Adams Ave, Kensington District, north of Hillcrest ⊕619/284-2848. Also known as "The Ken" – a great divey joint for beer, wine, and cocktails, but also for wide-ranging live music selections, from thumping dance DJs to head-banging rockers.

Live Wire 2103 El Cajon Blvd, just east of Hillcrest ⊕619/291-7450. An impressive selection of imported beers, pinball, pool, a great jukebox, and funky sub-bohemian atmosphere make this a fine choice for boozing, drawing an interesting, mixed crowd.

Martini Ranch 528 F St, Downtown ⊕619/235-6100. Prime poseur bar where yuppies and dapper meat-marketeers go to swill fancy cocktails for upwards of $10 amid smooth and precious decor. Worth a go if you want to try your luck at the swanky-skanky singles scene.

O'Hungry's 2547 San Diego Ave, Old Town ⊕619/298-0133. Tall, strong beers in cylinder glasses and a boisterous crowd, enlivened by a cheesy nautical theme and cheap and tasty comfort food, which all goes down easy once you've gotten properly plastered.

Red Fox Room 2223 El Cajon Blvd, just east of Hillcrest ⊕619/297-1313. This old-style piano bar with good steaks offers a merry, sloshy crowd of regulars and a convivial atmosphere that draws nostalgia buffs of all ages.

Sunshine Company Ltd 5028 Newport Blvd, Ocean Beach ⊕610/222-0722. A friendly neighborhood joint that's a good place to sample the convivial spirit of "OB", load up on affordable beer and bar food, and mix with the area's surfer dudes, hippies, and hipsters – all within a few blocks of the water. Connected to *Livingston's Chicken Kitchen*; see p.220.

Taylor's 721 Grand Ave, Pacific Beach ⊕858/270-3596. Microbrews by the beach, boasting a prime location a short jump from the sands and prime selection of handcrafted ales, lagers, and the like. Freewheeling surfer-dude atmosphere as well.

Waterfront 2044 Kettner Blvd ⊕619/232-9656. A mixed bag of working-class boozers and slumming hipsters are drawn to this old-time Little Italy joint like a beacon – solid burgers, fish'n'chips and bar food, friendly neighborhood atmosphere, and a lively crowd of regulars make this an essential stop if you want to see the real drinker's San Diego.

Cafés

Caffè Calabria 3933 30th St, Hillcrest ⊕619/291-1795. Serious coffee drinks for serious coffee drinkers, serving up some fine espresso and French and Italian roasts from their own roasted beans, which you can also buy to take home. Closes at 3pm.

Café Lulu 419 F St, Downtown ⊕619/238-0114. Hipster joint with eye-catching, mildly freakish decor, and hookah pipes ($20) if you like the taste and aroma of fruit-flavored tobacco. Also a good selection of coffees and late-night food orders on weekends.

Claire de Lune 2906 University Ave, Hillcrest ⊕619/688-9845. The prototypical coffeehouse, with steaming java, teas, and sandwiches, comfy seating, and entertainment that runs mainly on the weekend.

Gelato Vero Caffè 3753 India St, at the southern end of Hillcrest ⊕619/295-9269. San Diego isn't exactly known for its gelato, but you can get it here – from straciatella to tiramisu to a bevy of fruit flavors – along with good espresso. Open late on weekends.

Jungle Java 5047 Newport Ave, Ocean Beach ⊕619/224-0249. If sipping espresso and munching on pastries while shopping for plants sounds like a good idea, this is the place for you – another of this burg's quirky shops, with a good range of hot teas and coffee drinks to go with your ferns and creepers.

Living Room Coffeehouse 1010 Prospect St, La Jolla ☎858/459-1187. One in a chain of local coffee joints, with great sandwiches, soups, quiches, and pastries with fresh ingredients, in an antique-laden living room – though space is often a problem in the too-cozy setting.

Pannikin Café 7467 Girard Ave, La Jolla ☎858/454-5453. Modest, friendly spot that feels warm and lived-in, where you can knock back a java, read the paper, and dine on a sandwich, and deal with a bit less of the attitude you might find elsewhere in this town.

Upstart Crow 835 W Harbor Drive, Downtown ☎619/232-4855. This coffee bar fused with a bookstore makes for one good reason to come to dreary Seaport Village, offering a lively cross-section of customers and a surfeit of well-chosen reading material.

Zanzibar 976 Garnet Ave, Pacific Beach ☎858/272-4762. Relatively serene retreat from the brash bars along this strip. Cheap and tasty lunches and breakfasts, plus coffee, tea, pastries, and muffins served late on weekends.

Clubs

Bar Dynamite 1808 W Washington St, Mission Hills ☎619/295-8743. Located between Hillcrest and the airport, a good draw for house, hip-hop, reggae, and other danceable beats, with a friendly crowd that's not quite as style-obsessed as some spots in the Gaslamp.

Bitter End 770 5th Ave, Downtown ☎619/338-9300. Three-story venue in the Gaslamp, complete with lower-level dance floor, martini bar, and upstars, private "VIP" lounge, for the sophisticated poseur who doesn't mind paying $10 for an appletini.

Café Sevilla 555 4th Ave, Downtown ☎619/233-5979. Traditional Spanish cuisine and tapas upstairs, hip Latin American-flavored club downstairs, with Latin rock, flamenco, house, and Spanish dance grooves to whet your musical appetite.

Henry's Pub 618 5th Ave, Downtown ☎619/238-2389. One of the better pubs for nightlife in town, where retro-pop DJs and occasional live music acts perform, and many domestic and European beers are on offer in bottles or on tap. A unique experience in the Gaslamp.

Olé Madrid 755 5th St, Downtown ☎619/557-0146. Spanish restaurant that becomes a very popular funk and dance club at night. Arrive before 11pm on weekends if you want to get in (see p.218).

On Broadway 615 Broadway, Downtown ☎619/231-0111. The apotheosis of posing in town, a velvet-rope scene in the Karma Lounge that attracts the local celebrity elite (such as they are) and sends you into booty-shaking, roof-raising overdrive with national-league DJs.

Onyx Room 852 5th Ave, Gaslamp District ☎619/235-6699. Groovy underground scene with lush decor and comfortable seating, where you can listen to torch songs, knock back a few cocktails, and hit the back room for live jazz and dance tunes. The swanky lounge upstairs, Thin, has pricier drinks and bigger attitudes. $10–15 cover on weekends (for both floors).

Thrusters Lounge 4633 Mission Blvd, Pacific Beach ☎858/483-6334. Cozy bar and club where the hip-hop and dance beats come hard and heavy, and jazz and rock make occasional appearances as well.

Whistle Stop Bar 2236 Fern St, South Park ☎619/284-6784. Sited in a neighborhood on the east side of Balboa Park, this is a hip and lively spot that presents a wide range of theme nights, from weekend DJs to Sunday "knitting jams" to found-film and avant-video shows – always an interesting scene, and well removed from the typical meat-market club scene.

Live music

When it comes to **live music**, San Diego has a number of good choices Downtown and in the Gaslamp, as well as a smattering along the coast. For listings, pick up the free *San Diego Reader* (Ⓦwww.sdreader.com), buy the Thursday edition of the *San Diego Union-Tribune* (Ⓦwww.signonsandiego.com), or seek out the youth-lifestyle-oriented *Slamm/San Diego CityBeat* (Ⓦwww .sdcitybeat.com) at some of the places listed below. **Cover charges** at live music venues range from nothing to $15, unless a big-name act is playing or a major DJ is spinning.

Major performance venues

Coors Amphitheatre 2050 Entertainment Circle, Chula Vista ⓣ935/671-3600, ⓦwww.hob.com/venues/concerts/coors.

Embarcadero Marina Park South Off Marina Park Way near Seaport Village ⓣ619/659-5300.

Open Air Theatre 5500 Campanile Drive, San Diego State University ⓣ619/594-6947, ⓦwww.hob.com/venues/concerts/openair.

Palomar Starlight Theatre At Pala Casino Resort on Hwy 76 ⓣ760/510-4555, ⓦwww.palacasino.com/entertainment.

San Diego Sports Arena 3500 Sports Arena Blvd, Mission Bay ⓣ619/224-4171, ⓦwww.sandiegoarena.com.

Rock and punk

🏃 **4th and B** 345 B St, Downtown ⓣ619/299-2583, www.4thandb.com. One of the city's premier venues for live pop, rock, Latin, and other types of music, with pretty good sight lines and atmosphere, and a mix of up-and-comers with frenetic energy and old-timers playing out the string.

Brick by Brick 1130 Buenos Ave, Mission Bay ⓣ619/675-5483, ⓦwww.brickbybrick.com. Aggressively hip lounge that's one of the better known indie spots around town, attracting nationally known alternative, blues, and hard rock acts.

Canes Bar & Grill 3105 Ocean Front Walk, Mission Beach ⓣ858/488-1780, ⓦwww.canesbarandgrill.com. Mexican diner with decent food and a nice rooftop bar with seaside views, and a schedule that includes dance music nights and a solid array of touring rock and punk acts.

🏃 **Casbah** 2501 Kettner Blvd, Downtown ⓣ619/232-4355, ⓦwww.casbahmusic.com. If you're up for a night of hipstering, this is a good spot to begin – a grungy joint that nevertheless hosts a solid, varying roster of blues, funk, reggae, rock, and indie bands. Local popularity contrasts with cramped environs.

Epicentre 8450 Mira Mesa Blvd, north of Downtown ⓣ858/271-4000, ⓦwww.epicentre.org. Cozy haunt that draws a range of ages for its prime lineups, often of the punk tilt, but including some nationally known rock and indie acts as well.

House of Blues 1055 Fifth Ave, Downtown ⓣ619/299-2583, ⓦwww.hob.com. The heavyweight on the local concert scene, drawing a predictable lineup of big-name rock and pop acts. The environment's a little too well scrubbed – as are the bands – but this is the inevitable apex of tourist rock.

SOMA 3350 Sports Arena Blvd, west of Old Town ⓣ619/226-7662, ⓦwww.somasandiego.com. Favorite all-ages spot for thrashing to punk acts or head-banging to rockers, set in a former moviehouse complex with two stages. A good spot to seek out what's bubbling up in the music scene.

Winston's Beach Club 1921 Bacon St, Ocean Beach ⓣ619/222-6822, ⓦwww.winstonsob.com. A former bowling alley with rock bands most nights, along with reggae, blues, and indie, and an occasional Sixties band to go with the matching decor. Close to the pier.

Zombie Lounge 3519 El Cajon Blvd, east of Hillcrest ⓣ619/284-3323. An engagingly grim joint for serious rock, punk, and metal acts, where you can get wrecked on cheap liquor and practice your head-banging or kung fu moves out on the floor.

Pop, folk, and eclectic

Belly Up Tavern 143 S Cedros Ave, Solana Beach ⓣ858/481-9022, ⓦwww.bellyup.com. Mid-sized hall that plays host nightly to an eclectic range of live music – anything from Fergie and Les Nubians to Leon Russell and They Might Be Giants.

Hot Monkey Love Cafe 6875 El Cajon Blvd ⓣ619/469-4318, ⓦwww.hotmonkeylovecafe.com. Music lovers may want to head northeast of town to La Mesa, where in a converted church this spirited club plays jazz on Thurs nights, rock and pop bands on the weekends, and swing, hip-hop, tango, and salsa on other nights.

Humphrey's Concerts by the Bay 2421 Shelter Island Drive, Point Loma ⓣ619/523-1010, ⓦwww.humphreysconcerts.com. Located near its eponymous restaurant (see p.220), this mainstream concert venue draws a range of mellow, agreeable pop, blues, jazz, country, folk, and lite-rock acts, often of national caliber.

Spreckels Theatre 121 Broadway, Downtown ⓣ619/235-0494. Former moviehouse since converted into elegant venue for pop and lite-rock acts, as well as comedy, world beat, jazz, and lecturers.

Jazz, blues, and reggae

Croce's Jazz Bar 802 5th Ave, Downtown ⓣ619/233-4355, ⓦwww.croces.com. Classy jazz in the backroom of a pricey restaurant (see p.218), with a solid roster of traditional, cool, and smooth acts, and occasionally more adventurous stylings as well.

Dizzy's 344 7th Ave, Downtown ⓣ858/270-7467, ⓦwww.dizzyssandiego.com. As the name suggests, this joint is devoted to straight-up jazz and little else – literally, because the place is as spartan as they come, forcing you to focus on the music instead of chatting over dinner and cocktails.

Performing arts and film

The **performing arts** in San Diego are represented by both provincial and national-quality venues, depending on the medium. **Theater** in town is variable, but can often be quite good: although not quite up to the level of LA's scene, it does attract a range of top-caliber actors and directors by virtue of its Hollywood proximity, and some performances can be inspired. **Comedy**, however, rather pales in comparison here to the other major California cities, with just a few engaging options. **Classical music** and **opera**, by contrast, have much to recommend them, though prices are predictably steeper than for other performing arts fare and attendance figures have tailed off in recent years, imperiling the future of some arts groups. Finally, San Diego has a handful of charming venues for classic, revival, and art **films**, with the first-run multiplexes thicker on the ground, devoted solely to the latest Tinseltown product.

Depending on availability, **half-price tickets** for theater and classical music events for that evening can be purchased at Arts Tix, Broadway at Third Avenue, at Broadway Circle (Tues–Thurs 11am–6pm, Fri & Sat 10am–6pm, Sun 10am–5pm; ☎619/497-5000, ⓦwww.sandiegoperforms.com), or, if you're up in Escondido (see p.233), at the San Diego Visitors Bureau, 360 N Escondido Blvd (Mon–Fri 8.30am–5pm; same contact info). Full-price advance sales are also available, and on Saturday, half-price tickets are issued for Sunday performances. Otherwise, tickets for major shows can be purchased from the venue directly or through Ticketmaster (☎619/220-8497, ⓦwww.ticketmaster.com); check the local papers for times and venues.

Classical music and opera

California Center for the Arts 340 N Escondido Blvd, Escondido ☎760/839-4138, ⓦwww.artcenter.org. You can expect to see soprano recitals, violin sonatas, and chamber music concerts here, as well as the odd jazz and comedy performance.

La Jolla Athenaeum 1008 Wall St ☎858/454-5872, ⓦwww.ljathenaeum.org. A delightful, esteemed music and arts library that has regular performances of highbrow music of all stripes, as well as a nice art gallery.

La Jolla Music Society ☎858/459-3728, ⓦwww.ljcms.org. Makes regular appearances at the Sherwood Auditorium, among other venues, and also puts on the odd sonata or jazz ensemble.

Mandeville Center On the campus UCSD, north of La Jolla ☎858/534-3230, ⓦwww.mandeville.ucsd.edu. Offers jazz, classical, and world music fare throughout the year, as well as dance performances.

Museum of Contemporary Art Downtown at 1100 Kettner Blvd, or in La Jolla at Sherwood Auditorium, 700 Prospect St ☎858/454-3541,

ⓦwww.mcasd.org. Regular performances of jazz, classical, and eclectic tunes, as well as more avant-garde offerings.

San Diego Lyric Opera Birch North Park Theatre, east of Hillcrest at 29th and University Ave ☎619/239-8836, ⓦwww.lyricoperasandiego.com. Presents a bevy of frothy, toe-tapping operetta favorites from Strauss to Weill.

San Diego Opera Based at the Civic Theatre, 1200 Third Ave, Downtown ☎619/533-7000, ⓦwww.sdopera.com. Puts on the familiar big-ticket fare (Mozart, Puccini, Verdi, etc) and frequently boasts top international guest performers during its Jan–May season.

San Diego Symphony Copley Symphony Hall, 750 B St, Downtown ☎619/235-0804, ⓦwww.sandiegosymphony.com. Despite financial struggles in recent years, the symphony presents a full schedule of Classical- and Romantic-era warhorses, with some lite-pops concerts to please the crowds. Performs at a beautifully renovated 1929 movie palace.

Comedy

The **comedy** club scene in San Diego can barely be called a scene, with most jokes cracked (periodically) at venues like the Civic Theatre (see below) or the Spreckels Theatre (see p.224), both Downtown, or at *Humphrey's by the Bay*, in Point Loma (see p.224). The few dedicated comedy joints are listed below; tickets are generally $10–20.

Comedy Co-Op 1211 Sorrento Valley Rd, Sorrento Valley ☏ 1-888/567-4464, ⓦ www.comedycoop .org. Out in the middle of nowhere, this comedy site provides workshops for emerging talent, regular shows, and a wide spectrum of quality – from unbridled hilarity to humorless hamminess.
Comedy Store South 916 Pearl St, La Jolla ☏ 858/454-9176, ⓦ www.thecomedystore .com/2000/lajolla.htm. San Diego branch of the national chain, whose comics aren't quite up to the standard of those in Hollywood (see p.173), but are good enough for a snicker or two.
National Comedy Theatre At Marquis Theatre, 3717 India St, Mission Hills ☏ 619/295-4999, ⓦ www.nationalcomedy.com. A good bet for improvisational comedy – involving much audience participation and berserk antics from a cast of hungry up-and-comers.

Theater

There's a thriving **theater** scene in San Diego, with several mid-sized venues and many smaller fringe venues putting on quality shows. Tickets are over $50 for a major production, or $10–25 for a night on the fringe. The *San Diego Reader* (ⓦ www.sdreader.com) carries full listings.

6th @ Penn 3704 6th Ave, Hillcrest ☏ 619/688-9210, ⓦ www.sixthatpenn.com. A solid alt-venue that puts on performances nightly – sometimes of varying quality, but often quite good and affordable.
Balboa Theatre 850 4th Ave, Downtown ⓦ www .thebalboa.org. Grandly restored Spanish Revival moviehouse from 1924 that has a range of theater, film, dance, and music events.
La Jolla Playhouse UCSD campus, 2910 La Jolla Village Circle ☏ 858/550-1010, ⓦ www .lajollaplayhouse.org. Splashy new modern complex that hosts a range of productions, typically a mix of off-Broadway favorites and a few contemporary dramatica and musical offerings.
Lyceum Stage Theatre 79 Horton Plaza, Downtown ☏ 619/544-1000, ⓦ www .sandiegorep.com. A central theatre that presents consciousness-raising productions about the African-American, Jewish, and other experiences, along with a mix of classics and traveling musicals.
North Coast Repertory Theatre 987 Lomas Sante Fe Drive, Solana Beach ☏ 858/481-2155, ⓦ www.northcoastrep.org. Raucous comedies and earnest dramas, and many local and world premier productions.
San Diego Civic Theatre 202 C St, Downtown ☏ 619/570-1100, ⓦ www.broadwaysd.com. Three-thousand seats geared for mainstream entertainment that mainly revolves around off-Broadway touring shows and musical revivals.
Simon Edison Complex for the Performing Arts In Balboa Park, 1363 Old Globe Way ☏ 619/239-2255, ⓦ www.theoldglobe.org. Three Elizabethan-style theatres ranging from 200 to 600 seats that offer shows friendly to the Bard and other classic and modern playwrights.
Sushi Performance and Visual Art Rotating venues around town ☏ 619/235-8466, ⓦ www .sushiart.org. Avant-garde troupe whose shows are sometimes pretentious, often groundbreaking, and sometimes chilling, but rarely boring.

Film

San Diego has many **cinemas**, most of them offering the usual Hollywood blockbusters. Scan the newspapers for full listings; admission is usually $6–10. For more adventurous programs – foreign-language films, monochrome classics, or cult favorites – try the Landmark Cinemas around town: The Ken, 4061 Adams Avenue (☏ 619/283-5909), the Hillcrest Cinemas, 3965 5th Avenue (☏ 619/299-2100), or the La Jolla Village Cinemas, 8879 Villa La Jolla Drive (☏ 858/453-7831). For an entirely different experience, the

IMAX films at the Reuben H. Fleet Science Center (☎619/238-1233; see p.205) offer the kids an eye-popping selection of nature films and special-effects reels on a giant curved screen. Finally, as a nostalgic alternative, the South Bay Drive-Inn, 2170 Coronado Avenue, in Imperial Beach (☎619/423-2727, ⓦwww.southbaydrivein.com), is one of the few venues of its kind left in Southern California, offering three outdoor screens showing mainstream flicks for $7 per person.

Gay and lesbian San Diego

Although central San Diego is generally welcoming to visitors of all orientations, several hotels and bed and breakfasts are noted for their friendliness toward **gay and lesbian** travelers. Hillcrest is the heart of San Diego's **gay** scene, and you can get information about it from a number of publications and resource centers, as well as various bars and clubs. For **accommodation**, the *Balboa Park Inn* (see p.194) and *Park Manor Suites* (see p.194) are both estimable choices, as is the bare-bones *Friendship Hotel*, 3942 8th Avenue, Hillcrest (☎619/298-9898, ⓦwww.friendshiphotel.net; ❶), one of the least expensive in the area, which still offers clean rooms with TVs and refrigerators.

Publications and resource centers

The primary source of gay and lesbian news and upcoming events is the free weekly *Gay & Lesbian Times* (ⓦwww.gaylesbiantimes.com), distributed through gay bars and clubs, many of the city's coffee bars, and gay-run businesses. You can learn more by contacting the **Lesbian and Gay Men's Community Center**, 3909 Centre Street, Hillcrest (Mon–Fri 9am–10pm, Sat 9am–7pm; ☎619/692-2077, ⓦwww.thecentersd.org), which has served the community for thirty years in several different locations.

Bars and clubs

Bourbon Street 4612 Park Blvd, University Heights ☎619/291-4043. A chic gay crowd gathers nightly around the piano bar at this elegant New Orleans-style club north of Hillcrest, also featuring weekly karaoke and bingo.

Brass Rail 3796 5th Ave, Hillcrest ☎619/298-2233. High-energy dancing every night at this longstanding neighborhood hangout, with a mixed gay and straight crowd, and disco, house and Latin music pumping from the speakers.

Chee-Chee Club 929 Broadway, Downtown ☎619/234-4404. Comfortable, rumpled gay bar with casual atmosphere, grizzled crowd of regulars, and much less attitude than at some of the Hillcrest dance clubs.

Flicks 1017 University Ave, Hillcrest ☎619/297-2056. Popular drinking joint that plays music videos on large screens and offers pinball, pool, and occasional comedy as well.

Hamburger Mary's 308 University Ave, Hillcrest ☎619/491-0400. The epicenter for casual socializing and pre-party drinking in the area, a restaurant and bar which sports a mixed crowd for lunch but gets increasingly cruisey as darkness falls.

Lips 2770 5th Ave, Hillcrest ☎619/295-7900. Drag central in San Diego, with regular performances from smart-aleck queens and elegant divas alike. Signature events include drag karaoke and bingo, and a curious Sunday Gospel Brunch as well.

Numbers 3811 Park Blvd, Hillcrest ☎619/294-9005. Lesbian-friendly spot that has various theme nights (retro-retro-Eighties, hi-NRG, etc) and a frenetic dance vibe that attracts a posey crowd.

Rich's 1051 University Ave, Hillcrest ☎619/295-2195. Originally a mainly gay club, *Rich's* now attracts numerous straights for the heavy dance grooves on weekends and colorful drag queens. Cover charge most nights.

Listings

AAA of Southern California 2440 Hotel Circle North ☎619/233-1000, ⊛www.aaa-calif.com. For maps, guides, and other auto information.

Airport information San Diego International Lindbergh Field Airport, 3225 N Harbor Drive, north of Downtown; ☎619/400-2400, ⊛www.san.org.

Amtrak Based out of Santa Fe Depot, 1050 Kettner Blvd, Downtown; information at ☎1-800/872-7245, ⊛www.amtrak.com.

Beach and surf conditions ☎619/221-8884

Crime Victims Crisis Hotline ☎619/688-9200

Disabled assistance Accessible San Diego (☎858/279-0704, ⊛www.accessandiego.org); Access Center of San Diego, 1295 University Ave, Suite 10 (☎619/293-3500, TDD ☎/293-7757, ⊛www.accesscentersd.org).

Emergencies ☎911

Flea market The huge Kobey's Swap Meet takes place at the San Diego Sports Arena, 3500 Sports Arena Blvd (Fri–Sun 7am–3pm; 50¢ admission Fri, $1 weekends; ☎619/523-2700, ⊛www.kobeyswap.com).

Hospitals For non-urgent treatment, the cheapest place is the Beach Area Family Health Center, 3705 Mission Blvd, Mission Beach (Mon–Wed & Fri 8.30am–5.30pm, Thurs 9am–6pm; ☎619/515-2444, ⊛www.fhcsd.org).

Information ☎411

Internet The Central Library, 820 E St, has free access (see p.199), as do various coffeehouses (see p.222).

Left luggage At the Greyhound terminal and, for ticketed train and trolley travelers, at the Santa Fe Depot.

Pharmacy 24-hour pharmacy at Walgreens, 3005 Midway Drive, north of the airport (☎619/221-0831, ⊛www.walgreens.com), and 3222 University Ave, east of Hillcrest (☎619/528-1793).

Post offices The Downtown post office is at 815 E St (Mon–Fri 8.30am–5pm; Zip code 92101; ☎619/232-6004), and 1125 5th Ave (Mon–Fri 8.30am–5pm; ☎619/239-4350).

Rape Crisis Center/Hotline 4508 Mission Bay Drive ☎619/233-3088.

Sports Baseball's San Diego Padres (☎619/283-4494, ⊛sandiego.padres.mlb.com) play at Petco Park, at the edge of the Gaslamp District, while football's Chargers (☎1-877/242-7437, ⊛www.chargers.com) play at Qualcomm Stadium in Mission Valley. Tickets are available at the stadiums' box offices.

Taxes Sales tax at 7.75%; hotel tax at 10.5%.

Traveler's Aid Available at Lindbergh Field Airport at Terminal 1 (☎619/231-7361) and Terminal 2 (☎619/231-5230).

North San Diego County

Away from the city itself, **North San Diego County** runs from small bedroom communities to more rugged undeveloped country, where camping out and following forest and desert trails provide surprisingly appealing options for an area so close to a metropolis. **Transportation** around the region is straightforward. By car, I-5 skirts along the coast and I-15 runs a little deeper inland, while I-8 heads east from San Diego towards the southern part of the Anza-Borrego Desert State Park (see p.275). East of I-15, throughout the scattered rural communities, the main options involve a network of smaller roads. Public transit is no problem between San Diego and the North County coast, with the San Diego Coaster running from Downtown San Diego up to Oceanside, from where you can transfer to LA's Metrolink commuter rail system. There are also frequent Greyhound buses and Amtrak trains between LA and San Diego.

The North County coast

The towns of the **North County coast** stretch forty miles north from San Diego to the Camp Pendleton marine base, which divides the county from the outskirts of Los Angeles. As they get farther from the city and closer to military installations, the communities generally become more working class and less bourgeois, but by and large attract a mix of tight-lipped business commuters, beach-bumming surfer dudes, and crewcut-sporting tough guys. The main attraction is, of course, the coast itself: miles of excellent beaches with great opportunities for swimming and surfing.

Del Mar and Solana Beach

On the northern edge of the city of San Diego, the tall bluff that contains Torrey Pines State Preserve (see p.217) marks the southern boundary of **DEL MAR**, a town known mainly for its **Del Mar Racetrack**, which stages horse races between late July and early September (☎858/755-1141, ⓦwww.dmtc .com), and has been going strong for seventy years, originally founded by investors including Bing Crosby and Jimmy Durante. It's still one of the most revered and popular tracks in the country, sited just a few blocks from the water's edge. Held throughout June until Independence Day at the San Diego County Fairgrounds, the **San Diego County Fair** (☎858/755-1161, ⓦwww .sdfair.com) is an old-fashioned event with barbecues, kiddie games and face-painting, and livestock shows, though it's mixed with a fair amount of contemporary arts and music events, including cinema showings, mild concerts by pop acts and lite-rockers, and the occasional haunted house. If you want to hit the track and fair overnight, you could pinch a penny at a chain **hotel**, or you could go in style at the *L'auberge Del Mar*, 1540 Camino del Mar (☎858/259-1515, ⓦwww.laubergedelmar.com; ⑨), loaded with chic restaurants, tennis courts, and swanky rooms ($335), and offering top-notch spa and massage services, too. Beyond this, Del Mar is mainly a place to **eat** and **shop** well – at a price. Notable restaurants include *Pacifica Del Mar*, 1555 Camino Del Mar (☎858/792-1803), for its tasty, mid-priced combination of fresh seafood, California cuisine, and prime ocean views; and the top-notch but affordable offerings of the *Fish Market*, 640 Via de la Valle (☎858/755-2277), which also has a scrumptious oyster bar and primo location across from the racetrack. The town's train station is a short walk from its inviting beach.

SOLANA BEACH, the next town north from Del Mar, was in 2003 the first US city to ban smoking from its coastline. It has some striking oceanside views from Solana Beach County Park (also known as "Pillbox" or "Fletcher Cove"), which offers good diving and surfing opportunities, and the town makes a reasonable place for an overnight stop. There's a smattering of antique shops, galleries, and watersports vendors, as well as some decent entertainment – the North Coast Repertory Theatre is up here (see p.226), as is the 🎵 *Belly Up Tavern*, 143 S Cedros Avenue (☎858/481-9022), one of the major mid-sized music venues in the area (see p.224). Standard-issue **motels** line the coastal road, or you can stay just inland at the chic *Rancho Valencia Resort*, 5921 Valencia Circle (☎858/756-1123, ⓦwww .ranchovalencia.com; ⑨), another upscale golf-and-tennis outpost with fine dining, spa services, and lush rooms ($425), or more affordably at *Courtyard by Marriott*, 717 S Highway 101 (☎858/792-8200, ⓦwww.marriott.com; ⑥), with pool, gym, hot tub, and high-speed Internet access.

For **food**, make sure to drop in on *Nobu*, 315 S Coast Highway (☎858/755-7787), a singular spot for sushi and sashimi – among the best in the region – in a stretch dominated by more conventional seafood diners; and *Pizza Nova*, 945 Lomas Santa Fe Drive (☎858/259-0666), a North Coast outpost of the excellent regional chain, with toppings like gorgonzola pear and garlic-and-alfredo sauce, among more conventional choices. If you're driving, take a quick, four-mile detour inland along Hwy-8, passing the town of **Fairbanks Ranch** (built by the film star Douglas Fairbanks Jr), to **Rancho Santa Fe**, an ultra-upscale small community with a distinctive Spanish architectural flavor from the 1920s and 1930s, whose design style is enforced by an all-powerful "Art Jury" that rigidly disallows any deviation from the quaint look.

Encinitas and Leucadia

The major flower-growing center of **ENCINITAS** is at its best during the spring, when its blooms of floral color are most radiant. It's no surprise that an Indian guru, Paramahansa Yogananda, chose the town as the headquarters of the Self-Realization Fellowship, near Sea Cliff Roadside Park, a popular surfing beach dubbed "Swami's" by the locals. The fellowship's serene **Meditation Gardens**, around the corner at 215 K Street (Tues–Sat 9am–5pm, Sun 11am–5pm; free; ☎760/753-2888, ⓦwww.yogananda-srf.org), are open to all, and revolve around an ecumenical philosophy with spiritual healing and cleansing themes. Nearby are the similarly relaxing **Quail Botanical Gardens**, 230 Quail Gardens Drive (daily 9am–5pm; $10; ☎760/436-3036, ⓦwww.qbgardens.org), which hosts thirty different gardens, including some rich in bamboo, California endemics, palms, and various selections of foliage from each continent, plus a pocket rainforest and a "Succulents Under the Sea" section that simulates the look of a coral reef using desert plants. Also compelling is **San Elijo Lagoon Ecological Reserve**, 2710 Manchester Avenue (☎760/436-3944, ⓦwww.sanelijo.org), one of the biggest remaining coastal wetlands in the state, a thousand acres rich with endemic plants, fish, and birds – and based around marshes, scrubland, and chapparal – which you can explore on seven miles of hiking trails. For more local information, call at the **visitor center**, 138 Encinitas Boulevard (Mon–Fri 9am–5pm, Sat 10am–4pm; ☎760/753-6041, ⓦwww.encinitaschamber.com). Throughout the area's beaches, **surfing** opportunities are numerous, and you can practice your longboard skills at Leucadia Surf School (☎760/635-7873, ⓦwww.leucadiasurfschool.com), an esteemed outfit that offers two-hour group or private lessons for $50 and $100, respectively, on Grandview Beach, with boards and wetsuits included. Otherwise, if you've taken a lesson, you can rent basic surfboards for $20 for the remainder of the day.

Encinitas and the adjoining community of **LEUCADIA**, three miles to the north, offer reasonably priced **accommodation**, such as the *Moonlight Beach Motel*, 233 2nd Street, Encinitas (☎1-800/323-1259; ⑤), nicely located near the beach with kitchenettes, fridges, and microwaves in all rooms, and the *Leucadia Inn*, 960 N Highway 101 (☎1-888/942-1668; ⓦwww.leucadiainn.com; ⑥), whose six rooms are loosely themed around styles like "African safari" and "calypso," with kitchenettes and fridges and beach access a block away. Otherwise, there's the landscaped **campground** at San Elijo Beach State Park ($25–34; ☎1-800/444-7275, ⓦwww.reserveamerica.com), near **Cardiff-by-the-Sea** just to the south, whose name comes from the whim of its founder's British wife.

Dining options in the towns consist of the usual seafood eateries along the highway and a slew of basic breakfast-and-lunch diners; what stands out are places such as *Trattoria I Trulli*, 830 S Coast Highway, Encinitas (℡760/943-6800), whose California-styled Italian cuisine with fresh and delicious ingredients is well worth a try; *Vigilucci's*, 505 S Coast Highway, Encinitas (℡760/942-7332), one of five area locations, another solid Italian entry with more straightforward pizza, pasta, and seafood; and *Ki's*, 2591 S Highway 101, Cardiff (℡760/436-5236), which appeals for its range of healthy salads, seafood wraps, smoothies, and pasta, with a number of vegetarian and vegan choices on offer.

Carlsbad

Surfers are the main visitors to **South Carlsbad State Beach**, with a busy cliff-top campground for RVs only ($25–35; ℡1-800/444-7275, ⓦwww.reserveamerica.com), which also features swimming, fishing, and scuba diving. The beach marks the edge of **CARLSBAD**, another upscale town, whose cutesy, pseudo-Teutonic architecture derives from the early-1880s belief that water from a local spring had the same invigorating qualities as the waters of Karlsbad, a spa town in Bohemia (now part of the Czech Republic). "Carlsbad" thus became a health resort, promoted by pioneer-turned-entrepreneur John Frazier, whose bronze image overlooks the (now dry) original springs near Carlsbad Boulevard and Carlsbad Village Drive. The town's **visitor center**, 5934 Priestly Drive (Mon–Fri 9am–5pm, Sat 10am–4pm, Sun 10am–3pm; ℡1-800/227-5722, ⓦwww.carlsbad.org), offers a look at this curious local history.

Though it's prominently promoted by the center, only visitors who need a refresher on the difference between a violin and a viola, or who enjoy sound clips of old pop songs, should visit the plodding **Museum of Making Music**, 5790 Armada Drive (Tues–Sun 10am–5pm; $5; ℡760/438-5996, ⓦwww.museumofmakingmusic.org); more appealing are the blooms of the **Flower Fields**, 5704 Paseo del Norte (early Mar to early May daily 9am–6pm; $9; ℡760/431-0352, ⓦwww.theflowerfields.com), which appear in the spring on fifty acres highlighted with plots of roses, poinsettias, and other eye-catching seasonal blossoms. Otherwise, the most popular attraction in Carlsbad these days is the curious theme park of **Legoland California** (1 Lego Drive, exit Cannon Road off I-5; $57, kids $44, parking $10; ℡760/918-5346, ⓦwww.legoland.com), where kids are encouraged to climb on larger-than-life Lego bricks, make their way through colorful mazes, ride the Coastersaurus rollercoaster and other pint-sized thrill rides, splash around in the Pirate Shores water park section, operate miniature cars and boats, and view assorted places built on a minuscule scale – among them New Orleans, Las Vegas, Washington DC, and the coastline of Southern California.

Other than the campground and the usual chain motels, you'll pay plenty to **stay** in one of Carlsbad's more distinctive options for lodging. One of the less expensive places is the *Carlsbad Inn,* 3075 Carlsbad Boulevard (℡760/434-7020, ⓦwww.carlsbadinn.com; ❼), whose rooms variously come with kitchenettes, spas, and fireplaces, with more expensive suites and condos available with wide views of the Pacific. Otherwise, you can splurge even more at the *Grand Pacific Palisades* resort, across from the Flower Fields at 5805 Armada Drive (℡760/827-3200, ⓦwww.grandpacificpalisades.com; ❼), whose rooms comes with balconies or patios, CD and DVD players, and wireless Internet, and which boasts an on-site pool, sauna, game room, and three spas. Good places to **eat** include ⅔ *Fidel's Norte,* 3003 Carlsbad Boulevard (℡760/729-0903), one of the better and more authentic spots for Mexican food in the area, from the usual enchiladas to more exotic fare like cooked cactus, and *The Armenian Café,* 3126 Carlsbad Boulevard (℡760/720-2233), where the American and Middle

Eastern dishes are presented at very affordable prices. To really get into the spirit of the town, though, and stuff your ribs like you mean it, check out *Tip Top Meats*, 6118 Paseo del Norte (℡760/438-2620), a butchery and deli whose hefty German fare features the likes of bratwurst, stuffed cabbage, and smoked Polish sausages.

Oceanside

The most northerly town on the coast of San Diego County, **Oceanside**, five miles north of Carlsbad, is dominated by the huge **Camp Pendleton** marine base, though its downtown is charming and its beaches are beautiful, decorated by the fetching town **pier** that extends nearly two thousand feet into the waves. Oceanside is also a major transit center (Amtrak, Greyhound, the Coaster, and Metrolink trains to LA pass through) and the easiest place from which to reach Mission San Luis Rey (see below).

The town's prime attractions include the **Buena Vista Audubon Nature Center**, 2202 S Coast Highway (Tues–Sat 10am–4pm, Sun 1–4pm; free; ℡760/439-2473, ⓦwww.bvaudubon.org), which can recommend area walks and arranges nature-oriented field trips, and is adjacent to a lagoon that's especially good for spotting grebes, terns, coots, and pelicans, and for relaxing walks. Engaging in a different way is the **California Surf Museum**, 223 N Coast Highway (daily 10am–4pm; free; ℡760/721-6876, ⓦwww.surfmuseum .org), with displays on some of the top local surfers and boards that tackled the most wicked breaks, and some of the most inventive board designers who gave shape to that quintessential California icon. Finally, the **Oceanside Museum of Art**, 704 Pier View Way (Tues–Sat 10am–4pm, Sun 1–4pm; $5; ℡760/721-2787, ⓦwww.oma-online.org), is housed in a spartan but elegant Irving Gill design from the early twentieth century, with a fine range of contemporary art from glassworks to photography to multimedia, typically shown in rotating exhibits during the year.

Oceanside is mostly given over to a predictable complement of chain **lodging**, but one of the exceptions is the *Oceanside Marina Suites*, 2800 Harbor Drive N (℡760/722-1561, ⓦwww.omihotel.com; rooms ❻, suites ❼), which offers fine views (on separate sides) of both the town marina and the Pacific, and has newly renovated suites with fireplaces and kitchens and on-site spa, pool, sauna, and complimentary breakfast. For **eating**, the *Hill Street Coffee House*, 524 S Coast Highway (℡760/966-0985), is a worthwhile choice amid the fast-food joints, an old Victorian home offering great coffee, cakes, sandwiches, and salads, including some vegetarian options, and weekend live music; and the *101 Café*, 631 S Coast Highway (℡760/722-5220), is the town's oldest eatery and long a fixture for its 1950s decor and classic American diner fare, served from nearly dawn to midnight.

Mission San Luis Rey and around

Four miles inland from Oceanside along Hwy-76, **Mission San Luis Rey**, 4050 Mission Avenue (daily 10am–4pm; $5; ℡760/757-3651, ⓦwww .sanluisrey.org), founded in 1798 by Padre Laséun, was the largest of the California missions and once the center for three thousand Native American converts. Franciscan monks still inhabit the mission, and there's a **museum** and a serene candle lit **chapel**. Even if you don't go inside, look around the foundations of the guards' barracks immediately outside the main building and, across the road, the remains of the mission's ornate **sunken gardens**, once *lavanderías* where the mission's inhabitants did their washing. If you're sufficiently inspired by all the holiness, you can even **stay** here on selected weekends for various religiously themed retreats and workshops; overnight visits with dinner run anywhere from \$25 to \$225, depending on the length and focus of the visit. Contact the mission's retreat center (℡760/757-3659) for more information.

Beyond the mission, push on another four miles to **Guajome County Park**, 3000 Guajome Lake Road (9.30am to an hour before dusk; \$5 per vehicle, camping \$20), whose centerpiece is a twenty-room adobe **rancho**, 2210 N Santa Fe Avenue (guided tours Sat & Sun 11am, 12.30pm & 2pm; donation; ℡760/724-4082, ⓦwww.historyandculture.com/guajome). The structure was erected in the mid-nineteenth century for newlyweds Cave Couts and Ysidora Bandini, socialites who later entertained celebrities like Helen Hunt Jackson – who, according to legend, based the title character of *Ramona*, her sentimental tale of Indian life in the mission era, on Ysidora's maid. After Couts' death in 1874, Ysidora tried to maintain the place but over the years it became dilapidated, until it was finally bought and restored by the county.

Hwy-76 continues inland to Mission San Antonio de Pala and Palomar Observatory (see p.236). Along the coast beyond Oceanside, the US military keeps its territory relatively undeveloped, creating a vivid impression of how stark the land was before commercialization took hold. The uncluttered **beach** around the San Onofre Nuclear Plant is popular with surfers, thanks to its slow-rolling, longboard-friendly waves, and very unpopular with environmentalists, who have been trying for decades to get the plant – built near a tectonic fault – shut down for good. Beyond is the town of San Clemente (see p.148) and the southern edge of the huge LA metropolis.

The North County inland

Unlike the coast, the **North County inland** has no sizeable towns and is mostly given over to farming, its terrain featuring dense forests, deep valleys, and mile-high mountain ranges. Besides a few reminders of the ancient indigenous cultures, remnants from the mission era, and just a few settlements, it's best to make for the area's state parks and enjoy some leisurely countryside walks, or venture further east to the dramatic Anza-Borrego Desert (see p.275).

Escondido and around

The pleasant burg of **ESCONDIDO** – Spanish for "hidden" – is one of the region's fastest-growing spots, where retirees and ex-urbanites mix with hip younger folk, well away from most of San Diego County's tourist traffic. Accessible via bus #20 from Downtown (connecting with bus #350), it's about forty miles north of San Diego on I-15, and is the terminus of the new SPRINTER rail service (information at ℡760/599-8332, ⓦwww.gonctd .com), which links to Oceanside, from where you can access the entire coast of the state on public transit.

The town is definitely worth a look for its **Heritage Walk** in Grape Day Park, offering a glimpse of several restored Victorian buildings (Thurs–Sat 1–4pm; free) and a 1925 railroad car with an elaborate scale model of the train that previously linked Escondido to Oceanside, as well as an old-fashioned blacksmith shop, a rustic barn, a windmill, and an antique train depot. For more information, check out the **History Center** devoted to the walk, 321 N Broadway (same hours; \$3; ℡760/743-8207, ⓦwww.escondidohistory.org). Nearby, the **California Center for the Arts**, 340 N Escondido Boulevard

(Tues–Sat 10am–4pm, Sun 1–4pm; $5; ☎760/839-4138, ⓦwww.artcenter.org), features a surprisingly good contemporary art museum, showcasing a range of traditional media as well as avant-garde video-art exhibitions, and two theaters that present comedy and dance performances along with jazz, classical, and world music offerings. The other big draw is the local branch of the **Mingei International Museum** (based in Balboa Park; see p.204), at 155 W Grand Avenue (Tues–Sat 1–4pm; $6; ☎760/735-3355, ⓦwww.mingei.org), which displays a broad array of folk art encompassing native artifacts, handcrafted art furniture, origami, woven garments, and ceremonial clothing, as well as contemporary sculpture and design and just about anything else you can imagine.

Finally, no trip to Escondido would be complete without a stop at the eye-opening **Queen Califia's Magical Circle**, Bear Valley Parkway at Mary Lane, in Kit Carson Park (daily dawn–dusk; free; ☎760/839-4691, ⓦwww .queencalifia.org), Niki de Saint Phalle's bizarre, strangely delightful art garden based around nine of her more fanciful mosaic sculptures, including such oddments as hissing snake heads and gilded humans riding multicolored birds. The comprehensive **visitor center**, 360 N Escondido Boulevard (Mon–Fri 8.30am–5pm; ☎1-800/848-3336, ⓦwww.sandiegonorth.com), provides information for the entire North County area.

Five miles south of Escondido amid stunning scenery, the **Orfila Winery**, 13455 San Pasqual Valley Road (daily 10am–6pm, tours at 2pm; ☎760/738-6500 ext. 22, ⓦwww.orfila.com), offers tastings of wine produced by a former Napa Valley vintner, as well as tours of the handsome facility. Eight miles north of town off I-15 (no public transit) is the Escondido area's most renowned – or depressing – attraction, the **Lawrence Welk Resort**, 8860 Lawrence Welk Drive (☎1-800/932-9355, ⓦwww.welkresort.com; ❼), a thousand-acre vacation complex of golf courses, spas and swimming pools (with a water slide), guest villas, and the musical-oriented Welk Dinner Theater. Rising from accordion-playing unknown to musical juggernaut, TV bandleader Welk was the inventor of "champagne music" – basically waltzes and polkas with a touch of sanitized swing. Displayed around the theater lobby, the Welk hagiography is

▲ Queen Califia's Magical Circle, Escondido

both disturbing and fascinating, following the peculiar career of the thick-accented, native North Dakotan who most people assumed was an immigrant fresh from central Europe.

Beyond the Welk Resort, Escondido is not really the ideal place to **stay**, with only a few reasonable options of the chain-motel variety. One exception is the pleasant *Zosa Gardens*, 9381 W Lilac Road (℡760/723-9093, ⓦwww .zosagardens.com; ❺–❽), a bed and breakfast set in a replica Spanish hacienda on 22 acres, with thirteen somewhat precious rooms and suites and an on-site pool, a Jacuzzi, and an abundance of surrounding flowers and greenery. For **dining**, the *150 Grand Café*, 150 W Grand Avenue (℡760/738-6868), is one of the bigger names in town for its succulent California cuisine, while the *Brigantine Escondido*, 421 W Felicita Street (℡760/743-4718), doles out good, if pricey, surf'n'turf and has a good oyster bar, too. The most exciting recent arrival to town, though, is the *Stone Brewing World Bistro*, 1999 Citracado Parkway (℡760/471-4999, ⓦwww.stoneworldbistro.com), presenting a range of some of the country's best microbrews, including such tasty offerings as Arrogant Bastard Ale and Stone Ruination IPA.

North from Escondido

Hwy-S6 leads fifteen miles north from Escondido to **Mission San Antonio de Pala** (Tues–Sun 10am–5pm; donation; ℡760/742-3317), near the junction of Hwy-76 from Oceanside. Built as an outpost of Mission San Luis Rey in 1816, it lay in ruins until the Cupa Indians were ousted from their tribal home at the turn of the twentieth century and moved to this site, where the mission was revived to serve as their church. Although the current buildings are just replicas of the originals, they do offer an eerie atmosphere, with an evocative cemetery, lovely gardens, and a single-room **museum** which contains artifacts created by the native Pala people and dating back to the days of the original mission.

The enormous, half-million acres of **Cleveland National Forest** (℡760/788-0250, ⓦwww.r5.fs.fed.us/cleveland), east from the mission on Hwy-76, are home to twenty state and federal **campgrounds** ($10–25) and stretch south almost to the Mexican border. There are plenty of trails to explore in the Palomar, Trabuco, and Descanso sections of the forest, most of them running from one to ten miles, with the exception of the daunting **Pacific Crest Trail**, which covers a hundred miles here – only a small fraction of its full 2650-mile length as its crosses the spine of the West Coast from Mexico to Canada. Otherwise, there's a nice range of activities available in the park, from fishing to pleasant scenic drives, but be careful during the summer or excessively hot and dry periods – Cleveland National Forest is known for its significant potential for **wildfires**, which can take light and spread very quickly if the conditions are right, forcing mass evacuations and emergency state and regional action. For more information on activities, safety, and current conditions, contact the **ranger stations** located in the region's small towns: Trabuco District, 1147 E Sixth Street, Corona (℡951/736-1811), Palomar District, 1634 Black Canyon Road, Ramona (℡760/788-0250), or Descanso District, 3348 Alpine Boulevard, Alpine (℡619/445-6235).

Less hearty backpackers tend to prefer the 1900-acre **Palomar Mountain State Park** (℡760/742-3462, ⓦwww.palomar.statepark.org), on Hwy-S7, for its cooler, higher altitude (some parts rise above five thousand feet) and easy hiking trails. You can camp ($15) at Doane Valley (first-come-first-served Dec–Mar, rest of year by reservation at ℡1-800/444-7275, ⓦwww.reserveamerica .com) or Cedar Grove (April–Nov by reservation only, same info). Eight miles east of the park on Hwy-S6 sits the two-hundred-inch Hale telescope of CalTech's **Palomar Observatory** (daily 9am–4pm; free; ℡760/742-2111, ⓦwww.astro.caltech.edu/palomarpublic), capable of seeing a billion light years into the cosmos. As a visitor, it's not possible to view the distant galaxies directly, though the apparatus is impressive enough by itself and, at the visitor center, you can look at the observatory's striking collection of deep-space photographs taken with the powerful lens.

East from Escondido

Ten miles east of Escondido on Hwy-78 (bus #386; Mon–Sat) and thirty miles north of San Diego (no direct bus access), the San Diego Zoo's **San Diego Wild Animal Park**, 15500 San Pasqual Valley Road (daily 9am–4pm, summer until 8pm; $28.50, kids $17.50, combined ticket with San Diego Zoo $59, kids $39; parking $8; ℡619/718-3000, ⓦwww.sandiegozoo.org/wap), is the major tourist attraction in the area. It's an 1800-acre enclosure packed with three thousand animals, featuring a sizeable tropical-bird aviary, mock African bush and Kilimanjaro hiking trail, elephant rides, and various films and exhibitions. The steep admission fee includes a fifty-minute ride on the **Wgasa Bush Line Monorail** (as well as on a motorized tram line), which skirts through the outer reaches of the park, where the animals – including lions, tigers, cheetahs, deer, and monkeys – roam about for your amusement. More historically minded visitors may, however, prefer a stop at the **San Pasqual Battlefield**, two miles away at 15808 San Pasqual Valley Road (Sat & Sun 10am–5pm; free; ℡760/737-2201), whose visitor center provides the details of this bloody and tumultuous 1846 battle in the Mexican-American War, which is enthusiastically re-created every year on the Sunday closest to December 6 by groups of war re-enactors. An outlying historic trail also offers information on the region's ecosystem and native cultures predating the arrival of white colonists.

The terrain becomes increasingly sparse as you press further east along Hwy-78 into a region that's difficult to access without a car. If you're coming this way directly from San Diego, use Hwy-67 and join Hwy-78 at Ramona, eighteen miles from Escondido, and continue east for sixteen miles to **Santa Ysabel**. While unexceptional, this tiny crossroads is enlivened by **Dudley's Bakery**, 30218 Hwy-78, just before the junction with Hwy-79 (Fri–Mon 8am–5pm; ℡760/225-3348, ⓦwww.dudleysbakery.com), famous for its home-baked breads and pastries – the date, nut, and raisin loaf for one – at giveaway prices, and the small **Mission Santa Ysabel Asistencia**, a mile and a half north of town at 23013 Hwy-79 (summer 8am–5.30pm; winter 8am–4pm; donation; ℡760/765-0810), a 1924 replacement of an 1818 original structure. Sitting in moody isolation, the mission has a small modern chapel and, around the side, a one-room **museum** detailing the history of the site. Outside is an Indian burial ground, and the church continues to serve several local Native American communities.

Julian and around

Seven miles southeast of Santa Ysabel on Hwy-78A, the hamlet of **JULIAN** was amazingly once the second biggest town in the San Diego area, thanks to an 1869 gold discovery here. Its population declined after that, and it nearly burned down in 2003 when the devastating, 280,000-acre **Cedar Fire** – the second largest in the state's recorded history – enveloped much of the surrounding forest. These days, the town's formidable cider and apple pies can draw a fair crowd of weekend visitors, and at an elevation of 4000ft, the town provides a temperate base from which to make forays into the Anza-Borrego Desert (see p.275), fewer than ten miles to the east. There are also plenty of antique shops and Western-themed boutiques, horseback rides, and access to worthwhile park sites, wineries, and scenic drives. To get a sense of the full scope of history and activities, drop by the **visitor center**, housed in the hundred-year-old **Julian Town Hall**, 2129 Main Street (daily 10am–5pm; ☎760/765-1857, ⓦwww.julianca.com), which has information, photos, and displays, and offers a walking-tour guide of the local highlights. Indeed, Julian has numerous old buildings in various states of preservation with various exhibits inside. The most notable include the Gold Rush-era mining equipment on display at the **Julian Pioneer Museum**, 2811 Washington Street (April–Nov Wed–Sun 10am–4pm; donation; ☎760/765-0227), also including a mildly interesting assortment of antiques and castoffs from the late Victorian era, among them pianos, an old-time buggy, lace craftworks and historic apparel, stuffed animals, and Native American relics — all housed in a former brewery-turned-blacksmith shop. More precarious is the creaky old gold mine of the **Eagle Peak Mining Company**, at the end of C Street (call for hours; $8; ☎760/735-0036), where hour-long tours give a sense of the subterranean perils faced by the town's early workers.

Overall, with its quaint buildings and rustic charm, Julian's appeal centers on its Main Street. For **accommodation**, the visitor center has details of the town's many attractive **B&Bs**. Among these, the *Julian Gold Rush Hotel*, 2032 Main Street (☎1-800/734-5854, ⓦwww.julianhotel.com; ⓺), is the oldest functioning hotel in the state, opened in 1897 by a freed slave; the pair of rooms, plus a cottage and small house, are decorated in period styles, and rates include afternoon tea and a full breakfast. The *Julian Lodge*, 2720 C Street (☎1-800/542-1420, ⓦwww.julianlodge.com; ⓸ weekdays, ⓹ weekends), is only a replica of a historic hotel, but has a similar country atmosphere and many more rooms, offering a buffet-style continental breakfast. However, the most distinctive digs are at the *Shadow Mountain Ranch*, 2771 Frisius Road (☎760/765-0323, ⓦwww.shadowmountainranch.net; ⓹), which has a conventional Victorian room and two cottages, as well as a more unusual "Grandma's Attic" done up in lace and satin, a storybook cottage, and a "Gnome Home" that's even more kitschy than it sounds. **Eating** options include the *Julian Café*, 2112 Main Street (☎760/765-2712), for a good old-time atmosphere and meals, including apple pie; *Bailey Woodpit Barbecue*, 2307 Main Street (☎760/765-3757), featuring fine grilled meat served falling-off-the-bone tender, as well as pies; and the ⚘ *Julian Pie Company*, 2225 Main Street (☎760/765-2449, ⓦwww.julianpie.com), with three kinds of old-fashioned apple pies, and wonderful fruit-pie combinations using cherries, raspberries, peaches, and boysenberries.

To the north, and rising above Julian off Farmer Road, the 5000-foot-high **Volcan Mountain Wilderness Preserve** (open 24hr; free; ☎760/765-2300, ⓦwww.volcanmt.org) makes for an interesting visit, covering some 25,000 acres. Whether self- or fully guided (monthly May–Oct), the main trek is a five-mile round trip to the summit, from where you can get an excellent overview of the region; shorter trails pass through orchards, oak groves, and manzanitas. For a natural experience of a very different kind, visit the **California Wolf Center**, four miles south of Julian at 18457 Hwy-79 ($10; by reservation only at ☎619/234-9653, ⓦwww.californiawolfcenter.org), whose Saturday programs (at 2pm) provide an introduction to all things lupine, giving you a ninety-minute look at the steely-eyed North American gray wolves in their packs and discussing the need and strategy to reintroduce them to the wild.

Cuyamaca Rancho State Park

No area of San Diego County was more devastated by the 2003 Cedar Fire than the oaks, willows, sycamores, and pines of **Cuyamaca Rancho State Park** (☏760/765-0755, ⓦwww.cuyamaca.us), nine miles south of Julian and nine miles east of I-8 along Hwy-79. From its lush subalpine meadows to stark mountain peaks, most of the park's 25,000 acres, including its wilderness area, campgrounds, and hundreds of miles of hiking trails, were damaged. In the years since then, an army of volunteers has rebuilt the park's facilities and reconstructed its trails, and nature has done the rest – the park is a marvel of adaptability and revival in the face of natural, cyclical catastrophe. Most of the trails, together stretching some one hundred miles, have now been reopened, as have the **campgrounds** ($15–20; reserve at ☏1-800/444-7275, ⓦwww .reserveamerica.com), which are highlighted by **Paso Picacho**, twelve miles south of Julian, and **Green Valley**, five miles further south. These grounds are the only accommodation available unless you're hiking into the backcountry sites: *Arroyo Seco*, a mile and a half northwest of *Green Valley*, and *Granite Spring*, almost five miles east. Pick up information and maps from **park headquarters**, 12551 Hwy-79 (Mon–Fri 8am–5pm), sixteen miles south of Julian in the heart of the park. If you're a birder, check out the excellent **museum** (same hours; free) in the park headquarters, which gives the rundown of the various feathered creatures in the park, among them native wrens, hawks, bluebirds, and woodpeckers. It also offers a historical backdrop on how the local Kumeyaay natives resisted Spanish attempts to cut down the area's forests, strongly fought the arrival of white American settlers, and were one of the last groups forced onto reservations.

Travel details

Amtrak trains

San Diego to: Anaheim (10 daily; 2hr); Los Angeles Downtown (10 daily; 2hr 45min); Oceanside (10 daily; 50min); San Juan Capistrano (10 daily; 1hr 25min); Santa Barbara (4 daily; 5hr 35min); Solana Beach (10 daily; 35min).

Buses

San Diego (Greyhound) to: Anaheim (6 daily; 2hr 5min); Long Beach (6 daily; 2hr 20min); Los Angeles Downtown (18 daily; 2hr 45min); Oceanside (10 daily; 50min); San Francisco (6 daily; 11–13hr); Santa Barbara (6 daily; 5–7hr). San Diego (Metropolitan Transit) to: Escondido (regular service; 1hr 45min); La Jolla (30–50min); Ramona (2–3hr); San Luis Rey (1hr 40min); Wild Animal Park (3hr).

3

The deserts

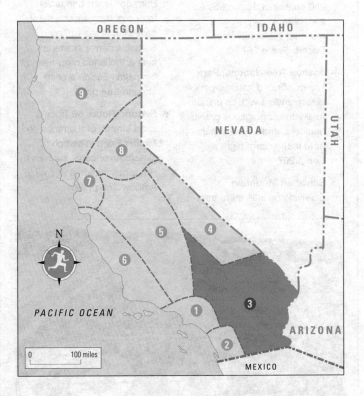

Highlights

✳ **Palm Springs Aerial Tramway**
Take a break from the scorching desert and ride the cable car up to the crisp pine forests to enjoy stupendous panoramic views. See p.255

✳ **Living Desert** Marvel at the desert's unique flora, fauna, and culture at this combined zoo, botanic garden, and museum in swanky Palm Desert. See p.257

✳ **Joshua Tree National Park**
The celebrated national park is resplendent with its unique freaky trees, gorgeous granite boulders, and coyotes that howl in the warm night air. See p.267

✳ **Salvation Mountain**
Surviving on little more than religious devotion, one man has produced his personal monument to God, a bizarrely colorful synthesis of found objects, straw bales, and paint. See p.274

✳ **Borrego Palm Canyon** An hour's stroll across the Anza-Borrego Desert brings you to one of the largest natural oases left in the United States, a dense cluster of over a thousand mop-headed fan palms beside a crisp stream. See p.277

✳ **Historic Route 66** Trace a short stretch of the renowned Mother Road in search of classic Americana, such as Roy's gas station and café in Amboy. See p.286

▲ Route 66, Amboy

The deserts

The **deserts** of Southern California represent only a fraction of the half a million square miles of North American desert that stretch away eastward into another four states and cross the border into Mexico to the south. Contrary to the monotonous landscape you might expect, California's deserts are a kaleidoscope of light, color, and texture, dotted with everything from ramshackle settlements to posh resorts. The one thing you can rely on is that, for a large part of the year, they will be uniformly hot and dry. In fact, during the hottest summer months temperatures in the deserts can reach such dangerous heights that you'd be well advised to give them a miss altogether. And don't count on rain to cool things off – rainfall in this landscape is highly irregular and a whole year's average of three or four inches may fall in a single storm.

Most of the 25 million acres that make up the desert are protected in state and national parks, but not all are entirely unspoiled. Three million acres are used by the US government as military bases for training and weapons testing, and when explosions aren't shaking up the desert's fragile ecosystem, the region's many fans flock here to do their own damage, many on off-road vehicles.

In spite of this, most of the desert remains a wilderness, and could easily be the highlight of your trip to California. Occupying a quarter of the state, it divides into two distinct regions: the **Colorado** or **Low Desert** in the south, stretching down to the Mexican border and east into Arizona, where it's an extension of the Sonoran Desert; and the **Mojave** or **High Desert**, which covers the south-central part of the state. The Colorado is easily reached from LA by passing through the extravagantly wealthy Coachella Valley, with **Palm Springs** serving as its gateway. It's the kind of town where it helps to have a bankroll for optimum enjoyment amid the plush resorts and swanky restaurants, but summer accommodation prices are remarkably low. And despite its glossy veneer, there's no shortage of moderately priced things to do: riding the **Palm Springs Aerial Tramway** to the cool of the San Jacinto mountains, learning about the region's pre-eminent habitat at the **Living Desert** ecological museum, and taking a **Celebrity Tour** past the homes of the rich and famous.

Serious desert enthusiasts should make a beeline for **Joshua Tree National Park**, which bridges the divide between the Colorado and Mojave deserts in a vast, silent area of craggy trees. Hiking during the day, then camping out amid the photogenic boulder stacks and the cries of coyotes, is an unforgettable experience. In contrast, the undiluted Colorado Desert of the **Imperial Valley** to the south is mostly given over to agricultural land, which you could pass through without realizing anyone lives there. Beyond is the **Salton Sea**, artificially created a century ago and now mostly a curiosity, though it is worth calling in at the bizarre

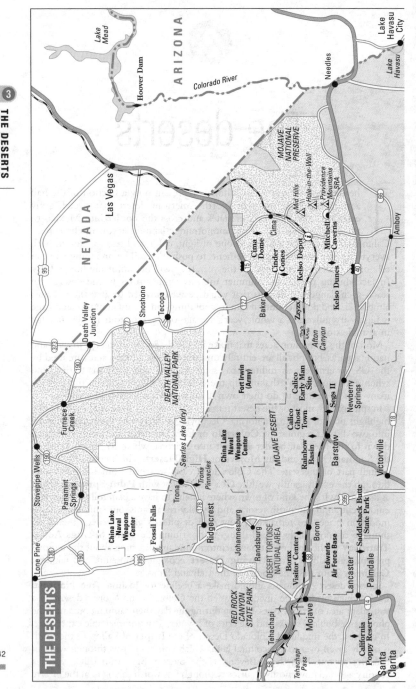

THE DESERTS

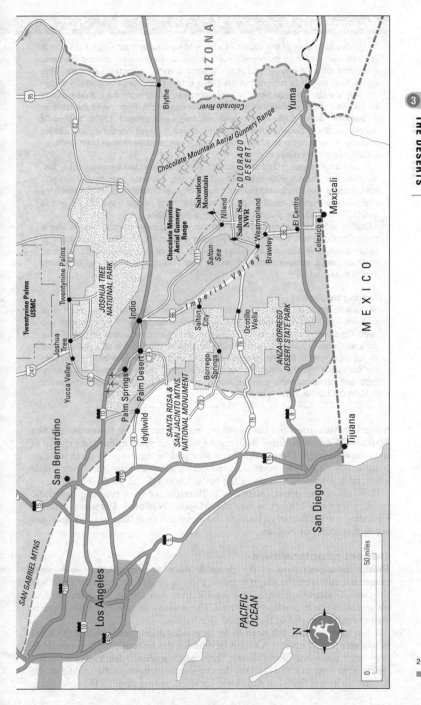

Desert survival

To survive the rigors of the desert you have to be cool in more ways than one. It is rarely conquered by pioneering spirit alone, and every year people die here. First, and most obviously, you're up against a pretty formidable **climate**. This varies from region to region, but the basic safety procedures remain the same: not only are you doing battle with incredible heat, but at night the high elevations can mean below-freezing temperatures. Lots of visitors do come to the deserts in summer, when daytime temperatures frequently exceed 120°F, but you'll appreciate the experience more if you time your travels here during the **cooler months**, from October to May, when daytime temperatures range from the mid-sixties to the low nineties.

At any time of year, you'll stay coolest and best protected wearing loose, full-length clothing and a wide-brimmed hat. Not only will such gear help shield you from the sun, but it may also prevent bites, stings, and scratches from desert flora and fauna, covered in detail on p.52. That said, many people travel the deserts in shorts, T-shirt, and sunglasses, and get by quite happily.

Bear in mind too that while the desert may be a danger to man, man is also a danger to the desert. Smog from Los Angeles drifts quickly eastward, and you may notice patches of it obscuring vistas here. To reduce your own impact, exercise common sense: remove nothing from the land except your trash, and leave only footprints behind.

Driving through

Sticking to the main highways, desert travel doesn't generally pose much of a problem, and filling your water jugs and gas tank should be all the preparation you need. On steep grades, there is a chance of getting an **overheated engine**. If your car's temperature needle rises alarmingly, turn the air conditioning off and the heater on full-blast to cool the engine quickly. If this fails and the engine blows, stop with the car facing into the wind and the engine running, pour water over the radiator grille, and top up the water reservoir. Also consider taking along a windshield reflector to keep the car cool when parked.

Salvation Mountain and the migratory birds at the **Sonny Bono Salton Sea National Wildlife Refuge**. Both can be visited en route to the vast expanse of the **Anza–Borrego Desert**, the largest state park in the lower 48 states, boasting multifarious varieties of vegetation and geological quirks that can, with a little effort, be as rewarding as those of the better-known deserts to the north.

The hub of the desert interstates is **Barstow**, often a first stop for those heading into the Mojave, where the **Mojave National Preserve** makes a rewarding natural detour en route to the unnatural neon oasis of **Las Vegas**, just across the border in Nevada.

Desert practicalities

Public transportation in the desert is poor to nonexistent. Los Angeles connects easily with the major points – Palm Springs, Barstow, Las Vegas – and the Anza–Borrego is marginally accessible from San Diego, but without your own vehicle you're stuck upon arrival. The region's scant rail and bus services are covered at the end of the chapter (see p.292).

If you have a car, it will need to be in good working order. While the $500 bomb you picked up in LA might be fine for the freeways, don't expect it to cope with the worst of the desert. Three major interstate **highways** cross the desert from west to east. I-15 cuts directly northeast through the middle of the Mojave on its way from Los Angeles to Las Vegas, passing through Barstow where

On less well-traveled routes, surfaces may not be well maintained, and it could be a long time before anyone comes along. In these areas, be sure you have plenty of food and drink, and consider carrying an **emergency pack** with flares, a first-aid kit, matches and a compass, a shovel, extra gas, and even a tire pump.

In an emergency, never leave the car: you'll be harder to find wandering around alone.

Hiking and camping

While heading off on a short walk doesn't require much preparation, **longer hikes** require far more forethought and your inability to carry enough water will seriously limit your range. The following pointers should help you get back safely.

Register your plans Register your itinerary with the local authorities, especially if hiking alone. If you get lost, find some shade and wait. So long as you've registered, the rangers will eventually come and fetch you. In areas where registration is not required, tell somebody where you are going and your expected time of return.

Take a map and compass And know how to use them.

Hike when it's cool Avoid hiking when the mercury goes over 90°F. Early morning and late afternoon are the best times, though you could even go at night, especially when moonlit.

Take enough water The body loses up to a gallon each day; even when you're not thirsty, you're continually dehydrating and you should keep drinking. On longer hikes, take two gallons of water per person per day (one is an absolute minimum), and don't save it for the walk back. Waiting for thirst, dizziness, nausea, or other signs of dehydration before doing anything can be dangerous. If you notice any of these symptoms, or feel weak and have stopped sweating, it's time to get to a doctor.

Take enough food Since any activity in this heat can be exhausting, you also need to eat well, packing in the carbohydrates.

Camp safely Never camp in a dry wash. Flash floods can appear from nowhere: an innocent-looking dark cloud can turn a dry wash into a raging river. And don't attempt to cross flooded areas until the water has receded.

I-40 heads eastwards to the Grand Canyon. I-10 takes you from LA through the Palm Springs and Joshua Tree area, heading into southern Arizona. Some fast, empty secondary roads can get you safely to all but the most remote areas of the desert, but be wary of using the lower-grade roads in between, which are likely to be unmaintained and are often only passable with four-wheel drive.

Other than in the Palm Springs area, **motels** in the California deserts are cheap, and you can generally budget for $40–50 per night. However, even if cost is no object, you'll get a greatly heightened sense of the desert experience by spending some time **camping** out.

The Colorado Desert

Despite the **Colorado Desert**'s hundreds of miles of beauty and empty highways, most visitors to the region have no intention of getting away from civilization. They're heading for where it's at – **Palm Springs**, a few square miles overrun with the famous, the star-struck, the aspirational, and, above all, the aging. It is said, not completely in jest, that the average age and average temperature of Palm Springs are about the same – a steady 88. It's the sort of town that fines homeowners who don't maintain their property to what local officials deem to be a suitable standard, and however much this turns you off, you'll find the place hard to avoid as it's the first stopping point east from LA on I-10. It's also the hub of the **Coachella Valley**, a resort area that stretches out for miles to the east along Hwy-111. The valley's farming communities have the distinction of forming part of the most productive irrigated agricultural center in the world, growing dates, oranges, lemons, and grapefruit in vast quantities, though sadly they're steadily giving way to the ever-expanding condos and golf courses of Palm Springs.

Fortunately you don't have to travel impossible distances to see the desert at its natural best. **Joshua Tree**, one of the most startling of California's national parks, lies less than an hour's drive east of Palm Springs, three from LA. A day-trip would give you a taste, but you really need a couple of days to fully appreciate Joshua Tree's sublime landscape, taking in the weird cactus formations and the crimson sunsets. East of the park, towards the Colorado River and Nevada, and south towards the Mexican border, only the highly saline **Salton Sea** breaks the arid monotony before you reach the **Anza–Borrego Desert**, whose starkly beautiful vistas are punctuated by several oases and unusual vegetation.

Palm Springs and the Coachella Valley

With its manicured golf courses, condominium complexes, and thousands of millionaires in residence, **Palm Springs** does not conform to any typical image of the desert. Purpose-built for luxury and leisure, it tends to attract conspicuous consumers and comfort seekers rather than the scruffier desert rats and low-rent retirees of less geographically desirable areas. But though it may seem harder to find the natural attractions and reasonably priced essentials among the glitz, they do exist.

Palm Springs and the adjacent resort towns of the **Coachella Valley** – Cathedral City, Desert Hot Springs, Rancho Mirage, Palm Desert, Indio, Indian Wells, and La Quinta – sit in the lushest agricultural pocket of the Colorado Desert, with the massive bulk of the snow-capped San Jacinto Mountains and neighboring ranges looming over the low-level buildings, casting an instantaneous and welcome shadow over the area in the late afternoon. Meteorologists have noted changes in the humidity of the desert climate around the town, which they attribute to the moisture absorbed from the hundreds of swimming pools – the consummate condo accoutrement, and the only place you're likely to want to be during the day if you come in the hotter months. When scarce water supplies aren't being used to fill the pools or nourish the nearby orchards, each of the Coachella Valley's hundred-plus **golf courses** receives around a million gallons daily to maintain their rolling green fairways.

Lovers of leisure have flocked to Palm Springs since the 1930s, when Hollywood stars were spotted enjoying a bit of mineral rejuvenation out here, and since then it's taken on a celebrity status all its own – a symbol of good LA living away from the amorphous, smoggy city. Most come for "**The Season**," the delightfully balmy months from January to May when all the golf and tennis tournaments are held. In recent years it has also become a major **gay** resort (see box, below), with many exclusively gay – and generally expensive – hotels, bars, and restaurants.

For years, high-school kids arrived in the thousands, too, for the drunken revelry of Spring Break (around the end of March and beginning of April). Local antipathy finally persuaded the city council, under the leadership of the late Sonny Bono, to ban the annual invasion in 1993, and the inebriated youth promptly decamped east to Lake Havasu City. The alcoholically inclined still flock to the area, but not to get drunk – the **Betty Ford Center**, smack in the middle of the valley at Rancho Mirage, draws a star-studded patient list to its booze- and drug-free environment, attempting to undo a lifetime's behavioral disorders.

Palm Springs wasn't always like this. Before the wealthy settlers moved in, it was the domain of the **Cahuilla**, who lived and hunted around the San Jacinto Mountains to escape the heat of the desert floor. They still own much of the town, and via an odd checkerboard system of land allotment, every other square

Gay Palm Springs

Palm Springs now claims to have overtaken Key West as America's largest **gay resort**, with dozens of exclusively gay clothing-optional inns and hotels flying the rainbow flag. With great weather almost all year round, it is hard to resist working on your tan by the pool all day while regaining your strength for dinner or a night around the clubs and bars.

The local gay press estimate that around forty percent of the town's residents are gay and you'll see evidence all over the place, but nowhere more so than along **Arenas Road**, near South Indian Canyon Drive, which has become something of a gay ghetto. Elsewhere businesses catering to a broader clientele are often gay-run and there's a general sense that the gay and straight communities coexist happily. That said, in 2003 conservative city officials tried to shut down the event of the gay men's year, the White Party (see p.261), but the election of an openly gay mayor, Ron Oden, in November of that year brought a considerably warmer welcome for the revelers.

Lesbians get their turn a couple of weeks earlier during what's still known as the Dinah Shore Week (see p.261), while later in the year the town hosts the Palm Springs Pride weekend (see p.262).

For information on other events, the local tourist machine puts out the free *Palm Springs Official Gay Visitors Guide*, though you'll get a better insight into the community from the free bi-monthly *The Bottom Line* (Ⓦwww.psbottomline.com) or the *Desert Post Weekly* (also free), which has listings and discussions of current issues.

Practicalities

Such is the power of the pink dollar in Palm Springs that virtually all hotels here are gay-friendly, though the Warm Sands district, half a mile southwest of downtown, contains around thirty exclusively **gay hotels**, most of them hedonistic fun palaces. More resorts populate the Deepwell neighborhood to the south along San Lorenzo Road and the Las Palmas area on North Palm Canyon Drive. Consult our listings on p.252, or check the town's website (Ⓦwww.palm-springs.org) for additional suggestions.

Hotel hosts are a mine of information about the trendiest restaurants and bars and will happily point you towards the sort of thing you're after, but restaurants with a strong gay following include *Shame on the Moon*, *Red Tomato*, and *John Henry's* (all listed from p.260). For predominantly gay bars and clubs try *Blame it on Midnight* and Oasis (see p.261).

mile of Palm Springs is theirs and forms part of the **Agua Caliente Indian Reservation** – a Spanish name which means "hot water," referring to the ancient mineral springs on which the town rests. The land was allocated to the tribe in the 1890s, but exact zoning was never settled until the 1940s, by which time the development of hotels and leisure complexes was well under way. The Cahuilla, finding their land built upon, were left with no option but to charge rent, a system that has made them one of the richest of the native tribes in America – and the money continues to pour in, thanks in part to revenue from a new **spa** and the **casinos** of Coachella Valley.

Arrival

Palm Springs lies 110 miles east of Los Angeles along the Hwy-111 turnoff from I-10. Arriving by **car**, you'll reach the town on North Palm Canyon Drive (Hwy-111), the main thoroughfare. Coming by **bus**, you'll alight downtown at the Greyhound terminus at 311 North Indian Canyon Drive (T 760/325-2053), linked with LA (4 daily; 2hr 30min to 3hr) and Phoenix, Arizona (3 daily; 5hr 30min). Amtrak **trains** arrive thrice-weekly from Los Angeles (Sun, Wed & Fri at 5pm) and Tucson, Arizona (Sun, Wed & Fri at 6.40am) at a desolate platform three miles north of Palm Springs at North Indian Avenue, just south of I-10.

Alaska, American, Continental, Delta, Northwest, United Express, and a handful of regional carriers **fly** into Palm Springs International Airport, 3400 E Tahquitz Canyon Way (T 760/318-3800), where you can catch bus #24 into town. Tickets are often expensive, and if you're flying to California it is usually cheaper to fly into Los Angeles and rent a car from there.

Information

On the approach to town from I-10 you can't miss the Palm Springs **visitor center**, 2901 N Palm Canyon Drive (daily 9am–5pm; T 1-800/347-7746, W www.palm-springs.org), installed in a revamped former gas station designed by Mid-Century Modern leading light Albert Frey. The sweeping roof over the forecourt shades the front of the center, where helpful staff dispense an exhaustive

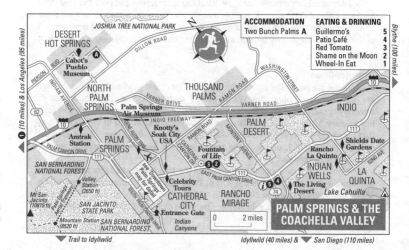

ACCOMMODATION	EATING & DRINKING	
Two Bunch Palms A	Guillermo's	5
	Patio Café	4
	Red Tomato	3
	Shame on the Moon	2
	Wheel-In Eat	1

PALM SPRINGS & THE COACHELLA VALLEY

0   2 miles

After trawling through the dull eastern suburbs of Los Angeles, I-10 throws you a surprise at the San Gorgonio Pass just before Palm Springs. Over four thousand **wind turbines** dot the valley, their glinting steel arms sending shimmering patterns across the desert floor. Along with Tehachapi Pass (see p.283), this is one of the largest concentrations of windmills in the country, generating enough electricity to service a small city, and the conditions are perfect. The sun beating down on the desert creates a low-pressure zone that sucks air up from the cooler coastal valleys, funneling it through the San Gorgonio Pass, the only break between two 10,000-foot-plus ranges of mountains. Strong winds often howl for days in spring and early summer, reaching an average speed of between fourteen and twenty miles per hour.

Companies running tours sporadically spring up, doing a quick circuit of the bases of the towers and plying you with facts, but are best left to the real enthusiasts. Casual observers will be happy just driving by or stopping for a few snaps.

selection of brochures including the *Palm Springs Official Visitors Guide* and the *Palm Springs Official Gay & Lesbian Visitors Guide* and matching map. Ask too for local maps, including the *Map of the Stars' Homes* ($5) that details the residences of the famous, and the *Palm Springs Modern* map (also $5) that guides you past homes exemplifying the Palm Springs Modern style of architecture (see p.254).

Getting around

Downtown Palm Springs is only a few blocks long and a couple of blocks wide and is manageable on foot. **Getting around** the rest of the Coachella Valley is possible with the natural-gas-powered fleet run by SunBus (℡1-800/347-8628, Ⓦwww.sunline.org), which operates daily from 6am to 8pm (until 11pm on some routes) and charges $1 per ride, plus an extra 25¢ for two transfers (good for two hours after purchase); a day pass costs $3. While the system is extensive and services fairly frequent, it is never a quick way to get about and you may prefer a **taxi**; call City Cab (℡760/416-2594).

To get the absolute best out of Palm Springs and the surrounding towns, though, you should think about **car rental**. All the majors are at the airport, but there are usually cheaper deals with Aztec Car Rental, 477 S Palm Canyon Drive (℡760/325-2294, Ⓦwww.azteccarrentals.com).

If you're not planning to stray too far, **rent a bike** from Palm Springs Bike Rentals, on Amado Road immediately west of Palm Canyon Drive, where you'll find city cruisers ($25 for half a day, $35/day; ℡760/779-1837).

Accommodation

Palm Springs was designed for the rich, and big luxury **resorts** and country clubs are abundant. Comfort and style also come in large doses at smaller and very tasteful hotels. Even if such places are outside your normal budget, you may find them surprisingly affordable if you **visit in summer** (May–Oct) when temperatures rise and prices drop dramatically. Many of the bigger places slash their prices by up to seventy percent, and even the smaller concerns give twenty to thirty percent off. The visitor center (see opposite) also offers special deals. If you couldn't care less about cachet, *Motel 6* and other **low-priced chains** are liberally represented. Regardless of where you stay, no Palm Springs lodging is without a **pool**.

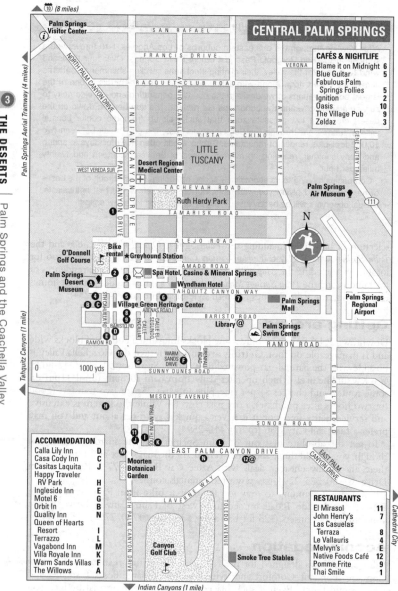

Bed and breakfasts are common, and with double-room rates at around $80–100 per night (more at weekends), they're a good deal. If you're traveling in a group, it may work out cheaper to rent an **apartment**: many of the homes in Palm Springs are used only for a brief spell and are let out for the rest of the year. Again, summer is the best time to look, but there is generally a good supply throughout the year. The Coachella Valley's daily paper, the

Desert Sun (ⓦ www.thedesertsun.com), has rental information, and the visitor center can point you to affordable agencies. **Camping** is not really a viable option unless you have an **RV**; the only campground accommodating tents is *Lake Cahuilla* (see below), and tent-carriers will have a better time exploring Joshua Tree or Anza-Borrego.

Listed here are some of the more reasonable and appealing options, with weeknight rates quoted; weekend prices are a price bracket or two higher than weeknights throughout the year. In winter you should always **book in advance**, but in summer this is rarely necessary and asking for a reduced rate is worthwhile.

For an introduction to the exclusively **gay hotels** listed below, see p.252.

Hotels, resorts, and B&Bs

🏃 **Calla Lily Inn** 350 S Belardo Rd ☏1-888/888-5787, ⓦ www .callalilypalmsprings.com. Intimate, restored 1950s inn with just nine rooms and suites set around a pool. It's comfortable and welcoming and offers all sorts of summer packages, which drop the rate further. Winter ❼, summer ❺

Casa Cody Inn 175 S Cahuilla Rd ☏1-800/231-2639, ⓦ www.casacody.com. Built in the 1920s by glamorous Hollywood pioneer Harriet Cody, this historic B&B offers tastefully furnished Southwestern-style rooms, a shady garden, great pool, and tasty buffet breakfasts in a good location two blocks from downtown. All options but the "rooms" have a kitchen. Families and small groups should go for the gorgeous two-bedroom adobe cottage (❼–❾). Winter: rooms and studios ❹–❺, suites ❼; summer: rooms and studios ❹–❺, suites ❻

Ingleside Inn 200 W Ramon Rd ☏1-800/772-6655, ⓦ www.inglesideinn.com. Set in a serene enclave a couple of blocks from downtown, this loosely Spanish-style inn is the last of Palm Spring's original hotels, dating from 1935. It once drew the likes of Garbo, Dalí, and Brando and still has enough real class to lure the glitterati. Each room is different, but all have a restrained elegance, often with antiques. Of course there are private patios and a lovely pool, and the excellent *Melvyn's Restaurant* is on site (see p.260). Winter: rooms ❺, villas ❼; summer: rooms ❹, villas ❺

🏃 **Orbit In** 562 W Arenas Rd ☏1-877/996-7248, ⓦ www.orbitin.com. If you're on the Mid-Century architectural trail or just fancy hanging poolside in your impeccably decorated 1950s-retro studio with private patio, you can't pass up this Modernist nirvana designed by Herbert Burns in 1957. Sip a complimentary Orbitini on arrival, cruise town on the free bikes, relax in rooms equipped with VCR and CD player, and languish over a continental breakfast. It is adults-only, and a two-night stay is required (three nights for their slightly cheaper "midweek escape" packages). Winter ❽, summer ❼

Villa Royale Inn 1620 S Indian Trail ☏1-800/245-2314, ⓦ www.villaroyale.com. Beautiful inn with individually designed and exquisitely furnished rooms and suites, most with Jacuzzi, situated around a pool. In the winter season meals and drinks are served from the bougainvillea-draped *Europa* restaurant. Winter: rooms ❼, villas from $350; summer: rooms ❺, villas ❽

The Willows 412 W Tahquitz Canyon ☏1-800/966-9597, ⓦ www .thewillowspalmsprings.com. The former estate of a US Secretary of State, whose friends – among them Clark Gable, Carole Lombard, and Albert Einstein – holed up here during the 1930s. Opulently decorated rooms, gorgeous lush grounds, a stunning Mount San Jacinto backdrop, sumptuous breakfasts, and an ideal downtown location make this well worth the splurge: starting around $300 in winter. Winter ❾, summer ❽

Motels and campgrounds

Happy Traveler RV Park 211 W Mesquite Drive, Palm Springs ☏760/325-8518. RV-only campground with 130 full-hookup sites and a pool close to the center of Palm Springs. $35 per site.

Lake Cahuilla 58075 Jefferson St, La Quinta ☏760/564-4712. Large campground for tents and RVs by a 135-acre stocked lake roughly fifteen miles east of Palm Springs. There are showers, a dump station for RVs, a summer-only swimming pool, and provision for horses. Electric hookup $18, tents $13.

Motel 6 660 S Palm Canyon Drive ☏760/327-4200, ⓦ www.motel6.com. The most central of the budget motels, with a good pool and outdoor hot tub. Winter ❸, summer ❷

Quality Inn 1269 E Palm Canyon Drive ☏1-877/474-6423, ⓦ www.qualityinn.com. Modern motel with spacious grounds, including a nice pool, kids' wading pool, free Wi-Fi, and a restaurant. Winter ❺, summer ❸

Vagabond Inn 1699 S Palm Canyon Drive ☎1-800/522-1555, ⓦwww.vagabondinn.com. Well-run three-story motel with free continental breakfast and high-speed Internet, a good pool, coffeemakers in each room, and refrigerators available. Winter ❹, summer ❺

Exclusively gay accommodation

Casitas Laquita 450 East Palm Canyon Drive, Palm Springs ☎760/416-9999, ⓦwww.casitaslaquita.com. A private women's resort in a rustic Southwestern-styled compound decorated with Native American crafts and motifs. All rooms have kitchen, private bathroom, and TV, and some come with a fireplace. Breakfast is taken in your room but there's plenty of opportunity to mingle over complimentary afternoon tapas. All year ❻

Queen of Hearts Resort 435 Avenida Olancha ☎1-888/275-9903, ⓦwww.queenofheartsps.com. On the site of Palm Springs' first lesbian hotel, this renovated resort has just nine rooms around a great pool, private mist-cooled patios, and gorgeous views of the Santa Rosa Mountains. Some rooms have kitchens (❻). All year ❺

Terrazzo 1600 E Palm Canyon Drive ☎1-866/837-7996, ⓦwww.terrazzo-ps.com. An intimate twelve-room, clothing-optional men's resort where comfort and service is such that you'll have trouble leaving the confines of the hotel. Sumptuous rooms around the pool, free airport transfer, on-site gym, fresh-baked goodies, and even complimentary sunscreen complete the deal. Winter ❼, summer ❺

Warm Sands Villas 555 Warms Sands Drive ☎1-800/357-5695, ⓦwww.warmsandsvillas.com. Renovated with marble floors and king-sized beds throughout, this men's inn comes with a big welcome and a generous continental breakfast. Some rooms have kitchenettes. Winter ❻, summer ❺

Palm Springs

Much of your time in the Coachella Valley is going to be spent in **PALM SPRINGS**, home to the majority of the recognized sights. It is a sprawling place but is focused on a fairly concentrated core.

Downtown Palm Springs stretches for about half a mile along Palm Canyon Drive, a wide, bright, and modern strip full of boutiques and restaurants that's engulfed the town's original Spanish village–style structures. With its celebrity stars embedded in the sidewalk and the neat rows of fan palms along Palm Canyon Drive, it makes for an attractive stroll through the valley's greatest concentration of places to eat, many with cooling misters to counteract the summer heat.

▲ Gay Pride Parade, Palm Springs

Palm Springs isn't all rampant consumerism, though. It's worth spending time in the **Palm Springs Desert Museum** and admiring the architecture of **Little Tuscany** (also known as the Heritage District and "the tennis club district"), just west of North Palm Canyon Drive, where some of the finest small hotels congregate. Further afield, cactus fans should spend an hour at **Moorten Botanical Garden**, while plane buffs are better served at the **Palm Springs Air Museum**.

You'll soon want to explore further, best done by spending half a day riding the **Palm Springs Aerial Tramway** into the San Jacinto Mountains and strolling the easy trails, then returning to explore the palm-filled **Indian Canyons**.

Downtown Palm Springs

Palm Springs owes its very existence to Hollywood, so it's no surprise that South Palm Canyon Drive has a **Walk of Fame** flanked by two life-size bronze statues honoring local leading lights: ex-mayor Sonny Bono stands guard over the junction of Arenas Road, while former resident Lucille Ball graces the intersection with Tahquitz Canyon Way.

Star-struck visitors could easily miss the **Village Green Heritage Center**, 219 South Palm Canyon Drive, a small brick plaza around a fountain and surrounded by a handful of buildings including the 1884 McCallum Adobe, "Miss Cornelia's Little House" (made of railroad ties), and the **Agua Caliente Cultural Museum** (June–Aug Fri–Sun 10am–4pm; Sept–April Wed–Sat 10am–5pm Sun noon–5pm; free; ⓦ www.accmuseum.org), with its collection of basketry and pottery.

Your time may be even better spent seeking out the attractive **Palm Springs Art Museum**, 101 Museum Drive (Oct–May Tues, Wed & Fri–Sun 10am–5pm, Thurs noon–8pm; June–Sept Wed & Fri–Sun 10am–5pm, Thurs noon–8pm; $12.50, but free Thurs 4–8pm; ☎ 760/325-7186, ⓦ www.psmuseum .org), which focuses on traditional and contemporary art, principally from California though with wider-ranging Native American and Southwestern art. The large, central space is dotted with works by major sculptors such as Henry Moore, Barbara Hepworth, and Alexander Calder, along with Duane Hanson's

---

Celebrity house tours

Knowing that they're in the thick of a megastar refugee camp, few can resist the opportunity to see the homes and country clubs of the international elite on a **celebrity tour**. As tacky as they are, these tours have some voyeuristic appeal, allowing you to spy on places like Bob Hope's enormous house and the star-studded area known as **Little Tuscany** – Palm Spring's prettiest quarter, where the famous keep their weekend homes. The tours only view the houses through the minibus window, but in the end it's not the homes that make the tours worthwhile but rather the fascinating trivia about the lives of those who live (or lived) in them. Most of the big names had their heyday fifty years ago so you'll need to be well up with your classic movies to really appreciate the fine detail.

Celebrity Tours, 4751 E Palm Canyon Drive (☎ 760/770-2700, ⓦ www.celebrity-tours .com), conduct entertaining one-hour jaunts around Palm Springs (daily; $30), driving past homes to satiate most people's celebrity craving. For the dedicated there are longer excursions (2.5hr; $35) around the country clubs and the Sinatra estate (where Frank used to bring Ava Gardner). Of course, if you've got a car, you can do it yourself with a $5 *Map of the Stars' Homes* from the visitor center (see p.248), but you'll miss the sharp anecdotal commentary that makes it such fun.

amazingly realistic *Old Couple on a Bench* – their watches even tell the time if the staff remember to change the batteries. Surrounding rooms highlight Western American art: note especially the Romantic works of Albert Bierstadt, Thomas Moran, and William Keith, who all brought the soft tones of their European homelands to rugged California landscapes – Yosemite looks more like the Alps than the Sierra, and raging snowmelt rivers have an English pastoral quality to them.

The mezzanine is devoted to Mesoamerican artworks such as the turquoise-inlaid human skull from the Mixtec classical period (550–950 AD) and the subtly realized, 2000-year-old armadillo effigy from Colima, Mexico. The top floor is all contemporary work and ever changing.

Once you've cooled off indoors, check out downtown's most anarchic piece of landscape gardening at **Moorten Botanical Garden**, 1701 S Palm Canyon Drive (Mon, Tues & Thurs–Sat 9am–4.30pm, Sun 10am–4pm; $3; ☎760/327-6555), a bizarre and somewhat shambolic cornucopia of just about every desert plant – cacti, succulents, dwarf trees, etc – lumped together in no particular order, but interesting for those who won't be venturing beyond town to see them in their natural habitat.

Out by the airport, the **Palm Springs Air Museum**, 745 N Gene Autry Trail (daily 10am–5pm; $10; ⓦwww.palmspringsairmuseum.org), contains an impressive collection of World War II European and US fighters and bombers, along with associated material on the campaigns they flew in and their pilots. The museum is easily identified by the F-14 and F-16 "Top Gun" fighters proudly displayed outside.

Palm Springs Aerial Tramway and Mount San Jacinto State Park

When the desert heat becomes simply too much to bear, you can travel through five climatic zones from the arid desert floor to (sometimes) snow-covered

Palm Springs architecture

Palm Springs' popularity among the rich and famous during the Forties, Fifties, and Sixties saw a massive building boom. Many newcomers opted for ostentatious palaces, but the more discerning employed young, Modernist architects such as Richard Neutra, who was "governed by the goal of building environmental harmony, functional efficiency, and human enhancement into the experience of everyday living." His work, and that of contemporaries Albert Frey and R.M. Schindler, became known as **Mid-Century Modern**, with its expression in these parts often dubbed Desert Modern or even Palm Springs Modern. After several decades in the architectural wilderness, Palm Springs has seen a surge of interest in its soaring rooflines, glass walls, unity of form, and sympathy for the desert setting. The town's renewed cachet means long-ignored houses by the movement's luminaries are now highly sought after. Many can be viewed from the road by driving the route on the Palm *Springs Modern* map ($5) from the visitor center, but you'll see a lot more (and learn fascinating details about the architects and their clients) by joining PS Modern Tours (☎760/318-6118, ⓔPSmoderntours@aol.com). Their three-hour minivan tours ($65) visit the exteriors of assorted residential, commercial, and civic buildings, including Richard Neutra's 1946 Kaufmann House (designed for Edgar Kaufmann, who commissioned Frank Lloyd Wright's Fallingwater in Pennsylvania); the 1968 Elrod Residence, with its spectacular living room used for scenes in the Bond flick *Diamonds are Forever*; and the 1962 House of Tomorrow, which later became Elvis and Priscilla's "Honeymoon Hideaway". Tours run all year on demand, but less frequently in summer.

alpine hiking trails atop Mount San Jacinto by riding the **Palm Springs Aerial Tramway** (Mon–Fri 10am–8pm, Sat & Sun 8am–8pm; last car down 9.45pm; $22, $34 with dinner; ☎1-888/515-8726, ⓦwww.pstramway.com), located on Tramway Road, four miles southwest of Hwy-111 on the northern edge of Palm Springs. Every thirty minutes a large cable car sets off up the rocky Chino Canyon, bound for the Mountain Station at 8516ft – a rise of almost six thousand feet. Each car is fitted with a rotating floor that makes two full revolutions on the twelve-minute journey, giving breathtaking 360-degree views outdone only by those from the top, which stretch 75 miles all the way to the Salton Sea. The temperature up here is a welcome 30°F cooler than in the valley, so bring something to keep warm or hide indoors, where you can watch a decent 18-minute video on the tramway's construction, visit the obligatory gift shop, or relax in the cafeteria-style restaurant, bar, or fine dining restaurant *Peaks*. Outside are viewing decks and access to a couple of forested **short trails**: the three-quarter-mile Discovery Trail loop and the mile-and-a-half Desert View Trail, with views down onto the Coachella Valley below. From November 15 through April 15, snow conditions permitting, the **Adventure Center** (Thurs & Fri 10am–4pm, Sat & Sun 9am–4pm; same contacts as Tramway office) offers cross-country **skiing** ($18 a day) and **snowshoeing** ($15 a day).

To stray further into the surrounding wilderness of the 14,000-acre **Mount San Jacinto State Park**, you'll need a permit from the State Park Ranger Station (Mon–Fri 1–5pm, Sat & Sun 9am–5pm) just outside the Mountain Station. This gives prepared hikers the freedom to summit the nearby peak of 10,834-foot Mount San Jacinto (six miles each way), trek down to Idyllwild (ten miles each way), or explore a number of other forest trails. See the Idyllwild account on p.262 for more details.

Exploring the canyons

Desert enthusiasts visit Palm Springs for the **hiking** and **horseback riding** opportunities in the canyons that incise the San Jacinto Mountains immediately west of town.

Indian Canyons

The best known and most accessible of the canyons are Palm Canyon, Andreas Canyon, and Murray Canyon, known collectively as **Indian Canyons** (Oct–May daily 8am–5pm; June–Sept Fri–Sun 8am–5pm, call to check; $8; ☎1-800/790-3398, ⓦwww.indian-canyons.com), on part of the Agua Caliente Indian Reservation to the south of downtown. Centuries ago, ancestors of the Cahuilla tribe settled in the canyons and developed extensive communities, made possible by the good water supply and animal stock. They grew crops of melons, squash, beans, and corn, hunted animals, and gathered plants and seeds for food and medicines. Evidence of this remains, and mountain sheep still roam the remoter areas despite the near extinction of some breeds. To reach the best of the remains, follow South Palm Canyon Drive about three miles south to the clearly signposted entrance, from where paved roads run to the entrances of each of the canyons.

The most popular is **Palm Canyon**, which comes choked with palms – some three thousand over seven miles – beside a seasonal stream along which runs the easy 1.5-mile Palm Canyon Trail. A one-mile loop visits the best of **Andreas Canyon**, noted for its rock formations and more popular than **Murray Canyon**, which is difficult to reach but offers a twelve-foot waterfall as a reward for those prepared to hike two miles.

A tiny trading post at Palm Canyon sells hiking maps, refreshments, and assorted native crafts, but to indulge in real Wild West fantasy you should see things on **horseback**. Smoke Tree Stables, 2500 Toledo Avenue (℡760/327-1372, ⓦwww.smoketreeranch.com), offers scheduled one- and two-hour riding tours of the canyons at $35 per hour – well worth it, especially if you go in the early morning (tours start at 8am) to escape the midday heat. Longer rides are available by advance arrangement.

Tahquitz Canyon

After years of hippy colonization and subsequent abandonment, the local tribe has in recent years re opened **Tahquitz Canyon**, 500 W Mesquite Avenue (Oct–June daily 7.30am–5pm; July–Sept Fri, Sat & Sun 7.30am–5pm; $12.50; ℡760/416-7044, ⓦwww.tahquitzcanyon.com), where the visitor center contains a small artifact-filled museum and a theater showing a video on the canyon's shamanic legend. Either take a self-guided hike in the palmless canyon itself, or join one of the free guided tours (at 8am, 10am, noon & 2pm), which spend around two and a half hours hiking through beautiful country and past a sixty-foot waterfall.

Swimming and spas

The desert sun will soon send you in search of a pool. In many cases you won't have to walk more than fifty feet from your room to the hotel pool, but these can be small and crowded and you may prefer the **Olympic-sized pool** at the Palm Springs Swim Center, Sunrise Way at Ramon Road (Mon, Wed & Fri 11am–5pm, all other days 11am–3pm; open later in July & Aug; $3.50; ℡760/323-8278).

Lots more water gets used at the 16-acre **Knott's Soak City USA**, 1500 Gene Autry Trail (daily 10am–5pm or 6pm; $28, kids $17, parking $8; ℡760/327-0499, ⓦwww.knotts.com), where you can surf on a one-acre wave pool and mess around on thirteen waterslides.

For a substantially more relaxing experience, visit one of Palm Springs' day spas, particularly the elaborate Spa Resort Casino, 401 Amado Road (daily 8am–7pm; ℡1-888/999-1995, ⓦwww.sparesortcasino.com), based around the **mineral spring** that the Cahuilla discovered on the desert floor over a century ago. Here, the basic "Taking of the Waters" ($40) gives you a sauna, spa, steam, eucalyptus rooms, and as much time in the swimming pool and fitness center as you desire. You're encouraged, of course, to spend a lot more on massages (from $65) and assorted skin and body care treatments (from $105), and at the on-site casino. You'll find more spas listed in the *Palm Springs Visitors Guide*.

The other Coachella Valley towns

Palm Springs may have the prestige, but it is the other towns of the **COACHELLA VALLEY** that now have the bulk of the swanky resorts, big-name shops, and elegant expense-account restaurants. On initial acquaintance, it is hard to tell one town from another as they form an amorphous twenty-mile sprawl of gated communities, country clubs, and over a hundred golf courses. Not all the boundaries between them are clearly marked, and on their main drags they tend to share faceless low-slung architecture – but differences become evident to those who have time to explore.

Hwy-111 runs the length of the valley through, or close to, most of the main points of interest, but if you've got a specific destination in mind and want to avoid endless stop lights, consider the faster **I-10** which runs parallel about four miles to the north.

Cathedral City and Rancho Mirage

About five miles east of Palm Springs along Hwy-111, **Cathedral City** ("Cat City") has no cathedral, but takes its name from the now-hidden Cathedral Canyon, which apparently reminded early explorers of some medieval minster. It boomed during prohibition when the absence of a police force encouraged bawdy establishments to set up shop. You may well come here to drink or dine, or to tap into the **gay scene** that's second only to the one in Palm Springs, but during the day there's not a lot to see except for Jennifer Johnson's fabulous *Fountain of Life* sculpture, complete with mosaic bighorn sheep, lizards, and tortoises. Local Hispanic mothers who spend their week tending the houses and swimming pools of the wealthy bring their kids to play in the fountain here on Sunday afternoons.

Further east along the valley, the generally staid **Rancho Mirage** tends to attract dignitaries – and high-profile substance abusers. This so-called "Playground of the Presidents" was home to former President Gerald Ford until his death in 2006, and is also host to the upscale rehab clinic the **Betty Ford Center**. Frank Sinatra was the first of the stars to move to Rancho Mirage in 1956, and others soon followed. The city now recognizes its more illustrious associations in its street names: Frank, Gerald, Bob Hope, and Dinah Shore all have drives named after them.

Palm Desert, Indian Wells, and La Quinta

Palm Desert, directly east along Hwy-111, is the safest place to witness the desert wildlife that flourishes in this inhospitable climate. Here, the ever-expanding **Living Desert**, 47900 Portola Avenue (daily: mid-June to Aug 8am–1.30pm; Sept to mid-June 9am–5pm; $12, summer $9; ☏760/346-5694, Ⓦwww.livingdesert.org), is the area's only essential sight, now encompassing over 1200 acres of irrigated and manicured sections of land. Basically a modern zoo, its various sections each represent a different desert region from around the world. Stroll among the cacti of the Mojave or the Chihuahua gardens, through an area specially designed to attract butterflies, or into a palm oasis. North American desert animals – coyotes, foxes, bighorn sheep, snakes, and mountain lions – have now been supplemented by sections devoted to African species, such as wild dogs, gazelles, zebras, cheetahs, and warthogs. There are shady palapas and cooling "mist stations" everywhere, but it is still best to arrive as the gates open for cool and fragrant morning air, particularly if you fancy the wilderness trail system, which penetrates the hill country behind the zoo. If you can't stand to walk around in the heat, hop on the shuttle ($5 all day), which makes frequent circuits of the park.

On nearby **El Paseo**, sometimes called the "Rodeo Drive of the Desert," you can glimpse a different species of local creature. The wealthy and the wishful thinkers flock to this mile-long strip of fashionable stores and galleries, which loops south off Hwy-111 and is one of the very few places in the whole Coachella Valley where you might leave your car and stroll. Come November (usually the first Sunday), the increasingly prevalent species *Homo golfus* turns out en masse for the nation's only **golf cart parade** (☏760/346-6111, Ⓦwww.golfcartparade.com), with decorated buggies proceeding along El Paseo.

For more on local events and sights, call at the **Palm Desert Visitor Center**, 72567 Hwy-111 near El Paseo (daily 9am–5pm; ☏1-800/873-2428, Ⓦwww.palm-desert.org), which is housed in a sustainable building – something this whole area needs a lot more of. For wilderness information, drive three miles south along Hwy-74 to the Santa Rosa and San Jacinto

Golf in the Coachella Valley

With over 110 courses, it's no surprise that the Coachella Valley has become synonymous with **golf**. Look at a detailed map of the valley and you could be forgiven for thinking that Rancho Mirage, Palm Desert, Indian Wells, and La Quinta are nothing but golf courses, and that a home beside the fairway proclaims your arrival among the Coachella Valley elite. The top courses are among the finest anywhere, the barren mountains all around in spectacular contrast to the lush, green fairways and placid water traps. Of course, watering all those fairways is completely unsustainable, but no one seems too concerned about the gradually draining aquifer that underlies most of the valley, as long as places like Palm Desert's Bighorn and Indian Wells' Vintage Club Mountain Course continue to grace the pages of golfing magazines. Throughout the year, celebrities, pros, and amateurs flock to tournaments like the Bob Hope Chrysler Classic (in late Jan), the Skins Game (in late Nov), and the Frank Sinatra Celebrity Invitational (in mid-Feb).

Many of the courses are **private**, with annual membership running up to $25,000 on top of a $350,000 initial joining fee. Semi-private and **public courses** are more accessible, though green fees can still be steep in winter: for bargains go in summer and play in the less fashionable afternoon or evening. One of the best public courses is the 36-hole Desert Willow Golf Resort, 38995 Desert Willow Drive, Palm Desert (℡760/346-0015, ⊛www.desertwillow.com), where morning green fees hit $135 in the popular winter season but drop as low as $30 in summer. Fees are slightly cheaper at Tahquitz Creek Golf Resort, 1885 Golf Club Drive, Palm Springs (℡328-1005, ⊛www.tahquitzcreek.com). You can book directly with the course up to around a week in advance, or try one of the reservation agents who book **tee times** at a range of courses. Try affordable Palm Springs Tee Times (℡760/324-5012, ⊛www.palmspringsteetimes.com), who have an online system that allows booking up to two months in advance.

Mountains National Monument Visitor Center (generally daily 9am–4pm, though reduced hours in summer).

Adjoining Palm Desert, the city of **Indian Wells** has one of the highest per-capita incomes in the US, as well as the largest concentration of the Coachella Valley's grand **resorts**. It's known for its four-day New Year **Jazz Festival**, its high profile **tennis tournaments**, and its prestigious Desert Town Hall **lecture series** (see p.261).

Heading east, next comes **La Quinta**, named for the Valley's first exclusive resort – *Rancho La Quinta* – which was built in 1927 and thrived during the Depression, when Hollywood's escapist popularity rose as the country suffered. Director Frank Capra wrote the script for multiple-Oscar-winner *It Happened One Night* at the resort in 1934, and considered the place so lucky he kept coming back, bringing stars like Greta Garbo in his wake. It's still so posh that it's not marked on the main road (take Washington Street south to Eisenhower to find it). The Santa Rosa Mountain backdrop is stunning, and the rich no longer get very duded up, so you won't feel out of place if you come for a drink at the piano lounge.

Indio

In stark contrast is neighboring **Indio**, a low-key town whose agricultural roots show in its many date and citrus outlets. Approaching from behind *Rancho La Quinta* along 50th Avenue, you'll pass so many date groves you'll think you're in Saudi Arabia. Back on Hwy-111, stop in at the **Shields Date Gardens**, no. 80225 (daily: June–Aug 9am–5pm; Sept–May 8am–6pm; free; ℡760/346-0996,

Ⓦ www.shieldsdates.com), built in 1924 but renovated in the 1950s, for a date crystal shake ($3.50) at the original soda fountain. Wander out to see the date palms (all with ladders attached for harvesting), and don't miss the free film, *The Romance and Sex Life of the Date*, with its cheesy commentary partly recorded in the 1950s by Floyd Shields, who set the place up. The town's huge February **Date Festival** draws people from as far as LA to its wonderfully goofy camel and ostrich races.

Desert Hot Springs

Isolated on the north side of I-10, twelve miles north of Palm Springs, **Desert Hot Springs** was honored in a 1999 competition for having the best-tasting water in the country. The underground wells for which the town is named supply water for the multitude of swimming pools as well as for drinking. A good jumping-off point for visiting Joshua Tree, it's somewhat more casual than the other Coachella Valley communities – except at **Two Bunch Palms** (Ⓣ 1-800/472-4334, Ⓦ www.twobunchpalms.com; rooms ➐, suites around $600), a luxury resort nestled in between trailer parks and a favorite of celebrities from Los Angeles. Normal people are also welcome if they can pay the price – spa treatments run about $100 per hour. However, spending your days soaking in the hot-springs pool with a book and a cocktail, with intermittent breaks for mud baths and massages, is not a bad way to pass the time.

Also be sure to check out **Cabot's Pueblo Museum**, 67616 E Desert View Avenue (call for hours; $6; Ⓣ 760/329-7610, Ⓦ ww.cabotsmuseum.org), in a four-story Hopi-style structure built by one Cabot Yerxa over a twenty-year period. After a peripatetic adulthood in Alaska, Cuba, and all over California, Cabot became Desert Hot Springs' first resident in 1913, then laboriously hand-dug the first well. He returned in his mid-50s in 1939 and began constructing what he intended to be both his house and a monument to the Indian people he had grown to love. Without formal plans and using homemade adobe bricks and any secondhand bits of wood he could get his hands on, he fashioned a wonderful, rambling, asymmetrical structure – adhering to the belief that symmetry retains evil spirits. Cabot died in 1965 having completed 35 rooms, several of which can now be visited on an entertaining guided tour.

Eating

Palm Springs **restaurants** run the gamut, from eminently posh to fast food, with some reasonable ethnic options in between. If you come in the low season, the desert sun may squelch your appetite sufficiently that you go without eating most of the day and find yourself ravenous at dusk. Although most of the famous restaurants in Palm Springs and Cat City are ultra-expensive, more affordable options can be found with a little effort. Dedicated diners should also sample what's on offer in the rest of the Coachella Valley; our recommendations merely scrape the surface of the huge selection that's out there. Only at the finest restaurants need you book in summer, but in winter places fill up quick and reservations are essential.

For the really budget-conscious, supermarket shopping is the best bet: try Von's (daily 6am–midnight) in the Palm Springs Mall, Tahquitz Canyon Way.

Palm Springs

🏃 **El Mirasol** 140 E Palm Canyon Drive Ⓣ 760/323-0721. Both literally and figuratively a mile away from the somewhat touristy *Las Casuelas* (see p.260), this Mexican restaurant is strong on regional dishes, producing an excellent chicken *mole* and *pollo en pipián*, a Zacatecan specialty made with ground pumpkin seeds and chilies. These and more mainstream enchilada and tamale plates go for $10–12.

John Henry's 1785 Tahquitz Canyon Way at Sunrise Way, Palm Springs ℡760/327-7667. Large portions of eclectic American fare, from rack of lamb to imaginative fish dishes, perfectly served and at half the price you'd expect. Dinner is around $20; reserve after 2pm. Closed Sundays and June–Sept.

Las Casuelas Terraza 222 S Palm Canyon Drive ℡760/323-1003. *Las Casuelas* opened its original establishment in 1958 (still going strong at 368 N Palm Canyon Drive), but you can't beat this Spanish Colonial-style sister restaurant for its bustling atmosphere, stacks of mist-cooled outdoor seating centered on a palm-roofed bar, and usually some live entertainment. The food suffers from north-of-the-border blanding but is still tasty, and with combination plates for $10–13 and $6 margaritas it's not too expensive.

Le Vallauris 385 W Tahquitz Canyon Way ℡760/325-5059, ⓦ www.levallauris.com. Palm Springs' best restaurant does not exactly hide its light under a bushel, describing itself as "*the* restaurant where the Stars entertain their friends;" you are indeed likely to run into one or two once-renowned artistes. Even if stargazing is not your style, the contemporary California-Mediterranean cuisine is excellent, the service impeccable, and the setting gorgeous. Main courses are in the $25–40 range. Open for lunch and dinner but closed July & Aug; reservations essential.

Melvyn's At the *Ingleside Inn* (see p.251). This classical continental restaurant is old-fashioned in the best possible way – elegant, understated, and serving beautifully prepared dishes such as their signature veal with avocado and mousseline sauce. Expect to part with $50 a head, or go for the four-course prix fixé dinner ($30). Book in advance and leave time for a cocktail or two in the intimate bar beforehand.

Native Foods Café 1775 E Palm Canyon Drive in the Smoke Tree Village Mall ℡760/318-1532. This totally vegan café puts a creative twist on traditional vegetarian fare. An eclectic menu, including tacos, pizzas, salads, and a variety of veggie burgers, and modest prices ($8–10) make it a worthwhile spot. The Jamaican jerk "steak" burger is highly recommended, as is the Save the Chicken salad. Mon–Sat 11.30am–9.30pm.

Pomme Frite 256 S Palm Canyon Drive ℡760/778-3727. Semi-casual French-Belgian joint that lends an air of Europe to downtown. Kick off with artichoke hearts and calamari ($11), perhaps followed by a pot of steamed mussels in lemongrass broth ($18) or a California bouillabaisse ($24). Closed Tues.

Thai Smile 651 N Palm Canyon Drive ℡760/320-5503. Mood lighting, Thai woodcuts, and a fish tank create an appealing ambience for getting stuck into authentic Thai green curries and the occasional Szechuan dish for $11–15. Lunch specials are $8 and takeouts are available.

The rest of the Coachella Valley

Guillermo's 72850 El Paseo, Palm Desert ℡760/341-0980. One of the top down-valley Mexicans; upscale without being particularly pricey, and with a wonderful selection of over 200 tequilas. Closed Sun & Mon lunch.

Patio Café 73200 El Paseo, Palm Desert ℡760/568-0733. Pleasant courtyard café providing a welcome break from window-shopping along El Paseo. Stop in for a poached salmon salad ($15) and one of their specialty cocktails ($5). A good range of breakfasts served to 11am.

Red Tomato 68784 E Palm Canyon Drive, Cathedral City ℡760/328-7518. Sit on the patio or indoors to dine on terrific thick-crust pizza, especially the garlicky "white" pies, plus Balkan-style lamb dishes, from 4pm nightly. Great early-bird specials until 5.30pm.

Shame on the Moon 69950 Frank Sinatra Drive at Hwy-111, Rancho Mirage ℡760/324-5515. Long-standing California-cuisine bistro with a dark, intimate bar, attracting a loyal, mature gay crowd. Drop in for an early evening martini or stay to eat the likes of sesame-crusted seared ahi tuna steak ($23). There are often three-course specials under $25 in summer; reservations a must in winter.

Wheel-Inn Eat 16 miles west on I-10 at the Cabazon exit (marked by two 50-foot concrete dinosaurs built in the 1960s and 1970s). Humble, 24-hour desert truck stop with a burly clientele and enormous portions – so unpretentious you'd think they'd never heard of Palm Springs. One of the dinosaurs houses a wonderfully kitschy gift shop, run by creationists: check out the labels on the toy dinosaurs.

Nightlife, bars, and clubs

The scattered nature of the Coachella Valley and the predominance of staid, moneyed residents does little to promote a thriving **nightlife**. Unless you're a member of one of the exclusive country clubs, you'll have to work to find much at all (let alone anything raucous), though you might stop in at one of the resort **piano lounges**, where, if you shell out for an overpriced drink, you can sometimes catch surprisingly good jazz.

The Palm Springs visitor center (see p.248) has details of **what's on** around town and stocks the seasonal **Palm Springs Visitors Guide** and the gay *The Bottom Line*. Pick up the monthly *Desert Guide* (Ⓦwww.desertguide.com) for news on the current nightlife situation. Unless you hear of something that warrants the journey, you're best staying around Palm Springs, where nightlife tends to the retro side, or nearby Cathedral City, which has some hipper options, especially for the gay crowd.

Palm Springs' main drag is particularly crowded on Thursday evenings, when the surprisingly funky **VillageFest street fair** (Oct–May 6–10pm; June–Sept 7–10pm) draws equal numbers of tourists and young locals. Traffic is temporarily barred from half a dozen blocks of North Palm Canyon Drive, which sprouts a kids' play zone and booths selling everything from fresh-baked bread to tacky souvenirs and local crafts.

The **Annenberg Theater** (☎760/325-4490), inside the Palm Springs Desert Museum, has a seasonal program of shows, films, and classical concerts, and there are a couple other film and arts festivals worth seeking out (see below).

Blame it on Midnight 777 E Tahquitz Canyon ☎760/323-1200. This predominantly gay establishment has a full restaurant but is best treated as a fun bar that draws a dressed up crowd. Very much a place to be seen.

Blue Guitar 120 S Palm Canyon Drive ☎760/327-1549. Mainly a blues and old-school R&B bar, often with no cover, though frequently $5–10 at weekends and up to $25 when someone special is playing. Happy hour 5–8pm nightly.

Fabulous Palm Springs Follies Plaza Theatre, 128 S Palm Canyon Drive ☎760/327-0225, Ⓦwww.psfollies.com. This historic theater hosts a long-running and enormously popular professional vaudeville show, with artists aged between 50 and 85. Nov–May daily at 1.30 & 7pm. From $42.

Ignition 123 N Palm Canyon Drive ☎760/778-4477. Small groups of slackers smoking hookahs

($10 apiece in a dozen flavors) on the front veranda distinguish this coffeehouse, which also has good espresso, free wireless Internet, and occasional live music.

Oasis 611 S Palm Canyon Drive ☎760/416-0950. Large and lively gay venue with pool tables, a patio, classic rock on Thurs, retro on Fri, and Hi-NRG on Sat. Wed–Sat only.

The Village Pub 266 S Palm Canyon Drive ☎760/323-3265. Worthwhile as a restaurant with lots of salads, pizzas, and burgers at reasonable prices, but best for a few drinks and a little dancing. Live music nightly and no cover.

Zeldaz Danceclub and Beachclub 169 N Indian Canyon Drive ☎760/325-2375. Lively and youthful, if a little cheesy, dance club playing Seventies, Eighties and current hits, with occasional theme nights. Thurs–Sat only 9pm–2am.

Festivals and events

If you're around in January, don't miss out on the **Palm Springs International Film Festival** (Ⓦwww.psfilmfest.org), which brings more nightlife to the city than the rest of the year combined. And in mid-March, the **La Quinta Arts Festival** (Ⓦwww.la-quinta-arts-found.org) serves up fine art and entertainment.

Desert Town Hall Lecture Series Ⓦwww.deserttownhall.com. Mid-February to mid-April. Indian Wells hosts four talks by high-profile speakers such as Newt Gingrich, Colin Powell, Rudi Giuliani, Garrison Keillor, and Jean-Michel Cousteau. Tickets start at around $65 for a single lecture.

Dinah Shore Week Ⓦwww.dinahshoreweekend.com. Late March or early April. Major lesbian fiesta officially known as the LPGA Kraft Nabisco Championship golf tournament. It's held at Mission Hills Country Club in Rancho Mirage on the Dinah Shore Tournament Course, named for her contribution to the game. The tournament ranks second only to the US Women's Open, but golf often plays second fiddle to the numerous hotel pool parties at what has become the nation's hottest lesbian vacation event.

White Party ☎1-888/777-8886, Ⓦwww.jeffreysanker.com. Third weekend in April. The single biggest event of the gay year, when over fifteen thousand gay men flock to Palm Springs for four days of hedonism centered on the *Wyndham Hotel*. It's been going since 1989 and has grown to the point where there are nonstop parties throughout the four days (often in and around hotel pools). The biggest event, an all-nighter of epic proportions, is held Sat at the Palm Springs Convention Center. A three-day weekend pass giving access to all eight major events goes for around $350.

Coachella Music and Arts ⓦ www.coachella.com. Late April. Massive three-day rock and alternative music festival packed with big-name artists. The 2007 event featured the Red Hot Chili Peppers, Rage Against the Machine, Arctic Monkeys, and many more.

Country Music Festival ⓦ www .stagecoachfestival.com. First weekend in May. The Empire Polo field in Indio draws many of the top names in country music – George Strait, Alan Jackson, Willie Nelson, and Emmylou Harris in 2007.

Palm Springs Pride ⓣ 760/416-8711, ⓦ www .pspride.org. First weekend in Nov. Draws gay crowds for three days of entertainment, a street parade, and more partying.

Listings

Bank Bank of America, 588 S Palm Canyon Drive ⓣ 760/340-1867.

Bookstore Barnes & Noble, 72840 Hwy-111, Palm Desert, or more conveniently at Peppertree Bookstore, 155 S Palm Canyon Drive (ⓣ 760/325-4821, ⓦ www.peppertreebookstore.com). with a good stock for a fairly small shop.

Cinema Film, 789 Tahquitz Canyon Way ⓣ 760/322-3456; alternative and foreign films at Camelot, 2300 Baristo Rd, Palm Springs, ⓣ 760/325-6565.

Hospital Desert Regional Medical Center, 1150 N Indian Canyon Drive ⓣ 760/323-6511.

Internet The Palm Springs Public Library (see opposite) offers free Internet access, and there's commercial access at Log-on, 1775 E Palm Canyon Drive, next to Native Foods Café (Mon–Fri 7am–10pm, Sat & Sun 9am–6pm; ⓣ 760/325-0077).

Library Palm Springs Public Library, 300 S Sunrise Way (Mon & Tues 9am–8pm, Wed & Thurs 9am–5.30pm, Fri 10am–5.30pm, Sat 9am–5.30pm; ⓣ 760/322-7323, ⓦ www .palmspringslibrary.org).

Pharmacy Rite Aid Drug Store, 366 S Palm Canyon Drive, is open 24/7.

Police ⓣ 760/323-8116 in Palm Springs; ⓣ 760/770-0300 in Cathedral City.

Post office 333 E Amado Road (Mon–Fri 8am–5pm, Sat 9am–3pm. Zip code 92262.

Around Palm Springs

As the largest desert community by far, the Coachella Valley towns, and Palm Springs in particular, make obvious bases for exploring the surrounding regions where urban comforts are often in short supply. Amenities can, however, be found in **Idyllwild**, a small mountain resort set among the pines high above Palm Springs that's ideal for weekend retreats from LA. The real desert starts to the north, where the **Morongo Basin** provides access to Joshua Tree National Park via the small roadside communities of **Yucca Valley**, **Joshua Tree**, and **Twentynine Palms**.

Idyllwild

Five thousand feet up the slopes of Mount San Jacinto, **Idyllwild** is the perfect antidote to the in-your-face success of Palm Springs, fifty road miles away. Pine-fresh, cool, and snow-covered in winter, this small alpine town of about two thousand inhabitants has only a few chalet-style restaurants and hotels, but it's a great place to slow up the cash drain inevitably incurred on a visit to Palm Springs. Get here by heading twenty miles west along I-10 to Banning, then taking the exit for Hwy-243, which sweeps you up the mountain on a good but sharply curving road.

The place is always busy at weekends when city escapees flood the town, but a more relaxed pace prevails midweek. At any time, there's considerable temptation to set out on the magnificent trails of **Mount San Jacinto State Park** or the surrounding wilderness areas. The permit rules are complicated and the best bet is to call first at the Forest Service's **Idyllwild Ranger Station**, 54270 Pine Crest Avenue (daily 8am–4.30pm; ☏951/382-2921), which has stacks of information about hiking and camping in the area. They'll sell you an **Adventure Pass** ($5 per day, $30 per year; America the Beautiful Annual Pass valid; ⓦwww.fs.fed.us/r5/sanbernardino/ap), which allows you to park at the region's trailheads.

Hikes to consider include the **Deer Springs Trail** (six miles round-trip; 3–4hr; 1700-foot ascent), which leads up to Suicide Rock, one of two distinctive peaks rising a couple thousand feet above the town. To get to the top of the Aerial Tramway (see p.255), follow the **Devil's Slide Trail** (sixteen miles round-trip; 7–9hr; 2300-foot ascent), for which permits are limited.

Practicalities

Places to stay are well scattered along the roads that fan out from Idyllwild's central shopping area. You can set up **camp** anywhere over two hundred feet away from trails and streams, or in designated Yellow Post Sites (Adventure Pass needed), which have fire rings but no water. There are also drive-in campgrounds run by the Forest Service (☏1-800/444-7275) and the county park (☏1-800/234-7275) at a cost of $10–16 per night.

The town center is where you'll find the bulk of the **restaurants** and the library, 5485 Pinecrest Avenue (Mon 10am–6pm, Wed 11am–7pm, Fri 10am–6pm, Sat 10am–4pm; ☏951/659-2300), which has **Internet access**.

Accommodation

Atipahato Lodge 25525 Hwy-243, half a mile north of the ranger station ☏1-888/400-0071, ⓦwww.atipahatolodge.com. About the best value around these parts, featuring wood-paneled rooms with an upscale cabin atmosphere. All have forest-view balconies and kitchenettes, and there's a range of luxury cabins with spa tub and fireplace. A continental breakfast is included. Luxury cabins ❺, standard cabins ❹
Idyllwild campground Hwy-243. Woodsy campground in the heart of Idyllwild with spacious tent sites ($15), a couple with hookups ($24), and a nature trail. Hikers and bikers pay $3.
Knotty Pine Cabins 54340 Pine Crest Ave ☏951/659-2933, ⓦwww.knottypinecabinsidyllwild.com. Idyllwild's cheapest accommodation, with cozy, wood-paneled cabins fitted with quilts, fireplace, and DVD player. ❸
Quiet Creek Inn 26345 Delano Drive ☏1-800/450-6110, ⓦwww.quietcreekinn.com. Beautifully appointed forest cabins set up for maximum relaxation. Most have a deck overlooking a creek

and a fireplace with wood provided. Follow Tollgate Road off Hwy-243, a mile east of the center. ❺
Strawberry Creek Inn 26370 Hwy-243 ☏951/659-3202, ⓦwww.strawberrycreekinn.com. Pampered luxury in B&B style a few hundred yards south of the center of town. Rooms are comfortable and well appointed, but vary in theme – Santa Fe, floral, autumn, etc – so ask to see a few. ❺

Eating

Bread Basket 54710 N Circle Drive, half a mile from the center ☏909/659-3506. Sit on the sunny deck and dine on French toast made with apple-nut loaf ($8), mushroom stroganoff ($12), or battered halibut ($12), all washed down with microbrews or espresso coffee. Closed Wed & Thurs evenings.
Java Lounge 54245 N Circle Drive ☏951/659-5282. Reliable espresso and free wireless Internet.
Red Kettle 54220 N Circle Drive ☏951/659-4063. A locals' favorite, this renovated diner serves fine all-day breakfasts, burgers, and sandwiches, and stays open for dinner at weekends. They also sell a $10 sack lunch ideal for days on the trail.

The Morongo Basin

Driving from Palm Springs (or Los Angeles) to Joshua Tree National Park, the easiest access is through the vast tract of high desert known as the **MORONGO**

BASIN, almost a thousand square miles of which is taken up by the Marine Corps Air Ground Combat Center, the world's largest marine base, just north of Twentynine Palms. Mostly useful for supplies and accommodation, the Morongo Basin does have a few points of minor interest, principally the wildlife haven of the **Big Morongo Canyon Preserve**, the oddball **Desert Christ Park**, and the Western charms of **Pioneertown**.

The Morongo Basin Transit Authority (☎1-800/794-6282, ⓦ www.mbtabus .com) runs a regular **bus service** between Palm Springs and Yucca Valley, but it's too infrequent to be of much use.

Yucca Valley and around

Heading north off I-10 along Twentynine Palms Highway (Hwy-62), the first point of interest is **Big Morongo Canyon Preserve**, 11055 East Drive (7.30am–sunset; donation; ⓦ www.bigmorongo.org), a wildlife refuge based around the cottonwoods and willows of a vast oasis that's one of the largest bodies of natural surface water for miles around. Consequently, it's a big hit with both wildlife and keen birders, who might hope to spot vermilion and brown-crested flycatchers, Bell's vireo, summer tanager, and a whole lot more – the preserve host keeps a list of current sightings. The numerous board-walks and trails meandering through the area can easily absorb a relaxing hour or two.

Much less appealing is **Yucca Valley**, nine miles east, the Morongo Basin's largest settlement but little more than a string of malls running for a few miles beside Hwy-62. Those driving through and in need of reliable **espresso**, snacks, and free wireless Internet should call at the *Water Canyon Coffee Co*, 55844 Twentynine Palms Highway.

From here, follow Pioneertown Drive north off Hwy-62 and, after half a mile, turn right onto Sunnyslope Drive and continue half a mile to the **Desert Christ Park** (7am–dusk; free; ⓦ www.desertchristpark.org). Displayed here are 37 of local sculptor Antone Martin's massive, fifteen-foot-tall white concrete figures, erected in the 1950s and depicting tales from the Bible – a fittingly bizarre addition to the region. Return to Pioneertown Drive and continue 3.5 miles north to **Pioneertown**, an Old West town created in the 1940s for the filming of movies and TV serials – a nice bit of synthetic cowboy country in case there isn't enough of the real thing around for you. It's nowhere near as tacky as it might sound, and has a bowling alley that's changed little since it was built. It also has the area's most interesting **accommodation** in the form of the *Pioneertown Motel* (☎760/365-4879, ⓦ www.pioneertownmotel.com; ❸), where clean but aging rooms are made more appealing by a full kitchen and a variety of decor: cowboy, pioneer, seascape, etc. There's good **food** and great atmosphere at *Pappy & Harriet's* (☎760/365-5956, ⓦ www.pappyandharriets.com), a Tex-Mex and mesquite barbecue, where there's live music pretty much every night of the week. Indeed, this place has become the area's main venue for touring bands, occasionally attracting the odd internationally recognized artist.

Joshua Tree

Six miles east of Yucca Valley, the town of **Joshua Tree** centers on the intersec-tion of Twentynine Palms Highway and Park Boulevard, which runs south to the national park's West Entrance. There's not much to it, but several decent places to stay and eat make it perhaps the best base for the park if you're not camping.

National Park information is best sought at the **visitor center**, 6554 Park Boulevard (see p.269), which also stocks books and has an attractive cactus garden outside. The cheapest **place to stay** is the pool-equipped *High Desert Motel*, 61310 Twentynine Palms Highway (T 1-888/367-3898; summer ❷, winter ❸), but you might prefer the bed-and-breakfast-style *Joshua Tree Inn* (T 760/366-1188, W www.joshuatreeinn.com; ❹, suites ❻), virtually opposite at 61259 Twentynine Palms Highway, where comfortable rooms and suites with kitchen are set around an attractive pool. Also consider *Spin and Margie's Desert Hideaway*, off Twentynine Palms Highway around three miles east of Joshua Tree (T 760/366-9124, W www.deserthideaway.com; ❺), with luxurious rooms vibrantly decorated in a desert style.

Several reliable **places to eat** huddle within a block or so of each other along Twentynine Palms Highway at its junction with Park Boulevard. Try ⌁ *Crossroads Café and Tavern*, no. 61715 (T 760/366-5414), for breakfasts, burgers, espresso, shakes, and microbrews; *Royal Siam*, no. 61599 (T 760/366-2923; closed Tues), for low-cost Thai and $7 lunch specials; or the *Beatnik Café*, no. 61597 (T 760/366-2090), a hip coffeehouse with tasty food and drink, Internet access, and live music most weekends.

Climbers and hikers needing to buy or **rent gear** should stop by Nomad Ventures, 61795 Twentynine Palms Highway (T 760/366-4684), or nip across the road to Coyote Corner, 6535 Park Boulevard (T 760/366-9683), where

Safe at Home – Gram Parsons in Joshua Tree

A relatively minor star in his lifetime, **Gram Parsons**, the wild country outlaw of early Seventies rock, has since become one of the era's icons. His musical influence spreads wide, from aging rockers like his old friend Keith Richards to Evan Dando, Beck, and the current breed of alt-country misfits, but his fame owes as much to his drug- and booze-fueled life and the bizarre circumstances surrounding his death at the age of 27. It is a story embellished over the years by myth, fabrication, and gossip.

Joshua Tree was Gram's escape from the LA music pressure cooker, and photos show him hanging out with Richards in pharmaceutically altered states, communing with nature, and scanning the night sky for UFOs. On his final visit, Gram and three friends spent September 18, 1973 consuming as much heroin, morphine, marijuana, and Jack Daniels as possible, with Gram finally ODing that night in Room 8 at the *Joshua Tree Inn*.

Parsons' stepfather stood to benefit from Gram's estate if he could get the body back to Louisiana for burial. However, Gram and his friend and tour manager, Phil Kaufman, had already agreed "the survivor would take the other guy's body out to Joshua Tree, have a few drinks and burn it." Three days after Gram's death, Kaufman persuaded an airline employee to release Gram's casket, drove out to Joshua Tree, doused his body in gasoline, and executed the wishes of his deceased friend. The body wasn't completely consumed, however, and Grams' remains now lie in a New Orleans cemetery. Kaufman was only charged with theft of a coffin and had to pay a $300 fine plus $708 for the coffin.

Fans come to stay in Room 8 at the *Joshua Tree Inn* (where you can inscribe your thoughts in a little book known as the Sacred Heart Journal, and add your guitar pick to the collection) and to attend the annual Gramfest (W www.gramfest.com), a devotional music festival held each September. The principal **point of pilgrimage**, though, is a makeshift fans' shrine near where his body was cremated. From the Cap Rock parking lot at the start of Keys View Road, follow a well-defined but unmarked trail around the west side of the rock to a point close to the road intersection. Here, a rock alcove is usually plastered with dedications, though the rangers consider it to be graffiti and periodically clean it off. For many years the spot was marked by a small concrete plinth daubed with "Gram – Safe at Home."

you can fill up your water jugs before heading into the park or have a **shower** ($3 for 7min) after several days of dust and sand.

The **library**, by the crossroads at 6465 Park Boulevard (Mon–Fri 10am–6pm, Sat 10am–2pm; ☎760/366-8615), has free **Internet access**.

Twentynine Palms

Fifteen miles east of the town of Joshua Tree and just two minutes' drive from the park's north entrance, the small highway-side desert town of **Twentynine Palms** (locally known as "two-nine") is a pleasant enough little place despite the occasional artillery booms from the nearby marine base. The climate has been considered perfect for convalescents ever since physicians sent World War I poison-gas victims here for treatment of their respiratory illnesses. The town is now billing itself as an "Oasis of Murals," and the Chamber of Commerce hands out maps of these hyperrealistic artworks, depicting scenes of local history such as the Dirty Sock Camp (named for a method used by miners to filter out gold).

The town runs for almost five miles along the highway and is divided into two sections separated by a small hill. The only sights to speak of are the national park's **Oasis Visitor Center** (see p.270) on the eastern edge of town, and the nearby **Old Schoolhouse Museum**, 6760 National Park Drive (June–Aug Sat & Sun 1–4pm; Oct–May Wed–Sun 1–4pm; free; ☎760/367-2366), whose partly restored schoolroom from 1927 has displays on the local mining industry, the military presence, and desert wildlife.

Pick up **information** at the Twentynine Palms Chamber of Commerce, 73660 Civic Center Drive (June–Aug Mon–Fri 9am–3pm; Sept–May Mon–Fri 9am–5pm; ☎760/367-3445, ⓦwww.29chamber.com), and get **Internet access** at the library, 6078 Adobe Road (Mon & Tues noon–8pm, Wed–Fri 10am–6pm, Sat 9am–5pm).

The best place in town to **stay** is the 🌂 *Twentynine Palms Inn*, 73950 Inn Avenue off National Park Drive (☎760/367-3505, ⓦwww.29palmsinn.com), where an array of cozy adobe bungalows and wood-framed cabins is set around attractively arid grounds and gardens, and a central pool area contains a restaurant and bar. Owned by the same large family since 1928, the inn was built on the Oasis of Mara (see p.271), and has cabins (winter ❺, summer ❹) which are comfortable but fairly basic. It's worth upgrading to a bungalow (winter ❻, summer ❺) or even the lovely Irene's Historic Adobe (winter $310, summer ❽), which sleeps four.

It's a only a small step down to the welcoming *Circle C Lodge*, 6340 El Rey Avenue, two miles west of town (☎1-800/545-9696, ⓦwww.circleclodge .com; ❺), where spacious and well-appointed rooms are ranged around a pool, spa, and barbecue area. Among the cheaper options nearby are the large *Motel 6*, 72562 Twentynine Palms Highway (☎760/367-2833; ❷), which has a pool.

There are low-cost lunches and early dinners at *Ramona's* (☎760/367-1929; closed Sun), a delicious and authentic Mexican joint at 72115 Twentynine Palms Highway, two miles west of town, but the best **place to eat** is the *Twentynine Palms Inn*, with excellent lunches ($8–10) and dinners ($15–20), with many of the ingredients grown in the oasis gardens. For good espresso, bagels, breakfast, wraps, and salads, try *WonderGarden Café*, 6257 Adobe Road (☎760/367-1238), which has a health-food store on site.

Campers in need of a cleanup should head along to 29 Palms Family Fitness, 73782 Two Mile Road at Adobe Road (☎760/361-8010), which has as-long-as-you-like **showers** with towels for $4.

Joshua Tree National Park

Spread over a transitional area where the high Mojave meets the lower Colorado Desert, **JOSHUA TREE NATIONAL PARK** is one of the most unusual and fascinating of California's national parks. Almost 800,000 acres have been set aside for the park's ragged and gnarled namesakes, which flourish in an otherwise sparsely vegetated landscape. If you're staying in Palm Springs, there's no excuse not to visit; if you've further to come, make the effort anyway.

The startling Joshua trees (see box below) are only found in the northwestern quarter of the park, where they form a perfect counterpoint to surreal clusters of monzogranite boulders, great rock piles pushed up from the earth by the movements of the Pinto Mountain Fault running directly below. Often as tall as a hundred feet, their edges are rounded and smooth from thousands of years of flash floods and winds, but there are enough nodules, fissures, and irregularities to make this superb **rock climbing** territory.

Throughout, it's a mystical, even unearthly, landscape, best appreciated at sunrise or sunset when the whole desert floor is bathed in red light. At noon it can feel like an alien and threatening furnace, with temperatures often reaching 125°F in summer, though dropping to a more bearable 70°F in winter. If you're visiting between May and October, you must stick to the higher elevations to enjoy Joshua Tree with any semblance of comfort. In the Low Desert part of the park, the Joshua trees thin out and the temperature rises as you descend below three thousand feet.

Some history

"Joshua Tree" may be a familiar name today, thanks in part to U2's 1987 album of that name, but previously it was almost unknown. Unlike the vast bulk of the

---

The Joshua tree

Unique to the Mojave Desert, the **Joshua tree** (*Yucca brevifolia*) is one of its oldest residents, with large examples probably over three hundred years old. The lack of growth rings makes their age difficult to determine. The Joshua tree isn't, in fact, a tree at all, but a type of yucca, itself a type of agave and therefore a giant member of the lily family.

Awkward-looking and ungainly, it got its unusual name from Mormons who traveled through the region in the 1850s and imagined the craggy branches to be the arms of Joshua leading them to the Promised Land. Of course, Native Americans had been familiar with Joshua trees for millennia, weaving the tough leaves into baskets and sandals, and eating the roasted seeds and flower buds. The trees became equally useful for homesteaders who arrived in the wake of the Mormons – the lack of better wood forced them to press the trunks of Joshua trees into use for fences and building material.

Joshua trees only grow at altitudes over **two thousand feet** and prefer extreme aridity and a bed of course sand and fine silt. By storing water in their spongy trunks, they can grow up to three inches a year, ultimately reaching heights of forty feet or more. To conserve energy, they only bloom when conditions are right, waiting for a crisp winter freeze, timely rains, and the pollinating attentions of the yucca moth before erupting in a springtime display of creamy white-green flowers, which cluster on long stalks at the tips of the branches. Successful young saplings start life as a single shoot, but eventually a terminal bud dies or is injured and the plant splits to form two branches, which in turn divide over time, producing the Joshua trees' distinctive shapes.

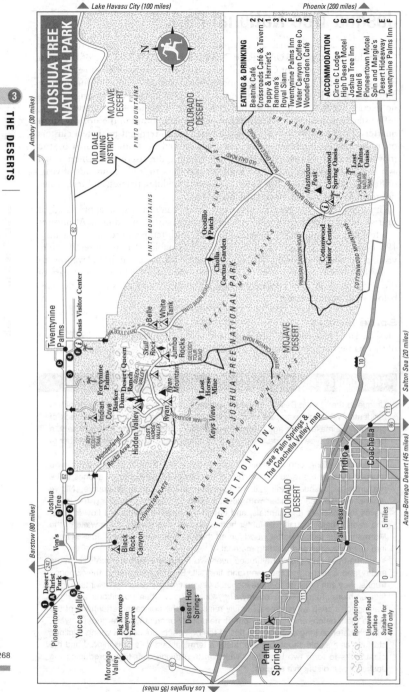

▲ *Lake Havasu City (100 miles)*

Phoenix (200 miles) ▲

JOSHUA TREE NATIONAL PARK

N

▲ *Amboy (30 miles)*

PINTO MOUNTAINS

OLD DALE MINING DISTRICT

MOJAVE DESERT

PINTO MOUNTAINS

COLORADO DESERT

EAGLE MOUNTAINS

EATING & DRINKING
Beatnik Café	2
Crossroads Café & Tavern	2
Pappy & Harriet's	1
Ramona's	2
Royal Siam	3
Twentynine Palms Inn	2
Water Canyon Coffee Co	5
WonderGarden Café	4

ACCOMMODATION
Circle C Lodge	C
High Desert Motel	B
Joshua Tree Inn	D
Motel 6	C
Pioneertown Motel	A
Spin and Margie's Desert Hideaway	E
Twentynine Palms Inn	F

OLD DALE ROAD

BLACK EAGLE MINE ROAD

PINTO BASIN

Mastodon Peak

Cottonwood Spring Oasis

Lost Palms Oasis

MASTODON NATURE TRAIL

PINTO BASIN ROAD

Cottonwood Visitor Center

COTTONWOOD MOUNTAINS

PINKHAM CANYON ROAD

Ocotillo Patch

Cholla Cactus Garden

PINTO MOUNTAINS

62

Oasis Visitor Center

Twentynine Palms

Belle

White Tank

HEXIE MOUNTAINS

PARK BOULEVARD

Skull Rock

Jumbo Rocks

GEOLOGY TOUR ROAD

Fortynine Palms

Indian Cove

Barker Dam

Desert Queen Ranch

QUEEN VALLEY

Ryan Mountain

Lost Horse Mine

PINTO BASIN ROAD

JOSHUA TREE NATIONAL PARK

MOJAVE DESERT

BOY SCOUT TRAIL

Wonderland of Rocks Area

Hidden Valley

LOST HORSE VALLEY

Ryan

Keys View

PARK BOULEVARD

LITTLE SAN BERNARDINO MOUNTAINS

COVINGTON FLATS

TRANSITION ZONE

TRANSITION ZONE

▲ *Barstow (80 miles)*

62

Joshua Tree

Von's

247

Pioneertown

Desert Christ Park

Yucca Valley

▲ *Yucca Valley*

Black Rock Canyon

Big Morongo Canyon Preserve

Morongo Valley

62

Desert Hot Springs

see 'Palm Springs & The Coachella Valley map'

COLORADO DESERT

SAN BERNARDINO MOUNTAINS

Indio

Coachella

Palm Desert

86

111

10

Palm Springs

10

111

▼ *Los Angeles (95 miles)*

▲ *Salton Sea (20 miles)*

Anza-Borrego Desert (45 miles) ▼

Rock Outcrops

Unpaved Road Surface

Suitable for 4WD only

0   5 miles

5 miles

state, nobody, save a few Native Americans, prospectors, and cowboys, had penetrated these remote environs. Despite receiving only around four inches of annual rainfall, the area is surprisingly lush, and it was grass that attracted the first significant pioneers. Forty-niners hurrying through on their way to the Sierra Nevada gold fields told tales of good pastures, and early cattlemen were quick to follow. Rustlers discovered that the natural rocky corrals made perfect sites for branding their illegitimate herds before moving them out to the coast for sale. Ambushes and gunfights drove the rustlers to seek refuge in the mountains, where they discovered small traces of gold and sparked vigorous mining operations that continued until the 1940s. In recognition of the uniqueness of the area, and the need for its preservation, the national park system took the land under its jurisdiction as a national monument in 1936 and has vigilantly maintained its beauty ever since. The park lost some of the original area to mining interests in the 1950s, but that was more than compensated for in 1994, when it was promoted to a **national park**, with the addition of 234,000 acres.

Park practicalities

Less than an hour's drive northeast from Palm Springs, Joshua Tree National Park (always open; $15 per vehicle for 7 days, $5 per cyclist or hiker; Ⓦwww .nps.gov/jotr) is best approached through the Morongo Basin (see p.263) along Hwy-62, which branches off I-10. Besides camping (see p.270), there is neither lodging nor anywhere to eat or buy supplies within the park, so the Morongo Basin towns of Yucca Valley, Joshua Tree, and Twentynine Palms are the main bases from which to explore. Visiting the park without your own **transport** is not really an option: at best, you're looking at a ten-mile desert walk to get to anything of interest.

You can enter the park via the West Entrance at the town of **Joshua Tree**, where there's a **visitor center**, 6554 Park Boulevard (daily 8am–5pm; Ⓣ760/367-5500), or the North Entrance at **Twentynine Palms**, where

▲ Joshua Tree National Park

you'll find the **Oasis Visitor Center** (daily 8am–5pm; ☏760/367-5500). Alternatively, if you're coming from the south, there's an entrance and the **Cottonwood Visitor Center** (generally daily 8am–4pm; ☏760/367-5500) seven miles north of I-10. It's worth stopping at one of the visitor centers to collect the free national park **map** and *Joshua Tree Guide*, which are fine for most purposes, though hikers will want a more **detailed map**, the best being Trails Illustrated's *Joshua Tree National Park* map ($10).

Park staff run free, campground-based **ranger programs** (generally mid-Feb to May and mid-Oct to mid-Dec, but also summer weekends), which might include campfire talks, discovery walks, and geology hikes: check at visitor centers for the current schedule.

Camping

Joshua Tree National Park has nine **campgrounds**, all concentrated in the northwest except for one at Cottonwood by the southern entrance. All have tables, fire rings (bring your own wood), and vault toilets, but only two (*Black Rock Canyon* and *Cottonwood*) have water supplies and flush toilets. The lack of showers and electrical and sewage hookups at any of the sites keeps the majority of RVs at bay, but in the popular winter months the place fills up quickly, especially at weekends. All campgrounds except *Black Rock Canyon* and *Indian Cove* are first-come-first-served, and are good for up to six people and two vehicles. **Winter** nights can be very cold, and campers here between November and March should come with warm jackets and sleeping bags or head for the lower (and warmer) *Cottonwood* campground.

Over eighty percent of the park is designated wilderness where **backcountry camping** is permitted, provided you register before you head out. Twelve backcountry boards are dotted through the park at the start of most trails. Here you can self-register, leave your vehicle, and study the regulations that include prohibition of camping within a mile of a road, five hundred feet of a trail, and a quarter-mile a water source.

The campgrounds are listed from northwest to southeast through the park.

Black Rock Canyon (100 sites; 4000ft) A large campground only accessible from outside the park. Reserve by calling ☏1-877/444-6777. Water available. $15.

Indian Cove (101 sites; 3200ft) Another large campground only accessible from outside the park. It's set among granite boulders and a trail from the eastern section of the campground road leads to Rattlesnake Canyon – its streams and waterfalls (depending on rainfall) breaking an otherwise eerie silence among the monoliths. Reservations on ☏1-877/444-6777. No water. $15.

Hidden Valley (45 sites; 4200ft) Popular campground that is almost entirely occupied by rock climbers in spring and fall. No water. $10.

Ryan (31 sites; 4300ft) Medium-sized campground amid some lovely rocks and trees. No water. $10.

Jumbo Rocks (125 sites; 4400ft) The highest and largest site in the park, often busy and with regular ranger programs including a free one on Sat evenings (spring–fall). No water. $10.

Belle (18 sites; 3800ft) Small, quiet site amid some lovely rocks. No water. $10.

White Tank (15 sites; 3800ft) Relatively small and quiet site with a short nature trail to Arch Rock. No water. $10.

Cottonwood (62 sites; 3000ft) Being lower down, this is the pick for the cooler winter months. Water available. $15.

Exploring the park

The best way to enjoy the park is to be selective, especially in the hotter months when you'll find an ambitious schedule impossible. Casual observers will find a day-trip plenty, most likely a leisurely drive along **Park Boulevard** and **Pinto Basin Road** – the paved roads which run right through the Park – perhaps

Nature trails and hikes in Joshua Tree National Park

To get a real feel for the majesty of the desert, you'll need to leave the main roads behind and hike, or at least follow one of the short (and mostly wheelchair-accessible) **nature trails** which have been set up throughout the park to help interpret something of desert ecology and plant life.

The more strenuous **hikes** outlined below are generally safe, but be sure to **stick to the trails:** Joshua Tree is full of abandoned gold mines, and although the rangers are fencing them as quickly as possible, they don't have the funds to take care of all of them.

Most of the listed trails are in the slightly cooler and higher Mojave Desert, but even on the easier trails allow around an hour per mile: there's very little shade and in summer you'll tire quickly. There's tougher stuff on the eastern side of the park around **Pinto Basin**, though this territory is purely for experienced groups of hikers well armed with maps and water. If you're thinking of heading out on anything more ambitious than the hikes described here, be sure to discuss your plans with a ranger; and anyone planning to stay out overnight in the wilderness must **register** at one of the trailhead backcountry boards.

Nature trails

These are listed northwest to southeast through the park.

Oasis of Mara (800-yard loop) A series of explanatory panels around a significant fan-palm oasis right by the Oasis Visitor Center.

Cholla Cactus Garden (400-yard loop) A beautiful stroll among these superbly photogenic cacti.

Bajada (400-yard loop) Investigate the flora of a naturally sloping drainage half a mile north of the South Entrance.

Recommended hikes

These are listed northwest to southeast through the park.

Fortynine Palms Oasis (3 miles; 2hr) Moderately strenuous, this leaves the badly signposted Canyon Road six miles west of the visitor center at Twentynine Palms. A barren, rocky trail leads to this densely clustered and partly fire-blackened oasis, which continues to flourish on the seepage down the canyon. There's not enough water to swim in, nor are you allowed to camp (the oasis is officially closed 8pm–7am), but a late afternoon or evening visit presents the best wildlife rewards.

Lost Horse Mine (4 miles; 3hr) Starting a mile east of Keys View Road, this moderately difficult trail climbs 450ft to the mine, which made an average of $20,000 a week in the 1890s. The hike takes you through abandoned mining sites, with building foundations and equipment still intact, to the top of Lost Horse Mountain.

Ryan Mountain (3 miles; 2hr) Some of the best views in the park are from the top of Ryan Mountain (5461ft), seven hundred strenuous feet above the desert floor. Start at the parking area near the *Sheep Pass* campground and follow the trail past the Indian Cave, which contains bedrock mortars once used by the Cahuilla and Serrano.

Mastodon Peak (3 miles; 2hr) Another peak climb, less strenuous than Ryan Mountain but with great views, especially south to the Salton Sea. Start from the *Cottonwood* campground.

Lost Palms Oasis (8 miles; 5hr) This moderate trail, starting from the *Cottonwood* campground or nearby trailhead, leads across desert washes and past palo verde, cottonwood, and ironwood trees to the largest stand of palms in the park. The trail offers a possible scrambling side-trip to Victory Palms. There's little surface water, but often enough to lure bighorn sheep.

joining a tour of the Desert Queen Ranch and driving up to Keys View. For desert-lovers a couple of nights camping out is a highlight that shouldn't be missed, and experienced hikers may want to take advantage of the park's excellent if strenuous trails and backcountry opportunities. The rangers and staff at the visitor centers will be able to recommend the most enjoyable itineraries, tailored to your requirements and abilities. And remember never to venture anywhere without a detailed **map** (see p.270).

Many of the roads are unmarked, hard to negotiate, and restricted to four-wheel-drive use. If a road is marked as such, don't even think about taking a normal car – you'll soon come to a grinding halt, and it could be quite a few panic-stricken hours before anybody finds you.

The northwest

Approaching from the township of Joshua Tree, you enter the park's north-western corner and immediately find yourself in the **Wonderland of Rocks** area, comprising giant, rounded granite boulders that draw **rock climbers** from all over the world. The various clusters flank the road for about ten miles, giving plenty of opportunity to stop for a little bouldering, or more adventurous routes for those suitably equipped and skilled.

A little further on, close to the *Hidden Valley* campground, a well-signposted one-mile nature trails loops into **Hidden Valley**, a near-complete natural circle of rock mounds where cattle rustlers used to hide out. To the north, a side road leads past the entrance to the Desert Queen Ranch (see below) to the rain-fed **Barker Dam**, Joshua Tree's crucial water supply, built around the turn of the century by cattlemen (and rustlers) to prevent their poor beasts from expiring halfway across the park. The route back from the dam passes a number of petroglyphs.

Desert Queen Ranch

Just northeast of the *Hidden Valley* campground sits the **Desert Queen Ranch** (aka Keys Ranch), only accessible by joining the informative and entertaining ranger-led **guided walking tour** (Oct–May daily 10am & 1pm; June–Sept check at the visitor centers; $5; reservations necessary March & April; ☏760/367-5555), which begins at the entrance to the ranch and takes around ninety minutes. You can buy tickets in advance at the Oasis Visitor Center, or just turn up and hope there is space. The ranch was once home to tough desert rat and indefatigable miner Bill Keys, a Russian by birth who lived here with his family from 1910 until his death (at age 89) in 1969 – long after less hardy men had abandoned the arid wasteland. He was briefly famous in 1943, when he was locked away for shooting one of his neighbors over a right-of-way argument, only to be bailed out by a friend, the mystery writer Erle Stanley Gardner. Keys and family made a spartan but surprisingly comfortable living from growing vegetables, mining, ranching, and working as a farrier and general trader for just about everything a desert dweller could desire. The tour visits their ramshackle home, orchard site, workshop, and even a schoolhouse that operated for seven years from 1935.

The center and southeast

Bill Keys is further remembered at **Keys View**, eight miles south, a 5185-foot-high vista offering the best views in the whole park. On a good day, you can see as far as the Salton Sea and beyond into Mexico – a brilliant desert panorama of badlands and mountains. The trouble is, "good" days are increasingly rare. Driven by prevailing winds, LA smog is funneled between the mountains straight to Joshua Tree National Park, with the result that **air pollution** is a significant issue.

Biking and rock climbing in Joshua Tree National Park

While driving through Joshua Tree lessens your contact with the desert, and the need to carry all your water limits the scope for hiking, **biking** strikes a nice balance. With cyclists restricted to roads open to motor vehicles, you shouldn't come expecting genuine off-road action, but there's an increasing number of bikeable and challenging dirt roads. Armed with your own set of wheels (there is no bike rental anywhere near the park), consider heading out on popular fifteen- to twenty-mile routes like the Geology Tour Road, Covington Flats Road, and Pinkham Canyon Road. These and more are listed in the *Joshua Tree Guide* (see p.270).

Since the 1970s, the fractured lumps of golden rock that pepper the northwestern corner of the park have become fabulously popular and world renowned for **rock climbing** and **bouldering**. Climbers keen to find a springtime training ground while the Sierra crags were still under snow began putting up routes which now see sticky-rubber traffic from October to May – the summer months are generally way too hot. In spring and fall, rock climbers sometimes base themselves here for weeks, usually at the *Hidden Valley* campground. Climbers should pick up the *Climber Ethics* leaflet from one of the visitor centers, and may want to call at the climbing shops in the township of Joshua Tree to obtain guidebooks; Coyote Corner rents guidebooks for $2.50 a day. The most comprehensive book is Randy Vogel's *Rock Climbing: Joshua Tree* (Falcon), though his condensed and much cheaper *Joshua Tree National Park: Classic Rock Climbs* (Falcon) may suit short-term visitors. Boulderers will want *A Complete Bouldering Guide to Joshua Tree National Park* by Robert Miramontes (K Daniels). Beginners or those after instruction and guiding should contact one of the climbing schools that operate here. Both Joshua Tree Rock Climbing School (℡1-800/890-4745, ⓦwww.joshuatreerockclimbing.com) and Uprising (℡1-888/254-6266, ⓦwww.uprising.com) offer a range of one-day courses for around $120 and improvers' weekends for around $225. Check the websites for course dates, or go for private guiding which costs around $285 a day for one person or $175 each for two.

Continue along Park Boulevard past the start of the Ryan Mountain hike (see box, p.271) and the turnoff for **Geology Tour Road**, which leads down through the best of Joshua Tree's rock formations. A little further on, the *Jumbo Rocks* campground is the start of a hiking loop (1.7 miles) through boulders and desert washes to **Skull Rock**, which can also be easily seen from the road immediately east of the campground.

Moving along eastward, now on Pinto Basin Road, you'll pass *White Tank* campground (see p.270), which is worth a short stop for its trail through huge granite domes to a photogenic **rock arch**; the trail starts by site 9.

Almost at the transition zone between the Colorado and Mojave deserts and on the fringes of the Pinto Basin, the **Cholla Cactus Garden** is a quarter-mile loop through an astonishing concentration of the "jumping" **cholla** cactus (see box, p.52), as well as creosote bushes, jojoba, and several other cactus species. It's a beautiful spot at any time, but come at dusk or dawn for the best chance of seeing the mainly nocturnal desert wood rat. Nearby, the almost barren desert at **Ocotillo Patch** comes stuffed with spindly ocotillo plants, most attractive in spring for their scarlet blooms.

The Imperial Valley and the Salton Sea

The patch of the Colorado Desert **south** of Joshua Tree and Palm Springs is one of the least friendly of all the California desert regions, and its foreboding aspect discourages exploration. It's best not to come between June and September, when intense heat makes journeys uncomfortable and services are greatly reduced; frankly, there's little reason to come here at all unless you're heading for Anza-Borrego Desert State Park or the Mexican border.

Sandwiched between Hwy-111 and Hwy-86, which branch off I-10 soon after Palm Springs and the Coachella Valley, the area from the **Salton Sea** down to the migrant-worker towns of the agricultural **Imperial Valley** lies in the two-thousand-square-mile Salton Basin: the largest area of dry land below sea level in the western hemisphere.

Created accidentally in 1905 (see box below), the Salton Sea and its shores were once extremely tony, attracting Frank Sinatra, Dean Martin, and others to its yacht clubs; in its 1940s heyday, the lake was actually a bigger tourist draw than Yosemite National Park. A series of mid-1970s storms caused the lake to rise and swallow shoreline developments, but pollution was already having a detrimental impact on tourism. Nestled 235ft below sea level, the Salton Sea has no natural outlet and has been plagued over the years by agricultural runoff and toxic wastes carried in by two rivers from Mexico, making it excessively saline. Local boosters are desperate to point out that the problems are exaggerated, but fish still carry a consumption warning, and people rarely swim and waterski here these days.

Still, the Salton Sea remains an important wintering area for shorebirds and waterfowl. Brown pelicans come by in summer, and terns and cormorants also nest here. The best place to see them is the **Sonny Bono Salton Sea National Wildlife Refuge** (daily dawn–dusk; free; ⓦ www.fws.gov/saltonsea) at the lake's southern tip. There's a viewing platform by the informative **visitor center** (April–Sept Mon–Fri 7am–3.30pm; Oct–March Mon–Fri 7am–3.30pm, Sat & Sun 8am–4.30pm; ⓣ 760/393-3052), or you can take the Rock Hill Trail for a closer look, a twenty-minute walk to the water's edge. To get to the refuge, take the poorly signposted backroads off Hwy-111 south of **Niland** or off Hwy-86 at **Westmorland**; both run past fields of alfalfa, cantaloupe, tomatoes, and other crop, proof that just about anything will grow in this fertile land provided it is suitably irrigated.

If you've come this far, it's worth turning east off Niland's Main Street and traveling three miles to see **Salvation Mountain** (ⓦ www.salvationmountain .us), a fantastic work of large-scale religious folk art built continuously since 1985 by friendly eccentric Leonard Knight. He has devoted his later life to this wildly colored mass of straw and adobe, liberally painted with extracts from the Bible and exhortations to "Repent" – there's even an abandoned motorboat used to represent Noah's Ark. Leonard adds to his structure – already thirty

---

The accidental sea

At 35 miles long by up to 15 miles wide, the **Salton Sea** is California's largest lake, but one which only came into existence a century ago. Over the millennia, the shallow Salton Basin has repeatedly filled with floodwaters that spilled over from the Colorado River some fifty miles to the east, but each time the lake has dried up. When European Americans started pushing into the West, they recognized that the fertile Salton Basin and the surrounding Imperial Valley could be made super-productive by channeling water from the Colorado. In 1901, a development company did just that, but river silt soon blocked the channel and in 1905 almost the entire flow from the Colorado River was pouring into the Salton Basin. The deluge wasn't stanched for almost two years, by which time it had formed the Salton Sea – a huge freshwater lake up to fifty feet deep.

feet high and a hundred feet wide – each morning, but spends much of the day guiding the trickle of visitors: a small donation is appreciated but never requested.

The only other reasons you might stop around here are to **camp** (primitive $7, developed sites $17, hookups $23) in the Salton Sea State Recreation Area, which encompasses a handful of sites along a fourteen-mile stretch of the eastern side of the lake from Bombay Beach to Mecca Beach. Agricultural work brings thousands of Mexicans north of the border, and the **restaurants** generally cater to them: practice your Spanish.

Anza-Borrego Desert State Park

Southwest of the Salton Sea, the **ANZA-BORREGO DESERT STATE PARK** is the largest state park in the country outside Alaska, covering 600,000 acres. In contrast to the Imperial Valley, it offers a diverse variety of plant and animal life as well as a legend-strewn history spanning Native American tribes, the first white trailfinders, and Gold Rush times. It takes its double-barreled name from Juan Baptista de Anza, a Spanish explorer who crossed the region in 1774, and the Spanish for the native bighorn sheep, **borrego cimarron**, which eats the brittlebrush and agave found here. Some of Anza-Borrego can be covered by car (confidence on gravel roads is handy), although you'll need four-wheel drive for the more obscure – and most interesting – routes, and there are over five hundred miles of hiking trails and dirt roads.

During the fiercely hot summer months, the place is best left to the lizards, although most campgrounds stay open all year. The most popular time to visit is the desert **blooming season** (typically a couple of weeks between late February and early April), though there's a fifty-percent chance in any given year that the wildflowers won't bloom at all. If you strike it lucky you'll be rewarded with scarlet ocotillo, orange poppies, white lilies, purple verbena, and other intensely colorful – and fragrant – wildflowers. For the latest information call the 24-hour Wildflower Hotline (℡760/767-4684). As well as taking the usual desert precautions (see box, p.244), you should read the comments on p.53 – this is mountain lion territory.

Though accessible from the Salton Sea along Hwy-178 or Hwy-S22, the Anza-Borrego is usually approached from San Diego, through Julian (see p.236). This way you'll hit the park at Scissors Crossing, with most of the developed facilities to the north and much of the more interesting historical debris to the south.

Borrego Springs

Human activity in Anza-Borrego revolves around **Borrego Springs**, a tiny town in the heart of the park centered on a large traffic island known as Christmas Circle. There's usually not much happening in Borrego Springs, but it's one of the most pleasant of all the desert towns, self-contained and remarkably uncommercialized. On a short visit to the park it's probably best to base yourself in Borrego Springs or camp at *Borrego Palm Canyon* campground, just outside of town, where there's an abundance of ranger-led hikes and campfire talks: check with the visitor center (see below) for the latest details. If you're camping out, it's the place to gather (expensive) supplies – but don't expect any big supermarket chains here.

Your first stop, two miles west of here, should be the excellent **State Park visitor center**, 200 Palm Canyon Drive (June–Sept Sat, Sun & holidays 9am–5pm;

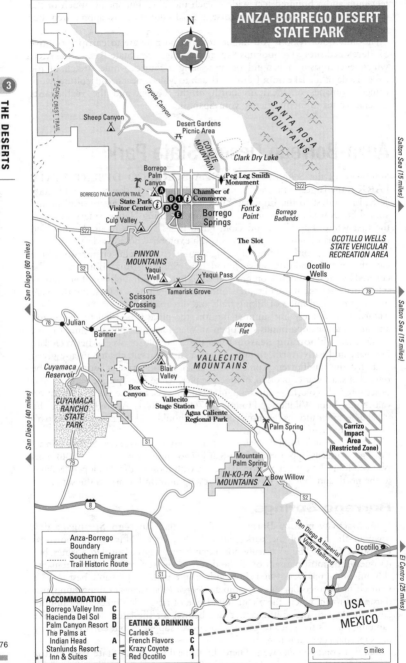

ANZA-BORREGO DESERT STATE PARK

N

PACIFIC CREST TRAIL

Sheep Canyon

Coyote Canyon

Desert Gardens Picnic Area

SANTA ROSA MOUNTAINS

COYOTE MOUNTAIN

Clark Dry Lake

S22 ◀ Salton Sea (15 miles) ▶

Borrego Palm Canyon

Peg Leg Smith Monument

BORREGO PALM CANYON TRAIL

A

State Park Visitor Center ⓘ

B 1 ⓘ Chamber of Commerce

D
E

Borrego Springs

Font's Point

Borrego Badlands

Culp Valley

PINYON MOUNTAINS

The Slot

OCOTILLO WELLS STATE VEHICULAR RECREATION AREA

◀ San Diego (60 miles)

S22

S2

Yaqui Well

S3

Yaqui Pass

Ocotillo Wells

78

Tamarisk Grove

◀ Salton Sea (15 miles) ▶

Scissors Crossing

Harper Flat

78 Julian

Banner

VALLECITO MOUNTAINS

◀ San Diego (40 miles)

Cuyamaca Reservoir

Blair Valley

CUYAMACA RANCHO STATE PARK

Box Canyon

Vallecito Stage Station

79

S1

Agua Caliente Regional Park

Palm Spring

Carrizo Impact Area (Restricted Zone)

Mountain Palm Spring

IN-KO-PA MOUNTAINS

Bow Willow

S2

San Diego & Imperial Valley Railroad

Ocotillo

◀ El Centro (25 miles) ▶

Anza-Borrego Boundary

Southern Emigrant Trail Historic Route

S1

8

94

USA

MEXICO

ACCOMMODATION
Borrego Valley Inn   C
Hacienda Del Sol   B
Palm Canyon Resort   D
The Palms at
  Indian Head   A
Stanlunds Resort
Inn & Suites   E

EATING & DRINKING
Carlee's   B
French Flavors   C
Krazy Coyote   A
Red Ocotillo   1

0   5 miles

Oct–May daily 9am–5pm; ☎760/767-5311, ⓦwww.anzaborrego.statepark.org), which is so well landscaped into the desert floor you barely notice it as you approach. Here you can also pick up an informative free newspaper, which contains a detailed map of the park along with numerous suggestions for hikes. Outside, the half-mile **All-Access Nature Trail** allows you to weave across the desert and identify the flora.

A mile to the north, the main *Borrego Palm Canyon* campground marks the start of the **Borrego Palm Canyon Trail** (3 miles round-trip; 2hr; 350-foot ascent), the most popular trail in the park (day-use fee $6 per vehicle). It follows a detailed nature trail to one of the largest oases left in the US, with a quarter-mile of stream densely flanked by around a thousand mop-

▲ Bighorn sheep, Anza-Borrego Desert State Park

topped California fan palms (sometimes known as Washingtonia palms from their Latin name, *Washingtonia filifera*) – the only palms native to the western United States.

Practicalities

Borrego Springs is accessible by **public transportation**: from San Diego, the Metropolitan Transit System (☎1-800/858-0291, ⓦwww.sdcommute.com; see p.188) makes the trip with a change in Ramona (currently Thurs & Fri only). Most of the town's commercial activity goes on either in The Center or The Mall, opposite each other on Palm Drive. Here you'll find the bulk of the restaurants, shops, and accommodation, but you'll need to head half a mile east for the **Chamber of Commerce**, 786 Palm Canyon Drive (daily 10am–4pm; ☎1-800/559-5524, ⓦwww.borregospringschamber.com), which has free wireless **Internet**. There's also Internet access at the library by the Mall (closed Sun & Mon).

There are some lovely primitive and developed campgrounds in the park (see box, p.278), but if you're not feeling adventurous enough, there's a handful of lovely **places to stay**. In season, even the basic motels seem quite expensive, though rates drop dramatically in summer. There are a few **places to eat**, some of which close or run reduced hours in summer.

Accommodation

Borrego Valley Inn 405 Palm Canyon Drive ☎1-800/333-5810, ⓦwww.borregovalleyinn.com. Probably the pick of the local accommodation, this lovely and centrally located cluster of Southwestern-style rooms is set in a cactus garden and comes with two heated pools (one clothing-optional), rooms with kitchenettes, afternoon snacks, and a hearty continental breakfast. Rooms are all tastefully decorated and well equipped, but step up to the deluxe rooms if you can. There's a two-night minimum stay on winter weekends. Summer ⑤, winter ⑦, deluxe rooms always ⑦

Hacienda del Sol 610 Palm Canyon Drive ☎760/767-5442. Central, budget motel with some kitchenettes and separate cottages (winter only). Rooms ③, kitchen units ⑤, cottages ⑥

Palm Canyon Resort 221 Palm Canyon Drive ☎1-800/242-0044, ⓦwww.pcresort.com. Modern hotel a mile west of town done in ersatz Old West style, with comfortable rooms and full-hookup RV sites ($36). Winter ⑤, summer ④

The Palms at Indian Head 2220 Hoberg Rd ☏760/767-7788, ⓦwww.thepalmsatindianhead .com. Stylish 1950s Modernist hotel – once the domain of Monroe, Brando, and other celebrities – with a great pool, all very tastefully done. After a period of neglect it's been steadily improving, and with no phones or alarm clocks in rooms the emphasis is very much on relaxation. Breakfast included. Winter ❻, summer ❺

🏃 Stanlunds Resort Inn & Suites 2771 Borrego Springs Road ☏760/767-5501, ⓦwww.stanlunds.com. The cheapest rooms around (some with kitchenettes), located three quarters of a mile south of town along Borrego Springs Road. There's a nice pool and continental breakfast is included. Winter ❸, summer ❷

Eating

Carlee's 660 Palm Canyon Drive ☏760/767-3262. Handy downtown restaurant and bar with a lively atmosphere and a menu covering burgers,

sandwiches, pizza ($14–16), and even tequila chicken fettucini ($16).

🏃 French Flavors 721 Avenida Sureste ☏760/767-4845. Informal French/Belgian-run crêperie and patisserie with French country decor that works surprisingly well in a Modernist desert building. A pair of savory or sweet crêpes goes for $10–12 and the crème brûlée is delicious. French wines start at $20 a bottle, and they do a hiker's lunch package ($14.50). Closed Tues & Wed.

Krazy Coyote Saloon & Grill At The Palms at Indian Head (see opposite). The pick of the area's more upscale restaurants with patio dining overlooking the pool. Expect the likes of French dip ($12), sesame garlic tenderloin ($17), and rack of lamb ($33). Open Nov to mid-May, dinner only.

Red Ocotillo 818 Palm Canyon Drive ☏760/767-3262. Diner-style place where you huddle in a Quonset hut or relax on the patio outside, perhaps tucking into a breakfast burrito ($7) or a Reuben sandwich ($9).

Northern Anza-Borrego

Six miles east of Borrego Springs along Hwy-S22, there's a memorial marker to Peg Leg Smith, an infamous local spinner of yarns from Gold Rush days who is further celebrated by a festival of tall tales – the **Peg Leg Liars Contest** – which takes place at this spot on the first Saturday in April. Anybody can get up before the judges and fib their hearts out for five minutes, with the most outrageous stories earning a modest prize. Roughly four miles further on, a fairly

Camping in Anza-Borrego

Anza-Borrego Desert State Park manages two developed and nine primitive campgrounds, but this is one of the few parks that allow **open camping**, giving you the freedom to pitch a tent pretty much anywhere without a permit, although it's advisable to let someone know your plans. The few provisos are that you don't drive off-road, don't camp near water holes, camp away from developed campgrounds, light fires only in fire rings or metal containers, collect no firewood, and leave the place as you found it, or cleaner.

The largest site, and the only one with RV hookups, is the Borrego Palm Canyon campground a mile from the visitor center (hookups $29, tents $20). Tamarisk Grove, thirteen miles south on Hwy-S3 ($20), is the only other developed site. Both charge $6 per vehicle for day-use of the facilities, which include water supply and coin-op **showers**. Both also organize **guided hikes** and have regular discussion and activity evenings led by a volunteer naturalist. Places can be reserved through ⓦwww .reserveamerica.com or at ☏1-800/444-7275 (essential for holidays and weekends, and in the March–April blooming season). The other primitive campgrounds fill on a first-come-first-served basis; those in the backcountry always have space. All are accessible by road vehicles and are free, except for Bow Willow, which charges $7 and is the only one with **drinking water**. Most sites are below 1500ft, which is fine in winter, but in the hotter months you might try Culp Valley, eight miles southwest of Borrego Springs, at a blissfully balmy 3400ft. In addition, there's a commercial campground at the Agua Caliente Regional Park (see opposite).

tough dirt road (check with the State Park visitor center or Chamber of Commerce for conditions) leads to **Font's Point** and a view over the **Borrego Badlands** – a long, sweeping plain devoid of vegetation, whose strange, stark charms are oddly inspiring. Sunset is the best time to fully appreciate the layered alluvial banding.

If you want to be outside but shaded from the sun's fierce rays, make for **The Slot**, a narrow fifty-foot-deep canyon carved from the soft rock by infrequent flooding – though frequent enough that you definitely shouldn't venture here if there's any sign of rain in the vicinity. You can walk down into the canyon and follow it downstream for five minutes to a quarter-mile-long section where it's just wide enough for one person to squeeze through. To get here, travel 1.5 miles east from the junction of Borrego Springs Road and Hwy-78, then follow the very sandy Buttes Pass Road for 1.8 miles, keeping left at the only junction. The road is usually passable for ordinary cars but if you have any doubts about your or your vehicle's abilities, turn back.

Southern Anza-Borrego

At Scissors Crossing, Hwy-78 from Julian intersects Hwy-S2, which heads towards the park's southeast corner. It follows the line of the old **Butterfield Stage Route**, which began service in 1857 and was the first regular line of communication between the eastern states and the newly settled West. Along the way you pass through **Blair Valley**, with its primitive campground, to **Box Canyon**, where the Mormon Battalion of 1847, following what is now known as the **Southern Emigrant Trail Historic Route**, forced a passage along the desert wash. It isn't especially spectacular, but makes for some safe desert walking, never more than a couple of hundred yards from the road. Five miles further on, the **Vallecito Stage Station** (Sept–May 9am–sunset; June–Aug closed) is an old adobe stagecoach rest stop that gives a good indication of the comforts – or lack of them – of early desert travel. The building is in the grounds of a county-run **campground** ($15), which requires you to pay a day-use fee of $2 per vehicle to see it.

A further three miles south, the **Agua Caliente Regional Park** (Sept–May daily 9.30am–5pm; $5 per vehicle) contains a couple of naturally fed pools, one large outdoor affair kept at its natural 96°F and one smaller indoor pool at a more modest temperature, fitted with water jets. Most visitors stay at the **campground** (tents $15, hookups $20–25; reservations ☎858/565-3600), which surrounds the pools and gives you longer access for evening soaking.

South of here lies the least-visited portion of Anza-Borrego, good for isolated exploration and undisturbed views around Imperial Valley, where there's a vivid and spectacular clash as gray rock rises from the edges of the red desert floor, and a primitive **campground** close to the small oasis at *Mountain Palm Spring*.

Hiking, biking, and other recreational activities

Recreational opportunities in the park are strictly controlled to preserve the fragile ecosystem. **Hiking** is perhaps the most obvious pursuit, with the Borrego Palm Canyon Trail (see p.277) being the most popular. If you'd prefer to have the desert to yourself, consider one of the other hikes listed in the park's free annual newspaper: the Pena Spring Trail (0.6 miles round-trip) is good for spotting bird and wildlife, or try the tougher Hellhole Canyon/Maidenhair Falls Trail (6 miles round-trip), which involves some rock scrambling and ends at a canyon oasis.

Mountain bikers are not allowed on hiking trails, but provided you bring your own set of wheels (there are no local rentals available) you've free rein on the dirt roads that cross the desert. If you'd rather have a larger saddle, try **desert horse trekking** with Smoketree Arabian Horse Rental (☎760/767-5850, ⓦ www.smoketreearabianranch.com), offering one-hour ($55) and two-hour ($95) rides, even in summer when they start at 7am.

The Mojave Desert

Desolate, silent, and virtually lifeless, the **MOJAVE DESERT**, mythic badland of the West, has no equal when it comes to hardship. Called the **High Desert** because its height above sea level averages around two thousand feet, the Mojave is very dry and for the most part deadly flat, dotted here and there with the shaggy form of a Joshua tree and an occasional abandoned miner's shed. For most, it's the barrier between LA and Las Vegas, an obstacle to get over before they reach either city; and, short on attractions as it is, you may want to follow their example. However, you should linger a little just to see – and smell – what a desert is really like: a vast, impersonal, extreme environment, sharp with its own peculiar fragrance, and alive in spring with acres of fiery orange poppies – the state flower of California – and other brightly colored wildflowers.

You will have relatively little company. If LA is the home of the sports car, the Mojave is the land of huge dust-covered trucks, carrying goods across the state to Nevada and beyond. Other signs of life include the grim military subculture marooned on huge weapons-testing sites. There is also a hardcore group of desert fans: backdrop for the legion of road movies spawned by the underground film culture in the late 1960s and early 1970s, the Mojave is a favorite with bikers and neo-hippies drawn by the barren panorama of sand dunes and mountain ranges. Nature lovers also find pockets of interest, but otherwise visitors are thin on the ground.

Access is mostly along I-15, which cuts through the heart of the Mojave, dividing it into two distinct regions. To the north are the Western Mojave and Death Valley (covered in Chapter Four); to the South lies Barstow the south lies **Barstow**, the lackluster capital of the Mojave, redeemed only by its location halfway between LA and Las Vegas on I-15. This makes it both a potential stopover between the two points and a good base for the surrounding attractions, such as the immense **Mojave National Preserve**. Here you can see spectacular sand dunes, striking rock formations, and a huge variety of plant life, including large concentrations of Joshua trees. Much of the preserve rises to about four thousand feet, so it also offers respite from the harshest of the area's heat.

The Western Mojave

The **western expanse** of the Mojave Desert spreads out on the north side of the San Gabriel Mountains, fifty miles from Los Angeles via Hwy-14. It is a barren plain that drivers have to cross in order to reach the alpine peaks of the eastern Sierra Nevada Mountains or Death Valley, at the Mojave's northern edge. The few towns that have taken root in this stretch of desert over the past few decades are populated by two sorts of people: retired couples who value the dry, clean air, and **aerospace** workers. The region's economy is wholly based on designing, building, and testing airplanes, from B-1 bombers for the military to the *Voyager*, which made the first nonstop flight around the globe in 1987. The post-world war II establishment of **Edwards Air Force Base**, on the desert and dry lakebeds east of the town of Mojave, has made the region the aerospace capital of the world, as well as one of the fastest growing regions in California.

Lancaster, near Edwards Air Force Base, is the largest town and one of the few places to pick up supplies; **Mojave**, thirty miles north, is a desert crossroads that caters mainly to drive-by tourists. **Tehachapi**, twenty miles west and a few thousand feet higher, offers a cool retreat. Hwy-14 joins up with US-395 another forty miles north, just west of the huge naval air base at **China Lake** and the faceless town of **Ridgecrest**, useful mainly as a jumping-off point for some interesting attractions.

Palmdale, Lancaster, and Mojave

Northbound travelers from Los Angeles hit the desert proper at the contiguous and equally soulless towns of **Palmdale** and **Lancaster**, the biggest places for miles. The nearby Edwards Air Force Base is the US military testing ground for experimental, high-speed, and high-altitude aircraft (such as the Blackbird; see below), and incorporates NASA's **Dryden Flight Research Center** and a backup space shuttle landing site. Even if you have no interest in military stuff, the region makes a reasonable base for exploring the desert hereabouts: Hwy-14 is the region's main artery and forays are best made from there. The area doesn't really warrant an overnight stop, but Lancaster and Palmdale have a full range of **lodging**, and **Mojave** has a number of $40–50 highwayside motels.

Palmdale

About the only thing of interest in **Palmdale** is the **Blackbird Airpark** (Fri–Sun 11am–4pm; free), three miles east of Hwy-14 along Avenue P. The two sinister-looking black planes standing by the roadside here are in fact the fastest and highest-flying planes ever created. The YA-12 was designed in the 1950s as a prototype for the SR-71 – the Blackbird – a reconnaissance plane that could reach 2100 miles per hour at 85,000ft. Unless you strike one of the infrequent "open cockpit" days, all you can do is circle the planes and admire their sleek lines and astonishing statistics. If you visit when the park's closed, you still get to see the key planes from outside the fence, though you won't get access to the small visitor center.

Lancaster and the poppy reserve

Five miles north of Palmdale you reach **Lancaster**, founded in 1876 when the Southern Pacific Railroad arrived. Signs at the Avenue K exit point to the informative **Mojave Desert State Parks visitor center**, 43779 15th Street West (Mon–Sat 10am–4pm; ☎661/942-0662), which has details of the poppy reserve and Saddleback Butte.

Two miles further north along Hwy-14, turn west onto Avenue I and follow it fourteen miles to reach the **Antelope Valley California Poppy Reserve** (daily sunrise–sunset in poppy season; $5 when there are poppies, otherwise $2). You can stroll the easy desert trails at any time of year, but the main reason to come is to witness the place blanketed in the bright orange of California's state flower, the Golden Poppy. It is a temperamental and unpredictable plant, but given enough rain it usually blooms (perhaps two or three years in every five) between mid-March and late May; for details, call the visitor center or the Wildflower Hotline (℡661/724-1180). During the blooming season you can also visit the excellent **interpretive center** (mid-March to mid-May daily 9am–5pm), which comes neatly embedded in the hillside and has displays of desert flora and fauna.

East of Lancaster: Saddleback Butte

Saddleback Butte State Park, seventeen miles east of Lancaster at the junction of Avenue J and 170th Street (daily dawn–dusk; $5 per vehicle), centers on a smallish hill whose slopes are home to a splendid collection of Joshua trees. It's also a likely spot to catch a glimpse of the desert tortoise, for whom the park provides a refuge from the motorcyclists and dune buggy enthusiasts who tear around the region. There's a half-mile nature trail and a simple **campground** ($12), which is mostly underused but is popular for stargazing on summer weekends. Three miles southwest, the **Antelope Valley Indian Museum** on Avenue M (closed until spring 2009; for hours contact ℡661/942-0662 or ⓦwww.avim.parks.ca.gov), housed in a mock Swiss chalet painted with Native American motifs, contains an extensive collection of ethnographic material from all over the state.

Mojave

MOJAVE, strung out along the highway thirty miles north of Lancaster, is a major junction on the interstate train network, though it's used solely by freight trains. The town itself – largely a mile-long highway strip of gas stations, $40-a-night motels, and franchised fast-food restaurants, open around the clock – is a good place to fill up on essentials before continuing north into the Owens Valley or Death Valley.

Mojave hit the headlines in October 2004 as the launch and landing site of **SpaceShipOne**, which became the first privately funded spaceship to achieve suborbital flight (around 62 miles above the earth) twice within fourteen days, thereby claiming the $10 million reward from the Santa Monica-based X Prize Foundation.

The same clear, dry conditions that favor space launching make the Mojave Airport (ⓦwww.mojaveairport.com), a mile east of town, the perfect parking lot for mothballed airplanes. Surplus commercial airliners are pastured here, often for years, and you can see the rows of Airbus and 747 tailplanes still decked out in the livery of their owners. Flight fans set up base camp at the airport's daytime *Voyager Restaurant*, where you can watch the activity of this working airport and listen in to the tower through radios at each table.

If you're heading north from here, consider a detour via the Desert Tortoise Natural Area (see p.284).

North of Mojave along Hwy-14

North from Mojave along Hwy-14 the desert is virtually uninhabited, the landscape marked only by the bald ridges of the foothills of the Sierra Nevada mountains that rise to the west, though you might see the odd ghostly sign of the prospectors who once roamed the region in search of gold and less precious minerals. Twenty-four miles north of Mojave, Hwy-14 passes through **Red Rock Canyon**, a brilliantly colored rocky badlands of wonderfully eroded formations.

The highway passes right through the center of the most impressive section, though if you walk just a hundred yards from the road you're more likely to see an eagle or coyote than another visitor. Better still, call at the **Red Rock Canyon State Park** (always open; $5 per vehicle), where the **visitor center** (open spring & fall Fri noon–8pm, Sat 9am–7pm, Sun 9am–3pm; closed summer and winter; ☎661/942-0662) can point you to a number of short trails. It also runs a weekend ranger program of nature walks and campfire talks, ranging from guest lectures by Native Americans to discussions on movie-filming in the area. The adjacent *Ricardo* **campground** ($12) is fairly primitive but beautifully sited amid Joshua trees and colorful rocks.

Around 25 miles north of Red Rock Canyon, Hwy-14 meets US-395, and after another twenty miles Cinder Rock Road leads east to **Fossil Falls**, a rather unearthly formation some 27 miles northwest of Ridgecrest. Relatively recent volcanic eruptions (about 20,000 years ago) drove lava through one of this region's dry river channels, creating what looks like a petrified cataract. Some remaining petroglyphs, as well as various small artifacts and polished indentations in the rocks, used for grinding grain, attest to widespread human habitation in this area.

Heading further north along US-395 brings you to the Owens Valley and the western entrance to Death Valley, regions covered in depth in Chapter Four.

Tehachapi

About twenty miles west from Mojave, Hwy-58 rises to the rolling hillsides of **Tehachapi**, an apple-growing center that, at an elevation of around 4000ft, offers a nice respite from the Mojave's heat. In addition to its pretty setting, the town has a couple of minor claims to fame. Some 4500 **wind generators** – built here since the early 1980s – make the Tehachapi Wind Resource Area, ranked along Cameron Ridge to the east, one of the world's most productive renewable energy stations. They're very visible from Hwy-58, but there are few places to stop so you may prefer to follow Tehachapi Willow Springs Road, a minor route between Tehachapi and Mojave running just south of Hwy-58.

Train enthusiasts cross states to see groaning diesels hauling their mile-long string of boxcars around the **Tehachapi Loop**, eight miles west of town. Built in 1876 as the only means of scaling the steep slopes of the region, the tracks double back on themselves to make a complete 360° loop. It's an impressive sight to watch a train over 85 boxcars long twisting around a mountain, its front end 77ft above its tail. For the best view, follow the signs three miles from the Keene exit to a roadside plaque commemorating the loop's engineers.

Practicalities

For **information** about these and other local attractions, including pick-your-own-fruit orchards, antiques shops, and ostrich farms, stop in at the **Chamber of Commerce**, 209 E Tehachapi Boulevard (Mon–Fri 9am–5pm; ☎661/822-4180), right by the train tracks in the older section of town. Nearby you'll find **accommodation** at the *Santa Fe Motel*, 120 W Tehachapi Boulevard (☎661/822-3184, ⓕ822-7905; ②), and the *Best Western Mountain Inn*, 420 W Tehachapi Boulevard (☎661/823-1800; ④). Eight miles southwest of town off Highline Road, there's **camping** (☎661/868-7000; $14) among the pines at a refreshing 6000ft in the *Tehachapi Mountain Park*, with toilets and water but no other facilities; it's sometimes snowbound in winter. Popular local **restaurants** include the daytime-only *Apple Shed*, 333 E Tehachapi Boulevard next to the visitor center (☎661/823-8333), good for country-style breakfasts, apple-pie breaks, and espresso, and *Domingo's*, 20416 Valley Boulevard (☎661/822-7611), a family-owned Mexican and seafood place in the newer section of town, a mile or so west.

Boron, the Rand Mining District, and Ridgecrest

Busy Hwy-58 runs east from Mojave, skirting the northern side of Edwards Air Force Base for thirty miles to a signed exit for the **Borax Visitor Center** (daily 9am–5pm; $2 per vehicle; ⊛ www.borax.com/borax6.html), a modern complex on a hill overlooking a processing plant and the vast open-cast borax mine – the largest mine in California. Borax is sodium borate, a crystalline mineral which was originally used as a flux to improve the working properties of gold and silver, but more recently has found applications in everything from washing detergents to heat-resistant glass and fiberglass. The center is primarily a promotional tool for the Borax Company, which owns the site, but call in if only to see the seventeen-minute video (complete with a 1960s snip of Ronald Reagan advertising hand cleaner), which finishes with curtains opening on a great view into the mile-wide, 650-foot-deep pit.

There's more on the history of boron extraction and the role of the twenty-mule teams, which hauled paired ten-ton wagons of borax out of Death Valley and elsewhere, at the **Boron Twenty Mule Team Museum**, 26962 Twenty Mule Team Road (daily 10am–4pm; donation; ⊛ www.20muleteammuseum .org), in the one-street town of **BORON** three miles further east. The museum also has coverage of movies filmed here – parts of *Erin Brockovich*, for one – and has a display on the Solar Energy Generating Station (SEGS), which spreads six miles across the desert at the junction of Hwy-58 and US-395. This vast array of shiny panels produces around thirty megawatts of electricity and is part of five such installations across the Mojave Desert.

The Desert Tortoise Natural Area

US-395 runs north from near Boron into the Rand Mining District, though you might fancy taking a detour to see California's state reptile at the **Desert Tortoise Natural Area** (8am–sunset, free; ☎951/683-3872, ⊛ www .tortoise-tracks.org), a forty-square-mile area of protected habitat amid desert torn up by off-roaders. To get there, follow Hwy-58 eight miles west from Boron, then turn north on California City Boulevard towards California City. After ten miles, turn left onto the dirt Randsberg-Mojave Road, which runs four miles to the site. Here you'll find panels explaining the area's significance, and a network of easy desert trails which spur off the quarter-mile Main Loop Trail. Free leaflets provide guidance.

The Rand Mining District

Following US-395 north of Boron, there's no reason to stop in the first thirty miles until you reach the **Rand Mining District**, a close cluster of three virtually deserted towns whose lifeblood is provided by the Yellow Aster and Baltic gold mines, the last to be commercially worked in California.

Red Mountain and **Johannesburg** are a couple of miles apart on US-395, but the area's real interest lies a mile to the west on a loop road between the two towns. Here you'll find **Randsburg**, a near ghost town of scruffy-looking shacks surrounded by the detritus of ancient mines. The streets are very quiet midweek, but the tempo picks up a little at weekends when a couple of antique-cum-knick-knack shops open up. This mild gentrification aside, the place retains a certain Wild West charm on its 200-yard-long main street, with two bars, a dozen shops, and the **Desert Museum**, 161 Butte Avenue (Sat & Sun 10am–5pm; free), which has displays on the glory days of the 1890s, when upwards of three thousand people lived in the town, mining gold, silver, and tungsten out of the arid, rocky hills. The nearby ⚘ **General Store**, at no.35

(☎760/374-2180), is a fascinating slice of history with its embossed tin ceiling, 1904 soda fountain (the super-thick chocolate shakes are locally celebrated), and a small restaurant surrounded by shelves of groceries and mining supplies. It's open daily, and is a good source of local **information** (☎760/374-2418). Also try the *White House Saloon*, 168 Butte Avenue (☎760/374-2464), one of the few surviving Wild West saloons with swing doors.

You're free to wander off and explore the nearby hills and old mine workings, but land-use conflict between off-roaders and the Bureau of Land Management, which is seeking to protect desert tortoise habitat, means you should ask locally about areas which may be closed.

For **accommodation** try *The Randsburg Inn* (☎760/374-2332, ⓦwww .randsburginn.com; ❷), opposite the General Store, which provides comfortable rooms, one with private bathroom (❹), a spacious lounge, and a full kitchen. **Eating** options in town are limited to low-cost burgers and sandwiches at the General Store and the *Opera House Café*, also on Butte Avenue.

Ridgecrest

Twenty miles north of Randsburg, Hwy-178 cuts east towards Death Valley, reaching the sprawling desert community of **Ridgecrest**, dominated by the huge China Lake Naval Weapons Center. Jet fighters scream past overhead, taking target practice on land that's chock-full of ancient **petroglyphs** – the largest grouping in the western hemisphere. Though access to the sites is strictly controlled, you can get some idea of the native culture of the Mojave Desert by visiting the **Maturango Museum**, on the corner of China Lake Boulevard and East Las Flores Avenue (daily 10am–5pm; $4; ☎760/375-6900, ⓦwww.maturango.org). Aside from being a **visitor center** (free), it has exhibits on both the natural and cultural history of the region, including examples of the rock-art figures pecked into dark basalt rocks. To get out and see the figures and designs in their natural surroundings, join a full-day, volunteer-led **tour** organized most Saturdays and Sunday during the season (mid-Feb to mid-June & mid-Sept to mid-Dec only; $35). The most concentrated collections of petroglyphs are on the military base, and in these security-conscious times, US citizens need access clearance, which can take at least ten days. Foreign nationals are currently banned. For the latest information call the museum or check its website (where you can download an application form), and be prepared to reserve a place several weeks in advance.

It may be more rewarding to stray four miles east of town to the Bureau of Land Management's **Wild Horse and Burro Corrals**, where sometimes over a thousand animals are kept while waiting for adoption. Even if you're not prepared to take one home, you can make an appointment to visit (Mon–Fri 8am–4pm; free; ☎1-800/951-8720, ⓦwww.wildhorseandburro.blm.gov); for an enthusiastic reception, bring along some apples or carrots, though the burros are often too wild to approach.

Ridgecrest has an abundance of **accommodation**, the vast majority being chain motels. Try the basic *Budget Inn & Suite*, 831 N China Lake Boulevard (☎760/375-1351, ⓦwww.budgetinnridgecrest.com; ❶), or the upscale *Carriage Inn*, 901 N China Lake Boulevard (☎1-800/772-8527, ⓦwww.carriageinn.biz; ❺), which has poolside cabanas and a good restaurant and includes a buffet breakfast. For something different, try the antique-furnished *BevLen Haus B&B*, 809 N Sanders Street (☎760/375-1988, ⓦwww.bevlen.com; ❷), with en-suite rooms, outdoor hot tub, and a hearty breakfast.

A wide range of **restaurant** choices includes casual Italian at *Nickoletti's*, 1110 N China Lake Boulevard (☎760/446-6425), and good espresso at *Casa Java*, 972 N Norma Street (☎760/446-5282), which also has free **wireless Internet**.

Trona Pinnacles and Searles Valley

Hwy-178 runs northeast from Randsburg past the burro corrals and out into the dry and desolate **Searles Valley**, which offers a back road into Death Valley with access to Telescope Peak (see p.310). Some sixteen miles northeast of Randsburg, a five-mile dirt road (passable except after rain) leads to the **Trona Pinnacles National Natural Landmark** (unrestricted access; free), where over five hundred tufa spires stretch up to 140ft. Mostly conical and grouped in clusters, these soft rock pinnacles were considered sufficiently extra-terrestrial-looking to form a backdrop for parts of *Star Trek V*, and are best viewed on the half-mile nature trail. There's free **camping** with a vault toilet but no water supply. You can find basic supplies six miles north on Hwy-178 at the industrial and substantially run-down borax-processing town of **Trona**.

Victorville, Barstow, and around

The long desert drive from LA to Las Vegas takes you along I-15, part of which follows the original line of Route 66. You'll see little of the old road – or anything else of great interest – from the freeway, so you should definitely consider taking time out to explore a few minor attractions. **Victorville** warrants a brief detour to view the highwayside Americana in the Route 66 Museum, and **Barstow** is better for what lies nearby, particularly the colored rocks of Rainbow Basin and the faux ghost town of Calico. Further east there are early human remains at the **Calico Dig**, and the etymological curiosity that is **Zzyzx**.

Victorville

I-15 heads north from the Los Angeles basin, slicing between the San Gabriel and San Bernardino mountains to reach the Mojave Desert. The first town of any size is **Victorville**, some eighty miles northeast of LA. It has all the motels, fast-food joints, and gas stations you could ask for along the freeway, but it's worth ducking off into the old town center for a quick look at the small **California Route 66 Museum**, 16825 D Street at Fifth Street (Mon & Thurs–Sat 10am–4pm, Sun 11am–3pm; free; ☎760/951-0436, ⓦwww.califrt66museum.org). Dedicated to

Route 66 in California

The advent of the interstates in the 1950s was the death knell for what John Steinbeck called **The Mother Road**. The umbilical cord between Chicago and Los Angeles, Route 66 was conceived in the 1920s when existing roads were stitched together to form a single 2400-mile route across eight states. It was just one of many such migration routes, but is the one that most captured the public imagination – not least through Nat King Cole's 1946 hit *(Get your kicks on) Route 66* – and became America's most famous highway. As freeways obliterated the old road and franchise hotels and restaurants populated their flanks, the old diners and mom-and-pop motels gradually disappeared, further enhancing its iconic status.

Large sections of the old route vanished long ago, but it was the realization that some of the last vestiges were about to disappear that kick-started a revival. Sections of the original route have since sprouted Route 66 signs, though these were promptly liberated by fans and you now tend to see "Historic Route 66" shields painted onto the asphalt. After considerable lobbying by Route 66 associations, Bill Clinton passed a National Preservation Bill benefiting the Route 66 Corridor in 1999,

▲ Roy's gas station and café, Amboy

American myth, it has devotional displays relating to the westernmost strip of the "Mother Road" (see box, below). Relics from an old roadside attraction called "Hulaville" are the museum's most interesting feature, but there are also various old-time videos and a stack of nostalgic merchandise.

There's more Mother Road Americana two miles north at *Emma Jean's Hollandburger Café*, 17143 D Street (Mon–Fri 5am–2.30pm, Sat 6am–12.30pm, closed Sun; ⊕760/243-9938), a 1940s diner serving straightforward breakfasts and burgers in classic style.

Barstow and around

Almost thirty miles northeast of Victorville along the thundering, seemingly endless I-15, **Barstow** looms up out of the desert, providing a welcome

and the tourist machine now promotes the old road vigorously. Some 320 miles of the original route ran through California, and Kingman, Barstow, and San Bernardino all get name-checked in the famous song, but the best-preserved section is in the Mojave Desert east of Barstow. Fans will want to visit the small **museums** in Victorville (see p.286) and Barstow (see p.288), or even try to track down San Bernardino's classic *Wigwam Motel*, at 2728 W Foothill Boulevard, Rialto (⊕909/875-3005, ⍟www.wigwammotel.com; ❸), but for most it's enough to drive the desert section that loops south off I-40 from Ludlow to Essex. One essential stop is **Amboy**, a place that seems instantly familiar from dozens of road-trip movies and car commercials principally because of the Modernist Atomic-Era sign for *Roy's* gas station and café. The whole minuscule town – including post office, abandoned church, and dirt airstrip – was bought in 2005 by fast-food chicken magnate Albert Okura, who plans to reopen the café, gas station, and motel in 2008.

To delve deeper, check out websites such as ⍟www.national66.com and ⍟www.historic66.com.

opportunity to get out of the car. Though situated at the crossroads of three major thoroughfares (I-40 and Hwy-58 also run through here), it's a small town, consisting of just one main road lined with a selection of motels and restaurants that make a budget overnight stop possible. This main street was once part of the famed **Route 66** (see box, p.286), so fans of neon will enjoy some classic examples. The town's appeal, however, ends there. For many months of the year, the relentless sun manages to keep people in their air-conditioned homes for a good part of the day, and Barstow can seem more like a ghost town than the capital of the Mojave.

Historical interest focuses on the grand 1911 **Harvey House**, also known as the Casa del Desierto (the "house of the desert"), built as a train station with associated restaurant and lodging. Trains still stop here and the building remains striking but is largely empty, with a forlorn air despite a couple of small museums inside. The **Western American Railroad Museum** (Fri–Sun 10am–4pm; donation suggested; ☎760/256-9276, ⊛www.barstowrailmuseum .org) is dedicated to preserving the history of southwest railroading, while the **Route 66 "Mother Road" Museum**, 681 N 1st Avenue (Fri–Sun 11am–4pm; free; ⊛www.route66museum.org), is full of highway Americana and some classic photos of yesteryear Barstow. For those with less specialized interests, there's the **Mojave River Valley Museum**, 270 E Virginia Way (daily 11am–4pm; free; ⊛www.mojaverivervalleymuseum.org), containing material on the social and natural history of the area, and a sizeable archeological collection including material from the Calico Dig (see opposite).

Getting out of town, make a stop at **Rainbow Basin** (unrestricted access), a rock formation cast in myriad shades, from vivid greens to deep reds, by thirty million years of wind erosion. It's best seen around dawn or dusk. To get there, take 1st Street north past the Harvey House, turn left into Irwin Road, and after six miles north turn west and continue four miles along Fossil Bed Road. From here, a winding four-mile loop road weaves around the canyon and you can marvel at the prettiness of it all. Camping is also available (see opposite).

Eight miles east on I-40, just past Dagget, the original Department of Energy's Solar One Power Plant has been replaced by the **SEGS II Solar Power Plant**, which, marked by a hundred-acre field of mirrors, is a surreal example of how California is putting its deserts to use. Anyone who has seen the film *Bagdad Café* (see opposite) will remember the light reflections the mirrors give off for miles around.

Practicalities

The **California Welcome Center** (daily 9am–6pm; ☎760/253-4782, ⊛www .visitcwc.com), four miles west of Barstow in the Tanger Outlet Mall off I-15 at the Lenwood Road exit, has a good selection of maps of the surrounding area, lodging and restaurant guides, and various flyers on local attractions.

Greyhound buses stop at 1611 E Main Street where it crosses I-15, a mile east of downtown, but arriving by **train**, you'll be dropped at the Amtrak station in the Casa del Desierto (see above) on First Street.

Numerous **motels** line Main Street. Rates start under $40 and they're generally only distinguished by the condition of the neon sign outside. Mainstream **restaurants** sit snugly between the many hotels on Main Street: visit your favorite franchise or try one of our suggestions.

Accommodation

Calico 7 miles east along I-15 ☎1-800/863-2542, ⊛www.calicotown.com. Camping at a re-created

ghost town (see opposite), with shaded canyons where you can pitch a tent for $18, hook up campers for $22 per night, or stay in one of the cabins (❶).

Economy Inn 1243 E Main St ☏ 760/256-5601. A little frayed around the edges, but a decent motel with comfortable a/c rooms, pool, and free Wi-Fi. ❶

Owl Canyon campground Rainbow Basin, 11 miles north (see opposite). Simple camping with a vault toilet but no water. $6

Ramada Inn 1511 E Main St ☏ 1-800/2726232. Upscale, corporate-style motel offering comfortable rooms with cable TV, pool, free Wi-Fi, and deluxe continental breakfast. Located 1.5 miles east of the centre near the East Main exit off I-15. ❹

Route 66 Motel 195 W Main St ☏ 760/256-7866. A genuine Route 66 motel, its yard dotted with hulks of 1940s and 1950s cars and decorated with old gas station signs. Rooms are old and a bit crummy, but some have round double beds. ❷

Eating and drinking

Bagdad Café 46548 National Trails Hwy, Newberry Springs, 23 miles southeast ☏ 760/257-3101, ⓦ www.bagdadcafeusa.com. Basic diner that's become an iconic stop along Route 66 on the back of the 1988 film of the same name. Browse the scrapbook as you tuck into burgers, chicken-fried steak, and seafood ($7–9), and take a look at the old Airstream trailer from the movie, which rots outside. Take the first Newberry Springs exit off I-40 and continue 3 miles east.

DiNapoli's Firehouse 1358 E Main St ☏ 760/256-1094. Rustic regional Italian joint decorated with fire fighting memorabilia and selling tasty hand-tossed pizza (from $13), hearty pasta dishes ($11–13), and seductive desserts ($5). Closed Sun.

Idle Spurs Steak House 690 Old Hwy-58, ☏ 760/256-8888. This Barstow institution just north of town has been serving the best steaks around, washed down with microbrews or something from their extensive wine list, since the 1950s. Try fillet mignon brochette ($18) or perhaps a prime rib and lobster tail combo ($40). To get there follow First Street 1.6 miles north, then left into Old Hwy-58.

Mollie's Pub 1309 Main St ☏ 760/256-1094. A lively downtown bar with sports TV and pool.

Rosita's 540 W Main St ☏ 760/256-9218. Freshly made tortilla chips and excellent salsa set the tone for this cavernous and authentic Mexican place. There's a massive range of combination dishes ($10–12) plus lunch and early dinner specials ($6–8). Closed Mon.

Slash X Ranch Café 28040 Barstow Rd ☏ 760/252-1179. Lively bar and café ten miles south of town on Hwy-247. A Barstow favorite since 1954 (and poplar with dirt bikers, who tear up the desert nearby), it's great for burgers or just a few cold beers.

East of Barstow: along I-15

Most people who stop in Barstow are not here to enjoy the desert, but to visit the contrived **Calico Ghost Town** (daily 8am–dusk; $6, admission free with camping; ☏ 1-800/863-2542, ⓦ www.calicotown.com), seven miles northeast along I-15, then three miles north. In the late nineteenth century, Calico produced millions of dollars of silver and borax and supported a population of almost four thousand. Attractively set in the color-streaked Calico Hills, but subject to the extreme heat of the Mojave, the town was quickly deserted when the silver ran out. It's since been rather insensitively restored, with souvenir shops, hot-dog stands, and a main thoroughfare lined with ersatz saloons, an old schoolhouse, a vaudeville playhouse, and shops kitted out in period styles. However, should you so desire, there are miles of mining shafts and tunnels open to crawl around in – until claustrophobia forces you up for air.

There's a more highbrow appeal to the **Calico Early Man Site** (Wed 12.30–4.30pm; Thurs–Sun 9am–4.30pm; guided tours on request; entry $5, tours free; ⓦ www.calicodig.com), at the Minneola Road exit off I-15, six miles northeast of the Calico exit, then 2.5 miles north. More popularly known as the "**Calico Dig**," it has become one of the most important archeological sites in North America since Louis Leakey excavated it in 1964. Some of the old tools found here have been dated at around 20,000 years old, controversially establishing mankind's presence here several thousand years earlier than was previously thought – and the debate rages on. The self-guided tour of the dig isn't very instructive, so try to get on a guided tour, which makes it all come alive.

After driving 23 miles further east of the site, take the Afton Road turnoff from I-15 to get to **Afton Canyon**, dubbed the "Grand Canyon of the

Mojave." At a couple hundred feet deep it's far less impressive than the Arizona original, but it's only three miles off I-15 and is striking nevertheless, with multicolored strata formed by erosion from an extinct lake. Though the lake is long gone, Afton Canyon is one of the three places where the **Mojave River** flows above ground throughout the year, making this a marshy mecca for almost two hundred types of desert creatures, including rare bird species such as the vermillion flycatcher and summer tanager. There's **camping** here on a first-come-first-served basis ($10).

Back on I-15 there's little of interest for twenty miles until Zzyzx Road. This leads five miles south to the western edge of the Mojave National Preserve and the oasis of **Zzyzx** (pronounced "zie-zics"), on the edge of the usually arid Soda Dry Lake, at the base of rocky hills. From 1905 to 1940, the site was on the Tonopah & Tidewater Railroad, and when the company decamped the charismatic quack, preacher, and LA radio personality **Curtis "Doc" Springer** set up a mineral springs resort. He renamed the spot Zzyzx, correctly surmising that the odd name would draw custom. Unfortunately, he never actually owned the land, and in 1974 he was evicted and the resort closed. Some dilapidated buildings continue to rot away, but most have been transformed into California State University's Desert Studies Center. If there are no happy-to-be-distracted researchers around, you can just stroll around the artificial palm-fringed lake on what is effectively a nature trail, and search for evidence of the area's colorful history.

From the Zzyzx Road junction on I-15 it is six miles to Baker.

Baker and the Eastern Mojave

There's not much to **Baker** – essentially a strip of fairly expensive gas stations and fast-food joints plus a couple of decent motels and restaurants – but it's a handy spot for refueling both body and rig, and as a base for exploring some of California's remoter corners. Death Valley lies immediately north, and it's in honor of the town's proximity to the country's hottest place that Baker has the **world's tallest functioning thermometer**, rising 134 feet to commemorate the highest temperature ever recorded in the US – 134°F in 1913. Baker is also a springboard for the Mojave National Preserve, so if you're not up for camping you may want to **stay** near the thermometer, either at the functional *Bun Boy Motel* (℡760/733-4363; midweek ❷, weekend ❸) or the *Wills Fargo Motel* (℡760/733-4477; midweek ❷, weekend ❸), which has a heart-shaped pool and slightly more character to its rooms. The supplies at the town's **general store** aren't cheap, but this is your last chance to stock up. Standing out from the fast-food joints, the Mexican-run ⚘ *Mad Greek* (℡760/733-4354) serves an eclectic and good-value range of choices, among them gyros, kebabs, burgers, Mexican dishes, espresso, pastries, and delicious fresh strawberry shakes – more a sundae than a drink. Most dishes cost $7–9.

Mojave National Preserve

In 1994, 1.4 million acres of undeveloped country wedged between I-15 and I-40 were set aside as the **MOJAVE NATIONAL PRESERVE**, a perfect spot to take a break from the freeway and maybe camp out a night or two to prepare for the excesses of Las Vegas, seventy miles ahead. It's a little higher than much of the desert hereabouts, making it a bit cooler in summer but also subject to winter snows.

The preserve's main roads all lead to the graceful Mission Revival-style **Kelso Depot**, built in 1924 for workers on the Union Pacific Railroad and now the main visitor center (see below). There's no roofed accommodation in the park, but several **campsites** are listed on p.292.

Preserve highlights

Approaching Kelso from Baker, Kelbaker Road shoots past a series of dramatic black-and-red **cinder cones**, created relatively recently (a thousand years ago). Visible to the south of the Kelso Depot are the spectacular **Kelso Dunes**, a golden five-mile stretch of sand reaching up as high as seven hundred feet. A sandy trail off Kelso Dunes Road wanders up to the dunes, where in half an hour you can be scrambling around and listening out for a faint booming sound caused by dry sand cascading down the steep upper slopes: apparently a rare phenomenon. There are free primitive camping spots nearby (see below).

Fourteen miles northeast of Kelso, the small town of **Cima** (there's a little store here, but no gas) heralds **Cima Dome**, a perfectly formed batholith rising some 1500ft above the desert floor and cloaked in dense stands of Joshua trees. These are best explored on the **Teutonia Peak Trail** (4 miles round-trip).

Southeast of Cima, Mojave Road and Black Canyon Road provide access to the *Mid Hills* campground, from where the moderately difficult **Mid Hills to Hole-in-the-Wall Trail** (eight miles each way; 1200-foot ascent) winds through Wild Horse Canyon and ends up at the *Hole-in-the-Wall* campground. You can also drive to *Hole-in-the-Wall* campground, where there's a **visitor center** (May–Sept Fri–Sun 9am–4pm, Oct–April Wed–Sun 9am–4pm) and another great hike along the **Rings Trail** (half-mile round-trip), which involves a little scrambling and a descent into Banshee Canyon using metal rings anchored to the rock wall.

A further ten miles south, then six miles west, the vegetation at the 5900-acre **Providence Mountain State Recreation Area** changes from scrubby bushes at lower desert elevations to the piñon pines that grow along rocky Fountain Peak (6996ft) and Edgar Peak (7171ft). Some people come to camp, but most are here to tour **Mitchell Caverns** (late May to early Sept daily at 1.30pm; early Sept to late May Mon–Fri 1.30pm, Sat & Sun 10am, 1.30pm & 3pm; $4; ☏760/928-2586), which were used for shelter by the Chemehuevi Indians for almost five hundred years. There's one brief claustrophobia-inducing part, but otherwise this ninety-minute walk through stalactites and stalagmites and rarer limestone formations is superb.

Practicalities

Mojave is a big preserve (larger than Yosemite) so be sure to **go prepared**: fill up and buy supplies before entering, as there's no gas, just one tiny shop at Cima, and only camping for accommodation.

Information is best sought in the heart of the preserve at the **Kelso Depot Visitor Center** (daily 9am–5pm; ☏760/733-4456, ⓦwww.nps.gov/moja), where you can obtain copies of the free park newspaper. Excellent displays include material on the region's geology, flora, fauna, and social history. They've even re-created the historic building's old dinner counter, a crew room, and a workers' room from its railroading heyday.

There are three formal **campgrounds**, all first-come-first-served and open year-round, and offering fire ring, table, toilets, and water. The authorities also allow limited, primitive, **roadside camping** at designated spots. Consult the park newspaper for full details, or head straight for Kelso Dunes Road, where there are numerous spots a mile beyond the hiking trailhead.

Mid Hills campground Beautifully sited at 5600ft in piñon-juniper woodland, this campground is cool (sometime snowy in winter) and the access road is unpaved. $12.

Hole-in-the-Wall campground Named by Bob Hollimon, a member of the Butch Cassidy gang, because it reminded him of his former hideout in Wyoming, this campground sits in at an elevation of 4500ft among striking volcanic rock formations. $12.

Providence Mountains State Recreation Area Located by Mitchell Caverns, this campground has just six sites. $12.

Travel details

Amtrak trains

The **Southwest Chief** runs daily from **LA** to Chicago via **Victorville** (3hr), **Barstow** (4hr), and **Flagstaff**, Arizona, with daily LA departures at 6.45pm and returns at 8.15am.

The **Sunset Limited** plies the southern route from LA to New Orleans with stops in **Palm Springs** (2hr 30min) and Tucson, Arizona. It departs LA at 2.30pm on Sun, Wed, and Fri, and the return journey finishes in LA at 10.10am on the same days.

Buses

Unless otherwise stated, all buses are direct Greyhound services.

Barstow to: Las Vegas (10 daily; 2hr 40min); Los Angeles (11 daily; 3–4hr).

Las Vegas to: Barstow (11 daily; 2hr 40min).

Los Angeles to: Barstow (10 daily; 3–4hr); Las Vegas (13 daily; 6–8hr); Palm Springs (4 daily; 2hr 40min).

Palm Springs to: Joshua Tree (Morongo Basin Transit Authority: 1 on Fri, Sat & Sun; 50min); Los Angeles (4 daily; 2hr 40min); Phoenix, Arizona (1 daily; 6hr).

San Diego to: Borrego Springs (Metropolitan Transit System: 2 weekly; 2hr 50min).

4

Death Valley, the Owens Valley, and the Eastern Sierra

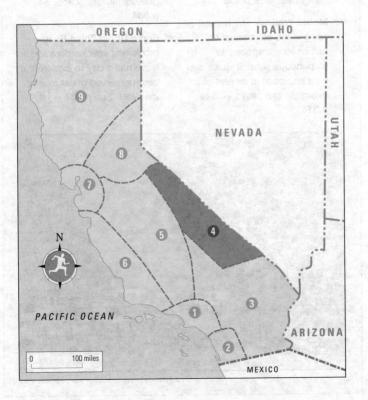

CHAPTER 4

Highlights

✳ **Rhyolite** Assorted Gold Rush ruins, a house made from bottles, a weird collection of fiberglass sculptures, and a location on the fringes of Death Valley make this an essential stop. See p.301

✳ **Scotty's Castle** The beautiful interiors of this Chicago millionaire's chateau make a cool respite from the Death Valley heat. See p.308

✳ **Mount Whitney** The highest point in the continental US has an iconic appeal; its stupendous summit views are best appreciated as part of an overnight camping trip. See p.314

✳ **Bristlecone Pine Forest** The gnarled and wizened forms of the world's most ancient living things – some nearly five millennia old – are on display in this alpine forest. See p.318

✳ **Mono Lake** Take a canoe or kayak trip amid the lakeside tufa towers, which create an otherworldly and highly photogenic landscape. See p.334

✳ **Bodie Ghost Town** Bring a picnic and your camera and leave half a day to explore the best-preserved ghost town in the West. See p.337

▲ Furnace Creek Inn, Death Valley National Park

Death Valley, the Owens Valley, and the Eastern Sierra

T
he far eastern edge of California, rising up from the Mojave Desert and cleaving to the border with Nevada, is a long narrow strip as scenically dramatic as anywhere else in the state, veering from blistering desert to ski country in the lee of the mighty Sierra Nevada Mountains. It's a region devoid of interstates, scarcely populated, and, but for the scant reminders of gold-hungry pioneers, developed in only the most tentative way.

At the region's base, technically forming the Mojave's northern reach, is **Death Valley**. With the highest average summer temperatures on earth, and so remote that it's almost a region unto itself, this vast national park is a distillation of the classic desert landscape: an arid, otherworldly terrain of brilliantly colored, bizarrely eroded rocks, mountains, and sand dunes, all a hundred miles from the nearest town.

North of here, the towering **eastern** peaks of the Sierra Nevada are perfectly described by their Spanish name, **Sierra Nevada**, which literally translates as "snowcapped saw." Virtually the entire range is preserved as wilderness, and hikers and mountaineers can get to higher altitudes quicker here than almost anywhere else in California: well-maintained roads lead to trailheads at over eight thousand feet, providing swift access to spires, glaciers, and clear mountain lakes. **Mount Whitney**, the highest point in the continental US, marks the southernmost point of the chain, which continues north for an uninterrupted 150 miles to the backcountry of Yosemite National Park, and beyond.

At the foot of Mount Whitney, the five-mile-wide **Owens Valley** starts, hemmed in to the east by the **White Mountains**, nearly as high but drier and less hospitable than the High Sierra, and home to the ancient, gnarled **bristle-cone pines**. In between the two mountain ranges, US-395 runs the length of the valley, which has few signs of settlement at all beyond the sporadic roadside towns and the larger **Bishop**.

An hour's drive further north, **Mammoth Lakes** is the Eastern Sierra's busiest resort, thick with skiers in winter and fishers and mountain bikers in

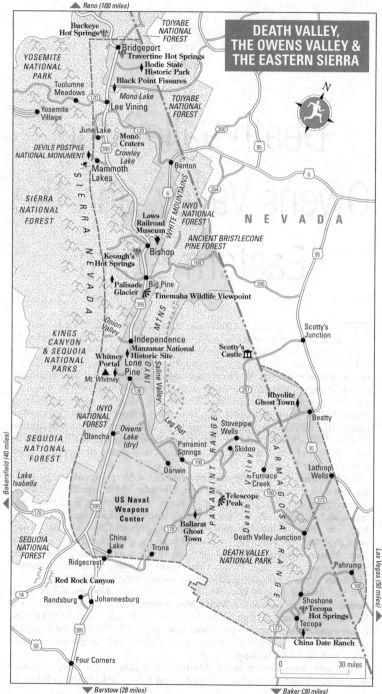

DEATH VALLEY, THE OWENS VALLEY & THE EASTERN SIERRA

N

▲ Reno (100 miles)

TOIYABE NATIONAL FOREST

Buckeye Hot Springs

Bridgeport
Travertine Hot Springs
Bodie State Historic Park
Black Point Fissures

YOSEMITE NATIONAL PARK

Tuolumne Meadows

Mono Lake
Lee Vining

TOIYABE NATIONAL FOREST

Yosemite Village

June Lake

Mono Craters
Crowley Lake

DEVILS POSTPILE NATIONAL MONUMENT

Mammoth Lakes

Benton

WHITE MOUNTAINS

INYO NATIONAL FOREST

NEVADA

SIERRA NATIONAL FOREST

Laws Railroad Museum

Bishop

ANCIENT BRISTLECONE PINE FOREST

SIERRA NEVADA

Keough's Hot Springs

Palisade Glacier

Big Pine
Tinemaha Wildlife Viewpoint

Onion Valley

KINGS CANYON & SEQUOIA NATIONAL PARKS

INYO MTNS

Independence
Manzanar National Historic Site

Scotty's Junction

Whitney Portal
Mt. Whitney
Lone Pine

Saline Valley

Scotty's Castle

Leg Flat

Rhyolite Ghost Town

Beatty

INYO NATIONAL FOREST

Olancha

Owens Lake (dry)

Stovepipe Wells

Panamint Springs

Skidoo

Furnace Creek

Lathrop Wells

SEQUOIA NATIONAL FOREST

Lake Isabella

Darwin

US Naval Weapons Center

China Lake

Trona

PANAMINT RANGE

Telescope Peak

Ballarat Ghost Town

Death Valley

ARMAGOSA RANGE

Death Valley Junction

DEATH VALLEY NATIONAL PARK

Pahrump

SEQUOIA NATIONAL FOREST

Ridgecrest

Red Rock Canyon

Randsburg Johannesburg

Shoshone
Tecopa Hot Springs
Tecopa

China Date Ranch

Four Corners

0   30 miles

Bakersfield (40 miles)

Las Vegas (50 miles)

▼ Barstow (28 miles)

▼ Baker (30 miles)

What makes Death Valley so hot and dry

It's no surprise that **Death Valley** is **hot and dry** – it's part of the northern Mojave Desert, after all – but certain factors combine to make this small patch of land hotter than anywhere else on earth, based on a year-round average.

Perhaps the biggest contributor to its unforgiving heat is its location: Death Valley sits at sea level in the **rain shadow** of four mountain ranges, so it receives an average precipitation of only an inch and a half each year. Moisture in wind from the Pacific Ocean is lost as rainfall in the Coast Ranges, or as snowfall when the air struggles over the 14,000-foot Sierra Nevada. Very little moisture is left by the time the air gets east of the Sierra, and the last of it is squeezed out as it climbs over the Angus Range and the 11,000-foot Panamint Range.

As this very dry air descends from these heights it compresses, causing it to heat up until it finds itself trapped in a narrow basin where the beating sun, the lack of shade-giving plants, and the low altitude allows the air temperature to reach unbearable levels. Even overnight the air doesn't get much chance to cool, as the surrounding mountains trap it to create strong, hot winds; at times it can feel like you're standing in front of a hairdryer.

summer. Finally, at the point where many turn west for Yosemite, bizarre rock formations rise from the placid blue waters of primordial **Mono Lake**, set in a dramatic desert basin of volcanoes and steaming hot pools. Beyond, and far enough out of most people's way to deter the crowds, lies the wonderful ghost town of **Bodie**, which preserves a palpable sense of gold-town life eight thousand feet up in a parched, windswept valley.

Getting around

Getting around the region is best done by car, primarily using **US-395** – the lifeline of the Owens Valley and pretty much the only access to the area from within California. Once north of Mojave, where Hwy-58 branches west to Bakersfield, no road crosses the Sierra Nevada until Hwy-120, a spur over the 10,000-foot Tioga Pass into Yosemite. Hwy-190, heading east from US-395 just south of Mount Whitney, cuts through the Panamint Range to Death Valley.

Neither Amtrak nor Greyhound runs any services in the region, and the only long-distance **public transportation** is the bus service by CREST (☏1-800/922-1930), which travels along the Owens Valley linking Ridgecrest in the south (see p.284) and Reno, Nevada in the north (see p.663). Both towns have onward connections, and buses generally have racks or space onboard to accommodate bikes.

A couple of small companies operate what are effectively taxi services up to mountain trailheads, but are finding it increasingly hard to stay in business.

Death Valley National Park

Initially **Death Valley** seems an inhuman environment: burning hot, apparently lifeless, and almost entirely without shade, much less water. If you just drive through in half a day, it can appear barren and monotonous, but longer acquaintance reveals multiple layers of interest. Death Valley itself is just the central portion (but very much the focal point) of the much larger **DEATH VALLEY NATIONAL PARK**, which extends a hundred miles from north to south and is almost as wide in some parts. Grand vistas sweep down from the sub-alpine slopes of the 11,000-foot **Telescope Peak** to **Badwater**, the lowest point in the western hemisphere at 282ft below sea level; sharply silhouetted hills are folded and eroded into deeply shadowed crevices, their exotic mineral content turning million-year-old mud flats into rainbows of sunlit phosphorescence; and stark hills harbor the bleached ruins of mining enterprises that briefly flourished against all odds.

On the face of it, it seems impossible that such a hot and dry landscape could support any kind of life, yet it is home to a great variety of creatures, from snakes and giant eagles to tiny fish and bighorn sheep. What little vegetation there is can be fascinating both for its adaptation to the rigors of the environment and the almost sculptural effect it has on the landscape.

Most people visit Death Valley in the **winter**, when daytime temperatures average around 70–80°F (21–27°C); at this time, visiting the sights is quite manageable and even lowland hikes are a pleasure. But the park is really known for its **summer air temperatures**, which average 112°F (44°C) and in 1913 peaked at 134°F (57°C), the highest temperature ever recorded in the US, and only ever beaten by two degrees in Libya in 1922. There are frequent periods when the temperature tops 120°F daily, and at such times the ground can reach near boiling point, so it's best to stay away. Visitors still come though, joining the car manufacturers who have been bringing their latest models out here for **extreme testing** ever since Dodge paved the way in 1913.

Unless you're a real glutton for scorching, potentially fatal punishment, it's best to come during the spring, especially March and early April, when wildflowers may be in bloom (though many years they refuse to play ball) and daytime temperatures average a manageable 83°F, dropping to the mid-fifties at night. At any time between October and May it's generally mild and dry, with occasional rainfall on the surrounding mountains causing flash floods through otherwise bone-dry gullies and washes.

Throughout the park, roads and services are sparse, mostly concentrated in the central north-south valley for which the park is named. Hwy-190 runs the length of the valley, linking **Furnace Creek** and **Stovepipe Wells**, the park's two main outposts for provisions and accommodation. Forays from these bases give access to extensive **sand dunes**, intriguing **ghost towns**, cool high-country camping in the **Panamint Range**, and the incongruous mansion known as **Scotty's Castle**.

Some history

The sculpted rock layers exposed in Death Valley, tinted by oxidized traces of various **mineral deposits**, comprise a nearly complete record of the earth's past. Relatively young **fossils** lie at the feet of 500-million-year-old mountains, and the valley floors hold deposits left behind by Ice Age lakes, which covered most of the park's low-lying areas. There's also dramatic evidence of volcanic activity, particularly at the massive **Ubehebe Crater** on the north side of the park.

Humans have lived in and around Death Valley since around ten thousand years ago, when the region was still filled by a massive lake; the climate was then quite mild and wildlife was more abundant than it is today. Later, wandering tribes of desert **Shoshone** wintered near perennial freshwater springs in the warm valley, spending the long, hot summers at cooler, higher elevations in the surrounding mountains; some of their descendents still live at Furnace Creek.

For advice on getting through the desert **safely**, see box, p.308. Flora and fauna dangers are covered on p.52.

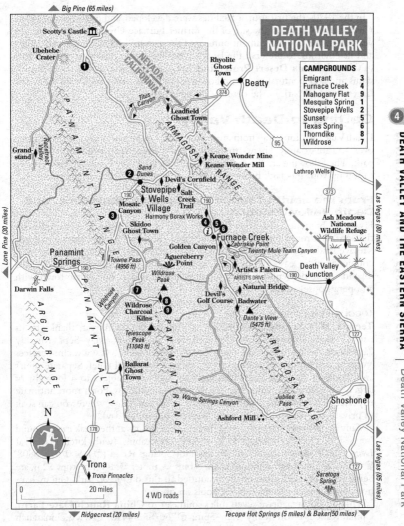

The first non-natives passed through in 1849, looking for a shortcut to the Gold Rush towns on the other side of the Sierra Nevada; they ran out of food and water but most managed to survive, though the death of one of their number encouraged a survivor to dub the place Death Valley. For the next 75 years, the only people willing to brave the hardships of the desert were miners, who searched for and found deposits of gold, silver, and copper. The most successful mining endeavors, though, were centered on **borates**, a harsh alkaline used in detergent soaps (and, eventually, in a variety of industries – everything from cosmetics to nuclear reactors). In the late nineteenth century, borate miners developed twenty-mule-team wagons to haul the borate ore across the deserts to the railroad line at Mojave.

In the 1920s, the first tourist facilities were developed, and in 1927 the *Furnace Creek Inn* was built on the site of the former Furnace Creek mining camp. Six years later, the US government purchased the two million acres of Death Valley and its environs, to preserve the land as a national monument. In 1994, as part of the **California Desert Protection Act**, Congress accorded it national park status and added a further 1.3 million acres to its area, making Death Valley the largest national park in the country outside Alaska.

④ Getting to Death Valley

Death Valley is a long way from anywhere, with **Las Vegas** being the nearest city, over 130 miles away. There's **no scheduled public transportation** into the park. The following are the main routes into Death Valley National Park; be sure to top up your **gas** tank before you head in, as it is expensive in the park.

From the south: Tecopa Hot Springs, Shoshone, and Death Valley Junction

Hwy-127 branches off I-15 at Baker (see p.290) – the last stop for supplies on the southern route into Death Valley – and cuts across fifty miles of desolate Mojave landscape into the Amargosa Valley before reaching any civilization. A couple of miles east of Hwy-127 and fifty-odd miles north of Baker, two dilapidated settlements of scrappy trailer homes (plus a one-horse town with an opera house) make unexpectedly decent places to stop off.

Tecopa Hot Springs

Tecopa Hot Springs has become a popular winter retreat, thanks to its natural **hot springs** (Oct–April daily 7am–10pm; May–Sept roughly 7am–noon & 6–10pm; day pass $5; ☎760/852-4481, ⓦwww.clm-services .com/tecopa.html), bequeathed to the people by a local chief. Separate men's and women's clothing-free bathhouses are ugly and subject to a long list of largely commonsense rules, but are relaxing nonetheless. For a more intimate experience head for the nearby *Delight's Hot Springs Resort*, where you can soak in private, odor-free mineral pools ($10 per person all day).

Many people **stay** across the road from the hot springs at the bleak campground (tents $14, electric hookup $17), though the cabins (with kitchenettes) at *Delight's Hot Springs Resort*, 368 Tecopa Hot Springs Road (☎1-800/928-8808, ⓦwww.delightshotspringsresort.com; cabins ❸, motel ❷, RV hookups $25), are being gradually and substantially beautified in this dusty RV park. Guests have free 24-hour access to private hot pools on site.

While in the area, drive seven miles southeast to **China Ranch Date Farm**, China Ranch Road (daily 9am–5pm; ☎760/852-4415, ⓦwww.chinaranch .com), where you're free to wander among the mostly young groves, follow a shady streamside nature path, explore more widely along the Old Spanish Trail (a pack route between old mission stations), or repair to the cactus garden to enjoy a refreshing date shake and, of course, to buy some dates. Amid the groves, *⚘ Ranch House Inn* (☎760/852-4360, ⓦwww.ranchhouseinn.com; $98 in winter) is an attractive, peaceful, and welcoming B&B in a 1920s cottage that's been imaginatively furnished. A full breakfast served on the screened porch is included; dinner is also available ($18) and you can bring your own wine.

Shoshone

The hamlet of **Shoshone**, eight miles north of Tecopa Hot Springs, wouldn't really rate a mention but for a gas station, a decent motel, and a few date palms and tamarisk trees within striking distance of the park.

While you're here it's worth spending a few minutes at the small **Shoshone Museum** and the Death Valley **Chamber of Commerce** (daily 8.30am–4pm; ☎760/852-4524, ⓦwww.deathvalleychamber.org); ask them to direct you to **Doublin Gulch**, a series of hand-hewn cave homes once used by miners and so named because early in the twentieth century the area was so popular it kept "doublin" in size. The last resident moved out in 1986.

Though you're still an hour south of Furnace Creek, consider a **stay** at the simple but pleasant *Shoshone Inn*, Hwy-127 (☎760/852-4335; ❸), a remodeled motel with its own warm-spring-fed pool and free **wireless Internet**. The only alternative is the *Shoshone RV Park*, Hwy-127 (☎760/852-4569; $25), which has electric and water hookup and access to the local warm springs.

For eating, the *Crowbar Café and Saloon* (☎760/852-4180) serves standard diner fare with antique photos around the walls, but don't miss *C'est Si Bon* (closed Tues & Wed), the best **café** for miles around. Located in a former railroad building now tastefully decorated with artwork and photos, it has Internet access and sells good espresso, Thai iced tea, smoothies, granola and yoghurt breakfasts, cheese platters, crêpes, home-made cakes, and more.

The route into Death Valley continues north through Death Valley Junction (see below).

Death Valley Junction

Some 25 miles north of Shoshone you reach the tiny and virtually abandoned settlement of **Death Valley Junction**. It offers no fuel or supplies, but it does have the **Amargosa Opera House**, the creation of Marta Becket, a New York dancer and artist who settled here in 1967. The inside of the theater is painted with trompe l'oeil balconies peopled by sixteenth-century Spanish nobles and revelers, apparently a confidence-building gesture for when audiences dwindled. Ballet-pantomimes, in which Ms Becket takes almost all the parts herself, have been staged here through the winter, but she is now well into her 80s and her dancing days are pretty much over. Still, she puts on a seated show discussing her life (typically Oct to early May Sat at 8.15pm only; $15; book a couple of months in advance on ☎760/852-4441, ⓦwww.amargosa-opera-house.com). Come for the spirit of the enterprise rather than the show itself, or just stop by for the **tour** (all year except performance days, on request; $5).

The Opera House is part of the *Amargosa Hotel* (☎760/852-4441, ⓦwww.amargosa-opera-house.com; ❷), a pleasantly run-down adobe **hotel** built by the Pacific Coast Borax Company in 1924. It has no TVs or phones, but many of the rooms have been hand-painted by Marta. Ask to see a few before choosing – there's a trompe l'oeil wardrobe in the Jezebel room and cherubs in the Baroque.

From Death Valley Junction it's an easy thirty-mile drive to **Furnace Creek**, passing Zabriskie Point and the junction for Dante's View (see p.307 for both) along the way.

From the northeast: Rhyolite, Beatty, and Titus Canyon Road

If you're heading into Death Valley from Las Vegas, don't pass up the opportunity to detour via the appealing ghost town of **Rhyolite** (ⓦwww.rhyolitesite.com), up a side road three miles west of Beatty, Nevada. Rhyolite was a gold-mining town whose mines were prematurely closed in 1912, after just six boom years. Mismanagement and a lack of technological know-how were largely to blame, and the working Bullfrog Mine just outside the town attests to the area's continuing mineral wealth. By the time of its demise, the town had spread over

the hillside (made of the town's namesake mineral) and had its own train station. The station is still the dominant structure, but the remains of other buildings, including a jail, schoolhouse, and bank, still stand, as does Tom Kelly's **bottle house**, built of some thirty thousand beer and spirit bottles in 1906. A more recent attraction is the roadside Goldwell Open Air Museum (unrestricted access; Ⓦ www.goldwellmuseum.org), a distinctly oddball **sculpture garden** that was the brainchild of Belgian artist Albert Szukalski, who died in 2000 after getting other artists to contribute. It's filled with structures built from car parts and an arresting series of white fiberglass figures arranged in imitation of *The Last Supper*, and you can't help but notice the huge sheet-metal miner and similarly proportioned

▲ Albert Szukalski's sculpture garden, Rhyolite

penguin that greet you as you enter town. Check the website for workshops and upcoming projects.

At nearby **Beatty** there's gas, a casino, the small **Chamber of Commerce**, at 119 Main Street (Tues–Sat 9am–2.30pm; ☎775/553-2424), and the folksy **Beatty Museum**, 417 Main Street (daily 10am–4pm; free; ☎775/553-2303), which tells tales of the local Bullfrog Mining District.

You can **eat** good American breakfasts and cheap Mexican all day at *Ensenada Grill*, 600 Second Street, and if you want to **stay**, try the basic and quiet *Phoenix Inn*, 350 First Street (☎1-800/845-7401; ❶), with HBO and continental breakfast. *Motel 6*, 550 Main Street (☎1-800/466-8356, Ⓦ www.motel6.com; ❷), is more modern, comfortable, and clean, with phone and TV.

From Rhyolite and Beatty you'll coast down into the park on Hwy-374, watching Death Valley unfold from above. There's also the chance to explore the one-way **Titus Canyon Road** (high-clearance vehicles recommended), a three-hour, 26-mile epic which winds past a handful of rusty corrugated iron shacks – all that's left of **Leadfield**, a 1926 mining boom town that never boomed. The highlight is **Titus Canyon** itself, a narrow defile where the road is forced to follow a dry riverbed between steep walls only thirty feet apart. The best of this can be seen from a parking area three miles east of the Scotty's Castle road.

From the southwest: the Panamint Range and Ballarat

Probably the least-used access road to Death Valley is from the southwest, leading from Ridgecrest, past the Trona Pinnacles (see p.286) and the industrial borax town of **Trona**, and into the park. This provides the quickest approach into the more mountainous backcountry on the western slopes of the **Panamint Range**.

Twenty miles north of Trona, a signposted road heads three miles east to the scant, eroded adobe ruins of the former gold-mining town of **Ballarat**. Here, *The Outpost* sells sodas, has information and artifacts (including Charles Manson's 1942 Dodge pickup), and manages a primitive **campground** ($2 per person).

Four-wheel-drive roads head further into the hills, where one fairly popular destination is Barker Ranch in Goler Wash, the site where Charles Manson and his "family" holed up after the notorious Tate-LaBianca murders in 1969.

Almost ten miles north of the Ballarat junction, the highway splits: left to Panamint Springs on a good road, or right along the winding **Emigrant Canyon Road** towards Telescope Peak (see p.310) in the park itself.

From the west: Owens Lake and Darwin

From the west, two routes (Hwy-136 and Hwy-190) spur off US-395 towards Death Valley. They run on either side of the dry bed of what, until the 1920s, used to be **Owens Lake**, which for part of the nineteenth century carried steamships loaded with gold bullion. The water that would naturally flow into the lake has been diverted to Los Angeles via the aqueduct that parallels US-395, leaving a pan of toxic alkali dust. Schemes are currently under way to control this by planting native vegetation and drip-feeding a quarter of the water flow back into the ecosystem.

Around thirty miles east of Owens Lake you pass through **Panamint Springs**, with accommodation and a restaurant (see p.304 and 311), then reach junctions for roads heading up into the pine-clad Panamint Range.

Park entrance information and orientation

Entrance to the park is $20 per vehicle, or $10 per person if you are mad enough to walk or cycle (see box, p.309). You'll get unrestricted entry for seven days, an excellent map, the park newspaper with up-to-date details on campgrounds and visitor services, and a glossy booklet on the national park. There are no staffed entrance stations, so pay at one of the self-serve machines near park entrances, or at one of the visitor centers and ranger stations.

Most visitor facilities are concentrated in Furnace Creek and Stovepipe Wells, neither of which are towns in the usual sense, just resorts with a motel, a restaurant or two, a gas station, and a grocery store. The busier of the two, **Furnace Creek**, is right in the center of the valley and has an excellent **visitor center** (daily 8am–6pm; ☏760/786-3200, ⊛www.nps.gov/deva) with a small but interesting **museum** (same hours; free) and a twelve-minute slideshow orientation. The only other significant sources of information are the ranger stations at Stovepipe Wells and Scotty's Castle.

There are **no banks** in the park, but Furnace Creek and Stovepipe Wells both have ATMs. Note that there is virtually no **cell phone** coverage in the park.

Accommodation

While the main sights of Death Valley can be seen in a day, you really should try to stay the night. To get the full impact of a desert visit, **camping** is the most rewarding option. For most of the year you don't even need a tent – it isn't going to rain – though you'll need a sleeping bag, especially in winter, when nights can be cold. If camping isn't a possibility, you're limited to fairly expensive **hotels** and **motels** inside the park, or lower-cost choices in towns on the fringes such as Tecopa, Shoshone, and Beatty. These places are covered in the respective town accounts starting on p.300.

Hotels and motels

Within the park, only the *Furnace Creek Inn* is worthy of special praise. Otherwise you have a choice of fairly overpriced **motel**-style accommodation at Furnace Creek, Stovepipe Wells, and Panamint Springs. Beyond the park boundaries the range of options expands and prices come down, though you lose the chance to wake up with Death Valley all around you.

You should make reservations as early as possible, especially during peak winter holiday periods.

Furnace Creek Inn Furnace Creek ☏1-888/297-2757, ⓦwww .furnacecreekresort.com. A beautiful Mission-style adobe hotel, built in the 1920s amid date palms and tended lawns, and the place to stay if you're in the valley with money to burn. Rooms are modern but tastefully done, many with great views across the valley to the Panamint Range. It's only open in the more fashionable cooler months when you can laze by the pool, which has bar service and is fed by naturally heated mineral spring. The on-site restaurant (see p.311) is the best around. Open early Oct to mid-May and especially busy mid-Feb to mid-April. Rooms ❽, suites ❾

Furnace Creek Ranch Furnace Creek ☏1-888/297-2757, ⓦwww.furnacecreekresort .com. Functional, family-oriented, and cheaper than the *Furnace Creek Inn*, but lacking much of its

atmosphere. The comfortable motel rooms are rather overpriced but at least you get free access to the chlorine-free mineral swimming pool. Cabins and rooms: summer ❺, winter ❻

Panamint Springs Resort Panamint Springs ☏775/482-7680, ⓦwww.deathvalley.com. Aging and pretty basic motel rooms (and no pool) 35 miles west of Stovepipe Wells, made more appealing by its restaurant and bar (see p.311) and free Wi-Fi. There's an adjacent campground (see opposite). ❹

Stovepipe Wells Motel Stovepipe Wells ☏760/786-2387, ⓦwww.stovepipewells.com. The best-priced option that's close to most of the park's main attractions, offering comfortable rooms, a mineral-water pool, a restaurant with buffet meals, and a bar. Nonguests can use the pool for $4. Rooms ❹, deluxe rooms ❺

Campgrounds and RV parks

Almost all the campgrounds in Death Valley National Park are operated by the National Park Service, most costing $12–14 a night, while sites without a water supply are free. The majority of National Park sites cannot be reserved and stays are limited to thirty days (so that people don't move in for the winter). Take note of the **altitude** listed for each, as this gives an idea of the temperatures you might expect, and remember that the only places with guaranteed shade are the canyons on the forested slopes of Telescope Peak, on the western edge of the park.

RV drivers will only find hookups inside the park at Stovepipe Wells and Panamint Springs, though most surrounding towns have facilities for RVs.

Free **backcountry camping** is allowed in most areas of the park, provided you keep two miles away from any roads (paved or otherwise) and two hundred yards from water sources. No permits are required, but voluntary backcountry **registration** is strongly recommended.

In the lowlands

Emigrant Open all year; 2100ft. Eight miles west of Stovepipe Wells, this is the only free lowland campground, and is tent-only. Fires are not allowed but there are flush toilets and water. Free.

Furnace Creek ☏1-877/444-6777, ⓦwww .recreation.gov. Open all year and reservable up to

six months in advance in the winter months; 196ft. Though one of the largest campgrounds in the park, it still fills up very early on winter weekends. Comes equipped with water, flush toilets, and a dump station. Mid-Oct to mid-April $18, mid-April to mid-Oct $12.

Mesquite Spring Open all year; 1800ft. Fairly small, pleasant, and relatively shady site near

Scotty's Castle on the north side of the park. Has water, flush toilets, and a dump station. $12.

Panamint Springs Resort Panamint Springs ⊙775/482-7680, ⓦwww.deathvalley.com. Restaurant and motel (see opposite) with adjacent campground, which has tent sites ($15), water, and electric hookups ($30), and $3 nonguest showers.

Stovepipe Wells Campground Open mid-Oct to late April; sea level. Moderate-sized campground close to the Stovepipe Wells restaurant and pool. Comes with water, flush toilets, and some fire pits. $12.

Stovepipe Wells RV Park Open all year; sea level. Run by the *Stovepipe Wells Motel* (see opposite), this bare lot has RV hookups for electricity, water, and sewer. $24.

Sunset Open Oct–April; -196ft. This enormous site, right in Furnace Creek, is virtually an RV parking lot. Fires are not allowed but there's water,

flush toilets, and a dump station. First-come-first-served. $12.

Texas Spring Open mid-Oct to late April; sea level. Furnace Creek's quietest site with water, flush toilets, and fires permitted. First-come-first-served. $14.

In the hills

Mahogany Flat Open March–Nov; 8200ft. The remotest and coolest campground in the park; virtually identical to *Thorndike* (see below). Free.

Thorndike Open March–Nov; 7400ft. Small site in the pines which is usually only accessible in high-clearance or four-wheel-drive vehicles. There are pit toilets, but bring your own water. Free.

Wildrose Open all year; 4100ft. Expect moderate temperatures at this site on the way to the charcoal kilns. There are pit toilets, but drinking water is only available April–Nov. Free.

Exploring Death Valley

You can get an unforgettable feel for Death Valley just by passing through, and you could quite easily see almost all the essential sights in a day. If you have the time, though, aim to spend at least a night here, if possible camped out somewhere far from the main centers of activity. Even if you've got your own car, the best way to experience the huge, empty spaces and the unique landforms of Death Valley is to leave the roads (and virtually all other visitors) behind and wander off – taking care to remember the way back. Sunrise and sunset are the best times to experience the color that's bleached out by the midday sun, and they're also the most likely times for seeing **wildlife**, mostly lizards, snakes, and small rodents, which hide out through the heat of the day.

Most of the park's recognized sights lie south of Furnace Creek **along the Badwater road**, where colorful rocks line Artist's Drive and a small pond marks the lowest point in the western hemisphere. The hills immediately to the east offer a couple of great viewpoints – **Dante's View** and **Zabriskie Point** – but the bulk of visitors head swiftly north past the **Keane Wonder Mine** to the ever popular **Scotty's Castle**. It's out on a limb, so leave time to explore **Ubehebe Crater** and perhaps **Racetrack Valley** while you're up here. On Death Valley's western flank rises **Telescope Peak**, a much cooler place to go hiking or exploring the **Wildrose Charcoal Kilns**.

Furnace Creek

Though by no means a big place, **Furnace Creek** is the hub of Death Valley for most visitors, with the park's only significant **visitor center** (see p.303), three campgrounds, the *Furnace Creek Inn* and *Ranch* (for both, see opposite), three restaurants, a couple of bars, a general store, a **post office** (Mon–Fri 10am–5pm), and a **gas station** (gas available 24hr with a credit card). Here you'll find the small **Borax Museum** (daily 9am–4pm; free), located in an 1883 wooden building, the valley's oldest structure. The story of the mineral and its excavation is rather ploddingly told through geological exhibits, a diorama of a twenty-mule-team, and plenty of old photos, but don't overlook the fine collection of arrow points, some dating back two thousand years. Outside, heavy-wheeled borax wagons and an old steam locomotive are arranged around an 1880s *arrastre* used for grinding up gold ore. Armed with a little background knowledge, head two miles north to the old **Harmony Borax Works** (unrestricted entry), where a quarter-mile interpretive trail tells of the mine and processing plant.

The *Furnace Creek Ranch* is the only place in the national park offering organized **outdoor activities**. Palms and tamarisk trees line the fairways of the *Ranch's* 18-hole **golf course** (℡760/786-2301) – the world's lowest grass course, at 214ft below sea level. It's open to anyone keen to pay the green fees (Oct–May $55 plus $13 if you want a cart; June–Sept $30 including cart). To check out the scenery and get a sense of how pioneers might have experienced Death Valley, join one of the walking-pace **horseback rides** offered at the *Ranch* (mid-Oct to early May; $45 for 1hr, $60 for 2hr; ℡760/786-3339). Even better, join one of the hour-long "full moon" rides ($45), which take place several nights a month.

Perhaps best of all is the large **swimming pool** (guests free, others $4 and entry only allowed 7am–1pm & 5–11pm), which is constantly fed hot mineral water and kept at 85ºC – a little warm for real swimming, but great for wallowing.

Furnace Creek has the tenor of an extended resort, but there is still a small, inhabited **Timbisha Shoshone village** on a forty-acre patch of land just southwest of *Furnace Creek Ranch* (see p.304). Displaced and then virtually ignored for decades, the tribe finally gained federal recognition in 1983, and in 2001 was granted seven thousand acres of park and nearby land. They keep largely to themselves.

The road to Badwater

Many of the park's most unusual sights are located south of Furnace Creek along the road to Badwater, which forks off Hwy-190 by the *Furnace Creek Inn*. A good first stop, two miles along, is **Golden Canyon**. Periodic rainstorms over the centuries have washed a fifty-foot-deep, slot-shaped gully through the clay and silt here, revealing golden-hued walls that are particularly vibrant in the early evening. A three-quarter-mile-long interpretive trail winds into the U-shaped upper canyon, and a loop hike (see box, p.309) continues from there.

Five miles further on, signs point to **Artist's Drive**, a twisting one-way loop road. It's perhaps best left until the drive back, especially if this means catching the afternoon sun on the **Artist's Palette**, an evocatively eroded hillside covered in an intense mosaic of reds, golds, blacks, and greens.

A couple of miles south, a dirt road heading west leads a mile to the **Devil's Golf Course**, a weird field of salt pinnacles and hummocks protruding a couple of feet from the desert floor. Capillary action draws saline solutions from below the surface, where alternating layers of salt and alluvial deposits from ancient lakes have been laid down over the millennia. As the occasional rainfall evaporates, the salt accretes to form a landscape as little like a golf course as you could imagine: small golf-hole-sized apertures in the mounds apparently give the place its name.

It's another five miles south to **Badwater**, an unpalatable but non-poisonous thirty-foot-wide pool of water, loaded with chloride and sulphates the only home of the endangered, soft-shelled Badwater Snail. Notice how much hotter it feels in the humid air beside the water, and take a look up on the hill behind where a sign marks sea level. From the pool, two rather uninteresting hikes, both around four miles long, lead across the hot, flat valley floor to the two **lowest points in the western hemisphere**, both at 282ft below sea level. Neither are marked and there's little satisfaction in being just two feet lower than you were at the roadside, though it is worth wandering half a mile out to where the salt deposits form polygonal shapes on the valley floor.

Badwater Ultramarathon

Driving through Death Valley in mid-July can seem like madness even in an air-conditioned vehicle, but an international field of almost a hundred masochists choose this time of year to run the grueling **Badwater Ultramarathon** (Ⓦ www.badwaterultra .com). Billed as "The World's Toughest Foot Race," it is undoubtedly one of the most demanding, extreme, and prestigious in the world. Searing heat and draining dehydration are constant threats on this 135-mile road race, which kicks off 282ft below sea level at Badwater and, after a total elevation gain of around 14,000ft, finishes at the 8360-foot **Whitney Portal**, the trailhead for ascents of Mount Whitney. Around four fifths of the field typically finish, the slowest finishers taking considerably more than two days.

Al Arnold was the first to run the course in 1977, but the race didn't actually get under way until 1987; it has been run every year since. The current men's record, set in 2005 by American Scott Jurek, is 24hr 36min, while in the 2002 event, American Pam Reed knocked almost two hours off the women's record (and beat all the men in the field) to record a time of just under 27hr 57min.

Zabriskie Point and Dante's View

The badlands around **Zabriskie Point**, four miles south of Furnace Creek off Hwy-190 and overlooking Badwater and the Artist's Palette, were the inspiration for Antonioni's eponymous 1970 movie. Proximity to Furnace Creek makes this a popular sunrise destination, as photographers try to capture the early rays catching **Manly Beacon**, an eminence rising above the badlands.

The point's sculpted spires of banded rock are less interesting than **Dante's View**, a further 21 miles south off Hwy-190 and then ten miles on a very steep (and very hot) road. From this point almost six thousand feet above the blinding white saltpan of Badwater, the valley floor does indeed look infernal. The view is best in the early morning, when the pink-and-gold Panamint Range across the valley is highlighted by the rising sun.

North from Furnace Creek

Twelve miles to the north, the **Keane Wonder Mine** and **Keane Wonder Mill** (unrestricted entry to both) were indeed wonderful during their heyday. Between 1904, when the mine was discovered by Jack Keane, and 1916, gold and silver worth $1.1 million was extracted at the mountainside mine. The ore was then carried to the valley-floor mill using a three-quarter-mile-long aerial tramway, which is still more or less intact. From the parking lot by the remains of the mill, a very steep path climbs (an ascent of 1500ft) alongside the thirteen tramway towers to the lowest of the mineshafts. It's only a mile but seems a lot more in the noonday heat. Don't be tempted to seek shelter in the adits and shafts leading off the path; all are dangerous and most unfenced.

Just off Hwy-190, fourteen miles north of Furnace Creek, the **Salt Creek Interpretive Trail** comprises a half-mile boardwalk loop through a spring-fed wash. As usual, dawn and dusk offer your best chances of spotting the likes of bobcats, foxes, coyotes, and great blue herons that come here to drink.

Just east of Stovepipe Wells and north of Hwy-190, the most extensive of the valley's **Mesquite Flat Dunes** spread out, fifteen rippled and contoured square miles of ever-changing sand dunes, some over a hundred feet high. Most people are happy to photograph them from the road (best in late afternoon), but while there are no formal trails, it is easy enough to pick a route out to the nearest of

DEATH VALLEY AND THE EASTERN SIERRA | Death Valley National Park

4

307

the dunes (about half a mile away) or even to the top of the highest dune (3–4 miles round-trip). On the opposite side of Hwy-190 stands the **Devil's Cornfield**, an expanse of tufted arrowweed grasses perched on mounds that make them look like corn shocks.

Stovepipe Wells, a couple of miles on from the dunes, is really just a motel (see p.304) with associated restaurant and RV park, a ranger station, a grocery store, a campground, and a gas station. It's a good place to take a break with views of the dunes, and is handy for trips to **Mosaic Canyon** (see box, opposite). The *Stovepipe Wells Motel* **pool** is open to the public ($4).

Scotty's Castle

On the northern edge of the park, 45 miles from the visitor center, stands **Scotty's Castle** (tours depart daily on the hour 9am–5pm; $11). It's well out of the way of most other attractions but its popularity here is unsurpassed; hordes of tourists wait in long lines for the chance to wander through this surreal, unfinished, yet still luxurious mansion. Executed in extravagant Spanish Revival style, the castle was built during the 1920s – at a cost of $2 million – as the desert retreat of wealthy Chicago insurance broker Albert Johnson, and has been left pretty much as it was when Johnson died in 1948. He was seldom there, so local cowboy, prospector, and publicity hound "Death Valley" Scotty claimed the house was his own, financed by his hidden gold mine – a fantasy Johnson was happy to indulge. The house features intricately carved wooden ceilings, waterfalls in the living room, beautifully crafted tiled floors and, most entertaining of all, a remote-controlled 1121-pipe organ. In winter, it's best to arrive as the doors open to avoid long waits for the fifty-minute **tours** (reservations on ⊤760/786-2392 ext. 224) of the opulently furnished house, left pretty much as it was when Johnson died in 1948. Scotty himself lived here until 1954 and is buried on the hill just behind the house: a good place to wander while waiting for your tour.

To achieve city comforts in such an inhospitable environment, Johnson arranged for the latest conveniences to be installed: primitive air conditioning, a hydro-electric generating system, and other minor marvels can be seen on the one-hour **Underground Mysteries Tour** (Nov–April 4–8 tours daily; May–Sept small groups by reservation a week in advance; $11). There's also the **Lower Vine Ranch Tour** (generally winter weekends, see current activities schedule in the visitor center; $15), which visits the wooden cabin that was Scotty's official home for twenty years.

Exploring the backcountry

The paved roads visit just a small fraction of what the park has to offer, and minor dirt roads (many not shown on the map the park provides on entry) thread into a backcountry full of abandoned mines and dramatic (if parched) scenery.

Going backcountry, however, involves increased **risk**. Even if you're only visiting established sights such as Racetrack Valley or driving Titus Canyon Road, the threat of sharp rocks causing flat tires is increased. While high-clearance vehicles with heavy-duty tires are recommended for these roads, ordinary cars can often get by quite happily, with care. That said, one flat is an inconvenience; two can mean a towing fee well into the hundreds of dollars, if not thousands.

If you're keen to do some real exploring, pick up the *Death Valley Backcountry Roads* map (free from the visitor center), which shows all back roads and ranks them in five levels of difficulty. Most really do need a high-clearance **four-by-four**, and if you are renting, be sure to check that the insurance will cover you.

Ubehebe Crater, Racetrack Valley, and the Eureka Sand Dunes

Eight miles southwest of Scotty's Castle – though it might as well be five hundred miles for all the people who venture here – gapes the half-mile-wide, 500-foot-deep **Ubehebe Crater**, the rust-colored result of a massive volcanic explosion some three thousand years ago; a half-mile south sits its thousand-year-old younger brother, **Little Hebe**. Beyond the craters, the road (high-clearance vehicles recommended, but ordinary cars usually sufficient; see box, opposite) continues twenty dusty miles south to **Teakettle Junction**, where visitors hang teakettles, many of them elaborately decorated, on a signpost. From here it's a further seven miles to **Racetrack Valley**, a 2.5-mile-long mud flat punctuated

---

Hiking and biking around Death Valley

Anything more than a short **hike** in the oppressive heat of Death Valley can become an ordeal. This is less true on the trails around Telescope Peak and Wildrose Peak in the Panamint Range, but you still need to carry all your **water** with you and will want a wide-brimmed hat.

While Death Valley National Park offers ample opportunities for **mountain biking**, only roads open to vehicles are accessible to cyclists; hiking trails are off limits. This still leaves plenty to go at for those who bring their wheels along (there are no rentals available). The map provided with your entry ticket shows the major four-wheel-drive routes: Echo Canyon into the Funeral Mountains and the Inyo Mine, Cottonwood Canyon from Stovepipe Wells, and the Warm Springs Canyon/Butte Valley road in the south of the park are all worthwhile.

Whatever you do, always register your intended route at the visitor center or any of the ranger stations, and for anything a little more adventurous than the walks listed here, get yourself a **topographic map** from the visitor center.

Top hikes

Golden Canyon to Zabriskie Point (5 miles round-trip; 3hr; 500-foot ascent). An unmaintained, moderately strenuous trail along ridges and through badlands to Zabriskie Point. Done in reverse, it's all downhill.

Gower Gulch Loop (4 miles round-trip; 2–3hr; 200-foot ascent). Loop walk starting at Golden Canyon and following the interpretive trail to marker #10. From there follow a trail down Gower Gulch back to the start, including an easy scramble down a couple of dry falls. A leaflet on the hike is available from the visitor center.

Mosaic Canyon (2 miles round-trip; 1hr; 100-foot ascent). A rough three-mile access road just west of Stovepipe Wells leads to the trailhead for a relatively easy hike through this narrow canyon, full of water-polished marble and mosaic-patterned walls. Beyond this most heavily trafficked section, the canyon carries on for another mile, with some scrambling at the upper end.

Telescope Peak (14 miles round-trip; 8hr; 3000-foot ascent). The easy-to-follow but moderately strenuous trail climbs from the trailhead by *Mahogany Flat* campground. It skirts a pair of 10,000-foot peaks and continues through bristlecone pines to the summit and its grand panorama of Death Valley, Mount Whitney, and the eastern face of the Sierra Nevada Mountains. Sign the summit register while you admire the view. There's no water en route except for snowmelt (often well into June), which should be treated. Crampons and ice axes may be required in harsh winters, and at all times you should self-register in the book a short way along the trail.

Wildrose Peak (8 miles round-trip; 5hr; 2000-foot ascent). If winter conditions or your own level of fitness rule out Telescope Peak, this hike makes a perfect, easier alternative. Start by the Charcoal Kilns on Wildrose Canyon Road and wind up through piñon pines and juniper to a stunning summit panorama.

by **The Grandstand**, a weird black-rock intrusion that breaks up the place's symmetry. Park two miles south of The Grandstand, then walk half a mile southeast for the best view of **The Racetrack**, where small boulders seem slowly to be racing, leaving faint trails in their wake. Scientists believe that the boulders are pushed along the sometimes icy surface by very high winds, though no one has ever seen them move. Two miles further on there's a very primitive, waterless **campsite**.

The expansion of Death Valley when it became a national park claimed several features formerly outside its boundaries. The **Eureka Sand Dunes**, forty miles northwest of Scotty's Castle, are the most exciting, but only accessible in a high-clearance vehicle. Far higher than the Mesquite Flat Dunes around Stovepipe Wells, these stand up to seven hundred feet above the surrounding land, making them the highest dunes in California and a dramatic place to witness sunrise or sunset. While here, keep your eyes open for the Eureka Dunes grass and evening primrose, both indigenous to the area and federally protected.

Aguereberry Point, Wildrose Charcoal Kilns, and Telescope Peak

To escape the heat and dust of the desert floor, head south along Emigrant Canyon Road from Stovepipe Wells into the **Panamint Range**. Ten miles up the canyon, a nine-mile dirt track turns off to the east toward the very meager remains of **Skidoo Ghost Town**, a 1915 gold-mining camp of seven hundred people that was watered by snowmelt from Telescope Peak, 23 miles away, and kept informed by telegraph from Rhyolite. There's very little to see, so a better side trip is to **Aguereberry Point**, a wonderful viewpoint looking six thousand feet down into Death Valley, and reached along a six-mile dirt road off Emigrant Canyon Road.

Further south, the *Wildrose* campground (see p.305) marks the start of a steep, five-mile road up Wildrose Canyon to the **Wildrose Charcoal Kilns**. This series of ten massive, beehive-shaped stone kilns, each some 25ft tall, was used in the 1880s to make charcoal from piñon and juniper logs for use in the smelters of local silver mines. Beyond here, the road deteriorates (high-clearance recommended) and climbs through juniper and pine forests past the free *Thorndike* campground (see p.305) to its end at *Mahogany Flat*, where there's another free campground and the trailhead for the strenuous hike up **Telescope Peak**, which at 11,049ft is the highest – and coolest – point in the park (see box, p.309). From the summit you can see both the highest (Mount Whitney) and the lowest (near Badwater) points in the continental United States.

Darwin Falls, Lee Flat, and Saline Valley

A mile west of Panamint Springs along Hwy-190, a two-mile dirt road south brings you to the start of a mile-long creekside trail to the thirty-foot, spring-fed **Darwin Falls**. It's hardly dramatic, but it does feed a welcome and shady cottonwood oasis, though because it supplies Panamint Springs with water, swimming here is not allowed.

You might not expect to see Joshua trees in Death Valley, but **Lee Flat**, a dozen miles west of Panamint Springs, has a whole forest of them on its higher slopes. At this point most visitors continue west towards US-395 (see p.297), but adventurous drivers with sturdy vehicles might fancy exploring the north-western corner of the park. A dirt road leads north past more Joshua trees at Lower Lee Flat, then continues on a very rough and unsigned fifty-mile trek out to **Saline Valley** – get the *Death Valley Backcountry Roads* map (free from the visitor center) and ask for local advice about road conditions. Old mine workings and the remains of a dilapidated salt tramway can be seen along the way, but the highlights are the generally clothing-free **hot springs** at Saline Warm Spring and the adjacent Palm Hot Spring, both easily spotted by the palm trees. Other than hot water, vault toilets, and a free, primitive campground there are no facilities, so take everything you might need. After a dip it's possible to continue north to meet US-395 at Big Pine.

Eating and drinking

There's not a great variety of **eating and drinking places** in Death Valley and you'll almost certainly find yourself eating very close to where you sleep. Furnace Creek has easily the best selection, though there are restaurants at both Stovepipe Wells and Panamint Springs – all somewhat overpriced. Beatty, with restaurants attached to all-night casinos, offers a couple of inexpensive diners, though it's quite a long drive back to the park after dark.

Expensive **grocery stores** with a limited supply are located at Furnace Creek and Stovepipe Wells.

49er Café At *Furnace Creek Ranch*. Diner-style family restaurant with sandwiches and burgers ($10–12), pasta ($15), and steak and fish mains ($15–19). Open 7–9pm in winter, 11am–9pm in summer.

Corkscrew Saloon At *Furnace Creek Ranch*. To quench a thirst after a day in the sun, join the few locals at this basic bar with pool table, jukebox, draft beer, espresso, a limited selection of light meals, and pizza to go (2–9pm only). Open until around midnight.

Inn Dining Room At *Furnace Creek Inn* ☎760/786-2345. Gourmet dining in a beautiful room almost unchanged since the 1920s. Soups, salads, sandwiches, and pizza are available for lunch (when dress is casual), but at dinner expect the likes of tortilla lime soup ($7), rattle-snake empanada ($15), and grilled venison ($28), and be prepared to dress up; shorts and T-shirts are banned. Open early Oct to mid-May; call ahead for dinner and Sun brunch reservations.

Lobby Lounge At *Furnace Creek Inn*. Pop up to the *Inn* for afternoon tea (served daily 3.30–5pm in

season; $17) or call in for an evening cocktail. Open early Oct to mid-May.

Panamint Springs Resort Relaxing restaurant and bar serving breakfast to 11am ($8–13), daytime sandwiches and burgers ($11–13), and good pasta ($14–16), salad, and steak dinners ($18–27). Eat either inside or out on the shady terrace, which is cool enough for outdoor summer dining or sipping a beer in the night air.

Stovepipe Wells Family restaurant and adjacent saloon serving three à la carte meals a day in winter, and buffet breakfast and dinner (but no lunch) in summer. Choose from chicken taquitos ($8), pork medallions ($18), and various other options.

Wrangler Buffet and Steakhouse At *Furnace Creek Ranch*. The *Ranch*'s main restaurant, serving buffet breakfast (6–9am or 10am; $10), buffet lunch (11am–2pm; $12.50), and dinners (5–10pm), including Greek salad ($7.50), chicken pasta ($24), or assorted steaks ($24–33) served with pepper-corn-brandy or mushroom-burgundy sauce.

The Owens Valley

Rising out of the northern reaches of the Mojave Desert, the Sierra Nevada Mountains announce themselves with a bang. Two hundred miles north of Los Angeles, **Mount Whitney** is the highest point on a silver-gray knifelike ridge of pinnacles that forms an eleven-thousand-foot rampart of granite. It provides a wonderful backdrop to the **OWENS VALLEY**, a hot, dry, and numinously thrilling stretch of desolate, semi-desert landscape, running north from **Lone Pine** to beyond **Bishop**.

The small towns along its length don't really amount to much, and if you're intent on visiting California's more cultural sights, you could easily drive through in half a day. However, for scenic beauty and access to a range of

Sierra pass and trailhead closures

After coming through the Mojave or Death Valley, it seems hard to imagine that many of the passes across the Sierra Nevada can remain closed well into June. The authorities try to open **Tioga Pass** (Hwy-120 from Mono Lake into Yosemite) by Memorial Day weekend (at the end of May), but harsh winters sometimes leave it closed until late June. Passes to the north of here, **Hwy-108** and **Hwy-4**, tend to open a couple of weeks earlier, in mid-May. All three close again with the first heavy snowfall, perhaps around late October or early November. **Hwy-88**, yet further north, stays open all year. For information on the state of the highways contact CalTrans (℡1-800/427-7623, ⊚www.dot.ca.gov).

Eastern Sierra **trailheads** are equally affected by snow, with most only accessible from May until early November. Even in June and early July the trails leading from the trailheads can be impassable without an ice axe and crampons.

outdoor activities, the Owens Valley is hard to beat. Twisting mountain roads rise quickly from the hot valley floor to cool, 10,000-foot-high trailheads ideal for **hiking** among Sierra lakes and forests or setting out for the summit of Mount Whitney or other peaks.

The Owens Valley is billed as the deepest valley in the US, and with its floor averaging 4000ft of elevation and the mountains on either side topping out above 14,000ft, that seems completely believable. Its eastern wall is formed by the contiguous **Inyo Mountains** and **White Mountains**; rounded and weathered in comparison with the Sierra and less dramatic, they have their own beauty, especially around the wonderful **Ancient Bristlecone Pine Forest**, which contains the world's oldest trees.

US-395 runs the length of the Owens Valley, a vital lifeline through a region that's almost entirely unpopulated outside of a handful of small towns, though a few solitary souls live in old sheds and caravans off the many dirt roads and tracks that cross the valley floor. Naturally a semi-desert with only around five inches of rain a year, the region relies on Sierra snowmelt, which once made it a prime spot for growing apples and pears. Since 1913, though, its plentiful natural water supply has been drained away to fill the swimming pools of Los Angeles (for more on this topic, read the box on p.335).

Lone Pine, Mount Whitney, and around

LONE PINE isn't much more than a single-street rural town strung with motels, gas stations, and restaurants, but it's lent a more vibrant air by being at the crossroads of desert and mountains. Any night of the week, there'll be desert rats mixing with Mount Whitney wilderness hikers and tourists recovering from the rigors of Death Valley. It also makes a good base and supply post for exploring the area, particularly if you're not prepared to camp out.

Part of what really makes it special is the unparalleled access it provides to the 14,497-foot summit of **MOUNT WHITNEY** – the highest point in the US outside Alaska. The view of the sharply pointed High Sierra peaks which dominate the town – captured by photographer Ansel Adams in a much-reproduced shot of the full moon suspended above stark cliffs – is fantastic.

The town and the Alabama Hills

Lone Pine loves to celebrate its **movie heritage**. The Alabama Hills immediately west of town were used extensively as the backdrop for Westerns from the 1940s and 1950s, then Western TV series in the 1960s, and more recently the occasional science fiction movie and car commercial. You'll see photos of stars of yesteryear all over town, but the place to key into the scene is the **Museum of Lone Pine Film History** at the corner of US-395 and Hopalong Cassidy Lane at the southern end of town (daily except Tues 10am–4pm; donation; Ⓦ www.lonepinefilmhistorymuseum .org). Watch the twelve-minute film, then browse the memorabilia, including an impressive collection of old movie posters and the 1937 Plymouth driven by Humphrey Bogart through the Alabama Hills in *High Sierra*. Look out for **screenings** of movies filmed in the area (usually Thursday and Saturday evenings) or time your visit to coincide with the **Lone Pine Film Festival** (Ⓦ www.lonepinefilmfestival.org), held over Columbus Day weekend (the second weekend in October).

Between Lone Pine and the Sierra Nevada stand the **Alabama Hills**, a rugged expanse of brown, tan, orange, and black granite and some metamorphic rock that's been sculpted into bizarre shapes by 160 million years of erosive wind and rain. Some of the oddest formations are linked by the **Picture Rocks Circle**, a paved road that loops around from Whitney Portal Road, passing rocks apparently shaped like bullfrogs, walruses, and baboons; it takes a degree of imagination and precise positioning to pick them all out, but it is an attractive drive nonetheless, especially at sunset. A map (free from the visitor centers; see below) details the best spots and marks the sites used as backdrops for many early Westerns, including the 1939 epic *Gunga Din*.

There's also plenty of scope for exploration, either mountain biking along the dirt roads and narrow trails (the loose sand is firmest in fall after the first rains), or hiking and scrambling among the rocks. A couple of fairly unspectacular but photogenic natural **rock arches** act as a focus for your wanderings; dusk is particularly pleasant, with the scent of sagebrush in the air. The visitor centers have rough explanatory maps, but the best of the arches is off Movie Road, just west of Lone Pine, where a ten-minute walk should find you at an eight-foot span.

Practicalities

CREST **buses** stop outside Statham Hall at 138 Jackson Street, not far from the **Chamber of Commerce**, 120 S Main Street (May–Sept Mon–Sat 8.30am–5pm; Nov–April Mon–Fri 8.30am–4.30pm; ℡ 1-877/253-8981, Ⓦ www.lonepinechamber.org), which is fine for local information. For details of hiking and camping throughout eastern California, visit the excellent **Eastern Sierra Interagency Visitor Center** (daily 8am–5pm, 6pm in summer; ℡ 760/876-6222, Ⓦ www.r5.fs.fed.us/inyo), two miles south of town on US-395 at the junction of Hwy-136, the Death Valley road. Most of the region is protected within the massive **Inyo National Forest** and covered by the very helpful Inyo National Forest **map** ($9), which covers everything between Mount Whitney and Yosemite National Park, including all hiking routes and campgrounds. Interestingly, this is the only map that makes clear the extent of the City of Los Angeles's holdings in the Owens Valley – basically the entire valley floor, bought in the early years of the twentieth century to slake the thirst of the expanding city (see box, p.335).

Accommodation is limited to a few motel-style places in town and plenty of **campgrounds**, all off Whitney Portal Road, which heads west from town at the lights. There's an adequate range of **restaurants** for the night or two you're going to be here.

In summer, the **swimming pool** at the high school on Muir Street south of town is open daily ($2).

Motels

Best Western Frontier Motel 1008 S Main St, half a mile south of town, ⓣ1-800/231-4071. Upscale motel which offers a heated pool, basic continental breakfast, and some rooms with mountain views. ❹

Budget Inn Motel 138 Willow St ⓣ1-877/283-4381. Simple budget motel with fridge, microwave, and a/c, located in the center of town, just off US-395. Midweek ❸, weekend ❹

Dow Villa Motel 310 S Main St ⓣ1-800/824-9317, ⓦwww.dowvillamotel.com. Large complex with an older section (the original Dow Hotel) built in 1923 to house movie industry visitors (though John Wayne always requested Room 20 in the newer motel section). There's an impressive range of accommodation, from basic bathless rooms in the hotel (❶), rooms with bath (❷), and plush motel units (❹), some with VCR and whirlpool (❺). ❶–❺

Campgrounds

Portagee Joe Campground Tuttle Creek Road (all year; 3800ft). Handily sited just three quarters of a mile outside Lone Pine, with toilets and water. Follow Whitney Portal Road for half a mile, then turn left into Tuttle Creek Road. $10.

Tuttle Creek Campground (early March to Oct; 5100ft). Basic waterless campground three miles out on Horseshoe Meadow Road. $5.

Whitney Portal Campground 12 miles west of Lone Pine (late May to late Oct; 8100ft). Family-oriented site at the base of the Mount Whitney trail. Reservable on ⓣ1-877/444-6777, ⓦwww.recreation.gov. $17.

Whitney Portal Trailhead Campground 12 miles west of Lone Pine (mid-May to late Oct; 8300ft). Hiker-oriented site perfect for the night before your Whitney ascent; maximum one-night stay. $8.

Eating

Bonanza 104 N Main St ⓣ760/876-4768. Authentic Mexican serving basic but filling dishes such as ranchero steak ($12), plus several vegetarian options.

The Espresso Parlor 123 N Main St. Good coffee and muffins plus Internet access and Wi-Fi (both $7 an hour).

Hiking Mount Whitney

Hiking up to the 14,497-foot **summit** of Mount Whitney is a real challenge: it's a very strenuous, 22-mile round-trip, made especially difficult by the lack of oxygen atop the highest point in the 48 contiguous states (see p.52 for advice on Acute Mountain Sickness). Vigorous hikers starting before dawn from the 8365-foot trailhead can be up and back before dark, but a couple of days spent acclimatizing up here is advisable, and the whole experience is enhanced by camping out at least one night along the route. The trail gains over a mile in elevation, cutting up past alpine lakes to boulder-strewn Trail Crest Pass – the southern end of the 211-mile John Muir Trail that heads north to Yosemite. From the pass it ascends along the cliff-tops, finally reaching the rounded hump of the summit itself, where there's a **stone cabin** – not a place you'd choose to be during a lightning storm. Water is available along the first half of the route but must be filtered or treated.

Ambitious hikers with experience in scrambling or technical rock climbing will enjoy the "**Mountaineers' Route**," which follows the North Fork of Lone Pine Creek, taking a more direct and much steeper (though no quicker) route to the summit past the bases of the numerous rock climbs on the mountain's east face. Ropes aren't generally needed, but a head for heights definitely is. Ask for directions and current advice at the ranger station and at the Whitney Portal store.

The **Inyo National Forest**, which manages Mount Whitney, also controls permits for various other sections of the 78,000-acre wilderness area detailed in this chapter. Except for the Whitney Trail and the North Fork of Lone Pine Creek (the Mountaineers' Route), day-use permits are not required, but a permit (free; reservations $5) is needed if you want to spend the night; inquire at the Eastern Sierra Interagency Visitor Center (see p.313) for the ranger station nearest the region you'd like to hike. Sixty percent of permits can be reserved. Out of season (Nov–April), self-issue permits are available at local ranger stations and the Eastern Sierra Interagency Visitor Center (see p.313).

Mt Whitney Restaurant 227 S Main St ☎760/876-5751. Reliable diner that backs up its claim to serve "the best burgers in town" with half a dozen types of patties – chicken, ostrich, venison, veggie – on which to build your creation.

Seasons 206 S Main St ☎760/876-8927. Lone Pine's best restaurant, serving excellent homemade pasta dishes ($15–19) and great steaks ($20–30), including elk. Dinner only; closed Sun.

Whitney Portal

Ten miles west of the Alabama Hills lies **Whitney Portal** (usually accessible May to early Nov), the 8000-foot-high trailhead for hiking up Mount Whitney. Even if a full-on slog to the summit is furthest from your mind, you might appreciate a refreshing break from the valley frazzle in the cool shade of the pines and hemlocks. What's more, there's a small café and general store for when you need fortifying between strolls around the trout-stocked pond, along the cascading stream, or up the Mount Whitney Trail to Lone Pine Lake (five miles round-trip; no permit required).

Manzanar National Historic Site

Just west of US-395, twelve miles north of Lone Pine, on the former site of the most productive of the Owens Valley apple and pear orchards, stand the concrete foundations of the **Manzanar National Historic Site** (daytime access; free; ☎760/878-2194, ⓦwww.nps.gov/manz), where more than ten thousand Americans of Japanese descent were corralled during World War II.

Obtaining permits

Such is the popularity of Whitney that from May to October **overnight and day-hikers** must obtain a permit ($15 reservation fee) through the Whitney Zone **lottery**, which takes place in February. Dates in July, August, and September (the only time the trail is generally totally free of snow) fill up fast, so May (when you may need an ice axe), June, and October (when there may be some snow on the ground) are better bets. The permit quota used for day-hikers is less competitive, though you should seriously consider your ability and fitness.

Apply for an overnight or day-use **wilderness permit** by fax or mail (not phone) through Inyo National Forest Wilderness Permit Office, 351 Pacu Lane, Suite 200, Bishop, CA 93514 (☎760/873-2483, ⒻF760-/873-2484, ⓦwww.r5.fs.fed.us/inyo), making sure it is postmarked or dated in February. Application forms can be downloaded from the website. If you're not that organized (or miss out), your best shot is to hope for a **cancellation** – unlikely, but possible, and more so for single hikers. Starting from mid-April you can apply for any spaces at least two days before your planned ascent (fax, mail, or phone in this instance); check availability on the website. Free **last-minute permits** can be obtained from the Eastern Sierra Interagency Visitor Center a day in advance of your planned ascent after 11am: avoid weekends when demand is highest. Overnight hikers are also required to pack their food in a **bear-resistant food canister**, which can be rented from the ranger station ($2.50 per day; min $5), the Whitney Portal Store (ⓦwww.whitneyportalstore.com), and local sporting goods stores. Once armed with a permit, drive to Whitney Portal, where you can park for the duration of your hike. Unfortunately there are no shuttle services currently running, so if you don't have your own wheels you'll have to hitch.

Day-hikers will want to **camp** at the small, first-come-first-served *Whitney Portal Trailhead* campground ($8) and be ready for an early start. Overnight hikers have more leisure and can plan to hike to one of two designated campgrounds (both first-come-first-served and free): *Outpost Camp* at 3.8 miles and *Trail Camp* at 6.2 miles.

Considering them a threat to national security, the US government uprooted whole families, confiscated all their property, and brought them to what was known as the Manzanar War Relocation Center. They were released at the end of the war, though claims for compensation were only settled in 1988 when President Reagan finally offered the sixty thousand survivors of the state's internment camps an official apology and agreed to pay millions of dollars in damages. Ringed by barbed wire, the one-square-mile camp was filled with row upon row of wooden barracks but, as part of an agreement with the landowner, everything was razed when the camp was closed in late 1945. Now only a couple of pagoda-like sentry posts, an auditorium, and a small cemetery remain among the sagebrush and scraggy cottonwoods. As the bronze plaque on the guardhouse says: "May the injustices and humiliation suffered here as a result of hysteria, racism, and economic exploitation never emerge again." Oddly poignant, in times when it can seem that anyone of Arab descent is considered suspicious.

Nonetheless, many shared the sentiment at the time, and photographer **Ansel Adams** (see box, p.399) spent several weeks here in 1943 depicting the prisoners as industrious and loyal Americans. Some of the former internees return each year, on the last Saturday in April, in a sort of pilgrimage. They often leave mementos on a kind of cenotaph in the cemetery, which is inscribed with Japanese characters meaning "soul-consoling tower."

Manzanar is now managed by the National Park Service, which has turned the auditorium into an excellent **Interpretive Center** (daily: April–Oct 9am–5.30pm; Nov–March 9am–4.30pm; free) where the moving 22-minute film "Remembering Manzanar" runs every half-hour. Pick up a leaflet for the three-mile **auto tour** past 27 points of interest around the camp, including remaining examples of Japanese gardens. Thirty- to ninety-minute **walking tours** (check website for current times; free) stick closer to the interpretive center and may include a visit to a former mess hall, which has been returned to the site and is under restoration.

Independence and around

Six miles north of Manzanar, the sleepy town of **INDEPENDENCE** takes its heroic name not from any great libertarian tradition but from a Civil War fort that was founded north of the town on the Fourth of July, 1862. Every year on that day, there's a parade down Edwards Street (US-395) followed by a mass barbecue and fireworks show in **Dehy Park**, along tree-shaded Independence Creek on the north side of town. The park is marked by a large steam locomotive, which once ran from here to Nevada on narrow-gauge tracks.

The main reason to stop is to visit the **Eastern California Museum** at 155 N Grant Street (daily except Tues 10am–5pm; donation; ☏760/878-0364), three blocks west of the porticoed County Courthouse, which contains an evocative and affecting exhibit detailing the experiences of many of the young children who were held at Manzanar. In the absence of any remaining barracks at the site, the museum has reconstructed part of a family-sized unit, and also holds an extensive collection of photos of camp life (not always on show) taken by Toyo Miyatake, who was interned at Manzanar and managed to smuggle in a lens and film holders.

The museum also has displays on the region's history, from native Paiute basketry to old mining and farming equipment, and on the natural environment of the Owens Valley, including the **California bighorn sheep**, a protected species which inhabits the mountains to the west of Independence. Nimble

4

creatures that roam around the steep, rocky slopes and sport massive, curling horns, they now number only around a hundred and fifty, and efforts to establish new populations are thwarted by appreciative mountain lions, who promptly eat them.

Outside the museum, there's a reconstructed pioneer village made up of old buildings from all over the Owens Valley that have been brought together and restored, and a fledgling **Native Plant Garden**. Honoring the work of local botanist Mary DeDecker, this collection of shrubs beside Independence Creek makes a nice spot to rest for a few minutes.

Practicalities

Local information is available from the Independence **Chamber of Commerce**, 139 N Edwards Street (Mon, Tues, Fri & Sat 9am–noon & 1–4pm; ☎760/878-0084, ⓦwww.independence-ca.com). If you're in the anti-camping camp, Independence offers a few **places to stay** indoors. Try the inexpensive *Courthouse Motel*, at 157 N Edwards Street (☎1-800/801-0703; ❷), or the 1927 *Winnedumah Hotel*, 211 N Edwards Street (☎760/878-2040, ⓦwww.winnedumah.com; shared bath ❸, private bath ❹), once a film-star haven that has retained its atmosphere, especially in the comfy lounge, which comes decorated with local paintings and native crafts. A good breakfast is included. There's also the *Independence Creek* campground ($10), half a mile west of town on Onion Valley Road.

The choice of **restaurants** is very limited, though the wonderful 🎋 *Still Life Café*, 135 S Edwards Street (daily except Mon or Tues 11am–2pm & 5.30–9pm; ☎760/878-2555, ⓦwww.stilllifecafe.com), serves burgers and sandwiches for lunch and excels with its evening French menu, which might extend to entrecôtes of pork with caramelized onions ($22), or a delicious tuna-packed pasta puttanesca ($20). Wines are mostly French, many available by the glass.

Around Independence

West from Independence, the minor Onion Valley Road twists up the mountains to the pine-shrouded trailhead at **Onion Valley**, fifteen miles away. The *Onion Valley* **campground** (June–Sept; 9200ft; $17; ☎1-877/444-6777) marks the start of **hiking** trails across the Sierra Nevada into Kings Canyon National Park, a sixteen-mile journey over Kearsarge Pass to Cedar Grove (see p.377). This is the easiest and shortest route across the Sierra, and you can get the required **wilderness permit** from the Inyo National Forest wilderness reservation service (see box, p.315) or at local ranger stations in the low season.

On the opposite side of the Owens Valley, a small blip on the Inyo Mountains ridgeline turns out to be a seventy-foot-high granite monolith known as **Winnedumah**. Sacred to the local Paiute, it is apparently the body of a brave who was turned to stone when an enemy warrior yelled "Winnedumah," or "stand right where you are." Legend has it that he awaits release by the Great Spirit. An exhausting, full-day boulder-hopping hike will get you to the rock: pick up instructions from the Eastern California Museum (see opposite) if you are keen.

A further ten miles north of Independence is the actual start of the **LA Aqueduct**, though the waters that flow into it have been channeled through a long pipe from around Mono Lake. Follow any of the dirt tracks that head east from US-395 and you can't fail to spot the traces of the railroads built to haul in the material needed to construct the great ditch – which Space Shuttle astronauts claim to have seen while orbiting the globe.

The **Tinemaha Wildlife Viewpoint**, a further twenty miles north, warrants a brief pause for spotting members of the five-hundred-strong herd of **tule elk**, now-protected California natives which were nearly wiped out by the end of the nineteenth century. A few dozen were relocated here from the San Joaquin Valley in 1914, and they seem to be thriving.

Big Pine and around

The town of **Big Pine**, 28 miles to the north of Independence, is slightly larger but doesn't have much more in the way of services. It does, however, act as a gateway to three of the most impressive natural phenomena in California: the **Palisade Glacier**, in the Sierra Nevada to the west of town; the Ancient Bristlecone Pine Forest, in the barren **White Mountains** to the east; and the northern reaches of Death Valley, in particular the Eureka Sand Dunes (see p.310) and the hot springs of the Saline Valley (see p.310).

Just off US-395 some eight miles north of Big Pine, there's a worthwhile diversion to **Keough's Hot Springs**, Keough's Hot Springs Road (daily 9am–7pm or later; $7.50; ☎760/872-4670, ⓦwww.keoughshotsprings.com), a mineral-water-fed swimming pool and hot soaking pool that was once the social center of the region, now restored to something of its former glory. A couple of hundred yards before the springs' entrance a dirt road cuts north to some **natural hot springs**, where locals have created a couple of clothing-optional bathing pools, their idyllic setting only slightly marred by the overhead power wires and indiscriminate littering.

Practicalities

Information about these destinations can be gleaned from the **visitor center**, 126 S Main Street (daily 8am–4.30pm; ☎760/938-2114, ⓦwww.bigpine.com). There are a couple of affordable **motels** along US-395 – the *Big Pine Motel*, 370 S Main Street (☎760/938-2282; ❷), and the slightly nicer *Starlight Motel*, 511 S Main Street (☎760/938-2011; ❸), which has cable, fridges and a little patio. There's also the *Glacier View* **campground** (tents $12, hookup $20) half a mile north of town at the junction of Hwy-168, and several more camping spots up Glacier Lodge Road (see p.320). Good diner **food** is available at the *Country Kitchen*, 181 S Main Street, almost opposite the visitor center.

The White Mountains

Rising to the east of Big Pine, the intimidating **WHITE MOUNTAINS** are effectively an alpine desert: bald, dry, and little visited, yet almost as high as the Sierra. The range is made up of some of the oldest, most fossil-filled rock in California, and geologically has more in common with the Great Basin to the east than the spiky Sierra, which came into being several hundred million years later. It looks like it, too: the scrubby, undulating high country appears more Scottish than Californian. The mountains are accessible only by car (or bike) via Hwy-168. Be sure to fill up on gas and **drinking water**, both of which are unavailable east of US-395.

On the mountains' lower slopes stand the prime reason for coming here – the gnarled trees of the **Ancient Bristlecone Pine Forest** – but snow renders them inaccessible for all but three or four months in the summer. **Schulman Grove** ($2.50 per person or $5 per car) is the most accessible collection, some 23 miles from Big Pine along a paved road that twists up from Hwy-168. The grove is split up into two self-guided nature trails, both at 10,000ft and therefore tougher than their length would indicate. The mile-long Discovery Trail passes by a number of splendid examples, while the four-mile Methuselah Trail loops around past the

▲ Ancient Bristlecone Pine Forest

oldest tree, the 4700-year-old Methuselah, though you'll have to guess which of the trees it is since it is unmarked due to fears of vandalism. Both trails start at the **visitor center** (June–Sept daily 10am–5pm; late May & Oct call for hours; ⊤760/873-2500), which explains the importance of the grove's namesake, Dr Edmund Schulman. An early practitioner of dendrochronology, he revealed the

Bristlecone pines

Great Basin **bristlecone pines** (*Pinus longaeva*) are the oldest known living things on earth. Some of them have been alive for over 4500 years (1500 years more than any sequoia), earning them a place in the *Guinness Book of Records*. The oldest examples cling to thin alkaline soils (predominantly dolomite) between 10,000 and 11,000 feet, where the low precipitation keeps the growing season to only 45 days a year. But such conditions, which limit the trees' girth expansion to an inch every hundred years, promotes the dense resin-rich and rot-resistant wood that lasts for millennia. Battered and beaten by the harsh environment into bizarrely beautiful shapes and forms, they look like nothing so much as twenty-foot lumps of driftwood. The most photogenic examples comprise mostly **dead wood**, the live section often sustained by a thin ribbon of bark. Even when dead, the wind-scoured trunks and twisted limbs hang on without decaying for upwards of another thousand years, slowly being eroded by wind-driven ice and sand.

Bristlecones thrive at lower altitudes and in richer soils than those in the White Mountains, growing tall and wide. But they seldom live as long as specimens subjected to the harsher conditions and, in fact, they're hardly recognizable as bristlecone pines – only the five-needle bundles, and the egg-shaped, barbed cone which lends the tree its name, give the game away.

For more information, consult the Inyo Forest website at ⓦwww.r5.fs.fed.us/inyo or, better still, the excellent ⓦwww.sonic.net/bristlecone.

extreme age of these trees in the mid-1950s and applied the knowledge gained from core samples to correct a puzzling error in early carbon-dating techniques. It turned out that artifacts from the Balkans, previously thought of as stylistic variations on Middle Eastern wares, were in fact a thousand years older and thereby changed scholars' perception of history. If you want to know more, show up at one of the free ranger talks scheduled frequently through July and August, or join one of the ranger-led walks typically held on Saturdays.

Patriarch Grove, twelve miles further on, along a dusty dirt road that gives spectacular views of the Sierra Nevada to the west and the Great Basin ranges of the deserts to the east, contains the Patriarch Tree, the largest of the bristlecone pines. Four miles beyond here, a research station (closed to the public) studies the physiology of high-altitude plant and animal life, which is in many ways similar to that of the arctic regions. From here you can hike to the summit of **White Mountain** (15 miles round-trip; 6–8 hr; 2500-foot ascent), the highest point in the range, and at 14,246ft the third highest in California.

There is **camping** (but no water) at the 8600-foot *Grandview* campground (all year; $3 donation), two miles south of Schulman Grove. Backcountry camping is not permitted in the Ancient Bristlecone Pine Forest, but is allowed in the surrounding forest provided you have a campfire permit for your stove. The ranger station in Bishop can provide this and tell you which springs and small creeks (if any) are flowing.

The Palisade Glacier

The **Palisade Glacier** is the southernmost glacier in the US and the largest in California. It sits at the foot of the impressive Palisade Crest, center of one of the greatest concentrations of enjoyable alpine climbing in the Eastern Sierra: Norman Clyde Peak in the south is named after California's most prolific early mountaineer; the immense bulk of Temple Crag offers a range of routes unparalleled outside of Yosemite Valley; and, to the north, Thunderbolt Peak and Mount Agassiz are highlights of the Inconsolable Range. The Palisade Glacier itself is an excellent introduction to snow and ice climbing.

Hikers not suitably equipped for technical climbing can still get a sense of this wondrous area by hiking from the trailhead at Big Pine Canyon, ten miles west of Big Pine at the end of Glacier Lodge Road; follow Crocker Street from Big Pine. July, August, and September are generally snow-free and best for hiking along the trail to **First Lake** (9 miles round-trip; 5–7hr; 2300-foot ascent). From here a network of shorter trails diverges to six more lakes and to the base of the **Palisade Glacier** (18 miles round-trip from the parking lot; 10–12hr; 4600-foot ascent). Backcountry campers must obtain a **permit** (see box, p.315).

At the trailhead, you'll find three **campgrounds** (late April–Oct; $18) – *Sage Flat*, *Upper Sage Flat*, and *Big Pine Creek* – all above seven thousand feet and with water and toilets; and the free *First Falls* walk-in site at 8300ft, a mile beyond the trailhead. *Glacier Lodge* (☎760/938-2837, ⓦwww.jewelofthesierra.com; ⑤), right at the end of the road, is a slightly more luxurious option, with cabins, RV parking ($35–50), overnight parking for hikers ($5), a limited general store, and showers ($4).

Bishop

BISHOP, fifteen miles north of Big Pine, rivals Mammoth Lakes as the **outdoor pursuits** capital of the Eastern Sierra. It may not have downhill skiing on its doorstep, but its proximity to the wilderness makes it an excellent base from which to explore the surrounding mountains; if you want to try cross-country skiing, fly-fishing, and especially rock climbing, there's no better place to be, with some of the world's best mountaineers offering their services through lessons and guided trips. With an urban population of 3500 and several thousand more in outlying districts, it's the largest town in the Owens Valley, yet maintains a laid-back ambience which makes it worth hanging about to enjoy. There's even a real town center, though the pleasure of strolling around it is mitigated by eighteen-wheelers thundering through.

Arrival and information

Almost everything of interest lies along or just off Main Street (US-395), where you'll find the CREST **bus stop** at 201 S Warren Street (℡760/872-1901) and the main **visitor center**, 690 N Main Street (Mon–Fri 9am–5pm, Sat & Sun 10am–4pm; ℡1-888/395-3952, ⓦwww.bishopvisitor.com), which hands out a comprehensive town visitor guide. For specific information on **hiking** and **camping** in the area, and permission to visit the local petroglyphs, contact the **Public Lands Information Center** (aka the White Mountain Ranger Station), 798 N Main Street (June–Sept daily 8am–5pm; Oct–May Mon–Fri 8am–4.30pm; ℡760/873-2500), which also issues the first-come-first-served wilderness permits.

Accommodation

There's a reasonable range of **accommodation**, for which booking in advance is advised on summer weekends (especially during **festivals**; see p.323). There a **campground** in town (see below) and plenty of Inyo National Forest sites all around.

Best Western Creekside Inn 725 N Main St ℡1-800/273-3550, ⓦwww.bishopcreekside.com. Modern, upscale hotel in the center of town offering large rooms (some with kitchenette for $10–20 extra), complimentary breakfast, free Wi-Fi, and an outdoor pool. ❻

Brown's Town Campground Schober Lane, off US-395, a mile south of town ℡760/873-8522. Large Old West-themed RV and tent campground, with kids' play area and other facilities, costing $17 for tents and $20 for water and electric hookup.

Chalfant House 213 Academy Ave ℡1-800/641-2996, ⓦwww.chalfanthouse.com. Antique-filled, Victorian-era B&B just off the 200 block of North Main Street. Rooms all have private bath, ceiling fans, and a/c, and there's a full gourmet breakfast. ❹

El Rancho Motel 274 W Lagoon St ℡1-888/872-9251. Well-maintained budget motel on the south

side of town with cable TV, free Wi-Fi, ceiling fans, and some rooms with kitchenette ($8 extra). Popular with fishers, so book well in advance for weekends. ❷

Joseph House Inn 376 W Yaney St ℡760-872-3389, ⓦwww.josephhouseinn .com. Upscale five-room B&B in three acres of gardens, with nicely decorated rooms, outdoor hot tub, free Wi-Fi, wine and cheese on arrival, and a full gourmet breakfast served either inside or on the terrace. ❻

The Village Motel 286 W Elm St ℡1-888/668-5546, ⓦwww.bishopvillagemotel.com. Budget motel with renovated rooms, all with microwave and fridge (some with fully equipped kitchen) and access to the outdoor pool (heated in summer and fall). Peacefully sited off the busy main drag. Rooms ❷, kitchen suites ❸

The Town

Specific sights in town are few, though anyone interested in gorgeous images of the Sierra and beyond have a pair of top class **photo galleries** to visit. Mountain Light Gallery, 106 S Main Street at Line Street (Mon–Thurs & Sun 10am–6pm, Fri & Sat 10am–9pm; free; ℡760/873-7700, ⓦwww.mountainlight.com), is lined with works by Galen Rowell, one of the world's foremost landscape photojournalists until his untimely death in a plane crash in 2002. Also a talented rock climber and mountaineer, Rowell photographed the region for over thirty years and extended his oeuvre to Patagonia, the Himalayas, northern Canada, Alaska, Antarctica, and elsewhere. You'll have to part with well over $500 to obtain one of the large-scale framed photos that line the walls, but it is well worth half an hour's browsing.

Similar themes are explored with impressive definition at Vern Clevenger Gallery, 905 N Main Street (☎1-888/224-8376, ⓦwww.vernclevenger.com). Clevenger goes to great lengths to render the Sierra and Owens Valley on wonderfully crisp large-scale prints; prices for smaller images start around $50.

Outdoor activities

Outdoor enthusiasts congregate in Bishop, their rigs laden with tents, sleeping bags, mountain bikes, rock-climbing gear, fishing tackle, crampons, and ice axes.

All year round there is somewhere to **rock climb**: in winter the sport climbs of the Owens River Gorge (see p.324) see a good deal of traffic, as do bouldering areas such as the nearby Happy Boulders and the Buttermilk Boulders (see opposite). As the daytime temperature pushes a hundred, climbers decamp to the High Sierra peaks, particularly Rock Creek, about twenty miles north of Bishop, and Tuolumne in Yosemite (see p.401). For more information, visit Wilson's Eastside Sports, 224 N Main Street (☎760/873-7520, ⓦwww.eastsidesports.com), an excellent mountaineering and sporting goods supply shop with gear rental and a climbers' notice board.

Much more of the money that flows into Bishop comes from the brigades of **fishing** enthusiasts, who spend their summer vacations angling for rainbow trout placed in the streams and lakes by the state government. Even when the high country lakes and streams are frozen or inaccessible there's still good fishing around Bishop, though the main trout season generally runs from late April to late October. As a taster of things to come, the Blake Jones Trout Derby takes place in mid-March at the Pleasant Valley Reservoir, six miles north along US-395; then there's a huge assembly of fisherfolk on the last Saturday in April around **Crowley Lake**, an artificial reservoir built thirty miles north of town to hold water diverted from Mono Lake.

Eating and drinking

With a huge 24-hour Vons store at 1190 N Main Street, as well as a number of good cafés and diners, Bishop is a good place to feast after a few days in the hills and to buy **food** and **supplies** for the next leg.

Amigo's Mexican Restaurant 285 N Main St ☎760/872-2189. Mainstream Mexican with a good range of Tex-Mex staples at good prices, and $10 daily specials.

Erick Schat's Bakkery 736 N Main St ☎760/873-7156. Huge and bustling pseudo-Dutch bakery that's been making its "Original Sheepherder Bread" since early in the twentieth century. There are dozens of other varieties – such as multigrain and sourdough – tables for tucking into their sandwiches ($8), and a huge range of cakes and pastries.

Jack's Restaurant and Bakery 437 N Main St. Well-regarded diner that bakes its own bread, used in their extensive range of burgers and sandwiches.

Leave space for a plate of their locally famous waffles or a slice of fruit pie. Open from 6am for breakfast.

Looney Bean Coffeehouse 399 N Main St ☎760/872-2326. Relaxed coffeehouse with good espresso, a limited selection of bagels and pastries, Internet access ($2 for 15min), and free Wi-Fi.

Whiskey Creek 524 N Main St ☎760/873-7174. Among Bishop's more upscale restaurants, with a sunny deck and an attached bar (where you can also eat) serving Whiskey Creek microbrews. Start with tempura shrimp ($10) and follow with ribs or halibut ($19–22) and a warm, apple bread pudding ($6).

Listings

Climbing and hiking guides For expert instruction or guided rock climbing, alpine climbing, and ski mountaineering contact: Sierra Mountain Guides (☎760/648-1122, ⓦwww.sierramtnguides.com); Sierra Mountain Center, 174 W Line St (☎760/873-8526, ⓦwww.sierramountaincenter.com); or Sierra Mountaineering International, 236 N Main St (☎760/872-4929, ⓦwww.sierramountaineering .com).

Festivals Bishop comes alive over Memorial Day weekend for Mule Days (☎760/872-4263, ⓦwww .muledays.org), with a huge parade, mule-drawn chariot racing, a country hoedown, an arts and crafts fair, and much more. The Tri-County Fair over Labor Day weekend includes a Wild West Rodeo.

Internet Schat.net 174 N Main St ($5/hr).

Library 210 Academy St (☎760/873-5115) has speedy Internet access and is open Mon, Wed & Fri 10am–6pm, Tues & Thurs noon–8pm, Sat 10am–1pm.

Medical treatment Northern Inyo Hospital, 150 Pioneer Lane (☎760/873-5811) has 24-hour emergency and intensive care.

Movies Bishop Twin Theatre, 237 N Main St, shows the latest Hollywood offerings.

Post office 595 W Line St (☎760/873-3526). For general delivery use Zip code 93514.

Showers and laundry There are showers at the City of Bishop Park Pool, 688 N Main St, behind the visitor center (June–Aug Tues–Sun noon–7pm; $2), and showers and laundry at the Wash Tub, 236 Warren St (daily 7am–9pm; $5).

Around Bishop and north towards Mammoth

You may well stay and eat in Bishop, but the main attractions lie outside town, such as along **South Lake Road** (Hwy-168), which climbs some fifteen miles to the west through aspens and cottonwoods to a cluster of alpine lakes and 10,000-foot trailheads. Alternatively, head north onto the so-called volcanic tablelands to see **native petroglyphs**, or northwest towards the **Owens River Gorge**.

If you don't have your own vehicle, you can still access the surrounding area using High Sierra Transportation (☎760/258-6060), which effectively operates as a trailhead taxi service and charges according to distance and number of passengers.

West along Hwy-168

Roughly six miles west of Bishop the narrow, unpaved Buttermilk Road leads northwest off the highway into an arid land of lumpy hills and large, golden granite rocks known as the **Buttermilk Boulders**. Year-round, rock climbers from around the state pit themselves against an almost limitless selection of low-lying boulder problems in this beautiful setting. Visit Wilson's Eastside Sports (see opposite) for details and guidebooks.

Hwy-168 ends at the dammed **Lake Sabrina**, where there's a restaurant that sells fishing tackle and rents boats. Nearby, **South Lake**, also nineteen miles from Bishop, is flanked by *Bishop Creek Lodge* (☎760/873-4484, ⓦwww .bishopcreekresort.com; ❺), with a general store, fishing shop, boat rentals, cabins, and $4 public showers. A number of **hiking routes** set off up into the High Sierra wilderness from trailheads at these lakes.

The trail from South Lake over Bishop Pass heads into Dusy Basin, where you can see the effects of centuries of glaciation in the bowl-like cirques and giant "erratic" boulders left by the receding masses of ice. Another path follows the northern fork of Bishop Creek under the rust-colored cliffs of the Paiute Crags, before climbing over Paiute Pass into the Desolation Lakes area of the John Muir Wilderness. There are a number of **campgrounds** between 7500 and 9000 feet up – almost all with water and costing $19 a night. The shady *Sabrina* site, right by the lake of the same name, is one of the best.

Laws and the Red Rock Canyon petroglyphs

On the northern edge of Bishop, US-395 divides from US-6, which runs north and east into Nevada. Four miles along US-6 is the **Laws Railroad Museum** (daily 10am–4pm; donation; ⓦ www.lawsmuseum.org), a handful of relocated old buildings and a slender black train known as the "Slim Princess" arranged in the restored old town of **Laws**. From 1883 to 1959 this was an important way station on the narrow-gauge Carson and Colorado Railroad, which ran along the eastern side of the Owens Valley from Carson City to the northern shores of Owens Lake, just south of Lone Pine.

Northwest of Laws, a stark desert plateau harbors the **Red Rock Canyon Petroglyphs**, where ancient native peoples have carved mysterious designs – spirals, geometric forms, even spacey figures – onto the rocks. Many beautiful examples exist, but several have been vandalized (and even stolen) over the years, so to help protect them the Bureau of Lands Management, in conjunction with the native owners, requires visitors to sign in at the White Mountain Ranger Station in Bishop (see p.321). There are no permits, fees, or gates to open, but they'll give you a map that pinpoints three petroglyph concentrations, the most interesting being at Chidago and Red Rock Canyon.

North along US-395

Around ten miles north of Bishop, US-395 starts up the **Sherwin Grade**, twelve miles of steady climbing which brings you from 4000ft to the 6500-foot **Mono Basin**. As you ascend the grade, Power Plant Road heads off on the right to the precipitously steep **Owens River Gorge**, another excellent rock-climbing spot in an area which until recently was completely dry. Since 1994, the Los Angeles Department of Water and Power has been forced to allow water to flow down the gorge, and the flora and fauna is slowly returning along with trout fishers and hikers.

Mammoth Lakes and around

Mammoth Lakes, forty miles north of Bishop, and the associated skiing, snowboarding, and mountain-biking hotspot of **Mammoth Mountain**, jointly make up the Eastern Sierra's biggest resort, and one that is challenged in California only by those around Lake Tahoe. During the winter months, masses of weekend skiers speed through the Owens Valley on their way to some of the state's premiere pistes, which rise above this pine-shrouded town. Although skiing and summer fishing are Mammoth's traditional attractions, the town is now increasingly hyped for its accessible mountain-biking terrain and a number of on- and off-road bike races.

Despite its popularity with weekenders from LA (just four hours away), Mammoth has always been a fairly low-key resort, but in recent years the involvement of a major corporate resort owner has propelled Mammoth into the ranks of the winter sports mega-resorts, such as Vail in the Rockies and Whistler/Blackcomb in Canada. A single company now owns the ski operation, large chunks of Mammoth real estate, and the new **Village at Mammoth** development, complete with pricey hotels, swanky stores, and direct access to the mountain via the Village Gondola. Lots of new lodging has been built along with Mammoth's second golf course, and there are advanced plans for a much-expanded airport with scheduled flights.

Residents are torn between enthusiasm for the new opportunities presented and nostalgia for the way things used to be, but for the moment Mammoth

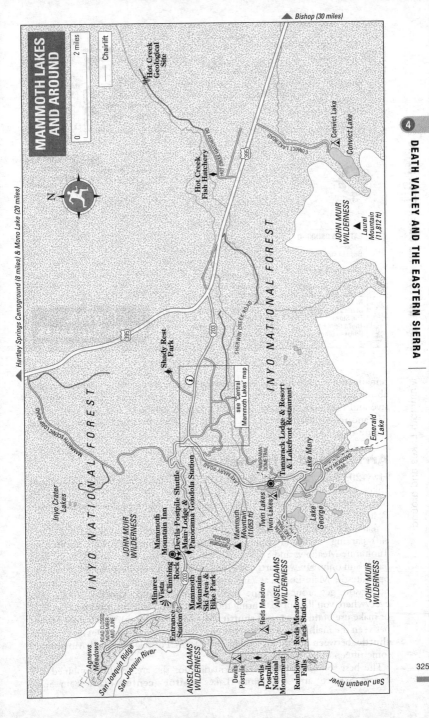

MAMMOTH LAKES AND AROUND

— Chairlift

0   2 miles

Bishop (30 miles)

Hot Creek Geological Site

HOT CREEK HATCHERY RD

395

Hot Creek Fish Hatchery

Convict Lake

CONVICT LAKE ROAD

Convict Lake

JOHN MUIR WILDERNESS

Laurel Mountain (11,812 ft)

Hartley Springs Campground (8 miles) & Mono Lake (20 miles)

N

INYO NATIONAL FOREST

MAMMOTH SCENIC LOOP ROAD

Inyo Crater Lakes

JOHN MUIR WILDERNESS

395

Shady Rest Park

203

SHERWIN CREEK ROAD

i

see 'Central Mammoth Lakes' map

INYO NATIONAL FOREST

PANORAMA DOME TRAIL

LAKE MARY ROAD

Tamarack Lodge & Resort & Lakefront Restaurant

Lake Mary

SKY MEADOWS TRAIL

Emerald Lake

Devils Postpile Shuttle

Main Lodge & Panorama Gondola Station

Mammoth Mountain Inn

Mammoth Mountain (11,053 ft)

Panorama Gondola

Twin Lakes

Twin Lakes

Lake George

CRYSTAL LAKE TRAIL

Minaret Vista

Climbing Rock

203

Mammoth Mountain Ski Area & Bike Park

Entrance Station

ROAD CLOSED NOVEMBER–MID JUNE

Agnews Meadows

San Joaquin Ridge

San Joaquin River

ANSEL ADAMS WILDERNESS

Reds Meadow

ANSEL ADAMS WILDERNESS

Devils Postpile

Devils Postpile National Monument

Rainbow Falls

Reds Meadow Pack Station

JOHN MUIR WILDERNESS

San Joaquin River

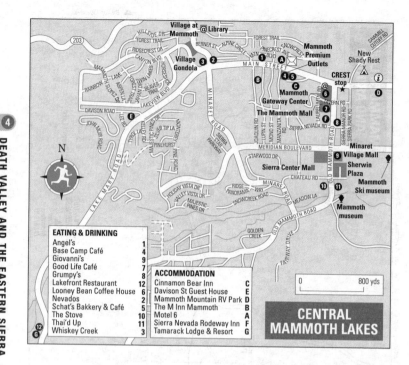

EATING & DRINKING

Angel's	1
Base Camp Café	4
Giovanni's	9
Good Life Café	7
Grumpy's	8
Lakefront Restaurant	12
Looney Bean Coffee House	6
Nevados	2
Schat's Bakkery & Café	5
The Stove	10
Thai'd Up	11
Whiskey Creek	3

ACCOMMODATION

Cinnamon Bear Inn	C
Davison St Guest House	E
Mammoth Mountain RV Park	D
The M Inn Mammoth	B
Motel 6	A
Sierra Nevada Rodeway Inn	F
Tamarack Lodge & Resort	G

CENTRAL MAMMOTH LAKES

remains unbeatable for outdoor activities and is scenically as dramatic as just about anywhere in the Sierra. You may find the testosterone overload oppressive and the town overpriced, but it's easy to escape to the hills during the day and return each evening to good food, lively bars, and even a couple of movie theaters.

Arrival and information

Hwy-203 runs three miles west from US-395 into the town of Mammoth Lakes, from where it continues six miles to the Main Lodge for Mammoth Mountain, then ascends the San Joaquin Ridge and drops down to the Devils Postpile National Monument.

Year-round **CREST buses** (see p.297) stop three times a week in the *McDonald's* parking lot on Hwy-203. There's also a seasonal **YARTS service** to Tuolumne Meadows and Yosemite Valley (July & Aug once daily; June & Sept Sat & Sun only; ⓦwww.yarts.com), which departs from *Mammoth Mountain Inn*, opposite the Main Lodge, at 7am and returns that evening around 9pm. In the ski season, get around on the five-route **Mammoth Shuttle**, which goes everywhere you'll want to. During the warmer months, **rent a bike** (see p.332) or make use of the free **town shuttle** (Mon–Fri 7am–8pm), which plies a route between the malls along Old Mammoth Road. There's also the **Devils Postpile shuttle** between the Main Lodge and Devils Postpile National Monument, some fifteen miles west of town.

The best source of practical information for the area is the combined US Forest Service and Mammoth Lakes **visitor center** (daily 8am–5pm;

(⊤760/924-5500, ⓦwww.visitmammoth.com), on the main highway half a mile east of the town center.

Accommodation

About every second building in Mammoth is a condo, but there are numerous other **accommodation** opportunities (including a hostel and some welcoming B&Bs), so beds are at a premium only during ski-season weekends. Winter prices are highest, summer rates (quoted here, and still fairly high) come next, and some relative bargains can be found in the months between. If you fancy staying in a **condo** try contacting Mammoth Mountain Reservations (⊤1-800/223-3032, ⓦwww.mammothreservations.com).

There is also mile upon mile of backcountry in which to pitch a tent, and so many established sites that you'll be almost overwhelmed by choice. Some twenty **campgrounds** lie within a ten-mile radius of town, the two main concentrations being around Twin Lakes and along Minaret Road. Almost all come with water, cost $15–16, and are let on a first-come-first-served basis. The Mammoth Lakes Welcome Center Visitor Guide (available free from the visitor center) has full details along with rules for free dispersed camping on the surrounding national forest lands.

Motels, B&Bs, and condos

Cinnamon Bear Inn 113 Center St ⊤1-800/845-2873, ⓦwww.cinnamonbearinn.com. Reasonably priced, 22-room B&B inn close to downtown, with comfortable rooms, all with TV and phone (and some with VCR), use of hot tub, wine-and-nibbles happy hour on arrival, and a full breakfast. Check the web for low-cost specials. Midweek ❺, weekends ❻

Davison Street Guest House 19 Davison St ⊤760/924-2188, ⓦwww.mammoth-guest.com. Mammoth's only backpacker hostel is in a wooden A-frame chalet with mountain views from its deck. There's a spacious lounge, good communal cooking facilities, bunks in fairly compact dorms (summer $28, winter weekdays $40, winter weekends $50), three-bed rooms (summer ❷, winter weekdays ❸, winter weekends ❹), and one en-suite room for an extra $25–$35.

The M Inn Mammoth 75 Joaquin Rd ⊤760/934-2710, ⓦwww.mammothcountryinn.com. Welcoming boutique inn located in a quiet neighborhood, with ten modern and tastefully themed rooms, all with private baths and some with Jacuzzis. There's wine and hors d'oeuvres on arrival, and full and delicious breakfasts. Midweek ❺, weekend ❻

Motel 6 3372 Main St ⊤1-800/466-8356, ⓦwww.motel6.com. Basic, modern motel close to the town center, with all you really need at an affordable price. ❸

Sierra Nevada Rodeway Inn 164 Old Mammoth Rd ⊤1-800/824-5132, ⓦwww.mammothsnri.com.

At the cheaper end of Mammoth motels but still with large, comfy rooms, pool, spa, and sauna, and on-site restaurant. ❺

Tamarack Lodge & Resort Lake Mary Rd ⊤1-800/626-6684, ⓦwww.tamaracklodge.com. Away from the town in a woodsy setting right by Twin Lake, on the edge of a cross-country ski area, this luxurious lodge in rustic style offers rooms (shared bath ❹, private bath ❻), rustic cabins (❻) with fully-equipped kitchens, refurbished cabins (❼), and some gorgeous deluxe cabins costing around $320 (❾).

Camping and RVs

Convict Lake Open late-April to Oct; 7600ft. Wooded, lakeside national forest campground just west of US-395, around four miles south of the Mammoth turnoff, with the longest open season in the area. Showers are available at the nearby *Convict Lake Resort* (⊤760/934-3800, ⓦwww.convictlake.com; $2 for two minutes). $18.

Devils Postpile Open July–Sept; 7500ft. National Park Service campground along Minaret Road, half a mile from the rocks themselves and a good base for hikes to Rainbow Falls or along the John Muir Trail. $16.

Hartley Springs Open early May–Oct; 8400ft. Just one of several primitive waterless campgrounds in the area, this one located 1.5 miles west of US-395 along Glass Flow Road, around eleven miles north of the Mammoth turnoff. Free.

Mammoth Mountain RV Park Hwy-203 ⊤1-800/582-4603, ⓦwww.mammothrv.com. Year-round, all-mod-cons RV park right in town opposite the visitor center, with indoor spas, kids' play areas, tent sites ($28), and a range of partial and full hookup sites ($45–51).

New Shady Rest Open mid-May to Oct; 7800ft. Large and busy campground close to town with flush toilets and a dump station. Several sites can be reserved on ☏1-877/444-6777 or ⓦwww .recreation.gov. $18.

Reds Meadow Open mid-June to Oct; 7600ft. National forest campground along Minaret Road

and within easy hiking distance of Devils Postpile, Rainbow Falls, and a nice nature trail around Sotcher Lake. It also comes with a natural hot spring bathhouse open to all (donations appreciated). $16.

Twin Lakes Open mid-May to Oct; 8700ft. The longest-open of five near-identical sites in this area of glacially scooped lakebeds, a mile southwest of Mammoth Lakes township. Lakeside setting among the pines and plenty of hiking trails nearby. $19.

Mammoth Mountain: biking and hiking

Mammoth is all about getting into the **outdoors**. Aside from eating, drinking, and mooching around the sports shops and factory clothing outlets, you'll find little reason to spend much time in town, though anyone interested in Mammoth's gold-mining and timber-milling origins may fancy a visit to the small **Mammoth Museum**, 5489 Sherwin Creek Road (June–Sept daily 10am–6pm; free), located in a 1920s log cabin. Winter sports fans will find more of interest in the **Mammoth Ski Museum**, 100 College Parkway (Tues–Sun noon–5pm; $3; ☏760/934-6592, ⓦwww.mammothskimuseum .org), a small but well-presented collection of skiing-related paraphernalia, most of it amassed over sixty years by one Mason Beekley. Inside are the expected racks of old skis, a chair from the original Mammoth chairlift, and a 450-year-old book by a Swedish monk which illustrates skiing. But the museum's strength is in the graphic arts: the walls come lined with vintage ski posters, photos (some by Ansel Adams), and even woodcuts, and many are reproduced and available at the gift shop.

There's more fun to be had four miles west of the center, up on the slopes of the dormant volcano called **MAMMOTH MOUNTAIN**, where the **Panorama Gondola** (all year except Oct to mid-Nov daily 9am–4.30pm; $20 round-trip) will whisk you to the top in eight minutes. A new interpretive center here lets you enjoy the fine mountain views through telescopes.

If you'd rather work up a sweat, there are a number of ways to do just that: mountain biking, hiking (see below and opposite for both), plus stacks of people willing to get you mobile: **kayaking** (see p.336) and **rock climbing** (p.332) are both covered.

Mountain biking

Once the ski runs have shed their winter snow, the slopes transform into the 3500-acre **Mammoth Mountain Bike Park** (late June to Sept daily 9am–4.30pm; ☏760/934-0706, ⓦwww.mammothmountain.com), with over eighty miles of groomed singletrack trails. Chairlifts quickly give you and your bike an altitude boost, allowing you to hurtle down the twisting sandy trails, brushing pines and negotiating small jumps and tree roots. The emphasis here is definitely on downhill, and when you're transported to the rarefied, eleven-thousand-foot air at the top of the chairlift, you very quickly appreciate the logic of this. The bike park produces a color map of the mountain showing the lifts and trails in three grades of difficulty, and indicates "X-Zones" of enhanced freeriding terrain for more aggressive riders. Beginners often take the **Downtown** run into Mammoth (from where a bike shuttle bus returns you to the bike park), while those with a little more skill or ambition might opt for the **Beach Cruiser**, which carves its way down the western side of the mountain from near the summit. Experts and those with a death wish can tackle the **Kamikaze**, scene of the ultimate downhill race which has traditionally formed the centerpiece of the annual World Cup racing weekend (usually around late Sept), when competitors hit speeds of sixty miles per hour.

The basic **park-use fee** ($10) gives you access to the trails, and you can rent bikes for $39 a day. In addition, there's a complex selection of deals such as the Park Pass (one day $37, two days $66), which gives all-day access to the Panorama Gondola and the bike shuttle from town. Gondola and bike-rental combos include a two-hour package ($40) giving bike rental and gondola access, and a full-day unlimited deal ($76).

If you don't fancy forking out for use of the bike park, or just prefer something a little gentler, there's plenty more **trail riding** around the resort, made comfortable by mid-summer temperatures reliably in the seventies. Several bike stores around town will point you in the right direction and rent bikes (see p.332), which can also be taken to the bike park. Likely candidates include the relatively gentle Shady Rest Park, close to central Mammoth; the Lakes Basin area near *Tamarack Resort*; and Inyo and Mono craters. The visitor center offers free trail maps and a brochure on route descriptions and trail ethics.

Hiking

Interwoven among the bike trails on Mammoth Mountain are a couple of **hiking paths** which top out at the summit. The views are stupendous but, as with many volcanoes, the hiking isn't the best and you're better off riding the gondola (see opposite) and saving your legs for hikes elsewhere.

Listed in the box below are some of the best of the **short hikes** around Mammoth. No permits are required for these, though you'll need to obtain a free **wilderness permit** if you want to spend the night in the Ansel Adams or John Muir wilderness areas to the west. The number of overnight hikers allowed to set off from each trailhead is limited during the **quota season** from May to October. Call the Public Lands Information Center in Bishop (℡760/873-2483, ℻873-2484, ⓦwww.r5.fs.fed.us/inyo) up to six months and at least two days in advance; there is a $5 reservation fee.

Short hikes around Mammoth Lakes

Crystal Lake (3.5 miles round-trip; 2hr; 650-foot ascent). From the Lake George trailhead the path skirts high above Lake George, revealing increasingly dramatic views as you climb towards Crystal Lake, hunkered below Crystal Crag. Fit hikers can tack on the Mammoth Crest Trail (a further 2.5 miles round-trip; 2–3hr; 1000-foot ascent).

Panorama Dome Trail (1 mile round-trip; 30min; 100-foot ascent). Great views over the town and the Owens Valley reward hikers of this short sylvan trail, from Twin Lakes on Lake Mary Road (see map, p.326).

Rainbow Falls Trail (5 miles; 2hr; 300-foot ascent). Moderate hike that combines the two key features of the Devils Postpile National Monument. Start from the *Devils Postpile* campground and stroll to the monument itself, then continue to the top of Rainbow Falls.

Sky Meadows Trail (4 miles; 1.5–2hr; 1200-foot ascent). Starting at the southern end of Lake Mary, this delightful hike along the wildflower-flanked Coldwater Creek passes Emerald Lake on its way to Sky Meadow, at the foot of the striking Blue Crag.

Along Minaret Road: Devils Postpile National Monument

From the ski area, the narrow and winding **Minaret Road** (typically open mid-June to Oct) climbs briefly to a nine-thousand-foot pass in the San Joaquin Ridge, then plummets toward the headwaters of the Middle Fork of the San Joaquin River, ending some eight miles beyond at the Reds Meadow pack station. This is the only road access into the evocatively named **Devils Postpile National Monument** (free but see "shuttle bus," below; ⑭www .nps.gov/depo), which centers on a collection of slender, blue–gray basalt columns ranged like hundreds of pencils stood on end. Some are as tall as sixty feet and others are twisted and warped; vulnerable sections are shorter, where the brittle rock has cracked and the upper sections have fallen forward to form a talus slope of shattered rubble. It was formed as lava from a vent near Mammoth Mountain cooled and fractured into multisided forms, a phenomenon best appreciated by skirting round to the top of the columns. The Postpile itself is a half-mile stroll from the *Devils Postpile* campground and its small **visitor center** (mid-June to mid-Sept daily 9am–4pm), where you can join daily ranger-led walks at 11am and free evening campfire programs (twice weekly at 8pm).

The second highlight of the National Monument is **Rainbow Falls**, where the Middle Fork of the San Joaquin River plunges 101ft into a deep pool, the spray refracting to give the falls its name, especially at midday. It's two miles from the Postpile through Reds Meadow, reached on a pleasant hike (see box, p.329).

Throughout the summer, Minaret Road is closed to private vehicles during the day and you must access Devils Postpile by **shuttle bus** (daily 7.15am–8.30pm, last bus leaves the Postpile 7.45pm; day-pass $7 per person, three-day pass $14, America the Beautiful Senior and Annual passes not accepted), which

---

Skiing at Mammoth

With one of the longest ski seasons in California (from early November often until well into June), three thousand vertical feet of skiing, and more than its fair share of deep, dreamy powder, **Mammoth Mountain** (daily 8.30am–4pm; ☏1-800/626-6684, lift and snow conditions ☏1-888/766-9778, ⑭www.mammothmountain.com) ranks as one of California's premier ski mountains. It's well balanced, too, with roughly equal areas of beginner, intermediate, and expert terrain, plus snow parks and halfpipes. Add to that a cat's cradle of intersecting gondolas and chairlifts – seemingly being added to each year and now numbering over thirty – bundles of snowmaking equipment, and a whole resort of bars and restaurants designed with après-ski in mind, and you can hardly go wrong. As if this weren't enough, your lift ticket is also valid at June Lake (see p.333), a few miles north.

Pick up **lift tickets** ($78) from the Main Lodge on Minaret Road, where you can also rent **equipment** ($32 for basic skis, boots, and poles; $25 for snowboard and boots), and book **lessons** ($55–67 per half-day).

Off the mountain there are stacks of **cross-country skiing** trails; *Tamarack Lodge & Resort* (see p.327) offers ski packages, including instruction, tours, and rentals, and charges $25 a day for access to the trails.

If you prefer a motorized approach to the white stuff, you can rent gear and clothing from DJ's Snowmobile Adventures (☏760/935-4480, ⑭www.snowmobilemammoth .com), which has one-hour (single $65, double $85), two-hour ($116/156), and half-day ($232/312) rentals.

leaves every thirty minutes from the Mammoth Mountain Main Lodge Gondola Building. Campers are allowed vehicular access at all times, and in the early morning (before 7am) and evening (after 7.30pm) others can drive along Minaret Road; drive over before 7am and you can leave whenever you wish. In theory, drivers and their passengers still have to pay, but there is unlikely to be anyone to take your money.

During the day, the furthest you can drive without taking the shuttle bus is **Minaret Vista**, a parking lot high on the San Joaquin Ridge with wonderful views of the **Minaret Peaks**, a spiky volcanic ridge just south of pointed Mount Ritter – one of the Sierra's most enticing high peaks.

Eating, drinking, and nightlife

Mammoth offers by far the widest selection – and some of the best examples – of **restaurants**, **cafés**, and **bars** (some with **live music**) on this side of the Sierra. That may be reason enough to stick around for a while, but if you've gotten used to the relative austerity elsewhere in the mountains, the drain on your finances may come as a shock. If all you're after is replenishing your cooler, pick up **groceries** at Von's, in the Minaret Village mall, and healthy goodies at Sierra Sundance Earth Foods in The Mammoth Mall.

Angel's Main St at Sierra Blvd ☎760/934-7427. The menu has a Southwestern kick at this broadly appealing and family-friendly restaurant. The *Angel's* salad ($4) and jalapeño corn fritters ($6) are very good, and there's a decent selection of burgers ($8–9) and $10 mains, such as spinach and mushroom lasagna and chicken pot pie, all washed down with Mammoth Brewing Company microbrews.

Base Camp Café 3325 Main St ☎760/934-3900. Great low-cost café usually bustling with the outdoors and active set, here for the hearty breakfasts ($4–7), tasty soups and sandwiches, bargain daily specials, organic espresso coffees, and microbrews. Also open for dinner (Thurs–Sun to around 8pm).

Giovanni's Minaret Village Mall, Old Mammoth Rd ☎760/934-7563. The favorite local stop for low-cost dining; three out of ten for decor and ambience, but very good pasta and pizza (a 12-inch from $13), and great lunchtime deals.

Good Life Café The Mammoth Mall ☎760/934-1734. Doesn't cater to vegetarians and vegans as well as they'd like you to believe, but probably the best around with freshly made veggie burritos ($9), good salads ($7–9), and vegetable wraps, as well as plenty of burgers and egg dishes ($8–9), all served inside or on the sunny deck. Daily 6.30am–3pm.

Grumpy's 361 Old Mammoth Rd ☎760/934-8587, ⓦwww.grumpysmammoth.com. Sports bar with 35 TVs, a pool table, and a good grill serving the likes of the half-pound Grumpy Melt with ortega chilies and grilled onions ($11), and a fine halibut and chips ($12).

Lakefront Restaurant *Tamarack Lodge* ☎760/934-2442. Superb lake views accompany dishes from a menu with French-Californian leanings, which might include wild mushroom strudel ($12), walnut-crusted chicken breast ($24), and a sumptuous selection of desserts and ports.

Looney Bean Coffee House The Mammoth Mall ☎760/934-1345. The most vibrant of Mammoth's coffee bars, with good coffee, muffins, and more, served up to dedicated regulars either inside (where there's a stack of magazines) or out front. Stays open late in the ski season and the free Wi-Fi is very popular.

Nevados Main St and Minaret Rd ☎760/934-4466. Another favorite with the foodies, with an eclectic menu featuring anything from crisp, nori-wrapped shrimp with wasabi to hazelnut-crusted rack of lamb; there's also a $38 prix fixé deal for an appetizer, main, and dessert.

Schat's Bakery & Café 3305 Main St ☎760/934-6055. Easily the best range of baked goods in town, either to take out or eat in with a coffee. The crisp Danishes, baklava, and hand-made chocolates are all toothsome.

The Stove 644 Old Mammoth Rd ☎760/934-2821. Long-standing Mammoth favorite for its traditional country cooking, serving egg, waffle, and pancake breakfasts (around $8), sandwiches, and full meals later on – all in massive portions.

Thai'd Up 587 Old Mammoth Rd ☎760/934-7355. Terrible name, but tasty food is served in this diminutive Thai restaurant. Try summer rolls (served cold; $5) followed by Panang curry ($10). Lunch Wed–Sun, dinner daily except Tues.

Whiskey Creek Main St at Minaret Rd ☎760/934-2555. Traditional American dining in one of the town's better restaurants, which particularly excels with its seafood, Sierra Ranch salad ($6.50), and meatloaf ($19). The upstairs bar is among the town's livelier ones, serving its own Mammoth Brewing Company beers (daily happy hour June–Oct 5–6.30pm, rest of year 4–5.30pm), and often hosting bands on winter weekends.

Listings

Banks Several around town (all with ATMs), including Bank of America, Main Street at Old Mammoth Road.

Bookstores Booky Joint in the Minaret Village Mall (☎760/934-2176) has the best all-around selection.

Festivals During the annual Jazz Jubilee, held over four days around the second weekend in July (details on ☎760/934-2478, ⊛www .mammothjazz.org), bars, restaurants, and impromptu venues around town pack out with predominantly trad-jazz types. Blues fans should come later for the Festival of Beers and Bluesapalooza (☎760/934-0606, ⊛ww.mammothevents .com), held over the first weekend in Aug.

Film First-run Hollywood fare at the Minaret Cinema in the Minaret Village Mall (☎760/934-3131).

Fishing Rent gear, get fly and spinner advice, and gather the latest news at Kittredge Sports, 3218 Main St (☎760/943-7566, ⊛www.kittredgesports. com). Mary Lake and Crowley Lake (see p.322) are popular (sometimes crowded) spots, as is the trout-filled San Joaquin River near the Devils Postpile.

Internet The library (see below) has free surfing for an hour at a time, and unlimited Wi-Fi. There's also access and Wi-Fi at the Stellar Brew coffee-house, 3280 Main St (☎760/924-3559).

Laundry Aloha Sudz, corner of Main Street and Old Mammoth Road. Also coin-op machines at Mammoth Mountain Inn (7am–9pm).

Library The public library is located at 960 Forest Trail (Mon–Fri 10am–7pm, Sat 9am–5.30pm) and has Internet access.

Mountain biking Footloose Sports, Main Street at Old Mammoth Road (☎760/934-2400, ⊛www .footloosesports.com), rents front- and full-suspension bikes ($6–9/hr, $32–39/day), plus the latest demo models ($18/78), and organizes weekly group rides; Mammoth Sporting Goods, Sierra Center Mall (☎760/934-3239, ⊛www .mammothsportinggoods.com), offers slightly better rates for a similar range of machines and also runs summer-only group rides (July–Oct Wed 5.30pm & Sat 9am) and a Friday evening night ride starting at 9pm.

Photographic supplies Speed of Light Photo & Video, Minaret Village Mall)☎760/934-8415).

Post office 3330 Main St (Mon–Fri 8.30am–5pm). The Zip code is 93546.

Rock and alpine climbing Mammoth Mountain runs family-oriented sessions on a 32-foot artificial climbing rock (late June to Sept daily 10am–5pm; single climb $10, or $20 an hour, shoes $5) in front of the Mammoth Mountain Inn. To get out on the real stuff, contact Southern Yosemite Mountain Guides (☎1-800/231-4575, ⊛www.symg.com), who offer a rock and alpine guiding service at $365 a day for up to six people. The Bishop-based guide services (see p.323) also run trips in the Mammoth area.

Showers In Mammoth township try Mammoth Mountain RV Park (daily 9am–5pm; $5). In the Devils Postpile area, head for the natural hot-spring bathhouse at the Reds Meadow campground (donations appreciated).

Around Mammoth

Mammoth makes a good base for exploring a little of the **surrounding area**, even as far as Mono Lake and Bodie Ghost Town (see p.337). Closer at hand, there's active geology and a mass of fine alpine scenery around the June Lake Loop.

Hot Creek Geological Site

Three miles east of US-395, on Hot Creek Hatchery Road three miles south of the exit for Mammoth Lakes, the **Hot Creek Geological Site** (daily dawn–dusk; free) is one of the more easily accessible examples of the region's volcanic activity. Jets of boiling water mix with the otherwise chilly snowmelt water to form pools ranging from tepid to scalding. This was once a popular warm bathing spot, but after a geyser erupted in the pool in June 2006 the US Forest Service banned swimming. It's still worth a quick detour, though. For more on the region's hot springs, see the box below.

June Lake Loop

The popularity of the Mammoth Mountain slopes sends some skiers and summer visitors a few miles further north to the relative solitude of **June Lake** and its neighbors, Grant, Silver, and Gull lakes. Reached by way of the sixteen-mile **June Lake Loop** road, which branches off US-395 fifteen miles north of the Mammoth exit, this cluster of high-altitude lakes is one of the most striking in the region, and offers Mammoth's attractions on a more manageable scale.

The small township of **June Lake**, two miles off US-395, is the most alpine-looking of any Sierra community and a place where imitation Swiss chalets don't seem entirely out of place. There's a reasonable range of roofed accommodation here, but the region is primarily a place for **camping**, easily done at one of several $15 Forest Service campgrounds scattered beside the various lakes. These include the relatively busy *June Lake* and *Oh! Ridge* locations (both reservable at ⓦwww.recreation.gov, ☎1-877/444-6777) and the more serene first-come-first-served *Grant Lake*, nine miles further on, where there is boat and fishing-tackle rental.

When the June Lake Loop road hits US-395 at its northern end, turn left for Lee Vining or right to directly access Mono Lake's tufa formations at South Tufa.

Vulcanism and hot springs in the Eastern Sierra

One of the pleasures of any extended visit to the Owens Valley is soaking your bones in one of the numerous **hot springs**. None is well signposted, and most are primarily used by locals who are welcoming enough if you are respectful. Springs tend to be tucked miles away down some rutted dirt road, and often comprise little more than a ring of rocks or a hollowed-out tub into which people have diverted the waters to create pools of differing temperatures. Most are **clothing-optional**, but you'll stand out as a tourist if you don't strip off. We've mentioned several springs in the text – those in the Saline Valley (p.310), Keough's Hot Springs (p.318), Travertine Hot Springs, and Buckeye Hot Springs (both p.339) – but aficionados will want to get hold of either *Hot Springs of the Eastern Sierra* by George Williams III or *Touring California and Nevada Hot Springs* by Matt Bischoff (Falcon). Both have full descriptions and detailed directions.

All the springs are the result of groundwater being heated by magma, which rises close to the surface in these parts. In fact, Mammoth Mountain stands on the edge of a geologically volatile region known as the **Long Valley Caldera**. A vast oval some eighteen miles by twelve, the Caldera was formed 760,000 years ago when a massive eruption spread ash as far away as Nebraska. Vulcanism has continued with the creation of Mammoth Mountain around 50,000 years ago, the Mono Craters and, most recently, **Paoha Island** in Mono Lake, only 300 years back.

In the last couple of decades, scientists have been alerted to swarms of earthquakes and measurable ground-swelling, both of which normally precede eruptions. One cluster of earthquakes in 1989 is thought to have triggered the release of carbon dioxide from an underground gas reservoir, and since 1994 this gas seeping up through the soil has killed 120 acres of trees near Horseshoe Lake.

An **eruption** is not likely in the near future, but the United States Geological Survey continues to monitor the region extensively for ground-temperature changes, land deformation, and frequency and amplitude of quakes. For more, visit the relevant section of the USGS website (ⓦlvo.wr.usgs.gov).

Mono Lake and around

North of Mammoth the landscapes become more open. The Sierra still provides the western backdrop, but as the White Mountains drop away to the south you enter the fringes of the Great Basin, which stretches away across Nevada towards Utah. Mostly sagebrush semi-desert, it's inhospitable territory but a fascinating area centered on the freakish **Mono Lake**. The few people who live hereabouts cluster in the lakeside **Lee Vining** or the peaceful town of **Bridgeport**, but a century ago the place to be was **Bodie**, now a fascinating ghost town.

Mono Lake and Lee Vining

The blue expanse of **MONO LAKE** sits in the middle of a volcanic desert tableland, its sixty square miles reflecting the statuesque, snowcapped mass of the Eastern Sierra Nevada. At over a million years old, it's an ancient lake with two large volcanic islands – the light-colored **Paoha** and the black **Negit** – surrounded by salty, alkaline water. It resembles nothing more than a science-fiction landscape, with great towers and spires formed by mineral deposits ringing the shores; hot springs surround the lake, and all around the basin are signs of lava flows and volcanic activity, especially in the cones of the Mono Craters, just to the south.

The lake's most distinctive feature, the strange, sandcastle-like **tufa** formations, were increasingly exposed from the early 1940s to the mid-1990s as the City of Los Angeles drained away the waters that flow into the lake (see box, opposite). The towers of tufa were formed underwater, where calcium-bearing freshwater springs well up through the carbonate-rich lake water; the calcium and carbonate combine as limestone, slowly growing into the weird formations you can see today.

Lee Vining overlooking Mono Lake, is the only settlement anywhere nearby, offering the usual range of visitor services but not a great deal more.

Arrival and information
Before striking out for a close look at the lake and its tufa, call in at both of the excellent visitor centers. In the heart of Lee Vining sits the town's **Mono Lake Committee Information Center** (daily: July & Aug 9am–10pm; rest of year 9am–5pm; ☎760/647-6595, ⓦwww.leevining.com and ⓦwww.monolake .org); it's partly the showcase for the committee's battle for Mono Lake, featuring an excellent twenty-minute video presentation, but also has helpful staff and an excellent bookstore concentrating on the environment and the Eastern Sierra. There's even a tasteful gift shop and **Internet access**.

A mile north along US-395, the **Mono Basin Scenic Area Visitor Center** (daily: May–Oct 9am–4.30pm; Nov–April generally closed; ☎760/873-2408, ⓦwww.r5.fs.fed.us/inyo) features lake-related exhibits, a good short film about geology, and ecology lectures by rangers.

Exploring Mono Lake
Everyone's first stop is **South Tufa**, five miles east of US-395 via Hwy-120 ($3 for a week's access), the single best place to admire the tufa spires. Boardwalks

---

Yosemite-bound?

Lee Vining is more than two hours by car from Yosemite Valley but makes an affordable base for exploring the eastern reaches of **Yosemite National Park**, particularly the Tuolumne Meadows area, only about twenty miles distant.

and trails lead you among these twenty-foot high limestone cathedrals and along the lakeshore, where photo ops turn up around every corner. About a mile to the east lies **Navy Beach** (free), where there are a few more (less spectacular) spires, and you can float in water at least twice as buoyant as (and a thousand times more alkaline than) sea water. Even towards the end of summer the water is chilly, however, and some find that the salt stings.

A thirsty city and the battle for Mono Lake

4

Mono Lake is one of the oldest on the continent and has survived several ice ages and all the volcanic activity that the area can throw at it, but the lake's biggest threat has been the City of Los Angeles, which owns the riparian rights to Mono Lake's catchment.

From 1892 to 1904, the fledgling city of Los Angeles experienced a twelve-year drought and started looking to the Owens River as a reliable source of water that could be easily channeled to the city. Under the auspices of the Los Angeles Department of Water and Power, the city bought up almost the entire Owens Valley, then diverted the river and its tributaries into a 223-mile, gravity-fed **aqueduct** to take this water to LA. Farms and orchards in the once-productive Owens Valley were rendered useless without water, and Owens Lake near Lone Pine was left to dry up entirely.

The aqueduct was completed in 1913, but the growing city demanded ever more water. Consequently, in 1941, LA diverted four of the five streams that fed Mono Lake through an eleven-mile tunnel into its Owens Valley Aqueduct. This was an engineering marvel, dug through the volcanically active Mono Craters, but it has been overshadowed by the legal battle surrounding the depletion of the lake itself, long one of the biggest **environmental controversies** raging in California.

Over the next fifty years, the **water level** in Mono Lake dropped over forty feet, a disaster not only because of the lake's unique beauty, but also because Mono Lake is the primary nesting ground for **California gulls** and a critical resting point for hundreds of thousands of migratory eared **grebes** and **phalaropes**. The lake was down to roughly half its natural size, and as the levels dropped, the islands in the middle of the lake where the gulls lay their eggs became peninsulas, and the colonies fell prey to coyotes and other mainland predators. Also, as less fresh water reached the lake, the landlocked water became increasingly saline, threatening the unique local ecosystem. About all that will thrive in the harsh conditions are brine shrimp and alkali flies, both essential food sources for the birdlife. Humans, too, are affected by the changes the lake is experiencing: winds blowing across the saltpans left behind by the receding water create alkaline clouds containing selenium and arsenic, both contributors to lung disease.

Seemingly oblivious to the plight of the lake, the City of Los Angeles built a second aqueduct in 1970 and the water level dropped even faster, sometimes falling eighteen inches in a single year. Prompted by scientific reports of an impending ecological disaster, a small group of activists set up the **Mono Lake Committee** (ⓦwww .monolake.org) in 1978, fighting for the preservation of this unique ecosystem partly through the courts and partly through publicity campaigns – "Save Mono Lake" bumper stickers were once de rigueur for concerned citizens. Though the California Supreme Court declared in 1983 that Mono Lake must be saved, it wasn't until 1994 that emergency action was taken. A target water height of 6377ft above sea level (later raised to 6392ft) was grudgingly agreed upon to make **Negit Island** safe for nesting birds. Streams dry for decades are now flowing again, and warm springs formerly located by lakeside interpretive trails are submerged. The target level – 18ft higher than its recorded minimum, but still 25ft below its pre-diversion level – won't be reached at least until the agreement is up for re-negotiation in 2014, something that concentrates the ongoing efforts of the Mono Lake Committee.

To add an educational component to your explorations, join one of the **guided walks** (July to early Sept daily 10am, 1pm & 6pm) around the tufa formations, run by the Mono Basin Scenic Area Visitor Center. You can also sign up for one of the Mono Lake Committee's regular hour-long **canoe trips** (mid-June to early Sept Sat & Sun 8am, 9.30am & 11am; $24; reservations recommended ☎760/647-6595), on which you'll paddle around the tufa towers, learning about their formation, and hear details of migrating birdlife and the brine shrimp they feed off.

You could also go by kayak with Mammoth Lakes-based Caldera Kayaks (reservations on ☎760/934-1691, ⓦwww.calderakayak.com), which runs natural history tours on Mono Lake ($75, or $65 each for groups of 3 or more) and rents sit-on-top kayaks for $40 a day (doubles $60).

Adjacent to the south shore of the lake stands **Panum Crater**, a 700-year-old volcano riddled with deep fissures and fifty-foot towers of lava, accessed by the short and fairly easy **Plug Trail** and **Rim Trail**. This is the most recent of the **Mono Craters**, a series of volcanic cones stretching twelve miles south from here towards Crowley Lake. It constitutes the youngest mountain range in North America, formed entirely over the last forty thousand years.

On the north shore of the lake, three miles along US-395, a side road leads to **Mono County Park**, where a guided boardwalk trail heads down to the lakefront and the best examples of mushroom-shaped tufa towers. A further five miles along this (mostly washboard gravel) side road is the trailhead for the **Black Point Fissures**, the result of a massive underwater eruption of molten lava some thirteen thousand years ago. As the lava cooled and contracted, cracks and fissures formed on the top, some only a few feet wide but as deep as fifty feet. You can explore their depths, but pick up a directions sheet from the visitor center and be prepared for hot, dry, and sandy conditions.

Practicalities

Roofed **accommodation** is concentrated in Lee Vining, where you'll also find a small selection of **places to eat**. There are a number of $15 Forest Service **campgrounds** along Lee Vining Creek off Tioga Pass Road, Hwy-120, or you could consider the county-run *Lundy Canyon* campground ($7; no water) on Lundy Lake Road, about eight miles north of Lee Vining off US-395.

Motels and an RV park

El Mono Motel US-395 ☎760/647-6310, ⓦwww .elmonomotel.com. Basic motel that's the place to go if you're looking for the cheapest roof over your head around Lee Vining. ❸

Mono Vista RV Park US-395 ☎760/647-6401. Central spot catering to RVs ($24–30) and tents ($17), and with showers for nonguests ($2.25 for 5min; daily 9am–6pm).

Murphey's Motel 51493 US-395 ☎1-800/334-6316, ⓦwww.murpheysyosemite.com. Very clean and well-presented motel in the center of town, with cable TV and a/c. Some units have a kitchen at no extra cost, and there are bathrooms with both shower and tub. ❹

Eating

Mono Inn Restaurant Almost five miles north along US-395 ☎760/647-6581, ⓦwww.monoinn

.com. Classy but relaxed restaurant owned by Ansel Adams' granddaughter, featuring lovingly prepared meals served on the patio or inside, both with a superb lake view. Expect the likes of roasted artichoke and goat's cheese tart with leeks ($11), followed by salmon with wild boar tenderloin ($31). Dinner only; closed Tues and Nov to mid-May.

Nicely's On US-395 in Lee Vining ☎760/647-6477. Great Fifties vinyl palace serving up reliable diner food to tourists and dedicated locals. All your favorites are here, including a three-egg omelet ($8), Jumbo burger and fries ($8), breaded steak ($11), and the obligatory slice of one of their many fruit pies ($3.50). Daily 6am–9pm, closed Tues & Wed in winter.

Whoa Nellie Deli Inside the Tioga Gas Mart, Hwy-120 East at US-395 ☎760/647 1088. The best quick food for miles around is served in the unlikely setting of the Mobil gas station, though in summer you can sit at tables outside. There's always a lively atmosphere, and they dish up great tortilla soup, jambalaya ($10), fish tacos ($10), burgers, and steaks, along with espresso, microbrews, and margaritas. There's also pizza by the slice and often live music outside on evenings in July and Aug. Closed Nov–March.

Bodie Ghost Town

In the 1880s, the gold-mining town of **Bodie**, eighteen miles north of Lee Vining and then thirteen miles (three of them dirt) east of US-395, boasted three breweries, some sixty saloons and dance halls, and a population of nearly

▲ Bodie State Historic Park

ten thousand. It also had a well-earned reputation as the raunchiest and most lawless mining camp in the West. Contemporary accounts describe a town that ended each day with a shootout on Main Street, while the firehouse bell, rung once for every year of a murdered man's life, seemed never to stop sounding. The town hit the headlines in 1877, when a rather unproductive mine collapsed and exposed an enormously rich vein. Within four years this was the second largest town in the state after San Francisco, even supporting its own Chinatown. By 1885, **gold and silver** currently valued at around $1.2 billion had been extracted, but a drop in the gold price made mining largely unprofitable. The town dwindled and then was virtually destroyed by two disastrous fires, the second in 1932. The school finally closed in 1942, but a few hardly souls stuck it out until the early 1960s, when the site was taken over by the State of California.

What remains has been turned into **Bodie State Historic Park** (daily: June to early Sept 8am–7pm; early Sept–May 9am–4pm; $3; ☎760/647-6445, Ⓦwww.parks.ca.gov), where the lack of theme-park tampering gives the place an authentically eerie atmosphere absent from other US ghost towns. Bodie is almost 8400ft above sea level and, although the park is open throughout the year, snow often prevents vehicular access between December and April; call for road conditions. If you can get in during that time, bundle up: Bodie is often cited on the national weather report as having the lowest temperature in the US. Whenever you go, remember to bring all you need, as there are no services at the site.

A good self-guided tour booklet ($1) leads you around many of the 150-odd wooden buildings – about six percent of the original town – surviving in a state of arrested decay around the intact town center. Some buildings have been re-roofed and others supported in some way, but it is by and large a faithful preservation: even the dirty dishes are much as they were in the 1940s, little damaged by sixty years of weathering. The **Miner's Union Building** on Main Street was the center of the town's social life; founded in 1877, the union was the first in California, organized by workers at the Standard and Midnight mines. The building now houses a small **museum** (daily: June–Aug 9am–6pm; May & Sept 9am–5pm; free), which paints a graphic picture of the mining life. Various **tours** depart from here in the summer, particularly on weekends, though schedules are flexible and you should call ahead if you have specific interests.

The history talk is free, but there's also a fifty-minute tour of the **Standard Consolidated Stamp Mill** (generally June–Aug daily 11am & 2pm; $5), otherwise off limits, and one along a ridge ($5) which offers some of the best views of Bodie. Other highlights of the town include the **Methodist church** with its intact pipe organ, the **general store** with its beautiful pressed-steel ceiling, the **saloon**, and the **cemetery** on the hill, where lie the remains of Bill Bodey, after whom the town was (sort of) named.

Bridgeport

Seven miles north of the Bodie road junction along US-395 is tiny **Bridgeport**, an isolated village in the middle of a mountain-girt plain that provided the new start in life for fugitive Robert Mitchum in the film-noir masterpiece *Out of the Past*. The gas station he owned in the film is long gone, though the place is otherwise little changed from a pretty high-country ranching community typically full of **fishermen** through the summer. If you want to join their ranks, head to Ken's Sporting Goods, 258 Main Street (☎760/9332-7707, ⓦwww.kenssport.com), for local information and all the tackle you could desire. Otherwise it's only worth stopping here to stroll Bridgeport's small and time-warped Main Street past the dainty white 1880 **County Courthouse**, and to visit the small local history **museum** (late May to Sept Mon–Sat 10am–4pm, Sun noon–4pm; $2), behind the town park in a restored schoolhouse.

Consider sticking around the region long enough to enjoy the local hot springs, one of the most popular ways to wind down after a day wrestling trout. The handiest are **Travertine Hot Springs**: follow US-395 half a mile south of town, turn left into Jack Sawyer Road, then fork left at the first junction and keep right for just over a mile. Many prefer the streamside setting of the lovely **Buckeye Hot Springs**, reached by following US-395 four miles north of Bridgeport, turning left for *Buckeye Campground* and continuing 4.6 miles to where a rough track leads from a dirt parking area to three small pools beside the river.

With the lure of the springs, you may want to stay overnight, and **accommodation** options include a beautifully furnished B&B, *The Cain House*, 340 Main Street (☎1-800/433-2246, ⓦwww.cainhouse.com; closed Nov–May; ❺). There are a couple decent motels, such as the *Silver Maple Inn*, 310 Main Street (☎760/932-7383, ⓦwww.silvermapleinn.com; closed Nov–May; ❹), as well as the decidedly decrepit *Victoria House* across the street (☎760/932-7020; closed Nov–May; ❶), a building which, like several in Bridgeport, is said to have been transported here from Bodie. One of the handful of places open year-round is the *Bridgeport Inn*, US-395 (☎760/932-1160, ⓦwww.thebridgeportinn.com; ❸), which has comfortable hotel and motel rooms and its own restaurant.

For **eating**, there are good breakfasts and lunches at *Hays Street Café*, 21 Hays Street, on the southern approach to town; decent espresso at *The Pony Expresso Coffee Co.*, 157 Main Street (☎760/932-7798); reasonably priced grills, sandwiches, and specialty pizzas at *Rhino's Bar & Grill*, 226 Main Street (☎760/932-7345); and top-rated fine dining at *1881*, 362 Main Street (☎760/932-1918; mid-April to Oct daily; Nov & Dec Thurs–Sun; rest of year closed), where local trout ($25) might be followed by vanilla crème brûlée ($7). A drive six miles south along US-395 is rewarded by reliably excellent dining at *Virginia Creek Settlement* (☎760/932-7780, ⓦwww.virginiacrksettlement.com; closed Mon), renowned in the region for its fresh and tasty steaks (from $19), pasta dishes ($13–15), and pizzas (from $13) – particularly the excellent gorgonzola.

From Bridgeport, US-395 continues north into Nevada, through the capital Carson City and the gambling hotspot of Reno, both described fully in Chapter Eight.

Travel details

Neither Greyhound buses nor Amtrak trains run any services within this region. The only long-distance bus services are the CREST bus along the Owens Valley (see p.297) and the summer-only YARTS service from Mammoth Lakes to Yosemite (see p.326).

Buses

Bishop to: Big Pine (3 weekly; 15min); Bridgeport (3 weekly; 2hr); Independence (3 weekly; 45min); Lee Vining (3 weekly; 1hr 25min); Lone Pine (3 weekly; 1hr 10min); Mammoth Lakes (3 weekly; 50min); Reno (3 weekly; 4hr 45min); Ridgecrest (3 weekly; 2hr 30min).

Mammoth Lakes to: Bishop (3 weekly; 50min); Lee Vining (3–5 weekly; 30min); Tuolumne Meadows (summer 2–7 weekly; 1hr); Yosemite Valley (summer 2–7 weekly; 3hr).

Reno to: Bishop (3 weekly; 4hr 45min); Bridgeport (3 weekly; 2hr 50min); Lee Vining (3 weekly; 3hr 20min); Mammoth Lakes (3 weekly; 4hr).

Ridgecrest to: Big Pine (3 weekly; 2hr); Bishop (3 weekly; 2hr 20min); Independence (3 weekly; 1hr 35min); Lone Pine (3 weekly; 1hr 20min).

5

The San Joaquin Valley, Yosemite, and the Western Sierra

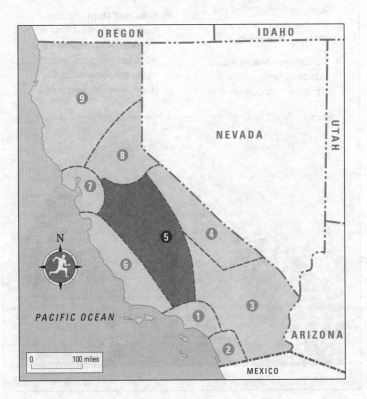

CHAPTER 5 # Highlights

* **Basque cuisine** Sample one of Bakersfield's Basque restaurants, notably the *Noriega Hotel*, where groaning dishes and jugs of wine are served at long, communal tables. See p.349

* **Kern River** Experience some of California's finest and most accessible whitewater rafting on the Kern, which spills off the lofty slopes of Mount Whitney. See p.349

* **Forestiere Underground Gardens** Delve below the baked hardpan into a labyrinth of rooms where an Italian subway tunneler carved out his home and fruit orchard. See p.356

* **Giant Forest** The densest collection of the world's largest trees, the mighty sequoias, looms in this section of Sequoia National Park, accessible by a panoply of trails. See p.370

* **Hike Half Dome** Follow the wonderful Mist Trail to the summit of Yosemite's most famous peak, which forms the sheerest cliff in North America. See p.402

▲ Half Dome, Yosemite National Park

The San Joaquin Valley, Yosemite, and the Western Sierra

The vast interior of California – stretching three hundred miles from the edges of the Mojave Desert in the south right up to the Gold Country and Northern California – is covered by the wide floor of the agricultural **San Joaquin Valley**, flanked on the east by the massive Sierra Nevada Mountains. It's a region of unparalleled beauty, yet the ninety percent of Californians who live on the coast are barely aware of the area, encountering it only while driving between LA and San Francisco on the admittedly tedious I-5, and consider it the height of hicksville.

The San Joaquin Valley is radically different from the rest of California. During the 1940s, this arid land was made super-fertile by a massive program of aqueduct building, using water flowing from the mountains to irrigate the area. The valley, as flat as a pancake, now almost totally comprises farmland, periodically enlivened by scattered cities that offer a taste of ordinary California life away from the glitz of LA and San Francisco. More than anywhere else in the state, the abundance of low-paying agricultural jobs has encouraged decades of immigration from south of the border, and there are now towns in the San Joaquin Valley where Spanish is the first language and **taquerias** outnumber burger joints ten to one. Fertile land and cheap labor have brought relative wealth to large numbers of San Joaquin Valley residents, who have responded by becoming increasingly mobile. This, and town planning which dictates that everyone must drive everywhere, has led to a dense photochemical haze – trapped by mountains on both flanks – that is so thick the pristine peaks once visible throughout the year are now seldom seen.

If coastal Californians pass through the San Joaquin Valley, it is to reach the **national parks** that cover the foothills and upper reaches of the Sierra Nevada Mountains. From the valley, a gentle ascent through rolling, grassy foothills takes you into dense forests of huge pine and fir trees, interspersed with tranquil lakes and cut by deep rocky canyons. The most impressive sections are protected

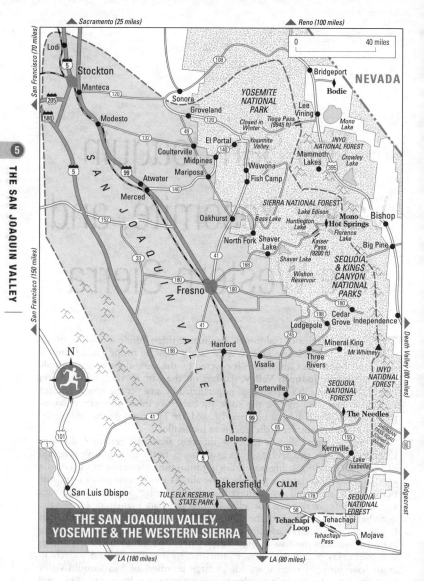

Sacramento (25 miles)

Reno (100 miles)

0   40 miles

NEVADA

Bridgeport

Bodie

Lodi

Stockton

Manteca

Sonora

Groveland

YOSEMITE NATIONAL PARK

Lee Vining

Mono Lake

Modesto

Closed in Winter

Tioga Pass (9945 ft)

INYO NATIONAL FOREST

Coulterville

El Portal

Yosemite Valley

Mammoth Lakes

Crowley Lake

Midpines

Wawona

Mariposa

Atwater

Fish Camp

Merced

SIERRA NATIONAL FOREST

Lake Edison

Oakhurst

Bass Lake

Huntington Lake

Mono Hot Springs

Bishop

North Fork

Shaver Lake

Florence Lake

Kaiser Pass (9200 ft)

Big Pine

Shaver Lake

SEQUOIA & KINGS CANYON NATIONAL PARKS

Wishon Reservoir

Fresno

Cedar Grove

Independence

Lodgepole

Hanford

Mineral King

Three Rivers

Mt Whitney

Visalia

INYO NATIONAL FOREST

Porterville

SEQUOIA NATIONAL FOREST

The Needles

Delano

SHERMAN PASS ROAD (Closed in Winter)

Kernville

Lake Isabella

Bakersfield

CALM

San Luis Obispo

TULE ELK RESERVE STATE PARK

SEQUOIA NATIONAL FOREST

THE SAN JOAQUIN VALLEY, YOSEMITE & THE WESTERN SIERRA

Tehachapi Loop

Tehachapi

Tehachapi Pass

Mojave

San Francisco (70 miles)

San Francisco (150 miles)

San Joaquin Valley

Death Valley (80 miles)

Ridgecrest

LA (180 miles)

LA (80 miles)

within three national parks. **Sequoia** is home to the last few stands of huge prehistoric trees, giant sequoias that form the centerpiece of a rich natural landscape. **Kings Canyon** shares a common border with Sequoia – together they make up one huge park – and presents a similar, slightly wilder array of Sierra wonders. **Yosemite**, with its towering walls of silvery granite artfully sculpted by Ice Age glaciers, is the most famous of the parks and one of the absolute must-sees in California. While only a few narrow, twisting roads penetrate the hundred miles of wilderness in between these three parks, the entire region is crisscrossed by hiking trails leading up into the pristine alpine backcountry of the **Sierra Nevada**, which contains the glistening summits of some of the highest mountains in the country.

Getting around
Drivers who aren't particularly interested in exploring the wilds can simply barrel through on I-5, an arrow-straight interstate through the western edge of the San Joaquin Valley that's the quickest route between LA and San Francisco. Six daily **trains** and frequent Greyhound **buses** run through the valley, stopping at the larger cities and towns along Hwy-99 – Merced being the most useful with its bus connections to Yosemite. Otherwise, getting to the mountains is all but impossible without your own vehicle, though with a bit of advance planning you can join one of the many camping trips organized by the Sierra Club, the California-based environmentalist group (see box, p.386).

The San Joaquin Valley

The **SAN JOAQUIN VALLEY** grows more fruit and vegetables than any other agricultural region of its size in the world – a fact that touches the lives, in one way or another, of every one of its inhabitants. The area is much more conservative and Midwestern in feel than the rest of California, but even if the nightlife begins and ends with the local ice cream parlor, it can all be refreshingly small-scale and enjoyable after visiting the big coastal cities. Admittedly, none of the towns has the energy to detain you long, and, between the settlements, the drab hundred-mile vistas of almond groves and vineyards can be sheer torture. The weather, too, can be a challenge – summers in the San Joaquin are frequently scorching and winters bring the cold and thick tule fog, so aim to visit in spring or fall, particularly March, when the fruit trees are in full bloom.

    Bakersfield, the first town you come to across the rocky peaks north of Los Angeles, is hardly the most prepossessing destination, but its **country music** scene has long been the best in the state. And, surprisingly enough, there are few better places on this side of the Atlantic to sample **Basque cuisine**. Bakersfield also offers a museum recording the beginnings of the local population, and the chance to sample some of the state's finest **whitewater rafting** on the nearby Kern River. Further on lies likeable **Visalia** and the well-restored turn-of-the-20th century town of **Hanford**. In many ways the region's linchpin, **Fresno** is the closest thing the valley has to a bustling urban center. Though economically thriving, it's frequently cited as one of the least desirable place to live in the US, and on arrival it's easy to see why. Its redeeming features, such as they are, take a bit of time to discover, though you shouldn't pass up the opportunity to visit the bizarre labyrinth of **Forestiere Underground Gardens**.

    Beyond Fresno, in the northern reaches of the valley, lie sedate **Merced** and slightly more boisterous **Modesto**, the inspiration for George Lucas's movie *American Graffiti*. At the top end of the valley, **Stockton** is scenically improved by the delta that connects the city to the sea, but is otherwise a place of few pleasures, though you may pass through on your way from San Francisco to the Gold Country or the national parks.

Bakersfield and around

BAKERSFIELD's flat and featureless look, surrounded by nodding-donkey oil pumps, does nothing to suggest that this is one of the nation's liveliest country music communities, with a batch of venues where locally and nationally rated musicians perform. It also has the country's largest community of Basque descent, making it *the* place to taste Basque cuisine, at its best in one of the specialist restaurants run by descendants of sheepherders who migrated to the San Joaquin Valley in the early twentieth century.

The town was founded in 1851 when Colonel Thomas Baker made his field available as a stagecoach rest stop. Since then the place has had its ups and downs, and the formerly moribund downtown area is currently seeing something of a renaissance, with half a dozen new bars opening up. On the outskirts of town a progressive small **zoo** warrants a visit, and if the hills are calling out, it's only an hour's drive east to **Lake Isabella**, a reservoir in the Sierra foothills that's well geared to family camping and watersports. Without your own equipment, you're better off making for **Kernville**, a few miles up the Kern River, which provides the venue for a full range of springtime **whitewater rafting**.

The Town

Bakersfield owes its existence to the fertile soil around the Kern River – once the longest river in the state but now dammed to form Lake Isabella – and to the discovery of local oil and gas deposits. The **Kern County Museum**, a mile north of downtown at 3801 Chester Avenue (Mon–Sat 10am–5pm, Sun

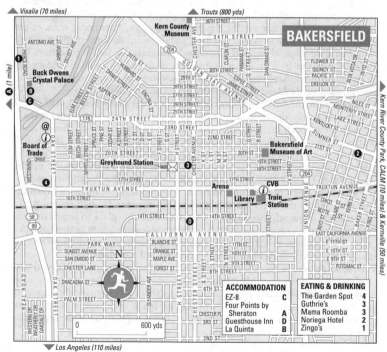

noon–5pm, last admission 3pm; $8; ⓦ www.kcmuseum.org), documents the town's petrochemical roots through "Black Gold: The Oil Experience," a modern science, technology, and history exhibit complete with 1922 nodding-donkey pump, a moderately enlightening 18-minute movie, and an unconvincing mock-up "undersea journey" in a diving bell. Leave a little time to browse the fifty-plus (mostly) restored rail wagons and assorted buildings, many dating from the late nineteenth or early twentieth century. Visitors needing to get kids out of the heat will want to check out the hands-on science exhibits in the site's **Lori Brock Children's Discovery Center**.

For something a little more highbrow, visit the **Bakersfield Museum of Art**, 1930 R Street (Tues–Fri 10am–4pm and Thurs to 7.30pm, Sat & Sun noon–4pm; $5; ⓦ www.bmoa.org), which usually has interesting touring exhibits, along with its own collection with works by Georgia O'Keeffe and Diego Rivera.

Wildlife fans will have to stray a little further out, where the greatest interest is at the **California Living Museum (CALM)**, 10500 Alfred Harrell Way

Country music in Bakersfield

The main reason to dally for more than a few hours in Bakersfield is to hear **country music** – on any weekend the town's honky-tonks reverberate to the sounds of some of the best country musicians in the US, many of them local residents.

The roots of Bakersfield's country music scene are with the dust bowl Okies who arrived in the San Joaquin Valley during the Depression, bringing their hillbilly instruments and campfire songs with them. This rustic entertainment quickly broadened into more contemporary styles, developed in the bars and clubs where future legends such as Merle Haggard and Buck Owens cut their teeth. A failed attempt to turn Bakersfield into "Nashville West" during the 1960s left the town eager to promote the distinctive "**Bakersfield Sound**," a far less slick and commercial affair than its Tennessee counterpart. You can gain an inkling of the Bakersfield Sound from the 1988 hit *Streets of Bakersfield*, a duet by Buck Owens and Dwight Yoakam, but you really need to get out and listen to some live music.

Venues

To find out **what's on**, read the Thursday Entertainment section of the *Bakersfield Californian*, or phone one of the venues we've listed. Fridays and Saturdays are the liveliest nights, although there's often something to enjoy during the week. There's seldom a cover charge for someone spinning platters, and only a small one for live sets (perhaps $5), usually entailing one band playing for four or five hours from around 8pm and taking a fifteen-minute break every hour. Stetson hats and Nudie shirts are the sartorial order of the day, and audiences span generations.

One venue not to be missed is ⚘ *Trouts*, 805 N Chester Avenue (☏ 661/399-6700), a slightly seedy country music bar a couple of miles north of downtown that's been in business for over forty years. Closer to town, the ersatz-Western *Buck Owens' Crystal Palace*, 2800 Buck Owens Boulevard (☏ 661/328-7560, ⓦ www.buckowens .com), is very much the showpiece for the Buck Owens empire, though the master himself died in 2006. It's a cabaret-style setup (Tues–Thurs free, Fri & Sat $5) with burgers and grills available while local and touring bands perform on Wednesday and Thursday; Tuesday is karaoke night. Buck's band, The Buckeroos (sometime fronted by his son Buddy), perform on Friday and Saturday nights at 7.30pm, playing numbers from Buck's back catalogue, classic country tunes, and beyond.

Cases around the walls make up a small **museum** (Tues–Sat 11am–4pm; $5, but visible for nothing during any show) of knick-knacks Buck picked up over the years – promo photos, Buck Rogers bolo tie clasps, platinum records, red-white-and-blue guitars, and a glittering display of rhinestone jackets.

(daily: Feb–Oct 9am–5pm; Nov–Jan 9am–4pm; $6.50; Ⓦ www.calmzoo.org), some twelve miles east of town off the road to Kernville. It's effectively a small zoo, but one focusing solely on California's native species and only those animals that have been injured and cannot be returned to the wild. Stroll around the landscaped grounds past the golden and bald eagles, pause to admire the black bears and bobcats, then repair to the reptile house with its array of snakes and lizards. The animals tend to hide from the heat of the day, so come early. Half an hour west of Bakersfield is the **Tule Elk Reserve State Park**, Morris Road (daily 8am–sunset; free), where around thirty of these beasts can be seen from a viewing platform, best at 3pm when they are fed nearby. Large herds used to roam hereabouts, but hunting and loss of habitat forced them to the brink of extinction early in the twentieth century; only projects like this and a major relocation to the Owens Valley (see p.310) have saved them. To get here, follow Stockdale Highway west for twenty miles, and then just after crossing I-5, follow the signs a mile or so south on Morris Road.

Practicalities

Bakersfield is an important public transportation hub and the downtown area – half a dozen blocks each way from the junction of 19th Street and Chester Avenue – is home to both the **Amtrak station**, 601 Truxton Avenue, the southern terminus of Amtrak's San Joaquins route from San Francisco (connections to LA via Thruway bus), and the **Greyhound station**, 1820 18th Street (Ⓣ661/327-5617). Traveling by bus, you may need to change routes here – although overnight stops are rarely necessary. The best source of information is the **Convention and Visitors Bureau (CVB)**, 515 Truxton Avenue (Mon–Fri 8.30am–5.30pm; Ⓣ661/425-7353, Ⓦ www.bakersfieldcvb.org), right by the Amtrak station. There's also the **Kern County Board of Trade**, 2101 Oak Street (Mon–Fri 8am–5pm; Ⓣ1-800/500-5376, Ⓦ www.visitkern.com), which has free **Internet access** on a single computer, and Wi-Fi. Free Internet access is likewise available at the **library**, 710 Truxton Avenue (Mon & Tues 10am–9pm, Weds & Thurs noon–9pm, Fri & Sat 10am–6pm; Ⓣ661/868-0701).

Bakersfield is dotted with clusters of mainstream **motels** and **hotels** (all excellent value), but little else. Though there are plenty of other worthwhile options for **eating**, you shouldn't pass through without trying Basque food. **Nightlife** now extends beyond slide-guitar and torch songs, with a number of places downtown offering local rock bands several nights a week, usually with no cover charge. Stroll 19th Street and see what turns up.

Accommodation

EZ-8 2604 Buck Owens Blvd Ⓣ661/322-1901, Ⓦ www.ez8motels.com. One of Bakersfield's cheapest motels, with a pool and handily placed a short stagger from *Buck Owens' Crystal Palace*. ❷

Four Points by Sheraton 5101 California Ave Ⓣ1-800/368-7764, Ⓦ www.fourpoints.com. One of the nicest places in town, with acres of attractive grounds, a swanky restaurant, and very comfy rooms. ❻

GuestHouse Inn 1301 Chester Ave Ⓣ661/327-7122, Ⓦ www.guesthouseintl.com. This comfortable and tidy downtown motel has been substantially revamped, making it the best bet in the center of town. Far nicer than it looks from outside. ❹

Kern River County Park 15 miles east of downtown, Ⓣ661/868-7000. On the shores of Lake Ming are Bakersfield's nearest tent sites, grassy and reasonably shaded sites but with no hookups. Mid-March to mid-Oct $22 per vehicle; mid-Oct to mid-March $11 per vehicle.

La Quinta 3232 Riverside Drive Ⓣ1-800/642-4271, Ⓦ www.lq.com. Comfortable midrange hotel close to *Buck Owens' Crystal Palace*, with pool, free Wi-Fi, and complimentary continental breakfast. ❹

Eating and drinking

Buck Owens' Crystal Palace 2800 Buck Owens Drive Ⓣ661/328-7560, Ⓦ www.buckowens.com.

Eat a meal while you watch a show (see p.347) or come for the extensive Sunday brunch (9.30am–2pm; $20).

The Garden Spot 3320 Truxton Ave. Makes healthy eating a pleasure with an all-you-can-eat salad bar buffet for around $8 for lunch, $10 for dinner. Closed Sat.

Guthrie's Alley Cat 1525 Wall St. In an alley parallel to 19th St, this dim bar with pool table is a long-standing Bakersfield favorite.

Mama Roomba 1814 Eye St ☎661/322-6262. Cuban and Mexican touches add interest to this small tapas restaurant, where you might sample garlic octopus ($9), corn-and-cheese empanadas ($7.25), or a larger dish like Havana-style pork chops with fried onions ($13). Wash it down with a jug of sangria or repair to the intimate bar.

Noriega Hotel 525 Summer St ☎661/322-8419. The most authentic Basque place is this century-old restaurant, where louvered shutters and ceiling fans cool diners at long, communal tables. They serve an all-you-can-eat set menu of soup, salad, beans, pasta, a meat dish, and cheese to finish, along with jug wine to keep you going. There are three sittings ($10 breakfast from 7–9am, $13 lunch at noon sharp, and $19 dinner at 7pm), and reservations are recommended for dinner, which will include the Basque specialty of pickled tongue. Closed Mon.

Zingo's 3201 Buck Owens Blvd. To stay in tune with Bakersfield's country music persona, eat at this 24-hour truck stop whose frilly-aproned waitresses deliver plates of diner staples. Closed Sat & Sun 1–5am.

Lake Isabella, Kernville, and the Kern River

After a night spent in Bakersfield's honky-tonks, clear your head by driving forty-five miles east to the mile-wide **LAKE ISABELLA**, typically alive with windsurfers, jet skiers, and anglers. Mountain biking and rock climbing are also popular activities here, and the place is heaving in the summer. Information on activities and rental outlets are available from the lakeside **visitor center** (mid-May to Oct daily 8am–5pm; Nov to mid-May Mon–Fri 8am–4.30pm; ☎760/379-5646), half a mile north of Hwy-178 along Hwy-155. Developed though barely shaded **campsites** ring the dry, sagebrush lakeside, almost all costing $19 a pitch: you can reserve at least a week in advance (☎1-877/444-6777, ⓦwww.recreation.gov), but first-come-first-served sites are typically available. If the frenetic lake activity doesn't suit, backtrack to the riverside *Hobo* campground ($17) on Old Fern Canyon Road, parallel to Hwy-178.

Lake Isabella is fed by the **Kern River**, which churns down from the slopes of Mount Whitney and spills into the lake at the small, appealing town of **KERNVILLE** on its northern shore. It's a peaceful, retiree-dominated place, but come on a summer weekend, or anytime in July and August, and it's full of adrenaline junkies blasting mountain bikes along the local trails or negotiating the rapids in all manner of aquatic paraphernalia. Most people come to ride the Kern, which ranks as one of the steepest "navigable" rivers in the United States, dropping over 12,000ft in 150 miles and producing some truly exhilarating **whitewater** opportunities, especially along a forty-mile section around Kernville. The tougher stuff is generally left to the experts, but during the season, which usually runs from May until early August (longer after heavy winters), commercial rafting operators vie for custom (see box, p.350). If you've got time to kill while friends raft, delve into the native, gold mining, and lumbering history in the **Kern Valley Museum**, 49 Big Blue Road (Thurs–Sun 10am–4pm; free), or take a look at their film room of movies shot in the area, mostly Westerns: John Wayne features prominently.

Practicalities

For general information contact the central **Chamber of Commerce**, 11447 Kernville Rd (Mon–Sat 9am–noon & 2–4pm; ☎760/376-2629, ⓦwww .kernvillechamber.org); for details on the wooded country to the north, call in at the **Kernville Ranger Station**, 105 Whitney Road (mid-May to Oct daily 8am–5pm; Nov to mid-May Mon–Fri 8am–4.30pm; ☎760/376-3781, ⊛www .fs.fed.us/r5/sequoia), next to the museum.

Kernville is big enough to have a bank, ATM, post office, and supermarket, but there isn't a very wide range of **accommodation**. Central motels start at around $85, and tent **campers** can stay in the various RV parks around town, but are better off in the string of riverside campgrounds to the north (see opposite).

Accommodation

Falling Waters River Resort 15729 Sierra Way, 3 miles north of town ☎1-888/376-2242, ⊛www .chuckrichards.com. Low-key, child- and dog-friendly complex with a range of accommodation: simple lodge rooms (❸), more spacious motel-style rooms (❺), and cottages slightly marred by overenthusiastic decor (❺). ❸–❺
Kern River Inn B&B 119 Kern River Drive ☎1-800/986-4382, ⊛www.kernriverinn.com. Sumptuous B&B with individually decorated river-view rooms featuring whirlpool tub or fireplace. Midweek ❺, weekends ❻

The Kernville Inn 11042 Kernville Rd ☎1-877/393-7900, ⊛www.kernvilleinn.com. The best-value motel, right in the center and with a pool and comfortable rooms, some with kitchens. Rooms ❹, with kitchen ❺
Whispering Pines Lodge 13745 Sierra Way, a mile north of town ☎1-877/241-4100, ⊛www .kernvalley.com/inns. Luxurious cottages, many with balconies overlooking the river, plus a nice pool and a delicious breakfast served on the terrace. Midweek ❻, weekend ❼

Kern River adventures

Three main sections of the Kern River are regularly rafted: the **Lower Kern**, downstream of Lake Isabella (Class III–IV; generally June–Aug); the **Upper Kern**, immediately upstream of Kernville (Class III–IV; early May to June); and **The Forks**, fifteen miles upstream of Kernville (Class V; early May to June), which drops an impressive sixty feet per mile.

By far the most popular section is the Upper Kern, the site for the **Lickety-Split** rafting trip – one for families and first-timers, with some long, bouncy rapids. This one-hour excursion (including the bus ride to the put-in) costs around $28, and with over half a dozen operators running trips throughout the day, there is little need to book ahead. Other trips run less frequently, and you should reserve in advance, though you've got a better chance midweek when crowds are thinner and prices a few dollars lower. The pick of these are the day-trips on the Upper Kern, which run close to the $150 mark ($180 at weekends), the two-day Lower Kern trip ($310, weekends $340), and the two- or three-day backcountry trips on The Forks, which range around $700–900. Wetsuits (essential early in the season and for the longer trips) usually cost extra. Within this basic framework there are any number of permutations: check with Chuck Richards' Whitewater (☎1-800/624-5950, ⊛www.chuckrichards.com) or Whitewater Voyages (☎1-800/488-7238, ⊛www.whitewatervoyages.com).

As you'd expect, kayaking is also big here, and Sierra South, 11300 Kernville Road (☎1-800/457-2082, ⊛www.sierrasouth.com), supplement their rafting operation with one of southern California's top **kayaking** schools, offering Eskimo rolling sessions, instruction at all levels, and guided multiday river trips, all generally costing around $150 a day. They also offer full-day beginner **rock climbing** lessons ($120) on the nearby Kernville Slab, as do Mountain & River Adventures, 11113 Kernville Road (☎1-800/861-6553, ⊛www.mtnriver.com), who stretch up to intermediate grades and have their own outdoor climbing wall three miles north along Sierra Way.

Permits, available free from the Kernville Ranger Station and any of the area's other Forest Service offices, are necessary even if you have your own equipment for private rafting or kayaking expeditions.

Eating and drinking

Big Blue Bear Gift Shop 101 Piute Drive
℡760/376-2442. Espresso haven with free Wi-Fi.
Johnny McNally's Sierra Way, 15 miles north of
Kernville ℡760/376-2430. Great steaks in an
unpretentious family-dining setting. The 40-ounce
porterhouse ($45) will see you through the next day
as well.
Kern River Brewing Co 13415 Sierra Way
℡760/376-2337, ⓦwww.kernriverbrewing.com.

Lively restaurant and bar serving burgers, salads,
stuffed pitas, and great fish'n'chips (all $8–10),
plus four toothsome microbrews. It's all eased
down with occasional live music (particularly on
summer weekends).
That's Italian 9 Big Blue Rd ℡760/376-6020.
Reliable restaurant by the central park serving
northern Italian cuisine. Closed Mon & weekday
lunches.

Sequoia National Forest

Wedged between Lake Isabella and Sequoia National Park lies **SEQUOIA
NATIONAL FOREST**, a vast canopy of pine trees punctuated by massive,
glacier-polished domes and gleaming granite spires. Much of it is untouched
wilderness that's barely less stunning than the national parks to the north, and
in recognition of this a large section was re-designated the **Giant Sequoia
National Monument** (unrestricted access) as one of Bill Clinton's final
gestures before leaving office. True to its name, it's packed with giant sequoias
(in 38 small groves), and, as the forest is far less visited than the national parks,
it's perfect for those seeking total solitude; hiking trails run virtually everywhere.
Camping only requires a free permit for your stove or fire, available from the
ranger stations dotted around the perimeter of the forest, which also have details
of the scores of drive-in campsites – some free, others up to $17 a pitch.

There's **no public transportation** through here, but the roads are in good
shape, though subject to **snow closure** in winter (mid-Nov to mid-May). To
find out about conditions and closures, visit ⓦwww.dot.ca.gov/hq/roadinfo or
call ℡1-800/427-7623.

Sierra Way and the Western Divide Highway

The best access into the forest is along Sierra Way from Lake Isabella, which
passes through Kernville and follows the Upper Kern River past numerous basic
camping sites (free) and half a dozen shaded, waterside campgrounds ($17;
reserve for summer weekends on ℡1-877/444-6777), eventually reaching
Johnsondale Bridge, twenty miles north of Kernville. From the bridge, hikers
can follow the **River Trail** upstream, passing the numerous rapids of The Forks
section of the Kern, great for spotting rafters and kayakers on weekend afternoons and even for camping at one of several free walk-in sites along the river;
the first is about a ten-minute hike.

Beyond Johnsondale Bridge the road splits. The eastern branch follows the
Sherman Pass Road, which cuts through the Golden Trout Wilderness to Hwy-
395 and the Owens Valley, passing numerous free "dispersed" **campgrounds**:
essentially just designated sites with no toilets or piped water. Staying instead on
Sierra Way, you turn west and start climbing to tiny Johnsondale – just a seasonal
store and restaurant – where a trail access road cuts 23 miles north to the Jerkey
Meadow trailhead. The access road gives great views of The Needles (see p.352)
and abundant dispersed **camping**, best four miles along at *Camping Area 4*,
where the stream has sculpted a lovely series of **bathing pools** and smooth
rocks for sunning yourself. A few miles further along, the *Lower Peppermint*
campground ($14) has toilets and water.

Continuing along Sierra Way, it's seven miles to a road junction where you
join the twisting and narrow **Western Divide Highway** (Hwy-190) which,
after a couple of miles, passes the **Trail of a Hundred Giants** ($5 per vehicle),

an easy, shaded interpretive trail around a stand of huge sequoias. Among more giant trees across the road is the *Redwood Meadow* campground (early April to mid-Nov; $17; book at ☏1-877/444-6777 or ⓦwww.recreation.gov).

Further north, you catch glimpses of magnificent Sierra vistas as the road climbs above the 7000-foot mark, but for the best views it's worth pressing on five miles to the 7200-foot exfoliated scalp of **Dome Rock**, just half a mile off the highway, or **The Needles**, a further three miles on. This series of tall pinnacles – the Magician, the Wizard, and the Warlock, among others – presents some of America's most demanding crack climbs, and can be visited on the moderate, undulating hiking and biking **Needles Lookout Trail** (5 miles round-trip; 2hr), which starts three miles off the highway up a dirt road. The final switchback leads to a fire-lookout station (generally open to visitors Wed–Sun 9am–6pm during the June–Oct fire season), precariously perched atop the Magician with supreme views over the Kern Valley and across to Mount Whitney. Nearby **accommodation** includes the *Quaking Aspen* campground (early April to mid-Nov; $15), half a mile to the north of The Needles; the woodsy *Mountain Top B&B*, half a mile to the south (☏1-888/867-4784, ⓦwww.mountaintopbnb. com; $125); and the adjacent *Ponderosa Lodge* (☏559/542-2579; ❹), with pleasant motel rooms, a restaurant, bar, grocery store, and expensive gas. From here onward, the Western Divide Highway executes endless twists and turns forty miles down to the valley town of Porterville, where you can turn right for Sequoia and Kings Canyon national parks or continue straight to rejoin Hwy-99 and head north to Visalia.

Visalia

From Bakersfield north towards Fresno on Hwy-99, the oil wells fade into full-blown agricultural territory. Only a couple of towns warrant your time, the first and largest being **VISALIA**, seventy miles north of Bakersfield and just east of Hwy-99 on Hwy-198. As the closest substantial town to the southern entrance of Sequoia National Park – less than an hour's drive away along Hwy-198 – Visalia makes a comfortable base for exploring the untrameled surrounding wilderness. It also has the only **bus service** into the parks.

Owing to a large oak forest that offered both shade and timber for home-building, Visalia was the first place in the San Joaquin Valley to be settled. Although the forest is gone, large numbers of oaks and sycamores are still planted around the city, and locals put an extraordinary amount of care into the upkeep of parks and gardens. In short, it's a pretty place, with a compact and leafy town center that invites strolls in the relative cool of the evening.

Central Visalia is best seen on foot: self-guided walking tours of the grand old houses in its older parts can be obtained free from the **CVB** (see opposite). Further out, **Mooney Grove Park**, three miles down South Mooney Boulevard (daily except Tues & Weds; nominally $6 per vehicle, though often free midweek), contains a huge slice of a giant sequoia which marks the **Tulare County Museum** (Mon, Thurs & Fri 10am–4pm, Sat 1–4pm; free), packed with intricate Yokuts basketry and a collection of buildings and agricultural equipment brought here from around the region.

Close to the park's south entrance, and visible from South Mooney Boulevard, you'll find a bronze replica of the *End of the Trail* statue, which was made for the 1915 Panama-Pacific International Exposition in San Francisco and was intended to mark the closing of the western frontier. It portrays the defeat of Native Americans at the hands of advancing white settlers and is intentionally gloomy. The statue became well known throughout the West, and still inspires a host of copies; the original was situated here for fifty years before being given to the National Cowboy & Western Heritage Museum near Oklahoma City.

Practicalities

Greyhound buses, along with KART buses from Hanford (℡559/584-0101) and the shuttle to Sequoia and Kings Canyon national parks (see p.362), arrive at the downtown **transit center**, 425 E Oak Street (℡559/734-3507), adjacent to the **CVB**, 220 N Santa Fe Avenue (Mon & Wed–Fri 8am–5pm, Tues 10am–5pm; ℡1-800/524-0303, @www.visitvisalia.org). There's free **Internet access** at the Tulare County Library, 200 W Oak Avenue (℡559/733-6954).

Accommodation here is a bargain; if you're on a budget, this is a good place to splash out on a B&B. Visalia also has some of the best places to **eat** for miles around.

Accommodation

Ben Maddox House B&B 601 N Encina St ℡1-800/401-9800, @www .benmaddoxhouse.com. Sumptuous accommodation in a large, pool- and spa-equipped redwood house built in 1876 for Ben Maddox, the man who brought hydroelectricity to the San Joaquin Valley. **❺**

Econo Lodge 1400 S Mooney Boulevard ℡1-800/242-4261. The pick of several motels along this stretch, recently renovated, with pool and a light breakfast included. **❷**

Lamp Liter Inn 3300 W Mineral King Ave ℡1-800/662-6692, @www.lampliter.net. Pleasant 100-room hotel surrounded by lawns and featuring a very nice pool, sports bar, and grill. **❹**

The Spalding House 631 N Encina ℡559/739-7877, @www.thespaldinghouse.com. Local lumberman W.R. Spalding built this fine Colonial Revival home, now a beautifully appointed B&B. Suites all have separate bathroom and sitting room and come with a gourmet breakfast. **❹**

Eating and drinking

Brewbakers 219 E Main St ℡559/627-2739. Dine among the polished steel and brass tanks of this lively brewpub, which serves tempting burgers, salads, and thick, chewy pizza, all for under $10. There's often live music to encourage you to sample their half-dozen brews.

Café 225 225 W Main St ℡559/733-2967. A modern bistro and tapas bar with an eclectic menu that features artichoke fritters ($5), baked red snapper ($17), and prosciutto and roasted garlic pizza ($12).

Tazzaria 208 W Main St ℡559/732-5282. Relaxed spot for good espresso and tea. Open 6am–6pm.

The Vintage Press 216 N Willis St ℡559/733-3033, @www.thevintagepress .com. Serving California continental cuisine, this fine restaurant has ranked as one of the best in the San Joaquin Valley for four decades. Succumb to wild mushrooms in puff pastry with cognac, followed by red snapper with toasted almonds and capers, and finally a dessert and coffee, all for around $55 a head – or much more if you explore the vast and wonderful wine list.

Hanford

HANFORD, twenty miles west of Visalia on Hwy-198, was named after James Hanford, a paymaster on the Southern Pacific Railroad who became popular with his employees when he took to paying them in gold. The town formed part of a spur on the railroad and remains a stop on the Amtrak route between Los Angeles and San Francisco. Today it exhibits a calm and restful air – if you're seeking anything more active, you'll be disappointed.

Hanford's **visitor center** (see p.354) can give you a map of the town detailing the now spotless and spruced-up buildings around Courthouse Square, once the core of local life at the beginning of the twentieth century. The honey-colored **Courthouse** retains many of its Neoclassical features, including a magnificent staircase. As you'd expect, the old Hanford jail, rather pretentiously modeled on the Paris Bastille, is only a ball-and-chain's throw away. It was used until 1968 and is now *The Bastille* restaurant (see opposite), which you can wander through to see the old cells.

Much less ostentatious are the rows of two-story porched dwellings, four blocks east of the square (between 7th & 8th), marking the district that was home to most of the eight hundred or so Chinese families who came to Hanford to work on the railroad. At the center of the community was the **Taoist Temple** on China Alley (open for groups of 6–20 only and by appointment; more details from the visitor center or call ☎559/582-4508). Built in 1893, the temple served both a spiritual and a social function, providing free lodging to work-seeking Chinese immigrants, and was used as a Chinese school during the early 1920s. Everything inside is original, from the teak burl figurines to the marble chairs, and it's a shame that entry is so restricted.

Mildly absorbing oddments from Hanford's past are gathered at the **Hanford Carnegie Museum**, 108 E Eighth Street (Weds–Sat 10am–2pm, closed Aug; $2; ☎559/584-1367), filling part of the interior of the town's elegant 1905 library – one of many small-town libraries financed by altruistic millionaire industrialist Andrew Carnegie.

For a bit more diversion, head six miles south of town to the **Clark Center for Japanese Art & Culture**, 15770 Tenth Avenue (Tues–Sat 1–5pm, closed Aug; $5; ⓦwww.ccjac.org), incongruously located on the land of local cattle rancher Bill Clark. With the guidance of friends and mentors Ruth and Sherman Lee, Clark has been amassing Japanese scrolls, folding screens, lacquerware, and sculpture since the 1970s and even designed the institute's Japanese-inspired building and his adjacent house and garden. Slip off your shoes and admire the dragon-in-clouds temple ceiling before entering the main room, where you can sit on tatami mats to view the works up close. Only a small portion of the collection is on show at one time but there are always outstanding pieces, some dating back to the tenth century and many from the Edo Period (1615–1868). In particular, look out for two superb thirteenth-century sculptural pieces: the *Bodhisattva of the Wish-granting Jewel* and the *Daiitoko Myoo* – the institute's signature piece – with its multi-limbed figure astride a kneeling ox. Docent-led tours (Sat 1pm; free) are particularly illuminating.

Practicalities

KART **buses** (☎559/584-0101) run from Visalia (3 daily Mon–Fri) and Fresno (2 daily Mon, Weds & Fri). They arrive on 7th Street near the town's **visitor center** (Mon–Fri 9am–5pm; ☎559/582-5024, ⓦwww.visithanford.com), which is conveniently located inside the handsomely restored Amtrak depot at 200 Santa Fe Avenue. Free **Internet access** is available at the library, 401 Douty Street (closed Sun).

Should you decide to stay a while, you'll find Hanford's **accommodation** and **eating** options limited but adequate.

Accommodation

Comfort Inn 10 N Irwin St ☎1-800/228-5150. Midrange motel right downtown with gym, heated outdoor pool, and continental breakfast. ❹

Downtown Motel 101 N Redington ☎559/582-9036. Basic motel, mainly of interest for its central location. ❷

Irwin Street Inn 522 N Irwin ☎1-866/583-7378. A cluster of four restored Victorian homes, furnished with antiques. Central location and a restaurant on site. Rooms ❹, suites ❻

Eating and drinking

Art Works 120 W Sixth St ☎559/583-8379. A relaxed espresso café with a great range of soups, sandwiches (mostly $6–7), and smoothies. They sometimes put on live music and there's free Wi-Fi.

The Bastille 113 Court St ☎ 559/583-9544. Fun bar and grill housed in the former jail and serving mountainous lean burgers and sandwiches until late. There's a pool table and plenty of high jinks as the week wears on.

Imperial Dynasty 406 China Alley ☎ 559/582–0196. Closed at last visit but promised to reopen, this institution of Hanford's Chinese community is just two doors on from the temple and still run by the family who opened it fifty years ago. The interior is rich with paper lanterns and painted screens, but the cooking, oddly, is mostly French rather than Chinese. Mains are in the $16–26 range and reservations are necessary.

Superior Dairy 325 N Douty St, just across from *The Bastille*. Classic diner notable for the rich creaminess of the made-on-the-premises ice cream.

Fresno

FRESNO, with its population of 400,000, is the largest city between LA and San Francisco, and an increasingly Hispanic one. In some ways it feels little more than an overgrown farming town, but it's very much the hub of business in the San Joaquin Valley, and is experiencing ongoing urban renewal. Witness such stridently modern buildings as the delta-winged, steel-and-glass **Fresno City Hall**, close to the Amtrak station, and the stadium for Fresno's Minor League baseball team, the Grizzlies, right downtown. Still, there's an odd mix of civic pride and urban decay, the latter fueling Fresno's status as one of the US's crime hotspots. Despite this, the city does have its good points, and you could spend a night here to take in the fascinating **Forestiere Underground Gardens** in the northern suburbs, and perhaps something of the nightlife in the vibrant **Tower District**.

If you're in the region in late February and early March you should also consider following at least part of the 62-mile **Blossom Trail** (free map from

Fresno Art Museum (1 mile) & Yosemite (60 miles)

FRESNO

0   800 yds

TOWER DISTRICT

ACCOMMODATION	
Days Inn	B
La Quinta Inn	C
Motel 6	A
Super 8	D

EATING & DRINKING	
Chicken Pie Shop	4
Kern St Coffee Company	6
Roger Rocka's	3
Sequoia Brewing Company	2
Thaiphoon	1
Veni Vidi Vici	5

& Merced (55 miles)

Forestiere Underground Gardens (4 miles)

Roeding Park

Chaffee Zoo

Kearney Mansion (5 miles)

City Airport

Farmers Market

Metropolita Museum

Meux Home Museum

City Hall

Train Station

Library

Fulton Mall

Greyhound Station

Kings Canyon & Sequoia National Parks (75 miles)

Visalia (40 miles)

the visitor center; see below), which weaves among fruit orchards, citrus groves, and the vineyards that make Fresno the world's raisin capital. Allow at least a couple of hours.

Arrival, information, and accommodation

The **bus** and **train** terminals are downtown – Greyhound at 1033 H Street (℡559/268-1829) and Amtrak at 2650 Tulare Street – both an easy walk from the **visitor center**, on the corner of Fresno and O streets (Mon–Fri 10am–4pm, Sat 11am–3pm; ℡559/237-0988, ⓦwww.fresnocvb.org), housed in a distinctive, conical-roofed water tower dating back to 1894. The nearby Fresno County Library, 2420 Mariposa Street (Mon–Thurs 9am–9pm, Fri & Sat 9am–6pm, Sun 1–6pm; ℡559/488-3195), has free **Internet access**.

Downtown is just small enough to walk around if you don't mind the heat, but non-drivers will want to make use of the Fresno Area Express **buses** ($1, exact change; ℡559/621-7433), if only to reach Forestiere Underground Gardens. Route #20, picked up downtown on Van Ness (every 30–60min), comes within a mile of the gardens, and you can transfer to the #9 for the last stretch. Routes #22, #26, and #28 travel between Van Ness and the Tower District.

If you decide to **stay**, you'll appreciate the low prices at numerous **motels** clustered together near the junction of Olive Avenue (the Tower District's main drag) and Hwy-99. Some charge rock-bottom rates but the rooms are well below par and are best avoided.

Days Inn 1101 N Parkway Drive ℡1-800/329-7466, ⓦwww.daysinn.com. Marginally nicer than *Motel 6* for not much more money. Free Wi-Fi and a pool. ❷
La Quinta Inn 2926 Tulare St ℡1-800/725-1661, ⓦwww.lq.com. Upscale motel with spacious rooms, fitness center, free Wi-Fi, and complimentary continental breakfast. ❹

Motel 6 1240 N Crystal Ave ℡559/237-0855, ⓦwww.motel6.com. Basic but comfortable budget motel with pool. ❷
Super 8 2127 Inyo St at L St ℡1-800/800-8000, ⓦwww.super8.com. Downtown motel with a pool and free continental breakfast. ❸

The town and around

To get the best of Fresno, you'll have to leave the center, and if time is short, the place to start is Forestiere Underground Gardens, a one-of-a-kind warren of rooms hewn out of the hardpan to protect one man and his crops from the heat. The Kearney Mansion also warrants an hour of your time before you return to the lesser attractions of downtown.

Forestiere Underground Gardens and Kearney Mansion

The one place which turns Fresno into a destination in its own right is **Forestiere Underground Gardens**, 5021 W Shaw Avenue (four to five 45-minute tours Easter to early Sept Sat & Sun; $10; check website or call for tour times ℡559/271-0734, ⓦwww.undergroundgardens.com), seven miles northwest of the center, a block east of the Shaw Avenue exit off Hwy-99. A subterranean labyrinth of over fifty rooms, the gardens were constructed by Sicilian émigré and former Boston and New York subway tunneler Baldassare Forestiere, who came to Fresno in 1905. In a fanatical attempt to stay cool and protect his crops, Forestiere put his digging know-how to work, building underground living quarters and skylit orchards with just a shovel and wheelbarrow. He gradually improved techniques for maximizing his yield but wasn't above playful twists like a glass-bottomed underground aquarium and a subterranean bathtub fed by water heated in the midday sun. He died in 1946, his forty years of work producing a vast earth honeycomb, part of which was destroyed by the construction of Hwy-99 next door, while another section awaits restoration. Wandering around the remainder of what he achieved is a fascinating way to pass an hour out of the heat of the day, enlivened by the tour guide's homespun anecdotes.

With more time to spare, head seven miles west from downtown along Kearney Boulevard, a long, straight, palm-lined avenue that was once the private driveway through the huge Kearney Park ($5 per vehicle; free with Mansion entry) to the **Kearney Mansion** (Fri–Sun tours at 1pm, 2pm & 3pm; $5). It was built between 1900 and 1903 for M. Theo Kearney, an English-born agricultural pioneer and raisin mogul, who maintained it in the opulent French Renaissance style to which he seemed addicted. He had even grander plans to grace Fresno with a French chateau, the mind-boggling designs for which are displayed here. Regarded locally as something of a mystery man, Kearney apparently led a busy social life on both sides of the Atlantic, which may explain why he died during an ocean crossing following a heart attack.

Downtown Fresno

Once you've hit Forestiere Underground Gardens and the Kearney Mansion, you've seen the best of the town: downtown sights are limited to a trio of fairly minor museums. The **Meux Home Museum**, 1007 R Street at Tulare Street (guided tours Fri–Sun noon–3.30pm; $5; ⑦559/233-8007, ⓦwww.meux.mus.ca.us), is Fresno's only surviving late nineteenth-century house, built for what was then the staggering sum of $12,000. This was the home of a doctor who arrived from the Deep South, bringing with him the novelty of a two-story house and a plethora of trendy Victorian features. What isn't original is a convincing reconstruction, and the turrets, arches, and octagonal master bedroom help make the place stylish and absorbing – quite out of sync with the Fresno that has sprawled up around it.

In 2007, the **Fresno Metropolitan Museum**, 1555 Van Ness Avenue (Tues–Sun 11am–5pm; $8, 2-for-1 admission on Thurs; ⑦559/441-1444, ⓦwww.fresnomet.org), mainly hosts temporary exhibitions, but it has a small collection of jigsaw puzzles dating back a century and a half and a delightful display of over two hundred mostly nineteenth-century Chinese snuffboxes arranged thematically – flowers, deities, mythological creatures, and so on. There's also coverage of Fresno's most famous son, the novelist, scriptwriter, and Pulitzer Prize-winner **William Saroyan**, who created a fictional identity for Fresno in his writing and died here in 1981 at the age of 72.

A couple of miles north of downtown, the **Fresno Art Museum**, 2233 N First Street in Radio Park (Tues–Sun 11am–5pm; $4, Sun free; ⑦559/441-4221, ⓦwww.fresnoartmuseum.org), has a changing roster of high-quality modern art that's usually worth browsing. In addition to an attractive sculpture garden, there are rooms devoted to pre-Columbian Mexican art spanning Mesoamerican styles from 2500 years ago until the arrival of the Spanish in the early sixteenth century. There's also a relatively minor but beautiful 1926 Diego Rivera canvas, *El Dia de las Flores, Xochimilco*, along with an explanation of how it came to be here.

Eating and drinking

To pick up fresh, good **food**, head for the **farmers' market** at Fulton and San Joaquin, downtown (Tues, Thurs & Sat 7am–2pm). There are decent places to eat downtown, but in general you're better off in the **Tower District**, three miles north, once something of a hippy hangout due to its proximity to the City College campus. Today it has a well-scrubbed liberal feel, plus several blocks of antique shops, bookstores, ethnic restaurants, bars, coffeehouses, and even a cabaret show to help fill a few relaxing hours.

Chicken Pie Shop 861 E Olive Ave ☎559/237-5042. This busy diner is locally famed for its chicken (and fruit) pies at bargain prices.

Kern St Coffee Company 2134 Kern St. Downtown spot for good java, soups, and bagels.

Roger Rocka's Dinner Theater 1226 N Wishon ☎559/266-9494, ⓦwww.gcplayers.com. Broadway-style shows in this 250-seat theater are preceded either by a sumptuous buffet (Wed, Thurs & Sun matinee; $40 all up) or a table-service meal (Fri & Sat; $45). Closed Mon & Tues.

Sequoia Brewing Company 777 E Olive Ave ☎559/264-5521. There's always plenty happening at this brewpub (with 8 excellent beers), including live music every Fri and Sat night. Good-value lunches and dinners extend to brick-oven pizzas, pasta dishes, and salads.

Thaiphoon 609 E Olive Ave ☎559/486-2445. Reasonable Thai with tasty versions of the usual noodle and curry dishes. Everything under $10.

Veni Vidi Vici 1116 N Fulton St ☎559/266-5510. For something special visit this dim and moody restaurant (with a patio for outdoor dining) for dishes like beef Thai rolls ($13) and chicken breast on bok choy with shiitake mushrooms ($25). After 10pm it becomes a lively bar. Lunch Tues–Fri & dinner daily except Mon.

Northern San Joaquin Valley

The towns of the northern San Joaquin Valley largely follow the pattern of those strung along Hwy-99 further south. Founded on agriculture, all had the hearts ripped out of them by suburban sprawl in the latter half of the twentieth century, leaving only winos, crazies, and a lot of poor Mexican immigrants. But in recent years the town centers have rebounded. Enough of the old downtown streets remain to evoke something out of an Edward Hopper painting, but the smartened-up cityscapes are all increasingly pleasant places to stroll, the ubiquitous taquerias now joined by java joints.

None of the three main towns warrant more than a few hours' exploration. You may spend the night in **Merced**, especially if **Yosemite-bound**; **Modesto** offers a couple of interesting sites and vestiges of the 1950s; and **Stockton** has a certain down-at-heel charm.

Merced

The best thing about sluggish **MERCED**, fifty miles north of Fresno, is its courthouse, a gem of a building in the main square that's maintained as the **County Courthouse Museum**, N Street at W 20th Street (Wed–Sun 1–4pm; free; ⓦwww.mercedmuseum.org). This striking Italian Renaissance-style structure, with columns, elaborately sculptured window frames, and a cupola topped by a statue of the Goddess of Justice (minus her customary blindfold), was raised in 1875 when it completely dominated the few dozen shacks that comprised the town. Impressively restored in period style, the courtroom retained a legal function until 1951, while the equally sumptuous offices were vacated in the 1970s, leaving the place to serve as storage space for local memorabilia – the most exotic item being an 1870s Taoist shrine, found by chance in a makeshift temple above a Chinese restaurant. Once you're through here, pass a pleasant half-hour in the mostly contemporary galleries in the **Merced Multicultural Arts Center**, 645 W Main Street (Mon–Fri 9am–4.30pm, Sat 10am–2pm; free; ⓦwww.artsmerced.org).

Six miles north of Merced, close to the bedroom community of **Atwater** – and signposted off Hwy-99 – lies the **Castle Air Museum** (daily: May–Sept 9am–5pm; Oct–April 10am–4pm; $8; ⓦwww.elite.net/castle-air). Forty-odd military aircraft dating from World War II to Vietnam – mostly bulky bombers with a few fighters thrown in, including the world's fastest plane, the SR-71 – are scattered outdoors, while inside there's a static B52 simulator, assorted military paraphernalia, and a collection of some 120 model planes crafted by one enthusiast from redwood. Route #8 of Merced's transit system, "The Bus" (Mon–Sat only; ⓣ1-800/345-3111), runs out here about every ninety minutes for $2 each way.

Practicalities

If none of these sights is much of a reason to visit Merced, the convenient **bus links to Yosemite** are. Greyhounds from Bakersfield, Sacramento, and San Francisco stop downtown at the **Transpo Center** on W 16th Street at N Street, where you'll find the **Merced California Welcome Center**, 710 W 16th Street (Mon–Sat 8.30am–5pm, Sun 9.30am–3.30pm; ⓣ1-800/446-5353, ⓦwww.yosemite-gateway.org), which covers the region but has some local info. The **Amtrak station** is somewhat isolated at 24th and K streets, about ten blocks away on the opposite side of the town center: follow K Street off W 16th Street. Train and bus stations are both stops for the four daily **YARTS buses** (ⓣ1-877/989-2787, ⓦwww.yarts.com) to Yosemite: see p.386 for more on getting to the national park.

If you're relying on public transportation, the best **place to stay** by far is the reservations-only *HI–Merced Home Hostel*. Drivers in need of a motel should take the Mariposa/Yosemite exit from Hwy-99, where there are a couple of good options. There are several good **places to eat** downtown, and if you're looking to **rent a car** to head up to Yosemite, try Enterprise, 1334 W Main Street (ⓣ209/722-4413), which usually has vehicles from as little as $40 a day.

Accommodation

HI–Merced Home Hostel ⓣ209/725-0407, ⓔmerced-hostel@juno.com. Reservations-only hostel that has limited check-in and access hours (7–9am & 5–10pm), but this is a small price to pay for a ride to and from the stations, an enthusiastic welcome, as much information as you can handle, and a free dessert every evening. It's a great place to hook up with Yosemite-bound travelers, who frequently rent cars together (see p.386). $15, nonmembers $18.

Holiday Inn Express 730 Motel Drive ⓣ1-800/465-4329. High-standard motel with all the expected facilities, including HBO, pool, sauna, & free Wi-Fi. ❺

The Hooper House - Bear Creek Inn 575 W N Bear Creek Drive ⓣ209/723-3991, ⓦwww.hooperhouse.com. B&B in a lovely Colonial-style house furnished with polished floors, plain painted walls, and an understated smattering of antique furnishings. It's all tastefully done and breakfast is served in a grand dining room. ❻

Slumber Motel 1315 W 16th St ⓣ209/722-5783 ⓔbhaktavb@yahoo.com. The pick of a string of basic, budget motels half a mile west of the Transpo Center (left as you step out of the door), with a small pool, cable TV, and free Wi-Fi. ❷

Eating and drinking

La Nita's 1327 18th St at T ⓣ209/723-2291. Authentic Mexican dining about ten blocks from the bus station, offering all the expected south-of-the-border staples along with *menudo* (tripe and hominy soup) and *albondigas*, or Mexican meatballs (both $7). Lunch specials change daily and there are hearty combination plates for under $10.

Paul's Place 2991 G St at Alexander ⓣ209/723-1339. Popular establishment boasting a broad range of ethnic and American dishes at very reasonable prices; try the Portuguese linguisa sausage omelet.

Wired 450 W 18th St ⓣ209/386-0206. Muffins plus good espresso (made from fair-traded organic beans) and fast Internet access. Closed Sat & Sun.

Modesto

Forty miles north of Merced along Hwy-99 you reach the town of **MODESTO**, which got its unusual name after prominent San Francisco

▲ Lucas Plaza Statue, Modesto

banker William Ralston was too modest to accept the new town being named after him. Much later, it was the childhood home of movie director George Lucas, and became the inspiration (though not the location) for his movie *American Graffiti*, the classic portrayal of growing up in small-town America during the late 1950s. The movie contains a number of references to local people, particularly the teachers who rubbed Lucas the wrong way in his formative years. Sadly, local ordinances (enacted in 1992 after several years of bad behavior) put an end to the fine art of **cruising**, though in recent years the American Graffiti Classic Car Show (middle weekend in June) has stepped in with hundreds of classic cars from all over the state and beyond, dusted off and cruised through the city.

About the only other reminder of those heady days is the **Lucas Plaza Statue**, a rather token duck-tail, bobby-sox, and '57 Chevy affair at the corner of J Street and McHenry Avenue. A more evocative celebration of the era is the ⚓ **A&W Root Beer Drive-In**, 1404 G Street, which has roller-skating "car-hop" waitresses serving root beer floats ordered from illuminated car-side menus. Despite the cruising ban, you'll still see the better-kept rigs parked here on Friday and Saturday nights (until 10pm), when Elvis and Marilyn impersonators are often in evidence.

It may seem hard to believe, but as a fairly typical valley town, Modesto does have a history stretching back beyond the Fifties. Its (comparatively) distant past is encapsulated by the shabbily grand **Modesto Arch** – erected in 1912 over Ninth and I to attract attention to the city's expanding economy. The slogan "Water, Wealth, Contentment, Health" clearly lays out the priorities of the city fathers in a time where the need for irrigation was paramount.

More imposingly, the Victorian **McHenry Mansion** at 906 15th Street (Sun–Thurs 1–4pm, Fri noon–3pm; donation; Ⓦ www.mchenrymuseum.org) is jam-packed with fixtures, fittings, and the personal features of a family whose fate was linked with Modesto's for years. Robert McHenry was a successful wheat rancher in the mid-nineteenth century who did much to bring about a general uplift in the agricultural well being of the area. Surprisingly, his luxurious dwelling was still being rented out as apartments, at quite low rates, as recently as the early 1970s. Docent-led tours enhance appreciation of the house, its history, and restoration.

A block from the mansion, a fine Victorian building originally financed by the McHenry family as the fledgling city's library now operates as the **McHenry Museum**, 1402 I Street (Tues–Sun noon–4pm; free; same contact info as mansion), which sports mock-ups of a doctor's office, blacksmith's shop, dentist's surgery, and gathering of cattle brands, revealing something of bygone days, although lacking the period atmosphere of the mansion.

Practicalities

You can find out more about the town and pick up maps at Modesto's **visitor center**, 1150 9th Street at L Street (Mon–Fri 8am–5pm; ☏1-888/640-8467, ⓦwww.visitmodesto.com). Greyhound **buses** stop downtown at the Modesto Transportation Center, 1001 Ninth Street at J Street, handy for such **accommodation** as the huge, upscale *Doubletree Hotel*, 1150 9th Street (☏1-800/222-8733; ➐), which includes a pool, sauna, and exercise room. It's a considerable step downmarket to the basic but clean *El Capitan Motel*, 1121 Needham Street (☏209/522-1021; ➋), half a mile northwest of the Doubletree along 9th Street.

You'll find downtown liberally supplied with decent **places to eat**. The ✦ *Queen Bean*, 1126 14th Street at K Street (open 7am–10pm or midnight; ☏209/521-8000), serves breakfast, espresso, cakes, and great sandwiches in a converted house, and often has bands playing at weekends; there's free wireless **Internet**, too. Beer drinkers will want to seek out *St Stan's Brewery, Pub and Restaurant*, 821 L Street (☏209/524-2337), where you've a choice of a dozen draught beers to wash down a burger or more substantial meal.

Stockton

The immediately striking thing about **STOCKTON**, perched at the far northern limit of the San Joaquin Valley some thirty miles north of Modesto, is the occasional sight of ocean-going freighters so far inland. The San Joaquin and Sacramento rivers converge here, creating a vast delta with thousands of inlets and bays, and a sixty-mile deep-water canal (built in the early 1930s) enables vessels to carry the produce of the valley's farms (especially Japan-bound bagged rice) past San Francisco and directly out to sea. But the geography that aided commerce also saddled Stockton with the image of a grim place to live and a tough city to work in. During the Gold Rush it was a supply stop en route to the mines, and it became a gigantic flophouse for broken and dispirited ex-miners who gave up their dreams of fortune and returned here to toil on the waterfront. Though valiant efforts have been made to shed this reputation and beautify the less attractive districts of this city of a quarter of a million, it's still primarily a hard-working, sleeves-rolled-up place.

A smattering of buildings downtown evokes the early decades of the twentieth century and makes Stockton an oft-demanded film set. John Huston's downbeat boxing picture *Fat City*, for example, was shot here. Marginally more appealing are the blocks bordered by Harding Way and Park, El Dorado, and California streets, a short way north of the center. This area has been preserved as the **Magnolia Historical District**, with sixteen intriguing specimens of domestic architecture spanning seven decades from the 1860s.

Roughly a mile west of the Magnolia District, in Victory Park, Stockton gathers totems of its past in the varied and large stock of the **Haggin Museum**, 1201 N Pershing Avenue (Wed–Sun 1.30–5pm; $5; ☏209/940-6300, ⓦwww .hagginmuseum.org). Not surprisingly, much is given over to agriculture, including the city's finest moment: the invention by local farmers of a caterpillar tread to enable tractors to travel over muddy ground, adapted by the British for use on tanks and in standard use since for militaries everywhere. In tremendous contrast, the museum also contains a batch of nineteenth-century French paintings, including works by Renoir and Gauguin, as well as Bouguereau's monumental 1878 painting of nymphs bathing, *The Nymphaeum*.

Practicalities

Stockton's **Greyhound station** is downtown at 121 S Center Street, a third of a mile east of the **Chamber of Commerce**, Waterfront Warehouse, 445 W Weber Avenue (Mon–Fri 9am–noon & 1–5pm; ☏209/547-2770, ⓦwww .visitstockton.org), which has limited information but stocks a free leaflet on the Magnolia District. **Amtrak** has two stops: downtown at 735 S San Joaquin Street, and half a mile northeast at the corner of N Aurora and E Weber streets.

Even traveling by public transportation doesn't mean you have to stay overnight in Stockton, but it can be worth stopping here to eat. For Chinese, the essential stop near downtown is *On Lock Sam*, 333 S Sutter Street (☏209/466-4561), standing here since 1898. Nearby *Yasoo Yani*, 326 E Main Street (☏209/464-3108; closed Sat & Sun), does a fine souvlaki, salad, and fries for about $8; while the Mexican-Southwestern *Fernando's Santa Fe Café*, 1005 N El Dorado Street (☏209/462-0165), turns out tasty fajitas for $15. There's more choice along the so-called **Miracle Mile**, a stretch of Pacific Avenue starting around a mile north of downtown where, among the bookshops, espresso bars, and restaurants, you'll find the *Valley Brewing Company*, 157 W Adams Street (☏209/948-2537). For **entertainment**, you may be able to catch stars of yesteryear performing downtown at the recently restored Bob Hope Fox Theater, 220 Main Street.

If you're forced to stay over, you can choose among the plentiful midrange chain **hotels** and budget motels, mostly near the Waterloo Road exit off Hwy-99. Downtown, try the *Stockton Travelers Motel*, 631 N Center Street (☏209/466-8554; ❷), or if this seems a little unsavory, go for the pool-equipped *Howard Johnson Express Inn*, 33 N Center Street (☏1-800/446-4656, ⓦwww.hojo.com; ❸), close to the Greyhound station.

Sequoia and Kings Canyon national parks

Separate parks but jointly run and with a long common border, **SEQUOIA AND KINGS CANYON NATIONAL PARKS** contain an immense variety of geology, flora, and fauna. **Sequoia National Park**, as you might expect from its name, boasts the thickest concentration – and the biggest individual specimens – of giant sequoia trees to be found anywhere. These ancient trees tend to outshine (and certainly outgrow) the other features of the park – an assortment of meadows, peaks, canyons, and caves. Notwithstanding a few notable exceptions, **Kings Canyon National Park** doesn't have the big trees but compensates with a gaping canyon gored out of the rock by the Kings

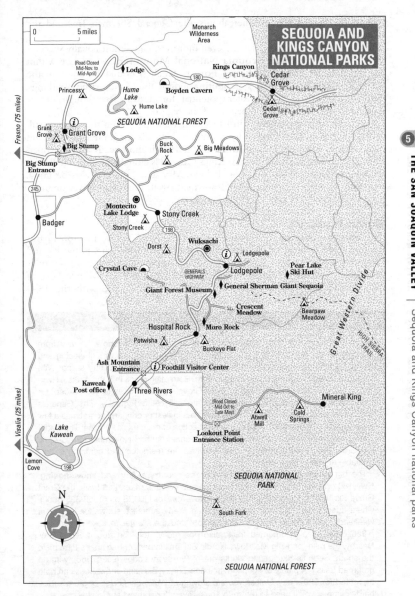

SEQUOIA AND KINGS CANYON NATIONAL PARKS

0   5 miles

Monarch
Wilderness
Area

(Road Closed
Mid-Nov. to
Mid-April) ▼ Lodge

Kings Canyon   Cedar
Grove

Princess╳   Hume
Lake   **Boyden Cavern**

Hume Lake   Cedar
Grove

SEQUOIA NATIONAL FOREST

Fresno (75 miles)

Grant
Grove ╳ Grant Grove   Buck
Rock   ╳ Big Meadows
Big Stump

**Big Stump
Entrance**

Montecito
Lake Lodge   Stony Creek

Badger   Stony Creek

Dorst ╳   **Wuksachi**

Crystal Cave   Lodgepole

GENERALS
HIGHWAY   Lodgepole

Pear Lake
Ski Hut

Giant Forest Museum   **General Sherman Giant Sequoia**

Crescent
Meadow   Bearpaw
Meadow

Hospital Rock   **Moro Rock**

Potwisha ╳   Buckeye Flat

**Ash Mountain
Entrance**   ⓘ Foothill Visitor Center

Kaweah
Post office   Three Rivers

Mineral King

(Road Closed
Mid-Oct to
Late May)

Atwell
Mill   Cold
Springs

**Lookout Point
Entrance Station**

Lake
Kaweah

Lemon
Cove

*SEQUOIA NATIONAL
PARK*

Visalia (25 miles)

N

╳ South Fork

SEQUOIA NATIONAL FOREST

Great Western Divide

HIGH SIERRA TRAIL

River, which cascades in torrents down from the High Sierra during the spring
snowmelt period. There's less of a packaged tourism feel here than in Yosemite:
the few established sights (principally the big trees) are near the main roads and
concentrate the crowds, leaving the vast majority of the landscape untrammeled
and unspoiled, but well within reach for willing hikers. Through it all runs the
Generals Highway, actually a fairly slow and winding paved road which links

two of the biggest sequoias hereabouts, the General Sherman Tree and the General Grant Tree.

To the north of the parks lies the even more vast and almost equally spectacular section of the **Giant Sequoia National Monument**, an enclave within the much larger **Sierra National Forest**, which is bound by fewer of the national park-style restrictions on hunting and the use of motorized playthings. Consequently there is a greater potential for disturbance, though this is counteracted by the sheer immensity of the region.

The **best time to come** is in late summer and fall, when the days are still warm, the nights are getting chilly at altitude, the roads remain free of snow, and most visitors have left. Bear in mind that although most roads are kept open through the winter, Hwy-180 into Kings Canyon is closed and snow blocks the road into Mineral King (see box, below). May and June can also be good, especially in Kings Canyon, where snowmelt swells the Kings River dramatically and the canyon-side yuccas are in bloom.

Some history

The land now encompassed by the Sequoia and Kings Canyon national parks was once the domain of **Yokuts sub-tribes** – the Monache, Potwisha, and Kaweah peoples – who made summer forays into the high country from their permanent settlements in the lowlands, especially along the Middle Fork of the Kaweah River. The first real European contact came with the 1849

> ### Winter in the parks
>
> The high country of both parks is covered in a blanket of **snow**, usually from November until April or May, and while this limits a great deal of sightseeing and walking it also opens up opportunities for some superb cross-country skiing. With chains, **access** is seldom much of a problem. Both main roads into the parks – Hwy-198 to Giant Forest and Hwy-180 to Grant Grove – are kept open all year, except for extraordinary circumstances, when they are still cleared quickly. The Generals Highway is also plowed after snowfall, but takes lowest priority and sometimes a few days to clear: it's best, then, to choose one section of the parks as a base. The Cedar Grove section of Kings Canyon is off limits to cars from mid-November to mid-April, but Grant Grove stays open all year. Facilities are restricted and camping is only available at snow-free lowland sites.
>
> The big winter activities up here are **cross-country skiing** and **snowshoeing**. Hwy-180 gives access to two places at the hub of miles of marked trails: the Grant Grove Ski Touring Center at Grant Grove (Nov–April; call KCPS on ℡559/335-5500), where there's ski and snowshoe rental, guided naturalist snowshoe walks at weekends, restaurants, and accommodation; and the *Montecito Lake Resort* (see p.366), with its own groomed trails, also open to visitors for around $15 a day. Nearby, the mile-long Big Meadows Nordic Ski Trail is perfect beginner's terrain. To the south, Sequoia Ski Touring works out of *Wuksachi Lodge* (see p.366), with no groomed trails but plenty of scope in the backcountry: skis and snowshoes can both be rented for $20 a day. Unless you are staying at *Wuksachi Lodge* or are a super-hardy camper, you'll need to return to Three Rivers for somewhere to stay.
>
> Experienced skiers and snowshoers should spend the night 9200ft up at the ten-berth **Pear Lake Ski Hut** (mid-Dec to mid-May; $24 per person), beautifully sited at the end of a steep six-mile trail from Wolverton Meadow: contact the Sequoia Natural History Association (℡559/565-3759, ⊛www.sequoiahistory.org) for reservations.
>
> **Snowmobiles** are banned in the national parks, but can be used on designated routes in the national forest, such as Big Meadows, Quail Flat, and Cherry Gap.

California **Gold Rush**, when prospectors penetrated the area in search of pasture and a direct route through the mountains. Word of abundant lumber soon got out and loggers came to stake their claims in the lowlands. The high country was widely ignored until, in 1858, local natives led **Hale Tharp**, a cattleman from Three Rivers, up to the sequoias around Moro Rock. Tharp spent the next thirty summers up there in his log home; John Muir visited him and wrote about the area, bringing it to the attention of the general public and the loggers. Before long, narrow-gauge railways and log flumes littered the area, mainly for clearing fir and pine rather than the sequoias, which tended to shatter when felled. Nonetheless, Visalia conservationist George Stewart campaigned in Washington for some degree of **preservation** for the big trees and, in 1890, four square miles around Grant Grove became Grant Grove National Park, the country's **third national park** after Yellowstone and Sequoia. In 1940 this was incorporated into the newly formed Kings Canyon National Park.

Arrival and information

Three **shuttle buses** run into and around Sequoia and Kings Canyon in the summer season (last week in May to early Sept). One service makes the two-hour run from **Visalia to Giant Forest** ($15 round-trip, including park entrance fee; ☏559/713-4100); the **Green Route** (#1: 9am–6pm every 15min; free) plies the Generals Highway between Giant Forest, the Sherman Tree, Lodgepole, and Wuksachi; and a third, the **Gray Route** (#2: 9am–6pm every 15min; free), links Giant Forest with Crescent Meadow via Moro Rock.

The twin parks are also easy to reach by **car**. The fastest approach is along Hwy-180 from Fresno, though it's slightly shorter following Hwy-198 from Visalia, a 55-mile drive including a tortuous 15-mile ascent on which RVs longer than 22ft and anything with a trailer are strongly discouraged. Those not bound by this limitation generally loop in one entrance and out the other. Make sure you prepare by stocking up with **cash** and **gas** before entering the parks, though some of both is available (see p.377).

The parks are always open: **park entry** costs $20 per car, or $10 per hiker or biker, and is valid for seven days. Fees are collected at the entrance stations, where you'll be given an excellent map and a copy of the free quarterly newspaper with the latest listings of ranger programs, **guided hikes**, and other interpretive activities, as well as general information on the parks.

For information, consult the parks' **website** (Ⓦwww.nps.gov/seki), or call at one of the five **visitor centers**: the park headquarters at **Foothills**, a mile north of the southern (Hwy-198) entrance (daily: June–Aug 8am–5pm; Sept–May 8am–4.30pm); and others at Lodgepole (summer only), Giant Forest Museum, Grant Grove Village, and Cedar Grove Village (summer only). There's also a useful **ranger station** at Mineral King; see the relevant accounts for details on all of these. For details of hikes and campground in the surrounding Sequoia National Forest, visit the **Hume Lake Ranger District Office**, 35860 Hwy-180 at Clingan's Junction, seventeen miles west of the Big Stump entrance (Mon–Fri 8am–4.30pm; ☏559/338-2251, Ⓦwww.r5.fs.fed.us/sequoia). You could also check the comprehensive, 24-hour recorded **information line** (☏559/565-3341), with details on camping, lodging, and road conditions, and the facility to order information by mail.

Accommodation

Inside the parks, all facilities, including accommodation, are managed by one of two concessionaires: Kings Canyon Park Services (KCPS; ☎559/335-5500 or 1-866/522-6986, ⊛www.sequoia-kingscanyon.com), who operate in Cedar Grove and Grant Grove; and Delaware North (DN ☎559/565-4070 or 1-888/252-5757, ⊛www.visitsequoia.com), who cover Lodgepole and Wuksachi. Upgrading in recent years has raised the standard of **accommodation**, shifting away from rustic towards greater luxury, though simple cabins are still available at Grant Grove. You can occasionally pick up cancellations upon arrival, but space is at a premium during the summer, when booking a couple of months in advance is advisable. Rates quoted are for the summer season, but huge savings can be had outside peak times, especially at the pricier places.

Heavy demand and the relatively high price of accommodation forces many to stay **outside the parks**, in the motels and B&Bs lining the approach roads a few miles from the entrances. The best selection is in the south at Three Rivers, where booking ahead is advised at **weekends** through the summer and holidays. Rates can also be up to one price code higher on Friday and Saturday nights, though this varies with demand.

Under the first heading below, all available roofed accommodation has been included, with just a selection of the best places to stay listed under the final two headings. For **camping**, see the box opposite.

In the parks and national forest

Bearpaw Meadow Camp Mid-June to mid-Sept; call DN. Soft beds, fluffy towels, hot showers, and hearty meals served up in magnificent wilderness are the trump cards for this cluster of six wooden-floored permanent tents (each with two single beds and floor space for one additional person). At 7800ft on the High Sierra Trail, it's an 11-mile walk east of Giant Forest Village: just follow the High Sierra Trail from Crescent Meadow. There's no electricity, everything is helicoptered in for the season, and all meals are included in the price. Most weekends and holidays are taken immediately after booking opens on Jan 2, though you've a reasonable chance of an on-spec place on weeknights in June and Sept. $175 per person; $75 for additional adult in tent.

Cedar Grove Late May to mid-Oct; call KCPS. Cozy lodge with private bathroom and a/c, right by the Kings River and in the same block as the fast-food restaurant and shops. ⑤, patio rooms ⑥

Grant Grove and John Muir Lodge All year; call KCPS. The parks' widest selection of ways to sleep under a roof, with most options accommodating up to four people. The most basic are the summer-only canvas-roofed cabins (early June to early Sept; ③), with cook stove, propane heater, and linen service. More solid rustic cabins (late May to late Nov; ③) were mostly built in the 1920s, and many have been nicely restored and

modernized; but for a private bath step up to the bath cabins (all year; ⑤), or the swanky, modern *John Muir Lodge*, with very comfortable hotel rooms (⑥).

Montecito Lake Resort For reservations ☎1-800/227-9900, for the lodge ☎1-800/843 8677, ⊛www.mslodge.com. On the Generals Hwy (Hwy-198) between Grant Grove Village and Giant Forest Village, this large but low-key family resort is tastefully set next to an artificial lake with all manner of activities: canoeing, swimming, horseback riding, wakeboarding, and volleyball in summer; and snowshoeing, skating, and cross-country skiing in winter. It's booked in six-night blocks from mid-June to early Sept (though you can book Saturday night separately), but at other times you can almost always stay in rustic cabins ($99 per person, weekends $129) or lodge rooms with private bath ($129 per person, weekends $159). Rates include all meals, which are pretty good.

Stony Creek Generals Hwy; late May to early Oct; call KCPS. Plain, comfortable motel-style rooms with TVs and showers in a block with a good restaurant and a grocery store. A generous continental breakfast is included. ⑥

Wuksachi Lodge All year; call DN. Directly competing with the *John Muir Lodge* for the best rooms in the park, the *Wuksachi* consists of several blocks of rooms (ask for mountain views on the upper floor) widely scattered in the woods around an elegant central lounge and restaurant area. Rooms ⑦, suites ⑧

Except during public holidays, there's always plenty of **camping space** in the parks and the surrounding national forest. All sites operate on a first-come-first-served basis except for *Lodgepole*, *Dorst*, *Princess*, and *Hume* (reserve through the Forest Service on ☏1-877/444-6777, ⓦwww.recreation.gov). RV drivers won't find any hookups, but there are summer-only dump stations at *Potwisha*, *Lodgepole*, *Dorst*, and *Princess*. Collecting "dead and down" firewood is permitted in both the national park and the national forest, but for cooking you really want to bring along a portable stove. There are public **showers** at several locations (see p.378). For **backcountry** camping, see the box on p.374.

Campsites are listed south to north, and the nighttime temperatures you can expect are indicated by the site's altitude. **Fees** are sometimes reduced or waived outside the main summer season and when piped water is disconnected, especially in winter.

South Fork (all year; $12; 3600ft). Trailer-free site a twisting thirteen miles east of Lake Kaweah on the very southwestern tip of the park. Non-potable piped water available.

Cold Springs Mineral King (late May to Oct; $12; 7500ft). Excellent shaded riverside site 25 miles west of Hwy-198, with some very quiet walk-in sites. Drinking water available.

Atwell Mill Mineral King (late May to Oct; $12; 6650ft). Quiet and pleasant campground on the site of a former Potwisha summer camp. Slightly less appealing than *Cold Springs*, but five miles closer to the highway. Some tent-only sites. Water available.

Potwisha (all year; $18; 2100ft). Smallish, RV-dominated site close to Hwy-198, three miles northeast of the park's southern entrance and beside the Marble Fork of the Kaweah River. Water available.

Buckeye Flat (late May to mid-Oct; $18; 2800ft). Peaceful, trailer-free site six miles east of Hwy-198, close to the park's southern entrance and beside the Middle Fork of the Kaweah River. Water available.

Lodgepole (all year; $18, or $20 if reserved; 6700ft). Largest and busiest of the sites, four miles north of Giant Forest Village and close to the highway. Reserve through the Forest Service in the high season, when pay showers, a camp store, water, and flush toilets are all made available.

Dorst (late May to early Sept; $20; 6700ft). Another large site, eight miles north of Lodgepole, with flush toilets and water during the season. Reserve through the Forest Service in summer.

Buck Rock (late May to Oct; free; 7500ft). Excellent and underutilized national forest site three miles east of the highway, midway between Lodgepole and Grant Grove Village. No water.

Big Meadow (late May to Oct; free; 7500ft). Similar site to *Buck Rock*, a mile further east among exfoliated granite domes. Mosquitoes in summer. Stream water.

Sunset, **Azalea**, and **Crystal Spring** Grant Grove Village. (*Azalea* year-round, others as needed; $18; 6500ft). Comparable large sites all within a few hundred yards of the Grant Grove visitor center.

Princess (late May to Sept; $15, or $17 if reserved; 5900ft). National forest campground with water and toilets, handily sited on the way into Kings Canyon. Reserve through the Forest Service.

Hume Lake (mid-May to Oct; $17, or $19 if reserved; 5200ft). Reservable national forest site with water, toilets, and lake-swimming for the brave.

Sheep Creek, **Sentinel**, **Canyon View**, and **Moraine** Cedar Grove Village (early May to Oct; $18; 4600ft). A series of all-but-contiguous forest sites around the Cedar Grove visitor center. *Canyon View* is tents-only.

South of the parks: Lemon Cove, Three Rivers, and Mineral King

Buckeye Tree Lodge 46000 Hwy-198, Three Rivers, just south of the park entrance ☏559/561-5900, ⓦwww.buckeyetree.com. Small but comfortable modern rooms with TV, private bathrooms, and verandas overlooking the foaming river, plus a seven-berth cottage (❼), all located right by the park entrance and equipped with a nice pool and free Wi-Fi. ❺

The Gateway 45978 Hwy-198, Three Rivers, just south of the park entrance ☏559/561-4133, ⓦwww.gateway-sequoia.com. Old but clean and perfectly functional motel-style rooms with satellite TV, plus a honeymoon cabin with dry sauna and patio (❻) and a large house sleeping eight with self-catering facilities ($265–325). It's located right beside the Kaweah River and the better rooms have a deck overlooking the water. ❺

Plantation B&B 33038 Hwy-198, Lemon Cove, 17 miles south of the park entrance ☏1-800/240-1466, ⓦwww.theplantation.net. Luxurious 8-room B&B with comfortable en-suite rooms (some with balconies) and truly delicious breakfasts, located on a citrus orchard twenty minutes' drive from the park entrance. Rooms follow a *Gone with the Wind* theme to the extent that the Belle Watling room comes bordello-hued with a crystal chandelier. Outside there's a heated pool, hot tub, and an acre of aging orange trees and youthful palms that's ideal for relaxing. Rooms ❻, suites ❼

Sierra Lodge 43175 Hwy-198, Three Rivers, 4 miles south of the park entrance ☏1-888/575-2555, ⓦwww.sierra-lodge.com. An old but spacious and clean lodge with pool and modern-ized en-suite rooms, many with decks and some featuring wood-burning fireplaces. Also suites, some of which have cooking facilities. Free Internet and Wi-Fi. Rooms ❸, suites ❺

🏃 **Silver City Mountain Resort** Mineral King, 20 miles east of Three Rivers ☏559/561-3223, ⓦwww.silvercityresort.com. A bucolic bolt hole in the woods that has been catering to committed regulars and casual visitors since the early 1930s. The rustic cabins are gorgeous with potbelly stoves, kitchen and propane lighting, and some come with a toilet. The more modern chalets have full bathroom and electric lighting whenever the generator is running. Sheets and towels are provided for out-of-state guests (otherwise bring your own) and the chalets (but not cabins) have a two-night minimum stay. Bring food for self-catering, though there is a store with limited supplies, and the resort has a restaurant attached (see p.370). Open late May–early Oct. Deluxe chalets one ❽ but mostly ❾, comfy cabins sleeping six ❼, rustic cabins sleeping four ❹

Three Rivers Hideaway 43365 Hwy-198, 3.7 miles south of the park entrance ☏559/561-4413, ⓦwww.threerivershideaway.com. Small RV and tent site with aging but renovated cabins (some with kitchens) at the lowest prices in the district. Tents $20, RV hookups $29–34, cabins ❹, kitchen cabins ❺

Along Hwy-180

Sequoia View Vineyard B&B 1384 S Frankwood Ave, Sanger, just off Hwy-180 ☏1-866/738 6420, ⓦwww.svbnb.com. A small winery, 20 miles east of Fresno and 35 miles west of the park entrance, with three large and tastefully furnished luxury suites, one with king-sized sleigh bed and balcony above the tasting room. A full country breakfast is served. ❻

Sierra Inn Motel 37692 Hwy-180, Dunlap ☏559/338-0678. Small and functional motel rooms with TV and a/c, located 14 miles west of the Big Stump entrance and next to a sandwiches-and-steaks restaurant and bar. ❷

Snowline Lodge 44138 Hwy-180 ☏559/336 2300, ⓦwww.snowlinecabin.com. Just six old – but clean and well-kept – rooms with ceiling fans in a wayside lodge eight miles west of the park entrance. There are a couple of family rooms, and some have access to a wide veranda. No TV or phones, but there is the option of a comfy self-contained cabin in the woods. Rooms ❸–❹, cabin ❻

Eating

There are **food** markets and fairly basic summer-only cafeterias at Lodgepole (the most extensive), Stony Creek, and Cedar Grove Village, though none of them are spectacular and prices will be higher than places outside the park, such as Three Rivers. Much the same applies to **restaurants**, with Three Rivers offering the best local selection at reasonable prices. In the restaurants inside the parks, diner fare prevails, with the exception of the restaurant at *Wuksachi*.

In the parks and national forest

Grant Grove Restaurant Basic diner fare – burgers, sandwiches, and breakfasts – plus fish, chicken, and steak dinners for $13–19 and pizza to stay or go ($14 for a 14-inch; summer only). There's also an espresso kiosk with seating out on the umbrella-shaded terrace.

Montecito Lake Resort See p.366. Hearty buffet breakfasts (7.30–9am; $9), lunches (noon–1.30pm; $10), and dinners (5.30–7.pm; $20) are all served communally at large tables, and there's a bar until 9pm.

Stony Creek Generals Hwy (late May to Oct; call KCPS). Fairly mainstream diner/restaurant serving decent burgers ($8–10), grilled chicken ($17), and steak ($20). Open daily 11am–2pm & 4–8pm.

Watchtower Deli Lodgepole. The best of the parks' budget eating places with respectable low-cost breakfasts, sandwiches, and coffee. Closed in winter.

Wuksachi Lodge Dining Room ☎559/565-4070. The finest dining in the twin parks, with Baja chicken sandwiches ($8), steaks ($20), and crusted mahi mahi ($20), plus a full buffet breakfast for $10, all served in a modern baronial-style room. The bar is open daily until 11pm; reserve for dinner.

Three Rivers

Gateway Restaurant 45978 Hwy-198, just south of the park entrance. Superbly set restaurant with a shady deck hung out over the Kaweah River. Great for a lunch of chicken tostadas ($12), salmon burgers ($12), or eggplant parmigiana ($15), or else the Sunday Champagne brunch ($20). Also open for meat and fish dinners ($18–35).

Nectar Java and Juice 42251 Hwy-198, 5.3 miles south of the park entrance ☎559/561-4785. The best espresso hereabouts.

We Three Bakery 43368 Hwy-198, 3.7 miles south of the park entrance. A good and friendly stop for breakfast or lunch either inside or out, or for their freshly baked cakes and pastries. Open Wed–Sun 7.30am–2.30pm.

Sequoia National Park

The two main centers in **SEQUOIA NATIONAL PARK** are **Giant Forest** and **Lodgepole**, the starting points for most of the hiking trails. To the south there's also the more isolated Mineral King area. While trees are seldom scarce – areas where the giant sequoias can't grow are thickly swathed with pine and fir – the scenery varies throughout the park: sometimes subtly, sometimes abruptly. Everywhere paths lead through deep forests and around meadows, and the longer treks rise above the tree line to reveal the barren peaks and superb sights of the High Sierra.

The history of the park is laced with political intrigue. In the 1880s, the Giant Forest area was bought by the Co-operative Land Purchase and Colonization Association, a group of individuals known as the **Kaweah Colony** that had the idea of forming a workers' colony here. They began what became the four-year task of building a road from Three Rivers up to Giant Forest, intending to start commercial logging of the huge trees there. Owing to legal technicalities, however, their rights to the area were disputed, and in 1890 the Senate passed a bill (probably instigated by a combination of agricultural and railroad interests) that effected the preservation of all sequoia groves. The colony lost everything and received no compensation for the road, which remained in use for thirty years – although decades later the ex-leader of the colony acknowledged that the eventual outcome was of far greater benefit to society as a whole than his own scheme would have been.

Three Rivers, Kaweah, and Mineral King

Approaching the park from the south, you pass through **Three Rivers**, a lowland community strung out for seven miles along Hwy-198 and providing the greatest concentration of accommodation and places to eat anywhere near the parks. As you approach the center of town, six miles south of the park entrance, a sign directs you three miles west to what remains of the Kaweah Colony, essentially just the **Kaweah Post Office**, the smallest still operating in California, with its original brass-and-glass private boxes.

A couple of miles north of Three Rivers, the twisting, early-1880s Mineral King Road (open late-May to October) branches 25 miles east into the southern section of the park to **Mineral King**, sitting in a scalloped bowl at 7800ft surrounded by snowy peaks and glacial lakes. This is the only part of the high country accessible by car (but not RVs, buses, or trailers) and makes a superb hiking base when you can reach it. Eager prospectors built the thorough-fare hoping the area would yield silver. It didn't, the mines were abandoned, and the region was left in peace until the mid-1960s, when Disney threatened to build a huge ski resort here. Thankfully the plan was defeated by the conserva-tion lobby that campaigned for the region's inclusion in Sequoia National Park, something finally achieved in 1978. Today there are just a few small stands of sequoias, a couple of basic campgrounds, one quaint resort, and near-complete tranquility. Having negotiated the seven-hundred-odd twists and turns from the highway, you can relax by the river before hiking up over steep Sawtooth Pass and into the alpine bowls of the glaciated basins beyond. There's also a gentler introduction to the flora and fauna of Mineral King by way of a short **nature trail** from the *Cold Springs* campground.

Pick up practical information and wilderness permits from the **ranger station** (June to early Sept daily 7.30am–4pm; ☎559/565-3768) opposite the *Cold Springs* campground. No permits are required for day-walks but overnight permits ($8 per person) are issued until late September (and self-issued there-after). They're in great demand in July and August: reservations can be made in advance from March 1, and some permits are offered on a first-come-first-served basis.

Unless you're committed to camping, the place to stay is the *Silver City Mountain Resort* (see p.368), five miles before the end of the road, which has a small, low-cost **restaurant** (daily except Tues & Wed) and excellent homemade fruit pies. The *Atwell* campground is nearby.

Giant Forest

Entering the park on **Hwy-180 from Visalia**, you pass **Hospital Rock**, easily spotted by the side of the road and decorated with rock drawings and acorn-grinding holes from an ancient Monache settlement. The rock got its name from a trapper who accidentally shot himself in the leg and was treated by the local tribe – who are further remembered by a small outdoor exhibition telling something of their evolution and culture. The road opposite leads to the small and appealing *Buckeye Flat* campground.

From Hospital Rock, the **Generals Highway** twists rapidly uphill into **GIANT FOREST**, the world's greatest accessible concentration of giant sequoias. A major tourist draw, Giant Forest contained a small village until 1998, but concerns over the health of the sequoias prompted the Park Service to raze the settlement. Almost three hundred hotel and restaurant structures built virtually on top of the sequoias' root systems have been removed, intrusive paths have been re-routed, and the whole area has been restored and re-seeded. The former shop, restaurant, and gas station have been transformed into the **Giant Forest Museum** (daily: July & Aug 8am–6pm; June & Sept 8am–5pm; Oct–May 9am–4.30pm; free), which admirably illustrates the life and times of

▲ Giant Forest, Sequoia National Park

the giant sequoias and shows some great footage of sequoia-felling and early tourism. Outside, the fire-damaged Sentinel Tree is barricaded to allow seedlings a chance to get established.

Various short hikes fan out from here through the trees, including the **Beetle Rock Trail** (5min round-trip), which affords a view down to the San Joaquin

Valley, and the **Big Trees Trail** (0.6-mile loop; 30min–1hr), which follows a well-formed boardwalk along the perimeter of Round Meadow.

Along Crescent Meadow Road

The densest concentration of sights (many specifically engineered for that purpose) is along **Crescent Meadow Road**, which spurs off the main highway just before the Giant Forest Museum and comes with abundant photo opportunities. The first attraction is the **Auto Log**, a fallen trunk originally chiseled flat enough for motorists to nose up onto it, though rot has now put an end to this practice. Beyond here, a side loop leads to the dramatic **Moro Rock**, a granite monolith streaking wildly upward from the green hillside. Views from its remarkably level top can stretch 150 miles across the San Joaquin Valley and, in the other direction, to the towering Sierra. Thanks to a concrete staircase, it's a comparatively easy climb to the summit, although at nearly 7000ft the altitude can be a strain.

Back on the road, you pass under the **Tunnel Log**: a tree that fell across the road in 1937 and has since had a vehicle-sized hole cut through its lower half. Further on, **Crescent Meadow** is, like other grassy fields in the area, more accurately a marsh, and too wet for the sequoias that form an impressive boundary around. Looking across the meadow gives the best opportunity to appreciate the changing shape of the aging sequoia. The trail circling its perimeter (1.5 miles; 1hr; mainly flat) leads to **Log Meadow**, to which a farmer, Hale Tharp, searching for a summer grazing ground for his sheep, was led by local Native Americans in 1856. He became one of the first white men to see the giant sequoias, and the first to actually live in one – a hollowed-out specimen which still exists, remembered as **Tharp's Log**. Peer inside to appreciate the hewn-out shelves. From here the loop presses on to the still-living

The life of the giant sequoia

Call it what you will – the sierra redwood, *Sequoiadendron giganteum*, or just "big tree" – the **giant sequoia** is the earth's most massive living thing. Some of these arboreal monsters weigh in at a whopping one thousand tons, courtesy of a thick trunk that barely tapers from base to crown. They're also among the oldest trees found anywhere, many reaching 2000 or even 3000 years of age.

Sequoias are only found in around 75 isolated groves on the western slopes of California's **Sierra Nevada** and grow naturally between elevations of 5000ft and 8500ft from just south of Sequoia National Park to just north of Yosemite National Park. Specimens planted all over the world during the nineteenth century seem to thrive but haven't yet reached the enormous dimensions seen here.

The cinnamon-colored bark of young sequoias is easily confused with that of the incense cedar, but as they age, there's no mistaking the thick spongy outer layer that protects the sapwood from the fires that periodically sweep through the forests. **Fire** is, in fact, a critical element in the propagation of sequoias; the hen-egg-sized female cones pack hundreds of seeds but require intense heat to open them. Few seeds ever sprout as they need perfect conditions, usually where an old tree has fallen and left a hole in the canopy, allowing plenty of light to fall on rich mineral soil.

Young trees are conical, but as they mature the lower branches drop off to leave a top-heavy crown. A shallow, **wide root system** keeps them upright, but eventually heavy snowfall or high winds topple aging trees. With its tannin-rich timber, a giant sequoia may lie where it fell for hundreds of years. John Muir discovered one still largely intact with a 380-year-old silver fir growing out of the depression it had created.

Chimney Tree, its center completely burnt out so that the sky is visible from its hollow base. Hardy backpackers can pick up the John Muir Trail here and hike the 74 miles to Mount Whitney (the tallest mountain in the continental US; see box, p.314).

The General Sherman Tree and Crystal Cave

North of Crescent Meadow Road, the Generals Highway enters the thickest section of Giant Forest and the biggest sequoia of them all (reachable on foot by various connecting trails). The 3000-year-old **General Sherman Tree** is 275ft high, has a base diameter of 36ft, and was, for a time, renamed the Karl Marx Tree by the Kaweah Colony. While it's certainly a thrill to be face-to-bark with what is widely held to be the largest living thing on earth, its extraordinary dimensions are hard to grasp in the midst of all the almost equally monstrous sequoias around – not to mention the other tremendous batch that can be seen on the **Congress Trail** (2 miles; 1–2hr; negligible ascent), which starts from the General Sherman Tree itself. Parking is several hundred yards from the General Sherman Tree, so consider catching the **free shuttle bus** from Giant Forest.

When you've had your fill of the magnificent trees, consider a trip nine miles from Giant Forest along a minor road to **Crystal Cave** (45-minute guided tours mid-May to Sept daily 11am–4pm; $11), which has a fairly diverting batch of stalagmites and stalactites. The early morning tours are not usually full, and whatever time you go, remember to take a jacket as the cave is at a constant 50°F. Those with a deeper interest in the cave's origins and features should join the ninety-minute **Discovery Tour** (mid-June to Aug daily 4.15pm except Sat; $19), or even **Wild Cave Tours** (check ⓦwww.sequoiahistory.org for dates and details; $129), which involves four to six hours of crawling and climbing away from the normal tourist route.

Tickets for cave trips cannot be bought at the caves themselves, but must be purchased at the Lodgepole or Foothills visitor centers at least a couple of hours beforehand.

Lodgepole and around

Whatever your plans, make sure you stop at **Lodgepole Village** – three miles north of the General Sherman Tree – for the geological displays, film shows, and general information at the **visitor center** (July & Aug daily 8am–6pm; May, June & Sept daily 8am–5pm; Oct–April Fri–Mon 9am–4.30pm; ⓣ559/565-4436). With its grocery store, burger bar, showers, laundromat, and campground, Lodgepole is very much at the center of Sequoia's visitor activities, and its situation at one end of the Tokopah Valley, a glacially formed canyon (not unlike the much larger Yosemite Valley), makes it an ideal starting point to explore a number of hiking trails (see box, p.374). Foremost among these is the **Tokopah Valley Trail** – leading from Lodgepole through the valley to the base of Tokopah Falls, beneath **The Watchtower**, a 1600-foot cliff. The top of The Watchtower and its great view of the valley are accessible by way of the **Lakes Trail**, or try the sharpest ascent of all the Lodgepole hikes, the **Alta Peak and Alta Meadows Trail**, which rises four thousand feet over seven miles.

Beyond Lodgepole the Generals Highway turns west and runs four miles to **Wuksachi**, just a fancy modern lodge and restaurant. The road soon swings north again and passes into the Giant Sequoia National Monument – where there is accommodation and food to be had at both **Stony Creek** (closed in winter) and the *Montecito Lake Resort*, and free camping at a couple of primitive sites – before striking into Kings Canyon National Park.

Kings Canyon National Park

KINGS CANYON NATIONAL PARK is wilder and less visited than Sequoia, with just two small settlements containing the park's main visitor facilities: **Grant Grove** lies close to the Big Stump entrance, and **Cedar Grove** huddles in the bottom of the canyon some 25 miles to the east, at the start of most of the marked hikes. The one real road (closed in winter; usually mid-Nov to mid-April) links the two, spectacularly skirting the colossal canyon. Away from these two places, you're on your own. The vast untamed park has a maze

Exploring the Sequoia and Kings Canyon backcountry

The **trails** in Kings Canyon and Sequoia see far less traffic than those in Yosemite, but can still get busy in high summer. Almost all those leaving from Mineral King and Kings Canyon climb very steeply, so if you're looking for easy and moderate hikes, jump to the second sub-heading below.

There are **no restrictions on day-walks**, but a quota system (operational late May to late Sept) applies if you are planning to camp in the backcountry. A quarter of the places are offered on a first-come-first-served basis and, provided you are fairly flexible, you should be able to land something by turning up at the ranger station nearest your proposed trailhead from 1pm on the day before you wish to start. Details for advance **wilderness permits** are given at ⓦ www.nps.gov/seki/planyourvisit /wilderness_permits.htm, where you can download an application form. There is a one-off $15 **wilderness camping fee** per person which entitles you to camp more or less anywhere in the backcountry, though the authorities prefer you to use already impacted sites. Reservations are accepted after March 1 and at least two weeks before your start date, and outside the quota period permits can be self-issued at trailheads. Park visitor centers stock the free *Backcountry Basics* newspaper, sell localized hiking maps ($3.50 each) and have a more detailed **topographical map** of the parks ($9).

Remember that this is **bear country**: read the box on p.388. Bear canisters can be rented ($5 per trip) at Mineral King, Foothills, Lodgepole, Grant Grove, and Cedar Grove; and bought ($66) at the Lodgepole store and most visitor centers.

From Mineral King, Sequoia
Eagle Lake Trail (7 miles round-trip; 4–6hr; 2200-foot ascent) Starting from the parking area a mile beyond the ranger station, this trail begins gently but gets tougher towards the lovely Eagle Lake. Highlights include the Eagle Sink Hole (where the river vanishes) and some fantastic views.

Mosquito Lakes No. 1 Trail (7 miles round-trip; 4–5hr; 1150-foot ascent) Follows the first half of the Eagle Lake Trail, then branches left to the lowest of the Mosquito Lakes at 9000ft.

Paradise Peak via Paradise Ridge Trail (9 miles round-trip; 9hr; 2800-foot ascent) Superb walk starting opposite the *Atwell Mill* campground and climbing steeply to Paradise Ridge, which affords views of Moro Rock. From there it's a fairly flat stroll to Paradise Peak (9300ft).

From Giant Forest, Wolverton, and Lodgepole
Alta Peak and Alta Meadows Trail (14 miles round-trip; 8–10hr; 4000-foot ascent) Starting at the Wolverton trailhead, this strenuous but rewarding hike rises 4000ft

of canyons and a sprinkling of isolated lakes – the perfect environment for careful self-guided exploration.

Grant Grove and the Big Stump Area

Unless you're planning a major backcountry hike across the parks' boundaries, you'll have to pass through **Grant Grove** to get to Kings Canyon. Indeed, this cluster of visitor facilities – including accommodation, post office, restaurant, and small supermarket, all set amid concentrated stands of sequoias, sugar pines, incense cedar, black oak, and mountain dogwoods – makes a good base for exploring Kings Canyon National Park. Grant Grove's useful **visitor center** (daily: June–Aug 8am–6pm; May & Sept 8am–5pm; Oct–April 9am–4.30pm; T559/565-4307) can supply all the background information you'll need, and contains a small **museum** (free entry) with old-time photos, logging parapher-

over seven miles. Initially following the Lakes Trail (see below), it eventually starts on a daunting near-vertical hike to the stunning Alta Peak.

Little Baldy Trail (3.5 miles round-trip; 2–3hr; 700-foot ascent) Starting from Little Baldy Saddle, six miles north of Lodgepole, this loop trail leads to a rocky summit with spectacular views.

Tokopah Falls Trail (3 miles round-trip; 2–3hr; 500-foot ascent) Fairly easy valley walk beside the Marble Fork of the Kaweah River and leading to impressive granite cliffs and the Tokopah Falls, which cascades into a cool pool, perfect for a bracing dip. Starts at the eastern end of the *Lodgepole* campground.

The Watchtower and Lakes Trail (13 miles round-trip; 6–8hr; 2300-foot ascent) A popular if fatiguing trail leading up from the Wolverton trailhead to The Watchtower (3–5hr round-trip), an exposed tower of granite overlooking Tokapah Falls far below. From there the path leads past three lakes in increasingly gorgeous and stark glacial cirques. The two furthest lakes, Emerald Lake (9200ft) and Pear Lake (9500ft), have campgrounds that, for the adventurous and experienced, make good starting points for self-guided trekking into the mountains.

From Kings Canyon

Cedar Grove Overlook Trail (5 miles round-trip; 3–4hr; 1200-foot ascent) Starting half a mile north of Cedar Grove Village on Pack Station Road, this trail switchbacks steeply through forest and chaparral to a viewpoint overlooking Kings Canyon.

Don Cecil Trail to Lookout Peak (13 miles round-trip; 7–9hr; 4000-foot ascent) Starting 400yd east of Cedar Grove Village, a strenuous trail that largely follows the pre-highway route into King's Canyon. After two miles you reach the shady glen of Sheep Creek Cascade before pressing on up the canyon to the wonderfully panoramic summit.

Mist Falls Trail (9 miles round-trip; 3–5hr; 600-foot ascent). This easy, sandy trail starts from Road's End, eventually climbing steeply past numerous thundering cataracts to Mist Falls, one of the largest waterfalls in the twin parks.

Rae Lakes Loop (4–5 days round-trip) One of the best of the multiday hikes in these parts, following the Kings River up past Mist Falls and beyond, through Paradise Valley and Castle Domes Meadow to Woods Creek Crossing, where the route meets the John Muir Trail. It follows this for eight miles, passing Rae Lakes before returning to Kings Canyon along Bubbs Creek and the South Fork of the Kings River. Permits are available from the Road's End ranger station.

nalia, and a cross-section of a tree. Grant Grove is home to a couple of trees that rival the General Sherman for bulk, the **Robert E. Lee Tree** and the **General Grant Tree**, after which the area is named. The General Grant is the world's second largest tree and was proclaimed as "The Nation's Christmas Tree" by President Coolidge in 1926. Every year, on the second Sunday in December, the people of the nearby town of Sanger hold a yuletide celebration with carols sung under its snow-weighted boughs. It's also the nation's only living shrine, dedicated to all those who have died in war. A half-mile trail wends its way among these and other giants, calling in at the **Fallen Monarch**, which you can walk through, and the **Gamlin Cabin**, where Israel and Thomas Gamlin lived while exploiting their timber claim until 1878. The massive stump of one of the trees' scalps remains after a slice was shipped to the 1876 Centennial Exhibition in Philadelphia – an attempt to convince cynical easterners that such enormous trees really existed.

Two miles south of Grant Grove, the **BIG STUMP AREA** unsurprisingly gets its name from the gargantuan stumps that litter the place – remnants from early logging of sequoias carried out during the 1880s. An easy trail (one to two miles depending on how many sad stumps you can bear to see) leads through this scene of devastation to the **Mark Twain Stump**, the headstone of another monster killed to impress: a sliver of this one resides in the American Museum of Natural History and another was sent to London's British Museum. Look too for hollows in the ground (known as feather beds), where pine boughs were laid on the ground to break the fall of huge trees, and check out the meager foundations of the sawmill which once processed all the lumber.

Before leaving the area, consider a twisting, two-mile drive east from the visitor center up to **Panoramic Point** for long views over Kings Canyon.

Hume Lake

About eight miles north of Grant Grove, a minor road spurs off three miles to **Hume Lake**, actually a reservoir built in 1908 to provide water for logging flumes, and now forming the heart of an underpopulated area of the Sequoia National Forest. Handily placed for local hiking trails, it's also a delightful spot to swim or launch your canoe and makes a good place to spend a night beside the lake at the comparatively large *Hume Lake* **campground** (see p.367). At the head of the lake, the facilities of the *Hume Lake Christian Camp* provide expensive gas, groceries, a post office, and a coffee shop.

Kings Canyon Highway

For most, Hume Lake doesn't even warrant a diversion from the northern park's main attraction, **Kings Canyon**, which some measurements make the deepest canyon in the US, at some 7900ft. Whatever the facts, its walls of granite and gleaming blue marble, and the white pockmarks of spectacularly blooming yucca plants (particularly in May and early June), are visually outstanding. A vast area of the wilderness beyond is drained by the South Fork of the Kings River, a raging torrent during the springtime snowmelt spate, and perilous for wading at any time: people have been swept away even when paddling close to the bank in a seemingly placid section.

The approach to the canyon leads through a section of the Giant Sequoia National Monument with two rewarding excursions. The first is a short drive to the **Chicago Stump**, yet another epitaph to a felled giant, this one carted in numbered sections to Chicago in 1893 where it was reassembled for the World's Columbian Exposition. A more alluring diversion leads past another sequoia graveyard, **Stump Meadow**, to a trailhead for the **Boole Tree**, the world's fattest sequoia and one that towers above the forest where all other sequoias were felled. The loggers apparently appreciated its girth and spared it, naming it after their boss, Frank Boole. Despite this and some fine examples of fire scarring, it's seldom visited, perhaps on account of its position on a two-mile loop trail: take the gentler left-hand trail and you'll be there in around half an hour.

Near the foot of the canyon, the road passes the less compelling of the region's two show caves, the **Boyden Cavern** (daily: June–Aug 10am–5pm; late April to May & Sept to early Nov 11am–4pm; 45-minute tours on the hour; $11; Ⓦwww.caverntours.com), whose interior has a number of bizarre formations growing out of the 40,000-year-old rock, their impact intensified by the cave's cool, still interior.

Cedar Grove

Once properly into the national park, the canyon sheds its V-shape and gains a floor, where the settlement of **Cedar Grove** sprawls among incense cedars. With a lodge, a food store and snack bar, several campgrounds, and a **visitor center** (mid-June to Aug daily 9am–5pm; ℡559/565-3793), this is as close to a built-up area as the park gets.

Three miles east are the **Roaring River Falls** which, when in spate, undoubtedly merit their name. Apart from the obvious appeal of the scenery, the main things to see around here are the **flowers** – leopard lilies, shooting stars, violets, Indian paintbrush, lupines, and others – and a variety of birdlife. The longer hikes through the creeks, many of them seven or eight miles long (see box, p.375), are fairly stiff challenges and you must carry drinking water. An easy alternative is to potter along the **nature trail** (1.5 miles; 1–2hr; flat) around the edge of **Zumwalt Meadow**, a beckoning green carpet a mile beyond the falls and a short walk from the road, beneath the forbidding gray walls of Grand Sentinel and North Dome mountains. The meadow boasts a collection of big-leaf maple, cat's-tails, and creek dogwood, and there's often a chance for an eyeful of animal life.

Just a mile further, Kings Canyon Road comes to an end at **Road's End**, from where a network of hiking trails penetrates the multitude of canyons and peaks that constitute the Kings River Sierra. Almost all are best enjoyed with a tent and some provisions. To obtain **wilderness permits** in this area, call at the Road's End Wilderness Permit Station (June to mid-Sept daily 7am–4pm; rest of Sept Fri & Sat 7am–2pm) at the end of Hwy-180. The less ambitious only need to venture a hundred yards riverward to **Muir Rock** to see where John Muir (see box, p.386) conducted early meetings of the Sierra Club. On the way back down the valley, cut right just before the road crosses the Kings River and follow the unmarked **River Road** (westbound only) along the north side of the river back to Cedar Grove.

Listings

Banks There are no banks in either park, but credit cards and travelers' checks are widely accepted. Lodgepole, Stony Creek, Grant Grove, and Cedar Grove have ATMs.

Cycling Bikes are not permitted on trails within the parks, limiting you to park roads, many of which are very steep and have limited space for passing.

A better bet is the network of trails in the surrounding national forest.

Gas There's no gas available in the parks, so drivers should fill up in Visalia or Fresno, or with slightly pricier stuff at Three Rivers. In desperation, you can get expensive gas at Stony Creek Village, the *Hume Lake Christian Camp* (see opposite), or sometimes at *Kings Canyon Lodge* on Hwy-180, which claims to have the oldest gravity-fed pumps in the country, dating back to the 1920s.

Horseback riding Stables and pack stations exist in three locations through the national parks and surrounding forest, mostly open from mid- or late May to early September: the Horse Corral between Lodgepole and Grant Grove (☏ 559/565-3404; ⊛ www.horsecorralpackers.com), Grant Grove (☏ 559/335-9292), and Cedar Grove (☏ 559/565-3464). All offer anything from two hours in the saddle ($60) to multiday backcountry excursions.

Internet access No public facilities in the parks. The closest is Three Rivers Library, 42052 Eggers Drive (Tues noon–5pm & 6–8pm, Thurs & Fri 10am–1pm & 2–5pm), five miles south of the park entrance. Also try the high-speed connections at *3 Rivers Cyber Café*, 41763 Hwy-198 (Mon–Fri 11am–6pm, Sat 11am–5pm; ☏ 559/561-4165).

Laundry Lodgepole, Cedar Grove Village, and Stony Creek have coin-operated laundries open daily 8am–8pm in summer.

Phones Many public phones in the two parks don't accept coins; make sure you have some kind of phonecard. Cell phone coverage is patchy at best.

Post offices Both post offices accept General Delivery mail: at Lodgepole (Mon–Fri 8am–1pm & 2–4pm) write to c/o General Delivery, Sequoia National Park, CA 93262; and at Grant Grove (Mon–Fri 9am–4.30pm, Sat 10–11.45am) write to Kings Canyon National Park, CA 93633.

Rafting From mid-April to the end of June, Three Rivers-based Kaweah Whitewater Adventures (☏ 1-800/229-8658, ⊛ www.kaweah-whitewater .com) runs a series of rafting trips on the Kaweah River between Three Rivers and Lake Kaweah. Trips range from a relatively gentle two hours ($50) to serious Class IV and V full-day trips ($130).

Roads For road conditions call ☏ 559/565-3341.

Showers There are showers at Lodgepole (summer daily 8am–1pm & 3–8pm; coin-op, min $3), Stony Creek (mid-May to Sept daily 8am–7.30pm; $4), Grant Grove Village (all year daily 11am–4pm; $4), and Cedar Grove Village (summer daily 9am–5pm; $4).

The Sierra National Forest

Consuming almost the entire gaping tract of land between Kings Canyon and Yosemite, the **SIERRA NATIONAL FOREST** boasts some of the California interior's most beautiful mountain scenery, though it's less well known than either of its national park neighbors. Lacking the environmental protection given to the parks, many of the rivers within the federally run area have been dammed and much of the forest developed into resort areas that are better for fishing and boating than hiking. Residents of the San Joaquin Valley are well aware of this, and stream up here throughout the summer for weekend getaways. That said, there are far fewer people and any number of remote corners to explore, not least the rugged, unspoilt terrain of the vast **John Muir Wilderness** and the neighboring **Ansel Adams Wilderness**, which contain some of the starkest peaks and lushest alpine meadows of the High Sierra. If you want to discover complete solitude and hike and camp in isolation, this is the place to do it, though you'll need a vehicle: public transportation is virtually nonexistent. We haven't highlighted any walks in this area: there are hundreds of them and any of the **ranger stations** can suggest suitable hikes, supply free permits (necessary for any overnight hikes into most of the forest), and sell you the detailed *Sierra National Forest Map* ($10), useful even if you are only driving.

The paltry network of roads effectively divides the forest into three main areas: the more southerly **Pineridge District**, accessible by way of Hwy-168; the **Bass Lake** and **Mariposa districts**, just off Hwy-41 between Fresno and Yosemite; and the **Sierra Vista National Scenic Byway**, which reaches out into the Sierra to the southeast of Yosemite. Call ☏ 559/855-5360 for road information.

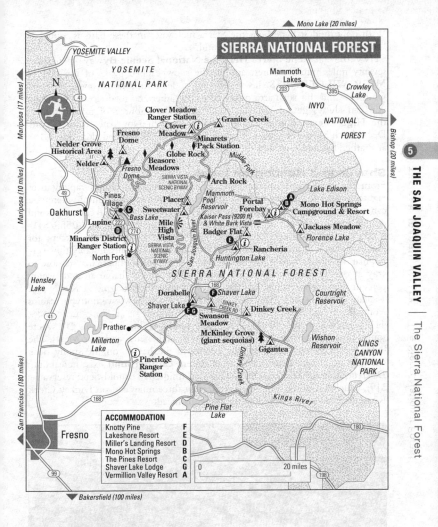

Mono Lake (20 miles)

SIERRA NATIONAL FOREST

ACCOMMODATION

Knotty Pine	F
Lakeshore Resort	E
Miller's Landing Resort	D
Mono Hot Springs	B
The Pines Resort	C
Shaver Lake Lodge	G
Vermillion Valley Resort	A

Bakersfield (100 miles)

The Pineridge District and the John Muir Wilderness

A forty-mile drive from Fresno along Hwy-168 through a parched and knobbly landscape dotted with blue, live, and scrub oak soon brings you to the best place for adventurous hiking, the **PINERIDGE DISTRICT**. Around **Kaiser Pass**, which scrapes 9200ft, you'll find isolated alpine landscapes served by decent campgrounds, a couple of minor resorts, and even some relaxing hot springs. The western section of the district is dominated by the weekend boating and fishing playgrounds of Huntington and Shaver lakes, while the east, up and over Kaiser Pass and around three hours' drive from Fresno, is big-time hiking territory. The region is swamped by **reservoirs** built as part of the "Big Creek" project that helped made the San Joaquin the agricultural heart of California.

With only modest hyperbole, the Sierra meltwater in these parts is touted as "the hardest-working water in the world."

Hwy-168 – aka **The Sierra Heritage National Scenic Byway** – penetrates seventy miles into the forest among the snow capped peaks of the **JOHN MUIR WILDERNESS**. It's a drive of at least four hours, even in good weather – and this is an area prone to bad weather and road closure, although you can always get to the lakes. The best-placed source of information is the **High Sierra Ranger District** office (April–Nov daily 8am–4.30pm; Dec–March Mon–Fri 8am–4.30pm; ℡559/855-5355), located along Hwy-168 at Prather, five miles west of the forest entrance.

Shaver and Huntington lakes

From the ranger station, the good and fast Hwy-168 climbs rapidly over eighteen miles to **Shaver Lake**, a mile-high, pine-girt community, where you can spend an afternoon dodging the jet skiers out on the lake. Rent canoes and double kayaks ($10–15 an hour) from Shaver Lake Watersports (℡559/841-8222), on the highway. Otherwise, there's little reason to stop except for groceries, gas, and meals at one of the half-dozen restaurants, notably the ever-popular *Village Restaurant and Bakery*, Hwy-168. Non-campers may choose to **stay** at one of several lodges and cabins, all of which charge around twenty percent more at weekends. Try the fully self-contained lodging at *Knotty Pine Vacation Cabins*, 41851 Hwy-168 (℡559/779-8426, ⓦwww.knottypinecabins .com; ❹), or the wide range of cabins three miles east at *Shaver Lake Lodge*, 44185 Hwy-168 (℡559/811-3326; basic rooms ❹, luxury rooms ❻), where some units come with queen-sized beds, a kitchenette, and lake views. The lodge serves burger-and-fries-type **meals** in the bar or on the sunny deck overlooking Shaver Lake. A couple of decent **campground** exist hereabouts: *Dorabelle*, near the lake on Dorabelle Road (mid-May to mid-Sept; reservable; $19), which has water; and *Swanson Meadow*, three miles east on Dinkey Creek Road ($15; no water) beside some gorgeous meadows.

▲ Shaver Lake, Sierra National Forest

Beyond Shaver Lake, Hwy-168 heads twenty miles east over the 7500-foot Tamarack Ridge to **Huntington Lake**. Effectively separated from the San Joaquin Valley, Huntington Lake feels more isolated than its neighbor over the hill, but is almost equally popular; again, watersports and angling are the pastimes of choice. Just before the lake, the *Rancheria* campground (open all year; reservable; $19) marks the turnoff to **Rancheria Falls**. A side road, east off Hwy-168, leads a mile to the head of the mile-long **Rancheria Falls Trail** (350-foot ascent), which winds through broadleaf woods to the 150-foot falls. A mile beyond the turnoff, Hwy-168 reaches the lake by the **Eastwood Visitor Center** (late May to early Sept daily 8am–4.30pm except Tues & Wed; Ⓣ559/893-6611), where the Kaiser Pass Road splits east over Kaiser Pass (see p.379). Continuing west around Huntington Lake, you soon hit the 1920s *Lakeshore Resort* (Ⓣ559/893-3193, Ⓦwww.lakeshoreresort.com; RV parking $30, rooms ❹, suites ❺), with rustic, knotty pine **cabins**, most sleeping four or five. There's a great **restaurant**, a lively bar, a gas station, post office, and general store all a few yards from the lake, and from here on the lakeshore is almost entirely taken up by $19 campsites.

Beyond Kaiser Pass: Mono Hot Springs and around

Beyond the Eastwood Visitor Center you're into true wild country, climbing Kaiser Pass (open June–Oct only) on a rapidly deteriorating road up to 9200ft and passing the *Badger Flat* campground ($17; no water) along the way. Eight miles from Eastwood, a mile-long side road (passable in a high-clearance vehicle) leads to **White Bark Vista**, one of the best mountain views in these parts. Over the pass is a vast basin, draining the south fork of the San Joaquin River. The lumpy single-lane road drops past the beautiful *Portal Forebay* campground ($15; lake water), and the **High Sierra Visitor Information Station** (June to early Sept Thurs–Sun 8am–4.30pm; Ⓣ559/877-7173) heralds a fork from where two very narrow and winding seven-mile roads split: north to Lake Edison, its approach marred by a huge earth dam, and west to Florence Lake.

Mono Hot Springs, two miles north of the junction on the road to Lake Edison, is the best thing about the region and a great place to relax and clean up after hikes. For the full hot springs experience, head for the ⚛ *Mono Hot Springs Resort* (mid-May to Oct; Ⓣ559/325-1710, Ⓦwww.monohotsprings.com; RV parking $25, tent cabins sleeping up to five ❸, rustic cabins ❸ for up to four, modern cabins ❹), where all cabin prices include free use of the therapeutic mineral pools and spa. Right on the banks of the San Joaquin River, the resort is a modest affair with individual mineral baths ($5 for nonguests), showers ($4), and massages ($40 per half-hour). Outside, there's a chlorinated spa filled with spring water, costing $5 for an all-day pass. Accommodation ranges from simple cabins with communal ablutions and no linen to more commodious affairs with toilets and kitchen. Typically there's a three-night minimum but you may be able to slot into a shorter gap, especially at either end of the season.

The resort also has a small restaurant, a limited general store, the *Mono Hot Springs* campground (early June to late Sept; Ⓦwww.recreation.gov; $17), and a post office used for mail and food pickups by hikers on the nearby John Muir and Pacific Crest trails (the latter being an epic, 2650-mile trek from the Mexican border to the Canadian frontier, typically taking around five months).

Better still, across the river there's a five-foot-deep concrete **bathing tank** (unrestricted access) that's perfect for soaking your bones while stargazing. This is just one of many pools on this side of the river; ask around.

Beyond Mono Hot Springs the wonderfully scenic road continues to **Lake Edison** and the *Vermillion Valley Reso*rt (T559/259-4000, W www.edisonlake .com; tent cabins ➋, motel units ➍), mainly geared towards boaters and anglers but also useful for entry into the John Muir Wilderness, easily accessed by a small **ferry** across the lake (June–Sept twice daily; $9 each way).

Florence Lake is more immediately appealing than Lake Edison: there's a greater sense of being hemmed in by mountains, and it's reached through an unearthly landscape of wrinkled granite shattered over the centuries by contorted junipers. There's a small store, the *Jackass Meadow* campground (June–Sept; reservable; $17), located unnervingly below the dam, and another **ferry** across the lake (late May to late Sept; 5 daily; $9 each way) which opens up multi day hikes along the John Muir and Pacific Crest trails.

Bass Lake

The northern reaches of the Sierra National Forest are most easily reached from **Oakhurst** (see p.389), the center of the Mariposa District and just seven miles west of the biggest tourist attraction in the area – the pine-fringed **Bass Lake**. A stamping ground of Hell's Angels in the 1960s – the leather and licentiousness memorably described in Hunter S. Thompson's *Hell's Angels* – Bass Lake is nowadays a family resort, crowded with boaters and anglers in summer, but a good spot to rest for a day or two. For detailed campground and hiking infor- mation, consult the Bass Lake Ranger District office (see opposite).

Road 222 runs right around the lake, though not always within sight of it. At the main settlement, **Pines Village**, you can buy groceries, eat well, and **spend the night** at the swanky *Pines Resort* (T1-800/350-7463, W www.basslake.com; chalets ➏–➐ suites ➐–➑) in luxurious two-story chalets with kitchens or even more palatial lakeside suites. By the southwestern tip of the lake, *Miller's Landing Resort*, 37976 Road 222 (T1-866/657-4386, W www.millerslanding; cabins ➋, deluxe cabins ➐), offers cabins without bathrooms right up to fancy chalets and suites. *Miller's Landing* is also the best place to rent aquatic equipment – including fishing boats ($60 for 6hr) and jet skis ($100 an hour) – and they have public showers and laundry.

The western side of Bass Lake is slung with $21-a-night family **campgrounds**, most oriented towards long stays beside your camper. In summer, book well in advance (see box, p.381), though no-shows are sometimes available at the Bass Lake Recreation Area office, 39900 Road 222, on the southwest side of the lake (late May to early Sept daily 8am–8pm; T559/642-3212). For tent campers, the best site is *Lupine* ($21), just north of Miller's Landing.

Sierra Vista Scenic Byway

If Bass Lake is too commercial and overcrowded for you, the antidote starts immediately to the north. The **SIERRA VISTA SCENIC BYWAY** makes a ninety-mile circuit east of Hwy-41, topping out at the Clover Meadow Wilder- ness Ranger Station (7000ft), the trailhead for much of the magnificent **Ansel Adams Wilderness**. Apart from a lot of trailheads and campgrounds, there's not a great deal to the road, though the views are fantastic and people are scarce. A straight circuit (snow-free July–Oct) takes five hours, and is especially slow going on the rough dirt roads of the north side. Stock up on supplies before you start: there are a couple of stores and gas stations dotted along the way, but they're not cheap and the range is limited. Accommodation on the circuit is largely limited to campgrounds, all (except three free sites) costing $16.

The best source of information on the circuit is the **Bass Lake Ranger District** office (Mon–Fri 8am–4.30pm; ℡559/877-2218), in the hamlet of North Fork at the southern end of Bass Lake, where you can pick up a **map** – important, as there are numerous confusing forestry roads and few signposts. Tackle the route in the direction described as route-finding is easier.

Before setting off, consider a **meal** at *La Cabaña*, 32762 Road 222 in North Fork (℡559/877-3311), a nondescript shack serving excellent and authentic Mexican dishes and burgers, most for under $7.

The south side

Before setting out from North Fork, check out the **Sierra Mono Indian Museum** (Tues–Sat 9am–4pm; $5), with some good examples of local Native American basketry and beadwork, as well as a lot of stuffed animals in glass cases. Once on your way, the first point of interest is the **Jesse Ross Cabin**, fifteen miles along, an 1860s hewn-log original that has been restored and brought to the site, and left open so you can poke around inside. Ten miles later, **Mile High Vista** reveals endless views of muscle-bound mountain ranges and bursting granite domes stretching back to Mammoth Mountain (see p.328). Further on, an eight-mile side road cuts south to the dammed **Mammoth Pool**, where anglers boat on the lake and smoke their catch at one of the four lake- and streamside **campgrounds** (all $16).

Back on the Scenic Byway, you'll pass the rather disappointing **Arch Rock**, where the earth under a slab of granite has been undermined to leave a kind of bridge, and continue climbing to a small ranger outpost (late June to Sept occasionally staffed; ℡559/877-2218) and the Minarets Pack Station (mid-June to Sept; ℡559/868-3405, Ⓦwww.highsierrapackers.org/min.htm). Apart from a general store and reasonable meals, the station offers simple lodging ($13 a night) and **horseback trips** from $55 a day. It's a great base for wilderness trips, many of which start by the **Clover Meadow Wilderness Ranger Station**, a couple of miles up a spur road (late June to mid-Sept daily 9am–5pm; permits available). Nearby are two wonderful free campgrounds, *Clover Meadow* and *Granite Creek*, both at 7000ft, the former with potable water.

The north side

The Minarets Pack Station marks the start of the descent from the backcountry and the end of the asphalt; for the next few miles you're on rough dirt, generally navigable in ordinary passenger vehicles when clear of snow. The hulking form of **Globe Rock** heralds the return to asphalt, which runs down to **Beasore Meadow**, where the summer-only **Jones Store** (open mid-June to mid-Oct) has supplied groceries, gas, and basic meals (8am–8pm) for the best part of a century, and offers showers to hikers. A short distance further on you reach Cold Springs Meadow, the junction with Sky Ranch Road (follow it left to continue the loop) and a spur to the wonderful *Fresno Dome* campground ($16; no water; 6400ft), a great base for a moderately strenuous walk to the top of the exfoliated granite namesake.

The Scenic Byway then passes several $16 campgrounds, most without running water, en route to the **Nelder Grove Historical Area** (unrestricted entry), a couple of miles north along a dirt road. Over a hundred giant sequoias are scattered through the forest here, though the overall impression is of devastation evidenced by the number of enormous stumps among the second-growth sugar pine, white fir, and cedar. The mile-long "Shadow of the Giants" interpretive walk explains the logging activities that took place here in the 1880s and early 1890s and, with its low visitor count, offers a more serene communion with these majestic trees than in Yosemite. A second interpretive trail leads from the nearby wooded *Nelder Grove* campground (free; stream water; 3500ft) to **Bull Buck Tree**, which, with its base circumference of 99ft, was once a serious contender for the world's largest tree. Though slimmer in the base, Sequoia National Park's General Sherman Tree is taller and broader at the top and so takes the prize. From here it's seven twisting miles back to Hwy-41, reached at a point around four miles north of Oakhurst.

Yosemite National Park

No temple made with hands can compare with the Yosemite. Every rock in its walls seems to glow with life. Some lean back in majestic repose; others, absolutely sheer or nearly so for thousands of feet, advance beyond their companions in thoughtful attitudes, giving welcome to storms and calms alike, seemingly aware, yet heedless, of everything going on about them.

John Muir, *The Yosemite*

More gushing adjectives have been thrown at **YOSEMITE NATIONAL PARK** than at any other part of California. But however excessive the hyperbole may seem, once you enter the park and turn the corner that reveals Yosemite Valley – only a small part of the park but the one at which most of the verbiage is aimed – you realize it's actually an understatement. For many, **Yosemite Valley** is the single most dramatic piece of geology to be found anywhere in the world. Just seven miles long and one mile across at its widest point, the Valley is walled by nearly vertical, three-thousand-foot cliffs whose sides are streaked by cascading waterfalls and whose tops, a variety of domes and pinnacles, form a jagged silhouette against the sky. At ground level, too, the sights can be staggeringly impressive. Grassy meadows are framed by oak, cedar, maple, and fir trees, with a variety of wildflowers and animals in attendance – deer, coyotes, and even black bears are not uncommon. As if that wasn't enough, in the southern reaches of the park near **Wawona**, sequoias grow almost as densely and to dimensions as vast as those in Sequoia National Park.

Understandably, you're not the first to appreciate Yosemite's appeal. Each year Yosemite has to cope with three and a half million visitors, and if you're looking for peace it's advisable to avoid Yosemite Valley and Wawona on weekends and holidays. That said, the whole park is diverse and massive enough to endure the crowds: you can visit at any time of year, even in winter when the waterfalls turn to ice and the trails are blocked by snow, and out of high summer even the valley itself resists getting crammed. Further-flung reaches of the park, especially around the crisp alpine **Tuolumne Meadows** (pronounced "too-OL-uh-mee") and the completely wild backcountry

Yosemite National Park is covered in further detail – along with the fifty best hikes – in the **Rough Guide to Yosemite National Park**.

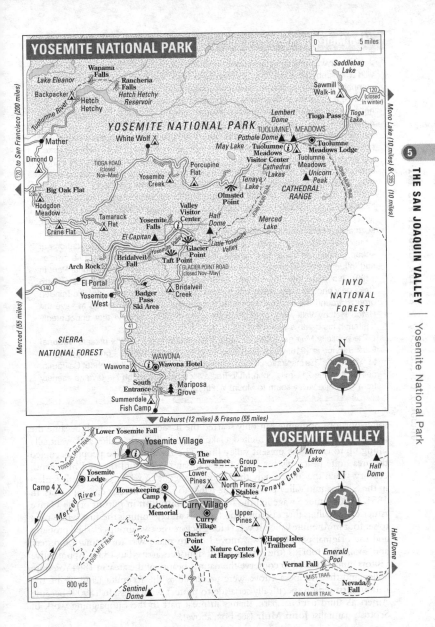

beyond them, are much less busy all year round, providing just about the most peaceful and elemental settings you could imagine.

Some history

Yosemite Valley was created over thousands of years by glaciers gouging through and enlarging the canyon of the Merced River; the ice scraped away much of the

John Muir and the Sierra Club

John Muir was one of nature's most eloquent advocates, a champion of all things wild who spent ten years living in Yosemite Valley in the 1870s, and the rest of his life campaigning for its preservation. Born in Scotland in 1838, he grew up in Wisconsin, became a mechanical inventor, and embarked on his first journey at the age of 27, noting in his diary, "All drawbacks overcome ... joyful and free ... I chose to become a tramp."

After walking a thousand miles to Florida with little more than a volume of Keats' poems and a plant press for company, he wound up in California in 1868 and asked for "anywhere that is wild." Working in Yosemite Valley as a sheepherder, mill worker, and hotel clerk, he spent every waking moment exploring the mountains and waterfalls, traveling light, and usually going to sleep hungry under the stars.

He dubbed the Sierra Nevada the **"Range of Light,"** and spent years developing his theory of how glaciers shaped the range. His articles gradually won him academic acceptance, and the general public was soon devouring his journal-based books, such as *My First Summer in the Sierra* and *The Yosemite*, which became classics.

Muir was desperate to protect his beloved landscape from the depredations of sheep grazing, timber cutting, and homesteading, and through magazine articles and influential contacts goaded Congress into creating Yosemite National Park in 1890. Two years later, he set up the **Sierra Club**, an organization whose motto "take only photographs; leave only footprints" has become a model for like-minded groups around the world. Despite his successes, in 1913 Muir failed to save the Hetch Hetchy Valley from being dammed (see p.401), a blow that undoubtedly hastened his death a year later.

The publicity Muir generated actually aided the formation of the present **National Park Service** in 1916, which promised – and has since provided – greater protection for Yosemite. This inspirational man is honored in place-names throughout California, not least in the 211-mile John Muir Trail, which twists through his favorite scenery from Yosemite Valley south to Mount Whitney.

softer portions of granite but only scarred the harder sections, which became the present cliffs. As the glaciers melted a lake formed, filling the valley and eventually silting up to create the present valley floor. The **Awahneechee** people occupied the area quite peaceably for some four thousand years until the mid-nineteenth century, when the increasingly threatening presence of white Gold Rush settlers in the San Joaquin Valley provoked the tribes to raid the nearest encampments. In 1851, Major James Savage led the **Mariposa Battalion** in pursuit of the Native Americans, trailing them beyond the foothills and becoming the first white men to set foot in Yosemite Valley. It wasn't long before the two groups clashed properly, and the original population was moved out to make way for farmers, foresters, and, soon after, tourists (the first group of sightseers arrived in 1855). Appreciative visitors quickly rallied to conserve the natural beauty of the area: in 1864 Yosemite Valley and the Mariposa Grove were preserved as the Yosemite Land Grant, the nation's first region specifically set aside to protect wilderness. In 1890 it became America's third national park, thanks in great part to the campaigning work of Scottish naturalist **John Muir** (see box, above).

Approaching Yosemite

Getting to Yosemite by car is straightforward, though on summer weekends parking can be a problem. Three roads from the San Joaquin Valley end up at

Yosemite Valley, roughly in the center of the park's 1200 square miles and home to its most dramatic scenery: Hwy-120 from Stockton and the San Francisco Bay Area; Hwy-140 from Merced; and Hwy-41 from Fresno, which passes the **Mariposa Grove** and **Wawona**, from where it's 27 miles further to the valley. All these roads are generally kept open throughout the year as far as the valley, though in extreme circumstances Hwy-120 is the first to close. The only road into the eastern side of the park is Hwy-120, the 10,000-foot Tioga Road, which branches off US-395 close to Lee Vining – though this is usually closed from late October to late May and in bad weather. Fill up with **gas** (see p.407) before heading into the park.

In an effort to encourage visitors to arrive by **public transportation**, the Park Service and local authorities maintain the YARTS bus system (℡1-877/989-2787, ⓦ www.yarts.com), running a useful service along Hwy-140 from Merced (see p.358), which has Amtrak and Greyhound connections. There are four departures daily picking up at both the Merced Transpo Center and the Amtrak station and arriving (after brief stops en route at all towns and significant accommodation) in the valley almost three hours later. A couple more services run into the valley from Mariposa along the same route, and there's a limited summer service from Mammoth Lakes (see p.324) and Lee Vining over Tioga Pass and through Tuolumne Meadows to Yosemite Valley. **Timetables** are available on the YARTS website and from visitor centers in the area. **Tickets** can be bought on board, and the round-trip **fare** (which includes the park entrance fee) to Yosemite from Merced is $25, from Mariposa and Midpines $12, and from El Portal just $7.

Tours to Yosemite

Generally speaking, anything called a **sightseeing tour** that begins outside the park will take you on an unsatisfying race through the valley. An alternative to this trend is **Yosemite Bug Bus Tours** (℡1-866/826-7108, ⓦ www.yosemitebugbus.com), which offers a range of trips, usually with accommodation and meals just outside the park at the *Yosemite Bug* (see p.394). The most frequent trip is the Two-Day-Two-Night Tour (all-year Mon, Wed & Fri; dorm $155, private room $175, en suite $195) starting in San Francisco and spending both nights at the *Bug*. Visits to Mariposa Grove, Sentinel Dome, Yosemite Valley, and the Mist Trail are supplemented by swimming, biking or gold panning, meals (included for an extra $26), and campfires at the *Bug*. For something more adventurous, go for the five-day Yosemite Backcountry Backpacking trips (June–Sept; $320–400), which involve exploring the high country and camping out in spectacular locations: see the website for details.

San Francisco-based tours in converted "communal" buses are run by **Green Tortoise** (℡1-800/867-8647, ⓦ www.greentortoise.com). These are geared towards active, outdoorsy types who enjoy camping out and pitching in. Their weekend trip (April–Sept; departs 9pm Fri returns 7am Mon; $129 plus $41 food fund) heads to the valley and the Mariposa Grove; a slightly more expensive three-day trip (June to mid-Oct; Mon & Fri evening departures; $181 plus $49 food fund) also allows half a day in Tuolumne Meadows and time around nearby Mono Lake and some hot springs. **Incredible Adventures** (℡1-800/777-8464, ⓦ www.incadventures.com), likewise San Francisco-based, offers another line of enjoyable minibus tours. The one-day trip ($129) includes a quick jaunt around the main Yosemite Valley sights and three hours to explore and hike. The more satisfying three-day camping tour ($240) includes high-country hiking around Tuolumne and visiting the sequoias.

The gateway towns

The heavy demand for accommodation within the park drives many to consider staying in one of the small, mostly former gold-mining towns along the main access roads. These are increasingly gearing themselves to park-bound tourists and do a reasonable job offering both lodging and food, though they are a poor substitute for actually staying in the park.

Approaching from the east: Lee Vining

From sometime around late May or early June until late October you can approach Yosemite from the east over the 10,000-foot Tioga Pass from US-395 and the town of **Lee Vining** (see p.334). You're almost two hours' drive from the Yosemite Valley heartland, but this area provides unparalleled access to the Tuolumne Meadows high country. Unless you want to stay in Lee Vining, or at the lodge or campground in Tuolumne Meadows (see pp.393 & 395, respectively), your best bet is to **camp** just outside the park at the *Sawmill Walk-in* campground or at *Lee Vining Creek* (see p.396 for all).

Approaching from the west: Groveland and Mariposa

Better bets for bases outside of the park are the western towns, particularly tiny **Groveland**, forty miles from the valley on Hwy-120, which retains wooden sidewalks with verandas and exudes a liberal air. Stop in at the Mountain Sage shop, 18653 Hwy-120 (ⓦ www.mtnsage.com), for an espresso while you browse their excellent stock of fair-trade crafts, natural history books, and an excellent photo gallery.

Further south, Hwy-140 runs through the bustling Gold Rush town of **Mariposa**, 45 miles from the valley, which boasts the oldest law-enforcement establishment west of the Mississippi still in continuous use: the **Mariposa County Courthouse**, on Jones Street at 10th Street (45-minute tours late May to early Sept Fri 5.30–8.30pm, Sat 10am–8.30pm, Sun 10am–4pm; free; reservations essential at ⓣ 209/966-7081). Built without nails, the lumber was rough-cut from a nearby stand of white pine, and you can still see the saw marks on the hand-planed spectator benches. The town's heritage is further celebrated at the **Museum and History Center**, on Jesse Street at 12th Street (daily: March–Oct 10am–4.30pm; Feb, Nov & Dec 10am–4pm; Jan closed; $3; ⓣ 209/966-2924), mildly diverting for its mock-up of a Gold Rush-era store and the large-scale mining paraphernalia scattered outside. In truth, you're better off at the **California State Mining and Mineral Museum**, two miles south on Hwy-49 (May–Sept

---

Smarter than the average bear

Yosemite **bears** (see p.52 for more on these beasts) may not be smarter than their cousins outside the park, but their familiarity with humans makes them more determined to get a free meal. They're not deterred by tent walls or car doors, and safe **food storage** is now mandatory in the park. As they say, "a fed bear is a dead bear," so do them and yourself a favor by keeping all food and smelly items – deodorant, sunscreen, toothpaste – either inside your room or in the metal lockers at campgrounds, parking lots, and trailheads.

Out in the backcountry, campers must use portable plastic **bear canisters** to store food. Sows have taught their cubs to climb along slender branches, so the old method of hanging food in trees seldom works.

You are encouraged to **report bear-related problems** and sightings on ⓣ 209/372-0322.

daily 10am–6pm; Oct–April daily except Tues 10am–4pm; $3; ℡209/742-7625, ⓦwww.parks.ca.gov), which revels in the glory days of the mid-nineteenth century with realistic reconstructions of a mine and stamp mill plus a vault where, among the assorted treasures, lies the largest existing gold nugget ever uncovered in California, a thirteen-pound chunk valued at over $1 million.

You'll find all you need to know about Yosemite and its surroundings at the very helpful **Mariposa County Visitor Center**, 5158 Hwy-140 (mid-May to mid-Sept Mon–Sat 7am–8pm, Sun 8am–5pm; mid-Sept to mid-May Mon–Sat 8am–5pm; ℡209/966-7081, ⓦwww.mariposa.org). Free **Internet access** is available at the library, beside the courthouse at Jones and 10th streets (Mon & Sat 9.30am–2pm, Tues & Thurs 9.30am–6pm, Wed & Fri 9.30am–5pm).

Further east along Hwy-140, on the way to Yosemite, the small towns of **Midpines** and **El Portal** also offer affordable lodging outside of the park (see p.394).

Approaching from the south: Oakhurst and Fish Camp

Yosemite visitors arriving from the south will come through **Oakhurst**, fifteen miles south of the southern park entrance, a small but booming sprawl of strip malls and sky-high signs for chain hotels and fast-food joints. Despite its lack of atmosphere, it makes a handy base for the southern section of the park and, with your own transport, day-trips into Yosemite Valley, fifty miles distant. The relocated buildings of the **Fresno Flats Historical Park**, almost a mile from the center on Road 427 (unrestricted access), won't detain you for long, but armloads of information on Yosemite are available at the **Yosemite Sierra Visitors Bureau**, 41969 Hwy-41 (Mon–Sat 8.30am–5pm, Sun 9am–1pm; ℡559/683-4636, ⓦwww.yosemite.travel).

The tiny huddle of hotels which makes up **Fish Camp** lies ten miles north of Oakhurst, handy for Wawona and the Mariposa Grove and good for keeping the kids quiet with the **Yosemite Mountain Sugar Pine Railroad**, 56001

Winter in Yosemite

From December to April, those prepared to cope with blocked roads – the Tioga Pass is always closed in winter – and below-freezing temperatures are amply rewarded at Yosemite; thick snow, frozen waterfalls, and far fewer people make for almost unimaginable beauty and silence. **Accommodation** is cheaper at these times, too (check ⓦwww.yosemitepark.com for special deals), and much easier to obtain, though weekends can still get pretty full. Many low-country **campgrounds** are open, and restrictions on backcountry camping are eased – you'll want a good sleeping bag and tent.

Much of Yosemite is fabulous **skiing** territory. Lessons, equipment rental, tows, and 25 miles of groomed cross-country trails are available at the **Badger Pass Ski Area** (ⓦwww.badgerpass.com) on the road to Glacier Point, accessible via the free bus from the valley. All-day lift tickets for the modest downhill ski area cost $38, and daily equipment rental will set you back $24 for downhill, $22 for cross-country, and $35 for snowboards. Lessons start from $60. If you want someone to take you out on Badger Pass's groomed trails, contact the Cross-Country Center (℡209/372-8444), which runs all manner of beginner, intermediate, and telemark and skating lessons, and leads overnight ski tours. **Ice skating** is a popular pastime at the open-air Curry Village rink in Yosemite Valley (normally $6.50, plus $3.25 skate rental).

Be aware if driving into the park that **tire chains** are recommended from November to April and can be rented in towns approaching the park. Inside the park, they are only available for sale.

Rock climbing in Yosemite

Rock climbers around the world flock to Yosemite, drawn by the challenge of inching up 3000-foot walls of sheer granite that soar up towards the California sun. Acres of superb, clean rock, easily accessible world-class routes, and reliable summer weather draw a vibrant climbing community bubbling over with campfire tales.

The best place to marvel at climbers' antics is from the roadside next to **El Cap Meadows**, always dotted with tourists training binoculars at the park's biggest slab of granite, **El Capitan**. The apparently featureless face hides hairline crack systems a thousand feet long and seemingly insurmountable overhangs whose scale is made apparent only by the flea-like figures of climbers.

The world's most famous climb, **The Nose**, traces a line up the prow of El Capitan. Climbers typically spend three to five nights on the route, but speed attempts have brought the record down to an astounding 2 hours 48 minutes 50 seconds. The **North American Wall** route lies to the right, passing directly through a massive stain on the rock that looks remarkably like a map of North America.

Some history

Technical rock climbing kicked off here in 1933, when four Bay Area climbers reached what is now known as the Lunch Ledge, 1000ft up Washington Column – the tower opposite Half Dome. With the aid of heavy steel **pitons** for driving into cracks, and equally weighty **karabiners** for attaching the ropes to the pitons, climbers began to knock off climbs such as the **Royal Arches** route, which weaves its way up the ledges and slabs behind *The Ahwahnee*.

After World War II, Swiss-born blacksmith **John Salathé** pushed standards to new levels by climbing **Lost Arrow Spire**, which rises to the right of Yosemite Falls and casts an afternoon shadow on the wall nearby. He even fashioned tough carbon-steel pitons from the axles of a Model A Ford.

For the next twenty years Salathé's mantle was assumed by classical purist **Royal Robbins** and goal-oriented **Warren Harding**. Little love was lost between them but when Robbins' team first scaled the face of **Half Dome** in 1957, Harding was on the summit to congratulate them. The climb ranked as the hardest in North America, and Yosemite became an international forcing ground for aid climbing. Now even the mighty El Cap seemed possible. **The Nose** refused to submit for seventeen months, even after Warren Harding drove four massive pitons fashioned from stove legs scavenged from the Berkeley city dump and drove them into what are still known as the Stoveleg Cracks. Harding and two colleagues finally topped

Hwy-41 (mid-March to Oct daily; $17; ☏559/683-7273, ⓦwww.ymsprr.com), a two-mile track into the forest plied by an oil-burning steam locomotive that once carted hewn timber. In the height of summer, several trains run each day, giving you the option of spending some time at the picnic area in the woods at the far end.

Arrival, information, and park transport

Yosemite National Park (general information ☏209/372-0200, ⓦwww.nps .gov/yose) is always open: **park entry** costs $20 per vehicle including passengers, or $10 for each cyclist and hiker, and is valid for seven days. Pay at the ranger stations when you enter, or if they're closed, at the visitor center in the valley or when you leave. To encourage use of public transportation, bus passengers pay no entry fees.

out in 1958 after a single thirteen-day push, the culmination of 47 days' work on the route.

The demands of ever harder climbs have pushed the development of an extensive **armory** of bathooks, birdbeaks, bongs, bugaboos, circleheads, fifi hooks, lost arrows, and RURPs, all employed either to grapple a ledge or wedge into cracks of different sizes. Climbers employ death-defying **pendulums**, and repeatedly sweep across the face to gain momentum until they can lunge out at a tiny flake or fingertip hold. They are forced to spend nights slung in a kind of lightweight camp bed known as a **portaledge** and haul food, gallons of water, sleeping bags, warm clothing, and wet-weather gear. As Yosemite veteran John Long writes: "Climbing a wall can be a monumental pain in the ass. No one could pay you enough to do it. A thousand dollars would be too little by far. But you wouldn't sell the least of the memories for ten times that sum."

The 1960s became the **Golden Age** of climbing, when Yosemite Valley drew a motley collection of dropouts and misfits, many ranking among the world's finest climbers. Purists at the top of their sport became disenchanted with the artificiality of aid ascents and began to "free" pitches: not hauling up on all the hardware, but using it only for protection in case of a fall. The culmination of years of cutting-edge climbing and months of route-specific training was Lynn Hill's ground-breaking free ascent of The Nose in 1993, praised and admired by all, if ruefully by some in Yosemite's traditionally macho climbing community.

Practicalities

The **best months** for climbing in Yosemite Valley are April, May, September, and October. In summer, the climbs on the domes around Tuolumne Meadows are cooler and usually considered a better bet. In the valley, everyone stays at the bohemian **Camp 4** (see p.395), where there's a great sense of camaraderie and an excellent **bulletin board** for teaming up with climbing partners, selling gear, organizing a ride, or just meeting friends.

The best stock of climbing gear is the Mountain Shop in Curry Village (daily 8am–6pm), also home to the Yosemite Mountaineering School (℡209/372-8344, ⓦwww .yosemitemountaineering.com), which runs daily courses ranging from the one-day beginners' classes (from $120) through various intermediate classes to private full-day guided climbs (one person $285, two people $210 each).

To catch something of the spirit of the scene, read *Camp 4: Recollections of a Yosemite Rockclimber* (The Mountaineers) by Steve Roper.

On arrival at any of the park entrances, you'll be given an excellent map of the park, the glossy annual *Yosemite* booklet, and the current *Yosemite Today* listings paper, which comes out every two to four weeks and covers current events and the extensive range of (mostly free) ranger programs. If you have more specific inquiries, try the park's most useful **visitor center** at **Yosemite Village** (daily: June–Sept 9am–7pm; Oct–May 9am–5pm; ℡209/372-0299), where you can pick up information and maps, including a topographic map ($10) essential for any adventurous hikes. The other main visitor centers are at **Tuolumne Meadows** (mid-June to Sept daily 9am–5pm and later in mid-season; ℡209/372-0263) and **Wawona** (mid-May to mid-Sept daily 8.30am–4.30pm; ℡209/375-9501). For **free** hiking permits and all the route-planning help you could ask for, pop next door to the **Wilderness Center** (mid-May to June and early Sept to mid-Oct daily 8am–5pm; July to early Sept daily 7.30am–6pm; closed in winter; ℡209/372-0745).

Park transport

While having your own vehicle is a boon for exploring the wider park, traffic congestion spoils everyone's fun on the valley floor, and if you're driving in just for the day, leave your vehicle in the day-use parking lots at Yosemite and Curry villages. You can then use the free and frequent **Yosemite Valley Shuttle Bus** that operates on the valley floor, running counterclockwise on a loop that passes through, or close to, all the main points of interest, trailheads, and accommodation areas. In high season, service runs roughly every twenty minutes between 7am and 10pm to most sections of the valley, with slightly reduced hours at other times.

Although bicycles are not allowed off paved surfaces, **cycling** around the twelve miles of dedicated bike paths is an excellent way to get around the valley. Yosemite Lodge

▲ El Capitan, Yosemite National Park

and Curry Village (April–Nov only) both rent city bikes for $7.50 per hour or $24.50 per day.

To stray further afield use the **hikers buses** (reservations ☎209/372-1240), which call at roadside trailheads on the way to Tuolumne Meadows and Glacier Point, and double as round-trip narrated tours for those on a tighter schedule. The **Tuolumne Meadows Tour and Hikers Bus** (mid-June to early Sept; $14.50 one way, $23 round-trip) makes a 2.5-hour run, leaving Yosemite Lodge at 8.20am and departing Tuolumne at 2pm, giving just over three hours at the meadows. The **Glacier Point Tour and Hikers Bus** (June–Oct 2–3 daily; $20 one way, $32.50 round-trip) runs up to Glacier Point, where it stays for around an hour.

There are always **guided tours** (☎209/372-1240, ⓦwww.yosemitepark .com), which range from the rather dull two-hour valley floor spin, costing $22, to the all-day Mariposa and Glacier Point Grand Tour (June–Oct), at $60; all are bookable through accommodation reception areas.

Accommodation

Once in the park, **accommodation** can be a problem; it's almost essential to book well in advance and anything other than camping can be expensive. Even canvas tents cost what you would pay for a reasonable motel elsewhere. All accommodation in the national park – the majority of it right in the valley – is operated by **DNC** (☎559/253-2003, ⓦwww.yosemitepark.com) and should be booked a few weeks ahead, even earlier for holiday weekends. Places generally reduce their rates in winter, though weekend prices remain close to high-season levels. One solution to the problem is to stay just outside the park (see opposite) and commute into it daily.

In the valley

The Ahwahnee A short distance from Yosemite Village at shuttle stop 3 (call DNC). Undoubtedly the finest place to stay in Yosemite, with rooms decorated in the hotel's Native American motif. Usually booked months in advance despite room rates starting close to $400, but worth visiting to view the wonderfully grand public areas, or for a drink or a meal. **❾**

Curry Village A mile from Yosemite Village at shuttle stops 13b and 20 (call DNC). A large family-oriented area dotted mostly with canvas tent cabins, each fitted with four beds on a wooden plinth. There are also cramped solid-walled cabins, spacious motel-style rooms, and some attractive cottages. Cottages **❼**, rooms **❻**, cabins with bath **❺**, cabins without bath **❹**, tent cabins **❸**

Housekeeping Camp Half a mile from Yosemite Village at shuttle stop 12 (call DNC). Ranks of simple concrete-walled plastic-roofed cabins with beds on sleeping platforms and the use of a fire grate and picnic table. April to mid-Oct only. **❸**

Yosemite Lodge Half a mile west of Yosemite Village at shuttle stop 8 (call DNC). Sprawling middle-market accommodation popular with tour groups, its proximity to restaurants, grocery stores, and a pool making it perhaps the most convenient choice in the valley. Rooms are motel-style, all with private bath, TV, and phone, but no a/c. Standard rooms **❻**, deluxe **❼**

Outside the valley

Tuolumne Meadows Lodge Tuolumne Meadows (call DNC). Seventy canvas tent cabins, each with four beds and a wood-burning stove but no electricity, located at nearly 9000ft and perfect for the first or last night of a long hiking trip. Open July to mid-Sept only; meals and showers available. **❹**

Wawona Hotel Wawona (call DNC; front desk ☏209/375-6556). An elegant New England-style hotel, parts of which date from 1879, with attractive public areas, distinctive wooden verandas dotted with white wicker chairs, and grounds that include a pool, tennis courts, and a nine-hole golf course. Rooms all lack phone, TV, and a/c, but have been gracefully restored with old-style furniture, Victoria-patterned wallpaper, and ceiling fans – though those in the main lodge are fairly small and lack bathrooms. Rooms with bath **❼**, without bath **❻**

White Wolf Lodge About halfway from the valley to Tuolumne Meadows (call DNC). Spacious four-berth tent cabins with wood-burning stove and candles, perfectly sited for day-hikes to Lukens and Harden lakes and the Grand Canyon of the Tuolumne River. Also four motel-style cabins. Open July to mid-Sept only. Cabins **❺**, tent cabins **❸**

Hwy-120: Groveland

Accommodation is listed by increasing distance from Yosemite.

Yosemite Lakes 31191 Hwy-120, 5 miles from the Big Oak Flat Entrance ☏1-800/533-1001, ⊛www.stayatyosemite.com. Reasonably priced family-oriented resort quite close to the park. Tent sites are well spaced ($29.50; full hookup $37) and there are rustic shared-bath bunkhouse cabins, rooms with communal kitchen and lounge, and conical canvas-walled yurts – with polished wood floors, a deck, cooking facilities, shower, and toilet – which sleep four in considerable comfort. Cabins **❸**, rooms **❸**, yurts **❺**

Yosemite Westgate Lodge 7633 Hwy-120, 15 miles from the Big Oak Flat Entrance ☏1-888/315-2378, ⊛www.yosemitewestgate .com. The closest standard motel to the park on Hwy-120, with the comforts of satellite TV, phone, pool, and hot tub. There's a decent restaurant next door and two kids under twelve stay free with two adults; rates drop dramatically in winter. Midweek **❺**, weekend **❻**

Groveland Motel & Indian Village 18933 Hwy-120, Groveland, 25 miles from the Big Oak Flat Entrance ☏1-888/849-3529, ⊛www .grovelandmotel.net. Either pitch your own tent ($15), use one of their tents supplied with airbeds (**❶**), try a concrete-floored teepee with a double bed (**❶**), or step up to some fairly basic a/c cabins with cable TV (**❹**) or even mobile homes with small kitchens (**❺**). **❶–❺**

Hotel Charlotte 18736 Hwy-120, Groveland, 25 miles from the Big Oak Flat Entrance ☏1-800/961-7799, ⊛www .hotelcharlotte.com. This charming ten-room hotel, dating back to 1921, has been lovingly updated. Rooms are mostly small and lack phones, but all have beautiful old-fashioned bathrooms and a/c and some have TV. Rates (at the bottom of this price code) include a good continental breakfast, and there's free Wi-Fi throughout the hotel. **❺**

Groveland Hotel 18767 Hwy-120, Groveland, 25 miles from the Big Oak Flat Entrance ☏1-800/273-3314, ⊛www.groveland.com. Gorgeous mining-era hotel with luxurious, individually styled, antique-filled rooms, most with deep baths. Suites (**❾**) feature spa tubs and real fires. **❻**

Hwy-140: Mariposa, Midpines, and El Portal

Accommodation is listed by increasing distance from Yosemite.

Cedar Lodge 9966 Hwy-140, El Portal, 8 miles west of the Arch Rock Entrance ⊤1-800/321-5261, ⓦwww.yosemiteresorts.us. Large hotel complex with indoor and outdoor pools, on-site restaurant, and 200 rooms and suites. There's a fair chance of getting something when everywhere else is full. Suites with kitchenettes ⑥, rooms ⑤

Bear Creek Cabins 6993 Hwy-140, Midpines, 10 miles east of Mariposa, 23 miles west of the Arch Rock Entrance; ⊤1-888/303-6993, ⓦwww.yosemitecabins.com. Well-maintained series of cabins, including standard cabin-rooms (④) with log finish, kitchenette, tub, and shower, larger cabins with full kitchen sleeping up to four (⑤), and very spacious suites (⑥) with a separate living room, gas fireplace, and full kitchen. All have access to a deck and barbecue area. ④–⑤

🏃 **Yosemite Bug Rustic Mountain Resort** 6979 Hwy-140, Midpines, 23 miles west of the Arch Rock Entrance. ⊤209/966-6666, ⓦwww.yosemitebug.com. Set in twenty acres of woodland, this low- to midrange lodge, HI-USA hostel, and campground is the handiest budget accommodation near Yosemite. Basic self-catering facilities exist for those staying in dorms, but there's also the excellent, licensed *Café at the Bug* (see p.406). Comfortable mixed and single-sex dorms ($15, nonmembers $18) are supplemented by tent cabins (②), shared-bath private rooms (③), and very cozy and distinctively decorated en-suite rooms with decks but no phone or TV (⑤). Pitching your own tent costs $17 per site. There's free Internet and Wi-Fi, a lounge with books and games, access to a good summer swimming hole, hot tub, sauna, massage, and yoga classes, and a YARTS bus stop outside. Reservations essential June–Sept. ②–⑤

Muir Lodge 6833 Hwy-140, Midpines, 8.6 miles east of Mariposa, 23.2 miles west of the Arch Rock Entrance ⊤209/966-2468, ⓦwww.yosemitemuirlodge.com. Old and fairly basic motel units (with TV and microwave) that haven't been upgraded for years, but are at least clean and cheap. ②.

River Rock Inn 4993 Seventh St, Mariposa, 35 miles from the Arch Rock Entrance ⊤209/966-5793, ⓦwww.riverrockncafe.com. Peaceful and welcoming seven-room budget motel just off Mariposa's main drag, with attractively decorated smallish rooms (and a couple of larger suites; ④)

all equipped with a/c, fridge, and coffee pot. Continental breakfast (included) is served in the adjacent River Rock Deli. ③

Comfort Inn 4994 Bullion St, Mariposa, 35 miles from the Arch Rock Entrance ⊤1-800/221-2222, ⓦwww.yosemite-motels.com. Modern midrange motel with Wi-Fi and a/c in all rooms, access to an outdoor pool and hot tub, and a continental breakfast included. Some suites with cooking facilities. ⑤

🏃 **Highland House B&B Inn** 3125 Wild Dove Lane, Mariposa, 35 miles from the Arch Rock Entrance ⊤209/966-3737, ⓦwww.highlandhouseinn.com. It's worth the effort to reach this superb B&B, tranquilly tucked away amid ponderosa pines and incense cedars around twelve miles northeast of Mariposa. The three elegantly furnished rooms all have private bathroom with tub and shower, and the suite (⑤) has a four-poster bed, fireplace, and VCR. Breakfasts are delicious, there's a full kitchen for guests' use, and the common area even has a pool table. Located off Jerseydale Road, but call for detailed directions. Reserve well ahead in summer. ④

Hwy-41: Oakhurst and Fish Camp

Accommodation is listed by increasing distance from Yosemite.

Owl's Nest Lodging 1235 Hwy-41, Fish Camp ⊤559/683-3484, ⓦwww.owlsnestlodging.com. Nicely decorated, friendly, and right by a stream, this lodge has large guest rooms for two (⑤) and self-contained chalets (⑥) that sleep up to seven, making them an excellent deal for small groups or large families. Closed mid-Oct to April. ⑤–⑥

Narrow Gauge Inn 48571 Hwy-41, Fish Camp ⊤1-888/644-9050, ⓦwww.narrowgaugeinn.com. Attractive lodge with a wide selection of rooms, many with a balcony and views over the forest, and a fine on-site restaurant (see p.407). All rooms come with phone, TV, and continental breakfast, and the inn has a pool and spa. ⑤

Sierra Sky Ranch 50552 Rd 632, Oakhurst, 12 miles from the South Entrance ⊤559/683-8040, ⓦwww.sierraskyranch.com. This woodsy lodge was started in 1875 and has a spacious feel, with a veranda-girt main lodge, large cozy lounge, and sunny library, plus a pool, creek-swimming, and fishing on site. Aging rooms come without a phone but do have cable TV and Wi-Fi. ⑤

Hounds Tooth Inn 42071 Hwy-41, 3 miles north of Oakhurst ⊤1-888/642-6610,

@www.houndstoothinn.com. Luxurious B&B with a dozen individually decorated rooms, most with either a fireplace or spa bath (or both) and all with a/c. The friendly hosts provide complimentary wine each evening and delicious buffet breakfasts. Rooms ⑤, deluxe ⑥
Days Inn 40662 Hwy-41, Oakhurst ☎1-800/329-7644, @www.daysinn.com. One of the cheapest of Oakhurst's franchise motels but still kept to a high standard, with comfortable rooms, a pool,

HBO, free Wi-Fi, and continental breakfast. Winter ❷, summer ⑤
The Homestead 41110 Rd 600, 2.5 miles off Hwy-49 in Ahwahnee, near Oakhurst ☎1-800/483-0495, @www.homesteadcottages .com. Just a handful of beautifully outfitted adobe cottages – a/c, TV, gas grill – each with full self-catering facilities, comfortable lounge area, and a nice deck. Two-night minimum stay at weekends. Loft ⑥, cottages ⑦

Camping

As with any national park, **camping** is the best way to really feel part of your surroundings, though this is less true in the large and crowded campgrounds of Yosemite Valley. In summer it's almost essential to book beforehand (☎1-877/444-6777, @www.recreation.gov): reservations open in one-month chunks, six months in advance, so to book for the month beginning July 15 you should call from February 15. Otherwise you'll need to show up at the Curry Village Reservations Office very early in the morning and hope for cancellations. Other than *Camp 4* (see below), all valley sites cost $20 and none have **showers** or **laundry** facilities (see pp.407 & 408). Between May and mid-September you're only allowed to camp for one week in Yosemite Valley and a total of two weeks in the whole park; outside this summer season you can move in for up to a month. Camping outside recognized sites in the valley is strictly forbidden.

In addition to the main campgrounds, there are **backpacker campgrounds** in Yosemite Valley, Tuolumne Meadows, and Hetch Hetchy, designed for hikers about to start (or just finishing) a wilderness trip and costing $5 per night – you must have a wilderness permit to use these.

Finally, with enough time you'll want to get out to one of several **primitive campgrounds** in the backcountry. Designed specifically for hikers, these have fire rings and some source of water, which must be treated. To use them, or to camp elsewhere in the backcountry, you must get a **free wilderness permit** (see p.391) – as ever, you must camp a mile from any road, four miles from a populated area, and at least a hundred yards from water sources and trails. Camping on the summit of Half Dome is not permitted. Remember to carry a stove and fuel, as indiscriminate use of trees could jeopardize future visitors' freedom to camp in the backcountry.

In the valley

Camp 4 Walk-in (all year; $5 per person; 4000ft). First-come-first-served campground west of and away from the other valley sites, popular with dirtbag rock climbers. It's a fairly bohemian (some would say squalid) place, with six-person sites just a few yards from a dusty parking lot. It's often full by 9am, especially in spring and fall, so join the line early.
North Pines, Upper Pines, Lower Pines (March–Oct, *Upper Pines* all year; $20; 4000ft). Largely indistinguishable, pine-shrouded sites, all with toilets, water, and fire rings. Popular with RV users. Reservations essential.

The rest of the park

Bridalveil Creek (July to early Sept; $14; 7200ft). High-country, first-come-first-served campground off Glacier Point Rd, with good access to wilderness trails.
Crane Flat (June–Sept; $20; 6200ft). Large campground northwest of the valley, at the start of Hwy-120 and close to a stand of sequoias. Reservations required.
Hodgdon Meadow (all year; $20; 4900ft). Relatively quiet campground right on the park's western boundary just off Hwy-120. Take Old Big Oak Flat Rd for half a mile. Reservations required May–Sept, first-come-first-served ($14) at other times.

Porcupine Flat (July to early Sept; $10; 8100ft). Attractive and small first-come-first-served campground near the road to Tuolumne Meadows, almost forty miles from the valley. Stream water available.

Tamarack Flat (June–Sept; $10; 6300ft). Small campground two miles off Hwy-120 Tioga Rd, 23 miles from the valley and with only limited RV access. Stream water available.

Tuolumne Meadows (July–Sept; $20; 8600ft). Large and popular streamside campground, effectively three campgrounds in one, beside a subalpine meadow. Half the sites are available by advance reservation, half by same-day reservation, and a further 25 sites ($5 per person) are available for backpackers with wilderness permits. There are flush toilets, piped water, and showers ($4) nearby at *Tuolumne Meadows Lodge*.

Wawona (all year; $20; 4000ft). The only site in the southern sector of the park, approximately a mile north of the *Wawona Hotel*. Some walk-in sites are reserved for car-free campers. Reservations required May–Sept; rest of year $14.

White Wolf (July to mid-Sept; $14; 8000ft). First-come-first-served tent and RV site a mile north of Hwy-120, midway between the valley and Tuolumne Meadows.

Yosemite Creek (July to early Sept; $10; 7600ft). First-come-first-served tent-only site ideal for escaping the crowds, though it can fill up very quickly in the summer. Inconveniently sited five miles off Hwy-120, but almost equidistant between the valley and Tuolumne Meadows. Stream water available.

Outside the park

Dimond O Evergreen Rd, off Hwy-120 West (late April to mid-Oct; $19; 4400ft). National forest campground one mile west of the Big Oak Flat Entrance, with tent and RV sites, piped water, and pit toilets.

Lee Vining Creek Off Hwy-120 East (late April to Oct; $14; 7800ft). A series of almost identical streamside national forest campgrounds along Poole Power Plant Rd, nine miles west of the Tioga Pass Entrance.

Sawmill Walk-in Mile 1.5 Saddlebag Lake Road, 3.7 miles east of the Tioga Pass Entrance (June to mid-Oct; $12; 9800ft). Primitive walk-in campground around 400yd from its parking lot, superbly sited amid jagged peaks that feel a world away from the glaciated domes around Tuolumne.

Summerdale Hwy-41 (June–Oct; $19; 5000ft). National forest campground 1.5 miles south of the park's South Entrance and handy for both Wawona and the Mariposa Grove.

Yosemite Valley

Even the most evocative photography can only hint at the pleasure of simply gazing at **YOSEMITE VALLEY**. From massive hunks of granite rising three thousand feet up from the four-thousand-foot valley floor to the subtle colorings of wildflowers, the variations in the valley can be both enormous and discreet. Aside from just looking, you can take many easy walks around the lush fields to waterfalls and lakes, and much tougher treks up the enormous cliffs (see box, p.402).

The valley's defining features are its enormous cliffs and thundering waterfalls; in fact, nowhere else in the world is there such an array of cascades concentrated in such a small area, though a mild winter can cause many of these falls to dry up as early as July.

If there is any drawback to the valley, it's that this is the busiest part of Yosemite, and you're rarely far from other visitors or the park's commercial trappings, notably in **Yosemite Village** and **Curry Village**, the two main concentrations of shops and restaurants. Most of the crowds can be easily left behind by taking any path which contains much of a slope, but a couple of days exploring the valley leaves you more than ready to press on to the park's less populated regions.

The big cliffs

However you approach the valley, your view will be partially blocked by **El Capitan**, a vast monolith jutting forward from the adjacent cliffs and looming

3593ft above the valley floor. One of the largest pieces of exposed granite in the world, "The Captain" is a full 320 acres of gray-tan granite, seemingly devoid of vegetation and almost vertical. Its enormous size draws rock climbers from all over the world; read more on p.390.

Impressive though El Capitan is, for most people it's the arching **Half Dome** that instantly grabs their attention. A stunning sight topping out at 8842ft, it rises almost 5000ft above the valley floor, with its 2000-foot northwest face only seven degrees off the vertical, making it the sheerest cliff in North America. Though stunning from the valley, the best views of Half Dome are from Glacier Point (see p.404), especially around sunset.

Ambitious day-hikers (see p.402) wanting to get up close and personal can make it to the shallow saddle of the dome's thirteen-acre summit, tackling the final four hundred feet by way of a steep steel-cable staircase (late May to mid-October only) hooked onto the rock's curving back. Once at the nearly flat summit, the brave (or foolish) can inch out towards the edge of the projecting lip for a vertiginous look straight down the face.

The major waterfalls

At 2425ft, **Yosemite Falls** is widely claimed to be the fifth highest waterfall in the world, and the highest in North America. It's a somewhat spurious assertion, since it is actually two falls separated by 675ft of churning rapids and chutes known as **Middle Cascade**. Nonetheless, the 1430-foot **Upper Yosemite Fall** and the 320-foot **Lower Yosemite Fall** are magnificent, especially in May and early June when runoff from melting snow turns them into a foaming torrent. The flow typically dries up by mid-August, leaving a dark stain of algae and lichen to mark the spot. A quarter-mile asphalt trail (from shuttle bus stop 6) leads towards the falls along an avenue of incense cedars and ponderosa pines, creating a perfect photo op.

Perhaps the most sensual waterfall in the park is the 620-foot **Bridalveil Fall**, a slender ribbon at the valley's western end, which in Ahwahneechee goes by the name of *Pohono* or "spirit of the puffing wind." While Bridalveil seldom completely dries up, it's best seen from April to June when winds blow the cascade outward up to twenty feet away from its base, drawing the spray into a delicate lacy veil. The quarter-mile trail from the parking lot is four miles west of the village and not accessible by shuttle bus.

Two of the park's most striking falls are guaranteed to still be active year-round, but are sequestered away from the road up the Merced River canyon, near Happy Isles (see p.399). It's a relatively easy walk to get a glimpse of the distant 317-foot **Vernal Fall**, a curtain of water about eighty feet wide that casts bright rainbows as you walk along the wonderful Mist Trail (see box, p.402). It requires much more commitment to hike steeply upstream as far as the 594-foot **Nevada Fall**, but it's worth the effort for a close look at this sweeping cascade that free-falls for half its height, then fans out onto the apron below.

Yosemite Village

Very much the heart of the valley, **Yosemite Village** is not really a cohesive "village" at all, but a settlement of scattered low buildings where mule deer wander freely. You'll find yourself returning time and again to visit shops, restaurants, banking facilities, Internet access points, the post office (see p.407 for the last three), and one of the park's **main visitor centers** (see p.391 for hours). Here you can watch the 23-minute *Spirit of Yosemite* (every 30min), which has great footage of the park through the seasons. For more great images walk a few steps east to the **Ansel Adams Gallery** and its collection of fine-art prints, posters, and postcards.

Immediately west of the visitor center a hefty nine-foot slice of a giant sequoia trunk marks the **Yosemite Museum** (daily: July & Aug 9am–5pm; Sept–June 10am–4pm; free), home to a small selection of artifacts focusing on Native American heritage, specifically the local Ahwahneechee and the neighboring Mono Lake Paiute, with whom they traded and intermarried. One of the few crafts to flourish after contact with whites was **basketwork**: fine examples on display include a superbly detailed 1930s Mono Lake Paiute basket almost three feet in diameter, and its even larger Miwok/Paiute equivalent, painstakingly created by famed basket-maker Lucy Telles. Basket-making demonstrations are given by Ahwahneechee practitioners throughout the day. A couple of **feather-trimmed dance capes** warrant a look, as does the buckskin dress worn by natives in the 1920s and 1930s during tourist demonstrations of basket-weaving and dance. Though completely alien to the Miwok tradition, the Plains-style buckskin clothing and feather headdresses fulfilled the expectations of the whites who came to watch. Outside, a self-guided trail weaves around the **Indian Village of Ahwahneechee** (always open; free), with its cluster of reconstructed Indian buildings.

Fifty yards west of the museum, the **Yosemite Cemetery** (always open; free) holds just three-dozen graves of early white settlers. Among the simple headstones are those of early orchardist **James Lamon** and park guardian **Galen Clark**, both marked with century-old sequoias.

Worth a quick look even if you don't intend to stay or eat, **The Ahwahnee** is a short signposted walk or shuttle bus ride from Yosemite Village. It was built in grand style in 1927 from local rock and is decorated with Native American motifs and some wonderful oriental rugs and carpets. Originally intended to blend into its surroundings and attract the richer type of tourist, it still does both fairly effortlessly – pop in for a few minutes to sink into the deep sofas and view the collection of paintings of Yosemite's early days.

Curry Village and the eastern valley

At some point, almost everyone finds themselves at the eastern end of the valley, which has the densest concentration of accommodation: all the main campgrounds are here, along with the permanent cabins of *Housekeeping Camp* and the tent cabin complex of **Curry Village**. This is a direct descendant of **Camp Curry**, started in 1899 by David and Jeannie Curry, who were keen to share their adopted home in the valley and charged just $12 a week for a "good bed, and a clean napkin every meal." It's now a rambling area of tent cabins and wooden chalets centered on a small complex of restaurants, shops, pay showers, a post office, and an outdoor amphitheater hosting ranger programs and evening shows. There's also a winter ice rink, bike rental, and a kiosk that rents rafts for use on the nearby Merced River.

The western end of Curry Village is marked by the **LeConte Memorial Lodge** (May–Sept Wed–Sun 10am–4pm; free; shuttle stop 12), a small, rough-hewn granite-block structure where the **Sierra Club** maintains displays on its history, runs a conservation library, and has a fascinating relief map of the valley dating back to around 1885. The Lodge itself was built by the Sierra Club in 1903 to commemorate the eminent geologist and early supporter of John Muir, **Joseph LeConte** (1823–1901), and as the Sierra Club's Yosemite headquarters, it was managed for a couple of summers in the early 1920s by **Ansel Adams**, who was happy to do anything if it meant he could spend more time in the valley. Their evening programs (usually Fri–Sun; free) are a little more highbrow than those elsewhere in the park and might include a slide show or talk by some luminary; check *Yosemite Today* for details.

Shuttle buses head east from Curry Village to the **Nature Center at Happy Isles** (early May to mid-Sept daily 10am–4pm; free; shuttle stop 16), containing a family-friendly set of displays on flora and fauna, a hands-on exhibit allowing you to feel how hunks of rough granite get weathered down to sand, and an exhibit on a year in the life of a bear. At the rear of the Nature Center be sure to check out the **rockfall exhibit**, where a number of explanatory panels highlight the pulverized rock and flattened trees that resulted from a massive rockfall in 1996.

Ansel Adams

Few photographers have stamped their vision on a place as unforgettably as **Ansel Adams** did with Yosemite Valley. While he worked all over the American West, Yosemite was Adams' home and the subject of his most celebrated works, icons of American landscape photography such as 1940's *Jeffrey Pine – Sentinel Dome*; *Clearing Winter Storm* from 1944; and *Moon and Half Dome* from 1960.

Born in 1902 into a moderately wealthy San Francisco family, Adams was given a Box Brownie when he was fourteen, on his first trip to Yosemite. He claimed that he knew his "destiny" on that first visit to Yosemite, and soon turned his attentions to the mountains.

He first made a mark in 1927 with *Monolith, The Face of Half Dome*, his first successful **visualization**: Adams believed that, before pressing the shutter, the photographer should have a clear idea of the final image and think through the entire photographic process, considering how lenses, filters, exposure, development, and printing need to be used to achieve that visualization. This approach may seem obvious today, but compared to the hit-and-miss methods of the time, it was little short of revolutionary.

As Adams fine-tuned his artistic theories through the 1930s, the idea of photography as fine art was still considered novel, and he spent much of his time lobbying for more respect for his craft. Adams was therefore delighted when, in 1940, he was made vice-chairman of the newly established **Department of Photography** at the Museum of Modern Art (MoMA) in New York City. Even so, there was still very little money in photography, and Adams continued to take commercial assignments, including shooting menu photos for *The Ahwahnee*. While still demanding the highest standard of reproduction, the artist had tempered his perfectionism by the 1950s and allowed his work to appear on postcards, calendars, and posters. By now he was virtually a household name, and for the first time in his life he began making money to match his status as the grand old man of Western photography. His final triumph came in 1979, when MoMA put on the huge "Yosemite and the Range of Light" exhibition. That same year, he was asked to make an official portrait of President Jimmy Carter – the first time a photographer had been assigned an official presidential portrait – and was subsequently awarded the nation's highest civilian honor, the Medal of Freedom.

Throughout his life, Adams was equally passionate about **conservation**. Back in 1932, he had a direct hand in creating Kings Canyon National Park, and two years later he became a director of the **Sierra Club**, overseeing several successful environmental campaigns until 1971. He never quit campaigning for conservation, and, after an interview in which he suggested he'd like to drown Ronald Reagan in his own martini, agreed to meet the president to promote the environmental cause.

Adams died on April 22, 1984, aged 82, and posthumously lent his name to both Mount Ansel Adams and a huge chunk of the High Sierra south of Yosemite National Park, now known as the Ansel Adams Wilderness.

▲ Riding near Mirror Lake, Yosemite National Park

One of the most rewarding of the easy trails near Curry Village leads from shuttle stop 17 around the edge of the valley floor to **Mirror Lake** (2 miles; 1hr; 100-foot ascent). This compellingly calm lake (typically dry in late summer) lies beneath and reflects the great bulk of Half Dome; it's best seen in the early morning before too many others arrive. Most visitors to Mirror Lake follow the traffic-free paved road from the shuttle stop, but several smaller parallel paths (easily found to the left of the main track) will steer you clear of the asphalt and the crowds.

Northern Yosemite

From the valley, Big Oak Flat Road climbs rapidly to Crane Flat, where there's a store and the closest gas station to the valley. From here Hwy-120 West runs to the Big Oak Flat Entrance and **Hetch Hetchy**, once a scenic rival for Yosemite Valley, though now partially filled with a water supply for San Francisco.

East of Crane Flat, **Tioga Road** (Hwy-120 East) climbs through dense forests into the Yosemite high country around Tenaya Lake, Tuolumne Meadows, and Tioga Pass – open grasslands pocked by polished granite domes and with a southern horizon delineated by the sawtooth crest of the **Cathedral Range**.

Hetch Hetchy

John Muir's passion for Yosemite Valley was matched, if not exceeded, by his desire to preserve the beauty of **Hetch Hetchy**, eighteen miles north of the valley and close to the Big Oak Flat entrance. Once a near replica of Yosemite Valley, with grassy, oak-filled meadows and soaring granite walls, it's now largely under the dammed waters of the slender Hetch Hetchy reservoir. When it came under threat from power- and water-supply interests in San Francisco in 1901, Muir battled for twelve years, instigating the first environmental letter-writing campaign to Congress. Eventually, in 1913, the cause was lost to a federal bill that paved the way for the Tuolumne River to be blocked by the **O'Shaughnessey Dam**. Hetch Hetchy is no longer a match for its southern kin, but the view of granite domes and waterfalls from the path crossing the dam gives some sense of what it must have been like. All this is best seen on a short and mostly flat hike which initially crosses the dam, passes through a short tunnel, and follows the north bank of the reservoir to **Wapama Falls** (five miles round-trip) and on to **Rancheria Falls** (a further four miles each way). Both falls are at their best in May and June but are dry by August.

Tioga Road and Tuolumne Meadows

From Crane Flat, the eastbound **Tioga Road** soon passes a parking lot from where there's a mile-long walking trail to the **Tuolumne Grove** of giant sequoias, nowhere near as spectacular as the Mariposa Grove (see p.404), but easier to reach – and it's always an honor to be among these giants. The road then climbs steadily through deep pine forests past the *White Wolf* and *Porcupine* campgrounds, rising above 8000ft just before **Olmsted Point** – right up there with Glacier Point as one of Yosemite's finest roadside views – which looks down Tenaya Creek towards Half Dome. In the late 1950s, when the Tioga Road was being upgraded, Ansel Adams fruitlessly fought against its re-routing past here and along the gorgeous shores of **Tenaya Lake** to Tuolumne.

The alpine area around **Tuolumne Meadows** (literally "meadow in the sky") has an atmosphere quite different from the valley, 55 miles (about a ninety-minute drive) away. The landscape here, at 8600ft, is much more open; the light is more intense, and the air always has a fresh, crisp bite. That said, there can still be good-sized blasts of carbon monoxide at peak times in the vicinity of the campground and *Tuolumne Meadows Lodge* (see p.393) – the only accommodation base in the area.

Being almost five thousand feet higher than Yosemite Valley makes Tuolumne Meadows a better starting point for **hiking** (see box, p.402) into the surrounding High Sierra wilderness. The meadows themselves are the largest in the entire Sierra: twelve miles long, between a quarter- and half-mile wide, and threaded by the meandering Tuolumne River. Snow usually lingers here until the end of

There are no restrictions on **day-hiking** in Yosemite, so for all the following hikes you need only equip yourself properly – map, raingear, food, etc – get to the trailhead, and set off. Unless otherwise noted, the following distances and times are for a round-trip.

Day-hikes from Yosemite Valley

Four-mile Trail to Glacier Point (10 miles; 5–6hr; 3200-foot ascent). The steep asphalt path from the valley floor to Glacier Point doesn't give much of a sense of being in the wilderness, but the magnificent views make this one of the valley's more popular day-walks. Generally open mid-May to Oct.

Half Dome (17 miles; 9–12hr; 4800-foot ascent). This is one of the valley's finest and most arduous walks, initially following the Mist Trail (see below) and continuing around the back of Half Dome. The final 400ft ascends over the huge, smooth, humped back, aided by a pair of steel cables and wooden steps which are partly removed in winter (mid-Nov to late May) to discourage hikers. There's usually a pile of free-use gloves at the base of the cables to protect tender hands. Once at the summit, anyone concerned about their outdoor credibility will want to edge out to the very lip of the abyss and peer down the sheer, 2000-foot northwest face. If you plan a one-day assault, you'll need to start at the crack of dawn.

Mist Trail to the top of Vernal Fall (3 miles; 2–3hr; 1100-foot ascent). If you only do one hike in Yosemite, this is it, especially during the spring snowmelt, when Vernal Fall is often framed by a rainbow and hikers get drenched in spray; bring a raincoat or plan to get wet. Start at shuttle stop 16 and head uphill, crossing a footbridge with great views of the fall. Then follow the Mist Trail along a narrow path which, though hardly dangerous, demands sure footing and a head for heights. At the top of the fall, either retrace your steps to the trailhead or return via the John Muir Trail.

Upper Yosemite Fall (7 miles; 4–7hr; 2700-foot ascent). This perennially popular, energy-sapping hike climbs steeply to the north rim of the valley, with great views of Upper Yosemite Fall for much of the way and the opportunity to sit virtually on the edge of the fall, gazing down at the Lilliputian activity below in Yosemite Village. Its northern aspect keeps the trail open longer than most (April–Dec) but is best done during the spring snowmelt: start before 7am to avoid the worst of the midday heat. The trailhead is just by the *Camp 4* campground (shuttle stop 7).

Day-hikes from Tuolumne Meadows

Soda Springs and Parsons Lodge (4-mile loop; 2hr; negligible ascent). An easy meander around some of Tuolumne Meadows' best and most accessible features, especially good in the late June and July wildflower season. Cross the meadow from a trailhead 300yd east of the visitor center to reach the Soda Springs and Parsons

June, forcing the **wildflowers** to contend with a short growing season. They respond with a glorious burst of color in July, a wonderful time for a wander.

The distinctively glaciated granite form of **Lembert Dome** squats at the eastern end of the meadows, gazing across the grasslands towards its western twin, **Pothole Dome**, which makes a great sunset destination. The mountain scenery is particularly striking to the south, where the **Cathedral Range** offers a horizon of slender spires and knife-blade ridges. Look out for the appropriately named **Unicorn Peak** and **Cathedral Peak**, a textbook example of a glaciated "Matterhorn," where glaciers have carved away the rock on all sides and left a sharp, pointed summit. Some of the best views are from the naturally carbonated **Soda Springs** (see box, above), described in 1863 as "pungent and delightful to the taste." And so it is, though the Park Service discourages drinking from it.

Lodge, then follow a broad trail to the base of Lembert Dome; either walk back along Tioga Road or use the shuttle bus.

Lembert Dome (3.7-mile loop; 2–3hr; 850-foot ascent). This hike up the meadows' most prominent feature offers expansive views from the summit and examples of glacially polished rock and "erratic" boulders left behind by retreating glaciers. Start at the parking lot at the dome's base and follow signs for Dog Lake, then head right to ascend via the bare rock of the dome's northeast corner. Descend, then turn right to complete a loop around the dome.

Cathedral Lakes (8 miles; 4–6hr; 1000-foot ascent). A candidate for the best Tuolumne day-hike, this route follows several miles of the John Muir Trail as far as a pair of gorgeous tarns in open alpine country with long views to a serrated skyline. Hike from the trailhead just west of the Tuolumne Meadows visitor center and enjoy the gradually improving views of the twin spires of Cathedral Peak. Near its base are Upper Cathedral Lake (with excellent camping) and Lower Cathedral Lake, a divine spot lodged in a cirque now partly filled with lush meadows, and split by a ridge of hard rock polished smooth by ancient glaciers.

Multiday hikes

Camping out overnight opens up the majority of Yosemite's eight hundred miles of backcountry trails. Choosing from the enormous range of paths is almost impossible, though some of the most popular are those running between Yosemite Valley and Tuolumne Meadows, a two-day hike for anyone with reasonable fitness. Further suggestions are outlined in the *Rough Guide to Yosemite National Park*.

To camp out overnight you need a **wilderness permit**, available free from ranger stations – at Wawona, Big Oak Flat, Hetch Hetchy, and Tuolumne – and the Wilderness Center in Yosemite Village (mid-May to June & early Sept to mid-Oct daily 8am–5pm; July to early Sept daily 7.30am–6pm). In winter, when the wilderness centers are closed, you can get a permit at the nearest visitor center. Numbers are limited by a quota system, but with a little flexibility you'll often find you can get a permit the day before you wish to start your hike. Large groups, people with tight schedules, and anyone hiking at busy times should **reserve in advance** (T 209/372-0740, W www.nps.gov/archive/yose/wilderness/permits.htm; $5 per person) from 24 weeks to two days ahead of your trip. Don't despair if you have trouble landing the trail you want: paths are so numerous that you may start at a less popular trailhead but end up doing largely the same hike.

When obtaining your permit you'll be instructed in **backcountry etiquette** (see p.51), especially water purification, waste disposal, and proper use of the required **bear-resistant food canister** (rentals $5 per trip). **Camping gear** can be rented quite reasonably from Yosemite Mountaineering School (see p.407).

The Tuolumne Meadows Tour and Hikers Bus (see p.392) runs up here once a day from Yosemite Valley, stopping at trailheads along the journey and at various points around Tuolumne Meadows, including the **visitor center** (see p.391). There's also a **free shuttle** service linking Tuolumne to Olmsted Point, just west of Tenaya Lake (June to mid-Sept daily 7am–6pm).

Southern Yosemite

The southern end of the park contains a broad swathe of sharply peaked mountains extending twenty miles from the foothills in the west to the Sierra crest in the east. In summer, visitors congregate at **Wawona**, where the hotel and campground provide most services, or at the nearby **Mariposa Grove**, the most impressive of the park's stands of giant sequoias. Roughly midway between Yosemite Valley and Wawona, Glacier Point Road carves its way to the park's **viewpoint** *par excellence* at **Glacier Point**, right on the rim of Yosemite Valley and on a level with the face of Half Dome.

Glacier Point, Sentinel Dome, and Taft Point

The most spectacular views of Yosemite Valley are from **Glacier Point**, the top of an almost sheer, 3200-foot cliff, 32 miles by road (usually open mid-May to late Oct) from Yosemite Valley. The valley floor lies directly beneath the viewing point, and there are tremendous views across to Half Dome (easy from here to see how it got its name) and to the distant snow capped summits of the High Sierra. It's possible to get here on foot along the very steep Four-Mile Trail (see box, p.402), though you may prefer to use the **Glacier Point Tour and Hikers Bus** (see p.392) from the valley and then hike down.

The road to Glacier Point passes the **Badger Pass Ski Area** (generally open mid-Dec to early April; ☎209/372-8444, ⊛www.badgerpass.com), which has a few short tows and a ski school that runs excellent **cross-country ski** trips eleven miles to the viewpoint. You'll also pass a number of signposted trailheads for easy and longer hikes. One of the best is to the 8122-foot summit of **Sentinel Dome** (two miles round-trip), a gleaming granite scalp topped by the rotting remains of a Jeffrey pine made famous by Ansel Adams photos from the 1940s. From the Sentinel Dome parking lot, a second dusty, undulating trail leads west to **Taft Point** (2 miles round-trip), which trades Glacier Point's Half Dome vista for a view across the valley to the top of El Capitan and Yosemite Falls. Far fewer people follow this trail, perhaps because of the vertiginous drops all around, protected only by the flimsiest of barriers in one spot. Here, the granite edges of the valley rim have been deeply incised to form what are known as the **Taft Point Fissures**.

Wawona and the Mariposa Grove

There's a decidedly relaxed pace at **Wawona**, 27 miles (or an hour's drive) south of Yosemite Village on Hwy-41. Most people spend their time here strolling the grounds of the landmark *Wawona Hotel* (see p.393), surrounded by a nine-hole golf course where $30 will get you a full eighteen-hole round (plus $10 for club rental, if needed) on the Sierra's oldest course. Fans of faster-paced pastimes can opt for the free tennis courts instead. Close by is the **Pioneer Yosemite History Center**, a collection of buildings culled from the early times of white habitation, which can be visited on a self-guided walking tour (free). The jail, homesteads, and covered bridge are good for a scoot around, and through the summer months (particularly weekends) the buildings are open and interpreted by attendant rangers. Once away from the main road, the area makes a quiet spot for a picnic.

The **Mariposa Grove**, three miles east of Hwy-41 on a small road that cuts off just past the park's southern entrance, is the biggest and best of Yosemite's groves of giant sequoia trees. To get to the towering growths, walk the 2.5-mile loop trail from the parking lot at the end of the road, or take the narrated **Big Trees Tour** around the grove (June–Oct 9am–5pm; $11), which follows a paved road to the major sights. There's also a free shuttle to the parking area from Wawona.

Trails around the sequoia groves call first at the **Fallen Monarch**, familiar from the 1899 photo, widely reproduced on postcards, in which cavalry officers and their horses stand atop the prostrate tree. The most renowned of the grouping, well marked along the route, is the **Grizzly Giant**, thought to be 2700 years old and with a lower branch thicker than the trunk of any non-sequoia in the grove. Other highlights include the **Wawona Tunnel Tree**, through which people drove their cars until it fell in 1969, the similarly bored **California Tunnel Tree**, which you can walk through, and all manner of trees which have grown together, split apart, been struck by lightning, or are simply staggeringly large. It's also worth dropping into the **Mariposa Grove Museum** (summer daily 9am–4pm; free), towards the top end of the trail, which has modest displays and photos of the mighty trees. For more on the life of the sequoia, see the box on p.372.

Eating, drinking, and entertainment

With a couple of notable exceptions, **eating** in Yosemite is more a function than a pleasure. Food, whether in restaurants or in the grocery stores around Yosemite Village (where there's a well-stocked supermarket), Curry Village, Wawona, and Tuolumne Meadows, is at least twenty percent more expensive than outside the park. Restaurants serve beer and wine, plus there's a lively **bar** at *Yosemite Lodge*, a swankier affair at *The Ahwahnee*, and a lounge with occasional piano entertainment at the *Wawona Hotel*. **Outside the park** the dining options are considerably better, with plenty of good restaurants and a smattering of bars in the gateway towns of Groveland, Mariposa, and Oakhurst.

To help visitors interpret Yosemite, the Park Service and related organizations run a number of **ranger programs** – nature hikes, photo walks, talks about bears, etc – most of which are free. In addition, there's **evening entertainment** in the form of ranger-led campfire talks at most of the campgrounds, occasional stargazing sessions, natural history slide shows, and music shows. The *Yosemite Today* newspaper carries a full catalog of events, along with listings of the *Yosemite Theater* program ($8), which presents two ninety-minute one-man shows featuring the talents of actor Lee Stetson, who has been impersonating John Muir since 1982.

In the valley

Ahwahnee Bar *The Ahwahnee* (11am–11pm). Intimate piano bar perfect for indulging in something from their selection of Armagnacs, ports, and classic martinis ($9–15), and perhaps an antipasto plate for two ($21). There's live music most Fri and Sat nights, usually something subdued.

Ahwahnee Dining Room *The Ahwahnee* ⊕209/372-1489. One of the most beautiful restaurants in the US, built in baronial style with 34-foot-high ceilings of exposed beams, rustic iron chandeliers, and floor-to-ceiling leaded windows. The food is by far the best in Yosemite: eggs Benedict ($17), smoked duck caesar salad ($15), and Kobe beef short rib pot roast with mushrooms and baby fennel ($35). The Sunday brunch ($35) is particularly stupendous. Casual dress is permitted during the day, but formal wear is expected for dinner (sports coats are available free of charge).

Degnan's Café, Deli & Loft Yosemite Village. Three eating spots in one building. There's a daytime café (with Internet kiosks) serving reasonable espresso, specialty teas, and cinnamon rolls; a takeout deli with bowls of soup ($2.75–3.75) and chili ($4–5), and massive sandwiches, burritos, and salads at under $7; and a gourmet pizza restaurant ($14–18 for medium; $17–22 for a large).

Pavilion Buffet Curry Village. Lively cafeteria serving great-value all-you-can-eat breakfasts ($10) with plenty of fresh fruit, juices, eggs, bacon, hash browns, waffles, yoghurt, and more. Dinner ($12) suffers a little from overcooked vegetables and sloppy preparation, but you can still fill up on salads, build-your-own tacos, chicken-fried steak, simple pasta dishes, cakes, and sodas. Buy a beer or wine at the adjacent bar and carry it through.

Pizza Deck and Curry Bar Curry Village. Very much the place to repair to on balmy evenings after a hard day in the hills. Fight for an outdoor table while you wait for a pretty decent build-your-own pizza (from $18 for twelve slices), and maybe a pint of good draft beer ($4.50) or a margarita ($6.50).

Yosemite Lodge Food Court *Yosemite Lodge*. Bright and cheerful self-serve café/restaurant with a full range of cold and cooked breakfasts ($3–7), muffins, Danishes, and coffee, plus lunches and dinners that range from a grilled chicken sandwich, pizza, or gyro platter (all $7) to pasta and meatballs ($9) or chicken, vegetables, and rice ($9). There is some outdoor seating.

The rest of the park

Tuolumne Meadows Grill Tuolumne Meadows. Basically a burger joint, also serving small and pricey breakfasts and sandwich lunches.

Tuolumne Meadows Lodge ☎209/372-8413. Family-style breakfasts ($5–10) and burgers, steak, chicken, and fish dinners ($14–24) served in a large tent beside the Tuolumne River.

Wawona Hotel Dining Room Semi-formal dining off white linen tablecloths, though the food is neither very expensive nor particularly special. Still, you can lunch on chicken alfredo, ratatouille, or a club sandwich ($9), then dress smart for dinner, such as pan-fried trout ($21) and a raspberry nut cake ($5). There's also a wonderful Sunday brunch buffet (Easter–Thanksgiving 7.30am–1.30pm; $19) and a Saturday barbecue (late May to early Sept 5–7pm).

White Wolf Lodge Just off Hwy-120 ☎209/252-4848. Large portions of good-value American food in rustic surroundings for $16–22. Open for breakfast and dinner only.

Hwy-120: Groveland

Café Charlotte 18959 Hwy-120, Groveland ☎209/962-6455. Excellent little restaurant where the casualness of the atmosphere belies a serious approach to the quality of the food. There's every-thing from pasta (including vegan and kid's dishes) to chicken Jerusalem (with artichokes and mushrooms) and succulent steaks (all $13–23), plus lip-smacking desserts. Licensed and BYO with $8 corkage.

Cocina Michoacana 18370 Hwy-120, Groveland. Authentic and low-priced Mexican spot; $8 will get you either a great breakfast of scrambled eggs with strips of steak or one of the daily lunch specials, and later they serve a full range of favorites including great fajitas ($21–25 for two) and melt-in-your-mouth breaded shrimps.

Iron Door 18761 Main St, Groveland. With its grill and soda fountain, the *Iron Door* is a fine place to eat, with a locally famous garlic soup

and fine ribeye steak ($22), all beautifully prepared and presented. But what makes it special is the atmospheric bar, reliably claimed to be the oldest saloon in California. It comes with pool table and all manner of paraphernalia on the walls, plus a live band most weekends.

Victorian Room Groveland Hotel, 18767 Hwy-120 ☎209/962-4000. The best restaurant in town, with a seasonally changing menu and nightly chef's specials – perhaps crab cakes with cilantro and caper sauce, or honey-glazed baby back pork ribs. Expect to pay $40–45 for three courses, including a glass or two from their extensive wine list.

Hwy-140: Mariposa, Midpines, and El Portal

Café at the Bug *Yosemite Bug Rustic Mountain Resort*, Midpines. Licensed café with quality food at a good price: wholesome breakfasts ($4.50–6.50), packed lunches ($6), and dinners ($8–14). If you don't mind the slightly frenetic hostel atmosphere, it's definitely worth the drive out for slow-roasted Cajun pork or baked trout filet with butter pecan sauce. Good microbrews on tap as well.

Happy Burger 5120 Hwy-140 at 12th St ☎209/966-2719. A huge array of good, cheap diner food – breakfast burrito ($4.50), tuna melt ($5.50), teriyaki chicken salad ($6) – to take out or eat in at Formica booths. There's a fine jukebox and the entire place is decorated with tragic Seventies album covers.

High Country Café Hwy-140 & Hwy-49, Mariposa. Daytime health-food café with sandwiches ($6–7), salads, burritos, and fruit smoothies. There's also a health-food store next door offering good bread, organic fruit, and goodies in bulk bins that are perfect for trail mix. Closed Sun.

Savoury's 5027 Hwy-140, Mariposa ☎209/966-7677. The pick of Mariposa's midrange restaurants, offering a relaxed atmosphere with a touch of class: modern decor, black linen tablecloths, and a secluded patio out back for those warm summer evenings. Choose from chipotle chicken ($16), roasted garlic cream scallops ($23), and spinach and pine nut pasta ($16), perhaps followed by chocolate bread pudding ($5). Wine is available by the glass.

Hwy-41: Oakhurst and Fish Camp

Mountain House Junction of Hwy-41 & Bass Lake Road, 3 miles north of Oakhurst. Reliable, friendly, and efficient diner that's the best place around for burgers, sandwiches, and pasta dishes, along with breakfast blintzes ($8), locally renowned New York steak ($24), and charbroiled trout ($17).

The Narrow Gauge Inn 48571 Hwy-41, Fish Camp ☏559/683-6446. Fine dining in an Old World setting with candlelight and a warming fire. Start by dipping sourdough into a rich fondue and continue with charbroiled swordfish or filet mignon. Expect to pay $40 each, more with wine. Open mid-April to mid-Oct Wed–Sun 5.30–9pm.

🚶 Three Sisters Café 40291 Junction Drive, off Hwy-49 behind Raley's supermarket, Oakhurst ☏559/642-2253. Classy but casual restaurant whose husband-and-wife owners run a tight ship. Check out the $12 Earlybird dinner specials (Weds & Thurs 4–5.30pm) or come later for pork medallions in a blue cheese sauce ($23) or braised lamb shanks ($22). Closed Mon & Tues in winter.

Yosemite Coffee & Roasting Company 40879 Hwy-41, a mile north of Oakhurst. Relaxed java joint with mismatched chairs and newspapers, ideal for breakfast burritos, toothsome muffins, sandwiches, cakes, and good espresso at modest prices. Also operates as a bar, often with live music at weekends.

Listings

Banks There are no banks in Yosemite, though there are several 24-hour ATMs, all charging a transaction fee of $3 on US accounts. There is no foreign currency exchange.

Bike rental Bikes are only allowed on the valley's flat, paved roads and bikeways, so the basic single-speed bikes ($7.50/hr, $24.50/day) available at Yosemite Lodge (all year) and Curry Village (summer only) are quite adequate.

Books The Yosemite Bookstore, by the Valley Visitor Center, has a good selection of Yosemite-related books and maps; the Ansel Adams Gallery specializes in photography and nature publications; and the Mountain Shop at Curry Village stocks climbing guides.

Campfires Summertime air-quality restrictions limit campfires to between 5pm and 10pm from May to mid-Oct. For ecological reasons, firewood must not be gathered in the valley or above 9600ft, but is available for sale at stores throughout the park.

Camping equipment Head for the Mountain Shop in Curry Village to buy gear or rent. Expect to pay $13 to rent a sleeping bag, $15.50 for an overnight pack, and comparable rates for tents, snowshoes, etc. The store in Tuolumne Meadows also stocks camping equipment, climbing gear, and lightweight food.

Gas Available at good prices in Oakhurst, moderate prices in Mariposa and Groveland, and expensive prices in the park; year-round at Wawona and Crane Flat, and seasonally at Tuolumne Meadows. There are no gas stations in Yosemite Valley.

Guided trips The Yosemite Mountaineering School (☏209/372-8344, ⊛www.yosemitemountaineering.com) runs guided backpacking, rock climbing, and alpine trips from around $125 each per day for groups of four or more.

Horseback riding Saddle trips accommodating riders of all standards are run from stables in Yosemite Valley (April–Oct; ☏209/372-8348), Tuolumne Meadows (early June to Sept; ☏209/372-8427), and Wawona (May–Sept; ☏209/375-5602): scenic rides cost $53 for two hours, $96 for the day.

Internet One first-come-first-served 30-minute session per week at the Yosemite Village public library (see below): they're popular so get there early. Also five feed-in-the-dollar-bills computers at Degnan's Café in Yosemite Village, free Wi-Fi at the Ahwahnee, and Wi-Fi (free for guests) in the lobby of Yosemite Lodge.

Laundry There's a coin-op affair at Housekeeping Camp (8am–8pm).

Library The Yosemite Village public library (Mon 8.30–11.30am, Tues 10am–2pm, Wed 8.30am–12.30pm, Thurs 4–7pm) is located just west of the Yosemite Museum in a building signed "Girls Club."

Medical assistance Yosemite Medical Clinic, between Yosemite Village and The Ahwahnee (☏209/372-4637) has 24-hour emergency care and drop-in and urgent care (daily 8am–7pm), and accepts appointments (Mon–Fri 8am–5pm). Dental treatment (☏209/372-4200) is also available.

Photography The Ansel Adams Gallery in Yosemite Village stocks slide, professional, and ordinary print film at reasonable prices, and runs free two-hour guided photography walks. There are also year-round photography walks run by the park concessionaire in Yosemite Valley: check Yosemite Today for all times.

Post office In Yosemite Village (Mon–Fri 8.30am–5pm, Sat 10am–noon) and accepting General Delivery (aka poste restante). Also year-round services in Wawona (Mon–Fri 9am–5pm, Sat 9am–1pm) and summer-only service in Tuolumne Meadows (Mon–Fri 9am–5pm, Sat 9am–1pm). The park's Zip code is 95389.

Rafting Inside the park itself, Curry Village rents six-berth rafts ($20.50 per person; minimum 2;

June & July only) allowing you to float gently along the placid and relatively gentle section of the Merced River – the cost includes a return bus ride. Outside the park, from April to June, far more rugged (Class III–IV) one-day stretches are run in the traditional guided fashion by Mariah Wilderness Expeditions (☏1-800/462-7424, ⓦwww.mariahwe.com), Whitewater Voyages (☏1-800/400-7238, ⓦwww.whitewatervoyages.com), Zephyr Whitewater Expeditions (☏1-800/431-3636, ⓦwww.zrafting.com), and others, all charging around $120–140 midweek and $130–160 at weekends.

Recycling Most items are accepted at the Yosemite Village Store Recycling Center, east of the supermarket.

RVs Campers can use all the main campgrounds, but there are no hookups in Yosemite. Dump stations are in Yosemite Valley, Wawona, and Tuolumne Meadows (summer only).

Showers In Yosemite Valley at Curry Village (24 hours; $3), where outside the peak summer season there's often nobody to either provide a towel or take your money. Outside the valley the only public showers are at *Tuolumne Meadows Lodge* (see p.393; $4).

Swimming There are pools in the valley at *Yosemite Lodge* and Curry Village (both free to hotel guests and $5 for others), the *Wawona Hotel* and *The Ahwahnee* both have pools for guests, and there are numerous small river beaches throughout the valley and at Wawona.

Travel details

Trains

The **San Joaquins** service runs six times daily between Bakersfield and Emeryville, near Oakland, from where Amtrak Thruway buses run into San Francisco. Amtrak Thruway bus connections from San Diego, Orange County, and Los Angeles link with the train at Bakersfield.

Bakersfield to: Emeryville (6hr); Fresno (1hr 45min); Hanford (1hr 15min); Merced (3hr); Stockton (4hr).

Buses

Buses are either Greyhound or Orange Belt Stages (☏1-800/266-7433, ⓦwww.orangebelt.com), which often use Amtrak and Greyhound stations as hubs for their network.

Bakersfield to: Hanford (1 daily, 2hr 30min); Los Angeles (15 daily; 2–3hr); Merced (8 daily; 3hr 30min–4hr 30min).

Fresno to: Merced (7 daily; 1hr 10min); Modesto (10 daily; 2hr); Stockton (7 daily; 3hr).

Hanford to: Bakersfield (1 daily; 2hr 30min); San Luis Obispo (2 daily; 4hr); Visalia (2 daily; 30min).

Los Angeles to: Bakersfield (15 daily; 2–3hr); Fresno (14 daily; 4–6hr); Merced (7 daily; 6–7hr); Modesto (10 daily; 6–8hr); Stockton (9 daily; 6hr–8hr 30min); Visalia (6 daily; 4–5hr).

Merced to: Bakersfield (8 daily; 3hr 30min–4hr 30min); Fresno (7 daily; 1hr 10min); Los Angeles (7 daily; 6–7hr); Modesto (7 daily; 1hr); Sacramento (6 daily; 3hr); San Francisco (3 daily; 4–6hr); Stockton (6 daily; 1hr 30min–2hr); Yosemite (3–5 daily; 2hr 45min).

Modesto to: Fresno (10 daily; 2hr); Merced (7 daily; 1hr).

San Francisco to: Bakersfield (6 daily; 7–8hr); Fresno (7 daily; 5hr); Merced (4 daily; 4hr); Modesto (4 daily; 3hr); Stockton (9 daily; 4–6hr); Visalia (2 daily; 7hr).

Stockton to: Fresno (7 daily; 3hr); Merced (4 daily; 1hr 30min); Sacramento (10 daily; 1hr); San Francisco (9 daily; 4–6hr).

Visalia to: Hanford (2 daily; 30min); San Francisco (2 daily; 7hr); San Luis Obispo (2 daily; 4hr 30min).

West Coast sounds

An astonishing number of famous acts and trends have emerged from California's musical tradition. The West Coast sound may have been born on the blues-soaked banks of the Mississippi, but as an infant in the 1960s it learned to surf the Pacific with the Beach Boys, and during 1967's Summer of Love the precocious flower child was daring the world to drop out, drop acid, and float to a unique soundtrack of psychedelia. After mellowing and going mainstream in the 1970s with the radio-friendly fare of Jackson Browne and the Doobie Brothers, the California music scene reacted to the Reaganite Eighties through the political diatribes of hardcore bands like Black Flag. In more recent years, these seemingly divergent styles – one slick, the other abrasive – have found common ground in lyrical West Coast rap and bittersweet pop-punk.

The psychedelic explosion

▲ Janis Joplin

"It's a wild time, I'm doing things that haven't got a name yet" – Jefferson Airplane from *Wild Tyme*

If Brian Wilson's soaring harmonies and the surf sounds of the Beach Boys were the prototypical California sound, the real revolution started in the mid-1960s with the inception of the hippy drug culture in **San Francisco** and the formation of such legendary groups as the Grateful Dead and Jefferson Airplane, who questioned accepted musical and political norms. Armed only with flowers, buckets of **LSD**, and peculiar instruments like sitars alongside their guitars, these and other luminaries – Quicksilver Messenger Service, It's a Beautiful Day, Janis Joplin's Big Brother & the Holding Company – led a peaceful brigade whose extended instrumental passages and visionary lyrics took music into uncharted territory. Nor did LA miss out on the fun for long, producing equally iconic acts like The Doors and Love. Over the years since, California has continued to nurture exponents of the far-out, including Dream Syndicate and other members of the Eighties' "Paisley Underground," the Warlocks (which also happened to be the original name of the Grateful Dead), and the Loud Family.

Top ten California music venues

924 Gilman Berkeley. Underground hardcore and punk. p.584
Boom Boom Room San Francisco. Great blues acts. p.547
Buck Owens' Crystal Palace Bakersfield. Prime spot for country. p.347
El Floridita Los Angeles. Live Cuban music and dancing. p.153
The Fillmore San Francisco. Major rock headliners. p.547
The Hollywood Bowl Hollywood. Open-air classical concerts. p.172
Spaceland Los Angeles. Independent punk and alternative. p.170
Sweetwater Mill Valley. Mellow hangout sometimes hosting Sixties legends. p.612
Whisky-a-Go-Go West Hollywood. Mainly hard rock. p.170
Yoshi's World Class Jazz House Oakland. Top international jazz artists. p.585

▼ The Hollywood Bowl

▲ Green Day

Punk and hardcore

"Pay attention to the back streets and the broken homes" – Green Day from *Welcome to Paradise*

Although **punk** kicked off in New York City and London, angry kids in laid-back California soon picked up instruments and got vocal, especially in and around LA. Seminal bands like the Germs were followed by the Dead Kennedys and Black Flag, who were at the forefront of the **hardcore** explosion and used a scathing mix of aggression, earnestness, and black humor to attack Reaganomics and the materialistic 1980s. Although the genre has grown lighter and poppier over the years, its tenets are still being upheld, with Bay Area natives Green Day helping to bring a healthy measure of political dialogue to the iPod generation.

Jazz, R&B, and rap

"Now let me welcome everybody to the wild, wild West" – 2Pac featuring Dr Dre from *California Love*

California has been one of the leaders in popular African American musical styles. LA in particular once had an exemplary **jazz** scene, with legends like Charles Mingus playing regularly for diverse audiences, and the Bay Area's Sly Stone was a DJ and producer before he helped develop the **funk** sound with his Family Stone. However, the most potent force in black popular music was the emergence in the late Eighties of West Coast **hip-hop**, whose angry "gangsta" attitudes were first developed by Ice Cube and Eazy-E of NWA. Over the next decade, producer Dr Dre (another NWA alumnus) and collaborators like Snoop Dogg perfected the form, developing a genre of lazy beats and casually violent and misogynistic lyrics that portrayed the menacing realities of inner-city life.

▼ Snoop Dogg

▲ The Eagles

Country and Latin

"I came here lookin' for something I couldn't find anywhere else" – Buck Owens from *Streets of Bakersfield*

Not surprisingly for a state with a huge and growing Latino population, **Hispanic music** is a constant, exotic element of the California playlist; as you travel south, more and more Spanish-language stations churn out a stream of hits from Mexico and other parts of Latin America. While the music's home is still below the border, various local bands – East LA's Los Lobos the most prominent among them – have contributed to its songbook.

Somewhat incongruously, Bakersfield – right in the middle of migrant farm-worker territory – is **country music**'s California outpost, far to the west of its original heartland. Country sounds influenced some of California's best known 1970s rock acts, such as the Eagles and grievous angel Gram Parsons.

Ten classic tunes about California

California Dreamin' – The Mamas & the Papas (1966). Summer of Love gem about homesick hippies lost in the cold of an East Coast winter.

California Über Alles – The Dead Kennedys (1980). Scathing attack on the pernicious state of affairs during Governor Jerry Brown's 1980s.

Californication – Red Hot Chili Peppers (1999). A slice of melancholia lamenting the state's stereotyped superficiality and pop-culture obsessions.

Fake Tales of San Francisco – Arctic Monkeys (2005). Pithy dig at cultural pseuds, where a lad from Rotheram fakes Stateside credentials.

Going to California – Led Zeppelin (1971). One of Zep's gentler songs, about an English exile in search of love out west.

If You're Going to San Francisco – Scott McKenzie (1967). Unashamed paean to the hippy generation and Sixties counterculture.

LA Woman – The Doors (1971). This epic track chronicled the story of Jim's latest romantic conquest.

Redondo Beach – Patti Smith (1975). Punk-reggae tale of the poetess having a lover's tiff beside the waves.

▼ The Doors

Saturday Afternoon – Jefferson Airplane (1967). Psychedelic anthem exalting one of Golden Gate Park's massive 1967 "be-ins."

Straight Outta Compton – N.W.A. (1989). Early gangsta rap single that paints a terrifying portrait of street warfare in LA.

The Central Coast

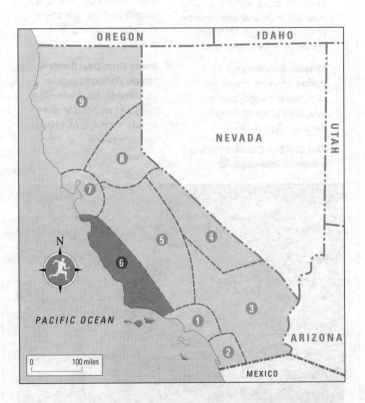

CHAPTER 6 # Highlights

✳ **Channel Islands National Park** This beguiling chain of desert islands off the coast of Los Angeles offers spectacular hiking and the chance to spot passing whales. See p.416

✳ **Hearst Castle** One of the most intriguing sights in America: a palatial monument to the life and ego of William Randolph Hearst. See p.441

✳ **Mission San Antonio de Padua** The best conserved of all the missions, and an evocative place to imagine the past. See p.446

✳ **The Big Sur Coast** Boasting a rugged, eye-popping coastline and, in the interior, some of the most stunning waterfalls in the state, this is still very much a wild and rewarding region. See p.449

✳ **Monterey Bay Aquarium** A world-class museum in a small California town – the enormous Outer Bay tank is superb and the sea otters are ever charming. See p.463

✳ **Santa Cruz Boardwalk** A classic California seaside promenade, filled with old rides and an amusement arcade – irresistible, cheesy fun. See p.474

▲ Santa Cruz Boardwalk

The Central Coast

The four hundred miles of the **CENTRAL COAST** between LA and San Francisco cover one of the most beautiful oceanside stretches anywhere in the world, a blend of sandy beaches and rocky cliffs, rural charm and urban energy. Sparsely populated outside a few medium-sized towns, much of the area is barely disturbed by the frenetic pressures of modern life. Indeed, first-time visitors may be surprised to find just how much of the region survives in its natural state, despite nestling snugly between two of the world's largest and richest cities. The mountain ranges that separate the shore from the farms of the inland valleys are for the most part pristine wilderness, sometimes covered in thick forests of tall and slender redwood trees, while, in winter especially, fast-flowing rivers and streams course down valleys to the sea. All along the shore, sea otters and seals play in the waves, and endangered gray whales pass close by on their annual migration from Alaska to Mexico.

Big Sur, where the brooding Santa Lucia Mountains rise steeply out of the thundering Pacific surf, is the heart of the region, and **Point Lobos**, at its northern tip, is the best place to experience this untouched environment at its most dramatic. Nature aside, though, the Central Coast also marks the gradual transition from Southern to Northern California. The two largest towns here are **Santa Barbara**, a conservative, wealthy resort a hundred miles north of Los Angeles, and **Santa Cruz**, 75 miles south of San Francisco, where long hair and tie-dyes blend with yuppie refugees from the Bay Area. What the two towns have in common is miles of broad, clean **beaches**, with chilly waters but excellent surf, and a branch of the University of California energizing the local nightlife. In between, small **San Luis Obispo** provides a feasible base for the Central Coast's biggest tourist attraction, **Hearst Castle**, an opulent hilltop palace that was once the estate of publishing magnate William Randolph Hearst.

The Central Coast also contains the bulk and the best of the late eighteenth-century Spanish Colonial **missions** – the first European settlements on the West Coast, set up to convert the natives to Christianity while co-opting their labor. Almost all of the major towns that exist here today grew up around the adobe walls and red-tiled roofs of these Catholic military and religious outposts. Each was deliberately situated a long day's walk from the next and typically comprised a church and a cloistered monastery, enclosed within thick walls to prevent attack by native tribes. **Monterey**, a hundred miles south of San Francisco, was the capital of California under Spain, and later Mexico, and today retains more of its early nineteenth-century architecture than any other city in the state; it's also a good base for one of the most beautiful of the missions, which stands three miles south in the upper-crust seaside resort of **Carmel**.

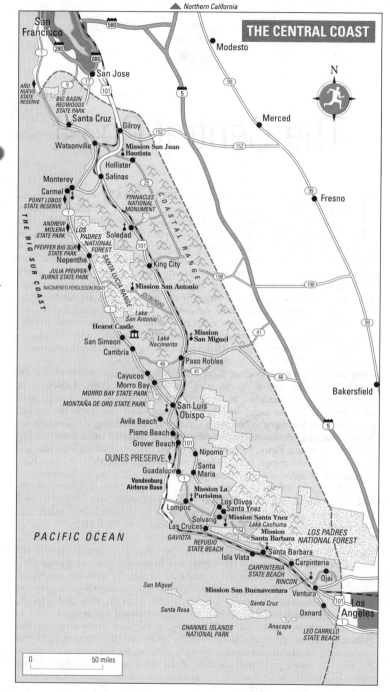

THE CENTRAL COAST

Northern California

San Francisco

Modesto

N

Merced

San Jose

Santa Cruz

Gilroy

Watsonville

Mission San Juan Bautista

Hollister

Salinas

Fresno

Monterey

Carmel

POINT LOBOS STATE RESERVE

PINNACLES NATIONAL MONUMENT

AÑO NUEVO STATE RESERVE

BIG BASIN REDWOODS STATE PARK

THE BIG SUR COAST

ANDREW MOLERA STATE PARK

LOS PADRES NATIONAL FOREST

Soledad

PFEIFFER BIG SUR STATE PARK

Nepenthe

JULIA PFEIFFER BURNS STATE PARK

King City

SANTA LUCIA RANGE

COASTAL RANGE

NACIMIENTO-FERGUSSON ROAD

JOLON ROAD

Mission San Antonio

Lake San Antonio

Hearst Castle

San Simeon

Cambria

Lake Nacimiento

Mission San Miguel

Paso Robles

Bakersfield

Cayucos

Morro Bay

MORRO BAY STATE PARK

MONTAÑA DE ORO STATE PARK

San Luis Obispo

Avila Beach

Pismo Beach

Grover Beach

DUNES PRESERVE

Nipomo

Santa Maria

Guadalupe

Vandenburg Airforce Base

Mission La Purisima

Los Olivos

Santa Ynez

Lompoc

Solvang

Mission Santa Ynez

Lake Cachuma

Las Cruces

GAVIOTA

REFUGIO STATE BEACH

Mission Santa Barbara

LOS PADRES NATIONAL FOREST

PACIFIC OCEAN

Isla Vista

Santa Barbara

Carpinteria

CARPINTERIA STATE BEACH

RINCON

Ojai

San Miguel

Mission San Buenaventura

Ventura

Los Angeles

Santa Cruz

Santa Rosa

Oxnard

Anacapa Is.

CHANNEL ISLANDS NATIONAL PARK

LEO CARRILLO STATE BEACH

0   50 miles

Getting around the Central Coast is easy enough: some of the best views in the state can be had from Amtrak's Coast Starlight train, which runs right along the coast up to San Luis Obispo before cutting inland north to San Francisco. The Pacific Surfliner, by contrast, is a shorter jaunt along the southern coastal section, linking San Luis Obispo with LA and San Diego. Greyhound buses stop at most of the towns, particularly those along the main highway, US-101 – though the best route, if you've got a car, is the smaller Hwy-1, which follows the coast all the way but takes twice as long. **Places to stay** are relatively easy to find, at least outside summer weekends when otherwise quiet towns and beaches are packed solid with vacationers. Opportunities for **camping** are plentiful, too, in a string of state parks, beaches, and forests.

Ventura

Suburban Los Angeles meets the Pacific Ocean at **VENTURA**, an agricultural town now being submerged beneath the LA metroplex and swallowed by spillover from the larger industrial city of **Oxnard** to the south (useful mainly for its Metrolink train connections to Downtown LA; see p.78). Ventura offers a few good reasons to stop if you're in the area, including buying fresh strawberries and other seasonal produce from the roadside stalls and catching a boat out to the offshore Channel Islands (see p.416) from the harbor, four miles southwest of town. There's also a scattering of relics from the Spanish, Mexican, and early American past; tour these and the town's selection of galleries and boutiques with the aid of brochures from the **visitor center**, 89 S California Street, Suite C (☎1-800/483-6214, ⓦwww.ventura-usa.com). The most interesting sight, though, is just north of the US-101 and Hwy-1 intersection, where the restored **Mission San Buenaventura**, 211 E Main Street (Mon–Fri 10am–5pm, Sat 9am–5pm, Sun 10am–4pm; $2; ☎805/643-4318, ⓦwww.sanbuenaventuramission.org), was raised in 1782 as the ninth of the 21 California missions and the last founded by Junípero Serra. Although it's been repeatedly damaged by neglect or earthquakes and then restored, it still retains a quaint parochial charm that makes it a worthwhile stop for passers-by or more intrepid "mission tourists" – though if you're looking for truly inspired church architecture, this unassuming Spanish Colonial relic probably won't fit the bill. Nearby, the **Ortega Adobe**, 215 W Main Street (daily summer 9am–4pm, rest of year Sat & Sun only; ☎805/658-4726), is best known as the original site of a well-known chili producer, but stands out for its early American adobe design, which gives a hint of the style that used to dominate the town but has since given away to more modern construction.

Main Street is also home to two small but engaging museums. The **Albinger Archaeological Museum**, 113 E Main Street (Wed–Fri 10am–2pm, Sat & Sun 10am–4pm; free; ☎805/648-5823), has displays on 3500 years of local history, from ancient Native American cultures to the Spanish era – including parts of the nearby mission's original foundation, dating from the 1780s. Across the street, the **Ventura County Museum of History and Art**, 100 E Main Street (Tues–Sun 10am–5pm; $4; ☎805/653-0323, ⓦwww.venturamuseum.org), takes up where the former leaves off, with exhibits on local pioneer families and antique agricultural machinery, plus preserved old saddles, Catholic devotional paintings, and more contemporary native artifacts from key tribes such as the Chumash. Another glimpse of early life in California can be found at **Olivas Adobe Historical Park**, further out at 4200 Olivas Park Drive (tours Sat & Sun 10am–4pm; donation; ☎805/644-6542), where the titular adobe was once the centerpiece of land baron Jose Olivas's estate in the 1840s, before the Mexican-American War altered the balance of power in the region. Still, Olivas, his wife, and their 21 kids lived out the century here, and today it's decorated in the rustic style of the mid-nineteenth century, with antique tools and a family chapel on display, as well as decor appropriate to the era.

To engage in the local outdoor activities, start at the restored 1872 **San Buenaventura Pier**, located where California Street ends, for fishing or light snacks, then head a mile north along a beachside promenade to **Surfer's Point**, a prime location to put a surfboard or windsurfer in the waves. You can rent boards for $35 per day at Walden Surfboards, 853 E Front Street (☎805/653-1717).

Before you launch an expedition to the Channel Islands, visit the **Channel Islands National Park visitor center**, 1901 Spinnaker Drive (daily 8.30am–5pm; ☎805/658-5730, ⓦwww.nps.gov/chis), next to the ferry landing in Ventura Harbor, which covers the geology and plant and animal life of the islands, including seals, sea lions, pelicans, and giant kelp forests. It also has current information on arranging trips, and an **observation tower** from which, on fine days, you can view the islands.

Practicalities

Amtrak **trains** (Pacific Surfliner only) pull in near Harbor Boulevard and Figueroa Street, three blocks from the Greyhound **bus** stop at 291 E Thompson Boulevard at Palm Street. The **visitor center** (see p.413) has local maps and lists of tour bus and shuttle operators. To help you get around the area, the local **transportation** service, Gold Coast Transit (transit center at 201 E Fourth Street, Oxnard; tickets $1.25; ☎805/487-4222, ⓦwww.goldcoasttransit.org), connects Ventura with Oxnard, Ojai, and other towns in the county.

Ventura is a clear choice for **accommodation** between LA and Santa Barbara. If you're looking for something beyond the usual chain lodging, the *Bella Maggiore Inn*, 67 S California Street (☎805/652-0277; ⑤), has two dozen rooms that variously come with balconies, Jacuzzis, or fireplaces, in a fetching space with a courtyard and fountains. Alternately, the *Victorian Rose* (☎805/641-1888, ⓦwww.victorian-rose.com; ⑤–⑥) is a fascinating B&B with five rooms housed in an 1890s Carpenter Gothic church, designed in high Victorian style, loaded with antiques and bric-a-brac, and offering a classic spiral staircase, barber shop and, of course, steeple. For **eating**, the *Taj Cafe*, 574 E Main Street (☎805/652-1521), has better Indian fare than you might expect, with an appealing array of masala and tandoori dishes, while *Yolanda's Mexican Cafe*, 2753 E Main Street (☎805/643-2700), presents a tasty, if Americanized, version of the cuisine. The best choice for breakfast, for its hearty pancakes, hash, and home fries, is *Allison's Country Cafe*, 3429 Telegraph Road (☎805/644-9072).

Moving on: Oxnard to Carpinteria

Ventura is obviously the major point of interest between LA and Santa Barbara, but if you're intent on exploring the Central Coast in detail, you may find yourself just south in **Oxnard**, regularly the butt of Angeleno jokes for its ungainly name. There's not much to detain you for more than a half-day, although **Heritage Square**, between A, B, 7th, and 8th streets (guided tours Sat 10am–2pm; donation; ☎805/483-7960), does offer a re-sited collection of a dozen Victorian structures, highlighted by a stately water tower, the Queen

Anne-styled Justin Petit Ranch House, and the Carpenter Gothic-flavored Pfeiler Ranch House. Just as appealing, the **Carnegie Art Museum** is housed in a historic 1907 Neoclassical library at 424 South C Street (Thurs–Sun 10am–5pm, Sun 1–5pm; $3; ☏805/385-8157, ⓦwww.vcnet.com/carnart), and showcases the work of local glassmakers, painters, and other artisans in temporary exhibits. The copious holdings of the **Murphy Auto Museum**, 2230 Statham Boulevard (Sat & Sun 10am–4pm; $6; ☏805/487-4333, ⓦwww.murphyautomuseum.com), on the other hand, are best suited for those interested in exploring classic cars, namely a decent selection of vintage Packards, a Model T, a Rolls, a Bentley, and more. Contact the **visitor center**, 1000 Town Center Road, Suite 130 (☏1-800/269-6273, ⓦwww.visitoxnard.com), for more information on any of these sites, the town's pedestrian array of hotels and restaurants, its many worthwhile fruit stands and farmers markets, or the interesting autumn tours of the area's classic early twentieth-century homes.

Thirteen miles north of Ventura, the best area surfers head to **Rincon Beach Park** (daily 8am–dusk), a legendary point off Hwy-101 on the Ventura County line that's best surfed in the winter at low tide to take advantage of its killer reef-break. Many LA surf gods have ventured this far north to get away from the Malibu crowds, and you're encouraged to do the same if you have any interest (and appropriate skill) in this quintessential California sport. Three miles west, **Carpinteria** is a beachside hamlet that's good for its laid-back southern California beach vibe, a small but high-quality farmers' market, at 800 Linden Avenue (Thurs 4–7pm; ☏805/962-5354), an early-October **avocado festival** (ⓦwww.avofest.com) that presents the subtropical fruit in all its glory, and several long, uncluttered **beaches** largely free from tourist traffic, with regular closures along part of the shoreline in the winter and spring to allow for bird and seal activity. The **Chamber of Commerce**, 1056-B Eugenia Place (☏805/684-5479, ⓦwww.carpchamber.org), has more information on surfing rentals and town listings. For a distinctive **stay** in town, camp at **Carpinteria State Beach** ($25; ☏1-800/444-7275, ⓦwww.reserveamerica.com), one of the better stretches of sand in these parts, or stop at *Prufrock's Garden Inn*, 600 Linden Avenue (☏1-877/837-6257, ⓦwww.prufrocks.com; ❼), whose seven quaint rooms are themed in mild Victoriana, some featuring claw-foot tubs, sitting rooms, and French doors, as well as Jacuzzis.

Ojai

Nestled in the hills above Ventura, the hamlet of **OJAI** (pronounced "O-hi") is a wealthy resort community frequented by weekend jet-setters and celebrities from LA, replete with exclusive spas and tennis clubs dotting the surrounding countryside. Consequently, perhaps, it's also a New Age hub that's the headquarters of the Krishnamurti Society, honoring the theosophist who, in the 1920s, lived and lectured in the Ojai Valley, which he considered "a vessel of comprehension, intelligence and truth." The **Krishnamurti Library and Archives**, four miles northeast of town at 1070 McAndrew Road (Wed–Sun 1–5pm; free; ☏805/646-4948, ⓦwww.kfa.org), details his progressive ideas on spirituality, while a mellow **retreat** in a classic ranch house, nearby at no. 1130 ($55, $85 double, two-night minimum; ☏805/646-4773), lets you get into the holistic spirit by taking nature walks in a shaded glade and reading up on the master's teachings. From here you can also access the numerous hiking trails that lead up into the marvelous preserve of **Los Padres National Forest**, whose nearest ranger station is at 1190 E Ojai

Avenue (Mon–Fri 8am–4.30pm; ☎805/646-3866, ⓦwww.fs.fed.us/r5/lospadres) and stocks maps, passes, camping information, and other materials for exploring the outback of this two-million acre expanse. The nearest campsite to Ojai, eight miles away off Hwy-33, is Wheeler Gorge (sites $14–20, day-use $6; ☎831/674-5726, ⓦwww.rockymountainrec.com), sited among the majestic forest peaks, with plenty of options for fishing and hiking.

The town itself is adorned by the graceful Spanish Revival architecture that glassworks magnate Edward Drummond Libbey introduced here a century ago after a devastating fire, exemplified best by the post office's iconic **bell tower** and the adjoining, curvaceous **pergola** at Libbey Park, E Ojai Avenue at S Signal Street. The **Ojai Valley Museum**, 130 W Ojai Avenue (Thurs–Fri 1–4pm, Sat 10am–4pm, Sun noon–4pm; $3; ☎805/640-1390, ⓦwww .ojaivalleymuseum.org), housed in a former Mission Revival church built in 1919, has ambitious exhibits on history, agriculture, oil prospecting, and art, highlighted by a Chumash garden that recalls the local peoples who predated the American settlers.

Practicalities

You can reach Ojai from Ventura or Oxnard on Gold Coast Transit (see p.414). Near Libbey Park, the **visitor center**, 201 S Signal Street (Mon–Fri 9am–4pm; ☎805/646-8126, ⓦwww.ojaichamber.org), is a good place for information on the town's historical architecture and numerous old-fashioned **B&Bs**. On a country farm ten minutes from downtown, the friendly *Farm Hostel* (☎805/646-0311, ⓦwww.hostelhandbook.com/farmhostel/default.htm) offers free pickup from the Greyhound and Amtrak stations in nearby Ventura, and dorm beds for $15, but you must have an international air-travel ticket or current visa (3- or 6-month period) to stay. For any kind of visitors but particularly golfers, the cushy, Mission-flavored *Ojai Valley Inn & Spa*, 905 Country Club Road (☎1-800/422-6524, ⓦwww.ojairesort.com; two-night weekend minimum; ⓭), has numerous elegant rooms and suites for $350 a night; the more central *Ojai Rancho Inn*, 615 W Ojai Avenue (☎1-800/799-1881, ⓦwww.ojairanchoinn.com; ⓭), offers nice entry-level rooms with fridges, microwaves, and kitchenettes, as well as cottages with fireplaces, DVD players, and pool and spa access. Also appealing is the *Su Nido Inn*, 301 N Montgomery Street (☎805/646-7080, ⓦwww.sunidoinn. com; ⓭), an attractive, Spanish Colonial-themed inn whose best suites boast fireplaces and large-screen TVs, some with balconies as well.

The top of the local **food** chain is the French high dining of ⚑ *Auberge at Ojai*, 314 El Paseo Road (☎805/646-2288), where you might spot a well-heeled bigwig nibbling on frogs' legs, foie gras, lamb sirloin, and similar continental delights. Another smart eatery is *Suzanne's Cuisine*, 502 W Ojai Avenue (☎805/640-1961), whose eclectic Cal-cuisine offerings include affordable lunchtime fare like calamari sandwiches, poached salmon, and reubens, while among the pricier dinners are rack of lamb, Cornish game hen, and a number of savory pastas. The more affordable *Ojai Cafe Emporium*, 108 S Montgomery Street (☎805/646-2723), is good for its breakfasts, muffins, scones, and other scrumptious treats to begin your day.

Channel Islands National Park

Stretching north from Santa Catalina Island off the coast of Los Angeles, a chain of fascinating desert islands is preserved as the 250,000-acre **CHANNEL**

ISLANDS NATIONAL PARK, offering excellent hiking trails and splendid views of marine life (with two thousand species present), as well as fishing and scuba and skin diving through the many caves, coves, and shipwrecks in the crystal-clear Pacific waters. Five of the eight islands are accessible as part of the park, though the closest, Anacapa, some fourteen miles south of Ventura, sees the most ecotourist traffic. The best time to visit is between February and April, when you can engage in **whale watching**. Inland **hiking** requires a permit (℡805/658-5711, ⊛www.nps.gov/chis) and **divers** can explore the two exposed wrecks on either side of the island.

Park practicalities

If you're considering visiting the Channel Islands, the best introduction to their unique geology, flora, and fauna – endemic to the islands – can be found in Ventura at the park's **visitor center**, 1901 Spinnaker Drive (daily 8.30am–5pm; free; ℡805/658-5730), which also offers models, films, and telescopes to view the islands at a distance.

The Nature Conservancy acquired ninety percent of the islands in 1988 and has made them accessible to the public on **day-trip tours**; nearly the only way to visit the park is by boat, through operators that run from Ventura Harbor. Anacapa is served by several tours run by Island Packers, 1691 Spinnaker Drive, three miles west of US-101 and a mile south of Ventura (℡805/642-7688 for 24-hour recorded information, ℡805/642-1393 for reservations 9am–5pm, ⊛www.islandpackers.com). Packages include all-day trips with two to five hours on the given island ($42–70, depending on the island), half-day cruises without landings ($27), two-day camping excursions ($54–102), and whale watching outings that last about three hours and start at $27. The trip over takes ninety minutes to three hours each way (or four to five hours for San Miguel), and boats don't run every day and often fill up, so reserve ahead. Truth Aquatics, 301 W Cabrillo Boulevard, Santa Barbara (℡805/962-1127, ⊛www.truthaquatics .com), has alternative itineraries to all the islands on smaller vessels at higher prices, including two-day hiking, diving, and kayaking excursions.

You can also reach Santa Rosa Island on a half-hour **flight** from Channel Islands Aviation (℡805/987-1301, ⊛www.flycia.com), which runs half-day weekend excursions ($160) from Camarillo Airport (off US-101, 20 miles south of Ventura). Santa Cruz Island is also the destination for kayak trips from Ventura and Santa Barbara (see p.418).

There are a number of free, primitive **campgrounds** (permits $15 per night; make reservations at ℡1-877/444-6777 or ⊛reservations.nps.gov) on each island if you want to rough it. Bring plenty of food and especially water, as none is available on the island.

The Islands

Tiny **Anacapa** (Chumash for "mirage") is actually two islets: **West Anacapa** is largely a refuge for nesting brown pelicans, most of it off limits except **Frenchy's Cove**, a pristine beach and good base for scuba or snorkeling expeditions; **East Anacapa** has a small visitor center and a 1.5-mile nature trail, and is known for its signature **Arch Rock**, encompassing a thin rocky bridge over the waves. There are no beaches here, but swimming in the cove where the boats dock is allowed. West of Anacapa, **Santa Cruz** is the largest and highest of the islands and is owned by the Nature Conservancy, which has recently managed the reintroduction of bald eagles to the terrain. Throughout the island, you can hike or even camp in the remote landscapes.

Almost as big as Santa Cruz, **Santa Rosa** has many grasslands, canyons, and steep ravines, but overall contains gentler terrain — though it's still compelling for its hiking and kayaking opportunities. Especially interesting are its archeological sites, some of which date back 11,000 years and are still being investigated for their Chumash settlement relics. The most distant island – windswept **San Miguel**, fifty miles offshore – is alive with elephant seals and sea lions, and is thought to be the burial place of sixteenth-century Spanish explorer Juan Cabrillo. No grave has been found, but a monument has been erected at Cuyler Harbor on the island's eastern end. Seasoned hikers may also wish to make the rugged cross-island trip to Point Bennett to spy on the plentiful wildlife. Keep in mind, though, that the island's perilous location — amid a low shelf riddled with hazardous rocks — can lead to regular cancellations of seagoing trips there. South of the main islands lies the smallest of the Channel group, **Santa Barbara**, named by Sebastian Vizcaíno, who dropped by on St Barbara's Day, December 4, 1602. The island's appeal these days is largely due to its sea lions, kestrels, larks, and meadowlarks, which can be seen on land gradually recovering its native flora after years of destruction by now-extinct rabbits.

Of the three other islands in the full chain, **San Clemente** (the furthest south) and **San Nicolas** are controlled by the US Navy, while the most urbanized, **Santa Catalina**, is a different sort of experience that constitutes its own weekend trip from LA (see p.136 for information).

Santa Barbara

The speedy US-101 that whips along the coast above Ventura slows to a more leisurely pace a hundred miles north of Los Angeles at **SANTA BARBARA**, a seaside resort beautifully situated on the gently sloping hills above the Pacific – though oddly named after the patron saint of firefighters and artillerymen. The town's low-rise Spanish Colonial Revival buildings feature red-tiled roofs and white stucco walls, a lovely background to the golden, palm-lined **beaches** below, winding along a gently curving bay.

Once home to Ronald Reagan, and a weekend escape for much of the old money of Los Angeles, Santa Barbara has both a traditional conservative side, as well as a more relaxed libertarian character among the younger set. Still, it's a fairly provincial place; local culture is confined to playing volleyball, surfing, cycling, sipping coffee, or cruising in expensive convertibles along the shore. After an essential visit to **Mission Santa Barbara** and a leisurely walk along the pier, most visitors will quickly get a sense of the place and move on, though there's more to the town and the area if you have the time to explore.

Arrival, information, and transportation

Greyhound **buses** arrive from LA and San Francisco every few hours, stopping downtown at 34 W Carrillo Street, while Amtrak **trains** stop at 209 State Street, a block west of US-101. Santa Barbara **airport** (℡805/683-4011, Ⓦwww.flysba.com), eight miles north of the town center at 500 Fowler Road (near UC Santa Barbara), has a limited and often expensive scheduled service to other cities in the Western US, hosting airlines such as American, United, Delta, and Alaska.

For more information on Santa Barbara, or for help with finding a place to stay, contact the **visitor center**, 1 Garden Street (Mon–Sat 9am–5pm, Sun 10am–5pm; ℡805/965-3021, Ⓦwww.santabarbara.com). The US Forest Service office, 3505 Paradise Road (Mon–Fri 8am–4.30pm; ℡805/967-7337,

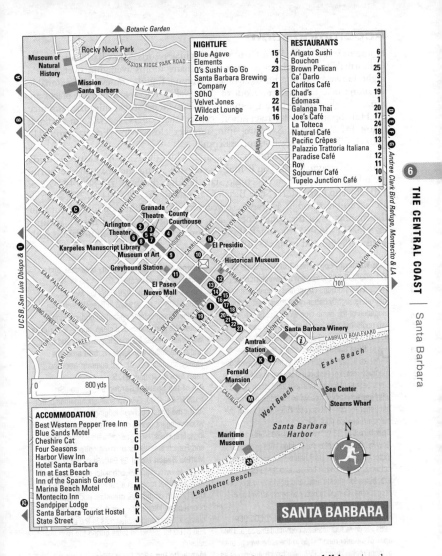

NIGHTLIFE
Blue Agave	15
Elements	4
Q's Sushi a Go Go	23
Santa Barbara Brewing Company	21
SOhO	8
Velvet Jones	22
Wildcat Lounge	14
Zelo	16

RESTAURANTS
Arigato Sushi	6
Bouchon	7
Brown Pelican	25
Ca' Darlo	3
Carlitos Café	2
Chad's	19
Edomasa	1
Galanga Thai	20
Joe's Café	17
La Tolteca	24
Natural Café	18
Pacific Crêpes	13
Palazzio Trattoria Italiana	9
Paradise Café	12
Roy	11
Sojourner Café	10
Tupelo Junction Café	5

ACCOMMODATION
Best Western Pepper Tree Inn	B
Blue Sands Motel	E
Cheshire Cat	C
Four Seasons	D
Harbor View Inn	L
Hotel Santa Barbara	I
Inn at East Beach	F
Inn of the Spanish Garden	H
Marina Beach Motel	M
Montecito Inn	G
Sandpiper Lodge	A
Santa Barbara Tourist Hostel	K
State Street	J

SANTA BARBARA

Ⓦwww.r5.fs.fed.us/lospadres), can provide information on **hiking** in the adjoining Los Padres National Forest, steering you toward the many trails accessible from town.

Getting around Santa Barbara mainly involves walking, though there's a 25¢ **shuttle** that loops between downtown and the beach on the "Downtown" route, and from the harbor to the zoo on the "Waterfront" line. Other areas are covered by Santa Barbara Metropolitan Transit District (SBMTD) **buses** (fares $1.25; Ⓣ805/683-3702, Ⓦwww.sbmtd.gov). If you want to **rent a car**, the best value is U-SAVE Auto Rental, in town at 510 Anacapa Street (Ⓣ805/963-3499, Ⓦwww.usavesantabarbara.com), and at the airport at 310 S Fairview Avenue (Ⓣ805/964-5436), where you can rent late-model cars for as little as $22 a day. Several major car-rental firms have offices at the airport, too.

Accommodation

Home to some of the West Coast's most deluxe resorts, Santa Barbara is among California's priciest places to **stay**, with many rooms averaging over $200 a night. However, with a bit of advance planning, finding somewhere reasonable shouldn't take too big a bite out of your wallet. The less expensive places are usually booked throughout the summer, but if you get stuck, enlist the assistance of Hot Spots, a hotel-reservation center that offers specials on lodging (Mon–Fri 9am–5pm, Sat 9am–4pm, summer closes Mon–Fri at 7pm; ☎1-800/793-7666, ⓦ www.hotspotsusa.com).

There is a **hostel** in Santa Barbara, and, while there are no **campgrounds** within the town limits, you'll find several sites along the coast to the north, including El Capitan and Refugio state beaches (both at ☎1-800/444-7275; $20–25), and Carpinteria State Beach to the south (☎1-800/444-7275; $25); all are accessible through ⓦ www.reserveamerica.com. Other options abound in the mountains of the Santa Ynez Valley, including sites around Lake Cachuma (☎805/688-4658; $18), which also has more comfortable accommodation with yurts ($45–65) and cabins ($145–165).

Best Western Pepper Tree Inn 3850 State St ☎1-800/338-0030, ⓦ www.bestwestern.com. Three miles from the city center, a comfortable inn that offers slightly better rates than most accommodation of the same type along the beach, with two pools, hot tubs, and a gym. Rates can jump by $50 on summer weekends, otherwise ⑥

Blue Sands Motel 421 S Milpas St ☎805/965-1624. Looks like your average roadside motel at first, but this spot is actually the city's best deal for accommodation: clean rooms with gas fireplaces, free wireless Internet access, kitchenettes, and flat-screen TVs – along with the standard heated pool. ⑤

Cheshire Cat 36 W Valerio St ☎805/569-1610, ⓦ www.cheshirecat.com. Loaded with precious Victorian decor, this B&B has twelve rooms, two cottages, and a coach house, and features a hot tub, bikes for guests' use, and an *Alice in Wonderland* theme. Complimentary wine on arrival and breakfast under a palm tree. ⑦

Four Seasons 1260 Channel Drive ☎805/969-2261, ⓦ www.fourseasons.com/santabarbara. The apex of swanky resort style in the area, where the opulent rooms (from $550) boast such amenities as fireplaces and wrought-iron balconies, the suites have two to four bedrooms, and the site has a spa, pool, and fitness center. ⑨

Harbor View Inn 28 W Cabrillo Blvd ☎1-800/755-0222, ⓦ www.harborviewinnsb.com. One of the more appealing luxury hotels around, offering on-site restaurant and bar, pool and Jacuzzis, and elegant rooms ($335; suites from $495) with patios or balconies. ⑨

Hotel Santa Barbara 533 State St ☎1-888/259-7700, ⓦ www.hotelsantabarbara.com. Surprisingly good rates for comfortable, well-decorated rooms,

Internet access, complimentary breakfast, and a prime downtown location. ⑥

Inn at East Beach 1029 Orilla del Mar ☎805/965-0546, ⓦ www.innateastbeach.com. Another unexpectedly appealing find, offering a motel-like appearance but clean, good-value rooms with free wireless Internet, microwaves and fridges, and some suites with kitchens, built around a kidney-shaped pool. ⑥, but summer weekend rates tack on another $125.

Inn of the Spanish Garden 915 Garden St ☎805/564-4700, ⓦ www.spanishgardeninn.com. About the finest boutique lodgings the city offers, whose elegant rooms come with designer furnishings, fireplaces, high-speed Internet connections, and French presses for morning coffee. ⑨

Marina Beach Motel 21 Bath St ☎1-877/627-4621, ⓦ www.marinabeachmotel.com. Clean and modern motel rooms in a recently remodeled facility, with continental breakfast and options for bike rentals, kitchenettes, and Jacuzzis. A bit cheaper than comparable spots in the area. ⑤, but add $100 for weekend rates during the high season.

Montecito Inn 1295 Coast Village Rd ☎1-800/843-2017, ⓦ www.montecitoinn.com. Charming Spanish Revival inn with a wide range of rooms and rates, from quaint, basic units to elaborate suites, plus pool, sauna, and Jacuzzi. Sometimes has summer discounts of $50 or so. Otherwise ⑧

Sandpiper Lodge 3525 State St ☎805/687-5326, ⓦ www.sandpiperlodge.com. Adequate motel lodging in uptown part of the city, with basic and clean rooms, pool, spa, and complimentary breakfast. ④, though summer rates can be around $50 more.

Santa Barbara Tourist Hostel 134 Chapala St ☎805/963-0154, ⓦwww.sbhostel.com. Centrally located hostel near the beach and State Street, with bicycle and surfboard rentals, complimentary breakfast, and Internet access. Dorm rooms go for $20–29, with private rooms also available ($55–89), some with private bath (extra $10).

State Street 121 State St ☎805/966-6586. Low-end digs near the wharf and beach in a colorful old Mission-style building, though it's subject to some noise from the nearby railway and only offers communal bathrooms. Cheap rates include breakfast. ❹

The Town

Up until the 1920s, Santa Barbara was a fairly typical California beachside community, with lingering bits of Victoriana and historic-revival styles mixed with a handful of Spanish Colonial castoffs from the nineteenth century – with the Presidio and Mission among the more conspicuous examples. Somewhat ironically, Santa Barbara owes its current Mission-era atmosphere, with its attendant quaintness and historical "authenticity," to a devastating **earthquake** in 1925, after which the city authorities decided to rebuild virtually the entire town as an apocryphal Mission-era village – even the massive "historic" El Paseo shopping mall has a whitewashed adobe facade. The planning scheme has become surprisingly successful, and Santa Barbara is now synonymous through California (and the nation) with genteel oceanside living. The square-mile **town center**, squeezed between the south-facing **beaches** and the foothills of the Santa Ynez Mountains, has one of the region's liveliest street scenes. The main drag, **State Street**, is home to an assortment of diners, bookstores, coffee bars, and nightclubs catering as much to the needs of locals – among them twenty thousand UC Santa Barbara students – as to visitors.

The historic center

The **historic center** of Santa Barbara lies mostly along State Street a few blocks inland from the highway, where the town's few genuine Mission-era structures are preserved as **El Presidio de Santa Barbara** (daily 10.30am–4.30pm; $3; ⓦwww.sbthp.org/presidio.htm), built around the fourth and last of the Spanish military garrisons in the region, though only the living quarters of the soldiers who once guarded the site remain. One of these structures, the modest **El Cuartel**, two blocks east of State Street at 123 Canon Perdido Street,

---

Santa Barbara County wineries

Wine fanatics – doubtless seduced by the 2004 film *Sideways* (see p.793) – shouldn't miss a visit to Santa Barbara County's copious vineyards, of which there are more than one hundred. Although it's not the Napa Valley per se, the area does offer plenty of **wineries** with the requisite tastings and merchandise for sale. Slightly beyond the town's center, not far from US-101, the **Santa Barbara Winery**, 202 Anacapa Street at Yanonali Street (daily 10am–5pm; tastings $5; ☎805/963-3633, ⓦwww.sbwinery.com), is worth a stop to see one of the oldest commercial wineries in the county, built in 1962. You can get more information on this and other wineries by contacting the Santa Barbara Vintners' Association (☎805/688-0881, ⓦwww.sbcountywines.com) or the similar WineCountry site (☎707/265-1835, ⓦwww.santabarbara.winecountry.com), which also has information on winery-related lodging and restaurants throughout the state. True fanatics may enjoy a more extensive trip courtesy of **Cloud Climbers** (by reservation only at ☎805/646-3200, ⓦwww.ccjeeps.com), who for $110 will take you on a six-hour jeep tour of local wineries, with lunch and four tasting fees included.

is the second oldest building in California, dating from 1782, and now houses historical exhibits and a scale model of the small Spanish colony. A block away, at 136 E De la Guerra Street, the **Santa Barbara Historical Museum** (Tues–Sat 10am–5pm, Sun noon–5pm; donation; ☎805/966-1601, ⊛www .santabarbaramuseum.com), built around an 1817 adobe, contains displays on Spanish- and Mexican-era life and presents other aspects of the city's past, from Ice Age geology to artifacts from native settlements to modern photographs. The museum can also point you in the direction of some of the area's more important old structures from the Mexican and early American periods, among them the Victorian **Fernald Mansion** and a nearby adobe, both at 414 W Montecito Street and tourable every Saturday (1 & 2pm; free; contact museum for info). Near the museum, where De la Guerra Street meets State Street, the **Casa de la Guerra** (Thurs–Sun noon–4pm; $3; ☎805/966-6961, ⊛www .sbthp.org/casa.htm) preserves what was, in the 1820s, one of the more upscale residences in town (though still built in the spartan Spanish Colonial style), home to one of the Presidio's commanders. These days, it holds spurs, saddles, toys, and weapons, plus exhibits of antique tools, furniture, and religious icons. After it survived the 1925 earthquake that otherwise obliterated much of downtown, the Casa became a template for the type of Spanish Colonial style that, in its revival form, continues to dominate the town's design.

On the corner of State and Anapamu, at 1130 State Street, the fine **Santa Barbara Museum of Art** (Tues–Sun 11am–5pm; $9; ☎805/963-4364, ⊛www.sbmuseart.org) features some classical Greek and Egyptian statuary, a smattering of French Impressionists, an Asian collection of some note, and interesting modern photography. There's an appealing if scattershot selection of European greats, from minor works of Picasso and Matisse to more engaging pieces from Chagall, Kandinsky, and Miró. Its main features, though, come from its **American collection**, which is particularly strong in nineteenth-century landscape painters such as Albert Bierstadt and postwar California modernists like Richard Diebenkorn. Just east, the still-functioning **County Courthouse**, at 1100 Anacapa Street (Mon–Fri 8.30am–4.30pm, Sat & Sun 10am–4.30pm; free tours Mon–Sat 2pm, also Mon, Tues & Fri 10.30am; ☎805/962-6464), is a Spanish Revival gem, an idiosyncratic 1929 variation on the Mission theme that's widely known as one of the finest public buildings in the US, with striking murals, tilework, and fountain. Take a break in the sunken gardens, explore the quirky staircases, or climb the seventy-foot "**El Mirador**" clock-tower for a nice view out over the town. From here you can get a fine perspective on how successful this little burg has been in transforming its California beach-town look into a homegrown version of early-modern Spain.

Two blocks up State Street, at no. 1317, the landmark 1930s **Arlington Theater** (☎805/963-4408) is an intact and functional movie palace and performance venue, with a trompe l'oeil interior modeled after an atmospheric Spanish village plaza. It is also home to the modest but respected Santa Barbara Symphony (tickets $28–60; ☎805/898-9526, ⊛www.thesymphony.org). Keep in mind that in 2008 the symphony is making its long-awaited move a block away to the 1924 Moorish-flavored **Granada Theatre**, 1216 State Street, gloriously renovated to serve as the town's main performing arts center (information at ☎805/899-3000, ⊛www.granadasb.org). Nearby, at 21 W Anapamu Street, the beautifully decorated **Karpeles Manuscript Library** (daily 10am–4pm; free; ☎805/962-5322, ⊛www.rain.org/~karpeles) is home to a diverse array of original documents such as the Constitution of the Confederate States of America, Napoleon's battle plans for his Russian invasion, and the manuscripts of famous figures such as Mark Twain, Thomas Edison, John Locke, and Jorge

Luis Borges. The library's other focus is its temporary exhibits, which range widely from handwritten orchestral scores to the testimony of Holocaust survivors to the computer program used for the first Apollo moon flight.

The beaches and around

Half a mile down State Street from the town center, Cabrillo Boulevard runs along the south-facing shore, a long, clean strip stretching from the yacht and fishing harbor beyond palm-lined **West Beach** to the volleyball courts and golden sands of **East Beach**. In the vicinity of 1 State Street, an outdoor **arts and crafts market** (Sun 10am–dusk; free) presents the work of some 250 local artisans every week. At the foot of State Street, take a stroll among the pelicans on the 1872 **Stearns Wharf** (ⓌWwww.stearnswharf.org), the oldest wooden pier in the state. The victim of several earthquakes and fires, it was nearly destroyed most recently in November 1998 when a third of it was engulfed in flames, but it has since been restored to its former glory. The wharf is lined with knick-knack shops, seafood restaurants, ice cream stands, and the **Ty Warner Sea Center** (daily 10am–5pm; $7; Ⓣ805/962-2526), an annex of the Museum of Natural History (see p.424), offering a tot-friendly selection of touch tanks, interactive exhibits, whale bones, and tide pools.

Just west, the **Santa Barbara Maritime Museum**, 113 Harbor Way, Suite 190 (daily except Wed 10am–5pm, summer closes 6pm; $7; Ⓣ805/962-8404, ⓌWwww.sbmm.org), is the town's newest museum, occupying the site of the old Naval Reserve Center and showcasing old-fashioned ship models and exhibits on the whaling and tallow trade, seal hunting, native Chumash canoes, and the current nautical practices of recovering shipwrecks and communicating with shore. A few vessels are outside, including a bathyscaphe submersible for plumbing the deep.

Outdoor fun in Santa Barbara

Just west of the pier, athletes keep in shape in the fifty-meter Los Baños del Mar swimming pool, 401 Shoreline Drive (dawn–10pm; $5; Ⓣ805/966-6110), an open-air, year-round facility. Windsurfers can be rented from beachfront stalls, and kayaks are available from Paddle Sports, 117 Harbor Way (Ⓣ805/899-4925, ⓌWwww.kayaksb.com), starting at $20 for two hours and $40 for a full day, or $30 and $48 for **surfboards**. This outfit can also arrange trips to the Channel Islands via Island Packers (see p.417). If you're interested in exploring the town by bicycle, Wheel Fun Rentals, 101 State Street (daily 9am–5pm; Ⓣ805/962-2585, ⓌWwww.wheelfunrentals.com), and 23 E Cabrillo Boulevard (Ⓣ805/966-2282), has a variety of models from tandems to tricycles, with basic two-wheelers going for around $20–35 a day, and provides a map of Santa Barbara's extensive system of bike paths. Get good **hiking** information from Santa Barbara Hikes (ⓌWwww.santabarbarahikes.com); the longest and most satisfying path leads west twelve miles along the bluffs to Isla Vista and UC Santa Barbara, passing a mile or so back from the rarely crowded, creekside Arroyo Burro Beach (locally known as "Hendry's"), four miles west of the wharf at the end of Las Positas Road. Alternatively, head along the beachfront bike path two miles east past the small but worthwhile Santa Barbara Zoo, 500 Niños Drive (daily 10am–5pm; $10; Ⓣ805/962-6310, ⓌWwww.santabarbarazoo.org) – notable for its sharks, stingrays, and turtles, plus a handful of monkeys and excellent display of sea lions – and cycle around the Andree Clark Bird Refuge, 1400 E Cabrillo Boulevard (daily dawn–10pm), a 42-acre saltwater marsh where you can see many interesting seabirds, including egrets, herons, and cormorants.

Mission Santa Barbara and beyond

The mission from which the city takes its name, **Mission Santa Barbara** (daily 9am–5pm; donation; ☎805/682-4713 ext. 121, ⓦwww.sbmission.org), is

located in the hills above town at 2201 Laguna Street. Known as the "Queen of the Missions," its imposing twin-towered facade – facing out over a perfectly manicured garden towards the sea – combines Romanesque and Mission styles, giving it a formidable character lacking in some of the prettier outposts in the chain. The present structure, built to replace a series of three adobe churches that had been destroyed by earthquakes, was finished and dedicated in 1820 by Franciscan friars, but the huge 1925 earthquake damaged the mission, and the ensuing restoration cost nearly $400,000. Today, a small **museum** displays artifacts from the mission archives, and the cemetery contains the remains of some four thousand Native Americans, many of

▲ Mission Santa Barbara

whom helped build the original complex, which includes aqueducts, waterworks, a grist mill, and two reservoirs, with the old pottery kiln and tanning vats now in ruin. To get to the mission, take SBMTD bus #22 from the Courthouse along Anapamu Street downtown, or walk or drive the half-mile from State Street up Mission Street and Mission Canyon.

Just beyond the mission at 2559 Puerta del Sol Road, the **Museum of Natural History** (daily 10am–5pm; $8; ☎805/682-4711, ⓦwww.sbnature .org) showcases intriguing artifacts from Chumash culture, various dioramas of mammals, birds, reptiles, and insects, a planetarium, and actual skeletons of such extinct creatures as the pygmy mammoth, taken from Santa Rosa Island in 1994. For a closer glimpse of nature, continue on into the hills from the mission until you come to the splendid **Botanic Garden**, 1212 Mission Canyon Road (Mar–Oct daily 9am–6pm, rest of year closes 5pm; $8; ☎805/682-4726, ⓦwww.sbbg.org), whose 65 acres feature pleasant hiking trails amid endemic cacti, manzanita, trees, and wildflowers – a relaxing respite among hillside meadows and glades.

Eating

Santa Barbara has a number of very good and very expensive **restaurants**, but it also has many more affordable options offering a range of cuisines. Since it's right on the Pacific, you'll find a lot of seafood and sushi; Mexican places are also numerous, and smoothies – blended fruit shakes – are everywhere, a welcome snack on a hot summer day.

Arigato Sushi 1225 State St ☎805/965-6074. The main draw for sushi in town, a boutique Japanese spot that's a bit on the pricey side – with the requisite modernist chic and hipster diners – but the fresh, delicious raw fish tends to justify the expense.

Bouchon 9 W Victoria St ☎805/730-1160. Among the town's top choices for elite dining, a California cuisine favorite that presents such rotating items as citrus-marinated quail, rack of lamb or venison, maple-glazed duck breast, and a full selection of fresh seafood.

Brown Pelican 2981 Cliff Drive ☎805/687-4550. Of the better eateries in town, this one's more affordable, offering a good array of seafood and wine from the local region, plus enjoyable breakfasts and lunches, all in a pleasant seafront location.

Ca' Dario 37 E Victoria St ☎805/884-9419. Although there are a number of upscale Italian haunts in town, this is one of the few that lives up to its prices, with a fine set of pastas from bocconcini to ziti, and mains that include roasted quail, veal chops, and fresh fish.

Carlitos Café y Cantina 1234 State St ☎805/962-7117. Good, affordable Mexican fare in a somewhat touristy spot, with the usual staples plus more enjoyable items like shrimp empanadas, stuffed chilies, and grilled giant prawns.

Chad's 625 Chapala St ☎805/568-1876. A popular local favorite, serving modern American cuisine – with seafood and steak among the highlights – in the intimate atmosphere of a historic Victorian home.

Cold Spring Tavern 5995 Stagecoach Rd ☎805/967-0066. Tucked away in the hills, this is the place for fresh regional game presented in a clubby lodge setting, with favorites like rabbit medallions, rack of venison, pork ribs, and duck breast regularly on the menu. Dinner can be expensive, but lunch and breakfast are more affordable.

Edomasa 2710 De La Vina ☎805/687–0210. Affordable, cozy sushi joint with a good menu and nice presentation – the salmon and marina rolls are top-notch. Frequented more by locals than tourist interlopers. Open until midnight.

Galanga Thai 507 State St ☎805/963-6799. Not much in the way of atmosphere, but this Southeast Asian joint still has cheap and well-prepared soups, curries, noodles, and pad Thai.

Joe's Café 536 State St ☎805/966-4638. Long-established bar and grill, still a great place to stop off for a burger, chowder, and a strong drink. More or less midway between the beach and the downtown museums.

La Tolteca 600 N Milpas St ☎805/899-4857. Fine Mexican food in a casual atmosphere for lunch or dinner, at a long-standing neighborhood fave that's been serving authentic tacos and *rellenos* for many decades.

Natural Café 508 State St ☎805/962-9494. Scrumptious, cheap veggie meals – with pasta, sandwiches, salads, falafel, and desserts – in a prime spot for people watching. Also at 361 Hitchcock Way (☎805/563-1163).

Pacific Crêpes 705 Anacapa St ☎805/882-1123. About as close to a decent crêpe as you're going to get between San Francisco and LA, in this case authentically prepared by real French cooks, who do an especially good job on the dessert crêpes. Expect to wait for service.

Palazzio Trattoria Italiana 1026 State St ☎805/564-1985. One of the better Italian restaurants in town, with old-fashioned sauce-heavy cuisine, gut-buster-sized portions, moderate prices, and one mean *tiramisu*.

Paradise Café 702 Anacapa St ☎805/962-4416. Stylish, mid-level indoor/outdoor grill, with good steaks, fresh seafood, solid pies, and burgers. Service can be marginal at times.

Restaurant Roy 7 W Carrillo St ☎805/966-5636. Tasting, tempting little restaurant whose mains include savory items like bacon-wrapped filet mignon, grilled ahi tuna, honey-glazed lamb chops, and various homemade pastas. There's also a variety of art, cocktails, and backgammon contests.

Sojourner Café 134 E Cañon Perdido ☎805/965-7922. A range of vegetarian food in a friendly bohemian setting, with occasional art shows as well.

Tupelo Junction Cafe 1218 State St ☎805/899-3100. One of the town's best spots for breakfast, in this case heavily in the Southern vein, focusing on such rib-stuffing items as bacon-spinach-onion scrambles, crab cake and potato hash, vanilla French toast, and pumpkin waffles. Also with affordable lunches and more expensive dinners.

Bars and clubs

There are quite a few **bars** and **clubs** along State Street, especially downtown; for the most up-to-date **nightlife** listings, check out a copy of the free weekly *Santa Barbara Independent* (Ⓦ www.independent.com), available at area bookstores, record stores, and convenience marts.

Blue Agave 20 E Cota St ☎805/899-4694. The mojitos, margaritas, and other fiery cocktails here, emphasizing rum and tequila, are outstanding. There's also mid-to-high-priced nouveau Latino fare, mixed with a healthy dose of Cal cuisine.
Elements 129 E Anapamu St ☎805/884-9218. If money's no object and you're a fan of inventive cocktails, then have your limo driver drop you off at this top-shelf bar and restaurant, where the regional cuisine is also excellent. Prices are a bit more affordable during Happy Hour.
Q's Sushi a Go Go 409 State St ☎805/966-9177. Four bars – including one for sushi – plus a dance floor in a three-story location make this lounge and restaurant a big draw if you're ready to drink and boogie; the sushi, though, is just average.
Santa Barbara Brewing Company 501 State St ☎805/730-1040. Serviceable American fare – burgers, seafood, and sandwiches – with solid microbrewed beers and live music on weekends. The Rincon Red and State Street Stout are both worth a swig.

SOhO 1221 State St ☎805/962-7776, ⓦwww .sohosb.com. Favorite local place to catch a jazz show, with nightly performances and the occasional big name. Mixes the vibe with frequent rock, acoustic, and world-beat artists and bands.
Velvet Jones 423 State St ☎805/965-8676, ⓦwww.velvet-jones.com. Among the few good places in town to catch a show, typically of the indie variety on the weekends and perhaps comedy and reggae at other times, drawing the usual crowd of students and would-be hellraisers.
Wildcat Lounge 15 W Ortega St ☎805/962-7970, ⓦwww.wildcatlounge.com. A good spot for seeing electronica DJs, and various other bands, in a chic atmosphere with a mix of locals, students, and out-of-towners.
Zelo 630 State St ☎805/966-5792, ⓦwww.zelo .net. One of Santa Barbara's more fashionable bars and restaurants, the *Zelo* evolves into a dance club as the night wears on, offering alternative, Latin, retro, and other eclectic rhythms throughout the week.

On from Santa Barbara

Continuing north from Santa Barbara you can either cut inland through the wine region of the Santa Ynez Valley (see opposite) or continue along the coast, where you'll pass **Goleta Beach** – popular with families – as well as the unassuming town of **Isla Vista**, which borders the campus of the **University of California, Santa Barbara**. Isla Vista Beach has some good tide pools and, at the west end, a popular surfing area at **Coal Oil Point** ("Devereux Beach" to locals), named after the natural tar deposits that seep through onto the sands. The estuary nearby has been preserved as a botanical study center and nature refuge, where birders will find much of interest on a walk around the perimeter of the reserve; one-hour guided tours are given monthly (first Sat of month 10am; info at ⓔstroh@lifesci.ucsb.edu).

All along this part of the coast **the beaches** face almost due south, so the surf is very lively, and in winter the sun both rises and sets over the Pacific. Almost twenty miles outside Santa Barbara, **El Capitan State Beach** (dawn–dusk; ☎805/968-1033) is a popular surfing beach with some tide pools as well, while **Refugio State Beach**, another three miles along, is one of the prettiest in California, with palm trees dotting the sands at the mouth of a small creek, giving the area a tropical feel. Inland on Refugio Road, up the canyon high in the hills, stands **Rancho El Cielo**, the one-time Western White House of Ronald Reagan, now a center for right-wing student activism. Ten miles west, the beach at **Gaviota State Park** is not as pretty, but there's a fishing pier and a large wooden railway viaduct that bridges the mouth of the canyon. All the beaches have **campgrounds**, and reservations can be made through Reserve America ($25; ☎1-800/444-7275, ⓦwww.reserveamerica.com).

Just beyond, the highways split, US-101 heading inland and the more spectac-ular Hwy-1 branching off nearer the coast. Half a mile off the highway in Gaviota State Park, but a world away from the speeding traffic, is the small **Las Cruces hot spring** (dawn–dusk), a pool of 100°F mineral water set in a shady, peaceful ravine. To get there, take the turnoff for Hwy-1, but stay on the east side of the freeway and double back onto a small road, continuing a quarter-mile to the parking lot at the end. Walk half a mile or so up the trail until you smell the sulfur.

The Santa Ynez Valley

An alternative to the coastal route out of Santa Barbara is to take Hwy-154 over the very steep **San Marcos Pass** and into the **Santa Ynez Valley**, a pleasant route through a prime wine-growing region that's popular with motorbikers and gung-ho bicyclists.

Three miles out of Santa Barbara, the walls of the **Chumash Painted Cave State Historic Park** (dawn–dusk; ☏805/733-3713), on the narrow Painted Caves Road, are colored with pre-conquest Native American art. You can't actually enter the sandstone cave, as it has been closed off to protect against vandalism, but peering through the bars will give you a good look at the vivid paintings inside. Their eye-opening shapes and perspective give a view of the afterlife and supernatural forces, with some images up to 1000 years old.

Several miles further, beyond the San Marcos Pass, Paradise Road follows the Santa Ynez River before the road ends at **Red Rocks**, an excellent swimming area amidst stony outcrops. It's a two-mile round-trip hike from the parking lot; for official access, buy an Adventure Pass ($5) from the ranger station or a kiosk along Paradise Road. **Lake Cachuma**, six miles further along Hwy-154, is a popular recreation area with a large **campground** (daily 8am–dusk; day-use $6, campsites $18, yurts $45–55; ☏805/686-5054, ⓦwww.sbparks.org). It's not actually a lake but a massive reservoir that holds the overstretched water supply for Santa Barbara and allows for biking, fishing, and horseback riding, among other activities.

Beyond the lake, Hwy-246 cuts off to Solvang, while Hwy-154 continues on through the vineyards around the hamlet of **Los Olivos**. The Santa Barbara County Vintners' Association (☏805/688-0881, ⓦwww.sbcountywines.com) publishes a handy wine-touring map of the area that includes each winery's address and hours. Although the town would prefer you focus on vino, it's also known as the site of Michael Jackson's 2800-acre **Neverland Ranch**, five miles north at 5225 Figueroa Mountain Road (though not visible from the roadside), where the forbidding pop icon once resided along with Bubbles the Chimp in an amusement-park setting, with a Ferris wheel, hundreds of zoo animals, and a museum devoted to himself. Following Jackson's legal troubles – he was accused and acquitted of pedophilia in 2005 – the singer closed the mansion on the property for good, and forty acres of the property burned down a year later.

Solvang and around

It's difficult to imagine anyone falling for the sham windmills and plastic storks that fill the saccharine-sweet town of **Solvang** ("sunny fields" in Danish), but people come by the busloads to see the community, featured prominently in the 2004 film *Sideways* and established in 1911 by expat Danish teachers from the Midwest looking for a place to found a Danish folk school. The town, three miles off US-101 on Hwy-246, now lives on tourism, and locals dress in "traditional" costume to entertain all comers. Besides indulging in a Scandinavian fantasyland, though, visitors can take advantage of Solvang's proximity to Santa Barbara wine country (see p.421).

You can **stay** in a grubby, Danish-themed motel or spend a little extra for the sleek and elegant *Inn at Petersen Village*, 1576 Mission Drive (☏1-800/321-8985,

@www.peterseninn.com; ❽), whose basic rooms are pricey but include canopy beds (sans Victoriana) and wireless Internet, while the tower suite ($380) is three levels with a fireplace and Jacuzzi. The cheapest adequate accommodation can be found at the *King Frederik Motel*, 1617 Copenhagen Drive (☎805/688-5515, @www.bwkingfrederik.com; ❺, add $40 for summer weekends), a clunky, ultra-basic "Old World" property with standard motel units, pool, hot tub, and continental breakfast. For **eating**, *Paula's Pancake House*, 1531 Mission Drive (☎805/688-2867), is the reliable choice for its Dutch pancakes, while *Cafe Angelica*, 490 First Street (☎805/686-9970), is the most solid spot for dinner, featuring serviceable pasta, seafood, and a mean stuffed filet mignon, each under $20. For other lodging and dining options, and information on minor Danish-themed museums – such as the **Hans Christian Andersen Museum**, upstairs at 1680 Mission Drive (daily 10am–5pm; donation; ☎805/688-2052), which has displays and volumes related to the Danish writer's life and fairy tales, including first editions of *Thumbelina* and *The Ugly Duckling* – there are **visitor information** stands run by the local CVB (☎1-800/468-6765, @www.solvangusa.com).

Mission Santa Inés, at 1760 Mission Drive (daily: June–Sept 9am–7pm; Oct–May 9am–5pm; $3; ☎805/688-4815, @www.missionsantaines.org), is hidden away behind the rows of gingerbread buildings on the eastern edge of town. A century before the Danes tried to make the place look like home, the Spanish erected the nineteenth mission in their chain here in 1804. Though the structure has undergone numerous restorations, the buildings are original, and the trompe l'oeil green-marble trim on the church's interior walls is one of the best surviving examples of mission-era decorative art. One of the better mission museums is also on the grounds, displaying furnishings, art, vestments, and documents, including a set of plaques praising the Franciscan fathers for improving the lives of the native Chumash.

Six miles from Solvang off US-101, **Nojoqui** (pronounced No-ho-kee) **Falls County Park** (daily 8am–dusk; ☎805/934-6123, @www.sbparks.org) offers a gentle ten-minute walk that brings you to a 75-foot waterfall. The route to the park is gorgeous, winding along Alisal Road under thick garlands of Spanish moss that dangle from a canopy of oak trees.

Lompoc

Hwy-1 splits off US-101 near Gaviota on a marvelous route through the inland valleys of the Santa Ynez Mountains. **LOMPOC** (pronounced Lom-POKE), the only town for miles, calls itself the "flower seed-growing capital of the world" and claims to produce as much as three-quarters of the flower seeds sold on earth. In summer, you'll see a thick carpet of color over the gently rolling landscape of the surrounding countryside. For a leaflet detailing where particular species have been planted this season, contact the **Lompoc Valley Chamber of Commerce**, 111 South I Street (Mon–Fri 9am–5pm; ☎1-800/240-0999, @www.lompoc.com), where you can also find out about the 75 folksy **murals** which, in recent years, have sprung up to beautify an otherwise faceless downtown. There are a few oddballs in the bunch, including one on the side of the Chamber of Commerce in fantastic praise of "Diatomaceous Mining" and the eerie "Patriotism" mural, 140 South H Street, painted by inmates of the nearby federal prison, featuring a phallic missile blasting off in front of a glowing American-flag horizon.

For tourist information at weekends, head to **Lompoc Museum**, 200 South H Street (Tues–Fri 1–5pm, Sat & Sun 1–4pm; $1; ☎805/736-3888). As for the collection here, it's strong on local archeology, with a number of Chumash and other Native American artifacts. It also has material on the town's **original mission site**, the scant remains of which can be found three blocks to the south on F Street off Locust Avenue.

Lompoc is also the home of **Vandenberg Air Force Base**, sprawled along the western side of town, where various new missiles and guidance systems get put through their paces over the Pacific Ocean, keeping interlopers from using the gorgeous beach for gentler pursuits like surfing. The missiles' vapor trails are visible for miles, particularly at sunset, though the only way to see any of it up close is by the Amtrak Coast Starlight train (see p.33), which runs along the coast. The route was **Jack Kerouac**'s favorite rail journey – he worked for a while as a brakeman on the train and subsequently used the "Midnight Ghost" for a free ride between LA and the Bay Area. Aerospace enthusiasts who plan at least two weeks ahead can visit the air base on four-hour **tours** (2nd Wed of month 10am–2pm; free; by reservation at ☎805/606-3595, ⓦwww.vandenberg .af.mil) that visit launch pads and a missile silo.

One accessible stretch of sand in the area, **Jalama Beach**, at the end of Jalama Road, twisting fourteen miles off Hwy-1 (daily 8am–dusk; $6; ☎805/736-3504, ⓦwww.sbparks.org), spreads beneath coastal bluffs, where you can camp overnight ($18–25). If you're only planning on stopping by during the day, head to the large sand dunes of **Ocean Beach** (free), a broad strand at the mouth of the Santa Ynez River thirteen miles west of Lompoc, the nesting grounds of many seabirds. If you're not camping and are interested in exploring the flowers or the mission (see below), Lompoc's most reasonable **accommodation** can be found at the *O'Cairns Inn*, 940 E Ocean Drive (☎805/735-7731, ⓦwww.bestwestern.com; ⑤), with clean, modern rooms and continental breakfast. Lompoc isn't exactly known for its quality **dining**, but *Sissy's Uptown Cafe*, 112 South I Street (☎805/735-4877), is one exception, good for its homemade soups, sandwiches, and veggie options, with a number of more expensive steaks for dinner.

La Purísima Mission State Park

Four miles east of Lompoc and signposted off Hwy-246, **La Purísima Mission State Park** (daily 9am–5pm; $4 per family vehicle, up to nine people; ☎805/733-3713, ⓦwww.lapurisimamission.org) is the most complete and authentic reconstruction of any of the 21 Spanish missions in California and one of the best places to get an idea of what life might have been like in these early settlements. La Mision la Purísima Concepción de Maria Santísima was founded in 1787 on a site three miles north of here, and by 1804 had converted around 1500 Chumash, five hundred of whom died in a smallpox epidemic over the next two years. In 1812, an earthquake destroyed all the buildings, and the fathers decided to move to the present site. This new design was the only mission in the chain to be built in a linear fashion rather than in a defensive quadrangle, normally used both to confine Native Americans and to keep them out – an especially important detail as the number of able-bodied residents had been slashed by the epidemic. The complex did not last long, however, after the missions were secularized in 1834; like all the rest, it was soon abandoned and gradually fell into disrepair.

The buildings that stand here today were rebuilt on the ruins of the mission as part of a Depression-era work project. From 1933 to 1940 over two hundred men lived and worked on the site, studying the remaining ruins and rebuilding the church and outbuildings using period tools and methods. Workers made adobe bricks from straw and mud, shaped roof timbers with handtools, and even took the colors of their paints from native plants.

The heart of the mission is a narrow church, decorated as it would have been in the 1820s; nearby, at the entrance, small but engaging displays of documents and artifacts from the mission era and photographs of the reconstruction are housed in the old wagon house that serves as a **museum** and gift shop, though a brand-new **visitor center** is also taking shape that will doubtless encompass many of the current exhibits. Once a month in summer you might catch a "Purisima People's Day," when volunteers switch back the clock to 1822, docents dressing as padres and natives holding a traditional Mass.

Pismo Beach and Avila Beach

Most of the land along the Santa Maria River, 75 miles north of Santa Barbara, is given over to agriculture, and both Hwy-1 and US-101 pass through a number of farm towns and villages. **Santa Maria** is the largest and most developed, though it's hardly worth stopping except to refuel or for a peek at the historic planes on display at the **Museum of Flight**, 3015 Airpark Drive (Fri–Sun 10am–4pm; $5; ☏805/922-8758, ⓦwww.smmof.org). Other towns seem hardly to have changed since the 1930s, when thousands of Okies, as they were known, fled to the region from the Dust Bowl of the Midwest.

Twenty-five miles north of Lompoc, Hwy-1 passes through the center of **Guadalupe**, a small farming village where Spanish signs and advertisements far outnumber those in English, and ramshackle saloons, cafés, and vegetable stalls line the dusty streets. Several miles west along the coast lies the **Guadalupe/Nipomo Dunes Preserve** (daily 8am–sunset, visitor center Thurs–Sun 10am–4pm; free; ☏805/343-2455, ⓦwww.dunescenter.org), where you can look for whales out at sea or climb the 500-foot sand dunes. The highest on the California coast, the dunes surround wetlands that are habitat for endangered seabirds. More bizarrely, buried within these dunes is much of the movie set for Cecil B. DeMille's original 1924 silent epic, *The Ten Commandments* (later remade with Charlton Heston), when the sands stood in for ancient Egypt in the director's monumental re-creation of "The City of Pharaoh." Disinterred relics from the set, which was buried instead of taken apart to save money, are on view in the visitor center, and if you're lucky you may even spot a Hollywood film crew using the dunes as a backdrop for a blockbuster production – the most recent was Johnny Depp's *Pirates of the Caribbean: At World's End*.

Pismo Beach

The dunes stretch ten miles up the coast, reaching as far as two miles inland and ending just south of **PISMO BEACH**, where the two highways merge. The portion of the dunes three miles south of the town is open to off-road-vehicle enthusiasts, who tear over the sandpiles of the **Pismo Dunes State Vehicle Recreation Area** in dune buggies and four-wheel-drives, motoring along the beach to reach them. This is California's only drive-on beach, bringing millions of dollars in tourist revenue to the area. Thankfully, another portion of the dunes inland is protected as a **nature reserve**.

North of the nature reserve, between the town and the dune-buggy area, a number of beachfront **campgrounds** line Hwy-1; mostly RV-packed, they all charge around $25 a site. **Pismo State Beach** has hot showers and beach camping (☏805/489-1869, reserve camping at ☏1-800/444-7275, ⓦwww.reserveamerica.com), and is a good place to see the black-and-orange monarch butterflies that winter in the eucalyptus trees here from October to February in their own designated grove, leaving before the summer crowds. For more information, see ⓦwww.monarchbutterfly.org. However, the once-plentiful **Pismo clams** that gave the town its name (from the Chumash word *pismu*, or "blobs of tar" that the shells resemble) have been so depleted that any you might dig up nowadays are probably under the 4.5-inch legal minimum size – a far cry from making the burg the "Clam Capital of the World." To try your luck at clamming, you'll need a fishing license from the Department of Fish and Game (day-pass $12.10; info at ⓣ916/928-5805, ⓦwww.dfg.ca.gov).

Most of the town's commercial activity happens at the junction where Pomeroy Avenue crosses Hwy-1. If you have no interest in dunes or watersports, you're in the wrong place, as the dozens of surf shops around you will attest. Beach Cycle Rentals, 150 Hinds Avenue (ⓣ805/773-5518), one of several similar dealers, rents boards and bikes. You can also walk out on the sizable pier for views back to town over the heads of surfers riding the waves.

If you continue just north of town to Shell Beach, you'll come to the redoubtable **Dinosaur Caves Park** (dawn–dusk; free; ⓦwww.dinosaur cavespark.org), whose craggy sea stacks dot the landscape and poke out in the waves, their various caves, coves, arches, and passages making for a geologist's and kayaker's delight. All kinds of rock are mashed together in this dramatic, mottled seascape, from mica to serpentine, and the best way to view the site is to paddle out into the protected inlet. Despite the park's moniker, you won't see any extinct reptiles – the place was named for a short-lived tourist attraction in the form of a concrete dinosaur. You can rent kayaks for $15–20 per hour or $40–50 per half-day. Central Coast Kayaks, 1879 Shell Beach Road (ⓣ805/773-3500, ⓦwww.centralcoastkayaks.com), is one reliable operator.

Practicalities

The **visitor center**, 581 Dolliver Street (Mon–Sat 9am–5pm, Sun 10am–4pm; ⓣ1-800/443-7778, ⓦwww.classiccalifornia.com), will help with maps and accommodation, and there are a number of affordable **motels**, including the *Sea Gypsy*, 1020 Cypress Street (ⓣ1-800/592-5923, ⓦwww.seagypsy motel.com; ❸), which has clean, modern decor and, for a small premium, natty studio apartments with kitchens and balconies. Right on the beach, the *Kon Tiki Inn*, 1621 Price Street (ⓣ805/773-4833, ⓦwww.kontikiinn.com; ❺), has a gym, decent restaurant, pool, Jacuzzis, and nice rooms with balconies and sea views. If you have a little more to spend, the *SeaVenture Resort*, 100 Ocean View Avenue (ⓣ805/773-4994, ⓦwww.seaventure.com; ❻), offers stylish rooms with fireplaces, balconies, and some designer furnishings, with in-room continental breakfast and expansive oceanside views, as well as a decent restaurant. During summer, rooms without views can be up to $50 cheaper.

Your **dining** options are similarly attractive: people have been known to drive fair distances just to sample the clam chowder at the ⅄ *Cracked Crab*, 751 Price Street (ⓣ805/773-2722), as well as its excellent crab, shrimp, and many other delicious, inexpensive crustaceans and fish. *Rosa's*, 491 Price Street (ⓣ805/773-0551), serves up good and affordable pasta, pizza, and seafood, while for fancier dining, *Giuseppe's*, 891 Price Street (ⓣ805/773-2870), is an Old World-styled Italian eatery with hearty, simple food.

For **transportation** needs, South County Area Transit (tickets $1; ⓣ805/481-7801, ⓦwww.scattransit.org) can get you around the local part of the coast, including Grover Beach, from where you can transfer to Amtrak's Pacific Surfliner train (see p.33).

Avila Beach

North of Pismo Beach the coastline becomes more rugged, with caves and tide pools below ever-eroding bluffs, and sea lions in the many coves. The three-mile-long strand in front of the summer resort town of **AVILA BEACH**, the last outpost of Southern California beach life, is finally recovering from a devastating ecological disaster caused by a 1990s spill from the nearby Unocal Refinery. The ambitious cleanup and reconstruction project that began soon after the spill has helped restore much of the area to its pre-disaster status.

The area has numerous golf courses, resorts, tourist shops, and **motels** with ocean views, the cheapest of which is the *Inn at Avila Beach*, 256 Front Street (℡805/595-2300, Ⓦwww.avilabeachca.com; ❻), with a faded beachfront style; the swanky *Avila Lighthouse Suites*, 550 Front Street (℡805/627-1900, Ⓦwww .avilalighthousesuites.com; ❽, or $329 for summer weekends), has ocean-view units which variously come with fireplaces, parlors, and wet bars. The *Olde Port Inn* (℡805/595-2515), dramatically perched out on Port San Luis, is *the* spot to **eat** in Avila and has magnificent views: of course, the menu's mostly fish – try the fish tacos for lunch or the spicy cioppino stew of fish and shellfish for dinner.

On the beach, you'll find teenagers on the loose from families cruising the boardwalk, while anyone old enough takes refuge in the loud local **bars**. The party atmosphere continues all summer long, and no one seems to mind the presence of the Diablo Canyon Nuclear Plant, which straddles an earthquake fault six miles up the coast. The scenic route north from here to San Luis Obispo, **See Canyon Road**, cuts off north a mile from US-101, climbing gradually up the narrow, overgrown canyon between sharply profiled volcanic cones, with great views out over the Pacific.

The world's first motel

The Milestone Mo-Tel opened in San Luis Obispo at 2223 Monterey Street in 1925, designed to take advantage of growing car ownership among Americans. Initially, enthusiastic Model–T drivers had used automobile "campgrounds" for overnight stays, pitching tents alongside their cars, and since San Luis Obispo is halfway between San Francisco and Los Angeles, it became an especially popular place to stop. Savvy architect **Arthur Heineman**, who'd recently overseen the development of residential bungalows, recognized the potential of adapting the bungalow concept for the travel industry, combining the convenience of a campground with the comfort and respectability (not to mention higher prices) of a hotel – a "motor hotel," which, because those words couldn't fit on the sign, became a "mo-tel."

Heineman and his brother Alfred opened the first motel in the auto nexus of San Luis Obispo, but envisaged a chain stretching from San Diego to Seattle, each one day's journey from the next, much like the first European settlements along the Camino Real – hence the Mission-style architecture of the existing *Milestone* building. Unfortunately, only one motel was built, and Heineman didn't even manage to copyright the word he'd coined. It entered the dictionary in 1950, long after hundreds of copycats had sprung up across America.

The *Milestone*, later the *Motel Inn*, closed in 1991 and, despite some promise of restoration from its new owners – the adjoining *Apple Farm Inn* (see p.434) – it's still falling into decay, a faded relic from the glory days of California car culture.

San Luis Obispo

Almost exactly halfway between LA and San Francisco, **SAN LUIS OBISPO** (locally, "SLO") is a main stopoff for both Amtrak and Greyhound. It's an underappreciated gem: primarily an agricultural town, but with a perked-up nightlife thanks to an influx of college students, and a pleasant place to dawdle and browse. The town center boasts well-preserved architecture, from turreted Victorian residences along **Buchon Street**, south of the town center, to the Art Deco Fremont Theater on Monterey Street. There are a number of good places to eat, a couple of decent pubs and nightclubs, and – outside summer holiday weekends – affordable accommodation. All these factors make it a smart base from which to explore Hearst Castle, too (see p.441).

Arrival and information

The Greyhound terminal is at 150 South Street (℡805/543-2121), half a mile down Higuera Street from the center of town near US-101; there are regular **bus connections** with both LA and San Francisco. Amtrak **trains** stop several times each day at the end of Santa Rosa Street, half a mile south of the business district. This is the northern terminus of the Pacific Surfliner route, from which you can transfer to Coast Starlight trains covering the entire coast. You can **get around** on the local shuttle services, SLO Transit (tickets $1; ℡805/541-2877) or the wider Regional Transit Authority ($1–2.50; ℡805/781-4472, Ⓦwww

.slorta.org), which links to Morro Bay and Pismo Beach, among other places.

Pick up a free walking-tour map highlighting much of the town's best architecture from the **visitor center** at 1039 Chorro Street (Sun–Wed 10am–5pm, Thurs–Sat 10am–7pm; ℡805/781-2670, Ⓦwww.visitslo.com), which will also help with finding accommo-dation. To find out what's on and where, check out the free weekly *New Times* (Ⓦwww.newtimesslo .com) or the "Ticket" supplement every Friday in the *San Luis Obispo Tribune* (Ⓦwww.sanluisobispo .com).

Accommodation

Monterey Street was the site of the world's first (now closed) **motel** – the *Milestone Mo-Tel* (see box, opposite). Rates at its modern counterparts are generally low. The best **camping** nearby is south of town beyond Pismo Beach, or north off Hwy-1 in Morro Bay.

▲ Fremont Theater, San Luis Obispo

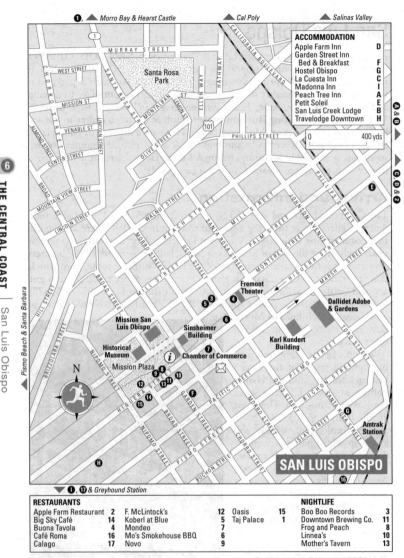

ACCOMMODATION

Apple Farm Inn	D
Garden Street Inn Bed & Breakfast	F
Hostel Obispo	G
La Cuesta Inn	C
Madonna Inn	I
Peach Tree Inn	A
Petit Soleil	E
San Luis Creek Lodge	B
Travelodge Downtown	H

SAN LUIS OBISPO

● ❶, ⑰ & Greyhound Station

RESTAURANTS					
Apple Farm Restaurant	2	F. McLintock's		Oasis	15
Big Sky Café	14	Koberl at Blue		Taj Palace	1
Buona Tavola	4	Mondeo	7		
Café Roma	16	Mo's Smokehouse BBQ	6		
Calago	17	Novo	9		

NIGHTLIFE	
Boo Boo Records	3
Downtown Brewing Co.	11
Frog and Peach	8
Linnea's	10
Mother's Tavern	13

Apple Farm Inn 2015 Monterey St ☎1-800/255-2040, ⓦwww.applefarm.com. Agreeable inn with homely Victoriana furnishings, including canopy beds and fireplaces, and excellent B&B-style breakfasts. Rates are lower in the Trellis Court building than the *Inn* proper. ⑤–⑦

Garden Street Inn Bed & Breakfast 1212 Garden St ☎1-800/488-2045, ⓦwww.gardenstreetinn.com. Very central B&B in a restored 1887 Victorian with comfortable, mildly themed rooms and suites (Ireland, China, Mozart, etc). There's complimentary wine on arrival and gourmet cooked breakfasts. ⑥

Hostel Obispo 1617 Santa Rosa St ☎805/544-4678 ⓦwww.hostelobispo.com. Comfortable hostel with lounge, patio, bike rentals, and dorm beds at $20 for HI members, $23 for others. A small number of private rooms are also available ($55–80).

La Cuesta Inn 2074 Monterey St ☎1-800/543-2777, ⓦwww.lacuestainn.com. As popular with businesspeople as vacationers, a decent motel with spacious modern rooms with fridges, continental breakfast, free Internet access, and a good-sized swimming pool and spa. **⑥** , add $30 for summer weekends.

Madonna Inn 100 Madonna Rd ☎1-800/543-9666, ⓦwww.madonnainn.com. Local landmark set in over 2000 acres, but the standard "theme" rooms (see p.436) in this shocking kitsch monstrosity are a big disappointment at such inflated rates, especially after touring the imposing pink, chalet-style lobby. Still, for many tourists, essential. **⑥**

Peach Tree Inn 2001 Monterey St ☎1-800/227-6396, ⓦwww.peachtreeinn.com. One of the town's better budget offerings, whose rooms feature wireless Internet access, VCRs, and a good continental breakfast. **④** , add $30 for summer weekends.

Petit Soleil 1473 Monterey St ☎805/549-0321, ⓦwww.petitsoleilslo.com. Very stylish French-themed B&B offering modish decor in each uniquely designed room, an even more elegant "Joie de Vivre" suite, and truly continental breakfasts that can be quite tasty. **⑦**

San Luis Creek Lodge 1941 Monterey St ☎1-800/593-0333, ⓦwww.sanluiscreeklodge.com. Offers 25 smart rooms in three buildings, each in a vaguely Greek Revival, Tudor, and Craftsman style, with microwaves and Internet access. Some units have fireplaces, Jacuzzis, or balconies. **⑦** , rates jump by $60 on summer weekends.

Travelodge Downtown 345 Marsh St ☎1-800/458-8848. Ultra-basic motel but good for location and value. There's another franchise at 1825 Monterey St (☎805/543-5110). **④**

The Town

San Luis is eminently walkable, with a compact core centered on the late eighteenth-century **Mission San Luis Obispo de Tolosa**, 751 Palm Street (daily: Jan–May 9am–4pm; June–Dec 9am–5pm; free; ☎805/781-8220, ⓦwww.missionsanluisobispo.org). A fairly plain church, it was the fifth structure in the mission trail and the prototype for the now-ubiquitous red-tiled roof – developed as a replacement for the original, flammable thatch, which caught fire here in 1776 during an attack by Native Americans. Wander through the garden and find grapevines of the sort used in the production of some of California's earliest wines, a native Chumash oven, and a statue of mission founder Padre Junípero Serra. Between the mission and the visitor center, **Mission Plaza**'s terraces step down along San Luis Creek. It's a leafy, restful spot adorned with endemic California trees and plants, crisscrossed by footpaths and bridges and overlooked by a number of stores and outdoor restaurants on the south bank – a delightful place to dawdle with a book.

Downstream and across a small park are a few minor museums, the focus of which is the **San Luis Obispo County Historical Museum**, 696 Monterey Street (Wed–Sun 10am–4pm; free; ☎805/543-0638, ⓦwww.slochs.org), holding a low-key collection of local, primarily domestic artifacts housed in a richly detailed 1904 Carnegie library. The main drag, **Higuera Street** (pronounced "hee-GEHR-ah"), a block south of Mission Plaza, springs to life for the **Farmers' Market** (Thurs 5–9pm; free), when it's closed to cars and filled with fruit and vegetable stalls, barbecues, and street-corner musicians. All of SLO (and a fair smattering of tourists) comes out to sample the food and entertainment of this weekly funfest.

Though a number of commercial buildings of minor architectural note are detailed on the Chamber of Commerce's **self-guided walking tour**, the only one not to be missed is the **Karl Kundert Building**, a doctor's surgery (no admittance except for patients) designed by Frank Lloyd Wright at Santa Rosa and Pacific streets. Though built in 1956, it resembles a truncated chunk of Wright's much earlier Robie House, with oddball window cutouts amid the red brick design. Close by, at the end of Pacific Street, stands the **Dallidet Adobe and Gardens**, at no. 1185 (gardens open year-round Thurs 2.30–5.30pm & Memorial Day to Labor Day Sun 1–4pm, docent-led tours of house Sun 1–4pm; donation; ☎805/543-6762), one of the county's oldest buildings.

Constructed by a disillusioned French forty-niner who, eluded by a fortune in the Mother Lode, ended up living in town, it's set among manicured grounds with two redwoods that are more than 125ft tall. Also not to be missed, particularly if you're on your way to Julia Morgan's Hearst Castle (see p.441), is the architect's **Monday Club**, 1815 Monterey Street (private building), exemplifying a more modest approach to the Mission Revival style, with a tiled roof, stucco walls, and tasteful geometry.

If you have neither the time nor the inclination to sample the worthwhile architecture of SLO, drop by the **Madonna Inn** (see p.435), whose rooms are decorated in a variety of themes from fairy-tale cutesy to Stone Age caveman; its signature shocking pink has been known to induce a headache or two. A very different sort of place is the **Shakespeare Press Museum** on the California Polytechnic State University campus (Mon–Fri by appointment; free; ☎805/756-2495, ⓦwww.grc.calpoly.edu/pages/spm) – nothing to do with the Bard (Shakespeare was the nickname given to Charles Palmer, owner of the donated collection, for his obsessive book-loving habits), but a great collection of old printing presses and lead typefaces collected mainly from the frontier newspapers of California's Gold Rush towns.

Eating

Higuera Street is the place to **eat**, especially during the Thursday afternoon Farmers' Market, when barbecues and food stalls are set up amidst the jostling crowds.

Apple Farm Restaurant 2015 Monterey St ☎805/544-6100. In the *Apple Farm Inn*, this casual family-style restaurant serves traditional American dishes and straight-up breakfasts of pancakes, French toast, and more.

Big Sky Café 1121 Broad St ☎805/545-5401. An airy, modern place with an emphasis on both vegetarian fare and seafood. Popular for items such as *pozole* stew, yam risotto, ginger noodles, and carnivore-friendly choices like braised lamb shank and sirloin sandwiches.

Buona Tavola 1037 Monterey St ☎805/545-8000. Small and stylish bistro with good range of moderately priced northern Italian wine and food – from *agnolotti di scampi* to *zuppa di pollo*.

Café Roma 1020 Railroad Ave ☎805/541-6800. Popular family-owned Italian restaurant with excellent pasta dishes, plus numerous seafood, steak, and veal mains, all served in a pleasant, romantic setting.

Calago 450 Marsh St ☎805/541-5393. Upscale Italian food in a restored Victorian house. The pastas, from crab ravioli to linguini mussels, are fairly good, and mains include items like osso bucco, poached venison, and plenty of seafood.

F. McLintock's 686 Higuera St ☎805/541-0686. Mainstream bar/restaurant with an Old West atmosphere, part of a local chain doling out solid burgers, pasta, and sandwiches for around $10 each – try the taco salad in a crispy shell or the gooey tri-tip French dip.

Koberl at Blue 988 Monterey St ☎805/783-1135. Swanky lounge/bar/restaurant with bare brick walls, dark wood fixtures, and a trendier, dressier crowd than most spots in town. Graze on snacks in the lounge or, in the restaurant, opt for dinner portions of items like coriander scallops, strip steak, and rack of lamb.

Mondeo 893 Higuera St #D4 ☎805/544-2956. Asian-fusion-inflected fast-food joint with an inventive, made-to-order menu. Every recipe can be served as a wrap or bowl: try an Americana with swordfish or meatloaf, or a Mediterraneo with basil scampi. The homemade ginger ale's also good.

Mo's Smokehouse BBQ 970 Higuera St ☎805/544-6193. Although no one will confuse SLO with Texas, the barbeque at this joint is as good as you're going to get for the Central Coast. The pulled pork and ribs are meaty and tender, and you can knock back your grease with a side of beans, slaw, or fried green tomatoes.

Novo 726 Higuera St ☎805/543-3986. The epitome of (affordable) fusion dining, mixing and matching international cuisines – from Moroccan quail salad to Singapore satay to tandoori salmon – though results may vary.

Oasis 675 Higuera St ☎805/543-1155. Delicious Middle Eastern eatery that features weekend belly dancing. Try the chicken with sweet potatoes and raisins, or the excellent-value set lunches.

Taj Palace 795 E Foothill Blvd ☎805/543-0722. SLO's main Indian choice is slightly pricier than you'd expect, but still good: the buffet lunch, including staples like chicken tikka and *aloo gobi*

(spicy cauliflower and potatoes) is the cheapest way to go.

Bars and live music

San Luis Obispo's sizeable student population supports more **nightlife** than you might expect for a small California town. You'll also find a couple of popular **bars** and **cafés** on and just off Higuera Street, around the Mission Plaza area.

Boo Boo Records 978 Monterey St ☎805/541-0657, ⊛www.booboorecords.com. One of the true holdouts in the tradition of great, independent record stores, with regular live in-store performances.
Christopher Cohan Performing Arts Center At Cal Polytechnic Institute, off Grand Ave ☎1-888/233-2787, ⊛www.pacslo.org. A considerable concert hall that presents a wide variety of music and arts, including classical, opera, choral, dance, and jazz.
Downtown Brewing Company 1119 Garden St ☎805/543-1843, ⊛www.downtownbrew.com. The major venue in the SLO nightlife scene, featuring two bars spread over two floors and hosting regular performances by Southern California bands and DJs.

Frog and Peach 728 Higuera St ☎805/595-3764. A popular local pub with cheap drinks and performers across a wide variety of genres.
Linnaea's 1110 Garden St ☎805/541-5888, ⊛www.linnaeas.com. Café that serves good espresso and offers live music, from indie rock and acoustic to variety shows, on its small stage on Thursday through Sunday nights.
Mother's Tavern 725 Higuera St ☎805/541-8733, ⊛www.motherstavern.com. Serves up burgers and pasta for lunch and dinner, and has a good bar with drink specials and regular performances by rockers, DJs, and local karaoke wizards.

Morro Bay and the coast to San Simeon

North of San Luis Obispo the highways diverge as US-101 – favored by trains and buses – speeds up through the Salinas Valley (see p.444), while Hwy-1 takes the more scenic route along the coast. The first dozen miles of Hwy-1 follow a series of hills rising around the plugs of extinct volcanoes, the most prominent of which have been dubbed the **Seven Sisters**, dormant for twenty million years and ranging from 500 to 1500ft high. Outdoor enthusiasts can trudge up these hills themselves, or go on a hike sponsored by a group such as Los Osos Fitness, (☎805/235-5402, ⊛www.losososfitness.com), which arranges monthly jaunts up the peaks and to other locations. The eighth volcano in the series, **Morro Rock**, is in the sea close to the coast, while the ninth is invisible under the sea. According to local lore, Morro Rock was named by the sixteenth-century explorer Juan Cabrillo, who thought it looked like the Moorish turbans in southern Spain. Later road-builders thought it looked more like a quarry for gathering stone, changing its look for the worse. Nowadays, it's off limits to the public in order to protect the nesting areas of the endangered peregrine falcon.

Morro Bay

The rock is most impressive from a distance, dominating the fine harbor at **MORRO BAY**, a collection of wetlands, mud flats, and a seawater inlet, where the local fishing boats unload their catches to sell in the many fish markets along the waterfront. This easy-paced resort town is accessible from San Luis Obispo via Regional Transit Authority bus #12 ($1.50; day-pass $4; ☎805/781-4472, ⊛www.slorta.org), though apart from the many seafood restaurants the only places worth coming here for are spread around the bay, miles from public transportation. One of the best views of the rock and surrounding coastline is from atop **Cerro Alto**, a 2620-foot volcanic cone with good hiking and camping ($18 per night), eight miles east of Morro Bay off Hwy-41. Closer in, on a point above the bay a mile south of town at the end of Main Street, but providing a good view of Morro Rock, the **Museum of Natural History** (daily 10am–5pm; $2; ☎805/772-2694, ⓦwww .morrobaymuseum.org) is a state-of-the-art interactive ecology museum aimed squarely at curious kids – the best display offers visitors the chance to build their own sand dune. North of the museum, a kayak (see below) is the best way to see the **Blue Heron Rookery**, with eucalyptus trees for attracting the great seabirds, as well as egrets and cormorants, though you're not allowed to land here since it's a protected reserve. Opposite the museum, there's a campground in **Morro Bay State Park** ($25; reserve at ☎1-800/444-7275, ⓦwww.reserveamerica.com), which also has a lagoon, marina, golf course, and opportunities for hiking, fishing, and birding. Across the bay, the thin sandy peninsula that protects the harbor is hard to reach except by boat – it's entirely undeveloped and about the only place where you stand a chance of finding Pismo clams (see p.431). Another intriguing site, on the bay's southeastern shore, is the **El Moro Elfin Forest**, at the end of 16th Street in Los Osos (dawn–dusk; free), a 90-acre preserve of pygmy oak trees that offers good strolling over walkways and paths amid its copious sand dunes. For accessing many of these places you can rent **kayaks**, which cost $9–12 per hour and $23–30 per half-day, or **canoes** for $16 per hour and $39 per half-day, from outfitters like Kayak Horizons, in town at 551 Embarcadero (☎805/772-6444, ⓦwww.kayakhorizons.com).

A few miles from the Elfin Forest near the southwest corner of the bay, **Montaña de Oro State Park** (daily dawn–dusk; free; ☎805/772-7434, ⓦwww.parks.ca.gov), at the end of Los Osos Valley Road (which turns into Pecho Valley Road), is much more primitive than Morro Bay State Park, and has some excellent tide pools as well as a good beach at Spooner's Cove. The windswept promontory stands solidly against the crashing sea, offering excellent hiking along the shore and through the sagebrush and eucalyptus trees of the upland hillsides, which in spring are covered in golden poppies – giving rise to the park's name, Spanish for "gold mountain." The dramatic landscape also makes an interesting and worthwhile spot for **camping** ($15–30; reserve at ☎1-800/444-7275, ⓦwww.reserveamerica.com).

Practicalities

For **accommodation** closer to town, there are many affordable chain **motels** around, though it's worth trying the more enjoyable *El Morro Masterpiece Motel*, 1206 Main Street (☎805/772-5633, ⓦwww.masterpiecemotels.com; ❸, add $60–80 for summer weekends), which has rooms with microwaves and fridges, some with balconies and fireplaces, and various classical artworks showcased on the walls – hence the name. The *Pleasant Inn*, 235 Harbor Street (☎805/772-8521, ⓦwww.pleasantinnmotel.com; ❸), has the cheapest decent digs in town, with attached kitchens for an extra $10; if you want a fancier spot, *Ascot Suites*, 260 Morro Bay Boulevard (☎805/772-0279, ⓦwww.ascotinn.com; ❻), will more than suffice with its elegant rooms and suites that offer hot tubs, fireplaces, and in some units, balconies – though rates jump by $90 on summer weekends. For **eating** try *Hofbrau Der Albatross*, 901 Embarcadero (☎805/772-2411), a deluxe burger joint with bratwurst and dipped sandwiches also on the menu; *Lolo's*, 2848 Main Street (☎805/772-5686), for authentic Mexican cuisine with plenty of rib-stuffing staples; and *The Coffee Pot*, 1001 Front Street (☎805/772-3176), for hearty breakfasts and lunches, with especially notable omelets. For more information, the **visitor center** is at 845 Embarcadero Road, Suite D (Mon–Sat 10–6pm; ☎1-800/231-0592, ⓦwww.morrobay.org).

Cayucos

The next town north is **Cayucos**, four miles along Hwy-1, originally a small port built by Englishman James Cass in the 1870s and now a sleepy place ranged along sandy beaches with a nice pier: a pleasant enough pit stop on a journey along the coast. *The Cypress Tree Inn*, 125 S Ocean Avenue (☎805/995-3917, ⓦwww.cypresstreemotel.com; ④), is just one block from the beach, with clean, old-fashioned rooms loosely themed around birds, Route 66, the Wild West, and more. Even better is the *Seaside Motel*, 42 S Ocean Avenue (☎1-800/549-0900,

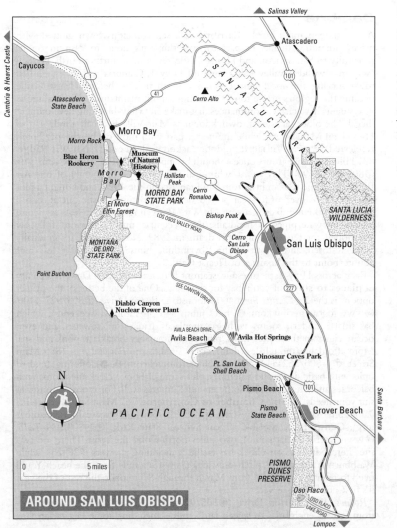

AROUND SAN LUIS OBISPO

www.seasidemotel.com; ❹), whose decor is a bit twee but which does have affordable suites and units with kitchenettes, and an oceanfront location. For coffee, muffins, and pastries, you can't beat *Kelley's*, 155 N Ocean Avenue (☎805/995-2980), and don't miss *Hoppe's Garden Bistro*, 78 N Ocean Avenue (☎805/995-1006), with a seasonal menu that focuses on fresh ingredients – venison, prime rib, lobster, and even the rare abalone – to create delicious California cuisine that goes down well with the region's estimable wines. Surprisingly, the town also has some of the area's best **nightlife** in the *Old Cayucos Tavern and Card Room*, in the heart of the two-block-long ramshackle center at 130 N Ocean Avenue (☎805/995-3209), with live bands on weekends and late-night poker games. For more information, contract the **Chamber of Commerce** (☎805/995-1200, www.cayucoschamber.com).

Cambria

About sixteen miles north, **Cambria** is a self-conscious town glutted with pricey amenities thanks in part to everything it's done to cash in on its proximity to San Simeon and Hearst Castle, seven miles further north. Hidden away in a wooded valley half a mile off Hwy-1, Cambria was an established town serving the local ranchers and fishermen long before Hearst Castle became the region's prime tourist attraction, and it maintains a certain allure as its residents have enacted ordinances that make any view-blocking development illegal. The older section of town, known as Main Village, is half a mile east of Hwy-1 on Main Street, while the newer part with most of the cheaper hotels is referred to as East Village. It holds one acknowledged oddity: **Nit Wit Ridge**, 881 Hillcrest Drive (tours once a month by appointment; Sat 10am & 1pm; $10; ☎805/927-2690). This weird, whimsical folly was the brainchild of one Art Beal, who came to Cambria from San Francisco in the 1920s and bought a plot of land where, over a fifty-year period, he built a Baroque castle out of trash – giving him the moniker "Captain Nit Wit." Recycling old toilet seats as picture frames or waterpipes as handrails, this eccentric misfit's glorious folly lay abandoned for ten years after his death in 1989. Now, though, it's gradually being restored, and a tour of the labyrinthine house is an offbeat, low-rent counterpoint to the luxuries of Hearst Castle.

Back across Hwy-1, picturesque, seafront Moonstone Beach Drive has plenty of **places to stay**, but you'll pay for the views. One of the better of the pricier options is the *FogCatcher Inn*, 6400 Moonstone Beach Drive (☎805/927-1400, www.fogcatcherinn.com; ❻, rates jump $40 on summer weekends), which has smart, modern rooms with gas fireplaces, fridges, microwaves, and even ocean views in the better units, plus complimentary breakfast, pool, and spa. More affordable, though less dramatically sited, is the *Bluebird Inn,* 1880 Main Street (☎1-800/552-5434, www.bluebirdmotel.com; ❸–❻), offering standard units with basic decor and amenities, plus more elaborate creekside rooms with balconies and fireplaces, and some en-suite units as well. For more options that suit your needs, visit the **Chamber of Commerce**, 767 Main Street (Mon–Fri 9am–5pm, Sat & Sun noon–4pm; ☎805/927-3624, www.cambriachamber .org). **Camping** is available at San Simeon State Park (☎1-800/444-7275, www.reserveamerica.com), two miles north along the coast. There are two sites here: San Simeon Creek has facilities including showers ($20–25), while Washburn is a primitive, pitch-only area ($11–15) a mile from the beach. You'll need to reserve a spot here from March through September; the rest of the year it's first-come-first-served.

Robin's, 4095 Burton Drive (☎805/927-5007), serves California cuisine – from lobster enchiladas to spiced lamb rolls – including some vegetarian fare,

Born in 1863, **William Randolph Hearst** was the only son of a multimillionaire mining engineer, though he was avidly devoted to his mother, Phoebe Apperson Hearst, one of California's most sincere and generous philanthropists, a founder of the University of California and the Traveler's Aid Society. Hearst learned his trade in New York City working for the inventor of inflammatory "**yellow journalism**," Joseph Pulitzer, who had four rules for how to sell newspapers: emphasize the sensational, elaborate the facts, manufacture the news, and use games and contests. When he published his own newspaper, Hearst took this advice to heart, his *Morning Journal* fanning the flames of American imperialism to help ignite the **Spanish-American War** of 1898. As he told his correspondents in Cuba: "You provide the pictures, and I'll provide the war." Hearst eventually controlled an empire that, at its peak during the 1930s, sold 25 percent of the newspapers in the entire country, including two other New York papers, the *Washington Times*, and the *Detroit News* – as well as *Cosmopolitan* and *Good Housekeeping* magazines. In California, Hearst's power was even more pronounced, with his San Francisco and Los Angeles papers controlling over sixty percent of the total market. Besides his many newspapers, Hearst owned eleven radio stations and two movie studios.

It was through his movie-studio proprietorship that he made his mistress **Marion Davies** a star. Although Hearst was married, his estranged wife Millicent disliked Hearst Castle, so Marion was queen-consort there; the only time Mrs Hearst spent here was as hostess whenever a head of state, like Churchill or Coolidge, was a visitor (while Davies was billeted at a mansion in LA). Marion's relationship with Hearst endured despite constant accusations of gold-digging and rumors swirling around a mysterious death onboard Hearst's boat (allegedly, Hearst murdered film-studio pioneer Thomas Ince and covered it up). When the Depression hit, Hearst was forced to sell off most of his holdings but remained a wealthy man; he continued to exert power and influence until his death, aged 88, at Marion Davies' ranch in 1951. She stuck by him until the end, despite the private sniggers of his upper-crust cohorts; in explanation, Davies is said to have shrugged "My mother raised me to be a gold-digger, but I fell in love."

most at moderate prices. For lunch, grab a tasty doorstop sandwich at the *Courtyard Deli*, 604 Main Street (☏805/927-3833), so crammed with filling it's almost impossible to eat whole, while the *Sow's Ear Cafe*, 2248 Main Street (☏805/927-4865), is a local favorite for its range of mid-priced and upscale beef and seafood, with some oddball items like lobster pot pie, honey–pecan catfish, and Danish pork ribs.

Hearst Castle and San Simeon

Forty-five miles northwest of San Luis Obispo, **HEARST CASTLE** sits on a hilltop overlooking rolling ranchlands and the Pacific Ocean. Far and away the biggest attraction for miles, the former holiday home of publishing magnate **William Randolph Hearst** is one of the most opulent and extravagant houses in the world. Its interior combines walls, floors, and ceilings torn from European churches and castles with Gothic fireplaces and Moorish tiles. Nearly every room is bursting with Greek vases and medieval tapestries, and even the many pools are lined with works of art. Ironically, the same financial power and lust for collecting that allowed Hearst to hoard these artifacts to himself have made them viewable to more people than ever would have seen them had they stayed in their respective lands. Though the castle was once a weekend retreat for only the most famous politicians and movie stars of the 1920s and 1930s – Hearst's highly selective range of guests included Winston Churchill, Walt Disney, and Charles Lindbergh, while the most frequent weekenders were Cary Grant and Charlie Chaplin (known here as "the Court Jester") – it now brings in more than a million visitors a year, and it would be unthinkable to visit the region without stopping off here.

The Castle

Hearst Castle, which Hearst himself referred to as "the ranch" (the official name is now "Hearst San Simeon State Historic Monument"), is the extravagant palace one would expect from the man whose grandstanding character and domination of the national media inspired Orson Welles's classic film *Citizen Kane*. The structure is actually more a complex of buildings than a "castle;" three guesthouses circle the hundred-room main **Casa Grande**, in which Hearst himself held court. What may come as a surprise is the harmony with which the many diverse art treasures that he collected were brought together by his mother's favorite architect **Julia Morgan** – herself a pioneer in the use of Spanish Mission elements in California architecture, from the Monday Club in San Luis Obispo (see p.436) to LA's landmark Herald-Examiner Building (Broadway and 11th Street). Here, Morgan designed each room and building in the spirit of the masterpieces destined to be housed inside – and received only $80,000 for her efforts. This paltry sum didn't keep her from acting as Hearst's personal architect for several decades after, though.

The ranchland had been in the family since 1865, bought by Hearst's father, mining magnate and senator George Hearst, and after the death of Hearst's mother Phoebe in 1919, construction began in earnest on his fantasies. This started on the southern edge of the 250,000-acre ranch, which became Hearst's own private free-roaming zoo with lions, tigers, zebras, and bears. Though it kept on for another three decades, the work was never truly completed, since rooms would often be torn out as soon as they were finished in order to accommodate more acquired treasure. It's no wonder that the castle looks more like a church than a mansion: the main facade is a twin-towered copy of a Mudejar cathedral in Ronda, Spain, while the main door was pilfered from a convent there. Casa Grande stands at the top of steps that curve up from an expansive **Neptune Pool** (one of the most photographed in the world), which is filled with pure spring water and lined by a Greek colonnade and marble statues. Indoors the **Roman Pool** is lined with blue Venetian glass and gold tiles, its soft lights reflecting in the water's steamy surface.

Highlights inside the castle include the **Refectory**, the great man's stunning dining chamber, lined with choir stalls removed from Spanish and Italian churches and bedecked pompously with heraldic flags; the **Library**, stuffed with thousands of rare and musty volumes; and the **Gothic Suite**, where Hearst conducted his daily business in medieval splendor, and whose grand, gloomy fireplace may have served as the inspiration for Kane's more colossal, jaw-like hearth. The **private cinema** shouldn't be missed, either; inside, Hearst saw first cuts of Hollywood films before they were released to the general public. The one disappointing element of the interior is its art collection: there are plenty of cherry-cheeked Madonnas and minor Old Masters, but not a single standout work – Hearst's taste was more decorative than artistic.

Outside the castle proper there are several other major buildings, including the seventeen Neptune Pool dressing rooms, still hung with period swimwear and sports equipment, and the elaborate **guesthouses**, highlighted by the Eastern-themed **Casa del Mar**, which Marion Davies claimed to be Hearst's favorite spot on the whole estate, and **Casa del Monte**, a smaller guesthouse loaded with tapestries, overlooking the Santa Lucia Mountains. The estate's extensive Italian- and Spanish-influenced gardens, terraces, and walkways require a full tour in themselves as they feature hundreds of species of rare and imported flowers and trees.

Castle practicalities

To see Hearst Castle, you must take one of the guided **tours** (1hr 45min daily 8.20am–3.20pm; $24; ☎1-800/444-4445, outside US ☎1-916/414-8400 ext. 4100, ⓦwww.hearstcastle.com). **Tour #1**, the Experience Tour, which includes a lush film on the building's construction plus an introductory spin around the Casa del Sol guesthouse and the main rooms of the Casa Grande, is usually recommended for the first visit – to guarantee a spot on the tour, make a **reservation**. More worthwhile is **Tour #2**, around the **Casa Grande Upper Floors**: instead of ambling around in a group of forty or more, you'll be with just a handful of other visitors. The docent's narrative about Hearst is just as informative as you poke around the Gothic Suite, with Hearst's library and office, and the Doge's Suite, his Venetian-flavored bedroom, and gives a more personal insight into the man than gawping at the staterooms seen on Tour #1 (the only difference is that you won't be able to catch that biopic). If you're fascinated enough to stay for the whole day, **Tour #3** is strictly for aficionados, concentrating as it does on the Casa del Monte guesthouse and the North Wing of Casa Grande, while **Tour #4** (spring and summer only) focuses on Casa del Mar and the gardens, including the estimable wine cellar. **Tour #5** (April–Oct; 2hr 10min; $30) runs on selected evenings, in which docents in period dress take visitors through the castle on a visit that combines elements of tours #1, 2, and 4. They speak of Hearst in the present tense, ending the visit at the lamplit Neptune Pool, with stories of the legends who frolicked there after dark. All tours include stops at the Neptune and Roman pools; for schedules, call the recorded information line at ☎805/927-2020 or book online or via ☎1-800/444-4445.

For each tour, budget around two hours, including the trundling ride via bus from the visitor center to the hilltop; all tours leave from the same depot at the rear of the center, through double doors past the ticket office. Make sure to collect your tickets before lining up for the tour. If you've arrived early, you can find out more about Hearst and his castle from the mildly diverting **museum** (daily 9am–5pm; free) in the rear half of the visitor center, beyond the point where you board the buses.

A final word of advice: try to visit the castle first thing in the **morning**, when coastal fogs often hide it from the world below. After a long bus ride from the visitor center to the top of the steep hill on which the mansion sits, you poke through the clouds into sunlight, as if entering one man's idea of heaven.

San Simeon and north

The old fishing pier at **San Simeon**, the remains of a harbor town along the coast just north of Hearst Castle, is where all of Hearst's treasures were unloaded, along with the many tons of concrete and steel that went into the building of the house. Before the Hearsts bought up the land, San Simeon was a whaling and shipping port, of which all that remains is a one-room schoolhouse and the 1852 *Sebastian's Store*, 442 San Simeon Road (☎805/927-4217), a combination post office, café,

▲ Elephant seals near San Simeon

history museum, and souvenir shop. The beach south of the pier is protected by San Simeon Point, which hooks out into the Pacific, making it safe for swimming. Along the highway three miles south, and still marked as part of San Simeon, there are some basic **motels**, mostly overpriced with the exception of a few along Castillo Drive, such as *Motel 6*, no. 9070 (℡1-800/466-8356, Ⓦwww.motel6.com; ❷), and *Inns of California-San Simeon*, no. 9280 (℡1-800/556-0400, Ⓦwww .innsofcal.com; ❸–❺). Both have heated pools, while the latter has some balconies and fireplaces and rates that tend to double on weekends in summer. There are more choices in Cambria, and there's **camping** four miles south along the beach at San Simeon State Park (see p.440 for both).

North of Hearst Castle the **coastline** is mostly rolling grasslands and cattle ranches, still owned and run by the Hearst family, with few buildings on the distant hills. About three miles past San Simeon, a small strip of sand provides a resting point for a large colony of **elephant seals**; trails lead past a gate near the car park down to the beach, where you can watch the huge piles of blubber cuddle one another and frolic in the waves. Beyond here the highway seems to drop off in mid-air, marking the southern edge of Big Sur (see p.449), one of the most dramatic stretches of coastline in America.

The Salinas Valley and Steinbeck Country

If you're in a hurry, US-101 through the **SALINAS VALLEY** takes four hours to cover the 220 miles between San Luis Obispo and San Francisco, compared to the full day it takes to drive the more scenic coast along Hwy-1 through Big Sur. Unless you have your own wheels, you may not have the choice, as both Greyhound and Amtrak take the inland route. The four-lane freeway closely follows the path of El Camino Real, the trail that linked the 21 Spanish **missions** along the Salinas River. It runs through farmland that's so fertile it's earned the nickname the "Salad Bowl of the World," thanks to the millions of lettuces (known as "green gold") produced here each summer. They're largely picked by Mexican immigrants, who populate the small rural towns that dot the valley.

This region is also popularly known as **STEINBECK COUNTRY** for having nurtured the imagination of Nobel Prize-winning author John Steinbeck, whose naturalistic stories and novels, including the epic *East of Eden*, were set in and around the valley.

Paso Robles

Paso Robles (pronounced "ROBE-ulls") is a thriving little town surrounded by horse ranches and nut farms. Despite a 6.5 magnitude earthquake in 2003, the town has rebounded quickly and there's little evidence of destruction other than a large pit just off the town square. Casualties were limited to two women killed when the nineteenth-century clocktower collapsed downtown.

The **visitor center**, 1225 Park Street (Mon–Fri 8.30am–5pm, Sat 10am–4pm; ☎805/238-0506, ⓦwww.pasorobleschamber.com), stocks a free map of the surrounding 150-odd **wineries** (ⓦwww.pasowine.com), many regarded as among the finest in the state. Some of the best string out along ten miles of Hwy-46 just east of town.

Try Turley Wine Cellars, 2900 Vineyard Drive (☎805/434-1030, ⓦwww.turleywinecellars.com), who make superb Zinfandel from vines over eighty years old; and Tablas Creek Vineyard, 9339 Adelaida Road (☎805/237-1231, ⓦwww.tablascreek.com), which was founded by the Perrin family of Châteauneuf-du-Pape fame.

Central **accommodation** includes the *Paso Robles Inn*, on the town square at 1103 Spring Street (☎1-800/676-1713, ⓦwww.pasoroblesinn.com; rooms ❻, spa rooms ❼), which has comfortable rooms, some with two-person tubs on the balconies, with water fed by local hot springs. The nearby *Melody Ranch Motel*, 939 Spring Street (☎805/238-3911; ❸) is cheap and clean, and the *Holiday Inn Express Hotel*, 2455 Riverside Avenue (☎1-800/465-4329, ⓦwww.holidayinn.com; ❺) fills the middle ground.

Out among the vines, try *Ann & George's B&B*, 1965 Niderer Road (☎805/423-2760, ⓦwww.voladoresvineyard.com; ❼), offering very comfortable lodging in the grounds of the Voladores Vineyard, five miles southwest of Paso Robles. The visitor center can point you to other bucolic options.

Restaurants cluster on and around the town square: try *Lombardi's*, 836 11th Street (☎805/237-7786), which serves tasty pastas and pizzas, many with lashings of gorgonzola, for $13–15 in a casual setting. *Café Vio*, 1111 Riverside Avenue (☎805/237-2722; closed Sun), brews good espresso and has free **Internet access** (and Wi-Fi).

About thirty miles east of town, on Hwy-46 past the junction of Hwy-41 near Cholame, you can pay your respects at the stainless-steel monument near the site where **James Dean** crashed in a silver Porsche Speedster on September 30, 1955.

Mission San Miguel Arcangel and Mission San Antonio de Padua

Even if you're racing up US-101, set aside half an hour for an essential peek at one of the least visited yet most intact and authentic of California's Spanish missions, **Mission San Miguel Arcangel**, 801 Mission Street (daily 9.30am–4.30pm; $2 donation; ☎805/469-3256), just off the freeway in the small town of **San Miguel**. Founded in 1797 as the sixteenth mission in the chain, the current building dates from 1816; it's the only mission not to have suffered from heavy-handed restorations. It was actually used for awhile as a saloon and dancehall, though the chapel was left pretty much unscathed, with colorful painted decoration and a marvelous sunburst reredos, complete with a striking Eye of God – all painted by Native Americans. The other buildings are notable, too, for their rough imprecision, with irregularly arched openings and unplastered walls forming a courtyard around a cactus garden. The mission was the most high-profile casualty of Paso Robles' 2003 earthquake; it didn't topple, but both the main chapel and quadrangle are closed to the public until $15 million can be found to shore up the place. A self-guided tour visits what's accessible, namely the old living quarters. The *Western States Inn*, right off Hwy-101 at 1099 K Street (☎805/467-3674, ⓦwww.westernstatesinn.com; ❸), is the only hotel in town and has plain but comfortable rooms.

If you're so inspired, venture west of US-101 to another fascinating mission. Ten miles north of San Miguel at Bradley, take Jolon Road (G18) twenty miles to the entrance of the Hunter Liggett Army Base. After inspecting your driver's license and vehicle registration they'll grant passage five miles into the base to **Mission San Antonio de Padua** (daily 8am–5pm; grounds and church free; museum $5 donation; ☎831/385-4478). This rarely visited restoration of the 1771 original settlement is less sanitized than some of the other California missions, and gives a very good idea of what life might have been like for the missionaries and their converts. Third to be founded, this mission was among the most prosperous of the entire chain, and around the extensive grounds, in a wide valley of oak trees and tall grasses, a number of scattered exhibits describe the work that went on in the long-abandoned vineyard, tannery, and gristmill. There's a monastic peace to Mission San Antonio these days, especially around the inner courtyard and dim church with flickering candles.

The large house across the valley from the mission used to belong to Hearst, who sold it and most of the land between here and Hearst Castle to the government in 1940 to help clear a $120-million debt. Today, the *Hacienda Guest Lodge* (☎831/386-2900; ❷), as it's now called, offers rather ascetic **accommodation**.

Soledad and Mission Soledad

Jolon Road loops back to US-101 at nondescript **King City**, from where those headed to the eastern entrance for the Pinnacles National Monument (and its campground) should follow road G13 to the northeast. Otherwise rejoin US-101 and follow it twenty miles north of King City to **Soledad**, a quiet, predominantly Mexican farming town principally of interest for its proximity to the Pinnacles. Its *panaderías*, selling cakes and fresh tortillas, make it a good place to stock up on food and drink for a trip to the monument, but the main reason to drop in is **Mission Nuestra Señora de la Soledad** (daily 10am–4pm; free; ☎831/678-2586), three miles west of US-101 on the south side of town. This, the thirteenth mission in the chain, lay neglected for over a hundred years until it was little more than a pile of mud. Never a great success, it suffered through a history of epidemics, floods, and crop failures. First restored in 1951, and again more recently, it now contain a museum on mission life, but the ruins adjacent to the rebuilt church are the most evocative section. **Accommodation** is best either at *Soledad Motel 8*, 1013 Front Street (☎831/678-3814; midweek ❸, weekends ❹), or at the swanky *Inn at the Pinnacles*, 32025 Stonewall Canyon Road (☎831/678-2400, ⓦwww.innatthepinnacles.com; ❼), on Hwy-146 just a mile short of the park's western entrance. There's excellent Mexican **food** in Soledad at *La Fuente*, 101 Oak Street (☎831/678-3130).

The Pinnacles National Monument

The major natural attraction of the region is the **Pinnacles National Monument** ($5 per vehicle, good for 7 days; ☎831/389-4485, ⓦwww.nps .gov/pinn), a compact region of startling volcanic spires and brilliant reds and golds against the blue sky. It's best visited in spring (especially mid-March to mid-April), when the air is still cool and the chaparral hillsides are lushly sprinkled with wildflowers. In particular look out for the beautiful mariposa lily,

6

the orange stinky monkeyflower, and the California buckeye, wonderfully sweet-smelling in late May. Also present here are legions of bees: apparently the Pinnacles have the highest known bee diversity in the world, some four hundred species in all.

For most people the main attraction is a day or two spent **hiking** some of the 35 miles of lovely and only moderately taxing trails. The place is so small that it's quite possible to hike from one side to the other and back in one long day: indeed, the east and west road ends are only three miles apart. The trails are exposed so avoid hiking in the middle of the day in summer, and remember to carry plenty of water. Backcountry camping is not permitted.

One of the best hikes is the **Balconies Trail** (2.4-mile loop; 1hr; 100-foot ascent), most easily accessed from the west, which skirts the multicolored, 600-foot face of the Balconies outcrop, then returns via a series of talus **caves** (take a flashlight) formed by huge boulders that have become wedged between the walls of the narrow canyons. An excellent **Park loop** (10 miles; 5–7hr; 1600-foot ascent) can be done from either entrance, and, by combining several trails (including the Balconies), takes in the best of the park's high and low country.

Practicalities

The park has east and west entrances: contrary to what appears on some maps, no road goes right through the monument. Several trails do, however, allowing you to explore the whole compact park from either entrance. Most of the park's facilities are around the **eastern entrance** (open 24hr; accessed along G13 and Hwy-25), which gives access to the Bear Gulch Visitor Center (daily 9am–5pm) and **camping** at the swimming-pool-equipped *Pinnacles Campground* ($10 per person up to a maximum of $35; reservations office open Tues–Thurs 4–6pm, Fri 4–9pm, Sat & Sun 9am–5pm; ☎831/389-4462, Ⓦwww.pinncamp.com) – reservations are essential in spring.

At the **western entrance** (gates open 7.30am–8pm) there's just a ranger station and toilets, and overnight stays are not allowed. Still, for day-visits it's the better option and is accessed off Hwy-101 from Soledad, from where Hwy-146 runs eleven winding miles to the park.

Salinas and around

The seat of Monterey County, **SALINAS**, twenty-five miles north of Soledad, is a sprawling agricultural town of 150,000 inhabitants. It's best known for the **California Rodeo** (tickets $19–76; ☎1-800/549-4989, Ⓦwww.carodeo.com), held during the third week in July and the biggest in the state, and as the birth-place of writer **John Steinbeck**. Salinas and the agricultural valley to the south are often bracketed together as Steinbeck Country: John Steinbeck was born in 1902 and raised in Salinas, but left the town in his mid-20s to live in Monterey and later in New York City.

Today, much as in Steinbeck's day, Salinas is a hotbed of labor disputes, with the gap between the low-paid manual laborers who pick the produce and the wealthy owners of agribusiness empires who run the giant farms still unbridged. In the 1960s and early 1970s, the United Farm Workers union, under the leadership of **César Chávez** and Dolores Huerta, had great success in organizing and demanding better pay and working conditions for the almost exclusively Latino workforce, masterminding a very effective boycott of the valley's main product, lettuce. But workers are once again under siege, with wages less than half of what they were two decades ago amidst increasing worries about the dangers of exposure to pesticides and agricultural chemicals.

The best introduction to the region is the big, modern **National Steinbeck Center**, 1 Main Street (daily 10am–5pm; $10.95; ☏831/796-3833, ⓦwww .steinbeck.org), which takes you on a sprightly, interactive journey through the author's life and work. A fifteen-minute **biographical film** offers an informative and lively approach to Steinbeck and sets the tone for the rest of the museum, throughout which snippets of films and material from sound archives play prominent roles. It's inspiring enough that you may well find yourself purchasing a novel or two from the center's excellent store. A new wing is devoted to the **Agriculture Museum**, which explores the history of vegetable growing in the region, the arrival of Latinos during World War II when labor was short, and more, all presented in both English and Spanish.

Further exploration of Steinbeck's Salinas connections is best done using the center's free Oldtown Walking Tour **map**, which highlights locales in the surrounding area that were influential in the writer's life. An obvious highlight is the author's childhood home, **Steinbeck House**, two blocks west of the museum at 132 Central Avenue (Tues–Sat 11.30am–2pm; ☏831/424-2735, ⓦwww.steinbeckhouse.com), which has been turned into an English-style tearoom. Docents will give a brief tour on request. Before leaving downtown, stroll the tree-lined Main Street with its prettified Victorian buildings, clothing boutiques, and craft stores, as well as the 1921 Art Deco **Fox Theater** at no. 239.

If you're heading for Monterey, call in at **Spreckels**, on Hwy-68 three miles southwest of Salinas, a small town raised in 1898 for employees of the Spreckels sugar factory (whose scion was Adolph, husband of the wild, art-loving beauty Alma – see p.517). Parts of the movie *East of Eden* were filmed here, including the famous scene when James Dean – playing Cal – hurls blocks of ice down a chute to get his father's attention.

Practicalities

Greyhound buses between LA and San Francisco (roughly five daily) stop in the center of town at 19 W Gabilan Street (☏831/424-4418) near Salinas Street,

---

The novels of John Steinbeck

John Steinbeck's novels and short stories are as remarkable for their historical content as for their narratives; he had a newspaperman's eye for the hardships of working-class life. **The Grapes of Wrath**, his best-known work, was made into a film starring Henry Fonda while still at the top of the bestseller lists, having captured the popular imagination for its portrayal of the Depression Era-miseries of the Joad family on their migration to California from the Oklahoma Dust Bowl. *Cannery Row* followed in 1945, a nostalgic portrait of the Monterey fisheries, which ironically went into steep decline the year the book was published. Steinbeck spent the next four years writing *East of Eden*, an allegorical retelling of the biblical story of Cain and Abel against the landscape of the Salinas Valley; in this book, which he saw as his masterpiece, Steinbeck expresses many of the values that underlie the rest of his works.

Much of Steinbeck's writing is concerned with the dignity of labor, and with the inequalities of an economic system that "allows children to go hungry in the midst of rotting plenty." Although he was circumspect about his own political stance, when *The Grapes of Wrath* became a bestseller in 1939 there was a violent backlash against Steinbeck in Salinas for what were seen as his Communist sympathies. Later, he was so wounded at the outcry over his worthiness of the Nobel Prize for Literature in 1962 that he never wrote another word. He died in New York City in 1968; today his ashes are buried in Salinas in the **Garden of Memories Cemetery**, 768 Abbott Street.

while Amtrak Coast Starlight trains leave once a day in each direction, two blocks away at 30 Railroad Avenue.

The **Chamber of Commerce** at 119 E Alisal Street (Mon 9.30am–5pm, Tues–Fri 8.30am–5pm; ☎831/424-7611, ⓦwww.salinaschamber.com) can help with accommodation, sometimes useful in summer when Monterey, twenty miles west, is packed and Salinas takes the overspill, though rates here start around $80. The MST bus #20 makes the 55-minute trip every hour from the Transit Center (see opposite).

Franchise **motel** signs are visible from Hwy-101; try the *Comfort Inn*, 181 Kern Street (☎831/770-1400, ⓦwww.choicehotels.com; ❹). There are quite a few good Mexican **restaurants** around the city, the best, oldest, and most central being *Rosita's Armory Café*, 231 Salinas Street (☎831/424-7039): settle into one of the big green booths here alongside old men chowing down on the super-cheap but delicious food – lunch specials are $6.25, mains around $9.

The Big Sur Coast

BIG SUR is not really a defined place, just the nebulous name used to describe the ninety miles of rocky cliffs and crashing seas along the California coast just south of the Monterey Peninsula. You'll know you're in Big Sur, however, when the estuaries and beaches of the Central Coast give way to craggy rock faces and distant redwood groves. Named by the Spanish *El País Grande del Sur* (the "big country to the south" of their colony at Monterey), it's still a wild and undeveloped region that's breathtakingly unspoilt given its proximity to San Francisco and other cities.

Before Hwy-1 was completed in 1937, the few inhabitants of Big Sur had to be almost entirely self-sufficient, farming, raising cattle, and trapping sea otters for their furs. The only connections with the rest of the world were by infrequent steamship to Monterey, or by a nearly impassable trail over the mountains to the Salinas Valley. Despite the better transport links, the area is growing more remote as each year passes, with fewer people living here today than a hundred years ago; most of the land is still owned by a handful of families, many of whom are descendents of Big Sur's original pioneers. Locals have banded together to protect the land from obtrusive development and to fight government plans to allow offshore oil drilling, and their ornery determination seems to be paying off.

The Big Sur Coast is also the protected habitat of the **sea otter**, and **gray whales** pass by close to the shore on their annual winter migration. Visit in April or May to see the vibrant **wildflowers** and lilac-colored ceanothus bushes, though the sun shines longest, without the morning coastal fog, in early autumn through until November. Summer weekends see the roads and campgrounds packed to overflowing and the wildness of the area dampened by hundreds of eager visitors.

Resist the temptation to try and see Big Sur in a single day: the best way to enjoy its isolation and beauty is slowly. Leave the car behind as often as you can and wander through parks and wilderness preserves, where a ten-minute walk takes you from any sign of the rest of the world.

Arrival, information, and getting around

The only public transportation through Big Sur is the summer-only (May–Oct) MST bus #22 from Monterey, which runs as far south as the *Nepenthe* restaurant (3 daily Mon–Fri, 2 daily Sat & Sun).

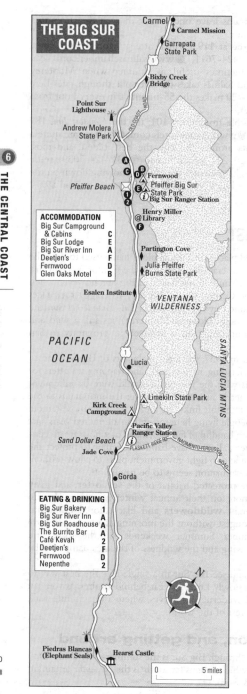

THE BIG SUR COAST

Carmel
Carmel Mission
Garrapata State Park
Bixby Creek Bridge
Point Sur Lighthouse
Andrew Molera State Park
Fernwood
Pfeiffer Beach
Pfeiffer Big Sur State Park
Big Sur Ranger Station
Henry Miller @ Library
Partington Cove
Julia Pfeiffer Burns State Park
Esalen Institute

ACCOMMODATION

Big Sur Campground & Cabins	C
Big Sur Lodge	E
Big Sur River Inn	A
Deetjen's	F
Fernwood	D
Glen Oaks Motel	B

VENTANA WILDERNESS

PACIFIC OCEAN

SANTA LUCIA MTNS

Lucia

Kirk Creek Campground

Limekiln State Park

Pacific Valley Ranger Station

Sand Dollar Beach
Jade Cove

PLASKETT RIDGE RD — NACIMIENTO-FERGUSON ROAD

Gorda

EATING & DRINKING

Big Sur Bakery	1
Big Sur River Inn	A
Big Sur Roadhouse	A
The Burrito Bar	A
Café Kevah	2
Deetjen's	F
Fernwood	D
Nepenthe	2

N

Piedras Blancas (Elephant Seals)
Hearst Castle

0   5 miles

There is no Big Sur town as such, and facilities like gas stations and grocery stores are scattered and surprisingly scarce – expect those you do find to be premium priced, so it's best to fill your gas tank and go shopping before you hit the deserted coastline. Note, too, that cell phone coverage here is patchy at best, so buy a phone card if you have calls to make; as for **Internet access**, it's available at most lodging and at public terminals at the Henry Miller Library (see p.453). Pick up a copy of the free *Big Sur Guide* newspaper as soon as you can, since its comprehensive listings are an invaluable resource: you'll find it at park information offices and some stores along the route. Otherwise, call the **Chamber of Commerce** (Mon, Wed, Fri 9am–1pm; ☎831/667-2100, ⍟www.bigsurcalifornia.org) or stop by the ranger station near Pfeiffer Big Sur State Park headquarters (see below).

While the narrow Hwy-1 is a perennial favorite with cyclists, most visitors will need a car to travel through the area, following the dramatic coast road as it winds a tortuous, exhilarating route through bedrock cliffs five hundred feet above the Pacific Ocean. The northern end of Big Sur around Hwy-1 is the most developed and most interesting for first-time visitors, with the three main inhabited areas close to **Pfeiffer Big Sur State Park**: around the post office two miles south of the park; at Fernwood, a mile north past the main entrance; and at The Village, a further mile and a half north. Pfeiffer Big Sur

State Park is a fantastic base for exploring; you can swim among giant boulders, hike up redwood canyons to a waterfall, or sunbathe on a fine sandy beach. Note that the state park day-use fee is valid at Julia Pfeiffer Burns, Pfeiffer Big Sur, and Andrew Molera, but none of the other parks.

Accommodation

In keeping with Big Sur's backwoodsy qualities, most of the available **accommodation** is in rustic (but typically expensive) mountain lodges, and the very few rooms on offer are full most nights throughout the summer, especially on weekends.

Public campgrounds are dotted all along the Big Sur Coast, in addition to a few less developed ones in the **Santa Lucia Mountains** above, where you can also see deer, bobcats, and (rarely) mountain lions. Sites along the coast are popular year-round, and all, unless otherwise stated, are available for $18–25 a night. Some are reservable; others are first-come-first-served, so get there early in the day to ensure a space. For additional **information** on camping in Big Sur, but not for reservations, phone the park directly (☎831/667-2315).

The following accommodation and campground listings are ordered from south to north. There's no official notation for addresses in Big Sur, so distances from major landmarks are used here as approximate guides.

Hotels, resorts, and RV parks

Deetjen's Big Sur Inn Hwy-1, 7 miles north of Julia Pfeiffer Burns State Park ☎831/667-2377, ⓦwww.deetjens.com. Built by Norwegian immigrant "Grandpa" Deetjen, this laid-back compound (with great restaurant and bar) offers comfortably rustic lodging in ski-lodge-style log cabins, with fireplaces, rocking chairs, old-fashioned leaded windows, and lots of wood paneling. Shared bath ④, private ⑥, fireplace rooms ⑦

Big Sur Lodge In Pfeiffer Big Sur State Park ☎1-800/424-4787, ⓦwww.bigsurlodge.com. Sixty-odd plushly furnished rooms, each with porch and enormous sit-down showers but no phones, TVs, alarm clocks, or radios; the park entrance fee's included in the rate. There are also rooms with fireplace and all have access to a nice outdoor pool and a pricey restaurant (mains around $25). ⑦

Fernwood Hwy-1, just over half a mile north of Pfeiffer Big Sur State Park ☎831/667-2422, ⓦwww.fernwoodbigsur.com. Basic motel rooms (⑤) are at least fairly cheap for these parts, though rooms with hot tub and fireplace (⑥) are much nicer. Down toward the river there are wooded sites for tents ($30) and RVs with electric hookup ($35), plus some tent cabins (③). ③–⑥

Glen Oaks Motel Hwy-1, a mile north of Pfeiffer Big Sur State Park ☎831/667-2105, ⓦwww.glenoaksbigsur.com. Redwood posts and adobe bricks form the framework for classily remodeled rooms, each with a modern gas fireplace. Clean lines and strong colors make a refreshing change in these

parts. There are two separate cottages with kitchen, and there's free Wi-Fi and use of computer. ⑥

Big Sur Campgrounds and Cabins Hwy-1, a mile north of Pfeiffer Big Sur State Park ☎831/667-2322, ⓦwww.bigsurcamp.com. Swanky campground with the best of the cabins: wooden tent affairs sleeping up to three (④) and fancier places (⑥). Tent sites $35, RV sites $45. Riverside sites $10 extra. ④–⑥

Big Sur River Inn Hwy-1, 2.5 miles north of Pfeiffer Big Sur State Park ☎1-800/548-3610, ⓦwww.bigsurriverinn.com. Woodsy lodge with a handful of very nice suites with down comforters and verandas, overlooking the river. There are cheaper, more basic motel-style rooms across Hwy-1, plus a handy on-site grocery store and reasonable restaurant. Rooms ⑥, suites ⑧

Camping

Kirk Creek ☎805/434-1996, ⓦwww.campone.com. First-come-first-served national forest campground five miles north of Pacific Valley ranger station and more exposed, but the only one in these parts that's right on the ocean and with hiker/biker sites ($5). $22.

Limekiln State Park Reservations ☎1-800/444-7275, ⓦwww.reserveamerica.com. State park campground two miles north of *Kirk Creek*, with hot showers and developed a trail to the limekilns, redwoods, and a waterfall. $25.

Pfeiffer Big Sur State Park reservations ☎1-800/444-7275, ⓦwww.reserveamerica.com. The main campground in the area, with spacious and well-shaded sites, many among the redwoods. Hot showers, a well-stocked store, a launderette, but no hookups. Also some hiker/biker-only sites for $5. Sites $25, riverside $35.

Andrew Molera State Park The only walk-in site around. Just a quarter-mile from the parking lot

and half a mile from the beach, this vast ten-acre meadow comes with water and latrines. First-come-first-served basis, so show up early. Camping payment waives day-use fee. $10.

Southern Big Sur

The southern coastline of Big Sur is the region at its most gentle – with sandy beaches hidden away below eroding yellow-ochre cliffs. Another thirty miles north of Hearst Castle, the cliffs get steeper and the road more tortuous around the vista point at **Willow Creek**, where you can watch the surfers and the sea otters playing in the waves. **Jade Cove**, a mile north, takes its name from the translucent California jade stones that are sometimes found here, mainly by scuba divers offshore. The rocky cove is a ten-minute walk from the highway, along a brambly trail marked by a wooden stile in the cattle fence: the close-up views of the crashing waves reinforce the awesome power of the sea.

Half a mile to the north is **Sand Dollar Beach**, a good place to enjoy the surf or watch for **hang-gliders**, launched from sites in the mountains off the one-lane Plaskett Ridge Road. This steep road is good fun on a mountain bike, and passes by a number of free, basic campgrounds along the ridge, ending at the paved Nacimiento–Fergusson Road. Check at the **Pacific Valley ranger station** a mile north (irregular hours; ☎805/927-4211) for up-to-date information on backcountry camping.

Kirk Creek to Julia Pfeiffer Burns State Park

The coastal **campground** at **Kirk Creek** (see p.451) sits at the foot of the Nacimiento–Fergusson Road, which twists over the Santa Lucia Mountains to the Salinas Valley via the excellent Mission San Antonio de Padua (see p.446). **Limekiln Creek**, two miles north of the junction, is named after the 100-year-old kilns that survive in good condition along the creek behind the state **campground**. In the 1880s local limestone was burned in these kilns to extract lime powder for use as cement, then carried on a complex aerial tramway to be loaded onto ships at Rockland Landing. The ships that carried the lime to Monterey brought in most of the supplies to this isolated area.

Esalen (ESS-allun), ten miles further north, is named after the local Native Americans. Before they were wiped out, they frequented the healing waters of the natural **hot spring** here, at the top of a cliff two hundred feet above the raging Pacific surf – now owned and operated by the Esalen Institute (☎831/667-3000, ⊛www.esalen.org). Since the 1960s, when all sorts of people came to Big Sur to smoke dope and get back to nature, Esalen has been at the forefront of the "New Age" human-potential movement. Today's devotees tend to arrive in BMWs on Friday nights for the expensive, reservation-only massage treatments, yoga workshops, and seminars on "potentialities and values of human existence." Drop-ins are not really welcome, so if you want to join them, make sure to reserve a place well in advance.

Julia Pfeiffer Burns State Park (daily dawn–dusk; parking $8; ☎831/667-2315, ⊛www.parks.ca.gov), three miles north of Esalen along McWay Creek, has some of the best day-hikes in the Big Sur area: a ten-minute walk from the parking area leads under the highway along the edge of the cliff to an overlook of McWay Falls, which crash onto a beach below Saddle Rock. A less-traveled path leads down from Hwy-1 two miles north of the waterfall (at milepost 37.85) through a 200-foot-long tunnel to the wave-washed remains of a small wharf at **Partington Cove**, one of the few places in Big Sur where you can get to the sea.

Nepenthe and Pfeiffer Beach

Seven miles north, just before you reach **Nepenthe**, you'll pass *Deetjen's*, a great place to stop for a meal (see p.454) or overnight (see p.451). Half a mile on, call at the **Henry Miller Library** (daily except Tues 11am–6pm; ☎831/667-2574, ⓦwww.henrymiller.org). Miller's own home, further south on the Big Sur Coast, is now a private residence, but this house was owned by his old friend Emil White, and stands as a ramshackle bookshop-cum-monument to the work of the author who lived in the area on and off until the 1960s: there's little Millerabilia on display, but they'll show you plenty if you ask. The secluded front lawn is a pleasant place to grab a free coffee; leave a small donation for **Internet access**, or use the free Wi-Fi.

It's with Nepenthe (☎831/667-2345, ⓦwww.nepenthebigsur.com) that Big Sur's commercial development starts in earnest. It's not a town proper, but rather a complex of expensive but dramatically sited restaurants, gallery, and bookstore heavy with works by Miller that's named after the mythical drug that induces forgetfulness. The one point of interest is its location: this is the hilltop site where star-crossed lovers Orson Welles and Rita Hayworth once shared a cabin.

Just over a mile north, the region's post office marks a **gas station** and the *Big Sur Bakery Restaurant* (see p.454). Nearby, the unmarked Sycamore Canyon Road leads a mile west to Big Sur's best strand, **Pfeiffer Beach** (dawn–dusk; $5 per car; ☎831/667-2315) – a sometimes windy, white-sand stretch dominated by a charismatic hump of rock whose color varies from brown to red to orange in the changing light. Park where you can at the end of the road and walk through an archway of cypress trees along the lagoon to the sands.

The Big Sur River Valley

A mile north of the post office, Hwy-1 drops down behind a coastal ridge into the valley of the Big Sur River, where most of the accommodation and eating options are located. Stop first at the **Big Sur Ranger Station** (daily: summer 8am–6pm; winter 8am–4.30pm; ☎831/667-2315), which handles the camping permits for the Ventana Wilderness in the mountains above and is the center for information on all the other parks in the area. A popular hike leads steeply up from the Pine Ridge trailhead behind the station, ten miles into the mountains to **Sykes Hot Springs** (unrestricted entry), just downstream from the free campground at *Sykes Camp* along the Big Sur River. This is an overnight expedition, at least five hours' walk each way; don't forget to pick up a fire permit if you plan to cook.

Plumb in the middle of the valley, the **Pfeiffer Big Sur State Park** (daily dawn–dusk; $8 per vehicle; ☎831/667-2315, ⓦwww.parks.ca.gov) is one of the most beautiful and enjoyable parks in California, with miles of hiking trails and excellent swimming along the Big Sur River. In late spring and summer, the river has deep swimming holes among the large boulders in the bottom of the narrow, steep-walled gorge, and the water is clean and clear. Nude sunbathing is tolerated (except on national holidays, when the park tends to be overrun with swarms of screaming children) and, since the park is sheltered a mile or so inland, the weather is warmer and sunnier than elsewhere along the coast. This is also the main **campground** (see p.451) in the Big Sur region.

The most popular hiking trail in the park leads to the sixty-foot **Pfeiffer Falls**, half a mile up a narrow canyon shaded by redwood trees, starting at a trailhead opposite the park entrance. The bridges over the river have an understated grace, as does the nearby amphitheater – built by the Civilian Conservation Corps during the Depression – where rangers give excellent campfire talks and slide shows about Big Sur during the summer season.

Eating and drinking

Most of the places to **eat and drink** in Big Sur are attached to the inns and resorts listed on p.451. Many of these are fairly basic burger-and-beer bars right along the highway, but there are a few special ones worth searching out, some for their good food and others for their views of the Pacific. Because of Big Sur's isolation, prices here are around 25 percent higher than you'd pay in a town. The following are listed from south to north.

Deetjen's Big Sur Inn On Hwy-1, 7 miles north of Julia Pfeiffer Burns State Park ☎831/667-2378. Excellent, unhurried breakfasts ($8) and a variety of top-quality fish and vegetarian dinners ($13–25) in a snug, redwood-paneled room.

Café Kevah Nepenthe ☎831/667-2344. Tasty, if slightly overpriced, organic concoctions served up café-style on a sunny outdoor terrace: some of the best views around, but stick to the snacks. March–Dec 9am–4pm.

Nepenthe Nepenthe ☎831/667-2345, @www .nepenthebigsur.com. Above the *Café Kevah*, this overpriced steak-and-seafood place has raging fires, an amazing view (with possible sunset whale watching in season), and a James Bond-ish après-ski atmosphere; mains $25–35.

Big Sur Bakery Restaurant 1.5 miles north of Nepenthe ☎831/667-0520, @www.bigsurbakery .com. Far from just churning out cakes and pastries, this moderately priced café has an on-site rotisserie where all the meats are cooked. Lunch is largely pizza (try the butternut squash and prosciutto; $18) and sandwiches, while the dinner menu's fancier, with grilled steak and pork from well-known Niman Ranch nearby (around $30).

Fernwood Hwy-1, just over half a mile north of Pfeiffer Big Sur State Park ☎831/667-2422. This budget diner is the place for salads, burgers, and

sandwiches for $10–12. There's a small grocery store/deli for picnic supplies, an espresso stand, and a bar with live music most Saturdays. Dining 11am–9pm.

Big Sur River Inn Restaurant The Village, Hwy-1, 2.5 miles north of Pfeiffer Big Sur State Park ☎831/667-2700. The slightly upscale restaurant features a creative range of sautéed and grilled seafood starters and hearty main dishes served in a spacious, redwood-log dining room. In summer, you can linger over lunch and cocktails on the sunny terrace or in the riverside garden; in winter, the fireplace attracts locals and visitors alike. Lunches $10–18, dinner mains $20–30. Live entertainment on the weekend.

Big Sur Roadhouse The Village, Hwy-1, 2.5 miles north of Pfeiffer Big Sur State Park ☎831/667-2264. Cal-Mex cuisine – think tortillas, burritos, and spicy salads – served in a cozy, flower-filled cottage. Make sure to order the chunky guacamole ($5). Closed Tues.

The Burrito Bar Inside the *Big Sur River Inn* (see p.451). Sandwich bar stashed in the rear of the store that's one of the scant few places to pick up dinner for under $10 – just make sure to eat early as it's only open 11am–7pm. Order an overstuffed Mexican burrito to go – the choices and ingredients are standard chilies and cheeses – then eat it by the river on the grounds of the inn.

North to Monterey

Andrew Molera State Park (daily dawn–dusk; parking $8; ☎831/667-2315, @www.parks.ca.gov), five miles north of Pfeiffer Big Sur State Park, is the largest park in Big Sur, with two and a half miles of rocky oceanfront reached by a mile-long trail. It occupies the site of what was once the El Sur Ranch, one of the earliest and most successful Big Sur cattle ranches, initially run in the early nineteenth century by Juan Bautista Alvarado, who became California governor in 1836; later, it was overseen by English sea captain Roger Cooper, whose cabin is preserved here. Although the cabin itself isn't open to the

▲ Bixby Creek Bridge, Big Sur

public, you can reach the site on some of the fifteen miles of hiking trails also used for guided two-hour **horseback rides** from the stables ($25–59; ☏1-800/942-5486, ⓦwww.molerahorsebacktours.com). There's also walk-in **camping** (see p.452).

Opposite the state park entrance, the Old Coast Road takes off inland from Hwy-1 up over the steep hills, affording panoramic views out over miles of coastline. The partly paved, roughly ten-mile road winds over wide-open ranchlands and through deep, slender canyons until it rejoins the main highway at Bixby Creek Bridge (see below).

Three miles north of the park entrance along Hwy-1, the **Point Sur Lighthouse** perches on a volcanic outcrop. It can be visited on walking **tours** (Sat 10am & 2pm, Sun 10am, additional tours April–Oct Wed 10am & 2pm, July & Aug Thurs 10am; $8; no reservations, ⓦwww.pointsur.org), which spend three hours exploring the lighthouse and its ancillary buildings.

Five miles on, **Bixby Creek Bridge** was ranked as the longest single-span concrete bridge in the world when constructed in 1932. It's the most impressive (and photogenic) engineering feat of the Coast Road project, a local construction program sponsored by the Works Progress Administration during the Depression.

The northernmost stop on the Big Sur Coast is the wildflower-crammed **Garrapata State Park** (daily dawn–dusk; free; ⓦwww.parks.ca.gov), three miles south of Point Lobos and the Monterey Peninsula. A mile-long trail leads from Hwy-1 out to the tip of **Soberanes Point**, about ten miles south of Carmel – a good place to watch for sea otters and gray whales.

The Monterey Peninsula

At the northern edge of the spectacular Big Sur Coast, the rocky promontory and gnarled cypress trees of the **MONTEREY PENINSULA** amplify the collision between the cliffs and the thundering sea. Though the manicured towns here now

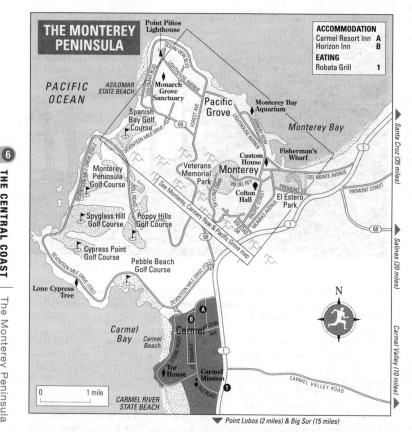

THE MONTEREY PENINSULA

ACCOMMODATION
Carmel Resort Inn **A**
Horizon Inn **B**
EATING
Robata Grill **1**

PACIFIC OCEAN

Point Piños Lighthouse

Monarch Grove Sanctuary

ASILOMAR STATE BEACH

Pacific Grove

Monterey Bay Aquarium

Monterey Bay

Spanish Bay Golf Course

Fisherman's Wharf

Monterey Peninsula Golf Course

Veterans Memorial Park

Custom House

Monterey

See Monterey, Cannery Row & Pacific Grove map

Colton Hall

El Estero Park

Spyglass Hill Golf Course

Poppy Hills Golf Course

DEL MONTE AVENUE

FREMONT STREET

Cypress Point Golf Course

Pebble Beach Golf Course

N

Lone Cypress Tree

Carmel Bay

Carmel Beach

Carmel

OCEAN AVE

Tor House

Carmel Mission

CARMEL VALLEY ROAD

0   1 mile

CARMEL RIVER STATE BEACH

▼ Point Lobos (2 miles) & Big Sur (15 miles)

▶ Santa Cruz (35 miles)

▶ Salinas (20 miles)

▶ Carmel Valley (10 miles)

thrive thanks to the regular flow of tourists, they still retain their individual characters. **Carmel** (officially **Carmel-by-the-Sea**) is by far the toniest: it's secluded and a little sniffy, though the election of Clint Eastwood as mayor in 1986 showed its starstruck side. To the west, the small, upscale village of **Pebble Beach** is primarily known for its golf courses (due to host the US Open in 2010), while at the tip of the Peninsula, with spectacular views out across the ocean, stands **Pacific Grove**, a pleasant if rather sleepy place known for its butterflies and Victorian architecture. The most convenient and practical base on the Peninsula is **Monterey** itself: the largest town, it was the capital of California under the Spanish and the Mexicans, and retains many old adobe houses and places of genuine historic appeal. The local population is a little younger than in the other towns, which gives Monterey the liveliest nightlife and restaurant scenes.

Arrival, information, and getting around

The Monterey Peninsula juts out into the Pacific to form the Monterey Bay, a hundred miles south of San Francisco; coastal Hwy-1 cuts across its neck, and Hwy-68 links up with US-101 at Salinas, twenty miles east. Greyhound **buses** and Amtrak **trains** stop in Salinas, connecting with MST bus #20 for the 55-minute trip (every hour) to Monterey.

Monterey's **visitor center**, 401 Camino El Estero at Franklin Street (April–Oct Mon–Sat 9am–6pm, Sun 9am–5pm; Nov–March Mon–Sat 9am–5pm, Sun 10am–4pm; ☎1-888/221-1010, ⓦwww.montereyinfo.org), has free parking, lots of advertiser-based brochures, and hotlines to local hotels.

The **Pacific Grove Chamber of Commerce**, 584 Central Avenue at Forest (Mon–Fri 9.30am–5pm, Sat 10am–3pm; ☎1-800/656-6650, ⓦwww.pacificgrove.org), across from the Natural History Museum, has walking-tour maps of Pacific Grove's historic buildings and can help find a room in the many local bed-and-breakfast inns. The best guide to what's on in the area is the widely available freebie *Monterey County Weekly* (ⓦwww.coastweekly.com), with listings of movies, music, and art galleries.

Getting around is surprisingly easy. Monterey-Salinas Transit (MST) buses (☎1-888/678-2871, ⓦwww.mst.org) run between 7am and 6pm (11pm on some routes), radiating out from Transit Plaza in the historic core of Monterey, and covering the entire region from Nepenthe on the Big Sur Coast north to Watsonville near Santa Cruz and inland to the Salinas Valley. The region is divided into six zones and fares are $2 per zone. One-way journeys throughout the Monterey Peninsula cost $2 (all-day pass $4.50); journeys to Nepenthe or Salinas are $4 (all zone one-day pass $9). Buy tickets and passes on board – exact change is required. The most useful routes are buses #4 and #5, which link Monterey with Carmel; #20, which runs between Monterey and Salinas; and #1, which runs along Lighthouse Avenue past the main sights and out to Pacific Grove. There's also a **free trolley** running every ten minutes from downtown to the Monterey Bay Aquarium on Cannery Row, and from Cannery Row to Pacific Grove (Memorial Day to Labor Day daily 10am–7pm). The only way to get to the Big Sur Coast on public transportation is on bus #22 (Memorial Day to Labor Day 2–3 daily). Alternatively, **rent a bike** (see p.469) to get around town and the peninsula.

Accommodation

The Monterey Peninsula is among the most exclusive and expensive resort locales in California, with **hotel** and **bed-and-breakfast** room rates averaging $120 a night. This may tempt you to stay elsewhere – in Santa Cruz, for example – and come here on day-trips; the other budget option is to avail yourself of one of the many motels along North Fremont Street (also a good place for cheap eats) or Munras Avenue, about one mile from the center. From mid-June to early September the place is usually packed, especially on **weekends**, when room rates shoot up massively (particularly at motels) and there's often a two-night minimum stay (particularly at B&Bs). Summer **prices** are quoted: rates at motels and some inns drop considerably out of season.

Monterey and Cannery Row

Cypress Gardens Resort Inn 1150 Munras Ave ☎1-877/922-1150, ⓦwww.cypressgardensinn.com. One of the better Munras motels, with a leafy garden, a large pool, Jacuzzi, gym, and free continental breakfast. Midweek ❸, weekends ❻

Econolodge 2042 N Fremont St ☎831/372-5851. Comfortable, standard rooms with free local calls, Wi-Fi, and continental breakfasts. Midweek ❷, weekends ❺

El Dorado Inn 900 Munras Ave ☎1-800/722-1836, www.eldoradoinnmonterey.com. Cheap, basic accommodation at budget rates in a motel-style, two-story building. Midweek ❹, weekend ❺

HI–Monterey 778 Hawthorne St ☎831/649-0375, ⓦwww.montereyhostel.org. Pleasant, well-managed hostel with a spacious common room, near Cannery Row. There's a six-day maximum stay and a 1am curfew. There's Internet access and free Wi-Fi. Members $21, nonmembers $24, rooms ❷

Mariposa Inn 1386 Munras Ave ☎1-800/824-2295, ⓦwww.mariposamonterey.com. Rambling complex offering cozy rooms with fireplaces and full amenities, including balconies and a heated pool. Larger groups should opt for one of the stand-alone townhouses, which are great value. Midweek ❺, weekend ❻

Veteran's Memorial Park Jefferson Street, just over a mile west of downtown ☎831/646-3865. The only camping close to Monterey is the site of Steinbeck's fictional Tortilla Flat, in the hills above town. First-come-first-served, it's set in the trees with picnic table and fire rings for each site. It's only $5 a night if you're on foot or bike, or $20 per car. RVs up to 21ft permitted.

Pacific Grove

Anton Inn 1095 Lighthouse Ave ☎1-888/242-6866, ⓦwww.antoninn.com. The clean lines and understated modern decor make a refreshing change from the Victoriana elsewhere in Pacific Grove. All rooms have fireplaces and some come with a soaking tub. Midweek ❺, weekend ❻

Bide-a-Wee Inn & Cottages 221 Asilomar Blvd ☎831/372-2330, ⓦwww.bideaweeinn.com. Nicely spruced-up rooms with modern, homely furnishings, including fridge and microwave. Also some cottages with kitchen. Rooms midweek ❺, weekend ❻; cottages ❻/❼

Borg's Ocean Front Motel 635 Ocean View Blvd ☎831/375-2406, ⓦwww.borgsoceanfrontmotel .com. Basic motel rooms come with TV and phone, and ocean views if you are prepared to pay the $35 premium. ❺

Green Gables Inn 301 Ocean View Blvd ☎1-800/722-1774, ⓦwww.greengablesinnpg. com. Plush doubles in one of the prettiest houses

in a town of fine homes, on the waterfront just a few blocks from the Monterey Bay Aquarium. Evening wine and buffet breakfast are served in the ocean-view lounge with fireplace. Shared bath ❺, private bath ❼

Lovers Point Inn 625 Ocean View Blvd ☎831/373-4771, ⓦwww.loverspointinnpg.com. Look past the shocking salmon-and-white exterior decor to find tidy but bland motel rooms with phone and coffeemaker. Some have sea glimpses. Midweek ❸, weekend ❹

Pacific Grove Inn 581 Pine Ave at Forest ☎1-800/732-2825, ⓦwww.pacificgrove-inn.com. Five blocks from the shore, this thoughtfully modernized 1904 mansion has 16 spacious rooms, some with fireplace and some with sea view. Continental breakfast and free Wi-Fi. Midweek ❺, weekend ❼

Rosedale Inn 775 Asilomar Blvd ☎1-800/822-5606, ⓦwww.rosedaleinn.com. These log-cabin-style rooms are refreshingly modern, with ceiling fans and pine furniture, as well as fireplaces and Jacuzzi baths. The real standout, though, is the affable, easy-going staff. ❻

Carmel

Carmel Resort Inn Carpenter and 2nd Ave, Carmel ☎1-800/454-3700, ⓦwww .carmelresortinn.com. One of the least expensive lodgings in Carmel; motel-style cottage rooms all have microwave, fridge, TV, and fireplace, and a continental breakfast is served. Midweek ❹, weekend ❺

Horizon Inn 3rd St and Junípero, Carmel ☎1-800/350-7723, ⓦwww.horizoninncarmel.com. Comfy bed-and-breakfast place with cozy rooms (all with microwave, toaster, and coffeemaker), a breakfast basket delivered to your door, and access to an outdoor hot tub. ❼

Monterey

The town of **MONTEREY** rests in a quiet niche along the bay formed by the forested Monterey Peninsula, proudly proclaiming itself the most historic city in California, a boast that, for once, may be true. Its compact center features some of the best vernacular **buildings** of California's Spanish and Mexican colonial past, most of which stand unassumingly within a few blocks of the tourist-thronged waterfront. The single best stop – and one of the unmissable highlights of the region – is the **Monterey Bay Aquarium**, a mile west of town at the end of Cannery Row.

Monterey was named by the Spanish merchant and explorer Vizcaíno, who landed in 1602 to find an abundant supply of fresh water and wild game after a seven-month voyage from Mexico. Despite Vizcaíno's enthusiasm for the site, the area was not colonized until 1770, when the second mission in the chain – the headquarters of the whole operation – was built in Monterey before being moved to its permanent site in Carmel. Under the Spanish, the Presidio de

Robert Louis Stevenson and Monterey

The Gold Rush of 1849 bypassed Monterey for San Francisco, leaving the community little more than a somnolent Mexican fishing village – which was pretty much how the town looked in the fall of 1879, when a 29-year-old, feverishly ill Scotsman arrived by stagecoach, flat broke and desperately in love with a married woman. **Robert Louis Stevenson** came to Monterey for fresh air and to see **Fanny Osbourne**, whom he had met while traveling in France two years before. He stayed here for three months, writing occasional articles for the local newspaper and telling stories in exchange for his meals at the saloon-restaurant run by Frenchman Jules Simoneau, behind what is now the **Stevenson House** (currently closed for a major refit) halfway between the Larkin House and the Royal Presidio Chapel (see p.462). It's said that he started *Treasure Island* here and used Point Lobos (see p.466) as inspiration for Spyglass Hill.

Stevenson witnessed Monterey (no longer politically important but not yet a tourist attraction) in transition, something he wrote about in his essay *The Old and New Pacific Capitals*. He foresaw that the lifestyle that had endured since the Mexican era was no match for the "Yankee craft" of the "millionaire vulgarians of the Big Bonanza," such as Charles Crocker, whose lavish Hotel Del Monte, which opened a year later (the site is now the Naval Postgraduate School, east of downtown), turned the sleepy town into a seaside resort of international renown almost overnight.

Monterey was also the military headquarters for the whole of Alta California, and thereafter Monterey continued to be the leading administrative and commercial center of a territory that extended east to the Rocky Mountains and north to Canada, but had a total population, excluding Native Americans, of less than seven thousand.

American interest in Monterey was purely commercial until 1842, when an American naval commodore received a false report that the US and Mexico were at war, and that the English were poised to take California. Commodore Catesby Jones anchored at Monterey and demanded the peaceful surrender of the port, and two days later, the American flag was raised. The armed but cordial US occupation lasted only until Jones examined the official documents closely and realized he'd got it all wrong (and his exuberance cost him his job). When the Mexican-American War began in earnest in 1846, the United States took possession of Monterey without resistance. The discovery of gold in the Sierra Nevada foothills soon focused attention upon San Francisco, and Monterey became something of a backwater, hardly affected by the waves of immigration that followed.

The waterfront and Old Monterey

More than half a century ago, when Monterey first tried to pass itself off to wealthy visitors from San Francisco and beyond as an upscale resort, there was a great deal of doubt whether or not the demand would ever match the supply. Today, those worries have been put neatly to bed along with the visiting mass that stays here nightly, and tourism is now Monterey's main livelihood.

Old Monterey extends half a mile inland from the waterfront, but many of its most interesting buildings are concentrated along tacky **Fisherman's Wharf**, where the catch of the day is more likely to be families from San Jose than the formerly abundant sardines. Most of the commercial fishermen moved out long ago, leaving the old wharves and canneries as relics of a once-prosperous industry; fat sea lions float by under the piers.

The most prominent building near the wharf, at the foot of Pacific Street, is the modern **Maritime Museum of Monterey** (daily except Wed 10am–5pm;

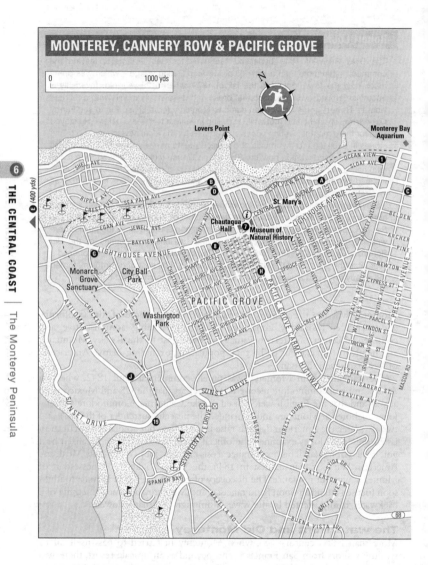

MONTEREY, CANNERY ROW & PACIFIC GROVE

0   1000 yds

N

Lovers Point

Monterey Bay
Aquarium

OCEAN VIEW
SLOAT AVE.

B
D

SHELL AVE.

RIPPLE AVE.

SEA PALM AVE.

St. Mary's

CRESS AVE.

OCEAN VIEW BLVD

CENTRAL

Chautaqua
Hall

EGAN AVE.

JEWELL AVE.

Museum of
Natural History

LIGHTHOUSE AVENUE

ARCHER

PINE

BELDEN

BAYVIEW AVE.

LIGHTHOUSE AVENUE

NEWTON

Monarch
Grove
Sanctuary

City Hall
Park

CYPRESS ST.

SPRUCE

H

PACIFIC GROVE

Washington
Park

JUNIPERO AVE.

GIBSON AVE.

PARCEL ST.

LYNDON ST.

SINEX AVE.

HILLCREST AVENUE

TAYLOR

ST.

JESSIE   ST.

DIVISADERO ST.

J

SUNSET DRIVE

SEAVIEW AVE.

19

CONGRESS AVE.

FOREST LODGE

DAVID AVE.

PATTERSON LN.

SUNSET DRIVE

SPANISH BAY

MAJELLA RD.

BENITO AVE.

BUENA VISTA AVE.

68

$3; ☎831/372-2608) with well-displayed but essentially mundane collections
of ships in glass cases enlivened by interesting background on the town's defunct
sardine industry.

Drop in on the foyer of the Maritime Museum to see the fourteen-minute
film on Monterey history (free), a good preparation for a stroll on the **Path of
History**. This loosely organized, roughly 1.5-mile trail connects 37 sites
scattered throughout the quarter-mile square of the modern city, an area designated as **Monterey State Historic Park**. The path is marked with small yellow
discs at regular intervals on the sidewalk. Many of Monterey's historic buildings
have survived in pristine condition: to see inside, join one of the 45-minute

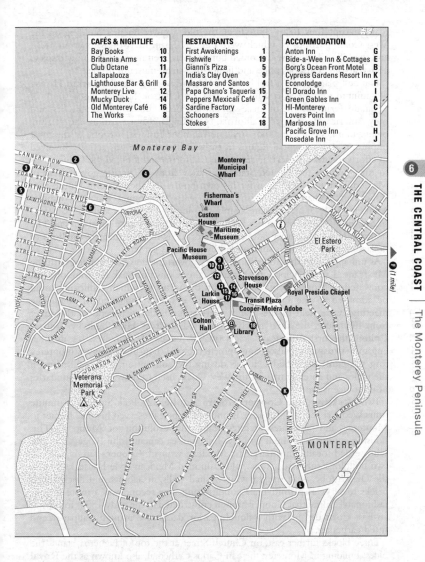

CAFÉS & NIGHTLIFE

Bay Books	10
Britannia Arms	13
Club Octane	11
Lallapalooza	17
Lighthouse Bar & Grill	6
Monterey Live	12
Mucky Duck	14
Old Monterey Café	16
The Works	8

RESTAURANTS

First Awakenings	1
Fishwife	19
Gianni's Pizza	5
India's Clay Oven	9
Massaro and Santos	4
Papa Chano's Taqueria	15
Peppers Mexicali Café	7
Sardine Factory	3
Schooners	2
Stokes	18

ACCOMMODATION

Anton Inn	G
Bide-a-Wee Inn & Cottages	E
Borg's Ocean Front Motel	B
Cypress Gardens Resort Inn	K
Econolodge	F
El Dorado Inn	I
Green Gables Inn	A
HI-Monterey	C
Lovers Point Inn	D
Mariposa Inn	L
Pacific Grove Inn	H
Rosedale Inn	J

guided **walking tours** of the Path of History (currently Wed at noon & Fri 10.30am; but call to check; free; ℡831/649-7118, ⓦwww.parks.ca.gov), which leave from the Pacific House Museum.

Among the essential buildings to visit, the **Pacific House Museum** (daily 10am–3pm; free) stands on the east side of the plaza outside the Maritime Museum; since its construction in 1847, it has been a courthouse, a rooming house, and a dancehall. It is now the best of the local **museums**, with displays on Monterey history and a fair collection of Native American artifacts; the lobby is an informal information center for the whole of the Monterey State Historic Park. While in the area, be sure to wander by the **Custom House**

461

(daily except Tues 10am–3pm; free), the oldest governmental building on the West Coast, portions of which were built by Spain in 1814, Mexico in 1827, and the US in 1846. The balconied building has been restored and now displays 150-year-old crates of coffee and liquor in a small museum inside.

The best place to get a feel for life in Old Monterey is at the **Larkin House** (45-minute tours Wed & Sat 2pm; free), on Jefferson Street a block south of Alvarado, former home of successful entrepreneur Thomas Larkin, the first and only American Consul to California. New England-born Larkin, the wealthy owner of a general store and a redwood lumber business, was one of the most important and influential figures in early California. He was actively involved in efforts to attract American settlers to California and lobbied the Californians to turn towards the United States and away from the erratic government of Mexico. Through his designs for his own house, and the Customs House near Fisherman's Wharf, Larkin is credited with developing the now-familiar Monterey style of architecture, combining local adobe walls and the balconies of Southern plantation homes with a puritan Yankee's taste in ornament. The house, the first two-story adobe in California, is filled with many millions of dollars of antiques and is surrounded by gorgeous gardens.

As unhappy with the American military government as he had been with the Mexicans, Larkin helped to organize the Constitutional Convention that convened in Monterey in 1849 to draft the terms by which California could be admitted to the US as the 31st state – which happened in 1850. The meetings were held in the grand white stone building just down the street from his house, the then newly completed **Colton Hall**, built by William Colton, the first American *alcalde* (mayor-judge) of Monterey. It's now an engaging **museum** (daily 10am–4pm; free; ☎831/646-5648, @www.monterey .org/museum), furnished as it was during the convention, with quill pens on the tables and an early map of the West Coast, used to draw up the boundaries of the nascent state.

Two blocks east, the **Cooper–Molera Adobe**, 525 Polk Street (45-minute tours Wed, Fri & Sat 1pm; free), is one of the best preserved historic homes in Monterey and illustrates architecturally the evolution of Monterey. This housing complex was built by New England sea captain John Rogers Cooper, who settled locally and married a Mexican woman. Cooper's family lived in two buildings: the first, a squat, old-fashioned Mexican-style house, known as the Diaz Adobe, with simple, whitewashed walls, no closets, and thick adobe bricks to serve as primitive air-conditioning. The second was a more formal, fashionable home that Cooper himself constructed in the early 1850s following an East Coast design, with a double parlor, decorative printed wallpaper, and fitted carpeting.

Three blocks further east, on Church Street at the top of Figueroa, stands the oldest building in Monterey, the San Carlos Cathedral, also known as the **Royal Presidio Chapel** (Mon–Fri 7.45am–12.15pm; free; ☎831/373-2628, @www .sancarloscathedral.com). This small and much-restored Spanish Colonial church was built in 1795 as part of a mission founded here by Junípero Serra in 1770, the rest of which was soon removed to a better site along the Carmel River.

Cannery Row and the Monterey Bay Aquarium

A waterfront **bike path** runs from Fisherman's Wharf along the disused railroad two miles out to Pacific Grove. It parallels the one-time Ocean View Avenue, renamed **Cannery Row** after John Steinbeck's evocative portrait of the rough-and-ready men and women who worked in and around the thirty-odd fish canneries here. During World War II, Monterey was the sardine capital of the western world, catching and canning some 200,000 tons of the fish each year. However, overfishing ensured that by 1945 the sardines were more or less all gone, and the canneries were abandoned, falling into disrepair until the 1970s, when they were rebuilt, redecorated, and converted into shopping malls and flashy restaurants, many with names adopted from Steinbeck's tales.

Ride, walk, or take the free trolley from a mile west of Fisherman's Wharf to visit the magnificent **Monterey Bay Aquarium** (daily 10am–6pm plus summer weekends to 8pm; $24.95, $3 audio tour; ⊤831/648-4800, Ⓦwww .montereybayaquarium.org), one of the largest, most stunning displays of underwater life in the world. The place can be very busy in summer, and reserving online beforehand saves you from waiting in line. It's built upon the foundations of an old sardine cannery and housed in industrial-style buildings that blend a sense of adventure with pleasant promenades along the bay.

The eastern end is largely devoted to the **Outer Bay** section, an enormous tank with vast windows providing matchless views of the species that populate the deep waters just beyond the bay. Lazy hammerhead sharks glide amongst the foul-tempered tuna, while barracuda dart past and massive sunfish weighing up to a ton make their stately circuit of the tank perimeter.

Towards the middle of the building the **sea otters** always draw a crowd, particularly at feeding time (usually 10.30am, 1.30pm & 3.30pm). These playful critters are now relatively common out in the bay, but were once hunted nearly to extinction for their fur – said to be the softest in the world, with some one million hairs per square inch.

At the western end of the building, habitats close to shore are presented in the **kelp forest**, where mesmerizing, ever-circling schools of silver anchovies avoid the lazy sharks. Nearby you can watch murres use their wings to effectively "fly" underwater, and upstairs there's the kid-friendly **Splash Zone** with touch tanks and penguin exhibits.

The complex also opens directly onto the bay, so you can step right out and peer into wild tide pools after wandering around the captive tanks.

Pacific Grove

PACIFIC GROVE – or "Butterfly Town USA," as it likes to call itself – stands curiously apart from the rest of the peninsula, less known but more impressively situated than its two famous neighbors. The town began as a campground and Methodist retreat in 1875, a summertime tent city for revivalist Christians in which strong drink, naked flesh, and reading the Sunday papers were firmly prohibited. The Methodists have long since gone, but otherwise the town is little changed. Its quiet streets, lined by pine trees and grand old Victorian wooden houses, are enlivened each year by hundreds of thousands of orange-and-black **monarch butterflies**, which arrive here each winter from all over the western US and Canada to escape the cold and have become the town's main tourist attraction. In fact, the migration of these butterflies is so important to the local economy that they're protected by local law: there's a $1000 fine for "molesting a butterfly in any way."

Downtown Pacific Grove centers upon the intersection of Forest Avenue and Lighthouse Avenue, two miles northwest of central Monterey. A block down Forest Avenue, on the corner of Central Avenue, the **Pacific Grove Museum of Natural History** (Tues–Sat 10am–5pm; free; ⊤831/648-5716, Ⓦwww .pgmuseum.org) has an informative collection of local wildlife, including lots of butterflies, over four hundred stuffed birds, a relief model of the Monterey Peninsula and Big Sur, and exhibits on the ways of life of the native Costanoan and Salinan peoples. A block west, **Chautauqua Hall** was, in the 1880s, the focus of town life as the West Coast headquarters of the instructional and populist Chautauqua Movement, a left-leaning, traveling university that reached thousands of Americans long before there was any accessible form of higher education. Nowadays, the plain white building is used as a dancehall, with a three-piece band playing favorites from the Thirties and Forties every Saturday night (Ⓦwww.pgdance.org).

About the only reminder of the Methodist camp meetings are the tiny, intricately detailed wooden cottages, along 16th and 17th streets, which date from the revival days; in some cases wooden boards were simply nailed over the frames of canvas tents to make them habitable year-round. Down Central Avenue at 12th Street stands the deep-red Gothic wooden church of **Saint Mary's By-The-Sea** (Mon, Wed & Fri 12.30–2pm; free), Pacific Grove's first substantial church, built in 1887, with a simple interior of redwood beams polished to a shimmering glow, and an authentic signed Tiffany stained-glass window, nearest the altar on the left.

Ocean View Boulevard, which runs between the church and the ocean, circles the town along the coast, passing the headland of **Lovers Point** – originally called Lovers of Jesus Point – where preachers used to hold sunrise services. Surrounded in early summer by the colorful red-and-purple blankets of blooming ice plants, it's one of the peninsula's best beaches, where you can lounge around and swim from the intimate, protected strand – if you're lucky enough to have arrived on one of the rare fog-free days in summer. Ocean View Boulevard runs another mile along the coast out to the tip of the peninsula, where the 1855 **Point Piños Lighthouse**, Asilomar Boulevard (Thurs–Mon 1–4pm; $2 donation; Ⓣ831/648-5716, Ⓦwww.pgmuseum.org), is the oldest continuously operating lighthouse on the California coast.

Duck a couple of blocks inland here to visit the **Monarch Grove Sanctuary**, Ridge Road off Lighthouse Avenue (dawn–dusk; free), where from mid-October to mid-February you should be able to spot giant brown clumps of monarchs discreetly congregating high up in the eucalyptus treetops.

Ocean View Boulevard continues from here but changes its name to Sunset Drive, leading on to **Asilomar State Beach**, a wild stretch with dramatic surf. It's too dangerous for swimming, though the rocky shore provides homes for all sorts of tide pool life.

The logical extension is to continue your explorations along **Seventeen Mile Drive** (daily dawn–dusk; $9 per car, bicycles free, no motorcycles allowed; Ⓣ831/649-8500), a privately owned, scenic toll road which loops from Pacific Grove along the coast south to Carmel; on the way, it swoops past the golf courses and country clubs of Pebble Beach. Don't miss the trussed-up figure of the **Lone Cypress** halfway along the route, as it's the subject of many a postcard; there are enough beautiful vistas of the rugged coastline to make it almost worth braving the hordes that pack the roads on holiday weekends.

Carmel and around

Set on gently rising headlands above a sculpted and largely untouched rocky shore, **CARMEL** is confined to a few neat rows of quaint shops along Ocean Avenue surrounded by assorted posh mansions. Besides all the rampant cuteness, Carmel's only real crime is its ridiculously inflated price scale; think of it as the West Coast's middle-aged answer to New York's Hamptons.

The town's reputation as a rich resort belies its origins: there was nothing much here until the San Francisco earthquake and fire of 1906 led a number of artists and writers from the city to take refuge in the area, forming a bohemian colony on the wild and uninhabited slopes that soon became infamous throughout the state for its free-spirited excess. The figurehead of the group was the poet George Sterling, and part-time members included Jack London, Mary Austin, and the young Sinclair Lewis. But it was a short-lived alliance, and by the 1920s the group had broken up, and an influx of wealthy San Franciscans had put Carmel well on its way to becoming the exclusive corner it is today.

Despite continued growth of tourism in the area, Carmel still seems the epitome of parochial snobbishness. Franchise businesses are banned outright within the city limits, while there's an array of laws enacted to stringently maintain the gingerbread charm of the town's central district: parking meters and street addresses are prohibited, for instance. One long-term byproduct of this bizarre rebellion against street numbers was that all mail had to be picked up in person from the post office – at least until recently, when a local resident sued for home delivery and was rewarded with the chance to pay a premium to have mail delivered.

Carmel's center, fifteen minutes south of Monterey on MST bus #4 or #5, is largely designer-shopping territory: Carmel Plaza Mall at Ocean Avenue and Mission Street holds branches of Tiffany and Louis Vuitton, and there are a number of tacky, overpriced art **galleries** along Dolores Street (there's even a clothing store for pampered lap dogs on Ocean Avenue). The Weston Gallery on Sixth Street between Dolores and Lincoln (summer daily 10.30am–5.30pm; ☎831/624-4453, ⓦwww.westongallery.com) is worth a look, however, hosting regular shows of the best contemporary photographers and featuring a permanent display of works by Fox Talbot, Ansel Adams, and Edward Weston – who lived in Carmel for most of his life. To get the lowdown on the other galleries, check out the free, widely available *Carmel Gallery Guide*.

The town's best feature, however, is the largely untouched coastline nearby, among the most beautiful in California. **Carmel Beach** is a tranquil cove of emerald blue water bordered by soft white sand and cypress-covered cliffs; the tides are deceptively strong and dangerous, so be careful if you chance a swim.

A mile south from Carmel Beach along Carmel Bay, **Tor House** was, when built in 1919, the only building on a then treeless headland. The poet Robinson Jeffers (whose very long, starkly tragic narrative poems were far more popular in his time than they are today) built the small cottage and adjacent tower by hand, out of granite boulders he carried up from the cove below. There are hourly guided tours of the house and gardens (Fri & Sat 10am–3pm; $7; ☎831/624-1813, ⓦwww.torhouse.org), and though they overload visitors with an obsequious account of the now-forgotten writer's life and work, the house itself is pleasant enough. Each tour only takes six people, so reserve a week in advance. Note that the entrance is at 26304 Ocean View Avenue, one block back from the cliff-top. Also, there's little parking in this residential neighborhood, so allow ample time to find a spot.

Another quarter of a mile along Scenic Road, around the tip of Carmel Point, you'll find the idyllic, mile-long **Carmel River State Beach** (☎831/649-2836, ⓦwww.parks.ca.gov). It's less visited than the city beach, and includes a bird sanctuary on a freshwater lagoon that offers safe and sometimes warm swimming. Again, if you brave the waves, beware of the strong tides and currents, especially at the south end of the beach, where the sand falls away at a very steep angle, causing big and potentially hazardous surf.

The Carmel Mission

Half a mile or so up the Carmel River from the beach, also reachable by following Junípero Avenue from downtown, **Carmel Mission Basilica**

(Mon–Sat 9.30am–5pm, Sun 10.30am–5pm; $5; ☎831/624-3600, ⓦwww
.carmelmission.org) was founded in 1770 by Junípero Serra as the second of the
California missions and the headquarters of the chain. Father Serra never got to
see the finished church – he died before its completion and is buried under the
floor in front of the altar. Finally completed by Father Lasuen in 1797,
the sandstone church has undergone one of the most painstakingly authentic
restorations in the entire mission chain, a process well detailed in one of the
three excellent **museums** in the mission compound. By 1937, when the reconstruction began, the mission had lain derelict for more than eighty years and was
little more than its foundations and a few feet of wall; but today the whimsically
ornate structure stands firmly as the most romantic mission in the chain.

Point Lobos State Reserve

Two miles south of the mission along Hwy-1, accessible in summer on MST
bus #22, the **Point Lobos State Reserve** (daily: summer 9am–7pm or later;
winter 9am–5pm; $9 parking; ☎831/624-4909, ⓦwww.parks.ca.gov) has
plenty of natural justifications to support its claim of being "the greatest
meeting of land and water in the world." There are over 250 bird and animal
species along the **hiking trails** in the area, and the sea here is one of the
richest underwater habitats in California. Because the point juts so far out into
the ocean, it has some of the earth's best undisturbed views of the sea: craggy
granite pinnacles, landforms that inspired Robert Louis Stevenson's *Treasure
Island*, reach out of jagged blue coves. Sea lions and otters frolic in the crashing
surf, just below the many vantage points along the park's coastal trail. Gray
whales are often seen offshore – sometimes as close as a hundred yards away –
migrating south in January and
returning with young calves in
April and early May. The park,
named after the *lobos marinos* –
the noisy, barking sea lions that
group on the rocks off the
reserve's tip – protects some of
the few remaining Monterey
cypress trees on its knife-edged
headland, despite being
buffeted by relentless winds.

It's a popular spot, so expect
to wait for a parking space at
busy times. A worthwhile guide
and map is included in the
admission fee.

Carmel Valley

About fifteen miles inland, east
along route G16, lies **Carmel
Valley Village**, where the
weather is warmer and more
predictable than the coast: that's
one of the reasons this country
hamlet can bill itself as the
epicenter of Monterey County's
wine country, a cluster of
vineyards encompassing an area

▲ Point Lobos State Reserve

that stretches as far as King City to the south on Hwy-101. In the **Carmel Valley** that surrounds the village, you'll find a number of vineyards in a quiet pastoral setting – a big breath of relief after crowded, coastal Carmel: most are known for their red wines, since the searing summer heat (up to 105°F) suits hardier varietals better. The Monterey County Vintners and Growers Association (☎831/375-9400, ⓦwww.montereywines.org) publishes a map of the area, and the **Chamber of Commerce** (Mon–Fri 10am–4pm; ☎831/659-4000, ⓦwww.carmelvalleychamber.com) lures visitors from Carmel with a local map – available from any visitor center in Monterey County – crammed with shopping and dining possibilities. One of the most pleasant wineries for tastings is Joullian, 2 Village Drive (daily 11am–5pm; ☎831/659-8100, ⓦwww.joullian.com), where the friendly, knowledgeable staff will be happy to talk at length about the region's history and current winemaking strengths.

Eating

The peninsula has many excellent **places to eat**, and though prices tend to float near resort level, the competition for tourist dollars ensures quality. For a full list of the hundreds of eating options in the area, check out a copy of the free, weekly, and widely available *Go!* or *Monterey County Weekly*. If you're on a tight budget, the best eats are on the north side of Monterey along North Fremont Street, on and around Lighthouse Avenue (just south of Cannery Row), and in the shopping malls along Hwy-1 south of Carmel.

Monterey and Cannery Row

First Awakenings 125 Oceanview Blvd, Cannery Row ☎832/372-1125. Located inside the American Tin Cannery building, this is an excellent spot for egg-and-pancake breakfasts, as well as their excellent "bombero" sausage burrito ($8.25). Also salads and sandwiches, served inside or out on the terrace.

Gianni's Pizza 725 Lighthouse Ave ☎831/649-1500. Lively pizza and pasta joint where you order at the counter, grab a beer at the bar, seat yourself and wait for tasty, no-nonsense dishes such as veggie lasagna ($9), linguini and clams ($9), or a 12-inch pizza ($15).

India's Clay Oven 150 Del Monte Ave, 2nd Floor ☎831/373-2529. All your tandoori favorites are here, though if you're feeling especially hungry aim to arrive for the $16 dinner buffet.

Massaro and Santos 32 Cannery Row #H-1, Coast Guard Pier ☎831/649-6700. Dine here for views out across the bay and the fish-crammed bouillabaisse, not to mention dozens of daily specials – mains are $15–20 but save room for the gorgeous desserts.

Papa Chano's Taqueria 462 Alvarado St ☎831/646-9587. One of the few bargain eateries in town, this fast-food-style taqueria serves juicy, authentic Mexican specialties – the chorizo is particularly tender. Tacos from $2.50; full meals around $9.

Sardine Factory 701 Wave St, Cannery Row ☎831/373-3775. California seafood served in French chateau splendor at less-than-expected prices, although you'll still pay $15 for a lump crab and prawn cocktail, and $30 for swordfish on a champagne vinaigrette sauce.

Schooners In the *Monterey Plaza Hotel*, 400 Cannery Row ☎831/372-2628. Colorful upscale bistro in a historic hotel with great views over the bay. Try a grilled, local Castroville artichoke served with herb mayonnaise ($7), perhaps followed by seafood pasta ($18).

Stokes 500 Hartnell St ☎831/373-1110, ⓦwww.stokesrestaurant.com. Built in 1833, this historic former home is now an elegant restaurant and bar serving Mediterranean cuisine with a California flair. Try crispy duck confit on warm spinach salad ($12.50), followed by lamb shoulder and artichoke mushroom risotto ($25).

Pacific Grove

Fishwife 1996 Sunset Drive at Asilomar ☎831/375-7107. Long-standing local favorite by Asilomar Beach, serving great California Caribbean food at reasonable prices in cozy, unpretentious surroundings. Try the king prawns sautéed in red onions, chilies, and lime juice for $17.

Pepper's Mexicali Café 170 Forest Ave ☎831/373-6892. Gigantic plates of Mexican food for around $10 per person, piled high with fresh, local produce: less healthful than it sounds but guaranteed to fill even the biggest stomach – try the classic Veracruz snapper ($14)

Carmel

La Bicyclette Dolores St between Ocean and 7th streets ⊤831/622-9899, ⓦwww
.labicycletterestaurant.com. Wooden tables and copper pots hanging from the ceiling set a suitably rustic tone for this lovely, dinner-only French country restaurant. Mains (mostly $25) come with a complimentary antipasto plate and soup.

Little Napoli Dolores St between Ocean and 7th streets ⊤831/626-6335. One of the town's many excellent midrange Italian restaurants, this tiny eatery serves oversized portions of fresh pasta with original sauces amid all the romantic charm you'd expect from a Carmel address. Dinner mains $16–27.

Paolina's San Carlos between Ocean and 7th streets ⊤831/624-5599 Fresh home-made pastas are served up in a casual courtyard setting at half the price of other Carmel dining.

Porta Bella Ocean Ave between Lincoln and Monte Verde ⊤831/624-4395. Popular with ladies who lunch, this upscale, flower-filled bistro serves fancy French food in a pleasant setting, with crisp white tablecloths and a charming garden tucked away beneath a vine-filled trellis at the back.

Robata Grill & Sake Bar 3658 The Barnyard, at the corner of Hwy-1 and Carmel Valley Rd ⊤831/624-2643. Local favorite for sushi and tempura in a warm, wood-paneled setting. Not cheap, but tasty and unpretentious for its locale.

Cafés and nightlife

The Peninsula has always been better known as a sleepy, romantic getaway than as a hub of hip coffee culture and nightlife. However, the best selection of bars is in Monterey, and the local **Jazz Festival** in mid-September (ⓦwww
.montereyjazzfestival.org) is the oldest continuous festival in the world, drawing crowds from afar. Check out the widely available *Monterey County Weekly* for the most current listings.

Cafés

Bay Books 316 Alvarado St, Monterey ⊤831/375-1855. Sip coffee until 10pm while browsing in one of Monterey's better bookshops.

Carmel Bakery Ocean Ave between Lincoln and Dolores, Carmel ⊤831/626-8885. Refreshing, low-key café on the main drag, serving old-fashioned gooey cakes and coffee to browsing locals.

Old Monterey Café 489 Alvarado St, Monterey ⊤831/646-1021. Reasonably priced, more-than-you-can-eat breakfasts ($7–10), with great omelets and buckwheat pancakes, plus tasty sandwiches. Breakfast and lunch only.

Patisserie Boissière Mission St between Ocean and 7th, Carmel ⊤831/624-5008. This combination patisserie and midrange restaurant serves sumptuous pastries you'd expect along with savory quiches, salads, and even Coquille Saint Jacques ($18). Picnic lunches available with advance notice. Closed Mon & Tues.

Tuck Box Tearoom Dolores St between Ocean and 7th, Carmel ⊤831/624-6365. Breakfast, lunch, and afternoon tea in this half-timbered, mock-Tudor Old England cottage; costly, kitschy, and fun.

The Works 667 Lighthouse Ave, Pacific Grove ⊤831/372-2242, ⓦwww.theworkspg.com. Relaxed bookstore and daytime café that's a bit of a Pacific Grove hangout. There's free Wi-Fi, and live entertainment most Sat (7.30–9.30pm).

Bars and nightlife

Britannia Arms 444 Alvarado St, Monterey ⊤831/656-9543, ⓦwww.britanniaarms.com. This authentic-feeling British pub is oddly incongruous in the heart of Monterey; it's filled with a largely local, laid-back crowd and serves greasily tasty traditional grub (around $10) plus two dozen beers on tap, including several English favorites.

Club Octane 321 Alvarado St, Monterey ⊤831/646-9244, ⓦwww.cluboctane.com. Lively downtown club with three dance floors and a youngish, collegiate crowd – more fun than hip. Closed Tues & Wed.

Lallapalooza 474 Alvarado St, Monterey ⊤831/645-9036. Smooth martini bar with olive-themed art on the walls, a small sidewalk terrace, and stylish oval bar – the dressiest place to drink in town. There's a reasonable restaurant attached, too.

Lighthouse Bar & Grill 281 Lighthouse Ave, Monterey ⊤831/373-4488. Rather dilapidated gay bar with a low-key pub atmosphere, pool tables, and an older crowd. Closed Sun & Mon.

Monterey Live 414 Alvarado St ⊤831/646-1415, ⓦwww.montereylive.org. Intimate performing arts venue with live music, dance, theater, or comedy every night of the week, plus meals and drinks served at your table. Often no cover, though sometimes up to $10; check the website.

The Mucky Duck 479 Alvarado St, Monterey ⊤831/655-3031. The menu at this friendly and popular Tudor-style bar/restaurant features British

food with a California flair. Occasional live music and DJ dancing on back patio.

Listings

Bike rental In Monterey try Adventures by the Sea, 299 Cannery Row or 201 Alvarado St ($6/hour, $24/day; ⊤831/372-1807, ⓦwww .adventuresbythesea.com), or Bay Bikes, 585 Cannery Row ($18/4hr, $24/day; ⊤831/655-2453, ⓦwww.baybikes.com).

Internet Free machines and Wi-Fi at the library.

Library 625 Pacific St (Mon 1–9pm, Tues & Weds 10am–9pm, Thurs & Fri 10am–6pm, Sat & Sun

1–5pm; ⊤831/646-3932, ⓦwww.monterey .org/library).

Movies Osio Cinemas, 350 Alvarado St, Monterey ⊤831/644-8171, www.osiocinemas.com. First-run movies downtown.

Post Office 565 Hartnell St (Mon–Fri 8.30am– 5pm, Sat 10am–2pm). For General Delivery the Zip code is 93940

North from Monterey

The landscape around **Monterey Bay**, between the Peninsula and the beach town of Santa Cruz, 45 miles north, is almost entirely given over to agriculture. **Castro-ville**, ten miles north along Hwy-1, has two claims to fame, one more glamorous than the other. Today, surrounded by farmland, it produces more than 85 percent of the nation's artichokes (try them deep-fried in one of the local cafés); in 1947, the first woman to be crowned Artichoke Queen was one Norma Jean Baker, later known as Marilyn Monroe. The wide **Pajaro Valley**, five miles further north, is covered with apple orchards, blossoming white in the spring. At the mouths of the Pajaro and Salinas rivers, the marshlands that ring the bay are habitats for many of California's endangered species of coastal wildlife and migratory birds.

Four miles northwest of Castroville, **Moss Landing** is an excellent place to stop for seafood – try *Phil's Fish Market*, 7600 Sandholtd Road (⊤831/633-2152), dramatically poised on a small island linked by a short bridge to the mainland, where you can pick from the catch of the day, then fish a bottle of white wine for yourself from the cooler. At the nearby **Elkhorn Slough National Estuarine Research Reserve** (Wed–Sun 9am–5pm, free guided tours Sat & Sun 10am & 1pm; $2.50; ⊤831/728-2822, ⓦwww.elkhornslough .org) you may spot a falcon or eagle among the 340 species of bird that call it home. Guided boat tours can be booked through Elkhorn Slough Safari on the harbor ($26; ⊤831/633-5555, ⓦwww.elkhornslough.com). The beaches along the bay to Santa Cruz are often windy and not very exciting, though they're lined by sand dunes that can provide hours of exploration.

Four miles inland, **Watsonville** is really only of interest as a transfer point where the Monterey and Santa Cruz **bus** systems connect.

San Juan Bautista

Inland from the Monterey Bay area, on US-101 between Salinas and San Francisco, tiny **San Juan Bautista** is an old Mexican town that, but for a modest smattering of collectibles shops, has hardly changed since it was bypassed by the railroad in 1876. The early nineteenth-century **Mission San Juan Bautista** (daily 9.30am–4.30pm; $4; ⊤831/623-4528, ⓦwww .oldmissionsjb.org), the largest of the California mission churches – and still the parish church of San Juan Bautista – stands on the north side of the town's central plaza, its original bells still ringing out from the bell tower. The arcaded monastery wing that stretches out to the left of the church contains relics and historical exhibits, including a vast collection of ceremonial robes. If it all looks a bit familiar, you may have seen it before – the climactic stairway chase scene in Alfred Hitchcock's *Vertigo* was filmed here.

The town that grew up around the mission was once the largest in central California and has been preserved as a **state historic park** (daily 10am–4.30pm; $2; ℡831/623-4526, ⓦwww.parks.ca.gov) with exhibits around the spacious central square interpreting the restored buildings. On the west side of the plaza, the two-story, balconied adobe Plaza Hotel was a popular stopping place on the stagecoach route between San Francisco and Los Angeles; next door, the 1840 **Castro-Breen Adobe**, administrative headquarters of Mexican California, later belonged to the Breen family – survivors of the ill-fated Donner Party (see box, p.662) – who made a small fortune in the Gold Rush.

Across from the mission, the large **Plaza Hall** was built to serve as the seat of the emergent county government, but when the county seat was awarded instead to Hollister – a small farming community eight miles east, and scene of a motorcycle gang's rampage that inspired the movie *The Wild One* – the building was turned into a dancehall and saloon. The adjacent stables display a range of old stagecoaches and wagons, and explain how to decipher an array of cattle brands, from "lazy H" to "rockin' double B."

The commercial center of San Juan Bautista, a block south of the plaza, lines Third Street in a row of evocatively decaying facades. If you're hungry, the best of the half-dozen **places to eat** is *Jardines de San Juan*, 115 Third Street (℡831/632-4466), a high-quality Mexican joint with champion margaritas and shady seating out under the arbor. Alternatively try the unfussy and friendly *Mission Café* at 300 Third Street (℡831/623-2635), which serves breakfast and lunch, or for dinner, pull up a chair in *Joan & Peter's German Restaurant*, 322 Third Street (℡831/623-4521), with its hearty bratwurst lunches ($9) and *wursteller* diner mains ($19). For **information** contact the Chamber of Commerce, 33 Washington Street (Mon–Fri 10am–noon and generally later; ℡831/623-2454, ⓦwww.sjbchamber.com).

Santa Cruz

Seventy-five miles south of San Francisco, the unassuming yet edgy community of **SANTA CRUZ** is a hard place to pin down. In many ways it's the quintessential California coastal town, with miles of beaches for sunning and superb surfing, thousands of acres of mountaintop forests for hiking, and a lively, historic boardwalk amusement park complete with a wild wooden rollercoaster. It's also home to a great number of homeless people who've spilled over from San Francisco and neighboring communities to benefit from the town's numerous liberal resources, joining with its hippy past to bring out the crustier side of local life. Santa Cruz enjoyed – or, rather, endured – a growth spurt in the late 1990s: it was commandeered as a dormitory suburb for San Jose and Silicon Valley during the dot-com boom, which pushed up its property prices significantly and drove some long-term locals away; that boom's stabilized but prices have yet to drop. Even so, some of its suburbs still have a conservative, almost redneck feel more akin to the Central Valley than the languid, laid-back coast. All this means that you rarely get an impression of a resort totally at ease with itself: the underlying conflicts are one of the many reasons why the town is so slow to change and makes an intriguingly schizophrenic place to visit.

The area has a reputation as a holdout from the 1960s, and is still considered among the most politically and socially progressive in California – one reason

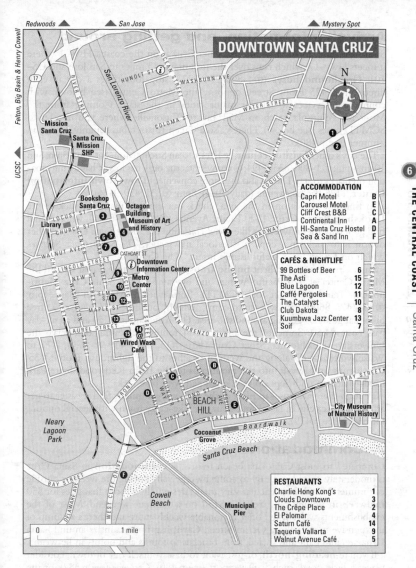

DOWNTOWN SANTA CRUZ

N

Felton, Big Basin & Henry Cowell

UCSC

Mission Santa Cruz

Santa Cruz Mission SHP

Bookshop Santa Cruz 3

Library

Octagon Building Museum of Art and History

Downtown Information Center

Metro Center

Wired Wash Café

BEACH HILL

Cocoanut Grove

City Museum of Natural History

Neary Lagoon Park

Santa Cruz Beach

Boardwalk

Cowell Beach

Municipal Pier

ACCOMMODATION	
Capri Motel	B
Carousel Motel	E
Cliff Crest B&B	C
Continental Inn	A
HI-Santa Cruz Hostel	D
Sea & Sand Inn	F

CAFÉS & NIGHTLIFE	
99 Bottles of Beer	6
The Asti	15
Blue Lagoon	12
Caffé Pergolesi	11
The Catalyst	10
Club Dakota	8
Kuumbwa Jazz Center	13
Soif	7

RESTAURANTS	
Charlie Hong Kong's	1
Clouds Downtown	3
The Crêpe Place	2
El Palomar	4
Saturn Café	14
Taqueria Vallarta	9
Walnut Avenue Café	5

0   1 mile

6

THE CENTRAL COAST | Santa Cruz

that Santa Cruz has become known, in recent years, as a **lesbian** haven (see p.480) – and there are still a few freaky holdouts from its hippy heyday. The town is also surprisingly untouristy: no hotels spoil the miles of wave-beaten coastline – in fact, most of the surrounding land is used for growing fruit and vegetables, and roadside stalls are more likely to be selling apples or sprouts than postcards and souvenirs. Places to stay are for once good-value and easy to find, and the town sports a range of bookstores and coffeehouses, as well as some lively bars and nightclubs where the music varies from hardcore surf-punk to long-time local Neil Young and friends.

Arrival, information, and getting around

Some 45 miles north of Monterey, Santa Cruz is on the coastal Hwy-1 where it meets Hwy-17, which runs over the mountains 33 miles to San Jose and US-101. **Greyhound buses** (T 1-800/231-2222) stop four times a day in each direction at 425 Front Street, opposite the Metro Center (see below), with connecting services to all the major cities in the state. Coming from the Monterey Peninsula, catch an MST bus to Watsonville where you transfer to SCMTD buses (see below). There's also a Green Tortoise bus roughly weekly in summer (see p.480).

The city's official **visitor center**, at 1211 Ocean Street (Mon–Sat 9am–5pm, Sun 10am–4pm; T 1-800/833-3494, W www.santacruz.org), has lots of handy information on places to stay. There's also the more convenient **Downtown Information Center**, 1126 Pacific Avenue (daily 10am–8pm; T 831/459-9486).

To find out what's on in the area, check out the free magazine rack at the **Bookshop Santa Cruz**, 1520 Pacific Avenue (T 831/423-0900), where you'll find generally useful weeklies like *Good Times* and the *Metro Santa Cruz*; another option is to pick up a copy of the local newspaper, *The Santa Cruz Sentinel*, which on Friday has a useful listings insert, "The Guide."

Santa Cruz has an excellent **public transportation** system, based around the Metro Center at 920 Pacific Avenue and operated by the Santa Cruz Metropolitan Transit District or SCMTD (information Mon–Fri 8am–4pm; T 831/425-8600, W www.scmtd.com), which publishes *Headways*, a free bilingual guide to getting around the area. The basic fare is $1.50 and an all-day pass costs $4.50. Some of the most useful routes are several that serve the University of California, Santa Cruz (#10, #15, #16, #19 & #20); #71 to Watsonville; and #7 along the western beaches to the lighthouse. Route #35, which runs up Hwy-9 into the mountains to Big Basin Redwoods State Park (mid-March to mid-Sept only), is equipped with bike racks.

Though there are buses to most of the beaches, you might find it easier to get around by **bicycle**. In fact, Santa Cruz is a bike-crazy town with several options for rental (see p.479).

Accommodation

Compared to most California beach resorts, **accommodation** in Santa Cruz is moderately priced and easy to come by, especially during the week or outside of summer. Motels in particular vary their rates wildly: a room that goes for $50 midweek in winter can easily be $150 on a summer weekend. Most of the establishments we've listed offer reasonable weekly rates, and there's a clump of inexpensive motels along Ocean Street. **Camping** opportunities around Santa Cruz are abundant and varied, from beaches to forests and points in between.

If you're **heading north**, or just want to base yourself out of town, consider places a little north such as Davenport (see p.480), *Costanoa* (see p.587), or the wonderful hostel at Pigeon Point (see also p.588).

Hotels, motels, and B&Bs

Capitola Venetian Hotel 1500 Wharf Rd, Capitola T 1-800/332-2780, W www.capitolavenetian.com. Quirky, aging beachfront hotel just across the bridge from Capitola's lively esplanade. All rooms have kitchens, and some are two-bedroom suites. Rates vary wildly with season: as low as ❷ in winter. Midweek ❼, weekend ❽

Capri Motel 337 Riverside Ave T 831/426-4611. The cheapest of a dozen or so budget motels near the beach and the boardwalk: it's clean, with microwave and fridge in room, a/c, a pool, on-site parking, and free Wi-Fi, but don't expect deluxe facilities. Midweek ❷, weekend ❸

Carousel Motel 110 Riverside Ave T 1-800/214-7400, W www.santacruzmotels.com. Sparklingly clean bargain, its simple rooms fitted out with blond wood furniture and loud, 1980s-inspired bedcovers; each room has a large TV and microwave, and there's free continental breakfast included. Even better, it's directly across from the boardwalk. Down to ❷ midweek in winter. ❻

🏃 **Cliff Crest B&B Inn** 407 Cliff St ☎831/427-2609, ⓦwww.cliffcrestinn.com. Eclectically furnished 1887 Queen Anne-style Victorian home with just five guestrooms and a self-contained carriage house, set in lovely gardens at the top of Beach Hill. It's within walking distance of downtown and the boardwalk, and rates include a full breakfast served in the solarium. Rooms ❼, carriage house ❽

Continental Inn 414 Ocean St ☎1-800/343-6941, ⓦwww.continentalinnsantacruz.com. Top value for a midrange motel. Comfortable if basic rooms and an easy walk to everything, with a heated pool, hot tub, and free Wi-Fi. Midweek ❹, weekend ❻

Historic Sand Rock Farm 6901 Freedom Blvd, Aptos ☎831/688-8005, ⓦwww.sandrockfarm .com. Owned by a local chef, this five-room guesthouse has been lovingly restored (look for details like rare panels of curly redwood) and filled with arts and crafts antiques; the multi-course made-to-order breakfasts are lavish and filling. A secluded bolt hole away from the beach and highly recommended. ❼

Pleasure Point Inn 2-3665 E Cliff Drive ☎1-877/557-2567, ⓦwww.pleasurepointinn.com. A well-designed, hip B&B with cliff-top views, a roof sundeck, and hot tub: rooms have built-in stereos, Jacuzzi baths, and all amenities. Highly recommended for those allergic to chintz. ❽

Sea and Sand Inn 201 W Cliff Drive ☎831/427-3400, ⓦwww.santacruzmotels.com. This small, upscale motel is overlooks the wharf with great views of the bay; flowerboxes burst with color under every window and the subtle, floral rooms are lushly decorated. Larger groups can opt for one of the individual cottages (❺) with private patio and outdoor Jacuzzi. Complimentary breakfast and free Wi-Fi. ❻

Hostel and campgrounds

Big Basin Redwoods State Park 21600 Big Basin Way on Hwy-236, Boulder Creek ☎831/338-8860, ⓦwww.santacruzstateparks.org; reservations ☎1-800/444-7275, ⓦwww.reserveamerica .com. High up in the hills around 12 miles north of Santa Cruz; sites with showers for $25, and $3 hiker/biker sites.

Henry Cowell Redwoods State Park 101 N Big Trees Park Rd, Felton ☎831/335-4598, ⓦwww .santacruzstateparks.org; reservations ☎1-800/444-7275, ⓦwww.reserveamerica.com. In the hills above UC Santa Cruz, around four miles north of town in a redwood grove along the San Lorenzo River. Bus #35 serves the park, and sites cost $25 a night.

HI–Santa Cruz 321 Main St ☎831/423-8304, ⓦwww.hi-santacruz.org. Well-situated hostel in a set of 1870s cottages just a couple of blocks from the beach. The atmosphere is informal but the place is closed during the day (10am–5pm) and is often booked up in advance. Office open 8–11am, 5–10pm for reservations. Members $20, nonmembers $23, rooms $50 and up, en-suite $75 and up.

New Brighton State Beach 1500 Park Ave, Capitola ☎831/464-6330, ⓦwww .santacruzstateparks.org; reservations ☎1-800/444-7275, ⓦwww.reserveamerica.com. Three miles south of Santa Cruz on the edge of the beachfront village of Capitola, set on bluffs above a lengthy strand. Hot showers available and reservations essential. Sites $25, hookups $35.

The Town

Santa Cruz provides a sharp contrast to the upscale resort sophistication of Monterey Peninsula across the bay. This sleepy community of 45,000 residents, along with 10,000 students, is spread out at the foot of thickly wooded mountains along a clean, sandy shore. There's not a lot to see in the town, almost all of which is within a ten-minute walk of the beach, apart from the many blocks of Victorian wooden houses.

The sluggish San Lorenzo River wraps around the town center, two blocks east of **Pacific Avenue**, a landscaped, prettified, and pedestrianized stretch that's Santa Cruz's main street, lined with bookstores, record and beachwear shops, and cafés. Disheveled hippies, trapped forever in their favorite decade, wander ceaselessly along the mall's length, brushing shoulders with wealthy shoppers who dodge occasionally into clothing and furniture stores. The homeless and the practically homeless cluster around park benches in the area, playing instruments, distributing literature, or simply dozing off.

One place that survived the massive 1989 earthquake, which damaged a large portion of the town, is the ornate brick-and-stone **Octagon Building**, 118 Cooper Street, at the north end of Pacific Avenue. Completed in 1882 as the Santa Cruz Hall of Records, it now houses a café. Adjacent is the **Museum of Art and History**, 705 Front Street (Tues–Sun 11am–5pm; $5, free first Fri of month; ℡831/429-1964, Ⓦwww.santacruzmah.org), with a sprightly display on the region's checkered history, plus a new sculpture garden and a rooftop gallery with great town views.

Several blocks away, past the clocktower fountain on Pacific and up Mission Street, **Santa Cruz Mission State Historic Park**, 144 School Street (Thurs–Sat 10am–4pm; free), displays fragments dating from the region's earlier Spanish colonial days in a restored army barracks. Around the corner is a half-scale replica of **Mission Santa Cruz**, 126 High Street (daily 9am–5pm; free; ℡831/426-5686, Ⓦwww.geocities.com/athens/aegean/7151/). The original adobe church, the sixteenth in the mission chain, was destroyed by an earthquake in 1857 and this replacement was built in the twentieth century.

Between the town center and the beach, **Beach Hill** rises at the foot of Pacific Avenue, its slopes lined with some of Santa Cruz's finest turn-of-the-century homes, such as the striking Queen Anne-style house at 417 Cliff Street, and the slightly odd structure around the corner at 912 3rd Street, constructed out of the remains of a shipwreck.

The beach, the boardwalk, and around

The **beach** closest to town, along the boardwalk, is wide and sandy, with lots of volleyball courts and water that's warm enough for swimming in summer. Not surprisingly, it can get crowded and rowdy, so for a bit more peace and quiet, or to catch the largest waves, simply follow the coastline east or west of town to one of the smaller beaches hidden away at the foot of the cliffs: most are undeveloped and easily accessible.

The main beach is dominated by the **Santa Cruz Boardwalk** (June–Aug open daily, fall and spring open Sat & Sun only, call for hours; closed Dec; $3–4.50 per ride, unlimited rides $29; ℡831/423-5590, Ⓦwww.beachboardwalk.com),

stretching half a mile along the sands. Packed with bumper cars, shooting galleries, log flume rides, and Ferris wheels, this is one of the last surviving beachfront amusement parks on the West Coast. Packed solid on weekends with teenagers on the prowl, most of the time it's a friendly funfair where barefoot hippies mix with farmers and their families. The newest ride is the 125-foot-tall Double Shot, which shoots riders in seconds from the ground to the top of its tower; but the star attraction is still the 80-year-old **Giant Dipper**, a wild wooden rollercoaster that's been ridden by more than 45 million people and is listed on the National Register of Historic Places; it often doubles for a Coney Island attraction in the movies. The boardwalk first

▲ Beach volleyball, Santa Cruz

opened in 1907 as a gambling casino:

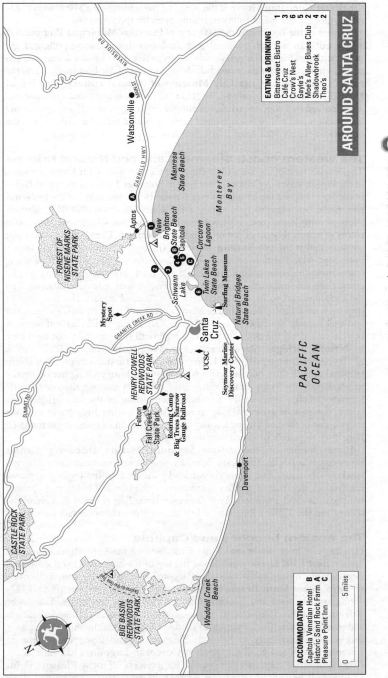

EATING & DRINKING

Bittersweet Bistro	1
Café Cruz	3
Crow's Nest	6
Gayle's	5
Moe's Alley Blues Club	2
Shadowbrook	4
Theo's	2

AROUND SANTA CRUZ

Watsonville

CABRILLO HWY

RIVERSIDE DR

MAIN ST

Monterey Bay

Manresa
State Beach

FOREST OF
NISENE MARKS
STATE PARK

Aptos

New
Brighton
State Beach

Capitola

Corcoran
Lagoon

Schwann
Lake

Twin Lakes
State Beach

Surfing Museum

Natural Bridges
State Beach

*PACIFIC
OCEAN*

Mystery
Spot

GRANITE CREEK RD

Santa
Cruz

UCSC

Seymour Marine
Discovery Center

HENRY COWELL
REDWOODS
STATE PARK

SUMMIT RD

Felton

Fall Creek
State Park

Roaring Camp
& Big Trees Narrow
Gauge Railroad

Davenport

CASTLE ROCK
STATE PARK

BIG BASIN
REDWOODS
STATE PARK

Skyline-to-the-Sea Trail

Waddell Creek
Beach

ACCOMMODATION

Capitola Venetian Hotel	B
Historic Sand Rock Farm	A
Pleasure Point Inn	C

N

0   5 miles

the elegant **Cocoanut Grove** at the west end has undergone a $10 million restoration, thought the grand ballroom is only open for special events.

Just west of the boardwalk, the 100-year-old wooden **Municipal Pier** juts half a mile out into the bay, crammed with fresh-fish shops, seafood grills, and gift stores, at the end of which people fish for crabs. You don't need a license and can rent tackle from one of the many bait shops. Just east of the boardwalk, across the river, the small **Santa Cruz City Museum of Natural History**, 1305 E Cliff Drive (Tues–Sun 10am–5pm; $2.50; ☏831/420-6115, ⓦwww.santacruzmuseums .org), marked by a concrete whale, has concise displays describing local animals and sea creatures, and a brief description of the local Native American culture with the opportunity to try your hand at grinding acorns in a mortar and pestle.

The western coast: Steamer Lane and Natural Bridges

The beaches west of the Santa Cruz Boardwalk, along **West Cliff Drive**, see some of the biggest waves in California, not least at **Steamer Lane**, off the tip of Lighthouse Point beyond the Municipal Pier. Cowell Beach, just north of the municipal pier, is the best place to give surfing a try; Club Ed (☏831/464-0177, ⓦwww .club-ed.com), in the parking lot, will rent boards and assist with lessons. Otherwise, plenty of surfers also gather just off Pleasure Point Beach. The ghosts of surfers past are animated at the tiny **Surfing Museum** (June–Aug daily except Tues 10am–5pm; Sept–May Thurs–Mon noon–4pm; $1 donation; ☏831/420-6289, ⓦwww .santacruzsurfingmuseum.org), in the old red-brick lighthouse building on the point; there are surfboards ranging from the twelve-foot redwood planks used by the early pioneers to modern, high-tech, multi-finned cutters. The best time to stop by is on a Friday, when Harry Mayo, a local surf pioneer, staffs the museum and will happily reminisce about the early days of the California surf scene. A bicycle path along the cliffs and the coast road both run two miles out from here to **Natural Bridges State Beach** (8am–dusk; $6 per car; ☏831/423-4609, ⓦwww.santsacruzstateparks.org). There's a $6 per car parking charge, but if you're prepared to walk three hundred yards you can usually leave your rig free on nearby streets. Beside the sandy beach, waves have cut holes through the coastal cliffs, forming delicate arches in the remaining stone; three of the four bridges after which the park was named have since collapsed, leaving large stacks of stone sticking out of the surf. The park is also famous for its annual gathering of monarch butterflies, thousands of which return each winter.

A mile further on, the cliff-top **Seymour Marine Discovery Center** (Tues–Sat 10am–5pm, Sun noon–5pm; $6; ⓦwww.seymourcenter.ucsc.edu) is a working laboratory that offers child-friendly insight into the region's undersea life through informative displays, windows into the labs, and touch tanks packed with sea stars and anemones. Free **tours** (at 1pm, 2pm & 3pm) go behind the scenes, and the 87-foot-long blue whale skeleton outside never fails to impress.

The eastern beaches and Capitola

Heading east from downtown Santa Cruz, beyond the City Museum and the harbor, **East Cliff Drive** winds along the top of the bluffs past many coves and estuaries. The nearest of the two coastal lagoons that border the volleyball courts of **Twin Lakes State Beach**, half a mile east at Seventh Avenue (☏831/427-4868), was dredged and converted into a marina in the 1960s. The other, **Schwann Lake**, is still intact, its marshy wetlands serving as a refuge for seabirds and migrating waterfowl. Twin Lakes is often warmer than the surrounding area, thanks to its proximity to Schwann Lagoon; beyond here, you'll come to **Lincoln Beach** and good tide pools at **Corcoran Lagoon**, a half-mile on.

East Cliff Drive continues past popular surfing spots off rocky **Pleasure Point** to the small beachfront resort of **Capitola**, its quiet conservativeness a sharp contrast with the alt-rock vibe of Santa Cruz. The town, three miles east of central Santa Cruz, began as a fishing village, living off the many giant tuna that populated the Monterey Bay, but soon became popular as a holiday spot with its own rail line. The large wooden trestle of the now-disused railroad still dominates what is now a moneyed town, rising over the soft and peaceful sands of **Hooper Beach**, west of the small fishing pier. Capitola is especially attractive in late summer, when the hundreds of begonias – the town's main produce – are in bloom; at any time of year, it's a relaxing escape from the rowdier Santa Cruz crowd. The **Chamber of Commerce**, 716-G Capitola Avenue (Mon–Fri 10am–4pm; ☎831/475-6522, ⓦwww.capitolachamber.com), has all the usual information.

Above Santa Cruz: UCSC and the mountains

The **University of California, Santa Cruz (UCSC)**, on the hills above the town (served by SCMTD bus #10 and others), is very much a product of the 1960s: until the early 2000s students didn't take exams or get grades, though the demands of grad schools have forced change. Still, the academic program continues to stress individual exploration of topics rather than rote learning. Architecturally, too, it's deliberately different. Its 2000-acre park-like campus is divided into small, autonomous colleges, where deer stroll among the redwood trees overlooking Monterey Bay – a decentralized plan drawn up under then-governor Ronald Reagan, which cynics claim was intended as much to diffuse protests as to provide a peaceful backdrop for study. You can judge for yourself by taking one of the free guided tours that start from the **visitor center** at the foot of campus (☎831/459-0111, ⓦwww.admissions.ucsc.edu/see/campustour). If you don't have time to visit the entire campus, at least stop by the **UCSC Arboretum** (daily 9am–5pm; free; ☎831/427-2998, ⓦwww2.ucsc.edu /arboretum), world-famous for its experimental cultivation techniques and its collections of plants from New Zealand, South Africa, Australia, and South America, all landscaped as they would be in their original habitats.

On the south side of the San Lorenzo River, three miles up Branciforte Drive from the center of town, there's a point within the woods where normal laws of gravity no longer apply. Here, trees grow at odd angles, pendulums swing counter-clockwise and balls roll uphill – and it's all thanks to the **Mystery Spot** (frequent 30-minute tours; Memorial Day to Labor Day daily 9am–7pm; Sept–May daily 9am–5pm; $5 per person plus $5 parking; ☎831/423-8897, ⓦwww.mysteryspot .com). The tours of this freaky, inexplicable place are hokey yet amusing; guides lead groups up and down the hill via a small toolshed that teeters on the edge of the hill, demonstrating in seven different ways how the laws of physics seem not to apply here. Much of the amusement's more reliant on canny perspective tricks than metaphysical skullduggery; it's a diverting treat even so, as guides posit the various theories about what caused the Mystery Spot, including everything from extraterrestrial interference to excess carbon dioxide seeping up from the earth.

High up in the mountains that separate Santa Cruz from Silicon Valley and the San Francisco Bay Area, SCMTD bus #35/35A (every 30min) runs to the village of **Felton**, six miles north of Santa Cruz on Hwy-9. This village is home to the **Roaring Camp Railroads** (parking $6; ☎831/335-4484, ⓦwww .roaringcamp.com), a depot based around buildings established here in the 1880s. The 100-year-old **Roaring Camp and Big Trees Narrow Gauge Railroad** (summer 1–3 daily; rest of year departures on most weekdays at 11am, Sat & Sun at 11am, 12.30pm & 2pm; $19) steams over trestle bridges on a six-mile run among the massive redwoods that cover the slopes of Bear Mountain, taking a little over an hour. From the same station the diesel-hauled, standard-gauge **Beach Train** (2 daily mid-June to mid-Aug plus weekends from late May to Sept; $21) powers down to the Santa Cruz Boardwalk and back in around two and a half hours.

The #35 bus (Sat & Sun 2 daily) continues further up the mountains to the **Big Basin Redwoods State Park** (dawn–dusk; $6 per vehicle; ☏831/338-8860, ⓦ www.santacruzstateparks.org), an hour's ride from Santa Cruz, where acres of 300-foot-tall redwood trees cover some 25 square miles of untouched wilderness, with excellent hiking and camping. The popular "Skyline-to-the-Sea" backpacking **trail** (12 miles one-way; 4hr; all downhill) steps down through cool, moist canyons ten miles to the coast, putting you fifteen miles north of Santa Cruz at Waddell Creek Beach (see p.480). From there, SCMTD bus #40 (2 daily) can take you back to town.

Eating

Restaurants in and around Santa Cruz are surprisingly diverse: from vegetarian cafés and all-American burger joints to elegant dining options, including a number of good seafood establishments on the wharf. The Wednesday-afternoon **Farmers' Market** downtown at the corner of Cedar and Lincoln, popular with local hippies, is a good place to pick up fresh produce.

Bittersweet Bistro 787 Rio Del Mar Blvd, Rio Del Mar ☏831/662-9799. Delicately prepared gourmet fish and pasta dishes for $15–20. Don't miss the beautifully presented desserts. Around five miles east of Santa Cruz along Hwy-1, but worth the trip.

Café Cruz 2621 41st Ave ☏831/476-3801. Tasty, reasonably priced Italian food in a Tuscan-inspired courtyard setting, inauspiciously located across from K-Mart. Delicious smoked chicken specials.

Charlie Hong Kong's 1141 Soquel Ave ☏831/426-5664. Small, pagoda-like hut with limited outdoor seating serving organic, mostly vegetarian noodle dishes for under $6.

Clouds Downtown 110 Church St ☏831/429-2000. Well-seasoned meats and Cal-Italian dishes in a pleasantly upbeat environment. The stuffed portobello mushrooms are especially good. Mains go for $16–25.

The Crêpe Place 1134 Soquel Ave ☏831/429-6994. Thirty-year local institution that serves bargain stuffed crêpes with savory and sweet fillings – try the Crêpe Gatsby, stuffed with pesto, mushrooms, feta, mozzarella, and chicken. The flower-filled, tumbleweed back garden is a groovy place to lounge on a warm summer evening.

Crow's Nest Santa Cruz Yacht Harbor, 2218 E Cliff Drive ☏831/476-4560. The modern American, fish-dominated menu here's tasty, if a little overpriced, but the real reason to come is for the spectacular views across the bay: eat dinner early and catch a fiery sunset. There's also a pub upstairs.

El Palomar 1336 Pacific Ave ☏831/425-7575. Don't be put off by the location (on the ground floor of a historic building that was once a resort hotel and now houses government-subsidized apartments). This midrange Mexican is probably the best in town, doing all the usual dishes well, plus several specialties with a fishy twist. Mains

$12–19. Assorted happy hour drinks Mon–Thurs 4–9pm.

Gayle's 504 Bay Ave, Capitola ☏831/462-1200. Ever-popular bakery and deli where you can sit in or out to tuck into freshly made sandwiches and wraps ($7), a huge range of salads (bought by weight), plus espresso coffee and delicious cakes such as the wonderful "crocodile," stuffed with pecans.

Saturn Café 145 Laurel St ☏831/429-8505. Wacky vegetarian diner set in a round building and decorated with red vinyl banquettes and Formica tables. There are burgers and sandwiches for $7.50–9, as well as specialties like vegan breakfasts with tofu ($6.50). It's open until 3am Sun–Thurs and 4am Fri & Sat, so it's a terrific option for late-night eats.

Shadowbrook 1750 Wharf Rd, Capitola ☏831/475-1511, ⓦ www.shadowbrook-capitola .com. The classic venue for a romantic dinner, this upscale steak and seafood place has mains costing $20–25, served on terraces which step down to the banks of a creek.

Taqueria Vallarta 1101A Pacific Ave ☏831/471-2655. It looks like a fast-food joint, but the large portions are cooked to order and authentic, and they even serve rice and tangy tamarind drinks. Don't be shy to ask for plenty of tortilla chips with your order – the self-service salsa bar has a delicious range to try. Everything is under $9.

Theo's 3101 N Main St, Soquel ☏831/462-3657. Upscale, anniversary-friendly restaurant with an all-organic menu, crisp white tablecloths, and hushed but attentive staff. In summer, many of the ingredients come from the owner's garden out back, while all fish and meats are from sustainable sources. A guilt-free gourmet treat (mains hover around $30) – just make sure to dress up.

Walnut Avenue Café 106 Walnut Ave ☎831/457-2307. This diner is a local favorite, dishing up massive breakfasts and lunches (sandwiches $7.50–9) only a block from Pacific Avenue Mall.

Cafés and nightlife

Santa Cruz has the Central Coast's rowdiest **nightlife**, ranging from coffee-houses to bars and nightclubs where the music varies from surf-thrash to reggae to rowdy rock, sometimes all on the same dance floor. For hanging out, your best bet is the range of espresso bars and coffeehouses lining Pacific Avenue; otherwise, we've listed a range of nightlife options – check with *Good Times* for the latest listings or pick up flyers at Streetlight Records, 939 Pacific Avenue (☎831/421-9200). The Rio Theatre, 1205 Soquel Avenue (☎831/423-8209, ⊛www.riotheatre.com), is a performance venue that focuses on an eclectic selection of live bands; for first-run foreign and indie films, head to the Del Mar, 1124 Pacific Avenue (☎831/469-3220, ⊛www.thenick.com), or Nickelodeon movie theaters, 210 Lincoln Street (☎831/426-7500, ⊛www.thenick.com).

99 Bottles of Beer 110 Walnut Ave ☎831/459-9999. This airy pub offers more than 40 beers on tap: the crowd's friendly and more mainstream than in many other local drinking holes. Great California burgers along with quiz, karaoke, and music nights.

The Asti 715 Pacific Ave ☎831/423-7337. Divey old-timers' cocktail lounge that now attracts Postmodern artsy types who enjoy its retro grittiness.

Blue Lagoon 923 Pacific Ave ☎831/423-7117, ⊛www.thebluelagoon.com. Lively bar and nightclub where good DJs spin anything from Top 40 to industrial (check the website for details). There are local live bands Wed and Fri, rarely a cover, and frequent early-evening drink specials.

Caffè Pergolesi 418A Cedar St ☎831/426-1775. Fun, friendly coffee-house in an old wooden villa with a garden. Open until around midnight. There's free Wi-Fi so it's often full of students hunched over laptops.

The Catalyst 1011 Pacific Ave ☎831/423-1336, ⊛www.catalystclub.com. The main venue for big-name touring artists and up-and-coming locals, this medium-sized club has something happening nearly every night. Usually 21 and over only; cover varies.

Club Dakota 1209 Pacific Ave ☎831/454-9030, ⊛www.clubdakota.net. Fun and fairly low-key dance club mainly playing house and hip-hop. There's a strong gay following, especially on Wed for women and Thurs for men. Open Mon–Fri 6pm–2am, Sat 4pm–2am, Sun 6pm to midnight.

Kuumbwa Jazz Center 320 Cedar St ☎831/427-2227, ⊛www.kuumbwajazz.org. The Santa Cruz showcase for traditional and modern jazz, in a friendly and intimate garden setting tucked back in a small alley. Mon and Thurs nights usually see big names like Chick Corea. Cover generally $10–25.

Moe's Alley Blues Club 1535 Commercial Way ☎831/479-1854, ⊛www.moesalley.com. Live entertainment nightly except Mon. Obviously blues is big, but also expect salsa, reggae, or just about anything else. Cover usually $10–20.

Soif 105 Walnut Ave ☎831/423-2020, ⊛www.soifwine.com. Young-professional hotspot, bathed in warm light with varnished wooden tables, serving small plates alongside more than fifty different wines by the glass. Live piano on Tues, jazz on Weds, and wine tasting Sat after-noons (3–5pm; $7).

Listings

Bicycle Rental Several places charge around $25 a day. Try Another Bike Shop, 2361 Mission Street (☎831/427-2232, ⊛www.anotherbikeshop.com), or Electric Sierra Cycles, 302 Pacific Avenue (☎1-877/372-8773, ⊛www.electricrecbikes.com).

Festivals The Santa Cruz Film Festival lasts ten days in late April (www.santacruzfilmfestival.com).

Internet Wired Wash Café (see below) has Wi-Fi and computers for $10/hr. Also at the library for $3/hr.

Kayak rental Venture Quest, on the wharf at 125 Beach Street (summer daily 10am–7pm; ☎831/427-2267, ⊛www.kayaksantacruz.com), rents sea kayaks for $25 for 3hr or $50 all day.

Laundry Wired Wash Café, 135 Laurel Street ☎831/429-9475. This handy laundromat,

espresso bar, and Internet café, open until midnight daily, also has a notice board detailing upcoming events.
Library 224 Church Street (Mon–Thurs 10am–9pm, Fri 10am–6pm, Sat 10am–5pm, Sun 1–5pm; ☎831/420-5700).
Post Office 850 Front Street (Mon–Fri 9am–5pm). Zip 95060.

The coast north to San Francisco

Heading eleven miles north from Santa Cruz along Hwy-1, the road mostly stays within sight of the coast until the former whaling town of **Davenport**, a blink-and-you'll-miss-it community that's home to the *Davenport Roadhouse*, 1 Davenport Avenue (☎831/426-8801, ⓦwww.davenportroadhouse.com; ⑥), a funky inn with small but tastefully decorated rooms. It sits above an excellent restaurant that specializes in transfat-free and organic dishes including wood-fired pizza, pasta, burgers, and chowders. It's decorated with local artworks and there's live folk, jazz, or blues most nights of the week and a roaring fire in winter.

Around seven miles north of Davenport, **Waddell Creek Beach** is the favorite spot for watching world-class windsurfers and kiteboarders negotiate the waves, and marks the end of the "Skyline-to-the-Sea" hike (see p.478).

The coast from here on – Año Nuevo State Reserve, Butano State Park, Half Moon Bay, and on into San Francisco – is covered in detail in Chapter Seven.

Travel details

Trains

LA to: Amtrak's Coast Starlight leaves at 10.15am for Oakland (1 daily; 11hr; a shuttle bus connects to San Francisco, stopping at Salinas (8hr 15min); San Jose (10hr 15min); San Luis Obispo (5hr 20min); Santa Barbara (2hr 30min); and continuing on through Sacramento, Chico, Redding, and Oregon to Seattle.
One train a day leaves Oakland at 8.50am on the return route.

Buses

All buses are Greyhound unless otherwise stated.

LA to: Salinas (5 daily; 8hr); San Francisco (14 daily; 8–12hr; also one Green Tortoise per week in each direction along the coast); San Luis Obispo (6 daily; 4–5hr); Santa Barbara (7 daily; 3hr); Santa Cruz (5 daily; 9–10hr).
Oakland to: Santa Cruz (4 daily; 2hr).
San Francisco to: LA (14 daily; 8–12hr); Salinas (6 daily; 2–4hr); San Luis Obispo (4 daily; 7hr); Santa Barbara (4 daily; 10hr); Santa Cruz (4 daily; 2hr 45min); San Jose (10 daily; 1hr 30min).
San Jose to: Santa Cruz (4 daily; 1hr).

San Francisco and the Bay Area

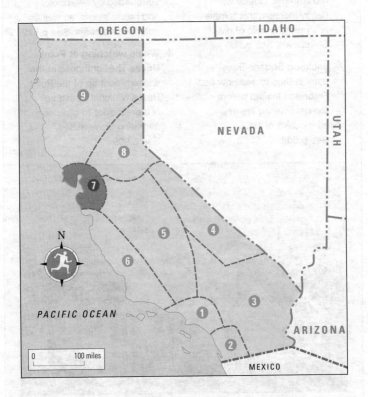

CHAPTER 7

Highlights

* **Cable cars** Famous for a good reason, these glorious old trams offer both irresistible photo opportunities and a leisurely way to avoid climbing Downtown San Francisco's heftiest hills. See p.500

* **Tien Hou temple, Chinatown** Festooned with gold and red lanterns, cloudy with heady incense, this temple is a precious relic of old Chinatown. See p.506

* **Jackson Square** Travel back in time to see how San Francisco looked before the devastating fire and earthquake of 1906. See p.508

* **Valencia Street** Check out the hipster artery of the Mission, where Anglo and Latino cultures collide. See p.525

* **University of California, Berkeley** The lively and attractive campus, renowned for political activism and scientific innovation, is surrounded by fine book and music stores, as well as eateries and cafés. See p.572

* **Whale watching at Point Reyes** The lighthouse at the westernmost tip of the Point Reyes National Seashore is a great spot to glimpse migrating gray whales. See p.609

▲ Painted Ladies, Alamo Square, San Francisco

San Francisco and the Bay Area

One of the prettiest and most liberal cities in the US – it certainly has had more platitudes heaped upon it than any other – **SAN FRANCISCO** is in serious danger of being clichéd to death. In the past three decades, though, the city has undergone a steady transition: the iconoclasm that made it famous has been glossed with a palpable air of affluence that's created a swanky, high-end town. One by one, the central neighborhoods have been smartened up, with poorer families edged out into the suburbs, leaving only a couple of areas that could still be considered transitional. Ironically, some of the groups who began on the margins, like the gay and lesbian community, are now wealthy and influential – even a little conservative.

For all the change, however, San Francisco remains an outdoorsy, surprisingly small city whose people pride themselves on being the cultured counterparts to their cousins in LA, as if this place were the last bastion of civilization on the lunatic fringe of America. A steadfast rivalry exists between the two cities: San Franciscans like to think of themselves as less obsessed with money, less riddled with status than those in the south – a rare kind of inverted snobbery, which Angelenos sniffily dismiss and which you'll detect almost immediately.

But San Francisco has its own narcissism, rooted in the sheer physical aspect of the place. Downtown streets lean upwards on impossible gradients to reveal stunning views of the city, the bay, and beyond. It has a romantic weather pattern, as blanket fogs roll in unexpectedly to envelop the city in mist, adding a surreal quality to an already unique appearance. This is not the California of monotonous blue skies – the temperatures rarely exceed the seventies, and even during summer they can drop much lower. Autumn is the best time to visit, as warm temperatures and cloudless skies fill the days of September and October.

San Francisco proper occupies just 48 hilly square miles at the tip of a slender peninsula, almost perfectly centered on the California coast. But its metropolitan area sprawls out far beyond these narrow confines, east and north across to the far sides of the San Francisco bay, and south back down the coastal strip. This is the **BAY AREA**, one of the most rapidly growing regions in the US: fewer than 750,000 people live in the actual city, but there are nearly seven million in the Bay Area as a whole. In the East Bay, across one of the two great bridges that connect San Francisco with its hinterland, are industrial **Oakland** and the

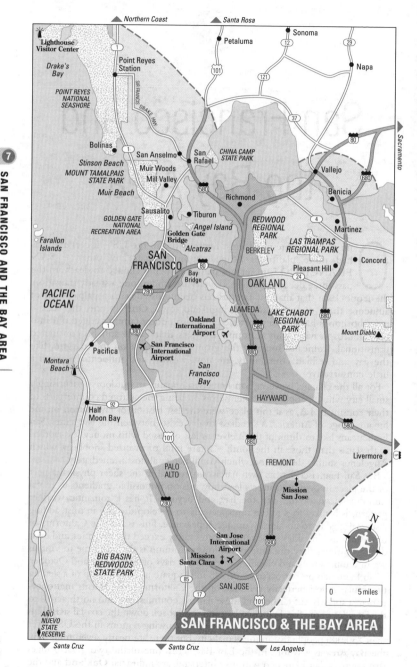

Lighthouse
Visitor Center

Drake's
Bay

POINT REYES
NATIONAL
SEASHORE

Point Reyes
Station

Bolinas

Stinson Beach
MOUNT TAMALPAIS
STATE PARK

Muir Beach

Sausalito

GOLDEN GATE
NATIONAL
RECREATION AREA

San Anselmo

Muir Woods

Mill Valley

Tiburon

Angel Island

San
Rafael

CHINA CAMP
STATE PARK

Richmond

Golden Gate
Bridge

Alcatraz

Farallon
Islands

PACIFIC
OCEAN

SAN
FRANCISCO

Bay
Bridge

Montara
Beach

Pacifica

San Francisco
International
Airport

Oakland
International
Airport

San
Francisco
Bay

Half
Moon Bay

REDWOOD
REGIONAL
PARK

BERKELEY

OAKLAND

ALAMEDA

LAKE CHABOT
REGIONAL
PARK

HAYWARD

Sonoma

Petaluma

Napa

Vallejo

Benicia

Martinez

LAS TRAMPAS
REGIONAL PARK

Concord

Pleasant Hill

Mount Diablo

Sacramento ▶

PALO
ALTO

BIG BASIN
REDWOODS
STATE PARK

AÑO
NUEVO
STATE
RESERVE

FREMONT

Mission
San Jose

Livermore

San Jose
International
Airport

Mission
Santa Clara

SAN JOSE

N

0   5 miles

SAN FRANCISCO & THE BAY AREA

radical locus of **Berkeley**; while to the south lies the gloating new wealth of **the Peninsula**, known as "Silicon Valley" for the multi-billion-dollar computer industries that wiped out the agriculture which dominated as recently as thirty years ago. Across the Golden Gate Bridge to the north, **Marin County** contains some of the Bay Area's wealthiest suburbs, its woody, leafy landscape and rugged coastline a bucolic – though in places very chic – harbinger of the delights of California's earthy northern coast.

San Francisco

A compact and highly approachable place of some four dozen or so hills by the bay, San Francisco is one of the few US cities where you can survive comfortably without a car. Indeed, given how expensive and time-consuming parking can be – not to mention how agreeable the city's year-round climate is – walking is the ideal daytime mode for taking in the renowned museums, stately Victorian homes, sophisticated and historic neighborhoods, and stirring hilltop vistas. After dark, San Francisco is quite safe for visitors exercising reasonable caution; it's best known for its astonishing assortment of first-class restaurants and its vibrant nightlife, both gay and straight.

Some history

The original inhabitants of San Francisco were **Ohlone Indians**, who lived in roughly 35 villages spread out around the bay. In 1776, **Mission Dolores**, the sixth in the chain of Spanish Catholic missions that ran the length of California, was established; harsh mission life, combined with the spread of European diseases, killed off the natives within a few generations. Mexicans took over from the Spanish in the early 1820s, but their hold was tenuous, and the area finally came under American rule after the **Bear Flag Revolt** of 1846, which took place around fifty miles north of San Francisco in Sonoma. The bloodless coup was supported by local land-owning *alcaldes* (a hybrid of judge and mayor), who recognized the land's huge economic potential. The coup brought US Marines, sailing on the USS *Portsmouth*, into the San Francisco Bay that year, prompting one soldier, John Fremont, to christen its spectacular entrance the "**Golden Gate**." The Marines docked their boat at the tiny town plaza founded in 1835 by British sailor William Richardson and renamed it **Portsmouth Square**, raising an American flag and claiming the city for the United States. The following year, the hamlet known as Yerba Buena was rechristened San Francisco, honoring the dying wish of Father Junípero Serra, the Franciscan founder of Mission Dolores.

Just over ten years later, in 1848, San Francisco's population exploded when pioneer Sam Brannan bounded across Portsmouth Square waving bottles of gold dust he claimed came from the Sierra foothills, thereby igniting the **Gold Rush**. Within a year, fifty thousand pioneers had arrived from all over the country as well as overseas, especially China, turning San Francisco from a muddy village and wasteland of dunes into a thriving supply center and transit town. By the time the **transcontinental railroad** was completed in 1869, San

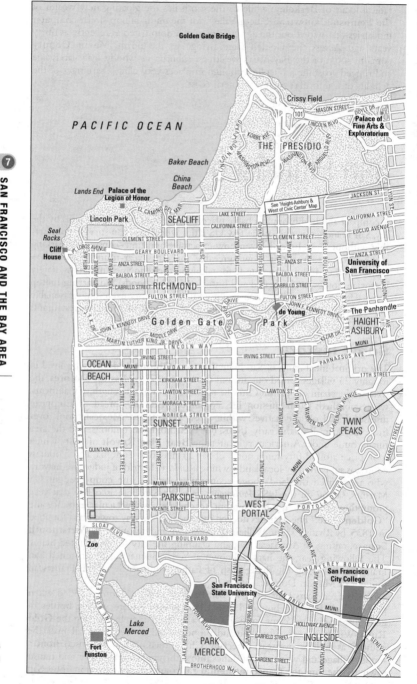

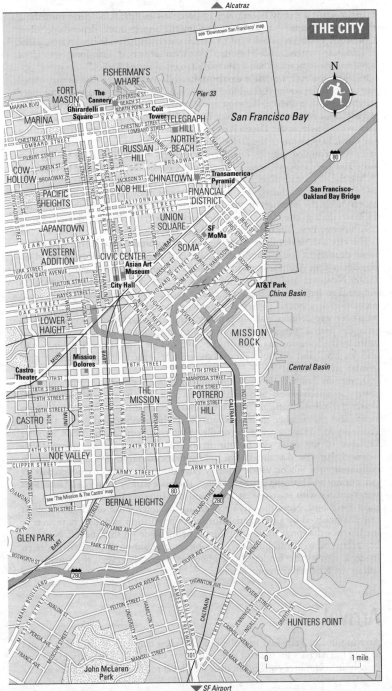

Francisco was a rowdy boomtown of bordellos and drinking dens, something the moneyed elite – who hit it big on the much more dependable silver Comstock Lode – worked hard to mend, constructing wide boulevards, parks, a cable-car system, and elaborate Victorian redwood mansions, the latter replacing the whores as San Francisco's famed "Painted Ladies."

In 1906, however, a massive **earthquake**, followed by three days of fire, wiped out most of the town. Rebuilding began immediately, resulting in a city more magnificent than before, drawing anew writers, artists, and free spirits. In the decades that followed, authors like Dashiell Hammett and Jack London lived and worked here, as did Diego Rivera and other WPA-sponsored artists. During the Great Depression of the 1930s, San Francisco's position as the nexus of trade with Asia, coupled with its engineering projects – including both the Golden Gate and Bay bridges – lessened the agonies of the Depression for its residents. While the strict anti-immigration laws against the Chinese and the internment of Japanese citizens during World War II remains in memory, people here prefer to canonize the exploits of the Beat Generation in North Beach and Cow Hollow during the 1950s and the message of the hippies during 1967's "Summer of Love" in the Haight-Ashbury neighborhood.

The city also prides itself on being the **gay capital** of the world: one of the most prominent local democratic politicians is openly gay former stand-up comedian Tom Ammiano; and the current mayor, the toothy and photogenic Gavin Newsom, made national headlines in 2004 as the first elected official in America to legalize gay weddings, albeit abortively. San Francisco basks in its reputation as a liberal oasis and a model of tolerance – there's nowhere you won't see gay couples walking proudly hand in hand, for instance. But it also struggles with a certain smugness thanks to that self-consciously open-minded attitude: the local mantra seems to be "live and let live" rather than "live with and let live," and different groups are tribally separated along lines of race, gender, and sexuality.

Despite its boldface fame as the hub of counterculture, San Francisco has always meant business and wealth, evinced today by a walk through the skyscraper-filled Financial District. Exquisite restaurants, art museums, designer malls, and the further gentrification of neighborhoods point to a thriving economy. San Francisco was the cradle of Internet mania in the 1990s, another example of the city's eye for the main chance – for a while many locals worried that one day they'd live in "SanFrancisco.com," a soulless bedroom community for Silicon Valley. Tenancy rates throughout the city hovered at 99 percent full and housing prices rocketed: the once shabby South of Market area was bursting with start-ups, at least until the Internet bubble itself burst and most went bust. Now the city's reclaiming a calmer sense of self, although it remains troubled by a substantial **homeless** population and local bureaucratic inefficiency that prevents much progress being made on their behalf. Newsom has promised to battle both these problems, and although progress has been made, a visit to the Tenderloin neighborhood quickly reveals the situation is still in need of major improvement.

Arrival

Arriving in San Francisco isn't the trafficky mess that finding your way in and around Los Angeles for the first time can prove. Of course, as in every major city, rush-hour commuter congestion does clog local roadways, but San Francisco's a place that firmly believes in public transport; and especially if you're touching down at either Bay Area airport, the journey into the city proper is usually quick and painless.

By plane

All international and most domestic flights arrive at **San Francisco International Airport** (SFO), located about fifteen miles south of the city (☎650/821-8211or 1-800/435-9736, ⑩www.flysfo.com). There are several ways of getting into town from here, each of which is clearly signed from the baggage-reclaim areas. The best option's the BART link: the effortless thirty-minute journey whisks you from the airport to the heart of downtown for only $5.15 (⑩www .bart.gov) and leaves every fifteen to twenty minutes. Otherwise, the SFO Airporter bus ($15) makes pick ups outside each baggage-claim area every thirty minutes; the only snag is that it just serves major hotels downtown – look for signs saying "Airporter" on the lower Arrivals level. The SuperShuttle and American Airporter Shuttle, along with other **minibuses**, depart every five minutes or so on the Departures/Ticketing level from the center island of the circular road and take passengers to any city-center destination for around $16 a head. They're signposted on the lower Arrivals level as "Door to Door Vans." **Taxis** from the airport cost $35–45 (plus tip) for any downtown location, more for East Bay and Marin County – definitely worth it if you're in a group or too tired to care. If you plan to rent a car, take the convenient AirTrain's Blue Line (24hr; free) to the **car rental** agencies' depots. Driving from SFO, head north on gritty US-101 for the twenty-to-thirty-minute drive downtown.

Several domestic airlines fly into **Oakland International Airport** (OAK; see p.560 for details), across the bay. Not quite as convenient to downtown San Francisco as SFO, OAK is nonetheless efficiently connected with the city by the $3 AirBART shuttle bus, which drops you at the Coliseum/Oakland Airport BART station. Get on BART and San Francisco's downtown stops are fifteen minutes away ($3.35).

Festivals in San Francisco

Like most major cities, San Francisco has a huge range of special festivals – the biggest of which are detailed below (for gay-and-lesbian-geared events, see box, p.553). Note that hotels and hostels will book up quickly during most of these festivals, especially Pride (see p.553), so plan ahead.

Chinese New Year ☎415/982-3071, ⑩www.chineseparade.com. End of Jan or early Feb. A month-long celebration around the lunar New Year, which culminates in the Golden Dragon Parade headed by the namesake 201-foot-long dragon.

Cherry Blossom Festival ☎415/563-2313, ⑩www.nccbf.org. Late April. The normally sedate Japantown's transformed into a riot of life and rowdy parades for two consecutive weekends; it culminates in a parade from Civic Center.

Bay to Breakers ☎415/359-2800. Third Sun in May. Only in San Francisco: this kooky, campy fun-run is a 12-kilometer footrace from the Embarcadero to Ocean Beach. But it's the costumes, not the contest, that really count here – it's also known for a sizeable contingent of nude joggers.

Halloween Oct 31. Wild fun is guaranteed during this holiday, although incidents of violence have soured the festivities a bit in recent years; dress up and watch the parade along Market Street – or better still, just hang out in the Castro for the evening to catch the best of the stuff-strutting.

By bus, train, and car

All of San Francisco's **Greyhound** services use the Transbay Terminal at 425 Mission Street, near the Embarcadero BART station in the South of Market (SoMa) neighborhood. Green Tortoise buses stop behind the Transbay Terminal on First and Natoma. Amtrak **trains** stop across the bay in Oakland, from where free Thruway shuttle buses run across the Bay Bridge to the Transbay Terminal; you can also take BART. An efficient alternative is to get off the train at Richmond, where a transfer to the nearby BART station can get you into San Francisco more quickly.

From the east, the main route **by car** into San Francisco is I-80, which runs via Sacramento all the way from Chicago. I-5, fifty miles east of San Francisco, serves as the main north–south route, connecting Los Angeles with Seattle. From I-5, I-580 takes you to the Bay Area. US-101 also runs the length of

Walking tours

A great way to get to know the quieter, historical side of San Francisco is to take a **walking tour**. The better ones keep group size small and are run by natives who truly love their subject matter and jobs. Some, like those sponsored by the library, are free. Reservations are recommended for all walks. The Visitor Information Center can give you a full list of available walks – every neighborhood has at least one – but do consider the following guides:

City Guides (ⓣ415/557-4266, ⓦwww.sfcityguides.com). A terrific free series sponsored by the library and covering every San Francisco neighborhood, also offering themed walks on topics ranging from the Gold Rush to the Beat Generation. Its wide-ranging subject matter means you'll often be trekking alongside locals instead of fellow tourists. Schedule varies – call for details.

Cruisin' the Castro (ⓣ415/255-1821, ⓦwww.webcastro.com/castrotour). Founded by the grand dame of San Francisco walks, Ms Trevor Hailey, the tour explains how and why San Francisco became the gay capital of the world. It's as much a history lesson as a sightseeing tour. $35 per person.

Haight-Ashbury Flower Power Walking Tour (Tues & Sat 9.30am; ⓣ415/863-1621, ⓦwww.hippiegourmet.com). Learn about the Human Be-in, Grateful Dead, Summer of Love, and also the Haight's distant past as a Victorian resort destination. $20 per person.

HobNob Tours (Mon–Fri 10am & 1.30pm; ⓣ650/814-6303; ⓦwww.hobnobtours .com). Terrific, information-crammed ramble round the haunts of Silver Kings and Robber Barons, mostly in and around Grace Cathedral. Highly recommended. $30 per person.

Mangia! North Beach (Sat 10am; ⓣ415/925-9013, ⓔgaw@sbcglobal.net). Culinary tour of North Beach's Italian nooks, run by larger-than-life local food writer GraceAnn Walden. $80 including lunch.

Mission Mural Walk (Sat & Sun 11am & 1.30pm; ⓣ415/285-2287, ⓦwww.precitaeyes .org). Two-hour presentation by mural artists leads around the Mission neighborhood's outdoor paintings. $10–12 per person.

Victorian Home Walk (daily 11am; ⓣ415/252-9485, ⓦwww.victorianwalk.com). Leisurely tour through Pacific Heights, where you'll learn to tell the difference between a Queen Anne, Italianate, and Stick-Style Vic. $20 per person for a 2.5-hour tour. Meet in Union Square at Powell and Post streets.

Wok Wiz Tours (daily 10am; ⓣ650/355-9657, ⓦwww.wokwiz.com). A walk through Chinatown run by chef-writer Shirley Fong-Torres and her team. Plenty of anecdotes but a little thin on historical information. $28 per person, $40 per person including lunch.

California from north to south, but if you have time and a tolerance of winding roads, take Hwy-1, the stunningly scenic Pacific Coast Highway, which traces the edge of California.

Information

The **San Francisco Visitor Information Center**, on the lower level of Hallidie Plaza at the end of the cable-car line on Market Street (Mon–Fri 9am–5pm, Sat & Sun 9am–3pm; closed Sun Nov–April; ☎415/391-2000, Ⓦwww.sfvisitor.org), has free maps of the city and the Bay Area, oodles of pamphlets on hotels and restaurants, and can help with lodging and travel plans. Its free *San Francisco Book* and *Visitors Planning Guide* provide detailed, if somewhat selective, information about accommodation, entertainment, exhibitions, and stores. The center also sells the **City Pass** ($54, $39 for ages 5–17; Ⓦwww.citypass.net), a half-price ticket valid for entry to the Exploratorium, California Palace of the Legion of Honor, de Young Museum, Steinhart Aquarium and Academy of Sciences, Asian Art Museum, and Museum of Modern Art, and passage on a Blue and Gold Fleet San Francisco Bay cruise – all that, plus a week's pass on MUNI transit (see below).

The city's several **newspapers** are indispensable sources of information. Two dailies have competed for decades – the *Chronicle* (Ⓦwww.sfgate.com) and the *Examiner* (Ⓦwww.examiner.com). Although neither paper is considered among the better US dailies, both are handy for getting up to speed on life in the Bay Area. For comprehensive arts and food listings, check the *Chronicle's* Thursday edition supplement, "96Hours," a four-day weekend entertainment guide, and the Sunday edition's *Datebook*, which contains previews and reviews for the coming week. The city's alternative press picks up the slack the more conservative dailies leave behind, resulting in two fine free weekly papers, *The Bay Guardian* (Ⓦwww.sfbg.com) and *SF Weekly* (Ⓦwww.sfweekly.com), available from streetside boxes around town. Both offer in-depth features on local life and better music and club listings than the dailies. **Online**, check out Ⓦwww.sfstation.com for the best of the many websites that cover the Bay Area.

City transportation

San Francisco is a rare American city where you don't need a car to see everything. The **public transportation** system, MUNI, though much maligned by locals for its unpredictable schedule, covers every neighborhood inexpensively via a system of cable cars, buses, and streetcars. **Cycling** is a good option, though you'll need strong legs to tackle those hills. **Walking** the compact downtown is still the best bet, with each turn revealing surprises.

Muni

The city's public transportation system is known as the San Francisco Municipal Railway, or most commonly **Muni**, and run by the San Francisco Municipal Transportation Agency (☎311, Ⓦwww.sfmta.com). A comprehensive network of buses, trolleys, and cable cars run up and over the city's hills,

Main MUNI routes

Useful bus routes

#5 From the Transbay Terminal, west alongside Haight-Ashbury and Golden Gate Park to the ocean.

#7 From the Ferry Building (Market Street) to the end of Haight Street and to Golden Gate Park.

#15 From Third Street (SoMa) to Pier 39, Fisherman's Wharf, via the Financial District and North Beach.

#20 (Golden Gate Transit) From Civic Center to the Golden Gate Bridge.

#22 From the Marina up Pacific Heights and north on Fillmore.

#28 & #29 From the Marina through the Presidio, north through Golden Gate Park, the Richmond, and Sunset.

#30 From the CalTrain depot on Third Street, north to Ghirardelli Square, via Chinatown and North Beach, and out to Chestnut Street in the Marina neighborhood.

#38 From Geary Street via Civic Center, west to the ocean along Geary Boulevard through Japantown and the Richmond, ending at Cliff House.

MUNI train lines

MUNI F-Market Line Restored vintage trolleys from around the world run downtown from the Transbay Terminal up Market Street and into the heart of the Castro. The

while the underground trains become streetcars when they emerge from the downtown metro system to split off and serve the outlying neighborhoods. On buses and trains the flat fare (correct change only) is $1.50; with each ticket you buy, ask for a transfer – good for travel on any Muni vehicle (except cable cars) within ninety minutes to two hours of purchase. Even if you don't plan on transferring, hang onto the slip of paper as it serves as proof that you've paid your fare. Note that cable cars cost $5 one way, with an all-day pass available for $10.

The best option if you're in town for a while is to buy a Muni **Passport pass**, available in one-day, three-day, and seven-day denominations ($11, $18, $24). It's valid for unlimited travel on the Muni system and on BART (see below) within the city limits. A Fast pass costs $45 for a full calendar month and also offers unlimited travel within the city limits. Most Muni trains and buses run throughout the night on a limited service. For more information, pick up the handy Muni map ($3) from the Visitor Information Center or bookstores.

BART and other train services

Along Market Street downtown, Muni shares station concourses with **BART** (Bay Area Rapid Transit; ☎415/989-2278, ⓦwww.bart.gov), which is the fastest way to get to the East Bay – including downtown Oakland and Berkeley – and outer suburbs east and south of San Francisco. Tickets aren't cheap ($1.40–6.30 depending on how far you ride), but the trains feature five routes that follow a fixed schedule, usually arriving every ten minutes. Trains run from 4am weekdays, 6am Saturdays, 8am Sundays until midnight, and tickets can be purchased on the station concourse; save your ticket after entering the station, as it is also needed when exiting the train. Free schedules are available at BART stations.

The CalTrain commuter railway (depot at Fourth and Townsend, South of Market) links San Francisco south to San Jose and is a fine option if you're new extension along the refurbished Embarcadero to Fisherman's Wharf is one of MUNI's most popular routes.

MUNI J-Church Line From downtown to Mission and the edge of the Castro.

MUNI K-Ingleside Line From downtown through the Castro to Balboa Park.

MUNI L-Taraval Line West from downtown through the Sunset to the zoo and Ocean Beach.

MUNI M-Ocean View West from downtown, by the Stonestown Galleria shopping center and San Francisco State University.

MUNI N-Judah Line From the CalTrain station, past the new baseball stadium, along South Beach to downtown and west through the Inner Sunset to Ocean Beach.

Cable car routes

California Street From the foot of California Street at Robert Frost Plaza in the Financial District through Nob Hill to Polk Street.

Powell-Hyde From Powell Street/Market along Hyde through Russian Hill to Fisherman's Wharf.

Powell-Mason From Powell Street/Market along Mason via Chinatown and North Beach to Fisherman's Wharf.

traveling along the Peninsula beyond the final BART stop at Millbrae; call ☏1-800/660-4287 or visit ⓦwww.caltrain.com for schedules and fares.

Driving: taxis and cars

Taxis ply the streets but, while you can flag them down (especially downtown), finding one can be difficult. You can instead schedule one by phone: try DeSoto (☏415/970-1300), Luxor (☏415/282-4141), or Yellow Cab (☏415/333-3333, ⓦwww.yellowcabsf.com).

The only reason to **rent a car** in San Francisco is if you want to explore the Bay Area, the Wine Country, or the landscape north or south along the coast. Driving in town, pay attention to San Francisco's attempts to control downtown traffic: the posted speed limit is 30mph, speeding through a yellow light is illegal, and pedestrians waiting in a crosswalk have the right of way. In addition, it's almost impossible to make a left turn anywhere in the city center because of one-way streets, meaning you'll have to get used to looping the block, making three rights instead of one left. Cheap, available parking is even rarer than a left-turn arrow, but it's worth playing by the rules: police issue multiple tickets for illegally parked vehicles and won't hesitate to tow your car if it's violating any posted laws. Downtown, plenty of garages exist, many advertising rates beginning at $2.50 per hour. Take care to observe the San Francisco law of curbing wheels – turn wheels into the curb if the car points downhill and away from the curb if it points up; violators are subject to a $35 ticket. Bridge tolls are collected only when entering San Francisco by car: the Golden Gate Bridge toll costs $5, while the Bay Bridge runs $4.

Cycling

Cycling is a great way to experience San Francisco. Golden Gate Park, the Marina and Presidio, and Ocean Beach all have excellent paved trails and some off-road routes. Throughout the city, marked bike routes – with lanes – direct

▲ Golden Gate Bridge

riders to all major points of interest, but note that officials picked the routes for their lack of car traffic, not for the easiest ride. Blazing Saddles, which rents bicycles, has several locations ($28 per day; ☎415/202-8888, ⓦwww .blazingsaddlessanfrancisco. com) – two of the most convenient are 1095 Columbus Avenue at Francisco in North Beach, and Pier 41. Another option, with similar rates, is Bike and Roll, 899 Columbus Avenue (☎415/229-2000, ⓦwww.bikerental.com). For a tranquil trek through undeveloped nature, head north over the Golden Gate Bridge (the western side is reserved solely for bikes) into the Marin Headlands for a series of off-road trails along cliffs, ocean, and into valleys (see p.602); alternatively, ride across the bridge to quaint Sausalito (see p.603) and catch a ferry back to the city.

Organized tours

One way to orient yourself is an **organized tour**. Gray Line Tours (☎1-888/428-6937, ⓦwww.graylinesanfrancisco .com) putters along for a fairly tedious three and a half hours for $44 a head; there are also deals that combine city stops with Muir Woods and Sausalito, as well as tours of Monterey, the Wine Country, and Yosemite. Considerably more exciting is El Camión Mexicano, the Mexican Bus Tour ($38; call for itineraries and reservations; ☎415/546-3747, ⓦwww .mexicanbus.com) through the Mission, which takes in local salsa clubs for drinking and dancing.

For breathtaking views of the bay, join a chilly 75-minute cruise with the Blue & Gold Fleet (☎415/773-1188, ⓦwww.blueandgoldfleet.com) from Pier 39 and Pier 41 – though be warned that everything may be shrouded in fog, making the price ($21) a little excessive. Undoubtedly the most impressive – and expensive – tours are aerial: the best operator is San Francisco Helicopter Tours (☎1-800/400-2404, ⓦwww.sfhelicoptertours.com), which offer a variety of spectacular flights over the Bay Area beginning at $140 per passenger for a twenty-minute flight.

For information on guided walking tours, see the box on p.490.

Accommodation

Full-time residents of San Francisco complain constantly about skyrocketing rents, and it's no different for the visitor. Expect accommodation to cost around $100 per night in a reasonable hotel or motel, slightly less out of season. We've listed some smart bargains below (some as cheap as $50 a night in the low season), but if you want to snag one of these cheaper rooms, it's essential to call around and book ahead.

San Francisco Reservations (℡510/628-4450 or 1-800/677-1570, ⓦwww.hotelres.com) can find you a room from around $100 for a double, and the Visitor Information Center (℡415/391-2000, ⓦwww.sfvisitor.org) can provide details on the latest accommodation options.

For **B&Bs**, the city's fastest-growing source of accommodation, contact a specialist agency such as Bed and Breakfast San Francisco (Mon–Fri 9am–5.30pm; ℡415/899-0060, ⓦwww.bbsf.com). If funds are tight, look into one of the many excellent **hostels** (see p.498), where beds start at around $25. Specifically gay and lesbian accommodation is listed on p.552; there are some mixed gay-straight places, too, which we've included here.

Hotels, motels, and B&Bs

Downtown and Union Square

See map on pp.502–503.

Adagio 550 Geary St at Jones, Theater District ℡1-800/228-8830, ⓦwww.jdvhospitality.com. The decor at this hotel echoes its ornate Spanish Revival facade with deep reds and ochres, and the large rooms are well appointed with all mod cons. The *Adagio* also provides high-speed Internet access and even free printing facilities. ❼

Clift 495 Geary St at Taylor, Theater District ℡1-800/697-1791, ⓦwww.morganshotelgroup.com. The old-school *Clift Hotel* is yet another postmodern Ian Schrager-Philippe Starck conversion. The rooms ($375 and up) are vaguely oriental and vintage Starck, with quirky touches like the Louis XIV-style chairs with mirrors on the seat and back, and sleigh beds. ❾

Golden Gate Hotel 775 Bush St at Mason, Union Square ℡1-800/835-1118, ⓦwww.goldengatehotel.com. Friendly European-style B&B with cozy, warmly furnished rooms, some with shared bathrooms (❹). Beautiful original iron elevator. ❻

Grant Hotel 753 Bush St at Mason, Union Square ℡1-800/522-0979, ⓦwww.granthotel.net. A good deal for its location, this hotel has small but clean rooms, overpowered a little by the relentlessly maroon carpets. Basic but convenient. ❷

Hotel Diva 440 Geary at Mason, Union Square ℡1-800/553-1900. A block from Union Square, this good-value boutique hotel has spacious rooms with cobalt carpeting and modern stylings, as well as a complimentary business center and a handful of Internet lounges decorated by local designers. The colorful "little divas" suite is an added bonus for families, with a karaoke machine, a drawing table, and a trunk stuffed with feather boas, hats, and jewelry. ❻

Mark Hopkins InterContinental One Nob Hill Circle, Nob Hill ℡415/392-3434, ⓦwww.markhopkins.net. Grand, castle-like hotel that was once the chic choice of writers and movie stars: it's more corporate these days in both clientele and design. All rooms are identical, but rates rise as the floors do. The *Top of the Mark* rooftop bar has one of the best views in town. ❾

Monaco 501 Geary St at Taylor, Union Square ℡1-866/622-5284, ⓦwww.monaco-sf.com. Quirky boutique hotel, part of a small national chain, that's housed in a historic Beaux Arts building. There are canopied beds in each room, and the rest of the decor's equally riotous, colorful, and a little over the top. Ask about the complimentary goldfish. ❽

Orchard Hotel 665 Bush St at Powell, Union Square ℡1-888/717-2881, ⓦwww.theorchardhotel.com. A little-known gem, this hotel's rates are lower than its ample amenities would suggest: every room has a DVD player with free movies on loan, free breakfast, and larger-than-average rooms, decorated like a clubby study in dark teak woods and striped fabrics. ❽

The Phoenix 601 Eddy St at Larkin, Tenderloin ℡1-800/248-9466, ⓦwww.jdvhotels.com. This raucous retro motel conversion is a favorite with up-and-coming bands when they're in town. There's a small pool, and the 44 rooms are eclectically decorated in tropical colors with changing local artwork on the walls – ask for the "Tour Manager Room," which has a fridge, fax, and microwave. ⑤

The Renoir 45 McAllister St at Seventh, Civic Center ☏ 1-800/576-3388, ⓦ www.renoirhotel .com. This wedge-shaped building is a landmark. The superior rooms cost $20 more than standard – worth the extra if you can snag one of the oddly shaped large ones at the building's apex. Especially popular during Gay Pride for its Market Street views along the parade route. ⑤

Sir Francis Drake 450 Powell St at Sutter, Union Square ☏ 1-800/795-7129, ⓦ www .sirfrancisdrake.com. The lobby here's a hallucinogenic evocation of all things heraldic: it's crammed with faux British memorabilia, chandeliers, and drippingly ornate gold plasterwork. Thankfully, the rooms are calmer, with a gentle apple-green color scheme and full facilities. The hotel's known for its classic bar *Harry Denton's Starlight Room* on the 21st floor. ❼

Triton 342 Grant Ave at Bush, Union Square ☏ 1-800/800-1299, ⓦ www.hotel-tritonsf.com. Trippy, eco-friendly hotel that offers modern amenities like a 24-hour gym and Nintendo, as well as weirder services like nightly tarot-card readings and a round-the-clock yoga channel. The rooms themselves are stylish but gaudy, painted in rich, clashing colors and plenty of gold. ❼

Westin St Francis 335 Powell St at Sutter, Union Square ☏ 1-866/500-0338, ⓦ www .westinstfrancis.com. This historic hotel has a sumptuous lobby, four restaurants and lounges, a fitness center, and a spa. The rooms in the historic main building, which dates to the early 1900s, have high ceilings and chandeliers, while those in the tower are contemporary and have views across the city. It's worth entering the lobby to see the famous clock, ornate ceiling, painting of Queen Elizabeth amidst American celebs, and the steps where President Gerald Ford almost met his end from a would-be assassin's bullet. ❼

SoMa

See map on pp.502–503 for locations.

Four Seasons 757 Market St at Third ☏ 415/633-3000, ⓦ www.fourseasons.com. Sparkling hotel with spectacular views across the city: its plush rooms ($480 and up) are the ultimate indulgence, from the soft, luxurious comforters to the standalone two-person shower stocked with Bulgari beauty products. There's an enormous on-site health club with a pool and vast gym that's free to guests. The place to stay if you win the lottery or someone else is paying. ❾

Hotel Griffon 155 Steuart St at Mission ☏ 1-800/321-2201, ⓦ www.hotelgriffon.com. Secluded hotel close to the waterfront: rooms are elegant and understated, with exposed brick walls, window seats, wireless Internet and flat-screen TVs, and refrigerator. ❼

🏃 **Hotel Vitale** 8 Mission St, Embarcadero ☏ 1-888/890-8688. Steps from the Ferry Building, this boutique newcomer boasts 199 elegant contemporary rooms ($300 and up), many with bay views, and an on-site spa with rooftop soaking tubs. The bar at the *Americano* restaurant is a happy-hour favorite of the downtown crowd, with patio seating along the Embarcadero. ❾

The Mosser 54 Fourth St at Market ☏ 1-800/227-3804, ⓦ www.themosser.com. This hotel is a funky conversion fusing Victorian touches like ornamental molding with mod leather sofas. The chocolate-and-olive rooms may be tiny but each is artfully crammed with amenities including multidisc CD players. There's even an on-site recording studio. Shared bath ❹, en suite ❼

Palace Hotel 2 New Montgomery St at Market ☏ 415/512-1111, ⓦ www.sfpalace.com. Hushed, opulent landmark building, known for its fabulous, historic Garden Court tearoom: the grand lobby and corridors are mismatched with rooms that are small for the sky-high prices ($389 and up), decorated in lush golds and greens like an English country house. Stay here for snob value rather than good value. ❾

North Beach and Chinatown

See map on pp.502–503 for locations.

Argonaut 495 Jefferson St at Hyde, Fisherman's Wharf ☏ 1-866/415-0704, ⓦ www.argonauthotel .com. This nautical-themed hotel in the Cannery complex has large, lush, blue-and-gold rooms that feature flat-screen TVs, DVD players, stereos, and impressive views. Surprisingly quiet for its location. ❾

Baldwin Hotel 321 Grant Ave at Bush, Chinatown ☏ 1-800/622-5394, ⓦ www.baldwinhotel.com. Surprisingly quiet, given its hub location in the heart of Chinatown, the *Baldwin*'s rooms are oatmeal and taupe, outfitted in neutral colors with simple furnishings and ceiling fans. Rooms are rented weekly out of season, so negotiate hard if you're staying fewer than seven nights. ❾ per week, ❹ per night

Boheme 444 Columbus Ave at Vallejo, North Beach ☏ 415/433-9111, ⓦ www.hotelboheme.com. Smack in the middle of Beat heartland, this small,

15-room hotel has tiny but dramatic rooms done in rich, dark colors, with Art Deco-ish bathrooms and free Wi-Fi. Columbus Ave can be noisy, so if you're a light sleeper, ask for a room at the back. ⑥

Hotel Astoria 510 Bush St at Grant, Chinatown ☎1-800/666-6696, ⓦwww.hotelastoria-sf.com. Located right next to the arch at the entrance to Chinatown, the *Hotel Astoria*'s decor is friskier than many other budget hotels, with TV and full in-room amenities; continental breakfast is included in the rate and there's discounted parking nearby ($20 for 24hr). ③, shared bath ②

San Remo 2237 Mason St at Chestnut, North Beach ☎1-800/352-7366, ⓦwww.sanremohotel .com. Quirky option close to Fisherman's Wharf. Rooms in this warren-like converted house are cozy and chintzy: all share spotless bathrooms and a few have sinks. There are no phones or TVs in the bedrooms and no elevator. ③

SW Hotel 615 Broadway at Grant, North Beach ☎415/362-2999, ⓦwww.swhotel.com. On the boundary between Chinatown and Little Italy. The decor in the large rooms is modern Asian with carved armoires and headboards and bright yellow bedspreads. ⑤

Washington Square Inn 1660 Stockton St at Union, North Beach ☎1-800/388-0220, ⓦwww .wsisf.com. This B&B-style hotel overlooking Washington Square has large, airy rooms, decorated in modern shades of taupe and cream, and friendly, amenable staff. ⑥

Pacific Heights and Cow Hollow

Cow Hollow Motor Inn 2190 Lombard St at Steiner, Cow Hollow ☎415/921-5800, ⓦwww .cowhollowmotorinn.com. Swiss-chalet-style inn, with plentiful parking and charmingly dated common areas. The rooms, though, are bland, if enormous. ⑤

🏃 **Del Sol** 3100 Webster St at Lombard, Cow Hollow ☎1-877/433-5765, ⓦwww .thehoteldelsol.com. Funky, offbeat, updated motor lodge with a tropical theme, plus a swimming pool. The color scheme combines zesty walls with chunky mosaics and palm trees wrapped in fairy lights: the best place for budget cool in the city. ⑥

Greenwich Inn 3201 Steiner St at Greenwich, Cow Hollow ☎415/921-5162, ⓦwww .greenwichinn.com. Formerly a *Travelodge*, this sprightly option in the Marina offers 32 rooms, all a little dark but made up for by the friendly owners. There's free on-site parking, too. ④

Laurel Inn 444 Presidio Ave at California, Laurel Heights ☎1-800/552-8735, ⓦwww.thelaurelinn .com. This Laurel Heights hotel is steps from

Sacramento Street's antique shops and eight blocks from the bustling Fillmore strip of cafés and stores. All rooms come with a VCR and CD player; the decor's a stylish update of 1950s Americana, with muted graphic prints and simple fixtures. ⑥

Queen Anne 1590 Sutter St at Octavia, Pacific Heights ☎1-800/227-3970, ⓦwww.queenanne .com. Gloriously excessive restored Victorian that began as a girls' school before becoming a bordello. Each room is stuffed with gold-accented Rococo furniture and bunches of silk flowers: the parlor (where afternoon sherry is served) is over-filled with museum-quality period furniture. Miss Mary Lake, former principal of the school, is said to still make periodic, supernatural appearances in Room 410. See map on p.527 for location. ⑤

Surf Motel 2265 Lombard St at Pierce, Cow Hollow ☎415/922-1950, ⓦwww.surfmotorinn .com. This old-school motel has two tiers of bright, simple rooms that are sparklingly clean. Ask for a room at the back, since the busy Lombard St thoroughfare roars past the main entrance. ②

The Mission and the Castro

See map on p.524 for locations.

Beck's Motor Lodge 2222 Market St at Sanchez, Castro ☎1-800/227-4360, ⓦwww .becksmotorlodgesf.com. This is one of only two accommodation options in the area that aren't B&Bs. The clientele's more mixed than you'd expect from its location, and the soft, bluish rooms are plusher than the gaudy yellow motel exterior might suggest. If you're a light sleeper, ask for a room well away from the road, as it can be noisy. ⑤

🏃 **Elements** 2524 Mission St, Mission ☎1-866/327-8407, ⓦwww.elementssf .com. Newbie that's one of the only places to stay in the heart of the Mission. The en-suite rooms are light-filled and modern, and there are women-only, men-only, and mixed dorm rooms ($27.50), plus free Internet access, complimentary continental breakfast, and stunning city views from the rooftop bar, *Medjool* (see p.544). ③

Inn San Francisco 943 S Van Ness at 20th, Mission ☎1-800/359-0913, ⓦwww.innsf.com. Superb, sprawling B&B in two adjoining historic Victorians on the Mission's edge. The 1872 mansion has fifteen dark and stylish rooms, and the 1904 extension next door holds six more. Breakfast buffet, redwood hot tub, on-site parking, and rooftop sun deck with stunning views are all major pluses. ⑤

Travelodge Central 1707 Market at Valencia, Mission ☎1-800/578-7878, ⓦwww .sanfranciscocentralhotel.com. Very basic motel-style lodging, but couldn't be more conveniently located – the free on-site parking makes up for the slightly worn, floral motel rooms. ⑤

Hayes Valley to Haight-Ashbury

See map on p.527 for locations.

Archbishop's Mansion 1000 Fulton St at Steiner, Alamo Square ☎415/563-7872. The last word in camp elegance, this B&B stands on the corner of Alamo Square and is crammed with $1 million worth of antiques, including Noël Coward's baby grand piano and the very chandelier that featured in the ballroom of *Gone With the Wind*. Built to house an archbishop, it's also served as a school for wayward Catholic boys. ⑦

Best Western Hotel Tomo 1800 Sutter St at Buchanan, Japantown ☎1-888/822-8666, ⓦwww.jdvhotels.com. This recently renovated hotel has been ripped straight from the pages of a comic book: the 125 rooms feature anime murals and contemporary Japanese decor, with iPod docking stations, bean bag chairs, and flat LCD TVs, plus some with private balconies. There are also gaming suites outfitted with Nintendo Wii, six-foot projection screens, and bean-bag chairs. Across the street from the Japan Center and convenient to the boutiques and restaurants of Fillmore St. ⑥

The Carl 198 Carl St at Stanyan, Haight-Ashbury ☎1-888/661-5679, ⓦwww.carlhotel.ypguides.net. Plainer than many of the surrounding B&Bs, this hotel is a bargain for its Golden Gate Park location. Small but florally pretty rooms, with microwaves and fridges; the six with shared bath are especially well-priced. En-suite ④, shared bath ③

Château Tivoli 1057 Steiner St at Fulton, Alamo Square ☎1-800/228-1647, ⓦwww.chateautivoli.com. Rooms in this lavishly furnished Victorian mansion are named after artists like Isadora Duncan and Mark Twain: there's history everywhere, whether in the building itself (built for an early local lumber baron) or the furniture (one of the beds was owned by Charles de Gaulle). Grand, and very serious, but a luxurious alternative to many of the cozy B&Bs elsewhere. En-suite ⑦, shared bath ⑤

Hayes Valley Inn 417 Gough St at Hayes, Hayes Valley ☎1-800/930-7999, ⓦwww.hayesvalleyinn.com. Homely rooms in a secluded location: furnishings are minimal, and baths are shared, but the friendly, well-stocked kitchen/breakfast room is a major plus. ④

The Red Victorian Bed, Breakfast and Art 1665 Haight St at Cole, Haight-Ashbury ☎415/864-1978, ⓦwww.redvic.com. Quirky B&B and Peace Center owned by Sami Sunchild and decorated with her ethnic arts. The TV-free rooms vary from simple to opulent: the best feature is the shared bathrooms, including a goldfish-filled toilet cistern. Breakfast's a lavish but highly communal affair, so be prepared to chat with your neighbors while you eat. En-suite ⑥, shared bath ④

Stanyan Park Hotel 750 Stanyan St at Waller, Haight-Ashbury ☎415/751-1000, ⓦwww.stanyanpark.com. Overlooking Golden Gate Park, this small hotel has 35 sumptuous rooms that are oddly incongruous in its counterculture neighborhood, busily decorated in country florals with heavy drapes and junior four-poster beds. Continental breakfast and an ample, cookie-filled afternoon tea are included. ⑥

Hostels

See map on pp.502–503 for locations.

Green Tortoise 494 Broadway at Montgomery, North Beach ☎-800/867-8647, ⓦwww.greentortoise.com. This laid-back hostel is the choicest option if money's tight: there's room for 130 people in dorm beds and double rooms (with shared bath). Both options include free Internet access, use of the small on-site sauna, and complimentary breakfast, as well as free dinner three times a week. There's no curfew, and the front desk is staffed 24hr: there's a ten-night maximum stay. Dorms $25, private doubles from $65. Green Tortoise also runs popular bus trips around the state; see p.34.

HI–San Francisco City Center 685 Ellis St at Larkin, Tenderloin ☎415/474-5721, ⓦwww.sfhostels.com. Spiffy hostel with 272 beds divided

into four-person dorms, each with en-suite bath. There's no curfew, and overall it's friendly, funky, and California cool: good for meeting other travelers, since there are plenty of activities laid on (nightly movies, communal pancake breakfast). Its only downside is the location in a sketchier part of the Tenderloin. Dorms from $23, private rooms from $67. Nonmembers pay $3 extra.

HI–San Francisco Downtown 312 Mason St at Geary, Union Square ☎415/788-5604, ⓦwww.sfhostels.com. With almost 300 beds, this downtown hostel still fills up quickly in peak season: four-person dorms are spotless, sharing bathroom facilities between eight people. The private rooms are pricier and sleep two people.

There's a kitchen with microwave and vending machines, a funky little reading room, and Internet access, all open 24hr. Dorms from $23, private rooms $60. Nonmembers pay $3 extra.

HI–San Francisco Fisherman's Wharf Building 240, Fort Mason ☎415/771-7277, ⓦwww .sfhostels.com. On the waterfront between the Golden Gate Bridge and Fisherman's Wharf, this is a choice option for the outdoorsy traveler, mostly thanks to its location in a historic former Civil War barracks in a rolling park. Be aware that although public transport connects the hostel with the main sights, it's a little out of the way on the federal complex at Fort Mason. Dorms $26–30, private rooms $75–100.

Pacific Tradewinds Guesthouse 680 Sacramento St at Kearny, Chinatown ☎1-888/734-6783, ⓦwww.pactradewinds.com. The best budget option in the center of town, this small hostel offers free, high-speed Internet access, a clean kitchen, and a large communal dining table that makes meeting fellow travelers easy. It's certainly an international hub – house rules are posted in almost forty languages, including Afrikaans and Catalan. There are only 38 beds so book ahead in high season. $24.

YMCA Central Branch 220 Golden Gate Ave at Leavenworth, Tenderloin ☎415/345-6700, ⓦwww.ymcasf.org. Rooms may be simple, but are a great deal: $12 overnight parking, free breakfast, free use of YMCA gym, Internet access at a nominal fee, and on-site laundry. Private rooms have either en-suite or shared baths, and dorms are available for groups of four or more (in summer only). Be aware of the YMCA's location in a grimy part of the Tenderloin. Prices include tax: dorms $26, shared-bath single $44, en-suite single $74.

The City

The first thing that strikes visitors to San Francisco is that it is a city of hills and distinct neighborhoods. Here, as a general rule, geographical elevation is a stout indicator of wealth – the higher you live, the better off you are. Commercial square-footage is surprisingly small and mostly confined to the downtown area, and the rest of the city is made up of primarily residential districts with street-level shopping, easily explored on foot. Armed with a good map and strong legs, you could plough through much of the city in a couple of days, but frankly the best way to get to know San Francisco is to dawdle, unbound by itineraries; the most interesting neighborhoods merit – at the very least – half a day each of just hanging out.

Most of the forty-odd hills that rise above the town serve as geographic barriers between neighborhoods. The flattest stretch of land, created by landfill and bulldozing, is **downtown**, at the top right-hand corner of the Peninsula, bordered by I-80 to the south, US-101 to the west, and the water. The city center is bisected by the wide, diagonal thoroughfare of **Market Street**, which is the main reference point for your wanderings. Lined with stores and office buildings, Market Street begins at the water's edge of the **Embarcadero** and runs southwest along the corporate high-rises of the **Financial District**, the shopping quarter of **Union Square**, and the scruffy **Tenderloin** and chic **Hayes Valley**, finally reaching the primarily gay district of the **Castro**. It then spirals around **Twin Peaks**, the most prominent of San Francisco's heights.

South and east of Market Street stands **SoMa**, which used to be one of the city center's few industrial enclaves until the artsy, nightclubbing crowd discovered it. Development poured in during the dot-com boom, funding the glorious waterfalls at **Yerba Buena Gardens** and the **San Francisco Museum of Modern Art**, but the neighborhood suffered after the bursting of the Internet bubble, and more than six years later, many of its sparkling new office buildings still lie empty, vacated by vanished companies. SoMa's waterfront, the long-neglected **South Beach**, has been re-zoned for housing and businesses, and is anchored by **AT&T Park**, the waterfront stadium built for baseball's San Francisco Giants.

Southwest of SoMa sits San Francisco's largest, and one of its most vibrant, neighborhoods: the **Mission**. Built around the wedding cake-like Mission Dolores and, thanks to fog-blocking hills, almost always sunny, the largely Hispanic neighborhood offers enough food, cinema, nightclubs, and shops to fill a separate vacation – or at least a day off the well-trodden tourist path around downtown.

North and west of Market Street, the land rises dramatically, and with it property values, as evinced by the stunning mansions atop the province of robber barons, **Nob Hill**. Beside this posh residential quarter, a short cable-car ride or walk down the hill, rests cluttered **Chinatown**, a thriving neighborhood of apartments, restaurants, temples, and stores built around **Portsmouth Square**, the spiritual heart of San Francisco. The land east of the square, towards the bay, used to be entirely water before hundreds of sailors heading for the Gold Rush abandoned their ships, resulting in an unnatural extension of the waterfront. The beached boats rapidly piled up along the shore of Portsmouth Square, until merchants began using the dry-docked vessels as hotels, bars, and shops. Now it's filled by the towering Transamerica Pyramid, which shadows the **Jackson Square** historical neighborhood of restored redbrick businesses. The diagonal artery **Columbus Avenue**, which separates Portsmouth from Jackson Square, is the spine of the Italian enclave of **North Beach**, much loved by Beat writers and espresso drinkers. North Beach extends to the northernmost tip of the city, the tourist-trap waterfront known as **Fisherman's Wharf**, but not before passing the peaks of **Russian Hill**, home to the famously curvy Lombard Street, and **Telegraph Hill**, perch of the celebrated Coit Tower.

SAN FRANCISCO AND THE BAY AREA | The City

7

The cable cars

San Francisco's **cable cars** first appeared in 1873, the brainchild of Andrew Hallidie, an enterprising engineer with a taste for moneymaking schemes. Scots-born Hallidie is said to have been inspired to find an alternative to horse-drawn carriages when he saw a team of horses badly injured while trying to pull a dray up a steep hill in the rain. More than equine welfare was under threat – his father had patented a strong wire rope that had been extensively used in the mines of eastern California but, as the Gold Rush there slowed, Hallidie needed a new application for his family's signature product and a privately owned transit system like the cable cars was the ideal solution.

The cable-car **pulley system** was dubbed "Hallidie's Folly" by unconvinced locals, but doubters were soon proved wrong as high sections of San Francisco like Nob Hill suddenly became accessible, and businesses and homes were constructed along cable-car routes. At their peak, just before the 1906 earthquake, more than six hundred cable cars plied eight lines and 112 miles of track throughout the city, traveling at a maximum of 9.5mph.

Unfortunately, though, the cable system was hit hard by the onset of the automobile, thanks to the devastation of the 1906 earthquake, when large chunks of the tracks were wrecked. However, when it was rumored in 1947 that the ailing system would be phased out altogether, a local activist organized a citizens' committee to save the cable cars. The protests worked, and seventeen years later the cars were put on the National Register of Historic Places and the remaining seventeen miles of track (now down to ten) was saved. Today there are 44 cars in use – each unique – and around 23 miles of moving cable underground. Since the mid-1980s, MUNI has been rebuilding the cars by hand: the process has taken far longer than the ten years originally estimated, requiring as much as 3000 hours and $275,000 per car.

New paved trails along the northern water's edge lead west towards the **Golden Gate Bridge**, passing the expansive green parkland of **Fort Mason** and **Crissy Field** and through the ritzy **Marina** neighborhood, home to the Palace of Fine Arts. High above, the mansions and Victorians of **Pacific Heights** snuggle up against neighborhood cafés and designer boutiques, along with spectacular views of the bridges and bay. The Heights slope down to the south to workaday **Japantown** and residential **Western Addition**. Directly west of here, you'll come to **Haight-Ashbury**, once San Francisco's Victorian resort quarter before the flower children took over. Today it's a rag-tag collection of used-clothing stores and hippies squeezing as much money as they can out of their fading past.

The western and southern sides of San Francisco are where most of the city's residents live, and – much to their dismay – the area is experiencing skyrocketing housing prices. **Geary Boulevard**, the main east-west passage, begins in the Financial District and ends at the Pacific Ocean in the **Richmond** neighborhood. Geary's lined with some of the city's best Asian and Russian restaurants, while a block north, the Clement Street area is known as "New Chinatown" for its collection of Chinese groceries, hot-pot restaurants, and dumpling cafeterias. The Richmond is hugged by nature on three of its sides: the beaches, the Golden Gate Bridge, and **Presidio** to the north; Ocean Beach to the west; and the expansive Golden Gate Park to the south. On the other side of Golden Gate Park, the **Sunset** neighborhood stretches south in suburban sameness, though the Irving Street strip of restaurants at Ninth Avenue is worth a detour for a fine selection of boutique eateries.

Union Square and around

The focus of downtown San Francisco, **UNION SQUARE** is a sixteen-block area filled with stores, hotels, and flocks of tourists. Thanks to a grueling and lengthy refit, the plaza itself, on the block north of Geary between Powell and Stockton streets, is more welcoming and much less shabby than it once was. The benches here are a good place to take a break from trekking around, and there's a handy café on its eastern rim (see p.542). In the center of the square, the 97-foot-tall Corinthian column commemorates Admiral Dewey's success in the Spanish-American War: the voluptuous female figure on top of the monument was modeled on **Alma de Bretteville Spreckels**, who founded the California Palace of the Legion of Honor art museum (see p.532). Though the site takes its name from its role as the gathering place for pro-Unionist speechmakers on the eve of the Civil War, these days it's remembered more for the attempted assassination of President Gerald Ford outside the bordering *Westin St Francis* hotel in 1975. The opulent hotel also featured prominently in many of Dashiell Hammett's detective stories, including *The Maltese Falcon* – in fact, during the 1920s Hammett worked there as a Pinkerton detective, investigating the notorious rape and murder case against silent film star Fatty Arbuckle.

The southern side of the plaza is dominated by a gigantic **Macy's** department store, but if you're looking for more interesting, albeit pricier, browsing, head east to **Maiden Lane**, ground zero for designer-label chasers. Before the 1906 earthquake and fire, it was known as Morton Street, one of San Francisco's lowest-class red-light districts; an average of around ten homicides a month occurred here, and prostitutes used to lean out low-hung windows of "cribs" that bore signs reading "Men taken in and done for." Today there's one major sight other than shopping: the only **Frank Lloyd Wright**-designed building in San Francisco, at no. 140. From the outside, it's a squat orange-brick edifice,

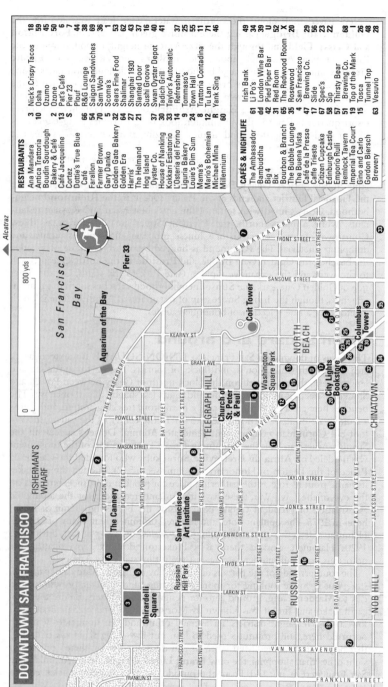

DOWNTOWN SAN FRANCISCO

RESTAURANTS

Ana Mandara	3
Antica Trattoria	10
Boudin Sourdough Bakery & Café	2
Café Jacqueline	13
Cortez	S
Dottie's True Blue Café	66
Farallon	54
Farmer Brown	70
Gary Danko	5
Golden Gate Bakery	32
Golden Era	64
Harris'	27
The Helmand	21
Hog Island Oyster Co.	37
House of Nanking	30
Kokkari Estiatorio	33
L'Osteria del Forno	14
Liguria Bakery	9
Louie's Dim Sum	24
Mama's	8
Mario's Bohemian	12
Michael Mina	R
Millennium	60

Nick's Crispy Tacos	18
Osha	59
Ozone	45
Ozumo	50
Pat's Café	6
Pier 23	7
Plouf	44
R&G Lounge	38
Saigon Sandwiches	69
Sam Woh	36
Scoma's	1
Sears Fine Food	53
Shalimar	62
Shanghai 1930	43
Slanted Door	37
Sushi Groove	16
Swan Oyster Depot	40
Tadich Grill	41
Taylor's Automatic Refresher	37
Tommaso's	25
Town Hall	55
Trattoria Contadina	11
Tu Lan	71
Yank Sing	46

CAFÉS & NIGHTLIFE

The Ambassador	49
Bambuddha	34
Big 4	39
Bix	U
Bourbon & Branch	52
The Bubble Lounge	31
The Buena Vista	65
Café de la Presse	35
Caffe Trieste	4
Citizen Cupcake	47
Edinburgh Castle	17
Emporio Rulli	67
Hemlock Tavern	58
Imperial Tea Court	57
Gino and Carlo	51
Gordon Biersch Brewery	15

Irish Bank	61
Li Po's	29
London Wine Bar	56
Pied Piper Bar	23
Red Room	22
The Redwood Room	68
Rosewood	I
San Francisco Brewing Co.	26
Slide	48
Spec's	28
Thirsty Bear	57
Top of the Mark	19
Tosca	15
Tunnel Top	
Vesuvio	63

800 yds

Alcatraz

Pier 33

San Francisco Bay

Aquarium of the Bay

Coit Tower

FISHERMAN'S WHARF

The Cannery

Ghirardelli Square

Russian Hill Park

San Francisco Art Institute

Church of St. Peter & Paul

Washington Square Park

City Lights Bookstore

Columbus Tower

NORTH BEACH

TELEGRAPH HILL

RUSSIAN HILL

NOB HILL

CHINATOWN

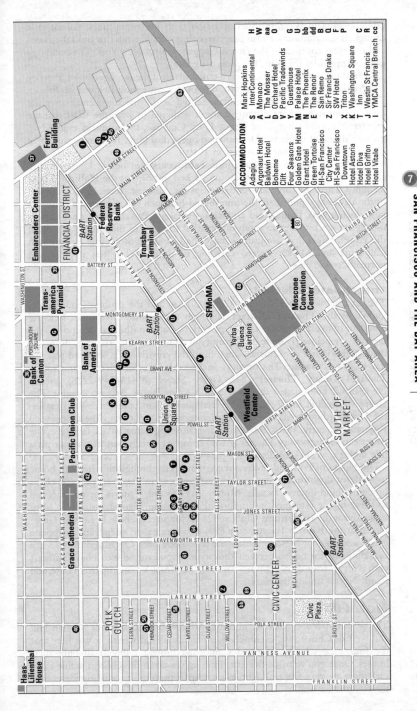

Ferry Building

Embarcadero Center

FINANCIAL DISTRICT

BART Station

Federal Reserve Bank

Transbay Terminal

Transamerica Pyramid

SFMoMA

Bank of Canton

Portsmouth Square

Bank of America

Moscone Convention Center

Yerba Buena Gardens

Pacific Union Club

Grace Cathedral

Union Square

Westfield Center

POLK GULCH

SOUTH OF MARKET

CIVIC CENTER

Civic Plaza

Haas-Lilienthal House

ACCOMMODATION

Adagio		Mark Hopkins	
Argonaut Hotel		InterContinental	H
Baldwin Hotel		Monaco	W
Boheme		The Mosser	aa
Clift		Orchard Hotel	
Four Seasons		Pacific Tradewinds	O
Golden Gate Hotel		Palace Hotel	G
Grant Hotel		The Phoenix	U
Green Tortoise		The Renoir	bb
HI-San Francisco		San Remo	dd
City Center		Sir Francis Drake	B
HI-San Francisco		SW Hotel	Q
Downtown		Triton	F
Hotel Astoria		Washington Square	P
Hotel Diva		Inn	
Hotel Griffon		Westin St Francis	C
Hotel Vitale		YMCA Central Branch	R
			cc

oddly lacking in Wright's usual obsession with horizontal lines; the interior, though, is extraordinary, a swooping, sweeping, curved ramp that links the floors and is a clear ancestor of the famed Guggenheim in New York. The building's now occupied by the Xanadu ethnic art gallery.

Around the corner, marooned on a traffic island at the intersection of Kearney and Market, lies **Lotta's Fountain**, one of the city's most beloved landmarks. This ornate caramel-colored fountain served as the message center after the 1906 earthquake, where distraught locals gathered to hear the latest damage reports. Named in honor of actress Lotta Crabtree, the fountain enjoyed its greatest moment when world-renowned opera diva Luisa Tetrazinni sang a free Christmas Eve performance atop it in 1910.

If you're heading to the waterfront, **cable cars** run beside Union Square along Powell Street but are usually too packed to board at the **Hallidie Plaza** terminus. There are three line-dodging tips for cable-car riders. First, come late in the day – by 7pm or so, the line should be much shorter; second, if you're here during peak hours, head a block north along Powell Street since drivers usually leave a bit of extra room on board at the start of the journey. Finally, if the Powell Street lines are just too busy, the California Street line (terminus at California and Market streets) crawling up Nob Hill is less popular and normally crowd-free.

The Theater District

The area between tourist-heavy Union Square and the grubby Tenderloin is known as the **Theater District**, although most of the playhouses lack the grandeur of many old theaters in New York or London (the one exception's the Geary – see below). Despite its proximity to a number of tourist attractions, this neighborhood is a convenient escape from the crowds and a secluded place to stay in the city center. The district's anchored by the American Conservatory Theater's **Geary Theater**, 415 Geary Street (☎415/749-2228), whose Neoclassical colonnaded facade is a nod to its Beaux Arts-era origins. The Geary was rebuilt in 1909 after the earthquake catastrophe three years earlier; the 1989 earthquake damaged the structure again, and it was closed for several years in the early 1990s for retrofitting and upgrading of its facilities. The American Conservatory Theater (ACT) company usually performs major plays five nights a week – for details, see p.549.

The blocks of Post and Sutter streets, which cut through this area, are home to some of downtown's least visible landmarks: some fourteen **private clubs** hidden behind discreet facades. Money isn't the only criteria for membership to these highly esteemed institutions, though being *somebody* usually is. Most notorious is the **Bohemian Club**, at 624 Taylor Street, whose Bohemian Grove retreat at the Russian River (see p.699) is where ex-presidents and corporate giants assemble for Masonic rituals and schoolboy larks. Organized in 1872 as a breakfast club for newspapermen, the city location evolved into a businessmen's club with an artsy slant, counting Ambrose Bierce, Jack London, Bret Harte, and Frank Norris among its members.

Nob Hill

The posh hotels and Masonic institutions of **Nob Hill**, south of Russian Hill and west of Chinatown, exemplify San Francisco's old wealth: it was here that the four men who transformed California through railroads all built their houses. Once you've made the stiff climb up (or taken the California line cable car), there are very few real sights as such, apart from the astounding views over the city and beyond.

Originally called California Street Hill, the 376-foot-high knoll used to be scrubland occupied by sheep. The invention of the cable car made it accessible to Gold Rush millionaires, and the area became known as Nob Hill (from "nabob," a Moghul prince, or "snob," or "knob" as in rounded hill) after the **Big Four** – Leland Stanford, Collis P. Huntington, Mark Hopkins, and Charles Crocker – came to the area to construct the Central Pacific Railroad and built their mansions here.

Ostentatious designs created out of Marin-headlands redwood were the fashion: unfortunately, after the earthquake and fire of 1906, all the mansions on Nob Hill had burned to the ground, with a single exception. James C. Flood had bucked local fashions and instead emulated the brownstone style popular on New York's Fifth Avenue: the stone weathered the fire, as did the burnt-out shell of the then-incomplete Fairmont Hotel. Flood's mansion, constructed in 1886 at the cost of a cool $1 million, is now the private **Pacific Union Club**, a retreat for the rich and closed to the public. Across California Street, you'll find another jaw-dropping view and even more startling prices at San Francisco's most famous vista-bar, *The Top of the Mark*, in the **Mark Hopkins Hotel** (see p.495), supposedly where Tony Bennett found his inspiration for *I Left My Heart in San Francisco*.

Overlooking Huntington Park, the manicured green space at the summit of Nob Hill, is one of the biggest hunks of sham-Gothic architecture in the US: **Grace Cathedral**, 1100 California Street (Mon–Fri 7am–6pm, Sat 8am–6pm, Sun 7am–7pm; free tours Mon–Fri 1–3pm, Sat 11.30am–1.30pm, Sun 12.30–2pm; ☎415/749-6300, ⓦ www.gracecathedral.org). Although this pale copy of Notre Dame in Paris was begun after the 1906 fire on land donated by the wealthy Crocker family, it took until the early 1960s to finish – and it suffers from a hodgepodge of styles as a result. The cathedral gives an impression of unloved hugeness, despite florid touches like the faithful replicas of Ghiberti's Renaissance doors from the Florence Baptistry adorning the main entrance. Utterly out of place, they're included simply because they were available: during construction, the first commercial copies of the fifteenth-century masterpiece were produced, and the supervising architect snapped them up. Inside, check out the AIDS Interfaith Chapel to the right of the main entrance, with an altarpiece designed by the late Pop artist Keith Haring. The triptych, titled *The Life of Christ*, was the last work Haring completed before his death 1990 from AIDS.

Chinatown

CHINATOWN's twenty-four square blocks smack in the middle of San Francisco make up the second largest (after New York City) Chinese community outside Asia. Its roots lie in the migration of Chinese laborers to the city after the completion of the transcontinental railroad, and the arrival of Chinese sailors keen to benefit from the Gold Rush. San Francisco is still known in China as "Old Gold Mountain," its storied moniker from the nineteenth century. The city didn't extend much of a welcome to Chinese immigrants: they were met by a tide of vicious racial attacks and the 1882 Chinese Exclusion Act that banned new immigration, a law that resulted in thousands of single Chinese men being forbidden from both dating local women and bringing wives from China. A rip-roaring prostitution and gambling quarter developed, controlled by gangs known as tongs. With the loosening of immigration rules due to China's partnership with the US during World War II, and decades of hard work by its residents, Chinatown has grown into a self-made success.

Many visitors assume that the neighborhood remains autonomous – cut off from San Francisco by language and cultural barriers. But Chinatown's residents are as American as the rest of the city's citizens, and the district has one of its highest voter turnouts on election days. The population nowadays, descendants of Cantonese- and Fujianese-speaking southern mainlanders, as well as Taiwanese, has been joined by Mandarin-speaking northerners, Vietnamese, Koreans, Thais, and Laotians, turning the area into **Asiatown**. Though sleepy by night, during the day the area bustles with activity. Overcrowding is compounded by a brisk tourist trade – sadly, however, Chinatown boasts some of the tackiest stores and facades in the city, more evocative of a cheesy part of Hong Kong than Beijing. Indeed, Chinese visitors are often disappointed by the neighborhood's disorder and pandering to tourists – for a truer sense of everyday Chinese life in San Francisco, you're better off heading to the Richmond (see p.531).

One major improvement to Chinatown – an attempt to keep tourists coming – is the new **night market** that happens under the stars every Saturday evening from 6pm to 11pm in Portsmouth Square, June to October (☎415/397-8000 for more information). Stalls pitching everything from fresh honey to leather jackets surround free performances of classical opera and traditional music.

The best way to approach Chinatown is through the dramatic **Chinatown Gate**, on the southern end of Grant Avenue at Bush. Facing south, per feng shui precepts, it's a large dragon-clad arch with a four-character inscription that translates to "The reason to exist is to serve the public good," given by the People's Republic of China to the city in 1969. It's hard to see how that idea is carried out on the blocks ahead: Grant's sidewalks are paved with plastic Buddhas, cloisonné "health balls," noisemakers, and chirping mechanical crickets that assault the ear and eye from every doorway. One of the oldest thoroughfares in the city, **Grant Avenue** – originally called Dupont Street – was a wicked ensemble of opium dens, bordellos, and gambling huts policed, if not terrorized, by tong hatchet-men. After the 1906 fire, though, the city decided to rename it in honor of president and Civil War hero Ulysses S. Grant and so in the process excise the seedy excesses for which it had been famous. Note the two pagoda-topped buildings on the corner of Grant and California streets, the Sing Fat and Sing Chong, important because they were the first to be constructed after the 1906 fire, signaling Chinese resolve to remain on the much-coveted land.

A few blocks west, running parallel to Grant Avenue, refreshingly undertouristed **Stockton Street** is the commercial artery of the area for locals, packed with grocery stores and dim sum shops, as well as herbalists and fishmongers. Between Stockton Street and Grant Avenue, narrow Waverly Place also runs north-south and holds two opulent but skillfully hidden temples: **Norras**, on the third floor of no. 109, and **Tien Hou** (pronounced "TEE-en how") on the fourth floor of no. 125. The latter is especially impressive, a Taoist temple dedicated to the Goddess of Heaven, its ornate interior splashed with gold and vermilion and its ceiling dripping with tassels and red lanterns. Both temples are still in use and open to visitors (daily 10am–5pm): note the pyramids of oranges, considered lucky because the Cantonese pronunciation of orange sounds similar to the word for wealth. Although the temples don't charge admission, it's respectful to leave a donation and not use cameras or camcorders inside. Note, too, the tiny mirrors fastened to the balcony of 829 Sacramento Street at the eastern end of Waverley Place: they're intended to ward off evil spirits.

Detour east along Washington Street from Grant Avenue to find the eye-catching **United Commercial Bank**, no. 743, a small, red, pagoda-like structure built in 1909 for the Chinese American Telephone Exchange: notice how the roof curves out and then back on itself, keeping evil spirits at bay since they travel in a straight line. It stands on the original site of the offices of Sam Brannan's *California Star* newspaper, which carried the news of the earliest ore discoveries back to the East Coast in 1848 and so played a major role in sparking the Gold Rush.

Portsmouth Square

One block downhill from the telephone exchange building, **Portsmouth Square** was San Francisco's original city center and its first port of entry. The plaza has been swallowed up by Chinatown, and whatever the time of day, it's filled with elderly Chinese practicing tai chi, playing cards, or watching their grandchildren climb the playground equipment. Indeed, it's hard to imagine the city springing up from this once dusty patch of land nestled between Nob, Telegraph, and Rincon hills, but it was here that Englishman William Richardson received permission from Mexican rulers to begin a trading post on the coast of the Bay. John Montgomery came ashore in 1846 to claim the hamlet for the United States, raising a flag in the same spot where the Stars and Stripes flies today.

There are four points of interest in Portsmouth Square aside from the American flag. The first is a monument to writer **Robert Louis Stevenson**, featuring a replica of the galleon *Hispaniola* from his novel *Treasure Island*: Stevenson spent much time observing the locals in Portsmouth Square during his brief sojourn in San Francisco and the Monterey Peninsula in the late 1870s. The plaque nearby honors California's first public school, built here in 1848, while the third monument is a tribute to cable-car poobah **Andrew Hallidie**, whose first line ran on Clay Street. The most recent addition to the square recognizes its role in the modern Chinatown: Thomas Marsh's bronze *Goddess of Democracy*, erected in memory of the 1989 Tiananmen Square protests.

On the edge of Chinatown is the tiny **Pacific Heritage Museum**, 608 Commercial Street (Tues–Sat 10am–4pm; free; ☏ 415/399-1124, ⓦ www .pacificheritage.citysearch.com). The rolling exhibits of Asian art are fine, but the real draw is the structure itself – a late nineteenth-century US Subtreasury building, now neatly incorporated into a modern skyscraper.

The Financial District

Stretching along Market Street between Chinatown and the waterfront, the **Financial District** is San Francisco's business hub, clogged with banks and home to the city's two signature skyscrapers. The famous **Bank of America Center**, 555 California Street, was used by disaster-minded 1970s filmmakers for the exterior shots of camp classic *The Towering Inferno* and was also featured at the beginning of *Dirty Harry*, a classic San Francisco flick starring a young Clint Eastwood as a hardened police inspector. A few blocks away stands San Francisco's tallest and most recognizable building, the **Transamerica Pyramid**, 600 Montgomery Street, a glossy, controversial landmark designed by LA-based architect William Pereira in 1972. Nicknamed "Pereira's Prick" thanks to its phallic shape, it's so tall and thin it looks more like a squared-off rocket than a pyramid. The building does have four triangular sides, rising from a square city block to a lofty point high above; it's fully earthquake-proof and was unscathed by the earthquake of 1989, although there's no longer public access to the viewing platform on the 27th floor.

As with most central business zones, the Financial District isn't a place that hums at the weekends: to see it at its liveliest, wander through on a weekday lunch hour.

Jackson Square historic district

Confusingly, there's no plaza in **Jackson Square**. The area bordered by Washington, Columbus, Sansome, and Pacific streets wasn't known by that name until the 1960s, when interior designers who'd recently opened showrooms here decided on a suitably artsy yet old-fashioned tag to replace the notorious **Barbary Coast**, San Francisco's district of vice during the nineteenth century. Then, a constant stream of sailors provided unrivaled demand for illicit entertainment, and the area was nicknamed "Baghdad by the Bay" for its unsavory reputation as a nexus for shanghai'ing: hapless young males were given Mickey Finns and, unconscious, taken aboard sailing ships into involuntary servitude. Though buildings here remarkably survived the 1906 disaster, the rowdy, raunchy businesses were hugely affected as nearby residential areas were leveled. The double whammy of fire and fury (chiefly, the relentless campaigning from William Randolph Hearst's *Examiner* newspaper against the district) soon put an end to most illicit fun here.

Remains of San Francisco's earliest days can be seen today in the restored redbrick buildings of Jackson Square's **historic district**. The **Hotaling Building** (pronounced hote-UH-ling), at nos. 451–455, was a distillery that was saved by a savvy manager at the height of the 1906 fire. Afterward, local wags came up with the doggerel: "If as they say God spanked the town for being so over frisky, why did he burn the churches down and spare Hotaling's whiskey?"

Montgomery Street, on the district's western flank, has retained much of its historic character, and several of the buildings have interesting pasts. No. 732 was the home of San Francisco's first literary magazine, the *Golden Era*, founded in the 1850s; it helped launch the careers of Bret Harte and Mark Twain. Later, John Steinbeck and William Saroyan spent many a night drinking in the vanished Black Cat Café down the street. In the middle of the block, nos. 722–728 (the Belli and Genella buildings) have been stripped of their original stucco and done up in overwrought Victorian mode. Together they were at various times a theater, a Turkish bath, a tobacco warehouse, and an auction room. It was bought by the flamboyant San Francisco lawyer Melvin Belli, but his widow's plans to turn the site into a museum have come to nothing. It has now fallen into disuse, hidden from view by shuttered windows, encroaching ivy, and gnarled tree branches, and has a sadly ruined feel.

As the district merges with North Beach and Chinatown, at the intersection of Jackson Street and Columbus Avenue stands the distinctive green-copper siding of the **Columbus Tower** (also known as the **Sentinel Building**), 916 Kearney Street. It's now owned by director and San Francisco native Francis Ford Coppola, and houses *Café Zoetrope*, named for Coppola's production company, American Zoetrope, and decorated with mementos from the director's career.

North Beach

Bordering Chinatown at the junction of Grant Avenue and Broadway, and Fisherman's Wharf to the south, bustling **NORTH BEACH** has always been a gateway for immigrants. Italian immigration to San Francisco was ignited, unsurprisingly, by the Gold Rush, although it gained momentum at the end of the nineteenth century, when this area began to develop the characteristics – delis, wine bars, salami grocers – of a true "Little Italy." The freewheeling European flavor here, coupled with a robust nightlife and wide availability of housing, attracted rebel writers like Lawrence Ferlinghetti, Allen Ginsberg, and

Jack Kerouac in the 1950s, making North Beach the nexus of the **Beat movement** (see box below).

The main drag of North Beach is **Columbus Avenue**, proudly tagged as Little Italy by the flags painted on each lamppost, and now one of San Francisco's liveliest nocturnal drags. At its southern end at the crossroads of **Columbus and Broadway**, you'll find the former site of many old bars and comedy clubs from the 1950s, where politically conscious comedians like Mort Sahl and Lenny Bruce performed. Many of the venues are now porno stores, which took over spaces here during the death throes of the Beat movement. As it turns out, one of the city's legacies is the topless waitress phenomenon: at the Condor Club in 1964, Carol "44 Inches" Doda slipped out of her top one night and into the history books. The club's now reincarnated as *Andrew Jaeger's House of Seafood & Jazz* at the Condor, 300 Columbus Avenue, but the current owners have preserved photos and clippings from the Condor Club's heyday. The area's one notable sex joint, The Lusty Lady, 1033 Kearney Street at Columbus (box office ☎415/391-3991), is an employee-owned-and-operated strip club with unionized workers, successful enough to be opening satellite branches around the country.

The Beats in North Beach

Beat literature didn't begin in San Francisco, but emerged a decade earlier in New York, where bohemian **Jack Kerouac** had joined with the Ivy League-educated Allen Ginsberg, as well as William Burroughs, to bemoan the conservative political climate there. The group quickly grew frustrated with New York and moved out West, most of them settling in North Beach and securing jobs at the docks to help longshoremen unload the fishing boats. The initial rumblings of interest in the movement were signaled by the opening, in 1953, of the first bookstore in America dedicated solely to paperbacks: Lawrence Ferlinghetti's City Lights Bookstore (see p.510) drew attention to the area as the latest literary capital of California.

But it wasn't until the publication four years later of Ginsberg's pornographic protest poem **Howl** – originally written simply for his own pleasure rather than for printing – that mainstream America took notice. Police moved in on City Lights to prevent the sale of the book, inadvertently catapulting the Beats to national notoriety – assisted by press hysteria over their hedonistic antics, including heavy drinking and an immense fondness for pot – that matched the fame earned by the literary merits of their work. Ginsberg's case went all the way to the Supreme Court, which eventually ruled that so long as a work has "redeeming social value" it could not be considered pornographic. Within six months, Jack Kerouac's **On the Road**, inspired by his friend Neal Cassady's benzedrine monologues and several cross-country trips, had shot to the top of the bestseller lists, cementing the Beats' fame.

It's said that the word **Beatnik** was coined by legendary local newspaper columnist Herb Caen, who noted that the writers were as far out as the recently launched Soviet rocket, Sputnik, and so jokily christened them Beatniks. Soon, North Beach was synonymous across America with a wild and subversive lifestyle, an image that drove away the original artsy intelligentsia, many of whom ended up in **Haight-Ashbury**. Instead heat-seeking libertines swamped the area, accompanied by tourists on "Beatnik Tours," who were promised sidewalks clogged with black-bereted, goateed trendsetters banging bongos. (The more enterprising fringes of bohemia responded in kind with "The Squaresville Tour" of the Financial District, dressed in Bermuda shorts and carrying plaques that read "Hi, Squares.") It wasn't long before the Italians who'd once dominated North Beach moved back in and reclaimed it from the dwindling Beat movement.

Most people don't make a pilgrimage here for the porn, though; rather, they want to visit a beacon of San Francisco culture, **City Lights Bookstore**, 261 Columbus Avenue at Broadway (daily 10am–midnight; ☎415/362-8193, ⓦwww.citylights.com). This was the heart of Beat North Beach and struggles on as an independent bookstore, despite the encroachment of big-name chains and a surfeit of surly, Beat-inspired staff. The place is still owned by Ferlinghetti, who's now in his late 80s: aside from its kooky section dividers – books filed under "Anarchism" and "Muckraking," for instance – the best reason to come here is the upstairs poetry room, where you'll find everything from $1 mini-books and poster-sized poems from Beatnik legends to various collections and anthologies.

The area grows more Italian as you head north along Columbus Avenue: from Vallejo Street to the waterfront, expect plenty of cafés, delis, and restaurants selling strong coffee and salami. One exception is the section of **Grant Avenue** north of Vallejo, where you'll find one of the best emerging shopping streets in the city, lined with clothing stores and scruffy cafés. It's also the site of San Francisco's oldest bar, *The Saloon*, at no. 1232 (☎415/989-7666) – a rare North Beach survivor of the 1906 fire, now a lively dive bursting with nightly blues acts.

The soul of North Beach is **Washington Square Park**, a grassy plaza that plays host to dozens of older, local Chinese each morning, clumped in exercise groups across the lawn. Delightfully loopy local legend Lillie Coit's not-so-subtle fascination with firefighters (see below) can be seen on the Columbus side of the park, in the form of a big, bronze, macho monument with men holding hoses. On the north side of the park, the white lacy spires of the **Church of St Peter and Paul** look like a pair of fairytale castles rising beneath the shadow of Telegraph Hill's Coit Tower: unfortunately, the interior's an unremarkable nineteenth-century confection with little to recommend it. In 1954, local baseball phenom Joe DiMaggio and Marilyn Monroe had their wedding pictures taken here (though the actual marriage took place earlier at City Hall since both were divorced). Note how masses here are celebrated in three languages: Italian, English, and Cantonese, reflecting the shift in the neighborhood's population.

Telegraph Hill

Dominated by Coit Tower, **Telegraph Hill** is a quiet cluster of slope-hugging homes. The most direct path up its slope is Filbert Street, but be aware that the gradient east of Grant Avenue is very steep. The ten-minute walk's pleasant enough, though, past clapboard houses and flowery gardens on a terraced sidewalk – make sure to keep turning around to catch the breathtaking views. Since there are few parking spots at the tower, non-walkers are better off waiting for the (infallibly infrequent) MUNI bus #39 to the top. Once you reach the summit, it's easy to see why it was used as a signal tower for ships entering the Golden Gate. A watchman on the hill would identify the boat's origin and name by the flags flying on the mast, and relay the information via telegraph to the docks along Fisherman's Wharf. A plaque in front of a statue honoring Christopher Columbus in **Pioneer Park**, which lies at the foot of the tower, marks the watchman's spot.

The park, which was donated to the city by private citizens in 1875, contains the best viewpoint in all of Telegraph Hill, **Coit Tower** (daily 10am–5pm; $4.50; ☎415/362-0808). Built with money bequeathed by Lillie Coit in 1929 as a tribute to the city's firemen, the tower is an attractive component of the city's skyline, and rewards those who trudge uphill with sweeping views from its observation deck. Legend has it that as a young girl, Lillie answered the cries of "Help!" and assisted the Knickerbocker Engine Company No. 5 of the Volunteer Fire Department as they towed their engine up Telegraph Hill. Grateful firefighters made her their mascot, and even after she married wealthy easterner Howard Coit in 1868, Lillie continued attending firemen's balls and playing poker over cigars with "her" men of Company No. 5. Local stories abound of her character and exploits, including scenes of dashing away from society balls and chasing clanging fire engines. Upon her death, she left behind $125,000 "to be expended in an appropriate manner for the purpose of adding to the beauty of the city, which I have always loved." The result is the 212-foot pillar that looks alarmingly like a firehose nozzle. Coit's rumored liaisons with firemen add fuel to the speculation that the tower was actually her parting memorial to another part of a fireman's equipment.

While waiting to ascend to the top, take some time to admire the frescoes at the interior's base. They were an early project overseen by the Public Works of Art Authority, a predecessor of the WPA that employed artists to decorate public and government buildings during the Depression. Those chosen for this project were students of the famous Mexican artist **Diego Rivera**, who was both artistically and politically influenced by Russian Communism. As in his work, the figures are typically muscular and somber, emphasizing the glory of labor, although there's a wide variation in style and quality between panels, despite their thematic cohesion. You can take a free tour of the murals Saturday at 11am as part of the City Guides series (Ⓦwww.sfcityguides.com).

The best way down Telegraph Hill is on the eastern side, where the Greenwich Steps cling to the hill at a 45-degree angle, one of several walkways and pedestrian streets. Another equally lovely walkway is the **Filbert Steps**, dropping down even more steeply before plateauing at Montgomery Street in a leafy garden surrounded by simple cottages. These single-story houses were built in the 1850s by Gold Rush immigrants, who needed quick, temporary homes while they sought their fortunes.

Russian Hill

West of North Beach, elegant **Russian Hill**, named for six unknown Russian sailors who died on an expedition here in the early 1800s and were buried on its southeastern tip, has the odd point of interest. The modest high-rises that you see at the top of the hill were fiercely contested when they were first built in the 1920s, prompting many of San Francisco's stringent zoning laws. Most people, though, come here for the white-knuckle drive down Lombard Street, a terracotta-tiled waterchute for cars. Its tight, narrow curves swoop down one block, and there's a 5mph speed limit here – not that you'll be able to drive much faster given the usual lines to enjoy the drive. Wealthy owners of the manicured houses along its edges have petitioned numerous times to close the road, but given how often this cutesy block is featured in San Francisco publicity shots, they're unlikely to succeed. The best time to enjoy it is early morning or, better still, late at night when the city lights twinkle below and the tourists have gone.

It's easy to get your bearings in the neighborhood, as the cable-car tracks along **Hyde Street** neatly divide the district in two. Two blocks east down the hill, the low-rise Mission-style building of the **San Francisco Art Institute**, 800 Chestnut Street at Leavenworth (gallery hours Mon–Sat 11am–6pm; free; Ⓣ415/771-7020, Ⓦwww.sanfranciscoart.edu), clings to the side of a steep

San Francisco's steepest streets

Though no street can match Lombard for its fabled curves, the wait to go down it may force you to consider another itinerary if pressed for time. The city's second twistiest street lies coiled in the outer Potrero Hill neighborhood, on Vermont Street between McKinley and 22nd streets: it has five full and two half-turns (compared with Lombard's eight), and its location keeps traffic flowing. Another San Francisco thrill that'll test the brakes of your car is to take a ride down any of the city's **steepest streets**. Since most locals prefer not to brave these – even if that forces them to make an elaborate detour – you won't normally have to wait to freewheel down one of the following.

	degree
• Filbert between Leavenworth and Hyde, Russian Hill	31.5
• 22nd Street between Church and Vicksburg, Castro/Noe Valley	31.5
• Jones between Union and Filbert, Russian Hill	29.0
• Duboce between Buena Vista and Alpine, Lower Haight	27.9
• Jones between Green and Union, Russian Hill	26.0
• Webster between Vallejo and Broadway, Pacific Heights	26.0
• Duboce between Alpine and Divisadero, Lower Haight	25.0
• Jones between Pine and California, Nob Hill	24.8
• Fillmore between Vallejo and Broadway, Pacific Heights	24.0

street. It's easy to miss this place, which is in fact the oldest art school in the West (past students include Jerry Garcia and Lawrence Ferlinghetti, and Ansel Adams started its photography department). Unfortunately, many of its galleries are often closed, since it's still a working school. The one unmissable sight is the **Diego Rivera Gallery**, with an outstanding mural called *The Making of a Fresco Showing the Building of a City*, executed by the painter in 1931 at the height of his fame.

The Embarcadero

The thin, long waterfront district known as **THE EMBARCADERO** is centered on the **Ferry Building** (Mon–Fri 10am–6pm, Sat 9am–6pm, Sun 11am–5pm; ☎415/693-0996, ⓦwww.ferrybuildingmarketplace.com) and extends from the city's ballpark, AT&T Park, to Fisherman's Wharf. Once cut off from the rest of San Francisco by the double-decker Embarcadero Freeway – damaged in the 1989 earthquake and torn down in 1991 – the Ferry Building, at the foot of Market Street, was modeled on the cathedral tower in Seville, Spain. Before the bridges were built in the 1930s, it was the arrival point for fifty thousand daily cross-Bay commuters, and a few ferries still dock here. But in 2003 it received a multi-million-dollar facelift to turn it into a food lovers' mall, filled with artisanal cheese shops and wine merchants – for details, see p.555. It's also home to the **Ferry Plaza Farmers' Market** (Tues 10am–2pm, Sat 8am–2pm; ☎415/291-3276, ⓦwww.ferryplazafarmersmarket .com), a good place for local produce. On Saturdays, San Francisco foodies make pilgrimages here to snap up fruits and veggies and enjoy a sunny outdoor meal from the city's pricey restaurants, which often set up temporary stalls among the fruit and vegetables.

Nearby **Justin Herman Plaza** was named in honor of the pasha of urban renewal who tore down acres of historic buildings in the Western Addition in the 1960s. It's perhaps fitting that it should be home to one of the ugliest modernist sights in the city, the **Vaillancourt Fountain**, a tangled mass of concrete tubing clearly inspired by air-conditioning ducts. The fountain's best known, though, as the meeting place for Critical Mass, the bike rally that convenes here on the last Friday of each month and then rides around the city en masse to help gum up car traffic and in the process promote cycling as a more environmentally friendly alternative.

▲ Ferry Plaza Farmers' Market

Fisherman's Wharf

San Francisco doesn't go dramatically out of its way to court and fleece the tourist, but with **Fisherman's Wharf** it makes a rare exception (ⓦ www.fishermanswharf.org). This is the one place in town guaranteed to produce shudders of embarrassment from most locals and, even for visitors with kids, there are better places (like Golden Gate Park; see p.530) to dawdle for an afternoon. Despite its tacky reputation, though, the wharf is massively popular. If you want to enjoy the waterfront, a better option is a stroll through the parks in the Marina; but if you're determined to see the wharf, avoid weekends and try to get there as early as possible before the crowds descend.

Hard as it might be to believe now, Fisherman's Wharf was once a serious fishing port. The few fishermen that can afford the exorbitant mooring charges these days are usually finished by early morning and are gone before visitors arrive. You can still find some decent seafood here at some of the better restaurants (see p.534), but worthwhile sights or remnants of the fishing trade are few and far between. The most endearing diversion at the wharf is a large colony of boisterous **sea lions** (no feeding allowed) that has taken over a number of floating platforms at sea level between piers 39 and 41. To see more aquatic life, check out **Aquarium of the Bay** at Pier 39 (summer daily 9am–8pm; rest of year Mon–Fri 10am–6pm, Sat & Sun 10am–7pm; $13.95, $7 kids; ☏ 1-888/732-3483, ⓦ www.aquariumofthebay.com). Here you'll get spectacular close-up views of fish and crustaceans that surround you as you trundle slowly along a 400-foot acrylic viewing tunnel – it's just a pity about the throbbing muzak. It isn't a patch on the Monterey Bay Aquarium, though (see p.458), so if you have time, you're better off heading down the coast instead of spending money here. Close by at Pier 45 is the eccentric **Musée Mécanique** (Mon–Fri 10am–7pm, Sat & Sun 10am–8pm; ☏ 415/346-2000, ⓦ www.museemecanique.com), an appealing collection of historic arcade games; if you want to play, bring plenty of quarters. The machines range from old-school classics like a 1980s Pac Man to a freakish, gap-toothed clown who'll cackle forever in return for 25¢.

Dozens of tacky souvenir shops and bland malls expose the wharf's mission to rake in disposable tourist dollars. An exception is the sensitively converted **Ghirardelli Square**, 900 N Point Street at Larkin (℡415/775-5500, ⓦwww .ghirardellisq.com): originally a wool mill, it was purchased by Domenico Ghirardelli to house his expanding chocolate empire. Ghirardelli was a gold prospector-turned-grocer who made a fortune through his 1865 discovery of the Broma process, which sweats butter out of raw cocoa. There are a few pricey shops here, and some fine restaurants, although there's no manufacturing on site now – Ghirardelli's has moved across the Bay to cheaper premises in Oakland.

Bay cruises depart from piers 39, 41, and 43½ several times a day; they're run by various operators and usually cost around $20 per person. Provided the fog isn't too heavy (which, even in summer, is often an issue), they give worthwhile city views. Cruises to Alcatraz leave from Pier 33 (see below).

Alcatraz

The rocky little islet of **Alcatraz**, rising out of San Francisco Bay north of Fisherman's Wharf, was originally home to nothing more than the odd pelican. In the mid-nineteenth century the island became a military fortress, first to help defend the coastline of the newly created state of California and later, during the Civil War, to protect the state from falling into confederate hands. But military technology soon improved enough that fortresses such as this became obsolete; eventually, in 1934, the rock was put to use again and converted into one of America's most dreaded **high-security prisons**. Surrounded by freezing, impassable water, Alcatraz was an ideal place for a jail: this is where many of America's brand-name criminals like Al Capone and Machine Gun Kelly were held. Although conditions were softened as time passed – look for the radio jacks installed in each cell in the 1950s – a stay in one of the tiny, lonely rooms must have been psychologically grueling, especially given the islet's proximity to the glittering lights of San Francisco. Escape, of course, was impossible, thanks to the violent currents that churn constantly in the icy bay: in all, nine men managed to get off "The Rock," but no one managed to swim to freedom.

Alcatraz's curious name is part corruption, part mistake. An early explorer christened one island in the bay *Isla de Alcatraces* ("island of pelicans") in honor of the hundreds of birds that lived on it; however, the island he was referring to is not the one we now know as Alcatraz. The pelicans' old home is currently called Yerba Buena Island because a clumsy English sea captain got confused when mapping the bay in 1826. He assumed (wrongly) that the rock he saw covered with guano must be where the birds lived; so he marked that in mangled Spanglish as Alcatraz, then assigned the name Yerba Buena to the other pelican-dotted islet.

These days the island's only function is as a tourist attraction, and at least 750,000 visitors each year take the excellent hour-long, self-guided audio **tours** of the abandoned prison. These include some sharp anecdotal commentary as well as campy re-enactments of prison life featuring improvised voices of characters like Capone and Kelly. Skip the dull twelve-minute introductory film at the dock – you're far better joining one of the lively, free ranger talks on a variety of themes (check the schedule when you arrive or call ℡415/561-4900, ⓦwww.nps.gov/alcatraz). Alcatraz Cruises runs enormous **boats** to the island, leaving from Pier 33 (frequent departures from 9.30am, last boat back at 4.30pm, 6.25pm in summer; times vary for evening cruises; $21.75 with audio tour, $28.75 with audio and guided tour; ℡415/981-7625, ⓦwww.alcatrazcruises.com). Advance reservations are essential: expect a two-week wait in peak season, although tickets can be reserved up to 90 days in advance. In summer, the company also runs a day-tour that combines a visit to Alcatraz with a stop at Angel Island ($51.25).

Aquatic Park
A little way west of the wharf, the **Aquatic Park** complex of buildings groups around the foot of Hyde Street, at its center the "bathhouse" – a bold, Art Deco piece of architecture now home to the **Maritime Museum**, 900 Beach Street (℡415/561-6662, Ⓦwww.maritime.org), which has been closed for renovations; call for opening times. The rest of the complex includes a maritime library and a forgettable collection of ocean-going memorabilia. Better, in fact, is the small selection of naval knick-knacks at the Visitor Center inside the nearby Cannery complex, 499 Jefferson Street (daily 9.30am–5pm; free; ℡415/447-5000, Ⓦwww.nps.gov/safr). There's a relief map of the treacherous ridges along the seabed around San Francisco showing where dozens of ships have wrecked over the years, as well as the original lamp from the Farallon Island lighthouse in the bay. At the adjacent **Hyde Street Pier** (late May through Sept daily 9.30am–5.30pm; Oct to late May daily 9am–5pm; $5; ℡415/561-7170, Ⓦwww.maritime.org), the museum has restored a number of old wooden ships that are worth clambering around on to get a sense of the boats that voyagers like Richard Henry Dana entrusted with their lives. The best is the square-rigger *Balclutha*, built in 1886 and the sole survivor of the great sailing ships that journeyed around Cape Horn in the 1800s. Of course, being that it's now in California, the boat also had a second career in the movies, playing bit parts in 1930s films like *Mutiny on the Bounty*.

The Marina and around

West of Fisherman's Wharf, the **MARINA** is one of the city's greenest neighborhoods and enjoys a prime location on a stretch of waterfront that boasts the Golden Gate Bridge and the Marin Headlands as a backdrop. The neighborhood itself is homogeneously young, white, professional, and straight, prompting derision from artier locals, who pinpoint the Marina, with its swanky yacht clubs and jogger-laden paths, as the local yuppie mother lode. Although it was built specifically to celebrate the rebirth of the city after the massive earthquake of 1906, the Marina was the worst casualty of the earthquake in 1989 – tremors tore through fragile landfill and a good number of homes collapsed into smoldering heaps. The neighborhood's commercial center runs along Chestnut Street between Broderick and Fillmore, and most of the amenities are geared to swinging singles.

On the Marina's eastern side and just uphill from Fisherman's Wharf, **Fort Mason** (Ⓦwww.fortmason.org) was a Civil War defense installation whose old buildings are now occupied by around fifty nonprofit groups including theaters, galleries, and museums, plus a youth hostel (see p.499). San Francisco's most theatrical piece of architecture lies about a mile west at Marina Boulevard and Baker Street. **The Palace of Fine Arts**, 3301 Lyon Street (Ⓦwww.palaceoffinearts.org), is not the museum its name suggests, but a huge, freely interpreted classical ruin by Bernard Maybeck that anyone can wander around. It was erected for the Panama Pacific International Exhibition in 1915 and, when all the other buildings were torn down, the palace was saved simply because locals thought it too beautiful to destroy. Unfortunately, since it was built of wood, plaster, and burlap, it crumbled with dignity until the late 1950s when a wealthy resident put up money for the structure to be recast in reinforced concrete. To a modern eye, the palace is a moody and mournfully sentimental piece of Victoriana, complete with weeping figures on the colonnade by sculptor Ulric Ellerhusen, said to represent the melancholy of life without art (the originals are now in the Exploratorium nearby).

Next door, the **Exploratorium**, 3601 Lyon Street at Baker, is the best kids' museum in San Francisco (Tues–Sun 10am–5pm; $14, kids ages 13–17 $11, kids 4–12 $9, free first Wed of the month; ☎415/561-0360, ⊚www.exploratorium .edu). It crams in more than 650 hands-on exhibits, including the famous Tactile Dome ($17 including museum admission, reservations essential ☎415/561-0362), a total sensory-deprivation dome, explored on hands and knees, which is not for the claustrophobic. Plan to visit as early as possible since it can get very busy later in the day, especially during school holidays.

From here, the waterfront stretches west along **Crissy Field**, a former military airfield that's now popular with joggers and picnickers who come to enjoy some of the city's best views of the Golden Gate Bridge (see below). It's one of the most pleasant places in the city for a stroll. At the field's western edge is the **Warming Hut**, an old army shed turned café and bookstore where you can recharge with a coffee and a sandwich before pressing on a few more hundred yards to the base of the Golden Gate Bridge. Here you'll find **Fort Point National Historic Site** (Fri–Sun 10am–5pm; free; ☎415/556-1693, ⊚www .nps.gov/fopo), a brick fortress built in the 1850s to guard the bay on the initial landing place of the city's first Spanish settlers. Formerly part of the Presidio Army Base (now a national park), it was to have been demolished to make way for the Golden Gate, but the redesign of the bridge's southern approach – note the additional arch overhead – left it intact. It's a dramatic site, the surf pounding away beneath the great span of the bridge high above – a view made famous by Kim Novak's suicide attempt in Alfred Hitchcock's *Vertigo*.

Cow Hollow

A few blocks inland from the Marina, **Cow Hollow** was originally a small valley of pastures and dairies in the post-Gold Rush years. The area languished until the 1950s, when problems with open sewage and complaints from

---

The Golden Gate Bridge

The orange towers of the **Golden Gate Bridge** – arguably the most photographed bridge in the world – are visible from almost every point of elevation in San Francisco. As much an architectural as an engineering feat, the Golden Gate was begun in January 1933 and took only 52 months to build, opening in May 1937. Overseen by Chicago-born Joseph Strauss, the final design was in fact the brainchild of his local-born assistant, Irving Morrow. The first massive suspension bridge in the world, with a span of 4200ft, it ranked until 1959 as the world's longest. Connecting the Peninsula's northwesterly point to Marin County and Northern California, the bridge rendered the hitherto essential ferry crossing redundant, and was designed to stand winds of up to a hundred miles an hour. Handsome on a clear day, the bridge takes on an eerie quality when the thick white fogs pour in and hide it almost completely. Note that its ruddy color was originally intended as a temporary undercoat before the grey topcoat was applied, but locals liked it so much, the bridge has stayed orange ever since – and it takes more than 5000 gallons of paint annually to keep it that way.

You can either drive, bike, or walk across. The **toll** for southbound cars is $5, although biking is more thrilling since you teeter along under the bridge's towers. Note that cyclists headed south across the bridge are always routed along the east side, while northbound cyclists must take the west side Monday to Friday, and the east side on weekends. The half-hour walk across, though, really gives you time to take in the bridge's enormous size and absorb the views of the city in one direction and the headlands of Northern California in the other.

neighbors up on prestigious Pacific Heights about the smell of the cows allowed enterprising merchants to transform the area. The gorgeous old Victorian houses have since been refitted, especially around Filbert and Green streets, and the stretch of Union between Van Ness and Divisadero now holds one of the city's densest concentrations of boutiques and cafés. This street is alive with neighborhood shoppers and the dearth of tourist sights is what keeps it appealing.

Pacific Heights

Perched on steep hills between Cow Hollow and Japantown, wealthy **PACIFIC HEIGHTS** is home to some of the city's most monumental Victorian piles and stone mansions – a millionaires' ghetto, beautifully poised around two windswept parks. The lavishly proportioned houses that teeter precipitously atop these hills today are the chosen domains of stockbrokers, business magnates, and the odd bestselling novelist, like Danielle Steel (see below), who lives in one of the largest houses in the city.

Pacific Heights is neatly divided by Fillmore Street: to the west are the large dwellings that earned the neighborhood its reputation, and **Alta Plaza Park**, at Clay and Steiner streets, where local dog-walkers earn their keep by exercising pampered pooches. East of Fillmore are swanky Art Deco apartment buildings and, facing the cypress-dotted peak of **Lafayette Park**, several noteworthy mansions: the squat brownstone at 2150 Washington Street at Laguna is known as the **Phelan Mansion** and was built by former mayor James Phelan. Not far away stands the **Spreckels Mansion**, 2080 Washington Street at Octavia: this gaudily decadent white-stone palace was constructed for sugar magnate Adolph Spreckels and his wayward wife, Alma, a former nude model who posed for the statue at the center of Union Square (see p.532). Auguste Rodin's first US patron, Alma donated her spectacular collection of his work to the California Palace of the Legion of Honor, a museum she built (see p.501). The home she and Adolph shared is now owned by romance pulpist Steel, who pumped a not-so-small fortune into the structure's restoration and upkeep. Neither the Phelan nor the Spreckels mansion is open to the public – for admission to a Pacific Heights home, you'll have to head two blocks east to the ornate **Haas-Lilienthal House** at 2007 Franklin Street at Washington (compulsory 1-hour tours leave every 20–30min, Wed & Sat noon–3pm, Sun 11am–4pm; $8; ℡415/441-3004, Ⓦwww.sfheritage.org). This double-sized Queen Anne Victorian was built by wealthy merchant William Haas, and the talky tours are more illuminating about his family's day-to-day life than about the architecture of the building. Even so, it's a grand symbol of old wealth, with intricate wooden towers outside, and Tiffany art-glass and stenciled leather paneling inside.

The Victorians

Constructed from redwood culled from the Marin Headlands across the Golden Gate, San Francisco's **Victorians** enjoyed their greatest popularity in the late nineteenth century, preferred by homeowners who could use "signature details" in crafting the facade to differentiate their house from every other. This ostentation came at a price: unlike many of the stone-built homes, the earthquake and fire of 1906 easily destroyed most of the city's grandest Victorians on Nob Hill, and the axe-ravaged hillsides of Marin County made replacing them difficult. Also, the trend after 1906 eschewed embellishment, instead ushering in an era of muted stone or stucco designs still seen around town today.

7

SAN FRANCISCO AND THE BAY AREA | The City

517

Japantown

Those looking to satisfy a jones for a steaming bowl of ramen or Hello Kitty contraband can push south along Fillmore to reach **Japantown**, a once thriving neighborhood that never recovered from World War II, when its entire community was hauled off to internment camps. Although a handful of the district's shops have roots in the early 1900s, Japantown today is basically a shopping mall with an eastern flavor – the Japan Center – around which only a small percentage of San Francisco's Japanese Americans now live. Its one notable sight is the 100-foot **Peace Pagoda**, standing in the central plaza like a stack of poured-concrete space-age mushrooms. Nearby are the **Kabuki Hot Springs**, 1750 Geary Street at Fillmore (daily 10am–9.45pm; $20 weekdays, $25 weekends; ☎415/922-6000, ⓦwww.kabukisprings.com), refurbished and funked up but retaining at least some of the original spa's eccentricity. The communal baths alternate days for men and women, with one day set aside for co-ed bathing; call for details.

SoMa, the Tenderloin, and the Civic Center

While parts of San Francisco can almost seem to be an urban utopia, the adjoining districts of the **Tenderloin** and the **Civic Center** reveal harsher realities. Particularly in the Tenderloin, the homeless and disaffected are very much in evidence and their constant presence in front of City Hall is a reminder of governmental failures. Thus far, sporadic attempts to improve the areas have been at best well-meaning hit-and-misses or, at worst, patently cosmetic gestures bound to fail; Gavin Newsom, who took office as mayor in 2004, guaranteed that this problem would be one of his priorities if elected, though so far he's made little visible headway. In contrast, the once shabby **SoMa** took an unimaginable upswing in recent years, thanks in part to Internet start-up companies attracted to the district's low rents. When the dot-com crash came, the techies fled and the neighborhood slowly sank back into its grimier former appearance. Slowly the district's reviving once more: at night it booms with the muffled reverberations of underground dance clubs and slick wine bars, and **Yerba Buena**, a museum and entertainment complex nearer to downtown, draws daytime visitors, as does the baseball stadium along the waterfront to the east.

South of Market

SOMA, the distinctly urban district **So**uth of **Ma**rket Street, stretches diagonally from the Mission in the southwest to the waterfront in the northeast. While the western sections have always been a working-class community, it's ironic, given the area's grubby recent history, that the waterfront **Rincon Hill** – not to mention the South Park neighborhood – were home to the first of the city's banking elite. By the 1870s, they were drawn away to Nob Hill by the newly invented cable car, and within thirty years South of Market had been turned over to industrial development and warehouses. The poorer community that remained was largely driven out by fires following the 1906 earthquake, and Rincon Hill was eventually cleared in 1930 to make way for the new Bay Bridge. Despite the Web boom and bust of the 1990s, there are still parts of SoMa that are downright dangerous: the most notorious is Sixth Street (where you're quite likely to see drug deals go down in broad daylight). Stay accordingly alert and keep valuables hidden.

Wealthier residents have begun to return, at long last, to SoMa's bayfront, where an array of new upscale condominium complexes has sprung up in the nascent **South Beach** neighborhood, aided by public works aimed at improving transportation and beautifying a waterfront long hidden in the shadows of the thankfully departed Embarcadero Freeway. A block inland from the waterfront is the **Rincon Center**, at 101 Spear Street and Mission. Originally a US Post Office, it was constructed in 1939, and the building is a fine example of Depression Moderne architecture, with its smooth, imposing lines, outer simplicity, and ornamented interior. The lobby is lavishly decorated with murals about California history, the largest commission ever by the WPA, painted by Russian expat artist Anton Refregier in 1941. It became a yuppified shopping center in the 1980s and still has a few good lunch spots, such as dim sum palace *Yank Sing* (see p.535).

Unfortunately, the area of SoMa around Second Street was especially doomed by the dot-com bust, and many of the companies that energized the local real-estate market are gone, leaving nothing but chic office furniture and "For Rent" signs in their wake. One noteworthy attraction, though, deserves a detour: the **California Historical Society**, at 678 Mission Street at Second (Wed–Sat noon–4.30pm; $3; ℡415/357-1848, ⊛www.californiahistoricalsociety.org). A tiny, offbeat gem, it showcases ephemera from the state's history, including maps and photographs, and is especially strong on the cultural and political fallout from early Spanish settlement.

SFMOMA and Third Street

Until it was finally socially fumigated over a decade ago, Third Street symbolized San Francisco's urban issues: a crime-ridden strip minutes from the tourist trail along Market Street. A recent wave of development, centered on Yerba Buena Gardens, is an indication of how seriously San Francisco has tried to spiff up the neighborhood. **Yerba Buena Gardens** has inviting lawns that are often packed with office workers on warm weekday lunchtimes: don't miss the fifty-foot granite waterfall memorial to Martin Luther King Jr, inscribed with extracts from his speeches, which stretches along its eastern edge. On the terrace above the waterfall, a Sister Cities garden features flora from each of the thirteen cities worldwide that are twinned with San Francisco: look for camellias from Shanghai and cyclamen from Haifa, among others.

New attractions radiate from the gardens on each side: to the east stands the **Yerba Buena Center for the Arts**, 701 Mission Street at Third (galleries: Tues–Sun noon–5pm, Thurs until 8pm; $7; ℡415/978-2700, ⊛www.ybca.org). The center was initially conceived as a forum for community art projects but has recently expanded its repertoire, hosting international touring exhibitions and performances in its two main spaces. The small second-floor screening room shows works by local experimental filmmakers, as well as themed programs of cult and underground films – call or check the center's website for the latest schedules.

Opposite the Center for the Arts is one of the Bay Area's marquee museums: the **SF Museum of Modern Art** at 151 Third Street (Fri–Tues 11am–5.45pm, Thurs 11am–8.45pm, closed Wed; June–Aug opens at 10am; $12.50, free first Tues of every month, half-price Thurs 6–9pm; ℡415/357-4000, ⊛www .sfmoma.org), an attraction so adored that it risks suffocating under the weight of superlatives piled on it since its construction in 1995. Certainly, it's a striking structure. Designed by Swiss architect Mario Botta at a reported cost of $62 million, SFMOMA vies to be the West Coast's premier exhibition space. It hosts touring shows from New York and Europe while struggling to assemble a collection worthy of its housing. Frankly, the traveling exhibits are more impressive than the patchy permanent work: head to the upper floors for temporary exhibits and make sure to stop by the fine outdoor sculpture garden on the fourth floor. The best permanent holdings are of the **California school**, with works by Richard Diebenkorn and others, plus a notable collection of **abstract expressionist** works by Mark Rothko, Jackson Pollock, and Robert Rauschenberg. Whatever the quality of work within, the building steals the show and is itself worth visiting: a huge central skylight floods the space with light, while the upper galleries are connected by a vertigo-inducing metal catwalk made up of tiny slats.

A few blocks away on Fifth Street, the California Academy of Sciences adds further cultural cache to the area, having decamped to 875 Howard Street while its original site in Golden Gate Park undergoes a radical makeover (see p.530).

AT&T Park and around

Walking further south along the entirely unscenic Third Street might not seem to promise much, but hidden down a short alley between Bryant and Brannan streets is the surprising sanctuary of **South Park**, a picturesque European-style common. The park was the nexus of SoMa's multimedia community and locals have been able to gauge the health of the ailing industry by the diminishing numbers of office workers eating lunches in the park. Its shops and cafés are pricey, but it's still an extremely pleasant place to get a meal or lounge for the afternoon.

The name may not be pretty, but **AT&T Park**, the San Francisco Giants' new stadium south of South Park, is one of the finest ballparks in the country and a major improvement over their much-maligned old home at Candlestick Park. Prone to gusts of brutally cold wind, the "Stick" (as it was semi-affectionately known) was everything you didn't want in a baseball stadium, making an afternoon at the ballgame feel like leisure time in a meat locker (although the city's NFL team, the 49ers, still toughs it out there for now). The new stadium, in one of the sunniest parts of town, has an outfield that opens onto the bay and concession stands featuring local microbrews and the stadium's signature garlic fries.

If you want to see the stadium but not the team, terrific tours leave from the dugout store on Third Street (daily, except when day games are scheduled, 10.30am & 12.30pm; ☎415/972-2400, ⓦwww.sfgiants.com). Tickets cost $10 – about half the price of a cheap seat, and you'll not only get to sit in the padded dugout and wander on the turf, but you'll also snag some superb views out across the city to the Bay Bridge from the upper balconies. For information on catching a game, see p.47.

The Tenderloin

The **Tenderloin**, sandwiched between Civic Center and Union Square on the north side of Market Street, is one of the poorest, most dangerous places in San Francisco, just minutes from the tourist center. This small, uninviting area – no more than four blocks by five – remains a blemish on the heart of the city, though you should be safe as long as you keep your wits about you and don't mind vagrants asking you for money. Exercise extra caution at night, and the vicinity of Taylor Street, particularly around Turk and Eddy, is best avoided altogether.

The area's oddball name has never been definitively explained. One tale is that nineteenth-century police were rewarded with choice cuts of steak for serving a particularly perilous tour of duty here. A less flattering version is that, thanks to the constant bribes they collected from the gambling houses and brothels, those same policemen were able to dine in the city's finest restaurants. Yet others say that the name is based on the district's shank shape or even its notoriety for flesh-flashing brothels: whatever the answer, it's always been the seediest part of town and the heart of San Francisco's vigorous sex industry. Recent waves of South and Southeast Asian immigrants have begun transforming the neighborhood, establishing numerous spots for a cheap bowl of curry or Vietnamese *pho* soup. If you're not too busy hurrying to your destination, there are a few sights worth seeing tucked into the neighborhood's dark corners, the best of which is **Glide Memorial Church** at 330 Ellis Street at Taylor (℡415/674-6000, Ⓦwww.glide.org). The church provides a wide range of social services for the neighborhood's downtrodden but it's best known for its rollicking Sunday service, which attracts a gloriously diverse crowd ranging from pious locals to drag queens (Sun 9am & 11am). Be sure to arrive at least an hour ahead if you want a seat in the main church – the overflow usually has to make do with watching the proceedings via CCTV in a smaller room nearby.

At the western limits of the Tenderloin, on Polk Street between Farrell and California, lies **Polk Gulch**, a congregating point for the city's transgender community and a hub for the flesh trade. The intersection of O'Farrell and Polk is home to a neighborhood landmark of sorts, the raunchy strip club known as **Mitchell Brother's O'Farrell Theater** (11.30am–2am; $15–40; ℡415/776-6686, Ⓦwww.ofarrell.com). The Mitchell boys achieved considerable notoriety in the 1970s when they persuaded a young Ivory Snow soap model named Marilyn Chambers to star in their porno film *Behind the Green Door*, which they debuted at the Cannes Film Festival. While the pair slowly slipped back into obscurity over the ensuing decades, they made a tragic return to tabloid fame when Jim Mitchell shot and killed his brother Artie in 1991.

The Civic Center

To the immediate southwest of the grubby Tenderloin stands San Francisco's grandest architectural gesture: the complex of Beaux Arts buildings known as the **CIVIC CENTER**. This cluster was the brainchild of brilliant urban planner Daniel Burnham: even before 1906, he proposed leveling San Francisco and building a grand civic plaza, extensive subways, and boulevard-like traffic arteries fanning out like spokes across the city. Unfortunately, after the earthquake, the city was choked in bureaucracy, and his plan was heavily diluted until only the civic plaza was approved. Even then, it wasn't finished until several years after his death. Despite Burnham's beliefs that grand architectural answers would silence social questions, the Civic Center today is simply the Tenderloin with better buildings.

Most people arrive at the Civic Center MUNI and BART station at the corner of Market and Leavenworth streets and are immediately disgorged into the **United Nations Plaza**, built to commemorate the founding of the UN here in 1945 – look for the UN Charter etched on a black stone shard. It's filled with fountains and homeless people: not somewhere to dawdle.

The first building you'll see is the **San Francisco Public Library**, 100 Larkin Street at Grove (Mon & Sat 10am–6pm, Tues–Thurs 9am–8pm, Fri noon–6pm, Sun noon–5pm; free; ℡415/557-4400, Ⓦwww.sfpl.org), which moved into its current location in 1996 from its original site, now the Asian Art Museum (see p.521). The library contains the James C. Hormel Gay and Lesbian Center (named in honor of the gay activist and meat magnate), the first of its kind in the nation, topped by a dome with a mural depicting leading figures in gay rights and literary movements.

Next door stands the **Asian Art Museum**, 200 Larkin Street at McAllister (Tues, Wed, Fri–Sun 10am–5pm, Thurs 10am–9pm; $12, $5 after 5pm Thurs, free first Tues of every month; ℡415/581-3500, Ⓦwww.asianart.org), relocated from its original, earthquake-crippled quarters next to the M.H. de Young Museum in Golden Gate Park (see p.530). The building conversion was masterminded by Gae Aulenti, the same woman who whipped up the fabulous Musée d'Orsay in Paris from a dingy old train station; here, Aulenti opened the musty, bookstack-crammed interior and created a welcoming, airy space that's ideal for the massive collection on show. With more than 10,000 paintings, sculptures, ceramics, and textiles from all over Asia, this museum is almost overwhelming in its size, so it's well worth picking up an audio guide to navigate the highlights. The museum's most precious holding is undoubtedly the oldest known Chinese Buddha image, dating back to 338 AD. There's also a superb, well-priced café accessible to both visitors and passers-by.

The central plaza in front of these buildings is usually filled with a combination of political protesters and the homeless. Grand **City Hall** stands on the other side of the plaza (Mon–Fri 8am–8pm; ☎415/554-4933, ⓦwww.ci.sf.ca .us/cityhall). After the first city hall was destroyed in 1906, a contest with a prize of $25,000 was announced for local architectural firms to design a new building. The winning design was by Bakewell and Brown, former students of the Ecole des Beaux Arts in Paris, who wanted to create a structure inspired by the haughty, gilded dome of Les Invalides there. City Hall cost an astonishing $3.5m to build, and includes more than ten acres of marble, shipped in from Vermont, New Hampshire, and Italy. It was here in 1978 that conservative ex-Supervisor Dan White got past security and assassinated Mayor George Moscone and gay City Supervisor Harvey Milk; later, when White was found guilty of manslaughter (not murder), it was the scene of violent demonstrations as protesters set fire to police vehicles and stormed the doors of the building (see box, p.526). The best way to see the interior is on one of the frequent, free tours (Mon–Fri 10am, noon, 2pm; ☎415/554-6139) – sign up at the Docent Tour kiosk on the Van Ness Avenue side of the main building.

Directly behind City Hall on Van Ness Avenue are San Francisco's cultural mainstays, most elegant of which is the **War Memorial Opera House**, where the United Nations Charter was signed in 1945. Today, it's home to the

▲ San Francisco City Hall

San Francisco Opera and Ballet, and its understated grandeur is a sharp contrast to the giant modernist fishbowl of the **Louise M. Davies Symphony Hall** one block down. Built in 1980, at a cost of almost $35 million, the hall has some fans in the progressive architecture camp, though the general consensus is that it's an aberration of the otherwise tastefully harmonious scheme of the Civic Center. Both buildings enjoy a healthy patronage, and San Francisco's hidden elite gather here regularly: unfortunately, few performances are subsidized, so don't expect budget ticket prices. (For full details of ballet and opera schedules, see p.549).

Be sure to detour west from here to reach **Hayes Valley**, reborn when the freeway that once overshadowed it was demolished after the 1989 earthquake. The heart of the neighborhood is **Hayes Street** between Franklin and Octavia streets, although the district is swelling daily as new shops open. Hayes Valley is more racially integrated than many older neighborhoods, and the chichi boutiques sit alongside earthy remnants of the area's past. Lined with shady trees and cafés, not to mention some of the funkiest homeware and clothing stores around, Hayes Street is an outstanding place to wander aimlessly and browse.

The Mission

San Franciscans often speak of the **MISSION** today as a "neighborhood in transition," but the phrase could easily be applied throughout much of the district's 200-year history. After California's annexation, the area became home to succeeding waves of immigrants: first Scandinavians, followed by a significant Irish influx, and then a sizeable Latin American settlement. Though long heavily Spanish, this tangled melting pot is now a trendy destination for local Anglos; they're headed to the hip bars and restaurants, notably along Valencia Street, that jostle for space with old taquerias and grocery stores (and, of course, crowd them out); rising rents have engendered a certain amount of ill will toward newcomers. Still, at various points in its history the Mission has been one of the city's richest neighborhoods and one of its poorest, making this latest transformation but one in a long line of facelifts. What doesn't change is the Mission's gloriously sunny skies: the mass of Twin Peaks acts as a giant windbreak and even when the rest of the city is cold and foggy, the Mission is bright and (relatively) warm.

The area gets its name from the oldest building in the city, the **Misión San Francisco de Asis**, more commonly known as **Mission Dolores**, 3321 16th Street at Dolores (☎415/621-8203, ⓦ www.missiondolores.org). Its moniker dates back to the first European camp here, for the Spanish arrived on the Friday before Palm Sunday – the Friday of Sorrows – and finding an ample freshwater supply, decided to pitch their tents here, naming the site *Laguna de los Dolores*. The first mass celebrated at Mission Dolores on June 29, 1776 marks the official founding of the city, though the community was then known as Yerba Buena. The evolution of San Francisco is reflected in the mission's architecture: the original building, dating from 1782, is squat and relatively spare, while the more prominent basilica next door, built in 1913, is a riot of ornate design. Aside from periodic tour-bus herds, the building can be quite serene, with a stained-glass-lit interior offering a pleasant opportunity to gaze into the city's long-erased past. The backyard cemetery (made famous in Hitchcock's *Vertigo*) holds the graves of the mission's founders, as well as hundreds of "converted" Native Americans. Far removed from the plastic gimmickry of Fisherman's Wharf, this is one of the city's best historical icons, and is well worth a visit.

THE MISSION & THE CASTRO

CAFÉS & NIGHTLIFE

Amnesia	27
Badlands	21
Blondie's Bar & No Grill	15
Café Flore	11
Dalva	12
Doc's Clock	33
Esta Noche	14
La Rondalla	28
Latin American Club	35
Lazslo	32
Lexington Club	25
The Lone Palm	34
Lucky 13	7
Make-Out Room	37
Martuni's	1
Medjool	H
Midnight Sun	22
Pilsner Inn	6
Revolution Cafe	36
Ritual Coffee Roasters	31
Samovar Tea Lounge	18
Twin Peaks Tavern	17
Zeitgeist	2

ACCOMMODATION

24 Henry	B
Beck's Motor Lodge	C
Elements	H
Inn on Castro	D
Inn San Francisco	G
The Parker Guest House	F
Travelodge Central	A
Village House	E

RESTAURANTS

2223	5
Andalu	8
Bi-Rite Creamery	19
Bissap Baobab	26
Blue	16
Boogaloo's	35
Chow	4
Delfina	23
Dosa	30
Emmy's Spaghetti Shack	44
Foreign Cinema	32
The Front Porch	43
Herbivore	29
Home	3
Lime	10
Luna Park	20
Mitchell's	42
Papalote	38
Suriya	41
La Taqueria	40
Tartine Bakery	24
Ti Couz	9
El Trébol	39
Truly Mediterranean	13

A short walk from the mission down the stately, palm tree-lined Dolores Street, one of the most attractive stretches of asphalt in the city, brings you to the sunbather-covered slope of Dolores Park. Though during the week much of the park is little more than a glorified dog run, on weekends the southwest corner transforms into "Dolores Beach," where members of the Castro gay community come to bronze their gym-toned muscles. Aside from the mission itself, the other best known local landmark is much more recent: the **Women's Building**, 3543 18th Street at Guerrero (☎415/431-1180, ⓦwww.womensbuilding.org), is a community space housing workshops, drop-in daycare, and a resource center, all with a feminist slant. The building is tattooed with an enormous, sprawling mural, known by the awkwardly self-conscious name of *MaestraPeace*. It's the work of seven female designers and a hundred muralists; on one side there's an enormous mother-goddess figure, while on the other there's a gigantic portrait of Rigoberta Menchú, the Guatemalan woman who won the Nobel Peace Prize in 1992.

Heading east into the heart of the neighborhood, you'll hit **Valencia Street**, among the city's best shopping and dining strips, packed with upscale boutiques sitting next to thrift stores, taquerias, and chic new restaurants. Browsing this strip between 16th and 24th streets is one of the delights of San Francisco. At its northern end is the original **Levi's factory building**, 250 Valencia Street, a huge lemon-yellow structure set back from the road. While the pants Levi's makes today bear only a remote resemblance to the original item invented during the Gold Rush, the jeans have outlasted countless trends, and the company's flagship store is now a fixture of Union Square.

If Valencia Street is the hipster heart of the Mission, then **Mission Street** is the commercial hub of the **Latino community**: it's lined with five-and-dime shops selling a virtually identical stock of kitschy religious items, along with dozens of taquerias. It's mostly untouched by the gentrification that has bled into the northern edge of the district: there are a few groovy bars here, but this strip still primarily caters to the needs of local Latin families. The 200-odd **murals** you'll see everywhere underscore a strong sense of community pride and Hispanic heritage. The greatest concentration of work can be found on **Balmy Alley**, an unassuming back way between Treat and Harrison streets, where's there barely an inch of wall unadorned. The murals here are painted on wooden fences, rather than stucco walls, and consequently are regularly refreshed and replaced. The project began during a small community-organizing event in 1973, but the tiny street has become the spiritual center of a burgeoning Latino arts movement that has grown out of both the US civil rights struggle and pro-democracy movements in South America. Frankly, many of the murals are more heartfelt than either skilled or beautiful; it's worth stopping by for a peek, although the heavy-handed political imagery can be wearing. For a tour of the artwork, call the **Precita Eyes Mural Arts Center**, 2981 24th Street at Harrison (tours Sat & Sun 11am & 1.30pm; $10-12; ☎415/285-2287, ⓦwww .precitaeyes.org), which has sponsored most of the paintings since its founding in 1971. The center also sells maps of the neighborhood's murals ($3.95).

The Castro and Twin Peaks

Directly west of the Mission, the **Castro** was formerly a wild frontier, though it's settled down considerably in recent years, mellowing into middle age. Gentrified by the city's gay community during the 1970s as a primarily residential quarter, the Castro was part of the bacchanalian atmosphere that prevailed in San Francisco's gay culture during that decade. The assassination of gay City Supervisor Harvey Milk in 1978 (see box, p.526), which sparked some of the most intense rioting in the city's history, and the onset of the AIDS epidemic motivated many in the community to focus their energy on political organizing instead of the wild life. As a result, the community now finds itself increasingly wealthy and politically influential – adopting the self-consciously enlightened demeanor of what is probably the world's most prominent gay community. But with this comfort has come a certain conservatism, and while activists argue that residents must still lead the fight on human rights issues such as AIDS funding and legal recognition of gay couples, many in the area seem increasingly concerned about more immediate quality-of-life issues such as chain stores and rising rents.

Oddly enough, for a neighborhood bursting with energy, there's not an awful lot to do in the Castro and the best way to while away an afternoon or evening here is to wander around. The heart of the district is filled with stores, restaurants, and bars all flying the rainbow flag and it's usually packed with people whatever the time of day: it's especially throbbing on a Sunday afternoon, crammed with men strolling, cruising, and sipping a coffee on the sidewalk. If you're lucky, you might spot one of the **Sisters of Perpetual Indulgence**, volunteers who dress as white-faced nuns to promote safe-sex and HIV awareness in a camp parody of Catholic pageantry. If the crowds of people are too much, head for the neighborhood's side streets, scrupulously manicured and lined with neat rows of brightly painted Victorians – a world away from the stores and bars crammed along the Castro.

Back on the main drag, the **Castro Theater**, 429 Castro Street at Market, with its lovely Art Deco neon sign rising high above the street, is a landmark that shines brightly in a neighborhood where people, not places, are the star attractions. Screening a well-curated schedule of classic film revivals and unusual premieres, the unofficial "Castro Cathedral" manages to find quality cinema that's more than a match for the theater's ambience. The ornate balconies, wall-mounted busts of heroic figures, and massive ceiling ornament would provide ample visual stimulation even without a film showing on the gigantic screen.

After leaving the Castro, make an effort to go to **Twin Peaks**, about a mile and a half uphill along Market from Harvey Milk Plaza. Get here by traveling west until you hit Twin Peaks Boulevard; the #37 Corbett bus will take you to

The assassination of Harvey Milk

In 1977, eight years after New York's Stonewall riots brought gay political activism into the spotlight, Castro camera-shop owner **Harvey Milk** won election as the city's first openly gay supervisor (or councilor), and quickly became one of the most prominent gay officials in the country. Milk was a celebrated figure for the city's gay community, nicknamed the "Mayor of Castro Street," so it came as a horrifying shock when, in 1978, former Supervisor **Dan White** walked into City Hall and shot both Milk and Mayor George Moscone dead. White was an ex-cop who had resigned from the board, claiming he couldn't live on the small salary. In fact, he was angered that the liberal policies of Moscone and Milk didn't accord with his conservative views: a staunch Catholic, White saw himself as a spokesman for San Francisco's many blue-collar Irish families and, as an ex-policeman, the defender of the family values he believed gay rights were damaging. At his trial, White claimed that harmful additives in his fast-food-laden diet had driven him temporarily insane – a plea which came to be known as the **"Twinkie defense"** (Twinkies being synthetic-cream cakes) – and was sentenced to five years' imprisonment for manslaughter. The gay community exploded when the news of White's light sentence was announced and the "White Night" riots that followed were among the most violent San Francisco has ever witnessed, as protesters stormed City Hall, turning over and burning police cars as they went. White was released from prison in 1985 and moved to Los Angeles, where he committed suicide shortly after. In a happier coda, current City Supervisor Tom Ammiano, a former stand-up comedian, who has said that he found the courage to publicly come out as gay through Milk's activism, is a prominent political figure in the city.

Park Ridge. The highest point in the city, Twin Peaks gives a 360-degree view of the Peninsula. During the day, busloads of tourists arrive to point their cameras, and during the summer crowds often build up waiting for the fog to lift. It's better to go at night, picking out landmarks from either side of the shimmering artery of Market Street.

Haight-Ashbury

Two miles west of downtown San Francisco, the **HAIGHT-ASHBURY** neighborhood lent its name to an entire era, receiving in return a fame on which it has traded mercilessly ever since. Originally part of the Western

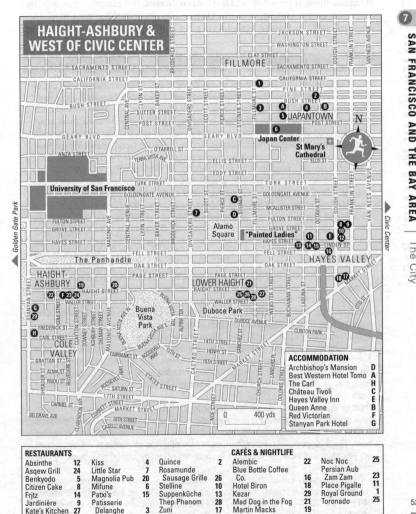

HAIGHT-ASHBURY & WEST OF CIVIC CENTER

Golden Gate Park

Civic Center

ACCOMMODATION

Archbishop's Mansion	D
Best Western Hotel Tomo	A
The Carl	H
Château Tivoli	C
Hayes Valley Inn	E
Queen Anne	B
Red Victorian	F
Stanyan Park Hotel	G

RESTAURANTS

Absinthe	12	Kiss	4	Quince	2
Asqew Grill	24	Little Star	7	Rosamunde	
Benkyodo	5	Magnolia Pub	20	Sausage Grille	26
Citizen Cake	8	Mifune	6	Stelline	10
Frjtz	14	Patxi's	15	Suppenküche	13
Jardinière	9	Patisserie		Thep Phanom	28
Kate's Kitchen	27	Delanghe	3	Zuni	17

CAFÉS & NIGHTLIFE

Alembic	22	Noc Noc	25
Blue Bottle Coffee		Persian Aub	
Co.	16	Zam Zam	23
Hotel Biron	18	Place Pigalle	11
Kezar	29	Royal Ground	1
Mad Dog in the Fog	21	Toronado	25
Martin Macks	19		

Addition, it was unofficially carved off following the widespread publication of a picture of the Grateful Dead posing at the sign for the intersection of Haight and Ashbury streets. For all its fame, "the Haight" proper is tiny, spanning no more than eight blocks of attractive Edwardian and Victorian buildings. Despite some locals' nostalgia, it's changed dramatically since it emerged in the 1960s as the focus of the countercultural scene. Haight-Ashbury in the 21st century is theme-park boho, crammed with shops offering hippy-themed souvenirs or trendy boutiques selling designer clothes. Look hard enough, though, and you can still unearth the embers of its radical past: a handful of stores selling leftist literature and vintage clothing, cafés filled with dawdling intellectuals, and a few surviving hippies.

Roughly divided into half by **Divisadero Street**, the Haight consists of the Upper and Lower Haight, with the **Upper Haight** stretching west to Golden Gate Park and the **Lower Haight** running east to Buchanan Street. Long an

Hippies

The first **hippies** were an offshoot of the Beats, many of whom had moved out of their increasingly expensive North Beach homes to take advantage of the low rents and large spaces in the Victorian houses of the Haight. The post-Beat bohemia that subsequently began to develop here in the early 1960s was initially a small affair, involving drug use and the embrace of Eastern religion and philosophy, together with a marked anti-American political stance and a desire for world peace. Where Beat philosophy had emphasized self-indulgence, the hippies, on the face of it at least, attempted to be more embracing, focusing on self-coined concepts such as "universal truth" and "cosmic awareness." Naturally it took a few big names to get the ball rolling, and characters like **Ken Kesey** and his Merry Pranksters soon set a precedent of wild living, challenging authority, and dropping (as they saw it) out of the established norms of society. Drugs were particularly important, and considered an integral – and positive – part of the movement. **LSD** especially, the affects of which were just being discovered and which at the time was not actually illegal, was claimed as an avant-garde art form. It was pumped out in private laboratories and distributed by Timothy Leary and his network of supporters with a prescription ("Turn on, tune in, drop out") that galvanized a generation into inactivity. An important group in the Haight at the time was the Diggers, who, famed for their parties and antics, truly believed LSD could be used to increase creativity.

Before long, life in the Haight began to take on a theatrical quality: Pop Art found mass appeal, light shows became legion, dress turned flamboyant, and the Grateful Dead, Jefferson Airplane, and Janis Joplin made names for themselves. Backed by the business weight of promoter Bill Graham, the **psychedelic music** scene became a genuine force nationwide, and it wasn't long before kids from all over America started turning up in Haight-Ashbury for the free food, free drugs, and free love. Money became a dirty word, the hip became "heads," and the rest of the world were "straights."

Other illustrious tenants of the Haight in the 1960s included Kenneth Rexroth (see opposite), who hosted a popular radio show and wrote for the *San Francisco Examiner*. Hunter S. Thompson, too, spent time here researching and writing his book *Hell's Angels*, and was notorious for inviting Angels round to his apartment on Parnassus Street for noisy, long, and occasionally dangerous drinking and drug-taking sessions.

Things inevitably turned sour towards the end of the decade, but during the heady days of the massive "be-in" in Golden Gate Park in 1966 and the so-called **Summer of Love** the following year, this busy little intersection became home to no less than 75,000 transitory pilgrims who saw it as the headquarters of alternative culture.

African-American neighborhood, the Lower Haight has been transformed over the past decade by youthful immigrants from Britain into the center of the city's rave culture. DJ shops line Haight Street between Webster and Divisadero, while bars blatantly capitalize on Old World nostalgia (even for the food). Though the Mission has stolen much of the Lower Haight's trend-hopping spotlight, the neighborhood remains very much torn between its older and newer identities – a conflict that has led to some tensions. It's best to exercise caution at night, particularly in the vicinity of Webster Street.

In much the same way that the Lower Haight tends to be overshadowed by its flashier neighbor up the hill, former resident **Kenneth Rexroth** (1905–82) has largely been overshadowed by the writers he inspired. As a poet, novelist, and translator of Chinese literature, Rexroth lived a wildly adventurous life that was an inspiration for Kerouac and crew. While not open to the public, you can take a walk past Rexroth's old apartment at 250 Scott Street, a place where several of the early Beats crashed upon first arriving in San Francisco.

Continuing uphill toward the heart of the Haight will bring you to **Buena Vista Park**, a mountainous forest of Monterey pines and California redwoods. Used by dog walkers in the daylight hours, come nightfall the park plays host to much sex-in-the-shrubbery; walk here accompanied by day and not at all at night. Continue past here along Haight Street, and the sidewalks become crowded by an increasing number of musicians, panhandlers, and hardcore hippy burnouts. Two blocks west, the **Grateful Dead House**, 710 Ashbury at Haight, was once ground zero for the counterculture. A 1967 drug bust only added to the band's myth, which survived countless tours and a rotating cast of keyboard players. Even the 1995 death of guitarist Jerry Garcia has done little to quell fans' devotion.

To the north of Haight Street, the **Panhandle** is a rivulet of greenery that runs like a tributary into Golden Gate Park. Though the grass is noticeably scraggly these days, it was once a ritzy thoroughfare catering to horse-drawn carriages, and the lovely houses speak of wealthier times; it's one of the trendier areas to live in the city, and the area north of the Panhandle now even boasts a trendy nickname, NoPa.

The Western Addition

Spreading north and east of the Haight, the **Western Addition** is one of the central city's few predominantly black neighborhoods and almost relentlessly poor – dangerous in parts and, but for one standout sight, certainly not tourist territory. The nadir for the neighborhood was in the 1960s, when the dual forces of urban renewal and blunderheaded civic planner **Justin Herman** – honored with a public park along the Embarcadero (see p.512) – led to the demolishing of blocks of precious Victorian housing. They were replaced with acres of monolithic concrete apartment blocks, leaving few vestiges of the Western Addition's history or character.

The exception to this rule is a small area surrounding **Alamo Square Park**, at Hayes and Scott – just uphill from the Lower Haight. A staple of every tour bus company in town, the park's southeast slope is home to small flocks of amateur photographers eager to snap a picture of "the Painted Ladies." These six Victorian houses, originally built in 1894 and colorfully and attractively restored, have been postcard subjects for years. Even if you've forgotten your camera, it's still worth the steep climb up here for the brilliant **views** across the city – on a clear day you can see across the bay all the way to the hills of North Berkeley.

Golden Gate Park and around

Unlike most American cities, San Francisco is not short on green space, and **GOLDEN GATE PARK** is its largest, simultaneously full of the bustle of urban living and hidden natural environments offering welcome respite to city residents. The park was designed in 1871 by Park Commissioner William Hall in the style of Frederick Law Olmsted, who was the man behind Central Park in New York. Spreading three miles or so west from the Haight as far as the Pacific shore, Golden Gate Park was constructed – on what was then an area of wild sand dunes buffeted by the spray of the nearby ocean – with the help of a dyke to protect the western side from the sea. Even so, the landscape still undergoes a natural transition as it approaches the ocean and, in contrast to the relatively placid bay, the strong winds blowing through the park and gusting up streets in the surrounding neighborhoods are a constant reminder of the sea's more turbulent temperament. It's generally best to visit in the late morning or early afternoon – even on seemingly sunny days, a chilly fog often rolls in before dusk. Although the original planners intended to keep the park free of buildings, that proved impossible and its eastern half is now dotted with city sights like the California Academy of Sciences. Most of them date from the 1894 World's Fair, the first held in California, which was designed as a recession-busting sideshow by local newspaperman M.H. de Young. It was so successful that de Young was honored with a permanent museum in his name (see below).

Exploration of the whole place could take days of footwork. Among its more obvious attractions, there's a Japanese Tea Garden, a giant greenhouse (allegedly modeled on the Palm House at Kew Gardens in London), and a Shakespeare Garden with every flower or plant mentioned in the writer's plays, not to mention the usual contingent of serious joggers, cyclists, and in-line skaters.

The park's new star attraction is the **M.H. de Young Museum** (Tues–Sun 9.30am–5.15pm, Fri until 8:45pm; $10, free first Tues of every month, $2 discount with valid MUNI transfer; ℡415/750-3600, ⓦwww.thinker.org). Reopened in 2005, the new space liberates the de Young from its former cramped confines, giving ample space to its varied collection, which wanders through sub-Saharan Africa and the Americas and includes some four hundred works of art from New Guinea. The museum's highlights are its **American paintings** – with more than a thousand works, they make up one of the best collections of its kind and include paintings by Georgia O'Keeffe, Edward Hopper, Thomas Eakins, and George Caleb Bingham. But like SFMOMA downtown, it's the building that's the main attraction here. An angular copper-clad structure designed by Swiss architects Jacques Herzog and Pierre de Meuron, the de Young looks like it landed in Golden Gate Park right out of a sci-fi flick. Spend some time here, though, and the interplay between modernist behemoth and outdoor public space becomes apparent, with interior courts filled with the park's trademark ferns and eucalyptus, and sculptures outside's the museum's walls.

The museum is well worth an entire morning, capped by lunch in the excellent cafeteria, which has outdoor seating next to a sculpture garden. Don't leave without visiting the ninth-floor observation tower (free) for sweeping views across the park and city at large. Dominating the view from here is the new home of the **California Academy of Sciences** (daily 10am–5pm; $10; ℡415/321-8000, ⓦwww.calacademy.org), whose exhibits are housed in a much smaller temporary site at 875 Howard Street at Fifth in SoMa (see p.518) until the refurbished, Renzo Piano-designed digs debut here in 2008. Unlikely to captivate adults but a delight for kids – expect it to be clogged with school groups during the week – the collection includes rotating science exhibits along with Nature Nest, a themed playroom for the under-5 set. Among the clearly labeled modular tanks at the **Steinhart Aquarium**, each holding a different species, look for the garishly furry pink-and-white anemones and the shy, oddly unscary piranhas which lurk at the bottom of their tank.

Nearby, the ever-crowded **Japanese Tea Garden** (daily 9am–6pm; $4; ⊤415/752-1171) was built in 1894 for the California Midwinter Exposition and beautifully landscaped by the Hagiwara family, who were also responsible for the invention of the fortune cookie during the Pan-Pacific Exposition of 1915 (despite the prevailing belief that fortune cookies are Chinese). The Hagiwaras looked after the garden until World War II, when, along with other Japanese Americans, they were sent to internment camps. A massive bronze Buddha dominates the garden, which is much larger than it at first appears; it's soothing to spend time exploring among the bridges, footpaths, pools filled with shiny oversized carp, and bonsai and cherry trees – as long as you can ignore the busloads of tourists that pour in regularly throughout the day. The best way to enjoy the garden is to get there around 9am when it first opens and have a breakfast of tea and fortune cookies in the teahouse.

Perhaps the most unusual thing about Golden Gate Park is its small herd of a dozen or so bison, roaming around the **Buffalo Paddock**, the sunken field north of JFK Drive near 38th Avenue. They're fenced in with hefty metal railings, and the closest you can get to the animals is in their feeding area at the far west end. Moving towards the edge of the park at Ocean Beach, passing a tulip garden and two crumbling windmills donated by the Queen of Holland, you'll come to the **Beach Chalet** (⊤415/386-8439, ⊛www .beachchalet.com). This two-story, white-pillared building was designed by Willis Polk and houses a series of 1930s frescoes depicting the growth of San Francisco as a city and the creation of Golden Gate Park. It also holds a small visitor center that provides information about the park's numerous guided walking tours, as well as a pair of lively restaurants, great for late weekend brunches or, on a sunny afternoon, chilling out in the back garden with beers from the on-site brewery.

Sunset, Richmond, and Ocean Beach

Golden Gate Park is hugged by the large, residential neighborhoods of **Richmond** to the north and **Sunset** to the south. As late as the 1940s, much of what comprises these two districts was still mile after mile of sand dunes, stretching to the ocean. And while residents of the city's more intensely urban eastern half might turn up their noses and say that, in terms of liveliness, not much has changed in the half-century since, the truth is that both neighborhoods – the multiethnic Richmond in particular – offer some rewarding oases of activity. More than the tourist-saturated downtown neighborhoods, this area is a window into the less seen side of San Francisco: a comfortable, though occasionally lethargic, blend of cultures. Numerous good, cheap restaurants, serving food from around the world, and the California Palace of the Legion of Honor's remote cultural outpost will reward those who stop here en route to the breathtaking (but often fog-bound) coastline at the city's edge.

Partly due to the weather and partly due to the coldness of the ocean water, beach culture doesn't exist in San Francisco the way it does in Southern California, and people here tend to watch the surf rather than ride it. Powerful currents and crashing waves dissuade all but the most fearless swimmers, and as a result the city's beaches remain blissfully uncrowded.

Across the street from the Beach Chalet and stretching to the city's southern border, buffeted by sea breezes and fog, the strip of **Ocean Beach** seems constantly on the brink of being either washed out to shore or blown into locals' backyards. Aside from a small community of particularly hearty surfers (most notably country-rock crooner Chris Isaak), the beach is the almost exclusive territory of joggers and dog walkers. Perched precipitously above the northern end of the beach, the original **Cliff House**, 1090 Point Lobos Road (T 415/386-3300, W www.cliffhouse.com), was built in 1863 and became a popular seaside resort for the city's wealthiest families. Twice destroyed by fire, the complex – today primarily restaurants – underwent a radical renovation in early 2004 to upgrade its rather faded interior, though most travelers would do better to skip the food and come only for the views or the small visitor center. On the lower landing is a rare **Camera Obscura** (11am–sunset, weather permitting; $2; T 415/750-0415). Using a rotating mirror – and a trick of light – it gives entrants a panoramic view of the surrounding area. Unfortunately, the camera is mostly surrounded by water, making the view less interesting than the presentation itself.

Down by the water you'll find the remains of another bygone amusement – the **Sutro Baths**. This collection of opulent recreational pools, gardens, and elegant sculptures, all covered with 100,000 feet of stained glass, was sadly destroyed by fire in the 1960s. From here you can explore the ramparts and tunnels of the fortified coastline – a bit frightening at night, when the surf really starts crashing, but there's a certain romance too, and on a rare warm evening it becomes one of the city's favorite make-out spots.

The Legion of Honor

The stately **California Palace of the Legion of Honor** (Tues–Sun 9.30am–5.15pm; $10, free first Tues of each month, $2 discount with valid MUNI transfer; T 415/750-3600, W www.legionofhonor.org) is one of the best museums in San Francisco. The building itself is no less staggering than its setting, built in 1920 by Alma de Bretteville Spreckels (see p.517), with a cast of Rodin's *The Thinker* set dramatically on a pedestal in the center of the front courtyard. The museum's Rodin holdings are breathtaking in their depth and range, although there are more bronzes than marble sculptures: with over eighty pieces, it's one of the best collections of its kind in the world. Sadly, the magnificent museum is somewhat let down by its lackluster collection of Old Masters – many of the artworks, including those by Giambologna, Cellini, and Cranach, are "attributed to" or from "the workshop of," rather than bona fide masterpieces. Reach the museum by taking the #38 bus from Geary Boulevard and transferring to the #18 at the Lincoln Park Golf Course; fitter types can skip the second bus and walk ten minutes uphill to the main entrance.

Eating

Surpassed only by Paris in number of restaurants per capita, San Francisco lives up to its hype as a food-crazed city. With so much agricultural land nearby it's not surprising that locals are ingredient snobs; indeed, menus regularly boast of their steak coming from Niman Ranch or of serving only veggies from this or that local farm. San Francisco's obsession with restaurants dates back to the Gold Rush days, when the city was overrun with single men staying in boarding-houses who had to find somewhere to eat every evening. Dozens of diners sprung up in response, and the city's been restaurant-obsessed ever since.

At the lower end of the scale, the **dim sum** houses of Chinatown and the **Mexican** places of the Mission are not only cheap, but cook up some of the

Bagdad Café 2295 Market St at 16th, Castro ☎415/621-4434. The best priced 24-hour option in the neighborhood.

Bruno's 2389 Mission St at 20th, Mission ☎415/648-7701. Jazz lounge serving modern American food until midnight.

Caffè Greco 423 Columbus Ave at Vallejo, North Beach ☎415/397-6261. Coffee and light meals at this old-fashioned Italian snack bar.

El Farolito 2779 Mission St at 24th, Mission ☎415/824-7877. A scruffy local institution, this 24-hour taqueria is pretty basic but the food is outstanding and cheap.

Magnolia Pub and Brewery 1398 Haight St at Masonic, Haight-Ashbury ☎415/864-7468. Pub food with a San Francisco twist. See p.539.

Osha 696 Geary St at Jones ☎415/673-2368. Yummy Thai noodles, convenient to Union Square. See p.534.

Yuet Lee 1300 Stockton St at Broadway, Chinatown ☎415/982-6020. Terrific Chinese seafood until 3am; daily except Tuesday.

best food in town. There are, inevitably, dozens of **Italian** restaurants in North Beach (though quality varies wildly), and **French** food is a perennial favorite, although nouvelle cuisine is finally beginning to loosen its grip on San Franciscan menus. **California cuisine** nowadays has grown away from its minimalist roots, but still features the freshest food, usually locally grown and beautifully presented. **Japanese** food is massively popular, as are an increasing number of **Thai and Vietnamese** eateries. Not surprisingly, health-conscious San Francisco also has a wide range of **vegetarian** and **wholefood** restaurants, and it's rare to find anywhere that doesn't have at least one meat-free item on the menu. It's also very worthwhile to plan on one splurge meal while in town – the high price you'll pay for a world-class meal here is still far below the big-city average.

Be warned: San Francisco closes up early and you'll be struggling to find places that will serve you much later than 10 or 11pm, unless they're of the 24-hour diner variety. As elsewhere in California, you cannot smoke in any restaurant in the city.

Downtown and Union Square

Cortez At the *Adagio*, 550 Geary St at Jones, Theater District ☎415/292-6360. Once one of the buzziest places in town, this restaurant's menu of mostly Mediterranean tapas still shines, with sharing plates of succulent treats like pan-roasted octopus and Monterey squid ($14) and katafi-wrapped crab cakes ($17). The swank bar, backlit by Mondrian-like panels, is a fine spot for a proper cocktail.

Dottie's True Blue Café 522 Jones St at O'Farrell, Theater District ☎415/885-2767. Hefty portions of homemade cakes, eggs, and other breakfast favorites are the draw at this inexpensive diner – along with quirky owner Kurt, who's always good for a gab. Breakfast and lunch only. Try the cinnamon-ginger pancakes with grilled sausage.

Farallon 450 Post St at Powell, Union Square ☎415/956-6969. Come for seafood prepared and served with great fanfare. Pity that the jellyfish-inspired decor with its dangling luminescent mobiles is so offputting.

Farmer Brown 35 Mason St at Turk (near Market), Tenderloin ☎415/409-3276. Outstanding new restaurant uses organic ingredients from local and African-American farmers to deliver on its promise of "farm-fresh soul food." Good tunes, a young, diverse crowd, and a smart copper-and-brick industrial space make this an equally good spot to settle in for a drink at the lively, often packed bar.

Golden Era 572 O'Farrell St at Leavenworth, Tenderloin ☎415/673-3136. Subterranean vegan eatery with a pan-Asian menu that swerves through Thai, Chinese, and Japanese: try the crispy mint-cilantro rolls and Thousand Layers Tofu Eggplant in pepper sauce.

Kokkari Estiatorio 200 Jackson St at Front, Financial District ☎415/981-0983. By far the best Greek restaurant in town. Though the decor is purely Northern California, the cuisine is classic Greek, relying on staples such as lamb and eggplant, served both separately and cooked together as moussaka.

Michael Mina *Westin St Francis*, 335 Powell St, Union Square ☎415/397-9222. Diners create their own prix fixe meal ($98) at Michael Mina's eponymous restaurant, choosing from seasonal selections that play off a main ingredient, say lamb, that's matched with a trio of accompaniments, or from "classic" dishes such as his lobster pot pie and ahi tuna tartare. It's American fare at the hands of a master chef and well worth breaking the bank for.

Millennium At the *Savoy Hotel*, 580 Geary St at Hyde, Theater District ☎415/345-3900. Legendary vegetarian restaurant, offering flavor-packed entrées ($20–24) like grilled portobello mushrooms, robust enough to please even avid meat eaters. The dark wood-paneled decor's gauzy and romantic, and the crowd's as much opera buff as eco-warrior.

Osha 696 Geary St at Jones ☎415/673-2368. Thai noodle shop smack in the heart of the Tenderloin that does the basics right and stays up late (Sun–Thurs until 1am, Fri & Sat until 3am). It has spawned several slicker siblings, including ones in the Mission (819 Valencia St) and Cow Hollow (2033 Union St).

Ozone 1160 Polk St at Sutter, Polk Gulch ☎415/440-9663. Young Thais pack this spacious upstairs eatery, where the modern vibe and Thai pop tunes create an ambience that's as authentic Bangkok as the food. It's some of the Bay Area's best Thai and offers a chance to indulge in hard-to-find dishes like *yaam blah duuk phoo* (spicy catfish salad) and *sai ua* (Thai style sausage). Open until 1.30am.

Plouf 40 Belden Lane at Bush, Financial District ☎415/986-6491. French seafood bistro, usually packed out with a yuppie crowd; the atmosphere's airy and the food is rustic and southern. *Plouf*, incidentally, is the French answer to "splash!"

Saigon Sandwiches 560 Larkin St at Eddy, Tenderloin ☎415/474-5698. Tiny store selling outstanding made-to-order Vietnamese sandwiches for $2.50 each: choose between BBQ chicken, BBQ pork, and meatballs, all served with lashings of fresh greens and tongue-curling hot pickles.

Sears Fine Food 439 Powell St at Post, Union Square ☎415/986-1160. This old-fashioned breakfast joint, founded in 1938, turns out great dollar-sized Swedish pancakes and hefty Denver omelets all day long.

Shalimar 532 Jones St at Geary, Tenderloin ☎415/928-0333. This hole in the wall serves delicious, cheap Indian and Pakistani fare, all of it made before your eyes in the *kulcha* oven: the chicken tikka is a fantastic deal at only $3.50 for an enormous portion. There are a few tables if you want to linger.

Tadich Grill 240 California St at Front, Downtown ☎415/391-1849. With its roots in the Gold Rush era, this San Francisco institution serves traditional seafood in a wood-paneled dining room. Gruff waiters in white coats and a classic bar complete the scene.

Embarcadero & Fisherman's Wharf

Ana Mandara Ghirardelli Square, 891 Beach St at Polk, Fisherman's Wharf ☎415/771-6800. Yes, it's co-owned by washed-up Eighties stars Don Johnson and Cheech Marin, but the modern Vietnamese menu is delicious (if pricey). If you're on a tighter budget, go for drinks and appetizers in the beautiful, bamboo-decorated lounge area and listen to the fine live jazz (Thurs–Sat).

Boudin Sourdough Bakery & Café 160 Jefferson St at Mason, Fisherman's Wharf ☎415/928-1849. The sourdough bread at this chain is the best around, made from a 150-year-old recipe and yeast that's descended from the first batch.

Gary Danko 800 North Point at Hyde, Fisherman's Wharf ☎415/749-2060. Don't let the location put you off – this understated eatery regularly vies for the title of best restaurant in this foodie city. Granted, it's performance food, served with a self-conscious flourish, but it's utterly splurgeworthy. Though the menu changes seasonally, expect dishes like horseradish-crusted salmon or lemon herb duck breast with port-glazed figs; order individually or go for the five-course tasting menu for $94 per person. Reserve well in advance.

Hog Island Oyster Co. 1 Ferry Building, Embarcadero ☎415/391-7117. Slurp down Hog Island oysters, brought in fresh daily from this eatery's Tomales Bay farm in Pt Reyes, while taking in a view of the bay at the U-shaped marble bar. A gourmet grilled cheese sandwich, local beers, and wine round out the menu.

Ozumo 161 Steuart St at Howard, Embarcadero ☎415/882-1333. Stylish, spacious Japanese, with good sushi; small plates, such as hamachi and avocado with a warm ginger-jalapeno *ponzu* sauce ($16) and beef carpaccio with an ume-plum *shiso* dressing ($18); and a robata grill, where veggies, meat, and fish are sizzled over imported *sumi* charcoal. The dimly lit sake lounge is often abuzz with the Financial District set.

Pat's Café 2330 Taylor St at Columbus, Fisherman's Wharf ☎415/776-8735. Bright and basic with simple Formica and a short menu of burgers and sandwiches.

Pier 23 Café Pier 23, Embarcadero ☎415/362-5125. Sit out on the bayside deck under the heat lamps and enjoy casual seafood and sandwiches, not to mention a gorgeous view of the Bay Bridge. At night, there's live music, ranging through jazz, reggae, and salsa.

Scoma's Pier 47, Fisherman's Wharf ☎415/771-4383. Still run by Al and Joe Scoma, this reliable seafood joint with views of local fishing boats in the heart of Fisherman's Wharf got its start as a six-stool stand in the 1960s. It's the place to come in the Wharf to get your fix of Dungeness crab. There's a second location in Sausalito, which boasts stunning views across the bay to the city.

Shanghai 1930 133 Steuart St at Howard, Embarcadero ☎415/896-5600. This swank subterranean spot evokes Shanghai from its days as "the Paris of the Orient," with live jazz acts in the Blue Bar and an elegant dining area. The food, if not cheap, is well priced for the scene, and includes standouts like minced duck in lettuce petals ($12), firecracker chicken ($14), and a wok-seared filet mignon in black pepper sauce ($20).

Slanted Door 1 Ferry Building, Embarcadero ☎415/861-8032. This understated restaurant has plenty of buzz and fills up quickly: book ahead or eat early. The menu, which changes daily, is light French-Vietnamese; there are several deliciously fragrant chicken dishes, and the tea list is impressive. Its more casual sibling, *Out the Door*, can be found in the food court of the Westfield shopping mall, at Market and Fifth streets.

Taylor's Automatic Refresher 1 Ferry Building, Embarcadero ☎1-866/328-3663. The city outpost of this casual, classic Napa joint serves excellent burgers, chicken sandwiches, and fish tacos, all made from fresh ingredients and best enjoyed with one of the super-thick milkshakes – try a "black and white" made from chocolate sauce and pure vanilla ice cream.

Yank Sing 101 Spear St at Mission, Embarcadero ☎415/957-9300. This revered restaurant – so popular that on weekends the tables spill out of the pleasant dining room into the atrium of the Rincon Center – is a must for dim sum aficionados. Don't leave without a taste of the exceptional Peking duck, served with scallions and a touch of sauce on a steamed bun.

SoMa

Acme Chop House 24 Willie Mays Plaza at King and Third ☎415/644-0240. Vegetarian hell, this

resoundingly old-style restaurant is another brainchild of local chef wunderkind Traci Des Jardins of *Jardinière* (see p.539). The place is enormous and usually packed with businessmen chowing down on chunky, choice cuts of steak.

COCO500 500 Brannan St at Fourth ☎415/543-2222. Chef Loretta Keller delivers deeply flavorful Cal-Med cuisine in a chic setting warmed by caramel and blue walls adorned with local artwork. Don't miss the beef cheeks — whether as a main with watercress and horseradish cream ($16) or as an app, whipped into tasty "tacos" with *mole* ($4) — or the inventive, expertly crafted cocktails, including the signature, made with Thai basil and kaffir lime vodka.

Fringale 570 Fourth St at Brannan ☎415/543-0573. Delightful, low-key charmer on a quiet SoMa block. The service is as exceptional as the food, predominantly French but with Basque touches like serrano ham. The decor is simple and romantic – just the place to feed your date one of the sumptuous after-dinner truffles.

Lulu 816 Folsom St at Fifth ☎415/495-5775. Famed California cuisine restaurant with a rustic, rather cramped dining room: the shared family-style dishes are hit and miss, although the pearl-sized gnocchi are meltingly fluffy; the spectacular wine list – many by the glass – is also impressive.

Town Hall 342 Howard St at Fremont, SoMa ☎415/908-3900. Upscale casual newcomer with a convivial atmosphere that's a great spot for a glass of wine or a martini at one of the communal tables in the bar. Savor a dinner of bacon-wrapped rainbow trout or the signature pan-roasted stuffed pork chop with sun-dried tomatoes, fontina, mozzarella, and spicy dirty rice (both $24.50).

Tu Lan 8 6th St at Market ☎415/626-0927. A legend ever since Julia Child first sampled the Vietnamese cooking in this cramped, dingy space on one of the seediest blocks in town. Should you sit at the sticky counter, you'll be nearly singed by the flames from the stove. Nevertheless, the food is consistently fresh, authentic, and flavorful – just don't look up at the grubby ceiling!

North Beach and Chinatown

Café Jacqueline 1454 Grant Ave at Union, North Beach ☎415/981-5565. A romantic, candlelit gourmet experience, this restaurant serves only chef-owner Jacqueline Margulis's signature soufflés, both savory and sweet (crab and chocolate are top picks). Since every dish is prepared fresh, don't plan on a quick bite here – and though it's pricey (around $40 per entrée), the food's more than worth it.

The Helmand 430 Broadway at Kearny, North Beach ☎415/362-0641. The decor here is simple and unassuming – unlike the food, which is unforgettable. The menu's filled with tangy and spicy Afghani staples: try the *kaddo borwani* (caramelized pumpkin) or the grilled beef tenderloin.

House of Nanking 919 Kearny at Jackson, Chinatown ☎415/421-1429. This tiny spot has become a legend: expect a long but rapidly moving line, curt service, and a fabulous, underpriced meal. Those in the know let the waiters do the ordering for them.

Golden Gate Bakery 1029 Grant Ave at Jackson, Chinatown ☎415/781-2627. This Chinese pastry shop's silky egg custards have a devoted following, as do its rich moon cakes, which are snapped up during the annual mid-autumn festival.

Liguria Bakery 1700 Stockton St at Filbert, North Beach ☎415/421-3786. Marvelous old-world Italian bakery overlooking Washington Square Park, with deliciously fresh focaccia – the raisin's superb if rather unorthodox. Get there early, as it simply closes when sold out.

L'Osteria del Forno 519 Columbus Ave at Green, North Beach ☎415/982-1124. Tiny, authentic North Italian eatery on the main drag of Little Italy that's a glorious refuge from the nearby tourist traps. The menu's small, and driven by whatever's freshest at the market: *focaccine* sandwiches (made with springy, fluffy Italian bread) are only $5-7. Try one of the bean salads.

Louie's Dim Sum 1242 Stockton St at Broadway, Chinatown ☎415/989-8380. The glistening, pearly dumplings are ranged in vast metal trays in front of you, and although variety is limited, they're all delicious and cheap ($1 for two).

Mama's 1701 Stockton St at Washington Square, North Beach ☎415/362-6421. There are cheery, bright yellow tablecloths and sunny staff at this homely diner: try the Dungeness crab Benedict or one of the gooey, cakey French toast specials. Expect gargantuan lines at the weekend, whatever the time, so bring a book. Tues–Sun 8am–3pm.

🏃 **Mario's Bohemian Cigar Store** 566 Columbus Ave at Union, North Beach ☎415/362-0536. The "bohemian" in the name is dead-on, even if there are no cigars now. Try one of the chunky, cheap house-made focaccia sandwiches or a fresh, pungent shot of espresso.

R&G Lounge 631 Kearny St at Clay, Chinatown ☎415/982-7877. This enormous Hong Kong–style restaurant is popular with both Chinese and westerners. Dishes come family style, and there's a heavy bias towards seafood; if you plan 24 hours ahead, though, you can order the house special, a whole chicken hollowed out, stuffed with rice, and deep fried.

Sam Woh 813 Washington St at Grant, Chinatown ☎415/982-0596. Cheap and popular late-night spot where Kerouac, Ginsberg, and others used to hold court – just don't expect smiley service. Walk through the kitchen and up the cramped stairs to reach the dining room.

🏃 **Tommaso's** 1042 Kearny St at Broadway, North Beach ☎415/398-9696. This restaurant claims to be home to the first pizza oven installed on the West Coast (in 1935). Whatever the origins, the crispy pizzas are delicious: ask for one topped with clams in the shell. The space is cavelike and comfy, decorated with splashy murals. It's well worth the wait.

Trattoria Contadina 1800 Mason St at Union, North Beach ☎415/982-5728. This tiny, family-owned trattoria still caters primarily to the local Italian community: the food, like rigatoni with eggplant and smoked mozzarella, is traditional and outstanding.

The Marina, Cow Hollow, and Russian Hill

A16 2355 Chestnut St at Division, Marina ☎415/771-2216. This Southern Italian restaurant (named for the freeway that bisects the region around Naples) serves terrific thin-crust pizzas, house-cured salumi, pastas, and entrées like roasted young chicken with radishes and salsa verde. The extensive wine list – with more than forty options by the glass – focuses on Southern Italian and Californian wines from small producers and can also be enjoyed at the wine bar at the front.

Antica Trattoria 2400 Polk St at Union, Russian Hill ☎415/928-5797. Chef-owner Ruggero Gadaldi offers a menu of rustic fare from his homeland in this neighborhood Italian, with deliciously tender pastas and house specialties like thin slices of beef with arugula and gorgonzola-filled parsley-potato pancakes.

Baker Street Bistro 2953 Baker St at Lombard, Cow Hollow ☎415/931-1475. Cramped but charming café with a few outdoor tables, where the slightly older local crowd enjoys simple food served by French staff. Wines are well-priced and the $14.50 prix fixe dinner is a bargain.

Barney's Gourmet Hamburgers 3344 Steiner St at Chestnut, Marina ☎415/563-0307. The Marina outpost of this local chain has patio seating and popular burgers – including meatless ones – smothered in dozens of different toppings. There's another in the Castro at 4138 24th St, and several in the East Bay (see p.580).

▲ Greens restaurant in Fort Mason

Betelnut 2030 Union St at Buchanan, Cow Hollow ☏415/929-8855. Sceney local hangout, known for its pan-Asian menu served in smaller portions in a hybrid of the dim sum and tapas traditions. Not cheap (around $8–10 per plate), but offerings such as the minced chicken and *lup cheong* with lettuce cups, not to mention delicious green beans, are well worth sampling.

Bistro Yoffi 2231 Chestnut St at Pierce, Marina ☏415/885-5133. Chef Sarah Lewington serves eclectic modern American dishes at this refreshingly quirky bistro, packed with potted ferns and mismatched chairs. Try to snag a table for brunch in the lush garden out back.

Greens Fort Mason Center, Building A, Marina ☏415/771-6222. The queen of San Francisco's vegetarian restaurants, this pricey gourmet spot perches on a picturesque pier at Fort Mason Center and offers spectacular views of the bay.

Harris' Restaurant 2100 Van Ness at Pacific, Russian Hill ☏415/673-1888. Clubby and proudly old-fashioned, *Harris'* is one of the premier steakhouses in the city: the staff is warm and welcoming (if a little over-assiduous at times), as is the decor, heavy on padded chairs and comfy booths. There's every cut of beef imaginable – from a $35 filet to a $65 Kobe rib-eye – and all are buttery, sweet, and tender.

Mamacita 2317 Chestnut St at Scott, Marina ☏415/346-8494. Traditional, beautifully presented Mexican cuisine with an emphasis on fresh, local ingredients. It can be loud – the bar is a Marina hotspot – but dishes like the signature *chilaquiles* – refried tortilla chips with shredded chicken,

peppers, queso fresco, and chipotle cream – make it well worth enduring the fray.

Nick's Crispy Tacos 1500 Broadway at Polk, Russian Hill ☏415/409-8226. Although oddly situated in the *Rouge* nightclub – complete with red banquettes and chandeliers – *Nick's* serves some of the best tacos and burritos north of Market St. Cash only.

Sushi Groove 1916 Hyde St at Union, Russian Hill ☏415/440-1905. Groovy, throbbing modern sushi restaurant with inventive and original maki rolls as well as a sprinkling of Asian fusion dishes (delicious sake martinis, too). The SoMa branch, which often hosts local DJs, is bigger and just as hip but hard to find, since there's no sign: *Sushi Groove South*,1516 Folsom St at 11th, SoMa ☏415/503-1950.

Swan Oyster Depot 1517 Polk at California, Polk Gulch ☏415/673-1101. No frills – and officially, no full meals – at this cheap seafood counter. Grab a stool and hang onto it (it gets crowded and competitive here) and suck down some cheap shellfish and seafood.

The Mission and the Castro

2223 2223 Market St at Noe, Castro ☏415/431-0692. This restaurant is one of the most mixed gay-straight venues in the neighborhood – likely both because of its friendly, chatty vibe and because everyone wants to sample the sumptuous, simple interpretations of California cuisine, like lightly roasted chicken topped with onion rings. The setting's a soft, pale yellow room with high ceilings and low lighting.

Andalu 3198 16th St at Guerrero, Mission ☎415/621-2211. Airy, upscale tapas bar with high ceilings, deep green walls, and huge paper chandeliers, serving an inventive blend of Californian, European, and comfort food – think ahi tartare tacos ($10) or mac'n'cheese ($5). Save room for a serving of donut holes for dessert.

Bi Rite Creamery 3692 18th St at Dolores St, Mission ☎415/626-5600. Artisanal ice-cream shop that's achieved cult status among local foodies with flavors like honey lavender, chai-spiced milk chocolate, and salted caramel.

Bissap Baobab 2323 Mission St at 19th, Mission ☎415/826-9287. Colorful Senegalese spot bringing a rare taste of West Africa to the San Francisco scene, with dishes such as *aloko* (fried plantains with tamarind sauce) and *yassa* (marinated chicken or fish in a lemon garlic mustard sauce), as well as homemade juices and infused rums. Around the corner, *Little Baobab*, at 3388 19th St, offers ginger cocktails, DJs, and dancing.

Blue 2337 Market St at Castro, Castro ☎415/863-2583. Small, retro diner/restaurant that's decked out in industrial chromes and blacks, but serves deliciously simple comfort food like chicken pot pie and chili to the early hours. Thanks to a restrictive liquor license, *Blue* also mixes up original martinis and cocktails with a sake base, or you can choose from a selection of root beers.

Boogaloo's 3296 22nd St at Valencia, Mission ☎415/824-4088. Breakfast's the big draw here: black beans and chorizo feature heavily in the Latinized versions of American diner classics, costing $6–8 per dish. The decor's basic, but perked up with bright orange and yellow tables. Daily 8am–3pm.

Chow 215 Church St at Market, Castro ☎415/552-2469. Unfussy comfort food, like bargain pastas and wood-fired pizzas, some with an Asian twist. No reservations accepted, and the wait can be long. There's a branch called *Park Chow* in the Sunset (see p.540).

Delfina 3621 18th Street at Guerrero, Mission ☎415/552-4055. Elegant and inventive Italian food served in an industrial-chic setting makes this neighborhood Mission gem one of the darlings of the San Francisco foodie circuit. Next door, *Pizzeria Delfina* serves up more casual fare and is well worth the wait.

Dosa 995 Valencia at 21st, Mission ☎415/642-3672. Stylish South Indian serving an array of curries and over a dozen takes on the restaurant's namesake dish, a savory crêpe served filled or plain, along with chutney and *sambar*, a lentil dipping soup ($8.50–11).

El Trébol 3324 24th St at Mission, Mission ☎415/285-6298. Run by a husband-and-wife team, this café serves excellent versions of Nicaraguan standards like *churrasco* (grilled beef) and *chancho con yucca* (fried pork) in a haphazard setting washed with Latin music. The mouth-puckering *tamarindo* drink is an experience; just don't plan on enjoying the menu to its full if you're dieting.

Emmy's Spaghetti Shack 18 Virginia St at Mission, Bernal Heights ☎415/206-2086. This funky café is filled nightly with local hipsters who give it a laid-back, neighborhoody vibe. The hearty food makes it even more appealing: try the house meatballs and spaghetti for around $9.

Foreign Cinema 2534 Mission St at 21st, Mission ☎415/648-7600. Originally, the dominant gimmick at this upscale Cal-French restaurant was its hybrid nature: part bistro, part drive-in with movies projected onto the large outdoor wall and speakers on each table. Now, the movies are secondary to the food, including an excellent oyster/raw bar selection and grilled Meyer Ranch steak. The *Laszlo* martini bar is on the same site.

The Front Porch 65a 29th St at Mission, Mission ☎415/695-7800. This dark, down-home eatery with pressed tin ceilings and a groovy Mission vibe dishes out stylish southern food with a West Indies' twist. The salt cod and sweet pepper fritters ($8) are not to be missed, and the house staples, a molasses brined pork chop ($18.50) and buckets of spicy fried chicken, are matched by outstanding sides like coconut red beans and rice and grits with chili oil.

Herbivore 983 Valencia at 21st, Mission ☎415/826-5657. Reliable vegan spot with seating on the sidewalk and the back patio. There's another location in the Western Addition at 531 Divisadero.

Home 2100 Market St at Church, Castro ☎415/503-0333. The menu at this upscale diner offers dishes that a chef might cook at home for his friends (hence the name) – expect fresh takes on comfort classics like meatloaf, pot roast, and mac'n'cheese. It's popular with a mixed crowd, and there's a patio bar with DJs at the weekend.

La Taqueria 2889 Mission St at 25th, Mission ☎415/285-7117. Simply put, this always bustlingly Mission taqueria serves the best tacos in town.

Lime 2247 Market St at Noe, Castro ☎415/621-5256. An in-house DJ and Sixties mod decor set the mood for mojitos and bellinis at the low-slung white-marble bar, or a dinner of small plates of unique, home-style food, like grilled cheese with tomato soup dipping sauce ($6) and mini-burgers ($8). Food available until midnight.

Luna Park 694 Valencia St at 18th, Mission ⓣ415/553-8584. Decked out like a lush bordello, with deep red walls and ornamental chandeliers, and menus in the shape of little black books. Most of the entrees, like a tuna salad niçoise or breaded pork chop stuffed with mushrooms and gruyere, hover around $15. Don't miss the offbeat but excellent goat cheese fondue appetizer with grilled bread and sliced apples, or the excellent cocktails.

Mitchell's 688 San Jose Ave at 29th, Mission ⓣ415/648-2300. In a fairly desolate southern corner of the neighborhood is the perfect spot for an after-dinner treat. *Mitchell's* serves home-made ice cream in an array of exotic tropical flavors – try the buko (baby coconut), avocado, or sweet bean.

Papalote 3409 24th St at Valencia, Mission ⓣ415/970-8815. Colorful taqueria whose fresh ingredients and high-quality meat place its burritos a cut above the competition. Vegetarians will delight in the marinated tofu burrito. Additional outpost at 1777 Fulton St at Masonic.

San Francisco Taqueria 2794 24th St at York, Mission ⓣ415/641-1770. On a leafy stretch of 24th, this unassuming taco shop makes some of the city's best burritos, wrapped in tortillas grilled to flaky perfection.

Suriya 1432 Valencia St at 25th, Mission ⓣ415/824-6655. You'll feel like you're in Bangkok at this tiny restaurant, which is crammed with antiques and palms. The flamboyant food rarely disappoints – try the emerald noodles, the pumpkin curry, or the deep-fried green papaya wedges in shredded coconut butter.

Tartine Bakery 600 Guerrero St at 18th, Mission ⓣ415/487-2600. It's well worth braving the long lines at the Bay Area's best bakery-café to sample the excellent pastries and bread, which forms the backbone of a delicious array of hot pressed sandwiches.

Ti Couz 3108 16th St at Valencia, Mission ⓣ415/252-7373. Friendly, hip, and gracious, this crêperie was one of the pioneers of today's Mission scene on Valencia. It still holds its place as one of the best cheaper restaurants around, serving savory buckwheat pancakes and lighter, fluffier dessert crêpes.

Truly Mediterranean 3109 16th St at Valencia, Mission ⓣ415/252-7482. *Truly Mediterranean's* version of the falafel is wrapped in thin, crispy *lavash* bread rather than a pita, though once you get it, you'll find barely anywhere to sit in the tiny windowfront restaurant. The busy staff's spontaneous singing and dancing comes free of charge.

Hayes Valley to Haight-Ashbury

Absinthe 398 Hayes St at Gough, Hayes Valley ⓣ415/551-1590. Brasserie-cum-bistro with two separate dining areas, both serving robust French food in an authentic, if trendy, atmosphere. The bar's a good option around here for drinks, since it's open until midnight (Fri–Sat til 2am) and does smallish snacks for $6 or so per plate.

Asqew Grill 1607 Haight St at Clayton, Haight-Ashbury ⓣ415/701-9301. Original location of this local café chain, with its wooden beams and knickknack-crammed surfaces, is a refreshing alternative to most fast food: it serves more than a dozen different kinds of grilled skewers, from pork apple and pear to shrimp, tomato, and squash.

Citizen Cake 399 Grove St at Franklin, Hayes Valley/Civic Center ⓣ415/861-2228. Stylish, pricey bakery-cum-restaurant with a soft jazz soundtrack serving delectable, delicate pastries. Weekend brunches are a standout – try the soufflé pancake with home-made jam for $9.50.

Frjtz 570 Hayes St at Laguna, Hayes Valley ⓣ415/864-7654. Hip little *friterie* serving cones of crunchy Belgian-style fries with dips like jalapeño ketchup or spicy yoghurt peanut. The overstuffed sofa in the tiny window is a great place to hunker down and listen to live DJs playing at the decks next to the main counter.

Jardinière 300 Grove St at Franklin, Civic Center ⓣ415/861-5555. Run by big-name chef Traci Des Jardins, this boxy brick space caters to a pre-theater crowd with valet parking and plenty of pizzazz. The French-Cal food's a splurge ($25–30 an entrée), but you'll get what you pay for; there's an emphasis on indulgence from beginning (foie gras) to end (aged cheese platter).

Kate's Kitchen 471 Haight St at Fillmore, Lower Haight ⓣ415/626-3984. Monstrously huge portions of hearty breakfast food and crunchy hushpuppies are the pluses at this small diner; the massive crowds at weekends are the minus.

Little Star Pizza 846 Divisadero St at McAllister, NoPa ⓣ415/441-1118. Dark, hipster pizzeria serving deep-dish and thin-crust pies. Additional location at 400 Valencia. Dinner only.

Magnolia Pub and Brewery 1398 Haight St at Masonic, Haight-Ashbury ⓣ415/864-7468. With an emphasis on local, seasonal ingredients, this popular corner spot serves pub food San Francisco-style. The menu bounces from bangers and mash ($15) to a portobello mushroom sandwich ($11), and the tasty burger is made with organic ground beef from Prather Ranch. A brewery in the basement produces American riffs on classic British ales.

Patxi's 511 Hayes St at Gough, Hayes Valley
☎415/558-9991. This bright, pleasant, family-style pizzeria is best known for its deep-dish pizzas and makes for a good pit stop while perusing Hayes Valley's trendy boutiques.

Rosamunde Sausage Grill 545 Haight St at Fillmore, Lower Haight ☎415/437-6851. Tiny storefront grill with a few stools at the bar, serving only grilled sausages on a sesame roll. Choose from a cherry-laced chicken link to the light flavors of a shrimp, scallop, and snapper version.

Stelline 330 Gough St at Hayes, Hayes Valley ☎415/626-4292. Red-checkered tablecloths, a handwritten and photocopied menu, plus affable, chatty staff make this a cheap, easy place to grab a pasta lunch.

Suppenküche 525 Laguna at Hayes, Hayes Valley ☎415/252-9289. Here you can pair traditional beer-garden fare, such as *spaetzle*, sausages, and sauerkraut, with a good selection of lagers and lemony wheat beers. There's a beer-hall theme, complete with bare walls, stark pine chairs, and long wood tables.

Thep Phanom 400 Waller St at Fillmore, Lower Haight ☎415/431-2526. One of the best Thai restaurants in the city, catering to both hippy holdouts and yuppies: the curries are fragrant, pungent, and cheap, and the spinach with peanut sauce is sweet and sharp.

Zuni 1658 Market St at Gough, Hayes Valley ☎415/552-2522. Once cutting edge and now an institution, *Zuni* features the most famous caesar salad in town – made with home-cured anchovies – and an equally legendary focaccia hamburger in a rustic California style. The oyster bar and signature roast chicken are also big hits with regulars. The loft-style dining area is light and airy with large glass windows opening onto the street; most entrees are in the $18–22 range.

Pacific Heights and Japantown

Benkyodo 1747 Buchanan St at Sutter, Japantown ☎415/922-1244. The Okamura family has been waking up before dawn since 1906 to make *manju*, the tradition Japanese sweet-bean-filled confection, and *mochi*, soft-rice cakes. One of Japantown's original businesses. Closed Sun.

Kiss 1700 Laguna St at Sutter, Japantown ☎415/474-2866. With seating for only nine, this intimate sushi restaurant is one of the jewels of Japantown. Reservations essential.

Mifune Japan Center, 1737 Post St at Fillmore, Japantown ☎415/922-0337. Everything at this noodle house in the Japan Center is just the right temperature – the beer's ice cold, and the tangy noodles piping hot. More elegant than most of its neighbors, with a large array of soup toppings and a small selection of sushi.

Patisserie Delanghe 1890 Fillmore St at Bush, Pacific Heights ☎415/923-0711. Gourmet French bakery run by two expats, who make flaky, buttery croissants and glistening fruit tarts for $2 or so – the fruit brioche is a good choice. There are a few tables in the window if you want to linger.

Quince 1701 Octavia St at Bush, Pacific Heights ☎415/775-8500. New rustic Italian restaurant nestled in Pacific Heights that's caught attention from local foodies, thanks both to the pedigree of its chef (he trained under Alice Waters, the guru of California cuisine) and its ever-changing, seasonal menu. Expensive, but worth it.

The Richmond and the Sunset

Aziza 5800 Geary Blvd at 22nd, Richmond ☎415/752-2222. Classy Moroccan eatery with opulent decor. Try the $49 tasters' menu, which boasts Middle Eastern specialties like hummus and baba ghanoush, or the *basteeya*, phyllo pie filled with saffron-braised chicken and almonds.

Burma Superstar 309 Clement St at Fourth Ave, Richmond ☎415/387-2147. Foodie fave draws long lines on the Richmond's multi-ethnic strip to sample authentic Burmese fare like tea leaf salad, pumpkin pork stew and coconut chicken noodle soup, as well as dishes that highlight the cuisine's influences from neighboring India, China, and Thailand.

Chapeau! 1408 Clement St at 15th, Richmond ☎415/750-9787. Downtown-quality French food at foggy Richmond prices, packed with locals enjoying a relaxed, provincial atmosphere.

Park Chow 1240 Ninth Ave at Lincoln, Sunset ☎415/665-9912. The sequel to popular *Chow* in the Castro. Reliable renditions of pizza and pasta, perfect for a post-park lunch.

Pizzetta 211 211 23rd Ave at California, Richmond ☎415/379-9880. You can rely on inventive and unusual pizza here: there's a different menu each week, offering whatever's fresh and seasonal as a topping.

Q 225 Clement St at Third, Richmond ☎415/752-2298. There's over-the-top decor – like a table with a tree growing through it – and outlandish portions of comfort food (think fish tacos and mac'n'cheese) at this hip outpost.

Spices! Sichuan Trendz 294 Eighth Ave at Clement, Richmond ☎415/752-8884. Tiny, vibrant Chinese spot with bright orange-and-yellow walls and an Asian pop vibe, where the excellent food is described on the wide-ranging, quirky menu as "explosive," "flaming," and "numbing."

Thanh Long 4101 Judah St at 46th Ave, Sunset ☎415/665-1146. The original restaurant by the owners of the (over)hyped *Crustacean* in Polk Gulch serves upscale French-Vietnamese food amid low-key ambience. Try the roasted Dungeness crab with garlic sauce.

White Caps Café 3738 Geary Blvd at Arguello, Richmond ☎415/221-1613. This casual café is known for its extensive list of British favorites: sample shepherd's pie or Cornish pasties and pick up some salt and vinegar crisps to go from the on-site grocery. There's a small patio area out back.

Bars, cafés, and clubs

While famous for its restaurants, San Francisco also has a huge number of **drinking** establishments, ranging from comfortably scruffy jukebox joints to the chic watering holes of social climbers. Though spread fairly evenly over the city, happening bars are particularly numerous in North Beach and the Mission, where they line up one after the other. Some of the seediest are to be found in the Tenderloin, while yuppie cruising zones populate the Marina and slick lounges speckle downtown and SoMa. According to California law, there's **no smoking** allowed in any bar unless its sole employees are the owners, though enforcement can be spotty. Unsurprisingly, the city has many specifically **gay bars** (see p.552), most plentifully in the Castro and the Mission – although gay men, lesbians, and women on their own are likely to feel welcome at any bar.

The city is also dotted with excellent **cafés** serving first-rate coffees, teas, and soft drinks, in addition to beer and wine. More social than utilitarian, people hang out in these generally lively venues as much to pass time as to refresh themselves.

A diverse range of affordable, small- to medium-sized **clubs** allow leather-clad goths to rub shoulders with the bearded and beaded, and a number of gay hangouts (listed on p.553) still rock to the sounds of high-energy funk and Motown. You'll find the occasional DJ hangout playing two-step and drum'n'bass, but what the city does best is all the old favorites, the songs you know the words to; clubbing is more of a party than a pose here. The greatest concentration of clubs is in **SoMa**, especially the area around 11th Street and Folsom, though the **Mission** is similarly well provided with spots to get your groove on.

Unlike most other cities, where the action never gets going until after midnight, many San Francisco clubs have to close at 2am during the week, so you can usually be sure of finding things well under way by 11.30pm. At weekends, most places stay open until 3 or 4am. Very few venues operate any kind of dress code or restrictive admission policy, and only on very busy nights are you likely to have to wait. Unfortunately, most live music and dancing opportunities are restricted to the 21-and-over crowd, forcing underage revellers to be more creative when it comes to late-night entertainment.

Bars

Downtown and Union Square

The Ambassador 673 Geary St at Jones, Tenderloin ☎415/563-8192. Crystal chandeliers, a marble bar, and red carpeting give this new Tenderloin cocktail lounge an air of old Vegas cool, while nightly DJs keep the scene firmly in the present. Reserve ahead for one of the high-backed black leather booths, which feature rotary phones to dial up the bar.

Bambuddha *The Phoenix*, 601 Eddy St at Larkin, Tenderloin ☎415/885-5088. Chilled-out lounge, with a New Age-meets-Asian vibe (think swirling, elemental decor and feng shui-favorable fountains).

Big 4 In the Huntington Hotel, 1075 California St at Taylor, Nob Hill ☏ 415/771-1140. The Huntington's wood-paneled homage to the four most famous railway titans of the nineteenth century is one of the city's best spots for a quiet cocktail.

Bix 56 Gold St at Montgomery, Jackson Square ☏ 415/433-6300. Hidden on a tiny side street, this bar-restaurant has a touch of 1940s glamor to its decor: the bar's packed after work with an office crowd, while music fans slip into the supper club later for dinner. It's famed for its gin martinis.

Bourbon & Branch 501 Jones St at O'Farrell, Tenderloin ⊚ www.bourbonandbranch.com. This reservations-only bar (book online) has garnered plenty of buzz with its re-creation of a Prohibition-era speakeasy and its exquisite cocktails, crafted from the finest ingredients. Give the password at the unmarked door, and you'll be whisked into a dimly lit space with wooden booths, burgundy velvet wallpaper, and a pressed tin ceiling. Just don't order a cosmo.

The Bubble Lounge 714 Montgomery St at Jackson, Financial District ☏ 415/434-4204. Champagne bar that attracts a young, label-touting crowd – surprisingly, the prices here are very reasonable.

Edinburgh Castle 950 Geary St at Polk, Tenderloin ☏ 415/885-4074. Just your average Scottish bar, filled with heraldic Highland memorabilia and offering a massive selection of beers on tap and tasty fish'n'chips. The room upstairs regularly hosts comedy and live music, plus there's a quiz night every Tues at 8.30pm.

Gordon Biersch Brewery 2 Harrison St at Embarcadero, SoMa ☏ 415/243-8246. Bayfront outpost of the successful Peninsula microbrewery, housed in a converted Hills Brothers coffee warehouse with a lovely view of the bridge, good bar food, and some of the best beers in San Francisco.

Hemlock Tavern 1131 Polk St at Post, Polk Gulch ☏ 415/923-0923. Neighborhood bar that hosts regular live sets from gigging bands ($7–10), most beloved by smokers for its handy, enclosed patio where you can puff and sip in peace.

The Irish Bank 10 Mark Lane at Bush, Financial District ☏ 415/788-7152. An appealingly dark and cozy respite from the shops of Union Square, with the requisite Irish artifacts and pub fare like fish'n'chips and burgers.

London Wine Bar 415 Sansome St at Sacramento, Financial District ☏ 415/788-4811. Claiming to be America's first wine bar, this clubby place has a worn mahogany bar and cozy paneled booths, and caters to an older crowd.

Red Room In the Commodore International Hotel, 827 Sutter St at Jones, Theater District ☏ 415/346-7666. This sexy bar is – as its name implies – completely red: walls, furniture, glasses, and even many of the drinks. The clientele's young and mixed gay-straight, and it can get crowded at weekends.

The Redwood Room *Clift Hotel*, 495 Geary St at Taylor, Theater District ☏ 415/929-2372. This clubby landmark bar was made over by Starck & Schrager, who added lightboxes on the walls displaying paintings that shift and fade. It's fun and hip – just don't choke on the drink prices.

Slide 430 Mason St at Geary, Theater District ☏ 415/421-1916. Access to this underground homage to the 1920s is via a serpentine slide, which leads to a swank cocktail lounge, a former speakeasy called Café Dan's.

Top of the Mark *Mark Hopkins InterContinental*, One Nob Hill, 999 California St at Mason ☏ 415/616-6916. Panoramic views of the city make the pricey cocktails worthwhile. There's a $5–10 cover when there's live jazz (Wed–Sat).

Tunnel Top 601 Bush St at Stockton, Union Square ☏ 415/986-8900. This grimy but groovy bar is hidden behind a seedy storefront on top of the Stockton Street tunnel. Inside is arty-industrial – check out the chandelier festooned with empty wine bottles – and there are movies projected on the walls. One of the few tobacco-friendly places downtown.

SoMa

21st Amendment 563 Second St at Brannan ☏ 415/369-0900. This bright, lively South Park brewpub, two blocks from the ballpark, turns out a dozen or so tasty microbrews, which it serves alongside decent burgers and other pub fare to a down-to-earth crowd.

Bacar Restaurant & Wine Salon 448 Brannan St at Fourth ☏ 415/904-4100. White-hot when it opened a few years back, this three-level bar-restaurant has settled into a mellower spot. It's still one of the best places in town for wine, with over sixty by the glass and 1400 by the bottle, and you can linger in overstuffed chairs, enjoying appetizers and live jazz, in the lounge downstairs (Fri–Sun).

Butter 354 11th St at Folsom ☏ 415/863-5964. Stylized "white trash" bar and diner featuring imitation trailer-park decor, like a bar covered with shingles. The serving window to one side serves only microwaveable junk food. Hip, fun, and ironic, if a little less supercool than it once was.

District 216 Townsend St at Third ☏ 415/896-2120. Rekindling the spirit of the dot-com days, this wine bar has high ceilings and exposed brick

While the surrounding countryside may be devoted to winemaking, the city of San Francisco is renowned for its beer, specifically its **microbreweries**: the best-known local product is so-called **steam** beer, a hybrid lager-bitter. It was invented when early local brewers, finding the ice needed for lager production too expensive, instead fermented their yeast at room temperature like an ale: the result was a beer with the lower ABV of lager but the hearty flavor of bitter. (The precise origin of the odd name, unfortunately, has never been established.) To find out more, head over to the **Anchor Steam Brewery**, 1705 Mariposa Street at Carolina, Potrero Hill, for a **tour** (weekday afternoons only; free; reservations essential ℡415/863-8350, ⓦwww .anchorbrewing.com), though the product is universally available at bars and stores. The pick of the local microbrewpubs are:

21st Amendment SoMa. See p.542.

Gordon Biersch Brewery SoMa. See p.542.

Magnolia Pub and Brewery Haight-Ashbury. See p.539.

San Francisco Brewing Company North Beach. See below.

Thirsty Bear Brewing Company SoMa. See below.

walls and draws a young, well-heeled crowd. There's an eclectic selection of over thirty wines by the glass, plus small plates such as pizzettas ($10–14) and salumi ($12).

Pied Piper Bar *Palace Hotel*, 2 New Montgomery St at Market ℡415/546-5020. Named after the famous mural of the Pied Piper by artist Maxfield Parrish that decorates the bar, this mahogany-paneled room is a secluded, elegant place for a martini.

The Ramp 855 China Basin St at Illinois, China Basin ℡415/621-2378. Way out on the old docks, this is well worth the half-mile trek from Downtown to sit out on the patio and sip beers while looking over the abandoned piers and boatyards.

Thirsty Bear Brewing Company 661 Howard St at Second ℡415/974-0905. A combination brewpub and tapas bar, packed in the evenings with local office workers; the food's well-priced ($7–12 a plate) and tasty (try the fried calamari).

North Beach and Chinatown

Gino and Carlo 548 Green St at Grant, North Beach ℡415/421-0896. Visitors wanting to stop by to play pinball or pool won't feel unwelcome at this classic drunken pressman's bar, filled all day with regulars and old-school locals.

Li Po's 916 Grant Ave at Jackson, Chinatown ℡415/982-0072. Named after the Chinese poet, *Li Po's* is a little grotty, although that's part of its charm. One of the few places to drink in Chinatown.

Rosewood 732 Broadway at Powell, North Beach ℡415/951-4886. Deliberately hidden bolt hole that doesn't even have a sign outside. The retro interior is complemented by great lounge-core DJs: the downside is the pricey drinks and the out-of-towners who pour in at weekends. Best on weeknights by far.

San Francisco Brewing Company 155 Columbus Ave at Pacific, North Beach ℡415/434-3344. Probably the most touristy of the various micro-brewpubs around town, with a bland crowd of nonlocals and big shining tanks of beer. Still, great happy-hour deals from 4 to 6pm.

Sip 787 Broadway St at Powell, North Beach ℡415/699-6545. Adding a splash of style to the North Beach scene, this friendly lounge has nightly DJs spinning everything from hip-hop to pop after 10pm.

Spec's 12 Saroyan Place at Columbus, North Beach ℡415/421-4112. Friendly dive bar in the heart of North Beach that's decked out with a museum's worth of oddities from the high seas. It's packed with an older, eccentric local crowd and known for its chatty barstaff, who'll often serve up cheese and crackers to regulars.

Tosca 242 Columbus Ave at Pacific, North Beach ℡415/986-9651. A bar so classic it feels like a Hollywood set: bartenders in white waistcoats; arias wafting out of the jukebox; and, along the 80-year-old wooden bar, a long line of cocktail glasses filled with the house drink, a brandy-laced cappuccino.

Vesuvio 255 Columbus Ave at Jack Kerouac Alley, North Beach ℡415/362-3370. Even if it weren't once the regular hangout of Jack Kerouac and the Beats, North Beach's most famous bar would still be one of the best spots in town to grab a pint.

The Marina, Cow Hollow, and Fisherman's Wharf

Balboa Café 3199 Fillmore St at Greenwich, Marina ☏ 415/921-3944. This dark-wood bar, with high ceilings and an excellent wine list, is packed most nights of the week with Marina singles on the prowl. The bartenders whip up a superb bloody mary, and the burger, served on a baguette, is one of the city's best.

Buena Vista Café 2765 Hyde St at Beach, Fisherman's Wharf ☏ 415/474-5044. Ever crowded with tourists and locals alike, this San Francisco landmark is still churning out its famed Irish coffee.

Liverpool Lil's 2942 Lyon St at Greenwich, on the edge of the Presidio ☏ 415/921-6664. Old-fashioned Brit-centric pub that's refreshingly rough-edged amid the Marina's hordes of wine bars. Come to drink pints of Bass ale and chow down on shepherd's pie until 1am most nights; for some reason, it's popular with local windsurfers at weekends.

Matrixfillmore 3138 Fillmore St at Greenwich, Marina ☏ 415/563-4180. Inspired by the original *Matrix* that opened on the same spot in 1965 and hosted big-name rock acts, this bar couldn't be more different now. It's glamorous and a little posey, with a Marina crowd sipping wine by the glass and dancing to mainstream house and disco.

The Mission and the Castro

Amnesia 853 Valencia St at 19th, Mission ☏ 415/970-0012. Small, red-lit bar serving micro-brews, wine, and soju cocktails, and hosting an eclectic array of nightly entertainment, from bluegrass (every Mon) to DJs laying down hip-hop beats, with the odd "drunk puppet" show thrown in for good measure. Admission for events ranges from free to $10.

Blondie's Bar & No Grill 540 Valencia St at 16th, Mission ☏ 415/864-2419. Always packed, this fun bar with a good-sized patio serves huge cocktails and often hosts live music. As a bonus, the Wetspot back room is smoker-friendly.

Dalva 3121 16th St at Valencia, Mission ☏ 415/252-7740. *Dalva's* divey and dark, and though the wafer-thin space is easy to miss, that doesn't stop a diverse crowd from packing in to lean against one of the narrow tables.

Doc's Clock 2575 Mission St at 21st, Mission ☏ 415/824-3627. Deco-style bar, easy to spot thanks to the hot-pink neon sign blazing out front; it attracts an artsy and alternative patronage.

La Rondalla 901 Valencia St at 20th, Mission ☏ 415/647-7474. It's always Christmas at this festive Mexican dive, decorated year-round with an orgy of tinsel and trinkets. There's a live mariachi band most nights.

Latin American Club 3286 22nd at Valencia, Mission ☏ 415/647-2732. This easy-going hipster joint is the Mission's answer to a friendly neighborhood watering hole, with seating at the tiny bar or at one of the 1950s Formica tables scattered about a room decorated with a bizarre array of cuckoo clocks, piñatas, and taxidermy.

Laszlo 2526 Mission St at 21st, Mission ☏ 415/401-0810. This industrial-chic bar, attached to the film-themed restaurant *Foreign Cinema*, is unsurprisingly named in homage to the movies – Jean-Paul Belmondo's character in *A Bout de Souffle*. There's a DJ nightly and the cocktails, especially the mojitos, are outstanding.

The Lone Palm 3394 22nd St at Guerrero, Mission ☏ 415/648-0109. Like a forgotten Vegas review bar from the 1950s, this dim, candlelit cocktail lounge is a secret gem. The namesake palm is actually metal and there's a TV above the bar playing classic American movies.

Lucky 13 2140 Market St at Church, Castro ☏ 415/487-1313. Divey rocker bar on the border between the Castro and the Lower Haight that's celebrated for its jukebox.

Make-Out Room 3225 22nd at Mission, Mission ☏ 415/647-2888, ⊛ www.makeoutroom.com. This small, dark space is primarily a place to drink at the enormous mahogany bar, but there are regular performances by local indie bands Fri–Sun. $5–8.

Medjool 2522 Mission St at 21st, Mission ☏ 415/550-9055. The Sky Terrace at this multilevel Mediterranean restaurant-lounge has a rare rooftop perch from which to enjoy sundowners with wraparound city views. What's more, the view comes without the touristy scene and stiff price tag found downtown.

Revolution Café 3248 22nd St at Valencia, Mission ☏ 415/642-0474. With seating overflowing onto the sidewalk, this café and art bar is a great spot to linger over coffee or drinks, soaking up the bohemian vibe and live tunes.

Zeitgeist 199 Valencia St at Duboce, Mission ☏ 415/255-7505. This friendly biker bar is a Mission institution, with an outdoor beer garden that's wildly popular on sunny afternoons. Come for punk tunes, tattooed bartenders, and some thirty beers on tap.

Hayes Valley to Haight-Ashbury

Alembic 1725 Haight St at Cole, Haight-Ashbury ☏ 415/666-0822. Offering a refreshing break from the dog-eared Haight scene, this small, stylish spot is serious about its liquor, with a wide selection of small-batch bourbons, ryes, and gins poured by knowledgeable, friendly bartenders. There's also a short menu of comfort food served with a twist – like Moroccan spiced lamb burgers with aioli and gin-drunken catfish cakes – along with beers brewed by its sister establishment, the *Magnolia* (see p.539).

Hotel Biron 45 Rose Street at Gough, Hayes Valley ⊤415/703-0403. Tucked away down an alley off Gough, this intimate wine bar has a quality selection of California and European wines, as well as a small menu of cheeses and olives. Revolving exhibitions of local art adorn the walls.

Kezar 770 Stanyan St at Beulah, Haight-Ashbury ⊤415/386-9292. Excellent neighborhood pub with pool, darts, and sports – be it American or Gaelic football.

Mad Dog in the Fog 530 Haight St at Fillmore, Lower Haight ⊤415/626-7279. Aptly named by the two lads from Birmingham who own the joint, this is one of the Lower Haight's most loyally patronized bars, with darts, English beer, copies of the *Sun* tabloid, and a typical pub menu that includes bangers'n'mash and ploughman's lunch.

Martin Macks 1568 Haight St at Ashbury, Haight-Ashbury ⊤415/864-0124. This neighborhood pub is popular for its simple, tasty food, but you can still grab a pint of Guinness by the bar – if you squeeze past the crowds that usually pack in by lunchtime.

Noc Noc 557 Haight St at Steiner, Lower Haight ⊤415/861-5811. Supergroovy, extra-dark bar with bizarre decor befitting a post-apocalyptic tribal cave. The bar doesn't have a license to sell hard alcohol, but it does make sake cocktails and boasts a solid range of beers. Worth the trip.

Persian Aub Zam Zam 1663 Haight St at Clayton, Haight-Ashbury ⊤415/861-2545. Bar regulars purchased this Casbah-style cocktail lounge after the death of its ornery owner, Bruno, and have just about managed to retain the surly but warm vibe, with a great jazz jukebox.

Place Pigalle 520 Hayes St at Octavia, Hayes Valley ⊤415/552-2671. Shabby-cool neighborhood joint with a good selection of beers on tap, a pool table, and work by local artists.

🏃 **Toronado** 547 Haight St at Fillmore, Lower Haight ⊤415/863-2276. A must for beer aficionados, with scores of beers on tap, many from small California brewers, and a rocker vibe.

The Richmond and the Sunset

The Abbey 4100 Geary Blvd at Fifth, Richmond ⊤415/221-7767. Quintessentially Irish, this sports bar is friendly and upscale, often hosting live Irish folk music when there aren't any important games on TV.

Pig & Whistle Pub 2801 Geary Blvd at Wood, Richmond ⊤415/885-4779. Thoroughly British pub serving a good selection of English and California microbrews, with a pool table, dartboards, and excellent pub food.

Yancy's Saloon 734 Irving St at Eighth, Sunset ⊤415/665-6551. Mellow, plant-festooned collegiate bar with free darts and cheap drinks.

Cafés

Blue Bottle Coffee Co. 315 Linden St at Gough, Hayes Valley. Oakland's Blue Bottle puts out some of the best coffee in the Bay Area, priding itself on its organic beans roasted in small batches. The Hayes Valley outpost is little more than a kiosk, as is the other branch in the city, which sets up on Saturdays at the Ferry Building farmers' market.

Café de la Presse 352 Grant Ave at Bush, Union Square ⊤415/398-2680. Parisian-inspired café with a good selection of European magazines and newspapers.

Café Flore 2298 Market St at Noe, Castro ⊤415/621-8579. Wedged into the triangle at the corner of Market and Noe streets, this café has a sunny, plant-filled courtyard that's a great place to grab a coffee and a gooey cake; it can be very cruisey, especially during the early evening.

Caffè Trieste 601 Vallejo St at Grant, North Beach ⊤415/392-6739. Opened in 1956, this small, crowded Italian coffeehouse claims to have served the first espresso on the West Coast. Its real attraction is the Sat-afternoon amateur opera hour, when old Italian ladies from the neighborhood come to gossip over a coffee and listen to charmingly off-key live singers.

Citizen Cupcake Café and Bar Virgin Megastore, 3rd Floor, 2 Stockton St at Market, Union Square ⊤415/399-1565. Downtown offshoot of the popular Hayes Valley café stashed inside a record store: there's coffee, tea, sake, and sandwiches and salads, as well as the namesake cupcakes. Try a Joe Cool (chocolate cake, chocolate cream, and mint frosting).

Emporio Rulli il Caffè Stockton Street Pavilion, Stockton St at Post St, Union Square ⊤415/433-1122. Café on Union Square that serves bracingly strong coffee and Italian pastries (try the cheesecake) and provides the best pit stop from the nearby shopping. There are tables outside if you want to lounge.

Imperial Tea Court 1411 Powell St at Broadway, Chinatown ⊤415/788-6080. Dart into this wood-paneled hideaway in the heart of Downtown to sit and sip a hot cup of tea – there are more than fifty varieties to choose from. Plan to linger.

Ritual Coffee Roasters 1026 Valencia St at 21st, Mission ⊤415/641-1024. Hipster coffee joint that's very serious about its java, all organic and fair trade. There's also Wi-Fi, though seating can be hard to come by.

Royal Ground 2060 Fillmore St at California, Pacific Heights ⊤415/567-8822. Situated among the boutiques and restaurants of Fillmore, this branch of a low-key local coffee chain has wireless Internet, sidewalk seating, and a laundromat next door.

Samovar Tea Lounge 498 Sanchez St at 18th, Castro ⊤415/626-4700. Earthy, cushion-filled café that serves more than 100 varieties of tea as well as tasty Asian-inflected snacks; the overstuffed wicker chairs are a great place to curl up with a book for the afternoon.

Clubs

330 Ritch St 330 Ritch St at Townsend, SoMa ⊤415/541-9574. The only constant at this small, out-of-the-way club is its location: different nights attract wildly varied crowds, but it's best known for the Popscene party on Thur, heaven for Modish Britpoppers in San Francisco. $5–15.

1015 Folsom 1015 Folsom St at Sixth, SoMa ⊤415/431-1200, ⊛www.1015.com. Multilevel superclub popular for late-night dancing. The music's largely house and garage, and expect marquee names like Sasha and Digweed on the main floor. $15.

Café Cocomo 650 Indiana St at Mariposa, Dogpatch ⊤415/824-6910, ⊛www.cafecocomo .com. The spot to hit if salsa's your thing. There's an outdoor patio for cooling off, plus salsa lessons (included in cover) most nights. $3–15.

DNA Lounge 375 11th St at Harrison, SoMa ⊤415/626-1409, ⊛www.dnalounge.com. Changes its music style nightly, but draws the same young, hip gay-straight crowd. Downstairs is a large dance floor, while the mezzanine is a comfy, sofa-packed lounge where you can chill. Check out the popular "Booty," the second Sat every month, devoted to the fine art of the mashup. $15–20.

The EndUp 401 Sixth St at Harrison, SoMa ⊤415/357-0827, ⊛www.theendup.com. Open all night (though you can only drink until 2am), this spot's where hardcore clubbers head for after-hours dancing on a cramped floor. If you want a break from the beats, there's an outdoor patio with plenty of seating. Club nights vary, but it's especially known for "Fag Fridays" (⊛www .fagfridays.com). $5.

Fluid 662 Mission St at Third, SoMa ⊤415/615-6888, ⊛www.fluidsf.com. Pricey, dressy bar-club, playing mostly hip-hop and mainstream house. The large first room is the lounge, its mirrored walls illuminated by the neon, flashing floor, while the rear room is home to a tiny dance floor.

Mezzanine 444 Jessie St at Fifth, SoMa ⊤415/625-8880, ⊛www.mezzaninesf.com. Massive megaclub with mainstream, brand-name DJs, as well as gigs by alt-rock and hip-hop acts – make a reservation for the VIP Ultra Lounge if you're feeling flush and flash. The music programming is unusually eclectic, taking in disco, electroclash, and even the occasional live rock show. $10 and up.

Mighty 119 Utah St at 15th, Potrero Hill ⊤415/762-0151, ⊛www.mighty119.com. Massive converted warehouse space huddled close to the freeway in Potrero Hill: it's a combination art gallery, performance venue, club, and lounge – check out the frozen vodka bar. As for the music, it's mostly live funk or DJs spinning old-school classic house. $10 and up.

Pink 2925 16th St at Capp, Mission ⊤415/431-8889, ⊛www.pinksf.com. You could walk right by without noticing it, but this tiny, fun club is a rare place for serious dancing in the Mission's otherwise loungey bar district; it's a friendly, mixed gay-straight place. $5–10.

Rickshaw Stop 155 Fell St at Van Ness, Hayes Valley ⊤415/861-2011. Hayes Valley bar-club known for its offbeat music programming and unusual themed parties like "Tots'n'Tonic," a cocktail bash where you can bring the kids. Wed–Sat only.

Ruby Skye 420 Mason St at Geary, Union Square ⊤415/693-0777. Set in a historic theater, this is one of the city's premier nightclubs, booking top DJs and live acts. Open Fri & Sat, with special events Wed, Thurs & Sun. $15.

Space 550 550 Barneveld Ave at Oakdale, Hunter's Point ⊤415/550-8286, ⊛www .space550.com. This enormous warehouse club is known for its trancey, industrial dance soundtrack: although it's a long way out in an iffy part of town, serious clubbers will find it's worth the trek. $5–15.

Live music

San Francisco's music scene reflects the character of the city as a whole: laid back and not a little nostalgic. The options for catching **live music** are wide and the scene is consistently progressive, characterized by the frequent emergence of good young bands. San Francisco has never recaptured its crucial 1960s role, though since then the city has helped launch acid jazz (beat-heavy jazz that's become de rigueur dinner-party music across the country), a classic swing revival, and the East Bay pop-punk sound.

Bands are extremely easy to catch. Many restaurants offer live music, so you can eat, drink, and dance all at once and often with no cover charge; ordinary neighborhood bars regularly host musicians, often for free, and there are any number of good and inexpensive small venues spread out across the city. Few fall into any particular camp, with most varying their bill throughout the week, and it can be hard to specify which of them cater to a certain music style.

To complement this fairly comprehensive list of established **venues**, be sure to check the weeklies. With these resources you'll find exhaustive listings of events in the city and Bay Area as a whole.

Large performance venues

Although San Francisco has a couple of major-league concert halls, bear in mind that some of the Bay Area's best large-scale venues, where the big names tend to play, are actually across the Bay in Oakland and Berkeley.

Bimbo's 365 Club 1025 Columbus at Chestnut, North Beach ☏ 415/474-0365, ⊛ www .bimbos365club.com. The savvy booker for this elegant, intimate club that dates to the 1930s schedules underground European acts, kitschy tribute bands, and big-name rock acts in equal proportion.

The Fillmore 1805 Geary St at Fillmore, Japantown ☏ 415/346-6000, ⊛ www.thefillmore .com. A national landmark, the *Fillmore* was at the heart of the 1960s counterculture, masterminded by the legendary Bill Graham. It reopened a decade ago after several years' hiatus and is home now to rock and alt-rock touring acts.

The Great American Music Hall 859 O'Farrell St at Polk, Tenderloin ☏ 415/885-0750, ⊛ www.musichallsf.com. Starting out as a bordello in the 1900s, the *Music Hall's* fortunes soon went into decline. It was resuscitated in the 1970s and now the gorgeous venue plays host to a wide variety of rock, country, and world music acts.

The Independent 628 Divisadero St at Hayes, Lower Haight ☏ 415/771-1422, ⊛ www .theindependentsf.com. Indie venue with strong sightlines, an impressive sound system, and eclectic booking policy, ranging from rock to rap.

The Warfield 982 Market St at Sixth, Tenderloin ☏ 415/775-7722, ⊛ www.thefillmore.com/warfield .asp. This old vaudeville venue is the sister to the Fillmore, with reserved balcony seating and general admission tickets that put you closer to the stage.

Rock, blues, folk, and country

12 Galaxies 2565 Mission St at 22nd, Mission ☏ 415/970-9777, ⊛ www.12galaxies.com. This ultra-hip spot with industrial decor centers on a low-rise stage, where there are live performances most nights ($5–25); the best views are from the mezzanine. There's also a pool table and a small snack menu.

Biscuits & Blues 401 Mason St at Geary, Union Square ☏ 415/292-2583, ⊛ www.biscuitsandblues .com. Certainly a tourist trap, but still one of the best spots in town to catch classic New Orleans jazz and delta blues, accompanied by delicious, if overpriced, soul food. Show times vary. From $15.

Boom Boom Room 1601 Fillmore St at Geary, Japantown ☏ 415/673-8000, ⊛ www.boomboom blues.com. Cose to the Japan Center, this Fillmore juke joint was owned by the late bluesman John Lee Hooker until he died in 2001: the dark, low-rise building plays host to a fine selection of touring blues and funk artists. $5–12.

Bottom of the Hill 1233 17th St at Missouri, Mission ☏ 415/621-4455, ⊛ www.bottomofthehill .com. The best place in town to catch up-and-coming or determinedly obscure rock acts.

Frequently packed for shows, there's a small patio out back to catch a breath of fresh air or, on Sundays, have a bite of barbecue. $6–10.

Café du Nord 2170 Market St at Sanchez, Castro ☏415/861-5016, ⊚www.cafedunord.com. The mahogany bar of this subterranean club (formerly a speakeasy) is a great place to enjoy cocktails, and

the varied booking provides constant surprises. $8–20.

Slim's 333 11th St at Folsom, SoMa ☏415/255-0333, ⊚www.slims-sf.com. Owned by local R&B artist Boz Skaggs, this is a prime venue to catch an array of punk, alternative, and world music. $10–30.

Jazz and Latin

Bruno's 2389 Mission St at 20th, Mission ☏415/643-5200, ⊚www.brunossf.com. Like something from a Scorsese movie, this retro restaurant has an intimate live venue attached, filled with 1960s-style white-vinyl furniture surrounding a tiny stage. The music's a mixture of jazz and nu-school R&B. If you eat in the (rather average) restaurant, there's no cover charge. $5–8.

Elbo Room 647 Valencia St at 17th, Mission ☏415/552-7788, ⊚www.elbo.com. The birthplace of acid jazz, a popular local variant that emphasizes a danceable groove over complex improvisation. The dark downstairs bar is a great spot for a low-key cocktail, and the Sun dub nights often feature world-class acts. $5–10.

Jazz at Pearl's 265 Columbus Ave at Pacific, North Beach ☏415/291-8255, ⊚www.jazzatpearls.com. The city's premier jazz club hosts two shows nightly in a plush, candlelit space that conjures the feel of an intimate 1930s supper club.

The Plough and Stars 116 Clement St at Second, Richmond ☏415/751-1122, ⊚www .theploughandstars.com. The Irish expat community crams into this terrific pub for hearty pints of Guinness, games of pool and darts, and live music six nights a week. Modest cover Fri & Sat.

Red Devil Lounge 1695 Polk St at Clay, Polk Gulch ☏415/921-1695, ⊚www.reddevillounge .com. Competing with the *Elbo Room* for fans of acid jazz and funk, this neo-Goth lounge is kitschly decorated with gargoyles. The music, though, is mainstream cool, making this a reliable option if you want to dance. $3–20.

Roccapulco 3140 Mission St at Cesar Chavez, Outer Mission ☏415/648-6611. Catering to the Mission's Latino population, this large club books salsa and Tejano music, including performers rarely heard in the US and big names like Celia Cruz. There are salsa lessons on Wed, while the live acts dominate Fri and Sat. $10–15.

Performing arts and film

San Francisco has a great reputation for **opera and classical music**; its orchestra and opera company are among the most highly regarded in the country. **Theater** is accessible and much less costly than elsewhere, with discount tickets available, but most of the mainstream downtown venues – barring a couple of exceptions – are mediocre, forever staging Broadway reruns, and you'd do better to take some time to explore the infinitely more interesting fringe circuit.

Cabaret and **comedy** are also lively, and **film** is almost as big an obsession as eating in San Francisco; you may well be surprised by the sheer number of movie theaters – repertory and current release – that flourish in this city.

Classical music, opera, and dance

San Francisco has an excellent reputation for the **performing arts** – there are five major symphonies based in the Bay Area, for example. It's also the only city on the West Coast to have its own professional **opera** and **ballet** companies – even if some observers sniff that quantity doesn't always guarantee quality. During the summer months, look out for the free concerts in Stern Grove (at 19th Avenue and Sloat Boulevard), where the symphony orchestra, opera, and ballet give open-air performances for ten successive Sundays beginning in June.

San Francisco Ballet War Memorial Opera House, 301 Van Ness Ave at Grove, Civic Center ☏415/865-2000, ⓦwww.sfballet.org. The city's ballet company, the oldest and one of the largest in the US, puts on an ambitious annual program (Feb–May) of both classical and contemporary dance. Founded in 1933, the ballet was the first American company to stage full-length productions of *Swan Lake* and *The Nutcracker*, which is still performed annually at Christmas.

San Francisco Opera War Memorial Opera House, 301 Van Ness Ave at Grove, Civic Center ☏415/864-3330, ⓦwww.sfopera.org. The Opera House, designed by architect Arthur Brown Jr, the creator of City Hall and Coit Tower, makes a very opulent venue for the San Francisco Opera Association, which has been performing here since the building opened in 1932. Still probably the strongest of San Francisco's cultural trio, the Opera Association has a main season that runs Sept through Dec plus a brief summer session in June; its opening night is one of the principal social events on the West Coast.

San Francisco Symphony Louise M. Davies Symphony Hall, 201 Van Ness Ave at Hayes, Civic Center ☏415/864-6000, ⓦwww.sfsymphony.org. The permanent home of the San Francisco Symphony Orchestra, which offers a year-round season of classical music and sometimes performances by other, often offbeat, touring groups. Established in 1909 as a small ensemble, the orchestra rose to international prominence in the 1950s when it began traveling and recording. Although not quite on a par with the New York Philharmonic or Chicago Symphony, the tenure of conductor Michael Tilson Thomas has catapulted it into the top half-dozen US orchestras.

Theater

The majority of the city's **theaters** congregate downtown around the Theater District. Most aren't especially innovative (although a handful of more inventive fringe places are scattered in other parts of town), but tickets are reasonably cheap, and there's usually good availability. Check the *Chronicle's* "96Hours" supplement on Thursday (or log on to ⓦwww.sfgate.com) to read up on the latest productions around town.

Most tickets can be purchased either through the individual theater's box offices or by calling **Ticketmaster** (☏415/421-8497, ⓦwww.ticketmaster.com). For last-minute bargains, try the **Tix Bay Area** booth on Powell Street, between Geary and Post streets (Tues–Thurs 11am–6pm, Fri 11am–7pm, Sat 10am–7pm, Sun 10am–3pm; ☏415/433-7827). Half-price tickets go on sale daily at 11am.

Downtown

American Conservatory Theater (ACT) Geary Theater, 415 Geary St at Taylor, Theater District ☏415/749-2228, ⓦwww.act-sfbay.org. San Francisco's flagship theater company, the Tony Award–winning ACT puts on eight major plays each season. Tickets start at $20.

Golden Gate Theater 1 Taylor St at Golden Gate Ave and Market St, Tenderloin ☏415/551-2000, ⓦwww.bestofbroadway-sf.com. Constructed during the 1920s and recently restored to its former splendor, the Golden Gate's marble flooring, Rococo ceilings, and gilt trimmings make it one of the city's most elegant theaters. It's a pity the programs don't live up to the surroundings – generally a mainstream diet of Broadway musicals.

Orpheum Theater 1192 Market St at Hyde, Tenderloin ☏415/551-2000, ⓦwww.bestofbroadway-sf.com. Arguably the top local space, in terms of seating capacity and glitz, hosting big-name Broadway productions.

Post Street Theatre 450 Post St at Powell, Union Square ☏415/771-6900, ⓦwww.poststreettheatre.com. Converted Gothic theater with drama, musicals, comedy, and mainstream theater pieces. Tickets from $35.

Yerba Buena Center for the Arts 701 Mission St at Third, SoMa. ☏415/978-2787, ⓦwww.yerbabuenaarts.org. Modern 750-seat performance space that hosts a wide-ranging, always high-quality mix of touring companies.

The rest of the city

Beach Blanket Babylon Club Fugazi, 678 Green St at Powell, North Beach ☏415/421-4222, ⓦwww.beachblanketbabylon.com. A 30-year local institution, this revue, based loosely on the story of Little Red Riding Hood, is a riotous evening, thanks to the spot-on celebrity pastiches and quick-fire wit of the mostly veteran cast. Camp, tacky, and highly recommended. Tickets $25–78.

Magic Theatre Fort Mason Center, Building D, Fort Mason ☎415/441-8822, ⓦwww.magictheatre.org. The busiest and largest company after ACT, and probably the most exciting, the Magic Theater specializes in the works of contemporary playwrights and emerging new talent; Sam Shepard traditionally premieres his work here.

Project Artaud Theater 450 Florida St at Mariposa, Mission ☎415/626-4370,

ⓦwww.artaud.org. Modern theater in a converted warehouse offering dance and theater performances, many less obscure than the theater's artsy name might imply. Tickets from $15.

Theater Rhinoceros 2926 16th St at S Van Ness, Mission ☎415/861-5079, ⓦwww.therhino.org. The city's prime gay-oriented theater space actually has two spaces, hosting everything from raunchy revues to issues-based dramas. Tickets start at $15.

Comedy

Comedians have always found a welcoming audience in San Francisco – after all, local political bigwig Tom Ammiano started out as a stand-up performer. Few of the comedians are likely to be familiar: as with any cabaret you take your chances, and whether you consider a particular club to be good will depend on who happens to be playing the week you go. You can expect to pay roughly the same kind of cover in most of the clubs ($7–15), and two-drink minimums are common. There are usually two shows per night, the first kicking off around 8pm and a late show starting at around 11pm. For bargains, check the press for "Open Mike" nights, when unknowns and members of the audience get up and have a go; there's rarely a cover charge for these evenings and, even if the acts are horrendous, it can be a fun night out.

Cobb's Comedy Club The Cannery, 915 Columbus Ave at Lombard, North Beach ☎415/928-4320, ⓦwww.cobbscomedy.com. Pricey and usually full of tourists, but the quality of the acts is fairly consistent. $13–35 with two-drink minimum.

The Marsh 1062 Valencia at 22nd, Mission ☎415/826-5750, ⓦwww.themarsh.org. Successful alternative space hosting solo shows, many with a political bent. $15–35.

The Punch Line 444 Battery St at Washington, Jackson Square ☎415/397-7573, ⓦwww .punchlinecomedyclub.com. Frontrunner of the city's "polished" cabaret venues, this place has an intimate feel that's ideal for downing expensive cocktails and laughing your head off. The club usually hosts the bigger names in the world of stand-up. $8–30.

Film

San Franciscans boasts a staggering assortment of current-release and repertory **film** houses, with programs that range from the latest films to Hollywood classics, iconoclastic Sixties pieces, and a selection of foreign and art films. For screening times and locations of current-run films, call ☎415/777-3456.

Film festivals

The **San Francisco International Film Festival**, specializing in political and short films you wouldn't normally see, is held at the Kabuki eight-screen movie theater, the Castro Theater, and the Pacific Film Archive in Berkeley (see p.574), at the end of April and first week or so of May. Tickets sell extremely fast and you'll need to book well in advance for all but the most obscure movies. If you know you're going to be in town, call ☎415/931-3456 or buy tickets on the Web at ⓦwww.sfiff.org. Just as popular is the **Lesbian, Gay, and Transgender Film Festival**, held in June at the Castro and other theaters. Call ☎415/703-8650 or check ⓦwww.frameline.org for program and ticket information.

The Castro Theatre 429 Castro St at Market, Castro ☎415/621-6120, ⓦwww.castrotheatre .com. San Francisco's most beautiful movie house, offering a steady stream of reruns, art films, Hollywood classics, and (best of all) a Wurlitzer organ played between films by a man who rises up from below the stage.

Four Star 2200 Clement St at 23rd, Richmond ☎415/666-3488, ⓦwww.hkinsf.com. Way out in the fog belt, but worth a visit for the interesting mix of Asian, international, and American culture films; two screens.

Landmark's Embarcadero Cinema One Embarcadero Center at Sansome, Financial District ☎415/267-4893. A good choice for independent and foreign language films. Five screens.

The Red Vic 1727 Haight St at Cole, Haight-Ashbury ☎415/668-3994, ⓦwww .redvicmoviehouse.com. Friendly collective, housed in a room full of ancient couches where you can put your feet up and munch organic popcorn.

The Roxie 3117 16th St at Valencia, Mission ☎415/863-1087, ⓦwww.roxie.com. An adventurous rep house and film distributor, the Roxie is one of the few theaters in the country willing to take a risk on documentaries and little-known foreign directors – and usually the risk pays off.

Gay and lesbian San Francisco

San Francisco's reputation as a city of **gay celebration** is not new – in fact it may be a bit outdated. Though still considered by many to be the gay capital of the world, the gay community here has made a definite move from the outrageous to the mainstream, a measure of its political success. The exuberant energy that went into the posturing and parading of the 1970s has taken on a much more sober, down-to-business attitude, and these days you'll find more political activists organizing conferences than drag queens throwing parties. Nowadays San Franciscans appreciate and recognize the huge economic and cultural impact of gays on the city, and openly gay politicians or businesspeople are not as much of an issue to locals as they would be anywhere else in the US, making it easy to forget things were not always this way.

San Francisco's gay scene has also mellowed socially, though in the city's increasingly conservative climate, gay parties, parades, and street fairs here still swing better than most. Like any well-organized section of society, the gay scene definitely has its social season – see the events listing on p.553 for highlights. Though **lesbian culture** flowered here in the 1980s and women's club nights still exist, the scene is more in evidence in bookstores than bars. Many lesbians have claimed Oakland for their own, though Bernal Heights and some areas of the Mission continue to be girl-friendly.

Details of gay accommodation, bars, and clubs appear on pp.552 & 553; gay bookstores and theater and film venues are listed under the relevant headings throughout this chapter.

Information and resources

The **LGBT Community Center**, 1800 Market Street at Octavia, Hayes Valley (Mon–Fri noon–10pm, Sat 9am–10pm; free; ☎415/865-5555, ⓦwww .sfcenter.org), not only has plenty of resources at the first-floor information desk, but also regularly hosts performances by comedy and theater groups on site – check the website or call for details. The **Golden Gate Business Association** promotes gay-owned businesses – check ⓦwww.ggba.com for a list of members.

The *Lavender Pages*, a telephone-cum-resource book, is available at A Different Light (see p.555) and other gay bookstores, as is the newly republished, always opinionated *Betty and Pansy's Severe Queer Review*, an offbeat guide to everything gay. Otherwise there are plenty of freesheets that provide entertainment and bar listings. For newspapers, check out the *San Francisco Spectrum* (Ⓦwww .sfspectrum.com), a monthly community newsletter, as well as the better-known *Bay Times* (Ⓦwww.sfbaytimes.com) and the *Bay Area Reporter* (Ⓦwww .ebar.com), which has a thorough entertainment and reviews supplement. For nightlife, check the biweekly *Gloss* (Ⓦwww.sfgloss.com).

Accommodation

Choose any hotel in San Francisco and a single-sex couple won't raise an eyebrow at check-in: some, like the *Queen Anne* and the *Archbishop's Mansion*, attract equal numbers of gay and straight visitors. There are, however, a few places that especially cater to gay and lesbian travelers that we've singled out here.

24 Henry 24 Henry St at Sanchez, Castro ☎1-800/900-5686, Ⓦwww.24henry.com. This small blue-and-white home tucked away on a leafy residential street north of Market is a predominantly gay male guesthouse with five simple rooms, one with private bath. It makes a friendly retreat from the cruisey Castro scene nearby. ❸

Inn on Castro 321 Castro St at Market, Castro ☎415/861-0321, Ⓦwww.innoncastro.com. This luxurious B&B is spread across two nearby houses. It has eight rooms and a handful of self-catering apartments available, all of which are brightly decorated in individual styles and have private baths and phones. There's a funky lounge where you can meet other guests. Two-night minimum at

weekends, three-night minimum on holidays, four-night minimum for gay holidays, but good midweek discounts. ❺

The Parker Guest House 520 Church St at 18th, Castro ☎1-888/520-7275, Ⓦwww.parkerguest house.com. This converted Edwardian mansion is set in beautiful gardens and has a friendly vibe, thanks to its ample, large common areas: there's a sunny breakfast room and on-site sauna. En-suite ❻, shared bath ❺

Village House 4080 18th St at Castro, Castro ☎1-800/900-5686, Ⓦwww.24henry.com. Mixed gay-straight B&B with rooms that are grand and a little gaudy. For camp extravagance, ask for Room 2, or take a trip back to the 1980s in Room 4. ❹

Bars

San Francisco's **gay bars** are many and varied, ranging from cozy cocktail lounges to no-holds-barred leather-and-chain hangouts. In the last few years, nearly every single lesbian bar has disappeared, with the notable exception of *Lexington Club* (see below). Otherwise, if you want exclusively female company you'll have to check out clubs that have lesbian nights. Many of the places in this section may turn up the music later and transform into miniclubs: for hardcore dancing, though, see opposite.

Badlands 4121 18th St at Castro, Castro ☎415/626-9320, Ⓦwww.sfbadlands.com. Decked out in distressed brick and shiny chrome, this video bar attracts a pretty, thirtysomething crowd and is usually packed at weekends. There's a wide selection of imported beer, and overall it's one of the less sceney places in the neighborhood.

The Eagle Tavern 398 12th St at Harrison, SoMa ☎415/626-0880. This good, old-fashioned leather bar is particularly popular on Sun, when it holds a late-afternoon "beer bust" for charity: all you can down for $8.

Esta Noche 3079 16th St at Valencia, Mission ☎415/861-5757. A gay Latin drag bar that's great fun and attracts a youngish, racially mixed clientele: there are shows nightly at 11.30pm, except on Sun (7pm, 10.30pm & midnight).

Lexington Club 3464 19th St at Lexington, Mission ☎415/863-2052, Ⓦwww.lexingtonclub .com. One of the few places in the city where the girls outnumber the boys (men must be accompanied by a woman to enter), this bustling lesbian bar attracts all sorts with its no-nonsense decor, friendly atmosphere, and excellent jukebox.

The Lone Star 1354 Harrison St at Tenth, SoMa ☎415/863-9999. One of the tamer biker bars in SoMa, the *Lone Star* attracts leather daddies, bears, cubs, and those who love them. It's large, friendly, and welcoming.

Martuni's 4 Valencia St at Market, Mission ☎415/241-0205. This piano bar draws a well-heeled, middle-aged crowd, all keen to sing along to classics from Judy, Liza, and Edith. There are regular open-mike evenings as well as a singles

Gay and lesbian events

AIDS Candlelight Memorial March & Vigil ☎415/863-4676. May. Procession from the Castro to Civic Center, commemorating all those who've died of AIDS.

San Francisco International LGBT Film Festival ☎415/703-8650, ⓦwww.frameline .org. June. Short films and features from amateurs and auteurs – usually at either the Castro or Roxie cinemas – at the oldest and largest event of its kind in the world.

San Francisco LGBT Pride Parade ☎415/864-3733, ⓦwww.sfpride.org. Late June. One of the largest Pride parades in the world – and also one of the longest (it can last up to four hours). Don't miss Pink Night, the evening when the Castro is virtually pedestrianized by thousands of revelers, or the Dyke March that takes place on Friday night.

Folsom Street Fair ☎415/777-3247, ⓦwww.folsomstreetfair.com. Late Sept. Hardcore leather fair, full of hairy-chested men in chaps. Surprisingly friendly and fun.

Castro Street Fair ☎415/841-1824, ⓦwww.castrostreetfair.org. Oct. Food and craft stalls take over the Castro.

---

evening on Wed. Try a martuni, the signature cocktail, made from Bombay Sapphire gin and dry vermouth with a lemon twist.

Midnight Sun 4067 18th St at Castro, Castro ☎415/861-4186. Long, narrow video bar, always busy with well-dressed white boys checking out the movies shown on the monitors, as well as each other: it's not a place to strike up a casual conversation. The weekly showings of popular television programs are a big draw.

Pilsner Inn 225 Church St at Market, Castro ☎415/621-7058. The best neighborhood gay bar in the Castro, filled with a diverse, slightly older crowd playing pool and darts. There's a large, smoker-friendly patio out back, and a generally welcoming, open vibe.

Powerhouse 1347 Folsom St at Doré Alley, SoMa ☎415/552-8689. One of the prime pickup joints in the city, this very cruisey old-school leather bar has plenty of convenient dark corners.

Twin Peaks Tavern 410 Castro St at Market, Castro ☎415/864-9470. Popular with an older crowd, this long-standing saloon has a prime location and full-length windows, making it a good spot for people watching.

Wild Side West 424 Cortland Ave at Wool, Bernal Heights ☎415/647-3099. Unpretentious, friendly lesbian pickup joint with a huge outdoor terrace – there are no heat lamps, though, so stay inside on a cold evening.

Clubs

There's currently a relative void of gay-centric places to dance; aside from the old favorites listed here, check local listings for up-to-date information and new venues.

The Café 2367 Market St at Castro, Castro ☎415/861-3846. There's a DJ here seven nights a week, and for a long time it was one of the few places to dance in the Castro, despite its postage-stamp-sized dance floor. The music's mainstream hi-NRG and house, while the crowd is dominated by lesbians and their swishy male friends. There's still usually a long line at weekends, inspired no doubt by the free entrance.

Cat Club 1190 Folsom St at Eighth, SoMa ☎415/703-8965. This dark, loud club is one of the lesbian hotspots of the city, mixing dancing and live performances. It's livelier the later you arrive. $5–10.

The EndUp 401 Sixth St at Harrison, SoMa ☎415/357-0827. Club nights vary, but it's especially known for "Fag Fridays." See p.546.

Pink 2925 16th St at Capp, Mission ☎415/431-8889. One of the city's best places to dance. See p.546.

The Stud 399 Folsom St at Ninth, SoMa ☎415/252-7883. Legendary gay club that's still as popular as ever, attracting a diverse, energetic, and uninhibited crowd. Check out the fabulously freaky drag-queen cabaret at "Trannyshack" (Tues) – an unmissable legend in local nightlife. Saturday's "Sugar," meanwhile, is one of the best underground gay dance nights in the city. $5–8.

Shopping

Aside from the retail palaces around **Union Square** (including Macy's, Saks, and practically every major designer label), San Francisco's shopping scene is refreshingly edgy, peppered with one-off boutiques selling locally designed clothes and stylish homeware stores. There's also a brilliantly varied selection of **independent booksellers** (including the world-famous Beat poet favorite, City Lights) as well as terrific **music stores**, some focusing solely on rarities and others jammed with DJs rifling through the latest import twelve-inch records from Europe. It's worth remembering that, unlike many other American cities, stores in San Francisco close relatively early – 6pm Monday to Saturday and 5pm on Sunday isn't unusual – so start a major shopping expedition early in the day.

Shopping streets

San Francisco's prime **shopping streets** are listed here, alphabetized by neighbourhood. These should be useful for any shopaholic planning a day of retail therapy, though there are many other great places to browse in addition to these.

The Castro Castro Street between 17th and 19th streets; Market Street between Castro and Church. Gay-oriented boutiques, clubwear, and shoes.

Cow Hollow Union Street between Steiner and Gough. Sweet if rather conservative boutiques (mostly for women), shoe stores, and cute homewares.

Haight-Ashbury Haight Street between Stanyan and Masonic. Clothing, especially vintage and secondhand.

Hayes Valley Hayes Street between Franklin and Laguna. Trendy but upscale, with edgy boutiques

for men and women, as well as jewelry galleries and other gorgeous, high-end goodies.

The Marina Chestnut Street between Broderick and Fillmore. Yuppified strip of health foods, wine shops, and women's clothing boutiques.

The Mission Valencia Street between 14th and 21st. The best choice for urban hipsters, with lots of used furniture and clothing stores, bookshops, and avant-garde designer gear.

North Beach/Telegraph Hill Grant Avenue between Filbert and Vallejo. Groovy boutiques, homewares, and divey cafés: one of the newest and freshest places to find cool clothes.

▲ Haight Street storefront

Bookstores

Unsurprisingly, for a city with such a rich literary history, San Francisco excels in terrific **specialty bookstores**: from the legendary City Lights in North Beach to the new literary hub in the Mission, home to some of the city's more energized – and politicized – bookstores. As for **secondhand booksellers**, there's a fine selection in the city, but rabid old book buyers should head across the Bay to Oakland and Berkeley for richer pickings. Most bookstores tend to open every day from roughly 10am to 8pm, though City Lights is open daily until midnight.

General

City Lights Bookstore 261 Columbus Ave at Broadway, North Beach ☏ 415/362-8193. Storied bookstore, renowned as the first place in the country to stock only paperbacks and headquarters of the Beat era. Oddball and thoroughly browsable – where else could you find books filed under sections like "Stolen Continents" and "Anarchism"? Pity about the belligerent staff.

A Clean, Well Lighted Place for Books Opera Plaza, 601 Van Ness Ave at Golden Gate, Civic Center ☏ 415/441-6670. The stock here is now more mainstream and less impressively exhaustive than it once was, but it's worth checking out for the regular readings by authors.

🏃 **Green Apple** 506 Clement St at Sixth Ave, Richmond ☏ 415/387-2272. Funky store with deft, eccentric touches like the regular section of "Books that will never be Oprah's picks." Not bargain prices, but a pleasure to rummage through the shelves. There's a smaller, less impressive music annex nearby.

Specialist and secondhand

Abandoned Planet Bookstore 518 Valencia at 16th, Mission ☏ 415/861-4695. Encouraging its customers to "Break the TV habit!" this eccentric and utterly San Francisco bookstore crams its black shelves with left-wing and anarchist volumes.

Argonaut Bookshop 786 Sutter St at Jones, Theater District ☏ 415/474-9067, ⓦ www.argonautbookshop.com. The best bookshop by far

for local history: it specializes in volumes on California and the West, from the Gold Rush era to the dot-com bomb. The knowledgeable staff are a major plus.

A Different Light 489 Castro St at 18th, Castro ☏ 415/431-0891, ⓦ www.adlbooks.com. This well-stocked bookshop features gay and lesbian titles, with an especially strong fiction section. Readings and events are held regularly.

Dog Eared Books 900 Valencia St at 20th, Mission ☏ 415/282-1901, ⓦ www.dogearedbooks .com. Smallish corner bookstore with a snappy selection of budget-priced remainders as well as an eclectic range of secondhand titles, all in terrific condition.

Get Lost 1825 Market St at Valencia, Hayes Valley/Mission ☏ 415/437-0529, ⓦ www.getlostbooks .com. Tiny, triangular travel bookstore, crammed with unusual titles alongside the standard guidebooks.

Kayo 814 Post St at Leavenworth, Theater District ☏ 415/749-0554, ⓦ www.kayobooks .com. Glorious vintage paperback store, crammed with bargain classics including pulpy mysteries, sci-fi, and campy 1950s sleaze fiction. Thurs–Sat only.

Modern Times 888 Valencia St at 20th, Mission ☏ 415/282-9246, ⓦ www.mtbs.com. Hefty stock of Latin American literature and progressive political publications, as well as a small but well-chosen selection of gay and lesbian literature and radical feminist magazines. Stages regular readings of authors' works.

Food and drink

Be sure to try **local specialties** such as Boudin's sourdough bread (see p.534), Gallo salami, and Anchor Steam beer – all of which are gourmet treats. The Ferry Building, on the Embarcadero, offers an easy way to graze the goods from some of North California's best specialty food producers, with everything from bread and cheese to wine and tea on offer. It's also home to the area's best farmers' market, held Tuesday and Saturday. If you're looking for everyday essentials, there are supermarkets across the city, including several branches of Whole Foods – the outposts on Fourth Street in SoMa and at California and Gough streets near Pacific Heights are both in easy reach of downtown. California **alcohol** laws are liberal: most stores carrying food sell alcohol too, provided you show ID proving you're at least 21 years of age.

Andronico's Market 1200 Irving St at Funston, Sunset ☏ 415/661-3220. The California gourmet's answer to Safeway. Pricey but gorgeous produce, microbrews, good wine, craft breads, fancy cheeses, an olive bar, and a pretty good deli. Not the cheapest, but much better quality than your average supermarket.

Cowgirl Creamery's Artisan Cheese Shop 1 Ferry Building, Embarcadero ☏ 415/362-9354, ⓦ www.cowgirlcreamery.com. Top-notch cheese shop featuring selections from small producers around the world, as well as the Point Reyes Station creamery's own award-winning cheeses.

Haig's Delicacies 642 Clement St at Seventh Ave, Richmond ☏415/752-6283, ⊛www .haigsdelicacies.com. In the heart of the New Chinatown, Haig's is one of the city's oldest international food shops, its shelves stocked with hard-to-find goods from around the globe. The excellent assortment of Mediterranean mezzes can be found in groceries around the Bay Area.

The Jug Shop 1567 Pacific Ave at Polk, Pacific Heights ☏415/885-2922, ⊛www.jugshop.com. The Jug Shop is famous for its cheap California wines – but it also has more than 200 varieties of beer that are similarly well-priced.

Molinari 373 Columbus Ave at Vallejo, North Beach ☏415/421-2337. Bustling veteran North Beach deli, jammed to the rafters with Italian goodies both familiar and exotic. Pick the bread of your choice and order a sandwich to go.

PlumpJack Wines 3201 Fillmore St at Greenwich, Cow Hollow ☏415/346-9870, ⊛www.plumpjack .com. If you're looking for an obscure California vintage for an oenophile relative, this is the place to come – it has an enormous, exhaustive selection of wines from across the state.

The Real Food Company 3060 Fillmore St at Filbert, Cow Hollow ☏415/567-6900, ⊛www .realfoodco.com. Smallish, artsy grocery store selling potions and vitamins alongside health foods. Excellent gourmet meat counter and whole-wheat pastries: grab a sandwich and sit outside on the terrace at one of the wrought-iron picnic tables. Also at 2140 Polk St, Russian Hill (☏415/673-7420).

Scharffen Berger Chocolate Maker 1 Ferry Building, Embarcadero, ☏415/981-9150, ⊛www .scharffenberger.com. A mouth-watering array of chocolate bars, sauces, and other goodies from the famed Berkeley chocolate maker.

Yum 1750 Market St at Gough, Hayes Valley ☏415/626-9866. Irresistible and fun hangar-like grocery store whose slogan is "Have you played with your food today?" Gourmet selections of cookies are especially delicious and the friendly staff will let you sample most items before you buy. Head to the back of the store for its best feature: refrigerators filled with a vast selection of sodas from across the world.

Record stores

Although San Francisco does have an outpost of Virgin, it's the specialty **record stores** that really shine: from old-school soul on vinyl to twelve-inch European imports for local DJs, there are some superb **independent** and **collectors'** haunts. And in Amoeba Records, Haight-Ashbury can lay claim to one of the best places to browse and buy music anywhere in the country.

Amoeba Records 1855 Haight St at Stanyan, Haight-Ashbury ☏415/831-1200, ⊛www.amoeba.com. This big sister to Berkeley's renowned emporium is one of the largest used-music retailers in America. Divided between new and secondhand CDs, this massive warehouse space hums with bargain hunters rifling through an encyclopedic selection of modern music. A treasure trove for any music fan. Branch at 2455 Telegraph, Berkeley (☏510/549-1125).

Aquarius Records 1055 Valencia St at 21st, Mission ☏415/647-2272, ⊛www.aquariusrecords .org. Friendly, ramshackle record store with hip, friendly staff: there's an emphasis on less mainstream music, including experimental, folk, and world.

Groove Merchant Records 687 Haight St at Pierce, Lower Haight ☏415/252-5766, ⊛www .groovemerchantrecords.com. Come here for secondhand soul, funk, and jazz: the owner's

passionate and knowledgeable, so don't be afraid to ask questions.

Medium Rare 2310 Market St at Noe, Castro ☏415/255-7273. This tiny store is crammed with CDs, ranging from camp classics like Peggy Lee and other 1950s cocktail lounge singers to throbbing hi-NRG stars like Donna Summer.

Taiyodo Record Shop Japan Center, 1737 Post St, Japantown ☏415/885-2818. One of several record stores in the mall selling the latest releases by Japanese singers, whether bubblegum pop or Asian alt-rock. Also great for hard-to-find anime DVDs.

Virgin Megastore 2 Stockton at Market St, Union Square ☏415/397-4525. Three floors packed with music in a wide variety of styles. The third floor has a good stock of current, popular books, videos, and a café with windows overlooking Market Street (see p.499).

Specialty stores and local labels

Flight 001 525 Hayes St at Octavia, Hayes Valley ☏415/487-1001, ⓦwww.flight001.com. This sleek, futuristic travel store sells books, funky accessories (including chunky, Day-Glo luggage tags and all-in-one shaving kits), and dapper carry-on bags. The place to stock up on sundries if you only travel first-class – or want to act like it.

Good Vibrations 603 Valencia St at 17th, Mission ☏415/522-5460, ⓦwww.goodvibes.com. Gloriously sexy store, run by a co-op of men and women, that's designed to destigmatize sex shops and make browsing fun and comfortable. It's packed with every imaginable sex toy, plus racks of erotica and candy-store-style jars of condoms. Branch at 1620 Polk St at Sacramento, Polk Gulch (☏415/345-0400).

Jeremys 2 South Park at Second, SoMa ☏415/882-4929. Local designer discount boutique, patronized by hipsters, where you just might find last spring's Prada dress for a fraction of the price.

Levi's 300 Post St at Stockton, Union Square ☏415/501-0100. Four levels of jeans, tops, and jackets set against a thumping backdrop of club music. This flagship offers the Levi's "Original Spin" service, where customers can order customized denim.

Paolo 524 Hayes St at Laguna, Hayes Valley ☏415/552-4580. Don't tell anyone but your best friends about this gem: designer Paolo Iantorno produces a limited edition (20–25 pairs) of his own men's and women's shoe designs in Italy, then sells them from his two stores here. Prices hover around $200, and every style is edgy but wearable.

Retro Fit Vintage 910 Valencia St at 20th, Mission ☏415/550-1530. Poppy, kitschy selection of smart vintage clothes: don't expect bargains, but well worth it for a spot-on shirt or just-right jacket. Check out the DIY vintage tees: pick a style, then flick through an enormous binder filled with transfers to customize the shirt, starting at $18. Closed Tues & Wed.

Wasteland 1660 Haight St at Belvedere, Haight-Ashbury ☏415/863-3150. Smart, high-end vintage selection, sorted by style and color: you'll pay for the ease of browsing, but it's one of the best places to find top condition, fashionable vintage.

Worn Out West 582 Castro St at 19th, Castro ☏415/431-6020. Gay secondhand fetish gear. Feel free to browse: there's plenty of Western wear, as well as leather-studded collars, cuffs, and even bow ties, plus a smattering of sex toys.

Listings

American Express 455 Market St at First, Financial District (Mon–Fri 9am–5.30pm, Sat 10am–2pm; ☏415/536-2600).

Car rental All the major firms have branches in the airport. Their offices in town are: Alamo, 687 Folsom St at Third, SoMa ☏415/882-9440; Avis, 675 Post St at Jones, Theater District ☏415/929-2555; Dollar, 364 O'Farrell St at Taylor, Theater District ☏1-866/434-2226; Enterprise, 1133 Van Ness Ave at Post, Tenderloin ☏415/441-3369; Hertz, 433 Mason St at Post, Union Square ☏415/771-2200.

Consulates Australia, 575 Market St at Second, Financial District ☏415/536-1970; Germany, 1960 Jackson St at Gough, Pacific Heights ☏415/775-1061; Ireland, 100 Pine St at Front, Financial District ☏415/392-4214; UK, 1 Sansome St at Market, Financial District ☏415/617-1300.

Dental treatment For a free referral to the nearest dentist, call the San Francisco Dental Society Referral Service (☏415/421-1435).

Disabled visitors Steep hills aside, the Bay Area is generally considered to be one of the most

barrier-free regions around, and physically challenged travelers are well catered for. Most public buildings have been modified for disabled access, all BART stations are wheelchair-accessible, and most buses have lowering platforms for wheelchairs – and, usually, understanding drivers. For more information, check ⓦwww.accessnca.com.

Drugstores Walgreens 24-hour pharmacies: 498 Castro St at 18th, Castro ☏415/861-3136; 3201 Divisadero St at Lombard, Marina ☏415/931-6417; and 459 Powell St at Sutter, Union Square ☏415/984-0793.

Ferries The Golden Gate Ferry, running commute hours to Sausalito and Larkspur in Marin County, leaves from the Ferry Building, east end of Market Street (☏511 toll free or 415/455-2000, ⓦwww.goldengate.org); Blue & Gold Fleet bay ferries to Angel Island, Oakland and Alameda, Sausalito, Tiburon, and Vallejo from Pier 39, Fisherman's Wharf (☏415/705-8200, ⓦwww.blueandgoldfleet.com). For Alcatraz ferry information, see p.514.

Hospitals The San Francisco General Hospital, 1001 Potrero Ave at 23rd, Potrero Hill (℡415/206-8000 or 206-8111 emergency), has a 24-hour emergency walk-in service. California Pacific Medical Center Davies Campus, Castro and Duboce streets, Lower Haight (℡415/600-6000), has 24-hour emergency care and a doctors' referral service.

Internet There's usually access at hostels, but there's often a wait to get on a machine; likewise, the public library has free access for 15min, often with a long wait: there are six terminals on the main floor and sign-up is first-come-first-served. Wi-Fi's becoming a citywide standard here, and most travelers with laptops will be able to find a café with free or low-cost access in any neighbourhood, if not in their hotel.

Legal advice The Bar Association of San Francisco runs a Lawyer Referral & Information Service, available by phone or online (℡415/989-1616, ⓦwww.sfbar.org).

Library Civic Center, 100 Larkin St at Grove ℡415/557-4400, ⓦwww.sfpl.org. Mon & Sat 10am–6pm, Tues–Thurs 9am–8pm, Fri noon–6pm, Sun noon–5pm.

Passport and visa office US Dept of Immigration, 630 Sansome St at Washington, Jackson Square ℡1-800/375-5283.

Post office You can collect General Delivery mail (bring your ID) from the main post office, 101 Hyde St at Fulton, Civic Center (Mon–Fri 9am–5pm; ℡1-800/275-8777), but letters will only be held for ten days before being returned to sender, so make sure there's a return address on the

envelope. Other post offices, with telephone and General Delivery facilities, include Sutter Street Station, 150 Sutter St at Montgomery, Financial District (Mon–Fri 8am–5pm), and Rincon Finance Station, 180 Steuart St at Mission, Embarcadero (Mon–Fri 8am–6pm, Sat 8am–2pm).

Rape Crisis Center and Hotline 24-hour switchboard ℡415/647-7273, ⓦwww.sfwar.org.

Religious services Grace Cathedral on Nob Hill, 1100 California St at Taylor, has an Episcopalian (Anglican) congregation (℡415/749-6300, ⓦwww.gracecathedral.org). Catholics can worship at St Mary's Cathedral, 660 California St at Grant (℡415/288-3800, ⓦwww.oldsaintmarys.org). The grandest synagogue is Congregation Emanu-El, 2 Lake St at Arguello Blvd, at the eastern edge of the Richmond district by the Presidio (℡415/751-2535, ⓦwww.emanuelsf.org).

Sports Advance tickets for all Bay Area sports events are available through Tickets.com (℡510/762-2277, ⓦwww.tickets.com) as well as from the teams themselves. **Baseball** The San Francisco Giants play in AT&T Park (℡415/972-2000, ⓦwww.sfgiants.com). **Football** The San Francisco 49ers appear at blustery Monster Park on Candlestick Point, south of town (℡415/656-4900, ⓦwww.sf49ers.com).

Suicide Crisis Hotline 24-hour ℡415/781-0500.

Tax Sales tax, added to virtually everything you buy in a store save for food, is 8.5 percent; hotel tax will add 14 percent to your bill.

Telegrams Western Union has numerous locations around the Bay Area; call ℡1-800/325-6000 or check ⓦwww.westernunion.com to find the nearest.

The Bay Area

Of the nearly seven million people who make their home in the San Francisco **Bay Area**, barely more than one in ten lives in the actual city of San Francisco. Everyone else is spread around one of the many less-renowned cities and suburbs that ring the bay, either down the Peninsula or across one of the two impressively engineered bridges that span the chilly waters of the world's most exquisite natural harbor. There's no doubt about the supporting role these places play in relation to San Francisco – always "the city" – but each has a distinctive character and contributes to the range of people and landscapes that makes the Bay Area one of the most desirable places in the US to live or visit.

Across the steel Bay Bridge, eight miles from downtown San Francisco, the **East Bay** is home to the lively, left-leaning cities of **Oakland** and **Berkeley**, which together have some of the best bookstores and restaurants in the greater Bay Area, as well as a good proportion of the live music venues. The weather's generally much sunnier and warmer here too, and it's easy to reach by way of the BART trains that race under the bay. The remainder of the East Bay is contained in Contra Costa County, which includes the short-lived early state capital of California, **Benicia**, as well as the former homes of writers John Muir and Eugene O'Neill.

South of the city, the **Peninsula** holds some of San Francisco's oldest and most upscale suburbs, spreading down through the computer-rich **Silicon Valley** and into **San Jose** – now America's tenth largest city, which easily surpasses San Francisco in both square mileage and population, though apart from a few excellent museums there's not a lot to see. The **beaches** to the west, however, are excellent – sandy, clean, and uncrowded – and a couple of youth hostels in old lighthouses perch on the edge of the Pacific.

For some of the most beautiful land- and seascapes in California, cross the Golden Gate Bridge or ride a ferry to **Marin County**, a mountainous peninsula that's half wealthy suburbia and half unspoiled hiking country, with **redwood forests** rising sheer out of the thundering Pacific Ocean. A range of 2500-foot peaks divides the county down the middle, separating the yacht clubs and plush bay-view houses of **Sausalito** and **Tiburon** from the nearly untouched wilderness that runs along the Pacific Coast, through Muir Woods and the **Point Reyes National Seashore**. North of Marin County at the top of the bay, and still within an hour's drive of San Francisco, the Wine Country regions of the Sonoma and Napa valleys make an excellent day-trip; they're detailed in Chapter Nine, beginning on p.681.

The East Bay

The largest and most traveled bridge in California, connecting Downtown San Francisco to the **EAST BAY**, the **Bay Bridge** is part graceful suspension bridge and part heavy-duty steel truss. Built in 1933 as an economic booster during the Depression, the bridge is made from enough steel cable to wrap around the earth three times. Completed just seven months before the more famous (and better loved) Golden Gate, it works a lot harder for a lot less respect: a hundred million vehicles cross it each year, though you'd have to search hard to find a postcard of it. Local scribe Herb Caen dubbed it "the car-strangled spanner," a reflection of its often-clogged lanes. Indeed, the bridge's only claim to fame – apart from the much-broadcast videotape of its partial collapse during the 1989 earthquake – is that **Treasure Island**, where the two halves of the bridge meet, hosted the 1939 World's Fair. During World War II the island became a Navy base, but since the end of the Cold War it has been undergoing a gradual transfer to the city of San Francisco. As the island offers great views of the city and the Golden Gate, the development authority has various plans to make it a tourist destination, including the reopening of its museum, closed since 1997.

The Bay Bridge eventually empties into **Oakland**, a hard-working, blue-collar city at the heart of the East Bay. The city traditionally earned its livelihood from shipping and transportation services, as evidenced by the enormous cranes in the massive Port of Oakland, but has been undergoing something of a renaissance as it lobbies to attract businesses and workers from the information technology industry. Oakland spreads north along wooded foothills to **Berkeley**, an image-conscious university town that looks out to the Golden Gate and collects a mixed bag of earnest young students, much-pierced dropouts, aging 1960s radicals, and Nobel Prize-winning nuclear physicists in its cafés and bookstores.

Berkeley and Oakland blend together so much as to be virtually the same city, and the hills above them are topped by a twenty-mile string of **regional parks**, providing much-needed fresh air and quick relief from the populated grids below. Spreading east and north of the hills is Contra Costa County, a huge area that contains some intriguing, historically important waterfront towns – well worth a stop if you're passing through on the way to the Wine Country – as well as some of the Bay Area's most inward-looking suburban sprawl. Across the narrow Carquinez Strait, further around the **North Bay** from the oil-refinery landscape of Richmond, lies the sleepy and little visited former state capital of **Benicia**, vitally important during California's first twenty years of existence after the 1849 Gold Rush. In contrast, standing out from the soulless dormitory communities that fill the often baking-hot **inland valleys** are the preserved homes of an unlikely pair of influential writers: the naturalist John Muir, who, when not out hiking around Yosemite and the High Sierra, lived most of his life near **Martinez**, and the playwright Eugene O'Neill, who wrote many of his angst-ridden works at the foot of **Mount Diablo**, the Bay Area's most significant peak.

Arrival

You're likely to be staying in San Francisco when you visit the East Bay, though it's just as convenient and sometimes better value to fly direct to **Oakland International Airport** (Ⓣ510/577-4015, automated flight info Ⓣ1-800/992-7433, Ⓦwww.oaklandairport.com), particularly if you're coming from elsewhere in the US. Most major domestic airlines serve the facility, which is less crowded and more accessible than its San Francisco counterpart. It's an easy trip from the airport into town: the **AirBART** shuttle van (every 15min; $2; Ⓣ510/577-4294) runs to the Coliseum BART station, from where you can hop on **BART** to Berkeley, Oakland, or San Francisco. Numerous door-to-door **shuttle buses** run from the airport to East Bay stops and into the city, such as A1 American (Ⓣ1-877/378-3596, Ⓦwww.a1americanshuttle.com) – expect to pay around $18 to Downtown Oakland, $30–35 to San Francisco. **Taxis** run about $20 into Oakland and $40 into San Francisco.

The **Greyhound** station is in an insalubrious part of northern Oakland, alongside the I-980 freeway at 2103 San Pablo Avenue (Ⓣ510/832-4730). **Amtrak** terminates at Second Street near Jack London Square, where a free Thruway shuttle bus heads across the Bay Bridge to the Transbay Terminal. A better option for heading into San Francisco, though, is to get off at Richmond and change onto the nearby BART trains. The most enjoyable way to arrive in the East Bay is aboard an Alameda-Oakland **ferry** ($6 each way; Ⓣ510/522-3300, Ⓦwww.eastbayferry.com), which sails every hour from San Francisco's Ferry Building and Pier 39 to Oakland's Jack London Square. The fleet also runs a service to Angel Island via Pier 41, departing from Oakland (mid-May to late Oct Sat & Sun 9am, returns 3.10pm; $14 round-trip, including park admission).

Information

The **Oakland CVB**, next to the enormous *Marriott Hotel* at 463 11th Street (Mon–Fri 8.30am–5pm; Ⓣ510/839-9000, Ⓦwww.oaklandcvb.com), is the best source for maps, brochures, and information on lodging and activities in the metropolitan area. In Berkeley, check in at the **Berkeley CVB**, 2015 Center

Street (Mon–Fri 9am–noon & 2–5pm; ☎510/549-7040, ✆www.visitberkeley
.com). The **University of California's Visitor Services**, 101 University Hall
(Mon–Fri 8.30am–4.30pm; ☎510/642-5215, ✆www.berkeley.edu/visitors), at
the corner of Oxford and University, has plenty of information about the
Berkeley campus, hands out free self-guided tour brochures, and conducts
ninety-minute tours (see p.572). For information on hiking or horseback riding
in the many parks that top the Oakland and Berkeley hills, contact the **East
Bay Regional Parks District**, 2950 Peralta Oaks Court, Oakland (☎510/562-
7275, ✆www.ebparks.org). The widely available *East Bay Express* (issued every
Wed; free) has the most comprehensive listings of what's on in the vibrant East
Bay music and arts scene, and the daily *Oakland Tribune* (50¢) is also worth a
look for its coverage of local politics and sporting events.

Getting around

The East Bay is linked to San Francisco via the underground BART Transbay
subway (Mon–Sat 6am–midnight, Sun 9am–midnight). Four lines (one of
which starts at Millbrae and stops at San Francisco airport) run from Daly City
through San Francisco and on to Downtown Oakland, before diverging to
service East Oakland out to Fremont, north to Berkeley and Richmond, and
northeast into Contra Costa County as far as Concord and Pittsburg/Bay Point.
A fifth line operates its entire length in the East Bay between Richmond and
Fremont. Fares range from $1.40 to $7.65, and the cost of each ride is deducted
from the total value of the ticket, purchased from machines on the station
concourse. If you're relying on BART to get around a lot, buy a **high-value
ticket** ($10 or $20) to avoid having to stand in line to buy a new ticket quite
so often. For $4.65, you can tour the entire system and get off at any of the 43
station platforms for up to three hours, so long as you enter and exit at the same
station; the same charge is made for lost tickets. To phone BART from San
Francisco, dial ☎415/989-2278; from the East Bay ☎510/465-2278, or check
✆www.bart.gov. Bikes are allowed on most trains.

From East Bay BART stations, pick up a **free transfer**, saving you 25¢ on the
$1.75 fares of the revamped AC Transit (☎510/817-1717 ext. 1111, ✆www
.actransit.org), which provides a good **bus service** around the entire East Bay,
especially Oakland and Berkeley. AC Transit also runs buses on a number of
routes to Oakland and Berkeley from the Transbay Terminal in San Francisco.
These operate all night and are the only way of getting across the bay by public
transport once BART has shut down. You can pick up excellent free maps of
both BART and the bus system from any station. A smaller-scale bus company
that also proves useful is the Contra Costa County Connection (☎925/676-
7500, ✆www.cccta.org), running buses to most of the inland areas, including
the John Muir and Eugene O'Neill historic houses.

One of the best ways to get around the East Bay is by **bike**. A fine cycle
route follows Skyline and Grizzly Peak boulevards along the wooded crest of
the hills between Berkeley and Lake Chabot. Within Berkeley itself, the
Ohlone Greenway makes for a pleasant cycling or walking route up through
North Berkeley to El Cerrito. Not many places rent bikes in the East Bay but
one exception is Solano Avenue Cyclery, 1554 Solano Avenue, Berkeley
(☎510/524-1094, ✆www.solanoavenuecyclery.com), whose rates are $40 for
24 hours or $140 per week for a standard bike, more for a fancy sports or
mountain model. For those interested in **walking tours**, the City of Oakland
sponsors free "discovery tours" (☎510/238-3234) of various neighborhoods;
a popular excursion is the Oakland Historical Landmark Tour (Sun 1–3.30pm;

free), beginning in front of the Oakland Museum at Tenth and Fallon, and covering areas like Chinatown, Lake Merritt, Preservation Park, and Jack London Square.

If you're **driving**, allow yourself plenty of time to get there: the East Bay has some of California's worst traffic, with the Bay Bridge and I-80 in particular jam-packed sixteen hours a day. Car-pool lanes are becoming increasingly popular, so having three or more people in your vehicle can speed things up, slightly at least.

Accommodation

The East Bay's **motels** and **hotels** are barely any better value than their San Francisco equivalents. However, they give visitors the chance to stay just outside of the city's hubbub whilst affording easy access to it. **Bed and breakfasts** often represent the best deals, tucked away as they are in Berkeley's leafy hills. Check with the Berkeley & Oakland Bed and Breakfast Network (℡510/547-6380, Ⓦwww.bbonline.com/ca/berkeley-oakland) for a complete list. A few **campgrounds** and **dorm beds** are available in summertime, such as the vacated summer-only student rooms in Stern Hall through the Summer Visitor Housing agency at 2601 Warring Street, Berkeley (℡510/642-4444, Ⓦwww.housing.berkeley.edu/conference/summervis).

Berkeley

Bancroft Hotel 2680 Bancroft Way, Berkeley ℡1-800/549-1002, Ⓦwww.bancrofthotel.com. Small hotel with 22 rooms with queen beds, a good location right by the campus, and fine service. Breakfast included. ❺

Berkeley City Club 2315 Durant Ave, Berkeley ℡510/848-7800, Ⓦwww.berkeleycityclub.com. Two blocks from the UC campus, this B&B was designed by Hearst Castle architect Julia Morgan, with an indoor swimming pool and exercise room. Each of the spacious rooms has a private bath. ❻

Berkeley YMCA 2001 Allston Way at Milvia St, a block from Berkeley BART ℡510/848-6400, Ⓦwww.baymca.org. Berkeley's best bargain accommodation; rates, starting at $39 for a single, include use of gym and pool. No dorms. ❷

🏃 **Claremont Resort & Spa** 41 Tunnel Rd, Berkeley ℡1-800/551-7266, Ⓦwww.claremontresort.com. Built in 1915, *The Claremont* is the lap of luxury among Berkeley hotels. Lavish rooms come with data ports for your laptop, hairdryers, cable TV, and big windows, some overlooking the large outdoor pool; spa sessions begin around $100 per hour for facials or massages. ❽

French Hotel 1538 Shattuck Ave, North Berkeley ℡510/548-9930. Small and comfortable hotel with 18 standard rooms in the heart of Berkeley's Gourmet Ghetto. ❺

Golden Bear Inn 1620 San Pablo Ave, West Berkeley ℡1-800/525-6770, Ⓦwww.goldenbearinn.com. The most pleasant of the many motels in the "flatlands" of West Berkeley, with smart furnishings, though somewhat out of the way. ❸

Nash Hotel 2045 University Ave, Berkeley ℡510/841-1163, Ⓦwww.nashhotel.com. Basic rooms with threadbare carpets in this Chinese-run hotel, but cheap and central. ❷

Rose Garden Inn 2740 Telegraph Ave, Berkeley ℡1-800/992-9005, Ⓦwww.rosegardeninn.com. All 40 rooms are stylishly decorated with fireplaces in this attractive mock-Tudor mansion half a mile south of UC Berkeley. ❻

Oakland

Jack London Inn 444 Embarcadero West, Oakland ℡510/444-2032 or 1-800/549-8780. Nicely revamped hotel/motel with a 1950s feel, located next to Jack London Square. ❸

Maya Motel 4715 Telegraph Ave, North Oakland ℡510/654-5850. Basic motel but tidy enough and better than most of those on nearby Macarthur Boulevard to the south. The trendy Rockridge shops and eateries are within walking distance. ❷

Waterfront Plaza Hotel Jack London Square, Oakland ℡1-800/729-3638, Ⓦwww.waterfrontplaza.com. Plush, modern hotel located on the best stretch of the Oakland waterfront, right among the square's amenities. ❻

Further out

East Brother Light Station 117 Park Place, Point Richmond ℡510/233-2385, Ⓦwww.ebls.org. A handful of rooms in a converted lighthouse, on an island in the straits linking the San Francisco and San Pablo bays. Not a handy base for seeing the sights, this is an adventurous retreat for an evening. Prices include highly rated gourmet dinners with wine as well as breakfast. Thursday to Sunday nights only. ❽

Union Hotel and Gardens 401 First St, Benicia ☎707/746-0100, ⓦwww.unionhotelbenicia.com. Historical hotel and once a bordello, now converted into a classy bed and breakfast with twelve rooms, all featuring a Jacuzzi. ❾

Campgrounds

Chabot Family Campground Off I-580 in East Oakland ☎1-888/327-2757, ⓦwww.ebparks.org. Year-round tent-only places, with hot showers and lots of good hiking nearby. Reservations wise in summer; $18 for one vehicle and up to ten people.

Mount Diablo State Park 20 miles east of Oakland off I-680 in Contra Costa County ☎510/837-2525. RV and tent places in three separate sites; book through on ☎1-800/444-7275 or ⓦwww.reserveamerica.com in summer; $20.

Oakland

What was the use of me having come from Oakland, it was not natural for me to have come from there yes write about it if I like or anything if I like but not there, there is no there there.

Gertrude Stein, *Everybody's Autobiography*

As the workhorse of the Bay Area, **OAKLAND** is commonly known as a place of little or no play. One of the busiest ports on the West Coast and the western terminal of the country's rail network, it's also the spawning ground of some of America's most unabashedly revolutionary **political movements**, such as the militant **Black Panthers**, who gave a radical voice to the African-American population, and the **Symbionese Liberation Army**, who demanded a ransom for kidnapped heiress Patty Hearst in the form of free food distribution to the poor.

The city is also the birthplace of literary legends **Gertrude Stein** and **Jack London**, who grew up here at approximately the same time, though in entirely different circumstances – Stein was a stockbroker's daughter, while London was an orphaned delinquent. Most of the waterfront where London used to steal oysters and lobsters is now named in his memory, while Stein, who was actually born in East Oakland, is all but ignored here, not surprising given her famously unflattering quote about the place. Still, until very recently, locals found it hard to come up with a better description: Oakland businesses have a long history of deserting the city once the going gets good, and even the iconic football team, the Raiders, defected to Los Angeles for thirteen years before returning in 1995.

But residents who've stuck by the city through its duller and darker days are pleased overall with recent efforts to revitalize (some say gentrify) the town and slash its infamous crime rate. These were initiated by former Mayor **Jerry "Moonbeam" Brown**, who drew in thousands of new residents by advertising the city's lower rents and consistently sunny climate, and have been continued in less flamboyant style by his successor, Ronald V. Dellums, who took office in late 2006. Already, rents in the increasingly popular **Rockridge** and **Lake Merritt** districts are approaching San Francisco prices. The city has also attracted a significant number of lesbians, who've left San Francisco's Castro and Mission, as well as a great number of artists pushed from their SoMa lofts by sky-high rents into the warehouses of West Oakland.

Perhaps, though, "Oaktown" (a local name for Oakland) is a better place to live in than to visit. Locals call San Francisco "the city" and will point visitors to its myriad attractions before recommending those in the East Bay. But given it's a short hop on BART or quick drive across the Bay Bridge, a day-trip to Oakland is worth it to get a feel for the East Bay's diversity and changing times.

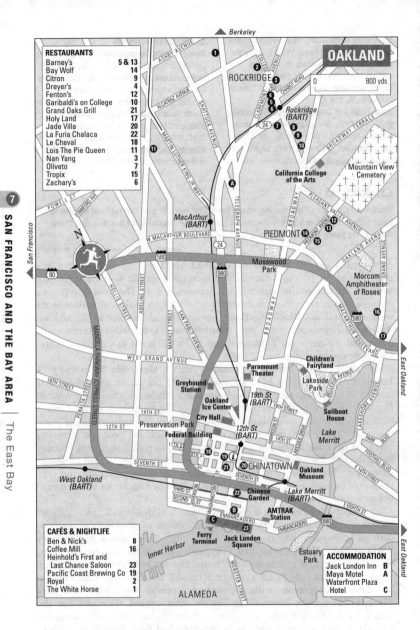

RESTAURANTS

Barney's	5 & 13
Bay Wolf	14
Citron	9
Dreyer's	4
Fenton's	12
Garibaldi's on College	10
Grand Oaks Grill	21
Holy Land	17
Jade Villa	20
La Furia Chalaca	22
Le Cheval	18
Lois The Pie Queen	11
Nan Yang	3
Oliveto	7
Tropix	15
Zachary's	6

OAKLAND

0 — 800 yds

CAFÉS & NIGHTLIFE

Ben & Nick's	8
Coffee Mill	16
Heinhold's First and Last Chance Saloon	23
Pacific Coast Brewing Co	19
Royal	2
The White Horse	1

ACCOMMODATION

Jack London Inn	B
Maya Motel	A
Waterfront Plaza Hotel	C

Downtown Oakland

Coming by BART from San Francisco, get off at the Twelfth Street–Civic Center station and you're at the open-air shopping and office space of **City Center** in the heart of **DOWNTOWN OAKLAND**. Bustling during weekdays with the nine-to-five contingent, the area can seem eerily deserted outside at other times. Downtown's compact district of spruced-up Victorian storefronts, overlooked by modern hotels and office buildings, has undergone an ambitious program of restoration and redevelopment for well over a decade. Fraught with allegations of illegal dealings and incompetent planning, the program has not been an unqualified success. One of the more controversial projects was the moat-like I-980 freeway, the main route through Oakland since the collapse of the Cypress Freeway in the 1989 earthquake; to make room, entire blocks were cleared of houses. Yet there were efforts to maintain the city's architectural heritage, most noticeably in the collection of charming properties of **Preservation Park** at 12th Street and Martin Luther King Jr Way. The late nineteenth-century commercial center along Ninth Street west of Broadway, now tagged **Old Oakland**, also underwent a major restoration some years ago, and nearly all premises are now occupied by tenants such as architecture and design firms, much like San Francisco's Jackson Square. Even better, the section between Broadway and Clay is home to a fine **farmers' market** every Friday between 8am and 2pm. By way of contrast with the generally subdued Old Oakland area, stroll a block east of Broadway, between Seventh and Ninth, to Oakland's **Chinatown**, whose bakeries and restaurants are more authentic and less tourist-trodden than their counterparts across the bay, even if they're neither as lively nor as picturesque.

The city experienced its greatest period of growth in the early twentieth century, and many of the grand buildings of this era survive a few blocks north along Broadway, centered on the gigantic grass triangle of **Frank Ogawa Plaza** and the awkwardly imposing 1914 **City Hall** on 14th Street. This area hosts the annual **Art and Soul Festival** over Labor Day weekend, featuring live music and art displays ($5). Two blocks away at 13th and Franklin stands Oakland's most unmistakable landmark, the chateauesque lantern of the **Tribune Tower**, the 1920s former home of the *Oakland Tribune* newspaper. A few blocks west at 659 14th Street, the **African American Museum & Library** (Tues–Sat noon–5.30pm; free; ℡510/238-6716) is housed in an elegant Neoclassical building whose upper floor has a permanent display on the history of African Americans in California from 1775 to 1900, and revolving art and photo exhibitions. Several blocks further on, the **Ebony Museum of Art**, 1034 14th Street (Tues–Sat 11am–6pm, Sun noon–6pm; free; ℡510/763-0141), is another showcase for black artists and promotes greater appreciation of African American heritage.

North of here, around the 19th Street BART station, are some of the Bay Area's finest early twentieth-century buildings, highlighted by the outstanding Art Deco interior of the 1931 **Paramount Theater** at 2025 Broadway (tours 10am first and third Sat of the month; $5; ℡510/465-6400, ⒲www.paramounttheatre.com). The West Coast's answer to New York's Radio City Music Hall, the Paramount shows Hollywood classics and hosts occasional concerts by rockers like Tom Waits and Neil Young and performances by stand-up comedians, ballet troupes, and the Oakland Symphony. Nearby buildings are equally flamboyant, ranging from the

▲ Paramount Theater, Oakland

wafer-thin Gothic "flatiron" office tower of the **Cathedral Building** at Broadway and Telegraph, to the Hindu-temple-like facade of the magnificent 3500-seat **Fox Oakland** (now closed) on Telegraph at 19th – the largest movie-house west of Chicago at the time it was built in 1928 – and, across the street, the 1931 **Floral Depot**, a group of small modern storefronts faced in black-and-blue terracotta tiles with shiny silver highlights. If you want to get your skates on, lace up at the nearby **Oakland Ice Center**, 519 18th Street (Mon & Wed noon–4pm, Tues, Thurs & Fri noon–5pm, Sat 12.30–5pm, Sun 1.30–5pm, also Tues & Thurs 7–8.30pm, Fri & Sat 7–10pm; $7.50 plus $2.50 skate rental; ℡510/268-9000, ⓦwww.oaklandice.com). The facility is the finest in the Bay Area, with a number of world-class instructors providing lessons here.

Lake Merritt and the Oakland Museum

Five blocks east of Broadway, the eastern third of Downtown Oakland comprises **Lake Merritt**, a three-mile-circumference tidal lagoon that was bridged and dammed in the 1860s to become the centerpiece of Oakland's most desirable neighborhood. All that remains of the many fine houses that once circled the lake is the elegant **Camron–Stanford House**, on the southwest shore at 1418 Lakeside Drive, a graceful Italianate mansion whose sumptuous interior is open for visits (2nd & 3rd Wed 11am–4pm, 1st & 3rd Sun 1–5pm; $5; ℡510/444-1876, ⓦwww.cshouse.org). The lake is also the nation's oldest wildlife refuge, and migrating flocks of ducks, geese, and herons break their journeys here. **Lakeside Park** lines the north shore, where you can rent canoes, rowboats, kayaks, pedal boats, and a range of sailboats and catamarans ($8–15 per hour, $10–20 deposit) from the **Sailboat House** (March–May Mon–Fri 10.30am–6pm, Sat & Sun 10.30am–5pm; summer Mon–Fri 9am–6pm, Sat & Sun 10am–6pm; ℡510/238-2196, ⓦwww .oaklandnet.com/parks) – provided you can convince the staff you know how to sail. A miniature Mississippi riverboat makes thirty-minute lake **cruises** ($1.50) on weekend afternoons, or you can be serenaded on the overpriced but romantic Gondola Servizio (from $45 for 30min; ℡1-866/737-8494, ⓦwww.gondolaservizio.com).

Kids will like the puppet shows and pony rides at the **Children's Fairyland** (summer Mon–Fri 10am–4pm, Sat & Sun 10am–5pm; times vary through rest of year; $6; ℡510/452-2259, ⓦwww.fairyland.org), along Grand Avenue on the northwest edge of the park. At night, the lake's lit up by the "Necklace of Lights," an elegant source of local pride. Once you reach the north side of the lake, be sure to stroll under the MacArthur Freeway to soak up the relaxed atmosphere of the cafés and shops along Grand and Lakeshore avenues. Note the huge Art Deco-cum-mock-Classical facade of the still-functioning **Grand Lake Movie Theater**, a bastion of subversive political films.

Two blocks south of the lake, or a block up Oak Street from the Lake Merritt BART station, the **Oakland Museum**, 1000 Oak Street (Wed–Sat 10am–5pm, Sun noon–5pm; $8, free every second Sun of month; ℡510/238-2200, ⓦwww.museumca.org), is undoubtedly Oakland's most worthwhile stop, not only for the exhibits but also for the superb modern building in which it's housed, topped by a terraced rooftop sculpture garden that gives great views out over the lake and the city. The museum covers many diverse areas: displays on the **ecology** of California, including a simulated walk from the seaside through various natural habitats up to the 14,000-foot summits of the Sierra Nevada Mountains; state history, ranging from old mining equipment to the guitar that Berkeley-born Country Joe MacDonald played at the Woodstock Festival in 1969; and a broad survey of works by California artists and craftspeople, some highlights of which are pieces of turn-of-the-twentieth century **arts and crafts furniture**. You'll also see excellent **photography** by Edward Muybridge, Dorothea Lange, Imogen Cunningham, and many others. Additionally, the museum also has a collector's gallery that rents and sells works by California artists.

Jack London Square

Half a mile south of Downtown Oakland on AC Transit bus #51, at the foot of Broadway on the waterfront, **Jack London Square** is Oakland's sole concession to the tourist trade. An erratically manned information booth on Broadway between Water and Embarcadero streets supplies maps detailing what the square has to offer. Also accessible by direct ferry from San Francisco (see p.494), this somewhat sterile complex of harborfront boutiques and restaurants, anchored by a huge Barnes and Noble bookstore, was named after the self-taught writer who grew up pirating shellfish around here, but is about as distant from the spirit of the man as it's possible to get. Jack London's best story, *The Call of the Wild*, was written about his adventures in the Alaskan Yukon, where he carved his initials in a small cabin that has been reconstructed here. The one sight worth stopping at is **Heinold's First and Last Chance Saloon**, a tiny, slanting bar at the eastern end of the promenade, built in 1883 from the hull of a whaling ship. Jack London really did drink here, and the collection of yellowed portraits of him on the wall are the only genuine thing about the writer you'll find on the square.

If you're not a keen fan of London (and if you are, you'd be better off visiting his Sonoma Valley ranch – see p.689), there are still a few interesting things to do here. At the western end of the square you can visit a couple of **historical vessels**; dockside tours are available for both the *Light Ship Relief* (Thurs & Fri 10am–3pm, Sat & Sun 11am–4pm; $3) and the USS *Potomac* (Wed & Fri 10.30am–2.30pm, Sun noon–3pm; $7; ☎510/627-1215, ⍟www.usspotomac.org), Franklin D. Roosevelt's famous "floating White House." On Sunday, the square bustles with the weekly farmers' market, where you can find all sorts of bargains and stock up on food. Otherwise, walk a few short blocks inland to the **Produce Market**, along Third and Fourth streets, where a couple of good places to eat and drink lurk among the rail tracks (see p.580). This bustling warehouse district has fruit and vegetables by the forklift-load, and is at its most lively early in the morning, from about 5am. On the Embarcadero between Clay and Washington, **Yoshi's World Class Jazz House** is the Bay Area's, if not the West Coast's, premier jazz club (see p.585), as well as a classy Japanese restaurant.

East Oakland

The bulk of Oakland spreads along foothills and flatlands to the east of Downtown, in neighborhoods running down the main thoroughfares of Foothill and MacArthur boulevards. Gertrude Stein grew up here, though when she returned years later in search of her childhood home it had been torn down and replaced by a dozen Craftsman-style bungalows – the simple 1920s wooden houses that cover most of **East Oakland**, each fronted by a patch of lawn and divided from its neighbor by a narrow concrete driveway. The main artery though the area is E 14th Street, whose string of cheap Mexican restaurants and Latino shops sums up its ethnic ambience.

A quick way out from the gridded streets and sidewalks of the city is to take AC Transit bus #64 from Downtown east up into the hills to **Joaquin Miller Park**, the most easily accessible of Oakland's hilltop open spaces. It stands on the former grounds of "The Hights," the misspelled home of the "Poet of the Sierras," Joaquin Miller, who made his name playing the eccentric frontier American in the literary salons of 1870s London. His poems weren't exactly acclaimed (his greatest poetic achievement was rhyming "teeth" with "Goethe"), although his prose account, *Life Amongst the Modocs*, documenting time spent with the Modoc people near Mount Shasta, has weathered the years well. It was more for his outrageous behavior that he became famous, wearing bizarre clothes and biting debutantes on the ankle. For years, Japanese poet Yone Noguchi also lived here, working the sprinkler as Miller impressed lady visitors with a rain dance he claimed to have learned from Native Americans.

Perched in the hills at the foot of the park, the pointed towers of the **Mormon Temple**, 4766 Lincoln Avenue, look like missile-launchers designed by the Wizard of Oz – unmissable by day or floodlit night. In December, speakers hidden in the landscaping make it seem as if the plants are singing Christmas carols. Though you can't go inside the main temple unless you're a confirmed Mormon, there are great views from its courtyard out over the entire Bay Area, and a small museum explains the tenets of the faith (daily 9am–9pm; free); expect to be greeted and offered a free personalized tour of the museum by one of the faithful upon entering. Several miles up in the hills behind the temple, the gigantic **Chabot Space & Science Center**, 10000 Skyline Boulevard (Wed & Thurs 10am–5pm, Fri & Sat 10am–10pm, Sun 11am–5pm; summer also Tues 10am–5pm; $13; ☎510/336-7300, ⓦwww.chabotspace.org), is a state-of-the-art museum with permanent interactive displays, temporary exhibitions, working telescopes, and a fine **planetarium** – daytime shows are included in the admission but the evening Sky Tonight costs extra (Fri & Sat 7.30pm; $8), as do screenings at the impressive **Megadome Theater** (various times; $8). The museum can be reached on AC Transit bus #53 from the Fruitvale BART station.

Out past the airport in the suburb of San Leandro, the **Oakland Zoo** (daily: summer 9am–5pm; winter 10am–4pm; $9.50; ☎510/632-9525, ⓦwww .oaklandzoo.org) is home to over three hundred species of animals, comfortably nestled in the rolling hills of 525-acre Knowland Park; AC Transit bus #56 heads out there from Oakland, or it costs $6 to park a car. The only other place of interest out in this direction is in **Fremont**, at the end of the BART line, where the peaceful and leafy **Mission San Jose de Guadalupe** (daily 10am–5pm; donation), which was completely rebuilt some years ago, stands on Mission Boulevard south of the I-680 freeway.

North Oakland and Rockridge

The high-priced hills of **North Oakland**, which lost three thousand homes and 26 people in a horrific fire in 1991, are still lush and green, though the thick foliage that made the area so attractive has never been allowed to grow back fully in order to prevent more fires. These bay-view homes, some of the area's most valuable real estate, look out across some of its poorest – the neglected flatlands below that in the 1960s were the proving grounds of Black Panthers Bobby Seale and Huey Newton.

Broadway is the dividing line between the two halves of North Oakland, and also gives access (via the handy AC Transit #51 bus) to most sights and activities. East of Broadway, **Piedmont Avenue**, one of Oakland's most neighborly streets, is lined by a number of small bookstores and cafés, and makes for a nice stroll or relaxing day out. At the north end of Piedmont Avenue, the **Mountain View Cemetery** was laid out in 1863 by Frederick Law Olmsted (designer of

New York's Central Park) and holds the elaborate dynastic tombs of San Francisco's most powerful families – the Crockers, the Bechtels, and the Ghirardellis. You can jog or ride a bike around the well-tended grounds, or just wonder at the enormous turtles in the pond. Next door, the columbarium, known as the **Chapel of the Chimes**, 4499 Piedmont Avenue (daily 9am–5pm; free; T510/654-0123), was designed by Julia Morgan of Hearst Castle fame during her decade-long involvement with the chapel, beginning in 1921. The structure is remarkable for its seemingly endless series of urn-filled rooms, grouped together around sky lit courtyards, bubbling fountains, and intimate sanctuaries – all connected by ornate staircases of every conceivable length. Morgan wanted the space to sing of life, not death, and she's succeeded – there's no better place in Oakland to wander about in peace, or even plop down with a book. Try to visit during one of the regular concerts held here for a completely unique – and distinctly California – experience.

Back on Broadway, just past College Avenue, Broadway Terrace climbs up along the edge of the fire area to small **Lake Temescal** – where you can swim in summer – and continues on up to the forested ridge at the **Robert Sibley Regional Preserve**. This includes the 1761-foot volcanic cone of Round Top Peak and offers panoramas of the entire Bay Area. The peak has been dubbed the "Volcanic Witch Project" by the local media due to the five mysterious mazes, carved into the dirt and lined with stones, located in the canyons around the crater. Nobody knows where they came from, but navigating the designs leads to their center, where visitors add to the pile of diverse offerings ranging from trinkets to cigarettes to poetry. Skyline Boulevard runs through the park and is popular with cyclists, who ride the twelve miles south to Lake Chabot or follow Grizzly Peak Boulevard five miles north through the Berkeley Hills to Tilden Park.

The majority of the Broadway traffic, including the AC Transit #51 bus, cuts off onto College Avenue through Oakland's most upscale shopping district, **Rockridge**, whose upper reaches merge into Berkeley. Spreading for half a mile on either side of the Rockridge BART station, the quirky stores and restaurants here, despite their undeniable yuppie overtones, are better than Piedmont's in variety and volume, and make for a pleasant afternoon's wander or night out.

Berkeley

This Berkeley was like no somnolent Siwash out of her own past at all, but more akin to those Far Eastern or Latin American universities you read about, those autonomous culture media where the most beloved of folklores may be brought into doubt, cataclysmic of dissents voiced, suicidal of commitments chosen – the sort that bring governments down.

Thomas Pynchon, *The Crying of Lot 49*

More than any other American city, **BERKELEY** conjures up an image of 1960s student dissent. When college campuses across the nation were **protesting** the Vietnam War, it was the students of the University of California, Berkeley, who led the charge – gaining a name as the vanguard of what was increasingly seen as a challenge to the authority of the state. Full-scale battles were fought almost daily here at one point, on the campus and its surrounding streets, and there were times when Berkeley looked almost on the brink of revolution itself: students (and others) throwing stones and gas bombs were met with tear-gas volleys and truncheons by National Guard troops under the nominal command of then-Governor Ronald Reagan.

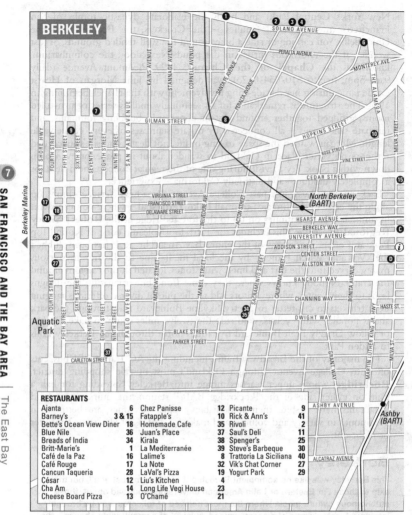

BERKELEY

SOLANO AVENUE

PERALTA AVENUE

KAINS AVENUE
STANNAGE AVENUE
CORNELL AVENUE
SANTA FE AVENUE
PERALTA AVENUE
MONTEREY AVE
THE ALAMEDA

GILMAN STREET

EAST SHORE HWY
FOURTH STREET
FIFTH STREET
SIXTH STREET
SEVENTH STREET
EIGHTH STREET
NINTH STREET
SAN PABLO AVENUE

HOPKINS STREET
MILVIA STREET

ROSE STREET

VINE STREET

CEDAR STREET

North Berkeley
(BART)

VIRGINIA STREET
FRANCISCO STREET
DELAWARE STREET
BELVEDERE AVE
ACTON STREET
HEARST AVENUE
BERKELEY WAY
UNIVERSITY AVENUE
ADDISON STREET
CENTER STREET
ALLSTON WAY
BANCROFT WAY
CHANNING WAY
DWIGHT WAY

MATHEWS STREET
MABEL STREET
SACRAMENTO STREET
CALIFORNIA STREET

FOURTH STREET
SIXTH STREET
EIGHTH STREET
NINTH STREET
SAN PABLO AVENUE

Aquatic
Park

BLAKE STREET

PARKER STREET

CARLETON STREET

FIFTH STREET
SEVENTH STREET

GRANT WAY
BONITA AVENUE
MARTIN LUTHER KING JR. WAY
HASTE ST.
MILVIA ST.

ASHBY AVENUE
Ashby
(BART)

ALCATRAZ AVENUE

RESTAURANTS

Ajanta	6	Chez Panisse	12	Picante	9	
Barney's	3 & 15	Fatapple's	10	Rick & Ann's	41	
Bette's Ocean View Diner	18	Homemade Cafe	35	Rivoli	2	
Blue Nile	36	Juan's Place	37	Saul's Deli	11	
Breads of India	34	Kirala	38	Spenger's	25	
Britt-Marie's	1	La Mediterranée	39	Steve's Barbeque	30	
Café de la Paz	16	Lalime's	8	Trattoria La Siciliana	40	
Café Rouge	17	La Note	32	Vik's Chat Corner	27	
Cancun Taqueria	28	LaVal's Pizza	19	Yogurt Park	29	
César	12	Liu's Kitchen	4			
Cha Am	14	Long Life Vegi House	23			
Cheese Board Pizza	13	O'Chamé	21			

Such action was inspired by the mood of the time and continued well into the 1970s, while during the conservative 1980s and Clinton-dominated 1990s, Berkeley politics became far less confrontational. But despite an influx of more conformist students, a surge in the number of exclusive restaurants, and the dismantling of the city's rent-control program, the progressive legacy has remained in the city's independent **bookstores** (see box, p.573) and at sporadic political demonstrations. Unsurprisingly, the increasing national political polarization caused by George W. Bush's uncompromising policies are particularly reflected in a town with such a strong radical heritage. Consequently, Berkeley has of late returned to being a bastion of the **anti–war movement** and streets like Telegraph Avenue are festooned with posters, stickers, badges, and T-shirts

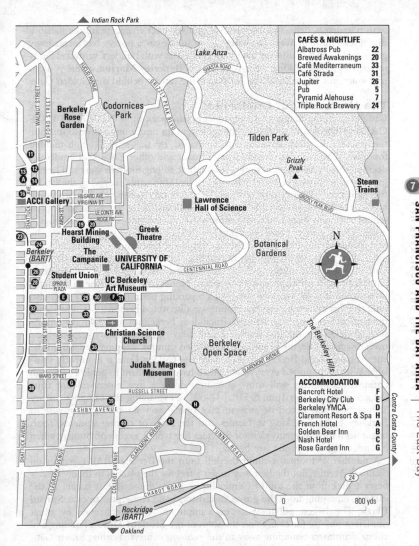

Lake Anza

SHASTA ROAD

Codornices
Park

Berkeley
Rose
Garden

Tilden Park

Grizzly
Peak ▲

Steam
Trains

GRIZZLY PEAK BLVD

WALNUT STREET
OXFORD STREET

Lawrence
Hall of Science

ACCI Gallery

HILGARD AVE.
VIRGINIA ST.
LE CONTE AVE.
RIDGE RD

Greek
Theatre

Botanical
Gardens

N

Hearst Mining
Building

The
Campanile

UNIVERSITY OF
CALIFORNIA

CENTENNIAL ROAD

Berkeley
(BART)

Student Union

SPROUL
PLAZA

UC Berkeley
Art Museum

The Berkeley Hills

FULTON STREET
ELLSWORTH STREET
DANA ST.

Christian Science
Church

Berkeley
Open Space

CLAREMONT AVENUE

Judah L Magnes
Museum

WARD STREET

RUSSELL STREET

ASHBY AVENUE

TUNNEL ROAD

SHATTUCK AVENUE
TELEGRAPH AVENUE
COLLEGE AVENUE
CLAREMONT AVENUE

CHABOT ROAD

24

0   800 yds

Rockridge
(BART)

▼ Oakland

Albatross Pub	22
Brewed Awakenings	20
Café Mediterraneum	33
Café Strada	31
Jupiter	26
Pub	5
Pyramid Alehouse	7
Triple Rock Brewery	24

ACCOMMODATION
Bancroft Hotel	F
Berkeley City Club	E
Berkeley YMCA	D
Claremont Resort & Spa	H
French Hotel	A
Golden Bear Inn	B
Nash Hotel	C
Rose Garden Inn	G

SAN FRANCISCO AND THE BAY AREA | The East Bay

Contra Costa County ▶

questioning the occupation of Iraq and the war against terrorism, or lampooning the "dunce-in-chief" in other ways.

The **University of California**, right in the center of town, completely dominates Berkeley and makes a logical starting point for a visit. Its many grand buildings and over 30,000 students give off a definite energy, which spills down the raucous stretch of Telegraph Avenue that runs south from the campus and holds most of the student hangouts, including a dozen or so lively cafés, as well as a number of fine bookstores. Older students, and a good percentage of the faculty, congregate in the **Northside** area, the part of **North Berkeley** just above the campus, popping down from their woodsy hillside homes to partake of goodies from the **Gourmet Ghetto**, a stretch of Shattuck Avenue crammed with restaurants, delis, and bakeries. Of quite distinct character are the flatlands that spread through **West Berkeley** down to the bay, a poorer but increasingly gentrified district that mixes old Victorian houses with builders' yards and light-industrial premises. Along the bay itself is the **Berkeley Marina**, where you can rent sailboards and sailboats or just watch the sun set behind the Golden Gate.

The University of California

Caught up in the frantic crush of students who pack the **UNIVERSITY OF CALIFORNIA** campus during the semesters, it's nearly impossible to imagine the bucolic learning environment envisaged by the school's high-minded founders. When the Reverend Henry Durant and other East Coast academics decided to set up shop here in the 1860s, these rolling foothills were still largely given over to dairy herds and wheatfields. In 1866, while surveying the land, a trustee recited "Westward the course of the empire takes its way," from a poem by George Berkeley. Moved by the moment, all assembled agreed to name their school after the bishop. Construction work on the two campus buildings – imaginatively named North Hall and South Hall – was still going on when the first 200 students, including 22 women, moved here from Oakland in 1873. Since then an increasing number of buildings have been squeezed into the half-mile-square main campus, and the state-funded university has become one of America's most prestigious, with so many Nobel laureates on the faculty that it's said you have to win one just to get a parking permit. University physicists built the first cyclotron, and plutonium was discovered here in 1941, along with thirteen other synthetic elements (including berkelium and californium). As such, sketches for the first atomic bomb began here. Nuclear weaponry and overcrowding aside, the beautifully landscaped campus, stepping down from the eucalyptus-covered Berkeley Hills toward the Golden Gate, is eminently strollable. With maps posted everywhere, you'd have to try hard to get lost – though enthusiastic students will show you around on a free ninety-minute **tour** (Mon–Sat 10am, Sun 1pm; ☏510/642-5215), explaining the campus's history, architecture, and flavor. Be sure to take one if you want a fuller picture of Berkeley beyond looking at facades and the faces of passing students. Tours begin from the University's Visitor Services (see p.561), except on Sunday, when it starts at the Campanile (see below).

A number of footpaths climb the hill from the Berkeley BART station on Shattuck Avenue, but the best way to get a feel for the place is to follow Strawberry Creek from the top of Center Street across the southeast corner of the campus, emerging from the groves of redwood and eucalyptus trees at **Sproul Plaza**. The largest public space on campus, it's often enlivened by street musicians playing for change on the steps of the **Student Union** building and conga drummers pounding away in the echoing courtyard below. Sather Gate, which bridges Strawberry Creek at the north end of Sproul Plaza, marks the entrance to the older part of the campus. Up the hill, past the imposing facade of Wheeler Hall, the 1914 landmark **Campanile** (Mon–Fri 10am–4pm; $2) is modeled after the one in the Piazza San Marco in Venice; take an elevator to the top for a great view of the campus and the entire Bay Area. At the foot of the tower stands the redbrick **South Hall**, the sole survivor of the original pair of buildings.

Higher up in the hills, above the 80,000-seat Memorial Stadium, the lushly landscaped **Botanical Garden** (daily 9am–5pm, closed first Tues; $3, free on first Thurs; ☏510/643-2755) defeats on-campus claustrophobia with its thirty acres of plants and cacti. Near the crest of the hills, with great views out over the bay, a full-sized fiberglass sculpture of a whale stretches out in front of the space-age **Lawrence Hall of Science** (daily 10am–5pm; $9.50; ☎510/642-5132, ⓦwww.lawrencehallofscience.org), an excellent museum and learning center that features earthquake simulations, model dinosaurs, and a planetarium, plus hands-on exhibits for kids in the Wizard's Lab. Both the gardens and the Lawrence Hall of Science are accessible on weekdays via the free UC Berkeley Shuttle bus from the campus or the Berkeley BART station.

In the southeast corner of the campus, the **Phoebe Hearst Museum of Anthropology** in Kroeber Hall (Wed–Sat 10am–4.30pm; free; ☎510/642-3682, ⓦwww.hearstmuseum.berkeley.edu) holds a variety of changing exhibits as well as an intriguing display of artifacts made by Ishi, the last surviving Yahi Indian who was found near Mount Lassen in Northern California in 1911. Anthropologist (and father of writer Ursula Le Guin) Alfred Kroeber brought

Berkeley's bookstores

Not surprising for a university town, Berkeley's **bookstores** are as exhaustive as they are exhausting. Perfect for browsing and taking your time, you won't be made to feel guilty or obliged to buy a book you've been poring over for ages. The CVB has a useful list of over fifty shops, of which the following are a representative selection:

Analog Books 1816 Euclid Ave ☎510/843-1816. A variety of quality books to choose from on graphics, art, and music, as well as a good stock of magazines.

Black Oak Books 1491 Shattuck Ave ☎510/486-0698. Huge selection of second-hand and new books for every interest; also holds regular evening readings by internationally acclaimed authors.

Cody's Books 1730 Fourth St at Virginia ☎510/559-9500. This newer branch is all that remains of this former icon of Bay Area booksellers, but it still offers a fine selection of titles on a broad range of subjects.

Comic Relief 2026 Shattuck Ave ☎510/843-5002. All the mainstream stuff, plus self-published mini-comics by locals.

Easy Going Travel Shop & Bookstore 1385 Shattuck Ave ☎510/843-3533. The essential bookstore for every traveler. Packed with travel paraphernalia, it offers a wide selection of guidebooks and maps for local, countrywide, and international exploration. Talks and slideshows by travel writers are also held on a regular basis.

Lewin's Metaphysical Books 2644 Ashby Ave ☎510/843-4491. The place to come for the best selection on spirituality, religion, astrology, and other arcane subjects.

Moe's Bookstore 2476 Telegraph Ave ☎510/849-2087. An enormous selection of new and used books on four floors, with esoteric surprises in every field of study; perfect for academics, book collectors, and browsers. There's also an excellent art section on the top floor (☎510/849-2133).

Mrs Dalloway's 2904 College Ave ☎510/704-8222. New store specializing in literature and gardening. Hosts regular readings and slideshows.

Revolution Books 2425c Channing Way ☎510/848-1196. Wide range of books on political themes with, as you might expect, an emphasis on leftist and anarchist thought.

Serendipity Books 1201 University Ave ☎510/841-7455. This vast, garage-like bookstore is off the loop of Berkeley bookstores, but is an absolute must for collectors of first-edition or obscure fiction and poetry, as well as black American writers. The prices are fair, and the owner – incredibly, given the towers of unshelved books – knows exactly where everything is to be found.

Shakespeare and Company 2499 Telegraph Ave ☎510/841-8916. Crammed with quality secondhand books at reasonable prices, Shakespeare and Company is the best place to linger and scour the shelves for finds, especially literature.

Ishi to the museum (then located on the UC San Francisco campus), where he lived under the scrutiny of scientists and journalists – in effect, in a state of captivity – until his death from tuberculosis a few years later.

The brutally modern, angular concrete of the **Berkeley Art Museum** at 2626 Bancroft Way (Wed & Fri–Sun 11am–5pm, Thurs 11am–7pm; $8, free on first Thurs; ⊤510/642-0808, ⓦwww.bampfa.berkeley.edu) is a stark contrast to the campus's older buildings. Its skylit, open-plan galleries hold works by Picasso, Cézanne, Rubens, and other notables, but the star of the show is the collection of 1950s American painter Hans Hofmann's energetic and colorful abstract paintings on the top floor. The museum is renowned for its cutting-edge, changing exhibitions: the main space hosts a range of major shows – such as Robert Mapplethorpe's controversial photographs – while the Matrix Gallery focuses on lesser-known, generally local artists. The new quarters of the **Pacific Film Archive**, diagonally opposite at 2575 Bancroft, feature nightly showings of classics and obscurities, while other artistic fare can be enjoyed at **Zellerbach Hall** (see p.584 & p.585, respectively).

Telegraph Avenue

Downtown Berkeley – basically two department stores, a few banks, a post office, and the City Hall building – lies west of the university campus around the Berkeley BART station on Shattuck Avenue, but the real activity centers on **Telegraph Avenue**, which runs south of the university from Sproul Plaza. This thoroughfare saw some of the worst of the 1960s riots and is still a frenetic bustle, especially the four short blocks closest to the university, which are packed with cafés and secondhand bookstores. Sidewalk vendors selling jewelry and subversive souvenirs are not as ubiquitous as they used to be, but down-and-outs still hustle for spare change and spout psychotic poetry. At no. 2455 the original Amoeba Records (⊤510/549-1125), whose vast younger sister is across the bay in Haight-Ashbury, still houses the East Bay's widest selection of used and new music.

People's Park, now a slightly seedy and partly overgrown plot of land half a block up behind Amoeba, was another battleground in the late 1960s, when organized and spirited resistance to the university's plans to develop the site into dormitories brought out the troops, who shot dead an onlooker by mistake. To many, the fact that the park is still a community-controlled open space (and outdoor flophouse for Berkeley's legions of pushers and homeless) symbolizes a small victory in the battle against the Establishment, though it's not a pleasant or particularly safe place to hang about, at least after dark. Though its message is rather undermined by its insalubrious surroundings, a mural along Haste Street recalls some of the reasons why the battles were fought, in the words of student leader Mario Savio: "There's a time when the operation of the machine becomes so odious, makes you so sick at heart, that you can't take part, you can't even tacitly take part. And you've got to put your bodies upon the gears and upon the wheels, upon the levers, upon all the apparatus, and you've got to make it stop."

Directly across Bowditch Street from People's Park stands one of the finest buildings in the Bay Area, Bernard Maybeck's **Christian Science Church**. Built in 1910, it's an eclectic and thoroughly modern structure, laid out in a simple Greek cross floor plan and spanned by a massive redwood truss with carved Gothic tracery and Byzantine painted decoration. The interior is only open on Sundays for worship and for tours at 11am, but the outside is worth lingering over, its cascade of gently pitched roofs and porticoes carrying the eye from one handcrafted detail to another. It's a clever building in many ways: while the overall image is one of tradition and craftsmanship, Maybeck also succeeded in inconspicuously incorporating such materials as industrial metal windows, concrete walls, and asbestos tiles into the structure – thereby cutting costs.

North Berkeley

North Berkeley is a subdued neighborhood of professors and postgraduate students, spreading from the flat leafy blocks around the BART lines to the steep, twisting streets that climb up the lushly overgrown hills north of the campus. At the foot of the hills, some of the Bay Area's finest **restaurants** and **delis** – most famously *Chez Panisse*, started and run by Alice Waters, the acclaimed inventor of California cuisine – have sprung up along **Shattuck Avenue** to form the so-called Gourmet Ghetto, a great place to pick up the makings of a tasty alfresco lunch. There are also a few **galleries**, most notably ACCI, 1652 Shattuck Avenue (Tues–Thurs 11am–6pm, Fri 11am–7pm, Sat 10am–6pm, Sun noon–5pm; free; ☏510/843-2527), an arts-and-crafts co-operative designed to exhibit and sell the work of local artists. Over a mile further northwest, where Berkeley meets Albany, **Solano Avenue** is fast catching up as a trendy shopping and dining area with a dazzling array of outlets, such as Tibetan craft shops, draped along its curved length.

Euclid Avenue, off Hearst and next to the north gate of the university, is a sort of antidote to Telegraph Avenue, a quiet grove of coffee joints and pizza parlors frequented by grad students, and the focal point of the largely academic enclave known as **Northside**. Above Euclid (if you want to avoid the fairly steep walk, take the daily #65 bus or the weekdays-only #8) there are few more pleasant places for a picnic than the **Berkeley Rose Garden** at the corner of Euclid Avenue and Bayview Place (daily dawn–dusk; free), a terraced amphitheater filled with some three thousand varieties of roses and looking out across the bay to San Francisco. Built as part of a WPA job-creation scheme during the Depression, a wooden pergola rings the top, stepping down to a small spring.

Tucked among the ridges of Berkeley Hills, a number of enticing parks give great views over the flatlands and the bay. The largest and highest of them, **Tilden Park**, spreads along the crest of the hills, encompassing some 2065 acres of near wilderness. Kids can enjoy a ride on the carved wooden horses of the carousel or through the redwood trees on the 1950s mini-steam train. In the warmer months, don't miss a swim in soothing **Lake Anza** (lifeguard on duty May–Sept daily, some weekends in Apr & Oct 11am–6pm; $3.50).

Nearer to town, between the north end of Shattuck Avenue and the east end of Solano Avenue, the gray basalt knob of **Indian Rock** stands out from the foothills, challenging rock climbers who hone their skills on its forty-foot vertical faces. Carved into similarly hard volcanic stone across the street are the mortar holes used by the Ohlone to grind acorns into flour. In between, and in stark contrast, stands the rusting hulk of a Cold War–era air-raid siren. Those who just want to appreciate the extraordinary view from the rock can take the steps around its back.

West Berkeley

From Downtown Berkeley and the UC campus, **University Avenue** runs in an almost imperceptible gradient downhill toward the bay, lined by increasingly shabby frontages of motels and massage parlors. The liveliest part of this **West Berkeley** area is around the intersection of University and San Pablo avenues, where a community of recent immigrants from India and Pakistan have set up stores and restaurants that serve some of the best of the Bay Area's curries.

The area between San Pablo Avenue and the bay is the oldest part of Berkeley, and a handful of 100-year-old houses and churches – such as the two white-spired Gothic Revival structures on Hearst Avenue – survive from the time when this district was a separate city, known as Ocean View. The neighborhood also holds remnants of Berkeley's industrial past, and many of the old warehouses and factory premises have been converted into living and working spaces for artists, craftspeople, and software companies. The newly polished and yuppified stretch of **Fourth Street** between Gilman and University features upscale furniture outlets and quaint gourmet delis, as well as some outstanding restaurants (see p.581). Just to the south of here at 708 Addison Street, you can take a tour of the huge Takara Sake USA Inc. brewery, whose tasting room and museum grant the opportunity to sample the company's products in elegant Japanese surroundings and learn about the process of sake-making (daily noon–6pm; free; ☎510/540-8250).

The North Bay and inland valleys

Compared to the urbanized bayfront cities of Oakland and Berkeley, the rest of the East Bay is sparsely populated, and places of interest are few and far between. The **North Bay** is home to some of the Bay Area's heaviest industry – oil refineries and chemical plants dominate the landscape – but also holds a few remarkably unchanged waterfront towns that merit a side trip if you're passing by. Away from the bay, the **inland valleys** are a whole other world of dry rolling hills dominated by the towering peak of **Mount Diablo**. Dozens of tract-home developments have made commuter suburbs out of what were once cattle ranches and farms, but so far the region has been able to absorb the numbers and still feels rural, despite having doubled in population in the past quarter-century.

The North Bay

North of Berkeley there's not a whole lot to see or do. Off the Eastshore Freeway in mostly mundane **Albany**, Golden Gate Fields has **horse racing** from October to June, and beyond it, the **Albany Mud Flats** are a fascinating place to stroll; impromptu works of art made from discarded materials vie with wild irises to attract the passer-by's eye in this reclaimed landfill jutting out into the bay. Back inland, San Pablo Avenue's strip of bars and clubs, including *Club Mallard* (no. 752, ☎510/524-8450) and *The Hotsy-Totsy* (no. 601, ☎510/524-1661), contain some of the best in the East Bay – that is, if you're looking for authentic, gritty saloons featuring live rock'n'roll on weekends, well-stocked jukeboxes, and pool tables reminiscent of San Francisco's Mission District. About a mile from Albany, **El Cerrito**'s main contribution to world culture was the band Creedence Clearwater Revival, who staged most of their *Born on the Bayou* publicity photographs in the wilds of Tilden Park in the hills above. The town is still home to one of the best record stores in California, Down Home Music, at 10341 San Pablo Avenue (☎510/525-2129), which stocks an eclectic array of blues, gospel, Cajun, Tex-Mex, old time, jazz, world, and rock.

Rough and depressing **Richmond**, at the top of the bay, was once a boomtown, whose Kaiser Shipyards built ships during World War II and employed 100,000 workers between 1940 and its closure in 1945. Now it's the proud home of the gigantic Standard Oil refinery, which you drive through before crossing the **Richmond-San Rafael Bridge** ($4) to Marin County. About the only reason to stop in Richmond is that it marks the north end of the BART line, and the adjacent Amtrak station is a better terminal for journeys to and from San Francisco than the end of the line in West Oakland.

Though not really worth a trip in itself, if you're heading from the East Bay to Marin County, **Point Richmond** merits a look. A cozy little town tucked away at the foot of the bridge between the refinery and the bay, its many Victorian houses have become commuter territory for upwardly mobile professionals from San Francisco. Through the narrow tunnel that cuts under the hill stands the most obvious sign of this gentrification: Brickyard Landing, an East Bay docklands development with modern bay-view condos, a private yacht harbor, and a token gesture to the area's industrial past – disused brick kilns, hulking next to the tennis courts on the front lawn. The rest of the waterfront is taken up by the broad and usually deserted strand of **Keller Beach**, which stretches for half a mile along the sometimes windy shoreline.

Benicia

On the north side of the Carquinez Straits, connected by the Carquinez Bridge ($4) and hard to get to without a car (turn right onto I-780 after the bridge), **Benicia** is the most substantial of the historic waterfront towns, but one that has definitely seen better days. Founded in 1847, it initially rivaled San Francisco as the major Bay Area port and was even the state capital for a time. Despite Benicia's better weather and fine deep-water harbor, San Francisco, which is closer to the ocean, eventually became the main transportation point for the fortunes of the Gold Rush, and the town very nearly faded away altogether. Examples of Benicia's efforts to become a major city stand poignantly around the very compact downtown area, most conspicuously the 1852 Greek Revival structure that was used as the **first State Capitol** for just thirteen months. The building has been restored as a **museum** (Wed–Sun 10am–5pm; $2), furnished in the legislative style of the time, complete with top hats on the tables and shining spittoons every few feet.

A walking-tour map of Benicia's many intact Victorian houses and churches is available from the **CVB**, 601 First Street (Mon–Fri 8.30am–5pm, Sat & Sun 11am–3pm; ☎707/745-2120, ⓦwww.beniciachamber.com). Included on the itinerary are the steeply pitched roofs and gingerbread eaves of the **Frisbie-Walsh house** at 235 East L Street, a prefabricated Gothic Revival building shipped here in pieces from Boston in 1849. Across the City Hall park, the arched ceiling beams of **St Paul's Episcopal Church** look like an upturned ship's hull; it was built by shipwrights from the Pacific Mail Steamship Company, one of Benicia's many successful nineteenth-century shipyards. Half a dozen former brothels and saloons stand in various stages of decay and restoration along First Street down near the waterfront, from where the world's largest train ferries used to ply the waters between Benicia and Port Costa until 1930. These days the only time this spot draws large crowds is during the annual **Waterfront Celebration** on the last weekend of July.

Since the early 1990s, Benicia has attracted a number of artists and craftspeople, and you can watch glassblowers and furniture makers at work in the **Benicia Glass Studios** at 675 East H Street (Mon–Sat 10am–4pm, Sun in summer noon–5pm; free). Ceramic artist Judy Chicago and sculptor Robert Arneson are among those who have worked in the converted studios and modern light-industrial parks around the sprawling fortifications of the old **Benicia Arsenal**, whose thickly walled sandstone buildings east of the downtown area formed the main army storage facility for weapons and ammunition from 1851 through the Korean Conflict. One of the oddest parts of the complex is the **Camel Barn** in the **Benicia Historical Museum** (Wed–Sun 1–4pm; free; ☎707/745-5435, ⓦwww.beniciahistoricalmuseum .org): the structure used to house camels that the army imported in 1856 to transport supplies across the deserts of the southwestern US. The experiment failed, and the camels were kept here until they were sold off in 1864.

The inland valleys

BART tunnels from Oakland through the Berkeley Hills to the leafy-green stockbroker settlement of **Orinda**, continuing east through the increasingly hot and dry landscape to **Concord**, site of a controversial nuclear-weapons depot. In the mid-Nineties, a civilly disobedient blockade here ended in protester Brian Wilson losing his legs under the wheels of a slow-moving munitions train. The event raised public awareness – before it happened few people knew of the depot's existence – and earned Wilson a place in the Lawrence Ferlinghetti poem *A Buddha in the Woodpile*. These days, however, it's business as usual at the depot.

From the Pleasant Hill BART station, one stop before the end of the line, Contra Costa County Connection buses leave every thirty minutes for **Martinez**, the seat of county government and a major Amtrak hub, passing the preserved home of naturalist **John Muir**, at 4202 Alhambra Avenue (Wed–Sun 10am–5pm; $3; ☎925/228-8860, ⓦwww.nps.gov/jomu), just off Hwy-4 two miles south of Martinez. Muir, an articulate, persuasive Scot whose writings and political activism were of vital importance in the preservation of America's wilderness, spent much of his life exploring and writing about the majestic Sierra Nevada, particularly Yosemite. He was also one of the founders of the **Sierra Club** – a wilderness lobby and education organization that retains a strong presence today (see p.386). Anyone familiar with the image of this thin, bearded man wandering the mountains with his knapsack, notebook, and packet of tea might be surprised to see his very conventional, upper-class Victorian home, now restored to its appearance when Muir died in 1914. Built by Muir's father-in-law, only those parts of the house Muir added himself reflect much of the personality of the man, not least the massive, rustic fireplace he had built in the East Parlor so he could have a "real mountain campfire." The bulk of Muir's personal belongings and artifacts are displayed in his study on the upper floor, and in the adjacent room an exhibition documents the history of the Sierra Club and Muir's battles to protect America's wilderness. Also included in the modest fee is entry to the still-productive orchard and the 1849 **Martinez Adobe**, homestead of the original Spanish land-grant settlers and now a small **museum** of Mexican colonial culture.

At the foot of Mount Diablo, fifteen miles south, playwright **Eugene O'Neill** used the money he received for winning the Nobel Prize for Literature in 1936 to build a home and sanctuary for himself, which he named **Tao House**. It was here, before 1944 when he was struck down with Parkinson's disease, that he wrote many of his best-known plays: *The Iceman Cometh*, *A Moon for the Misbegotten*, and *Long Day's Journey into Night*. Readings and performances of his works are sometimes given in the house, which is open to visitors, though you must reserve a place on one of the free guided **tours** (Wed–Sun 10am & 12.30pm; ☎925/838-0249, ⓦwww.nps.gov/euon). As it's now protected National Park Service land, there's no parking on site, so the tours pick you up in the tony town of **Danville**, at a location given when you book. Danville's richest neighborhood, Blackhawk, is the home of the **Blackhawk Automotive Museum**, 3700 Blackhawk Plaza Circle (Wed–Sun 10am–5pm; $8; ☎925/736-2277, ⓦwww.blackhawkmuseum.org), where you'll find an impressive collection of classic cars from Britain, Germany, Italy, and the US, along with artwork inspired by them.

Mount Diablo

Majestic **Mount Diablo** rises up from the rolling ranchlands at its foot to a height of nearly four thousand feet, its summit and flanks preserved within **Mount Diablo State Park** (daily 8am–sunset; $6 per vehicle). North Gate, the main road through the park, comes within three hundred feet of the top, so it's a popular place for an outing and you're unlikely to be alone to enjoy the marvelous view: on a clear day you can see over two hundred miles in every direction. There's no public transportation, though the Sierra Club sometimes organizes day-trips (see p.50).

Two main entrances lead into the park, both well marked off I-680. The one from the southwest by way of Danville passes by the **ranger station**, where you can pick up a trail map ($5) listing the best day-hikes. The other runs from the northwest by way of Walnut Creek, and the routes join together five miles from the summit, beside which the attractive **Visitor Center** (daily 10am–4pm; ☎925/837-6119) contains a free interpretive museum and observation deck. March and April, when the wildflowers are out, are the best months to come, and since mornings are ideal for getting the clearest view, you should drive to the top first and then head back down to a trailhead for a hike, or to one of the many picnic spots for a leisurely lunch. In summer it can get desperately hot and dry, and parts of the park are closed because of fire danger.

Eating

Home to **California cuisine** and some of the best restaurants in the state, Berkeley is an upmarket diner's paradise. But it's also a college town, and you can eat cheaply and well, especially around the southern end of the campus and along Telegraph Avenue. The rest of the East Bay is less remarkable, except when it comes to plain **American food** such as barbecued ribs, grilled steaks, or deli sandwiches, for which it's unbeatable.

Nemesis at Altamont

Uncannily timed at the dying embers of the Sixties and often referred to as "the nemesis of the Woodstock generation," the concert headlined by the **Rolling Stones** at the **Altamont Speedway**, fifteen miles southeast of Mount Diablo, on December 6, 1969 ended in total disaster. The free event was conceived to be a sort of second Woodstock, staged in order to counter allegations that the Stones had ripped off their fans during a long US tour. The band, however, inadvisably hired a chapter of Hell's Angels instead of professional security to maintain order and the result, predictably enough, was chaos. Three people ended up dead, one kicked and stabbed to death by the Hell's Angels themselves.

The whole sorry tale was remarkably captured on film by brothers David and Albert Maysles (plus co-director Charlotte Zerwin) and released the following year as their documentary *Gimme Shelter*. The footage of the concert clearly shows the deteriorating mood and growing menace in the crowd, exemplified by the scene when Jefferson Airplane vocalist Marty Balin jumped down into the fray to break up a fight, earning himself a broken jaw. By the time the Stones came on stage matters were patently out of hand, and after several interruptions and pleas for sanity by Mick Jagger, all hell broke loose during, ironically, *Sympathy for the Devil*. Jagger, Richards, and company are later shown watching footage of the incident with numb looks on their faces as the glint of a knife signals the fatal stabbing.

Those interested in NASCAR can still attend races at the site, now known as the Altamont Motorsports Park (☎925/423-3272, ⊛www.altamontmotorsportspark .com), while counterculture historians may find a pilgrimage to the scene of the crime oddly rewarding.

Oakland

Budget food: diners and delis

Barney's 4162 Piedmont Ave, North Oakland ☎510/655-7180; 5819 College Ave, Rockridge ☎510/601-0444; and 1591 Solano Ave, Berkeley ☎510/526-8185. The East Bay's most popular burgers – including meatless ones – smothered in dozens of different toppings.

Holy Land 677 Rand Ave, North Oakland ☎510/272-0535. Casual diner-style kosher restaurant just beyond the freeway north of Lake Merritt, serving moderately priced Israeli food, including excellent falafel.

Lois the Pie Queen 851 60th St at Adeline, North Oakland ☎510/658-5616. Famous around the bay for its southern-style sweet potato and fresh fruit pies, this cozy diner also serves massive breakfasts and Sun dinners, all for $10 or less.

American and California cuisine

Bay Wolf 3853 Piedmont Ave, North Oakland ☎510/655-6004. Comfortable restaurant serving grilled meat, fish dishes, and specialties such as duck-liver flan on an ever-changing, expensive menu.

Grand Oaks Grill 736 Washington St, Oakland ☎510/452-1258. Moderately priced meat and seafood dishes, such as chicken marsala and calamari dore, cooked in a mixture of European and Asian sauces.

Asian

Le Cheval 1007 Clay St, Oakland ☎510/763-8495. Serving exquisite Vietnamese in ample portions, the way it was meant to be; the chic, spacious surroundings and reasonable prices here won't let you down either.

Nan Yang 6048 College Ave, Rockridge ☎510/655-3298. Burmese food served in colorful, large, palate-exciting portions. The political refugee owner/chef is willing to discuss all his esoteric delicacies.

French and Italian

Citron 5484 College Ave, Rockridge ☎510/653-5484. Neighborhood gem of a bistro that rivals

San Francisco's best restaurants. Warm, unpretentious service and exquisite French-influenced food, but fairly expensive with entrées around $25.

Garibaldi's on College 5356 College Ave, Rockridge ☎510/595-4000. Quality upmarket Italian with delicious pasta dishes and an emphasis on fine wines. Some of the sauces have a spicy Arabic and Middle Eastern element.

Oliveto 5655 College Ave, Rockridge ☎510/547-5356. Chef Paul Canales creates appetizing gourmet Italian cuisine by using creative recipes and home grown ingredients. The main dining room is pretty expensive (entrées approaching $30), but there's a less pricey basement section with more stolid fare on offer.

Zachary's 5801 College Ave, Rockridge ☎510/655-6385 and 1853 Solano Ave, North Berkeley ☎510/525-5950. Zealously defended as the best pizza in the Bay Area, *Zachary's* is also one of the only places offering the rich, deep-dish Chicago-style pies.

Latin American and Caribbean

La Furia Chalaca 310 Broadway, Oakland ☎510/451-4206. Impressive range of seafood with pasta and various Peruvian sauces, as well as some meat dishes like the excellent braised pork.

Tropix 3814 Piedmont Ave, North Oakland ☎510/653-2444. Large portions of fruity Caribbean delicacies at reasonable prices, with authentic jerk sauce and thirst-quenching mango juice.

Ice cream and desserts

Dreyers 5925 College Ave, Rockridge ☎510/658-0502. Oakland's own rich ice cream, which is distributed throughout California, is served at this small, slightly dull Rockridge café.

Fenton's Creamery 4226 Piedmont Ave, North Oakland ☎510/658-7000. A brightly lit 1950s ice cream and sandwich shop, open until 11pm on weeknights, midnight on weekends.

Berkeley

Budget food: diners and delis

Bette's Ocean View Diner 1807 Fourth St, West Berkeley ☎510/644-3932. Named after the neighborhood, not after the vista, but serving up some of

the Bay Area's best breakfasts and lunches. Very popular on weekends, when you may have to wait an hour for a table, so plan accordingly.

Homemade Café 2454 Sacramento St, Berkeley ☎510/845-1940. Nontraditional, inexpensive

California-style Mexican and Jewish food served for breakfast and lunch, at shared tables when crowded.

Rick & Ann's 2922 Domingo Ave, Berkeley ☎510/649-8538. Even in Berkeley folks sometimes want meatloaf and mashed potatoes instead of arugula, and to get their fill of both the crowds line up outside this neighborhood diner every weekend.

Saul's Deli 1475 Shattuck Ave, North Berkeley ☎510/848-3354. For pastrami, corned beef, kreplach, or knishes, this is the place. Great sandwiches and picnic fixings to take away, plus a full range of sit-down evening meals.

American and California cuisine

Café Rouge 1782 Fourth St, West Berkeley ☎510/525-1440. Located along a short cul-de-sac, their specialty is delicately prepared organic meats, fresh from their own butcher shop. There are vegetarian pasta dishes for the less carnivorous.

Chez Panisse 1517 Shattuck Ave, North Berkekey ☎510/548-5525. The California restaurant to which all others are compared, its chef Alice Waters is widely credited for inventing California cuisine with delights like Monterey Bay sardine toast with arugula and fennel, or Sonoma County duck with roasted butternut squash, beets, and tatsoi. The set menu starts at $50 per head on Mon, rising to $85 at weekends.

Fatapple's 1346 Martin Luther King Jr Way, North Berkeley ☎510/526-2260. Crowded but pleasant family-oriented restaurant with excellent, cheap American breakfasts and an assortment of sandwiches and burgers for lunch or dinner.

Lalime's 1329 Gilman St, North Berkeley ☎510/527-9838. A culinary dissertation on irony, as rich leftist Berkeley professors chow down on rich veal, pâté de foie gras, and other distinctly un-PC fare, in a casual setting. Expect to pay $40–50 per person.

Rivoli 1539 Solano Ave, North Berkeley ☎510/526-2542. Delivers all that's wonderful about Berkeley dining: first-rate fresh food based on Italian and French cuisine, courteous service, and a casual, friendly atmosphere. It's all followed by a steep bill, as most entrées exceed $20.

Spenger's 1919 Fourth St, West Berkeley ☎510/845-7771. With a spacious sit-down restaurant and cheap takeout counter, this is a local institution. As one of the largest chains in the Bay Area, *Spenger's* serves up literally tons of simple but well-cooked seafood dishes to thousands of customers daily.

Asian, African, and Indian

Ajanta 1888 Solano Ave, North Berkeley ☎510/526-4373. Pretty upmarket curry house featuring an interesting array of dishes, such as duck curry Kerala and Dhaniwal *murg korma*, from different parts of India and Pakistan, not found in many other establishments.

Blue Nile 2525 Telegraph Ave, Berkeley ☎510/540-6777. Filling Ethiopian food, with an adequate range of meat and vegetarian choices all around $10, served with a smile amidst cozy African decor.

Breads of India 2448 Sacramento St, Berkeley ☎510/848-7648. This gourmet curry house turns out delicious, fresh daily specials for around $10.

Cha Am 1543 Shattuck Ave, North Berkeley ☎510/848-9664. Climb the stairs up to this unlikely, always crowded small restaurant for deliciously spicy Thai food at moderate prices. The adjacent *Dara's* is similar, with Laotian food as well.

Jade Villa 800 Broadway, Oakland ☎510/839-1688. For endless dim sum lunches or traditional Cantonese meals, this is one of the best places in Oakland's Chinatown.

Kirala 2100 Ward St, Berkeley ☎510/549-3486. Many argue that *Kirala* serves the best sushi in the Bay Area; others argue that it's simply the best in the world. Moderate pricing, too – expect to pay around $20 to get your fill.

▲ Chez Panisse restaurant, Berkeley

Liu's Kitchen 1593 Solano Ave, North Berkeley ☎510/525-8766. Huge helpings of tasty Chinese fare at very low prices – the filling pot stickers are a meal in themselves.

Long Life Vegi House 2129 University Ave, Berkeley ☎510/845-6072. Cheap vegetarian cooking (no surprises there) that's perpetually popular with Cal students, although the dishes' good value often exceeds their quality.

O'Chamé 1830 Fourth St, West Berkeley ☎510/841-8783. One of the top Japanese restaurants in the US, with beautifully prepared sashimi and sushi as well as a full range of authentic Japanese specialties. A treat in the $20–25 range.

Steve's Barbeque In the Durant Center, 2521 Durant Ave, Berkeley ☎510/848-6166. Excellent, low-priced Korean food (kimchee to die for); other cafés in the center sell Mexican food, sushi, healthy sandwiches, deep-fried donuts, and slices of pizza – not to mention bargain pitchers of beer.

Vik's Chaat Corner 726 Allston Way at Fourth St, West Berkeley ☎510/644-4412. A terrific lunchtime destination offering a wide array of south Indian snacks – expect long queues at weekends. The ambience is minimal, leaving nothing to distract you from the delights of *masala dosa* or *bhel puri*. Open until 6pm.

Italian and Mediterranean

Cheese Board Pizza 1512 Shattuck Ave, North Berkeley ☎510/549-3055. Tiny storefront selling some of the world's most delicious and unique pizza at very reasonable prices: $3 a slice, with a different topping every day. Well worth searching out, but keeps irregular hours: usually Tues–Sat 11.30am–2pm & 4.30–7pm.

La Mediterranée 2936 College Ave, Berkeley ☎510/540-7773. Good Greek and Middle Eastern dishes, such as Levantine meat tart or various kebabs for $10 or less, served indoors or on the large patio.

LaVal's Pizza 1834 Euclid Ave, Berkeley ☎510/843-5617. Lively graduate-student hangout near the North Gate of campus. Pool table, wide-screen TV broadcasting sports, wide selection of microbrews, and great pizza. Lunch specials often a feature.

Trattoria La Siciliana 2993 College Ave, Berkeley ☎510/704-1474. Intimate, family-run Italian place with a wide range of antipasti, pastas, risotti, and specialties like stuffed beef roll for under $20.

Latin American

Café de la Paz 1600 Shattuck Ave, North Berkeley ☎510/843-0662. Authentic South American cuisine, especially Brazilian, can be found in this large, attractive restaurant. Reasonable prices for such style appeal to the New-Agey and leftist clientele.

Cancun Taqueria 2134 Allston Way, Berkeley ☎510/549-0964. Popular and cheap Downtown self-service burrito joint, with huge portions of tasty food in lively and colorful surroundings.

Juan's Place 941 Carleton St, West Berkeley ☎510/845-6904. One of Berkeley's oldest Mexican restaurants, serving heaps of great food to an interesting mix of people at moderate prices – meat dishes cost around $10.

Picante 1328 Sixth St, West Berkeley ☎510/525-3121. Fine and very reasonably priced tacos with fresh salsa, plus live jazz on weekends. Nicely decorated, with an outdoor patio for fine weather.

French and Spanish

Britt-Marie's 1369 Solano Ave, Albany ☎510/527-1314. Along with a fine selection of mostly California wines by the glass, this place serves well-priced eclectic home cooking plus outstanding chocolate cake.

César 1515 Shattuck Ave, North Berkeley ☎510/883-0222. Perpetually crowded tapas bar serving small portions overflowing with taste. Loosely affiliated with *Chez Panisse*, the combination of quality and a relaxed atmosphere has made it a cultish destination for locals, though be mindful of the diminutive dishes – prices can add up.

La Note 2377 Shattuck Ave, Berkeley ☎510/843-1535. The appropriately sunny, light cuisine of Provence isn't the only flavor you'll find in this petite dining room: students and teachers from the Jazzschool (sic) next door routinely stop in for casual jam sessions.

Ice cream and desserts

Yogurt Park 2433a Durant Ave, Berkeley ☎510/549-0570. Frozen yoghurt is the specialty here; open until midnight for the student throngs.

Specialty shops and markets

Berkeley Bowl 2777 Shattuck Ave, Berkeley ☎510/841-6346. A converted bowling alley that's now an enormous produce, bulk, and health-food market. The least expensive grocery in town, with the largest selection of fresh food.

Cheese Board 1504 Shattuck Ave, North Berkeley ☎510/549-3183. Collectively owned and operated since 1967, this was one of the first outposts in Berkeley's Gourmet Ghetto, offering over 200 varieties of cheese and a range of delicious breads.

Epicurious Garden 1511 Shattuck Ave, North Berkeley. This new indoor mall of top-notch produce and takeout snacks includes half a dozen independent outlets, such as Alegio chocolate (☎510/548-2466) and Picoso Mexican (☎510/540-4811), as well as a Japanese tea garden at the back.

La Farine 6323 College Ave, Rockridge ☎510/654-0338. Small but extremely popular French-style bakery, with excellent *pain au chocolat*.

Monterey Foods 1550 Hopkins St, North Berkeley ☎510/526-6042. The main supplier of exotic produce to Berkeley's gourmet restaurants, this boisterous market also has the highest quality fresh fruit and vegetables available.

Vintage Berkeley 2113 Vine Street, North Berkeley ☎510/665-8600. Excellent outlet for quality domestic and imported wines, mostly under $20, housed in a cute old pump station. The highly knowledgable staff will match a wine with any meal.

Cafés and bars

One of the best things about visiting the East Bay is the opportunity to enjoy its many **cafés**. Concentrated most densely around the UC Berkeley campus, they're on par with the best of San Francisco's North Beach for bohemian atmosphere – heady with the smell of coffee, and from dawn to near midnight full of earnest characters wearing their intellects on their sleeves. If you're not after a caffeine fix, you can generally also get a glass of beer, wine, or fresh fruit juice, though for serious drinking you'll be better off in one of the many **bars**, particularly in rough-hewn Oakland. Grittier versions of what you'd find in San Francisco, they're mostly blue-collar, convivial, and almost always cheaper. Not surprisingly, Berkeley's bars are brimming with students and academics.

Cafés

Brewed Awakenings 1807 Euclid Ave, North Berkeley ☎510/540-8865. Spacious coffee- and teahouse near the North Gate of campus, frequented by professors and grad students. Friendly staff, plenty of seating, and lovely artwork on the redbrick walls explain why this is annually rated the "Best Café to Study In" by the student press.

Café Mediterraneum 2475 Telegraph Ave, Berkeley ☎510/841-5634. Berkeley's oldest café featuring sidewalk seating. Straight out of the Beat archives: beards and berets optional, battered paperbacks de rigueur.

Café Strada 2300 College Ave, Berkeley ☎510/843-5282. Spacious, open-air café where art and architecture students cross paths with would-be lawyers and chess wizards.

Coffee Mill 3363 Grand Ave, North Oakland ☎510/465-4224. Elongated room that doubles as an art gallery and often hosts poetry readings. Also a great bakery.

Royal 6255 College Ave, Rockridge ☎510/653-5458. Bright, modern, and relaxing spot in the Rockridge area, with outdoor seating. Perfect for a leisurely afternoon with the newspaper.

Bars

Albatross Pub 1822 San Pablo Ave, West Berkeley ☎510/843-2473. Popular student superbar, replete with darts, pool, board games, and fireplace. Serves a large selection of ales from around the world, including a pretty good pint of Guinness. Live jazz, flamenco, and blues music on weekends (free–$5).

Ben'n'Nick's 5612 College Ave, Rockridge ☎510/933-0327. Lively bar with good taped rock music and tasty food, if you're hungry.

Heinold's First and Last Chance Saloon 56 Jack London Square, Oakland ☎510/839-6761. Authentic waterfront bar that's hardly changed since the turn of the century, when Jack London was a regular. They still haven't bothered to fix the slanted floor caused by the 1906 earthquake.

Jupiter 2181 Shattuck Ave, Berkeley ☎510/843-8277. Many types of lager, ale, and cider to select from at this local favorite, which offers wood-fired pizza and an outdoor beer garden. There's a real buzz here, especially for the loud disco nights or live jazz at weekends.

Pacific Coast Brewing Co 906 Washington St, Oakland ☎510/836-2739. Oaktown's only real microbrewery, which conjures up a range of decent brews and offers quite an extensive menu too. Attracts Downtown office workers as well as a younger crowd later on.

Pub (Schmidt's Tobacco & Trading Co) 1492 Solano Ave, Albany ☎510/525-1900. Just past the official Berkeley limit, this small, relaxed bar lures a mixture of bookworms and game players with a good selection of beers. They even get away with a semi-open smoking area out back, perhaps because their other specialty is selling the evil weed.

Pyramid Alehouse 901 Gilman St, West Berkeley ☎510/528-9880. This huge, postindustrial space makes a surprisingly casual spot to sip the suds. Outdoor film screenings on weekend nights during summer.

Triple Rock Brewery 1920 Shattuck Ave, Berkeley ☎510/843-2739. Buzzing, all-American microbrewery with decent food: the decor is Edward Hopper–era retro, and the beers (brewed on the premises) are a bit fizzy unless you ask for one of the fine cask-conditioned ales at the end of the bar.

The White Horse 6560 Telegraph Ave at 66th St, Oakland ☎510/652-3820. Oakland's oldest gay bar – a smallish, friendly place, with mixed nightly dancing for men and women.

Nightlife and other entertainment

Nightlife is where the East Bay really comes into its own. Dancing to canned music and paying high prices for flashy decor is not a popular pastime here, although more venues have at least one dance/trance night these days, often Thursday. On the other hand, there are still dozens of **live music** venues, particularly in Oakland, covering a range of musical tastes and styles – from small, unpretentious jazz clubs to buzzing R&B venues. Berkeley's clubs tend more towards folk and world music, with other places dedicated to underground rock, and the university itself holds two of the best medium-sized venues in the entire Bay Area, both of which attract touring big-name stars. **Tickets** for most venues are available at their box office or, for a service charge, through BASS (☎510/762-2277).

Though not bad by US standards, the East Bay **theater** scene isn't exactly thriving, and shows tend to be politically inspired rather than dramatically innovative. By contrast, the range of **films** is first-class, with over a dozen movie theaters showing new releases and Berkeley's revamped Pacific Film Archive, one of the world's finest film libraries, filling its screens with obscure but brilliant art flicks. Check the free *East Bay Express* (ⓦwww.eastbayexpress.com) or the *SF Weekly* (ⓦwww.sfweekly.com) for details of what's on.

Major performance venues

Berkeley Community Theater 1930 Allston Way, Berkeley ☎510/845-2308. Jimi Hendrix played here, and the 3500-seat theater still hosts major rock concerts (Oasis to Sonic Youth) and community events. Tickets through major agents.

Center for Contemporary Music Mills College, 5000 MacArthur Blvd, Oakland ☎510/430-2191, ⓦwww.mills.edu. One of the prime centers in the world for experimental music.

McAfee Coliseum 7000 Coliseum Way, near the airport ☎510/639-7700, ⓦwww.coliseum.com. Mostly stadium shows here, inside the 18,000-seat arena or outdoors in the adjacent 55,000-seat coliseum. Used to be a favorite gig of the Grateful Dead's.

Paramount Theater 2025 Broadway, Downtown Oakland ☎510/465-6400, ⓦwww .paramounttheater.com. Beautifully restored Art Deco masterpiece, hosting classical concerts, big-name crooners, ballets, operas, and a growing roster of rap and rock shows. Ticket office Tues–Sat noon–5pm; $20–85. Some nights they play old Hollywood classics for $8.

Zellerbach Hall and the outdoor **Greek Theatre** on the UC Berkeley campus ☎510/642-9988, ⓦwww.calperfs.berkeley.edu. Two of the top spots for catching big names touring the Bay Area during the academic year. Zellerbach showcases drama, classical and world music, and dance, while the Greek welcomes more popular acts. Tickets $20–100.

Live music venues

924 Gilman 924 Gilman St, West Berkeley ☎510/525-9926, ⓦwww.924gilman.org. Part social project, part outer edge of the hardcore punk scene in a bare, squat-like old warehouse. Weekends only; cover $5–10.

The Alley 3325 Grand Ave, North Oakland ☎510/444-8505. Ramshackle black-timber piano bar, decorated with business cards and with live old-time blues merchants on the keyboards. No cover.

Ashkenaz 1317 San Pablo Ave, West Berkeley ⓣ510/525-5054, ⓦwww.ashkenaz.com. World-music and dance café. Acts range from modern Afrobeat to the best of the Balkans. Kids and under-21s welcome. Cover $10–15.

Blakes on Telegraph 2367 Telegraph Ave, Berkeley ⓣ510/848-0886, ⓦwww .blakesontelegraph.com. Student-patronized saloon with a funky roster of live music most nights of the week and DJs the rest. Latin, funk, soul, hip-hop, roots, rock, reggae, blues, and more. $3–12.

La Peña Cultural Center 3105 Shattuck Ave, Berkeley, near Ashby BART ⓣ510/849-2568, ⓦwww.lapena.org. More folk than rock, and some Latin, often politically charged – the website encourages cultural activism for social change. $8–20.

Mile High Club 3629 Martin Luther King Jr Way, North Oakland ⓣ510/654-4549, ⓦwww .oaklandmilehigh.com. The best of the Bay Area blues clubs. Waitresses balance pitchers of beer on their heads to facilitate a safer passage through the rocking crowds. Cover $8–20.

Starry Plough 3101 Shattuck Ave, Berkeley, near Ashby BART ⓣ510/841-2082, ⓦwww .starryploughpub.com. Music ranges from noisy punk to alternative pop to country to traditional Irish folk, and the crowd is just as varied. Doubles as a friendly saloon and restaurant in the afternoon and early evening. Free–$8.

Yoshi's World Class Jazz House 510 Embar-cadero West, Oakland ⓣ510/238-9200, ⓦwww .yoshis.com. The West Coast's premier jazz club near Jack London Square regularly attracts an impressive roster of performers nightly. The place is almost always full. Most shows $10–20, more for big names.

Film

Grand Lake Movie Theater 3200 Grand Ave, Oakland ⓣ510/452-3556. The grand dame of East Bay picture palaces, just above Lake Merritt, showing the best of the current major releases, with special emphasis on politically alternative works.

Oaks Theater 1875 Solano Ave, Berkeley ⓣ510/526-1836, ⓦwww.renaissancerialto.com /current/oaks. A mixture of mainstream and

political films are shown at this cozy, renovated Art Deco cinema, built in 1925.

Pacific Film Archive 2575 Bancroft at Bowditch St, Berkeley ⓣ510/642-5249, ⓦwww.bampfa .berkeley.edu. The archive's splendid new digs plays the West Coast's best selection of cinema. It features nightly showings of classics, Third World, and experimental films, plus revivals of otherwise forgotten favorites. Call for listings or pick up a free monthly calendar around campus. Two films a night; tickets $8.

UC Theater 2036 University Ave, Berkeley ⓣ510/843-6267. Popular revival house with a huge auditorium and a daily double-feature showcasing funky theme-weeks of noir, melodrama, and other genres. Matinees $5, $8 thereafter.

Theater

Berkeley Repertory Theater 2025 Addison St, Berkeley ⓣ510/845-4700, ⓦwww.berkeleyrep .org. One of the West Coast's most highly respected theater companies, presenting updated classics and contemporary plays in an intimate modern theater. Tickets $40–60; fifty percent discounts for students and under-30s with advance booking.

Black Repertory Group 3201 Adeline St, Berkeley ⓣ510/652-2120, ⓦwww.blackrepertorygroup .com. After years of struggling, this politically conscious company moved into its own specially built home near Ashby BART in 1987; since then they've encouraged new talent with great success. Tickets $15–30.

California Shakespeare Festival Siesta Valley, Orinda ⓣ510/548-3422, ⓦwww.calshakes.org. This annual, summer-long festival has a gorgeous open-air home in the wooded East Bay Hills. Tickets $32–60.

Julia Morgan Center for the Arts 2640 College Ave, Berkeley ⓣ510/845-8542, ⓦwww .juliamorgan.org. A variety of touring shows stop off in this cunningly converted old church. Tickets $10–30.

The Peninsula

The city of San Francisco sits at the tip of a five-mile-wide neck of land commonly referred to as **THE PENINSULA**. Home to old money and new technology, the Peninsula stretches for fifty miles of relentless suburbia south from San Francisco along the bay, past the wealthy enclaves of Hillsborough and Atherton, winding up in the futuristic roadside landscape of the **"Silicon**

Valley" near **San Jose**, the fastest-growing city in California and now tenth-largest in the US.

There was a time when the region was largely agricultural, but the computer boom – spurred by Stanford University in **Palo Alto** – has replaced orange groves and fig trees with office complexes and parking lots. Surprisingly, however, most of the land along the **coast** – separated from the bayfront sprawl by a spur of redwood-covered ridges – remains rural and largely undeveloped; it also contains some excellent **beaches** and a couple of affably down-to-earth communities, all well-served by public transportation.

Information

The **Palo Alto Chamber of Commerce**, 122 Hamilton Avenue (Mon–Fri 9am–5pm; ☎650/324-3121, ⓦwww.paloaltochamber.com), has lists of local restaurants and cycle routes; for information on Stanford University, contact its visitor center (Mon–Fri 8am–5pm, Sat & Sun 9am–5pm; ☎650/723-2560, ⓦwww.stanford.edu) in the Memorial Auditorium opposite Hoover Tower, or get a copy of the free *Stanford Daily*, published weekdays. To find out what's on in the area and where, pick up a free copy of the *Palo Alto Weekly*, available at most local shops, or log onto the paper's ⓦwww.paloaltoonline.com, a well-organized, rich databank of everything from local bike shops and restaurants to history and movie times.

At the southern end of the bay, the **San Jose CVB** is at 408 S Almaden (Mon–Fri 8am–5pm, Sat & Sun 11am–5pm; ☎1-800/726-5673, ⓦwww .sanjose.org), around the side of the massive Convention Center; it's rather more geared towards helping visiting businesspeople than the casual traveler, though. For a better idea of local news and events pick up a copy of the excellent *San Jose Mercury* daily newspaper (ⓦwww.mercurynews.com) or the free weekly *Metro* (ⓦwww.metroactive.com), although the latter usually lists as many events for San Francisco as it does for the South Bay. The website ⓦwww.siliconvalley .citysearch.com also holds a cache of reviews and features on the area.

Along the coast, the **Chamber of Commerce** in **Pacifica**, 225 Rockaway Beach Avenue (Mon–Fri 9am–5pm, Sat & Sun 10am–4.30pm; ☎650/355-4122, ⓦwww.pacificachamber.com), is the nearest to San Francisco on the Peninsula. Further south, the **Half Moon Bay Chamber of Commerce**, at 520 Kelly Avenue (Mon–Fri 9am–4pm; ☎650/726-8380, ⓦwww .halfmoonbaychamber.org), gives out walking-tour maps and information on accommodation. There's also a small kiosk under the clocktower at the corner of Kelly Avenue and Main Street that opens at weekends (Sat & Sun 10am–3pm). Another way of finding out what's happening is to log on to ⓦwww.visithalfmoonbay.org.

Getting around

BART only travels down the Peninsula as far as Daly City, from where you can catch SamTrans (☎1-800/660-4287, ⓦwww.samtrans.com) **buses** south to Palo Alto or along the coast to Half Moon Bay. For longer distances, **CalTrain** (☎1-800/660-4287, ⓦwww.caltrain.com) offers a rail service at least every half-hour from its terminal at Fourth and King streets in Downtown San Francisco, stopping at most bayside towns between the city and Gilroy ($2.25–11) via San Jose ($7.50); Greyhound runs regular buses along US-101 to and from its San Jose terminal at 70 S Almaden. Santa Clara Valley Transit Authority (VTA) ($1.75, day-pass $5.25; ☎408/321-2300, ⓦwww.vta.org) runs buses and modern trolleys around metropolitan San Jose. If you're going to be spending significant time there, most major domestic airlines fly direct into **Norman J. Mineta San Jose International Airport** (☎ 408/501-7600, ⓦ www.sjc.org), very close to Downtown San Jose; the VTA SJC Airport Flyer bus runs to Downtown San Jose and Santa Clara for $3.50, and there's the usual choice of taxis, limos, and shuttles for fancier rides to your destination.

Accommodation

Visitors to San Francisco often choose to stay on the Peninsula rather than in the city. Dozens of $60-a-night motels line Hwy-82 – "El Camino Real," the old main highway – and, with a bit of advance planning (and a car), sleeping here can save a lot of money. Also, if you're arriving late or departing on an early flight from SFO you might want to avail yourself of one of the many airport hotels. Perhaps the best reasons to spend the night down on the Peninsula are its low-priced, pleasant **hostels**, two of which are housed in old lighthouses right along the Pacific Coast. San Jose's **hotels** are largely overpriced during the week, catering more to the conventioneering corporate world than the tourist or traveler, though it's possible to find decent deals at weekends.

Hotels and motels

Bay Landing Hotel 1550 Bayshore Hwy, Burlingame ☎ 650/259-9000, ⓦ www .baylandinghotel.com. One of the best options at the north end of the Peninsula, with views of the bay and planes taking off from SFO. Refreshingly, it's a family-owned place with quality rooms and service. ❸

Beach House 4100 N Cabrillo Hwy, 3 miles north of Half Moon Bay ☎ 1-800/315-9366, ⓦ www .beach-house.com. Large, modern resort hotel with fully equipped loft-suites, all with balconies, overlooking Pillar Point Harbor and the ocean. An excellent value for this price range. ❻

Cardinal Hotel 235 Hamilton Ave, Palo Alto ☎ 650/323-5101, ⓦ www.cardinalhotel.com. Reasonably comfortable hotel in the heart of downtown Palo Alto. En-suite rooms cost almost double those with shared baths. ❸

Coronet Motel 2455 El Camino Real, Palo Alto ☎ 650/326-1081, ⓦ www.coronetmotel.com. Just around the corner from lively California Ave, this friendly motel has clean rooms and a pool. ❸

Costanoa 2001 Rossi Rd at Hwy-1, 3 miles north of Año Nuevo ☎ 650/879-1100, ⓦ www.costanoa .com. Unique and relaxed resort with an emphasis on communing with nature and spa treatments. Offers camping and RV sites (from $50), as well as top-notch canvas-walled cabins and swish lodges. ❼

Fairmont Hotel 170 S Market St, San Jose ☎ 1-800/441-1414, ⓦ www.fairmont.com. San Jose's finest hotel, part of the luxury chain which began in San Francisco, is located in the heart of Downtown on the plaza. All the expected amenities, such as room service, swimming pool, lounge, and sparkling rooms; half-price at weekends. ❽

Garden Court Hotel 520 Cowper St, Palo Alto ☎ 650/322-9000, ⓦ www.gardencourt.com. Very upmarket place, built in attractive Mission style, in a handy downtown location. All rooms boast full facilities and balconies. Suites go for nearly $700. ❻

Hotel De Anza 233 W Santa Clara St, San Jose ☎ 1-800/843-3700, ⓦ www.hoteldeanza.com. Plush business- and conference-oriented hotel with full amenities in one of the livelier sections of town. Special weekend rates and packages. ❼

Howard Johnson Express 1215 S First St, San Jose ☎ 1-800/509-7666, ⓦ www.hojo.com. Adequate if charmless rooms Downtown, within walking distance of the city's main nightspots. ❹

Pacifica Motor Inn 200 Rockaway Beach Ave, Pacifica ☎ 1-800/522-3772, ⓦ www .pacificamotorinn.com. Large rooms just a block off the beach in a hamlet alongside Hwy-1. ❸

Sea Breeze Motel 100 Rockaway Beach Ave, Pacifica ☎ 650/359-3903, ⓦ www.nicksrestaurant .net. Beachfront hotel with attached restaurant, *Nick's* (see p.597). Rooms are well kept, but standard motel-style. ❹

Bed and breakfasts

Farallone Inn 1410 Main St, Montara ☎ 1-800/818-7316, ⓦ www.faralloneinn.com. Restored mansion whose rooms vary in size from extremely cozy to penthouse suites – but all have Jacuzzis. ❸

Old Thyme Inn 779 Main St, Half Moon Bay ☎ 1-800/720-4277, ⓦ www.oldthymeinn .com. Seven incredibly quaint rooms, each with a private bath, in a lovely Victorian house surrounded by luxuriant herb and flower gardens and with paintings by the owner. ❺

Pillar Point B&B 380 Capistrano Rd, Princeton-By-The-Sea ⊤ 1-800/400-8281, ⓦ www .pillarpointinn.com. Pretty house with lovely rooms, a library, outdoor deck, and topiary garden. Close to Pillar Point harbor and a range of restaurants. ➏
San Benito House 356 Main St, Half Moon Bay ⊤ 650/726-3425, ⓦ www.sanbenitohouse.com. Twelve restful B&B rooms in a 100-year-old building, just a mile from the beach. Excellent restaurant downstairs. ➍

Hostels

HI–Hidden Villa 26807 Moody Rd, Los Altos Hills ⊤ 650/949-8648, ⓦ www.hiddenvilla.org. Located on a 1600-acre ranch in the foothills above Silicon Valley, with plenty of wilderness trails; closed June–Aug for an eco-summer camp; dorm $20 per night. Private cabins $40–56.

🏃 **HI–Pigeon Point Lighthouse** Hwy-1, just south of Pescadero ⊤ 650/879-0633, ⓦ www.norcalhostels.org. Worth planning a trip around, this beautiful hostel, fifty miles south of San Francisco, is ideally placed for exploring the redwood forests in the hills above, watching the wildlife in nearby Año Nuevo State Reserve, or just soaking in the outdoor hot tub. Office hours 7.30–10am & 5.30–10pm; check-in from 4.30pm, doors locked at 11pm. Members $20 per night, nonmembers $25; reservations essential in summer. Private rooms $55–63.

HI–Point Montara Lighthouse 16th St/Hwy-1, Montara ⊤ 650/728-7177, ⓦ www.norcalhostels .org. Dorm rooms in a converted 1875 lighthouse, 25 miles south of San Francisco and accessible by bike or SamTrans bus #1L or #1C (Mon–Fri until 5.50pm, Sat until 6.15pm). You can even see the ocean from the outdoor hot tub. Office hours 7.30–10am & 4.30–9.30pm; doors locked 11pm. Members $20 per night, nonmembers $25; reservations essential in summer. Private rooms $55–94.
Sanborn Park Hostel 15808 Sanborn Rd, Saratoga ⊤ 408/741-0166, ⓦ www .sanbornparkhostel.org. Independent hostel with comfortable rooms in a wooded 3600-acre park 15 minutes southwest of San Jose. Call from downtown Saratoga (bus #54 from Sunnyvale CalTrain station) and they'll arrange to pick you up. Open 7–9am & 5–11pm (curfew); dorm $14 per night.

Campgrounds

Butano State Park Pescadero ⊤ 650/879-2040. RV and tent spaces in a beautiful redwood forest; book on ⊤ 1-800/444-7275 on ⓦ www .reserveamerica.com. $25, off-season $20.
Half Moon Bay State Beach Half Moon Bay ⊤ 650/726-8820. Tent sites in the woods behind the beach; book on ⊤ 1-800/444-7275, ⓦ www .reserveamerica.com. $25.

South along the bay

US-101 runs south from San Francisco along the bay to San Jose, through over fifty miles of unmitigated sprawl lined by light-industrial estates and shopping malls. There's one place along the freeway in **San Mateo** worth a visit: the **Coyote Point Museum**, 1651 Coyote Point Drive (Tues–Sat 10am–5pm, Sun noon–5pm; $6; ⊤ 650/342-7755, ⓦ www.coyoteptmuseum.org), four miles south of the airport off Poplar Avenue. Surrounded by a large bayfront park, the museum showcases examples of the natural life of the San Francisco Bay, from tidal insects to birds of prey, all exhibited in engaging and informative displays and enhanced by interactive computers and documentary films.

Six-lane freeways don't usually qualify as scenic routes, but an exception is **I-280**, one of the newest and most expensive freeways in California. It runs parallel to US-101 but avoids the worst of the bayside mess by cutting through wooded valleys down the center of the Peninsula. Just beyond the San Francisco city limits the road passes through **Colma**, a unique place filled with cemeteries, which, other than the military burial grounds in the Presidio, are prohibited within San Francisco. Besides the expected roll call of deceased San Francisco luminaries like Levi Strauss and William Hearst are a few surprises, such as Wild West gunman Wyatt Earp.

Further south, beyond the vast Crystal Springs Reservoir, just off I-280 on Canada Road near the well-heeled town of **Woodside**, luscious gardens surround the palatial **Filoli Estate** (mid-Feb to late Oct Tues–Sat 10am–3.30pm, Sun 11am–3.30pm, last admission 2.30pm; tours by reservation only; $12; ☎650/364-8300 ext. 507, ⓦwww.filoli.org). The 45-room mansion, designed in 1915 in neo-Palladian style by architect Willis Polk, may look familiar – it was used in the TV series *Dynasty* as the Denver home of the Carrington clan. It's the only one of the many huge houses around here that you can visit, although the gardens are the real draw, especially in the spring when everything's in bloom.

Palo Alto and Stanford University

PALO ALTO, just south and three miles east of Woodside between I-280 and US-101, is a small, leafy community which, despite its proximity to Stanford, exudes little of the college-town vigor of its northern rival, Berkeley. In recent years, Palo Alto has become something of a social center for Silicon Valley's nouveau riche, as evidenced by the trendy cafés and chic new restaurants that have popped up along its main drag, **University Avenue**. The computer-industry-boom job market made more than a few people rich, and this is where many of them came to spend their cash; small houses in the quaint neighborhoods surrounding the downtown area can cost up to a million dollars.

In terms of sights, the town doesn't have a lot to offer other than Spanish Colonial homes, but it's a great place for a lazy stroll and a gourmet meal. Monthly historic tours of Palo Alto's neighborhoods take place during summer (☎650/299-8878), and otherwise the best of the city's designs can be seen along **Ramona Street**. Be aware, however, that **East Palo Alto**, on the bay side of US-101, has a well-deserved reputation for gang- and drug-related violence, with one of the highest per capita murder rates of any US city. The area was founded in the 1920s as the utopian Runnymeade Colony, an agricultural, poultry-raising co-operative, and the local preservation society (☎650/329-0294) can point out the surviving sites. East Palo Alto, where Grateful Dead guitarist Jerry Garcia grew up, is about as far as you can get off the San Francisco tourist trail.

STANFORD UNIVERSITY, spreading out from the west end of University Avenue, is by contrast one of the tamest places you could imagine. The university is among the top – and most expensive – in the US, though when it opened in 1891, founded by railroad magnate Leland Stanford in memory of his dead son, it offered free tuition. Stanford's reputation as an arch-conservative think-tank was enhanced by Ronald Reagan's offer to donate his video library to the school (though Stanford politely declined) but it hasn't always been an entirely boring place. Ken Kesey came here from Oregon in 1958 on a writing fellowship, working nights as an orderly on the psychiatric ward of one local hospital, and getting paid $75 a day to test experimental drugs (LSD among them) in another. Drawing on both experiences, Kesey wrote *One Flew over the Cuckoo's Nest* in 1960 and quickly became a counterculture hero. The period is admirably chronicled by Tom Wolfe in *The Electric Kool-aid Acid Test*.

Approaching from the Palo Alto CalTrain and SamTrans bus station, which acts as a buffer between the town and the university, you enter the campus via a half-mile-long, palm-tree-lined boulevard which deposits you at its heart, the **Quadrangle**, bordered by the colorful gold-leaf mosaics of the **Memorial Church** and the phallic **Hoover Tower**, whose observation platform (daily 10am–4.30pm; $2) is worth ascending for the view. Free hour-long walking tours of the campus leave from here daily at 11am and 3.15pm, though it's fairly big and best seen by car or bike. Indeed, driving tours in a golf cart are offered daily at 1pm during term ($5) from Memorial Auditorium.

While you're here, don't miss one of the finest museums in the Bay Area. The **Iris and B. Gerald Cantor Center for Visual Arts** comprises 27 galleries (spread over 120,000 square feet) of treasures from six continents, dating from 500 BC to the present (Wed–Sun 11am–5pm, Thurs 11am–8pm; free; ☎650/723-4177, ⊚www.museum.stanford.edu). Housed in the old Stanford Museum of Art at the intersection of Lomita Drive and Museum Way, the Cantor Center incorporates the former structure, damaged in the 1989 earthquake, with a new wing, including a bookshop and café. Visiting exhibitions have featured the work of such artists as Duchamp, Oldenburg, and Lucien Freud; one of the finest pieces in the permanent collection is the stunning *Plum Garden, Kameido*, by Japanese artist Hiroshige. Be sure to have a look at the distinguished collection of over two hundred **Rodin sculptures**, including a *Gates of Hell* flanked by a shamed *Adam and Eve*, displayed in an attractive outdoor setting on the museum's south side. There's a version of *The Thinker* here as well, forming a sort of bookend with the rendition that fronts the Palace of the Legion of Honor Museum in San Francisco.

San Jose

Burt Bacharach wouldn't need to ask the way to **SAN JOSE** today – heading south from San Francisco, it should take under an hour (avoiding peak times) to reach the heart of the heat and smog that collects below the bay. Sitting at the southern end of the Peninsula, San Jose has in the past 25 years emerged as the civic heart of Silicon Valley, spurred by the growth of local behemoths Apple, Cisco, Intel, and Hewlett-Packard. San Jose's current priority is the development of a culture outside the computer labs that surround the city, and new museums, shopping centers, restaurants, clubs, and performing arts companies have mushroomed throughout the compact Downtown area. However, the recent downturn in the economy has led to various ambitious downtown renewal plans being put on hold by the city council. Still, while the nightlife and cultural scene here can't begin to compete with San Francisco, there are enough attractions around the city's clean and sunny streets to warrant a day-trip.

Downtown San Jose

Though now rooted in the modern high-tech world, San Jose's 1777 founding actually makes it one of the oldest settlements – and the oldest city – in California. The only sign of that **Downtown** is the 1797 **Peralta Adobe**, at 184 W St John Street (tours by arrangement; $6; ☎408/918-1055, ⊚www .historysanjose.org), notable more for its having survived the encroaching suburbia than anything on display in its sparse, whitewashed interior. Admission includes a tour of the **Fallon House**, a Victorian mansion across the street, built by the city's seventh mayor in 1855, a one-time frontiersman in the Fremont expedition. The building is currently undergoing renovation so guided tours may not take you through all fifteen rooms furnished from the period, but you will be shown a comprehensive video presentation on the home and adobe's relationship to the development of the cityscape.

The two blocks of San Pedro Street that run south of the adobe form a restaurant row known as **San Pedro Square**. There's no central plaza as such, just a collection of some of San Jose's best eateries (see p.596). Further south, down Market Street, lies the pleasant and palm-dotted **Plaza de César Chávez**. The plaza is San Jose's town square and there's no better place to catch some rays on the grass, read while sitting on one of the many wooden benches, or play in the unique **fountain** whose shooting spumes are a favorite hangout for kids in the summer.

SAN JOSE

San Francisco ▲   San Jose Flea Market ▲

0   2 miles

Norman J Mineta
San Jose
International
Airport

GUADALUPE PARKWAY

TECHNOLOGY DRIVE

GISH RD

N 1ST STREET

N 4TH STREET

N 10TH STREET

101

N

LAFAYETTE STREET

EL CAMINO REAL
LEWIS ST

BENTON ST

Triton Museum
Santa Clara
University

Mission
Santa Clara
de Asis

MARKET STREET
BELLOMY STREET

WASHINGTON ST

ALVISO ST

COLEMAN AVENUE

HEDDING STREET

TAYLOR STREET

EMPIRE STREET

N 1ST STREET

N 13TH STREET

NEWHALL STREET

WINCHESTER BLVD

MONROE ST

HEDDING ST

FOREST AVE

DAVIS STREET

HEDDING STREET

PARK AVENUE

CHAPMAN ST

MORSE ST

DANA AVE

NAGLEE AVE

Municipal
Rose Garden

Rosicrucian
Egyptian
Museum

THE ALAMEDA

STOCKTON AVENUE

San Jose
Arena

see inset

DOWNTOWN
SAN JOSE

SANTA CLARA ST

N MARKET ST

N SAN PEDRO ST

N 3RD ST

N 4TH ST

S 3RD ST

N 13TH ST

N 10TH ST

S 10TH ST

San Fernando

San Jose
State
University

Santa Clara ◄

Winchester
Mystery House

STEVENS CREEK BLVD

SCOTT STREET

LELAND AVE

SAN CARLOS STREET

AVENUE

San Jose
Amtrak
Station

RACE STREET

PARK AVENUE

MERIDIAN AVE

SAN CARLOS STREET

AUZERAIS AVE

280

VIRGINIA ST

ALMADEN AVE

VINE STREET

S 6TH ST

S 5TH ST

MOORPARK   AVE

PARKMOOR AVE

WILLIAMS
ROAD

GENEVIEVE LANE

DANIEL WAY

WAY

THORNTON

MAYWOOD
AVE

DOWNING
AVE

FRUITDALE AVENUE

BASCOM AVENUE

LEIGH

PAULA ST

SOUTHWEST EXPWY

GLEN EYRIE RD

LINCOLN AVENUE

BIRD AVENUE

WILLOW STREET

87

ACCOMMODATION
Fairmont Hotel   **B**
Hotel De Anza   **A**
Howard Johnson
Express   **C**

Fallon
House

Peralta Adobe
❶

SAN PEDRO
SQUARE

❷ ❹ ❸
❺

Ⓐ

St Joseph's
Cathedral Basilica

❼

Greyhound
Station

N

Ⓑ

❽

Tech
Museum
of Innovation

DOWNTOWN SAN JOSE

SANTA CLARA ST

MARKET ST

ALMADEN BLVD

Downtown
Center
Plaza

❻

N SAN PEDRO ST

San Jose
Museum of Art

The
Pavilion

Montgomery
Theater

❾

❿
⓫ ⓬
⓭

SOFA

S 1ST ST

San Jose
State University

San Jose
Repertory
Theater

S 2ND ST

American
Museum of
Quilts &
Textiles

S 4TH ST

Convention
Center

Ⓒ

Institute of
Contemporary Art

ℹ

SAN CARLOS ST

0   200 yds

▼

RESTAURANTS
71 Saint Peter   **1**
AP Stump's   **4**
E & O Trading Co   **6**
Eulipia   **10**
Original Joe's   **9**
Peggy Sue's   **2 & 8**
Spiedo   **3**

NIGHTLIFE
Agenda   **13**
The Blank Club   **7**
Britannia Arms
Downtown   **5**
Emma's Club Miami   **5**
Glo   **12**
Hookah Nites Café   **11**
Wine Galleria   **11**

A block north of the plaza, the **Cathedral Basilica of St Joseph** stands
on the site of the first Catholic parish in California, circa 1803. The present
building was dedicated in 1997, and you should duck inside to see its painted
cupola, stained-glass windows, and Stations of the Cross. Masses are held
daily, often in Spanish. Next door to the church at 110 S Market, the fantastic
San Jose Museum of Art (Tues–Sun 11am–5pm; $8; ☎408/294-2787,

@www.sjmusart.org) is set in the old post office building built in 1892, to which a new wing was added in 1991. The museum contains more than one thousand twentieth-century works, with the spotlight falling on post-1980 Bay Area artists. A relationship with New York's Whitney Museum of American Art has recently been formed, allowing the museum to exhibit works from the Whitney's vast permanent collection. The sweeping, open galleries are flooded with light, as is the attached café, including its outdoor patio with a plaza view. On Sundays there are special workshops and activities to help make the art accessible to kids.

Facing the southwest corner of the plaza, Downtown's biggest draw is the **Tech Museum of Innovation**, at 201 S Market Street (daily 10am–5pm; $8; T 408/294-8324, @www.thetech.org), with its hands-on displays of high-tech engineering. There are three floors of exhibits, as well as the inevitable IMAX theater (one show included in entry; extra show $4). Highlights include a program that allows you to design a virtual rollercoaster, regular demonstrations of state-of-the-art surgical instruments, and the chance to communicate with interactive robots. Unfortunately, the lines to access many of the best exhibits can seem like a virtual hell, and, unless you're a computer junkie, you may leave the museum feeling more like you've attempted to read an impervious software manual than visited a popular museum.

Aside from the attractions around the plaza, San Jose's other area worth walking through is the buzzing **"SoFA"** entertainment district, short for South First Street. To get here from the southern tip of the plaza, turn east on San Carlos Street and walk one block to First Street. SoFA forms the heart of San Jose's nightlife, with half a dozen clubs and discos along with a popular wine bar (see p.597 & p.598). There's plenty to see during the day as well, including the **Institute of Contemporary Art** (Tues, Wed & Fri 10am–5pm, Thurs 10am–8pm, Sat noon–5pm; free; T 408/283-8155, @www.sjica.org) at 451 S First Street. The ICA's large, sunny room exhibits modern art, mainly Bay Area artists, but also work by international painters and sculptors. On the same street is Downtown San Jose's **art cinema** house, the Camera 1, no. 366 (T 408/998-3300, @www.cameracinemas.com), and at no. 490, one of its performing arts companies, **The Stage** (T 408/283-7142, @www.sanjosestage.com). Performances of contemporary work regularly run Wednesday to Saturday, with tickets available for $20–45.

Around San Jose

Head four miles northwest of Downtown and you'll come across two of San Jose's more intriguing, and relaxing, places to hang out. The first is the **Rosicrucian Egyptian Museum**, 1342 Naglee Avenue (Mon–Fri 10am–5pm, Sat & Sun 11am–6pm; $9; T 408/947-3636, @www.egyptianmuseum.org), a grand structure that contains a brilliant collection of Assyrian and Babylonian artifacts, with displays of mummies, amulets, a replica of a tomb, and ancient jewelry. Don't miss the mummies of baboons, birds, and fish on the left-hand side of the tomb wing. There's also a **planetarium**, whose shows (daily 2pm, Sat & Sun also 3.30pm; free) cover such esoteric subjects as "The Mithraic Mysteries." Aside from fascinating exhibits within, the best part about the Rosicrucian is its garden grounds, featuring a replica of the Akhenaten Temple from Luxor. Across the street and two blocks west of the museum is the second peaceful locale, San Jose's **Municipal Rose Garden** (daily 8am–sunset; free). This beautiful expanse of green and rows of rose bushes is perfect for a picnic, and the fountain in the garden's center is a popular wading pool for youngsters. Roll up your pants, soak your feet, and take in a nice view of the Santa Cruz Mountains to the west amidst the sweet scents.

Engulfed in the sprawl of northwestern San Jose, the small community of **Santa Clara** holds a few tourist attractions of its own. The late eighteenth-century **Mission Santa Clara de Asis** (daily sunrise–sunset; free), just south of The Alameda (Route 82) at 500 El Camino Real, is one of the least impressive structures in the mission chain, but it's interesting to note how the remnants have been subtly preserved and integrated into the campus of the Jesuit-run **University of Santa Clara**. The **de Saisset Museum** (Tues–Sun 11am–4pm; free; ☎408/554-4528, ⓦwww.scu.edu/desaisset) within the complex traces the history of the mission through a permanent display of objects recovered from its ruins – the mission burned in a 1926 fire – along with changing shows of contemporary art. The bell in the belfry is original, a gift from King Carlos IV of Spain in 1798. Overall, the university is a green, quiet place to stroll around and pass an afternoon.

A few miles south of Santa Clara is a true American tourist trap, unmissable if you're into a good yarn. The **Winchester Mystery House**, 525 S Winchester Boulevard, just off I-280 near Hwy-17 (daily summer 9am–7pm, winter 9am–5pm; $23.95; ☎408/247-1313, ⓦwww.winchestermysteryhouse.com), belonged to Sarah Winchester, heiress to the Winchester rifle fortune, who was convinced upon her husband's death in 1884 that he had been taken by the spirits of men killed with his weapons. The ghosts told her that unless a room was built for each of them, the same fate would befall her. She took them so literally that the sound of hammers never ceased – 24 hours a day for the next thirty years. Now, unfinished, the house is a hodgepodge of extensions and styles: extravagant staircases lead nowhere and windows open onto solid brick walls. It is also a shameless money maker, where visitors have to run a gauntlet of ghastly gift stores and soda stands to get in or out. If you're a real sucker for punishment you can take the extra Behind the Scenes tour for $20.95 (combo with admission $28.95).

The coast

The largely undeveloped **coastline** of the Peninsula south of San Francisco is worlds away from the inland valleys. A few small towns, countless beaches, and sea lions trace the way 75 miles south to the mellow summer fun of Santa Cruz and Capitola. Bluffs protect the many **nudist beaches** from prying eyes and make a popular launching pad for hang-glider pilots, particularly at **Fort Funston**, a mile south of the San Francisco Zoo – also the point where the earthquake-causing San Andreas Fault enters the sea, not to surface again until Point Reyes. **Skyline Boulevard** follows the coast from here past the repetitious tracts of proverbial ticky-tacky houses that make up Daly City, before heading inland toward Woodside at its intersection with Hwy-1, which continues south along the coast. Driving **Hwy-1** can be a relaxing jaunt providing jaw-dropping views of the ocean, as long as you avoid the masses. Summer and weekend afternoons find the route clogged with campers creeping along at 30mph and few opportunities to pass. Try hitting the road at sunrise if you can manage it and, provided the fog isn't obscuring everything, expect a magical ride.

Pacifica and around

San Pedro Point, a popular surfing beach fifteen miles south of San Francisco proper, and the town of **Pacifica** mark the southern extent of the city's suburban sprawl. Pacifica is a pleasant stopover for lunch and wave-gazing around Rockaway Beach. Visit the ultra-friendly **Chamber of Commerce**

(see p.586) for free maps of the area, including trail guides for **Sweeney Ridge**, from where Spanish explorer Gaspar de Portola discovered the San Francisco Bay in 1769. Pacifica's old **Ocean Shore Railroad Depot** here, now a private residence, is one of the few surviving remnants of an ill-advised train line between San Francisco and Santa Cruz. Wiped out during the 1906 earthquake, the line was in any case never more than a third complete. Its few patrons had to transfer back and forth by ferry to connect the stretches of track that were built, the traces of which you can still see scarring the face of the bluffs. The continually eroding cliffs make construction of any route along the coast difficult, as evidenced a mile south by the **Devil's Slide**, where a cement support has been added to lessen erosion during winter storms. The slide area was also a popular dumping spot for corpses of those who fell foul of rum-runners during Prohibition, and is featured under various names in many of Dashiell Hammett's detective stories.

Just south of the Devil's Slide, the sands of **Gray Whale Cove State Beach** (daily 8am–sunset; free) are clothing-optional. Despite the name, it's not an especially great place to look for migrating gray whales, but the stairway at the bus stop does lead down to a fine strand. Two miles south and a good half-mile off Hwy-1, the red-roofed buildings of the 1875 **Montara Lighthouse**, set among the windswept Monterey pine trees at the top of a steep cliff, have been converted into a youth hostel (see p.588). Just south of the turn to the light-house, at the end of California Street, the **Fitzgerald Marine Reserve** (T650/728-3584, W www.fitzgeraldreserve.org) has three miles of diverse oceanic habitat, peaceful trails, and, at low tide, the best tide pools in the Bay Area. The ranger often gives free interpretive walks through the reserve at low tide, the best time to explore, so call ahead or ask at one of the coast's tourist offices for low-tide times. At the south end of the reserve, Pillar Point juts out into the Pacific; just to the east, fishing boats dock at Pillar Point Harbor.

Captured in all its raging glory in the surfing documentary *Riding Giants*, **Mavericks Beach**, just off Pillar Point beyond the enormous communications dish, boasts the largest waves in North America and attracts some of the world's best (and craziest) surfers when conditions are right. Just watching them can be an exhilarating way to spend an hour or so, and hundreds of people do every day. There's a long breakwater you can walk out on, too, but remember never to turn your back to the ocean – rogue waves have crashed in and swept unsus-pecting tourists to their deaths. The surrounding villages of **Princeton-by-the-Sea**, whose main drag beside the marina is becoming increasingly trendy, and **El Grenada** both have good restaurants serving freshly caught fish and hamburgers. Further along, surfers also frequent the waters just offshore from the splendid long stretch of **Miramar Beach**. After a day in the water or on the beach, the place to head is the beachfront *Douglass Beach House* (see p.598), an informal jazz club and beer bar that faces the sands.

Half Moon Bay

Half Moof Bay, twenty miles south of the city and the only town of any size along the coast between San Francisco and Santa Cruz, takes its name from the crescent-shaped bay formed by Pillar Point. It was originally called Spanish-town, as it was founded when Spanish settlers forced the native Costonoa off the land in the 1840s and is thus the oldest European settlement in San Mateo County. Lined by miles of sandy beaches, the town is surprisingly rural consid-ering its proximity to San Francisco and Silicon Valley, and sports a number of ornate Victorian wooden houses clustered around its center. The oldest of these, at the north end of Main Street, was built in 1849 just across a little stone bridge over Pillarcitos Creek. The **Chamber of Commerce** (see p.586) on Hwy-1 has free walking-tour maps of the town and information on the two annual festivals for which the place is well known. The first is the **Holy Ghost and Pentecost Festival**, a parade and barbecue held on the seventh Sunday after Easter, while the other, the **Pumpkin Festival**, celebrates the harvest of the area's many pumpkin farms just in time for Halloween, when the fields around town are full of families searching for the perfect jack-o'-lantern to greet the hordes of trick-or-treaters. If you fancy an equine experience, the combined Sea Horse and Friendly Acres ranches, one mile north of town at 2150 N Cabrillo Highway (☎650/726-9903, ⓦwww.horserentals.com/seahorse.html), have trail **rides** for $40 per hour and ninety-minute beach rides for $50. Free, basic campgrounds line the coast in **Half Moon Bay State Park**, half a mile west of the town, although there is a parking fee for day-use (daily 8am–sunset; $6). The town is a good place to stop if you're low on gas, as the fifty-mile stretch of Hwy-1 to Santa Cruz doesn't offer many places to fill up.

The Butano redwoods, Pescadero, and the Año Nuevo State Reserve

If you've got a car and it's not a great day for the beach, head up into the hills above the coast, where the thousands of acres of the **Butano Redwood Forest** feel at their most ancient and primeval in the greyest, gloomiest weather. About half the land between San Jose and the coast is protected from development in a variety of state and county parks, all of which are virtually deserted despite being within a thirty-minute drive of the Silicon Valley sprawl. Any one of a dozen roads heads through endless stands of untouched forest, and even the briefest of walks will take you seemingly miles from any sign of civilization. Hwy-84 climbs up from San Gregorio through the Sam McDonald County Park to the hamlet of **La Honda**, where Ken Kesey had his ranch during the Sixties and once notoriously invited the Hell's Angels to a party. From here, you can continue on to Palo Alto, or, better, loop back to the coast via Pescadero Road.

A mile before you reach the quaint town of **Pescadero**, Cloverdale Road heads south to **Butano State Park**, where you can hike and camp overlooking the Pacific. Tiny Pescadero itself has one of the best places to eat on the Peninsula – *Duarte's* (see p.597), as well as a gas station. Just north of the turnoff to the village from Hwy-1, Pescadero State Beach is yet another fine spot for a dip, with no time restrictions or parking fee. The marsh between the beach and the town is a great place for watching waterfowl, especially at high tide. Pescadero, which was

▲ Pigeon Point Lighthouse

founded by Portuguese fishermen, celebrates the same **Holy Ghost Festival** as Half Moon Bay but a week earlier, on the sixth Sunday after Easter. The festival is also known by its Portuguese name of Chamarita.

Five miles south of Pescadero, you can stay the night in the old lighthouse-keeper's quarters and soak your bones in a marvelous hot tub at the *HI-Pigeon Point Lighthouse Hostel* (see p.588). The grounds of the light station are open to visitors (daily 8am–sunset; free; ☎650/879-2120) but the structure itself is closed. The calmest, most pleasant beach for wading is **Bean Hollow State Beach**, a mile north of the hostel; it's free but has very limited parking.

If you're here between December 15 and March 31, continue south another five miles to the **Año Nuevo State Reserve** for a chance to see one of nature's most bizarre spectacles – the mating rituals of **northern elephant seals**. These massive, ungainly creatures, fifteen feet long and weighing up to three tons, were once found all along the coast, though they were nearly hunted to extinction by whalers in the nineteenth century. During the mating season, the beach is literally a seething mass of blubbery bodies, with the trunk-nosed males fighting it out for the right to sire as many as fifty pups in a season. At any time of the year, you're likely to see a half-dozen or so dozing in the sands. The reserve is also good for birding, and in March you might even catch sight of migrating gray whales.

The slowly resurgent Año Nuevo elephant seal population is still carefully protected, and during the breeding season the obligatory guided tours – designed to protect spectators as much as to give the seals some privacy – begin booking in October (hourly 8am–4pm; $5 per person, $6 parking; ☎1-800/444-4445, ⓦwww.anonuevo.org). Otherwise tickets are usually made available to people staying at the *Pigeon Point Lighthouse Hostel*, and from April to November you can get a free permit from the park entrance to visit the point.

Eating

The **restaurants** on the Peninsula, particularly in pseudo-ritzy Palo Alto, are increasingly on a par with their San Franciscan counterparts. Many, filled with wealthy young computer executives, require dinner reservations every night of the week. In San Jose, consider dining around San Pedro Square for a good choice of cuisine. The following list concentrates primarily on establishments centrally located in the downtown areas of the main Peninsula cities and towns, with a few others that are worth almost any effort to get to.

71 Saint Peter 71 N San Pedro St, San Jose ☎408/971-8523. Patio dining and oyster bar centered on a menu of filet mignon, pork loin, chicken, and salads. Extremely hot with the in-crowd. Lunch Mon–Fri, dinner nightly.

AP Stump's 163 W Santa Clara St, San Jose ☎408/292-9928. The best place to go if you have an unlimited expense account. Pricey (entrées all over $20) California cuisine, but one of the spots to be seen in Silicon Valley. Great wine list.

Barbara's Fish Trap 281 Capistrano Rd off Hwy-1, Princeton-by-the-Sea ☎650/728-7049. Ocean-front seafood restaurant with good-value fish dinners and an unbeatable view.

Bistro Elan 448 S California Ave, Palo Alto ☎650/327-0284. Serving spiffy Cal cuisine, like duck confit and pan-seared Maine scallops,

to the cyber-elite. Prices are rather steep at over $20 per dinner entrée, so consider a lunchtime visit.

Café Capistrano 480 Capistrano Rd off Hwy-1, Princeton-by-the-Sea ☎650/728-7699. Inexpensive and authentic Mayan fare such as slow-roasted pork is on offer at this simple eatery.

Cetrella 845 Main St, Half Moon Bay ☎650/726-4090. Classy Italian/Mediteranean restaurant with a huge dining room, serving delights like Australian lamb sirloin in kalamata olive tapenade. Dinner entrées around $25 but there's a cheaper café/bar section too.

Château des Fleurs 523 Church St, Half Moon Bay ☎650/712-8837. An exquisite flower garden in front welcomes you to this small, reasonably priced French restaurant.

Duarte's 202 Stage Rd, Pescadero ☎650/879-0464. Platefuls of traditional American food (especially fish) for around $10 are served in this down-home find, connected to a bar full of locals in cowboy hats. Famous for their artichoke soup.

E&O Trading Company 96 S First St, San Jose ☎408/938-4100. Upscale Southeast Asian grill featuring curried fish and other Vietnamese/Indonesian fare. Entrées approaching $20.

Eulipia 374 S First St, San Jose ☎408/280-6161. Stylish dinner spot boasting well-prepared versions of California cuisine staples like grilled fish and fresh pastas. Mains $12–28. Closed Mon.

Evvia 420 Emerson St, Palo Alto ☎650/326-0983. Rather pricey California/Greek lamb dishes such as *paidakia arnisia* and *arni kapama*, as well as baked fish and other Hellenic faves, served in a cozy yet elegant dining room. Full bar.

Gin Wan 2810 Cabrillo Hwy, Half Moon Bay ☎650/726-6028. Copious portions of delicious Taiwanese and Szechuan cuisine at very reasonable prices in a simple dining room right on Hwy-1.

Hyderabad House 448 University Ave, Palo Alto ☎650/327-3455. Inexpensive Indian restaurant combining dishes from both north and south, with touches of ginger and coconut.

Joanie's Café 447 California Ave, Palo Alto ☎650/326-6505. Home-style breakfasts and lunches in a comfortable neighborhood restaurant.

Krung Siam 423 University Ave, Palo Alto ☎650/322-5900. Classy but not too expensive restaurant serving beautifully presented traditional Thai fare.

La Cheminée 530 Bryant St, Palo Alto ☎650/329-0695. Quality fare, such as lavender-encrusted halibut or pork Dijon, are among the delights at this French bistro. The prices, mostly under $20 per entrée, are not too outrageous either.

Los Gallos Taqueria 3726 Florence St, Redwood City ☎650/369-1864. Simply put, they make the best burritos on the Peninsula. Take the Marsh Road exit from Hwy-101 and look for the Marsh Manor shopping center.

Nick's Seashore Restaurant 101 Rockaway Beach, Pacifica ☎650/359-3903. Beloved enough to reel folks in from the city regularly, this all-purpose joint provides cheap brekky, moderate pasta, and pricier steak/seafood dishes.

Original Joe's 301 S First St, San Jose ☎408/292-7030. Grab a stool at the counter or settle into one of the comfy vinyl booths and enjoy a burger and fries or a plate of pasta at this San Jose institution, where $10 still goes a long way. Open until 1am.

Peggy Sue's 29 N San Pedro St, San Jose ☎408/298-6750. Inexpensive milkshakes, burgers, and fries served in a 1950s setting. Also has a vegetarian and kids' menu. Popular with Sharks' fans before ice hockey games. There's another outlet a few blocks away at 183 Park Ave ☎408/294-0252.

Rock'n'Rob's 450 Dundee Way, Rockaway Beach, Pacifica ☎650/359-3663. This new diner decorated in the old style churns out tons of burgers and fries all day, but no breakfast.

Sam's Chowder House 4210 Cabrillo Hwy, 3 miles north of Half Moon Bay ☎650/712-0245. Large, modern restaurant with wonderful ocean views, serving generous portions of seafood, fish, and steaks at around $20 a pop.

Spiedo 151 W Santa Clara St, San Jose ☎408/971-6096. Handmade pasta, pizza, calamari, salmon, and more delight the taste buds at lunch and dinner daily. Entrées begin at $16.

St Michael's Alley 806 Emerson St, Palo Alto ☎650/326-2530. This former student hangout has become one of Palo Alto's hottest bistros, serving "casual California" cuisine. A fine wine list and weekend brunch ($10–15) keeps guests coming back for seconds.

Cafés and nightlife

For a serious night out on the town, you're better off heading up to San Francisco, though many San Jose residents may try to convince you otherwise. Nevertheless, there are a number of good **bars** and **clubs** on the Peninsula – particularly in San Jose's SoFA district, but also in the studenty environs of Palo Alto. On the other hand, if you're in the mood for quiet conversation, check out one of the **cafés** listed here.

Bars and clubs

Agenda 399 S First St, San Jose ☎408/287-3991. A bar/restaurant/lounge in SoFA that heralded the arrival of nightlife in San Jose. DJ, dancing, and live jazz nightly.

The Blank Club 44 S Almaden, San Jose ☎408/292-5265. Live shows most nights and the only regular space for indie, punk and alternative sounds.

Blue Chalk Café 630 Ramona St, Palo Alto ☏ 650/326-1020. Yuppies and other young Silicon-ites have been flocking to this wildly successful bar/pool-hall/restaurant ever since it opened in 1993.

Brittania Arms Downtown 173 W Santa Clara St, San Jose ☏ 408/266-0550. The latest addition to the growing chain of British-themed pubs with fish'n'chips, real ale, footie (meaning soccer) on TV, and a trivia quiz night.

Cameron's Inn 1410 Cabrillo Hwy, 1 mile south of Half Moon Bay ☏ 650/726-5705. The other main UK-style joint on the Peninsula, with imported ales, pub grub, and games, as well as two London double-deckers outside, one for smoking and one for kids' videos.

Douglass Beach House Miramar Beach, 2.5 miles north of Half Moon Bay on Hwy-1, then west down Medio Ave ☏ 650/726-4143, ⊛ www.bachddsoc .org. Two-story country beach house with fireplace and outside deck; international jazz performers are frequently hosted by the Bach Dancing & Dynamite Society. The quieter *Ebb Tide Café* below is open Thurs–Sun.

Emma's Club Miami 177 W Santa Clara St, San Jose ☏ 408/279-3670. Huge San Pedro Square bar/Mexican restaurant with Latin music and dancing in the upstairs club at weekends. Great patio.

Glo 394 S First St, San Jose ☏ 408/280-1977. Dance music from light hip-hop to heavy disco is featured at this club, which imports top DJs from SF, LA, and Vegas on Sat nights.

Gordon Biersch Brewery 640 Emerson St, Palo Alto ☏ 650/323-7723. Among the first and still the best of the Bay Area's microbrewery-cum-restaurants. Also in San Francisco (see p.542) and in Downtown San Jose at 33 E San Fernando St ☏ 408/294-6785.

Half Moon Bay Brewing Co. 390 Capistrano Rd, Princeton-by-the-Sea ☏ 650/728-2739. Lively watering hole with a rock soundtrack, where you can get your kisser round a range of decent brews from blonde through amber to brown ale. Also has a popular restaurant serving California and American cuisine.

Moss Beach Distillery Beach and Ocean, Moss Beach ☏ 650/728-0220. If you don't feel like paying out $20 per entrée at the popular restaurant, snuggle up under a wool blanket, order a drink and an appetizer, and watch the sunset from the patio overlooking the ocean.

Wine Galleria 377 S First St, San Jose ☏ 408/298-1386. Large wine bar with plush sofas and a huge array of vintages for sale by the glass, with specials such as five glasses for $20.

Cafés

Caffè del Doge 419 University Ave, Palo Alto ☏ 650/326-9942. Relaxing, colorful hangout for Palo Alto's intellectual crowd, a branch of the Venice original.

Hookah Nites Café 371 S First St, San Jose ☏ 408/286-0800. Avant-garde art is showcased in this spacious and trendy venue, which serves fresh coffee and pastries.

Marin County

Across the Golden Gate from San Francisco, **MARIN COUNTY** (pronounced "Ma-RINN") is an unabashed introduction to California self-indulgence: an elitist pleasure zone of conspicuous luxury and abundant natural beauty, with sunshine, sandy beaches, high mountains, and thick redwood forests. Often ranked as the wealthiest county in the US, Marin has attracted a sizeable contingent of Northern California's rich young professionals, many of whom grew up during the Flower Power years of the 1960s and lend the place its New Age feel and reputation. Though many of the cocaine-and-hot-tub devotees who seemed to populate the swanky waterside towns in the 1970s have traded in their drug habits for mountain bikes – which were invented here – life in Marin still centers on personal pleasure, and the throngs you see hiking and cycling at weekends, not to mention the hundreds of esoteric self-help practitioners (rolfing, rebirthing, and soul-travel therapists fill up the classified ads of the local papers) prove that residents of Marin work hard to maintain their easy air of physical and mental well being.

Flashy modern ferries, appointed with fully stocked bars, sail across the bay from San Francisco and present a marvelous initial view of the county. As you head past desolate Alcatraz Island, curvaceous **Mount Tamalpais** looms larger until you land near its foot in one of the chic bayside settlements of **Sausalito** or **Tiburon**. **Angel Island**, in the middle of the bay but most easily accessed from Tiburon, provides relief from the excessive style-consciousness of both towns, retaining a wild, untouched feeling among the eerie ruins of derelict military fortifications.

Sausalito and Tiburon (and the lifestyles that go with them) are only a small part of Marin. The bulk of the county rests on the slopes of the ridge of peaks that divides the Peninsula down the middle, separating the sophisticated harbor-side towns in the east from the untrammeled wilderness of the Pacific coast to the west. The **Marin Headlands**, just across the Golden Gate Bridge from San Francisco, hold time-warped old battlements and gun emplacements that once protected San Francisco's harbor from would-be invaders, and now overlook hikers and cyclists enjoying the acres of open space and wildlife. Along the coastline that spreads north, the broad shore of **Stinson Beach** is the Bay Area's finest and widest stretch of sand, beyond which Hwy-1 clings to the coast past the counterculture village of **Bolinas** to seascapes around **Point Reyes**, where it's thought Sir Francis Drake may have landed in 1579 and claimed all of what is now California for England. Whale and seal watchers congregate here year-round for glimpses of migrations and matings.

Inland, the heights of Mount Tamalpais, and specifically **Muir Woods**, are a magnet to sightseers and nature lovers, who come to wander through one of the few surviving stands of the native coastal redwood trees. Such trees covered most of Marin before they were chopped down to build and rebuild the wooden houses of San Francisco. The long-vanished lumber mills of the rustic town of **Mill Valley**, overlooking the bay from the slopes of Mount Tam, as it's locally known, bear the guilt for much of this destruction; the oldest town in Marin County is now home to an eclectic bunch of art galleries and cafés. Further north, Marin's largest town, **San Rafael**, is rather bland, though its outskirts contain two of the most unusual attractions in the county: **Frank Lloyd Wright**'s peculiar Civic Center complex and the preserved remnants of an old Chinese fishing village in **China Camp State Park**. The northern reaches of Marin County border the bountiful wine-growing regions of the Sonoma and Napa valleys, detailed in Chapter Nine.

Arrival

Just getting to Marin County can be a great start to a day out from San Francisco. Golden Gate Transit **ferries** (℡415/923-2000 in San Francisco, ℡415/455-2000 in Marin, ⊛www.goldengate.org) leave from the Ferry Building on the Embarcadero, crossing the bay past Alcatraz Island to **Sausalito** (Mon–Fri 7.40am–7.55pm, Sat & Sun 10.40am–6.30pm) and **Larkspur** (Mon–Fri 6.25am–9.35pm, Sat & Sun 12.30–7pm); they run every thirty to forty minutes during the rush hour, roughly hourly during the rest of the day, and about every ninety minutes to two hours on weekends and holidays. Tickets cost $6.75 one way to both destinations and refreshments are sold on board. The slightly more expensive and less frequent Blue and Gold Fleet ($8.50 one way; ℡415/773-1188, ⊛www.blueandgoldfleet.com) sails from Pier 41 at Fisherman's Wharf to Sausalito (Mon–Fri 11am–2.45pm, Sat & Sun 10.35am–5.05pm) and **Tiburon** (Mon–Fri 7.15am–7.15pm, Sat & Sun 10.35am–5.05pm) – from where the Angel Island ferry (daily 10am–4pm; $10.25 round-trip, including state park entry fee; $1 per bicycle; ℡415/435-2131, ⊛www.angelislandferry .com) nips back and forth to **Angel Island State Park** daily in summer, weekends only in the winter. Blue and Gold Fleet provides additional weekday rush-hour crossings to Tiburon from the Ferry Building and a daily excursion service direct to Angel Island ($14.50 round-trip) from Pier 41. Note that the ferry timetables change quarterly, so it's best to check in advance.

Information

Three main on-the-spot sources can provide further information on Marin County: the **Marin County Visitors Bureau**, 1013 Larkspur Landing Circle, Larkspur (Mon–Fri 9am–5pm; ☎1-866/925-2060, ⓦwww.visitmarin.org), the **Sausalito Visitor Center**, occupying a modest hut at 780 Bridgeway Avenue (Tues–Sun 11.30am–4pm; ☎415/332-0505, ⓦwww.sausalito.org), and the **Mill Valley Chamber of Commerce**, 85 Throckmorton Avenue (Mon–Fri 10am–noon & 1–4pm; ☎415/388-9700, ⓦwww.millvalley.org), in the center of the town.

For information on hiking and camping in the wilderness and beach areas, depending on where you're heading, contact the **Golden Gate National Recreation Area**, Building 201, Fort Mason Center, San Francisco (Mon–Fri 9.30am–4.30pm; ☎415/561-3000), or the **Marin Headlands Visitor Center** (daily 9.30am–4.30pm; ☎415/331-1540, ⓦwww.nps.gov/goga); other outlets are the **Mount Tamalpais State Park Visitor Center**, 801 Panoramic Highway, Mill Valley (daily 8am–5.30pm; ☎415/388-2070, ⓦwww.mttam.net), and the Point Reyes National Seashore's **Bear Valley Visitors Center**, Point Reyes (Mon–Fri 9am–5pm, Sat & Sun 8am–5pm; ☎415/464-5100, ⓦwww.nps.gov /pore). Information on what's on in Marin can be found in the widely available local freesheets, such as the down-to-earth *Coastal Post* (ⓦwww.coastalpost.com) or the New-Agey *Pacific Sun* (ⓦwww.pacificsun.com).

Getting around

Golden Gate Transit runs a comprehensive **bus service** around Marin County and across the Golden Gate Bridge from the Transbay Terminal in San Francisco (same contacts as ferries above), and publishes a helpful and free system map and timetable, including all ferry services. Bus fares range from $2 to $8, with routes running every thirty minutes throughout the day, and once an hour late at night. Some areas can only be reached by GGT commuter services, which run during the morning and evening rush hours (call ahead to check schedules). On Sundays only, San Francisco's MUNI bus #76 runs hourly from San Francisco direct to the Marin Headlands. Golden Gate Transit bus #40, the only service available between Marin County and the East Bay, runs from the San Rafael Transit Center to the Del Norte BART station in El Cerrito ($3.40 each way).

If you'd rather avoid the hassle of bus connections, Gray Line (☎415/558-9400, ⓦwww.grayline.com) offers four-hour guided **bus tours** from the Transbay Terminal in San Francisco, taking in Sausalito and Muir Woods (daily year-round 9am, check for increased services in summer; $45, $63 with bay cruise); the Blue and Gold Fleet ferry also has a bus trip to Muir Woods (daily 9.15am & 2.15pm; 3.5hr; $50) with an option to return by ferry from Tiburon to Pier 41 in the city.

One of the best ways to get around Marin is by **bike**, particularly using a mountain bike to cruise the many trails that crisscross the county, especially in the Marin Headlands. If you want to ride on the road, Sir Francis Drake Highway – from Larkspur to Point Reyes – makes a good route, though it's best to avoid weekends, when the roads can get clogged up with cars. All ferry services to Marin allow bicycles.

Accommodation

You might prefer simply to dip into Marin County using San Francisco as a base, and if you've got a car or manage to time the bus connections right it's certainly possible, at least for the southernmost parts of the county. However, it can be nicer to take a more leisurely look at Marin, staying over for a couple of nights in some well-chosen spots. Sadly, there are few **hotels**, and those that there are often charge well in excess of $100 a night; **motels** are hardly ubiquitous, though there are a couple of attractively faded ones along the coast. If you want to stay in a B&B, contact Marin Bed and Breakfast (☎415/485-1971, ⍟www.marinbedandbreakfast.com), which can fix you up with rooms in comfortable private homes all over Marin County from $65 a night for two, ranging from courtyard hideaways on the beach in Tiburon to houseboats in Sausalito. The best bet for budget accommodation is a dorm bed in one of the beautifully situated **hostels** along the western beaches.

Hotels and motels

Casa Madrona 801 Bridgeway Ave, Sausalito ☎1-800/288-0502, ⍟www.casamadrona.com. Deluxe, European-style hotel with a new extension spreading up the hill above the bay. Spa facilities available and the *Mikayla* restaurant is highly rated. ⑦

Colonial Motel 1735 Lincoln Ave, San Rafael ☎1-888/785-2111, ⍟www.colonialinnmarin.com. Quiet, well-furnished, and friendly motel with decent rates in a residential neighborhood. ②

Grand Hotel 15 Brighton Ave, Bolinas ☎415/868-1757. Just two budget rooms in a funky, run-down old hotel above a secondhand shop. Sometimes only operates at weekends. ②

Hotel Sausalito 16 El Portal, Sausalito ☎1-888/442-0700, ⍟www.hotelsausalito.com. Sixteen stylish rooms with views across the park and harbor. Owned and run by an entertaining Scot. ⑥

The Lodge At Tiburon 1651 Tiburon Blvd, Tiburon ☎415/435-3133, ⍟www.thelodgeattiburon.com. Smart modern hotel with a rustic feel. Comfortable rooms, all with CD/DVD players, some with Jacuzzis. Rather inept staff. ⑤

🏃 **Mill Valley Inn** 165 Throckmorton Ave, Mill Valley ☎1-800/595-2100, ⍟www.millvalleyinn.com. By far the best hotel in Marin County, this gorgeous European-style inn boasts elegant rooms, two private cottages, and a central location. ⑥

Ocean Court Motel 18 Arenal St, Stinson Beach ☎415/868-0212, ⍟www.oceancourt.ws. Large simple rooms with kitchens, just a block from the beach and west of Hwy-1; you pay for the location though. ⑤

Stinson Beach Motel 3416 Shoreline Hwy, Stinson Beach ☎415/868-1712, ⍟www.stinsonbeachmotel.com. Average, slightly overpriced roadside motel right on Hwy-1, with tiny rooms. Five minutes' walk to the beach. ④

Bed and breakfasts

Blue Heron Inn 11 Wharf Rd, Bolinas ☎415/868-1102, ⍟www.blueheron-bolinas.com. Lovely double rooms in an unbeatable locale with ocean view. A friendly welcome, and its own restaurant serving good seafood and steaks help make this an excellent choice. ⑤

Lindisfarne Guest House Green Gulch Farm Zen Center, Muir Beach ☎415/383-3134, ⍟www.sfzc.org. Restful rooms in a meditation retreat set in a secluded valley above Muir Beach. Price includes three excellent vegetarian buffet meals. ⑥

Mountain Home Inn 810 Panoramic Hwy, Mill Valley ☎1-877/381-9001, ⍟www.mtnhomeinn.com. Romantically located near Mount Tamalpais's crest, this B&B offers great views and endless hiking opportunities. Some rooms with hot tubs. ⑥

Olema Inn 10000 Sir Francis Drake Blvd, Olema ☎1-800/532-9252, ⍟www.theolemainn.com. Wonderful little B&B with comfy rooms near the entrance to Point Reyes National Seashore, on a site that's been a hotel since 1876. Features a gourmet restaurant serving seafood and a full bar with heady wine list. Ideal for a break from the city. ⑥

Pelican Inn 10 Pacific Way, Muir Beach ☎415/383-6000, ⍟www.pelicaninn.com. Very comfortable rooms in a romantic pseudo-English country inn, with good bar and restaurant downstairs, serving full English breakfast and fine ales. A ten-minute walk from beautiful Muir Beach. ⑦

Ten Inverness Way 10 Inverness Way, Inverness ☎415/669-1648, ⍟www.teninvernessway.com. Quiet and restful, with a hot tub and complimentary evening wine, in a small village of good restaurants and bakeries on the fringes of Point Reyes. ⑥

Hostels

HI–Marin Headlands Building 941, Fort Barry, Marin Headlands ☎1-800/909-4776, ⍟www.norcalhostels.org. Hard to get to without a car –

it's near Rodeo Lagoon just off Bunker Road, five miles west of Sausalito – but worth the effort for its setting, in a cozy old army barracks near the ocean. On Sundays and holidays only, MUNI bus #76 from San Francisco stops right outside. Closed 10am–3.30pm, except for registration. Dorm beds $20 a night, private rooms from $60.

HI–Point Reyes In Point Reyes National Seashore T 415/663-8811, W www.norcalhostels.org. Also hard to reach without your own transportation: just off Limantour Road six miles west of the visitor center and two miles from the beach, it's located in an old ranch house and surrounded by meadows and forests. Closed 10am–4.30pm. Dorm beds $18–20 a night.

Campgrounds

Angel Island State Park Angel Island T 415/435-5390, W www.angelisland.org. Nine primitive walk-in sites (and one kayak-in site) with great views of San Francisco, which explains why they cost as much per night as more developed sites elsewhere ($20 summer/$15 winter). In summer it's essential to book.

China Camp State Park Off N San Pedro Rd, north of San Rafael T 415/456-0766. Walk-in plots (just 600ft from the parking lot) overlooking a lovely meadow. First-come-first-camped for $25 a night (winter $20). April–Oct reserve on T 1-800/444-7275, W www.reserveamerica.com.

Marin Headlands Just across the Golden Gate Bridge T 415/561-4304, W www.nps.gov/goga. Five campgrounds, the best of which is very popular *Kirby Cove* (open April–Oct only), at the northern foot of the Golden Gate Bridge (reservations T 1-877/444-6777, W www.recreation.gov; $25). Of the remaining sites, one is a group camp ($25), and the other three are free.

Mount Tamalpais State Park Above Mill Valley T 415/388-2070. Two separate campgrounds ($20) for backpackers, one on the slopes of the mountain ($20), and the other towards the coast at Steep Ravine, which also has a few rustic cabins ($65 a night). Reserve on T 1-800/444-7275, W www.reserveamerica.com.

Point Reyes National Seashore 40 miles northwest of San Francisco T 415/663-1092. A wide range of hike-in sites for backpackers, near the beach or in the forest. Reserve sites up to two months in advance (weekdays 9am–2pm; $15; T 415/663-8054).

Samuel P. Taylor State Park On Sir Francis Drake Blvd, 15 miles west of San Rafael T 415/488-9897. Deluxe, car-accessible plots with hot showers, spread along a river for $25 a night (winter $20); basic hiker/biker sites for $5. Don't miss the swimming hole or bat caves. In summer, reserve on T 1-800/444-7275, W www.reserveamerica.com.

Across the Golden Gate: the Marin Headlands and Sausalito

The largely undeveloped **MARIN HEADLANDS** of the Golden Gate National Recreation Area, across the Golden Gate Bridge from San Francisco, afford some of the most impressive views of the bridge and the city behind. As the regular fog rolls in, the breathtaking image of the bridge's stanchions tantalizingly drifting in and out of sight and the fleeting glimpses of downtown skyscrapers will abide long in the memory. Take the first turn as you exit the bridge (Alexander Avenue) and follow the sign back to San Francisco – the one-way circle trip back to the bridge heads first to the west along Conzelman Road and up a steep hill. You'll pass through a largely undeveloped land, dotted by the concrete remains of old forts and gun emplacements standing guard over the entrance to the bay, dating from as far back as the Civil War and as recent as World War II. The coastline here is much more rugged than it is on the San Francisco side, making it a great place for an aimless cliff-top hike or a stroll along one of the beaches at the bottom of treacherous footpaths.

The first installation as you climb the steep hill up the headlands is **Battery Wallace**, the largest and most impressive of the artillery sites along the rocky coast here, cut through a hillside above the southwestern tip of the Peninsula. The angular military geometry survives, framing views of the Pacific Ocean and the Golden Gate Bridge. Otherwise, continue along Conzelman for incredible views of the city from any of the many turnouts. For birding, walk from the Battery

Wallace parking lot through tunnels that lead five hundred yards to the opposite bluff, overlooking **Point Bonita Lighthouse** far below. To reach Point Bonita by vehicle, drive down the one-way lane that Conzelman becomes and keep winding down to the lighthouse. It stands sentry at the very end of the headlands and is open for tours (Sat–Mon 12.30–3.30pm; free). Conzelman comes to a "T" in the road; turn left and park your car on the side of the road or at the parking lot three hundred yards west, at the end of the drive. To reach the lighthouse, you have to walk the half-mile pathway down, a beautiful stroll that takes you through a tunnel cut into the cliff, and across a precarious suspension bridge.

Looping back around, you'll be heading northeast on Bunker Road. If you really want to relive holocaustic Cold War nightmares, you can visit the **Nike Missiles Site** (Wed–Fri and first Sun 12.30–3.30pm; ⓦ www.atomictourist .com/nike.htm) at **Fort Barry** and take a free guided tour of an abandoned 1950s ballistic-missile launchpad, complete with disarmed nuclear missiles. If you're after a more pacifistic pastime, stop off at the **Marin Headlands Visitor Center** (see below for details), alongside Rodeo Lagoon, for free maps of popular hiking trails in the area. Across the road and a bit further along, one of the largest of Fort Barry's old residential buildings has been converted into the spacious but homely *HI–Marin Headlands* hostel (see p.601), an excellent base for more extended explorations of the inland ridges and valleys.

Turn off to the left where Bunker Road snakes down to wide, sandy **Rodeo Beach** (#76 MUNI bus from San Francisco: Sun & holidays only). The beach separates the chilly ocean from the marshy warm water of **Rodeo Lagoon**, where swimming is prohibited to protect nesting seabirds. North of the lagoon, the **Marine Mammal Center** (ⓣ 415/289-7355, ⓦ www.tmmc.org) rescues and rehabilitates injured and orphaned sea creatures, such as dolphins and sea otters. The main building is currently closed to the public for renovations but a temporary **Visitor Center** at Building 1049 (daily 10am–4pm) gives a glimpse into their work and sells T-shirts and posters.

Sausalito

SAUSALITO, fronting the bay below US-101, is a picturesque, snug little town of exclusive restaurants and pricey boutiques along a pretty waterfront promenade. Expensive, quirkily designed houses climb the overgrown cliffs above **Bridgeway Avenue**, the main route through town. Sausalito used to be a fairly gritty community of fishermen and sea-traders, full of bars and bordellos, and despite its upscale modern face it still makes a fun day out from San Francisco by ferry, the boats arriving next to the Sausalito Yacht Club in the center of town. Hang out in one of the waterfront bars and watch the crowds strolling along the esplanade, or climb the stairways above Bridgeway Avenue and amble around the leafy hills. If you have sailing experience, split the $172–375 daily rental fee of a four- to ten-person sailboat at Cass's Marina, 1702 Bridgeway Avenue (ⓣ 415/332-6789, ⓦ www.cassmarina.com). The other main diversion is sea kayaking, and Sea Trek (ⓣ 415/488-1000, ⓦ www.seatrekkayak.com) rents single or double sea kayaks beginning at $15/25 for one hour's worth of superb paddling around the bay. They offer sit-on-top kayaks, lessons, and safe routes for first-timers, or closed kayaks and directions around Angel Island for the more experienced.

The old working wharves and warehouses that made Sausalito a haven for smugglers and Prohibition-era rum-runners are long gone; most have been taken over by dull strip malls. However, some stretches of it have, for the moment at least, survived the tourist onslaught. A mile north of the town center along Bridgeway Avenue, an ad hoc community of exotic **barges** and **houseboats**, some of which have been moored here since the 1950s, are still staving off eviction to make room for yet another luxury marina. In the meantime, many of the boats – one looks like a South Pacific island, another like the Taj Mahal – can be viewed at Waldo Point, half a mile beyond the cavernous concrete **Bay Model Visitor Center**, 2100 Bridgeway Avenue (spring Tues–Sat 9am–4pm; summer Tues–Fri 9am–4pm, Sat & Sun 10am–5pm; free; ☎415/332-3871, Ⓦwww.spc.usace.army.mil/bmvc). Inside the huge building, elevated walkways lead you around a scale model of the bay and its surrounding deltas and aquatic inhabitants, offering insight on the enormity and diversity of this area.

Back towards the Golden Gate Bridge at 557 McReynolds Road is the **Bay Area Discovery Museum** (Tues–Fri 9am–4pm, Sat & Sun 10am–5pm; $8.50, free every second Sat 1–5pm; ☎415/339-3900, Ⓦwww.baykidsmuseum.org). Within the remodelled barracks of **Fort Baker**, it holds a series of activities and workshops for youngsters up to 10 or so, including art and media rooms as well as the outdoor Lookout Cove area. Here kids can play in a mini-tide pool, on a shipwreck, or on the model of the Golden Gate Bridge as it was during construction – pretty cool, as the real one is visible in the distance if it's clear.

The Marin County Coast to Bolinas

The **Shoreline Highway**, Hwy-1, cuts off west from US-101 just north of Sausalito, following the old main highway towards Mill Valley (see p.606). The first turn on the left, Tennessee Valley Road, leads up to the less-visited northern expanses of the Golden Gate National Recreation Area. You can take a beautiful three-mile hike from the parking lot at the end of the road, heading down along the secluded and lushly green **Tennessee Valley** to a small beach along a rocky cove, or you can take a trail-ride lesson on horseback from Miwok Livery at 701 Tennessee Valley Road ($65 for 90min; ☎415/383-8048, Ⓦwww.miwokstables.com).

Hwy-1 twists up the canyon to a crest, where **Panoramic Highway** spears off to the right, following the ridge north to Muir Woods and Mount Tamalpais; Golden Gate Transit bus #63 to Stinson Beach follows this route every hour on weekends and holidays only. Be warned, however, that the hillsides are usually choked with fog until 11am, making the approach from San Francisco to Stinson Beach/Bolinas via Hwy-1 both dangerous and uninteresting. Two miles before you reach the crest, a small paved lane cuts off to the left, dropping down to the bottom of the broad canyon to the **Green Gulch Farm Zen Center** (☎415/383-3134, Ⓦwww.sfzc.org), an organic farm and Buddhist retreat with an authentic Japanese teahouse and a simple but refined prayer hall. On Sunday mornings the center is open from 8.15am for a public meditation period and an informal lecture on Zen Buddhism at 10.15am, after which you can stroll down to Muir Beach. If you're interested in learning more about Zen, inquire about the center's Guest Student Program, which enables initiates to stay from three days to several weeks at a time (it costs about $15 a night). Residents rise well before dawn for meditation and prayer, then work much of the day in the gardens, tending the vegetables that are eventually served in many of the Bay Area's finest restaurants (notably *Greens* in San Francisco – see p.537). If you just want a weekend retreat, you can also stay overnight in the far more upmarket *Lindisfarne Guest House* (see p.601) on the grounds.

Beyond the Zen Center, the road down from Muir Woods rejoins Hwy-1 at **Muir Beach**, usually uncrowded and beautifully secluded in a semicircular cove. Three miles north, **Steep Ravine** drops sharply down the cliffs to a small beach, past very rustic cabins and a campground, bookable through Mount Tamalpais State Park (see p.606). A mile on is the small and lovely **Red Rocks** nudist beach, down a steep trail from a parking area along the highway. **Stinson Beach**, which is bigger, and more popular despite the rather cold water (it's packed on weekends in summer, when the traffic can be nightmarish), is a mile further. You can rent kayaks at Off the Beach Boats, 15 Calle del Mar ($25 for two hours, $100 all weekend, cheaper in winter; ℡415/868-9445).

Bolinas and southern Point Reyes

At the tip of the headland, due west from Stinson Beach, is the laid-back village of **Bolinas**, though you may have a hard time finding it – road signs marking the turnoff from Hwy-1 are removed as soon as they're put up by locals hoping to keep the place to themselves. The campaign may have backfired, though, since press coverage of the "sign war" has done more to publicize the town than any road sign ever did; to get there, take the first left beyond the estuary and follow the road to the end. Bolinas is completely surrounded by federal property – the Golden Gate National Recreation Area and Point Reyes National Seashore – and even the lagoon was recently declared a National Bird Sanctuary. Known for its leftist hippy culture, the village itself has been home at different times to Grace Slick and Paul Kantner, a regular colony of artists, bearded handymen, writers (the late trout-fishing author Richard Brautigan and basketball diarist Jim Carroll among them), and stray dogs. There's not a lot to see apart from the small **Bolinas Museum**, 48 Wharf Road (Fri 1–5pm, Sat & Sun noon–5pm; free; ℡415/868-0330, ⓦwww.bolinasmuseum.org), which has a few historical displays and works by local artists in a set of converted cottages around a courtyard. Mostly, it's just a case of people watching and taking in the laid-back atmosphere.

Beyond Bolinas, there's a rocky beach at the end of Wharf Road west of the village and, half a mile west at the end of Elm Road, **Duxbury Reef Nature Reserve** lures visitors to its tide pools, full of sea stars, crabs, and sea anemones. Otherwise, Mesa Road heads north from Bolinas past the **Point Reyes Bird Observatory** (℡415/868-1221, ⓦwww.prbo.org) – open for informal tours all day, though best visited in the morning. The first bird observatory in the US, this is still an important research and study center, and if you time it right you may be able to watch, or even help, the staff as they put colored bands on the birds, such as cormorants and sandpipers, to keep track of them. Beyond here, the unpaved road leads on to the **Palomarin Trailhead**, the southern access into the Point Reyes National Seashore (see p.609). The best of the many beautiful hikes around the area takes you past a number of small lakes and meadows for three miles to **Alamere Falls**, which throughout the winter and spring cascade down the cliffs onto Wildcat Beach. **Bass Lake**, the first along the trail, is a great spot for a swim and is best entered from one of the two rope-swings that hang above its shore.

At the junction of Bolinas Road and Hwy-1, cross the highway and head due east. If there's no sign warning the road is closed (landslides and washouts are common), continue up this route, the **Bolinas–Fairfax Road**, for a superb, winding drive through redwoods and grassy hillsides. When you reach the "T" in the road, turn left to get to Fairfax, or right to scale Mount Tamalpais.

Mount Tamalpais and Muir Woods National Monument

Mount Tamalpais, fondly known as Mount Tam, dominates the skyline of Marin County, hulking over the cool canyons of the rest of the county and

▲ Muir Woods

dividing it into two distinct parts: the wild western slopes above the Pacific Coast and the increasingly suburban communities along the calmer bay frontage. Panoramic Highway branches off from Hwy-1 along the crest through the center of **Mount Tamalpais State Park** (℡415/388-2070, Ⓦwww .mttam.net), which has some thirty miles of hiking trails and many campgrounds, though most of the redwoods which once covered its slopes have long since been chopped down to form the posts and beams of San Francisco's Victorian houses. One grove of these towering trees does remain, however, protected as the **Muir Woods National Monument** (daily 8am– sunset; $5; ℡415/388-2595, Ⓦwww .nps.gov/muwo), a mile down Muir Woods Road from Panoramic Highway. It's a tranquil and majestic spot, with sunlight filtering through the 300-foot trees down to the laurel- and fern-covered canyon below. The canyon's steep sides are what saved it from Mill Valley's lumbermen, and today it's one of the few first-growth redwood groves between San Francisco and the fantastic forests of Redwood National Park (see p.722), up the coast towards the Oregon border.

One way to avoid the crowds that descend here at weekends, and the only way to get here on public transportation, is to enter the woods from the top by way of a two-mile hike from the **Pan Toll Ranger Station** (℡415/388-2070) on Panoramic Highway – which is a stop on the Golden Gate Transit #63 bus route. As the state park headquarters, the station has maps and information on hiking and camping, and rangers can suggest hikes to suit your mood and interests. From here the **Pan Toll Road** turns off to the right along the ridge to within a hundred yards of the 2571-foot summit of Mount Tamalpais, where red-necked turkey vultures listlessly circle against breathtaking views of the distant Sierra Nevada.

Mill Valley

From the east peak of Mount Tamalpais, a quick two-mile hike downhill follows the **Temelpa Trail** through velvety shrubs of chaparral to **Mill Valley**, the oldest and most enticing of Marin County's inland towns – also accessible every thirty minutes by Golden Gate Transit bus #10 from San Francisco and Sausalito. Originally a logging center, it was from here that the destruction of the surrounding redwoods was organized, though for many years the town has made a healthy living out of tourism. You can still follow the route of the defunct **Mill Valley and Mount Tamalpais Scenic Railroad** from the end of Summit Avenue in Mill Valley, a popular trip with daredevils on mountain bikes, which were, incidentally, invented here.

Though much of Mill Valley's attraction lies in its easy access to hiking and mountain-bike trails up Mount Tam, its compact yet relaxed center has a number of cafés and some good shops and galleries. The *Depot Bookstore and Café* (Mon– Sat 7am–10pm, Sun 8am–10pm; ℡415/383-2665) is a popular bookshop, café, and meeting place at 87 Throckmorton Avenue, next door to the Chamber of Commerce (see p.600), which has free maps of Mount Tam and area hiking trails. Across the street, the **Pleasure Principle** is a reminder of the Northern California eclecticism hidden beneath a posh surface – the store, the self-declared UFO headquarters of Mill Valley, is also the proud purveyor of a large vintage porn collection. If you're in the area in early October, don't miss the **Mill Valley Film Festival**, a world-class event that draws a host of up-and-coming directors, as well as Bay Area stars like Robin Williams and Sharon Stone; for program information, call ☎415/383-5346, or check ⓦwww.mvff.com.

Tiburon

Tiburon, at the tip of a narrow peninsula three miles east of US-101 and five miles from Mill Valley, is, like Sausalito, a ritzy harborside village to which hundreds of people come each weekend, many of them via direct Blue and Gold Fleet **ferries** from Pier 41 in San Francisco's Fisherman's Wharf. It's a relaxed place, less touristy than Sausalito, and if you're in the mood to take it easy and watch the boats sail across the bay, sitting out on the sunny deck of one of the many cafés and bars can be idyllic. There are few specific sights to look out for here, but it's pleasant enough to simply wander around, browsing the galleries and antique shops. The best of these are grouped together in **Ark Row**, at the west end of Main Street, where the quirky buildings are actually old houseboats that were beached here early in the century. Further along, you can get a taste of the Wine Country at the Windsor Vineyards tasting room, 72 Main Street (daily 10am–6pm; ☎415/435-3113, ⓦwww.windsorvineyards.com). On a hill above the town stands **Old St Hilary's Church** (April–Oct Wed–Sun 1–4pm; ☎415/789-0066), a Carpenter Gothic beauty best seen in the spring, when the surrounding fields are covered with multicolored buckwheat, flax, and paintbrush.

Cyclists can cruise around the many plush houses of **Belvedere Island**, just across the Beach Road Bridge from the west end of Main Street, enjoying the fine views of the bay and Golden Gate Bridge. More ambitious bikers can continue along the waterfront bike path, which winds from the bijou shops and galleries three miles west along undeveloped Richardson Bay frontage to a bird sanctuary at **Greenwood Cove**. The pristine Victorian house here is now the western headquarters of the National Audubon Society and open for tours on Sundays (10am–4pm; free; ☎415/388-2524, ⓦwww.audubon.org); a small interpretive center has displays on local and migratory birds and wildlife.

Angel Island

However appealing, the pleasures of Tiburon are soon exhausted, and you'd be well advised to take the Angel Island Ferry (see p.599 for details) a mile offshore to the largest island in the San Francisco Bay, ten times the size of Alcatraz. **Angel Island** is officially a state park, but over the years it has served a variety of purposes, everything from a home for Miwok Native Americans to a World War II prisoner-of-war camp. It's full of ghostly ruins of old military installations, but it's the nature that lures people to Angel Island nowadays, with its oak and eucalyptus trees and sagebrush covering the hills above rocky coves and sandy beaches, giving the island a feel quite apart from the mainland. It offers some pleasant biking opportunities as well: a five-mile road rings the island, and an unpaved track, along with a number of hiking trails, leads up to the 800-foot hump of **Mount Livermore**, with panoramic views of the Bay Area.

The ferry arrives at **Ayala Cove**, where a small snack bar selling hot dogs and cold drinks provides the only sustenance available on the island – bring a picnic if you plan to spend the day here. The nearby **visitor center** (daily 9am–4pm; ☎415/435-1915), in an old building that was built as a quarantine facility for soldiers returning from the Philippines after the Spanish-American War, has displays on the island's history. Around the point on the northwest corner of the island the **North Garrison**, built in 1905, was the site of a prisoner-of-war camp during World War II; while the larger **East Garrison**, on the bay half a mile beyond, was the major transfer point for soldiers bound for the South Pacific.

Quarry Beach around the point is the best on the island, a clean sandy shore that's protected from the winds blowing in through the Golden Gate; it's also a popular landing spot for kayakers and canoeists who paddle across the bay from Berkeley. **Camping** on Angel Island (see p.602 for details) is well worth considering for the views of San Francisco and the East Bay at night; the nine sites fill up fast, so make reservations well ahead. For **tours** of Angel Island, contact Angel Island TramTours (☎415/897-0715, ⊛www.angelisland.com), which gives one-hour tours ($13.50) and rents mountain bikes ($10/hour, $35/day).

Sir Francis Drake Boulevard and Central Marin County

The quickest route to the wilds of the Point Reyes National Seashore, and the only way to get there on public transportation, is by way of **Sir Francis Drake Boulevard**, which cuts across central Marin County through the inland towns of **San Anselmo** and **Fairfax**, reaching the coast thirty miles west at a crescent-shaped bay where, in 1579, Drake supposedly landed and claimed all of what he called Nova Albion for England. The route makes an excellent day-long cycling tour, with the reward of good beaches, a youth hostel, and some tasty restaurants at the end of the road.

The Larkspur Golden Gate Transit **ferry**, which leaves from the Ferry Building in San Francisco, is the longest of the bay crossings. Primarily a commuter route, it docks at the modern space-frame terminal at Larkspur Landing. The monolithic, red-tile-roofed complex you see on the bayfront a mile east is the maximum-security **San Quentin State Prison**, which houses the state's most violent and notorious criminals, and of which Johnny Cash sang so resonantly "I hate every stone of you." If you arrive by car over the Richmond–San Rafael Bridge, follow road signs off Hwy-101 for the **San Quentin Prison Museum**, Building 106, Dolores Way (Mon–Fri 10am–4pm, Sat 11.45am–3.15pm; $2; ☎415/454-8808).

San Anselmo and Point Reyes Station

San Anselmo, set in a broad valley two miles north of Mount Tam, calls itself "the antiques capital of Northern California" and sports a tiny center of specialty shops, furniture stores, and cafés that draws many San Francisco shoppers on weekends. The ivy-covered **San Francisco Theological Seminary** off Bolinas Avenue, which dominates the town from the hill above, is worth a quick peek for the view and mission-styled architecture. At serene **Robson-Harrington Park** on Crescent Avenue you can picnic among well-tended gardens, and the very green and leafy **Creek Park** follows the creek that winds through the town center, but otherwise there's not a lot to do other than stop in at a restaurant or café or browse through fine bookstores, such as Oliver's Books, at 645 San Anselmo Avenue (☎415/454-4421).

Ten miles beyond fairly nondescript Fairfax, which San Anselmo merges into, Sir Francis Drake Boulevard winds through gentle and increasingly pastoral hills, passing **Samuel P. Taylor State Park**, with excellent camping (see p.602).

Five miles more brings you to the coastal Hwy-1 and the hamlet of **Olema**, which has good food and lodging. A mile north of Olema sits the tourist town of **POINT REYES STATION**, another good place to stop off. Pick up a bite to eat or picnic supplies on the quaint main street before heading off to enjoy the wide open spaces of the Point Reyes National Seashore just beyond.

The Point Reyes National Seashore

From Point Reyes Station, Sir Francis Drake Boulevard heads out to the westernmost tip of Marin County at Point Reyes through the **POINT REYES NATIONAL SEASHORE**, a near-island of wilderness surrounded on three sides by more than fifty miles of isolated coastline – pine forests and sunny meadows bordered by rocky cliffs and sandy, windswept beaches. This wing-shaped landmass, something of an aberration along the generally straight coastline north of San Francisco, is in fact a rogue piece of the earth's crust that has been drifting slowly and steadily northward along the San Andreas Fault, having started some six million years ago as a suburb of Los Angeles. When the great earthquake of 1906 shattered San Francisco, the land here – the quake's epicenter – shifted over sixteen feet in an instant, though damage was confined to a few skewed cattle fences.

The park's **visitor center** (see p.600 for details), two miles southwest of Point Reyes Station near Olema, just off Hwy-1 on Bear Valley Road, holds engaging displays on the geology and natural history of the region. Rangers dish out excellent hiking and cycling itineraries, and have up-to-date information on the weather, which can change quickly and be cold and windy along the coast even when it's hot and sunny here, three miles inland. They also handle permits and reservations for the various hike-in **campgrounds** within the park. Nearby, a replica of a native Miwok village has an authentic religious **roundhouse**, and a popular hike follows the Bear Valley Trail along Coast Creek four miles to **Arch Rock**, a large tunnel in the seaside cliffs that you can walk through at low tide.

North of the visitor center, Limantour Road heads west six miles to the *HI-Point Reyes Hostel* (see p.602), continuing on another two miles to the coast at **Limantour Beach**, one of the best protected swimming beaches and a good place to watch the seabirds in the adjacent estuary. Bear Valley Road rejoins Sir Francis Drake Boulevard just past Limantour Road, leading north along Tomales Bay through the village of **Inverness**, so named because the landscape reminded an early settler of his home in the Scottish Highlands. Eight miles west of Inverness, a turn leads down past **Drakes's Bay Oyster Farm** (daily 8am–4.30pm; T415/669-1149) – which sells the bivalves for around $10 a dozen, less than half the price you'd pay in San Francisco – to **Drake's Beach**, the presumed landing spot of Sir Francis in 1579 (his voyage journal makes the exact location unclear). Appropriately, the coastline here resembles the southern coast of England, often cold, wet, and windy, with chalk-white cliffs rising above the wide, sandy beach. The road continues southwest another four miles to the very tip of Point Reyes. A precarious-looking **lighthouse** (Thurs–Sun 10am–4.30pm; free) stands firm against the crashing surf, and the bluffs are excellent for watching migrating **gray whales** from mid-March to April and late December to early February. Just over a mile back from the lighthouse a narrow road leads to **Chimney Rock**, where you can often see basking **elephant seals** or **sea lions** from the overlook. Keep in mind the distance and slow speeds it takes to reach these spots, which is hard to judge on a map. From the visitor center, it's 15 miles to Drakes Beach and 23 miles to the lighthouse.

Check with the rangers on weather conditions before setting out. From late December through April a shuttle bus (9.30am–5pm; $5) runs roughly every twenty minutes on weekends and holidays out to the lighthouse and Chimney Rock, and the roads are closed to private vehicles to avoid congestion.

The northern tip of the Point Reyes National Seashore, **Tomales Point**, is accessible via Pierce Point Road, which turns off Sir Francis Drake Boulevard two miles north of Inverness. Jutting out into Tomales Bay, it's the least-visited section of the park and a refuge for hefty **tule elk**; it's also a great place to admire the lupins, poppies, and other wildflowers that appear in the spring. The best swimming (at least the warmest water) is at **Heart's Desire Beach**, just before the end of the road. Down the bluffs from where the road comes to a dead end, there are excellent tidal pools at rocky **McClure's Beach**. North of Point Reyes Station, Hwy-1 continues past the famed oyster beds of Tomales Bay north along the crashing surf and up the Northern California coast.

San Rafael and around

You may pass through **San Rafael** on your way north from San Francisco on US-101, but there's little to detain you. The county seat and the only sizeable city in Marin County, it has none of the woodsy qualities that make the other towns special, though you'll come across a couple of good restaurants and bars along Fourth Street, the main drag. Its lone attraction is the old **Mission San Rafael Arcangel** (daily 11am–4pm; free), in fact a 1949 replica that was built near the site of the 1817 original on Fifth Avenue at A Street. The real point of interest, however, is well on the northern outskirts in the shape of the Marin County Civic Center.

The **Marin County Civic Center** (Mon–Fri 9am–5pm; tours Wed 10.30am; free; ☎415/499-6646), spanning the hills just east of US-101 a mile north of central San Rafael, is a strange, otherworldly complex of administrative offices, plus an excellent performance space that resembles a giant viaduct capped by a bright-blue-tiled roof. These buildings were architect **Frank Lloyd Wright**'s one and only government project, and although the huge circus tents and amusement park at the core of the designer's conception were never built, it does have some interesting touches, such as the atrium lobbies that open directly to the outdoors.

Six miles north of San Rafael, the **Lucas Valley Road** turns off west, twisting across Marin to Point Reyes. Although he lives and works here, it was not named after *Star Wars* filmmaker George Lucas, whose sprawling **Skywalker Ranch** studios are well hidden off the road. Hwy-37 cuts off east, eight miles north of San Rafael, heading around the top of the bay into the Wine Country of the Sonoma and Napa valleys (see p.681).

Eating

Marin's **restaurants** are as varied in personality as the people who inhabit the county – homely neighborhood **cafés** dish out nutritious portions to healthy mountain bikers, well-appointed waterside restaurants cater to tourists, and gourmet establishments serve delicate concoctions to affluent executives.

Avatar's Punjabi Burritos 15 Madrona St, Mill Valley ☎415/381-8293. A dastardly simple cross-cultural innovation: inexpensive burritos stuffed with delicious spicy curries. Does a brisk take out trade, as there are only two tables inside.
Broken Drum 1132 Fourth St, San Rafael ☎415/456-4677. Lively brewery/grill with

pavement seating, where you can tuck into cheapish fish tacos with mango salsa or mesquite grilled ribs.
Bubba's Diner 566 San Anselmo Ave, San Anselmo ☎415/459-6862. Hip little old-fashioned diner with a friendly and casual atmosphere; be sure to try a delicious biscuit with your meal.

Caffè Trieste 1000 Bridgeway Ave, Sausalito ☎ 415/332-7770. This distant relative of San Francisco's North Beach institution serves good coffee, a wide menu of pastas and salads, and great *gelato*.

Dipsea Café 200 Shoreline Hwy, Mill Valley ☎ 415/381-0298. Hearty pancakes, omelets, sandwiches, and salads, especially good before a day out hiking on Mount Tamalpais. Breakfast and lunch only.

Farmhouse Grill 10005 Hwy-1, Olema ☎ 415/663-1264. The farm-fresh ingredients that go into the down-home cooking make this a good stop for mostly meaty lunches or dinners. Also a friendly bar.

Guaymas 5 Main St, Tiburon ☎ 415/435-6300. Some of the most unique, inventive Cal-Mex cuisine in the Bay Area (and priced accordingly), paired with a spectacular view of the city.

The Lark Creek Inn 234 Magnolia Ave, Larkspur ☎ 415/924-7766. The place to go in Marin for fine dining. The contemporary American food at this classy restored Victorian is expensive, but not without reason: the food, such as pan-fried sweetbreads and gorgonzola soufflé, is exquisite, the service first-rate, and the atmosphere charming.

Mountain Home Inn 810 Panoramic Hwy, above Mill Valley ☎ 415/381-9000. A place that's as good for the view of the surrounding valleys as for the food, with broiled meat and fish dishes served up in a rustic lodge on the slopes of Mount Tamalpais.

New Morning Café 1696 Tiburon Blvd, Tiburon ☎ 415/435-4315. Lots of healthy wholegrain sandwiches, plus salads and omelets.

Piazza D'Angelo 22 Miller Ave, Mill Valley ☎ 415/388-2000. Good salads, tasty pasta, and affordable pizzas, served up in a lively but comfortable room right off the downtown plaza.

Rice Table 1617 Fourth St, San Rafael ☎ 415/456-1808. From the shrimp chips through the crab pancakes and noodles on to the fried plantain desserts, these fragrant and spicy Indonesian dishes are an excellent value and worth planning a day around. Dinners only.

Sam's Anchor Café 27 Main St, Tiburon ☎ 415/435-4527. This rough-hewn, amiable waterfront café and bar has been around for more than 75 years. Good burgers, sandwiches, and very popular Sun brunches are best enjoyed on the outdoor deck.

Sartaj India Cafe 43 Caledonia St, Sausalito ☎ 415/332-7103. Great, inexpensive Indian place that does a selection of meat and veggie dishes, including *thalis*, and, oddly enough, bagels for those who can't stomach a spicy breakfast.

Station House Café 11180 Hwy-1 (Main Street), Point Reyes Station ☎ 415/663-1515. Serving three meals daily, this friendly local favorite entices diners from miles around to sample their grilled seafood and top-notch steaks.

Stinson Beach Grill 3465 Shoreline Hwy, Stinson Beach ☎ 415/868-2002. Somewhat pricey, but relaxed, with outdoor dining – look out for the bright-blue building right in the heart of town. Mainly steaks and seafood, but leave room for the glorious puddings.

Sweet Ginger 400 Caledonia St, Sausalito ☎ 415/332-1683. Moderately priced small Japanese restaurant that serves sushi, sashimi, and main courses like tempura and teriyaki.

Thai Orchid 726 San Anselmo Ave, San Anselmo ☎ 415/457-9470. Family restaurant dishing up spicy Thai fare, including a fine range of curries and zesty salads.

Tommy's Wok 3001 Bridgeway, Sausalito ☎ 415/332-5818. This Chinese joint specializes in organic vegetables, free-range meats, and fresh seafood, cooked in Mandarin, Hunan, and Szechuan recipes.

Vladimir's Czech Restaurant 12785 Sir Francis Drake Blvd, Inverness ☎ 415/669-1021. This relic of rural Bohemia in the far West has been serving up tasty items like Moravian cabbage roll, roast duckling, and apple strudel since 1960.

Bars and cafés

While Marin County **nightlife** is never as charged as it gets in San Francisco, almost every town has at least a couple of **cafés** that are open long hours for a jolt of caffeine, and any number of saloon-like **bars** where you'll feel at home immediately. In addition, since most of the honchos of the Bay Area music scene and dozens of lesser-known but no less brilliant session musicians and songwriters live here, Marin's nightclubs are unsurpassed for catching big names in intimate locales.

Bars

The Bar With No Name 757 Bridgeway Ave, Sausalito ☎ 415/332-1392. An ex-haunt of the Beats, hosting live jazz several times per week beginning at 8pm and on Sun from 3–7pm.

Fourth Street Tavern 711 Fourth St, San Rafael ☎415/454-4044. Gutsy, no-frills beer bar with free, bluesy music most nights.

Marin Brewing Company 1809 Larkspur Landing, Larkspur ☎415/461-4677. Lively pub opposite the Larkspur ferry terminal, with half a dozen tasty ales – try the malty Albion Amber or the Marin Hefe Weiss – all brewed on the premises.

Smiley's Schooner Saloon 41 Wharf Rd, Bolinas ☎415/868-1311. The bartender calls the customers by name here at one of the oldest continually operating bars in the state.

Sweetwater 153 Throckmorton Ave, Mill Valley ☎415/388-3820. Large, open room full of beer-drinking locals that after dark evolves into Marin's prime live-music venue, bringing in some of the biggest names in music, from jazz and blues all-stars to Jefferson Airplane pioneers.

Cafés

Bridgeway Café 633 Bridgeway, Sausalito ☎415/332-3426. A good place to relax over a coffee or grab a gourmet egg breakfast at reasonable prices by local standards.

Depot Bookstore and Café 87 Throckmorton Ave, Mill Valley ☎415/383-2665. Lively café in an old train station, sharing space with a bookstore and newsstand. Weekly readings from local and nationally recognized authors.

Java Rama 546 San Anselmo Ave, San Anselmo ☎415/453-5282. Specialty coffees and pastries along with modern rock on the stereo attracts a young crowd.

Sweden House 35 Main St, Tiburon ☎415/435-9767. Great coffee and marvelous pastries on a jetty overlooking the yacht harbor, all for surprisingly reasonable prices.

Travel details

Trains

Free **Amtrak** shuttle buses depart San Francisco from the Ferry Building (where there's a full service ticket office, 6am–11pm), as well as six other points downtown and in SoMa, to the Emeryville depot, from where the **Coast Starlight** train departs at 10.15pm northeast to Sacramento, Portland, and Seattle, and 8.20am south to San Jose, Santa Barbara, Los Angeles, and San Diego. The **San Joaquins** route operates four times daily to Stockton, Modesto, Fresno, and Bakersfield, where there are Amtrak Thruway bus connections to Los Angeles. Amtrak's **Capitol Corridor** route links Oakland with San Jose.

San Francisco-San Jose commuters rely more on **CalTrain** (☎1-800/660-4287). About fifty trains make the trip each way daily, taking 1hr on the Baby Bullet or 1hr 30min or longer on the local ($7.50 each way). The main San Francisco station is at Fourth and King streets.

Oakland/Emeryville to: Bakersfield (2 daily; 6hr–6hr 30min); Fresno (2 daily; 4hr–4hr 15min); Los Angeles (3 daily; 9–11hr); Portland (2 daily; 18hr); Reno (3 daily; 6hr); Sacramento (11–16 daily; 2hr 30min); San Diego (3 daily; 12–14hr; San Jose (7 daily; 1hr); Santa Barbara (2 daily; 7hr 15min–8hr 30min); Seattle (2 daily; 23hr); Stockton (2 daily; 1hr 45min–2hr 10min).

Buses

Greyhound unless specified otherwise; note the number of services can vary during the course of the year.

San Francisco to: Eureka (1 daily; 6hr 45min); Los Angeles (17 daily; 7hr 25min–12hr 45min); Redding (4 daily; 5hr 10min–6hr 50min); Reno (2 daily; 6hr 10min–9hr 10min); Sacramento (9 daily; 2hr–2hr 20min); San Diego (7 daily; 10hr 50min–14hr 10min); San Jose (10 daily; 1hr–1hr 45min); San Rafael (1 daily; 1hr); Santa Rosa (1 daily; 1hr 45min).

The Gold Country and Lake Tahoe

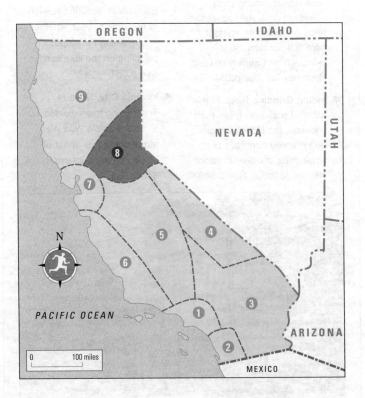

CHAPTER 8

Highlights

✳ **Sacramento Capitol building**
This elegant Classical Revival structure has some spectacular architectural detailing, and the comprehensive tours provide a glimpse of California's government innards. See p.623

✳ **The Empire Mine State Park**
Now retired among thick stands of pine, the impressive array of mining equipment here is a contemplative reflection on California's Gold Rush heyday. See p.634

✳ **Indian Grinding Rock** In this national park nine miles from Jackson, the Miwok Indians once carved hundreds of small cups into the limestone, still visible today. See p.643

✳ **Jamestown's Railtown 1897 State Historic Park** Even if you're not a trainspotter, it's worth stopping by to see the old engines, thanks to the enthusiastic, endlessly knowledgeable docents. See p.649

✳ **Lake Tahoe** This region guarantees beautiful scenery at any time of year, whether you're skiing the slopes or paddling on the lake itself. See p.651

✳ **Virginia City, Nevada** This mining town exudes a more tangible Wild West atmosphere than most of its California counterparts. See p.668

▲ Virginia City, Nevada

The Gold Country and Lake Tahoe

The gold of California is a touchstone which has betrayed the rottenness, the baseness, of mankind. Satan, from one of his elevations, showed mankind the kingdom of California, and they entered into a compact with him at once.

Henry David Thoreau, *Journal*, February 1, 1852

About 150 years before techies from all over the world rushed to California in search of Silicon Valley gold, the rough-and-ready forty-niners invaded the **GOLD COUNTRY** of the Sierra Nevada to pan for the real thing. The first prospectors on the scene – about 150 miles east of San Francisco – sometimes found large nuggets of solid gold sitting along the riverbanks. They worked all day in the hot sun, wading through fast-flowing, ice-cold rivers to recover trace amounts of the precious metal that had been eroded out of the hard-rock veins of the Mother Lode – the name miners gave to the rich sources of gold at the heart of the mining district.

The region ranges from the foothills near Yosemite National Park to the deep gorge of the Yuba River, two hundred miles north. In many parts throughout this area, little seems to have changed since the argonauts began their digging, and even in the air-conditioned comfort of your rental car – without one it's nearly impossible to navigate the area – distances from one town to the next may seem exponentially greater than they appear on the map: count on plenty of switchbacks and steep climbs.

The **Mother Lode** was first discovered in 1848 at Sutter's Mill in **Coloma**, forty miles east of **Sacramento**, the largest city in the Gold Country and the state capital. Once a tiny military outpost and farming community that boomed as a supply town for miners, Sacramento lies between two distinct mining areas to the north and south. The **northern mines**, around the twin towns of **Grass Valley** and **Nevada City**, were the richest fields, and today retain most of their Gold Rush buildings in an unspoiled, near-alpine setting halfway up the towering peaks of the Sierra Nevada. The hot and dusty **southern mines**, on the other hand, became depopulated faster than their northern neighbors. These towns were the rowdiest and wildest of all, and it's not too hard to imagine that many of the abandoned towns sprinkled over the area once supported upwards of fifty saloons and gambling parlors, each with

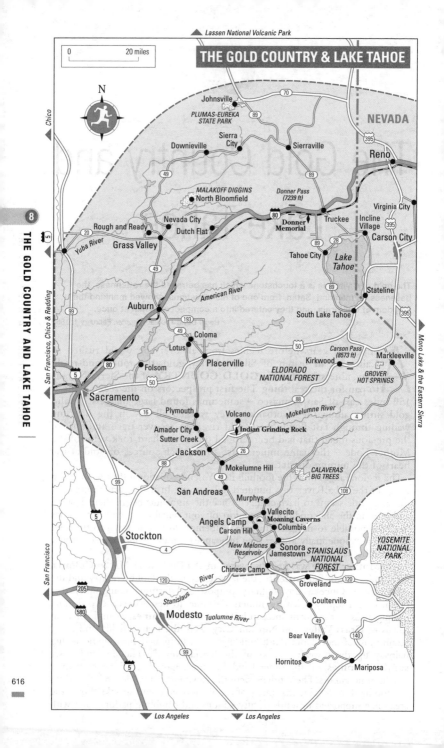

Lassen National Volcanic Park

0   20 miles

N

Chico

Johnsville

PLUMAS-EUREKA
STATE PARK

NEVADA

Downieville

Sierra
City

Sierraville

Reno

MALAKOFF DIGGINS
North Bloomfield

Donner Pass
(7239 ft)

Virginia City

Incline
Village

Carson City

Rough and Ready

Nevada City
Dutch Flat

Donner
Memorial

Truckee

Grass Valley

Tahoe City

Lake
Tahoe

Yuba River

Auburn

Stateline

American River

San Francisco, Chico & Redding

Coloma

South Lake Tahoe

Lotus

Folsom

Placerville

Carson Pass
(8573 ft)

Markleeville

Sacramento

Kirkwood

ELDORADO
NATIONAL FOREST

GROVER
HOT SPRINGS

Mono Lake & the Eastern Sierra

Plymouth

Volcano

Mokelumne River

Amador City

Indian Grinding Rock

Sutter Creek

Jackson

Mokelumne Hill

San Andreas

CALAVERAS
BIG TREES

Murphys

Stockton

Angels Camp

Vallecito
Moaning Caverns

Carson Hill

Columbia

New Melones
Reservoir

Sonora

STANISLAUS
NATIONAL
FOREST

YOSEMITE
NATIONAL
PARK

San Francisco

Jamestown

Chinese Camp

River

Groveland

Stanislaus

Coulterville

Modesto   Tuolumne River

Bear Valley

Hornitos

Mariposa

Los Angeles   Los Angeles

River rafting in the Gold Country

Although plenty of people come through the area to see the Gold Rush sights, at least as many come to enjoy the thrills and spills of **whitewater rafting** and **kayaking** on the various forks of the American, Stanislaus, Tuolumne, and Merced rivers, which wind down through the region from the Sierra crest towards Sacramento. Whether you just want to float in a leisurely manner downstream, or fancy careening through five-foot walls of water, contact one of the many river-trip operators, among them American River Recreation (☎1-800/333-7238, ⓦwww.arrafting.com), CBOC White-water Raft Adventures (☎1-800/356-2262, ⓦwww.cbocwhitewater.com), O.A.R.S., Inc. (☎1-800/346-6277, ⓦwww.oars.com), Tributary Whitewater Tours (☎1-800/672-3846, ⓦwww.whitewatertours.com), and Whitewater Adventures (☎1-800/977-4837, ⓦwww.gowhitewater.com). Trips run from late spring through early fall and start at about $90 per person per day midweek.

its own cast of cardsharps and thieves, as immortalized by writers like Bret Harte and Mark Twain.

Most of the mountainous forest along the Sierra crest is preserved as near-pristine wilderness, with excellent hiking, camping, and backpacking. There's great skiing in winter around the mountainous rim of **Lake Tahoe** – "lake of the sky" to the native Washoe – on the border between California and Nevada, aglow under the bright lights of the casinos that line its southeastern shore. East of the mountains, in the dry Nevada desert, sit the highway towns of **Reno**, famed for low-budget weddings and speedy divorces, and **Carson City**, the Nevada state capital and one-time boomtown of the Comstock silver mines.

Getting around

Hwy-49 runs north to south, linking most of the sights of the Gold Country; two main highways, US-50 and I-80, along with the transcontinental **railroad**, cross the Sierra Nevada through the heart of the region, and there is frequent Greyhound **bus** service to most of the major towns. To get a real feel for the Gold Country, however, and to reach the most evocative ghost towns, you'll need a **car**. Also, though it's all very scenic, **cycling** throughout the region is not a viable option: the distances between the sights are long, and the roads are far too hilly and narrow for comfort.

Sacramento and the Central Mother Lode

Roughly midway between San Francisco and the crest of the Sierra Nevada, and well connected by Greyhound, Amtrak, and the arterial I-5 highway, **Sacramento** is likely to be your first stop in the Gold Country. It's the quintessential American state capital, with sleepy tree-lined streets fanning out from the elegant State Capitol building. The city's waterfront quarter, restored to the style of Pony Express days, contains the region's largest collection of Gold Rush–era buildings. From Sacramento, two main routes climb east through the gentle foothills of the Mother Lode: US-50 passes through the old supply town of **Placerville** on its way to Lake Tahoe, while I-80 zooms by **Auburn** over the Donner Pass into Nevada. Both towns have retained enough of their Gold Rush past to merit at least a brief look if you're passing through, and both make good bases for the more picturesque towns of the northern mines.

Sacramento

Until recently, **SACRAMENTO** had the reputation of being decidedly dull, a suburban enclave of politicians and bureaucrats surrounded by miles of marshes and farmland. The government has long loomed large over the city, filling its streets on weekdays and emptying the center at weekends; but now residential neighborhoods are slowly reawakening, especially around the Midtown area, thanks to the cafés and restaurants that have mushroomed on many of the leafier blocks. The election of Arnold "the Governator" Schwarzenegger in a 2003 election didn't hurt either: his dash of Hollywood pizzazz (and Kennedy-grade connections courtesy of his wife, TV anchor Maria Shriver) has energized the city far more than his predecessor, the aptly named Gray Davis. Arnold has also proved a surprisingly popular and moderate governor, failing to fulfil many locals' early fears that he would turn state government into a media circus. Schwarzenegger aside, there's increasing local pride in the city's Gold Rush history, which has led to important historic preservation and restoration projects, injecting a hefty dose of tourist dollars into the local economy.

Some history

Before gold was discovered in 1848, the area around Sacramento belonged entirely to one man, **John Sutter**. He came here from Switzerland in 1839 to farm the flat, marshy lands at the foot of the Sierra Nevada, which were then within Mexican California. Sacramento, the prosperous community he founded, became a main stopping place for the few trappers and travelers who made their way inland or across the range of peaks. Yet it was after the discovery of flakes of **gold** in the foothills forty miles east that things really took off and the small trading post was transformed.

Sutter's 50,000-acre settlement, set at the confluence of the Sacramento and American rivers in the flatlands of the northern San Joaquin Valley, was granted to him by the Mexican government and he worked hard to build the colony into a busy trading center and cattle ranch. He was poised to become a wealthy man when his hopes were thwarted by the discovery of gold at a nearby sawmill. His workers quit their jobs to go prospecting, and many thousands more flocked to the goldfields, trampling over Sutter's land. The small colony was soon overrun: since ships could sail upriver from the San Francisco Bay, Sacramento quickly became the main supply point for miners bound for the isolated camps in the foothills above. The city prospered, and in 1854 Sacramento snagged the title of **California state capital**, thanks to its equidistance between the gold mines, the rich farmlands of the San Joaquin Valley, and the financial center of San Francisco. As the Gold Rush faded, Sacramento remained important as a transportation center, first as the western terminus of the Pony Express and later as the western headquarters of the transcontinental railroad.

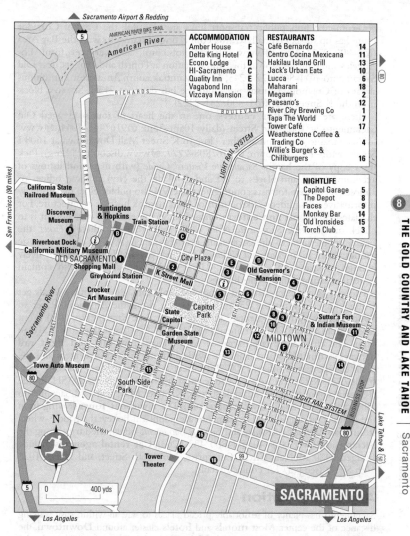

Sacramento Airport & Redding

AMERICAN RIVER BIKE TRAIL

American River

RICHARDS

BOULEVARD

JIBBOOM STREET

LIGHT RAIL SYSTEM

San Francisco (90 miles)

ACCOMMODATION
Amber House   F
Delta King Hotel   A
Econo Lodge   D
HI-Sacramento   C
Quality Inn   E
Vagabond Inn   B
Vizcaya Mansion   G

RESTAURANTS
Café Bernardo   14
Centro Cocina Mexicana   11
Hakilau Island Grill   13
Jack's Urban Eats   10
Lucca   6
Maharani   18
Megami   2
Paesano's   12
River City Brewing Co   1
Tapa The World   7
Tower Café   17
Weatherstone Coffee &
  Trading Co   4
Willie's Burger's &
  Chiliburgers   16

NIGHTLIFE
Capitol Garage   5
The Depot   8
Faces   9
Monkey Bar   14
Old Ironsides   15
Torch Club   3

California State
Railroad Museum

Discovery
Museum

Huntington
& Hopkins

Train Station

Riverboat Dock
California Military Museum

OLD SACRAMENTO
Shopping Mall

Greyhound Station

City Plaza

Old Governor's
Mansion

Crocker
Art Museum

Capitol
Park

State
Capitol

Garden State
Museum

MIDTOWN

Sutter's Fort
& Indian Museum

Towe Auto Museum

South Side
Park

Tower
Theater

N

BROADWAY

0   400 yds

SACRAMENTO

C STREET, D STREET, E STREET, F STREET, G STREET, H STREET, K STREET MALL, CAPITOL AVE, CAPITOL AVENUE, N STREET, O STREET, P STREET, Q STREET, R STREET, S STREET, BUSINESS LOOP

3RD STREET, 4TH STREET, 5TH STREET, 6TH STREET, 7TH STREET, 8TH STREET, 9TH STREET, 10TH STREET, 11TH STREET, 12TH STREET, 14TH STREET, 15TH STREET, 16TH STREET, 17TH STREET, 18TH STREET, 19TH STREET, 20TH STREET, 26TH STREET, 27TH STREET, 28TH STREET, 29TH STREET

Sacramento River

FRONT STREET

Los Angeles

Los Angeles

Lake Tahoe & 50

Sacramento

Although its administrative role saved the city when mining dollars dwindled, it also smothered much of its rough, pioneer edges and, even now, it's only slowly developing a distinct, urban personality.

Arrival, information, and city transportation

At the intersection of the I-5, I-80, US-50, and Hwy-99 freeways, Sacramento is the hub for many long-distance transportation networks. Sacramento International **airport** (☎916/874-0700, ⓦwww.sacairports.org), twelve miles northwest of Downtown, is served by most major domestic airlines. SuperShuttle Sacramento vans (☎1-800/258-3826, ⓦwww.supershuttle.com) can take you directly to any Downtown destination for $14. Thanks to the city's status as a governmental hub, public transport links are plentiful: the Capitol Corridor route has up to sixteen daily **trains** connecting Sacramento with the Bay Area (T 1-800/872-7245, W www.amtrakcapitols.com), and services from Los Angeles and Chicago stop at the Amtrak station at Fourth and I streets, near Old Sacramento (T 1-800/872-7245, W www.amtrak.com). An almost continuous stream of Greyhound **buses** pulls into the bus depot at 715 L Street, a block from the K Street Mall (T 1-800/231-2222).

There are two **visitor centers**: one in the heart of tourist-clogged Old Sacramento at 1002 2nd Street (daily 10am–5pm; T 916/442-7644, W www.oldsacramanto.com), and another close to K Street Mall Downtown at 1608 I Street (Mon–Fri 8am–5pm; T 916/808-7777, W www.discovergold.org). Pick up a copy of the handy *Sacramento Visitors' Guide* (with maps and listings of accommodation and places to eat and drink in the city) at these offices or almost everywhere tourists congregate; the CVB also publishes an exhaustively informative self-guided walking tour of Sacramento's historic architecture. For the latest on **events and entertainment** in Sacramento, the best option is to check out the free *Sacramento News & Review*; otherwise, there's *Ticket*, the Friday supplement to the *Sacramento Bee* newspaper (50¢), or the free music listings publication *Alive and Kicking*. The city's gay and lesbian scene is lively enough to spawn two freesheets, *MGW* and *Outword*, which also contain general restaurant and events listings.

The city is compact, flat, and somewhat **walkable**, though many locals get around (especially on the 25-mile cycle path along the American River to Folsom Lake) by **bike** – rentals are available at Bike Sacramento, 1050 Front Street, Suite 110, in Old Sacramento (T 916/444-0200), starting around $18 an hour. The city center is crisscrossed with an extensive **bus and light rail** network – timetables and maps are available from the visitor centers and the main transportation office, 1400 29th Street at N Street (Mon–Fri 8am–5pm; T 916/321-2877). The service you're most likely to use is the DASH shuttle (Rte-30) connecting the Amtrak station, K Street Mall, and Old Sacramento (50¢; T 916/321-2877, W www.sacrt.com). The **riverboat tours** leaving from the L Street landing in Old Sacramento are popular if hokey: the paddle-wheel steamboats *Matthew McKinley* and *Spirit of Sacramento* offer varied trips along the Sacramento River ($15–40; T 1-800/433-0263). **Car rental agencies** include Budget, 6420 McNair Circle, Enterprise, 1409 16th Street, and Hertz, 1025 16th Street (see p.37 for contact details).

Accommodation

Sacramento has plenty of reasonably priced places to stay, all within easy walking distance of the center. Most **motels** and **hotels** cluster around **Downtown**, the trendy **Midtown** area, where much of the city's nightlife is centered, or in the outskirts, particularly Richards Boulevard just off I-5. Choices are limited primarily to unexciting chains with a few B&Bs thrown in – rates at weekends are often steeply discounted thanks to the exodus of government workers. There's no good **camping** anywhere within easy reach of Sacramento, though KOA runs the RV-heavy *Sacramento Metro* site, 3951 Lake Road, West Sacramento (T 1-800/562-2747, W www.sacramentokoa.com; ❷), four miles west of the center.

Amber House Bed & Breakfast Inn 1315 22nd St at N, Midtown T 1-800/755-6526, W www.amberhouse.com. The pick of the city's B&Bs, with luxurious rooms, including marble baths, and sumptuous breakfasts – with rates to match. A worthwhile treat to avoid the endless chain motels nearby. ❻

Delta King Hotel 1000 Front St, Old Sacramento T 1-800/825-5464, W www.deltaking.com. A 1926 paddle-wheel riverboat now permanently moored on the waterfront: although the rooms fail to justify their "stateroom" advertising, the vessel makes an enjoyably unusual place to stay. Be aware the area is usually throbbing with visitors at weekends, and prices rise accordingly. ❺

Econo Lodge 711 16th St at H, Downtown ⊤1-800/553-2666, ⓦwww.econolodge.com. The best deal in town, with basic but comfortable rooms and complimentary continental breakfast. ❷

HI–Sacramento 925 H St at 10th, Downtown ⊤916/443-1691, ⓦwww.norcalhostels.org. This hostel is housed in a rambling 1885 mansion with all the usual facilities, plus free bike rental, but there's a daytime lockout and 11pm curfew. $23 for dorm beds plus a very limited number of private rooms starting at $57.

Quality Inn 818 15th St at I, Downtown ⊤1-800/228-5151, ⓦwww.qualityinn.com/hote /ca505. Refurbished rooms near the old Governor's Mansion in a standard chain hotel equipped with a pool. ❹

Vagabond Inn 909 3rd St at J, Old Town ⊤ -800/522-1555, ⓦwww.vagabondinns.com. Motor-lodge-style accommodation near the river and Old Sacramento: there's a pool and free shuttle to public transport hubs, plus free continental breakfast. ❹

Vizcaya Mansion 2019 21st St at T, Midtown ⊤1-800/456-2019, ⓦwww.sterlinghotel.com. A lavish, historic property with elegantly furnished rooms and marble-tiled bathrooms. ❻

The Town

Most of the local attractions in Sacramento are close together, in one of the three main areas that together comprise the city center: the I-5 highway quarantines **Old Sacramento** from the commercial hub of **Downtown**, centered on K Street Mall, as well as the funkier, residential **Midtown** district further east.

Old Sacramento and the riverfront

Sacramento grew up **along the riverfront**, where the wharves, warehouses, saloons, and stores of the city's historic core have been restored and converted into the novelty shops and theme restaurants of **OLD SACRAMENTO**. It's a shame that such a large collection of authentic Gold Rush–era architecture should be choked with such relentless fakery: costumed sales staff hawking souvenirs and tourist-chasing bars dressed up as faux Wild West saloons. In fact, although most of the buildings are original, some stood elsewhere until they were forcibly relocated here in the 1960s to make way for the massive I-5 highway that carves this area off from the rest of the city center. To avoid the stampede of tourists in search of taffy and souvenirs, it's best to avoid Old Sacramento completely at weekends, since that's when the place seems most inauthentic, its streets more like a Hollywood backlot than the real thing.

Three of the area's main historical attractions stand in a row along **I Street**: the smallest is the Huntington & Hopkins hardware store at no. 113. Here, the **Big Four** – Leland Stanford, Mark Hopkins, Collis P. Huntington, and Charles Crocker – held their first meeting to mastermind the Central Pacific and later Southern Pacific railroads (see box, p.624). It's now a **museum** (Tues–Sun 10am–5pm; free; ⊤916/323-7234) decked out as a spartan 1840s supply store, highlighting the humble beginnings of the ruthless Huntington and the henpecked Hopkins, a meeker man who joined him as partner in his grocery store and later in the railroad. Upstairs there's a low-key homage to the men, with a re-creation of their boardroom and an archive of rail history.

One of the city's highlights is the **California State Railroad Museum** at 111 I Street (daily 10am–5pm; $8; ⊤916/445-7387, ⓦwww.californiastaterail roadmuseum.org), which brings together a range of lavishly restored 1860s locomotives with "cow-catcher" front grilles and huge, bulbous smokestacks. Frankly, despite its exhaustive exhibits on early railroad technology, it's still more suited to dedicated trainspotters than casual tourists. Instead, catch a leisurely taste of railroad life by heading across to the old passenger station and freight depot a block south, which is also part of the museum. Here you can take a seven-mile, 45-minute jaunt beside the river on a vintage train (April–Sept Sat & Sun hourly 11am–5pm; $6).

For a broader view of the area's past, the **Discovery Museum of History, Science and Technology** at 101 I Street (June–Aug daily 10am–5pm; Sept–June Tues–Sun 10am–5pm; $5; ☎916/264-7057, ⓦwww.thediscovery.org) features a hands-on display about the early newspapers in California (including the *Sacramento Bee*, founded in 1857) as well as coverage of more recent history, like the Depression-era diner run by the pioneering African-American Dunlap family. The exhibits are hit and miss, but they have a wider appeal than the highly specialized Railroad Museum.

Two smaller museums are really only worth a look if you're desperate to escape the souvenir shops. The **California Military Museum**, 1119 2nd Street (Tues–Sun 10am–4pm; $5; ☎916/442-2883, ⓦwww.militarymuseum.org), provides an uninspiring chronicle – with documents, weaponry, and uniforms – of California's involvement in armed struggles from pre-statehood days to the present; there's even a section, albeit skimpy, on the 1992 race riots in Los Angeles. The **Wells Fargo Historical Museum**, 1000 2nd Street at J (daily 10am–5pm; free; ☎916/440-4263), is one of the many corporate museums run by the bank across California. Unfortunately, it's not one of the best, with a tiny collection of unremarkable ephemera. In fact, most people only pass through to use the ATMs inside this 1853 bank building, which also held the first State Supreme Court, the unassuming old chambers of which are sometimes open for public view on the top floor.

Pass over the highway to reach the nearby **Crocker Art Museum** at 216 O Street between Second and Third (Tues, Wed, Fri–Sun 10am–5pm, Thurs 10am–9pm; $6; ☎916/264-5423, ⓦwww.crockerartmuseum.org). Here, in an odd complex of Renaissance Revival and modern buildings, you'll see paintings collected by Supreme Court judge Edwin Crocker, brother of railroad baron Charles. Although there are a few pictures of early California life, the Eurocentric collection (mainly drawings by Dürer, Rembrandt, Boucher, and Fragonard, as well as some second-tier canvases from artists like Henry Raeburn) seems oddly incongruous in this city. More appropriate to its setting, in the shadow of the massive I-5 and I-80 interchange at 2200 Front Street, the **Towe Auto Museum** (daily 10am–6pm; $7; ☎916/442-6802, ⓦwww.toweautomuseum.org) offers an impressive collection of antique cars and trucks, from Model Ts and As to classic '57 T-birds and "woody" station wagons.

Downtown

Running east from the riverfront and Old Sacramento, past the Greyhound and Amtrak stations, the **K Street Mall** is the commercial heart of **DOWNTOWN SACRAMENTO**, with the end of the light rail network running through the center of a pedestrianized shopping precinct. While its western reaches are rather forlorn, with plenty of empty storefronts, the street grows livelier the closer it gets to the massive, open-air **Downtown Plaza** shopping complex. Every major retail name is here, along with a food court and an enormous movie theater; at its western end is a tunnel that takes pedestrians under the highway to connect with Old Sacramento.

Northeast of the mall, at 16th and H, stands the old **Governor's Mansion** (tours daily on the hour 10am–4pm; $4; ⓦwww.parks.ca.gov). Although built in 1877 as a private home, this enormous and elaborate Victorian house was home to California's governors for more than sixty years until 1967, when then-governor Ronald Reagan abandoned its high ceilings and narrow staircases in favor of a ranch-style house on the outskirts of town. His excuse was that the structure had been condemned as a firetrap, although it's likely that he simply craved better creature comforts than the traditional building could offer. Today, the meringue-like mansion has been restored to its former glory, and is a perfect place to begin a self-guided **walking tour** of Sacramento's historic architecture with one of the detailed free brochures published by the Sacramento CVB. And no, the Governor doesn't live here.

The city's most imposing edifice is the **State Capitol**, with its Classical Revival dome, built in the 1860s, although there have been several significant, if insensitive, additions since then. It was restored to nineteenth-century opulence in 1976 in what was then the largest such project in US history; it underwent another heavy restoration following a catastrophic incident in early 2001 when a mentally unstable truck driver ploughed his milk tanker into the southern facade and caused almost $15 million in damage, most of it smoke related. Unsurprisingly, security has been tightened, and you'll need a photo ID to enter the building: once inside, you're free to ramble around the main floor using the self-guided leaflets on offer in the rotunda. You'll see more, though, if you take one of the free **tours** (daily 9am–5pm, last tour 4pm; ☎916/324-0333, ⓦwww.capitolmuseum.ca.gov) that leave hourly from Room B-27 on the lower ground floor. These tours will take you through administrative rooms set up as if it were April 1906, when the devastating San Francisco earthquake occurred. You'll also visit the salmon-pink Senate Gallery and lush green Assembly Room; in the latter, note the gargoyle's face in the egg-and-dart ceiling molding, sticking its tongue out at whoever's at the podium (illicitly added, it's claimed, by disgruntled artisans during construction). Outside, the park around the Capitol is delightful, filled with rowdy flowerbeds, enormous trees, and a plague of friendly squirrels; it's often crowded on weekday lunch-times with office workers snacking in the sun.

The **California State History Museum**, 1020 O Street (Tues–Sat 10am–5pm, Sun noon–5pm; $7.50; ☎916/653-7524, ⓦwww.goldenstatemuseum.org),

▲ The State Capitol, Sacramento

is an enormous, cutting-edge facility that focuses on both the state's physical history and the development of the often lampooned, laid-back worldview of its inhabitants. The layout's rather confusing, since each exhibit bleeds into the next, but don't miss the eye-catching re-creation of an early Chinese herbalist store or the perky TV montage showing Californians' often amusing reflections on their home state.

Midtown

Sacramento's trendiest district is **Midtown**, a pleasant neighborhood for a leisurely, leafy stroll; city planners planted trees on almost every street, so there's ample shade from the relentless sunshine. Here, although there are few actual attractions, you'll find dozens of funky restaurants and cafés (see opposite) dotted among the old Victorian mansions, especially along Capitol Avenue, not to mention one of the city's best sights, **Sutter's Fort State Historic Park** (daily 10am–5pm; $3, free entry after 4.30pm; ☎916/445-4422, ⓦwww.parks.ca.gov). This re-creation of Sacramento's original settlement stands at 27th and L streets: the main entrance is on the south side. With its low, starkly whitewashed walls, the fort is strikingly simple amid the residential frippery of the many Victorians nearby. Inside, motion-triggered audio commentary describes each room, like the Blacksmith's and the Bakery, and an adobe house exhibits relics from the Gold Rush; its quiet atmosphere gives a vivid sense of early European life in California.

One block north, the small **Indian Museum** at 2618 K Street (daily 10am–5pm; $2; ☎916/324-0971) displays tools, handicrafts, and ceremonial objects of the Native Americans of the Central Valley and the Sierra Nevada, and recounts the story of Ishi, the last of the Yahi Indians, who was paraded around towns as a curiosity in the early twentieth century. Frankly, it's dark, a little threadbare, and disappointing – the display on the Miwoks at Indian Grinding Rock (see p.643) is much more impressive.

Eating

Dozens of fast-food stands, ice-cream shops, and overpriced Western-themed **restaurants** fill Old Sacramento, but you'd do better to steer clear of these and search out the places listed here. Many of the restaurants Downtown cater primarily to office workers and are therefore closed in the evening; for dinner, it's better to stroll over to Midtown, around 20th Street and Capitol Avenue, where you'll also find the odd good bar.

Café Bernardo 2726 Capitol Ave, Midtown ☏916/443-1180. Large refectory-style restaurant where you can order huge portions of cheap, healthy food from the walk-up counter and eat in the casual dining room, reminiscent of a Tuscan farmhouse. The menu's mainly Italian, with pastas, salads, and small pizzas; it's also open for breakfast, when the fare's more American, with French toast and pancakes. Also branches at 1415 L St and 1431 R St.

Centro Cocina Mexicana 2730 J St, Midtown ☏916/442-2552. This innovative, upscale Mexican restaurant offers regional cooking, like delicious chicken and *mole* enchiladas from Oaxaca. Lunch prices and dishes are lighter; the bar's especially impressive, since it stocks more than fifty aged tequilas.

Hukilau Island Grill 1501 16th St at O, Midtown ☏916/444-5850. Loud, garish, but fun restaurant, complete with cartoonish Hawaiian decor and an eclectic Pacific Rim menu: the simpler dishes, like grilled fish kebabs, are the most successful.

Jack's Urban Eats 1230 20th St at Capitol Ave, Midtown ☏916/444-0307. Groovy bargain rotisserie, serving slab-like sandwiches of juicy herbed chicken or steak for $5, with a starkly chic ambience and a few canvases by local artists on the walls. The urban-style fries, with blue cheese and spicy chili oil, are knockout.

Lucca 1615 J St at 16th, Midtown ☏916/669-5300. If you're hoping to spot the Governator, your best chance is here – he's a regular. The space is surprisingly low-key – bare brick walls, no table-cloths – as is the rustic, Tuscan food. Try the chicken, mushroom, and fontina risotto for $12 or a lavish fish stew for $16.

Maharani 1812 Broadway at 18th St, Downtown ☏916/441-2172. Slightly pricey California-style Indian that's light on oil, but still heavy on all the traditional spices – go with the tandoori chicken.

Megami 1010 10th St at J St, Downtown ☏916/448-4512. A bargain Japanese restaurant with lunch and combination sushi plates for under $5. The sesame chicken is also a good bet. Mon–Fri only.

Paesano's 1806 Capitol Ave at 18th St, Midtown ☏916/447-8646. Brick-walled pizzeria serving hearty portions of pasta and oven-baked sandwiches at reasonable prices.

River City Brewing Company 545 Downtown Plaza ☏916/447-2745. One of the few acceptable places to eat near Old Sacramento, this slick, modern brewpub at the west end of the K Street Mall serves standard food at regular prices, enhanced by tasty beers (some brewed on site).

Tapa the World 2115 J St at 20th St, Midtown ☏916/442-4353. Choose from twenty different tapas, including filet mignon tips sauteed in spicy plum and ginger sauce, or have a full meal of paella, lamb, or fresh fish, all while being serenaded by flamenco guitar.

Tower Café 1518 Broadway at 15th, Downtown ☏916/441-0222. The furnishings at this casual restaurant are as eclectic as the food – expect walls covered in masks and tapestries and a Caribbean-influenced menu. Try the jerk chicken or swing by for brunch for gooey and crispy French toast, soaked overnight in vanilla custard.

Weatherstone Coffee & Trading Co 812 21st St at H, Midtown ☏916/443-6340. Sacramento's oldest coffeehouse has a massive courtyard that's pleasant on a sunny afternoon; the interior's a little dilapidated, but it's unpretentious and easy-going. Tucked away on a largely residential block, it can be a bit hard to find.

Willie's Burgers and Chiliburger 2415 16th St at X St, Downtown ☏916/444-2006. Old-school burger joint serving up sloppy, unmissable cooked-to-order burgers and fries, as well as tamales and – best of all – hot, sweet *beignets* at breakfast time.

Bars and nightlife

Sacramento's **nightlife** can be rather flat, especially in the center of the city once the office workers have headed home to the suburbs. The best place to catch offbeat live music is *Old Ironsides*, 1901 10th Street (℡916/443-9751, Ⓦ www.theoldironsides.com), or at the *Torch Club*, 904 15th Street (℡916/443-2797, Ⓦ www.torchclub.net; closed Mon), the town's oldest blues haunt; another option is the *Capitol Garage*, 1427 L Street at 14th (℡916/444-3633, Ⓦ www .capitolgarage.com), a coffeehouse-cum-performance space featuring local bands with a nominal cover. For bigger touring names, try the Crest Theater, a refurbished Art Deco gem in the K Street Mall at no. 1013, which also hosts short runs of edgy indie **movies** (℡916/442-7378, Ⓦ www.thecrest.com). For more art-house films, try the Tower Theater at Broadway and 16th (℡916/442-4700).

The hip *Monkey Bar* at 2730 Capitol Avenue (℡916/442-8490), with its mosaic details and mixed preppy-indie crowd, is the best place to drink and serves bargain cocktails for around $3. The biggest dance club in the city center is *Faces*, on the corner of K and 20th streets (℡916/448-7798, Ⓦ www.facesnightclub.com), with two dance floors and nine bars; the cover hovers around $6, and there's a mixed gay/straight crowd. Opposite *Faces*, at 2001 K St, *The Depot* (℡916/441-6823, Ⓦ www.thedepot.net) is a friendly gay video bar.

The Central Mother Lode

From Sacramento, US-50 and I-80 head east through the heart of the Gold Country, up and over the mountains past Lake Tahoe and into the state of Nevada. The roads closely follow the old stagecoach routes over the Donner Pass, named in honor of the gruesomely tragic exploration (see box, p.662). In the mid-1860s, local citizens, seeking to improve dwindling fortunes after the Gold Rush subsided, joined forces with railroad engineer Theodore Judah to finance and build the first railroad crossing of the Sierra Nevada over much the same route – even along much of the same track – that Amtrak uses today. The area's less touristed than the northern or southern mines: either **Placerville** or **Auburn** make good bases, with affordable accommodation and some local points of interest in each. Placerville's especially handy if you want to cruise around and sample some of the vintages produced locally in the El Dorado wine country. And while the area's towns may not be nearly as postcard-perfect as those elsewhere in the region, **Coloma** and **Folsom**, in between the two highways on the American River, are both worth exploring for their less touristy Gold Rush feel.

Folsom

In 1995, just as the **Folsom** powerhouse was gearing up for the centennial celebration of its pioneering efforts in long-distance electricity transmission, one of the sluice gates on the Folsom Dam gave way, sending millions of gallons of water down the American River towards Sacramento, twenty miles downstream. The levees held, but Folsom Lake had to be almost completely drained before repairs could be undertaken.

The event sent shockwaves through California's extensive hydroelectric industry and brought a fame to Folsom unknown since Johnny Cash sang of being "stuck in Folsom Prison" after having "shot a man in Reno, just to watch him die." The stone-faced **Folsom State Prison**, two miles north of town on Green Valley Road, has an arts-and-crafts gallery (daily 8am–5pm) selling works by prisoners, who get the proceeds when released. It's more interesting stopping at the small **museum** across the road (daily 10am–4pm; donation; ℡916/985-2561), which

El Dorado wine country

In the 1860s, when the now-famous Napa and Sonoma valleys were growing potatoes, **vineyards** flourished in El Dorado County. However, the fields were neglected after the Gold Rush and killed off by phylloxera, a nasty yellow aphid that gorges itself on vine roots; it wasn't until 1972 that vineyards were systematically re-established. Since then, however, the **wineries** in El Dorado County, especially around Placerville, have rapidly gained a reputation that belies their diminutive size. Most are low-key affairs where no charge is levied for tasting or tours, and you're encouraged to enjoy a bottle out on the veranda. At quiet times, you may even be shown around by the winemaker, a far cry from the organized tours and rampant commercialism of Napa and Sonoma (see p.681 & 686, respectively).

The differences in altitude and soil types throughout the region lend themselves to a broad range of grape varieties, and the producers here are often criticized for being unfocused; regardless, in recent years local wineries have regularly snagged awards. Zinfandel and Sauvignon Blanc are big, but it's the Syrah/Merlot blends that attract the attention, and the Barbera (from a Piedmontese grape) is said to be one of the best in the world.

If you're out for a relaxed day's tasting, avoid the two consecutive **Passport Weekends** ($65; ⓣ1-800/306-3956, ⓦwww.eldoradowines.org), usually the last weekend in March and the first in April and booked out months in advance, although the purchase of this passport does entitle you to all manner of foodie extravagances to complement the tastings. Better to pick up the **El Dorado Wine Country Tour** leaflet from the El Dorado Chamber of Commerce (see p.629) and make your way to the Boeger Vineyard, 1709 Carson Road (daily 10am–5pm; ⓣ530/622-8094, ⓦwww.boegerwinery.com), less than a mile from the Greyhound stop (see p.628), where you can sit in an arbor of apples and pears. Also try the Lava Cap Vineyard, 2221 Fruitridge Road (daily 11am–5pm; ⓣ530/621-0175, ⓦwww.lavacap.com), which in recent years has produced some excellent Chardonnay and Muscat Canelli.

The quality of the local produce – not only grapes, but also apples, pears, peaches, cherries, and more – is widely celebrated around the district, especially during the **Apple Hill Festival** (ⓣ530/644-7692, ⓦwww.applehill.com) in October, when a shuttle bus runs from Placerville to the majority of the orchards and wineries situated in the Apple Hill region, along the winding country roads just north of I-50 and east of town. At other times, you'll have to make your own way. The Chamber of Commerce can also supply you with the *Cider Press Guide to Apple Hill* and *Farm Trails Harvest & Recreation Guide*, both of which have detailed information and maps leading to farms, ranches, wineries, and historic country inns in the most remote areas of the county.

is filled with grisly photographs, the medical records of murderers and thieves who were hanged for their crimes, and a whole arsenal of handmade escape tools recovered from prisoners over the years.

Folsom itself is attractive enough, with a single main street, Sutter Street, of restored homes and buildings that date from the days of the Pony Express. A reconstruction of the 1860 Wells Fargo office makes an imposing setting for the **Folsom History Museum**, no. 823 (Tues–Sun 11am–4pm; $3; ⓣ916/985-2707, ⓦwww.folsomhistorymuseum.org), whose prized possessions include a working scale-model of a steam-powered gold dredge, artifacts from the Chinese community that settled here in the 1850s, and a huge mural depicting the area's main native people, the Maidu.

In town, the Folsom **Chamber of Commerce**, 200 Wool Street (Mon–Fri 9am–5pm, Sat 11am–4pm; ⓣ1-800/377-1414, ⓦwww.folsomchamber.com), has the usual brochures. There are plenty of chain **eateries** around town;

otherwise, a good choice is the *Balcony Restaurant*, 801 Sutter Street (☎916/985-2605), where you can simultaneously enjoy a hearty meal and a view of the historic downtown. For **accommodation**, you'd do better heading back to Sacramento, though if you're particularly tired and have a flexible budget, stop at *Lake Natoma Inn*, 702 Gold Lake Drive (☎1-800/808-5253, ⓦwww .lakenatomainn.com; ❺), with full amenities, restaurant, and a spa.

Placerville

PLACERVILLE, twenty miles east of Folsom, takes a perverse delight in having been known originally as Hangtown for its practice of lynching alleged criminals in pairs and stringing them up from a tree in the center of town. Despite these gruesome beginnings, Placerville has always been more of a market than a mining town and is now a major crossroads, halfway between Sacramento and Lake Tahoe at the junction of US-50 and Hwy-49. For a time in the mid-1850s it was the third largest city in California, and many of the state's most powerful historical figures got their start here: railroad magnates Mark Hopkins and Collis P. Huntington were local merchants, while car mogul John Studebaker made wheelbarrows for the miners.

The modern town spreads out along the highways in a string of fast-food restaurants, gas stations, and motels. The old Main Street, running parallel to US-50, retains some of the Gold Rush architecture, with an effigy dangling by the neck in front of the *Hangman's Tree* bar, built over the site where the town's infamous tree once grew. At 441 Main Street is the oldest continuously operating hardware store west of the Mississippi, and you'll see many fine old houses scattered among the pine trees in the steep valleys to the north and south of the center. Nearby, one of the best of the Gold Country museums is in the sprawling El Dorado County Fairgrounds, just north of US-50. This, the **El Dorado County Historical Museum**, 104 Placerville Drive (Wed–Sat 10am–4pm, Sun noon–4pm; free; ☎530/621-5865, ⓦwww.co.el-dorado.ca .us/museum), gives a broad historical overview of the county from the Miwok to the modern day, including logging trains and a mock-up of a general store, plus pioneer wagons and Native American handicrafts. There's also a library and research center which is crammed with archival photographs of the area's golden era. For more on the days of the argonauts, head across US-50 to the **Gold Bug Mine Park** on Bedford Avenue (April–Oct daily 10am–4pm; Nov–March Sat & Sun noon–4pm, weather permitting; $4, $1 audio tour; ☎530/642-5207, ⓦwww.goldbugpark.org) for a self-guided tour of a typical Mother Lode mine, including a hard-rock mining site and a stamp mill showing the ore extraction process. If you want to try your luck hunting for gold, you can rent a pan for $2 an hour – though don't expect to find anything.

Practicalities

Greyhound buses on their way to South Lake Tahoe stop twice a day at 1750 Broadway, a mile and a half east of town. El Dorado Transit buses provide local transit service ($1.10–2.00; ☎530/642-5383, ⓦwww.eldoradotransit.com). Near the Greyhound stop are a number **accommodation** choices, such as the *Mother Lode Motel*, 1940 Broadway (☎530/622-0895, ⓔpatelat1940@aol.com; ❷), and *National 9 Inn*, 1500 Broadway (☎530/622-3884; ❸), with slightly larger, newer rooms. With more money, you're far better off at the landmark *Chichester-McKee House*, 800 Spring Street (☎530/626-1882 or 1-800/831-4008; ❺), a historic B&B offering guestrooms with period furnishings and home-baked breakfasts, reached by turning north off US-50 onto Hwy-49 at the traffic lights in town. The El Dorado County **Chamber of Commerce** office, 542 Main Street (Mon–Fri 9am–5pm; ☎530/621-5885, ⓦwww .eldoradocounty.org), has local information and can help set up **river-rafting** trips in Coloma (see below).

As for **eating** options, try the local concoction, "the Hangtown Fry," an omelet-like scramble of bacon, eggs, and breaded oysters. It's said to have been whipped up using ingredients that were scarce at the height of the Gold Rush for a wealthy miner who wanted the priciest dish on the menu: try one at *Chuck's Pancake House*, 1318 Broadway (☎530/622-2858). *Sweetie Pie's*, at 577 Main Street (☎530/642-0128), serves great breakfasts and what could be the finest cinnamon rolls on the planet. Grab an organic coffee or an authentic chai at the natural foods eatery *Cozmic Café*, housed inside the remnants of an actual gold mine, 594 Main Street (☎530/642-8481). If you've got a car, don't miss *Poor Red's Barbeque* (☎530/622-2901), housed in the old Adams and Co. stagecoach office on Hwy-49 three miles south of Placerville, serving the Gold Country's top barbecued dinners for under $7, with $1 beers and two-fisted margaritas. If none of these appeal, *Heyday*, 325 Main Street (☎530/626-9700), dishes up fine, affordable Italian food.

Coloma

Sights along Hwy-49 north of Placerville are few and far between, but it was here that gold fever began on January 24, 1848, when James Marshall discovered flakes of gold in the tailrace of a mill he was building for John Sutter along the south fork of the American River at **Coloma**. By the summer of that year, thousands had flocked to the area, and by the following year Coloma was a town of ten thousand – though most left quickly following news of richer strikes elsewhere in the region, and the town all but disappeared within a few years. The few surviving buildings, including two Chinese stores and the cabin where Marshall lived, have been preserved as the **Marshall Gold Discovery State Historic Park** (daily 8am–sunset, museum daily 10am–4.30pm; $5 per car; ☎530/622-3470, ⓦwww.parks.ca.gov). A reconstruction of **Sutter's Mill** stands along the river within the park and working demonstrations are held on most weekends at 10am and 1pm. There's a small historical museum across the road, and on a hill overlooking the town a statue marks the spot where Marshall is buried. Marshall never profited from his discovery, and in fact it came to haunt him. At first, he tried to charge miners for access to what he said was his land along the river (it wasn't), and he spent most of his later years in poverty, claiming supernatural powers had helped him to find gold.

Whether or not you believe in ghosts, Coloma certainly has one attraction that will still turn your knuckles white: it's the best place to begin a **whitewater rafting** journey on the American River. Tours can be booked with Mariah Wilderness Expeditions (☎1-800/462-7424, ⓦwww.mariahwe.com) or Current Adventures (☎1-888/452-9252, ⓦwww.currentadventures.com): expect to pay around $80–100 for a one-day excursion and at least $200 for overnight trips. If you decide to stay in town for the night, the choicest **accommodation** is the *Coloma Country Inn*, 345 High Street (☎530/622-6919, ⓦwww.colomacountryinn.com; ❺), adjacent to the state park, with antique-crammed rooms and 2.5 acres of gardens. Barely a mile west of Coloma, on the main road through tiny **Lotus** at 1006 Lotus Road, is the unexpected location for one of the region's newest and finest restaurants: ⚜ *Café Mahjaic*, where you can savor delights like chocolate chipotle prawns and *coulotte espanole* steak for around $20 (☎530/622-9587; closed Sun & Mon).

Auburn and Dutch Flat

Heading north thirty miles or so, the town of **Auburn**, built into a hillside on three levels, manages to preserve its Gold Rush-era charm, even though it's right at the crossroads of Hwy-49 and I-80. Greyhound **buses** heading from Sacramento to Reno stop at 246 Palm Avenue, and Amtrak **trains** depart from Nevada and Fulleiler streets. The outskirts are sprawling and modern, but the Old Town, on Auburn's lowest level just off Hwy-49, is one of the best preserved and most picturesque of the Gold Rush sights, with antique stores and saloons clustered around a Spanish-style plaza. You'll also find California's oldest post office, in continuous use since 1848, and the unmissable red-and-white tower of the 1891 **firehouse**. There are also a number of undervisited museums like the **Gold Country Museum**, 1273 High Streets (Tues–Sun 11am–4pm; free; ☎530/889-6500, ⓦ www.placer.ca.gov/museum/local-museums/goldctry). Of course, it's another mine of information with an authentic tunnel on site and a replica of a miners' camp. More offbeat and unusual is the **Bernhard Museum Complex** at 291 Auburn-Folsom Road (Tues–Sun 11am–4pm; free; ☎530/889-6500, ⓦ www.placer.ca.gov/museum/local-museums/bernhard), mostly since its former owner was looking for liquid, rather than nugget, gold: come here for guided tours of an amateur viticulturist's 1851 home, as well as his carriage barn and modest winery.

For a free map and information on places to stay, stop by the **California Welcome Center**, north of town at 13411 Lincoln Way (Mon–Sat 9.30am–4.30pm, Sun 11am–4.30pm; ☎530/887-2111, ⓦ www.visitplacer.com). Affordable **accommodation** is available at the *Super 8 Motel* at 140 E Hillcrest Drive in Auburn, which offers no-frills comfort (☎1-800/800-8000, ⓦ www.super8.com; ❸). For a good **meal**, try either *Bootlegger's Old Town Tavern and Grill*, 210 Washington Street (☎530/889-2229), where hearty fare is served in a stately brick building, or *Latitudes*, 130 Maple Street (☎530/885-9535), for California interpretations of multicultural cuisines like East Indian curried tofu or teriyaki tempeh.

The twenty or so miles of Hwy-49 north of Auburn are a dull but fast stretch of freeway to one of the best parts of the Gold Country – the twin cities of Grass Valley and Nevada City (see opposite). For an interesting side trip on the way there, or if you're heading for Lake Tahoe, take I-80 from Auburn 27 miles east to the small town of **Dutch Flat**, where old tin-roofed cottages are sprinkled among the pine- and aspen-covered slopes. Miners here used the profitable, but very destructive, method of hydraulic mining (see p.637) to get at the gold buried under the surface – with highly visible consequences.

The northern mines

The **northern section** of the Gold Country includes some of the most spectacularly beautiful scenery in California. Fast-flowing rivers cascade through steeply-walled canyons whose slopes are covered in the fall with the flaming reds and golds of poplars and sugar maples, highlighted against an evergreen background of pine and fir trees. Unlike the freelance placer mines of the south, where wandering prospectors picked nuggets of gold out of the streams and rivers, the gold here was (and is) buried deep underground and had, therefore, to be pounded out of hard-rock ore. In spite of that, the **northern mines** were the most profitable of the Mother Lode – more than half of California's gold originated in the mines of **Nevada County**, and most of that came from **Grass Valley**'s Empire Mine, now preserved as one of the region's many excellent museums. Just north, the quaint Victorian houses of **Nevada City** make it the most alluring Gold Rush town.

A few miles away, at the end of a steep and twisting back road, the scarred yet curiously beautiful landforms of the **Malakoff Diggins** stand as an exotic reminder of the destruction wrought by overzealous miners, who, as gold became harder to find, washed away entire hillsides to get at the precious metal. Hwy-49 winds further up into the mountains from Nevada City, along the Yuba River to the High Sierra hamlet of **Downieville**, at the foot of the towering Sierra Buttes, and even smaller **Sierra City**. From here you're within striking distance of the northernmost Gold Rush ghost town of **Johnsville**, which stands in an evocative state of arrested decay in the middle of the forests of Plumas-Eureka State Park, on the crest of the Sierra Nevada.

You need a **car** to get to any of the outlying sights, among which you'll find a few inexpensive motels and a handful of B&Bs, but there are no youth hostels; **camping** is an option too, often in unspoiled sites amid gorgeous mountain scenery.

Grass Valley and Nevada City

Twenty-five miles north of Auburn and I-80, the neighboring towns of **Grass Valley** and **Nevada City** were the most prosperous and substantial of the gold-mining towns and are still thriving communities, four miles apart in beautiful surroundings in the lower reaches of the Sierra Nevada. Together they make one of the better Gold Country destinations, with museums that successfully conjure up the era and many balconied, elaborately detailed buildings staggering up hills and hanging out over steep gorges.

Gold was the lifeblood of the area as recently as the mid-1950s, and both towns look largely unchanged since the Gold Rush. The locals have retained a bit of the fiery determination of their rough-and-ready ancestors, as evidenced by the booming downtown businesses that combine the Old West with big-city sophistication. Since the 1960s, a number of artists and craftspeople have also settled in the old houses in the hills around the area, tempering the rugged regional culture with a vaguely alternative feel that's reflected in the free weekly *Community Endeavor* newspaper, the noncommercial community radio station KVMR (99.3FM), the disproportionate number of bookshops, and the friendly throngs that turn out for the annual Bluegrass Festival in the middle of June. For a detailed rundown on the whole of Nevada County, including the mines, check out Ⓦwww.ncgold.com.

Both towns are very compact and connected every thirty minutes by the Gold Country Stage **minibus** (Mon–Fri 7am–6pm, Sat 10am–5pm; $1, $3 for a day-pass; ⓣ1-888/660-7433, Ⓦwww.goldcountrystage.com), which follows the same stretch of road that burro trains and stagecoaches frequented in the twin towns' heyday, when it was the busiest four-mile route in California.

Accommodation

There's a smattering of cheapish **motels** around but if you can fork out more for a **bed and breakfast**, Nevada City in particular has some excellent options.

Otherwise there are a couple of revamped Gold Rush **hotels**. See the box on p.637 for **camping** options.

Grass Valley

Coach 'N' Four Motel 628 S Auburn St, Grass Valley ℡530/273-8009, 🖷530/273-0827. Handy for Empire State Park, this clean and comfortable motel offers the best rates around. ❸

Holbrooke Hotel 212 W Main St, Grass Valley ℡1-800/933-7077, 🖱www.holbrooke.com. Right in the center of town, this historic hotel, where Mark Twain once stayed, has great rooms and an opulent bar-cum-restaurant. ❹

Holiday Lodge 1221 E Main St, Grass Valley ℡1-800/742-7125, 🖱www.holidaylodge.biz. Comfortable, no-frills rooms in a lodge featuring a swimming pool, free breakfast, and free local calls. ❸

Stagecoach Motel 405 S Auburn St, Grass Valley ℡530/272-3701. Decent rates and all the basic amenities, handily placed for the Empire Mine. ❸

Swan-Levine House 328 S Church St, Grass Valley ℡530/272-1873, 🖱www.swanlevinehouse.com. Attractively decorated, sunny en-suite rooms in an old Victorian hospital. There's original artwork on display, and the friendly owners give print-making lessons. ❹

Nevada City

Flume's End 317 S Pine St, Nevada City ℡530/265-9665, 🖱www.flumesend.com. A small inn across the Pine Creek Bridge from the center of town, overlooking a pretty waterfall and featuring lovely gardens ranged along Deer Creek. ❻

National Hotel 211 Broad St, Nevada City ℡530/265-4551, 🖱www.thenationalhotel.com. The oldest continuously operated hotel in the West and a state historic landmark, with plenty of Gold Rush charm in the rooms and lobby, which boasts original photographs, musty wallpaper, and a grand staircase. ❹

Northern Queen Inn 400 Railroad Ave, Nevada City ℡1-800/226-3090, 🖱www.northernqueeninn.com. Well-priced hotel with a heated pool. Attractive woodland cottages and chalets, along with simpler rooms in another building. ❹

Outside Inn 575 E Broad St, Nevada City ℡530/265-2233, 🖱www.outsideinn.com. Quiet 1940s motel with swimming pool, a 10-minute walk from the center of town. Credit cards not accepted. ❸

Piety Hill Cottages 523 Sacramento St, Nevada City ℡1-800/443-2245, 🖱www.pietyhillcottages.com. Cottages with kitchenettes, decorated in period furnishings in a garden setting; the smaller ones are an especially good deal. ❹

Grass Valley

There's nothing Gold Country folk love better than telling a long tale about their town's toughest days, making it virtually impossible to pass through **GRASS VALLEY** without getting at least one rendition of the **Lola Montez** story. This Irish dancer and entertainer – the former mistress of Ludwig of Bavaria, and friend of Victor Hugo and Franz Liszt – embarked on a highly successful tour of America in the 1850s, playing to packed houses from New York to San Francisco. Her provocative "Spider Dance," in which she wriggled about the stage shaking cork spiders out of her dress, didn't much impress the miners, but she liked the wild lifestyle of the town, gave up dancing, and retired to Grass Valley with her pet grizzly bear, which she kept tied up in the front yard. Max Ophüls' 1955 *Lola Montes*, which had the largest budget of any film in the history of French cinema at the time of its release, tells a surreal, fictionalized version of her life story.

A few mementoes of Lola's life, such as clothes and accessories, are displayed in the **Grass Valley Museum**, in the Old St Mary's Academy at the corner of Church and Chapel streets (Tues–Fri 12.30–3.30pm; donation; ℡530/273-5509). The town's **tourist office** (Mon–Fri 9.30am–5pm, Sat 10am–3pm; ℡1-800/655-4667, 🖱www.grassvalleychamber.com) is housed in a replica of her home, on the south side of town at 248 Mill Street. It also has reams of historical information, lists of accommodation, and a walking-tour map of the town, pointing out what used to be the oldest hardware store in California

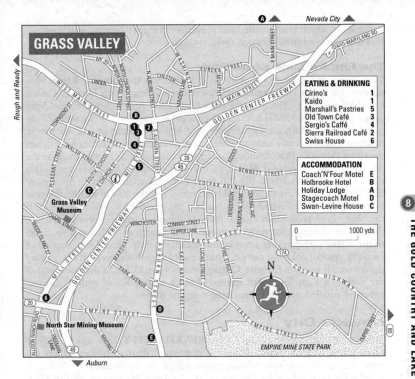

EATING & DRINKING

Cirino's	1
Kaido	1
Marshall's Pastries	5
Old Town Café	3
Sergio's Caffé	4
Sierra Railroad Café	2
Swiss House	6

ACCOMMODATION

Coach'N'Four Motel	E
Holbrooke Hotel	B
Holiday Lodge	A
Stagecoach Motel	D
Swan-Levine House	C

Grass Valley Museum

North Star Mining Museum

EMPIRE MINE STATE PARK

0   1000 yds

N

(now a tacky art gallery) among the wooden awnings and storefronts of the gas-lighted business district.

The North Star Mining Museum

The **North Star Mining Museum**, at the south end of Mill Street (early May to mid-Oct daily 10am–5pm; donation; ℡530/273-4255), is one of the most evocative Gold Country museums, with enthusiastic guides and interesting exhibits illustrating the days when Grass Valley was the richest and most important of all the California mining towns. Housed in what used to be the power station for the North Star Mine, the centerpiece is the giant **Pelton wheel**. Patented in 1878 and resembling nothing so much as a thirty-foot-diameter bicycle wheel, the wheel became one of the most important inventions to come out of the Gold Country. Many Pelton wheels were used to generate electricity, though the one here drove an air compressor that powered the drills and hoists of the mine.

A series of dioramas in the museum describes the day-to-day working life of the miners, three-quarters of whom had emigrated here from the depressed tin mines of Cornwall in England. Besides their expertise at working deep underground, the "Cousin Jacks," as they were called by the non-Cornish miners, introduced the **Cornish pump** (not to mention the Cornish pasty, a traditional pastry pie) to the mines. You can see a mock-up of one of these mammoth beasts, which were designed to extract water from underground, as well as a replica of the old surface mechanism.

The great machines are now at peace, but when they were in action the racket could be heard for miles around. The noisiest offenders were the thundering stamp mills, which once mashed and pulverized the gold-bearing quartz ore – a scaled-down version is operated upon request.

The Empire Mine State Park

The largest and richest gold mine in the state was the **Empire Mine**, now preserved as a state park a mile southeast of Grass Valley, just off Hwy-174 at the top of Empire Street. The 800-acre **park** (daily: May–Aug 9am–6pm; Sept–April 10am–5pm; $3; ☎530/273-8522, ⓦwww.empiremine.org) is surrounded by pines, amongst which are vast quantities of mining equipment and machinery, much of it only recently reinstated here after having been sold off for scrap when the mine closed in 1956. Standing among the machines, it's easy to imagine the din that shook the ground 24 hours a day, or the skips of fifty men descending the now-desolate shaft into the 350 miles of underground tunnels. After more than six million ounces of gold had been recovered, the cost of getting the gold out of the ground exceeded $35 an ounce – the government-controlled price at the time – and production ceased. Most of the mine has been dismantled, but there's a small, very informative **museum** at the entrance with a superb model of the whole underground system, built secretly to help predict the location of lucrative veins of gold. You can get some sense of the mine's prosperity by visiting the owner's house, the **Empire Cottage** (tours 1pm; $1.50), at the north end of the park – a vaguely English stone-and-brick manor house with a glowing, redwood-paneled interior overlooking a formal garden.

Nevada City

Towns don't get much quainter than **NEVADA CITY**, four miles north of Grass Valley, with its crooked rows of elaborate Victorian homes set on the winding, narrow, maple-tree-lined streets, which rise up from Hwy-49. It gets away with its cuteness by being one of the least changed of all the Gold Country towns, with a cluster of excellent shops and restaurants in the town center – all in all, a good, if pricey, base for following the many steep streets up into the surrounding forest.

A smart first stop is the **tourist office** (Mon–Fri 9am–5pm, Sat 11am–4pm; ☎1-800/655-6569, ⓦwww.nevadacitychamber.com) at 132 Main Street, a

▲ Broad Street, Nevada City

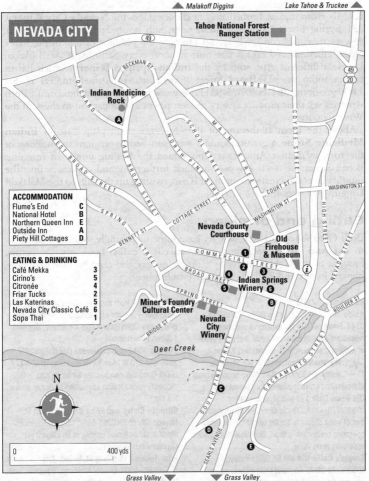

block north of Hwy-49, where you can pick up a free walking-tour **map** of the town. There aren't many specific points of interest, but one place to start is the restored, lacy-balconied and bell-towered **Old Firehouse**, at 214 Main Street, one block up from the tourist office, which houses a small **museum** (daily: May–Oct 11am–4pm; Nov–April Fri–Sun noon–3pm; donation) describing the social history of the region. The heart of town is Broad Street, which climbs up from the highway past the imposing 1854 **National Hotel** (see p.632) and a number of antique shops and restaurants, all decked out in Gold Country balconies and wooden awnings. Almost the only exception to the rule of picturesque nostalgia is the Art Deco 1937 **City Hall**, near the top of Broad Street.

The **Miner's Foundry Cultural Center** (Mon–Fri 10am–4pm; free), close to the Deer Creek Canyon at 325 Spring Street, is an old tool foundry converted into a multiuse cultural center, art gallery, performance space, and

KVMR radio studios. Immediately next door stands the **Nevada City Winery**, 321 Spring Street (Mon–Sat noon–6pm, Sun noon–5pm; ☎530/265-9463, Ⓦwww.ncwinery.com), where you can taste the produce of one of the state's oldest vineyards and take a free tour at noon every Saturday. If you'd like to sample a different glass, stop by the **Indian Springs Winery**, which has its tasting room at 303 Broad Street (Sun–Thurs 11.30am–5pm, Fri & Sat 11.30am–6pm; ☎1-800/375-9311, Ⓦwww.indianspringswines.com). Both wineries sell their product at very modest prices in comparison to those of the Wine Country.

Above the town at the top of Pine Street, a small plaque marks **Indian Medicine Stone**, a granite boulder with sun-beds worn into the hollows of the rock by Native Americans who valued the healing power of sunshine. Broad Street intersects Hwy-49 a block further on, and continues into the mountains as the North Bloomfield Road, twisting up the hills to the Malakoff Diggins (see opposite).

Eating and drinking

Both Grass Valley and Nevada City have some surprisingly sophisticated places to **eat and drink**, including a few excellent **cafés**. Look out for pasties, brought to the Gold Country by Cornish miners, and crisp Nevada City beer, brewed locally and available at better establishments.

Grass Valley

Kaido 207 W Main St, Grass Valley ☎530/274-0144. Smart but not too expensive Japanese restaurant serving excellent sushi and other dishes in authentic surroundings. Closed Sun & Mon.

Marshall's Pastries 203 Mill St, Grass Valley ☎530/272-2844. Mind-boggling array of fresh filled Cornish pasties, for takeout only.

Old Town Café 110 Mill St, Grass Valley ☎530/273-4303. Classic diner in a sharp renovation of what claims to be the oldest continuously operating restaurant in town. The breakfasts are an especially good value.

Sergio's Caffé 154 Mill St, Grass Valley ☎530/274-2600. Gourmet sandwiches, salads, and more substantial Italian entrées comprise the menu at this lively café/restaurant.

Sierra Railroad Café 111 W Main St, Grass Valley ☎530/274-2233. Decent diner food accompanied by the clatter of a model railroad continuously operating overhead. Breakfast & lunch only Sun–Thurs, all three meals Fri & Sat.

Swiss House 535 Mill St, Grass Valley ☎530/273-8272. The Central European decor in the heart of the Sierra foothills warrants at least a grin, and you might even be tempted to stay for one of the hearty, reasonably priced Swiss-German meals – try the schnitzel or apple strudel.

Nevada City

Café Mekka 237 Commercial St, Nevada City ☎530/478-1517. Relaxed, fabulously decorated

coffee shop – from exposed piping to trompe l'oeil wallpaper – popular with teenagers, trendies, and ex-hippies. Open 8am–11pm weekdays, and until 1.30am on weekends.

Cirino's 309 Broad St, Nevada City ☎530/265-2246 and 213 W Main St, Grass Valley ☎530/477-6000. Good deli sandwiches for lunch and modestly priced Italian specialties at dinner, plus a full bar.

Citronée Bistro and Wine Bar 320 Broad St, Nevada City ☎530/265-5697. Upscale American-Mediterranean fusion cuisine in an elegant yet unpretentious atmosphere.

Friar Tuck's 111 N Pine St, Nevada City ☎530/265-9093. Quality American, European, and Pacific Rim cuisine, including fondue dinners, are on the menu at this large and rather pricey establishment.

Las Katerinas 311 Broad St, Nevada City ☎530/478-0275. Huge portions of tasty Mexican favorites in cheerful, colorful surroundings. Closed Tues.

Nevada City Classic Café 216 Broad St, Nevada City ☎530/265-9440. Plain-looking all-American diner with eggs for breakfast and burgers for lunch.

Sopa Thai 312 Commercial St, Nevada City ☎530/470-0101. Wonderful, tasty, and moderately-priced Thai fare, served with a smile in a pleasantly decorated dining room.

Nevada County

Grass Valley, Nevada City, and the foothills of **NEVADA COUNTY** are as attractive now as they were productive in the gold heyday. Before the deep, hard-rock mines were established in the late 1860s, there were mining camps spread all over the northern Gold Country, with evocative names like "Red Dog" and "You Bet," that disappeared as soon as the easily recovered surface deposits gave out. **Rough and Ready**, five miles west of Grass Valley, survives on the tourist trade alone – visitors come to take a look at the only mining town ever to secede from the United States, which Rough and Ready did in 1850. The band of veterans who founded the town, fresh from the Mexican–American War, opted to quit the Union in protest against unfair taxation by the federal government, and although they declared their renewed allegiance in time for that summer's Fourth of July celebrations, the conflict was not officially resolved until 1948. Now the place – little more than a handful of ramshackle buildings, including a gas station and a general store – isn't really worth visiting, except perhaps for the old-time singalong with the Fruit Jar Pickers band that takes place every Sunday from 10am to noon in the town's tiny square. If you do pass through, the **Chamber of Commerce** (℡530/272-4320, Ⓦwww .roughandreadychamber.com) publishes a lengthy, well-written brochure on the town's history; you can usually find one at the post office or general store.

Six miles northwest of Rough and Ready, off the winding Bitney Springs Road in the **South Yuba River State Park**, stands the **Bridgeport covered bridge**, the longest single-span, wood-truss covered bridge in the world, spanning the Yuba River. The swimming spot underneath offers some relief from a hot summer's day, and the nearby visitor center (℡530/432-2546) has plenty of information on the area's hiking trails, guided wildflower, history, and birding tours, and the inevitable gold-panning demonstrations.

Malakoff Diggins State Park

The waters of the Yuba River are now crisp and clear, but when the Bridgeport Bridge was completed in 1862 they were being choked with mud and residue from the many **hydraulic mining** – or "hydraulicking" – operations upstream. Hydraulic mining was used here in the late 1850s to get at the trace deposits of gold that weren't worth recovering by orthodox methods. It was an unsophisticated technique: giant nozzles or monitors sprayed powerful jets of water against the gold-bearing hillsides, washing away tons of gravel, mud, and trees just to recover a few ounces of gold. It also required an elaborate system of flumes and canals – some still used to supply water to local communities – to collect the water, which was sprayed at a rate of over thirty thousand gallons a minute.

Camping in Nevada County

One of the easiest ways to get a feel for the day-to-day life of the miners is to "rough it" yourself, **camping** out in one of the many accessible campgrounds in the surrounding hills, which you can only reach by car. On Hwy-20, just east of Nevada City, *Gene's Pineaire Campground*, at 31041 Relief Hill Road, Washington (℡530/265-2832), and *Scott's Flat Lake*, on Scott's Flat Road (℡530/265-5302), are privately operated and have the best facilities; seven miles on, *White Cloud* is more remote – for details, contact the ranger station (℡530/265-4531) in Nevada City on Coyote Street, a quarter-mile north past the tourist office. Rates at all sites start at around $15, but can be more in the high season.

Worst of all, apart from the obvious destruction of the landscape, was the waste it caused, silting up rivers, causing floods, impairing navigation, and eventually turning the San Francisco Bay, nearly 150 miles away, a muddy brown.

Site of the worst offense, whose excesses caused hydraulic mining to be outlawed in 1884, was the **Malakoff Diggins**, sixteen miles up steep and winding North Bloomfield Road from Nevada City (or reachable via the sixteen-mile Tyler Foote Crossing Road, which turns off Hwy-49 twelve miles northwest of Nevada City). Here, a canyon more than a mile long, half a mile wide, and over six hundred feet deep was carved out of the red-and-gold earthen slopes. Natural erosion has softened the scars somewhat, sculpting pinnacles and towers into a miniature Grand Canyon, now preserved as a 3000-acre **state park** (summer daily; winter Sat & Sun sunrise–sunset; $5 per vehicle; ☎530/265-2740). While the park may seem just a short detour from Hwy-49 on your map, its interminable unmarked gravel roads and snaking bends may give you an eerie feeling. Old buildings from ghost towns around the Gold Country have been moved to the restored settlement of **North Bloomfield**, inside the park, where a small museum (June–Aug daily 10am–4pm; Sept–May Sat & Sun only; free with park entry; call ☎530/265-2740 for winter hours) shows a twenty-minute film on hydraulicking; there's a **campground** near the spooky cliffs ($20; ☎1-800/444-7275, ⊛www.reserveamerica.com). While in the area, those interested in yoga and spirituality mustn't miss **Ananda's Retreat Center** (☎1-800/346-5350, ⊛www.expandinglight.org), which occupies expansive mountainside grounds en route to the park at 14618 Tyler-Foote Road. Most of the grounds, shrines, and the visitor center are open to the public, and regular courses are scheduled.

Downieville and the High Sierra towns

From Nevada City, Hwy-49 climbs up along the Yuba River Gorge into some of the highest and most marvelous scenery in the Gold Country, where waterfalls tumble over sharp, black rocks bordered by tall pines and maple trees. In the middle of this wilderness, an hour's drive from Nevada City, **DOWNIEVILLE**, the most picturesque of the Gold Rush towns, spreads out along both banks of the river, crisscrossed by an assortment of narrow bridges. Hwy-49 runs right through the center of town, slowing to a near-stop to negotiate tight curves that have not been widened since stagecoaches passed through. Thick stone buildings, some enhanced with delicate wooden balconies and porches, others with heavy iron doors and shutters, face raised wooden sidewalks, as their backs dangle precipitously over the steep banks of the river.

For what is now a peaceful and quiet little hamlet of three hundred people, Downieville seems strangely proud of its fairly nasty history. It has the distinction of being the only mining camp ever to have hanged a woman, Juanita, "a fiery Mexican dancehall girl" who stabbed a miner in self-defense. A restored wooden gallows, last used in 1885, still stands next to the County Jail on the south bank of the river to mark this ghastly heritage. Across the river and two blocks north, at the end of a row of 1850s storefronts, the **Downieville Museum** (May–Oct daily 11am–4pm; donation; ☎530/289-3423) is packed full of odd bits and historical artifacts, including a set of snowshoes for horses and a scaled-down model of the local stamp mill, "made by the boys of the shop classes 1947–8." To ensure your visit is complete, pick up a walking-tour map of the town, which celebrated its 150th anniversary in the summer of 2002, from the phoneless and erratically opening **tourist kiosk** (May–Sept Sat & Sun only), on a prime grassy spot by the river.

For such a diminutive town there are several very decent **accommodation** options, including the *Riverside Inn* (℡1-888/883-5100, ⊛www.downieville .us; ❸) and the nicely refurbished *Carriage House Inn* (℡1-800/296-2289, ⊛www.downievillecarriagehouse.com; ❹), on opposite sides of the Yuba River where Hwy-49 crosses it. The *Sierra Shangri-La* (℡530/289-3455, ⊛www .sierrashangrila.com; ❸), 2.5 miles further northeast in thick woods above the river, has B&B rooms and fully fixtured cottages, the latter available by the week in summer.

Eating and drinking options can be found on Main Street at the family-style *Downieville Diner* (℡530/289-3616) or the inexpensive *Riverview Pizzeria* (℡530/289-3540), and the *Downieville Bakery & Café* (℡530/289-0108), on the corner of Commercial and Main streets, will prepare your favorite coffee drink.

The full-sized original of the museum's stamp mill model is maintained in working order at the **Kentucky Mine Museum** (summer Wed–Sun 10am–5pm; $2; ℡530/862-1310), a mile east of **Sierra City** further up Hwy-49, where a guided tour (11am & 2pm; $5) takes you inside a reconstructed miner's cabin and down a mineshaft to give you a look at various pieces of equipment used for retrieving gold-bearing ore. Until the mine was shut down during World War II, the ore was dug out from tunnels under the massive **Sierra Buttes**, the craggy granite peaks that dominate the surrounding landscape.

Sierra City is full of rustic charm and can be a useful base for visiting the surrounding area. Adequate **accommodation** is available year-round at *The Yuba River Inn* (℡530/862-1122, ⊛www.yubariverinn.com; ❸), a rustic, cabin-like spot east on Hwy-49 by the river, and in town at the *Old Sierra City Hotel*, 212 Main Street (℡530/862-1300, ✉oschotel@inreach.com; ❷). Seasonal places include the fairly plush *Busch & Heringlake Country Inn*, 231 Main Street (℡530/862-1501, ❹), and the more down-to-earth *Herrington's Sierra Pines* resort (℡1-800/682-9848, ⊛www.herringtonssierrapines.com; ❸), a little west of town. In the area you'll also find some of the most remote and attractive **campgrounds** in the Gold Country, including the *Sierra Campground*, seven miles beyond Sierra City, and *Chapman Creek*, another mile upstream on the Yuba River. All sites are $20 and can be reserved by calling High Sierra Campgrounds (℡530/993-1410). The best **place to eat** is the English-run *Red Moose Inn*, 224 Main Street (℡530/862-1990), which serves genuine fish'n'chips and filling sandwiches.

Hwy-49 continues east through the **Tahoe National Forest**, passing over the 6700-foot **Yuba Pass** on its way to join forces with Hwy-89 just north of Sattley at Bassett Junction. From here Hwy-89 heads north to Johnsville and south to Truckee and the Lake Tahoe area. Five miles south of the junction, there are basic facilities at **Sierraville**: at a pinch you could stay at the *Sierraville Motel* (℡530/994-3751; ❸) or stop for a quick meal or drink at *Los Dos Hermanos* (℡530/994-1058; closed Mon), both by the right-angle turn where the two highways separate again in the middle of the tiny town.

Johnsville

Founded in 1870, **Johnsville** is, after Bodie (see p.337), the best preserved and most isolated old mining town in California. Located 25 miles north of Bassett Junction and five miles off Hwy-89, the ghost town is surrounded by over seven thousand acres of pine forest and magnificent scenery and lies at the center of the **Plumas-Eureka State Park** – which has $20 campsites

(☎1-800/444-7275, ⓦwww.reserveamerica.com) and miles of **hiking** trails. Johnsville's huge stamp mill and mine buildings are being restored; in the meantime, a small museum (June–Sept daily 9am–4pm; donation) describes the difficult task of digging for gold in the High Sierra winters. Right in the center of the town's main road, the *Iron Door* (☎530/836-2376) serves up multinational cuisine, with an emphasis on steaks, schnitzel, and pasta, in the premises of the old general store. Back towards Hwy-89, the *Mohawk Café* (☎530/836-0901) offers quality bar food and snacks. For the rest of Plumas County and the Hwy-89 route northwest to Lassen Volcanic National Park, see p.736.

The southern mines

Though never as rich or successful as the diggings further north, the camps of the **southern mines** had a reputation for being the liveliest and most uproarious of all the Gold Rush settlements and inspired most of the popular images of the era: Wild West towns full of gambling halls, saloons, and gunfights in the streets. Certainly the southern settlements were more ethnically varied than those to the north, even if most groups firmly stuck together – Sonora, for instance, was established by Mexican immigrants and Chinese Camp was almost exclusively Asian. The mining methods here were also very different from those used north of here. Instead of digging out gold-bearing ore from deep underground, claims here were more often worked by itinerant, roving prospectors searching for bits of gold washed out of rocks by rivers and streams, known as **placer** gold (from the Spanish word meaning both "sand bar," where much of the gold was found, and – appropriately – "pleasure"). Nuggets were sometimes found sitting on the riverbanks, though most of the gold had to be laboriously separated from mud and gravel using handheld pans or larger sluices.

Mining wasn't a particularly lucrative existence: freelance miners roamed the countryside until they found a likely spot, and if and when they struck it rich they quickly spent most of their earnings, either in celebration or on the expensive supplies needed to carry on digging. Unsurprisingly, the boom towns that sprang up around the richest deposits were abandoned as soon as the gold ran out, but a few slowly decaying ghost towns have managed to survive more or less intact to the present day, hidden among the forests and rolling ranchland. Other sites were buried under the many **reservoirs** – built in the 1960s to provide a stable source of water for the agricultural San Joaquin Valley – that cover much of the lower elevations.

During spring, the hillsides are covered in fresh green grasses and brightly colored wildflowers, though by the end of summer the hot sun has baked everything to a dusty golden brown. Higher up, the free-flowing rivers rush through steep canyons lined by oak trees and cottonwoods, and the ten-thousand-foot granite peaks in the Sierra Nevada above offer excellent skiing in winter, and hiking and camping in the pine and redwood forests all year round. South from Placerville, Hwy-49 passes through **Jackson**, which makes a convenient, if unattractive, base for exploring the many dainty villages scattered around the wine-growing countryside of **Amador County**; then the highway continues on through the mining towns of **Calaveras County**. The center of **Tuolomne County** and the southern mining district is still **Sonora**, a small, prosperous town of ornate Victorian houses set on ridges above steep gorges. Once an archrival but now a ghost town, neighboring **Columbia** has a carefully restored Gold Rush-era Main Street. The gold-mining district actually extended as far south as **Mariposa**, but the mines here were comparatively worthless and little remains to make it worth the trip, except perhaps as a quick stop on the way to Yosemite National Park (see p.384).

You'll need your own **transportation** to see much of the southern Gold Country. Trains steer well clear of the hilly terrain and buses only pass through Mariposa on their way from Fresno and Merced to Yosemite. Drivers be warned – **speed traps** are rampant around the southern mines, particularly in Amador County and on any roads leading to Yosemite, where the speed limits tend to be a bit unrealistic and regional traffic police eagerly await to rake in tourist revenue.

Amador County

South from Placerville and US-50, the old mining landscape of **AMADOR COUNTY** has been given over to the vineyards of one of California's up-and-coming **wine-growing** regions, best known for its robust Zinfandel, a full-flavored vintage that thrives in the sun-baked soil. Most of the wineries are located above Hwy-49 in the Shenandoah Valley, near Plymouth on the north edge of the county. For a detailed map to all the local establishments, contact Amador Vintners in Plymouth (☎1-888/655-8614, ⓦwww.amadorwine.com).

Amador City and Sutter Creek

About thirty miles east of Sacramento, Hwy-16 joins Hwy-49 at **Amador City**, whose short strip of antique shops gives it a cutesy Old West look. The landmark *Imperial Hotel* at the northern edge dominates the town, its four-foot-thick brick walls standing at a sharp bend in Hwy-49 and enclosing sunny double **rooms** (☎209/267-9172, ⓦwww.imperialamador.com; ❺). Another option is the *Mine House Inn*, on the way to Sutter Creek (☎1-800/646-3473, ⓦwww.minehouseinn.com; ❺) – as its name suggests, this place is a fancy conversion of an old 1870s mining office and now boasts luxury rooms and a solar-heated pool. The secluded *Rancho Cicada Retreat*, at 10001 Bell Road near Plymouth (May–Oct only; ☎1-877/553-9481, ⓦwww.ranchocicadaretreat.com; tents ❹, cabins ❺), offers nature walks and group activities. A great place to grab a snack or picnic fixings is *Andrae's Bakery & Cheese Shop*, 14141 Hwy-49 (☎209/267-1352), which does gourmet sandwiches, cakes, and other tasty items.

Sutter Creek, two miles south, is much larger than Amador City, but still little more than a row of tidy antique shops and restaurants catering to tourists along Hwy-49. Though there are a number of surprisingly large Victorian wooden homes – many styled after Puritan New England farmhouses – the town lacks the disheveled spontaneity that animates many of the other Gold Rush towns, perhaps because its livelihood was never based on independent prospectors panning for placer gold, but on hired hands working underground in the more organized and capital-intensive hard-rock mines. It was a lucrative business for the mine owners. The **Eureka Mine** operated until 1958: it was owned by one

Black Bart

The mysterious man known as **Black Bart** made an unlikely highwayman: Charles E. Bowles – sometimes Bolton – was a prominent and respectable San Francisco citizen in his 50s who claimed to be a wealthy mining engineer. In fact, Charles' background was rather more checkered: born to a farmer father in England, he'd emigrated to America as a child and moved to California to try his luck in the Gold Rush. His luck failed and, now married with children, Bowles enlisted in the Union Army, fighting through the Civil War.

Unsurprisingly, it left him a changed man; and once discharged, he drifted around the West Coast, losing contact with his family and trying his hand at silver mining. Finally, in 1875, Charlie turned to crime: over the next eight years, he'd commit almost thirty **stagecoach robberies** and yield a then-staggering income of $6000 a year. But what set Bart apart wasn't his money but his manners. No brutal thug, he instead always addressed his victims as "Sir" and "Madam," never shot them, and in a waggish touch, sometimes recited fragments of poetry before escaping with the loot (his name was pinched from a fictional story published in a local paper that mythologized a merciless criminal known as Black Bart).

But Bart's luck only held so long: he was finally discovered after dropping a handkerchief at the scene of a hold-up, the police nabbing him by tracing the laundry mark back to a San Francisco laundry and from there to Bowles. He spent four years of a six-year sentence in **San Quentin** (of course, it was commuted for good behavior) and, after his release, disappeared without trace.

Hetty Green, the Warren Buffet of her day and at one time the richest woman in the world; at her death in 1916, her estate was worth $100 million. She, however, was notorious for her cheapness, wearing old shabby clothes and giving nothing to charity. Hetty earned her nickname "The Witch of Wall Street" from fellow investors who envied her savvy ruthlessness. Leland Stanford was more generous with the money he made from the **Lincoln Mine**, if no more personally endearing: he become a railroad magnate and governor of California, but used a chunk of his fortune to endow Stanford University (for more on Stanford and his cronies, see the box on p.589).

Sutter Creek holds the bulk of Amador County's **accommodation** and **eating** choices, with two central and very comfortable B&Bs: *The Foxes*, 77 Main Street (T 1-800/987-3344, W www.foxesinn.com; ❻), with well-appointed rooms and claw-foot baths; and the larger, more communally minded *Sutter Creek Inn*, 75 Main Street (T 209/267-5606, W www.suttercreekinn.com; ❹), with no TVs, no phones, and no fake Victoriana, but a nice garden with hammocks and a welcoming atmosphere. The *American Exchange Hotel*, 53 Main Street (T 1-800/892-2276, W www.americanexchangehotel.com; ❸), has the cheapest accommodation in town and *Belotti's* **restaurant** below (T 209/267-5211) serves full meals and pasta dishes for $13–15. *Susan's Place*, in the Eureka Street Courtyard, a half-block east of Hwy-49 (lunch only Thurs–Sun, dinner Fri & Sat; T 209/267-0945), serves sandwiches, soups, and salads under a shaded gazebo and, across the street, the *Sutter Creek Coffee Roasting Co.* (T 209/267-5550) serves the best coffee in town. For dessert, don't miss the *Sutter Creek Ice Cream Emporium*, 51 Main Street (T 209/267-0543), where the friendly owner will play Scott Joplin tunes on the piano while you sip a milkshake.

Jackson

After Sutter Creek, the town of **Jackson**, four miles south, can seem distinctly blue-collar, mainly because of the huge Georgia Pacific lumber mill that serves as its northern gateway. Nevertheless, it's a more affordable base for exploring the surrounding countryside. Most of the well-preserved buildings in the small historic downtown area were erected after a large fire in 1862, and today are a bit drowned out by the encroaching modern businesses that surround it. Note the lovely, if architecturally inappropriate, 1939 Art Deco front on the **County Courthouse** at the top of the hill, while further along the crest, the **Amador County Museum**, 225 Church Street (Wed–Sun 10am–4pm; donation; ℡209/223-6386), has displays of all the usual Gold Rush artifacts, but is worth a look most of all for its detailed models of the local hard-rock mines – with shafts over a mile deep – that were in use up until World War II. The headframes and some of the mining machinery are still standing a mile north of the museum on Jackson Gate Road, where two sixty-foot-diameter **tailing wheels** (8am–dusk; free), which carried away the waste from the Kennedy Mine, are accessible by way of short trails that lead up from a well-signposted parking area. The headframe of the 6000-foot shaft, the deepest in North America, stands out at the top of the slope, along Hwy-49. The other major mine in Jackson, the **Argonaut Mine** (of which nothing remains), was the scene of a tragedy in 1922, when 47 men were killed in an underground fire.

The **Amador County Chamber of Commerce**, 125 Peek Street (Mon–Fri 8am–5pm; ℡209/223-0350 or for lodging info 1-800/726-4667, Ⓦwww .amadorcountychamber.com), is rather awkwardly situated at the junction of Hwy-49 and Hwy-88, but offers a *Visitor's Guide to Amador County*, full of the usual maps and historical information. The best place to stay is the friendly, if slightly run-down, *National Hotel*, 2 Water Street (℡209/223-0500, Ⓔnationalhotel @volcano.net; ➍), an 1860s hotel with individually decorated rooms like the "Bordello Room" with flock wallpaper, a four-poster bed, and a freestanding bathtub on iron claw feet. Other options include the *Amador Motel* (℡209/223-0970; ➋) or the *Jackson Lodge* (℡1-888/333-0486; ➋), both on Hwy-49 north of town. *Mel and Faye's Diner*, 211 Mountain View Drive (℡209/223-0835), on Hwy-49 near the town center, is open all day for **breakfasts and burgers**, while *Café Max Swiss Bakery*, 140 Main Street (℡209/223-0174), serves pastries and a mean cup of coffee until 6pm Monday to Saturday. For **drinking**, the *Fargo Club*, 2 Main Street (℡209/223-3859), is the modern equivalent of a Wild West saloon, with cheap beers and all-night poker games.

Indian Grinding Rock and Volcano

Hwy-88 heads east from Jackson up the Sierra crest, through hills that contain one of the most fitting memorials to the Native Americans who lived here for thousands of years before the Gold Rush all but wiped them out. Nine miles from Jackson, off Hwy-88, a side road passes by the **Indian Grinding Rock State Historic Park** (daily dawn–dusk; $6 per car; ℡209/296-7488, Ⓦwww .parks.ca.gov), where eleven hundred small cups – *Chaw'Se* in Miwok – were carved into the marbleized limestone outcropping to be used as mortars for grinding acorns into flour. It's the largest collection of bedrock mortars in North America, and if you arrive near dawn or dusk and look closely from the small elevated platform next to the biggest of the flat rocks, you can just detect the faint outline of some of the 360 **petroglyphs** here. The state has developed the site into an interpretive center and has, with the close participation of tribal elders and community leaders, constructed replicas of Miwok dwellings and religious buildings. Descendants of the Miwok gather here during the weekend following the fourth Friday in September for **Big Time**, a celebration of the survival of their culture with traditional arts, crafts, and games. At the entrance to the site, the **Chaw'Se Regional Indian Museum** (Mon–Fri 11am–3pm, Sat & Sun 10am–6pm; ☎209/296-7488) explores the past and present state of the ten Sierra Nevada native groups in a building said to simulate a Miwok roundhouse. The full process of producing acorn flour is covered, but the lack of information on modern Miwok life is a sad testament to the extent of the devastation done to the culture. If you'd like to spend the night, a **campground** in the surrounding woods costs $20 per pitch; space is not reservable and is on a first-come-first-served basis. Note that the campground is closed for Native American gatherings on the third weekend in May, third weekend in June, and last weekend in September.

Named after the crater-like bowl in which it sits, **VOLCANO**, a tiny village a mile and a half north, once boasted over thirty saloons and dancehalls. Today, it claims nearly as many historic sites as Jackson but has been mercifully bypassed by all the latter's development and traffic. The densely forested countryside around the village makes it well worth a visit, especially during spring (particularly mid-March to mid-April) when **Daffodil Hill**, three miles north of Volcano, is carpeted with more than 300,000 of the bobbing heads. Signs directing you there are only displayed when the flowers are in bloom. Its other notable attraction is the creaky cannon known as "Old Abe": locals threatened to fire it at a rebellious band of confederate sympathizers during the Civil War – the sole skirmish to take place in California, even though not a single shot was actually exchanged. The only **accommodation** in the immediate area is the friendly *St George Hotel* on Main Street (☎209/296-4458, ⓦwww .stgeorgehotel.com; ❹), offering bed and breakfast without the comforts of televisions, phones, or private bathrooms. Guests congregate in the restaurant and bar, whose walls are decked with every office poster and wisecrack bumper sticker imaginable.

Highway-88

Highway-88 heads east beyond the Volcano turnoff to Pioneer, where it meets Hwy-26 from Mokelumne Hill (see opposite). Three miles east, the **Forest Ranger Station** (Mon–Fri 8am–4.30pm; ☎209/295-4251) supplies wilderness permits for overnighting in the **Mokelumne Wilderness**, a segment of the Stanislaus and Toiyabe national forests south of Hwy-88, which closely follows the route of many early settlers. The ranger station also has details of camping and hiking in the **Eldorado National Forest**, beautiful in the fall, just before the winter snows turn the Sierra Nevada around the 8500-foot Carson Pass into Kirkwood, one of California's best ski resorts (see box, p.653). For more off-the-beaten-path recreation, try the **Bear River Lake Resort** (☎209/295-4868; campsite $25, rooms ❹), just south of Hwy-88 on the way to Kirkwood and Tahoe, which offers camping, hiking, fishing, swimming, and boating, without all the hype of the better-known resorts.

Calaveras County

CALAVERAS COUNTY lies across the Mokelumne River, eight miles south of Jackson, and is best known for being the setting of Mark Twain's first published story, *The Celebrated Jumping Frog of Calaveras County*. Today, precious few sights of historic interest remain, though there are plenty of options in the country for rugged outdoor recreation. The most northerly town in the county,

Mokelumne Hill, or "Moke Hill," was as action-packed in its time as any of the southern Gold Rush towns, but tourism has been slower to take hold here, and today the town is an all-but-abandoned cluster of ruined and half-restored buildings, not without a certain melancholy appeal. The **Mokelumne Hill History Society**, 8367 East Center (Tues & Wed 10am–5pm, Thurs 1–5pm, Fri & Sat 10am–2pm; summer Sat & Sun 11am–3pm; donation; ℡209/286-0507, Ⓦwww.mokelumnehillhistory.org), has a modest exhibit on the history of the immediate area, once home to almost ten thousand people. The range of names and languages on the headstones of the **Protestant Cemetery**, on a hill a hundred yards west of town, gives a good idea of the mix of people who came from all over the world to the California mines.

San Andreas

Eight miles south, **San Andreas** hardly seems to warrant a second look: the biggest town for miles, it's now the Calaveras County seat, and has sacrificed historic character for commercial sprawl. The Calaveras County **Chamber of Commerce** publishes a handy map to the county that includes recreational activities in the area; it's available from the visitor center in Angels Camp (see p.646). What remains of old San Andreas survives along narrow Main Street, on a steep hill just east of the highway, where the 1893 granite-and-brick County Courthouse has been restored and now houses an interesting collection of Gold Rush memorabilia in the **Calaveras County Museum**, 30 N Main Street (daily 10am–4pm; $2; ℡209/754-4658). Local history buffs have put together a detailed and diverse show: there are gold nuggets and miners' tools, like sluice boxes and baskets, as well as Miwok artifacts and a replica of an 1880s general store. Local **nightlife** revolves around the *Black Bart Inn*, 35 N Main Street

---

The limestone caverns in the Gold Country

Limestone caverns abound in the southern Gold Country: three have been developed expressly for public tours, the largest of which is the **Moaning Caverns** in Vallecito, just south of Hwy-4 and five miles east of Angels Camp off Parrots Ferry Road (mid-May to mid-Sept daily 9am–6pm; rest of year Mon–Fri 10–5pm, Sat & Sun 9am–5pm; $12.95 walking tour, $59 rappeling tour; ℡1-866/732-2837, Ⓦwww .caverntours.com). Although discovered by gold miners in 1851, bones have been found here dating back 13,000 years. It didn't take long for locals to recognize the lucrative potential of the eerie, lacy rock formations, and the caves were opened as a tourist attraction in 1919. The owners first inserted a 234-step spiral staircase to facilitate access and then corked the cavern's opening by building a gift shop on top of it: ironically, these renovations wrecked the cave's natural acoustics and muted the moaning sounds after which it's named.

The same company oversees **California Cavern** in Calaveras (mid-May to mid-Sept daily 10am–5pm; rest of year Mon–Fri 11am–4pm, Sat & Sun 10am–4pm; $12.95; contact details above), a horizontal network of caves that's a better choice for vertigo sufferers unwilling to brave the precipitous stairs at Moaning Caverns. Here, you can even take a four-hour Middle Earth Expedition ($135, reservations essential) wearing coveralls and a lighted helmet, and following a professional guide through miles of craggy recesses. The last of the local commercially developed sites, **Mercer Caverns**, a mile north of Murphys on Sheep Ranch Road, is known for the spectacular stalagmite and stalactite formations in its 800-foot-long gallery, resembling swooping angels' wings and giant flowers (Memorial Day to Sept Sun–Thurs 9am–5pm, Fri & Sat 9am–6pm; Oct–April daily 10am–4.30pm; $12; ℡209/728-2101, Ⓦwww.mercercaverns.com).

(℡209/754-3808, ⓦwww.blackbartinn.com; ❶), across the street, which hosts bands on weekends and also offers inexpensive **accommodation**. It's named after the gentleman stagecoach robber who was captured and convicted here (see box, p.642).

Angels Camp and Carson Hill

The mining camps of southern Calaveras County were some of the richest in this part of Gold Country, both for the size of their nuggets and for the imaginations of their residents. The author Bret Harte spent an unhappy few years teaching in and around the mines in the mid-1850s and based his short story, *The Luck of Roaring Camp*, on his stay in **Angels Camp**, thirty miles south of Jackson. There isn't much to see here these days, though the downtown feels mildly authentic. The **visitor center** is in a single-story clapboard building with a wide veranda at 1211 S Main Street (Mon–Sat 9am–5pm, Sun 11am–3pm; ℡1-800/225-3764, ⓦwww.visitcalaveras.org) and has plenty of information on the surrounding area as well as copious frog-related memorabilia in honor of **Mark Twain**. The saloon in the *Angels Hotel* on Main Street is where 29-year-old Twain heard a tale that inspired him to write his famous story, *The Celebrated Jumping Frog of Calaveras County*, about a frog-jumping competition (the saloon is now a discount tire store). Aside from the relentless onslaught of frog-themed souvenirs, the most unfortunate legacy of Twain's story is the **Jumping Frog Jubilee**; it's held with the local state fair on the third weekend in May each year and inexplicably attended by thousands of people who come to watch as pet amphibians compete to see who can jump farthest. On the north side of town, the **Angels Camp Museum**, 753 Main Street (summer daily 10am–3pm; winter Weds–Sun 10am–3pm; $1; ℡209/736-2963), presents a cornucopia of gold-excavating equipment and memorabilia, as well

as a carriage barn filled with historic horse-drawn vehicles. Unsurprisingly, the place **to stay** is called the *Jumping Frog Motel* (℡1-888/850-3764, ⓦwww.jumpingfrogmotel.com; ❷), at 330 Murphy's Grade Road.

Carson Hill, now a ghost town along Hwy-49 four miles south of Angels Camp, boasted the largest single nugget ever unearthed in California: 195 pounds of solid gold fifteen inches long and six inches thick, worth $43,000 when it was discovered in 1854 and well over a million dollars today. Nearby, **New Melones Reservoir** is the third largest reservoir in California and has all the camping ($12 for tent-only, $16 for RV and tent site; reservations ℡1-877/444-6777, ⓦwww.reserveusa.com), swimming, hiking, boating, and other recreational possibilities you could hope for, not to mention spectacular, if man-made,

▲ Jumping frog, Angels Camp

views. It's seldom visited by the throngs who fly through the Gold Country on their way to pricier recreational areas: for more information, stop at the **visitor center** (daily 10am–4pm; ☎209/536-9094 ext. 22), just past Carson Hill on Hwy-49.

Murphys

Nine miles east of Angels Camp, up the fairly steep Hwy-4, **Murphys**' one and only street is shaded by locust trees and graced by rows of decaying monumental buildings. One of the Gold Country's few surviving wooden water flumes still stands on the town's northern edge, while the oldest structure here, at 470 Main Street, now houses the **Old Timer's Museum** (Fri–Sun 11am–4pm, Mon also in summer; donation; ☎209/728-1160), a small gathering of documents with a wall-full of rifles. You can take a free one-hour walking tour from here at 10am on Sundays. If you want to **stay** in town, head across the street to the old *Murphys Hotel*, 457 Main Street (☎1-800/532-7684, ⓦwww .murphyshotel.com; ❸), which hosted some of the leading lights of the boom days in its rustic double rooms. The **Calaveras Big Trees State Park** (visitor center open daily 11am–3pm; weekends only in winter 11am–3pm; park dawn–dusk; $6 per car; ☎209/795-3840, ⓦwww.parks.ca.gov), fifteen miles east, covers six thousand acres of gigantic sequoia trees, threaded with trails. It makes for fine ski touring in winter, with **hiking** and **camping** (no reservations; $20) the rest of the year. Murphys is also a mini gourmet paradise with a smattering of wine-tasting rooms and a disproportionate number of eateries for a town of its size. Try the swordfish, steaks, or pasta at slightly upscale *Grounds*, 402 Main Street (☎209/728-3248) or imaginative but pricey vegetarian fare at *Mineral* (☎209/728-9743).

Tuolomne County

The mountains get a little taller, the ravines sharper, and the scenery even more picturesque as Hwy-49 presses on south through **TUOLOMNE COUNTY**, which contains several more fascinating towns from the gold heyday.

Sonora

Sonora, fifteen miles southeast of Angels Camp, is the center of the southern mining district: it was the site of the **Bonanza Mine**, one of the most lucrative Gold Rush digs. Now a logging town set on steep ravines, it makes a good base for exploring the southern region: there are two settlement clusters, Historic Sonora and the commercial district known as East Sonora. There's little to see beyond the false-fronted buildings and Victorian houses on the main **Washington Street** and the Gothic **St James Episcopal Church** at its far end, but it's a friendly, animated place, worth spending an afternoon. The small **Tuolumne County Museum**, in the old County Jail at 158 W Bradford Avenue (Mon–Fri & Sun 10am–4pm, Sat 10am–3.30pm; free; ☎209/532-1317, ⓦwww.tchistory.org) is worth a look for the restored cellblock, if not for the collection of old clothes and photographs. There's also the superb Sonora Used Books at 21 S Washington Street (☎209/532-1884), with a vast selection of cheap paperbacks in good condition. Pick up architectural and historical walking-tour **maps** ($1) from the **Tuolumne County Visitors Bureau**, 542 W Stockton Street (April–Sept Mon–Fri 9am–7pm, Sat 10am–6pm, Sun

10am–5pm; Oct–March Mon–Fri 9am–6pm, Sat 10am–6pm; ☏1-800/446-1333, ⊛www.thegreatunfenced.com).

Washington Street contains just about all the town's facilities. One of the best-value **hotel** options in Sonora is the old adobe *Gunn House* at 286 S Washington Street (☏209/532-3421, ⊛www.gunnhousehotel.com; ❸), which has large, slightly dark rooms; for a few dollars more, the *Sonora Days Inn*, 160 S Washington Street, is more central, although its decor has seen better days (☏1-866/732-4010, ⊛www.sonoradaysinn.com; ❸).

For **lunch**, try *Café Soma*, at no. 230 (☏209/532-8858), which serves organic goodies including sandwiches and pancakes, or treat yourself to a delicious ice cream or smoothie in the classic parlor within Legends Books & Antiques at no.131 (☏209/532-8120). After dark, there are several good options: *Alfredo's*, at no. 123 (☏209/532-8332), is widely regarded as the best reasonably priced Mexican restaurant in these parts, serving standard burritos and enchiladas for $8 or so; otherwise, the *Diamondback Grill* at no.110 (☏209/532-6661) is a reliable option for hefty portions of meat for around $15. Of several **bars** on Washington, the retro *Iron Horse Lounge* at no. 97 (☏209/532-4482) is the best place to find a hint of the Wild West.

Columbia

Sonora's one-time archrival, tourist-loving **Columbia**, three miles north on Parrots Ferry Road, now passes itself off as a ghost town with a carefully restored Main Street that gives an excellent – if contrived – idea of what Gold Rush life might have been like, complete with period costumed staff in the local hotels and restaurants. The town experienced a brief burst of riches after Dr Thaddeus Hildreth and his party picked up thirty pounds of gold in just two days in March 1850. Within a month, over five thousand miners were working claims limited by local law to ten square feet, and by 1854 Columbia was California's second largest city, with fifteen thousand inhabitants supporting some forty saloons, eight hotels, and one school. Legend has it the town missed becoming the state capital by two votes – just as well, since by 1870 the gold had run out and Columbia was almost totally abandoned, but only after over two and a half million ounces of gold (worth nearly a billion dollars at today's prices) had been taken out of the surrounding area.

Thanks to agitation from locals, the entire town of Columbia is now preserved as a **State Historic Park** (daily 9am–5pm; ☏209/532-0150, ⊛www.parks .ca.gov), though it's also a genuine town with an active Main Street and year-round residents. Most of the surviving buildings date from the late 1850s, rebuilt in brick after fire destroyed the town a second time. Roughly half of them house historical exhibits – including a dramatized visit to the frontier dentist's office, complete with a 200-proof anesthetic and tape-recorded screams. The rest have been converted into shops, restaurants, and saloons, where you can sip a sarsaparilla or munch on a hot dog. Two notable structures are the **Claverie Mason Building**, once the heart of Columbia's Chinatown, and the atmospheric ruins of the **Bixel Brewery**, a mile or so north along Main Street from downtown: although there's little to see now, it's an evocative change from the staged Victoriana in the center. As you might imagine, the park/town can be nightmarishly crowded, especially on **Living History Days** (early June), when volunteers dress up and act out scenes from old times. If you want to escape the crowds, the hokey but fun stagecoach ride (April–Sept Tues–Sun, Oct–March Fri–Sun 10am–4.45pm; $5–6.50; ☏209/588-0808) leaves hourly from the Wells Fargo Building and zips along the old mining trails around the town. Alternatively, take a trip to the **Matelot Gulch gold mine**, where nuggets are still occasionally found: ninety-minute tours ($12; hours vary ☎209/532-9693) start from the shack at the south end of Main Street and are hosted by amusingly crabby former miners. The modest **museum** (daily 10am–4pm) on Main Street also houses the local **visitor center** (☎209/536-1672, ⓦwww.columbiacalifornia.com).

If you want to **stay**, the *Columbia City Hotel* on Main Street (☎1-800/532-1479, ⓦwww.cityhotel.com; ❹) is luxurious and central with a gourmet restaurant, while the *Columbia Inn Motel*, 22646 Broadway (☎209/533-0446, ⓦwww.columbiainnmotel.net; ❷), is basic but spotless, with a small pool and cheery staff. Alternatively, a mile south of town, the *Columbia Gem Motel*, 22131 Parrots Ferry Road (☎1-866/436-6685, ⓦwww.columbiagem.com /business/gem; ❷), offers basic accommodation in rustic cabins. The best **food** in town is served up at the ⅀ *Lickskillet Café*, 11256 State Street (☎209/536-9599; Thurs–Sun only), whose owner learned the recipes for his multiethnic fare during his wide travels.

Jamestown

Three miles south of Sonora on Hwy-49, **Jamestown** serves as the southern gateway to the Gold Country for drivers entering on Hwy-120 from the San Francisco Bay Area. Before 1966, when much of Jamestown burned down in a fire, it was used as a location for many well-known Westerns: the classic TV series *Little House on the Prairie* spent several seasons filming in town, and Clint Eastwood shot scenes for his Oscar-winning *Unforgiven* here. The train from that movie – also used forty years earlier in *High Noon*, starring Gary Cooper – can be found among many other steam giants in the **Railtown 1897 State Historic Park**, Jamestown's biggest attraction, five blocks east of Main Street at Fifth and Reservoir (daily: April–Oct 9.30am–4.30pm; Nov–March 10am–3pm; $2; ☎209/984-3953, ⓦwww.railtown1897.org). On weekends from April to October, you can ride one of the vintage trains for an additional fee (hourly 11am–3pm; $8). Along with its train collection, Jamestown is one of the few Gold Country towns that still has a **working mine** – the huge open-pit Sonora Mining Corporation west of town on Hwy-49 – and a number of outfits take visitors on gold-mining expeditions. Among them, Gold Prospecting Expeditions, 18170 Main Street (from $25 for 1hr; ☎1-800/596-0009, ⓦwww .goldprospecting.com), gives brief instruction in the arts of panning, sluicing, and sniping, and allows you to scrape what you can from its local stream – although don't expect to strike it rich. Main Street is the town's central thoroughfare, with a few **accommodation** choices: the *National Hotel*, 77 Main Street (☎1-800/252-8299, ⓦwww.national-hotel.com; ❹), has nine rooms and a casually elegant restaurant with a small bar. Nearby is the plush and historic ⅀ *Victorian Gold B&B* at 10382 Willow Street (☎1-888/551-1849, ⓦwww.victoriangoldbb.com; ❺): its antiquey rooms are a riot of Victoriana, most with claw-footed tubs and stained-glass windows. Otherwise, try the *Miner's Motel* (☎1-800/451-4176; ❷) on Hwy-108, almost halfway back towards Sonora.

For **food** on Main Street, try the popular diner, *Mother Lode Coffee Shop*, at no. 18169, which is open for breakfast or lunch (☎209/984-3386), or grab a gooey sundae at the old-fashioned *Here's the Scoop* ice-cream parlor, no. 18242 (☎209/984-4583). Nearby is the *Smoke Café* (☎209/984-3733), which serves tasty Southwestern-style Mexican food and huge margaritas in a touristy atmosphere; lunch specials hover around $6, and there's live music most nights.

Chinese Camp

Hwy-49 winds south from Sonora through some sixty miles of the sparsely populated, rolling foothills of **Mariposa County**, but first it passes the scant remains of the town of **Chinese Camp**. It was here that the worst of the Tong Wars between rival factions of Chinese miners took place in 1856, after the Chinese had been excluded from other mining camps in the area by white miners. Prejudice against all foreigners was rampant in the southern Gold Country, which accounts for its most enduring legend, that of the so-called Robin Hood of the Mother Lode, **Joaquin Murieta**. Though it's unlikely he ever existed, Murieta was an archetype representing the dispossessed Mexican miners driven to banditry by racist abuse at the hands of newly arrived white Americans. Today, amid the run-down shacks and trailers, there's little evidence of Chinese Camp's violent past, other than a historic marker on the main road.

Further south on Hwy-49 lie the southern Gold Rush towns of **Groveland** and **Mariposa**. Owing to their proximity to Yosemite National Park, they're covered in Chapter Five.

Lake Tahoe, Truckee, and into Nevada

High above the Gold Country, just east of the Sierra ridge, **Lake Tahoe** sits placidly in a dramatic alpine bowl, surrounded by high granite peaks and miles of thickly wooded forest. It's a big tourist area; the sandy beaches and surrounding pine-tree wilderness are overrun with thousands of fun-lovers (predominantly families) throughout the summer, and in winter, the snow-covered slopes of the nearby peaks are packed with skiers. The eastern third of the lake lies in Nevada, where gambling is legal, and therefore glows with light from the neon signs of the inevitable **Stateline casinos**.

Little visited beyond an influx of winter skiers, **Truckee**, fifteen miles north of Lake Tahoe, ranges along the Truckee River, which flows out of Lake Tahoe down into the desert of Nevada's Great Basin. **Donner Pass**, just west of town, was named in memory of the pioneer Donner family, many of whom lost their lives when trapped here by heavy winter snows.

Across the border in **Nevada**, **Reno**, at the eastern foot of the Sierra Nevada, is a downmarket version of Las Vegas, popular with slot-machine junkies and elderly gamblers; others come to take advantage of Nevada's lax marriage and divorce laws. Though far smaller than Reno, **Carson City**, thirty miles south, is the Nevada state capital, with a couple of engaging museums that recount the town's frontier history. Heading a little deeper into Nevada, and up into the arid mountains to the east, the silver mines of the **Comstock Lode**, whose wealth paid for the building of much of San Francisco, are buried deep below the evocative, if touristy, **Virginia City**.

Lake Tahoe

Fault-formed **LAKE TAHOE** is one of the highest, deepest, cleanest, coldest, and most beautiful lakes in the world. More than sixteen hundred feet deep, it is so cold – or so the story goes – that cowboys who drowned over a century ago have been recovered from its depths in perfectly preserved condition, gun holsters and all. The lake's position, straddling the border between California and Nevada, lends it a schizophrenic air, the dichotomy most evident at **South Lake Tahoe**, the lakeside's largest community, where ranks of restaurants, modest motels, and pine-bound cottages stand cheek by jowl with the high-rise gambling dens of **Stateline**, just across the border. **Tahoe City**, the hub of the lake's northwestern shore, does not escape the tourists but manages to retain a more relaxed – if somewhat exclusive – attitude. Expensive vacation homes and shabby family-oriented mini-resorts line much of the remainder of the lake. Tahoe is never truly off-season, luring weekenders from the Bay Area and beyond with clear, cool waters in the summer, snow-covered slopes in the winter, and slot machines all year round. On holiday weekends, expect traffic to reach maddening levels; convoys of cars and trucks spilling over with ski equipment and mountain bikes stretch throughout the area. To take advantage of the natural resources and still avoid at least some of the crowds, you might consider staying south of Tahoe near **Kirkwood**, though during peak times even that area can fill up quickly.

Arrival and information

One hundred miles east of Sacramento on both US-50 and I-80, Lake Tahoe is served by a number of coach **tours** but no longer Greyhound or Amtrak Thruway buses – coming from the Bay Area or Sacramento, you'll have to travel via Truckee (see p.661). South Tahoe Express **buses** ($24 one way, $43 round-trip; ☎1-866/898-2463, ⍟www.southtahoeexpress.com) run roughly every hour from 8.30am to midnight between Reno Airport and the Stateline casinos, while the North Lake Tahoe Express ($35 one way, $60 round trip; ☎1-866/216-5222, ⍟www.northlaketahoeexpress.com) links Reno Airport with Truckee, Tahoe City, and other North Shore destinations. If you're **driving**, expect to get here in a little over three hours from San Francisco, unless you join the Friday-night exodus, in which case you can add an hour or two, more in winter when you'll need to carry **chains**; call the Caltrans road phone (☎1-800/427-7623) to check on road conditions before you depart.

There are booths claiming to be visitor centers all over South Lake Tahoe, but most are just advertising outlets for the casinos or fronts for timeshare agents. For slightly more useful **information**, you can obtain maps and brochures, as well as some help with finding a place to stay, at one of the official visitor centers. The **South Lake Tahoe Chamber of Commerce**, 3066 US-50 (Mon–Fri 9am–5pm, Sat 9am–4pm; ☎530/541-5255, ⍟www.tahoeinfo.com), sits just before US-50 reaches the lake at El Dorado Beach. Just inside Nevada at 168 US-50, Stateline, lies the **Tahoe-Douglas Chamber & Visitor Center**, 195 US-50 (daily 9am–5pm; ☎775/588-4591, ⍟www.tahoechamber.org). The **Tahoe City Visitors Information Center**, 380 North Lake Boulevard in Tahoe City (daily 9am–5pm; ☎1-888/434-1262, ⍟www.gotahoenorth.com), is the best bet for information on the North Shore region. And lastly, the **Incline Village/Crystal Bay Visitors Bureau**, 969 Tahoe Boulevard (Mon–Fri 8am–5pm, Sat & Sun 10am–4pm; ☎1-800/468-2463, ⍟www.gotahoenorth.com), is another option on the Nevada side of the lake.

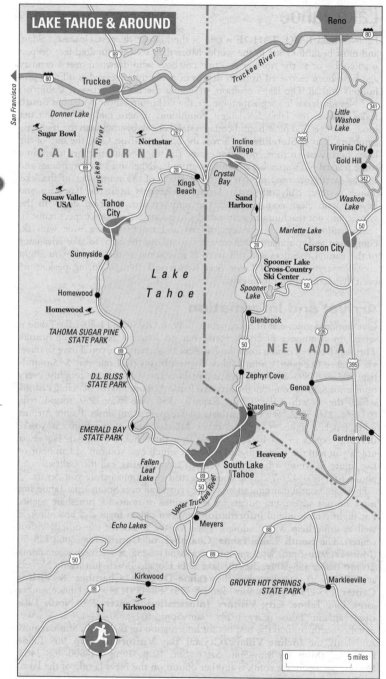

Reno

San Francisco

Truckee River

Truckee

Donner Lake

Sugar Bowl

Northstar

Little
Washoe
Lake

C A L I F O R N I A

Incline
Village

Virginia City

Gold Hill

Squaw Valley
USA

Kings
Beach

Crystal
Bay

Sand
Harbor

Washoe
Lake

Tahoe City

Marlette Lake

Carson City

Sunnyside

L a k e
T a h o e

Spooner Lake
Cross-Country
Ski Center

Homewood

Homewood

Spooner
Lake

TAHOMA SUGAR PINE
STATE PARK

Glenbrook

N E V A D A

D.L. BLISS
STATE PARK

Zephyr Cove

Genoa

EMERALD BAY
STATE PARK

Stateline

Gardnerville

Fallen
Leaf
Lake

Heavenly

South Lake
Tahoe

Upper Truckee River

Echo Lakes

Meyers

Kirkwood

GROVER HOT SPRINGS
STATE PARK

Markleeville

Kirkwood

N

0   5 miles

Lake Tahoe has some of the best **downhill skiing** in North America, and its larger resorts rival their Rocky Mountain counterparts. **Snowboarding** has, of course, caught on in a big way, and most resorts have now installed massive snow parks with radical halfpipes and jumps. The slopes are usually open from mid-November through April or later, with peak season January through March. Although skiing is certainly not cheap – the largest ski areas charge over $50 for the privilege of using their mountain for a single day at the busiest times – many resorts offer decent-value rental/lift ticket/lesson packages or multiday discounts.

The following list of ski resorts is not exhaustive, but highlights the best options for skiers of varying ability and financial standing. Skis can be rented at the resorts for about $28–32, and snowboards go for $35–40, but better deals for both can be found in the rental stores dotted around town. Pick up the *Reno–Tahoe Winter Vacation Guide for Skiers and Boarders* at any of the tourism information offices for a complete listing of resorts, along with prices and amenities. Rates below are for **high season** but even then discounts are available for multiple days, especially online.

Downhill skiing and snowboarding

Heavenly Reachable by shuttle from South Shore, 2 miles from the casinos (T1-800/243-2836, Wwww.skiheavenly.com). Prime location and sheer scale (82 runs, 27 lifts, 3500 vertical feet) make this one of the lake's most frequented resorts. Those not seeking to ski or snowboard can take the aerial tram for the view from the 8200-foot summit ($28). Lift tickets are $65.

Homewood Six miles north of Tahoe City on Hwy-89 (T1-800/824-6348, Wwww.skihomewood.com). Smaller and more relaxed than its massive neighbors, Homewood boasts some surprisingly good skiing with unbeatable views of the lake and reasonable prices. Lift tickets go for $44 with $25 "value days." Beginner package ($55) includes equipment, lesson, and beginner lift ticket.

Kirkwood Ski Resort South of Lake Tahoe on Hwy-88 (T1-877/547-5966, Wwww.kirkwood.com). Kirkwood manages to escape the overdeveloped feel of many of the Tahoe resorts while still providing some amazing skiing. Lift tickets are $59.

Squaw Valley USA Squaw Valley Road, halfway between Truckee and Tahoe City (T1-800/766-9321, Wwww.squaw.com). Thirty-one lifts service over 4000 acres of unbeatable terrain at the site of the 1960 Winter Olympics. Nonskiers can take the aerial tram ($19) and use the ice-skating/swimming pool complex ($27 including tram). Lift tickets including night skiing are $62; beginner packages from $62 include equipment and 2-hour lesson.

Sugar Bowl Ten miles west of Truckee at the Soda Springs–Norden exit (T530/426-9000, Wwww.sugarbowl.com). The closest ski area to San Francisco has ten lifts and newly expanded terrain. Inexplicably, this excellent mountain is often less crowded than others in the area. Lift tickets cost $59.

Cross-country skiing

Kirkwood Cross Country Center South of Lake Tahoe on Hwy-88 (T209/258-7248, Wwww.kirkwood.com). More than fifty miles of groomed track and skating lanes for cross-country enthusiasts. Trail fee is $18.

Royal Gorge In Soda Springs, 10 miles west of Truckee (T1-800/500-3871, Wwww.royalgorge.com). The largest and best of Tahoe's cross-country resorts has 204 miles of groomed trails. $28 trail fee, $19.50 rental fee, and $25–40 for lessons; good midweek discounts.

Spooner Lake In Nevada at the intersection of US-50 and Hwy-28 (T775/749-5349, Wwww.spoonerlake.com). The closest cross-country resort to South Lake Tahoe has lake views and 63 miles of groomed trails. Trail fees are $20, rentals $18.50, and lessons $42.50, including pass and rental.

Of the many wonderful hikes in the Lake Tahoe area, only one – the 150-mile **Tahoe Rim Trail** – makes the circuit of the lake, some of it on the **Pacific Crest Trail**, which follows the Sierra ridge from Canada to the Mexican border. Most people tackle only a tiny section of it, such as **Kingsbury Grade** to **Big Meadows** (22 miles), starting off Hwy-207 northwest of South Lake Tahoe and finishing on US-50, south of the lake.

There are also many **mountain-biking** trails around the lake: **Meiss County**, between Hwy-89 and Hwy-88 twenty miles south of South Lake Tahoe, is a favored area, where several beautiful lakes that escape most tourist itineraries are located. **Fallen Leaf Lake**, **Echo Lakes**, and **Angora Lake** are all pleasant, somewhat remote alternatives to the big T. Biking trails near the south shore include the three-mile loop of the **Pope-Baldwin Trail**, and you can pick up the popular **Marlett Lake/Flume Trail** in the Nevada State Park.

Ask at the **US Forest Service Visitor Center**, 870 Emerald Bay Road (summer daily 8am–5.30pm; ☏530/543-2674, ⊛www.fs.fed.us/r5), three miles northwest of the junction where Hwy-89 and US-50 separate to the west and east of the lake, for recommendations, free maps, and brochures on the entire area.

Camping

For overall range and quality of facilities, Lake Tahoe's best **campground** is *Campground by the Lake*, on the lakeshore three miles west of Stateline (☏530/542-6096; $23–31). Other South Shore sites include *Fallen Leaf* (☏530/544-0426, reserve through NRRS ☏1-877/444-6777, ⊛www.reserveusa.com; $20) and *Eagle Point* (☏530/541-3030, reserve on ☏1-800/444-7275, ⊛www.reserveamerica.com; $25), which is in Emerald Bay State Park. Details for sites at the *Camp Richardson* and *Zephyr Cove* resorts can be found in the accommodation listings on p.656. North Shore has several sites within striking distance of Tahoe City, including the nicely located *Tahoe State Recreation Area* (☏530/583-3074, reserve on ☏1-800/444-7275, ⊛www.reserveamerica.com; $25) right in the center, and just as crowded as you would expect. A mile and a half east, *Lake Forest* (☏530/583-3796; $15) is cheaper though further from the beach and cannot be reserved, and two miles southwest along Hwy-89, there's the large *William Kent* site (☏530/583-3642, reserve through NRRS ☏1-877/444-6777; $16). Halfway down the west shore, *Sugar Pine Point* (☏530/525-7982, reserve on ☏1-800/444-7275, ⊛www.reserveamerica.com; $25) has lovely sites in thick pine forest.

Along the western side of the lake, the Tahoe Rim Trail follows the Pacific Crest Trail through the glaciated valleys and granite peaks of the **Desolation Wilderness**. Here, **wilderness permits** ($5) are required by all users, though for day-users these are self-issued. For overnighters, a quota system operates in summer: fifty percent of these are first-come-first-served on the day of entry from the Forest Service visitor center; the remainder are reservable up to ninety days in advance (☏530/644-6048). Among the most strenuous trails here is the five-mile Bayview Trail to Fontanillis Lake. The other wilderness areas around Tahoe – Granite Chief to the northwest and Mount Rose to the northeast – are used much less and consequently no wilderness permits are needed, though campfire permits are.

Getting around

BlueGo **buses** (☏530/541-7149, ⊛www.bluego.org) run 24 hours a day all over the South Lake Tahoe area, and will take you anywhere within a ten-mile radius for a flat $1.75 fare ($3 buys you an all-day pass); the company runs trolleys for the same fares in summer. Tahoe Casino Express runs northeast from South Lake Tahoe to Glenbrook, then east to Carson City and Reno Airport. In the north, TART buses (roughly 6am–6pm; $1.50 flat fare, $3.50 for an all-day pass;

▲ Emerald Bay, Lake Tahoe

📞 1-800/736-6365, 🌐 www.laketahoetransit.com) run between Sugar Pine Point and Incline Village, with a branch route from Tahoe City up to Truckee. In addition, the Tahoe Trolley (same contacts and fares as TART) runs between Tahoe City and Crystal Bay (6am–6pm), and also between Sugar Pine Point and Emerald Bay (9am–6pm); in the evening there's a free service between Squaw Valley and Incline Village (6pm–midnight), with a short extra route between Sunnyside and Crystal Bay (7–10.30pm).

Car rental, starting at about $30 a day, is available through the Stateline outlets of most national chains – try Avis (📞 1-800/831-2847, 🌐 www.avis .com), Enterprise (📞 1-800/736-8222, 🌐 www.enterprise.com), and Hertz (📞 1-800/654-3131, 🌐 www.hertz.com). You could also **rent a bicycle** for around $24–40 a day from any of over a dozen lakeside shops in South Lake Tahoe – some of them offering a full range of **sports equipment rentals** – such as the Mountain Sports Center, Hwy-89 near the "Y" junction (📞 530/542-6584), Lakeview Sports, 3131 S Lake Boulevard (📞 530/544-0183), or the welter of outlets lining Ski Run Boulevard on the way to Heavenly. On North Lake Boulevard in Tahoe City, try Olympic Bike Shop, no. 620 (📞 530/581-2500), or The Back Country, no. 255 (📞 530/581-5861).

Accommodation

Most of the hundred or so **motels** that circle the lake are collected together along US-50 in South Lake Tahoe. During the week, except in summer, many have bargain rates, from around $45 for a double; however, these rates can easily double on weekends or in summer, so be sure to confirm – bear in mind the price codes below are based on the lowest high-season rates. Don't expect great deals at the **casinos**; there are fewer than in Las Vegas or Reno, and the casino hotels charge whatever the busy market will bear. If you're having trouble finding a room, try the tourist offices listed on p.651.

Tahoe City lacks the range and competition of its southerly neighbor, South Lake Tahoe, so you can expect to pay slightly more for a room there, although the reprieve from the Stateline bustle may just make the extra cost worth it if you're looking for peace and quiet. There are also a few other pleasant options dotted around the lake. **Camping** (see box, p.654) is only an option during summer.

South Shore

The Block 4143 Cedar Ave, South Lake Tahoe ☏1-888/544-4055, ⓦwww.theblockattahoe.com. Just off US-50, between the casinos and the lakeshore, this is the trendiest if not the cheapest motel in the area, with futuristic decor, a cybercafé, and games room. ❹

Camp Richardson Resort Hwy-89 between Emerald Bay and South Lake Tahoe ☏1-800/544-1801, ⓦwww.camprichardson.com. Hotel-style rooms and comfortable cabins with full kitchens on a 150-acre resort that also has campsites from $20. In summer, cabins are available by the week only from $940. ❹

Doug's Mellow Mountain Retreat 3787 Forest Ave, South Lake Tahoe ☏530/544-8065, ⓔhostelguy@hotmail.com. Essentially Doug's home, operating as a relaxed, if cramped, hostel with cooking facilities and occasional BBQs. Beds are $18 a night and double rooms are available. ❷

Driftwood Lodge 4115 Laurel Ave at Poplar, South Lake Tahoe ☏530/541-7400, ⓦwww.tahoedriftwood.com. The heated pool and private beach access make this otherwise very basic accommodation particularly appealing in summer; very close to Stateline. ❷

Harveys Lake Tahoe US-50, Stateline, Nevada ☏1-800/648-3353, ⓦwww.harrahs.com. Deluxe casino and resort; the best rooms overlook the lake. Packages include buffet brunches and spa discounts. ❻

Inn by the Lake 3300 Lake Tahoe Blvd, South Lake Tahoe ☏1-800/877-1466, ⓦwww.innbythelake.com. Nicely furnished rooms, a heated swimming pool and Jacuzzi, free breakfast, and use of bicycles render this relaxing spot good value for money. Free shuttle bus to the casinos. ❺

Pine Cone Acre 735 Emerald Bay Rd, between Emerald Bay and South Lake Tahoe ☏530/541-0375. Set in wooded grounds with a quieter location than most, the pleasant *Pine Cone Acre* offers a fridge and microwave in each room. ❸

Zephyr Cove Resort 760 US-50, Zephyr Cove, Nevada ☏1-800/238-2463, ⓦwww.zephyrcove.com. Run by the same management as the MS *Dixie II* (see opposite), its deluxe lodge rooms and lakeside cabins are away from the hubbub in a quiet, pine-clad nook. Also has expensive (around $60) RV sites. ❼

North Shore

Ferrari's Crown Motel 8200 N Lake Blvd, Kings Beach ☏1-800/645-2260, ⓦwww.tahoecrown.com. Relatively smart budget motel right by the lake, though you'll pay double for a room with a view. ❸

Lake of the Sky Motor Inn 955 N Lake Blvd, Tahoe City ☏530/583-3305, ⓦwww.lakeoftheskyinn.com. Better value than the slightly more expensive *Tahoe City Inn* opposite, with greater comfort and more pleasant decor. ❹

Mayfield House 236 Grove St, Tahoe City ☏1-888/518-8898, ⓦwww.mayfieldhouse.com. Quality B&B with plush rooms in the converted mansion and the quaint cottage behind. ❻

Parkside Inn at Incline 1003 Tahoe Blvd, Incline Village ☏1-800/824-6391, ⓦwww.innatincline.com. Nestled in a secluded forest setting, with private beach access, indoor pool, spa, and sauna. ❺

Pepper Tree Inn 645 N Lake Blvd, Tahoe City ☏1-800/624-8580, ⓦwww.peppertreetahoe.com. Heated pool and standard hotel accommodation in an otherwise rather characterless high-rise. ❹

Resort at Squaw Creek 400 Squaw Creek Rd, Olympic Valley ☏1-800/327-3353, ⓦwww.squawcreek.com. The area's most lavish resort with sweeping mountain views and luxurious accommodations, though rather a stilted atmosphere. There's a golf course, private ski lift, and shopping mall thrown in too. ❽

River Ranch Lodge Hwy-89 at Alpine Meadows Road, Alpine Meadows ☏1-800/535-9900, ⓦwww.riverranchlodge.com. Historic and casual lodge on the Truckee River with one of the lake's best restaurants (see p.660); the cheapest rooms are right above the dining room. ❸

🏃 **Sunnyside** 1850 W Lake Blvd, 1 mile south of Tahoe City ☏1-800/822-2754, ⓦwww.sunnysideresort.com. Large, comfortable mountain lodge right on the lakeshore. Unbeatable views of the lake from many rooms, and a popular restaurant on the ground floor (see p.660). ❹

Tahoma Meadows B&B 6821 W Lake Blvd, Tahoma ☏1-866/525-1553, ⓦwww.tahomameadows.com. Well-furnished rooms in a lovely setting on the west shore, 7 miles south of Tahoe City. ❺

Tamarack Lodge 2311 N Lake Blvd, 1 mile northeast of Tahoe City ☏1-888/824-6323,

@www.tamarackattahoe.com. Nestled on a pleasant wooded knoll, you'll get more for your money at this comfortable and clean lodging than almost anywhere else on the lake. ②

Further out

Sierrawood Guest House 12 miles from South Shore, Tahoe Paradise ☎1-800/700-3802, @www .sierrawoodbb.com. For that romantic getaway, a secluded chalet in the woods within a few minutes' drive of the casinos' glitter. Jacuzzi, exercise room, fireplace, and free snowmobiling on premises. Popular with gay and lesbian couples. ⑤

Sorensen's 14255 Hwy-88, Hope Valley ☎1-800/423-9949, @www.sorensensresort.com. Enveloped by the aspens of Hope Valley, about a half-hour drive away from South Shore on the west fork of the Carson River, *Sorensen's* features kitsch and cozy cabins with a Bavarian ski-lodge theme. ⑤

South Lake Tahoe and Stateline

Almost all of Tahoe's lakeshore is developed in some way or another, but nowhere is it as concentrated and overbearing as at the contiguous settlements of **South Lake Tahoe** and **Stateline**. The latter is compact, a clutch of gambling houses huddled, as you might expect, along the Nevada-California border. The half-dozen or so casinos compete for the attentions of tourists, almost all of whom base themselves in the much larger South Lake Tahoe on the California side. This is the best place to organize one of the many **outdoor activities** the lake has to offer. Power boating, water skiing, surfing, parasailing, scuba diving, canoeing, and mountain biking are just a few of the proposed activities on the menus of local sporting-equipment rental offices (see p.655). If you happen to lose your vacation allowance at the tables and slot machines, you can always explore the beautiful hiking trails, parks, and beaches that adorn the surrounding area.

Though many stretches of the route around Lake Tahoe are stunning, the entire 72-mile **drive** is perhaps not the most beautiful in America, as at least one locally produced brochure touts. A better way to see the lake is to take a **paddlewheel boat cruise**, on the *Tahoe Queen* from South Lake Tahoe or the MS *Dixie II* from Zephyr Cove, both reached on a free shuttle from South Lake Tahoe; they offer three to four cruises daily, the more expensive ones including dinner (call for times; $39–69; ☎1-800/238-2463, @www.zephyrcove.com /cruises). Even more impressive is the view of the lake from above, in one of the neighboring ski resort's **aerial trams**; the most convenient and popular is Heavenly's gondola (see p.653 for details), which runs from a smart terminal only a couple of blocks from Stateline. Finally, in lousy weather you can always visit the modest **Lake Tahoe Historical Museum**, next to the Chamber of Commerce at 3058 US-50 (Tues–Sat 10am–4pm; $2; ☎530/541-5458), which has a small collection of local artifacts and historical displays.

West around the lake

In summer, many enjoyable music and arts events take place at the **Tallac Historic Site** (mid-June to mid-Sept daily dawn-dusk; prices vary; ☎530/544-7383, @www.tahoeheritage.org), beside Hwy-89 on the western side of the lake just northwest of the "Y" (where Hwy-89 and US-50 separate to the west and east). Even when there's nothing special going on, the site's sumptuous wooden homes – constructed by wealthy San Franciscans as lakeside vacation retreats in the late 1800s – are well worth a look. You can also see the remains of the lavish casino-hotel erected by Elias "Lucky" Baldwin, which brought the rich and famous to Lake Tahoe's shores until it was destroyed by fire in 1914. Inside the former Baldwin house, the **Tallac Museum** (daily 10am–4pm; free) records the family's impact on the region.

The prettiest part of the lake, however, is along the southwest shore, where **Emerald Bay State Park**, ten miles from South Lake Tahoe (daily 8am–dusk; $6 per vehicle; ☎530/541-3030), surrounds a narrow, rock-strewn inlet. In the park, at the end of a steep, mile-long trail from the parking lot, is **Vikingsholm**, an authentic reproduction of a Viking castle built as a summer home in 1929 and open for half-hourly **tours** (summer daily 10am–4pm; $5). A short way out in the bay, diminutive **Fanette**, Lake Tahoe's only island, pokes pine-clad above the water. Its only structure is the defunct 1929 teahouse built by Vikingsholm's original owner, Lara Knight. From Vikingsholm, the stunning **Rubicon Trail** runs two miles north along the lakeside to **Rubicon Bay**, flanked by other grand old mansions dating from the days when Lake Tahoe was accessible only to the most well-heeled of travelers. You can also drive here on Hwy-89 and enter through the **D.L. Bliss State Park** (daily 8am–dusk; extremely limited parking $6; ☎530/525-7277), just to the north. Less than five miles further north, thickly pined **Sugar Pine Point State Park** (daily 8am–dusk; $6 per vehicle; ☎530/525-7982) offers more lakeside relaxation and has one of only two year-round campgrounds (see box, p.654) in the area. It also attracts crowds to see the 15,000-square-foot **Hellman–Ehrman Mansion** (guided tours daily 11am–4pm on the hour; $5), decorated in a happy blend of 1930s opulence and backcountry rustic, and surrounded by extensive lakefront grounds.

Lake Kirkwood and Grover Hot Springs State Park

About two dozen miles southwest of Tahoe, a dozen west of where Hwy-89 joins Hwy-88, **Lake Kirkwood** is home to a popular ski resort (see box, p.653) and is a destination in its own right, with plenty of **outdoor recreation** possibilities without all the Tahoe hype. Stop by the adventure center in Kirkwood Village (Mon–Fri 9am–5pm, Sat & Sun 9am–6pm; ☎209/258-6000) for information on accommodation, equipment rental, and hiking in the surrounding area, which holds nearly a dozen lakes, such as Winnemucca and Woods. For accommodation, try the *Lodge at Kirkwood* in the village, which must be booked through Kirkwood Central Reservations (☎1-800/967-7500, ⓦ www.kirkwood.com; ❹).

If you head a dozen miles southeast from the junction of Hwy-89 and Hwy-88, you'll come to **Markleeville**, a town of two hundred people on the Sierra crest. The major attraction here is the **Grover Hot Springs State Park**, four miles west (May to mid-Sept daily 9am–9pm; closed last two weeks in Sept; reduced hours through winter; $6 per vehicle; ☎530/694-2248), with two concrete, spring-filled tubs – one hot, one tepid – in which the water appears yellow-green due to mineral deposits on the pool bottom. There's a **campground** on site for $25 per night (book on ☎1-800/444-7275, ⓦ www .reserveamerica.com).

Tahoe City and around

TAHOE CITY, on the north end of the lake, is less developed and more compact than South Lake Tahoe, and a close-knit population of permanent residents coupled with a family-oriented atmosphere give it a more relaxed, peaceful disposition. Still, you're never far from the maddening tourist crowds who flock here all year long.

At the western end of town, Hwy-89 meets Hwy-28 at Fanny Bridge, named for the body part (posterior rather than anterior in American English) that greets drivers as people lean over the edge to view the giant trout in the **Truckee River**. Flow-regulating sluice gates at the mouth of the river are remotely controlled from Reno, but were once operated by a gatekeeper who lived in what is now the **Gatekeeper's Museum** (mid-June to early Sept daily 11am–5pm; May to mid-June & early to late Sept Wed–Sun 11am–5pm; $2; ☎530/583-1762), containing a well-presented hodgepodge of artifacts from the nineteenth century, and a good collection of native basketware. Nearby, the **Truckee River Bike Trail** begins its three-mile waterside meander west to the *River Ranch Lodge*, which is also the end of a popular river-rafting route. **Rafting** down the Truckee is the thing to do on warm summer days, though it's really more of a relaxing social affair than a serious or challenging adventure. Stop at one of several well-advertised boat-rental stands along the river across from the Chevron station, or call Tahoe White-water Tours (☎1-800/442-7238, ⓦwww.gowhitewater.com) for advance reservations. On the lake itself, an even more relaxed excursion is a **cruise** with the *Tahoe Gal* ($18–34; ☎1-800/218-2464, ⓦwww.tahoegal.com), leaving from the jetty at 850 N Lake Boulevard.

A couple of miles south along Hwy-89, five hundred yards past the Kaspian picnic grounds, it's well worth **hiking** ten minutes up the unmarked trail to the top of **Eagle Rock** (see box, p.654, for more ambitious hiking suggestions). The amazing panoramic views that surround you as you look down on the expansive royal-blue lake make this one of the world's greatest picnic spots. Several miles further south along Hwy-89 is **Chamber's Beach**, which, in summer, is as popular for sunning and **swimming** as it is for schmoozing.

You could also visit **Squaw Valley**, the site of the 1960 Winter Olympics, five miles west of Tahoe City off Hwy-89, although the original facilities (except the flame and the Olympic rings) are now swamped by the rampant develop-ment that has made this California's largest ski resort (see box, p.653). In the valley below, **hiking**, **horseback riding**, and **mountain biking** are all popular summertime activities.

East from Tahoe City are some unremarkable settlements but decent stretches of beach at **Tahoe Vista** and **King's Beach** on Carnelian Bay. As soon as you cross the Nevada state line from King's Beach into **Incline Village**, you're greeted by the predictable huddle of **casinos**, though they're not as numerous or in-your-face as at the south end of the lake. Consequently, the casual visitor might find having a flutter at the *Crystal Bay* or *Cal-Neva* somewhat less sordid and garish. Unfortunately the beaches here only open to guests at the casino hotels, but better swimming options are close at hand. Once you leave the buildings behind at the northeast corner of the lake and bear south, you enter one of the most appealing and quietest stretches. **Lake Tahoe Nevada State Park** boasts a great beach at **Sand Harbor**, though the water is always prohibi-tively cold, and has trails winding up through the backcountry to the Tahoe Rim Trail. Just south, **Secret Harbor** is an appropriate location for an idyllic nudist beach where gawkers are not tolerated.

Eating and drinking

South Lake Tahoe has few exceptional **restaurants**; average burger-and-steak places, rustic in decor with raging fireplaces, are commonplace. Far better are the **buffets** at the Nevada **casinos**, though they're not as cheap as in Reno or Vegas: *Harrah's*, for example, serves a wonderful, all-you-can-eat spread. The casinos are also good places to **drink** and hold most of the region's entertain-ment options: low-budget Vegas-style revues, by and large. For its size, Tahoe

City has a fair range of moderately priced restaurants as well as a couple of happening **bars**, all within a few minutes of each other.

South Shore

The Brewery at Lake Tahoe 3542 Lake Tahoe Blvd, South Lake Tahoe ⓣ 530/544-2739. Micro-brewery with decent ales ranging from pale to porter, and food specials such as beer-steamed shrimp and quality steaks.

Café Fiore 1169 Ski Run Blvd, South Lake Tahoe ⓣ 530/541-2908. Small and intimate, *Café Fiore* serves innovative, upscale Italian meals, accompanied by an extensive list of top-notch wines.

Nephele's 1169 Ski Run Blvd, South Lake Tahoe ⓣ 530/544-8130. Long-standing restaurant at the foot of the Heavenly ski resort, with a great selection of fairly expensive California cuisine: grilled meat, fish, and pasta dishes.

Red Hut Waffle Shop 2723 US-50, South Lake Tahoe ⓣ 530/541-9024. Ever-popular coffeeshop, justifiably crowded early winter mornings with skiers looking to load up on tasty carbs.

Rockwater Bar & Grill 787 Emerald Bay Rd ⓣ 530/544-8004. Big portions of appetizers, followed by a variety of Tex-Mex and seafood dishes at moderate to expensive prices, plus a decent bar.

Scusa! 1142 Ski Run Blvd ⓣ 530/542-0100. Subtly colorful decor and good service complement the fine seafood, steaks, and pasta at this well-respected Italian restaurant.

Six Bridges Bar & Grill 2500 Emerald Bay Rd, between South Lake Tahoe and Emerald Bay ⓣ 530/577-0788. Standard grill serving large portions of meaty fare in a quiet, wooded setting.

Sprouts 3123 US-50 near Alameda Ave, South Lake Tahoe ⓣ 530/541-6969. Almost, but not completely vegetarian, with excellent organic sandwiches, burritos, and smoothies.

Taj Mahal 3838 Lake Tahoe Blvd, South Lake Tahoe ⓣ 530/541-6495. Standard Indian fare with a cheap daily eleven-course lunch buffet.

Tep's Villa Roma 3450 Lake Tahoe Blvd, South Lake Tahoe ⓣ 530/541-8227. South Shore institution giving generous servings of hearty Italian food, including several simple yet superb vegetarian pasta dishes for about $10.

North Shore

Bridgetender Bar & Grill 30 W Lake Blvd, Tahoe City ⓣ 530/583-3342. Friendly rustic bar with good music, a fine range of beers, and huge portions of ribs, burgers, and more.

Hacienda del Lago 760 N Lake Blvd, Tahoe City ⓣ 530/583-0358. Tasty Mexican fare at moderate prices on the upper level of the Boatworks Mall; great lake views from the open deck. Margaritas and Latin or jazz music on many evenings.

Jasons' Beachside Grille 8338 N Lake Blvd, Kings Beach ⓣ 530/546-3315. Classic American fare with an emphasis on huge plates of meat, plus a salad bar and great desserts. Outside deck with lake views.

Lakehouse Pizza 120 Grove St, Tahoe City ⓣ 530/583-2222. In the Lakehouse Mall, Tahoe's best place for pizza is also a popular spot for cocktails on the lake at sundown. Be prepared to wait in winter.

Pierce Street Annex In the back of the Safeway complex, Tahoe City ⓣ 530/583-5800. The place for drinking and dancing on the North Shore. Packed with sunburned skiers or drunk beach-goers, depending on the season.

River Ranch Hwy-89 and Alpine Meadows Road, Tahoe City ⓣ 530/583-4264. A trendy place to watch whitewater rafters return from their adventures on the Truckee River as you kick back on the deck, nibbling moderately priced California cuisine.

Soule Domain Just before the state line and casinos at 9983 Cove Ave, King's Beach ⓣ 530/546-7529. Typical Tahoe rustic elegance in unexpected surroundings: Parisian chic in Davy Crockett territory. Lots of seafood and ethnic dishes, such as curried cashew chicken.

Spindleshanks 6873 N Lake Blvd, Tahoe Vista ⓣ 530/546-2191. American bistro and wine bar, serving imaginative dishes like pan-roasted artichokes and *chipotle* lime-marinated brick chicken at reasonable prices.

Sunnyside 1850 W Lake Blvd, Tahoe City ⓣ 530/583-7200. One of the most popular places to have cocktails at sunset, on the deck overlooking the lake.

Tahoe House Bakery Hwy-89, half a mile south of Tahoe City ⓣ 530/583-1377. Family-style bakery with lots of deli items for picnics. Popular with locals.

Yama Sushi and Robata Grill 950 North Lake Blvd, Tahoe City ⓣ 530/583-9262. An excellent range of tempura, sushi, and grilled *robata* dishes, all expertly prepared, makes this Lake Tahoe's top Japanese restaurant.

Za's 395 North Lake Blvd, Tahoe City ⓣ 530/583-1812. At the back of the friendly *Pete and Peter's* bar, this pizzeria also has a selection of pastas and a wide variety of sauces.

Truckee and around

Just off I-80 along the main transcontinental Amtrak route, **TRUCKEE**, fifteen miles north of Lake Tahoe, makes a refreshing change from the tourist-dependent towns around the lake. A small town mostly lining the north bank of the Truckee River, it retains a fair amount of its late nineteenth-century wooden architecture along the main section of Donner Pass Road, which many locals still refer to as Commercial Row; some of it appeared as backdrop in Charlie Chaplin's *The Gold Rush*. Truckee is usually viewed as more of a stopover than a destination in its own right, with a livelihood dependent on the logging industry and the railroad. However, the town's rough, lively edge makes it as good a base as any from which to see the Lake Tahoe area (public transport links the two; see p.654), a fact that hasn't escaped the businesses beginning to exploit the commercial opportunities.

Practicalities

Greyhound **buses** from San Francisco stop three times a day (four times heading west) in Truckee, from where five daily TART buses continue on to Tahoe City (see p.658). There's one daily Amtrak **train** in each direction from the station on Commercial Row in the middle of town. The **Chamber of Commerce**, 10065 Donner Pass Road (Mon–Fri 8.30am–5.30pm, Sat & Sun 9am–6pm; ☎530/587-2757, ⓦwww.truckee.com), has all the usual brochures and maps, as well as friendly staff; in addition, where Hwy-89 branches north off I-80, an easy-to-miss **Forest Service Ranger Station** (Mon–Fri 8am–4.30pm; ☎530/587-3558) offers details of camping and hiking in the surrounding countryside. To get around, rent a mountain bike for $25 a day (also kayaks, skiing, and climbing gear) from The Sports Exchange, 10095 W River Street (☎530/582-4520), or a car from Enterprise out at Albertson's Longs Shopping Center on Hwy-89 (☎530/550-1550, ⓦwww.enterprise.com).

Truckee's cheapest **place to stay** is the *Cottage Hotel*, 10178 Donner Pass Road (☎530/587-3108; ❶), central but a bit shabby with shared bathrooms. Much nicer is the *Truckee Hotel*, close to the train station at 10007 Bridge Street (☎1-800/659-6921, ⓦwww.thetruckeehotel.com; ❺), once decorated in the grand old railroad tradition and now decked out in Victorian B&B style; or the *The River Street Inn*, a quaint brick-and-wood building at 10009 E River Street (☎530/550-9290, ⓦwww.riverstreetinntruckee.com; ❹). At the top of the range is the splendid new alpine-style ⚡ *Cedar House Sport Hotel*, a few minutes' drive from downtown at 10918 Brockway Road (☎530/582-5655, ⓦwww.cedarhousesporthotel.com; ❻). A number of low-cost **campgrounds** line the Truckee River between the town and Lake Tahoe, off Hwy-89: the closest and largest is *Granite Flat*, three miles from Truckee; others are *Goose Meadows* and *Silver Creek*, five and nine miles south respectively (all three locations ☎530/587-3558; $13–15).

Commercial Row has a number of good **eating** options, especially the diner-style *Coffee And...* at 10106 Donner Pass Road (☎530/587-3123), while omelets are the specialty at the *Squeeze Inn*, 10060 Donner Pass Road (☎530/587-9814); both are only open until 2pm. For cheap all-day meals, try *The Truckee Diner*, on the other side of the tracks at 10144 W River Street (☎530/582-6925), or *El Toro Bravo*, a standard taqueria at 10186 Donner Pass Road (☎530/587-3557). The more expensive *Moody's Bistro & Lounge* in the *Truckee Hotel* (☎530/587-8688) serves upscale meat and fish such as pan-roasted wild Oregon sturgeon; and *Dragonfly*, 10118 Donner Pass Road (☎530/587-0557), is a refreshingly modern place providing a mixture of Pacific Rim, Southeast Asian, and American cuisine on its rooftop terrace. Though the old bucket-of-blood saloons of frontier lore are long gone, there are a few good places to stop for a **drink**, including the *Bar of America* (℡530/587-3110), at the corner of Hwy-26 and Donner Pass Road, offering free live music most nights, or *Ye Old Pastime Club*, 10096 Donner Pass Road (℡530/582-9219), which features great live blues and jazz. *OB's*, at 10046 Donner Pass Road (℡530/587-4164), is another relaxed pub with decent food. For chocolate so good that you might consider hibernating here through a brutal Truckee winter, try the award-winning cappuccino truffles at *Sweets*, 10118 Donner Pass Road (℡530/587-6556).

Donner Lake

Two miles west of Truckee, surrounded by alpine cliffs of silver-gray granite, **Donner Lake** was the site of one of the most gruesome and notorious tragedies of early California, when pioneers trapped by winter snows were forced to eat the bodies of their dead companions (see box, below).

The horrific tale of the Donner party is recounted in some detail in the small **Emigrant Trail Museum** (daily: summer 9am–5pm; rest of year 9am–4pm; donation; ℡530/582-7892) – just off Donner Pass Road, three miles west of Truckee in **Donner Memorial State Park** (8am–sunset; $6 per vehicle) – which shows a re-enactment of the events in the hourly, 26-minute video that's so over-the-top most viewers will have a hard time choking back their chuckles. Outside, the **Pioneer Monument** stands on a plinth as high as the snow was deep that fateful winter of 1846 – 22ft. From the museum, an easy nature trail winds through the forest past a memorial plaque marking the site where the majority of the Donner party built its simple cabins. Nearby, on the southeastern shore of the lake, there's a summer-only **campground** ($25, ℡1-800/444-7275, ⓦwww.reserveamerica.com).

Above Donner Lake, the Southern Pacific railroad tracks climb west over the **Donner Pass** through tunnels built by Chinese laborers during the nineteenth century – still one of the main rail routes across the Sierra Nevada. For much of the way, the tracks are protected from the usually heavy winter snow by a series of wooden sheds, which you can see from across the valley, where Donner Pass Road

---

The Donner party

The 91-member **Donner party**, named after one of the pioneer families among the group, set off for California in April 1846 from Illinois across the Great Plains, following a shortcut recommended by the first traveler's guide to the West Coast (the 1845 *Emigrant's Guide to California and Oregon*), which actually took three weeks longer than the established route. By October, they had reached what is now Reno and decided to rest a week to regain their strength for the arduous crossing of the Sierra Nevada Mountains – a delay that proved fatal. When at last they set off, early snowfall blocked their route beyond Donner Lake, and the group was forced to stop and build crude shelters, hoping that the snow would melt and allow them to complete their crossing; it didn't, and they were stuck.

Within a month, the pioneers were running out of provisions, and a party of fifteen set out across the mountains to try to reach **Sutter's Fort** in Sacramento. They struggled through yet another storm and, a month later, two men and five women stumbled into the fort, having survived by eating the bodies of the men who had died. A rescue party set off from Sutter's Fort immediately, only to find more of the same: thirty or so half-crazed survivors, living off the meat of their fellow travelers.

snakes up the steep cliffs. On well-signposted Hwy-40, there's a scenic overlook where you can get that prize-winning photo of Donner Lake and possibly a glimpse beyond to Tahoe. Further on, rock climbers from the nearby Alpine Skills Institute (☎530/426-9108, ⓦwww.alpineskills.com) can often be seen honing their talents on the 200-foot granite faces; the institute offers a variety of climbing and mountaineering courses and trips. At the crest, the road passes the Soda Springs, Sugar Bowl, and Royal Gorge **ski areas** before rejoining I-80, which runs east from Donner Pass to Reno, Nevada, and west to Sacramento.

Into Nevada: Reno and around

On I-80 at the foot of the Sierra Nevada, thirty miles east of Truckee, **RENO, NEVADA** has plenty of affordable places to stay and eat, making it a reasonable stopoff, especially if you enjoy gambling. The town itself, apart from the stream of blazing casino neon, may not be much to look at, having sprung up out of nowhere in the middle of the desert on the hopes that the gambling industry alone could sustain its existence. Nevertheless, its setting – with the snowcapped Sierra peaks as a distant backdrop and the Truckee River winding through – is nice enough, and unlike Las Vegas, to which it is most often compared, Reno maintains a small-town feel that residents are proud of. As the locals love to say – over and over again – Reno is the biggest little town in the world. Even if you don't like to gamble, you can still pass a pleasant afternoon here ambling in the dry desert heat or visiting one of the mildly diverting museums. Reno is also another good place from which to visit Lake Tahoe, and a suitable base for exploring the evocative mining towns of **Carson City** and **Virginia City**.

Arrival and information

Reno's Cannon International **airport** (☎775/328-6400, ⓦwww.renoairport .com) is served by most major domestic carriers. RTC/Citifare (6am–1am; $1.70 flat fare, $4 day-pass; ☎775/348-0480, ⓦwww.citifare.com) bus #13 makes the twenty-minute journey from the terminals to Reno's downtown Citicenter transit center, where you can connect to many of the company's other routes. Greyhound **buses** from San Francisco, via Sacramento and Truckee, and from LA, via the Owens Valley, use the terminal at 155 Stevenson Street, also used by KT Services (☎775/945-2282), which operates a daily bus to Las Vegas and Phoenix. The Amtrak *California Zephyr* **train** from Chicago stops in the center of town at 135 Commercial Row. To **rent a car**, try Alamo (☎1-800/327-9633, ⓦwww.alamo.com), Avis (☎1-800/831-2837, ⓦwww.avis.com), or Thrifty (☎1-800/367-2277, ⓦwww.thrifty.com), all at the airport.

The brand new **visitor center** is located inside the Reno Town Mall at 4001 S Virginia Street (Mon–Fri 8am–5pm; ☎1-800/367-7366, ⓦwww .visitrenotahoe.com). On the sixteenth floor of 1 E First Street, the **Chamber of Commerce** (Mon–Fri 8am–5pm; ☎775/337-3030, ⓦwww .reno-sparkschamber.org) can also dish out advice and brochures.

Accommodation

Inexpensive **accommodation** is plentiful, but if you arrive on a weekend you should book ahead and be prepared for rates to nearly double. A two-night minimum stay usually applies on weekends, especially at the **casinos**. You can also call the **Reno-Sparks Visitor and Convention Association**'s toll-free information and reservation line (☏1-800/367-7366) for help with finding a place to stay. **Camping** is an RV experience in Reno; for tent sites, head west to the numerous campgrounds around Lake Tahoe (see p.654).

Atlantis 3800 S Virginia St ☏1-800/723-6500, ⓦwww.atlantiscasino.com. One of the newer casinos on the scene, this hotel offers great rates and plush amenities for slightly less than casinos of the same class in the center of town, especially in its motor-lodge rooms. ❷

Circus Circus 500 N Sierra St ☏1-800/648-5010, ⓦwww.circusreno.com. One of the largest and tackiest casinos, with over 1600 popular rooms – check online for very low rates at slow times. ❷

Crest Inn 525 W Fourth St ☏775/329-0808, ⓔcrestinn@aol.com. Simple downtown motel with few trimmings and rock-bottom prices. ❶

Eldorado 345 N Virginia St ☏1-800/777-5325, ⓦwww.eldoradoreno.com. The nicer rooms are on the upper floors, while those lower down are cheaper in this bustling downtown casino. Lots of online specials. ❷

Peppermill 2707 S Virginia St ☏1-866/821-9996, ⓦwww.peppermillreno.com. Another large casino, slightly outside the center of town; cushier than most, with special rates offered frequently. ❸

Truckee River Lodge 501 W First St ☏1-800/635-8950, ⓦwww.truckeeriverlodge.com. Nonsmoking hotel near the river with an emphasis on recreation; it has its own fitness center. ❷

The Town

It may lack the glitz and the glamor that make Vegas a global draw, but **Reno** is northern Nevada's number one **gambling** spot, offering a 24-hour diet of slot machines, blackjack, craps, keno, roulette, and many more ways to win and lose a bundle. Gaming was only legalized in Nevada in 1931, but silver miners in Virginia City and Gold Hill regularly tried their hands at fortune's wheel back in the mid-nineteenth century, when a deck of cards was an almost mandatory part of a miner's kit. This tradition was revived with a vengeance when Reno came into being the following century.

While nowhere near as grand as the Vegas gambling institutions, most of Reno's **casinos** still warrant a quick tour. If you can only handle visiting a few, the best of the lot are: **Circus Circus**, 500 N Sierra Street, where a small circus performs every half-hour, giving patrons a reason to look up from their dwindling savings; it runs seamlessly into **Silver Legacy**, whose main entrance is around the corner at 407 N Virginia Street, revealing a planetarium-style dome with a makeshift 120-foot mining derrick underneath, appearing to draw silver ore out of the ground and spilling cascades of coins in the process. This is joined in turn with **Eldorado** and you can quite unwittingly wander between all three; the other main attraction for punters is **Harrah's**, a few blocks south at 219 N Center Street, the classiest casino downtown with row upon row of high-stakes slot machines and the occasional famous entertainer. If you want to compare these with one of the newer establishments further out, then the best bet is to head south towards the brash opulence of **Peppermill** at 2707 S Virginia Street. In order to learn more than you can glean from a solo jaunt through the casinos, contact the Reno–Tahoe Gaming Academy, 1313 S Virginia Street (☎775/329-5665), for an overview of some of the rules of the major games followed by a behind-the-scenes **tour** of Reno's major gambling dens (hours vary; $10) – lessons are also available from $5.

Once you're ready to cash in all the casino clatter and any remaining chips for some peace and quiet, take refuge in one of Reno's many **museums**. The

▲ Reno, Nevada

largest and most significant among them is the **National Automobile Museum** (The Harrah Collection), at Mill and Lake streets (Mon–Sat 9.30am–5.30pm, Sun 10am–4pm; $9; ☏775/333-9300,Ⓦwww.automuseum .org), which holds the most comprehensive public display of automobiles in the western hemisphere, with more than two hundred vintage and classic cars, some artfully arranged along re-created city streets of bygone decades. The sheer scale of the collection can't help but impress, even if you think you'd rather be pulling on the arm of a slot machine than admiring the shine on an 1892 Philion. The one time it's guaranteed to get crowded is during the Hot August Nites classic cars festival, when famous twentieth-century automobiles congregate and go on show. Those more into motifs than motors should take a look at the inventive contemporary exhibitions at the **E.L. Weigand Gallery and Nevada Museum of Art**, 160 W Liberty Street (Tues–Sun 10am–5pm, until 8pm on Thurs; $10; ☏775/329-3333, Ⓦwww.nevadaart.org).

You'll find Reno's most curious trove, however, at the **Wilbur D. May Great Basin Adventure** (hours and admission fees vary; ☏775/785-5961, Ⓦwww .maycenter.com), which sits on the edge of **Rancho San Rafael Park**, a mile north of downtown Reno off North Sierra Street. The collection outlines the eventful life of Wilbur May (1898–1982) – a traveler, hunter, military aviator, cattle-breeder, and heir to the May department store fortunes – with several rooms of furnishings, mounted animal heads, and plunder from his trips to Africa and South America; the museum also houses temporary exhibitions. In summer only, the complex opens its **Great Basin Adventure** (hours vary; $7–10; ☏775/785-4319), where kids can pet animals, ride on ponies, shoot down a flume, and learn about Native Americans and dinosaurs.

On the other side of US-395, the University of Nevada campus hosts the **Nevada Historical Society Museum**, 1650 N Virginia Street (Mon–Sat 10am–5pm; $3; ☏775/688-1190), full of items of local interest, especially Native American artifacts. Next door is the **Fleischmann Planetarium** (Mon–Fri 10.30am–8pm, Sat & Sun 10.30am–9pm; $8; ☏775/784-4811, Ⓦwww.planetarium.unr.nevada.edu), where, amongst the telescopes and solar system galleries, OMNIMAX-style films (2–4 shows daily; $5–8) are projected onto a huge dome; the museum contains all four meteorites recovered in Nevada and impressive six-foot globes of earth and the moon.

Getting married (and divorced) in Reno

If you've come to Reno to get **married**, you and your intended must be at least 18 years old and able to prove it, swear that you're not already married, and appear before a judge at the **Washoe County Court** (daily 8am–midnight; ☏775/328-3275), south of the main casino district at South Virginia and Court streets, to obtain a **marriage license** ($55). There is no waiting period or blood test required. Civil services are performed for an additional $50 at the **Commissioner for Civil Marriages**, behind the Courthouse at 195 S Sierra Street (☏775/328-3461). If you want something a bit more special, however, **wedding chapels** all around the city will help you tie the knot: over the crossroads from the courthouse, the Heart of Reno, 243 S Sierra Street (☏775/786-6882, Ⓦwww.heartofrenochapel.com), does the job quickly – "No Waiting, Just Drive In" – for around $80–100, providing a pink chintzy parlor full of plastic flowers. Fork out more cash, and you get the tux and dress and can invite a few guests. Other chapels include the Park Wedding Chapel, 136 S Virginia Street (☏775/323-1770), and the Silver Bells Wedding Chapel, 628 N Virginia Street (☏1-800/221-9336, Ⓦwww.silverbellsweddingchap.com). If it doesn't work out, you'll have to stay in Nevada for another six weeks before you can get a **divorce**.

Eating and nightlife

All-you-can-eat casino buffets are the order of the day for tourists in Reno, and seemingly everyone goes out and stuffs themselves to bursting. The buffets can be fun and of surprisingly good quality; the best are listed here along with locals' favorite alternatives, most of which are awkwardly spread over the south of the city. Tourists tend to stick to the shows in the casinos for **nightlife**, but occasionally the city holds an art or music festival, and there are some popular venues downtown like *Reno Live*, at Sierra and Second streets (☎775/329-1952), which claims to be the largest nightclub complex in Nevada. Check Reno's free independent weekly *Reno News and Review* for listings. There are a number of **gay and lesbian bars** in town, including the popular *Patio Bar* at 600 W Fifth Street (☎775/323-6565).

Buffets

Atlantis 3800 S Virginia St ☎775/825-4700. Consistently and justifiably voted best buffet in town by locals – well worth the extra couple of bucks. The casino also boasts the moderately priced *Café Alfresco* and more upscale *Seafood Steakhouse*, which has exceptional food, wine list, and service.

Circus Circus 500 N Sierra St ☎1-800/648-5010, ⓦ www.circusreno.com. The place to go for a buffet meal if your budget is of greater concern than your stomach, with all-you-can-eat dinners for little over $10.

Harrah's 219 N Center St ☎775/786-3232. The most lavish downtown casino buffet includes multiple entrées such as prime rib, crab legs, shrimp, and a fine Asian section for around $12 most days. Their à la carte *Café Napa* is also recommended.

Restaurants

Aloha Sushi In the Mervyns shopping center at 3338 Kietzke Lane ☎775/828-9611. A bit of a jump southeast from casino central, but reasonable and good; if you're staying for any length of time, you'll need to escape from the buffets eventually. Try their specialty "Mountain" roll.

Bangkok Cuisine 55 Mt Rose St ☎775/322-0299. Cozy Thai family restaurant offering spicy dinners and filling lunch specials for around $6.

Beto's 575 W 5th St ☎775/324-0632. Excellent and authentic self-service Mexican canteen, one of the best-value downtown eateries outside of the casinos.

Einstein's Quantum Café 6135 Lakeside Drive, near Virginia Lake Park ☎775/825-6611. An inexpensive vegetarian café that's a hit among locals tired of meat-dominated menus – well off course though.

La Vecchia Varese 130 West St ☎775/322-7486. Unfussy decor and an excellent, moderately priced selection of gourmet Italian dishes, with several vegetarian choices.

Liberty Belle Saloon & Restaurant 4250 S Virginia St ☎775/825-1776. Reasonably priced place famed for its prime rib with spinach salad and other meaty dishes. Established in 1958, it also houses a slot-machine collection and other memorabilia.

S.S. Super Indian Restaurant 1030 S Virginia St ☎775/322-5577. Fresh, primarily Northern Indian specialties and a daily $7 lunch buffet.

Carson City

US-395 heads south from Reno along the jagged spires of the High Sierra past Mono Lake, Mount Whitney, and Death Valley (see Chapter Four). Just thirty miles south of Reno, it briefly becomes Carson Street as it passes through **CARSON CITY**, the state capital of Nevada. It's small compared to Reno, and despite the sprawling mess of fast-food joints, strip malls, and car dealerships that surround its center, it's well worth a visit, especially if you're interested in the history of mining. The city has a number of elegant buildings, excellent historical museums, and a few world-weary casinos, populated mainly by old ladies armed with buckets of quarters.

Named, somewhat indirectly, after frontier explorer Kit Carson in 1858, Carson City is still redolent with Wild West history: you'll get a good introduction at the **Nevada State Museum & Mint** at 600 N Carson Street (daily 8.30am–4.30pm; $5; ☎775/687-4810). Housed in a sandstone structure built during the Civil War as the Carson Mint, the museum's exhibits deal with the geology and natural history of the Great Basin desert region, from prehistoric days up through the heyday of the 1860s, when the silver mines of the nearby Comstock Lode were at their peak. Amid the many guns and artifacts, the two best features of the museum are the reconstructed **Ghost Town** and a full-scale model of an **underground mine**, connected to the former by a tunnel and giving some sense of the cramped and constricted conditions in which miners worked. The **North Building** is home to the **Under One Sky** exhibition, featuring material about cowboys and Indians, natural history, and children's interactive displays.

Four blocks from the museum, on the other side of Carson Street, the impressively restored **State Capitol**, 101 N Carson Street (daily 9am–5pm; free), dating from 1871, merits a look for its stylish Neoclassical architecture and the commendable stock of artifacts relating to Nevada's past, housed in an upper-floor room.

The **Nevada State Railway Museum**, 2180 S Carson Street (daily 8.30am–4.30pm; $4; ☎775/687-6953), just a stone's throw away from the visitor center (see below), displays carefully restored locomotives and carriages, several of them from the long since defunct but fondly remembered Virginia & Truckee Railroad, founded in the nineteenth century.

Practicalities

Greyhound **buses** stop outside the Frontier Motel on North Carson Street. Amtrak Thruway services from Sacramento and South Lake Tahoe stop outside the Nugget casino at the junction of Robinson and Carson streets. For transport between Carson City and Reno Airport, make an advance reservation with No Stress Express ($40 one-way; ☎1-800/426-5644, ⓦwww.nostressexpress.com). The **Convention and Visitors Bureau**, on the south side of town at 1900 S Carson Street (Mon–Sat 9am–4pm, summer only Sun 9am–3pm; ☎1-800/638-2321, ⓦwww.visitcarsoncity.com), can help with practical details, and sells the *Kit Carson Trail Map* ($2.50), a leaflet detailing a **walking tour** of the town, taking in the main museums, the state capitol, and many of the fine 1870s Victorian wooden houses and churches on the west side.

There are a number of reasonably priced **motels** in town, among them the *Nugget Motel & Inn* at 651 N Stewart Street (☎775/882-7711, ⓦwww .nuggetmotel.com; ❷) behind the Nugget casino, and the more colorful *Plaza Hotel*, 801 S Carson Street (☎1-888/227-1499, ⓦwww.carsoncityplaza.com; ❸), not far from the capitol building. A little further out is the plusher *Piñon Plaza Resort Hotel and Casino* at 2171 US-50 (☎775/885-9000, ⓦwww .pinonplaza.com; ❹), a *Best Western* franchise. If exploring Carson City gives you an appetite, **places to eat** in town include *Heidi's Family Restaurant*, 1020 N Carson Street (☎775/882-0486), which serves generous breakfasts and lunches, the basic *Howlin' Good BBQ & Grill*, 1701 N Carson Street (☎775/885-2248), or the rather more ambient *Whiskey Creek Steakhouse & Saloon* in the *Piñon Plaza Resort* (☎775/885-9000).

Virginia City and Genoa

Much of the wealth on which Carson City – and indeed San Francisco – was built came from the silver mines of the Comstock Lode, a solid seam of pure silver discovered in 1859 underneath Mount Hamilton, fourteen miles east of Carson City off US-50. Raucous **VIRGINIA CITY** grew up on the steep slopes above the mines, and a young writer named Samuel Clemens made his way here in the 1860s with his older brother, who'd been appointed acting secretary to the governor of the Nevada Territory, to see what all the fuss was about. His descriptions of the wild life of the mining camp, and of the desperately hard work men put in to get at the valuable ore, were published years later under his adopted pseudonym, **Mark Twain**. Though Twain also spent some time in the Gold Rush towns of California's Mother Lode on the other side of the Sierra – which by then were all but abandoned – his accounts of Virginia City life, collected in *Roughing It*, give a hilarious, eyewitness account of the hard-drinking life of the frontier miners.

The miners have long since left, but Virginia City still exploits a rich vein, one which runs through the pocketbooks of tour parties bussed up here from Reno. But despite the camera-clicking throngs, there's a sense of authenticity to Virginia City missing from even the most evocative of the California mining towns. Perhaps it's the town's location, encircled by the barren Nevada Desert that so sharply contrasts with the diverse countryside of California's Gold Country, or perhaps it's the colorful advertisements that lure tourists to the many quirky museums. Then again, it could simply be the rambunctious spirit that seems to affect almost every sarsaparilla-sippin' tourist who sets foot here. Whatever the reason, it's hard not to get caught up in the infectious Wild West atmosphere and stay longer than you'd intended. Still, not everyone who floods into town is here for the Gold Rush nostalgia – many visitors are here to frequent the **legal brothels**, another reminder of the town's frontier days.

At the **Chamber of Commerce**, in the disused premises of the old *Crystal Bar Saloon* on the corner of Taylor and North C streets (daily 10am–5pm; ℡775/847-0311, ⓦwww.virginiacity-nv.org), you can pick up pamphlets and a self-guided walking-tour map, or you can just as easily wander around the town until you've bumped into all the sights in your own time. Historic highlights include the **Mackay Mansion Museum**, 129 South D Street (daily 11am–6pm; $4; ℡775/847-0173), a painstakingly preserved 1860s residence, and the **Nevada Gambling Museum**, 50 South C Street (daily: April–Sept 10.30am–5pm; Oct–March 10.30am–4pm; $1.50; ℡775/847-9022), with its historic roulette wheel and other period game-room accessories. You can also poke your head into the **Bucket of Blood Saloon** at 1 South C Street, which is delightfully crowded with period fixtures and crooked old furnishings. The mood of the era and current desire to cash in on it is summed up in **The Way It Was Museum**, 113 North C Street (daily 10am–5.30pm; $3; ℡775/847-0766), with its collection of mining equipment, rare photos and maps, and fully stocked gift shop.

If you'd like to **stay in town**, there are a few decent options, but no Reno-style resorts. The *Silver Queen*, at 28 North C Street (℡775/847-0468; ❶), and *Comstock Lodge Motel*, at 875 South C Street (℡775/847-0233; ❷), are two reasonable, if basic, options for spending the night on the main drag of an old boomtown. The converted 1861 *Chollar Mansion* B&B, 565 South D Street (℡1-877/246-5527, ⓦwww.chollarmansion.com; ❺), provides greater comfort and amenities. Decent **dining** options include good Chinese cuisine at *Mandarin Garden*, 30 North B Street (℡775/847-9288), whose outside deck affords great views, and cheaper bar food at the *Old Washoe Club*, 112 South C Street (℡775/847-7210), which claims to be the town's oldest saloon.

A 35-minute train ride ($7 diesel or $9 steam round-trip) from the town center on the **Virginia & Truckee Railroad** will take you a little over a mile up to the all-but-extinct town of **Gold Hill**, which consists primarily of the ⚔ *Gold Hill* hotel, restaurant, and tavern (℡775/847-0111, ⓦwww.goldhillhotel.net; ❷); Nevada's oldest hotel, with good rates and atmosphere, it also lets out half a dozen more expensive lodges in ex-miner's houses around the tiny town.

South of Carson City in the Carson Valley lies another evocative Wild West scene, **GENOA**, the oldest town in Nevada. Slightly less stampeded by tourists than Virginia City, the main draw here is the curious **Mormon Station**, 2295 Main Street (daily mid-May to mid-Oct 9am–5pm; free; ☎775/782-2590), a replica of the original trading post and fort built on the site in 1851. To learn about walking tours in town, stop by the information counter in the **Genoa Courthouse** at 2304 Main Street (daily May–Oct 10am–4.30pm; $3; ☎775/782-4325). You can **stay** in some comfort at *The Legend Country Inn*, 2292 Main Street (☎1-888/783-0906, ⓦwww.legendcountryinn.com; ❻), part of a complex mercifully built to blend in with the old architecture. Locals still congregate at the ⚑ *Genoa Bar & Saloon*, 2282 Main Street (☎775/782-3870), an atmospheric joint which claims to be Nevada's oldest continuously operating watering hole, open for business since 1853.

Travel details

Trains

Reno to: Oakland/Emeryville (1 daily; 7hr 45min); Sacramento (1 daily; 5hr 45min); Truckee (1 daily; 1hr).
Sacramento to: Oakland/Emeryville (11–16 daily; 1hr 40min); Reno (1 daily; 5hr); Truckee (1 daily; 3hr 30min).

Buses

All buses are Greyhound unless otherwise stated.

Reno to: Las Vegas (2 daily; 18–20hr); Los Angeles (6 daily; 10hr 25min–15hr 45min); Sacramento (7 daily; 2hr 40min–3hr 40min); San Francisco (7 daily; 5hr–6hr 50min).
Reno airport to: Stateline (11 daily South Tahoe Express; 1hr 30min).
Sacramento to: Los Angeles (11 daily; 7hr 10min–9hr 25min); Reno (7 daily; 2hr 50min–3hr 55min); San Francisco (8 daily; 2hr–2hr 35min); Truckee (2 daily; 2hr 55min).
South Lake Tahoe/Stateline to: Reno airport (11 daily South Tahoe Express; 1hr 30min).

9

Northern California

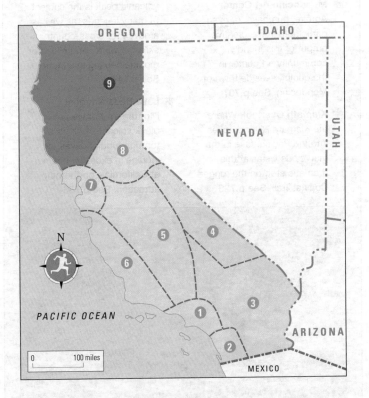

CHAPTER 9

Highlights

* **Russian River Valley wineries** Opportunities for leisurely wine-tasting against a glorious backdrop of vineyards and redwoods abound in this less commercialized part of Wine Country. **See p.698**

* **Mendocino Art Center** Admire, purchase, or even participate in the creative output of this friendly community art center in the quaint, seaside town of Mendocino. **See p.707**

* **Klamath Overlook** Where the Klamath River empties into the Pacific, take in the marvelous vistas at this dramatic stop on the rugged Coastal Trail. **See p.726**

* **Lassen Volcanic National Park** Visit this top wilderness area to enjoy steaming geysers, high-altitude lakes, bracing walks, and exhilarating campsites. **See p.736**

* **Mount Shasta** This huge volcanic peak is the subject of many legends, as well as a haven for cross-country skiing in winter and hiking or mountaineering in summer. **See p.747**

* **Lava Beds National Monument** Admire the black volcanic rock, crawl through tubular caves, or indulge in excellent birding at California's northernmost attraction. **See p.756**

▲ Elk in Redwood National Park

Northern California

The northern coast and interior of California covers about a third of the state, a gigantic area over four hundred miles long and three hundred wide, with a rugged rural landscape and an ethic far removed from the urban lifestyles to the south. It's a schizophrenic region of a schizophrenic state, coupling volcanoes with vineyards, fog-shrouded redwoods with scorched olive trees, loggers with environmentalists, and legends of Bigfoot with movies of Ewoks. Northern Californians are tied to the land, and agriculture dominates the economy as well as the vistas. Deep-rooted forestry, fishing, and cattle industries are also ever-present (even though the first two are in decline), along with the wild, crashing Pacific Coast and steady rain that supports a marijuana-growing region called the Emerald Triangle. Add only two major highways and the lack of a metropolis in favor of small, Main Street towns, and you have a region that has more in common with Oregon and Washington than Los Angeles or San Francisco. In that regard, Northern Californians have long rumbled about forming a state of their own. Indeed, in 1941 there was a proposal to form a state called Jefferson near Mount Shasta, an event that could have gained steam were it not for Japan's bombing of Pearl Harbor two days later, channeling collective energies into the war.

Immediately north of the Bay Area, the **Wine Country** might be your first – indeed your only – taste of Northern California, though it's by no means typical. The two valleys of **Napa** and **Sonoma** unfold along thirty miles of rolling hills and premium real estate, home to the California wine barons and San Franciscan weekenders wanting to escape in style. Napa is the reigning king of indulgence and high-caliber vintages, while Sonoma caters to a funkier set, with its interesting history and outdoor tours. The northwest corner of Sonoma County is the Wine Country's other "grape escape," an area of six varieties and resorts clustered around the **Russian River** and its tributaries. Further north and towards the coast, the **Anderson Valley** in Mendocino County holds another haven for vineyards. **Clear Lake**, to the north of the Wine Country, can be included in a longer itinerary.

It's the **northern coast** which provides the most appealing, and slowest, route through the region, beginning just north of Marin County and continuing for four hundred miles on Hwy-1 and US-101 along rugged bluffs and through dense forests as far as the Oregon border. The landscape varies little at first, but given time reveals tangible shifts from the flat oyster beds of **Sonoma County**, to the seal and surfer breeding grounds around the coastal elegance of **Mendocino**, and to the big logging country further north in **Humboldt**. Trees are the main attraction up here: some thousands of years old and hundreds of feet high, dominating a very sparsely populated landscape

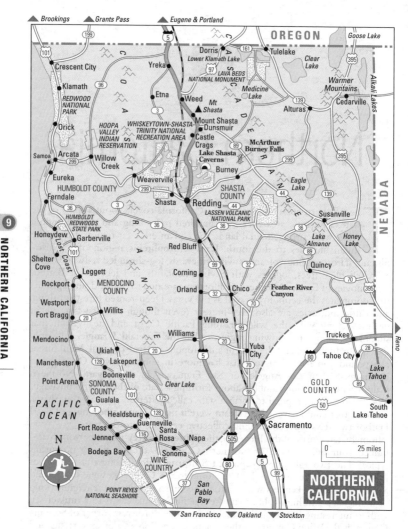

NORTHERN CALIFORNIA

swathed in swirling mists. In summer, areas like **Redwood National Park**, stretching into the most northerly **Del Norte County**, teem with campers and hikers, but out of season they can provide idyllic experiences and an opportunity to coexist with the area's woodland creatures – including, some say, Bigfoot. Although the nightlife is rarely swinging in these parts, the college town of **Arcata**, towards the top end of the northern coast, makes a lively refuge when the great outdoors begins to pall.

The **interior** is more remote still, an enchanting land whose mystery and sheer physical enormity can't help but leave a lasting impression. I-5 neatly divides the region, cutting through the forgettable Sacramento Valley north to the **Shasta Cascades**, a mountainous area of isolated towns, massive lakes, and a forbidding climate. In winter, much of this corner of the state is completely impassable, and the region's commercial activities are centered around the lower, warmer climes of the largest town and transportation hub of **Redding**. Now boasting an excellent museum and iconic new bridge, Redding is a major crossroads serving **Whiskeytown–Shasta–Trinity National Recreation Area**, **Lassen Volcanic National Park**, **McArthur–Burney Falls State Park** and, northward, the railroad towns in the shadows of towering **Mount Shasta**. Up at the top of the interior, the eerie, moonlike terrain of the **Lava Beds National Monument** rewards those who make the effort to get there, and the wetlands of the **Klamath Basin**, which straddles the Oregon border, are a must for birders. In the very northeast corner of the state, rugged **Modoc County** is another paradise for admirers of natural beauty.

Unlike the Wine Country and the coast, locals all over the Shasta Cascades are actually glad to see tourists, and visitor centers take the time to explain the many outdoor recreational options. Food and lodging costs are cheap by California standards, and the efficient network of highways – by-products of the logging industry – makes travel easy. Parts of the region fill up in summer, but given the sheer enormity of the forests and the plethora of lakes, waterfalls, parks, and bird sanctuaries, escaping the masses and finding peace isn't much of a task. Out of season, you may feel like you're the only one here at all.

Some history

As with elsewhere in California, the first inhabitants of the north were **Native Americans**, whose past has been all but erased, leaving only the odd desolate reservation or crafts museum. Much later, the **Russians** figured briefly in the region's history when they had a modest nineteenth-century settlement at Fort Ross on the coast, ostensibly to protect their interests in otter hunting and fur trading, though more likely to promote territorial claims. **Mexican** explorers and maintenance costs that exceeded revenues prevented them from extending their hunting activities further south, and in the 1840s they sold the fort to the **Americans**. It was the discovery of **gold** in 1848 that really put the north on the map, and much of the countryside bears the marks of this time, dotted with abandoned mining towns, deserted since the gold ran out. Not a lot has happened since, although in the 1980s New Ageism triggered a kind of future for the region, with low land prices pulling more and more devotees up here to sample the delights of a landscape they see as rich in rural symbolism. Hollywood has also been drawn to the region, using the north as a cost-effective way to travel to another place or time. *Robin Hood*, *Gone With the Wind*, *The Birds*, *The Return of the Jedi*, and *Jurassic Park: The Lost World* are just a few examples of movies filmed amongst the frozen-in-time beauty. In more recent years the spiralling rise in Bay Area property prices has led to a small but steady movement of more mainstream folk and retirees into some areas, searching for better value for money or a spacious second home. Many diehard locals are fearful of this influx of new homes and lifestyles spoiling the coast, in particular, and property prices have been creeping up as far north as Mendocino and beyond, though the Coastal Commission tightly controls development, and farmers have so far resisted selling out on a large scale.

Getting around

While most people see the Wine Country on a day-trip from San Francisco, it's also feasible to take in the area en route to the less manicured territory further north. **Public transportation** is sparse all over Northern California, and to enjoy the region you'll need to be independently mobile. Infrequent Greyhound

buses run from San Francisco and Sacramento up and down I-5, stopping in Chico, Redding, and Mount Shasta, and US-101, with halts in Garberville, Eureka, and Arcata. The complication is that none of these routes solves the problem of actually getting around once you've arrived. Frankly, your best bet is a **driving tour** with a reliable car, fixing on a few points. The Wine Country can be seen pretty comprehensively in a long weekend, while the rest of Northern California requires a week for just the sketchiest impression. Only the largest of the region's towns have any local bus service, although for some of the remoter spots you could, perhaps, consider an organized trip, notably Green Tortoise's one-week tours – see p.34 for details.

The Wine Country

"The coldest winter I ever spent was summer in San Francisco," quipped Mark Twain. Like Twain, many visitors to San Francisco can't get over the daily fog and winds that chill even the most promising August day. For this reason, heading into the golden, arid, and balmy **Napa** and **Sonoma valleys**, less than an hour's drive north of San Francisco, can feel like entering another country. Here, around thirty thousand acres of vineyards, feeding hundreds of wineries and their upscale patrons, make the area the heart of the American wine industry in reputation, if not in volume. In truth, less than five percent of California's wine comes from the region, but what it does produce is some of America's best.

Predictably, the region is also one of America's wealthiest and most provincial, a fact that draws – and repels – a steady stream of tourists. There seems to be a bed and breakfast or spa for every grape on the vine, and tourism is gaining on wine production as the Wine Country's leading industry. Expect clogged highways and full hotels during much of peak season (May–Oct), especially at weekends, as well as packed tastings in the more popular wineries. The main road through Napa, Hwy-29, can begin to feel like a monotonous chain of connecting towns anchored by rustic red-brick-facade antique stores.

However, there are two sides to the Napa and Sonoma valleys. One, of course, is its prominence for serious, quality **wine** experiences. Almost all of the region's many wineries offer tours and tastings, usually for a small charge (typically $5–10); this sometimes includes the wineglass and usually a credit towards the purchase of a bottle. Aside from the type and flavor of the drink, wineries all differ in what they offer visitors. Some delight enologists by explaining the process of growing grapes, some excite kids with tractor rides through the vineyard, and some please thirsty patrons with generous samples. The other side to the Wine Country is its **natural landscape**. Separated by the Mayacamas Mountains, the Napa and Sonoma valleys feature some of the most beautiful geography in the state, from the Valley of the Moon to Mount St Helena. Once you've tired of sipping, check out ballooning, biking, horseback riding, hiking, and myriad historical sights, including Spanish missions and Jack London's homestead.

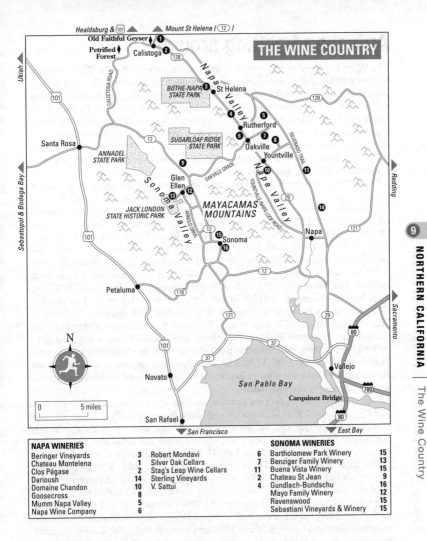

THE WINE COUNTRY

Old Faithful Geyser ❶
Petrified Forest ✦
Calistoga ❷
128

Ukiah
101

BOTHE-NAPA STATE PARK
St Helena ❸
❹
❺ Rutherford
❻ ❼ ❽
Oakville
Yountville
128

Napa Valley

Santa Rosa
ANNADEL STATE PARK
12
SUGARLOAF RIDGE STATE PARK
❽
Glen Ellen
OAKVILLE GRADE
❿
⓫

Redding

⓭ ⓬
JACK LONDON STATE HISTORIC PARK
MAYACAMAS MOUNTAINS
12
ARNOLD DRIVE
YOUNTVILLE-NAPA LOOP ROAD
29
⓮
Napa
121

Sonoma Valley
101
⓯ Sonoma
⓰
12

Petaluma
116
121
29

Sacramento

9

NORTHERN CALIFORNIA | The Wine Country

N
🏃

0   5 miles

101
37
San Pablo Bay
80
Vallejo
780

Novato
Carquinez Bridge
80

Sebastopol & Bodaga Bay

San Rafael ●
▼ San Francisco   ▼ East Bay

NAPA WINERIES			**SONOMA WINERIES**	
Beringer Vineyards	3	Robert Mondavi	6	Bartholomew Park Winery	15
Chateau Montelena	1	Silver Oak Cellars	7	Benziger Family Winery	13
Clos Pégase	2	Stag's Leap Wine Cellars	11	Buena Vista Winery	15
Darioush	14	Sterling Vineyards	2	Chateau St Jean	9
Domaine Chandon	10	V. Sattui	4	Gundlach-Bundschu	16
Goosecross	8			Mayo Family Winery	12
Mumm Napa Valley	5			Ravenswood	15
Napa Wine Company	6			Sebastiani Vineyards & Winery	15

Nothing comes cheap around **Napa**, and the town itself can be quickly done with unless you want to board the over-hyped Wine Train. But many small towns further up the valley, particularly **St Helena**, have retained enough of their early twentieth-century-homestead character to be a welcome relief. **Calistoga**, at the top of the valley, is famous for its hot springs, massages, and spas. On the western side of the dividing Mayacamas Mountains, the smaller backroad wineries of the Sonoma Valley reflect the down-to-earth nature of the place, which is more beautiful and less crowded than its neighbor to the east. The town of **Sonoma** itself is by far the prettiest of the Wine Country communities, retaining a number of fine Mission-era structures around its gracious central plaza. **Santa Rosa**, at the north end of the valley, is the region's sole urban center, handy for budget lodgings but otherwise unremarkable.

Arrival and getting around

The Wine Country region spreads north from the top of the San Francisco Bay in two parallel, thirty-mile-long valleys, **Napa** and **Sonoma**. As long as you avoid the rush-hour traffic, it's about an hour's drive from San Francisco along either of the two main routes: through Marin County via the Golden Gate Bridge and US-101, or through the East Bay via the Bay Bridge and I-80. Good highways ring the region, and a loop of the two valleys is conceivable in a day or so. Consider working against the flow of traffic by taking in Sonoma, Glen Ellen, and Santa Rosa first before crossing the Mayacamas and dropping into Calistoga, St Helena, and Napa.

As the Wine Country's attractions are spread over a fairly broad area, a **car** is pretty much essential. There are limited public bus options, however, from Golden Gate Transit (☎707/541-2000, ⓦwww.goldengate.org), Greyhound (☎1-800/231-2222, ⓦwww.greyhound.com), Sonoma County Transit (☎1-800/345-7433, ⓦwww.sctransit.com), Napa Valley's Vine bus system (Mon–Sat; ☎1-800/696-6443, ⓦwww.nctpa.net/vine.cfm), and the Mendocino Transit Authority (☎1-800/696-4682, ⓦwww.4mta.org); see p.704 for routes. Another option for the car-less is to sign up for a Gray Line **guided bus tour** ($63; ☎1-888/428-6937, ⓦwww.grayline.com) from San Francisco (9.15am; call ☎415/434-8687 the previous day for pickup details). The tour covers both valleys, visiting three wineries and stopping for lunch at Yountville's Vintage 1870 (see p.682). To bypass San Francisco altogether, take the Sonoma Airporter (6 daily; 1hr 30min; $40–45; reservations required ☎1-800/611-4246, ⓦwww.sonomaairporter.com) from the San Francisco airport directly to Sonoma City Hall. The bus also stops at the corner of Geary Boulevard and Park Presidio in San Francisco's Richmond District, and makes six return trips to the city daily.

Blue and Gold Fleet **ferries** travel from Pier 39 (11 daily; $11.50 one-way, $19.25 day-pass; ☎415/705-5500, ⓦwww.blueandgoldfleet.com) in San Francisco to Vallejo, and are met by hourly Vine buses (see above), which continue on to the city of Napa and beyond. Blue and Gold also runs a Wine Country tour leaving daily from Pier 41 (daily 9.15am; $63).

The three-hour **Wine Train** ($49.50 ticket only, plus $39.50–85.50 for various dining options; ☎1-800/427-4124, ⓦwww.winetrain.com) runs two or three times daily from Napa's station at 1275 McKinstry Street, east of downtown. The ten-car train of restored 1950s Pullman cars chugs up the valley to St Helena and back, usually with a stop at Grgich Hills or Domaine Chandon wineries (tour and tasting $24 and $39 extra respectively). The scenery en route is pleasant, but the ride is more of a wining-and-dining experience than a means of transportation.

Cycling

If you don't want to drive all day, **cycling** is a great way to get around. You can bring your own bike on Greyhound (though it costs $10, and the bike must be in a box) or rent one locally for around $25–60 per day and $120–200 per week. If renting, try Napa Valley Bike Tours, 6488 Washington Street, Yountville (☎1-800/707-2453, ⓦwww.napavalleybiketours.com); Getaway Bike Shop, 2228 North Point Parkway, Santa Rosa (☎1-800/499-2453, ⓦwww.getawayadventures.com); St Helena Cyclery, 1156 Main Street, St Helena (☎707/963-7736, ⓦsthelenacyclery.com); or the Sonoma Cyclery, 20093 Broadway, Sonoma (☎707/935-3377, ⓦwww.sonomacyclery.com).

Both valleys are generally flat, although the peaks in between are steep enough to challenge the hardiest of hill-climbers. If the main roads through the valleys are full of cars, as they are most summer weekends, try the smaller parallel routes: the **Silverado Trail** in Napa Valley and lovely **Arnold Drive** in Sonoma Valley. For the more athletically inclined, the **Oakville Grade** between Oakville in the Napa Valley and Glen Ellen in the Sonoma Valley has challenged the world's finest riders. Check with the Santa Rosa Cycling Club (T707/544-4803, W www.srcc.com) for itineraries.

Most local firms organize **tours**, providing bikes, helmets, food, and vans in case you get worn out. In Calistoga, Getaway Adventures offers trips of varying lengths, and Napa Valley Bike Tours sets up more leisurely tours – highlighted by gourmet lunches – all over the Napa area; see opposite for contact details on both. More ambitious (and quite expensive) overnight tours are run most weekends by Backroads, 801 Cedar Street, Berkeley (daily 7am–5pm, Sat 9am–3pm; T1-800/462-2848, W www.backroads.com).

By air

The most exciting way to see the region is on one of the widely touted **hot-air balloon rides**. These usually lift off at dawn, and last sixty to ninety magical minutes, winding up with a champagne brunch. The most established of the operators is Napa Valley Balloons (T1-800/253-2224, W www.napavalleyballoons.com), who fly out of Yountville. Other options in Napa include the slightly cheaper Balloons Above the Valley (T1-800/464-6824, W www.balloonrides.com) and Aerostat Adventures (T1-800/579-0183, W www.aerostat-adventures.com). The crunch comes when you realize the price – up around $200 a head whichever company you use – but it really is worth every cent. Make reservations a week in advance, especially in summer, though with the increasing number of balloon companies, same-day drop-bys are a possibility.

If it's thrills you're looking for, consider taking to the air in a World War II propeller **biplane**. Vintage Aircraft Company, 23982 Arnold Drive, Sonoma (T707/938-2444, W www.vintageaircraft.com), operates one- or two-person flights that take in both valleys. The basic choice is between the twenty-minute Scenic Flight ($150) and various forty-minute Explorer Flights ($295): add $50 to either for the extra thrill of some aerobatics.

Information

Not surprisingly for such a tourist-dependent area, the Wine Country has a well-developed network of **tourist information** outlets, though the rivalry between the two valleys makes it next to impossible to find out anything about Sonoma when you're in Napa, and vice versa. Both the **Napa Valley Visitors Bureau**, 1310 Napa Town Center off First Street in downtown Napa (daily 9am–5pm; T707/226-7459, W www.napavalley.com), and the **Sonoma Valley Visitors Bureau**, 453 First Street E at the center of Sonoma Plaza (daily: summer 9am–6pm; winter 9am–5pm; T707/996-1090, W www.sonomavalley.com), should be able to tell you all you need to know about their respective areas; the smaller towns usually have a tourist office, too. If you're keen on touring the wineries, both the above places hand out basic free **maps** and sell more detailed ones ($3–5) giving the lowdown on the hundreds of producers.

Accommodation

Most people are content to visit the Wine Country as a day-trip from San Francisco, stopping at a few of the wineries and maybe having a picnic or a meal before heading back to the city. But if you really want to absorb properly what the region has to offer, plan to spend at least one night here, pampering yourself in one of the many (generally pricey) **hotels** and **bed and breakfast inns** that provide the bulk of the area's accommodation options. In summer, the Sonoma Valley Visitors Bureau posts a daily list of available rooms in front of their downtown office, and the Napa Valley Visitors Bureau can also help out (see p.679 for both). During summer weekends, prices can rise as much as fifty percent, so call ahead; from November to March, on the other hand, lodging prices drop considerably, often by as much as half. At peak times, rooms of all descriptions get snapped up, so if you have a hard time finding a place, make use of one of the many **accommodation services**: Bed and Breakfast Inns of Napa Valley (☎707/944-4444, ⊛www.bbinv.com); Napa Valley Reservations Unlimited (☎1-800/251-6272, ⊛www.napavalleyreservations.com); or the Bed and Breakfast Association of Sonoma Valley (☎1-800/969-4667, ⊛www.sonomabb.com).

Campers can find a pitch eight miles north of Sonoma at the Sugar Loaf Ridge State Park, 2605 Adobe Canyon Road ($20; ☎707/833-5712), or outside Santa Rosa at the Spring Lake Regional Park, 391 Violetti Drive (May–Sept daily; Oct–April Sat & Sun; $19; ☎707/565-2267).

Hotels and motels

Astro Motel 323 Santa Rosa Ave, Santa Rosa ☎707/545-8555, ⊛www.sterba.com/astro. No frills here at this downtown Santa Rosa motel, but some of the cheapest Wine Country rooms available. ❷

Calistoga Inn 1250 Lincoln Ave, Calistoga ☎707/942-4101, ⊛www.calistogainn.com. Comfortable rooms with one bed, all with shared bathroom facilities, in a landmark building right on the main street, with its own restaurant and micro-brewery. ❸

Discovery Inn 500 Silverado Trail, Napa ☎707/253-0892, ⊛www.napadiscoveryinn.com. This small motel-style place has adequately furnished modern rooms and is well placed a short drive south of Napa and the Silverado Trail wineries. ❸

Dr Wilkinson's Hot Springs 1507 Lincoln Ave, Calistoga ☎707/942-4102, ⊛www.drwilkinson.com. Legendary health spa and hotel downtown. Choose from a variety of spacious, well-lit rooms with sparse furnishings, facing the courtyard or pool patio. TV and a/c standard. ❺

El Bonita Motel 195 Main St, St Helena ☎1-800/541-3284, ⊛www.elbonita.com. Old roadside motel lavishly done up in Art Deco style to suit wealthy weekenders, with a pool and hot tub. Surrounded by a 2.5-acre garden, the rooms here contain microwaves, refrigerators, and coffee-makers. ❺

Harvest Inn 1 Main St, St Helena ☎1-800/950-8466, ⊛www.harvestinn.com. English Tudor cottages at the edge of a vineyard. The place to stay if you can afford it, as the rooms ($399 and up) are huge and loaded with perks like a down-feather bed, fireplace, and private terrace overlooking the garden or 14-acre vineyard. Two outdoor heated pools, whirlpool spas, and jogging/biking trails on-site make the $2 million renovation seem like money well spent. ❾

Hotel La Rose 308 Wilson St, Santa Rosa ☎1-800/527-6738, ⊛www.hotellarose.com. Restored lodging on Railroad Square with Internet access in each of its clean, new rooms. ❻

Hotel St Helena 1309 Main St, St Helena ☎707/963-4388, ⊛www.hotelsthelena.com. Slightly claustrophobic (or cozy, depending on your mood) country-style hotel right downtown. European breakfast included each morning. ❻

Jack London Lodge 13740 Arnold Drive, Glen Ellen ☎707/938-8510, ⊛www.jacklondonlodge.com. Modern motel near the Jack London State Park, with a good restaurant and pool. A smart place to try if Napa and Sonoma hotels are booked, or if you want a truly rural setting and fine stargazing. ❺

Métro Hôtel 508 Petaluma Blvd S, Petaluma ☎707/773-4900, ⊛www.metrolodging.com. Handily placed for both the Sonoma Valley and the coast, this classily renovated hotel offers unexpected touches of European style, both in its decor and the French café, at unbeatable rates – especially the online deals. ❹

Mount View Hotel and Spa 1457 Lincoln Ave, Calistoga ☎1-800/816-6877, ⓦwww .mountviewspa.com. Lively Art Deco-style hotel with spacious rooms and stylish cottages, featuring nightly jazz and a Cajun restaurant, *Catahoula*, on the ground floor. ❼; cottage with patio and hot tub ❽

🏃 **Swiss Hotel** 18 W Spain St, Sonoma ☎707/938-2884, ⓦwww .swisshotelsonoma.com. A 90-year-old landmark building situated right on the plaza, with a fine restaurant. The five rather small rooms each have a view of either the garden patio or Sonoma's plaza, and come with a four-poster queen-sized bed. ❻

Travelodge Hotel & Suites 853 Coombs St, Napa ☎1-800/578-7878, ⓦwww.travelodge.com. Standard motel chain with several fancier suites featuring Jacuzzis. Not especially great value but as cheap as it gets in downtown Napa. ❺

Triple-S Ranch 4600 Mount Home Ranch Rd, Calistoga ☎707/942-6730. Up the hill from Calistoga, in the middle of the wilderness, these unpublicized cabins are decidedly no-frills, but clean and cheap, with a rustic steakhouse/bar on the premises. Take Hwy-128 north for one mile, turn left on Petrified Forest Road, follow it for five miles to Mount Home Road, turn right and continue one mile. ❺

Vintage Inn 6541 Washington St, Yountville ☎1-800/351-1133, ⓦwww.vintageinn.com. Huge luxury rooms from $340 in a modern hotel complex – all with fireplaces – plus swimming pool and free bike rental. Handy for Yountville's many fine restau-rants, and great for romantic getaways, though drastically overpriced. ❺

The Wine Country Inn 1152 Lodi Lane, St Helena ☎1-888/465-4608, ⓦwww.winecountryinn.com. Patios, strolling gardens, and vineyard-side swimming pool highlight this inn. The rooms are tasteful, open, and uncluttered with antiques. A fireplace comes with most rooms. ❽–❾

Bed and breakfasts

Ambrose Bierce House 1515 Main St, St Helena ☎707/963-3003, ⓦwww.ambrosebiercehouse .com. Luxury accommodation in the 1872 house

once inhabited by Bierce himself (see p.683). Breakfast is washed down with complimentary champagne. ❼

Candlelight Inn 1045 Easum Drive, Napa ☎1-800/624-0395, ⓦwww.candlelightinn.com. Spacious mock-Tudor mansion with a pool in its lovely grounds and luxurious interior, featuring rooms of varying sizes. Friendly and informal atmosphere with free drinks and snacks. ❻

Christopher's Inn 1010 Foothill Blvd, Calistoga ☎1-866/876-5755, ⓦwww.christophersinn.com. Sizeable yet friendly B&B, one block north of the center of town, with a lovely English-style garden and comfortable rooms, especially those in the luxurious new extension. ❻

Cottage Inn & Spa 302 1st St E, Sonoma ☎1-800/944-1490, ⓦwww.cottageinnandspa.com. Owned by two interior designers, this tranquil, downtown B&B comprises one room and six pricier suites, ranged around relaxing courtyard with hot tub. ❼

Gaige House Inn 13540 Arnold Drive, Glen Ellen ☎1-800/935-0237, ⓦwww.gaige.com. Beautifully restored Queen Anne farmhouse in a quiet and contemporary country setting. Unique, egg-shaped stone baths. No children under 12. ❽

Garnett Creek Inn 1139 Lincoln Ave, Calistoga ☎707/942-9797, ⓦwww.garnettcreekinn.com. Gaily decorated old house at the Hwy-29 end of the main street, recently converted into a B&B and one of the best deals in this price code. Friendly and knowledgeable innkeeper. ❻

Kenwood Inn & Spa 10400 Sonoma Hwy, Kenwood ☎1-800/353-6966, ⓦwww.kenwoodinn .com. Deluxe, beautiful, and secluded Italian-villa-style B&B with a fireplace in all suites – rooms range from $400 to $800 in high season. ❾

🏃 **Oleander House** 7433 St Helena Hwy (Hwy-29), Yountville ☎1-800/788-0357, ⓦwww.oleander.com. Cozy and friendly B&B in a handy mid-valley location. Quiet enough despite being on the main road, which also keeps prices a tad lower. ❻

Thistle Dew Inn 171 W Spain St, Sonoma ☎1-800/382-7895, ⓦwww.thistledew.com. Sonoma's most raved-about B&B. Near Sonoma Plaza, it features five elegantly restored rooms, an amazing full breakfast, and free bike rental. Some rooms come with a fireplace, private hot tub, and patio. ❻

Napa Valley

A thirty-mile strip of gently landscaped corridors and lush hillsides, **NAPA VALLEY** looks more like southern France than a near-neighbor of the Pacific

Ocean. In spring, the valley floor is covered with brilliant wildflowers that mellow into autumnal shades by grape-harvest time. Local Native Americans named the fish-rich river which flows through the valley "Napa," meaning "plenty"; the name was adopted by Spanish missionaries in the early nineteenth century, but the natives themselves were soon wiped out. The few ranches the Spanish and Mexicans managed to establish were in turn taken over by Yankee traders, and by the 1850s, with California part of the US, the town of Napa was soon swallowed by the Gold Rush. Its location also made it a thriving river port, sending agricultural goods to San Francisco and serving as a supply point for farmers and ranchers. The opening of White Sulphur Springs in 1852, California's first mineral-springs resort, made Napa the vacation choice for San Francisco's elite. Settlers came, too, including Jacob Beringer in 1870. The rocky, well-drained soil he saw resembled that of his hometown of Mainz, Germany, and by 1875 he and his brother had established Beringer Vineyards, today America's oldest continually operating winery. Before long, Napa was bypassed by the railroads and unable to compete with other deepwater Bay Area ports, but the area's fine climate saved it from oblivion. The main route through the valley is Hwy-29, along which all the towns described here are strung, but for a quieter alternative route between Napa and Calistoga, the **Silverado Trail** to the east is highly recommended.

Napa, Yountville, and Oakville

The town of **Napa** itself, at the southern end of the valley, is the anomaly of the region. The highway sprawl that greets travelers is fair warning to what the rest of this city of 60,000 has to offer: but for a proud courthouse and some intriguingly decrepit old warehouses along the Napa River, it's rather lacking in character. That said, Napa is worth a quick stop to visit the **Napa Valley Visitors Bureau** (see p.679 for details). It's the most helpful in the whole valley and a good place to load up on free maps and brochures. Across the street, the Napa County Historical Society (☎707/224-1739) has free, informative materials on the region's pre-wine era. The other reason to visit is the smart wine and arts center **Copia**, built as the showcase for an organization founded by Robert Mondavi, at 500 First Street (Wed–Mon 10am–5pm; $12.50; ☎1-888/512-6742, ☏www.copia.org). The somewhat steep entry fee grants access to a thirty-minute video, the exclusively wine- or food-themed art galleries, including an interesting wall display of spent matches ignited by one of the Mondavi clan, some original Greek and Roman pottery, and the obligatory gift shop and restaurant. You can also sign up for classes and special events. Smaller attractions include the **Napa Firefighters Museum** at 1201 Main Street (Wed–Sat 11am–4pm; free; ☎707/259-0609, ☏www.napafirefightersmuseum .org), which features an array of firefighting paraphernalia, or you might want to take in some culture at the newly refurbished **Opera House** at 1030 Main Street (☎707/226-7372, ☏www.napavalleyoperahouse.org).

Yountville, nine miles north on Hwy-29, is anchored by Vintage 1870, 6525 Washington Street (daily 10.30am–5.30pm; ☎707/944-2451, ☏www .vintage1870.com), a shopping complex in a converted winery that contains a range of touristic emporia. Aside from antique shops and a few restaurants, nothing in town exerts enough pull to merit a long stop, so push on three miles to tiny **Oakville**, further north along Hwy-29. Dominated by the massive Robert Mondavi winery (see box, p.685), Oakville features a dozen top-rated wineries, and almost all of them require an appointment and charge a tasting fee, ranging from $10 for a famous Silver Oak Cabernet Sauvignon to a whopping $25 for Opus One. Besides its high-caliber wines, Oakville is known for its wonderful Oakville Grocery, an unmissable deli packed with the finest local and imported foods.

St Helena

Eighteen miles from Napa and far more appealing, **St Helena** is the largest of all the antique-shop-filled villages you'll encounter heading north. Its main street, Hwy-29, is lined by some of the Wine Country's finest old buildings, many in pristine condition, and the town itself boasts some unlikely literary attractions. St Helena is also at the heart of a large concentration of wineries, and this combination of history and location make it the de facto tourism capital of Napa Valley, home to a large concentration of luxurious lodgings and restaurants, and with a chic appeal that you'll either love or hate.

If you're driving through, at least stop off to see the quaint Craftsman-style homes that line residential **Oak Avenue**, and also to see remnants of two unlikely past residents: Robert Louis Stevenson and Ambrose Bierce, both of whom lived in St Helena back in its days as a resort. The **Silverado Museum** (Tues–Sun noon–4pm; free; ☏707/963-3757, ⓦ www.silveradomuseum.org), just off Main Street at 1490 Library Lane, has a collection of over eight thousand articles relating to Stevenson, who spent just under a year in the area, honeymooning and recovering from an illness (see p.686). It's claimed to be the second most extensive collection of Stevenson artifacts in the US, though the only thing of interest to any but the most obsessed fan is a scribbled-on manuscript of *Dr Jekyll and Mr Hyde*. The other half of the building is taken up by the **Napa Valley Wine Library** (same hours), a briefly entertaining barrage of photos and clippings relating to the development of local viticulture. On the north side of town, at 1515 Main Street, Bierce's former residence has been converted into the **Ambrose Bierce House** bed and breakfast (see p.681). The inn houses a very small collection of memorabilia relating to the misanthropic ghost-story writer and author of *The Devil's Dictionary*, who lived here for some fifteen years before heading off to fight for Pancho Villa in the Mexican Revolution and mysteriously vanishing.

Calistoga and around

Beyond St Helena, towards the far northern end of the valley, the wineries become prettier and the traffic a little thinner. At the very tip of the valley, nestling at the foot of Mount St Helena, **CALISTOGA** is perhaps the most enjoyable Napa community, featuring around twenty wineries and some fancy bistros. The town, though, is better known for its mud baths and hot springs – and the mineral water that adorns every California supermarket shelf. Sam Brannan, a young Mormon entrepreneur who made a mint out of the Gold Rush, established a resort community here in 1860. In his groundbreaking speech he attempted to assert his desire to create the "Saratoga of California," modeled upon the Adirondack gem, but in the event got tongue-tied and coined the town's unique name.

Calistoga's main attraction, then as now, is the opportunity to soak in the soothing hot water that bubbles up here from deep in the earth. A multitude of **spas** and volcanic **mud baths**, together with a homely and health-conscious atmosphere, beckon city dwellers and tourists alike. The extravagant might enjoy *Dr Wilkinson's Hot Springs*, 1507 Lincoln Avenue (treatments from $77; ☏707/942-4102, ⓦ www.drwilkinson.com), a legendary health spa and hotel whose heated mineral water and volcanic ash tension-relieving treatments have

Napa Valley wineries

Almost all of Napa Valley's **wineries** offer tastings, though not all have tours. There are more than three hundred wineries in all, producing wines of a very high standard, so your taste should ultimately determine the ones you visit. The following selections are some long-standing favorites, plus a few lesser-known hopefuls. Keep in mind that the intention is for you to get a sense of a winery's product, and perhaps buy some, rather than get tipsy, so don't expect more than a sip or two of any one sort – though some wineries do sell wines by the glass. If you want to buy a bottle, particularly from the larger producers, you can usually get it cheaper in supermarkets than at the wineries themselves, unless you ship in bulk.

Beringer Vineyards 2000 Main St, St Helena ☎707/963-7115, ⊛www.beringer.com. Napa Valley's most famous piece of architecture, the gothic "Rhine House," modeled on the ancestral Rhine Valley home of Jacob Beringer, graces the cover of many a wine magazine. Expansive lawns and a grand tasting room, heavy on dark wood, make for a regal experience. Tasting $5, tours $10–35; daily summer 10am–6pm, winter 10am–5pm.

Chateau Montelena 1429 Tubbs Lane, 2 miles north of Calistoga ☎707/942-9105, ⊛www.montelena.com. Smaller but highly rated winery, nestled below Mount St Helena. The Cabernet Sauvignon in particular is acquiring a fine reputation. Tasting daily 9.30am–4pm; $15. Estate tour and tasting 2pm; $25.

Clos Pégase 1060 Dunaweal Lane, Calistoga ☎707/942-4981, ⊛www .clospegase.com. A flamboyant upstart at the north end of the valley, this high-profile winery amalgamates fine wine and fine art, with a sculpture garden around buildings designed by postmodern architect Michael Graves. Free tours daily at 11am and 2pm; tasting daily 10.30am–5pm; $5.

Darioush 4240 Silverado Trail, northeast of Napa ☎707/257-2345, ⊛www.darioush .com. Grandiose new winery modelled on Persepolis and contructed with stone blocks imported by the owner from his native Iran. Cabernet Sauvignon and Shiraz are the signature wines. Tasting daily 10.30am–5pm; $20; tour 2pm; $50.

Domaine Chandon 1 California Drive, Yountville ☎707/944-2280, ⊛www .chandon.com. Sparkling wines from this progeny of France's Moët & Chandon can challenge the authentic champagnes from France. Vast and modern, this winery and gallery is popular with connoisseurs and features a top-notch restaurant. Tasting daily 10am–6pm; $10–20; tours 11am, 1pm, 3pm & 5pm; $7.

Goosecross Cellars 1119 State Lane, east of Yountville ☎1-800/276-9210, ⊛www.goosecross.com. It's well worth taking time to locate this friendly family-run winery, tucked away off Yountville Cross Rd. Crush-time is fun and their Chardonnay especially good. Tasting daily 10am–4.30pm; $5. Tours May–Oct Fri 10.30am & Sat 2.30pm; $20.

been overseen by the same family for almost fifty years. *Mount View Spa*, 1457 Lincoln Avenue (☎1-800/772-8838, ⊛www.mountviewspa.com), can soothe you with a variety of combined herbal and mud treatments for over $100 and offers shorter but cheaper hydrotherapy sessions. If swaddled luxury isn't what you're after, a number of slightly more down-to-earth establishments are spread along and off the mile-long main drag, Lincoln Avenue. *Golden Haven Hot Springs Spa and Resort*, 1713 Lake Street (☎707/942-6793, ⊛www.goldenhaven .com), for example, offers a one-hour mud bath, hot mineral Jacuzzi, and blanket wrap for $75, and *Calistoga Spa*, 1006 Washington Street (☎1-866/822-5772, ⊛www.calistogaspa.com), has similar rates. If that's still too expensive, ask a local resident to spray you down with their garden hose – although even that might cost a few bucks given Calistoga water's restorative reputation.

Calistoga has one standard tourist attraction in the shape of the **Sharpsteen Museum and Sam Brannan Cottage**, 1113 Washington Street (daily

Mumm Napa Valley 8445 Silverado Trail, Rutherford ☏1-800/686-6272, ⓦwww .mummnapa.com. Opened in 1986 by G.H. Mumm, France's renowned champagne house, and Seagrams, the sparkling wines from this beautifully situated winery are good but superseded by sweeping views of the surrounding valleys. The tours are particularly engaging and fun, led by witty and informative guides. Tasting daily 10am–5pm, $5–20; free hourly tours 10am–3pm, on the hour.

Napa Wine Company 7830-40 St Helena Hwy, Oakville ☏1-800/848-9630, ⓦwww .napawineco.com. Modeled on the co-operative wineries of France, the Napa Wine Company offers 25 small-vineyard owners access to state-of-the-art crushing and fermentation machinery, and also acts as a sales outlet for their vintages. Their tasting room is one of the best – and certainly the broadest – in Wine Country; daily 10am–3.30pm; $10–25.

Robert Mondavi 7801 St Helena Hwy, Oakville ☏1-888/766-6328, ⓦwww .robertmondavi.com. Long the standard-bearer for Napa Valley wines ("Bob Red" and "Bob White" are house wines at many California restaurants), they have one of the most informative and least hard-sell tours. Tours and tasting daily 10am–5pm, reservations recommended. Tastings from $15, tours from $25.

Silver Oak Cellars 915 Oakville Cross Rd, Oakville ☏1-800/273-8809, ⓦwww .silveroak.com. Lovers of Cabernet Sauvignon mustn't miss a stop at Silver Oak, the crème de la crème of the heady red that costs over $100 a bottle in some San Francisco restaurants. Sadly, though, the original winery building burnt down in 2006. Tasting daily 9am–4pm; $10.

Stag's Leap Wine Cellars 5766 Silverado Trail, east of Yountville ☏1-866/422-7523, ⓦwww.stagsleapwinecellars.com. The winery that put Napa Valley on the international map by beating a bottle of Château Lafitte-Rothschild at a Paris tasting in 1976. Still quite highly rated. Tasting daily 10am–4.30pm; $15–40; tours by appointment; $40.

Sterling Vineyards 1111 Dunaweal Lane, Calistoga ☏1-800/726-6136, ⓦwww .sterlingvineyards.com. Famous for the aerial tram ride that brings visitors up the 300-foot knoll to the tasting room, with a gorgeous view of Napa Valley. The extravagant white mansion, modeled after a monastery on the Greek island of Mykonos, is Napa's most recognizable. Tasting their wide selection of wines on the View Terrace is a memorable experience. Aerial tram, tasting, and self-guided tour 10.30am–4.30pm; Mon–Fri $15, Sat & Sun $20.

V. Sattui 1111 White Lane, St Helena ☏1-800/799-2337, ⓦwww.vsattui.com. Small, family-owned winery right off Hwy-29 with award-winning wines – the Riesling and Gamay Rouge are particularly good. Sattui wines are only sold at the winery or through the mail. Gourmet deli next door to stock up for a picnic in the popular tree-shaded grove. Tastings daily summer 9am–6pm, winter 9am–5pm; $10–25.

11am–4pm; $3 donation; ☏707/942-5911, ⓦwww.sharpsteen-museum.org). Founded by long-serving Disney producer Ben Sharpsteen, the quaint little museum contains some of his personal effects, including his Oscar for the pearl-diving film *Ama Girls*, as well as a model of the original resort and lots of biographical material on Sam Brannan, plus a full-size re-creation of his cottage. You can check what else is going on in town and get maps at the friendly **Chamber of Commerce**, 1506 Lincoln Avenue (Mon–Fri 10am–5pm, Sat 10am–4pm, Sun 11am–3pm; ☏1-866/306-5588, ⓦwww.calistogachamber.com).

Heading northwest out of town on Hwy-128 takes you up the ridge of the **Mayacamas**, a picturesque and steep drive that winds to the summit and spirals southwest, depositing you in Santa Rosa. More evidence of Calistoga's lively underground activity can be seen on this route at the **Old Faithful Geyser** (daily: summer 9am–6pm; winter 9am–5pm; $8; ☏707/942-6463, ⓦwww .oldfaithfulgeyser.com), two miles north of town at 1299 Tubbs Lane, which spurts boiling water sixty feet into the air at nine- to forty-minute intervals, depending on the time of year. The water source was discovered during oil-drilling here in the 1920s, when search equipment struck a force estimated to be up to a thousand pounds per square foot; the equipment was blown away and, despite heroic efforts to control it, the geyser has continued to go off like clockwork ever since. Landowners finally realized that they'd never tame it and turned it into a high-yield tourist attraction, using the same name as the famous spouter at Yellowstone National Park. Just south of the geyser, stylish Venetian artist Carlo Marchiori conducts weekly guided tours of his imaginatively decorated house, **Villa Ca'Toga** (May–Oct Sat only 11.15am; $25 per person with minimum of 25 people). The Palladian villa is full of delicate whimsy – one room is painted as if you are a bird in a cage, another is adorned with painted cows – and the grounds secrete mock ruined temples, a Buddhist corner, and a shell-encrusted cave. An idea of his art can be gleaned, and tours arranged, through his gallery at 1206 Cedar Street (℡707/942-3900, ⓦwww .catoga.com).

The **Petrified Forest** (daily: summer 9am–7pm; winter 9am–5pm; $6; ℡707/942-6667, ⓦwww.petrifiedforest.org), five miles west of Calistoga, is a popular local tourist trap, but there's little worth stopping here for unless you're a geologist or really into hardened wood. After an entire redwood grove was toppled during an eruption of Mount St Helena some three million years ago, the forest here was petrified by the action of the silica-laden volcanic ash as it gradually seeped into the decomposing fibers of the uprooted trees.

Mount St Helena

The clearest sign of the local volcanic unrest is the massive conical mountain that marks the north end of the Napa Valley, **Mount St Helena**, some eight miles north of Calistoga. The 4343-foot summit is worth a climb for its great views – on a very clear day you can see Point Reyes and the Pacific Coast to the west, San Francisco to the south, the towering Sierra Nevada to the east, and impressive Mount Shasta to the north. It is, however, a long steep climb (ten miles round-trip) and you need to set off early in the morning to enjoy it – take plenty of water (and maybe a bottle of local wine).

The mountain and most of the surrounding land is protected and preserved as the **Robert Louis Stevenson Park** (daily 8am–sunset; free), though the connection is fairly weak: Stevenson spent his honeymoon here in 1880 in a bunkhouse with Fanny Osborne, recuperating from tuberculosis and exploring the valley – a plaque marks the spot where his bunkhouse once stood. Little else about the park's winding roads and dense shrub growth evokes its former notoriety, though it's a pretty enough place to take a break from the wineries and have a picnic. In Stevenson's novel, *Silverado Squatters*, he describes the highlight of the honeymoon as the day he managed to taste eighteen of local wine baron Jacob Schram's champagnes in one sitting. Quite an extravagance, especially considering that Schramsberg champagne is held in such high esteem that Richard Nixon took a few bottles with him when he went to visit Chairman Mao.

Sonoma Valley

On looks alone, the crescent-shaped **SONOMA VALLEY** beats Napa Valley hands down. This smaller, altogether more rustic stretch of land curves between oak-covered mountain ranges from the small town of **Sonoma** a few miles north along Hwy-12 to the hamlet of **Glen Ellen** and **Jack London State Park**, and ends at the booming bedroom community of **Santa Rosa**. The area is known as the "Valley of the Moon," a label that's mined by tour operators for its connection to former resident Jack London, whose book of the same name retold a Native American legend about how, as you move through the valley, the moon seems to rise several times from behind the various peaks. The area has long been a favorite with visitors: Spain, England, Russia, and Mexico have all raised their flags in Sonoma, proclaiming it their own. The US took over in 1846 during the Bear Flag Revolt against Mexico in Sonoma's central plaza and annexed all of California.

▲ Sonoma County vineyard

Sonoma Valley's **wineries** are generally smaller and more casual than their Napa counterparts, even though the Sonoma Valley fathered the wine industry from which Napa derives its fame. Colonel Agostin Haraszthy first started planting grapes here in the 1850s, and his Buena Vista Winery in Sonoma still operates today.

Sonoma

Behind a layer of somewhat touristy stores and restaurants, **Sonoma** retains a good deal of its Spanish and Mexican architecture. The town's charm emanates from the grassy square that acts as downtown's centerpiece, where visitors and locals alike linger over newspapers or lazy picnics. This is indicative of the town's welcoming and relaxed feel, although as a popular retirement spot with a median age of about fifty, it's not exactly bubbling with action.

Today, a number of historic buildings and relics stand in the sprawling **Sonoma State Historic Park** ($2 combined entry to all sites; all daily 10am–5pm). The restored **Mission San Francisco Solano de Sonoma** was the last and northernmost of the California missions, established by nervous Mexican rulers fearful of expansionist Russian fur traders. Half a mile west stands the **General Vallejo Home**, the leader's ornate former residence, dominated by decorated, filigreed eaves and slender, Gothic-revival arched windows. The chalet-style storehouse next door has been turned into a **museum** of artifacts from the general's reign.

There's more to Sonoma than historic buildings, though, and relaxing cafés, great restaurants, rare bookstores, and a 1930s-era movie house ring the plaza, making Sonoma a nice town to come back to after a day in the vineyards.

Sonoma wineries

Over 45 **wineries** are scattered across the Sonoma Valley, but there's a good concentration in a well-signposted group a mile east of Sonoma Plaza, down East Napa Street. Some are within walking distance, but often along quirky back roads, so take a winery map from the tourist office and follow the signs closely. If you're tired of driving around, visit the handy Wine Exchange of Sonoma, 452 First Street E (daily 10am–5.30pm; ☎707/938-1794), a commercial tasting room where, for a small fee, you can sample the best wines from all over California. There's also a selection of 300 beers.

Bartholomew Park Winery 1000 Vineyard Lane ☎707/935-9511, ⓦwww .bartholomewparkwinery.com. This lavish Spanish Colonial building is surrounded by some great topiary in the gardens and extensive vineyards. The wines are relatively inexpensive vintages that appeal to the pocket and palate alike; a safe bet for buying a case. There's a good little regional history museum, too, that also provides an introduction to local viticulture. Self-guided tours of the winery and $10 tastings daily 11am–4.30pm.

Benziger Family Winery 1883 London Ranch Rd, Glen Ellen ☎1-888/490-2739, ⓦwww.benziger.com. Beautiful vineyard perched on the side of an extinct volcano next to Jack London State Park. There are five or six daily tram tours through the fields ($10) with emphasis on viticulture, or a self-guided tour introducing trellis techniques. Tastings daily 10am–5pm; $10.

Buena Vista Carneros 18000 Old Winery Rd ☎1-800/926-1266, ⓦwww .buenavistacarneros.com. Oldest and grandest of the wineries, founded in 1857, whose wine is re-establishing a good reputation after some slim years. The tasting room, a restored state historical landmark, features a small art gallery. Tasting daily 10am–5pm; $5–10 including glass. Various tours available, ranging from free self-guided tours to a two-hour Sonoma Wine and Cheese Experience for $50.

Chateau St Jean 8555 Sonoma Hwy, Kenwood ☎1-800/543-7572, ⓦwww .chateaustjean.com. Attractive estate with an overwhelming aroma of wine throughout the buildings. Quirky tower to climb from where you can admire the view of the surrounding countryside. Tastings daily 10am–5pm; $5–10. Tours daily 11am & 2pm; $15.

Gundlach-Bundschu 2000 Denmark St, Sonoma ☎707/939-3015,

ⓦwww.gundlach-bundschu.com. Set back about a mile away from the main cluster, Gun-Bun, as it's known to locals, is highly regarded, having stealthily crept up from the lower ranks of the wine league. The plain, functional building is deceptive – this is premium stuff and definitely not to be overlooked. The winery also hosts various theatrical, cinematic, and musical events throughout the summer. Tasting daily 11am–4.30pm; $5–10. Tours Sat & Sun hourly noon–3pm, weekdays by appointment; free.

Mayo Family Winery 13101 Arnold Drive, Glen Ellen ☎707/938-9401, ⓦwww .mayofamilywinery.com. Relatively new winery with a cozy feel and friendly welcome, matching the small-time production of under 5000 cases annually. Complimentary tasting daily 10.30am–6.30pm; barrel tasting tours Fri–Sun 2 & 4pm. They also have a tasting room in the Duhring Building at the southwest corner of Sonoma Plaza; daily 11.30am–6pm.

Ravenswood 18701 Gehricke Rd, Sonoma ☎707/933-2332 or 1-888/669-4679, ⓦwww.ravenswood-wine .com. Noted for their "gutsy, unapologetic" Zinfandel and advertising a "no wimpy" approach to the wine business, the staff at this unpretentious winery is particularly friendly and easy-going. Well-known to locals for its summer barbecues. Tastings and tours daily 10.30am–4.30pm; $10.

Sebastiani Vineyards & Winery 389 4th St E, Sonoma ☎1-800/888-5532, ⓦwww .sebastiani.com. One of California's oldest family wineries, only four blocks from central Sonoma, it now boasts a newly renovated hospitality center, while the rest of the estate is being returned to its original appearance. There's another tasting room on the central square at 103 W Napa St (☎707/933-3291). Free tasting and tours via tram every half-hour. Daily 10am–5pm.

Sonoma Plaza was the site of the **Bear Flag Revolt**, the 1846 event that propelled California into independence from Mexico, and then statehood. In this much-romanticized episode, American settlers in the region, who had long lived in uneasy peace under the Spanish and, later, Mexican rulers, were threatened with expulsion from California along with all other non-Mexican immigrants. In response, a band of thirty armed settlers – including the infamous John Fremont and Kit Carson – descended upon the disused and unguarded presidio at Sonoma, taking the retired and much-respected commander, Colonel Mariano Guadalupe Vallejo, as their prisoner. Ironically, Vallejo had long advocated the American annexation of California and supported the aims of his rebel captors, but he was nonetheless bundled off to Sutter's Fort in Sacramento and held there while the militant settlers declared California an independent republic. The **Bear Flag**, which served as the model for the current state flag, was fashioned from a "feminine undergarment and muslin petticoat" and painted with a grizzly bear and single star. Raised on Sonoma Plaza, where a small plaque marks the spot today, the Bear Flag flew over the Republic of California for a short time. Three weeks later, the US declared war on Mexico and, without firing a shot, took possession of the entire Pacific Coast. While far from a frontier town now, Sonoma once had a much wilder side and in fact gave the English language a slang word for prostitutes. Not long after the Bear Flag revolt, General Lee Hooker arrived, bringing along a group of ladies employed to cheer up the troops. The ladies soon became known as "Hooker's girls," and then simply, "hookers."

Jack London State Park

Continuing north on Hwy-12, beautiful winding roads lead to the cozy hamlet of **Glen Ellen**, five miles from Sonoma, and more interestingly, **Jack London State Park** (daily: summer 9.30am–7pm; winter 10am–5pm; $6 per car; ℡707/938-5216, ⓦwww.jacklondonpark.com). A half-mile up London Ranch Road past the Benziger Family winery, the state park sits on the 140 acres of ranchland the famed author of *The Call of the Wild* owned with his wife Charmian. A one-mile walk through the woods leads to the ruins of the **Wolf House**, which was to be the London ancestral home: "My house will be standing, act of God permitting, for a thousand years," wrote the author. But in 1913, a month before they were to move in, the house burned to the ground, sparing only the boulder frame. Mounted blueprints point out the splendor that was to be: the mansion contained a manuscript room, sleeping tower, gun room, and indoor reflecting pool. Nearby lies the final resting place of London – a red boulder from the house's ruins under which his wife sprinkled his ashes. Just off the parking lot, the **House of Happy Walls** (daily 10am–5pm; free) is a jewel of a London museum, housing an interesting collection of souvenirs he picked up traveling the globe. Manuscripts, rejection letters (over six hundred before he was published the first time), and the note explaining his and Charmian's resignation from the Socialist Party fill the exhibits, along with reproductions of the Londons' rooms and plenty of photographs. A nearby trail leads past a picnic ground to **London's Cottage** (Sat & Sun noon–4pm; free), where he died. West of the cottage, a trail leads one mile toward the mountains and into the woods, ending at the lake London had built so he and Charmian could fish and swim. Bring a bottle of wine and soak in the sunny charm; given the hoopla of the Wine Country, the usually uncrowded museum and lovely park grounds feel like an oasis of tranquility.

Santa Rosa

Sixty miles due north of San Francisco on US-101, and about twenty miles from Sonoma on Hwy-12, **Santa Rosa**, the largest town in Sonoma County, sits at the top end of the valley and is more or less the hub of this part of the Wine Country. It's a very different world from the indulgence of other Wine Country towns, however; much of it is given over to shopping centers and roadside malls. In an attempt to form a central pedestrian-only hub, **Historic Railroad Square** – a strip of red-brick-facade boutiques – has been developed, but it will never be mistaken for St Helena's Main Street or Sonoma Plaza. With real estate prices higher than ever in the Bay Area, Santa Rosa is exploding with growth, making it both a bedroom community for San Francisco and site of the Wine Country's cheapest lodging, with major hotel and motel chains located around town. It also has a decent selection of restaurants and bars. Full listings of what the town has to offer can be found at the **CVB**, 9 Fourth Street (Mon–Sat 9am–5pm, Sun 10am–5pm; ℡1-800/404-7673, ⓦwww.visitsantarosa.com), by Railroad Square.

You can kill an hour or two at the **Luther Burbank Home and Gardens**, at the junction of Santa Rosa and Sonoma avenues (gardens daily 8am–dusk; free; guided tours Tues–Sun every half-hour 10am–3.30pm; $5; ℡707/524-5445, ⓦwww.lutherburbank.org), where California's best-known horticulturist is remembered in the house where he lived and the splendid gardens where he created some of his most unusual hybrids. The **Redwood Empire Ice Arena**, 1667 W Steele Lane (℡707/546-7147, ⓦwww.snoopyshomeice.com), was built by *Peanuts* creator Charles Schulz as a gift to the community. The arena actually comprises two buildings: the ice skating rink and the Charles M. Shulz Museum (summer Mon–Fri 11am–5pm, Sat & Sun 10am–5pm, closed Tues off season; $8; ℡707/546-3385, ⓦwww.schulzmuseum.org), a paean to all things *Peanuts* and a lasting tribute to the much-loved Schulz, who died in 2000.

One enterprise few people would expect to find tucked away in the Wine Country is a full-blown **wildlife refuge**, yet spreading over four hundred acres of the pristine hills between the two valleys, five miles northeast of Santa Rosa, is **Safari West**, 3115 Porter Creek Road (℡1-800/616-2695, ⓦwww.safariwest.com). Set up in 1989 by Peter Lang, son of *Daktari* producer Otto, the refuge runs breeding programs for hundreds of rare mammal and bird species. Three-hour African-style **jeep tours** (daily 9am, 1pm & 4pm in summer; 10am & 2pm in winter; $62) take you through vast open compounds of herd animals, and you can wander at leisure past large cages of cheetah and primates or the leafy aviary, while expert guides supply detailed background on the furry and feathered inhabitants. You can even feed the giraffe, if you're lucky. Accommodation in genuine African luxury tents, hung on stilted wooden decks, is available for a princely $225 per unit, and filling buffet meals are served in the mess tent.

Eating and drinking

Culinary satisfaction looms around every corner in the Wine Country. California cuisine is almost standard in both valleys, and freshness and innovative presentation are very much the order of the day. **Yountville**, in particular, is little more than a string of high-style restaurants, any of which is up there with the best San Francisco has to offer, with prices to match. **St Helena** and **Calistoga**, though more low-key, are both gourmet paradises. **Sonoma**, too, has its share and is strong on Italian food, while the size of **Santa Rosa** allows for a good deal of diversity. **Bars** are mostly locals' or immigrant Hispanic workers' hangouts, and nightlife nearly nonexistent, perhaps a result of the free booze on offer from the wineries.

Inexpensive to moderate restaurants

Armadillo's 1304 Main St, St Helena ☏ 707/963-8082. Good-value Mexican cuisine, such as fine quesadillas and burritos, in a brightly painted dining room.

Arrigoni's Deli 701 Fourth St, Santa Rosa ☏ 707/545-1297. The place to go for a tasty snack or picnic supplies, serving an array of gourmet meats, cheeses, and other savories.

Bosko's Trattoria 1364 Lincoln Ave, Calistoga ☏ 707/942-9088. Standard Italian restaurant preparing moderately priced, fresh pasta dishes. Cheerful, and popular with families.

Café Citti 9049 Sonoma Hwy, Kenwood ☏ 707/833-2690. Small, inexpensive trattoria with great Italian food and an intimate yet casual atmosphere.

Café Sarafornia 1413 Lincoln Ave, Calistoga ☏ 707/942-0555. Famous for delicious and enormous breakfasts and lunches, with lines around the block on weekends. Let the owner talk your ear off.

Coffee Garden Café 421 First St W, Sonoma ☏ 707/996-6645. Fresh sandwiches are served on the back patio of this 150-year-old adobe, which was converted into a café with small gift shop.

Cucina Viansa 400 E First St, Sonoma ☏ 707/935-5656. Very reasonably priced at $9–15, considering the small but creative and delicious selection of Italian specialties on offer.

Gary Chu's 611 Fifth St, Santa Rosa ☏ 707/526-5840. Large helpings of high-quality, award-winning Chinese food, like jade garden beef, at very reasonable prices. Closed Mon.

La Casa 121 E Spain St, Sonoma ☏ 707/996-3406. Friendly, festive, and inexpensive Mexican restaurant just across from the Sonoma Mission. Enjoy an enchilada or refreshing margarita on the sunny outdoor patio.

The Model Bakery 1357 Main St, St Helena ☏ 707/963-8192. Local hangout serving the best bread in Napa Valley, as well as sandwiches and pizza.

Peking Palace 1001 Second St, Napa ☏ 707/257-7197. Mandarin and Szechuan cuisine served up in a spacious and snazzy space in the heart of downtown Napa.

Piccolino's 1385 Napa Town Center, First St, Napa ☏ 707/251-0100. Roomy and light joint in the modern plaza, serving a wide variety of Italian faves at reasonable prices.

Puerto Vallerta 1473 Lincoln Ave, Calistoga ☏ 707/942-6563. Heaps of tasty and genuine Mexican grub can be consumed in the shady courtyard of this establishment, tucked in beside the Cal-Mart supermarket.

Rins Thai 139 E Napa St, Sonoma ☏ 707/938-1462. Good range of spicy curries and other Thai favorites available at this modest restaurant, right on the main square.

The Schellville Grill 22900 Broadway, Sonoma ☏ 707/996-5151. No longer the *Ford's Café* of yore but still an institution with locals, who flock here for the ample burgers and sandwiches, some with surprisingly imaginative touches thrown in.

Upmarket restaurants

All Seasons Bistro 1400 Lincoln Ave, Calistoga ☏ 707/942-9111. Exquisite main courses such as roasted monkfish with fava beans and Bohemian pheasant cost $20–30 in this upscale but relaxed bistro.

Bouchon 6534 Washington St, Yountville ☏ 707/944-8037. Parisian chic and haute cuisine at high prices – the terrine de fois gras de canard goes for $45, but most entrées are around $25–30.

Brannan's 1374 Lincoln Ave, Calistoga ☏ 707/942-2233. Pecan-stuffed quail, fresh steamed oysters, and a wonderful wooden interior make this rather expensive, high-profile eatery worth a visit.

Café La Haye 140 E Napa St, Sonoma ☏ 707/935-5994. Only eleven tables, and always packed for its lovely, lively interior and tasty Italian/California cuisine. Mains around $20.

Cole's Chop House 1122 Main St, Napa ☏ 707/224-6328. This is the place to come for huge chunks of well-prepared red meat. Very spacious inside and top service, but with a somewhat stilted atmosphere.

Culinary Institute of America Greystone Restaurant 2555 Main St, St Helena ☏ 707/967-1010. California/Mediterranean cuisine served in an elegant ivy-walled mansion just outside of town, with a tastefully wacky Art Deco interior. Reasonably priced considering the delicious, large portions of chicken, duck, fish, and venison.

The General's Daughter 400 W Spain St, Sonoma ☏ 707/938-4004. Creative California cuisine is served in three- to five-course meals for $45–65;

the Victorian building was formally owned by General Vallejo's daughter.

The Girl & The Fig 110 W Spain St, Sonoma ℡707/938-3634. On the ground floor of the *Sonoma Hotel*, this well-known restaurant offers French dinners and weekend brunch from a menu as eclectic as its name. Entrées mainly $20–25.

Glen Ellen Inn 13670 Arnold Drive, Glen Ellen ℡707/996-6409. Husband-and-wife team cook and serve slightly pricey gourmet dishes in an intimate, romantic dining room with half a dozen tables. Specializes in oysters and martinis.

Mustards Grill 7399 St Helena Hwy (Hwy-29), Yountville ℡707/944-2424. Huge range of starters and main dishes, like tea-smoked Peking duck with "100 almond-onion sauce." Reckon on spending well over $30 a head and waiting for a table if you come on a weekend.

Rutherford Grill 1180 Rutherford Rd, Rutherford ℡707/963-1920. Large portions of classic yet classy contemporary American food – the mashed potatoes should not be missed – served in a handsome new dining room popular for its martinis and as a meeting place.

Saffron Restaurant 13648 Arnold Drive, Glen Ellen ℡707/938-4844. The food has a Hispanic touch in this new establishment, which also stocks fine wines from Spain. The delicious lentil soup is indeed laced generously with saffron.

Tra Vigne 1050 Charter Oak Ave, St Helena ℡707/963-4444. On the south side of town, but it feels as if you've been transported to Tuscany. Excellent food and fine wines served up in a lovely vine-covered courtyard or elegant dining room, but

you pay for the privilege. They also have a small deli, where you can pick up picnic goodies.

Zuzu 829 Main St, Napa ℡707/224-5885. Not the place to come if ravenous, but this popular tapas bar offers tasty fare and a good wine list in its trendy interior.

Bars

Amigos Grill and Cantina 19315 Sonoma Hwy, Sonoma ℡707/939-0743. Award-winning margaritas using your choice of one of 20 tequilas and a home-made mix.

Ana's Cantina 1205 Main St, St Helena ℡707/963-4921. Long-standing, down-to-earth saloon and Mexican restaurant with billiards and darts tournaments.

Compadres Bar and Grill 6539 Washington St, Yountville ℡707/944-2406. Outdoor patio seating and amazing martinis and margaritas, with free salsa and chips.

Downtown Joe's 902 Main St at Second, Napa ℡707/258-2337. One of Napa's most popular and lively spots for sandwiches, ribs, and pasta, with outdoor dining by the river and beer brewed on the premises. About the only place in town open until midnight and a good spot to meet locals.

Murphy's Irish Pub 464 First St E, Sonoma ℡707/935-0660. Small bar with an eclectic interior and a few outdoor tables serving basic pub grub and European beers.

Third Street Aleworks 610 Third St, Santa Rosa ℡707/523-3060. Frequent live music and hearty American grub like burgers and pizza, washed down with microbrewed ale, are the order of the day at this lively joint.

The northern coast

The fog-bound towns and windswept, craggy beaches of the **NORTHERN COAST** couldn't be farther removed from Southern California's sandy, sunny strip of ocean. Stretching north of San Francisco to the Oregon border, the northern coast is better suited for hiking than sunbathing, with a climate of cool temperatures year-round and a huge network of national, state, and regional **parks** preserving magnificent redwood trees. **Wildlife** thrives here and is always in view, from seals lounging on rocks around Goat Rock Beach in the south to elk chomping on berry bushes in the north, all against a backdrop of spectacular scenery. Far rarer fauna has been spotted up here as well: the legendary Bigfoot supposedly leaves footprints through the forest, and Ewoks once battled the Galactic Empire under the direction of *Star Wars* creator George Lucas, who used areas north of Orick as the set for *The Return of the Jedi*.

The only way to see the coast properly is on the painfully slow but visually magnificent Hwy-1, which hugs the coast for two hundred miles through the wild counties of **Sonoma** and **Mendocino**, before turning sharply inland at Legget to join US-101 and **Humboldt County**. The hundred miles of wild coastline Hwy-1 never reaches has become known, appropriately, as the **Lost Coast**, a virgin territory of campsites and trails. If you're heading for the coast from the Wine Country, a pleasant route is via the quieter wineries of the **Russian River Valley**, or you can take US-101 and detour inland further north to placid **Clear Lake**, before cutting across to Mendocino. North of here, the redwoods take over, blanketing the landscape all the way to Oregon, doubling as raw material for the huge logging industries (the prime source of employment in the area) and the region's prime tourist attraction, most notably in the **Redwood National Park**. **Eureka**, the coast's largest city, is neighbored by lively **Arcata**, home to **Humboldt State University** and thousands of Birkenstock sandals. The last stretch of redwood coast before the Oregon state line lies in **Del Norte County**, whose functional seat of **Crescent City** offers little to detain the visitor for long.

You'll need to be fairly independent to **get around** this region: only one Amtrak Thruway and two Greyhound buses a day travel via US-101, which parallels the coastal highway, but they don't link up with the coast until Eureka and terminate just north of there. Consequently most visitors travel by car and should, in summertime, expect legions of slow-moving campers trying to negotiate the two-lane road's hairpin curves.

The Sonoma coast and Russian River Valley

Hwy-1 twists and winds along the edge of the **SONOMA COAST** through persistent fog that, once burned off by the sun, reveals oyster beds, seal breeding grounds, and twenty-foot-high rhododendrons. A spectacular introduction to the northern coast, Sonoma County's western rim is never short on visitors due to its proximity to San Francisco. But tourist activity is confined to a few narrow corridors at the height of summer, leaving behind a network of north coast villages and backwater wineries that for most of the year are all but asleep. The coast is colder and lonelier than the villages along the valley, and at some point most people head inland for a new scene and a break from the pervasive fog. What both areas have in common, though, is a reluctance to change. As wealthy San Franciscans cast their eyes towards the north for potential second-home sites, the California Coastal Commission's policy of beach access for all keeps the architects at bay, making the Sonoma coast one of the few remaining undeveloped coastal areas in California; the southern third of the coast is almost entirely state beach.

At the tiny town of Jenner, Hwy-116 heads inland along the Russian River, leading to the **RUSSIAN RIVER VALLEY**, an affluent summer recreation area popular for its canoeing, swimming, wineries, and gay resorts. This part of Sonoma County is also the center of the Farm Trails ecotourism effort – check out Ⓦ www.farmtrails.org for more details.

The Sonoma coast

Bodega Bay, about 65 miles north of San Francisco, is the first Sonoma County village you reach on Hwy-1. Pomo and Miwok Indians populated the area peacefully for centuries, until Captain Lt Juan Francisco de la Bodega y Quadra Mollineda anchored his ship in the bay and "discovered" it in 1775. Hitchcock filmed the waterside scenes for *The Birds* here; an unsettling number of his cast can still be found squawking down by the harbor. Not so long ago, a depleted fishing industry, a couple of restaurants, and some isolated seaside cottages were all there was to Bodega Bay, but in recent years San Franciscans have got wind of its appeal and holiday homes and modern retail developments now crowd the waterside.

If you're traveling the whole coast, Bodega Bay makes a tolerable first stop (although better beaches, weather, and services exist in Jenner, fourteen miles north). Of several **places to stay**, the *Bodega Harbor Inn*, 1345 Bodega Avenue (℡707/875-3594, Ⓦwww.bodegaharborinn.com; ❸), is the best value in town, while the extremely comfortable *Bodega Coast Inn*, 521 Hwy-1 (℡1-800/346-6999, Ⓦwww.bodegacoastinn.com; ❺), has beautifully refurbished rooms with fireplaces. Reservations are pretty much essential in summer and on weekends throughout the year. If you don't have a reservation, the **Sonoma Coast Visitor Center**, 850 Hwy-1 (Mon–Thurs 10am–6pm, Fri & Sat 10am–8pm, Sun 10am–7pm; ℡707/875-3866, Ⓦwww.bodegabay.com), has information on availability throughout the area. **Campsites** are available at the *Bodega Dunes Campground* (℡707/875-3483, reserve on ℡1-800/444-7275, Ⓦwww .reserveamerica.com; $25), two miles north of the village on Hwy-1 at the base of a windy peninsula known as **Bodega Head**, laid out across sand dunes that end in coastal cliffs behind the beach. There are **hiking** and **horseback riding** trails around the dunes behind the beach – though in summer these tend to be packed with picnicking families, and for less crowded routes you should head up the coast.

If you're looking for a **restaurant**, *Brisas del Mar*, 2001 Hwy-1 (℡707/875-9190), does inexpensive pastas and Mexican dishes, as well as seafood, while *Lucas Wharf*, 595 Hwy-1 (℡707/875-3522), specializes in crab (mid-Nov to June) and salmon (mid-May to Sept) dishes at around $20, and has a good menu of local wines. As part of the upscale *Inn at the Tides*, the equally pricey *Tides Wharf and Restaurant*, 835 Hwy-1 (℡707/875-3652), gives a good viewpoint for watching fishing boats unload their catch. Hearty breakfasts, sandwiches, and full meals can be enjoyed at the *Sandpiper Restaurant*, 1410 Bay Flat Road (℡707/875-2278). Nearby, at 1580 Eastshore Road, *The Seaweed Café* (℡707/875-2700) offers a rather limited menu of pricey California cuisine. Bodega Bay Surf Shack in Pelican Plaza, 1400 Hwy-1 (℡707/875-3944), rents out bikes, kayaks, and windsurfing equipment at standard rates. For a **tour** of the bay, head over to Wil's Fishing Adventures, 1580 Eastshore Road ($10; ℡707/875-2323), where boats leave daily at 6pm, if there are enough punters, and tour the locations where *The Birds* was filmed, the area where Sir Francis Drake supposedly really landed, and Bodega Rock, home to sea lions and oceanic birds.

North of Bodega Bay to Jenner

North of Bodega Bay, along the **Sonoma Coast State Beach** (actually a series of beaches separated by rocky bluffs), the coastline coarsens and the trails become more dramatic. It's a wonderful stretch to hike – quite possible in a day for an experienced hiker – although the shale formations are often unstable and you must stick to the trails, which are actually quite demanding. Of Sonoma's thirteen miles of beaches, the finest are surfer-friendly **Salmon Creek Beach**, a couple of miles north of Bodega Bay and site of the park headquarters, and **Goat Rock Beach**, at the top of the coast. The latter offers the chance to get

▲ Coastline near Bodega Bay

close to harbor seals. For **horseback riding**, *Chanslor Guest Ranch*, 2660 Hwy-1 (℡707/875-3333, ⓦwww.chanslor.com), requires a two-person minimum for their selection of rides, which range from a thirty-minute wetlands jaunt ($30 per person) to hour-long rides along Salmon Creek ($50) and on the beach of Sand Dune State Park (1hr 30min; $70). Located on the same property is a B&B (℡707/875-2721; ⑥); staying here takes ten percent off the price of a ride but is worth it only if you plan on doing a lot of riding.

Campgrounds are dotted along the coast (call ☎707/875-3483 for information), but the best **places to stay** are in the tiny seaside village of **Jenner**, which marks the turnoff for the Russian River Valley – a small, friendly place where you can stay in the salubrious rooms, cabins, and cottages of *The Jenner Inn*, 10400 Hwy-1 (☎1-800/732-2377, ⊛www.jennerinn.com; ❺), or the quaint cabins of *River's End Resort* (☎707/865-2484, ⊛www.ilovesunsets.com; ❺). The **Russian River** joins the ocean in Jenner, and a massive sand spit at its mouth provides a breeding ground for harbor seals from March to June. The *Seagull Deli*, 10439 Hwy-1, sells wonderful clam chowder on a deck along the river-mouth to accompany your viewing.

Fort Ross and beyond

North of Jenner, the population evaporates and Hwy-1 turns into a slalom course of hairpin bends and steep inclines for twelve miles as far as **Fort Ross State Historic Park** (daily 8am–sunset; $6 per car), which houses the **Fort Compound** (daily 10am–4.30pm; free). At the start of the nineteenth century, San Francisco was still the northernmost limit of Spanish occupation in Alta California, and from 1812 to 1841 Russian fur traders quietly settled this part of the coast, clubbing the California sea otter almost to extinction, building a fort to use as a trading outpost, and growing crops for the Russian stations in Alaska. Officially they posed no territorial claims, but by the time the Spanish had gauged the extent of the settlement, the fort was heavily armed and vigilantly manned with a view to continued eastward expansion. The Russians traded here for thirty years until over-hunting and the failure of their shipbuilding efforts led them to pull out of the region. They sold the fort and chattels to one John Sutter in 1841, who moved them to his holdings in the Sacramento Valley, so all you see is an accomplished reconstruction built using the original techniques. Among the empty bunkers and storage halls, the most interesting buildings are the Russian Orthodox chapel and the commandant's house, with its fine library and wine cellar. At the entrance, a potting shed, which labors under the delusion that it is a **museum**, provides cursory details on the history of the fort, with a few maps and diagrams.

Fort Ross has a small beach and picnicking facilities, and you can **camp** just south of the park entrance at *Reef Campground* (☎707/847-3286; $18) or in **Salt Point State Park** (☎707/847-3221, reserve on ☎1-800/444-7275, ⊛www.reserveamerica.com; $25), six miles north on Hwy-1. Two reasonable **hotel** options exist close to the two parks. *Fort Ross Lodge*, fifteen miles north of Jenner at 20705 Hwy-1 (☎707/847-3333, ⊛www.fortrosslodge.com; ❹), provides a VCR, microwave, coffeemaker, small refrigerator in all rooms, each of which have a private patio and barbecue, and some much pricier suites with hot tub. A little further north, the *Timber Cove Inn*, 21780 Hwy-1 (☎1-800/987-8319, ⊛www.timbercoveinn.com; ❸), is also comfortable, with splendid ocean views from the costlier rooms and an intimate **restaurant**. The restaurant at the *Salt Point Lodge*, 23255 Hwy-1 (☎707/847-3234), also serves fine seafood and steak dinners for $15–20, but the rooms are reported to be noisy.

One of Sonoma County's most accessible and beautiful beaches, part of Salt Point State Park, is at **Gerstle Cove** (daily 8am–sunset; $6 per car), which includes a paved, wheelchair-accessible path from the cove to Salt Point, past kelp beds, wave-battered rocks, and lounging harbor seals. The park's rainfall and habitat make mushrooms thrive, and Gerstle Cove is a popular place for **mushroom gatherers** to park their cars and begin foraging, which the park permits. Ask the ranger for the sheet of guidelines when you enter the lot. Just north of Salt Point and a little inland, the **Kruse Rhododendron State**

Epicurean California

The rich diversity of California's food and wine holds many contradictions. Los Angeles is the land of protein bars, salads, and the trendy diets of wannabe actresses, but it's also a destination for burgers and the home of innovative pizza from Wolfgang Puck. In the north, the San Francisco Bay Area spawned the state's signature California cuisine, a style of cooking that emphasizes the use of local, seasonal ingredients that is now the standard for fine dining in the US; it's also the birthplace of the modern-day burrito.

▲ Organic farm, Bolinas

California cuisine

California cuisine got its start in Berkeley in the 1970s, when **Alice Waters** began preparing French recipes using the best local ingredients, adjusting the menu of her restaurant, *Chez Panisse*, according to the seasons. LA's Puck, of the *Spago* restaurants and glitzy post-Oscar celebrity bashes, helped popularize the cuisine. Scan the day's

▼ Light California fare

menu at a fine California restaurant these days, and you might think you're reading a culinary sonnet to the state's myriad farms, as chefs carefully and colorfully chronicle whence every morsel of pork and each artichoke leaf hails. In addition to the emphasis on **local ingredients**, this practice also stems from the fact that many Northern Californians have long worked to make their food organic and cruelty-free. Other celebrated California chefs include Michael Mina and Gary Danko, both of whom have eponymous eateries in San Francisco, and Thomas Keller, whose *French Laundry* in Napa is widely considered the best restaurant in the country.

Burgers and fast food

What the Bay Area did for fine dining, southern California did for the US's iconic dish: the hamburger. The rise of this quintessentially American food is tied to the birth of car culture in 1940s LA, where the love of the automobile spawned a new type of restaurant, the **drive-in**. The world's most famous fast-food chain began in San Bernardino as a drive-in run by the McDonald brothers. Other California-born chains with roots in this era include *Jack in the Box*, *Taco Bell*, and *In-N-Out*. Among these, *In-N-Out* is perhaps the most loved

▲ A California favorite

by Californians, who queue up to order fast food from fresh ingredients – there are no microwaves or freezers, and you can watch nattily clad employees turn potatoes into fries right before your eyes.

A dash of spice

The burger aside, traditional California food draws inspiration from Latin America and Asia, hardly surprising considering the region's diverse population. The state also has its own style of Mexican cuisine, sometimes called **Cal-Mex**, which is lighter than the more commonly known Tex-Mex, and incorporates plenty of veggies and seafood. In San Francisco, Cal-Mex is exemplified by large Mission district burritos – bulging tortillas stuffed with rice, beans, zesty salsa, and meat – whose style has become the norm at burrito chains across the US. In the south, the influence from Baja California is more prevalent, showing itself in fish tacos and crispy tostadas.

Excellent Asian restaurants, too, are dotted throughout LA and the Bay Area. LA boasts the country's best **sushi** and a surfeit of top-notch Korean, Thai, and Vietnamese joints. The Bay Area also features delicious Thai and Vietnamese, the latter particularly in San Jose, while South Asian restaurants fill the strip malls of Silicon Valley.

▼ Quesadillas with salmon

Fruits of the vine

California is by far the largest and most famous wine-producing state in the US, and its vintners were the first among those of the New World to prove that great wine can be produced outside of Europe. In contrast to those of Europe, **California wines** are often bold and fruity, a natural result of the climate.

Winemaking in California traces its roots to Franciscan missionaries in the late 1700s, but the industry didn't really come into its own until the 1960s, when pioneers like **Robert Mondavi** began to transform the **Napa Valley**. The efforts of these winemakers culminated in 1976, when a red from Stag's Leap and a white from Chateau Montelena put Napa on the map by besting top French wines in a now-famous Paris tasting. California Cabernets were pitted with Bordeaux, and California Chardonnays went head-to-head against white Burgundies (in California wines are categorized by grape varietal rather than place of origin). As described by a writer from *Time*, the panel of French experts not only selected the two Napa wines as tops, but also punctuated its picks with remarks like "Ah, back to France!" while sipping a Napa Chard.

Although Napa remains the state's best-known wine region, it only represents about four percent of the state's total wine production. Nor is it alone in producing fine wines – regions like **Sonoma**, Santa Barbara, and Santa Cruz have won reputations for their superb wines as well.

▲ Robert Mondavi winery

◄ Grapevines in Sonoma

Major wine regions

Central Valley Three quarters of California's grapes come from the state's flat, hot agricultural heartland, although most of these are produced by the world's two biggest wine concerns – Gallo and Constellation. The best grapes are grown near Lodi and Clarksburg, with the former known for its Zinfandel, the latter its Chenin Blanc. p.343

Napa To avoid the crowds, skip the big-name wineries on Rte-29 and cruise the leafy Silverado Trail, or head to cooler Carneros, an area known for its Pinot Noir and Chardonnay. p.684

Sonoma Sprawling Sonoma's Russian River Valley produces some of the state's finest Pinot Noir, while nearby Dry Creek Valley is known for its Sauvignon Blanc and Zinfandel. p.688

South Central Coast Santa Barbara's grapes were romanced in the popular wine flick *Sideways*, and rightly so – Santa Maria and Santa Ynez produce delicious Pinot Noirs. p.421

North Central Coast Dominated by large companies in the Salinas Valley, the region's highlights are found among the smaller wineries in the Santa Cruz mountains, where the most notable wines are Chardonnays and Cabernets. See pp.445 & 466.

Reserve (☎707/847-3221) is a sanctuary for twenty-foot-high rhododen-drons, indigenous to this part of the coast and in bloom from April to June, and you can drive through or walk along a short trail. The beaches on this last stretch of the Sonoma coastline are usually deserted, save for a few abalone fishermen, driftwood, and the seal pups who rest here. As usual, they're good for hiking and beachcombing, but stick to the trails. From here you pass tiny and inconsequential Stewart's Point before entering the Mendocino coast (see p.704).

The Russian River Valley

Hwy-116 begins at Jenner (see opposite) and turns sharply inland, leaving behind the cool fogs of the coast and marking the western entrance to a relatively warm and pastoral area known as the **Russian River Valley**. The tree-lined highway follows the river's course through twenty miles of what appear to be lazy, backwater resorts but in fact are the major stomping grounds for partying weekend visitors from San Francisco. The valley's seat, **Guerneville**, has the most nightlife and lodging, while **Healdsburg** serves as the gatekeeper for the **wine area**, bordering US-101 and the Dry Creek and Alexander valleys.

The fortunes of the Russian River Valley have come full circle; back in the 1920s and 1930s, it was a recreational resort for well-to-do city folk who abandoned the area when newly constructed roads took them elsewhere. Drawn by low rents, city-saturated hippies started arriving in the late 1960s, and the Russian River took on a nonconformist flavor that lingers today. More recently, an injection of affluent Bay Area property seekers, many of them gay, has sustained the region's economy, and the funky mix of locals and wealthy weekenders gives it an offbeat cachet that has restored its former popularity.

The road that snakes through the valley is dotted with campgrounds every few miles, most with sites for the asking, although during the first weekend after Labor Day, when the region hosts the **Jazz on the River Festival**, things can get a bit tight. The festival is something of a wild weekend around here and a good time to come: bands set up on Johnson's Beach by the river and in the woods for impromptu jam sessions as well as regular scheduled events. The late-June **Russian River Blues Festival** has proven equally popular. Both events are now run by the same promoters in the East Bay, who can be contacted for details (☎510/655-9471, ⊛www.russianriverfestivals.com). Gourmets will enjoy the **Russian River Food and Wine Festival** on the last Sunday in September.

Sonoma County Transit (☎1-800/345-7433, ⊛www.sctransit.com) runs a fairly good weekday bus service (though patchy on weekends) between the Russian River resorts and Santa Rosa in the Wine Country, although to see much of the valley, you really need a car. You could also rent a bicycle from Russian River Bikes, 14070 Mill Street, Guerneville (☎707/869-1455).

Guerneville

The main town of the Russian River Valley, **GUERNEVILLE**, came out some time ago. No longer disguised by the tourist office as a place where "a mixture of people respect each other's lifestyles," it's quite clearly a **gay resort** and has been for a good twenty years: a lively retreat popular with tired city dwellers who come here to unwind. Gay men predominate during the summer, except during two **Women's Weekends** (☎707/869-9000) – in early May and late September – when many of the hotels take only women.

If you don't fancy venturing along the valley, there's plenty to keep you busy without leaving town. Weekend visitors flock here for the canoeing, swimming,

Russian River Valley wineries

The Guerneville Chamber of Commerce (see opposite) issues an excellent Russian River Wine Road map, which lists all the **wineries** that spread along the entire course of the Russian River – now numbering nearly a hundred. Unlike their counterparts in Napa and Sonoma, few of the wineries here either organize guided tours or charge for wine-tasting. You can usually wander around at ease, guzzling as many and as much of the wines as you please. Some of the wines are of remarkably good quality, if not as well known as their Wine Country rivals. By car, you could easily travel up from the Sonoma coast and check out a couple of Russian River wineries in a day, although the infectiously slow pace may well detain you longer.

Belvedere 4 miles south of Healdsburg at 4035 Westside Rd ☎1-800/433-8296, ⓦwww.belvederewinery.com. Pleasantly situated winery with good views from the terraced garden. Live jazz on summer Saturday afternoons. Tastings daily 11am–5pm.

Dry Creek Vineyard 3770 Lambert Bridge Rd, 4 miles northwest of Healdsburg at Dry Creek Rd ☎1-800/864-9463, ⓦwww .drycreekvineyard.com. This family-owned operation is well known for its consistently top-class wines – particularly the Cabernet Sauvignon and Chardonnay. Picnic facilities. Tastings daily 10.30am–4.30pm.

Ferrari Carano 8761 Dry Creek Rd, 6 miles northwest of Healdsburg ☎1-800/831-0381, ⓦwww.ferrari-carano.com. One of the smartest wineries in the region, Ferrari is housed in a Neoclassical mansion with beautiful landscaped grounds. They specialize in Italian-style wines. Tastings daily 10am–5pm; $5. Tours by appointment.

Hop Kiln 6050 Westside Rd, over 5 miles south of Healdsburg ☎707/433-6491, ⓦwww.hopkilnwinery.com. Recently estab-lished rustic winery with a traditional atmosphere but not a snobbish attitude. Ironically, a plaque marks the spot where kilns used to dry the hops when this was beer country. Picnic area. Tastings daily 10am–5pm.

Korbel Champagne Cellars 13250 River Rd, 2 miles east of Guerneville ☎707/824-7000, ⓦwww.korbel.com. The bubbly itself – America's best-selling premium champagne – can be found anywhere, but the wine and brandy are sold only from the cellars, and are of notable quality. The estate where they are produced is lovely, surrounded by hillside gardens covered in blossoming violets, coral bells, and hundreds of varieties of roses – perfect for quiet picnics. A microbrewery and upscale deli are also on the premises. Tastings daily summer 9am–5pm, winter 9am–4.30pm.

Lake Sonoma 9990 Dry Creek Rd, Geyserville ☎707/473-2999, ⓦwww .lakesonomawinery.net. In a fine elevated setting at the far end of Dry Creek Valley from Healdsburg, Lake Sonoma makes a good range of wines and a particularly fine port, and has a microbrewery on the premises. Tastings daily 10am–5pm.

Porter Creek 8735 Westside Rd, over 5 miles east of Guerneville ☎707/433-6321, ⓦwww.portercreekvineyards.com. Small winery with a cottagey feel, producing all organic wines; Pinot Noir a specialty. Tastings daily 10.30am–4.30pm.

Russian River Vineyards 5700 Gravenstein Hwy, Forestville, 5 miles from Guerneville along Hwy-116 ☎1-800/867-6567, ⓦwww .topolos.net. One of the Russian River Valley's most accessible wineries, special-izing in Zinfandels. The popular on-site restaurant *Stella's* (☎707/887-1562) serves Greek-inspired California dishes – dine on the patio and feast your eyes on the wildflower gardens. Tastings daily 11am–5.30pm; tours by appointment.

and sunbathing that comprise the bulk of local activities. **Johnson's Beach**, on a placid reach of the river in the center of town, is the prime spot, with canoes, pedal boats, and tubes for rent at reasonable rates. But Guerneville's biggest natural asset is the magnificent **Armstrong Redwoods State Reserve** (☎707/869-2015; $6 per vehicle), two miles north at the top of Armstrong

Woods Road – seven hundred acres of massive redwood trees, hiking and riding trails, and primitive campsites. The visitor center (daily 11am–3pm) can provide trail maps: take food and water and don't stray off the trails, as the densely forested central grove is quite forbidding and very easy to get lost in. One of the best ways to see it is on horseback; Horseback Adventures (℡707/887-2939, ⓦwww.redwoodhorses.com) offers guided horseback tours that range from a half-day trail ride ($70) to overnight pack trips ($250 per horse per day). A natural amphitheater provides the setting for the Redwood Forest Theater, once used for dramatic and musical productions during the summer but now simply a fine spot for rustic contemplations.

The **Chamber of Commerce & Visitor Center**, 16209 First Street (Mon–Sat 10am–5pm, Sun 10am–3pm; 24-hour info line ℡1-877/644-9001, ⓦwww.russianriver.com), is welcoming and has good free maps of the area plus **accommodation** listings. As with most of the valley, B&Bs are the staple; two choices are the comfortable *Creekside Inn and Resort*, 16180 Neely Road (℡1-800/776-6586, ⓦwww.creeksideinn.com; ❹), and more luxurious *Applewood Inn & Restaurant*, 13555 Hwy-116 (℡707/869-9093, ⓦwww.applewoodinn.com; ❼), which also features a highly acclaimed gourmet restaurant. Lower rates can be found at the *New Dynamic Inn*, 14030 Mill Street (℡707/869-5082, ⓦwww.newdynamicinn.com; ❹), a relaxed New Age establishment where "cosmic energies unite with you," while *The Highlands*, 14000 Woodland Road (℡707/869-0333; ❸), also caters primarily to the gay community and has campsites from $20. **Camping** is an easy option elsewhere, too: the *Austin Creek State Recreation Area*, Armstrong Woods Road (℡707/865-2391; $15), is guaranteed RV-free, while *Johnson's Beach and Resort*, 16241 First Street, also has cabins and rooms available ($15 per vehicle plus one person, extra people $3 each; ℡707/869-2022, ⓦwww.johnsonsbeach.com; ❸).

Guerneville has a generous selection of reasonably priced, reliable **restaurants**, among them *Wild Jane's*, 16440 Main Street (℡707/869-3600), which serves classic American/California cuisine and hosts live music. *Taqueria la Tapatia*, on the west side of town at 16632 Hwy-116 (℡707/869-1821), is an excellent, authentic, and cheap Mexican joint. Really, though, it's the **nightlife** that makes Guerneville a worthwhile stop. *Main Street Station*, 16280 Main Street (℡707/869-0501), slings pizzas and offers nightly live music, mostly jazz; while the lively gay bar *Rainbow Cattle Co*, 16220 Main Street (℡707/869-1916), gets livelier as the night draws on. Both the *Russian River Resort* ("*Triple R*"), 16390 Fourth Street (℡707/869-0691), and *Liquid Sky*, 16225 Main Street (℡707/869-9910), serve alcohol and food and are also popular with the gay crowd.

Monte Rio

The small town of **Monte Rio**, four miles west along the river from Guerneville, is definitely worth a look: a lovely, crumbling old resort with big Victorian houses in stages of graceful dilapidation. For years it has been the entrance to the 2500-acre **Bohemian Grove**, a private park that plays host to the San Francisco-based Bohemian Club. A grown-up summer camp, its membership includes a very rich and very powerful male elite – ex-presidents, financiers, politicians, and their peers. Every year in July they descend for "Bohemian Week" – the greatest men's party on earth, noted for its hijinks and high-priced hookers, away from prying cameras in the seclusion of the woods.

The most reasonable of Monte Rio's pricey **places to stay** is the expertly restored ⚘ *Highland Dell Resort*, 21050 River Boulevard (℡707/865-2300, ⓦwww.highlanddell.com; ❹), whose gourmet restaurant is highly praised, followed by the lovely *Rio Villa Beach Resort*, 20292 Hwy-116 (℡707/865-1143, www.riovilla.com; ⑤), and *Village Inn*, 20822 River Boulevard (☏707/865-2304, www.villageinn-ca.com; ⑤), all in beautiful spots on opposite banks of the Russian River. *Huckleberry Springs Country Inn and Spa* (☏1-800/822-2683, www.huckleberrysprings.com; ⑦) is a deluxe adult-pampering retreat with massages and a spa, just outside of town at 8105 Old Beedle Road. Fill your belly at *Northwood Restaurant*, 19400 Hwy-116 (☏707/865-2454), serving up tasty, high-priced California cuisine.

The lonely, narrow **Cazadero Highway** just to the west makes a nice drive from here, curving north through the wooded valley and leading back to Fort Ross on the coast. At the north end of the bridge over the Russian River in Monte Rio, **cyclists** can begin the world-renowned King Ridge–Meyers Grade ride, a 55-mile loop (and 4500ft of climb) that heads along the Cazadero Highway and into the hills, finally descending to the coast and Hwy-1. Contact the Santa Rosa Cycling Club (☏707/544-4803, www.srcc.com) for a complete itinerary.

Healdsburg

The peaceful modern town of **Healdsburg** straddles the invisible border between the Wine Country and the Russian River Valley, and in a quiet way manages to get the best of both worlds. While **Veterans Memorial Beach**, a mile south of the pleasant plaza along the banks of the Russian River, is a popular spot for swimming, picnicking, and canoeing in the summertime, there are also several dozen wineries, most of them family owned, within a few miles of the center of town. The only cultural diversion in town is the **Healdsburg Museum**, 221 Matheson Street (Tues–Sun 11am–4pm; free; ☏707/431-3325, www.healdsburgmuseum.org), which displays local history through a decent collection of Pomo Indian basketry, nineteenth-century tools and crafts, and eight thousand original photos. Romantic bed and breakfasts have sprung up all over the area, including in the neighboring village of **Geyserville**, and although the town's economic well being is almost exclusively dependent on tourism, it still manages to maintain a relaxed, backcountry feel. The Healdsburg Area **Chamber of Commerce**, 217 Healdsburg Avenue (Mon–Fri 9am–5pm, Sat 9am–3pm, Sun 10am–2pm; ☏1-800/648-9922, www.healdsburg.com), provides winery and lodging information.

If you have the money to spend it's hard to beat the *Madrona Manor*, 1001 Westside Road (☏1-800/258-4003, www.madronamanor.com; ⑦), a luxurious Victorian-style **bed and breakfast** mansion crowning a hilltop, with meticulously maintained gardens and a gourmet restaurant. A more economic, if less distinctive, option is the *Best Western Dry Creek Inn*, 198 Dry Creek Road (☏1-800/222-5784, www.drycreekinn.com; ⑤).

Of several gourmet **restaurants** that circle the green, wooded plaza, ⚔ *Bistro Ralph*, 109 Plaza Steet (☏707/433-1380; closed Sun), with sparse modern decor and well-crafted French/California cuisine dishes such as chicken *paillard* for around $20 a pop, is your best bet. For a cheaper meal accompanied by fine local ale, look no further than *Bear Republic Brewing Co*, 345 Healdsburg Avenue (☏707/433-2337). *Flying Goat Coffee Roastery and Café*, just off the main plaza at 324 Center Street (☏707/433-9081), is a great place to unwind with a newspaper and a good cup of coffee.

Lake County and Clear Lake

An alternative route to the northern coast along Hwy-29 from the Wine Country or via Hwy-20, if coming from the I-5 north of Sacramento, is through often-neglected **LAKE COUNTY** and its centerpiece, **Clear Lake**, the largest natural freshwater lake in California. With a basin that was lifted above sea level some fifty million years ago by the collision of the Pacific and North American crustal plates, it is also one of the most ancient lakes on the continent, possibly even the oldest. The earliest inhabitants of its shores were the Pomo Indians, attracted by the mild climate and abundance of fish, who traded peacefully with other tribes and remained here undisturbed until they were displaced by white settlers; now they number just two percent of the population. With a surface area of sixty-four square miles and over a hundred miles of shoreline, the lake is renowned among anglers as the best **bass-fishing** territory in the country. Mostly surrounded by rolling hills, the lake is dominated by the green twin cone of **Mount Konocti**, a 4500-foot dormant volcano, which looms above its south shore. The largest city, conveniently named **Clearlake**, which occupies the southeast corner of the lake, has plenty of tourist facilities but is rather modern and faceless, so you're better off concentrating on the lakefront areas around **Lakeport** to the west and along the **North Shore**.

Clear Lake

A popular playground for vacationing middle classes up until World War II, **CLEAR LAKE** is currently undergoing a drive to reinvent itself as a holiday destination after several slim decades, during which it gained an unflattering reputation among many Californians as "white trash central." Evidence of this period can still be found in the rather dowdy motels that line parts of the lakeshore, some of which have been turned into recovery houses. However, the locals are once again trying to harness the lake's undoubted natural beauty, sunny climate, and its location – a little over two hours from San Francisco – to make it an attractive destination. This effort is bolstered by promoting its suitability for all sorts of **water activities**: windsurfing, water skiing, boating, and fishing facilities are available all around the lake. Southeast of Lakeport, the adjacent attractions of **Clear Lake State Park** and **Soda Bay** provide ample opportunities to play or simply unwind, as do the string of small resorts on the lake's **North Shore**. As the revitalization process is still in its early stages, the visitor can easily find great deals on accommodation, dining, and entertainment. It is also, by Northern California standards, relatively easy to spend time here without your own vehicle, thanks to decent **public transport** connections once you arrive: sadly the Greyhound service has been suspended, but the efficient Lake Transit service (℡707/263-3334, ⊛www.laketransit.org) runs frequent buses all around the lake every day except Sunday, and operates a route to Calistoga and St Helena in the Napa Valley four times a week, with an onward service to Santa Rosa on Thursdays.

Lakeport and around

The county seat of **LAKEPORT** is the older and more picturesque of Clear Lake's two towns, dating from the latter part of the nineteenth century, when settlers moved into the picturesque area as gold fever began to wane. Although the suburban sprawl along the lakefront gives the impression of a larger town, it's home to fewer than five thousand people. If you arrive by Hwy-29, the first point of call is the smart **Lakeport Regional Chamber of Commerce**, perched on a green knoll right by the highway exit ramp at 875 Lakeport Boulevard (Mon–Fri 9am–5pm, Sat 10am–2pm; ℡1-800/525-3743, ⊛www.lakeportchamber .com). As well as providing the usual brochures, maps, and helpful info, it affords a splendid view across the lake. Downtown Lakeport still retains a good deal of

Victorian charm, with the original 1871 brick courthouse standing imperiously on the gentle slopes of the grassy main square right in the heart of town. The building now houses the **Lake County Museum**, 255 N Main Street (March–Dec Thurs & Fri 1pm–4.30pm, Sat 1pm–4pm; May–Sept also Tues & Wed 1pm–4.30pm; $2; ☎707/263-4555, ⊛www.lakecountymuseum.com). Exhibits concentrate on the area's native heritage, with a full-sized Pomo village diorama and large collection of baskets, arrowheads, and tools.

The dozen or so blocks of Main Street on either side of the square and the roads leading down from it to the waterfront contain most of the town's facilities. For **accommodation**, it's hard to beat *Mallard House Inn*, 970 N Main Street (☎707/262-1601, ⊛www.mallardhouse.com; ❷), a friendly English-style inn, while the posher *Lakeport English Inn*, 675 N Main Street (☎707/263-4317, ⊛www.lakeportenglishinn.com; ❻), is the best of the B&Bs around here. A little further north, *Skylark Shores*, 1120 N Main Street (☎707/263-6151, ⊛www.skylarkshoresmotel.com; ❸), is typical of the resort motels to be found in the vicinity, fairly uninspiring but in exquisite surroundings. Downtown **eating** options include *Park Place*, 50 Third Street (☎707/263-0444), the place for filling pastas, burgers, and steaks, and inexpensive Chinese food at *Chopstick*, 185 N Main Street (☎707/263-3310). To stock up on **fishing** gear, stop at The King Connection, 2470 Reeves Lane (☎707/263-8856), and for boat or jet ski rental contact Disney's Water Sports, 401 S Main Street ($40 per half-hour; ☎707/263-0969, ⊛www.disneyswatersports.com).

About six miles southeast of Lakeport, two adjacent areas are worthy of exploration. The first is **Clear Lake State Park** (daily 8am–sunset; $6 per vehicle; ☎707/279-4293), whose erratically opening visitor center houses displays on the lake's cultural and natural history, as well as a 700-gallon aquarium of indigenous fish. The park also offers forest trails, a swimming beach, and four developed campgrounds (book on ☎1-800/444-7275, ⊛www.reserveamerica.com; $20–30). Right below Mount Konocti, in the protected waters between the park and Buckingham Peninsula, which almost spans the lake, **Soda Bay** is another haven for swimming and watersports. The eastern shore of the bay is blessed with soda springs, hence the name, which bubble up from shafts over a hundred feet deep. Indian legend claims that the bubbling waters mark the spot where Chief Konocti's daughter Lupiyoma threw herself into the lake after her father and lover were killed in battle. A number of **places to stay** line the bay, such as *Edgewater Resort*, 6420 Soda Bay Road (☎1-800/396-6224, ⊛www.edgewaterresort.net; ❺), which offers tent and RV sites for $30, as well as a few spacious family cabins. Almost next door, ⚑ *The Lakeside Inn*, 6330 Soda Bay Road (☎707/279-1620; Thurs–Sun only), is a cozy English boozer serving meat pies and good ale; in fact it's an exact replica of its namesake in Southport, Lancashire, recorded in the *Guinness Book of Records* as the smallest pub in England.

Mount Konocti

Majestic **Mount Konocti**, clearly visible from just about anywhere on Clear Lake's circumference, is a multiple volcano, estimated to have first erupted some 600,000 years ago but inactive for the last several thousand years. Indeed, geologists have declared large parts of it officially extinct. Its name comes from the Pomo Indian words "kno" and "hatai," meaning "mountain" and "woman" respectively. Unfortunately, most of the mountain is under private ownership, so you can't wander its slopes at will. Visitors can, however, gain access by permission and guided tours are conducted on select days; call ☎707/972-1990 for information and reservations. The nearest amenities can be found at **Kelseyville** on the lower southern reaches. These include the biggest resort in the region, *Konocti Harbor Resort & Spa*, 8727 Soda Bay Road (℡1-800/660-5253, ⓦwww .konoctiharbor.com; ❸), with accommodation ranging from motel-style rooms through beach cottages to a VIP suite that nudges $600 on special event weekends, as well as a spa, marina, sports facilities, restaurants, and a concert hall that attracts famous acts such as Aerosmith and Bob Dylan.

Clearlake

Though somewhat anodyne and sprawling, with a population approaching twelve thousand, **Clearlake** and the town of **Lower Lake** with which it merges do hold some interest and certainly offer plenty of amenities. Culturally speaking, the one place to see is the **Lower Lake Historical Schoolhouse Museum**, 16435 Morgan Valley Road, Lower Lake (Wed–Sat 11am–4pm; free), which preserves one of the old grammar-school classrooms just as it was during the late nineteenth century.

If you decide **to stay** in Clearlake, you shouldn't have any problem finding somewhere adequate and economical by the waterside. The *Linger Longer Resort*, 14165 Lakeshore Drive (℡707/994-6427, ⓦwww.lingerlongerresort .com; ❹), has adequate motel-style cottages of varying sizes, while the *Highlands Inn* at no. 13865 (℡1-800/300-8982, ⓦwww.high-lands.com; ❺) offers smarter suites with perks like Wi-Fi. Decent breakfasts and simple, inexpensive **meals** are the norm at *Main Street Café*, 14084 Lakeshore Drive (℡707/994-6450), and there's hearty Mexican grub at *Cabo's*, 14868 Olympic Drive (℡707/995-2162), several hundred yards back from the lakefront. Funtime Watersports, at 6235 Old Hwy-53 (℡707/994-6267), rents out boats, fishing gear, and other equipment.

North Shore

Some five miles north of Clearlake, Hwy-53 ends at Hwy-20, which continues northwest along the lake's **North Shore** past a series of small resorts under the shade of white oak and pepperwood trees. The first place you come to once the road hits the lake is Clearlake Oaks, which doesn't really merit a stop, so it's best to press on towards **Glenhaven**. A mile or so before the town are the rustic cabins of *Blue Fish Cove*, 10573 E Hwy-20 (℡707/998-1769, ⓦwww .bluefishcove.com; ❷). At **Glenhaven** itself the *Sea Breeze Resort*, 9595 Harbor Drive (℡707/998-3327, ⓦwww.seabreeze-resort.com; ❹), has quaint, nicely decorated cottages; if you're seeking a **campsite**, try *Glenhaven Beach* at 9625 E Hwy-20 (℡707/998-3406), where sites cost from $18. Cheap boat rental is also available here.

There's more going on, however, up towards the lake's northwest corner, which also boasts the longest stretches of beach. Five miles beyond Glenhaven in the larger settlement of **Lucerne**, the *Lakeview Inn*, 5960 E Hwy-20 (℡707/274-5515; ❷), offers bargain rooms, while *The Beachcomber Resort*, 6345 E Hwy-20 (℡707/274-6639, ⓦwww.beachcomberresort.net; ❸), has slightly higher rates – and you can fish from their own pier. The best di ning option is *Taylor's Bar & Grill*, 6034 E Hwy-20 (℡707/274-8014). Lucerne is also home to the informative **Lake County Visitor Center** (summer Mon–Sat 9am–6pm & Sun 10am–5pm; winter Mon–Sat 9am–5pm & Sun noon–4pm; ℡1-800/525-3743, ⓦwww.lakecounty.com) at 6110 E Hwy-20.

Several miles further on, where Hwy-20 prepares to leave the lake behind as the shoreline dips south towards Lakeport, the pleasant town of **Nice** is the best base on the North Shore. Apart from more cheap cabins, there are a couple of attractive **B&Bs**: the unique railway-themed *Featherbed Railroad Company*, 2870

Lakeshore Boulevard (☎1-800/966-6322, ⓦwww.featherbedrailroad.com; ❺), where all the rooms are fashioned out of disused cabooses; and the more conventional *Gingerbread Cottages*, 4057 E Hwy-20 (☎707/274-0200, ⓦwww.gingerbreadcottages.com; 5). Nice is also the most fruitful part of North Shore for **eating**: try the delicious and inexpensive American classics served all day at *The Marina Grill*, 3707 E Hwy-20 (☎707/274-9114), the fresh seafood, steaks, and pasta at the *Harbor Bar & Grill*, 4561 E Hwy-20 (☎707/274-1637), or the well-prepared fish and barbecued meat at *The Boathouse*, 2685 Lakeshore Boulevard (☎707/274-3534).

The Mendocino coast

The coast of **Mendocino County**, 150 miles north of San Francisco, is a dramatic extension of the Sonoma coastline – the headlands a bit sharper, the surf a bit rougher, but otherwise more of the same. Sea stacks form a dotted line off the coast, and there's an abundance of tide pools, making the area a prime spot for exploring the secrets of the ocean, either on foot or in diving gear. Surfers love it, too, for the waves and sandy beaches to be found between **Gualala** and **Albion**, and March brings out droves of people to watch migrating **whales**. Tourists tend to mass in charming **Mendocino** and gritty **Fort Bragg**, leaving the other small former logging towns along Hwy-1 preserved in the salt air and welcoming to visitors. The county also thrives as a location spot for the movie industry, having featured in such illustrious titles as *East of Eden, Frenchman's Creek, Same Time Next Year,* and *The Fog*. Occasionally such films are supposed to be set on the East Coast, but make use of the New England-style architecture closer to Hollywood, so watch out for any suspicious sunsets over the ocean next time you're in the theater.

If you're already on the coast, you can continue to hug Hwy-1 all the way to Rockport when it turns east to join US-101, the last thirty miles constituting one of only two true wildernesses left on California's rim. The most direct route to Mendocino from the south, however, is to travel the length of the peaceful **Anderson Valley** by taking Hwy-128 north from US-101. The main coastal towns of Mendocino and Fort Bragg are connected to each other and the interior towns of **Willits** and Ukiah (both on US-101 and served by Greyhound) by two local **bus** operators: Mendocino Stage (☎707/964-0167) and Mendocino Transit Authority buses (☎1-800/696-4682, ⓦwww.4mta.org); the latter has additional routes south to Gualala and Santa Rosa. For general information about the county, visit the Mendocino County Alliance's website (ⓦwww.gomendo.com).

The coast from Gualala to Albion

The first oceanside stop of note, once you leave Sonoma County on Hwy-1, is **Gualala**, which has developed into quite an artistic community, as well as a spot for holidaymakers due to its fine stretch of sand. A handy brochure locating the dozen or so **galleries** can be found at any one of them – try the central Dolphin Gallery (☎707/884-3896, ⓦwww.gualalaarts.org) in Sundstrom Mall, directly off Hwy-1. If you decide **to stay** here, look no further than the old *Gualala Hotel*, on the corner of Hwy-1 and the main plaza (☎1-800/888-482-5252; ❷), whose cheaper rooms have shared baths and which runs a good restaurant and old-style saloon. A pricier option is the upscale *Surf Motel at Gualala* (℡1-888/451-7873; ⑤), opposite the far corner of the plaza. Steak, seafood, and pasta fills the menu at *Meza Grille* (℡707/884-3398), up the hill at 39080 Hwy-1.

Beyond Gualala the route is very appealing, as Hwy-1 climbs up through increasingly wooded hillsides that afford tantalizing glimpses of the crashing waves at the frequent bends. Eventually the road straightens out somewhat as it turns inland to become the main street of nondescript **Point Arena**, fifteen miles or so north. The town does have the cheapest **motel** on this stretch of coast, however, in the *Sea Shell Inn* at 135 Main Street (℡707/882-2000, ⓦwww.mendocinoseashellinn.com; ③), and a couple of reasonable **places to eat** – try the pasta and soups at *Carlini's Café* (℡707/882-2942) or Mexican fare at *El Burrito* (℡707/882-2910), located at nos. 206 and 165 Main Street, respectively. A turn on the north side of town leads two miles to the impressive **Point Arena Lighthouse** (daily 10am–3.30pm; $5; ℡1-877/725-4448, ⓦwww.pointarenalighthouse.com). Built in 1870 and rebuilt after the San Francisco earthquake of 1906 – think of the devastating effect from such a distance – the landmark contains a small museum, and the 115-foot tower is a great vantage point for viewing birds, whales, and other ocean life.

Hwy-1 continues north through a mixture of coastal scrub and grazing land, rejoining the ocean around **Manchester Beach State Park** (daily 8am–sunset; free); its cheap campsite ($10) is about half a mile inland from the largely deserted strand. Further on you reach the pretty village of **Elk**, which boasts an excellent driftwood-strewn beach and a couple of quaint but fairly pricey **accommodations**: the *Greenwood Pier Inn* at 5928 S Hwy-1 (℡1-800/807-3423, ⓦwww.greenwoodpierinn.com; ⑥) has a wide range of rooms and deluxe cabins made entirely of redwood, as well as a multicuisine restaurant; while the *Griffin House Inn*, almost next door at #5910 (℡707/877-3422, ⓦwww.griffinhouseinn.com; ⑤), is co-run with the adjoining, hearty *Bridget Dolan's Pub & Dinner House*. The road winds on through an extremely scenic stretch of cliffs counterpointed by sea stacks and crashing waves until it reaches **Albion**, a couple of miles north of the junction with Hwy-128. The small fishing village is only six miles south of Mendocino itself and has a couple of romantic **places to stay**: *Fensalden B&B Inn*, 33810 Navarro Ridge Road (℡1-800/959-3850, ⓦwww.fensalden.com; ⑥), offers comfortable rural surroundings and distant sea views; while the *Albion River Inn*, 3790 N Hwy-1 (℡1-800/479-7944, ⓦwww.albionriverinn.com; ⑦), perches on the edge of a cliff, and all the rooms except one face the ocean. The inn also has a first-class **restaurant**, serving pricey, wonderful food with a spectacular wine list and top service.

Mendocino

Continuing north, Hwy-1 passes the offshore kelp forests of Van Damme State Park before you reach the coast's most lauded stop, the decidedly touristy village of **MENDOCINO**. The quaint town sits on a broad-shouldered bluff with waves crashing on three sides; it's hard to find a spot here where you can't see the ocean sparkling in the distance. New England-style architecture is abundant, lending Mendo, as the locals call it, a down-home, almost cutesy air. Its appearance on the National Register of Historic Places and reputation as an artists' colony draw the curious up the coastal highway, and a fairly extensive network of bed and breakfasts, restaurants, and bars are more than happy to cater to their every need.

▲ Mendocino

Accommodation

Room rates in and around Mendocino are generally high, but provided you stay away from the chintzy hotels on the waterfront, it's possible to find more reasonably priced options on the streets behind. Mendocino Coast Accommodations (☎1-800/262-7801, ⓦwww.mendocinovacations.com) can book rooms at B&Bs, hotels, cottages, and vacation homes for free. There's $25 **camping** at Russian Gulch State Park and Van Damme State Park (book both at ☎1-800/444-7275, ⓦwww.reserveamerica.com).

Brewery Gulch Inn 9401 Hwy-1, 1 mile south ☎1-800/578-4454, ⓦwww.brewerygulchinn.com. Huge luxury inn made of redwood timber salvaged from the local river. Some rooms have Jacuzzis and evening wine and snacks are served as well as a quality breakfast. ⑥

Joshua Grindle Inn 44800 Little Lake Rd ☎1-800/474-6353, ⓦwww.joshgrin.com. Luxurious but intimate and friendly B&B, offering five standard and five deluxe rooms and serving excellent gourmet breakfasts. ⑦

Jughandle Creek Farm 3 miles north on Hwy-1, just beyond Caspar ☎707/964-4630, ⓦwww .jughandle.creek.org. Funky place with shared rooms ($30 per person), cabins ($38), and tent sites ($12); there's a $5 discount if you're willing to donate an hour's work. You can explore the trails in the woods and participate in nature-study programs. ③

Little River Inn 2 miles south on Hwy-1 at Little River ☎1-888/466-5683, ⓦwww .littleriverinn.com. Wonderful spot with views over a bay full of sea stacks. Accommodations range from cozy rooms to spacious seafront cottages. The restaurant/bar is excellent, too. ④

MacCallum House Inn 45020 Albion St ☎1-800/609-0492, ⓦwww.maccallumhouse.com. The largest B&B in town, with a range of smart rooms in the main house, as well as luxury suites, cottages, and two off-site properties. ⑥

Mendocino Hotel 45080 Main St ☎1-800/548-0513, ⓦwww.mendocinohotel.com. Luxurious, antique-filled rooms, the cheaper ones with shared baths, lend an air of class to this popular hotel. ④

Sea Gull Inn 44960 Albion St ☎1-888/937-5204, ⓦwww.seagullbb.com. The best of the more affordable B&Bs right in the center of town, with pastel-decorated rooms. ⑤

The Town

Like other small settlements along the coast, Mendocino was originally a mill site and shipping port, established in 1852 by merchants from Maine who thought the proximity to the redwoods and exposed location made it a good site for sawmill operations. The industry has now vanished, but the large community of artists has spawned craftsy commerce in the form of art galleries, gift shops, and boutique delicatessens. This preservation didn't come about by accident. The state of California traded a block of old-growth forest with the Boise–Cascade logging company in exchange for the headlands surrounding the town. The headlands became a state park, and Mendocino in turn became a living museum, with strict local ordinances mandating architectural design and upkeep.

The **visitor center**, 735 Main Street (daily 11am–4pm; ☎707/937-5397), is located in **Ford House**, one of many mansions built by the Maine lumbermen in the style of their home state. The **Kelley House Museum**, 45007 Albion Street (summer Thurs–Tues, winter Fri–Mon 11am–3pm; free; ☎707/937-5791, ⓦwww.mendocinohistory.org), has exhibits detailing the town's role as a center for shipping redwood lumber to the miners during the Gold Rush, and conducts **walking tours** of the town on Saturday mornings at 11am – though you could do it yourself in under an hour, collecting souvenirs from the galleries as you go. Chief among them, the **Mendocino Art Center**, 45200 Little Lake Street (daily 10am–5pm; ☎1-800/653-3328, ⓦwww.mendocinoartcenter.org), has a revolving gallery for mainly Mendocino-based artists and runs workshops in ceramics, weaving, jewelry, and metal sculpture. The **Mendocino Theatre Company** (☎707/937-4477, ⓦwww.mendocinotheatre.org) on the same premises puts on regular performances of both avant-garde and classic works.

There's plenty more to occupy you around the town, with a long stroll along the headlands topping the list. **Hiking** and **cycling** are popular, with bikes available for around $25 a day from Catch a Canoe & Bicycles, Too (☎1-800/320-2453), just south of Mendocino at the corner of Hwy-1 and Comptche–Ukiah Road. They also rent outriggers and kayaks. At the west end of Main Street, hiking trails lead out into the **Mendocino Headlands**, where you can explore the grassy cliffs and make your way down to the tide pools next to the breaking waves. The **Russian Gulch State Park** ($6 per car; ☎707/937-5804), two miles north of town, has bike trails, beautiful fern glens, and waterfalls. Just south of town, hiking and cycling trails weave through the unusual **Van Damme State Park** ($6 per car; ☎707/937-5804), which has a **Pygmy Forest** of ancient trees, stunted to waist-height because of poor drainage and soil chemicals. The coast of the park is punctuated with sea stacks and caves, carved by the pounding surf; two-hour sea-cave tours are available through Lost Coast Kayaking (9am, 11.30am & 2pm; $50; ☎707/937-2434, ⓦwww.lostcoastkayaking.com). After a day of hiking and shopping, you may want to pamper yourself with a massage and a hot tub at one of the town's spas, such as *Sweetwater Spa & Inn* at 44840 Main Street (☎1-800/300-4140, ⓦwww.sweetwaterspa.com).

Abalone diving is extremely popular along the coast here, particularly just south of town in the small cove beside Van Damme State Park. In an attempt to thwart poaching, the practice is strictly regulated – the delectable gastropods are not available commercially, and you can only have three in your possession at any given time or collect a total of 24 in one season. In early October, four hundred hungry judges pay a substantial fee for the opportunity to help choose the best abalone chef in the annual Abalone Cookoff. To catch your own, visit Sub-Surface Progression Dive Center, 18600 Hwy-1 in Fort Bragg (☎707/964-3793, ⓦwww.subsurfaceprogression.com), which leads all-inclusive, half-day diving expeditions.

Eating, drinking, and nightlife

Of Mendocino's **restaurants**, the best and most famous is *Café Beaujolais*, 961 Ukiah Street (℡707/937-5614), whose founder wrote a book on organic California cuisine and which serves up a frequently changing menu of such fare nightly. Almost next door, *955 Ukiah Street* (℡707/937-1955; closed Mon & Tues) serves slightly cheaper ($15–25) entrées that make it even more popular with many locals. For slightly cheaper fair, try the *Mendocino Café*, 10451 Lansing Street (℡707/937-0836), serving an eclectic mix of salads, pastas, and sandwiches. Meanwhile, the *Moose Café*, 390 Kasten Street (℡707/937-2611), is a good spot for filling breakfasts. If you don't have time to visit any of the Anderson Valley wineries (see p.711), Fetzer Vineyards Tasting Cellar, 45070 Main Street (daily: summer 11am–6pm; winter 11am–5pm; $4; ℡707/937-6191, Ⓦwww.fetzer.com), next to the *Mendocino Hotel*, stocks its vintages for sampling or perusing. If beer's your preferred tipple, *Dick's Place*, 45070 Main Street, is Mendocino's oldest bar, with all the robust conviviality you'd expect from a spit-and-sawdust saloon, while *Patterson's Pub*, 10485 Lansing Street (℡707/937-4782), is another friendly joint with fine ale.

The first weekend in March brings the **Mendocino Whale Festival** (℡1-800/726-2780), a celebration of food and headland views of whales returning to the Arctic. They can also be spotted in November, on the trip to the warmer waters of Baja California. Since 1999 Mendocino has also hosted a twelve-day **Wine and Mushroom Fest** every November, while another gastronomic event is the popular **Crab & Wine Days Festival** that lasts from late December through February – check with the tourist authorities for details of both. Moviegoers will enjoy the **Film Festival** every May (℡707/937-0171, Ⓦwww.mendocinofilmfestival.com), and music-lovers the two-week **Mendocino Music Festival** (℡1-800/937-2044, Ⓦwww.mendocinomusic.com) in the middle of July; although the emphasis is largely on classical music and opera, some blues and jazz bands from all over the state also perform.

Fort Bragg and around

FORT BRAGG, a mere nine miles north of Mendocino, is very much the blue-collar flipside to its comfortable neighbor, although some trendier enterprises are beginning to spring up. Still, for the most part, where Mendocino exists on wholefood, art, and peaceful ocean walks, Fort Bragg brings you the rib shack and tattoo parlor. Until recently the town sat beneath the perpetual cloud of steam choked out from the lumbermills of the massive Georgia Pacific Corporation, which used to monopolize California's logging industry and provide much of the town's employment. There was once a fort here, but it was only used for ten years until the 1860s, when it was abandoned and the land sold off cheaply. The otherwise attractive **Noyo Harbor** (south of town on Hwy-1) is these days crammed with an equal number of pleasure boats and diminishing commercial-fishing craft, as the town attempts to cash in on Mendocino's tourist trade. Indeed, its proximity to the more isolated reaches of the Mendocino coast, an abundance of budget accommodation, and a bevy of inexpensive restaurants make it a good alternative to Mendocino.

As for things to do, you can take a quick look at the historical exhibits of the **Guest House Museum** (Tues–Sun 10am–4pm; donation; ℡707/964-4251) in front of the train station at 343 Main Street. Spend a worthwhile hour or two rummaging on **Glass Beach**, a ten-minute walk north of downtown at the end of Elm Street, below an attractive overgrown headland. Used as the town's dump until the 1960s, the disposed articles have been smoothed by the ocean into a kaleidoscopic beachcomber's paradise of broken glassware and crockery fragments. Take an amusing day-trip on the **Skunk Trains** operated by the Californian Western Railroad ($45 round-trip; ☎1-800/777-5865, ⓦwww.skunktrain.com), which run twice daily during the summer months and once in the shoulder seasons from the terminus on Laurel Street, forty miles inland to the tiny halt at **Northspur** and back. Taking their name from the days when, piled up with timber from the redwood forests, they were powered by gas engines and could be smelled before they were seen, the trains now operate exclusively for the benefit of tourists. It's good fun to ride in the open observation car as it tunnels through mountains and rumbles across a series of high bridges on its route through the towering redwoods, taking almost three and a half hours to complete the trip. At Northspur you can connect with the tour from **Willits** (local depot ☎707/459-5248), on US-101 forty miles inland. Besides being the official county seat due to its central position, Willits is otherwise no different from other strip-developed, mid-sized American towns, and is hardly worth visiting. Its one advantage is that you can connect with interstate buses here, although it's far cheaper to get a bus to Ukiah further south.

A short drive or bus ride south of Fort Bragg will take you to the **Mendocino Coast Botanical Gardens**, 18220 N Hwy-1 (daily: Mar–Oct 9am–5pm; winter 9am–4pm; $10; ☎707/964-4352, ⓦwww.gardenbythesea .org), where you can see more or less every wild flower under the sun spread across 47 acres of prime coastal territory. It's particularly renowned for the many varieties of **rhododendron** that bloom in April and May. Heading north, the next stretch of Hwy-1 is the slowest, continuing for another twenty miles of road and windswept beach before leaving the coastline to turn inland and head over the mountains to meet US-101 at **Leggett**. Redwood country begins in earnest here: there's even a tree you can drive through (summer 8.30am–8pm; $3), though the best forests are further north. If you're peckish, stop for a filling all-American snack or meal at *Redwood Diner* (☎707/925-6442). Further on, just before you cross the Humboldt County line, you can pause briefly at **Confusion Hill** to see the "world's largest chainsaw sculpture," hewn from redwood.

Practicalities

Fort Bragg's **Chamber of Commerce** (Mon–Fri 9am–5pm, Sat 9am–3pm; ☎1-800/726-2780, ⓦwww.mendocinocoast.com) is almost directly across the street from the Guest House Museum, at 332 N Main Street. Most of the **motels** cluster along Hwy-1 close to the center of town, the cheapest of which is the renovated *Chelsea Inn*, 763 N Main Street (☎707/964-4787 or 1-800/253-9972; ❷). Another good option is the slightly smarter *Surf Motel*, 1220 S Main Street (☎1-800/339-5361, ⓦwww.surfmotelfortbragg.com; ❸). **B&Bs** are more upscale (as usual), but cheaper than those in Mendocino: the *Grey Whale Inn B&B*, 615 N Main Street (☎1-800/382-7244, ⓦwww .greywhaleinn.com; ❻), has great views from its rooms, while the *Old Coast Hotel*, 101 N Franklin (☎1-888/468-3550, ⓦwww.oldcoasthotel.com; ❺), has comfortable rooms in a restored 1892 building, with a steak-and-seafood restaurant attached. Finally, there's camping among six miles of coastal pines and sandy beach at **MacKerricher State Park** ($25; reserve on ☎1-800/444-7275, ⓦwww.reserveamerica.com), three miles north of Fort Bragg.

Restaurants in Fort Bragg (of which there are plenty) tend to cater to the ravenous carnivore: *Jenny's Giant Burger*, 940 N Main Street (☎707/964-2235), for example, is usually full of men from the mill scoffing large chunks of red meat. A more genteel option is the ✴ *Mendo Bistro*, upstairs in the converted old Union Lumber Store complex at 301 N Main Street (☏707/964-4974), which serves excellent, imaginative international cuisine, including gourmet pasta dishes, at very moderate prices. Otherwise, *The Restaurant*, at 418 Main Street (☏707/964-9800), has lovely fish entrees for around $20, and vegetarians can take refuge in the hearty Italian offerings at *Headlands Coffee*, 120 E Laurel Street (☏707/964-1987), which also serves wine, along with a full menu of espressos. For big breakfasts, try *Egghead's*, at 326 N Main Street (daily 7am–2pm), which lists 41 different omelets on their menu. If you're feeling thirsty, stop in for one of the "handmade ales" at the *North Coast Brewing Company*, 444 N Main Street (☏707/964-3400), voted one of the ten best breweries in the world by the Beverage Testing Institute of Chicago as part of their year-long World Beer Championships. Try the Acme California Brown Ale and the Old Rasputin Russian Imperial Stout. Free tours of the brewery itself, on the opposite side of Main Street, are conducted at 12.30pm on Saturday. To work up a gentle thirst first, All Aboard Adventures, down by the water at 32400 N Harbor Drive (☏707/964-1881, ⊛www.allaboardadventures.com), does fishing trips for $70–80 and whale watching expeditions from $35 per person.

The Anderson Valley

Running diagonally northwest for nearly twenty miles, from just south of its small main town of **Boonville** to within a few miles of the coast, is the fertile **ANDERSON VALLEY**, an amalgam of sunny rolling hills shaded by oaks and madrones that merge into dark redwood forest. Hwy-128, connecting US-101 near Cloverdale to the coast at Albion, is the sole artery through the valley, which has a long-standing reputation as a magnet for mavericks. The original settlers were sheep farmers who saw so few outsiders between the 1880s and 1920s that they developed their own language, **boontling**, snippets of which still survive today. A good sixth of this odd dialect was known as "nonch harpin's," meaning "objectionable talk," and largely referred to the then taboo subjects of sexual activity and bodily functions. You can see examples of boontling in the names of local beers and establishments, but if you want to know the full story, track down a copy of *Boontling, An American Lingo* in local stores. During the twentieth century, sheep farming gradually gave way to the cultivation of apples but, though many orchards still exist, they are fast being replaced by more lucrative vineyards, as the craze for California wine means this area is becoming a northern annex of the Wine Country, along with the **Yorkville Highlands**, the southeastern extension of the valley. Most of the Anderson Valley's existing wineries line Hwy-128 between the tiny settlements of **Philo** and **Navarro**. The area is also famous for the excellent beer produced at the Anderson Valley Brewing Co, 17700 Hwy-253 (tasting daily 11am–6pm; tours daily 1.30 & 4pm, except Tues in winter; $5 including sampling; ☏1-800/207-2337, ⊛www.avbc.com), just east of the junction with Hwy-128 on the south side of Boonville. Their Hop Ottin' IPA (an example of boontling) and rich amber ales are especially delicious.

Boonville and Philo

Despite having a population of little over seven hundred, **Boonville** still easily manages to be the largest town in the Anderson Valley. Strung along its widened half-mile section of Hwy-128 are some quaint shops, a hotel, and a few places to find sustenance. In terms of **accommodation**, the only choice in town is the grand nineteenth-century *Boonville Hotel*, Hwy-128 at Lambert Lane

There are now around thirty **wineries** dotted along the Anderson Valley, and the number increases year by year. The cooler temperatures, especially at the northwest end, which sees the coastal fogs roll in, are better suited mostly to white varieties such as Gewürztraminer, Chardonnay, and Riesling, but the hardy Pinot Noir fares equally well. For further details you can contact the Mendocino Winegrowers Alliance in Ukiah (℡707/468-9886, ⓦwww.mendowine.com). About a dozen of the wineries have **open tastings** and there's rarely a fee, as they remain for the time being far less commercialized than their cousins further south. Here are a handful that would repay a visit.

Christine Woods Vineyards 3155 Hwy-128, about 2 miles south of Navarro ℡707/895-2115, ⓦwww.christinewoods.com. The Chardonnay and Merlot from this family winery have received awards in Mendocino and San Francisco. All wines are made entirely from grapes grown on the estate, a relative rarity. Tastings daily 11am–5pm.

Goldeneye Winery 9200 Hwy-128, just south of Philo ℡707/895-3202, ⓦwww.goldeneyewinery.com. This offshoot of Napa's Duckhorn produces wines from the Pinot Noir variety exclusively, including an excellent rosé. Tastings daily 11am–4pm; $5.

Handley 3155 Hwy-128, about 2 miles south of Navarro ℡1-800/733-3151, ⓦwww.handleycellars.com. A fine range of white wines, dry, sweet, and sparkling, are produced at this family winery. The tasting room also has a nice little collection of oriental art. Tastings daily May–Oct 10am–6pm; winter 10am–5pm.

Husch Vineyards 4400 Hwy-128, almost 3 miles south of Navarro ℡1-800/554-8724, ⓦwww.huschvineyards.com. Founded in 1971, this small family winery is the oldest in the valley, and you're assured of a warm welcome at its rustic tasting room. Tastings daily summer 10am–6pm; winter 10am–5pm.

Navarro Vineyards 5601 Hwy-128, 3 miles north of Philo ℡1-800/537-9463, ⓦwww.navarrowine.com. This small winery specializes in Alsatian-style wines, which it only sells directly to the consumer and select restaurants. It also concocts a wicked grape juice, so even the kids can enjoy a free sip or two here. Tastings daily summer 10am–6pm; winter 11am–5pm.

Roederer Estate 4501 Hwy-128, about 3 miles south of Navarro ℡707/895-2288, ⓦwww.roederer-estate.com. One of the higher-profile Mendocino wineries, specializing in sparkling vintages. Tastings daily 10am–5pm; $3.

(℡707/895-2210, ⓦwww.boonvillehotel.com; ❺), although the *Anderson Creek Inn*, less than two miles northwest of town just off Anderson Valley Way (℡1-800/552-6202, ⓦwww.andersoncreekinn.com; ❻) is an extremely comfy and quiet ranch-style B&B. Apart from the spicy Mexican-influenced California **cuisine** on offer at the *Boonville Hotel*, you can get cheaper and more authentic Mexican food at *Lola's*, 14025 Hwy-128 (℡707/895-3857), or enjoy quality bar food and **drink** your way through the entire range of Boonville beers at the boontling-named *Highpockety Ox*, 14081 Hwy-128 (℡707/895-2792).

Six miles beyond Boonville, as you head northwest towards the coast, the village of **Philo** has alternative venues to spend the night or have a meal, although it's all rather cutesy. *The Philo Pottery Inn*, 8550 Hwy-128 (℡707/895-3069; ❺), is a plush **B&B** right in the village, but the best deal is at the nearby *Anderson Valley Inn*, 8480 Hwy-128 (℡707/895-3325, ⓦwww.avinn.com; ❹). *Libby's Restaurant*, 8651 Hwy-128 (℡707/895-2646), serves up excellent, inexpensive Mexican **food**, and you can grab a sandwich or picnic ingredients from Lemon's Market (℡707/895-3552), just down the road.

A great place to take your picnic is three miles northwest to **Hendy Woods State Park** (℡707/895-3141; $6 per car), clearly signposted off Hwy-128. The park features hiking trails through two sizeable redwood groves, fishing on the Navarro River, and camping for $25 (reserve on ☎1-800/444-7275, ⓦwww .reserveamerica.com) or six-person cabins for $60. A mile or so beyond the park entrance, another signposted left turn leads four miles up through more redwood-clad ridges to *Highland Ranch* (☎707/895-3600, ⓦwww .highlandranch.com; ❾). The $295-per-person overnight charge at this friendly guest ranch, set amidst a stunning three hundred acres, includes a luxury detached cabin, three meals, plus all drinks and most activities on offer, principally horseback riding and clay-pigeon shooting.

The Humboldt coast

Of the northern coastal counties, **HUMBOLDT** is by far the most beautiful, and also the one most at odds with development: the good folk of Eureka famously voted to bar chainstore-behemoth WalMart from erecting a huge waterfront outlet in 1999. This is logging land, and the drive up US-101 gives a tour of giant sawmills fenced in by stacks of felled trees. Yet Humboldt County also contains the largest preserves of giant redwoods in the world in **Humboldt Redwoods State Park** and, north, **Redwood National Park**. Both are peaceful, otherworldly experiences not to be missed, though the absence of sunlight within the groves and the mossy surfaces can be eerie.

Indeed, many locals hope that the forests are too creepy for visitors. Tourism, while good for business, encroaches on a lifestyle far removed from the glitz of Mendocino and Sonoma counties. Locals are worried that as more people discover the area, the rugged serve-yourself mentality here could quickly turn into a service economy. Locals still welcome outsiders but, beyond of the few more touristic spots, do so on their own terms. The coastal highway's inability to trace Humboldt's southern coast formerly guaranteed isolation and earned the region the name of the **Lost Coast**. The area, while still isolated, is not quite as "lost" any more thanks to the construction of an airstrip in Shelter Cove and an infusion of hotels, restaurants, and new homes.

Humboldt is perhaps most renowned for its "Emerald Triangle," which produces the majority of California's largest cash crop, **marijuana**. As the Humboldt coast's fishing and logging industries slide, more and more people have been turning to growing the stuff to make ends meet, and new hydroponic techniques ensure that the potency of the ultra-thick buds is extremely high. The occasional bouts of aggressive law enforcement and a steady stream of crop-poaching have been met with defiant, booby-trapped, and frequently armed protection of crops, and production goes on – the camouflage netting and irrigation pipes you find on sale in most stores clearly do their job.

Apart from considerable areas of this alternative agriculture, the county is almost entirely forestland. The highway rejoins the coast at **Eureka** and **Arcata**, Humboldt's two major towns and both jumping-off points for the redwoods. These "ambassadors from another time," as John Steinbeck dubbed them, are at their 300-foot best in the **Redwood National Park**, which contains three state parks and covers some 106,000 acres of skyscraping forest.

As usual in this part of the state, **getting around** is going to be your biggest problem. Although Greyhound and Amtrak Thruway buses run as far as Arcata along US-101, they're hardly a satisfactory way to see the trees, and you'll need a car to make the trip worthwhile. **Hitchhiking** still goes on up here, and gaggles of locals gather at the gas stations and freeway entrances begging for rides. This is part necessity, as public transportation is scarce, and part lifestyle, as the region is a throwback to the kinder decades when hitching was a normal practice on American roads. Still, remember that stopping on the highways is illegal, and that no matter the kind appearance of a hitcher or driver, hitch-hiking can be dangerous in the US. For information on **what's on** in Humboldt, two excellent, free county newspapers, *The Country Activist* and *North Coast Journal* (⊛www.northcoastjournal.com), detail the local scene and people, and where to go and what to do in the area. Look out, too, for the Humboldt-based, activist *Greenfuse* and *Econews*, which highlight the ecological plight of Northern California's wild country.

Southern Humboldt and the Lost Coast

The inaccessibility of the Humboldt's beautiful **LOST COAST** in the south of the county is ensured by the **Kings Range**, an area of impassable cliffs that shoots up several thousand feet from the ocean, so that even a road as sinuous as Hwy-1 can't negotiate a passage through. To get there, you have to travel US-101 through deep redwood territory as far as tiny **Garberville**.

Garberville

A one-street town with a few good bars and hotels, **Garberville** is the center of the cannabis industry and a lively break from the freeway. Each week, the local paper runs a "bust-barometer," which charts the week's pot raids, and every August, the town hosts the massive two-day **Reggae on the River** festival. Tickets cost over $100; contact ☏707/923-4583 or ⊛www.reggaeontheriver .com by early May to reserve them.

The town has no bus connections, unless you're linking straight to the train line at Martinez, in which case you can use the twice daily Amtrak Thruway service. The town's **Chamber of Commerce** (summer daily, winter Mon–Fri 10am–4pm; ☏1-800/923-2613, ⊛www.garberville.org) is located in the Redwood Drive Center at 782 Redwood Drive. For what you get, much of the town's **accommodation** is a bit overpriced. The *Benbow Inn*, several miles south of town at 445 Lake Benbow Drive (☏1-800/355-3301, ⊛www.benbowinn .com; ⑤), is a flash place for such a rural location (former guests include Eleanor Roosevelt and Herbert Hoover); the *Humboldt House Inn*, 701 Redwood Drive (☏1-800/862-7756, ⊛www.bestwestern.com/humboldthouse.inn; ④), and the more basic *Sherwood Forest Motel*, 814 Redwood Drive (☏707/923-2721, ⊛www.sherwoodforestmotel.com; ③), round out the better options. The closest **campground** is seven miles south at **Benbow Lake State Recreation Area** (☏707/923-3238), while five miles further south on US-101 the **Richardson Grove State Park** in Piercy (☏707/247-3318) spreads over 1400 acres along the Eel River. Sites cost $20–28 and can be reserved on ☏1-800/444-7275 or ⊛www.reserveamerica.com.

Even if you don't intend to stay in Garberville, at least stop off to sample some of the town's **restaurants** and **bars**, which turn out some of the best live bluegrass you're likely to hear in the state. Redwood Drive is lined with bars, cafés, and restaurants: the *Woodrose Café*, at no. 911 (☏707/923-3191), serves organic lunches, while *Treats Café*, at no. 764 (☏707/923-3554), offers snacks, drinks, and Internet access for 10¢ a minute. For an inexpensive eat-in or takeout meal, try *Calico's Café*, at no. 808 (☏707/923-2253). All the town bars tend to whoop it up in the evening; the noisiest of the lot is probably the *Branding Iron Saloon*, at no. 744 (☏707/923-2562), with a small cover for its live music at weekends. Subversive gifts and more innocent by-products of the region's industry can be obtained at The Hemp Connection, 412 Maple Lane (℡707/923-4851), on the corner of Redwood Drive.

Shelter Cove

From Garberville, via the adjoining village of **Redway**, where you can enjoy a gourmet meal on the terrace of the *Mateel Café*, 3342 Redwood Drive (℡707/923-3020), the Briceland and Shelter Cove roads wind 23 miles through territory populated by old hippies and New Agers beetling around in battered vehicles. You eventually emerge on the **Lost Coast** at **Shelter Cove**, set in a tiny bay neatly folded between sea cliffs and headlands. First settled in the 1850s when gold was struck inland, its isolated position at the far end of the **Kings Range** kept the village small until recent years. Now, thanks to a new airstrip, weekenders arrive in their hordes and modern houses are indiscriminately dotted across the headland. It's the closest real settlement to the **hiking** and **wildlife** explorations of the surrounding wilderness, which remains inhabited only by deer, river otter, mink, black bear, bald eagles, and falcons, so many travelers use either *Mario's Marina Motel*, 461 Machi Road (℡707/986-7595; ❹), or the *Beachcomber Inn*, 412 Machi Road (℡707/986-7551 or 1-800/718-4789; ❸), as a **base**; the former establishment also has an adequate restaurant (℡707/986-1401) with a sea view on its extensive grounds, and rents out various seafaring equipment.

Another fine spot to admire the ocean is from the Cape Mendocino Lighthouse, on Upper Pacific Drive (late May to late Sept daily 10.30am–3.30pm; free), which was reopened to the public in 1998 after being relocated from 25 miles further north, near Ferndale. The lighthouse operates limited hours during the rest of the year, but you can call for a docent to come and open it up for you (℡707/986-7112) when it's closed. To the north the 24-mile **Lost Coast Trail** runs along cliff-tops dotted with four primitive campgrounds ($10), all near streams and with access to black-sand beaches. Bring a tide book, as some points of the trail are impassable at high tide. Another trail takes you to the top of **Kings Peak** which, at 4086ft, is the highest point on the continental US shoreline. Cape Mendocino can also lay claim to being the **westernmost point** of the lower 48 states.

Humboldt Redwoods State Park

The heart of redwood country begins in earnest a few miles north of Garberville, along US-101, when you enter the **Humboldt Redwoods State Park** (unrestricted entry; ℡707/946-2409, ⓦwww.humboldtredwoods.org): over 53,000 acres of predominantly virgin timber, protected from lumber companies, make this the largest of the redwood parks – though it is the least used. Thanks to the Save-the-Redwoods League, which has been acquiring land privately for the park, it continues to slowly expand year after year. At the Phillipsville exit, the serpentine **Avenue of the Giants** follows an old stagecoach road, weaving for 32 miles through trees which block all but a few strands of sunlight. This is the habitat of *Sequoia sempervirens*, the coast redwood, with ancestors dating back to the days of the dinosaur. The Avenue parallels US-101, adding at least thirty minutes to your travel time, but there are several exits to the freeway if you're in a hurry. Pick up a free **Auto Tour** guide at the southern or northern entrances and, better still, stop at the **Visitor Center** (daily: summer 9am–5pm; winter 10am–4pm; ℡707/946-2263), halfway along at **Burlington**, a mile south of Weott, which has fascinating interpretive exhibits highlighting the redwoods, other flora and fauna, logging history, and a catastrophic flood in 1964. At sporadic points along the Avenue, small stalls selling lumber products and refreshments dot the course of the highway, chief among them the **Chimney Tree** (daily 9am–5pm; free), a wonderfully corny gift shop built into the burnt-out base of a still-living redwood. There's also another **Drive-Thru Tree** towards the southern end of the Avenue at Myers Flat ($1.50). Three developed campgrounds ($20; ☎1-800/444-7275, ⓦwww.reserveamerica.com), and a simpler environmental one ($12), comprise your accommodation options within the park. *The Riverwood Inn* (☎707/943-3333, ⓦwww.riverwoodinn.info; ❸), in **Phillipsville** itself, is a nice, rustic place to stay; the bar/restaurant showcases live bluegrass and other styles of music sporadically and serves good Mexican food, and you're assured a friendly welcome from the locals.

Honeydew and Scotia

The Avenue follows the south fork of the Eel River, eventually rejoining US-101 at **Pepperwood**. Ten miles before this junction, Mattole Road peels off to the left and provides the best **backcountry** access to the towering trees, which most visitors neglect, as well as further access to the Lost Coast. A few miles after the road emerges from the forest, it passes through **Honeydew** into a region thin on even small settlements. Honeydew is a postage-stamp-sized town popular with marijuana growers who appreciate its remote location – and the two hundred inches of annual rain that sustain the crops, making the town the wettest in California. Three miles west, you can get that middle-of-nowhere feeling by **staying** at *Mattole River Organic Farm's Country Cabins* (☎1-800/845-4607; ❸). If you continue up and over the treeless grazing country around **Petrolia**, you will descend to the ocean at a splendid driftwood-strewn beach just south of Cape Mendocino and are guaranteed that sheep and cattle will far outnumber fellow humans.

Back inland, any visitors awed by the majesty of the redwood forests will soon be brought back down to earth a few miles north of Pepperwood at **Scotia**, a one-industry town if ever there was one. In this case it's timber, and the stacks and stacks of logs that line the freeway are actually quite a sight. The Pacific Lumber Company has been here since 1869, but with the decline in the industry and the rise in environmental objections to clear-cutting of native forests, the company is throwing itself at the tourist market and parts of the complex have already ceased active operations. Boasting of being "The World's Largest Redwood Mill," it attempts to win you over to the loggers' cause on self-guided **sawmill tours** (call for hours; ☎707/764-2222, ⓦwww.palco.com), starting at the Scotia Museum on Main Street.

Ferndale

Just over ten miles north of Scotia, you should definitely take a detour a few miles west to **Ferndale**, unquestionably the Lost Coast's most attractive town, although with enough time on your hands an even better route is the stunningly scenic Lost Coast loop via Honeydew and Cape Mendocino. Promoting itself unabashedly as "California's best-preserved Victorian village," Ferndale certainly has its charms – for once the appealing architecture is not just confined to one quaint street, but continues for blocks on either side of Main Street in a picturesque townscape of nineteenth-century houses and churches. Indeed, the entire town, which celebrated its 150th birthday in 2002, has been designated a State Historical Landmark. You can learn more about its history at the **Ferndale Museum**, 515 Shaw Street (Feb–Dec Wed–Sat 11am–4pm, Sun 1–4pm; June–Sept also Tues 11am–4pm; $1; ☎707/786-4466, ⓦwww.ferndale-museum.org), by perusing the old newspaper cuttings, documents, photos, and equipment that was once used in bygone occupations. The much more contemporary **Kinetic Sculpture Race Museum**, 581 Main Street (daily 10am–5pm), within the Ferndale Art and Cultural Center, contains vehicles from the peculiar annual competition that takes place between Arcata and Ferndale (℡707/786-9259, www.kineticsculpturerace.org; see p.720) every Memorial Day weekend. Ferndale supports an active artistic community, so there are a disproportionate number of galleries and antique shops to browse through.

As you might expect, most of Ferndale's **accommodation** comes in the shape of stylish hotels and B&Bs, though the remote location keeps prices very reasonable. The *Victorian Inn*, 400 Ocean Avenue at Main Street (℡1-888/589-1808, www.victorianvillageinn.com; ⑤), has comfortable rooms above its classy, carpeted lobby and lounge. Almost directly opposite at 315 Main Street, *The Ivanhoe* (℡707/786-9000, www.ivanhoe-hotel.com; ④), claims to be the oldest hotel in town and the westernmost in the country; it also has a decent restaurant. Further along, the *Francis Creek Inn*, 577 Main Street (℡707/786-9611; ③), offers hotel comforts at motel rates. Finally, a great option on a quiet corner a couple of blocks off Main Street is the beautiful yellow ♣ *Gingerbread Mansion*, 400 Berding Street (℡1-800/952-4136, www.gingerbread-mansion .com; ⑤), with a range of plush rooms and lavish suites. *Curley's Grill* (℡707/786-9696), inside the *Victorian Inn*, serves quality California **cuisine** plus sandwiches and cocktails, while *Poppa Joe's*, 409 Main Street (℡707/786-4180), dishes up down-home breakfasts and lunches. The *Candystick Fountain & Grill*, 361 Main Street (℡707/786-9373), is the spot for a cheaper snack or a whopping ice cream. The **entertainment** scene is appropriately low-key but you can drink in one of the hotel bars or catch a performance of the renowned Ferndale Repertory Theatre at 477 Main Street (℡707/786-5483).

Eureka

Eureka may mean "I have found it!" but once you pull into the largest coastal settlement north of San Francisco you may wonder just what it was the first settlers were seeking. Near the top of the north coast of California between the Arcata and Humboldt bays, **EUREKA** feels – despite some rather attractive Victorian mansions and cutesy B&Bs – like an industrial, gritty, and often foggy lumbermill town, though its fishing industry carries the most economic weight, providing ninety percent of the state's catch of Pacific Ocean shrimp and Dungeness crab. There are a few worthwhile sights here, as well as an abundance of cheap motels along Broadway, the type of mall-lined strip that's ubiquitous across America, and a growing number of fine eateries.

Arrival, information, and accommodation

Eureka has fairly limited **transportation** links: Greyhound, 1603 Fourth Street, connects Eureka to San Francisco once a day but only goes as far north as nearby Arcata. For getting around town or up the coast as far as Trinidad and south as far as Scotia, Humboldt Transit Authority, 133 V Street (℡707/443-0826, www.hta.org), has a Monday-to-Saturday service. The Eureka **Visitor Center** is on the southern approach to town at 2112 Broadway (Mon–Fri 8.30am–5pm; ℡1-800/356-6381, www.eurekachamber.com).

The collection of **motels** dotted around town, mostly on the busiest through streets, make Eureka a reasonable option for a night, but nearby Arcata provides a much more laid-back environment. If you do decide to stay here, try the *Town House Motel*, 933 Fourth Street at K (℡1-800/445-6888, www .visithumboldt.com/townhouse; ③), one of the cleanest of the cluster heading

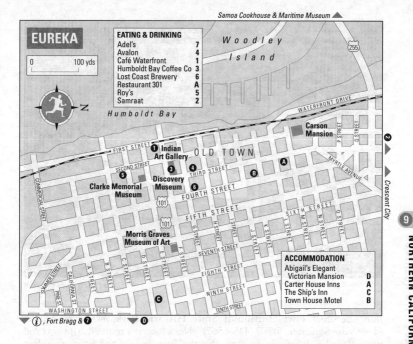

EUREKA

0   100 yds

N

Humboldt Bay

Woodley Island

255

WATERFRONT DRIVE

Carson Mansion

FIRST STREET

❶ Indian Art Gallery

O L D T O W N

SECOND STREET

❸ ❹

THIRD STREET Ⓑ

Ⓐ

MYRTLE AVENUE

Clarke Memorial Museum

❺

Discovery Museum

FOURTH STREET

101

FIFTH STREET

101

Morris Graves Museum of Art

SIXTH STREET

SEVENTH STREET

EIGHTH STREET

NINTH STREET

TENTH STREET

WASHINGTON STREET

ⓒ

COMMERCIAL STREET

SUMMER STREET

PINE STREET

CALIFORNIA STREET

A STREET

B STREET

C STREET

D STREET

E STREET

F STREET

G STREET

H STREET

I STREET

J STREET

K STREET

L STREET

M STREET

N STREET

O STREET

P STREET

Q STREET

2 ▶ *Crescent City*

ⓘ , Fort Bragg & ❼   ▼ ⓓ

EATING & DRINKING

Adel's	7
Avalon	4
Café Waterfront	1
Humboldt Bay Coffee Co	3
Lost Coast Brewery	6
Restaurant 301	A
Roy's	5
Samraat	2

ACCOMMODATION

Abigail's Elegant Victorian Mansion	D
Carter House Inns	A
The Ship's Inn	C
Town House Motel	B

north. If you want more than just a bed and a shower, head for *Abigail's Elegant Victorian Mansion B&B*, 1406 C Street at 14th Street (☎707/444-3144, ⓦwww.bnbweb.com/abigails; ⑤), which, as the name suggests, recalls the opulence and splendor of a past era and even offers complimentary vintage car rides and bicycles. Another plush and relaxing B&B is *The Ship's Inn* at 821 D Street (☎1-877/443-7583, ⓦwww.shipsinn.net; ⑤). At the top of the range are the exquisitely refurbished 🍴 *Carter House Inns* (☎1-800/404-1390, ⓦwww.carterhouse.com; ⑦), an enclave of four buildings arranged around the corner of L and Third streets, including a private $600-a-night cottage and a superb restaurant (see p.719). **Campgrounds** line US-101 between Eureka and Arcata; the best is the *KOA* (☎1-800/562-3136, ⓦwww.koa.com; from $26 per tent, RV hookups from $40, cabins $60), a large site with copious amenities four miles north of town at 4050 N US-101.

The City

Downtown Eureka is fairly short on charm, lit by the neon of motels and generic chain restaurants, and surrounded by rail and shipyards, although some colorful murals have brightened things up and the pretty, compact **Old Town**, bounded by C, G, First, and Third streets, at the edge of the bay, does its best to support a fledgling tourist economy. The peeling Victorian buildings and poky bars of the old sailors' district are pretty dingy – though they do have a certain seedy appeal, along with a handful of lively, mostly Italian restaurants. What few sights there are include the **Carson Mansion**, 143 M Street at Second, an opulent Gothic pile built in the 1880s by William Carson, who made and lost fortunes in both timber and oil. Carson designed the project to keep his millworkers busy during a slow period in the industry. It now operates as a private gentleman's club behind its gingerbread facade, and can only be enjoyed

▲ Fishing boats in Eureka

from the street. **Fort Humboldt State Historic Park**, 3431 Fort Avenue (daily 9am–5pm; free; ☎707/445-6567), gives a look at a restored army fort and not much else, disappointing given that the army general and future president Ulysses S. Grant used it for a headquarters in 1853. Visitors with children might be rewarded by dropping in at the **Discovery Museum**, 517 Third Street (Mon–Sat 10am–4pm, Sun noon–4pm; $4; ☎707/443-9694), which has hands-on kids' art and science displays, a puppet theatre, and planetarium.

The collection of Native American art at the **Clarke Memorial Museum**, Third and E streets (Tues–Sat 11am–4pm; free; ☎707/443-1947, ⊛www .clarkemuseum.org), can't hold a candle to the stuff at the **Indian Art Gallery**, 241 F Street (Mon–Sat 10am–4.30pm; free; ☎707/445-8451, ⊛www.ncidc .org), which affords a rare opportunity for Native American artists to show and market their works in a gallery setting, and an even rarer chance to get your hands on some incredibly good, inexpensive silver jewelry. If dragging yourself around town for these sights doesn't appeal, you might prefer the Eureka Health and Spa, 601 Fifth Street (☎707/445-2992), with its salt-rubs, tranquility tanks, and saunas. Completing an artistic trio, the **Morris Graves Museum of Art** at 636 F Street (Wed–Sun noon–5pm; $3 donation; ☎707/442-0278, ⊛www .humboldtarts.org) has six galleries of modern paintings and a sculpture garden. Back outdoors, LBJ Enterprises at 1707 E Street (Mon–Fri 10am–4pm; ☎707/442-0339, ⊛www.birdjobs.com), runs enthusiastic **birding** tours into the surrounding region for $50–100.

A few minutes by car from Eureka across the Samoa Bridge, squashed against the Louisiana–Pacific plywood mill, the tiny company town of **Samoa** is the site of the last remaining cookhouse in the West. The **Samoa Cookhouse** (daily 7am–3.30pm & 5–9pm; ☎707/442-1659) was where lumbermen would come to eat gargantuan meals after a day of felling redwoods, and although the oilskin tablecloths and burly workers have gone, the lumber-camp style remains, making the cookhouse something of an institution. Eating massive portions of red meat at its long tables is pure entertainment; you're served as much as you can eat of the daily fixed menu ($10–15) with a smile and a bit of history. Adjacent to the cookhouse, the one-room **Maritime Museum** (Tues–Sat noon–4pm; $4 donation; ℗707/444-9440) is chock-full of photos, maps, and relics from the days when Eureka was a whaling port.

Eating and drinking

In addition to the *Samoa Cookhouse* (see opposite), **eating** options are numerous. Eureka has a fair sprinkling of **nightlife** venues, though none stand out. For full listings, check out the free weekly *North Coast Journal*.

Adel's 1724 Broadway ℗707/445-9777. Basic meat-and-potato meals and salads for about $10 make this local hangout on the south side of town a good option.

Avalon Third St at G ℗707/445-0500. Parisian meets California cuisine at a price – expect to pay at least $50 for meal and drinks. Closed Sun & Mon.

Café Waterfront 102 F St ℗707/443-9190. Good spot for delicious seafood and burgers, where entrées cost around $15.

Humboldt Bay Coffee Company 211 F St ℗707/444-3969. Ranks as the coast's finest coffeeshop, with its beautiful red-brick interior and sock-it-to-me roasts. It's open until around 9pm and often features live music.

The Lost Coast Brewery and Café 617 Fourth St at G ℗707/445-4480. Serves large, hearty dishes to a rambunctious crowd of discerning microbrew drinkers and sports fans.

Restaurant 301 301 L St ℗707/444-8062. The *Carter House Inns'* classy dining room serves sumptuous set menus and à la carte dishes for around $25–30. The cuisine is mostly California with a French tinge, and you can choose from one of the most extensive wine lists in the country.

Roy's 218 D St ℗707/442-4574. The place to head if you want to try one of the Old Town Italian restaurants, with entrées costing around $20.

Samraat 1735 Fourth St ℗707/476-0930. Good, simple Indian curry house with a range of mild and spicy favorites, mostly under $10.

Arcata

ARCATA, only seven miles up the coast from Eureka, is by far the more appealing of the two towns, centered on a grassy central plaza that flies an Earth flag under those of the US and California. Beards and Birkenstocks are the norm in this small college town, with a large community of rat-race refugees and Sixties throwbacks, whose presence is manifest in some lively bars and the town's earthy, mellow pace. The beaches north of town are some of the best on the north coast, white-sanded, windswept, and known for their easy hikeability and random parties. But think twice about diving headlong into the surf without a wetsuit, as the ocean in these parts remains frigid throughout the year.

The main square is the focal point of the town's shops and bars, with everything you're likely to want to see and do within easy walking distance. In the middle of the square rests a statue of President McKinley. Originally intended for nearby McKinleyville, it fell off the train on the way and stayed put in Arcata. Just east of the town center, **Humboldt State University**, with its nationally known environmental education and natural resource management programs, attracts a decidedly liberal student body, which contributes considerably to Arcata's leftist feel. If you're interested in the college's history and programs, take a free student-led tour, which will give you much more insight than just wandering the campus's unflattering architecture. Free tours begin at the Plaza Avenue entrance on weekdays at 10am and 2pm and on Saturday at noon. Call ℗707/826-4402 for information. The **HSU Natural History Museum**, 1315 G Street (Tues–Sat 10am–5pm; $3 donation; ℗707/826-4479, ⓦwww.humboldt.edu/~natmus), houses interesting displays of fossils, live local fauna, and interactive exhibits.

At the foot of I Street, the **Arcata Marsh and Wildlife Sanctuary**, a restored former dump on 150 acres of wetland, is a peaceful place where you can lie on the boardwalk in the sun and listen to the birds. The Interpretive Center at 569 South G Street (daily 9am–5pm; ☎707/826-2359) runs **guided wildlife walks** (Sat 2pm), as does the Audubon Society, which meets at the very end of I Street at 8.30am every Saturday morning. For those who don't have time to explore the Redwood National Park, Arcata's own second-growth **community forest**, a beautiful 575-acre spot with manageable trails and ideal picnic areas, is accessible by going east on 14th Street to Redwood Park Drive.

If you're around over Memorial Day weekend, don't miss the three-day **Kinetic Sculpture Race**, a spectacular event in which competitors use human-powered contraptions of their own devising to propel themselves over land, water, dunes, and marsh from Arcata to Ferndale; call ☎707/786-9259 for information.

Practicalities

Greyhound **buses** only head south from the station at 925 E Street; there's also a Humboldt Transit Authority link with Eureka every day except Sunday. Going north, Redwood Coast Transit (☎707/464-6400, ⓦ www.redoodcoasttransit.org) runs a twice-daily service for $20 to Crescent City and on to Smith River. The **California Welcome Center**, over a mile north of town just off US-101 at 1635 Heindon Road (daily 9am–5pm; ☎707/822-3619, ⓦ www.arcatachamber.com), has free maps, brochures, and displays from all over the state, and lists of local accommodation and services.

Motels just out of town on US-101 are cheaper than the increasingly popular **bed and breakfasts**, if a little less inviting, but still cost $60–70 per night. You can get reasonable rooms at the *Fairwinds Motel*, 1674 G Street (☎1-866/352-5518, ⓦ www.fairwindsmotelarcata.com; ❸), though if you spend just a bit more, the *North Coast Inn* at 4975 Valley West Boulevard (☎1-800/446-4656, ⓦ www.northcoastinn.com; ❸) is a cut above in quality and comfort. Of the central establishments, the *Hotel Arcata*, 708 Ninth Street to the town's main square (☎1-800/344-1221, ⓦ www.hotelarcata.com; ❹), is pretty stylish, while among the B&Bs, *The Lady Anne*, between the plaza and the college at 902 14th Street (☎707/822-2797, ⓦ www.humboldt1.com/ladyanne; ❺), has been an Arcata favorite for years. There are several **campgrounds** north of Arcata along the coast, but none within easy reach of town unless you've got a car. The nearest and cheapest is at **Clam Beach County Park** (☎707/445-765), eight miles north of town on US-101, where showerless sites cost $10 per car or $3 per walk-in, making it quite a party venue for dishevelled youngsters staying long-term. See p.721 for options with better facilities.

Dotted around the plaza and tangential streets, Arcata's **bars** set the town apart. The best of the bunch, 🎋 *Jambalaya* at 915 H Street (☎707/822-4766), is more of a restaurant with a saucy cajun touch and an additional nightly diet of R&B, jazz, and rock bands. *Humboldt Brews*, 856 Tenth Street (☎707/822-2739), no longer produces its own beer but the bar has low-priced meals and hosts regular gigs. There's also the relaxed café at the *Finnish Country Sauna and Tubs* (☎707/822-2228), on the corner of Fifth and J streets, with live acoustic sets at the weekend and tubs in the garden for $15 an hour ($8 for 30min). Facing US-101 on 1603 G Street, *Muddy's Hot Cup* (☎707/826-2233) supports local music with weekly free concerts and is a pleasant place to relax and mingle with students. Good **restaurants** also abound – the *Wildflower Café and Bakery*, 1604 G Street (☎707/822-0360), turns out first-rate, cheap organic meals, while the *Big Blue Café*, 846 G Street, is a great place to watch proceedings on the square over a fine, leisurely breakfast. *Abruzzi*, 780 H Street (☎707/826-2345), serves top-quality Italian dinners at moderate prices, while the mainly takeout *Pacific*

Room Noodle House, at 359 G Street (℡707/826-7604), makes delicious, inexpensive Asian dishes, which can also be consumed in its courtyard.

Around Arcata

If you've got a car, take time to explore the coastline just north of Arcata along US-101. On the way, make a short detour east of the highway through the modern strip-mall town of **McKinleyville**, near Clam Beach, in order to see the world's tallest **totem pole**. The gaily decorated, 160-foot ex-redwood stands proudly at the back of the McKinleyville Shopping Center, halfway along Central Avenue near the junction with City Center Road. If you're peckish, you can't beat the gourmet sandwiches on the other side of the main road at *Tastebuds*, 2011 Central Avenue (℡707/839-2788).

Moonstone Beach, about twelve miles north of town, is a vast, sandy strip that, save for the odd beachcomber, remains empty during the day, but by night heats up with guitar-strumming student parties that rage for as long as the bracing climate allows. **Trinidad Harbor**, a few miles further on, is a good place to eat or drink, nose around the small shops, or just sit down by the sea wall and watch the fishing boats being tossed about beyond the harbor. Locals rave about the harbor's *Seascape Pier Restaurant* (℡707/677-3762), whose menu of fresh fish, steaks, and pasta tastes all the more delicious given its waterfront location. You'll find similar grub at more moderate prices back up in town at the *Trinidad Bay Eatery* (℡707/677-3777), on the corner of Parker and Trinity streets. There are several good **accommodation** options a little to the north: the *Trinidad Inn*, 1170 Patrick's Point Drive (℡707/677-3349, ⓦwww.trinidadinn.com; ❸), is a lovely motel in a quiet location, while the *Emerald Forest*, 733 Patrick's Point Drive (℡707/677-3554, ⓦwww.cabinsintheredwoods.com; ❺), offers secluded cabins and tent sites for $25. If money is no object, then one of the most romantic retreats along the entire coast is the *Lost Whale Inn*, 3452 Patrick's Point Drive (℡1-800/677-7849, ⓦwww.lostwhaleinn.com; ❼); this luxurious and friendly B&B has an outdoor hot tub and access to a secluded little beach where seals frolic. **Patrick's Point State Park**, five miles north of Trinidad, sports an agate beach below rocky coastal bluffs, and tours of a re-created Yurok village are conducted by appointment (℡707/677-3570), although you can wander alone at will. The park also offers reasonably secluded **camping** for $20 (reserve on ℡1-800/444-7275, ⓦwww.reserveamerica.com). Several miles further on, **Big Lagoon County Park** (℡707/445-7651; day-use $2) has tent spaces for $15 with a vehicle or $3 walk-in.

Hoopa Valley Indian Reservation and around

A more adventurous destination is **Hoopa Valley Indian Reservation**, sixty miles inland, the largest in California. In past years the site of often violent

---

The legend of Bigfoot

Reports of giant 350- to 800-pound humanoids wandering the forests of north-western California have circulated since the late nineteenth century, fueled by long-established Indian legends, though they weren't taken seriously until 1958, when a road maintenance crew found giant footprints in a remote area near Willow Creek. Photos were taken and the **Bigfoot** story went worldwide. Since then there have been more than fifty separate sightings of Bigfoot prints. At the crossroads in Willow Creek stands a huge wooden replica of the prehistoric-looking apeman, who in recent years has added kidnapping to his list of alleged activities.

confrontation between Native Americans and whites over fishing territory, Hoopa is seen by some as the badlands of Humboldt, and few take the time to check out the valley. Although some of the youth still hang around listlessly, the atmosphere has been improving of late and the local casino has reopened after a period of closure due to alcohol-induced violence. If you're here in the last week in July you should make an effort to catch the All Indian Rodeo, held southwest of the village. Otherwise it's enough to visit the **Hoopa Tribal Museum**, located in the Hoopa Shopping Center on Hwy-96 (Tues–Fri 8am–5pm, summer only Sat 10am–4pm; free; ℡530/625-4110) – full of crafts, baskets, and jewelry of the Hoopa (aka Natinixwe) and Yurok tribes.

To get to the reservation, take Hwy-299 west out of Arcata for forty miles until you hit **Willow Creek** – self-proclaimed gateway to **"Bigfoot Country"** – then take Hwy-96, the "Bigfoot Scenic Byway," north. Beside the Hwy-299 /Hwy-96 junction, a statue of Bigfoot marks the entrance to the small **Willow Creek–China Flat Museum** (mid-Apr to Oct Wed–Sun 10am–4pm, rest of year by appointment; free; ℡530/629-2653), which displays a modest collection of Indian quilts and settlers' possessions. Next door, a small **Chamber of Commerce** hut (summer only 9am–5pm; ℡530/629-2693, ⓦwww .willowcreekchamber.com) has details of Bigfoot's escapades, and information on **whitewater rafting** on the Smith, Klamath, and Trinity rivers near here. Among the numerous rafting companies in the area, Bigfoot Rafting Company (℡1-800/722-2223, ⓦwww.bigfootrafting.com) offers guided trips from $55. Otherwise, the town comprises a handful of grocery stores, diners, and cheap **motels**, such as the inevitably-named *Bigfoot Motel*, 39116 Hwy-299 (℡530/629-2142, ⓦwww.bigfootmotel.com; ❷). Of the **eateries**, *Cinnabar Sam's*, 19 Willow Way (℡530/629-3437), is the best bet for filling breakfast, sandwiches, and Mexican or American meals. Just north of town, the Lower Trinity Ranger Station (summer Mon–Sat 9am–4.30pm; rest of year Mon–Fri 9am–4.30pm; ℡530/629-2118) handles camping and wilderness permits for the immediate surroundings. Continue east on Hwy-299 and you'll arrive in the Weaverville/ Shasta area (see p.746), where you can join the super-speedy I-5 freeway.

The Redwood National and State parks

Way up in the top left-hand corner of California, the landscape is almost too spectacular for words, and the long drive up here is rewarded with a couple of tiny towns and thick, dense redwood forests perfect for hiking and camping. Some thirty miles north of Arcata, **Orick** marks the southernmost end of this landscape, a contiguous strip of forest jointly managed as the **REDWOOD NATIONAL AND STATE PARKS** (unrestricted access; free), a massive area that stretches up into Del Norte County at the very northernmost point of California, ending at the rather dull town of **Crescent City**. The fragmented Redwood National Park and the three state parks which plug the gaps – Prairie Creek Redwood, Del Norte Coast Redwood, and Jedediah Smith Redwood – together contain some of the tallest trees in the world: the pride of California's forestland, especially between June and September when every school in the state seems to organize its summer camp here. Increasingly, and despite being designated a World Heritage Site and International Biosphere Reserve, it's becoming a controversial area where campers wake to the sound of chainsaws and huge lumber trucks roaring up and down the highway. Despite this and other sustained cutting, local loggers are still dissatisfied, claiming that they've lost much of the prime timber they relied on to make their living before the days of the parks.

One word of caution: **bears** and **mountain lions** inhabit this area, and you should heed the warnings on p.52.

Practicalities

The parks' 58,000 acres divide into distinct areas: **Redwood National Park**, southwest of the Orick area; the Prairie Creek **Redwood State Park**, south of the riverside town of **Klamath**; and the area in the far north around the **Del Norte Coast Redwood** and **Jedediah Smith Redwood** state parks, in the environs of Crescent City in Del Norte County. The park **headquarters** are in Crescent City, at 1111 Second Street (summer daily 9am–5pm; winter Mon–Sat 9am–5pm; ☎707/464-6101, ⓦwww.nps.gov/redw), but the **visitor centers** and **ranger stations** throughout the parks are far better for maps and information, including up-to-date hiking conditions and the weather forecast. Most useful is the **Kuchel Visitor Center** (daily 9am–5pm; ☎707/465-7765), right by the southern entrance to Redwood National Park, before you get to Orick.

The two daily Redwood Coast Transit **buses** that run along US-101 to Crescent City and Smith River will, if asked, stop along forested stretches of the highway; if you're lucky, you can even flag them down. Still, unless you want to single out a specific area and stay there, which is hardly the best way to see the parks, you'll be stuck without a **car**.

As for accommodation, **camping** is your best bet. You can stay at the many primitive and free campgrounds all over the parks; for more comfort, head for the sites we've mentioned in the text below (all $20), along with a hostel and a few **motel/B&B** recommendations. Failing that, get onto US-101 and look for motels around Crescent City.

Orick and Tall Trees Grove

As the southernmost and most used entrance to the Redwood National Park, the Orick area is always busy. Its major attraction is **Tall Trees Grove**, home of one of the world's tallest trees – a mightily impressive specimen that stands at some 367ft. Incidentally, the tallest tree in the world, recently measured at 379ft, stands in an undisclosed location, inaccessible to the public. The easiest way to get to the Tall Trees Grove, with the least amount of trampling through thick undergrowth, is to drive yourself, although you'll need to get a free access permit (limited to fifty cars per day – only occasionally a problem even in high summer) at the visitor center. Here you can also pick up a free trail guide that explains why some redwood cutting is being done to balance the damages inflicted on old growth in the past. When you reach the parking lot, it takes about half an hour to hike down the steep trail to the grove itself and, unless you're exceptionally fit, somewhat longer to get back up. The best view of the tallest redwood and its companions is from the mostly dry riverbed nearby. Some people prefer to hike the 8.5-mile **Redwood Creek Trail** (permit needed if staying overnight in the backcountry) from near Orick: take a right off US-101 onto Bald Hills Road, then, six hundred yards along, fork off to the picnic area where the trail starts. The bridge, 1.5 miles down the trail, is passable in summer only. A bit further east another trail turns north off Bald Hills Road and winds for half a mile to **Lady Bird Johnson Grove** – a collection of trees dedicated to former US President LBJ's wife, "Lady Bird" Johnson, a big lover of flora and fauna right up to her death in 2007. A mile-long self-guided trail winds through the grove of these giant patriarchs. On the western side of US-101, across from the entrance to the Redwood Creek Trail, begins the **Coastal Trail**, which follows the coastline and takes backpackers up the entire length of all three state parks. An unpaved road leads in for a few hundred yards before petering out into the hikers-only path.

In **ORICK** itself, which actually lies two miles north of the entrance and ranger station, a couple of **stores** and **cafés**, along with two **motels**, string alongside US-101. On the right as you enter town from the south, the *Green Valley Motel* (☎707/488-2341; ❷) has bargain-rate rooms, while a little further along on the left the *Palm Motel & Café* (☎707/488-3381; ❷) also has adequate rooms and serves cheap burgers and sandwiches. You might also stop next door at the *Lumberjack* (aka *Hawgwild*; ☎707/488-5095) for a game of pool and an ice-cold beer. Three miles north of Orick, the narrow, gravel Davison Road turns coastwards for a bumpy eight miles to **Gold Bluffs Beach**, where you can camp in the stomping grounds of elk. The $6-per-vehicle fee also covers Fern Canyon, visited on an easy three-quarter-mile trail, its 45-foot walls slippery with mosses, fern, and lichen.

Prairie Creek Redwood State Park

Of the three state parks within the Redwood National Park area, **Prairie Creek** is the most varied and popular. Bear and elk often roam in plain sight, and you can take a ranger-led **tour** of the wild, dense redwood forest. Check with the **ranger station** (summer daily 9am–5pm; rest of year daily 10am–4pm; ☎707/465-7354) for details and informative displays. Whether you choose to go independently or opt for a tour, the main features of the park include the meadows of **Elk Prairie** in front of the ranger station, where herds of Roosevelt elk – massive beasts weighing up to four hundred pounds – wander freely, protected from poachers. Remember that elk, like all wildlife, are unpredictable and should not be approached. Day-use of the park is $6 per vehicle, but you can leave your car beside the road and wander at will; if you're pressed for time, there are some car-accessible routes through the woods. Overnighters can stay at a **campground** on the edge of Elk Prairie, at the hub of a network of hiking trails. Just south of the ranger station, on the east side of US-101, is the entrance to **Lost Man Creek**, an unpaved, 1.5-mile round-trip drive into a grove that passes by a cascade. To enter Prairie Creek Redwoods State Park, take the **Newton B. Drury Scenic Byway** off US-101 north of Lost Man Creek. Even if you're just passing through, the eight-mile byway is a worthwhile trip deep into the trees. A mile north of the ranger station, the magnificent **Big Tree Wayside** redwood, more than 300ft tall and, at over 21ft in diameter, one of the fattest of the coastal redwoods, overlooks the road. North of the Big Tree Wayside and before the byway rejoins US-101, the rough, gravel Coastal Drive branches off to the west following the Coastal Trail for 7.5 miles, leading to **High Bluff Overlook** and camping at **Flint Ridge**.

Prairie Creek also has a couple of **restaurants** on the southern approach on US-101. All do a good line in wild boar roasts, elk steaks, and other game, as well as a more traditional menu of burgers and breakfasts. *Rolf's Park Café*, on US-101 by the Fern Canyon turnoff, is one of the best, with outdoor seating and German entrées, as well as decent **accommodation** at the attached *Prairie Creek Motel* (☎707/488-3841; ❸).

Klamath and around

KLAMATH, in Del Norte County, isn't technically part of the Redwood area nor, by most definitions, does it qualify as a town, as most of the buildings were

▲ Rhododendrons and redwoods, Redwood National Park

washed away when the nearby Klamath River flooded in 1964. Nonetheless, there are spectacular coastal views from trails where the Klamath River meets the ocean, famed salmon and steelhead fishing in the river itself, a few decent accommodation options and, for a bit of fun, the **Trees of Mystery** (daily: summer 8am–7pm; winter 9am–5pm; $13.50; ☎1-800/638-3389, ⓦwww.treesofmystery .net) on US-101, where you'll notice two huge wooden sculptures of Paul Bunyan and Babe, his blue ox. Taped stories of Bunyan's adventures emanate periodically from within the redwood stands and ethereal choral music greets you at the most impressive specimen of all, the **Cathedral Tree**, where nine trees have grown from one root structure to form a spooky circle. Enterprising Californians hold wedding services here throughout the year. A recent addition to the site, which somewhat justifies the steep entry fee, is an aerial tram, which takes you from the top of the foot trail over the forest canopy to 750-foot **Ted's Ridge**.

Here you're provided with binoculars to enhance your enjoyment of the ocean views to the west and tree-clad ridges and valleys to the east – from March to October, look out for the active osprey nest atop one distant redwood. Back down in the gift shop, the free **End of the Trail Museum** highlights artwork from a number of the region's Indian tribes. Further south, where Hwy-169 peels off from US-101, the 725-year-old living **Tour Thru Tree** on Terwer Valley Road (daylight hours; $4) provides a cute photo opportunity. The most spectacular scenery in Klamath, however, is not the trees but the ocean: take Requa Road about three quarters of a mile down to the estuary, to a point known as the **Klamath Overlook**, from where, once the fog has burnt off, there's an awe-inspiring view of the estuary meeting the sea and the rugged coastline to the south. From here you can pick up the Coastal Trail on foot, which leads north for ten miles along some of California's most remote beaches, ending at Endert's Beach in Crescent City.

Practicalities

The *Historic Requa Inn*, 451 Requa Road (℡1-866/800-8777, ⓦwww .requainn.com; ❹), offers some of the best **accommodation** around. There are simple cabins at *Woodland Villa*, a mile and a half north of Requa (℡1-888/866-2466, ⓦwww.klamathusa.com; ❸), and small cottages with kitchenettes at *Camp Marigold* (℡1-800/621-8513, ⓔcampmar@tlk.net; ❷), just over one mile south of the Trees of Mystery. Three miles southeast of Klamath down Hwy-275, the *Rhode's End*, 115 Trobitz Road, Klamath Glen (℡707/482-1654, ⓦwww.rhodes-end.com; ❹), offers B&B accommodation along the Klamath River, and the beautifully situated, spotlessly clean, and friendly *HI–Redwood National Park Hostel*, several miles north of Trees of Mystery at 14480 Hwy-101 N (℡1-800/295-1905, ⓦwww.norcalhostels.org; ❷), has dorm beds for $20–22, whether you're a member or not, and rooms for $49–69. A couple of miles further north is the free, primitive *DeMartin* campground, and two miles west of US-101 on Klamath Beach Road, *River-woods Campground* (℡707/482-5591) has shady tent sites for $15 on the south bank of the Klamath River towards its mouth.

Pickings are slim in the **eating** department around Klamath, especially in the evening, but the *Sweet Street Café*, 164 Klamath Boulevard (℡707/482-3125), serves American standards throughout the day. For some river activity, Klamath River Jet Boat Tours, 17635 Hwy-101 S (℡1-800/887-5387, ⓦwww.jetboattours .com), runs two-hour tours for $38 and can arrange guided fishing trips.

Crescent City

The northernmost outposts of the Redwood National Park, the Del Norte and Jedediah Smith state parks, sit on either side of **Crescent City**, a rather forlorn place whose most attractive buildings were wiped out by a tsunami in 1964, leaving little to recommend it other than its proximity to the parks. That said, the city is the halfway point on US-101 between San Francisco (349 miles south) and Portland, Oregon (355 miles north) and is therefore often used as a rest stop, so there are plenty of places to stay and eat. Redwood Coast Transit (℡707/464-6400, ⓦwww.redoodcoasttransit.org) runs **buses** twice a day to Smith River, further inland, and down the coast to Arcata for $20. The **Visitor Center** is at 1001 Front Street (summer daily 9am–5pm; winter Mon–Fri 9am–5pm; ℡1-800/343-8300, ⓦwww.northerncalifornia.net).

Crescent City's most popular tourist attraction is **Ocean World** (daily 9am–7pm, later in summer; $7.95; ℡707/464-4900, ⓦwww.oceanworldonline.com), an unmissably large complex on US-101 south of town, which has a limited range of fish and other sea creatures. The guided tours that run every fifteen minutes are informative and give you the opportunity to handle many of the inmates – if you fancy picking up a starfish or stroking a shark or sea lion, this is the place for you. Take an hour to visit the **Battery Point Lighthouse** (April–Sept Wed–Sun 10am–4pm; tours sporadically during low tide; $3), reached by a causeway from the western end of town. The oldest working lighthouse on the West Coast, it houses a collection of artifacts from the *Brother Jonathan*, wrecked off Point St George in the 1870s. Because of this loss, the St George Lighthouse, the tallest and most expensive in the US, was built six miles north of Crescent City. The local history society maintains both this and the old-fashioned **Main Museum**, 577 H Street (May–Sept Mon–Sat 10am–3pm; $3; ☎707/464-3922, ⓦwww.delnortehistory.org), whose dusty interior contains some Indian artifacts, quilts, old musical instruments, a lens from the St George Lighthouse, historical displays and, most interesting of all, original cells from the building's earlier incarnation as the county jail.

Among the several passable **motels**, try the pleasant *Crescent Beach Motel*, on the beach two miles south of town at 1455 US-101 S (☎707/464-5436, ⓦwww.crescentbeachmotel.com; ❸), or the much cheaper *Gardenia Motel*, 119 L Street (☎707/464-2181; ❷), which offers no frills but is in a more central location. For a posher stay, try *Cottage By The Sea*, 205 South A Street (☎1-877/642-2254, ⓦwww.waterfrontvacationrental.com; ❺), a smart B&B perched on a bluff overlooking the ocean – you might even spot a migrating whale from your room. **Eating** options include the upmarket *Bistro Gardens*, 110 Anchor Way (☎707/464-5627), for great pasta and vegetarian dishes, or the excellent, moderately priced Italian, steak, and seafood at *Da Lucianna*, 575 Hwy-101 S (☎707/465-6566). Other fine ethnic choices are the Thai and Vietnamese cuisine at *Thai House*, 105 N Street (☎707/464-2427), the filling Chinese at *China Hut*, 928 Ninth Street (☎707/464-4921), or *Los Compadres*, a cheap Mexican diner opposite the marina at 457 Hwy-101 S (☎707/464-7871).

Del Norte and Jedediah Smith state parks

Del Norte State Park, seven miles south of Crescent City, is worth visiting less for its redwood forests (you've probably had enough of them by now anyway) than its fantastic beach area and hiking trails, most of which are an easy two miles or so along the coastal ridge where the redwoods meet the sea. From May to July, wild rhododendrons and azaleas shoot up everywhere, laying a floral blanket across the park's floor. The Mill Creek **campground** (reserve on ☎1-800/444-7275 or ⓦwww.reserveamerica.com; $20) here sits next to a lovely stream through the woods. **Jedediah Smith State Park** (☎707/465-2144), nine miles east of Crescent City, is named after the European explorer who was the first white man to trek overland from the Mississippi to the Pacific in 1828, before being killed by Comanche tribes in Kansas in 1831. Not surprisingly, his name is everywhere: no less than eighteen separate redwood groves are dedicated to his memory. Sitting on the south fork of the Smith River, the park attracts many people who canoe downstream or, more quietly, sit on the riverbank and fish. Of the hiking trails, the **Stout Grove Trail** is the most popular, a flat, one-hour walk leading down to a most imposing Goliath – a 345-foot-tall, 20-foot-diameter redwood.

If you're heading further east and can't face more highway, you could opt for the painfully slow but scenic six-mile route that follows Howland Hill Road from Crescent City through the forest to the **Hiouchi Information Center** (mid-June to mid-Sept 9am–5pm; ☎707/458-3944) on Hwy-199. Branching off this are several blissfully short and easy trails (roughly half a mile each) that are quieter than the routes through the major parts of the park. The **Little Bald Hills Trail** east of Hiouchi traces a strenuous ten-mile hike that should take about eight hours. At the end of the Howland Hill Road you'll find the *Jedediah Smith Redwoods* **campground** (reserve on ☎1-800/444-7275, ⓦwww .reserveamerica.com; $20) and picnicking facilities. Back on the main road at 2097 Hwy-199, the *Hiouchi Motel* (☎1-888/881-0819, ⓦwww.hiouchimotel .com; ❷) has basic but adequate rooms, and about ten miles further on, shortly before you leave the redwoods of the **Six Rivers National Forest** behind, the *Patrick Creek Lodge & Historical Inn*, 13950 Hwy-199 (☎707/457-3323, ⓦwww .patrickcreeklodge.net; ❹), is the last place to stay in California on this route; there are good single rates on the stylish rooms, rustic cabins, and an excellent but pricey restaurant. The apparent detour into Oregon on Hwy-199 to connect with I-5 back south is actually by far the quickest way to reach the interior of Northern California from the extreme north coast.

The northern interior

As big as Ohio, yet with a population of only 250,000, the **NORTHERN INTERIOR** of California is about as remote as the state gets. Cut off from the coast by the **Shasta Cascade** range, it's a region dominated by forests, lakes, some fair-sized mountains – and two thirds of the state's precipitation. It's largely uninhabited, and, for the most part, infrequently visited, which makes a spin up here all the more worthwhile. Locals take the time to chat and point out areas to explore, and the region's efficient network of hiking trails and roads usually remains empty of traffic jams.

I-5 leads through the very middle of this near wilderness, forging straight up the **Sacramento Valley** through acres of olive and nut trees, and past the college towns of **Chico** to **Redding**: the latter makes a useful base, with cheap lodging, from where you can venture out on loop trips a day or so at a time. Most accessible, immediately west and north of Redding, the **Whiskeytown-Shasta-Trinity National Recreation Area** is a series of three lakes and forests set aside for (heavy) public use, especially in summer, when it's hard to avoid the camper vans, windsurfers, jet skiers, and packs of happy holidaymakers. A better bet lies east at **Lassen Volcanic National Park**, a stunning alpine landscape of sulfur springs and peaks, or in the scenic environs of **Plumas County** to the southeast, between Lassen and Lake Tahoe. Traveling on state highways through national forests north of Lassen reveals numerous roadside surprises, including towering **Burney Falls** and access points to the **Pacific Crest Trail**, the 1200-mile path from Canada to Mexico.

Further north, the crowds swell a bit in the shadows of **Mount Shasta**, a 14,000-foot volcano whose reputation as both spiritual convergence point and climbing challenge brings together an interesting cast of characters in the small town of the same name. Train buffs should stop in the historical railroad town of **Dunsmuir**, just south of Shasta, and anglers will find trout streams filled to the gills all around the area. North of Shasta, the mountains and pines give way to cattle and caves; the latter are part of the stunning lava fields of **Lava Beds National Monument**, the site of one of the saddest Indian wars in US history. Trails and monuments mark the battle's history, while all around the desolate plain, migrating birds rest up in the gigantic sanctuary of the **Klamath Basin** before resuming their journeys on the **Pacific Flyway**. To the east, the scrubby volcanic landscape gradually transforms into the heavily wooded and mountainous terrain of **Modoc County**, where outdoor activities predominate.

It's the usual story with sparse **public transportation**: reasonably frequent Greyhound buses connect San Francisco and Sacramento to Portland via I-5, stopping off at the Sacramento Valley towns and Redding on the way, and trains from Oakland stop in Redding and Chico. However, neither route provides anything close to comprehensive access to the area, and if you're going to come here at all it should be in a **car**. Anything worth seeing lies at least five miles from the nearest bus stop, and the area is too big and the towns too far apart to make traveling by bus even faintly enjoyable.

The Sacramento Valley

The **SACRAMENTO VALLEY** lays fair claim to being California's most uninteresting region: a flat, largely agricultural corridor of small, sleepy towns and endless vistas of wheat fields and fruit trees. By far the best thing to do is pass straight through on I-5 – the half-empty, straight, and speedy freeway cuts an almost two-hundred-mile-long swathe through the region, and you could forge right ahead to the more enticing far north quite painlessly in half a day. If you're coming from San Francisco, save time by taking the I-505 byway around Sacramento.

Chico and around

Charming little **CHICO**, about midway between Sacramento and Redding and some twenty miles east of I-5 from the Orland exit, is a good stopoff if you don't want to attempt to cover the whole valley from top to bottom in one day, or if you're here to visit Lassen Volcanic National Park (see p.736) and need somewhere to stay. It's home to **Chico State University**, a grassy institution of sandal-wearing students renowned more for their devotion to partying than academic pursuits. Chico was once the grounds surrounding the mansion of General John Bidwell, one of the first men to cash in on the Gold Rush. As such, the city's traditional layout around a plaza, numerous college eateries, and surrounding expanse of parkland make it something of an oasis compared to the dusty fields and sleepy towns beyond, although the detour east to the **Butte Creek Canyon** is worth the effort.

Arrival, information, and getting around

Chico is right on Hwy-99. **Trains** stop at the unattended station at Fifth and Orange, as do Greyhound **buses**, which serve cities north and south along I-5 two or three times a day. The *Coast Starlight* train, from Los Angeles to Seattle, stops here once daily, though in the middle of the night.

Chico's **Chamber of Commerce**, 300 Salem Street (Mon–Fri 9am–5pm, Sat 10am–3pm; ☏1-800/852-8570, ⓦwww.chicochamber.com), has a terrific supply of information, from pamphlets outlining a historical walking tour through downtown to mountain-bike trails and swimming-hole locations

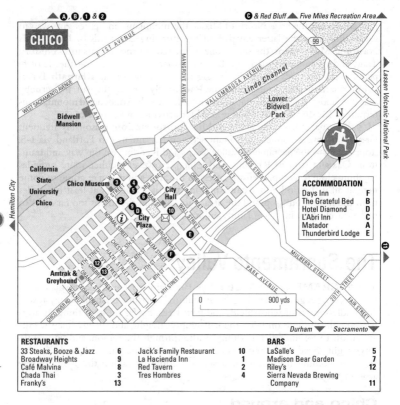

CHICO

ACCOMMODATION

Days Inn	F
The Grateful Bed	B
Hotel Diamond	D
L'Abri Inn	C
Matador	A
Thunderbird Lodge	E

Durham ▼   Sacramento ▼

RESTAURANTS				BARS	
33 Steaks, Booze & Jazz	6	Jack's Family Restaurant	10	LaSalle's	5
Broadway Heights	9	La Hacienda Inn	1	Madison Bear Garden	7
Café Malvina	8	Red Tavern	2	Riley's	12
Chada Thai	3	Tres Hombres	4	Sierra Nevada Brewing	
Franky's	13			Company	11

nearby. They also publish updated lists of lodging options with prices. To find out what's on, consult the free *Chico News & Review* (Ⓦ www.newsreview.com), published every Thursday, or tune in to KZFR (90.1 FM) or The Point (107.5 FM), both broadcasting eclectic local-community radio.

Parking is only 25¢ an hour all over downtown during weekday business hours, and free at weekends. The majority of places you're likely to want to visit are within walking distance of the town center, but the trails in Bidwell Park need to be biked to be appreciated. You can rent one for a rather exorbitant $35 per day from Campus Bicycles, right off the plaza at 330 Main Street (Ⓣ530/345-2081); the shop also provides free maps for cyclists.

Accommodation

Chico has much more in the way of **accommodation** than it does in sights, though for **camping** you'll need to head to the Plumas National Forest to the east or Lassen Volcanic National Park. Motels are everywhere in town, particularly in the Main Street and Broadway area, and there are a couple of good B&Bs.

Days Inn 740 Broadway Ⓣ1-800/329-7466, Ⓦ www.daysinn.com. Not the cheapest downtown motel, but a safe-bet chain franchise and just two blocks south of the plaza, with refrigerators in rooms and a pool. ❹

The Grateful Bed 1462 Arcadian Ave Ⓣ530/342-2464, Ⓦ www.chico.com/grateful. No tie-dye linen but a laid-back atmosphere at this plush and friendly B&B, two blocks west of The Esplanade. ❹

Hotel Diamond 220 W Fourth St ☎1-866/993-3100, ⓦwww.hoteldiamondchico.com. Imposing edifice with a range of swish rooms and suites, as well as an elegant lobby, restaurant, and full bar. ❺
L'Abri Inn 4350 Hwy-99 ☎1-800/489-3319, ⓦwww.now2000.com/labri. Five miles north of town, this place comprises three rooms in a ranch-style home with a serene country atmosphere. Enjoy a sumptuous breakfast, then go out and pet the barnyard animals. ❹

The Matador Motel 1934 The Esplanade ☎530/342-7543. A pretty Spanish Revival building ten blocks north of the plaza; the tasteful rooms have individual tiling. Set around a courtyard, with palms shading one of Chico's largest pools, this is among Northern California's best deals. ❶
Thunderbird Lodge 715 Main St ☎530/343-7911. Decent motel two blocks from the plaza. Some rooms have refrigerators and coffeemakers. ❶

The Town

Chico doesn't have much by way of sights, but strolling the leafy streets, college campus, and shady riverside feels great after the monotonous drive up I-5. The 1904 **Chico Museum**, housed in the former Carnegie Library at the corner of Second and Main streets (Wed–Sun noon–4pm; free; ☎530/891-4336, ⓦwww.chicomuseum.org), contains three distinct parts: a permanent historical section, a reconstruction of a Taoist temple altar, and a gallery for rotating shows. You might also try the three-story **Bidwell Mansion** at 525 The Esplanade, the continuation of Main Street (Wed–Fri noon–4pm, Sat & Sun 10am–4pm; tours on the hour until 3pm; $2; ☎530/895-6144). Built in 1868, it's an attractive Italian country villa filled with family paraphernalia, visited on 45-minute anecdotal tours that are reasonably interesting, though Bidwell Park (most sections open daylight hours; free) is a more pleasurable place to spend your time. Extending from the center of the town for ten miles to the northeast, this is a tongue of semi-wilderness and oak parkland where, incidentally, the first Robin Hood film, starring Errol Flynn, was made, a fair hike from Sherwood Forest. The busiest recreation areas are at One-Mile Dam and Five-Mile Dam, both reached via Vallombrosa Avenue, and Cedar Grove off East Eighth Street, but a half-hour stroll into Upper Park will earn you more solitude. Students frequent the **swimming holes** on Big Chico Creek in the Upper Park, including Bear Hole, Salmon Hole, and Brown's Hole, which has a small rope swing. For the holes, take Vallombrosa Avenue all the way east, turn left into Manzanita Avenue, then right on Wildwood Avenue, and continue on past the golf course to the creek. A stout pair of legs or a bicycle is the best way to get around the area.

Back downtown, vintage American car fans will enjoy **Cruces Classic Auto Sales** (☎530/345-9779), 720 Main St, a commercial showroom with a walk-through museum showing some of the really rare models that are brought here to be restored. Vintage airplane afficionados, meanwhile, won't want to miss the collection on display at **Chico Air Museum** (Sat 10am–4pm; free; ☎530/345-7985), in the municipal airport four miles north of downtown. The remodeled **Sierra Nevada Brewing Company**, 1075 E 20th Street (self-guided tours daily 10am–6pm; guided tours Tues–Fri & Sun 2.30pm, Sat noon–3pm; free; ☎530/893-3520, ⓦwww.sierranevada.com); there is no official tasting as such but you can sample the ten or so brews on tap for around $5 at the brewery's bar. Those nostalgic for the innocent days of childhood will enjoy the **National Yo-Yo Museum**, 320 Broadway (Mon–Sat 10am–5.30pm, Sun 11am–4pm; free; ☎530/892-1414, ⓦwww.nationalyoyo.org/museum), where enthusiasts enjoy showing visitors around the thousands of exhibits and photos.

The **Farmers' Market** closes off downtown every summer Thursday at 5.30pm for three hours of produce sales. Come for the almonds and other fresh nuts grown nearby. The **Gold Cup Races** at the Silver Dollar Speedway

NORTHERN CALIFORNIA | The Sacramento Valley

(☎530/969-7484), a stock-car extravaganza on the second weekend of September, is Chico's biggest weekend and fills all area hotels.

Eating and drinking

Chico does itself proud when it comes to **food**, and the listings here are just a sample of what is on offer. If you're in town on the second Sunday in September look out for the Taste of Chico **festival** (☎530/345-6000). Being a California State University town, there are many excellent places aimed at the younger customer, as well as a handful of lively **bars**, featuring live music by national acts. It's noticeably quieter when school's out, but on summer Friday evenings, **free concerts** by talented locals draw the crowds to the Downtown Park Plaza, beginning at 7pm.

Restaurants

33 Steaks, Booze & Jazz 305 Main St ☎530/893-1903. Entrées cost around $20–30 in this smart restaurant/bar, which specializes in martinis and hosts live jazz every evening. Closed Mon.

Broadway Heights 300 Broadway ☎530/899-8075. This modern upstairs establishment dishes up moderate California cuisine and healthy snacks.

Caffè Malvina 234 W Third St ☎530/895-1614. Italian restaurant with reasonably priced pasta and fish, plus some cheaper specials.

Chada Thai Downstairs at 117b W Second St ☎530/342-7121. Authentic and predominantly vegetarian Thai cuisine at very affordable prices, especially at lunchtime. Closed Sun.

Franky's 506 Ivy St ☎530/898-9948. Inexpensive, freshly made pasta and pizza, a staple diet for students and locals alike.

Jack's Family Restaurant 540 Main St ☎530/343-8383. This 24-hr diner's a bit on the greasy side, but good for breakfasts and late-night munchies.

La Hacienda Inn 2635 The Esplanade ☎530/893-8270. *Bon Appetit* and *Gourmet* magazines have done features on this Mexican restaurant's special pink sauce, known to locals as "Heroin Sauce" for its addictive sweet flavor. Try it on a tostada, but be warned – you may get hooked.

Red Tavern 1250 The Esplanade ☎530/894-3463. Quality California dishes such as chilled golden beet soup and caper-crusted sole are available for around $20 at this fairly upscale restaurant.

Tres Hombres 100 Broadway ☎530/342-0425. Large restaurant popular with students for the wide selection of margaritas. Reasonably priced burritos, quesadillas, tostadas, and tacos in a fun environment. Dinner until 10pm every night, drinks until 2am on weekends. Live jazz Sunday afternoons.

Bars

LaSalle's 229 Broadway ☎530/893-1891. The place in Chico to down large quantities of inexpensive beer, play pool, and listen to live rock bands.

Madison Bear Garden 316 W Second St ☎530/891-1639. A place for swigging beer with students from the nearby campus. Burgers, buffalo wings, and other bar food is served.

Riley's 702 W Fifth St ☎530/343-7459. Catch the ballgame on one of the many TV screens and hang out with the enthusiastic students at the most popular sports bar in Chico.

Sierra Nevada Brewing Company 1075 E 20th St ☎530/893-3520. The bar food is unexceptional, but the pale ale, porter, stout, and seasonal brews are a strong draw. There's usually jazz on Mondays and good local bands some weekends.

Around Chico

Ten miles outside Chico, south on Hwy-99 then east on Skyway to Humburg–Honey Run Road, the **Honey Run Covered Bridge** is one of the few remaining covered bridges in California. You can't drive on it, but its position in rugged Butte Creek Canyon over a riffling river leads to peaceful walking and swimming opportunities. Further east, the apple orchards of **Paradise** were used as a location for *Gone With the Wind*. You'll find the town's name quite apt if you **stay** at the unique ⚘ *Chapelle de l'Artiste*, 215 Wayland Road (☎530/228-0941, ⓦ www.chapelledartiste.com; ❼), a superb mansion in opulent grounds with a pool and llama pastures. A gourmet dinner, usually in the company of the hosts, is included in the price.

Red Bluff and Corning

The largest town in Tehama County is **Red Bluff**, 45 miles north of Chico on Hwy-99. The Greyhound **bus** stops in front of the Salt Creek Deli at the junction of Hwy-36 and Antelope Road (Hwy-99), but that leaves no reliable form of public transportation into Lassen itself. Despite its favorable location on the Sacramento River, Red Bluff today is known more as a gas-and-lodging stop before the fifty-mile drive into Lassen along Hwy-36 or the push north to Redding and Mount Shasta on I-5. You may consider visiting the **Kelly-Griggs House Museum**, 311 Washington Street (Thurs–Sun 1–4pm; donation; ☎530/527-1129), where there's an exhibit on Ishi, "the last wild Indian." There are a number of antique shops to browse in and Gaumer's, on the I-5 side of the bridge at 78 Belle Mill Road (Mon–Fri 9am–5pm; free; ☎530/527-6166), is really a jeweler's with an on-site **gemology museum**, displaying hundreds of precious stones, mining equipment, a lapidary workshop, and collection of corals and ammonites. The star exhibit is a sparkly four-foot-tall amethyst geode from Brazil.

If you find yourself staying over, there's a reasonable selection of **motels** for $50 per night or less along Main Street – among them the *Crystal Motel*, 333 S Main Street (☎530/527-1021, ⓦwww.redbluffcrystalmotel.com; ❶), and the *Lamplighter Lodge*, 210 S Main Street (☎530/527-1150, ⓦwww.lamplighterlodge.us; ❷) – and a handful of diners and burger joints around town. The one classier **restaurant** is the *Riverside Bar & Grille*, 500 Riverside Way (☎530/528-0370), which serves great grilled steak and ribs on its patio overlooking the river by the bridge into town. For any more information you need, visit the **Chamber of Commerce**, 100 Main Street (Mon–Fri 8.30am–5pm; ☎1-800/655-6225, ⓦwww.redbluffchamberofcommerce.com).

If you bypass Chico and enter Tehama County from the south on I-5, an alternative stop for gas and provisions is **Corning**, home of the celebrated **Olive Pit**, 2156 Solano Street, just east off the interstate (☎1-800/654-8374, ⓦwww.olivepit.com). This only-in-America store and restaurant sells jars of olives, olive oil, garlic, almonds, and pickles, and has a good grill and ice-cream bar as well. Martini-lovers can get bottles of olive-juice mixer, and a free tasting bar allows a trip around the world via olives – from Brine Greek wholes to Napa Valley Wine queens to French pitted and Sicilian cracked. The anchovy-stuffed greens are a must, and pint jars of all varieties go for around $3–6.

Plumas County

Many visitors traveling between Lake Tahoe and the Lassen/Mount Shasta region bypass the Sacramento Valley altogether by using Hwy-89, which winds its way through sparsely populated and scenically exquisite **PLUMAS COUNTY**. Although it boasts no major set-piece attraction, with only a couple of stoplights and constant vistas of pine-clad ridges, grassy valleys, sparkling lakes, and trout-rich rivers, the county is rural California at its best. Geographically, it's significant as the meeting point of the lofty Sierra and volcanic Cascade mountain ranges. The area was home to the hunter-gatherer **Maidu Indians** before white settlers flooded into the valleys when gold frenzy took hold in the mid-nineteenth century, followed by a substantial number of Chinese. The veins of the precious metal were never as rich as those to the south, however, so the prospectors left and the **timber** industry soon took over as the prime economy. That too has since gone into decline, leaving farming as the main source of income for the few inhabitants, along with a smattering of tourism.

Coming from the south, you pass through the missable golfing and retirement paradise of Graegle before Hwy-89 combines with Hwy-70 to form part of the **Feather River National Scenic Byway**; this leads to the county seat and commercial hub of **Quincy**, whose old town merits a wander. Further north, Hwy-89 continues solo through the cattle-grazing land of the **Indian Valley**, past the lazy town of **Greenville** to the recreational area of **Lake Almanor**, within easy striking distance of Lassen Volcanic National Park, whose snowcapped peaks are visible in the distance.

Quincy

Nestled on the lower western slopes of the northernmost reaches of the Sierra Nevada Mountains, **Quincy** is a pleasant town divided by a hill into two distinct halves. Modern and functional East Quincy is not especially appealing, but the blocks surrounding West Main Street in Quincy proper present some fine examples of Victorian architecture and are worth stopping at to look around. Behind the grand old Neoclassical **Courthouse**, which stands proudly near the junction where the highway through town veers from West Main Street into Crescent Street, you can visit the **Plumas County Museum**, 500 Jackson Street (summer only Tues–Sat 8am–5pm; $2; ☎530/283-6320, ⓦwww .countyofplumas.com). Inside you'll find informative displays on the area's Indian culture, the story of its settlement, and natural history, while the grounds contain an old buggy and an authentic 1890s gold miner's cabin.

For information, you have a choice between the **Chamber of Commerce**, 464 W Main Street (Mon–Fri 9am–noon & 1–4.30pm; ☎1-877/283-6320, ⓦwww.quincychamber.com), and the more comprehensive **Plumas County Visitors Bureau** on the northern edge of town at 550 Crescent Street (Mon–Sat 8am–5.30pm; ☎1-800/326-2247, ⓦwww.plumascounty.com). Of several **motels** around town, the best mix of location and economy is the *Gold Pan Motel*, 200 Crescent Street (☎1-800/804-6541; ❷), while among the **B&Bs** in the old town *The Feather Bed*, 542 Jackson Street (☎1-800/696-8624, ⓦwww.featherbed-inn .com; ❺), and *Ada's Place*, 562 Jackson Street (☎530/283-1954, ⓦwww.adasplace .com; ❹), are both comfortable and suitably atmospheric. *Greenhorn Creek Guest Ranch*, twelve miles east of town and a mile and a half from the highway at 2116 Greenhorn Ranch Road (☎1-800/334-6939, ⓦwww.greenhornranch.com; ❽), is the place to go for a Wild West experience – horseback riding, fishing, and hiking are all included in the cost of a night's stay. Though **eating** choices aren't spectacular in Quincy, you can grab a filling breakfast or lunch at the *Courthouse Café*, 525 W Main Street (☎530/283-3344), bang opposite – you guessed it – the courthouse, or enjoy a more upscale evening meal nearby at *Moon's* Italian steakhouse, 497 Lawrence Street (☎530/283-0765; closed Mon). East Quincy offers a few cheap and cheerful joints such as *Round Table Pizza*, 60 E Main Street (☎530/283-4545), and the *Mi Casita*, 875 E Main Street (☎530/283-4755), the latter serving authentic Mexican food.

Northern Plumas County

Leaving Quincy behind, Hwy-70 soon peels off to the left and continues to follow the middle fork of the Feather River southwest, while Hwy-89 meanders in a northerly direction through the rich grassy meadows, ranches, and farms of the **Indian Valley** towards the old mining town of **Greenville**, 23 miles on from Quincy. A further nine miles brings you close to the western shore of

Lake Almanor, an increasingly popular destination for boaters and families, and its main settlement of **Chester** at the northern end.

Greenville

Although it now depends more on cattle ranching and the felling of Christmas trees, sleepy **Greenville** still celebrates its mining heritage every summer with the **Gold Digger Days** festival on the third weekend of July. For the rest of the year it remains in its slumbers, but its quietude and idyllic countryside setting still make a pleasant spot to break your journey. Though there's not much to see, just wandering along Main Street can give you a sense of the town's workaday past. If you stop for a bite to **eat**, the bar food at the *Way Station Dinner House & Tiki Bar* (☎530/284-6018), at the central Hwy-89/Main Street junction, or burgers and pizza from *Mountain Valley Pizza* (☎530/284-6680) at 116 Ann Street (Hwy-89) will have to suffice. To use the town as an overnight base for some hiking in the surrounding picturesque **Indian Valley**, the most distinctive option is the English-literature-themed *Yorkshire House B&B*, 421 Main Street (☎530/284-1794, ⓦwww.yorkshirehousebb.com; ⑤).

Lake Almanor and Chester

Lake almanor, created in 1914 by the Great Western Power Company's damming of the north fork of the Feather River, stands at an elevation of 4500ft and covers fifty-two square miles, making it the largest of Plumas County's many lakes. This is also where the Cascades and the Sierras truly meet. The lake's clear blue waters reach a comfortable seventy-five degrees in summer, rendering it ideal for all sorts of **watersports**. Numerous resorts ring the pine-forested shoreline, and most rent equipment for all sorts of water-based activities, from high-speed water skiing to leisurely fishing, and provide a range of **accommodation** possibilities. Several such enterprises are, in counterclockwise order around the lake: *Plumas Pines Resort*, on the west shore at 3000 Almanor Drive West, Canyon Dam (☎530/259-4343, ⓦwww.plumaspinesresort.com; ③), with motel-style rooms, cabins, and RV slots ($25), as well as decent food at its own *Boathouse Grill*; the friendly *Dorado Inn*, on the east shore at 4379 Hwy-147 (☎530/284-7790, ⓦwww.doradoinn.com; ⑤), which offers great sunset views and a swimming pontoon; and on the peninsula that juts out from the north shore, *Knotty Pine Resort*, 430 Peninsula Drive (☎530/596-3348, ⓦwww.knottypine.net; ⑥), whose half-dozen two-bedroom cabins are ideal for groups of four or five. For **campers** there are simple sites all over the lake that are usually let on a first-come-first-served basis, though some can be booked through the US Forest Service (☎1-800/280-2267, ⓦwww.reserveusa.com). Of the reasonable **restaurants** dotted round the lake, *BJ's BBQ & Deli*, near Hamilton Branch at 3881 Hwy-A13 (☎530/596-4210), offers good home-style prime rib and halibut, while the *Peninsula Grill* at 401 Peninsula Drive (☎530/596-3538) does tasty seafood, steaks, and pasta.

At the northwest corner of the lake, the only town on its shores, **Chester**, is a relaxed place with a splendid setting and a selection of amenities. You can get information on the whole region at the **Chamber of Commerce**, 529 Main Street (Mon–Fri summer 9am–4pm, winter 10am–3pm; ☎1-800/350-4838, ⓦwww.chester-lakealmanor.com). The town's small **museum**, showcasing local history and Maidu Indian basketry, is inside the library at 210 First Avenue (Mon–Wed & Fri 10am–1pm & 1.30pm–5.30pm, Thurs noon–5pm & 6–8pm, Sat 10am–2pm; free; ☎530/258-2742). Among the dozen places to **stay**, the *Rose Quartz Inn*, 306 Main Street (☎530/258-2002, ⓦwww.rosequartzinn.com; ③) is a smartly refurbished motel, while *Antlers Motel*, 268 Main Street (☎530/258-2722 or 1-888/469-7829; ❷), is more basic despite a recent makeover. As you might expect, the *Cinnamon Teal B&B*, 227 Feather River Drive (☎530/258-3993, Ⓦwww.cinnamonteal.net; ❸), provides somewhat more ambience and great value. Two miles east of town on Hwy-36, *North Shore Campground* (☎530/258-3376, Ⓦwww.northshorecampground.com) is the biggest **campground** on the lake, with tent spaces for $32 and RV sites from $35. Once you've worked up an appetite on the lake, *Carol's Ranch House*, 669 Main Street (☎530/258-4226; Thurs–Sat), serves hearty down-home dinners, while the *Volcano Grill*, 384 Main Street (☎530/258-1000), fires up quality steaks and pasta and *Happy Garden*, 605 Main Street (☎530/258-2395), provides copious portions of Chinese favorites. *Three Beans Coffee House* at 150 Main Street (☎530/258-3312) is the place to head for a caffeine fix or a light snack like a bagel.

Lassen Volcanic National Park

About fifty miles over gently sloping plains east from Red Bluff on Hwy-36, the 106,000 acres that make up the pine forests, crystal-green lakes, and boiling

Camping in and around Lassen

During the few months of the year when conditions are suitable for camping, this is by far the best accommodation option. All **developed campgrounds** in the park are listed here and operate on a first-come-first-served basis, not a problem except on midsummer weekends. Most remain open from June to October and cost $16–18. Remember that Lassen is **bear country**; follow the posted precautions for food and waste storage, and make your presence known when hiking.

Primitive camping requires a free **wilderness permit** obtainable in advance from the park headquarters in Mineral (see opposite), or in person from the visitor centers and entrance stations. There is no self-registration and chosen sites must be a mile from developed campgrounds and a quarter-mile from most specific sites of interest. In the surrounding **Lassen National Forest**, camping is permitted anywhere, though you'll need a free permit to operate a cooking stove or to light a fire; these are sometimes refused in the dry summer months. In addition, there are a couple dozen developed sites strung along the highways within thirty miles of Lassen, most charging between $10 and $20.

Butte Lake 6100ft. In the far northeast corner of the park, accessed by Hwy-44. Can accommodate trailers and has a boat launch.

Juniper Lake 6800ft. In the far south-eastern corner of the park, with good hiking trails nearby and swimming in the lake. Drinking water must be boiled or treated.

Manzanita Lake 5900ft. By far the largest of the Lassen campgrounds and the only one with a camp store (8am–8pm), firewood for sale ($6), 24-hour showers (bring quarters), and a laundry. Trailers allowed and boat launch facilities available. Rangers run interpretive programs from here. Open May 23 to snow closure.

Southwest 6700ft. Small tent-only campground by the southwest entrance on

Hwy-89 with walk-in sites, water, and fire rings. Open year-round if you're equipped to brave it.

Summit Lake 6700ft. The pick of the Hwy-89 campgrounds, right in the center of the park and at the hub of numerous hiking trails. It's divided into two sections: the northern half can take trailers and is equipped with flush toilets, the southern half only holes. There's swimming in the lake for the steel-skinned.

Warner Valley 5700ft. Off Hwy-89 in the south of the park, this is a beautiful site, but its distance from the road makes it only worth heading for if you're planning extended hiking in the region.

thermal pools of the **LASSEN VOLCANIC NATIONAL PARK** are one of the most unearthly parts of California. A forbidding climate, which brings up to fifty feet of snowfall each year, keeps the area pretty much uninhabited, with the roads all blocked by snow and, apart from a brief June-to-October season, completely deserted. It lies at the southerly limit of the Cascades, a low, broad range which stretches six hundred miles north to Mount Garibaldi in British Columbia and is characterized by high volcanoes forming part of the Pacific Circle of Fire. Dominating the park at over 10,000ft is a fine example, **Mount Lassen** itself, which – although quiet in recent years – erupted in 1914, beginning a cycle of outbursts that climaxed in 1915, when the peak blew an enormous mushroom cloud some seven miles skyward, tearing the summit into chunks that landed as far away as Reno. Although nearly ninety years of geothermal inactivity have since made the mountain a safe and fascinating place, scientists predict that of all the Californian volcanoes, Lassen is the likeliest to erupt again.

Arrival and information

Lassen is always open ($10 per vehicle for seven days, $5 per hiker or biker), but you'll have a big job ahead of you if planning to get in or around without a car. During the winter, when the roads in the park are almost always shut down due to snow, a car won't do you much good either – snowshoes and cross-country skis take over as popular modes of transportation. Public transportation really isn't an option, seeing as Mount Lassen Motor Transit's "mail truck" from Red Bluff (Mon–Sat from 8am; ☎530/529-2722 or 1-800/427-9533) can only drop you short of the park's southwest entrance, where Hwy-89 turns up through Lassen to the north entrance at the junction with Hwy-44 near Manzanita Lake.

The Park Service has its **headquarters** in **Mineral** (summer daily 8am–4.30pm; winter Mon–Fri 8am–4.30pm; ☎530/595-4444, ⓦwww.nps.gov /lavo), where you can get free maps and information (there's a box outside when it's closed, and they'll leave your backcountry permits here if you arrive late), including the *Lassen Park Guide*. The main **visitor center** (June–Aug daily

9

▲ Bumpass Hell, Lassen Volcanic National Park

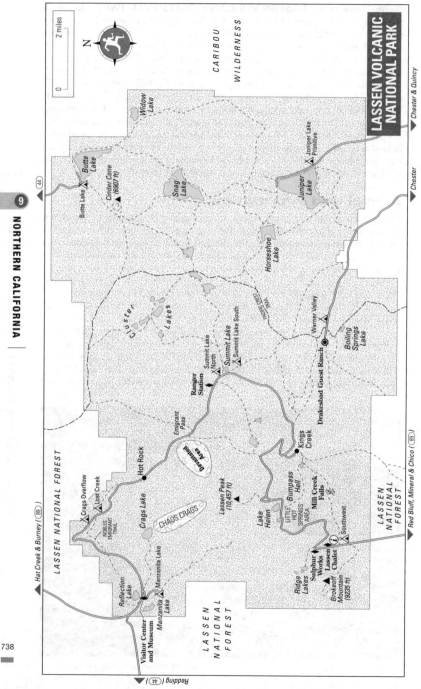

LASSEN VOLCANIC NATIONAL PARK

9am–5pm; May & Sept Wed–Sun 9am–5pm; ☏530/595-4444 ext. 5180) is at Manzanita Lake, just inside the north entrance, and occupies the same building as the Loomis Museum (see p.740).

Accommodation

The only way to **stay** inside Lassen is to camp (see box, p.736), but even in August night temperatures can hover around freezing, and many people prefer to stay in one of the resorts and lodges that pepper the surrounding forest. To be sure of a room in the popular summer months, it pays to book well ahead.

Childs Meadow Hwy-36, 9 miles southeast of southwest entrance ☏1-888/595-3383, ⊛www .childsmeadowresort.com. One of the few choices on this side of the park, scenic and friendly *Childs Meadow* offers basic motel accommodation, more comfy chalet rooms, tent sites for $15, and an on-site café. ❸

Hat Creek Resort Hwy-89, Old Station, 11 miles northeast of the north entrance ☏1-800/568-0109, ⊛www.hatcreekresortrv.com. A complex of motel units and fancier cabins with kitchens (two-day minimum stay), plus tent sites for $20, RV sites from $27, and a deli. ❸

Lassen Mineral Lodge Hwy-36, Mineral, 9 miles southwest of the southwest entrance on Hwy-36 ☏530/595-4422, ⊛www.minerallodge.com. Unspectacular base-rate rooms and considerably comfier family ones for not much more. There's a

general store, restaurant, and bar on site, as well as tent sites for $18. ❸

Mill Creek Resort Hwy-172, Mill Creek, 8 miles south of the southwest entrance ☏1-888/595-4449. Set amidst thick forest, there are cabins of different sizes and tent/RV spaces from $15. ❸

Padilla's Rim Rock Ranch Resort 13275 Hwy-89, Old Station, 11 miles northeast of the north entrance ☏530/335-7114. A collection of motel rooms and cabins of varying standards, the best sleeping up to six, dotted around a meadow. Closed Nov–March. ❷

Weston House Red Rock Road, Shingletown, 19 miles west of the north entrance ☏530/474-3738, ⊛www.westonhouse.com. An extremely pleasant B&B, with six elegant rooms perched on a beautiful volcanic ridge with pool and deck, overlooking the Ishi National Wilderness Area. ❻

The Park

Unlike most other wilderness areas, you don't actually need to get out of the car to appreciate Lassen, as some of the best features are visible from the paved Hwy-89 that traverses the park. A thorough tour should take no more than a few hours. Pick up a copy of the *Road Guide: Lassen Volcanic National Park* ($5) in the visitor center.

Starting from the southwest entrance, you'll pass the trailhead to **Brokeoff Mountain**, a six-mile round-trip hike through wildflowers. Next is the **Lassen Chalet**, the only place to get food and, in winter, limited skiing facilities in the park. The first self-guided trail is just up ahead – follow your nose and the **Sulfur Works** can be reached via a 200-foot boardwalk around its steaming fumaroles and burbling mud pots. The winding road climbs along the side of Diamond Peak before edging **Emerald Lake** and Lassen's show-stealer, **Bumpass Hell**, named after a man who lost a leg trying to cross it. This steaming valley of active pools and vents, bubbling away at a low rumble, can be traversed on a flat, well-tended trail that loops three miles to boardwalks that put you right in the middle of the stinky action. Recall the fate of Mr Bumpass, however, and stay on the trails; the crusts over the thermal features are brittle and easy to break through, leaving you, literally, in hot water. Across the road from Bumpass Hell's parking lot, the trails around the glassy surface of Emerald Lake are also spectacular, though in much quieter fashion; the lake itself resembles a sheet of green ice, perfectly still and clear but for the snow-covered rock mound which rises from its center. The lake approaches swimmable temperatures only during summer.

Just north of here, the road reaches its highest point (8512ft) at the trailhead for **Lassen Peak**. It then winds down to the flat meadows around **King's Creek**, whose trails along the winding water are popular for picnics. From road marker 32, a three-mile round-trip walk leads to the seventy-foot-tall **Kings Creek Falls**. At the halfway point you'll come to **Summit Lake**, a busy camping area set around a beautiful icy lake, from where you can start on the park's most manageable hiking trails. Press on further to the **Devastated Area**, where, in 1914, molten lava from Lassen poured down the valley, denuding the landscape as it went, ripping out every tree and patch of grass. Slowly the earth is recovering its green mantle, but the most vivid impression is still one of complete destruction. From here it's a gauntlet of pines to the northern entrance, site of **Manzanita Lake** and the **Loomis Museum** (summer daily 9am–5pm; winter Fri–Sun 9am–5pm; free), a memorial to Benjamin Loomis, whose documentary photos of the 1914 eruption form the centerpiece of an exhibition strong on flora and local geology – plug domes, composite cones, and cinder cones. An easy trail circles the lake, but so do many of the campers from the nearby campground: an early start is needed for any serious wildlife spotting.

Leaving Lassen, Hwy-44 heads forty miles west to Redding and I-5 or, alternatively, you can continue northwest on Hwy-89 one hundred miles to Mount Shasta, stopping halfway at the breathtaking **McArthur–Burney Falls State Park** ($6 per vehicle; ☏530/335-2777). The park's centerpiece is a 129-foot waterfall, unique for the way the water spills over the rim from two different

---

Hiking in Lassen National Park

For a volcanic landscape, a surprisingly large proportion of the walking trails in the park are predominantly flat, and the heavily glaciated terrain to the east of the main volcanic massif is pleasingly gentle. Rangers will point you toward the **hiking routes** best suited to your ability – the park's generally high elevations will leave all but the most experienced walker short of breath, and you should stick to the shorter trails at least until you're acclimatized. For anything but the most tentative explorations, pick up a copy of *Lassen Trails* ($4.25) or the better, color *Hiking Trails of Lassen* ($15.95), which describes the most popular hikes.

Chaos Crags Lake (3.5 miles round-trip; 2–3hr; 800-foot ascent). From the Manzanita Lake campground access road, the path leads gently up through pine and fir forest to the peaceful lake. An adventurous extension climbs a ridge of loose rock to the top of Chaos Crags, affording a view of the whole park.
Cinder Cone (13 miles round-trip; 1 day; 800-foot ascent). Check with the rangers for the best seasonal starting point for this, Lassen's most spectacular hike, through the Painted Dunes and Fantastic Lava Beds before reaching Snag Lake. Can also be done as a 4-hour hike from Butte Lake.
Lassen Peak (5 miles round-trip; 4hr; 2000-foot ascent). A fairly strenuous hike from road marker 22 to the highest point in the park. Be prepared with water and warm clothing.

Manzanita Lake (1.5 miles; 1hr; flat). Easy trails on level ground make this one of the most popular short walks in the park.
Nobles Emigrant Trail (2.5 miles; 1–2hr; 200-foot ascent). The most accessible and one of the more interesting sections of a trail forged in 1850 starts opposite the Manzanita Lake entrance station and meets Hwy-89 at marker 60. It isn't maintained, but is heavily compacted and easy going.
Paradise Meadows (3 miles round-trip; 3hr; 800-foot ascent). Starting either at the Hat Creek parking area (marker 42) or marker 27, and passing Terrace Lake on the way, this hike winds up at Paradise Meadows, ablaze with wildflowers in the summer and a marvelous spot to pass an afternoon.

levels. A paved trail leads to the misty base and pool, and a 1.5-mile steep loop takes you downstream and then back up the other side of the pool to a bridge over the falls' headwater. The Pacific Crest Trail passes alongside nearby **Lake Briton**, and paddleboats, canoes, and rowboats can be rented at the park entrance. Plentiful **camping** amongst the black oaks is available for $20 a night.

Eating

You don't have an awful lot to choose from in Lassen Volcanic National Park in terms of **food**. There's a reasonable general store at *Manzanita Lake* campground (see box, p.736), and Lassen Chalet, in the southwest corner of the park, has a surprisingly good café (daily 9am–6pm), but beyond that you'll have to go outside the park and even then it's slim pickings. Some of the accommodations listed on p.739 have food; otherwise, *JJ's Café* (☎530/335-7225) in tiny Old Station, eleven miles northeast of the park, does filling breakfasts, lunches, and pizza or barbecue dinners.

Redding and around

At the heart of northern interior California, the sizeable modern town of **Redding** is often viewed simply as a hub for the region, without much to merit more than refueling, grabbing a bite, or changing transportation. It does, however, hold a certain degree of interest, especially its revitalized central stretch on the Sacramento River. Its diminutive neighbor **Shasta**, a once-lively gold-mining town just to the west, provides a historical counterpoint and seems a world away from the urban sprawl nearby.

Redding

With a spreading expanse of strip malls along I-5 that have made its central shopping complex virtually obsolete, **REDDING** first appears to be a bit of an anomaly amidst the natural splendor of the northern interior. The region's largest city, with over 70,000 people, it's been a northern nexus since the late nineteenth century, when the Central Pacific Railroad came through. Today it remains a crossroads, bulging with cookie-cutter motels and diners that service traffic heading east to Lassen, west to Whiskeytown-Shasta-Trinity National Recreation Area, north to Mount Shasta, and south to San Francisco. In recent years, however, the opening of a major museum and iconic new bridge across the central stretch of the Sacramento River have done more to detain passers-through. The one annual event that has long attracted substantial crowds is the **Kool April Nites** classic-car meeting (☎1-800/874-7562, ⊛www.koolaprilnites.com) on the second or third weekend of April, the only time you're likely to encounter problems finding a room.

Though fiercely hot in summer (100°F even in late September), the temperature drops forbiddingly in some of the surrounding areas in winter. Bear in mind that what looks like a mild day in Redding could turn out to be blizzard conditions a few miles up the road (and several thousand feet up a mountainside).

Arrival, getting around, and information

Considering its position at the crossroads of Northern California, **public transportation** in Redding is woefully inadequate, though at least the various

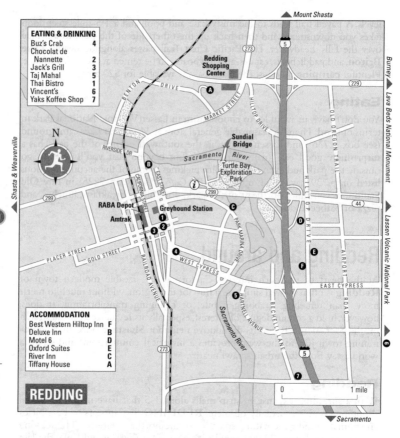

▲ Mount Shasta

EATING & DRINKING

Buz's Crab	4
Chocolat de Nannette	2
Jack's Grill	3
Taj Mahal	5
Thai Bistro	1
Vincent's	6
Yaks Koffee Shop	7

Redding Shopping Center

Sundial Bridge

Sacramento River

Turtle Bay Exploration Park

RABA Depot

Greyhound Station

Amtrak

ACCOMMODATION

Best Western Hilltop Inn	F
Deluxe Inn	B
Motel 6	D
Oxford Suites	E
River Inn	C
Tiffany House	A

REDDING

0   1 mile

▼ Sacramento

Shasta & Weaverville ◀ | ◀ Burney | Lava Beds National Monument ▶ | Lassen Volcanic National Park ▶

modes of ground transport available all stop within easy walking distance of each other downtown. The Greyhound station is at 1321 Butte Street (☎530/241-2070, ⓦ www.greyhound.com), while the local RABA **bus** system depot (☎530/241-2877, ⓦ www.ci.redding.ca.us/raba/rabahome.htm) is on California Street on the other side of the deserted shopping center, and the Amtrak station right beside it. If you're in a hurry to reach Northern California from elsewhere on the West Coast, there are at least six United Express (☎1-800/241-6522, ⓦ www.united.com) **flight** connections daily from SFO to **Redding Municipal Airport** (☎530/224-4321), plus one or two daily from Seattle via Portland and sometimes Arcata/Eureka with Horizon Air/Alaska Air (☎1-800/547-9308, ⓦ www.horizonair.alaskaair.com). Typically there's no public transportation from the airport (though some hotels have shuttles), and once here, you're not going to get to see much without a **car** anyway. Call Caltrans to check ahead for weather and road conditions (☎1-800/427-7623) and, if necessary, gather extra provisions (de-icer, tire chains, and so on) in case of snowstorms.

The **Redding CVB**, 777 Auditorium Drive (Mon–Fri 8.30am–6pm, Sat 10am–4pm; ☎1-800/874-7562, ⓦ www.visitredding.org), can give advice on accommodation, information on camping in the outlying areas, and details on where to rent camping equipment. For more specific information on the surrounding area and the whole of the northern interior and beyond, the new **California Welcome Center**, just off I-5 nine miles south of Redding at 1699 Hwy-273, Anderson (Mon–Fri 9am–5pm, Sat & Sun 10am–4pm; ☏1-800/474-2782, ⓦwww.shastacascade.com), has a huge collection of maps, information, and well-organized displays, and is staffed by helpful outdoor experts. As a general rule, Lassen National Volcanic Park is for hardier and more experienced hikers, and novices are pointed in the direction of the Whiskeytown-Shasta-Trinity National Recreation Area, where there are warmer climes and easier trails.

Accommodation

Motels are concentrated along Redding's old main strip, Market Street (Hwy-273), and Pine Street, while the smarter chain hotels tend to be along Hilltop Drive, Redding's newer service area east of I-5. A few B&Bs dotted around town round out the options.

Best Western Hilltop Inn 2300 Hilltop Drive ☏1-800/336-4880, ⓦwww.bestwestern.com. This comfortable franchise – with its pool, sauna, buffet breakfasts, and convivial grill – makes you feel you're staying somewhere more personal than your average chain. Specials available most of the year. ❺

Deluxe Inn 1135 Market St ☏530/243-5141. This ultra-cheapie is fine for a night but hardly lives up to its name, with rather poky rooms. ❶

Motel 6 1640 Hilltop Drive ☏1-800/466-8356, ⓦwww.motel6.com. The most central of three outlets in the Redding area, this one is basic but clean and efficient. ❸

Oxford Suites 1967 Hilltop Drive ☏1-800/762-0133, ⓦwww.oxfordsuites.com. This California chain offers smart and comfy suites at good rates. You can drink your two free happy-hour beverages in peace by the pool. ❹

River Inn 1835 Park Marina Drive ☏530/241-9500 or 1-800/995-4341. Glorified motel, perhaps a little overpriced for the area because of its prime riverside location. ❹

Tiffany House 1510 Barbara Rd ☏530/244-3225, ⓦwww.tiffanyhousebb.com Just over a mile north of downtown, the *Tiffany* is a plush yet good-value B&B in a converted Victorian house, with a pricier detached cottage behind. ❺

The Town

Redding has worked hard to improve its image in order to tempt visitors to spend a day or two in its leafy urban environment before sampling the surrounding natural delights. Tourists are encouraged to stay in the newer areas near the freeway rather than in the dowdy old **downtown** area, which has still not received the proposed injection of cash to spruce it up. Though in no way unsafe, walking around it gives the distinct impression that it has seen better days. One place to stop is the **Old City Hall Arts Center**, 1313 Market Street (Tues–Fri 9am–5pm, Sat 11am–3pm; free; ☏530/241-7320), which has rotating displays of works by local artists. Even more attractive as a building is the beautifully restored Art Deco **Cascade Theatre**, 1731 Market Street (☏530/243-8877), which hosts drama, concerts, and films.

The centerpiece of Redding's revitalization is the splendid **Turtle Bay Exploration Park**, 800 Auditorium Drive (June–Sept daily 9am–5pm; Oct–May Tues–Sun 9am–5pm; $12; ☏1-800/887-8532, ⓦwww.turtlebay.org), an ambitious $64 million project. The glass-and-wood structure blends seamlessly into the riverside environment and contains permanent displays on the region's natural history, resources, and Native American culture, including a full-scale replica of an Indian bark-house. The skillfully crafted **Visible River** exhibit, which allows you to enter a simulated limestone cave and view local water creatures in a 24-foot tank, creates the impression that you're below a riverbank – a huge cottonwood tree even starts within the "river" and protrudes upwards into the museum. The River Lab enables you to play with natural materials and learn by experience how processes like erosion work on a large tilted table covered in sand, while the Exploration Hall and Art Gallery display changing cultural and artistic exhibitions, among them detailed plans from the construction of the **Sundial Bridge** (see below). Also within the grounds, Paul Bunyan's Forest Camp includes logging and ecological displays and a summer butterfly house, while the 220-acre McConnell Arboretum (summer 7am–dusk; winter 9am–5pm; $6 but free with Turtle Bay entry) includes Mediterranean and other dry-climate flora and a fascinating medicinal herb garden arranged according to the parts of the human body each plant treats. The glass **café** at the west end of the main building gives uninterrupted views of the riverbank, which forms part of the newly extended **Sacramento River Trail**, a pleasant ten-mile loop through savannah and wetland sections, designed for walkers and cyclists. The central stretch of the river opposite the Exploration Park is dominated by the unique Sundial Bridge, designed by celebrated Spanish architect **Santiago Calatrava**, whose other works include the arched roof of the Olympic Stadium in Athens. Opened to great local fanfare on July 4, 2004, the gracefully curved and tapered 218-foot mast at the northern end of this slim, translucent, glass-floored footbridge forms a sundial and has already become a true icon for the region, even the state.

Eating

Redding's **restaurants** are as ubiquitous as its motels, some of them 24-hour, many of them greasy diners or fast-food outlets, limited in appeal. There are, however, some noble exceptions.

Buz's Crab 2159 East St ☏ 530/243-2120. Just south of downtown, this local institution rustles up a vast range of fish and seafood delights at very moderate prices.

Chocolat de Nannette 1777 Market St ☏ 530/241-4068. A fairly chic but inexpensive bistro serving imaginative salads and main courses, combined with a quality bakery and café.

Jack's Grill 1743 California St ☏ 530/241-9705. Popular restaurant that prepares fine grilled steak and shrimp and chicken dishes for $10–15. Reservations not accepted, and though you'll probably have to wait for a table, it's well worth it. Closed Sun.

Taj Mahal 40 Hartnell Ave ☏ 530/221-4655. Authentic North Indian cuisine in a modern dining room; quite pricey dinner entrees, but great lunch buffet seven days a week.

Thai Bistro 1270 Yuba St ☏ 530/244-4666. Small, brightly lit dining room, serving well-prepared spicy Thai fare at slightly inflated prices.

Vincent's 1647 Hartnell Ave ☏ 530/222-1307. Hidden in a castle-shaped mall, this is Redding's most upscale restaurant, with an eclectic seasonal menu of high-quality French, Italian, and American dishes. Most entrées over $20.

Yaks Koffee Shop 3274 Bechelli Lane ☏ 530/223-9999. Massive, colorful place with a full range of coffees, smoothies, savory snacks, and sweet pastries.

Shasta

Huddling four miles west of Redding, the ghost town of **Shasta** – not to be confused with Mount Shasta (see p.747) – is about the area's only option for historic entertainment, and it's a slim option at that. A booming gold-mining town when Redding was an insignificant dot on the map, Shasta's fortunes changed when the railroad tracks were laid to Redding in the late nineteenth century. Abandoned since then, it remains today a row of half-ruined brick buildings that were once part of a runaway prosperity, and literally the end of the road for prospectors. All roads from San Francisco, Sacramento, and other southerly points terminated at Shasta; beyond, rough and poorly marked trails made it almost impossible to find gold diggings along the Trinity, Salmon, and Upper Sacramento rivers, and diggers contented themselves with the rich pickings in the surrounding area, pushing out the local Native Americans in a brutal territorial quest for good mining land.

The **Courthouse**, on the east side of Main Street, has been turned into a museum (Wed–Sun 10am–5pm; $2), full of mining paraphernalia and paintings of past heroes, though best are the gallows at the back and the prison cells below – a grim reminder of the daily executions that went on here. The miners were a largely unruly lot, and in the main room of the Courthouse a charter lays down some basic rules of conduct:

IV Thou shalt neither remember what thy friends do at home on the Sabbath day, lest the remembrance may not compare favorably with what thou doest here.
VII Thou shalt not kill the body by working in the rain, even though thou shalt make enough money to buy psychic attendance. Neither shalt thou destroy thyself by "tight" nor "slewed" nor "high" nor "corned" nor "three sheets to the wind," by drinking smoothly down brandy slings, gin cocktails, whiskey punches, rum toddies and egg nogs.

From *The Miners' Ten Commandments*

The **Shasta State Historic Park** (unrestricted entry; ☎530/243-8194) straddles two blocks of Main Street, and is less grand than it sounds, though it's a good place to stretch your legs before moving further west. Indistinguishable ruins of brick buildings are identified by plaques as stores and hotels, and the central area, not much bigger than the average garden really, features miscellaneous mining machinery and a picnic area, along with a trail that loops around the back.

Whiskeytown-Shasta-Trinity National Recreation Area

To the west and north of Redding lies the **WHISKEYTOWN-SHASTA-TRINITY NATIONAL RECREATION AREA**. Assuming the roads are open – they're often blocked due to bad weather in winter – this huge chunk of land is open for public use daily, year-round. Its series of three impounded **lakes** – **Whiskeytown**, **Trinity**, and **Shasta** – have artificial beaches, forests, and camping facilities designed to meet the needs of anyone who has ever fancied themselves as a water skier, sailor, or wilderness hiker. Sadly, during summer the area becomes completely congested, as windsurfers, motorboats, jet skis, and recreational vehicles block the narrow routes which serve the lakes. But in the winter, when the weekenders have all gone, it can be supremely untouched, at least on the surface. In fact, there's an extensive system of tunnels, dams, and aqueducts directing the plentiful waters of the Sacramento River to California's Central Valley to irrigate cash crops for the huge agribusinesses. The lakes are pretty enough, but residents complain they're not a patch on the wild waters that used to flow from the mountains before the Central Valley Project came along in the 1960s.

Whiskeytown Lake

Of the three, **Whiskeytown Lake**, just beyond Shasta, is the smallest, easiest to get to, and inevitably the most popular. It's open all the time but day-use parking costs $5. Ideal for watersports, it hums with the sound of jet skis and powerboats ripping across the still waters. Those who don't spend their holiday in a wetsuit can usually be found four-wheel-driving and pulling action-man stunts on the primitive roads all around. The best place for **camping** and **hiking** is in the **Brandy Creek** area – a hairy five-mile drive along the narrow J.F. Kennedy Memorial Drive from the main entrance and **Whiskeytown Visitor Information Center** on Hwy-299 (daily: summer 9am–6pm; winter 10am–4pm; T530/246-1225, Wwww.nps.gov/whis), where you can pick up permits for primitive camping sites ($10) around the lake. There's a small store at the water's edge in Brandy Creek and three more developed campgrounds (summer $16–18) about a mile behind in the woods.

Trinity Lake and Weaverville

After Hwy-299 has climbed over the wooded, 3213-foot Buckhorn Summit, you can turn northeast on Hwy-3 around forty miles west of Whiskeytown to **Trinity Lake**, officially called Clair Engle Lake, but not locally referred to as such. This is much quieter, used by fewer in summer, and in winter primarily a picturesque stopoff for skiers on their way to the **Trinity Alps** area beyond, which in turn lead to the extensive **Salmon Mountains** range. There are several places to **stay** and enjoy the peaceful lapping waters. Of these, *Pinewood Cove*, 45110 Hwy-3 (T1-800/988-5253, Wwww.pinewoodcove.com; ⑤), rents out boats of various sizes and has $27.50 campsites and luxury cabins for four, as do *Trinity Lake Resorts*, further north at 45810 Hwy-3 (T1-800/255-5561, Wwww .trinitylakeresort.com; ⑤); they also have houseboats (minimum stay three days) and a full restaurant. At its southern end, Lake Trinity squeezes through a narrow bottleneck to form the much slimmer and smaller Lewiston Lake, which can be reached by the back road that cuts the corner between Hwy-299 and Hwy-3. Camp for free on the grassy banks of the lake or stay in greater comfort at the *Old Lewiston Inn* (T1-800/286-4441, Wwww.theoldlewistoninn.com; ④) in the diminutive old mining town of Lewiston itself, on the same road.

Weaverville

Sadly, many people don't bother to stop in the small Gold Rush town of **Weaverville**, 43 miles west of Redding, where Hwy-3 branches north to Trinity Lake, while Hwy-299 continues a further one hundred miles west to Eureka (see p.716) and the coast. The town's distinctive brick buildings, fitted with exterior spiral staircases, were built to withstand fires – indeed, the fire station itself is particularly noteworthy. The main draw, though, is the **Joss House** on Main Street (Wed–Sun 10am–5pm; $2; T530/623-5284), a small Taoist temple built in 1874 by indentured Chinese mineworkers. A beautiful shrine still in use today, it features a three-thousand-year-old altar and can be visited on a poor guided tour (last 4pm). Next door, the **J.J. Jake Jackson Museum** (May–Oct daily 10am–5pm; April, Nov & Dec daily noon–4pm; Jan–March Tues & Sat noon–4pm; donation; T530/623-5211, Wwww.trinitymuseum.org) exhibits artifacts from the Gold Rush. On the opposite side of the road look out for California's oldest still-functioning pharmacy, which stocks a brilliant selection of remedies in glass jars within original glass and wood cabinets.

You can **stay** in some style at the refurbished 1861 *Weaverville Hotel*, 481 Main Street (T530/623-2222, Wwww.weavervillehotel.com; ⑤). Alternatives include the renovated *49er Gold Country Inn*, 880 Main Street (T530/623-4937, Wwww.goldcountryinn.com; ②), or the friendly *Motel Trinity* (T1-877/623-5454, Wwww.moteltrinity.com; ②), south of Hwy-3 at 1270 Main Street, which has some rooms with Jacuzzis for twice the price of basic ones.

For **food**, try the pizza, sandwiches, and ice cream at the cozy *Christopher Robin's*, 529 Main Street (T530/623-2663), or delicious Chinese cuisine in the dark-red interior of the *Red Dragon*, 625 Main Street (℡530/623-3000), across from the Joss House, appropriately enough. The *New York Saloon*, 527 Main Street (℡530/623-3492), is a great place to mingle with the friendly locals over a glass of beer. For more information, consult the **Chamber of Commerce**, 501 Main Street (Mon–Sat 9am–5pm; ℡1-800/487-4648, Ⓦwww.trinitycounty.com), though there's not always staff to man it.

Shasta Lake

East of the other two lakes and eight miles north of Redding is **Shasta Lake**. The biggest of the three lakes – larger than the San Francisco Bay in fact – it's marred by the unsightly and enormous **Shasta Dam**, 465ft high and over half a mile long, bang in the middle. Twice the mass of the Hoover Dam, it's the second largest dam in America, made of enough concrete to send a foot-square strip round the planet several times. Built between 1938 and 1945 as part of the enormous Central Valley irrigation project, the dam backs up the Sacramento, McCloud, and Pit rivers to form the lake, the project's northern outpost. You can visit the **powerhouse visitor center** (daily 9am–4pm) via US-151, off I-5, and take one of the free **tours** (6 daily in summer, 3–4 other seasons), though security is tight and you cannot take cameras or mobile phones with you. Still, it's an entertaining 45 minutes, and the close-up views of the millions of gallons of water gushing down the face of the giant structure are memorable.

On the north side of the lake, the massive limestone formations of the **Shasta Caverns** (daily 2-hour tours: June–Aug every 30min 9am–4pm; April, May & Sept hourly 9am–3pm; winter 10am, noon & 2pm; $20; ℡1-800/795-2283, Ⓦwww.lakeshastacaverns.com) are the largest in California, jutting above ground and clearly visible from the freeway. The interior, however, conceals just a fairly standard series of caves and tunnels in which stalactite and stalagmite formations are studded with crystals, flowstone deposits, and miniature waterfalls. The admission price covers the short ferry journey from the ticket booth across an arm of Shasta Lake and the bus transfer on the other side.

If you turn west instead of east at the exit to the caverns, within a couple of miles you reach two great **places to stay**. First, in the small hillside settlement of **O'Brien**, the 🍴 *O'Brien Mountain Inn* (℡1-888/799-8026, Ⓦwww .obrienmountaininn.com; ❺) is a welcoming country B&B whose star room is the detached Luke's Tree House Suite on stilts over the forest ($300). A little further on, the *Bridge Bay Resort*, 10300 Bridge Bay Road (℡1-800/752-9669, Ⓦwww.sevencrown.com; ❺), provides the only accommodation right on the lake in the shape of motel rooms, suites, cabins, and houseboats; you can also dine with a view of the water at the resort's excellent *Tail of the Whale* restaurant. From Lake Shasta, I-5 crosses the world's highest double-decker bridge and races up towards Mount Shasta, an impressive drive against a staggering backdrop of mountains and lakes.

Mount Shasta and Mount Shasta City

When I first caught sight of it over the braided folds of the Sacramento Valley I was fifty miles away and afoot, alone and weary. Yet my blood turned to wine, and I have not been weary since.

John Muir, about Mount Shasta

The lone peak of the 14,179-foot **MOUNT SHASTA** dominates the landscape for a hundred miles all around, almost permanently snow-covered and hypnotically beautiful, but menacing in its potential for destruction: it last erupted over two hundred years ago, but is still considered an active volcano. Summing up its isolated magnificence, Joaquin Miller once described it as "lonely as God and as white as a winter moon." Local lore is rich with tales of Lemurians – tall, barefoot men dressed in white robes – living inside the mountain, alongside their legendary neighbors the Yakta- vians, who are said to be excellent bell-makers. Such tales have lent the mountain a bit of a Twilight Zone reputation, and numerous UFO sightings and otherworldly experiences have made Mount Shasta a center of the American **spiritualism** movement. This prominence was heightened in 1987 when five thousand people arrived to take part in the good vibes of the Harmonic Convergence, an attempt to channel the energies of sacred power spots into peace and harmony. Not all is peaceful on the mountain, however, as hundreds of climbers annually attempt to ascend its icy heights,

Climbing Mount Shasta

Even if you're only passing through the region, you'll be tempted to tackle Mount Shasta. Ambling among the pines of the lower slopes is rewarding enough, but the assault on the summit is the main challenge – and it can be done in a day with basic equipment and some determination.

Still, it's not a climb to be taken lightly, and every year several deaths occur and numerous injuries are sustained through inexperience and overambition. The wise stick to the routes prescribed by the **Mount Shasta Ranger District Office**, 204 W Alma Street (June–Aug daily 8am–4.30pm; Sept–May Mon–Fri 8am–4.30pm; ☎530/926-4511), which insists that you obtain a **summit pass** (also self-issued outside the office when closed and at the trailhead; $15) and enter your name in the **climbers' register** before and after your ascent. Those not planning to go above 10,000ft only require a free **wilderness permit**.

The mountain's isolation creates its own **weather**, which can change with alarming rapidity. In early summer, when most novice attempts are made, the snow cover is complete, and crampons and an ice axe are a requirement to get a good grip; later during the season, as the snow melts, patches of loose ash and cinder appear, making the going more difficult and the chance of falling rock greater. Only at the end of summer, with most of the snow melted, is there a chance of climbing safely without equipment. There are countless equipment rental agencies in town, such as The Fifth Season, 300 N Mount Shasta Boulevard (☎530/926-3606, ⓦwww.thefifthseason.com), which has the following rental prices for two/three-day trips: boots ($26), crampons and ice axe ($22), mountain tent ($75), and sleeping bag ($26). They also provide a mountain weather forecast on ☎530/926-5555. House of Ski & Board, 316 Chestnut Street (☎530/926-2359, ⓦwww.shastaski.com), offers much the same at equally competitive rates. To be prepared for **storms** on the mountain, you'll want to bring extra food, stove fuel, a good, wind-resistant shelter, and plenty of warm clothing.

Even for fit, acclimatized climbers, **the ascent**, from 7000ft to over 14,000ft, takes eight to ten utterly exhausting hours. The easiest, safest, and most popular way up is via **Avalanche Gulch** – just follow the footprints of the person in front of you. Drive up the mountain on the Everitt Memorial Highway to the **Bunny Flat** trailhead at 7000ft. A gentle hour's walk brings you to **Horse Camp** (7900ft), a good place to acclimatize and spend the night before your ascent – there's drinking water, toilet facilities, and a knowledgeable caretaker who can offer good advice about your impending climb. The return trip is done in four or five hours, depending on the recklessness of your descent: Mount Shasta is a renowned spot for **glissading** – careering down the slopes on a jacket or strong plastic sheet – a sport best left to those proficient in ice-axe arrests, but wonderfully exhilarating nonetheless.

an activity that has resulted in deaths, usually from falls or the ever-changing weather.

Just below the shadow of the behemoth sits the historic railroad town of **Dunsmuir** and, right up against the mountain, pleasant **Mount Shasta City**, a small town of shops, outfitters, spiritual bookstores, and fantastic restaurants. To the southeast, also commanding wonderful views of the mountain, is pretty little **McCloud**, while on the northern flank of the peak rests **Weed**, another tiny town that offers some of the clearest views of Mount Shasta in summertime and access to Lava Beds National Monument. Further north towards the Oregon border, **Yreka** is more useful as an I-5 service stop than as a place to visit in its own right.

Arrival and information

Merely getting to Mount Shasta City without a car is a complex but rewarding journey: the nearest Greyhound **buses** will bring you is Weed (see p.754), seven miles north, while Amtrak **trains** stop six miles south in Dunsmuir, unfortunately in the middle of the night; from both towns, half a dozen or so daily STAGE buses (℡530/842-8295 or 1-800/247-8243) run to the Mount Shasta Shopping Center next to the *Black Bear Diner*, although you'll have to wait at least three hours for the first bus from Dunsmuir. STAGE also operates five daily services to McCloud. The **Chamber of Commerce**, 300 Pine Street (daily: May–Sept 9am–5.30pm; Oct–April 10am–4pm; ℡1-800/926-4865, ⓦwww.mtshastachamber.com), has a rather limited selection of brochures; you can obtain more comprehensive information on the entire county from the **Siskiyou County Visitor Bureau** (℡1-877/847-8777, ⓦwww.visitsiskiyou.org), although there is no office to visit here.

Accommodation

Mount Shasta City has no shortage of **accommodation**, and reservations should only be necessary on weekends in the height of summer. Mount Shasta Cabins & Cottages, 500 S Mount Shasta Boulevard (℡1-888/565-9422, ⓦwww.mtshastacabins.com), is a useful agency with a wide range of cabins and houses in the area.

Hotels, motels, and B&Bs

Alpenrose Cottage Guesthouse 204 E Hinckley St ℡530/926-6724, ⓦwww.snowcrest.net/alpenrose. A top-quality and friendly hostel-style guesthouse with a relaxed atmosphere and a great deck for watching the sunset over Mount Shasta, immediately behind. Single people can stay for $60. Follow the KOA signs a mile north on N Mount Shasta Blvd. ❸

Best Western Tree House 111 Morgan Way ℡1-800/545-7164, ⓦwww.bestwestern.com. One of the more attractive and intimate members of the international chain, with all the usual amenities. Close to downtown, too. ❺

Cold Creek Inn 724 N Mount Shasta Blvd ℡1-800/292-9421, ⓦwww.coldcreekinn.com. Nicely refurbished motel, an easily walkable few blocks to downtown. Good Internet specials. ❸

Dream Inn 326 Chestnut St ℡1-877/375-4744, ⓦwww.dreaminnmtshastacity.com. Very central and reasonably priced B&B, a block east of Mount Shasta Blvd, in a Victorian house with all the usual trappings. ❸

Mount Shasta Ranch B&B 1008 W A Barr Rd ℡530/926-3870, ⓦwww.stayinshasta.com. A stylish ranch house with spacious rooms, a hot spring, and a great view of Mount Shasta. The cheaper rooms have shared bathrooms; $44 singles. ❷

Travel Inn 504 S Mt Shasta Blvd ℡530/926-4617, ⓦwww.shastaweb.com/travelinn. Decent, clean motel with basic rooms at bargain rates. ❷

Camping

Campgrounds abound in the surrounding area, but few have full amenities and hot showers are fairly essential when the mercury drops. The most picturesque campground in the area is the woodland *Lake Siskiyou Camp Resort* (Apr–Oct; $20; ☏1-888/926-2618, ⓦwww.lakesis.com), four miles southwest of town on a lake of the same name, where you can picnic, bathe, and go boating. More **primitive sites** tend to be free if there's no piped drinking water, though creek water is often available. The most useful of these is the walk-in *Panther Meadows* (7400ft; closed in winter), high up on the mountain at the end of the Everitt Memorial Highway, though *McBride Springs* ($10; 5000ft), being lower down the same road, tends to be open for longer. The fully equipped *KOA*, 900 N Mount Shasta Boulevard (☏530/926-4029 or 1-800/736-3617), a few blocks from downtown, charges from $21 per tent site and has basic cabins from $50.

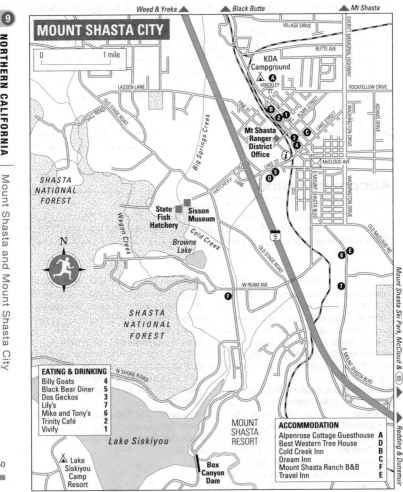

MOUNT SHASTA CITY

Weed & Yreka ▲   ▲ Black Butte   ▲ Mt Shasta

VILLAGE DRIVE
BUTTE AVE
EVERITT MEMORIAL HIGHWAY

KOA Campground ⚠ Ⓐ

HINCKLEY ST
ROCKFELLOW DRIVE
LASSEN LANE

HILL ROAD
OLD STAGE ROAD
PINE ST
CHESTNUT ST
Ⓑ ❷❶
ALMA STREET
LAKE STREET
WASHINGTON DRIVE
ADAMS DRIVE

Big Springs Creek

Mt Shasta Ranger District Office
Ⓒ
❸❹
ⓘ
LAKE ST
MCCLOUD AVE

HATCHERY LANE
LAKE ST
Ⓓ❺

S MOUNT SHASTA BLVD
WASHINGTON DRIVE

SHASTA NATIONAL FOREST

Wagon Creek

State Fish Hatchery
Sisson Museum

Cold Creek
Browns Lake

5

OLD STAGE ROAD
OLD McCLOUD RD

Ⓔ❻

W REAM AVE
Ⓕ
❼

SHASTA NATIONAL FOREST

N

0 —— 1 mile

Mount Shasta Ski Park, McCloud & ⑧⑨ ▶   ▼ Redding & Dunsmuir

S MOUNT SHASTA BLVD

EATING & DRINKING

Billy Goats	4
Black Bear Diner	5
Dos Geckos	3
Lily's	7
Mike and Tony's	6
Trinity Café	2
Vivify	1

N SHORE ROAD

Lake Siskiyou

⚠ Lake Siskiyou Camp Resort

MOUNT SHASTA RESORT

Box Canyon Dam

ACCOMMODATION

Alpenrose Cottage Guesthouse	A
Best Western Tree House	D
Cold Creek Inn	B
Dream Inn	C
Mount Shasta Ranch B&B	F
Travel Inn	E

The town and around

Quite rightly, few people come to Mount Shasta for its museums, but in bad weather you might visit the otherwise missable **Sisson Museum**, 1 N Old Stage Road (daily: June–Aug 10am–4pm; April, May & Sep–Dec 1–4pm; donation; ☏530/926-2440, ⊛www.mountshstasissonmuseum.org), with a few examples of native basketware, a fair bit on pioneering life in the region, and some more diverting material on the mountain itself. The brown, rainbow, and eastern brook trout in the **fish hatchery** outside (daily 8am–sunset; free) can be fed on food from a vending machine.

A couple of New Age **bookstores** along North Mount Shasta Boulevard provide the key to some of the town's more offbeat activities. Golden Bough Books at no. 219 (☏530/926-3228 or 1-877/674-7282), for example, has active bulletin boards and stacks of publications exhorting you to visit a sweat lodge or get in touch with the ascended masters. They provide an ever-changing list of metaphysics, astrology, and alternative-healing options as their practitioners and followers migrate in and out of town. Shasta Vortex Adventures, 310 N Mount Shasta Boulevard (☏530/926-4326), is an interesting outfit whose primary business is providing personalized spiritual tours of the mountain, but they also offer other esoteric services. For a bit of **culture**, the Stage Door, 414 N Mount Shasta Boulevard (☏530/926-1050, ⊛www.stagedoorcabaret.com), is a small theater showcasing drama and music at the back of a relaxed coffee shop. An increasing number of galleries and gift shops are sprouting up, too.

Mainly, though, Mount Shasta is full of outfits hoping to help you into the **outdoors**, from trout fishing to dog sledding to, of course, mountain climbing. Competition keeps prices reasonable and the options wide open. Obviously, there are a thousand ways to climb Mount Shasta, some of which are covered in the box on p.748. Otherwise, Shasta Mountain Guides, 1938 Hill Road (☏530/926-3117, ⊛www.shastaguides.com), arranges jeep trips up the mountain and conducts rock and ice climbing courses for all levels, as well as backcountry skiing trips, from around $100 per day. For real thrills, whitewater

▲ Mount Shasta

rafting trips on the churning Upper Sacramento are offered by Turtle River Rafting (☎1-800/726-3223, 🌐www.turtleriver.com) and River Dancers (☎1-800/926-5002, 🌐www.riverdancers.com), both starting at about $90 a day. Train enthusiasts should check out the elegant **Shasta Sunset Dinner Train**, which departs from the nearby town of McCloud (see p.754), nine miles southeast of Mount Shasta City on Hwy-89. Cars constructed in 1916 clack along east- and westbound routes while you sit back and enjoy a full-course meal (3hr; from $90; ☎1-800/733-2141, 🌐www.shastasunset.com). Shorter one-hour excursion-only trips (4pm Fri & Sat; $12) leave from McCloud in summer only.

Eating

Aside from a rash of fast-food outlets towards I-5, Mount Shasta's **eating** options are largely health-conscious, with vegetarian dishes featured on almost every menu. Hardy mountain types are amply catered for, too, with plenty of opportunities to stoke up on hearty fare before hitting the mountain heights. You can gather picnic supplies with the handcrafted loaves from *The Oven Bakery* at 214 N Mount Shasta Boulevard.

Billy Goats Tavern 107 Chestnut St ☎530/926-0209. Friendly bar/restaurant where you can wash down a generous meal with fine ale while chatting up the locals. Closed Sun & Mon.
Black Bear Diner 401 W Lake St ☎530/926-4669. Wholesome family diner, a great place for heaped breakfasts or classic American dinners.
Dos Geckos 401 N Mt Shasta Blvd ☎530/926-3796. Excellent build-your-own-burrito joint, with stunning views of the mountain from the patio.
Lily's 1013 S Mt Shasta Blvd ☎530/926-3372. Moderately priced and consistently good restaurant serving California cuisine, vegetarian, and Mexican dishes. Mains cost around $16–20, sandwiches $8–10.

Mike and Tony's 501 S Mt Shasta Blvd ☎530/926-4792. It may not look like much, but this excellent Italian restaurant specializes in homemade ravioli. It offers nice wines, figs, and goat cheese, plus great martinis. Dinner only; closed Tues & Wed.
Trinity Café 622 N Mt Shasta Blvd ☎530/926-6200. The best place for quality international cuisine made from local produce. The menu changes weekly and fine microbrewed ales are available on tap. Closed Sun & Mon.
Vivify 531 Chestnut St ☎530/926-1345. Stylish Japanese restaurant serving totally organic sushi and main meals at reasonable prices.

Around Mount Shasta

Apart from Mount Shasta itself and the surrounding towns covered here, there are several other natural delights to explore, which you'll certainly find less well-trodden in season than the main body of the mountain. Five miles north of town, the largely treeless cone of **Black Butte** (2.5 miles; 2–3hr; 1800-foot ascent) offers a more modest alternative to climbing Mount Shasta. The switchback trail to this 6325-foot volcanic plug dome is hard to find without the leaflet available from the ranger station or visitor center.

If you have time, you'd also be well advised to explore the beautiful trails that climb four thousand feet up to the 225-million-year-old, glacier-polished granite crags at the aptly named **Castle Crags State Park** (daily 8am–dusk; $6 per car; ☎530/235-2684), thirteen miles south of Mount Shasta along I-5. Campgrounds with full amenities are available for $20 per night (book on ☎1-800/444-7275, 🌐www.reserveamerica.com) and primitive ones for $10 in the often deserted, 6200-acre forested park.

Mount Shasta Ski Park (☎1-800/754-7478, 🌐www.skipark.com), near McCloud on Hwy-89, has yet to establish itself on the ski circuit, so its lift tickets (Mon–Thurs $25, Fri–Sun $39) and rental charges for skis ($23) and snowboards ($30) are quite reasonable. On the lower slopes, keep your eyes skinned for the inedible **watermelon snow**, its bright red appearance caused by a microbe which flourishes here – think Frank Zappa, just change the color.

After a day or two trudging around or up Mount Shasta, **Stewart Mineral Springs**, (Mon–Thurs & Sun 10am–6pm, Fri & Sat 10am–8pm; ☎530/938-2222, ⓦwww.stewartmineralsprings.com; ❷) at 4617 Stewart Springs Road off I-5 just north of Weed, provides welcome relief. Individual bathing rooms in a cedar and pine forest glade soothe your aches away for $25, less if you stay in the very affordable cabins, teepees ($30), or campground ($20) here. Just before you reach the springs, you can take Parks Creek Road to the top of the ridge, from where it's a ninety-minute hike along the **Pacific Coast Trail** to tranquil Dead Fall Lakes.

Dunsmuir

One example of how the Shasta area looked in the past can be seen in the hamlet of **Dunsmuir**, even quainter than Mount Shasta City. Situated ten miles south of Mount Shasta on a steep hill sloping down from I-5, Dunsmuir's downtown was bypassed by the freeway, essentially freezing the community in time. Now it makes its living as a historic railroad town, and the main drag, **Dunsmuir Avenue**, is lined with restored hotels and shops, many of them taking the train theme a bit too far; expect to see shopkeepers dressed as train engineers and business names like Billy Puffer Suites. Amtrak stops at the recently spruced-up railway station, its last California halt before continuing north to Oregon. The **Visitors Bureau**, at Suite 100 5915 Dunsmuir Avenue (daily 9.30am–5pm; ☎1-800/386-7684, ⓦwww.dunsmuir.com), has updated train and STAGE schedules. The best place for trails information is the **River Center**, 5819 Sacramento Avenue (Mon–Fri 10am–3pm; ☎530/235-2012), which also has some interpretive exhibits on local nature.

Dunsmuir used to bill itself as a day-trip from Shasta, but recently realized that it had quietude and natural wonders of its own. Foremost among these are the Mossbrae and Hedge Creek **waterfalls**, along the Sacramento River Canyon, beautiful spots for walks and picnics. To reach **Mossbrae**, drive north on Dunsmuir Avenue to Scarlet Way, crossing the bridge and railroad tracks to the parking area. Follow the walking trail along the train tracks for one mile until you get to the railroad bridge. Don't cross, but continue along the tracks through the trees and the falls are ahead. **Hedge Creek Falls** are accessible via the parking area at the North Dunsmuir exit on I-5.

If you plan **to stay**, several B&Bs ply their trade around town, the most central being *The Dunsmuir Inn*, 5423 Dunsmuir Avenue (☎530/235-4543 or 1-888/386-7684; ❸). Under a mile south, the *Dunsmuir Lodge*, 6604 Dunsmuir Avenue (☎1-877/235-2884, ⓦwww.dunsmuirlodge.net; ❸), is a little cheaper. The most unique lodging in the area is the *Railroad Park Resort* (☎530/235-0420, ⓦwww.rrpark.com; ❹), nearly three miles south at 100 Railroad Park Road; most of the accommodations are fashioned out of old railway cabooses, though there are also some cabins. Dunsmuir has been developing into a gourmet paradise of late, with a number of new upscale **restaurants**. The *Cornerstone Bakery Café*, 5759 Dunsmuir Avenue (☎530/235-2620; closed Tues), serves upmarket California-style breakfasts and lunches, while equally pricey is *Sengthong's*, 5855 Dunsmuir Avenue (☎530/235-4770), the place for quality Southeast Asian cuisine. Meanwhile, tasty Mediterranean evening meals are on the menu at *Café Maddalena*, 5801 Sacramento Avenue (☎530/235-2725;

Thurs–Sun only). Two places for a cheaper meal on Dunsmuir Avenue are *Gary's Pizza Factory*, no. 5804 (☎530/235-4849), and *Las Gringas Taqueria*, no. 5740 (☎530/235-9801).

McCloud

Home to the famous Sunset Dinner Train (see p.752 for details), **McCloud** is a delightful little town with stunning views of Mount Shasta, and it can make another good base for the area, especially if you plan to spend much time in the Ski Park (see p.752). The only cultural diversion is the small **Heritage Junction Museum** at 320 Main Street (May–Oct Mon–Sat 11am–3pm, Sun 1–3pm; free; ☎530/964-2604), loaded with a haphazard collection of bric-a-brac, memorabilia, and woodcutters' gear. In the **accommodation** stakes the *McCloud Hotel*, right in town at 408 Main Street (☎1-800/964-2823, ⓦwww.mccloudhotel.com; ⑤), has smart rooms in a classy restored building and a fine restaurant, while an excellent B&B option just up the road is *Stoney Brook Inn*, 309 W Colombero Drive (☎1-800/369-6118, ⓦwww.stoneybrookinn.com; ⓷), with some shared bathrooms and particularly good single rates. The only motel in the vicinity is the *McCloud Timber Inn*, 153 Squaw Valley Road (☎530/964-2893; ❷), which boasts an attractive location and roomier-than-average lodgings. For a **meal**, try the tasty barbeque dishes at the *McCloud River Grille & Bar*, on the south side of Hwy-89 at 140 Squaw Valley Road (☎530/964-2700), which is also the town's main watering hole. Grab a daytime snack *Floyd's Frosty*, 125 Broadway (☎530/964-9747), a Fifties-style joint offering hefty burgers, thick shakes, and ice cream.

There's not much to do in the town itself, but the nearby **McCloud River Falls**, five miles east on Hwy-89, is a great spot for a picnic or gentle stroll. The falls, set amidst thick woods, are divided into three distinct sections, each about one mile from the next and connected by a riverside walking trail, but also accessible by road. If you're short of time, head for the more dramatic Middle Falls; at *Fowlers*, near the Lower Falls, there's **camping**, often free because of the intermittent water supply, while the Upper Falls boast a lovely picnic area. Continuing southeast on Hwy-89, you'll eventually come to the more renowned and spectacular Burney Falls and, still further, Lassen Volcanic National Park (see p.736).

Weed

A gateway town to Klamath Falls, Oregon, and the Lava Beds National Monument, **Weed** can't compete with Mount Shasta City's hip charm. But, perhaps in a form of karmic justice, it gets the better view of the peak during the summertime. Too bad the tourism board couldn't leave it at that, instead of dressing up the place as a "historic lumber town" with the groaner of a slogan, "Weed love to see you." Those responsible can be found at the **Chamber of Commerce**, 34 Main Street (summer daily 9am–5pm; winter Mon–Fri 10am–4pm; ☎530/938-4624, ⓦwww.weedchamber.com), along with further information on the area. Just off Main Street at 303 Gilman Avenue, **Weed Historic Lumber Town Museum** (summer daily 10am–5pm; winter by appointment; donation; ☎530/938-0550, ⓦwww.snowcrest.net/whm) occupies the former courthouse and outlines local history, primarily that of the lumber industry; it also contains a couple of fine old vehicles. The Greyhound **bus** office is at 628 S Weed Boulevard (Mon–Sat 8.30am–4pm; ☎530/938-4454 or 1-800/231-2222) and is also the nearest stop to Mount Shasta City. A couple of good budget **motels** and **eateries** reside in town, as does the College of the

Siskiyous, which is certainly California's prettiest campus owing to its views of the peak. In town, the *Hi Lo Motel & Café*, 88 S Weed Boulevard (T530/938-2731; ❷), has decent rooms and a café that slings hash and eggs. On the northern end of Weed Boulevard, at no. 466, the *Motel 6* branch includes a nice outdoor pool and stunning sunrise views of Mount Shasta (T1-800/466-8356, Wwww.motel6.com; ❸). The best place for a meal is *Hungry Moose* (T530/938-4060), an excellent all-day diner located at 86 N Weed Boulevard, or you can chill out with a healthier snack at *Buddha Belly Kitchen*, 51 Main Street (T530/938-4366), which has a very loungeable lounge. *Papa's Place*, 203 Main Street (T530/938-2277), is a friendly bar for drinking beer with the locals and getting a basic bite to eat, but the best ales can be tasted for $1 and tours arranged at the Mt Shasta Brewing Company, 360 College Avenue (Thurs–Sun 2–6pm; T530/938-2394, Wwww.mtshastabrewingcompany.com).

Five miles outside of town, north on US-97 on the way to Oregon and Lava Beds, the **Living Memorial Sculpture Garden** experience (unrestricted entry; donation) is an intriguing remembrance of the Vietnam War. Artist Dennis Smith has created ten metal sculptures illustrating different aspects of an American soldier's experience in the war. Surrounding the art are about 53,000 pine trees, one for every American killed in Vietnam. The trees, art, silence, and position under Mount Shasta add up to a very moving experience.

Yreka

There's little to justify more than an hour or two in quiet, leafy **Yreka** (pronounced "why-REE-ka"), twenty-five miles north of Weed on I-5, but it makes a pleasant break. The reason most people come here is to ride the Yreka Western Railroad, better known as the **Blue Goose**, a 1915 Baldwin steam engine pulling attractive carriages to and from the nearby historic town of Montague, whose vintage depot is full of railroad memorabilia (summer Wed–Sun 11am; $20–23; T1-800/973-5277, Wwww.yrekawesternrr.com); apart from the regular schedule, the train runs on certain other weekends and for special events. The **Siskiyou County Museum**, 910 S Main Street (Tues–Fri 9am–5pm, Sat 9am–4pm; $2; T530/842-3836), deserves some attention, particularly the outdoor section (Tues–Fri 10am–3.30pm) with its historic buildings – church, houses, and shops – transported here from around the county. Finally, there's a valuable collection of gold nuggets in the **County Courthouse**, 311 Fourth Street (Mon–Fri 8am–5pm; free).

The **Chamber of Commerce**, 117 W Miner Street (summer daily 9am–5pm; winter Mon–Fri 9am–5pm; T530/842-1649, Wwww.yrekachamber.com), issues maps for a self-guided Historic Walking Tour around Yreka's numerous Victorian homes. It can also help you find **accommodation** – not that it's hard to find, with plenty of chain motels such as the *Econolodge*, 526 S Main Street (T530/842-4404, Wwww.econolodge.com; ❸), and independent ones like the *Klamath Motor Lodge*, 1111 S Main Street (T1-800/551-7255, Wwww.klamathmotorlodge.net; ❸). Smarter accommodations can be found for almost the same price at the town's only B&B, the *Yreka Third Street Inn*, 326 Third Street (T530/841-1120, Wwww.yrekabedandbreakfast.com; ❸). Good **eating** options exist along S Main Street at *Nature's Kitchen*, a decent diner at no. 412 (T530/842-1136; closed Sun), *Natalee*, a simple Thai joint at no. 1225 (T530/842-7939), or *China Dragon*, no. 520 (T530/842 3444), where you can get inexpensive Chinese and American food. For a more romantic setting, try the excellent Italian cuisine at *Angelini's*, 322 W Miner Street (T530/842-5000). Yreka can be reached by STAGE **bus** from Mount Shasta, Dunsmuir, and McCloud.

A worthwhile twenty-mile detour south of Yreka along Hwy-3 takes you to charming, turn-of-the-century **Etna**, recently voted one of twenty "dream towns" by *Outside* magazine, and it certainly does not disappoint. Its other great claim to fame is the Etna Brewing Company, 131 Callahan Street (Wed–Sun 11am–6pm; ☎530/467-5277), a tiny microbrewery producing around one thousand barrels a year for local distribution, although its increasing reputation has led to plans for expansion. Typically four or five of the malty real ales are available to taste, along with other beers, each and every one a drinker's dream, and you can usually take an impromptu tour; toothsome bar food is also available. While here, check out the 1950s soda fountain in the Scott Valley Drugstore at the top of Main Street. And if you're really struck by the place, you can **camp** for free in the town park on Diggles Street or **stay** at the basic but comfortable *Etna Motel*, 317 Collier Way (☎530/467-5388; ❷). For expert guidance around the local wilderness and the possibility of staying in a yurt, contact Rusty Coleman of Mountain Spirit Adventures (☎530/467-5444, Ⓦusers.sisqtel.net/mtspiritad), inside his *Corrigan's* bar at 412 Main Street.

Lava Beds National Monument and around

After seeing Mount Shasta, you really should push on to the **LAVA BEDS NATIONAL MONUMENT**, which commemorates a war between the US and Modoc Indians on the far northern border of the state. Carved out of the huge **Modoc National Forest**, it's actually a series of volcanic caves you can explore, and huge black lava flows with a history as violent as the natural forces that created them.

Lava Beds is one of the most remote, forgotten, and beautiful of California's parks, with pungent yellow rabbit-brush blooming around the burnt rocks in *autumn*. It's in the heart of Modoc country, a desolate outback where cowboys still ride the range, and where, as the territory of one of the last major battles with the Native Americans, there's still a suspicious relationship between the settlers and the native peoples.

Today the Lava Beds region is inhabited only by wild deer and three million migrating ducks who easily outnumber the trickle of tourists that make it this far. To the west and north, the **Klamath Basin National Wildlife Refuge**

The land of the Modoc

Until the 1850s Gold Rush, the area which now defines the Lava Beds National Monument was home to the **Modoc tribe**, but after their repeated and bloody confrontations with the miners, the government ordered them into a reservation with the Klamath, their traditional enemy. After only a few months, the Modoc drifted back to their homeland in the Lava Beds, and in 1872 the army was sent in to return them by force to the reservation. It was driven back by 52 Modoc warriors under the leadership of one **Kientpoos**, better known as "Captain Jack," who held back an army of US regulars and volunteers twenty times the size of his for five months, from a stronghold at the northern tip of the park (see p.760). Eventually Captain Jack was betrayed by a member of his tribe, captured, and hanged, and what remained of the tribe was sent off to a reservation in Oklahoma, where most of them died of malaria.

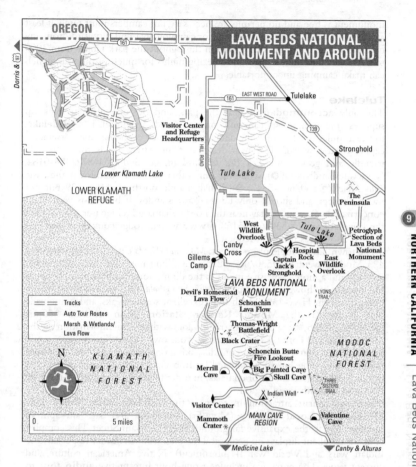

spreads over the border into Oregon. This stop on the Pacific Flyway draws birders and hunters alike, hoping to catch sight of a rare eagle among the millions of migratory guests.

Park practicalities

Lava Beds National Monument ($10 per vehicle for seven days) is 160 miles northeast of Redding, and inaccessible without a **car**. It's a day-trip from Mount Shasta, one and a half hours away, but can be combined with camping, spelunking, and birding for a much longer stay. The most tortuous route follows Hwy-89 to Bartle, then passes Medicine Lake (see p.760); the approach via Hwy-139 is easier, but the best and fastest is from Weed, following US-97 through Dorris and then via Hwy-161 through the Klamath Basin National Wildlife Refuge (see p.761).

Pick up an excellent **map** of the monument from the **visitor center**, just inside the southwestern entrance (daily: summer 8am–6pm; rest of year 8am–5pm; ☎530/667-2282, ⓦwww.nps.gov/labe). Close by, at Indian Wells, is the park's one **campground** ($10). All **wilderness camping** throughout the monument is free and no permits are necessary, but campers must pitch at least a quarter of a mile from any road, trail, or camping area, and fifty yards from any cave. Be warned, though, that elevation throughout the park ranges from 4000 to 5700 feet, and there's snow and freezing nights for much of the year, which can make camping uncomfortable.

Tulelake

The only **accommodation** near the park, and the one place to pick up supplies (the monument can only muster a soda machine), is at **Tulelake**, fourteen miles north, which incidentally prides itself on being "the horseradish capital of the world." The near-deserted Main Street holds the extremely friendly and good-value *Fe's Bed & Breakfast*, no. 660 (℡1-877/478-0184, Ⓦwww.fesbandb.com; ❸), while the only other option around town, the basic *Ellis Motel* (℡530/667-5342; ❷), is half a mile north on Hwy-139 but not much cheaper, and should only be used as a standby. If birding is your main concern and you want to stay near the Lower Klamath Refuge (see p.761), then the *Winema Lodge* (℡530/667-5158, Ⓦwww.winemalodge.com; ❷) is your best bet – it also serves meals on request.

The town has a couple places to **eat**: *Mike and Wanda's*, just off Main Street at 423 Modoc Avenue (℡530/667-3226), has filling meals in the café and bar sections and a more expensive menu in the dining room in between. The area's top restaurant, however, is *Captain Jack's Stronghold* (℡530/664-5566), seven miles south on Hwy-139, which does excellent soups, steaks, and homemade pies. Nearby is the **Modoc Ranger Station** (Mon–Fri 8am–4.30pm; ℡530/667-2246, Ⓦwww.fs.fed.us/r5/modoc) with general information on the Modoc National Forest. Even if you have your own car, and it's unlikely you'll be here if you don't, you might consider taking one of the expert guided **tours** ($50–60, including lunch) conducted by Bob Galeoto of LuCena West Tours out of *Fe's B&B* (see above for contacts) in order to get the most out of the Lava Beds and Klamath Basin region.

The one tourist attraction in town is the **Tulelake-Butte Valley Fair Museum of Local History** (Mon–Fri 9am–5pm, also Sat 9am–5pm in summer; $3), in the expansive fairgrounds at 800 S Main Street. This complex contains excellent displays on geological features, wildlife, history (especially the Indian wars and World War II internment), Native American culture, and current issues. The entry fee includes a one-hour interpretive **audio tour** to enhance your visit. Also within the grounds is the **Chamber of Commerce** information bureau (Mon–Fri 9am–5pm; ℡530/667-5312, Ⓦwww.tbvfair.com). The fairgrounds host an enormous annual **fair** during the week following Labor Day in September, and you can camp on the grounds for $12 at any time.

The Monument

A day spent in the **Lava Beds** is akin to exploring the innards of a volcano, scampering down hollow tubes through which molten lava once coursed. The youngest of them were formed 30,000 years ago when volcanic upwellings sent molten, basaltic magma careering across the Modoc Plateau. As the magma came into contact with cool air, it solidified, leaving a flowing molten core feeding the expanding lava field downhill. In time, the magma flow stopped and the molten lava drained out, leaving the world's largest concentration of such hollow tubes. Most remain unexplored, but where the casing has collapsed, access is possible and you're free to scramble through. Some of the caves are so small that you have to crawl along on all fours, while others are an enormous 75ft in diameter. Some contain Native American **petroglyphs** – not to be confused with the names painted on the cave walls by J.D. Howard, one of the first White men to explore and name the caves.

Pick up the free loaner flashlights from the visitor center and begin your explorations of the caves just outside. Initially, though, entering the darkness alone can be an unnerving experience, so most people prefer to take the **free guided ranger walks** (daily Memorial Day to Labor Day). Two-to-three-hour morning walks (9am) leave from the visitor center and explore little-known sections of the monument; afternoon tours (2pm) concentrate on ninety-minute guided cave trips; and in the evening (9pm) rangers lead hour-long campfire talks and slideshows, which shift to Mushpot Cave in bad weather.

If you insist on eschewing ranger guidance, you must abide by a few **rules**. Don't go alone, wear decent shoes, and take two flashlights each. Borrowed

Exploring the Lava Beds

Most of the interest in Lava Beds lies around the visitor center, where the largest concentration of caves can be visited on the short **Cave Loop** access road. For a confidence-building handle on your location in the twenty-five "developed" caves – less than a tenth of the known total – get the *Lava Caves Map* ($4.50) from the visitor center. New ones are discovered all the time, so the possibilities are almost endless, but for the moment, the tried and tested caves below should satisfy.

Catacombs Cave At over a mile long, this is the longest open tube in the monument, though you need perseverance, a slim body, and a cool head to get anywhere near the end. The profusion of interconnecting passageways makes it one of the most confusing; keep track of whether you are heading up- or downhill. On Cave Loop.

Golden Dome Cave The startling golden hues of the moist mossy roof lend the cave both its name and an otherworldly appearance. On Cave Loop.

Labyrinth Cave Striking geological features – lava pillars and lavacicles – and evidence of Native American habitation. At the entrance to Cave Loop.

Mushpot Cave Right by the visitor center near the start of Cave Loop, this is the most developed of the caves. It provides a good introduction, is lit during center opening hours, and has interpretive panels highlighting key features.

Skull Cave Named for bighorn skulls found when the cave was discovered by early explorer E.L. Hopkins, this has the largest entrance of any of the lava tubes and contains ice all year round. About two miles north of Cave Loop.

Symbol Bridge and **Big Painted Cave** (1.5-mile round-trip; almost flat) Two very

worthwhile caves adjacent to each other on a trail north of the visitor center. No flashlight is needed, though one could come in handy. Some of the best examples of pictographs in the monument – tentatively dated between 1000 AD and 1500 AD – show up as different angles of sunlight catch the rocks beside the entrance. Respecting Modoc sensibilities, make two clockwise turns before descending into a large cave, open at both ends (hence the "bridge" name), in which zigzags, squiggles, sunbursts, and human figures are depicted out in grease and charcoal on pumice-washed background. Make a single counterclockwise turn on departure for Big Painted Cave, where the pictographs are less impressive. In the mid-1920s, J.D. Howard excavated a small tunnel at the very back of the cave to reveal an ice flow in a cavity 15ft down: with a flashlight you can scramble down there. Two miles north of Cave Loop.

Valentine Cave Interesting because it combines various characteristic cave features, such as stalactites and catacombs. The ridges at the base of the walls leading down into the deep and wide chamber almost appear to be man-made, so even are their lines. About two miles southeast of Cave Loop.

flashlights must be returned by nightfall to ensure no one goes missing. For night explorations (the caves remain open), you'll need your own light source. Hard hats are strongly advised and can be purchased for $4 at the visitor center.

If caves don't do it for you, the other attraction of Lava Beds is its well-documented history. Begin at the visitor center for an exhibit on the Modoc War, including photos of its chief participants, including Modoc leader Captain Jack (see box, p.756), and scathing editorials from national papers condemning the US Army over its mission. You'll need a car to get to the northern reaches of the park, around **Captain Jack's Stronghold**, a natural fortress of craggy lava flows and shallow caves on the shores of Old Tule Lake. When you arrive, pick up a trail book (50¢) from the parking lot and enjoy one of two well-narrated **self-guided trails** (one half a mile, the other 1.5 miles) through a war that in many ways typified the conquest of the West. When you get here you'll see how the Modoc managed to hide and move around through the passageways of the hills. Two miles west, **Canby's Cross** marks a turning point in the war, when Captain Jack, coerced by the man who would later betray him, drew a gun during a council and murdered US General Canby and a pastor. Two miles east, the shallow lava bowl of **Hospital Rock** marks the point where one Lt Sherwood, wounded by the Modoc, was unsuccessfully tended in a makeshift field hospital towards the end of the siege on the stronghold.

Around the monument

Small volcanic craters, buttes, spatter cones, and chimneys dot Lava Beds, but the flows which produced most of the lava tubes came from **Mammoth Crater** on the southern perimeter of the monument, where a short path leads to a viewpoint overlooking the deep conical crater.

Underlying the most recent of Lava Beds' fabulous creations is a bed of basalt, the product of a huge shield volcano with a profile so flat it's barely noticeable. Its core is now filled by the subalpine **Medicine Lake**, ten miles southwest of Mammoth Crater. Formerly a Modoc healing center, the only therapies on offer today are fishing and swimming from the $10 campsites along the north shore. It's accessible via an unpaved road closed November to mid-May.

More volcanic spectacle lies just west at **Glass Mountain**, made almost entirely of glassy, black obsidian – source of Modoc arrowheads – but covered in fluffy, white pumice quarried for stonewashing jeans. A short and fairly easy trail leads in from the road. Just beyond the monument's northeast corner, a small outlier known as the Petroglyph Section contains **Petroglyph Point**, a 300-yard-long cliff face made of "tuff," volcanic rock formed when lava flows hit Old Tule Lake. The soft rock offers some fine, but cryptic, examples of ancient art: shields, female figures, and a series of small circles thought to represent travel. The crevices are home to various bird species, especially horned owls. Pick up an interpretive leaflet at the visitor center.

East of the Petroglyph Section, the road continues to Hwy-139 and the town of **Newell**, site of the **Tule Lake Camp**, where 110,000 people of Japanese descent, many of them American citizens, were interned without charge or trial between 1942 and 1946. There were as many as 18,000 inmates at any given time. Many of the camp buildings have been sold off to local farmers, but the wood-sided police and military barracks remain, and a simple plaque commemorates the disgraceful chapter and prays it will never be repeated. Nearby there was also a less well-known camp for internees of German and Italian origin.

The most rewarding excursion from the monument, though, is to the **Klamath Basin National Wildlife Refuge** (open daylight hours), just to the north along Hill Road (Hwy-161), leading to US-97, and spreading into Oregon. One of the last **wetlands** in California, with swathes of open water and emerging vegetation on the shoreline, it attracts an estimated eighty percent of birds following the Pacific Flyway, the major migration routes from Alaska and northern Canada to Baja California in Mexico. In spring and fall, almost a hundred species are present and the population tops a million. Bald eagles appear from December to January, bringing out hundreds of photographers trying to navigate the snowy road. Meanwhile, spring is the best time for migratory birds and autumn for waterfowl. The most accessible reaches of the reserve are the **Lower Klamath Refuge** and **Tule Lake**, an open body of water surrounded by reeds (*tule* in Modoc). At the north-western corner of the latter on Hill Road, the **visitor center** (Mon–Fri 8am–4.30pm, Sat & Sun 10am–4pm; ☏530/667-2231) contains some informative displays. Surprisingly, the best way of spotting the wildlife is by driving along designated routes ($3): getting out of the car and walking scares the birds off.

Heading south back towards Mount Shasta on US-97, your car will be stopped in otherwise droll **Dorris** by agriculture agents checking to see if you're transporting fruit or vegetables from out of state. Say "No" and they'll give you a nice color map to welcome you to California.

Modoc County

Occupying the far northeastern corner of California, wild and rugged **MODOC COUNTY** is bordered by equally thinly-populated areas of Oregon and Nevada, and is about as remote as it gets. Despite covering an immense area, the total population is only ten thousand, the majority of whom reside in the county seat of **Alturas**. Outside of that modest settlement, the mostly high-desert region is home to a lot more wildlife – bobcats, mule deer, antelope, elk, mountain lions, wolves, and birds such as sandhill cranes and bald eagles – than people, many of whom rely on cattle ranging and alfalfa cultivation for their livelihood. On the eastern side, the imposing **Warner Mountains** divide the rest of the county from **Surprise Valley**, home to several small communities within spitting distance of the Nevada state line.

Historically the area belonged to three native tribes – the Modoc, the Paiute, and the Pit River Indians. The creation of the Emigrant Trail in the late 1840s, the main east-west route into Northern California, brought white settlers to the region in increasing numbers and into all-too-common confrontation with indigenous people. For the next six decades, a series of violent conflicts earned the region the title of **Bloody Ground of the Pacific**. The settlers gradually took over, though the area's control was successively bounced around between Utah Territory, Nevada Territory, and California's Shasta and Siskiyou counties before Modoc County was created in 1874. It retains a frontier feel to this day and has the highest per capita gun ownership in the state, so it's no surprise that most locals and many of those who find their way here tend to occupy themselves with outdoor pursuits like hunting.

Alturas and around

Out-of-the-way **ALTURAS** is about sixty miles southeast of Tulelake via Hwy-137 and then Hwy-299, which you can also take all the way up from the Burney Falls area. Coming from Lava Beds, the black craggy rocks gradually give way to the increasingly pine-forested hills of the **Modoc National Forest**, which surround the town on three sides. The Modoc National Forest Service headquarters at 800 W 12th Street (Mon–Fri 7.30am–4.30pm; ☎530/233-5811, ⊛www.fs.fed.us/r5/modoc) provides a wealth of information on all the hiking, hunting, fishing, and camping possibilities in the region, as well as some useful maps. For more info on the town itself, visit the **Chamber of Commerce**, 522 S Main Street (Mon–Fri 9am–12.30pm & 1.30–4pm; ☎530/233-4434, ⊛www.alturaschamber.org), though it's not always manned. A glimpse into the region's turbulent past can be gained at the modest **Modoc County Historical Society Museum** (May–Oct Tues–Sat 10am–4pm; $2; ☎530/233-2944), which occupies a modern building by the park at 600 S Main Street; the displays concentrate on settler and Indian artifacts, as well as some of the county's natural history.

Though much of its dozen blocks are modern, Alturas, with its position by the mountains and the clear relation of the people to the land, manages to exude a Wild West atmosphere. The most obvious places **to stay** are basic motels such as the *Frontier Motel* at 1033 N Main Street (☎530/233-3383; ❷). Among the **eating** options, *Nipa's*, 1001 N Main Street (☎530/233-2520), dishes up a delightful combination of Thai and California cuisines in a laid-back setting; *Antonio's*, 220 S Main Street (☎530/233-5600), is a slightly smarter Italian restaurant serving filling pasta, pizza, and sandwiches; and *Norma's Taqueria*, 204 W 12th Street (☎530/233-5859), is the place for inexpensive and tasty Mexican fare.

Spreading out over thousands of acres south of Alturas, the **Modoc National Wildlife Refuge** (7am–sunset; free) is composed largely of unspoilt grasslands, incorporating some wetlands, and is home to many avian species, among them sandhill cranes, tundra swans, teal, pintail ducks, and warblers, as well as migratory visitors such as white-fronted geese, pelicans, cormorants, and egrets. The refuge starts only a couple of miles southeast of town – take the road between the Chamber of Commerce and the museum and turn right at the first main junction, after about half a mile, which takes you right there. Around twenty miles north of town, the **Devil's Garden** is a very different type of terrain, a densely forested plateau with more wetlands and a community of some four hundred wild horses – there are trails through the excellent hiking country but you should take a good map and be careful not to stray from the paths. A little further northeast, reachable by US-395, lies **Goose Lake**, which straddles the Oregon state line. Good for fishing and other recreational activities, its largest settlement, on the east shore, is New Pine Creek, nearly all of whose facilities lie on the Oregon side – making it a good place to head to for cheaper gas. Finally, nearby **Davis Creek**, just off US-395 towards the lake, is the site of numerous obsidian mines, and bucket-fuls of the jagged black rocks can be carried away if you obtain a free permit from the Forest Service headquarters in Alturas.

The Warner Mountains and Surprise Valley

Providing a dramatic backdrop to Alturas, the proud ridges of the **Warner Mountains**, snowcapped for two thirds of the year and prone to snowfall in any month, exert a magnetic pull on the few outsiders who venture this far. The range is divided into north and south by the valley that carries Hwy-299 east through the mountains. This road passes by the **Cedar Pass Snowpark** (☎530/233-3323, ⓦwww.cedarpasssnowpark.com), where you can ski during winter weekends – all-day rope tow and T-bar tickets range from $5–15 and ski and snowboard rental is very cheap at $10 per day. It is, however, nearby **South Warner Wilderness**, part of the extensive Modoc National Forest, which presents the most fruitful territory for exploration. Here 77 miles of trails spread over more than seventy thousand acres of slopes, steeper on the east side than the west, offer excellent hiking opportunities. Get maps and details from the Forest Service headquarters in Alturas, but make sure to carry provisions and all-weather gear. In the north, unpaved Route 9 ascends over the North Warners from US-395 near Goose Lake and climbs up over **Fandango Pass**, where the old Applegate Trail and Lassen forty-niner route converge. It's passable with care in a regular car and makes for a scenic alternative route east, with arresting views of Surprise Valley along the way.

On the sunrise side of the mountains, secretive **Surprise Valley** marks the border with Nevada and is hemmed in by more barren ridges to the east. Indeed, the fiercely independent types who live over here are said to feel more allegiance to the Silver State than the Golden State. Hwy-299 from Alturas ends in the pleasant small town of **Cedarville**, the largest in the valley, a modest claim though that may be. The **Chamber of Commerce** is in Warner Realty at 517 Main Street (only Tues & Thurs 9–11am; ☎530/279-2101), and a few brochures are available in the entrance to no. 519. Reasonable **accommodation** choices include the cutesy *J H Metzker House B&B*, 520 Main Street (☎530/279-2650; ④), and the cheaper *Sunrise Motel*, 54889 Hwy-299 (☎530/279-2161, ⓕ530/279-6261; ②). The finest place to stay, however, is a real hidden gem, five miles due east: ⚐ *Surprise Valley Hot Springs* (☎1-877/927-6426, ⓦwww.surprisevalleyhotsprings.com; 5), whose splendid themed suites each have a naturally heated outdoor tub and would cost double if the location was not so remote. If you're hungry, the *Suprise Café*, 540 Main Street (☎530/279-2065), serves up classic home-style breakfasts and lunches, while *Country Hearth*, opposite at no. 551 (☎530/279-2280), also serves dinners. From Cedarville you can branch south to even quieter Eagleville or, better yet, head north past a couple of white alkali lakes to pay a brief visit to **Fort Bidwell**, home to a thriving community of 150 Paiute Indians. Here you can pop into their modern community center (flexible hours) to see a collection of rocks, trophies, and an original peace pipe.

Travel details

Trains

Oakland to: Chico (1 daily; 4hr 8min); Dunsmuir (1 daily; 7hr 17min); Redding (1 daily; 5hr 27min).
Redding to: Chico (1 daily; 1hr 29min); Dunsmuir (1 daily; 1hr 50min); Oakland (1 daily; 6hr 14min).

Buses

Schedules listed below are mostly Greyhound, with some county services where applicable. Some routes require a transfer. See text for additional connecting local services.

Arcata to: Crescent City (2 daily; 2hr); Eureka (9–16 daily except Sun; 15min); San Francisco (1 daily; 7hr 30min); Santa Rosa (1 daily; 5hr 15min).

Chico to: Red Bluff (3 daily; 50min); Redding (3 daily; 1hr 30min); Sacramento (2 daily; 2hr 15min); San Francisco (2 daily; 6hr 35min–6hr 50min); Weed (1 daily; 3hr 20min).

Eureka to: Arcata (9–16 daily except Sun; 15min); San Francisco (1 daily; 7hr 10min); Santa Rosa (1 daily; 4hr 55min).

Redding to: Chico (2 daily; 1hr 30min); Red Bluff (2 daily; 40min); Sacramento (6 daily; 2hr 40min–3hr 50min); San Francisco (5 daily; 5hr 40min–8hr 25min).

San Francisco to: Arcata (1 daily; 7hr 5min); Chico (2 daily; 5hr 15min–5hr 40min); Eureka (1 daily; 6hr 45min); Redding (5 daily; 5hr 10min–7hr 15min); Santa Rosa (hourly; 1hr 45min–2hr 25min); Weed (3 daily; 7hr–9hr 5min).

Santa Rosa to: Arcata (1 daily; 5hr 10min); Eureka (1 daily; 4hr 50min); San Francisco (hourly; 2hr 5min).

Contexts

Contexts

History

To many people, California seems one of the least historic places on the planet. Unburdened by the past, it's a land where anything is possible, whose inhabitants live carefree lives, wholly in and for the present moment. Its very name, appropriately for all its idealized images, is a work of fiction, free of any historical significance. The word first appeared in a popular Spanish picaresque novel of the early 1500s, *Las Sergas de Esplandián* by García de Montalvo, as the name of an island, located "very near to the terrestrial paradise" and inhabited entirely by Amazons "without any men among them."

Native peoples

For thousands of years before the arrival of Europeans, the **aboriginal peoples** of California flourished in the naturally abundant land, living fairly peacefully in tribes along the coast and in the deserts and the forested mountains. Anthropologists estimate that nearly half the native population then living within the boundaries of the present-day US were spread throughout what's now California, in small, tribal villages of a few hundred people, each with a clearly defined territory and often its own distinct language. Since there was no political or social organization beyond the tribe, it was not difficult for the colonizing Spaniards to divide and to conquer, effectively wiping the natives out – though admittedly more died of epidemics than outright genocide.

Very little remains to mark the existence of California's Native Americans: they had no form of written language, relatively undeveloped craft skills, and built next to nothing that would last beyond the change of seasons. About the only signs of the coastal tribes are the piles of seashells and discarded arrowheads that have been found, from which anthropologists have deduced a bit about their cultures. Also, a few examples of **rock art** survive, as at the Chumash Painted Cave, near Santa Barbara on the Central Coast (see p.427). Similar sorts of petroglyph figures were drawn by the Paiute Native Americans, who lived in the deserts near Death Valley, and by the Miwok of the Sierra Nevada foothills.

Discovery and early exploration

The first Europeans to set foot in California were Spanish explorers, intent on extending their colony of New Spain, which, under the 1494 Treaty of Tordesillas, included all the New World lands west of Brazil and all of North America west of the Rocky Mountains. In 1535, **Hernán Cortés**, fresh from decimating the Aztecs, headed westward in search of a shortcut to Asia, which he believed to be adjacent to Mexico. Though he never reached what's now California, he set up a small colony at the southern tip of the Baja (or lower) California peninsula. Thinking it was an island, he named it Santa Cruz, writing in his journals that he soon expected to find the imagined island of the Amazons.

The first explorer to use the name California, and to reach what's now the US state, was **Juan Cabrillo**, who sighted San Diego Harbor in 1542, and continued north along the coast to the Channel Islands off Santa Barbara. He died there six months later, persistent headwinds having made it impossible to sail any further north. His crew later made it as far as what is now the state of Oregon, but were unable to find any safe anchorage and returned home starving and half-dead from scurvy. It was fifty years before another Spaniard braved the difficult journey: **Juan de Fuca**'s 1592 voyage caused great excitement when he claimed to have discovered the Northwest Passage, a potentially lucrative trade route across North America. It has long since turned out that there is really no such thing (de Fuca may have discovered the Puget Sound, outside Seattle), but Europeans continued to search for it for the next two hundred years.

The British explorer **Sir Francis Drake** arrived in the *Golden Hind* in 1579, taking a break from his piracy of Spanish vessels in order to make repairs. His landing spot, now called Drake's Bay, near Point Reyes north of San Francisco, had "white bancks and cliffes" that reminded him of Dover. Upon landing, he was met by a band of native Miwoks, who feted him with food and drink, and placed a feathered crown upon his head; in return, he claimed all of their lands – which he called Nova Albion (New England) – for Queen Elizabeth, supposedly leaving behind a brass plaque now on display in the Bancroft Library at the University of California.

Setting sail from Acapulco in 1602, **Sebastián Vizcaíno**, a Portuguese explorer under contract to Spain, made a more lasting impact than his predecessors, undertaking the most extensive exploration of the coast and bestowing most of the place names that survive. In order to impress his superiors he exaggerated the value of his discoveries, describing a perfect, sheltered harbor, which he named **Monterey** in honor of his patron in Mexico. Subsequent colonizers based their efforts on these fraudulent claims (the windy bay did not live up to Vizcaíno's estimation), and the headquarters of the missions and military and administrative center of the Spanish government remained at Monterey, one hundred miles south of San Francisco, for the next 75 years.

Colonization: the Spanish and the Russians

The Spanish occupation of California began in earnest in 1769, with a combination of military expediency (to prevent other powers from gaining a foothold) and Catholic missionary zeal (to convert the Native Americans). Father **Junípero Serra** and a company of three hundred soldiers and clergy set off from Mexico for Monterey, half of them by ship, the other half overland. In June 1770, after establishing a small mission and presidio (fort) at San Diego, the expedition arrived at Monterey, where another mission and small presidio were constructed.

The Spanish continued to build missions all along the coast, ostensibly to Catholicize the Native Americans, which they did with inquisitional fervor. The mission complexes were broadly similar, with a church and cloistered residential structure surrounded by irrigated fields, vineyards, and more extensive ranchlands. The labor of the Native American converts was co-opted: they were put to work making soap and candles, were often beaten, and never educated.

Objective accounts of the missionaries' treatment of the indigenous peoples are rare, though mission registries record twice as many deaths as they do births, and their cemeteries are packed with Native American dead. Not all of the Native Americans gave up without a fight: many missions suffered from raids, and the now-ubiquitous red-tiled roofs were originally a replacement for the earlier thatch to better resist arson attacks.

Most of the mission structures that survive today were built to the designs of Serra's successor, Father **Férmin de Lasuén**, who was in charge of the missions during the period of their greatest growth. By the time of his death in 1804, a chain of 21 missions, each a long day's walk from its neighbors and linked by the dirt path of **El Camino Real** ("The Royal Road"), ran from San Diego to San Francisco.

During this time the first towns, called **pueblos**, were established in order to attract settlers to what was still a distant and undesirable territory. The first was laid out in 1777 at San Jose, south of the new mission at San Francisco. Los Angeles, the second pueblo, was established in 1781, though neither had more than a hundred inhabitants until well into the nineteenth century.

One reason for Spain's military presence in California – which consisted of four presidios all told, with twelve cannon and only two hundred soldiers – was to prevent the expansion of the small **Russian** colony based in Alaska, mostly trappers collecting beaver and otter pelts in the northwestern states of Washington and Oregon. The two countries were at peace and relations friendly, and in any case the Spanish presidios were in no position to enforce their territorial claims. In fact, they were so short of supplies and ammunition that they had to borrow the gunpowder to fire welcoming salutes whenever the two forces came into contact. Well aware of the Spanish weakness, the Russians established the outpost of **Fort Ross** in 1812, sixty miles north of San Francisco. This further undermined Spanish sovereignty over the region, though the Russians abandoned the fort in 1841, selling it to John Sutter (who features prominently in later California history; see p.771).

The Mexican era

While Spain, France, and England were engaged in the bitter struggles of the Napoleonic Wars, the colonies of New Spain rebelled against imperial neglect, with Mexico finally gaining independence in 1821. The Mexican Republic, or the United States of Mexico as the new country called itself, governed California as a territory. However, the fifteen distinct administrations it set up lacked the money to pay for improvements and the soldiers needed to enforce the laws, and they were unable to exercise any degree of authority.

The most important effect of the Mexican era was the final **secularization** in 1834, after years of gradual diminution, of the Franciscan missions. As most of the missionaries were Spanish, under Mexican rule they had seen their position steadily eroded by the increasingly wealthy, close-knit families of the Californios – Mexican immigrants who'd been granted vast tracts of ranchland. The government's intention was that half of the missions' extensive lands should go to the Indian converts, but this was never carried out, and the few powerful families divided most of it up among themselves.

In many ways this was the most lawless and wantonly wasteful period of California's history, an era described by **Richard Henry Dana** – scion of a distinguished Boston family, who dropped out of Harvard to sail to California

– in his 1840 book *Two Years Before the Mast*. Most of the agriculture and cottage industries that had developed under the missionaries disappeared, and it was a point of pride amongst the Californios not to do any work that couldn't be done from horseback. Dana's Puritan values led him to heap scorn upon the "idle and thriftless people" who made nothing for themselves. For example, the large herds of cattle that lived on the mission lands were slaughtered for their hides and sold to Yankee traders, who turned the hides into leather which they sold back to the Californios at a tidy profit. "In the hands of an enterprising people," he wrote, "what a country this might be."

The first Americans

Throughout the Mexican and Spanish eras, foreigners were legally banned from settling, and the few who showed up, mostly sick or injured sailors dropped off to regain their health, were often jailed until they proved themselves useful, either as craftsmen or as traders able to supply needed goods. In the late 1820s, the first **Americans**, without exception males, began to make their way to California, tending to fit in with the existing Mexican culture, often marrying into established families, and converting to the Catholic faith. The American presence grew slowly but surely as more and more people emigrated, still mostly by way of a three-month sea voyage around Cape Horn. Among these was **Thomas Larkin**, a New England merchant who, in 1832, set up shop in Monterey, and later was instrumental in pointing the disgruntled Californios towards the more accommodating US; Larkin's wife Rachel was the first American woman on the West Coast.

The first people to make the four-month journey to California overland – in a covered wagon, just as in so many Hollywood Westerns – arrived in 1841, having forged a trail over the Sierra Nevada Mountains via Truckee Pass, just north of Lake Tahoe. Soon after, hundreds of people each year were following in their tracks. In 1846, however, forty migrants, collectively known as the **Donner party**, died when they were trapped in the mountains by early winter snowfall (see p.662). The immense difficulties involved in reaching California, over land and by sea, kept population levels at a minimum, and by 1846 just seven thousand people, not counting Native Americans but including all the Spanish and Mexicans, lived in the entire region.

The Mexican-American War

From the 1830s onwards – inspired by **Manifest Destiny**, the popular, almost religious, belief that the United States was meant to cover the continent from coast to coast – US government policy regarding California was to buy all of Mexico's land north of the Rio Grande, the river that now divides the US and Mexico. President Andrew Jackson was highly suspicious of British designs on the West Coast – he himself had been held as a (14-year-old) prisoner of war during the Revolutionary War of 1776 – and various diplomatic overtures were made to the Mexican Republic, all of which backfired. In April 1846, Jackson's protégé, President James Polk, offered forty million dollars for all of New Mexico and the California territory, but his simultaneous annexation of the newly independent Republic of Texas – which Mexico still claimed – resulted in the outbreak of war.

Almost all the fighting of the **Mexican–American War** took place in Texas; only one real battle was ever fought on California soil, at San Pasqual, northeast of San Diego, where a roving US battalion was surprised by a band of pro-Mexican Californios, who killed 22 soldiers and wounded another 15 before withdrawing south into Mexico. Monterey, still the territorial capital, was captured by the US Navy without a shot fired, and in January 1847, when the rebel Californios surrendered to the US forces at Cahuenga, near Los Angeles, the Americans controlled the entire West Coast.

Just before the war began, California had made a brief foray into the field of self-government: the short-lived **Bear Flag Republic**, whose only lasting effect was to create what's still the state flag, a prowling grizzly bear with the words "California Republic" written below. In June 1846, American settlers in the Sonoma Valley took over the local presidio – long abandoned by the Mexicans – and declared California independent, which lasted for all of three weeks until the US forces took command.

The Gold Rush

As part of the Treaty of Guadalupe Hidalgo, which formally ended the war in 1848, Mexico ceded all of the Alta California territory to the US. Nine days before the signing of the accord, in the distant foothills of the Sierra Nevada Mountains, flakes of **gold** were discovered by workmen building a sawmill along the American River at Coloma, though it was months before this momentous conjunction of events became known.

At the time, California's non-Native American population was mostly concentrated in the few small towns along the coastal strip. Early rumors of gold attracted a trickle of prospectors, and, following news of their subsequent success, by the middle of 1849 – eighteen months after the initial find – men were flooding into California from all over, in the most madcap migration in world history. **Sutter's Fort**, a small agricultural community, trading post, and stage stop which had been established six years earlier by John Sutter on the banks of the American River, was overrun by miners, who headed up into the nearby foothills to make their fortune. Some did, most didn't, but in any case, within fifteen years most of the gold had been picked clean. The miners moved on or went home and their camps vanished, prompting Mark Twain to write that "in no other land, in modern times, have towns so absolutely died and disappeared as in the old mining regions of California."

Statehood

Following the US takeover after the defeat of Mexico, a **Constitutional Convention** was held at Monterey in the autumn of 1849. The men who attended were not the miners – most of whom were more interested in searching for gold – but those who had been in California for some time (about three years on average). At the time, the Territory of California extended all the way east to Utah, so the main topic of discussion was where to place the eastern boundary of the intended state. The drawing up of a state constitution was also important, since it was the basis on which California applied for admission to the US. This constitution contained a couple of noteworthy inclusions – to protect the dignity of the manually laboring miners, **slavery** was prohibited; and to attract well-heeled **women** from the East Coast, California was the first state to recognize in legal terms the separate property of a married woman. In 1850, California was admitted to the US as the 31st state.

The Indian Wars

Though the US Civil War had little effect on California, throughout the 1850s and 1860s white settlers and US troops fought many bloody battles against the various Native American tribes whose lands the immigrants wanted. At first the government tried to move willing tribes to fairly large reservations, but as more settlers moved in, the tribes were pushed onto smaller and smaller tracts. The most powerful resistance to the well-armed invaders came in the mountainous northeast of California, where a band of **Modoc** fought a long-running guerrilla war, using their superior knowledge of the terrain to evade the US troops (see p.756).

Owing to a combination of disease and lack of food, as well as deliberate acts of violence, the Native American population was drastically reduced, and by 1870 almost ninety percent had been wiped out. The survivors were concentrated in small, relatively valueless reservations, where their descendants still live: the Cahuila near Palm Springs, the Paiute/Shoshone in the Owens Valley, and the Hupa on the northwest coast. All are naturally quite protective of their privacy.

The boom years: 1870–1900

After the Gold Rush, **San Francisco** boomed into a boisterous frontier town, exploding in population from five hundred to fifty thousand within five years. Though far removed from the mines themselves, the city was the main landing spot for ship-borne argonauts (as the prospectors were called), and the main supply town. Moreover, it was the place where successful miners went to blow their hard-earned cash on the whiskey and women of the **Barbary Coast**, then the raunchiest waterfront in the world, full of brothels, saloons, and opium dens. Ten years later, San Francisco enjoyed an even bigger boom as a result of the silver mines of the Comstock Lode in Nevada, owned mainly by San Franciscans, who displayed their wealth by building grand palaces and mansions on Nob Hill – still the city's most exclusive address (see p.504).

The completion in 1869 of the **transcontinental railroad**, built using imported Chinese laborers, was a major turning point in the settlement of California. Whereas the trip across the country by stagecoach took at least a month, and was subject to scorching hot weather and attacks by hostile natives, the crossing could now be completed in just five days.

In 1875, when the Santa Fe Railroad reached Los Angeles (the railroad company having extracted huge bribes from local officials to ensure the budding city wasn't bypassed), there were just ten thousand people living in the whole of **Southern California**, divided equally between San Diego and Los Angeles. A fare war developed between the two rival railroads, and ticket costs dropped to as little as $1 for a one-way ticket from New York. Land speculators placed advertisements in East Coast and European papers, offering cheap land for homesteaders in towns and suburbs all over the West Coast that, as often as not, existed only on paper. By the end of the nineteenth century, thousands of people, ranging from Midwestern farmers to the East Coast elite, had moved to California to take advantage of the fertile land and mild climate.

Hollywood, the war, and after

The greatest boost to California's fortunes was, of course, the **film industry**, which moved here from the East Coast in 1911, attracted by the temperate climate, in which directors could shoot outdoors year-round, and by the incredibly cheap land, on which large indoor studios could be built at comparatively little cost. Within three years, movies like D.W. Griffith's *Birth of a Nation* – most of which was filmed along the dry banks of the Los Angeles River – were being cranked out by the hundreds.

Hollywood, a suburb of Los Angeles that was the site of many of the early studios, and which has ever since been the buzzword for the entire entertainment industry, has done more to promote the mystique of California as a pleasure garden than any other medium, disseminating images of its glamorous lifestyles around the globe. Los Angeles is increasingly an international center for the music business as well.

This widespread, idealized image had a magnetic effect during the **Great Depression** of the 1930s, when thousands of people from all over the country descended upon California, which was perceived to be – and for the most part was – immune to the economic downturn that crippled the rest of the US. From the Dust Bowl Midwest, entire families, who came to be known as **Okies**, packed up everything they owned and set off for the farms of the Central Valley, an epic journey captured by John Steinbeck's bestselling novel *The Grapes of Wrath*, in the photographs of Dorothea Lange, and in the baleful tunes of folksinger Woody Guthrie. Some Californians who feared losing their jobs to the incoming Okies formed vigilante groups and, with the complicity of local and state police, set up roadblocks along the main highways to prevent unemployed outsiders from entering the state.

One Depression-era initiative to alleviate the poverty, and to get the economy moving again, were the government-sponsored **Works Progress Administration (WPA)** construction projects, ranging from restoring the California missions to building trails and park facilities, and commissioning artworks like the marvelous Social Realist murals in San Francisco's Coit Tower.

Things turned around when **World War II** brought heavy industry to California, as shipyards and airplane factories sprang up, providing well-paid employment in wartime factories. After the war, most stayed on, and today California companies – McDonnell Douglas, Lockheed, Rockwell, and General Dynamics, for example – still make up the roll call of suppliers to the US military and space programs.

After the war, many of the soldiers who'd passed through on their way to the battlegrounds of the South Pacific came back to California and decided to stay on. There was plenty of well-paid work, and the US government subsidized house purchases for war veterans and, most importantly, constructed the

freeways and interstate highways that enabled land speculators to build new commuter suburbs on land that had been used for farms and citrus orchards.

The **1950s** brought prosperity to the bulk of middle-class America (typified by President Dwight Eisenhower's goal of "two cars in every garage and a chicken in every pot"), and California, particularly San Francisco, became a nexus for alternative artists and writers, spurring an immigration of intellectuals that by the end of the decade had become manifest as the **Beat generation** – pegged "Beatniks" by San Francisco columnist Herb Caen, in honor of Sputnik, the Soviet space satellite.

The 1960s and 1970s

California remained at the forefront of youth and **social upheavals** into and throughout the **1960s**. In a series of drug tests carried out at Stanford University – paid for by the CIA, which was interested in developing a "truth drug" for interrogation purposes – unwitting students were dosed with **LSD**. One of the guinea pigs was the writer Ken Kesey, who had just published the highly acclaimed novel *One Flew Over the Cuckoo's Nest*. Kesey quite liked the experience and soon secured a personal supply of the drug (which was still legal) and toured the West Coast to spread the word of "acid." In and around San Francisco, Kesey and his crew, the Merry Pranksters, turned on huge crowds at **Electric Kool-Aid Acid Tests** – in which LSD was diluted into bowls of the soft drink Kool-Aid – complete with psychedelic light shows and music by the Grateful Dead. The acid craze reached its height during the **Summer of Love** in 1967, when the entire Haight-Ashbury district of San Francisco seemed populated by barefoot and drugged flower children.

Within a year the superficial peace of Flower Power was shattered, as protests mounted against US involvement in the **Vietnam War**; Martin Luther King Jr and Bobby Kennedy, heroes of left-leaning youth, were both gunned down – Kennedy in Los Angeles after winning the California primary of the 1968 presidential election. The militant **Black Panthers**, a group of black radical activists based in Oakland, terrorized a white population that had earlier been supporters of the civil rights movement. By the end of the 60s the "system," in California especially, seemed to be at breaking point, and the atrocities committed by **Charles Manson** and his "Family" seemed to signify a general collapse.

The antiwar protests, concentrated at the University of California campus in Berkeley, continued through the early **1970s**. Emerging from the milieu of revolutionary and radical groups, the Symbionese Liberation Army (SLA), a small, well-armed, and stridently revolutionary group, set about the overthrow of the US, attracting media (and FBI) attention by murdering civil servants, robbing banks, and, most famously, kidnapping 19-year-old heiress **Patty Hearst**. Amid much media attention, Hearst converted to the SLA's cause, changing her name to Tanya and, for the next two years – until her capture in 1977 – she went underground, provoking national debate about her motives and beliefs.

California **politics**, after Watergate and the end of American involvement in Vietnam, seemed to lose whatever idealistic fervor it might once have had, and popular culture withdrew into self-satisfaction, typified by the smug harmonies of musicians like the Eagles and Jackson Browne. While the 60s upheavals were overseen by California Governor Ronald Reagan, who was ready and willing to fight the long-haired hippies, the 70s saw the reign of "Governor Moonbeam"

Jerry Brown, under whose leadership California enacted some of the most stringent **antipollution** measures in the world. The state also actively encouraged the development of renewable forms of energy such as solar and wind power, and protected the entire coastline from despoliation and development. The possession of under an ounce of **marijuana** was decriminalized (though it remains an offense to sell it), and the harvesting of marijuana continues to account for over $1 billion each year, making it the number-one cash crop in the number-one agricultural region in the US.

The 1980s and 1990s

The easy money of **1980s** Reaganomics and the trickle-down economy, which unsurprisingly never quite trickled down to the state's poorest, ended in a messy downturn. Many saw this as a disgraceful but fitting finale to a decade when greed was elevated to a virtue. LA junk-bond king Michael Milkin was convicted of multibillion-dollar fraud, and the Savings and Loan banking scandals enmeshed such high-ranking politicos as California Senator Alan Cranston. Consequently, the **1990s** kicked off with a stagnant property market and rising unemployment.

In **Los Angeles**, the videotaped beating of black motorist Rodney King by officers of the LA Police Department, and the subsequent acquittal of those officers, sparked off destructive **rioting** in April 1992. State and federal authorities, forced into taking notice of LA's endemic poverty and violence, promised all sorts of new initiatives but achieved few concrete results. Race also dominated the year-long trial of former black football star **O.J. Simpson** – accused and finally acquitted of murdering his white ex-wife and her male friend – splitting public opinion into directly opposed camps of black and white.

All these factors combined to make the first five years of the 1990s perhaps the bleakest since the Great Depression, and **natural calamities** – regional flooding, Malibu fires and mudslides, and two dramatic earthquakes – only added to the general malaise. Mike Davis's *City of Quartz*, despite flaws and inaccuracies, served as a secular bible for the time, an artfully written work based on the inevitable doom LA was facing. And with LA's chronic interethnic hatred, natural disasters, bureaucratic inaction, and general public pessimism, it seemed that Davis was probably right.

The latter half of the decade saw **Richard Riordan**, a multimillionaire technocrat who served as LA mayor from 1992 to 2000, preside over a major **revival** in the city's fortunes and a restructuring of its economic base – aerospace and automotive giving way to tourism, real estate and, as always, Hollywood. New property developments attempted to revitalize deprived areas, and even crime and violence tailed off marginally. However, these improvements probably owed more to the national upswing during the Clinton years than to purely local initiatives.

San Francisco also suffered in the early 90s; on top of AIDS-related illnesses stretching health services, the area was hit by a series of natural disasters. An **earthquake** in October 1989 devastated much of the San Francisco Bay Area, followed two years later by a massive **fire** in the Oakland Hills, which burned over two thousand homes and killed two dozen people – the third worst fire in US history.

But even more so than LA, San Francisco's economic upswing turned the city around, replacing pre-millennium jitters with Information Age optimism. The

Silicon Valley industries boomed, with companies scrambling to find high-paid workers to fill their constantly growing rosters. San Jose, San Francisco's southern neighbor, surpassed the Golden Gate city in population, and even Oakland, the gritty East Bay port-town, started to receive a much-needed facelift. Still, not everyone in the Bay Area was happy with the apparent prosperity. **Gentrification** threatened to turn San Francisco from a province of activism into a playground for Silicon Valley's rich young things. Housing prices rocketed sky-high, and tenancy at 99 percent full, forcing out not only the city's poor, but the lower middle class as well.

Contemporary California

The optimism that had overridden many concerns at the tail end of the old millennium soon took a pummeling once the new one started. The world's computers may not have gone belly-up at zero hour on Y2K, but the high-tech industry became the biggest victim of a nationwide economic **recession** – the cause of it, in fact, according to many analysts. This immediately affected the Silicon Valley companies, which saw billions wiped off their stock values and had to offload employees faster than they had hired them. Over half a decade later the big players that survived the crash have stabilized and continue to grow steadily, fuelling the continuous rise of the NASDAQ. On the other hand, the Bay Area's notoriously inflated **property prices**, which originally slowed for the first time in a decade with the high-tech bust, have continued to cool off, though still not as badly as elsewhere in the nation, where the market is in severe crisis.

More gloom, literally, struck California in 2001, when gross mismanagement of the state's energy supplies led to a series of Third World-type **power cuts**, as the ailing grid system was unable to meet the enormous demands for electricity. The state was forced to fork out vast sums to import some of its shortfall in energy from other states and, although some of the management issues have been resolved, a true long-term solution to the problem has still to be found. Environmentalists maintain that there will not be a proper solution until serious money is invested in **renewable energy** sources, something the traditional lobbyists are not at all keen on.

Somewhat bravely then, and unusually for a Republican, Governor **Arnold Schwarzenegger**'s passing of a series of green measures towards this end and protecting the environment has become a centrepiece of his administration, which replaced Democrat Gray Davis's in a rare **recall** election (a vote of confidence, in effect) in October 2003 and was re-elected in 2006. The other main platform of the "Governator," as he is known to detractors and supporters alike, was to set about balancing the **state budget** by cutting down on certain programs, including funding for tourism. He also implemented various initiatives aimed at raising revenue, hence the sudden hike of day-use and camping fees in state parks, for example. Indeed, his mixture of old-style conservative fiscal responsibility (as opposed to Bush's bankruptcy-inducing economic policies) and more liberal (by GOP standards) social positions like supporting stem cell research, although he refused to support gay marriage, seem to have struck a happy medium with the voters. In the state that gave birth to film, many are also charmed by his Hollywood charisma, and being married to a member of the Kennedy clan does him no harm in courting Democrats either.

The governorship notwithstanding, California remains a staunch **Democrat stronghold**, voting overwhelmingly for John Kerry in the 2004 presidential elections and returning its large majority of Democratic representatives to the US House undiminished then and in 2006. Indeed, after the Democrat takeover of Congress in the 2006 midterms, **Nancy Pelosi** became the first-ever woman Speaker of the House, and other California Democrats have assumed key positions on committees in Washington DC, thus playing an important role in the gradual shift towards more progressive politics that seems to be happening nationwide. Meanwhile, back in San Francisco and Berkeley, grassroots political **activism** has continued to stir ever more vigorously and spread to other parts of the state in response to George W. Bush's hardline domestic and international policies. On the streets, California has hosted some of the largest antiwar demonstrations since the days of Vietnam, as the national **Peace Movement** began to quell much of the earlier flag waving and saber rattling over Iraq. One of the most public leaders of this effort has been bereaved military mother **Cindy Sheehan**, who hails from near Sacramento and, after a short break from activism in 2007, announced she would run for Pelosi's congressional seat, following the latter's failure to initiate impeachment proceedings against Bush.

In local politics, the most interesting developments have been at the southern end of the state. **Municipal corruption** in San Diego, California's one major city controlled by Republicans, reached such ludicrous proportions that the FBI were called in to investigate and mayor Dick Murphy forced to resign in 2005. At the same time, Democrat and former union leader **Antonio Villaraigosa** was being elected as LA's first Latino mayor in 133 years. He is also a co-chair on Hillary Clinton's 2008 presidential campaign and may well have aspirations to higher office himself. Set against a background of rising national concern about illegal immigration, principally from Mexico, his election emphasized the changing demographics of America and the power of the legal **Hispanic vote**. In this more conducive climate, the state's growing number of legitimate immigrant workers have also been leading the way in **union organization**, which some believe could energize the national labor movement, too long emasculated by neocon policies and even the indifference of the Clinton administration.

California has also been on the receiving end of extreme weather conditions, most likely attributable to climate change. These have mainly taken the form of **wildfires**, which have ravaged many different parts of the state in recent years, destroying hundreds of thousands of acres of forest and property and even causing considerable casualties. There have also been disastrous spates of **flooding** in certain areas. Yet, despite all these setbacks, California still manages to cling to its aura as a Promised Land. Barring its complete destruction by the **Big One** (the earthquake that's destined one day to drop half of the state into the Pacific and wipe out the rest under massive tidal waves), California seems set to continue much as it is, acting as the pot of gold at the end of the West's mythical rainbow and as the place where America forever reinvents itself.

Wildlife and the environment

Though popularly imagined as little more than palm trees and golden sand beaches, California is hard to beat for sheer range of landscape. With glaciated alpine peaks and meadows, desolate desert sand dunes, and flat, fertile agricultural plains, it's no wonder that Hollywood filmmakers have so often and successfully used California locations to simulate distant and exotic scenes. These diverse environments also support an immense variety of plant and animal life, much of which – due to the protection offered by the various state and national parks, forests, and wilderness areas – is both easily accessible and unspoiled by encroaching civilization.

Background: geology, earthquakes, and ecosystems

California's landscape has been formed over millions of years through the interaction of all the main geological processes: Ice Age glaciation, erosion, earthquakes, and volcanic eruptions. The most impressive results can be seen in **Yosemite National Park**, east of San Francisco, where solid walls of granite have been sliced and chiseled into unforgettable cliffs and chasms. In contrast, the sand dunes of **Death Valley** are being constantly shaped and reshaped by the dry desert winds, surrounded by foothills tinted by oxidized mineral deposits into every color of the spectrum.

Earthquakes – which earned Los Angeles the truck driver's nickname "Shakeytown" – are the most powerful expression of the volatile unrest underlying the placid surface. California sits on the Pacific "Ring of Fire," at the junction of two tectonic plates slowly drifting deep within the earth. Besides the occasional earthquake – like the 1906 one which flattened San Francisco, or the 1994 tremor which collapsed many of LA's freeways – this instability is also the cause of California's many volcanoes. Distinguished by their symmetrical, conical shape, almost all of them are now dormant, though Mount Lassen, in Northern California, did erupt in 1914 and 1915, destroying much of the surrounding forest. Along with the boiling mud pools that accompany even the dormant volcanoes, the most attractive features of volcanic regions are the bubbling **hot springs** – pools of water that flow up from underground, heated to a sybaritically soothing temperature. Hot springs occur naturally all over the state, and though some have now been developed into luxurious health spas, most remain in their natural condition, where you can soak your bones *au naturel* surrounded by mountain meadows or wide-open deserts. The best of these are listed throughout the guide.

Here you'll find details of the major **ecosystems** of California. The accounts are inevitably brief, as the area encompasses almost 320,000 square miles, ranging from moist coastal forests and the snowcapped Sierra Nevada peaks to Death Valley, 282ft below sea level and with an annual rainfall of two inches. These ecosystems are inhabited by a multitude of species. Native to California are 54 species of cactus, 123 species of amphibian and reptile, 260 species of bird, and 27,000–28,000 species of insect.

Some of the most fantastic **wildlife** is now extinct in its natural habitat: neither the grizzly bear (which still adorns the California state flag) nor the

▲ Hot springs near Mammoth Lakes, Eastern Sierra

California condor (one of the world's largest birds, with a wingspan of over eight feet) have been seen in the California wilds for over half a century. But plenty of other creatures are still alive and thriving, like the otters, elephant seals, and gray whales seen all along the coast, and the chubby marmots – shy mammals often found sunning themselves on rocks in higher reaches of the mountains. Plant life is equally varied, from the brilliant but short-lived desert wildflowers to the timeless bristlecone pine trees, which live for thousands of years on the arid peaks of the Great Basin desert.

The ocean

The **Pacific Ocean** determines California's climate, keeping the coastal temperatures moderate all year round. During the spring and summer, cold, nutrient-rich waters rise up to produce cooling banks of fog and abundant crops of phytoplankton (microscopic algae). The algae nourishes creatures such as krill (small shrimp), which in their turn provide sustenance for juvenile fish. This food chain offers fodder for millions of nesting **seabirds**, as well as harbor and elephant **seals**, California **sea lions**, and whales. **Gray whales**, the most common whale species spotted from land, were once almost hunted to the point of extinction, but have returned to the coast in large numbers. During their southward migration to their breeding grounds off Mexico, from December to January, it's easy to spy them from prominent headlands all along the coast, and most harbors have charter services offering whale watching tours. On their way back to the Arctic Ocean, in February and March, the newborn whale pups can sometimes be seen playfully leaping out of the water, or "breaching." Look for the whale's white-plumed spout – once at the surface, it will usually blow several times in succession.

Tide pools

California's shoreline is composed of three primary ecosystems: tide pools, sandy beaches, and estuaries. To explore the **tide pools**, first consult a local newspaper to see when the low tides (two daily) will occur. Be careful of waves, don't be out too far from the shore when the tide returns, and watch your step – there are many small lives underfoot. Miles of tide pool-strewn beaches line the coast, some of the best at Pacific Grove near Monterey. Here you'll find **sea anemones** (they look like green zinnias), hermit crabs, purple and green shore crabs, red sponges, purple sea urchins, starfish ranging from the size of a dime to the size of a hubcap, mussels, abalone, and Chinese-hat limpets – to name a few. You may also see black **oystercatchers**, their squawking easily heard over the surf, foraging for an unwary, lips-agape mussel. Gulls and black turnstones are also common, and during the summer brown pelicans dive for fish just offshore.

The life of the tide pool party is the **hermit crab**, who protects its soft and vulnerable hindquarters with scavenged shells, usually those of the aptly named black turban snail. Hermit crabs scurry busily around in search of a detritus snack, or scuffle with other hermit crabs over the proprietorship of vacant snail shells.

Pacific Grove is also home to large populations of **sea otters**. Unlike most marine mammals, sea otters keep themselves warm with a thick, soft coat rather than blubber. The trade in sea otter pelts brought entrepreneurial Russian and British fur hunters to the West Coast, and by the mid-nineteenth century the otters were virtually extinct. In 1938, a small population was discovered along the Big Sur coast, and with careful protection otters have re-established themselves in the southern part of their range. They are charming creatures with big rubbery noses and Groucho Marx moustaches. With binoculars, it's easy to spot them amongst the bobbing kelp, where they lie on their backs opening sea urchins with a rock, or sleep entwined within a seat belt of kelp, which keeps them from floating away. The bulk of the population resides between Monterey Bay and the Channel Islands, but – aside from Pacific Grove – the best places to see them are Point Lobos State Park, Seventeen-Mile Drive, and Monterey's Fisherman's Wharf, where, along with sea lions, they often come to beg for fish.

Many of the **seaweeds** you see growing from the rocks are edible. As one would expect from a Pacific beachfront, there are also palms – **sea palms**, with four-inch-long rubbery stems and flagella-like fronds. Their thick, root-like holdfasts provide shelter for small crabs. You'll also find giant **kelp** washed up on shore – harvested commercially for use in thickening ice cream.

Sand beaches

The long, golden **sandy beaches** for which California is so famous may look sterile from a distance. However, observe the margin of sand exposed as a gentle wave recedes, and you will see jet streams of small bubbles emerge from the holes of numerous clams and mole crabs. Small shorebirds called **sanderlings** race amongst the waves in search of these morsels, and sand dollars are often easy to find along the high-tide line.

The most unusual sandy-shore bathing beauties are the **northern elephant seals**, which will tolerate rocky beaches but favor soft sand mattresses for their rotund torsos. The males, or bulls, can reach lengths of over six meters and weigh upwards of four tons; the females, or cows, are petite by comparison –

four meters long, and averaging a mere two thousand pounds in weight. They have large eyes, adapted for spotting fish in deep or murky waters; indeed, elephant seals are the deepest diving mammals, capable of staying underwater for twenty minutes at a time, reaching depths of over four thousand feet, where the pressure is over a hundred times that at the surface. They have to dive so deeply in order to avoid the attentions of the great white sharks who lurk offshore, for whom they are a favorite meal.

Elephant seals were decimated by commercial whalers in the mid-nineteenth century for their blubber and hides. By the turn of the century fewer than a hundred remained, but careful protection has partially restored the California population, which is concentrated on the Channel and Farallon islands, at Piedras Blancas just north of San Simeon, and at Año Nuevo State Park.

Elephant seals only emerge from the ocean to breed or molt; their name comes from the male's long, trunk-like proboscis, through which it produces a resonant pinging sound that biologists call "trumpeting," which is how it attracts a mate. The Año Nuevo beach is the best place to observe this ritual. In December and January, the bulls haul themselves out of the water and battle for dominance. The dominant alpha male will do most of the mating, siring as many as fifty young pups, one per mating, in a season. Other males fight it out at the fringes, each managing one or two couplings with the hapless, defenseless females. During this time, the beach is a seething mass of ton upon ton of blubbery seals – flopping sand over their backs to keep cool, and squabbling with their neighbors while making rude snoring and belching sounds. The adults depart in March but the weaned pups hang around until May.

Different age groups of elephant seals continue to use the beach at different times throughout the summer for molting. Elephant seals are completely unafraid of people, but are huge enough to hurt or even kill you if you get in their way. Still, you're allowed to get close, except during mating season, when entry into the park is restricted to ranger-guided tours.

Estuaries

Throughout California, many **estuarine** or river-mouth habitats have been filled, diked, drained, "improved" with marinas, or contaminated by pollutants. Those that survive intact consist of a mixture of mud flats, exposed only at low tide, and salt marsh, together forming a critical wildlife area that provides nurseries for many kinds of invertebrates and fish, and nesting and wintering grounds for countless birds. Cord grass, a dominant wetlands plant, produces five to ten times as much oxygen and nutrients per acre as wheat.

Many interesting creatures live in the thick organic ooze, including the fat **innkeeper** (a revolting-looking pink hot-dog of a worm that sociably shares its burrow with a small crab and a fish), polychaete worms, clams, and other goodies. Most prominent of estuary birds are the **great blue herons** and **great egrets**. Estuaries are the best place to see wintering shorebirds such as dunlin, dowitchers, eastern and western sandpipers, and yellowlegs, and peregrine falcons and osprey are also found here.

Important California estuaries include Elkhorn Slough, near Monterey, San Francisco Bay, and Bolinas Lagoon, some fifteen miles north.

Coastal meadows, hills, and canyons

Along the shore, **coastal meadows** are bright with pink and yellow sand verbena, lupines, sea rocket, sea fig, and the bright orange **California poppy**, the state flower. Slightly inland, hills are covered with coastal scrub, which consists largely of coyote brush. Coastal canyons contain broadleaf trees such as California laurel, alder, buckeye, and oaks – and a tangle of sword ferns, horsetail, and cow parsnip.

Common rainy-season canyon inhabitants include four-inch-long banana slugs and rough-skinned newts. In winter, orange-and-black **Monarch butterflies** gather in large roosts in a few discreet locales, such as Bolinas, Santa Cruz, and Pacific Grove. Coastal thickets also provide homes to weasels, bobcats, gray fox, raccoons, black-tailed deer, California quail, and garter snakes. **Tule elk**, a once common member of the deer family, have also been reintroduced to the wild; good places to view them are on Tomales Point at the Point Reyes National Seashore (see p.609), and inland at reserves near Bakersfield (p.346) and in the Owens Valley (p.311).

River valleys

Like most fertile **river valleys**, the Sacramento and San Joaquin valleys – jointly known as the Central Valley – have both been greatly affected by agriculture. Riparian (streamside) vegetation has been logged, wetlands drained, and streams contaminated by agricultural runoff. Despite this, the habitat that does remain is a haven for wildlife. Wood ducks, kingfishers, swallows, and warblers are common, as are gray foxes, raccoons, and striped skunks. Regular winter migrants include snow and Canada geese, green-winged and cinnamon teals, pintail, shovelers, and widgeon. The refuges where many of these creatures live are well worth a visit, but don't be alarmed by large numbers of duck hunters – the term "refuge" is a misnomer. However, most have tour routes where hunting is prohibited.

Vernal pools are a valley community unique to California. Here, hardpan soils prevent the infiltration of winter rains, creating seasonal ponds. As these ponds slowly evaporate in April and May, sharply defined concentric floral rings come into bloom. The white is meadowfoam, the blue is the violet-like downingia, and the yellow is goldfields. Swallows, meadowlarks, yellowlegs, and stilts can also be found here.

Forests

One of the most notable indigenous features of California's forests are the wide expanses of **redwood** and **sequoia trees**. It's easy to confuse the coastal species, *Sequoia sempervirens*, or redwood, with the *Sequoiadendron giganteum*, or giant sequoia (pronounced *seh-KOY-uh*), as both have the same fibrous, reddish-brown bark. Redwoods are the world's tallest trees, while sequoias have the greatest base circumference and are the largest single organisms on earth; for more on the latter, see the box on p.372. Both species can live for over two thousand years, and recent research now indicates a maximum age of 3500 years for the sequoia. Their longevity is partially due to their bark: rich in tannin, it protects the tree from fungal and insect attack and inhibits fire damage. In fact, fire is beneficial to these trees and necessary for their germination; prescribed fires are set and controlled around them.

The wood of the redwood in particular is much sought after both for its resistance to decay and its beauty – near any coastal forest you'll see signs advertising redwood burl furniture.

Redwoods and sequoias are the only surviving members of a family of perhaps forty species of trees which, fossil records show, grew worldwide 175 million years ago. **Redwoods** are a relict species, meaning they flourished in a moister climate during the Arcto-Tertiary (just after the golden age of the dinosaurs), and, as weather patterns change, have retreated to their current near-coastal haunts. Today they are found in a few pockets from the border with Oregon to just south of Monterey, and a tremendous battle between environmentalists and loggers is being waged over the remaining acres. These **virgin forests** provide homes to unique creatures, such as the spotted owl and marbled murrelet.

The floor of the redwood forest is a hushed place with little sunlight, the air suffused with a rufous glow from the bark, which gives the trees its name. One of the most common ground covers in the redwood forest is the redwood sorrel, or oxalis, with its shamrock leaves and tubular pink flowers; ferns are also numerous. Birds are usually high in the canopy and hard to see, but you might hear the double-whistled song of the varied thrush, or the "chickadee" call from the bird of that name. Roosevelt elk, larger than the tule elk, also inhabit the humid northwest forests. Prairie Creek Redwoods State Park, near the border with Oregon, has a large herd.

Sequoias are found on the western slopes of the Sierra Nevada, most notably in Yosemite and Kings Canyon national parks – though trees from saplings given as state gifts can be found growing all over the world. The sequoia forest tends to be slightly more open than the redwood forest. Juvenile sequoias – say up to a thousand years old – exhibit a slender conical shape which, as the lower branches fall away, ages to the classic heavy-crowned figure, with its columnar trunk. For its bulk, its cones are astonishingly small, no bigger than a hen's egg, but they live on the tree for up to thirty years before falling.

The Sierra Nevada

In the late nineteenth century, the environmental movement was founded when John Muir fell in love with the **Sierra Nevada Mountains**, which he called the Range of Light. Muir fought a losing battle to save Hetch Hetchy, a valley said to be as beautiful as Yosemite, but in the process the **Sierra Club** was born and the move to save America's remaining wilderness began.

The Sierra Nevada, which run almost the entire length of the state, have a sharp, craggy, freshly glaciated look. Many of the same conifers can be found as in the forests further west, but ponderosa and lodgepole pines are two of the dominants, and the forests tend to be drier and more open. Lower-elevation forests contain incense cedar, sugar pine (whose eighteen-inch cones are the longest in the world), and black oak. The oaks, along with dogwood and willows, produce spectacular autumnal color. The east side of the range is drier and has large groves of aspen, a beautiful white-barked tree with small round leaves that tremble in the wind. **Wildflowers** flourish for a few short months here – shooting star, elephant's head, and wild onions in early spring, asters and yarrow later in the season.

The dominant campground scoundrels are two sorts of noisy, squawking bird: Steller's jays and Clark's nutcrackers. Black bears, who may make a raid on your camp, pose more danger to iceboxes than humans, but nonetheless you should treat them with caution. The friendly twenty-pound pot-bellied rodents that lounge around at the fringes of your encampment are **marmots**, who probably do more damage than bears: some specialize in chewing on radiator hoses of parked cars. For tips on dealing with wildlife safely and respectfully, see p.52.

Other common birds include mountain chickadees, yellow-rumped warblers, white-crowned sparrows, and juncos, and among the mammals, deer, golden-mantled ground squirrels, and chipmunks are plentiful.

The Great Basin

The little-known **Great Basin** stretches from the northernmost section of the state down almost to Death Valley, encompassing all of Nevada and parts of all the other bordering states. It's a land of many shrubs and few streams, and what streams do exist drain into saline lakes rather than the ocean.

Mono Lake, reflecting the 13,000-foot peaks of Yosemite National Park, is a spectacular example. Its salty waters support no fish but lots of algae, brine shrimp, and brine flies, the latter two providing a smorgasbord for nesting gulls (the term "seagull" isn't strictly correct – many gulls nest inland) and migrating phalaropes and grebes. Like many Great Basin lakes, Mono Lake has been damaged through diversion of its freshwater feeder streams, in this case to provide water for the swimming pools of Los Angeles.

Great Basin plants tolerate hot summers, cold winters, and little rain. The dominant Great Basin plant is **sagebrush**, whose dusky green leaves are wonderfully aromatic, especially after a summer thunderstorm. Other common plants include bitterbrush, desert peach, junipers, and piñon pine. Piñon cones contain tasty nuts that were a mainstay of the Paiute diet.

The **sage grouse** is one of the most distinctive Great Basin birds. These turkey-like fowl feed on sage during the winter and depend on it for nesting and courtship habitat. In March and April, males gather at dancing grounds called leks, where they puff out small pink balloons on their necks, make soft drum-banging calls, and in general succeed in looking and sounding rather silly. The hens coyly scout out the talent by feigning greater interest in imaginary seeds.

Pronghorns are beautiful tawny-gold antelope seen in many locales in the Great Basin. Watch for their twinkling white rumps as you drive. Other Great Basin denizens include golden eagles, piñon jays, black-billed magpies, coyotes, feral horses and burros, black-tailed jackrabbits, and western rattlesnakes. Large concentrations of waterfowl gather at Tule Lake in northeastern California, part of the Klamath Basin National Wildlife Refuge (see p.756), where hundreds of wintering **bald eagles** congregate in November before the cold really sets in.

The Mojave Desert

The **Mojave Desert** lies in the southeast corner of the state, near Death Valley. Like the Great Basin, the vegetation here consists primarily of drought-adapted shrubs, one of the commonest of which is creosote, with its olive-green leaves and puffy yellow flowers. Death Valley is renowned for its early spring wildflower shows. The alluvial fans are covered with desert trumpet, gravel ghost, and pebble pincushion. The quantity and timing of rainfall determines when the floral display peaks, but it's usually some time between mid-February and mid-April in the lower elevations, late April to early June higher up.

Besides shrubs, the Mojave has many interesting kinds of **cactus**. These include barrel, cottontop, cholla, and beavertail cactus, and many members of the yucca family. Yuccas have stiff, lance-like leaves with sharp tips, a conspicuous representative being the **Joshua tree** (see p.267), whose twisting, arm-like branches are covered with shaggy, upward-pointing leaf fronds, which can reach to thirty feet high.

Many Mojave Desert animals conserve body moisture by foraging at night, including the kit fox, wood rat, and various kinds of mice. The **kangaroo rat**, an appealing animal that hops rather than runs, has specially adapted kidneys that enable it to survive without drinking water. If you're lucky you might catch sight of the **bighorn sheep**, usually found in secluded canyons and on high ridges; the **desert fox**, a regular sight among the sand dunes; and the **coyote**, which frequently keeps cool in the shade. Other desert animals include birds like the roadrunner, ash-throated flycatcher, ladder-backed woodpecker, verdin, and Lucy's warbler; and reptiles like the Mojave rattlesnake, sidewinder, and chuckwalla.

California on film

n the early 1910s, attracted by the sunshine, cheap labor, and rich variety of California landscapes, a handful of independent movie producers left the East Coast and the stranglehold monopoly of Thomas Edison's Motion Picture Patents Company, and set up shop in the small Los Angeles suburb of Hollywood. Within a decade Hollywood had become the movie capital of the world, and Southern California the setting for everything from Keystone Kops car chases to Tom Mix Westerns, not to mention the odd Biblical epic or historic romance.

Not surprisingly, since then the list of **movies** set in California, and especially LA, has become almost endless. What follows are those that are the most memorable classics, make the most original use of California locations, and reflect the state's navel-gazing fascination with itself.

Hollywood does Hollywood

The Bad and the Beautiful (Vincente Minnelli, 1952). Bitter tale of the rise and fall of a ruthless Hollywood producer (Kirk Douglas), told in flashbacks by the star, writer, and director he launched and subsequently lost.

Barton Fink (Joel Coen, 1991). Tinseltown in the 1940s is depicted by the Coen brothers as a dark world of greedy movie bosses, belligerent screenwriters, and murderers disguised as traveling salesmen. Allegedly based on the experience of playwright Clifford Odets.

Ed Wood (Tim Burton, 1994). The ragged low-budget fringes of 50s Hollywood are beautifully re-created in this loving tribute to the much-derided auteur of *Plan Nine from Outer Space* and *Glen or Glenda*. Gorgeously shot in black and white, with a magnificent performance by Martin Landau as an ailing Bela Lugosi.

Get Shorty (Barry Sonnenfeld, 1995). Slick Miami gangster Chili Palmer, played by John Travolta, takes up residence in Tinseltown and decides he wants to become a movie producer, in this amusing adaptation of an Elmore Leonard novel.

Gods and Monsters (Bill Condon, 1998). An interesting tale of the final days of 1930s horror-film director James Whale (well portrayed by Ian McKellen), ignored by the Hollywood elite and slowly dying of malaise by his poolside. The title refers to a memorable Ernest Thesiger line from Whale's classic *Bride of Frankenstein*.

Good Morning, Babylon (Paolo and Vittorio Taviani, 1987). Two restorers of European cathedrals find themselves in 1910s Hollywood, working to build the monstrous Babylonian set for D.W. Griffith's *Intolerance*, in this Italian story of the contribution of immigrants in early Tinseltown.

In a Lonely Place (Nicholas Ray, 1950). A glamourless Hollywood peopled with alcoholic former matinee idols, star-struck hat-check girls, and desperate agents forms the cynical background for this doomed romance between Humphrey Bogart's hot-tempered screenwriter and his elegant neighbor Gloria Grahame.

The Player (Robert Altman, 1992). Tim Robbins is a studio shark who thinks a disgruntled screenwriter is out to get him; he kills the writer (at South Pasadena's Rialto Theater), steals his girlfriend, and waits for the cops to unravel it. A wickedly sharp satire about contemporary Hollywood, with some great celebrity cameos.

🏃 **Singin' in the Rain** (Stanley Donen & Gene Kelly, 1952). A merry trip through Hollywood set during the birth of the sound era. Gene Kelly, Donald O'Connor, and Debbie Reynolds sing and dance to many classic tunes, including "Good Morning," "Moses," "Broadway Melody," and countless others.

A Star Is Born (George Cukor, 1954). The story of the rise of a starlet mirroring the demise of her Svengali. Janet Gaynor and Fredric March star in the early version, Judy Garland and James Mason in the later. Both are worthwhile, while a 1977 remake with Barbra Streisand and Kris Kristofferson runs a distant third.

LA noir

The Big Sleep (Howard Hawks, 1946). One of the key noirs of the 1940s, with Humphrey Bogart as Philip Marlowe, and featuring a wildly confused plot that ends up being subordinate to the crackling chemistry between Bogie and Lauren Bacall.

🏃 **Chinatown** (Roman Polanski, 1974). One of the essential films about the city. Jack Nicholson hunts down corruption in this dark criticism of the forces that animate the town: venal politicians, black-hearted land barons, crooked cops, and a morally neutered populace. Great use of locations, from Echo Park to the San Fernando Valley.

Devil in a Blue Dress (Carl Franklin, 1995). Terrific modern

Sullivan's Travels (Preston Sturges, 1941). A high-spirited comedy about a director who wants to stop making schlock pictures and instead create gritty portrayals of what he thinks real life to be. The first two-thirds are great, the last third ends in mawkish fashion.

Sunset Boulevard (Billy Wilder, 1950). Award-winning film about a screenwriter falling into the clutches of a long-faded silent-movie star. William Holden was near the beginning of his career, Gloria Swanson well past the end of hers. Erich von Stroheim nicely fills in as Swanson's butler, and even Cecil B. DeMille makes a cameo.

Who Framed Roger Rabbit? (Robert Zemeckis, 1988). Despite being a live-action/cartoon hybrid, a revealing film about 1940s LA, where cartoon characters suffer abuse like everyone else and the big corporations seek to destroy the Red Car transit system.

noir, in which South Central detective Easy Rawlins (Denzel Washington) navigates the ethical squalor of elite 1940s white LA and discovers a few ugly truths about city leaders – most of which he already suspected.

Double Indemnity (Billy Wilder, 1944). The prototypical film noir. Greedy insurance salesman Fred MacMurray collaborates with harpy wife Barbara Stanwyck to murder her husband and cash in on the settlement. Edward G. Robinson lurks on the sidelines as MacMurray's boss.

Heat (Michael Mann, 1995). Stars big names like De Niro and Pacino, but this crime drama, which does include some stunning set pieces (eg a Downtown LA shootout), is ultimately less than the sum of its parts, with a frustratingly predictable ending.

Jackie Brown (Quentin Tarantino, 1997). A glorious return to form for Pam Grier who, as a tough airline stewardess, plays the perfect foil for Samuel Jackson's smooth gangster. LA itself provides the dark, menacing backdrop.

The Killing of a Chinese Bookie (John Cassavetes, 1976). Perfectly evoking the sleazy charms of the Sunset Strip, Cassavetes' behavioral crime story about a club owner (Ben Gazzara) in hock to the mob is just one of his many great LA-based character studies.

LA Confidential (Curtis Hanson, 1997). Easily the best of all the contemporary noir films, a perfectly realized adaptation of James Ellroy's novel about brutal cops, victimized prostitutes, and scheming politicians in 1950s LA. Even the good guys, Russell Crowe and Guy Pearce, are morally dubious.

The Long Goodbye (Robert Altman, 1973). Altman intentionally mangles noir conventions in this Chandler adaptation, which has Elliott Gould play Marlowe as a droning schlep who wanders across a desaturated landscape of casual corruption, encountering bizarre characters like nerdy mobster Marty

Augustine and Sterling Hayden as a hulking alcoholic writer.

One False Move (Carl Franklin, 1991). A disturbing early role for Billy Bob Thornton, as a murderous hick who kills some people in an LA bungalow with his girlfriend and psychotic, nerdy colleague Pluto, then gets pursued by the LAPD and a small-town Arkansas sheriff.

The Postman Always Rings Twice (Tay Garnett, 1946). Lana Turner and John Garfield star in this seamy – and excellent – adaptation of the James M. Cain novel, first brought to the screen as *Ossessione*, an Italian adaptation by Luchino Visconti. Awkwardly remade by Bob Rafelson in 1981 with Jessica Lange and Jack Nicholson.

Touch of Evil (Orson Welles, 1958). Supposedly set at a Mexican border town, this noir classic was actually shot in a seedy, decrepit Venice. A bizarre, baroque masterpiece with Charlton Heston playing a Mexican official, Janet Leigh as his beleaguered wife, and Welles himself as a bloated, corrupt cop addicted to candy bars.

True Romance (Tony Scott, 1993). With a Quentin Tarantino plot to guide them, Patricia Arquette and Christian Slater battle creeps and gangsters amid wonderful LA locations, from cruddy motels to *Rae's Diner* in Santa Monica.

Apocalyptic LA

Blade Runner (Ridley Scott, 1982). While the first theatrical version flopped (thanks to a slapped-on happy ending and annoying voiceover narration), the recut director's version establishes the film as a sci-fi classic, involving a dystopic future LA where "replicants" roam the streets and soulless corporations rule from pyramidal towers.

Earthquake (Mark Robson, 1974). Watch the Lake Hollywood dam collapse, people run for their lives, and chaos hold sway in the City of Angels. Originally presented in "Sensurround!"

Escape from LA (John Carpenter, 1996). LA is cut off from the mainland by an earthquake and declared so "ravaged by crime and immorality" that it's been turned into a dead zone for undesirables. Sent in to stop the insurrection, Kurt Russell battles psychotic plastic surgeons in Beverly Hills and surfs a tsunami to a showdown in a netherworld Disneyland.

Falling Down (Joel Schumacher, 1993). Fired defense-worker Michael Douglas tires of the traffic jams on the freeways and goes nuts in some of the city's poorer minority neighborhoods. A fitting reflection of the bleak attitudes of riot-era LA.

Kiss Me Deadly (Robert Aldrich, 1955). Perhaps the bleakest of all noirs, starring Ralph Meeker as brutal detective Mike Hammer, who tramples on friends and enemies alike in his search for the great "whatsit" – a mysterious and deadly suitcase.

Mulholland Drive (David Lynch, 2001). A frightening take on the city by director Lynch, who uses nonlinear storytelling to present a tale of love, death, glamour, and doom – in which elfin cowboys mutter cryptic threats, elegant chanteuses lip-sync to phantom melodies, and a blue key can unlock a shocking double identity.

Strange Days (Kathryn Bigelow, 1995). In a chaotic, nightmarish vision of LA, Ralph Fiennes, Angela Bassett, and Juliette Lewis run around the city screaming-in the new millennium. More interesting as a reflection of mid-1990s LA angst than as compelling cinema.

The Terminator (James Cameron, 1984). Modern sci-fi classic, with Arnold Schwarzenegger as a robot from the future sent to kill the mother of an unborn rebel leader. Bravura special effects and amazing set pieces here were successfully followed up with the director's 1989 sequel, *T2: Judgment Day*, with Arnold as a good robot.

Modern LA

Boyz N the Hood (John Singleton, 1991). An excellent period piece that cemented the LA stereotype as a land of gangs and guns, starring Cuba Gooding Jr in his first big role, and Lawrence Fishburne as his dad.

Clueless (Amy Heckerling, 1995). Jane Austen's *Emma* transplanted to a rich Southern California high school, with a fine performance by Alicia Silverstone as a frustrated matchmaker.

Dogtown and Z-Boys (Stacy Peralta, 2002). Even if you have no interest in skateboarding, this is a fun, high-spirited look at the glory times of the sport in the mid-1970s, when a daring group of LA kids took to using the empty swimming pools of the elite as their own private skate-parks.

Ghost World (Terry Zwigoff, 2001). An alienated teenager encounters LA (here, nameless) in all of its corporatized drabness, a soulless desert of identical mini-malls, cheap retro-50s diners, and desperate, lonely characters. Oddly enough, something of a dark comedy.

The Glass Shield (Charles Burnett, 1995). Institutionalized racism in the LAPD is brought under the harsh glare of Charles Burnett, who, with his masterpieces *Killer of Sheep* (1977) and *My Brother's Wedding* (1983), has long been one of the great chroniclers of black urban life in LA.

The Limey (Steven Soderbergh, 1999). Gangster Terence Stamp wanders into a morally adrift LA looking for his daughter's killer, and finds the burned-out husk of former hippy Peter Fonda.

Magnolia (Paul Thomas Anderson, 1999). A gut-wrenching travelogue of human misery. The San Fernando Valley serves as an emotional inferno of abusive parents, victimized children, haunted memories, plaintive songs, and a curious plague of frogs.

Mayor of the Sunset Strip (George Hickenlooper, 2003). Great, disturbing documentary about the titular character, a former stand-in for one of the Monkees, legendary DJ, lounge denizen, and apparent man-child who can't seem to get his life together, despite being pals with people like David Bowie.

Mi Vida Loca (Alison Anders, 1993). Depressing ensemble piece about the hard lives of Latinas in Echo Park girl-gangs and the central reason the director won a prestigious MacArthur Fellowship.

Nixon (Oliver Stone, 1996). A long, dark look at the first president from Southern California, starring

Anthony Hopkins, with James Woods as his henchman H.R. Haldeman.

Pulp Fiction (Quentin Tarantino, 1994). A successful collection of underworld stories presented in nonlinear fashion and set against a down-at-heel backdrop of LA streets, bars, diners, and would-be torture chambers. The film's most famous location, the *Jackrabbit Slim's* retro-diner, was actually a studio set, not a real-life restaurant.

Short Cuts (Robert Altman, 1993). Vaguely linked vignettes tracing the lives of LA suburbanites, from a trailer-park couple in Downey to an elite doctor in the Santa Monica Mountains. Strong ensemble cast bolsters the intentionally fractured narrative.

Slums of Beverly Hills (Tamara Jenkins, 1998). Troubled teen Natasha Lyonne deals with growing pains in a less glamorous section of town, far from Rodeo Drive, where a pill-popping cousin, manic uncle, weird neighbors, and her own expanding bustline are but a few of her worries.

Swingers (Doug Liman, 1996). Cocktail culture gets skewered in this flick about a couple of dudes who flit from club to club to eye "beautiful babies" and kibbitz like Rat Pack-era Sinatras. Many LA locales shown, such as the *Dresden Room* and *The Derby*.

To Sleep with Anger (Charles Burnett, 1990). An interesting view of LA's overlooked Black middle class, directed with polish by a very underrated African-American filmmaker.

Tupac and Biggie (Nick Broomfield, 2002). Eye-opening documentary about the murders of rappers Tupac Shakur and Notorious B.I.G., both of whom the director suggests may have been the victims of hip-hop producer Suge Knight, along with rogue elements of the LAPD.

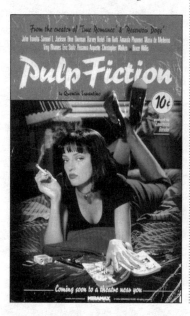

From the creators of *True Romance* & *Reservoir Dogs*

John Travolta Samuel L. Jackson Bruce Thurman Harvey Keitel Tim Roth Amanda Plummer Maria de Medeiros Ving Rhames Eric Stoltz Rosanna Arquette Christopher Walken Bruce Willis

Pulp Fiction

by Quentin Tarantino

10¢

Coming soon to a theatre near you

MIRAMAX

If you're going to San Francisco

Bullitt (Peter Yates, 1968). In the minds of many filmgoers, the classic portrait of San Francisco, presented at breakneck speed in cinema's most famous car chase, ripping up and down the city's steep hills at a frenetic, still-amazing pace. No modern special effects for this legendary sequence, either.

The Conversation (Francis Ford Coppola, 1974). Opening with a mesmerizing sequence of high-tech eavesdropping in Union Square, Coppola's chilling character study of San Francisco surveillance expert Harry Caul is one of the best films of the paranoid Watergate era.

Dim Sum: A Little Bit of Heart (Wayne Wang, 1985). Set among San Francisco's Chinese community, Wayne Wang's appealing comedy of manners about assimilation and family ties is a modest and rewarding treat. His earlier sleeper *Chan is Missing* (1982) also shows a Chinatown tourists don't usually see.

Dirty Harry (Don Siegel, 1971). Based on the infamous case of the Zodiac Killer, Siegel's morally dubious, sequel-spawning thriller casts Clint Eastwood in his most famous role as a vigilante San Francisco cop. The first and best in a long series.

Escape from Alcatraz (Don Siegel, 1979). Though evocatively portrayed in *Bird Man of Alcatraz*, *Point Blank*, *The Rock*, and many others, this is the ultimate movie about San Francisco's famously unbreachable offshore penitentiary. Starring Clint Eastwood (again) as a most resourceful con.

Gimme Shelter (Albert and David Maysles, 1969). Excellent documentary about the ill-fated Rolling Stones' concert at Altamont, in which Hell's Angels were hired to provide their own version of "security." Its

searing look at home grown American violence and Vietnam-era chaos at the end of the 1960s includes an on-camera stabbing.

Greed (Erich von Stroheim, 1924). Legendary silent masterpiece about the downfall of Polk Street dentist Doc McTeague was shot mostly on location in the Bay Area, and remains, even in its notoriously truncated version, a wonderful time capsule of working-class San Francisco in the 1920s.

Invasion of the Body Snatchers (Philip Kaufman, 1978). Great remake of a classic 1956 paranoid chiller, in which aliens replicate by taking the shape of humans in the form of "pod people." This quite atmospheric and eerie version is set in San Francisco, which is used to great effect, and has Donald Sutherland as the health-inspector protagonist.

Petulia (Richard Lester, 1968). Julie Christie is dazzling in this fragmented puzzle of a movie about a vivacious and unpredictable married woman who has an affair with a divorced doctor (George C. Scott). Set against the wittily described background of psychedelic-era San Francisco, and superbly shot by Nicolas Roeg.

Play It Again, Sam (Herbert Ross, 1972). A strike in Manhattan led to one of Woody Allen's uncommon visits to the West Coast for this hilarious film about a neurotic San Francisco film critic in love with his best friend's wife and obsessed with Humphrey Bogart in *Casablanca*.

The Times of Harvey Milk (Robert Epstein, 1984). This powerful and moving documentary about America's first openly gay politician chronicles his career in San Francisco and the aftermath of his

1978 assassination. Based on the book by Randy Shilts (see p.797).

🏃 **Vertigo** (Alfred Hitchcock, 1958). Hitchcock's somber, agonized, twisted love story is the San Francisco movie nonpareil, and one of the greatest films ever made. From James Stewart's wordless drives around the city to the film's climax at the San Juan Bautista Mission, Hitchcock takes us on a mesmerizing tour of a city haunted by its past.

The Wild Parrots of Telegraph Hill (Judy Irving, 2005). Cult documentary about the curious flock of cherry-headed conures that lives in the shadow of Coit Tower, and the fierce loyalty and debate they surprisingly inspire in the city.

Zodiac (David Fincher, 2007). Pulse-pounder covering a lone cartoonist's search for the infamous Zodiac Killer, who still hasn't been caught after almost forty years. Jake Gyllenhaal is good as the cartoonist; Robert Downey Jr is his usual brilliant and bizarre self as a crime reporter.

"Way out" West

24 Hours on Craigslist (Michael Ferris Gibson, 2005). Engaging and funny documentary about online communities, in this case in San Francisco, where the Craigslist website leads people to buy and exchange items, find emotional support, hunt down sexual-fetish partners, and even put together the film crew for the actual movie.

Beach Blanket Bingo (William Asher, 1965). A cult favorite – the epitome of sun-and-surf movies, with Frankie Avalon and Annette Funicello singing and cavorting amid hordes of wild-eyed teenagers.

Bob & Carol & Ted & Alice (Paul Mazursky, 1969). Once-daring, but still funny zeitgeist satire about wife-swapping and bed-hopping in hedonistic Southern California, starring Natalie Wood, Robert Culp, Elliott Gould, and Dyan Cannon as the titular foursome.

Boogie Nights (Paul Thomas Anderson, 1997). A suburban kid from Torrance hits the big time in LA – as a porn star. Mark Wahlberg, Julianne Moore, and Burt Reynolds tread through a sex-drenched San Fernando Valley landscape in the disco years.

House on Haunted Hill (William Castle, 1958). Not the clumsy remake, but the ghoulish Vincent Price original, with the King of Horror as a master of ceremonies for a scary party thrown at his Hollywood Hills estate – actually, Frank Lloyd Wright's Ennis House (see p.105).

Modern Romance (Albert Brooks, 1981). Brooks – the Woody Allen of the West Coast – stars in this comedy about a neurotic film editor who dumps his girlfriend and instantly regrets it. Full of early 80s LA signifiers, from Quaaludes to jogging suits to off-Hollywood parties with B-movie stars.

Point Break (Kathryn Bigelow, 1991). Pop favorite set in the surfer-dude world with Keanu Reeves as a robbery-investigating FBI agent and Patrick Swayze as his rebel-surfer quarry.

Rebel Without a Cause (Nicholas Ray, 1955). Fine, brash colors and widescreen composition in this troubled-youth film, starring, of course, James Dean. A Hollywood classic with many memorable images, notably the use of the Griffith Park Observatory as a shooting location.

Repo Man (Alex Cox, 1984). Emilio Estevez is a surly young punk who repossesses cars for Harry Dean Stanton. Very imaginative and fun, and darkly comic.

Shampoo (Hal Ashby, 1975). Using LA as his private playground, priapic hairdresser Warren Beatty freely acts on his formidable, though nonchalant, libido. A period piece memorable for its washed-out look.

Valley Girl (Martha Coolidge, 1983). Early Nicolas Cage flick, in which he winningly plays a new-wave freak trying to woo the title character (Debra Foreman) in a clash of LA cultures. Good soundtrack, too.

Off the beaten track

Bagdad Café (Percy Adlon, 1988). Inspiring fable about a German tourist who arrives at a dusty roadside diner in the Mojave Desert and magically transforms the place with her larger-than-life charm.

The Birds (Alfred Hitchcock, 1963). Set in Bodega Bay, just north of San Francisco, Hitchcock's terrifying allegory about a small town besieged by a plague of vicious birds, features indelible bird's-eye views of the Northern California coastline.

Citizen Kane (Orson Welles, 1941). In this pinnacle of American filmmaking, director Welles successfully copies the baroque splendor and frightful vulgarity of William Randolph Hearst's legendary prison-like palace in San Simon on the Central Coast (see p.441). Here, it's called "Xanadu" and shot in San Diego's Balboa Park.

Faster, Pussycat! Kill! Kill! (Russ Meyer, 1965). Meyer's wonderfully lurid, camp action flick unleashes a trio of depraved go-go girls upon an unsuspecting California desert. One of a kind.

Fat City (John Huston, 1972). Stacy Keach and Jeff Bridges star in one of the last great films from the old-line Hollywood master, this one a realistic, grim depiction of the lives of small-time Stockton boxers. Based on an equally acclaimed novel (see p.801).

The Graduate (Mike Nichols, 1967). Although usually more identified with youthful 1960s anomie than California per se, there are many evocative images in this generational comedy, including those of campus life at Berkeley and USC and middle-class suburban complacency.

High Plains Drifter (Clint Eastwood, 1972). Spooky Mono Lake is one of the bleak, disturbing settings for this tale of a mysterious gunslinger who comes back to a dusty burg to avenge a wrongful death – before drenching the town in blood and renaming it "Hell."

One-Eyed Jacks (Marlon Brando, 1961). Set, unusually for a Western, on the roaring shores of Monterey, where Brando tracks down Karl Malden – the bank-robbing partner who betrayed him five years earlier in Mexico – only to find him reformed and comfortably ensconced as sheriff.

Play Misty for Me (Clint Eastwood, 1971). Another Monterey movie, Eastwood's directorial debut, a thriller about the consequences of a DJ's affair with a psychotic fan, was shot in Clint's hometown of Carmel, and on his own two hundred acres of Monterey coastland.

Sideways (Alexander Payne, 2004). Two vino-slurping pals take a trip to the Central Coast's wine country, one of them seeking a last fling before he gets married, the other wallowing in shame and self-pity. The golden landscapes often resemble a two-hour ad by the California tourism board.

🏃 **Some Like It Hot** (Billy Wilder, 1959). The film some claim as the best comedy ever, set around a luxurious Florida resort that's actually San Diego's own *Hotel del Coronado* (see p.211), itself dripping with swank beachfront elegance.

Three Women (Robert Altman, 1977). A fascinating, hypnotic, and unique film in which Sissy Spacek and Shelley Duvall, co-workers at a geriatric center in Desert Springs, mysteriously absorb each other's identity.

Zabriskie Point (Michelangelo Antonioni, 1970). Muddled, pretentious misfire from the director that nonetheless features some promising early work by Jack Nicholson and visually interesting shots of the California desert.

Books

C
alifornia may well be the subject of more **books** than any other US state outside of New York, and for contemporary culture it's clearly drawn the most ink. Most of the state's stories tend to revolve around the Spanish Mission era, Gold Rush, movie industry, and modern politics and cultural mores. LA and San Francisco are predictably well covered, though other major cities appear much less often, with San Diego in particular yet to find an insightful chronicler on the order of Carey McWilliams (LA), Herb Caen (SF), or Kevin Starr (the entire state). In the following list, wherever a book is in print, the publisher's name is given in parentheses after the title, in the format: UK publisher; US publisher. Where books are published in only one of these countries, we have specified which one; when the same company publishes the book in both, it appears just once. The note "o/p" signifies an out-of-print title – which you may be able to find through one of the many used-book merchants in LA or on the Internet.

Travel and impressions

Umberto Eco *Travels in Hyperreality* (Vintage; Harvest). Influential examination of the still-potent concept of "simulacra," in which reality is denigrated in favor of its crass imitation. Examples are a bit dated now, though, including a now-closed museum in Orange County that re-created the great works of art as wax figurines.

Barney Hoskyns *Beneath the Diamond Sky: Haight–Ashbury 1965–1970* (o/p). A vivid account of the glory days of mid-1960s psychedelia, with evocative pictures of seminal rock bands such as the Jefferson Airplane, Grateful Dead, and Charlatans, and a narrative that describes how the hippy paradise was lost.

Robert Koenig *Mouse Tales* (Bonaventure Press). All the Disneyland dirt that's fit to print: a behind-the-scenes look at the ugly little secrets – from disenchanted workers to vermin infestations – that lurk behind the happy walls of the Magic Kingdom.

Leonard Pitt and Dale Pitt *Los Angeles A to Z* (University of California Press, US). If you're truly enthralled by the city, this is the tome for you: six-hundred pages of encyclopedic references covering everything from conquistadors to movie stars.

John Waters *Crackpot* (Simon & Schuster; Scribner). Odds and ends from the Pope of Trash, the mind behind cult film *Pink Flamingos*, including a personalized tour of LA.

Tom Wolfe *The Electric Kool-Aid Acid Test* (Black Swan; Bantam). Take an LSD-fueled bus trip with Ken Kesey and his Merry Pranksters as they travel through mid-1960s California, before the counterculture was discovered, and co-opted, by corporate America.

History

Oscar Zeta Acosta *Autobiography of a Brown Buffalo, Revolt of the Cockroach People* (Vintage). The legendary model for Hunter S. Thompson's bloated D. Gonzo, this author was in reality a trailblazing

Hispanic lawyer who used all manner of colorful tactics to defend oppressed and indigent defendants. Two vivid portraits of late-1960s California, written just before the author mysteriously vanished in 1971.

🏃 **Mark Arax and Rick Wartzman** *The King of California: J.G. Boswell and the Making of a Secret American Empire* (Public Affairs; o/p). Essential reading for anyone interested in the real history of the state, focusing on how a family of Georgia farmers migrated to the San Joaquin Valley and created the nation's biggest cotton empire with hardly anyone noticing.

H.W. Brands *The Age of Gold* (Arrow; Anchor). Excellent introduction to Gold Rush-era California, highlighting the immigrants from around the world who came to mine the ore, the unexpected fortunes of a lucky few, and the political and social repercussions of this unprecedented event – the first glimmer of the Gilded Age.

Gray Brechin *Imperial San Francisco: Urban Power, Earthly Ruin* (University of California Press, US). Long-overdue puncturing of myths about the City by the Bay, showing how dubious mining and financial schemes led to its rise, and how its history, strangely enough, parallels that of ancient Rome and other classical cities.

Vincent Bugliosi *Helter Skelter: The True Story of the Manson Murders* (WW Norton). The late 1960s wouldn't have been complete without the Manson Family, and here the prosecutor-author lays out the full story of the horrifying crimes carried out by the gang, inspired by their cult leader, formerly a Sunset Strip hippy and would-be pop songwriter.

James Conaway *Napa: the Story of an American Eden* (Mariner, US). Compelling tale of how Napa Valley vintners attained international glory through clever science and down-and-dirty politics. A follow-up volume, *The Far Side of Eden* (Clarion; Mariner), details how fame and fortune have led to corruption and malaise.

🏃 **Carey McWilliams** *Southern California: an Island on the Land* (Gibbs Smith). The bible of Southern California histories, focusing on the key years between the two world wars and written by a lawyer and social activist involved in much of the drama of the time. Evocatively written and richly detailed.

🏃 **Mark Reisner** *Cadillac Desert* (Penguin, US). An essential guide to water problems in the American West, with special emphasis on LA's schemes to bring upstate California water to the metropolis. One of the best renderings of this sordid tale.

Dennis Smith *San Francisco Is Burning: The Untold Story of the 1906 Earthquake and Fires* (Plume). An excellent, detailed examination – published on the hundredth anniversary of the event – of the infamous cataclysm, with a good mix of scientific and historical analysis and personal stories of some of the figures involved.

Kevin Starr *California: A History* (Modern Library). The latest round of Golden State history from the state's pre-eminent chronicler, this one more bite-sized and overarching than the other seven in the series, which focus on decades and details. Of those, the best overall are those covering the 1920s and 30s.

Politics and society

Erik Davis *Visionary State: A Journey Through California's Spiritual Landscape* (Chronicle Books, US). Quite a journey, indeed, focusing on the various cults, New Agers, and Zen philosophers that have illuminated the state in recent decades, along with older shamans and showmen, all highlighted by evocative, tantalizing photographs.

Mike Davis *City of Quartz* (Verso). The most important modern history of LA, in this case from a leftist perspective, vividly covering cops, riots, politicians, movies, and architecture. The latest edition provides a modern update. Other volumes, *Ecology of Fear* (Vintage, US) and *Under the Perfect Sun* (New Press, US), respectively tell of LA's apocalyptic bent and of the corruption at the core of sunny San Diego.

Joan Didion *Slouching Towards Bethlehem* (Farrar Straus & Giroux, US). One of California's most polarizing writers takes a critical look at 1960s California, from the acid culture of San Francisco to a profile of American tough guy John Wayne. In a similar style, *The White Album* (Flamingo, US) traces the West Coast characters and events that shaped the 1960s and 70s. The current, lesser memoir, *Where I Was From* (Harper Perennial; Vintage), may be too sour for many.

Lisa McGirr *Suburban Warriors: the Origins of the New American Right*

(Princeton University Press). The tale of how once-fringe right-wing activists in Southern California rose from the ashes of the 1960s to dominate state and, later, national politics, culminating with the presidency of Ronald Reagan and his acolytes.

Ethan Rarick *California Rising: The Life and Times of Pat Brown* (University of California Press, US). More than even Nixon or Reagan, Pat Brown was the most influential political figure for modern California, from building aqueducts and freeways to curbing racial discrimination, and this impressive volume serves the man and his empire-building legacy well, with appropriate criticism where necessary.

Randy Shilts *The Mayor of Castro Street: the Life and Times of Harvey Milk* (St. Martin's Griffin, US). Overview of the life, career, and martyrdom of one of America's most famous gay-rights advocates, presented as an emblem for the rise of identity politics and social activism in 1970s California.

Danny Sugarman *Wonderland Avenue* (Abacus; Little Brown). Publicist for The Doors and other seminal US rock bands from the late 60s on, Sugarman delivers a raunchy, autobiographical account of sex, drugs, and LA rock 'n' roll.

Architecture

Reyner Banham *Los Angeles: the Architecture of Four Ecologies* (University of California Press, US). The most lucid account of how LA's history has shaped its present form; the trenchant British author's enthusiasms are infectious.

David Gebhard and Robert Winter *Architectural Guidebook to Los Angeles* (Gibbs Smith, US). For many years the essential guide to LA architecture, from historical treasures to contemporary quirks. Some of the quality has been lost with Gebhard's death, so try the 1994 edition (his last) for the best writing on modernist structures.

Jim Heimann *California Crazy and Beyond: Roadside Vernacular Architecture* (Chronicle Books, US). This fun volume is still a favorite after twenty years, and has now been updated to include the latest of the state's bizarre-chitecture, from diners shaped liked hot dogs to wigwam motels, and the influence it has had nationally.

Randy Leffingwell *California Missions and Presidios* (Voyageur). Its attractive photos draw the eye, but this valuable pictorial is also good for its detailed story of the checkered history and architectural background of the state's signature spiritual outposts.

Esther McCoy *Five California Architects* (Hennessey & Ingalls). The still-relevant 1960s book that first drew attention to LA's Irving Gill, an early twentieth-century forerunner of the modern style in San Diego and LA,

along with Bernard Maybeck, R.M. Schindler, and the Greene brothers.

Elizabeth Pomada *Painted Ladies Revisited* (Studio Books, US). One in a series of volumes on Victorian mansions (in San Francisco and beyond) that you'll see in bookstores throughout the region, and well worth a look as a photo glossy and architecture guide.

Elizabeth A.T. Smith *Blueprints for Modern Living: History and Legacy of the Case Study Houses* (o/p). An excellent compendium of essays and articles about the built and unbuilt homes of California's renowned Case Study Program, with descriptions, diagrams, and photographs of each.

John and Sally Woodbridge *San Francisco Architecture: An Illustrated Guide* (Ten Speed). Although the Bay Area inexplicably lacks the number and quality of architectural books as those on LA, this volume will suffice for those with a yen to see and understand the better and more influential of the city's key structures.

Hollywood and the movies

Kenneth Anger *Hollywood Babylon* (Dell, US). A vicious yet high-spirited romp through Tinseltown's greatest scandals, written by one of the great avant-garde filmmakers. A second volume, *Hollywood Babylon II* (o/p), covers more recent times, but was hurriedly put together and not as well researched.

Jeanine Basinger *Silent Stars* (Wesleyan University Press). Great ode to the still-famous and long-forgotten Hollywood figures of the silent era, with brief biographies that outline the careers of movie cowboys, vamps, and sheiks.

Robert Berger *Last Remaining Seats* (Hennessey & Ingalls). An excellent photo guide to the extant movie

palaces of Los Angeles, particularly along the Broadway corridor, including many shots of theaters that are now closed to the public.

Robert Evans *The Kid Stays in the Picture* (Faber & Faber; Hyperion). Spellbinding insider's view of the machinations of Hollywood after the demise of the studio system, written with verve and flash by one of LA's biggest egos and, it turns out, most compelling authors – the head of Paramount when that company was at its modern peak.

Otto Friedrich *City of Nets* (University of California Press, US). Evocative descriptions of the major actors, directors, and studio bosses of the last good years of the studio system, before TV, antitrust actions, and Joe McCarthy ruined it all.

Julia Phillips *You'll Never Eat Lunch in This Town Again* (Faber & Faber, UK). Amusing and memorable, if somewhat self-serving, portrayal of the drugs and violence behind the Hollywood gloss.

Jerry Stahl *Permanent Midnight* (Process, UK). When his employers heard star scriptwriter Stahl (*Moonlighting*, *thirtysomething*) was spending his already-huge paycheck to support his heroin and other habits, they gave him a raise to cover the difference and keep him on the job. A gritty descent into Tinseltown drug hell.

Specialist guides

Steve Grody *Graffiti LA* (Abrams). If you're inclined to probe LA's poorer neighborhoods, you might discover many of the colorful pieces of home grown art depicted here, which the author dissects according to their ethnic, cultural, and (in places) gang affiliation. Includes CD-ROM.

Tom Kirkendall and Vicky Spring *Bicycling the Pacific Coast* (Mountaineers Books). Recently updated, detailed guide to the bike routes all the way along the coast, from Mexico up to Canada.

John J. Lamb *San Diego Specters* (Sunbelt, US). Looks into the ghosts, poltergeists, and other assorted spooks that populate San Diego County. An intriguing counterpart to the usual sun-and-surf books about the city.

Ray Riegert *Hidden Coast of California* (Ulysses). A detailed and interesting guide, now in its 11th edition, to the nooks and crannies along the California state beaches and parks, told from the perspective of a recreational enthusiast who tracks down all his favorite under-rated beachside gems.

John R. Soares *100 Classic Hikes in Northern California* (Mountaineers Books). An engaging presentation of wilderness hiking in the northern side of the state, from the Bay Area up to the Oregon border.

Surfer Magazine's Guide to Southern California Surf Spots (Chronicle Books, US). Along with the companion *Northern and Central California Surf Spots* (Chronicle Books, US), this is a handy, comprehensive reference to the best places in the state to ride the pipeline and find a killer break – even better, the pages are waterproof.

Walking the West Series *Walking Southern California*; *California Coast*; *California's State Parks*; and others (all o/p). Well-written paperbacks, each covering over a hundred excellent day-walks from two to twenty miles. Strong on practical details (maps, route descriptions, and so on), and boasting inspiring prose and historical background.

Fiction and literature

Eve Babitz *Eve's Hollywood*; *Slow Days, Fast Company*; *LA Woman* (all o/p). Eye-opening, thinly veiled autobiographical portraits of Southern California in the 1960s and 70s, with all the drugs, sex, and rock'n'roll you can imagine, but described in a relaxed, sometimes wistful manner. Only the first is difficult to find online.

T. Coraghessan Boyle *The Tortilla Curtain* (Bloomsbury; Penguin). Set in LA, this novel boldly borrows its premise – a privileged white man running down a member of the city's ethnic underclass – from Tom Wolfe's *The Bonfire of the Vanities*, and develops its plot with a similar intensity.

Richard Brautigan Tacoma-born writer often associated with the California Beat writers of the 50s and 60s. His surreal work seems overtly simple, but is overlaid with cultural references that question the direction the country was traveling in. His most successful book, *Trout Fishing in America* (Vintage, UK), although designed as a fishing handbook, stealthily creates a disturbing image of contemporary life. Other novels include *A Confederate General from Big Sur* (Mariner, US) and *In Watermelon Sugar* (Vintage, UK).

James Brown *The Los Angeles Diaries* (Bloomsbury; Harper Perennial). Difficult-to-stomach but strangely compelling memoir about life in the dark underbelly of the state, awash in drug abuse, child molestation, arson, suicide, and Hollywood striving. A memorable self-view from a talented author and screenwriter.

Charles Bukowski *Post Office* (Virgin; Ecco). An alcohol- and sex-soaked romp through some of LA's more festering back alleys, with a mailman surrogate for Bukowski as your guide. One of several books the author wrote exploring his encounters with the city's dark side.

James M. Cain *Double Indemnity*; *The Postman Always Rings Twice*; *Mildred Pierce* (all Orion; Everyman's

Library). Along with Raymond Chandler, Cain is one of the finest writers of dark, tough-guy novels. His entire oeuvre is excellent reading, but these three are the best explorations of LA.

Raymond Chandler *Farewell My Lovely*; *Lady in the Lake*; *The Big Sleep* (all Penguin; Library of America). Famous books adapted into classic movies, but Chandler's prose is still inimitable: terse, pointed, and vivid. More than just detective stories (centered on gumshoe detective Philip Marlowe), these are masterpieces of fiction.

Michael Connelly *Angels Flight* (Orion; Grand Central). One of several volumes focusing on LAPD investigator Harry Bosch, whose appropriate moniker casts him as a keen observer of LA's blood-curdling mix of corruption, public scandals, and violence.

Philip K. Dick *A Scanner Darkly* (Gollancz; Vintage). Erratic but brilliant author who evokes the mid-1990s split between the Straights, the Dopers, and the Narks – a dizzying study of identity, authority, and drugs. Among the pick of the rest of Dick's vast legacy is *Do Androids Dream of Electric Sheep?* (Gollancz; Library of America), set in San Francisco, which gave rise to the film *Blade Runner*, set in LA.

Joan Didion *Play It as It Lays* (Farrar, Straus & Giroux, US). Hollywood rendered in all its booze-guzzling, pill-popping, sex-craving terror. Oddly, the author went on to write the uninspired script for the third adaptation of *A Star Is Born*.

James Ellroy *The Black Dahlia*; *The Big Nowhere*; *LA Confidential*; *White Jazz* (all Arrow; Vintage). The LA Quartet: an excellent saga of city cops from the postwar era to the 1960s, with each novel progressively more complex and elliptical in style. The author's other LA-based works are also excellent – but start here.

John Fante *Ask the Dust* (Canongate; Harper Perennial). The third and still the best of the author's stories of itinerant poet Arturo Bandini, whose wanderings during the Depression highlight California's faded glory and struggling residents. Made into a subpar recent film.

F. Scott Fitzgerald *The Last Tycoon* (Penguin). The legendary author's unfinished final work, on the power and glory of Hollywood. Intriguing reading that gives a view of the studio system at its height.

James Gardner *Fat City* (University of California Press, US). Poignant account of small-time Stockton boxing, following the initiation and fitful progress of a young hopeful and the parallel decline of an old contender. Painfully exact on the confused, murky emotions of its men as their lives stagnate in the heat of the town and the surrounding country.

Molly Giles *Iron Shoes* (o/p). A sobering but fascinating look into the life of a Northern California woman, busy caring for her dying mother while trying to juggle the absurd and dismal characters in her life.

Dashiell Hammett *Complete Novels* (Library of America). Seminal detective novels featuring Sam Spade, the private investigator working out of San Francisco. Also track down the absorbing biography of Hammett: Diane Johnson's *Dashiell Hammett: A Life* (o/p).

Joseph Hansen *Gravedigger* (No Exit Press). Best in a series of entertaining tales of Dave Brandstetter, a gay insurance-claims investigator, set against a vivid Southern California backdrop.

Chester Himes *If He Hollers Let Him Go* (Serpent's Tail; Thunder's Mouth). A fine literary introduction to mid-twentieth-century race relations in LA, narrated by one Bob Jones, whose struggles mirrored those of author Himes, who eventually ended up living in Spain.

Helen Hunt Jackson *Ramona* (Signet Classics, US). Ultra-romanticized depiction of mission life that criticizes America's treatment of Indians while showing the natives to be noble savages and glorifying the Spanish exploiters. A valuable period piece – perhaps the most influential work of fiction ever written about California.

Jack Kerouac *Desolation Angels* (Riverhead, US); *The Dharma Bums* (Penguin). The most influential of the Beat writers on the rampage in California. See also his first novel *On the Road* (Penguin), which has a little of San Francisco and a lot of the rest of the US.

Elmore Leonard *Get Shorty* (Penguin). Ice-cool mobster Chili Palmer is a Miami debt collector who follows a client to Hollywood, and finds that the increasing intricacies of his own situation are translating themselves into a movie script.

David Levien *Wormwood* (Allison & Busby, UK) Get a glimpse of the seamier side of the contemporary movie biz, following an up-and-coming story editor through the corporate ranks until he achieves utter exhaustion and, curiously, an addiction to absinthe.

Ross MacDonald *Black Money* (Orion; Vintage); *The Blue Hammer* (o/p); *The Zebra-Striped Hearse* (Vintage, US); *The Doomsters*; *The Instant Enemy* (both o/p). Following in the footsteps of Spade and Marlowe, private detective Lew Archer looks behind the glitzy masks of Southern California life to reveal the underlying nastiness of creepy sexuality and manipulation.

Armistead Maupin *Tales of the City; Further Tales of the City; More Tales of the City* (all Black Swan; Harper Perennial). Lively and witty soap operas detailing the sexual antics of a select group of archetypal San Francisco characters of the late 70s and early 80s. See also *Babycakes* and *Significant Others*, which continue the story, though in more depth, and *Sure of You* – set several years later and more downbeat.

Walter Mosley *Devil in a Blue Dress; A Red Death; White Butterfly; Black Betty; A Little Yellow Dog; Bad Boy Brawly Brown* (all Mask Noir; Washington Square). Excellent modern noir novels that involve black private detective Easy Rawlins, who "does favors" from his South Central base. Mosley compellingly brings to life pre-riots Watts and, later, Compton.

Frank Norris *Novels and Essays* (Library of America). One of the great naturalist writers presents a bleak, uncompromising view of the state at the turn of the last century; *McTeague* has a San Francisco dentist face social struggle and his own violence, while *The Octopus* is an epic battle in the San Joaquin Valley between railroad robber barons and heroic wheat farmers.

Kem Nunn *Tapping the Source* (No Exit Press; Thunder's Mouth). One of the most unexpected novels to emerge from California beach culture, an eerie murder-mystery set among the surfing landscape of Orange County's Huntington Beach.

Thomas Pynchon *The Crying of Lot 49* (Vintage; Harper Perennial). Pynchon's celebrated – and most readable – excursion in modern paranoia follows the hilarious adventures of techno-freaks and potheads

in 60s California, and reveals the sexy side of stamp collecting. His later, lesser *Vineland* (Vintage; Penguin) is set in Northern California.

John Ridley *Love is a Racket* (o/p). A delightful slice of Hollywood hell, in which protagonist Jeffty Kittridge, slumming through the dregs of local society and being abused by countless predators, leads us on a darkly comic journey through LA's many bleak corners.

Luis J. Rodriguez *Republic of East LA* (Harper Perennial). Stark, memorable tales of life in the barrio, where struggling romantics and working-class strivers face the inequities of class and race, and gang crime looms ever-present.

Theodore Roszak *Flicker* (No Exit Press; Chicago Review Press). In an old LA movie house, Jonathan Gates discovers cinema and becomes obsessed by the director Max Castle – a genius of the silent era who disappeared under mysterious circumstances in the 40s – leading Gates into a labyrinthine conspiracy with its roots in medieval heresy.

Danny Santiago *Famous All Over Town* (Plume, US). Coming-of-age novel set among the street gangs of East LA, vividly depicting life in the Hispanic community.

Budd Schulberg *What Makes Sammy Run?* (Vintage, US). Classic anti-Hollywood vitriol by one of its insiders, a novelist and screenwriter whose acidic portrait of the movie business is unmatched.

Mona Simpson *Anywhere But Here* (Atlantic Books, UK). Bizarre and unforgettable saga of a young girl and her ambitious mother as they pursue LA stardom for the daughter.

Upton Sinclair *The Brass Check* (University of Illinois Press, US). The failed California gubernatorial candidate and activist vigorously criticizes LA's yellow journalism and its underhanded practices. Sinclair also wrote *Oil!* (o/p), about the city's 1920s oil rush.

Terry Southern *Blue Movie* (Grove Press, US). Sordid, frequently hilarious take on the overlap between high-budget moviemaking and pornography, with the author's vulgar themes and characters cheerfully slashing through politically correct literary conventions.

John Steinbeck *The Grapes of Wrath* (Penguin; Library of America). The classic account of a migrant family forsaking the Midwest for the Promised Land. The light-hearted but crisply observed novella, *Cannery Row*, captures daily life on the prewar Monterey waterfront, and the epic *East of Eden* (both Penguin; Library of America), updates and resets the Bible in the Salinas Valley and depicts three generations of family feuds.

Robert Louis Stevenson *The Silverado Squatters* (Wildside; Alan Rodgers). Portrays the splendor of the San Francisco hills and the cast of eccentrics and immigrants that populate them, as well as the strange atmosphere of Silverado itself, a deserted former Gold Rush settlement.

Amy Tan *The Joy Luck Club* (Vintage; Penguin). Huge bestseller in which four Chinese women – new arrivals in 1940s San Francisco – come together to play mahjong and tell their stories. They have four daughters, divided between Chinese and American identities, who also tell their tales, from childhood and from their often troubled present.

Michael Tolkin *The Player* (Grove, UK). A convincing look at the depravity and moral twilight of the filmmaking community, with special scorn for venal movie execs. Made into a classic flick by Robert Altman (see p.786).

Gore Vidal *Hollywood* (Abacus; Vintage). The fifth volume in the author's "Empire" series about emerging US power on the world stage, this one focusing on the movie industry, its interaction with Washington bigwigs, and its boundless capacity for propaganda.

Evelyn Waugh *The Loved One* (Penguin). The essential literary companion to take with you on a trip to Forest Lawn – here rendered as Whispering Glades, the apex of funerary pretension and a telling symbol of LA's postmortem status mania.

Nathanael West *The Day of the Locust* (Penguin; Signet). The best book about LA not involving detectives, an apocalyptic story of the fringe characters at the edge of the film industry, which culminates in a glorious riot and utter chaos.

Karen Tei Yamashita *Tropic of Orange* (Coffee House Press). Successful melding of the apocalyptic, noir, and surrealist styles that characterize LA, in the form of a vitriolic satire about the media, cultural dissonance, and social disintegration.

Travel store

UK & Ireland
Britain
Devon & Cornwall
Dublin D
Edinburgh D
England
Ireland
The Lake District
London
London D
London Mini Guide
Scotland
Scottish Highlands
  & Islands
Wales

Europe
Algarve D
Amsterdam
Amsterdam D
Andalucía
Athens D
Austria
Baltic States
Barcelona
Barcelona D
Belgium &
  Luxembourg
Berlin
Brittany & Normandy
Bruges D
Brussels
Budapest
Bulgaria
Copenhagen
Corfu
Corsica
Costa Brava D
Crete
Croatia
Cyprus
Czech & Slovak
  Republics
Denmark
Dodecanese & East
  Aegean Islands
Dordogne & The Lot
Europe
Florence & Siena
Florence D
France
Germany
Gran Canaria D
Greece
Greek Islands

Hungary
Ibiza & Formentera D
Iceland
Ionian Islands
Italy
The Italian Lakes
Languedoc &
  Roussillon
Lanzarote &
  Fuerteventura D
Lisbon D
The Loire Valley
Madeira D
Madrid D
Mallorca D
Mallorca & Menorca
Malta & Gozo D
Menorca
Moscow
The Netherlands
Norway
Paris
Paris D
Paris Mini Guide
Poland
Portugal
Prague
Prague D
Provence
  & the Côte D'Azur
Pyrenees
Romania
Rome
Rome D
Sardinia
Scandinavia
Sicily
Slovenia
Spain
St Petersburg
Sweden
Switzerland
Tenerife &
  La Gomera D
Turkey
Tuscany & Umbria
Venice & The Veneto
Venice D
Vienna

Asia
Bali & Lombok
Bangkok
Beijing

Cambodia
China
Goa
Hong Kong & Macau
Hong Kong
  & Macau D
India
Indonesia
Japan
Kerala
Laos
Malaysia, Singapore
  & Brunei
Nepal
The Philippines
Rajasthan, Dehli
  & Agra
Singapore
Singapore D
South India
Southeast Asia
Sri Lanka
Taiwan
Thailand
Thailand's Beaches
  & Islands
Tokyo
Vietnam

Australasia
Australia
Melbourne
New Zealand
Sydney

North America
Alaska
Baja California
Boston
California
Canada
Chicago
Colorado
Florida
The Grand Canyon
Hawaii
Honolulu D
Las Vegas D
Los Angeles
Maui D
Miami & South Florida
Montréal
New England
New Orleans D
New York City

New York City D
New York City Mini
  Guide
Orlando & Walt
  Disney World® D
Pacific Northwest
San Francisco
San Francisco D
Seattle
Southwest USA
Toronto
USA
Vancouver
Washington DC
Washington DC D
Yellowstone & The
  Grand Tetons
Yosemite

**Caribbean
& Latin America**
Antigua & Barbuda D
Argentina
Bahamas
Barbados D
Belize
Bolivia
Brazil
Cancùn & Cozumel D
Caribbean
Central America
Chile
Costa Rica
Cuba
Dominican Republic
Dominican Republic D
Ecuador
Guatemala
Jamaica
Mexico
Peru
St Lucia D
South America
Trinidad & Tobago
Yúcatan

Africa & Middle East
Cape Town & the
  Garden Route
Dubai D
Egypt
Gambia
Jordan

D: Rough Guide
DIRECTIONS for
short breaks

Available from all good bookstores

Kenya
Marrakesh **D**
Morocco
South Africa, Lesotho
& Swaziland
Syria
Tanzania
Tunisia
West Africa
Zanzibar

Travel Specials
First-Time Africa
First-Time Around
the World
First-Time Asia
First-Time Europe
First-Time Latin
America
Travel Health
Travel Online
Travel Survival
Walks in London
& SE England
Women Travel
World Party

Maps
Algarve
Amsterdam
Andalucia
& Costa del Sol
Argentina
Athens
Australia
Barcelona
Berlin
Boston & Cambridge
Brittany
Brussels
California
Chicago
Chile
Corsica
Costa Rica
& Panama
Crete
Croatia
Cuba
Cyprus
Czech Republic
Dominican Republic
Dubai & UAE
Dublin
Egypt

Florence & Siena
Florida
France
Frankfurt
Germany
Greece
Guatemala & Belize
Iceland
India
Ireland
Italy
Kenya & Northern
Tanzania
Lisbon
London
Los Angeles
Madrid
Malaysia
Mallorca
Marrakesh
Mexico
Miami & Key West
Morocco
New England
New York City
New Zealand
Northern Spain
Paris
Peru
Portugal
Prague
Pyrenees & Andorra
Rome
San Francisco
Sicily
South Africa
South India
Spain & Portugal
Sri Lanka
Tenerife
Thailand
Toronto
Trinidad & Tobago
Tunisia
Turkey
Tuscany
Venice
Vietnam, Laos
& Cambodia
Washington DC
Yucatán Peninsula

**Dictionary
Phrasebooks**
Croatian
Czech
Dutch
Egyptian Arabic
French
German
Greek
Hindi & Urdu
Italian
Japanese
Latin American
Spanish
Mandarin Chinese
Mexican Spanish
Polish
Portuguese
Russian
Spanish
Swahili
Thai
Turkish
Vietnamese

Computers
Blogging
eBay
iPhone
iPods, iTunes
& music online
The Internet
Macs & OS X
MySpace
PCs and Windows
PlayStation Portable
Website Directory

Film & TV
American
Independent Film
British Cult Comedy
Chick Flicks
Comedy Movies
Cult Movies
Film
Film Musicals
Film Noir
Gangster Movies
Horror Movies
Kids' Movies
Sci-Fi Movies
Westerns

Lifestyle
Babies
Ethical Living
Pregnancy & Birth
Running

Music Guides
The Beatles
Blues
Bob Dylan
Book of Playlists
Classical Music
Elvis
Frank Sinatra
Heavy Metal
Hip-Hop
Jazz
Led Zeppelin
Opera
Pink Floyd
Punk
Reggae
Rock
The Rolling Stones
Soul and R&B
Velvet Underground
World Music
(2 vols)

Popular Culture
Books for Teenagers
Children's Books,
5-11
Conspiracy Theories
Crime Fiction
Cult Fiction
The Da Vinci Code
His Dark Materials
Lord of the Rings
Shakespeare
Superheroes
The Templars
Unexplained
Phenomena

Science
The Brain
Climate Change
The Earth
Genes & Cloning
The Universe
Weather

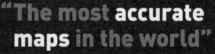

A Rough Guide to Rough Guides

Published in 1982, the first Rough Guide – to Greece – was a student scheme that became a publishing phenomenon. Mark Ellingham, a recent graduate in English from Bristol University, had been traveling in Greece the previous summer and couldn't find the right guidebook. With a small group of friends he wrote his own guide, combining a highly contemporary, journalistic style with a thoroughly practical approach to travellers' needs.

The immediate success of the book spawned a series that rapidly covered dozens of destinations. And, in addition to impecunious backpackers, Rough Guides soon acquired a much broader and older readership that relished the guides' wit and inquisitiveness as much as their enthusiastic, critical approach and value-for-money ethos.

These days, Rough Guides include recommendations from shoestring to luxury and cover more than 200 destinations around the globe, including almost every country in the Americas and Europe, more than half of Africa and most of Asia and Australasia. Our ever-growing team of authors and photographers is spread all over the world, particularly in Europe, the USA and Australia.

In the early 1990s, Rough Guides branched out of travel, with the publication of Rough Guides to World Music, Classical Music and the Internet. All three have become benchmark titles in their fields, spearheading the publication of a wide range of books under the Rough Guide name.

Including the travel series, Rough Guides now number more than 350 titles, covering: phrasebooks, waterproof maps, music guides from Opera to Heavy Metal, reference works as diverse as Conspiracy Theories and Shakespeare, and popular culture books from iPods to Poker. Rough Guides also produce a series of more than 120 World Music CDs in partnership with World Music Network.

Visit www.roughguides.com to see our latest publications.

Rough Guide travel images are available for commercial licensing at www.roughguidespictures.com

Rough Guide credits

Text editor: Seph Petta
Layout: Ajay Verma
Cartography: Rajesh Mishra
Picture editor: Nicole Newman
Production: Rebecca Short
Proofreader: Amanda Jones
Cover design: Chloë Roberts
Editorial: **London** Kate Berens, Claire Saunders, Ruth Blackmore, Alison Murchie, Karoline Densley, Andy Turner, Keith Drew, Edward Aves, Nikki Birrell, Alice Park, Sarah Eno, Lucy White, Jo Kirby, James Smart, Natasha Foges, Róisín Cameron, Emma Traynor, Emma Gibbs, Kathryn Lane, Joe Staines, Duncan Clark, Peter Buckley, Matthew Milton, Tracy Hopkins, Ruth Tidball; **New York** Andrew Rosenberg, Steven Horak, AnneLise Sorensen, Amy Hegarty, April Isaacs, Ella Steim, Anna Owens, Sean Mahoney; **Delhi** Madhavi Singh, Karen D'Souza
Design & Pictures: **London** Scott Stickland, Dan May, Diana Jarvis, Mark Thomas, Sarah Cummins; **Delhi** Umesh Aggarwal, Jessica Subramanian, Ankur Guha, Pradeep Thapliyal, Sachin Tanwar, Anita Singh, Nikhil Agarwal

Production: Vicky Baldwin
Cartography: **London** Maxine Repath, Ed Wright, Katie Lloyd-Jones; **Delhi** Jai Prakash Mishra, Rajesh Chhibber, Ashutosh Bharti, Animesh Pathak, Jasbir Sandhu, Karobi Gogoi, Amod Singh, Alakananda Bhattacharya, Swati Handoo
Online: Narender Kumar, Rakesh Kumar, Amit Verma, Rahul Kumar, Ganesh Sharma, Debojit Borah
Marketing & Publicity: **London** Liz Statham, Niki Hanmer, Louise Maher, Jess Carter, Vanessa Godden, Vivienne Watton, Anna Paynton, Rachel Sprackett; **New York** Geoff Colquitt, Megan Kennedy, Katy Ball; **Delhi** Ragini Govind
Manager India: Punita Singh
Series Editor: Mark Ellingham
Reference Director: Andrew Lockett
Publishing Coordinator: Helen Phillips
Publishing Director: Martin Dunford
Commercial Manager: Gino Magnotta
Managing Director: John Duhigg

Publishing information

This ninth edition published March 2008 by
Rough Guides Ltd,
80 Strand, London WC2R 0RL
345 Hudson St, 4th Floor,
New York, NY 10014, USA
14 Local Shopping Centre, Panchsheel Park,
New Delhi 110017, India
Distributed by the Penguin Group
Penguin Books Ltd,
80 Strand, London WC2R 0RL
Penguin Group (USA)
375 Hudson Street, NY 10014, USA
Penguin Group (Australia)
250 Camberwell Road, Camberwell,
Victoria 3124, Australia
Penguin Books Canada Ltd,
10 Alcorn Avenue, Toronto, Ontario,
Canada M4V 1E4
Penguin Group (NZ)
67 Apollo Drive, Mairangi Bay, Auckland 1310,
New Zealand

Cover concept by Peter Dyer.

Typeset in Bembo and Helvetica to an original design by Henry Iles.

Printed and bound in China

© Rough Guides 2008

No part of this book may be reproduced in any form without permission from the publisher except for the quotation of brief passages in reviews.

824pp includes index

A catalogue record for this book is available from the British Library

ISBN: 978-1-84353-999-5

The publishers and authors have done their best to ensure the accuracy and currency of all the information in **The Rough Guide to California**, however, they can accept no responsibility for any loss, injury, or inconvenience sustained by any traveller as a result of information or advice contained in the guide.

1 3 5 7 9 8 6 4 2

Help us update

We've gone to a lot of effort to ensure that the ninth edition of **The Rough Guide to California** is accurate and up to date. However, things change – places get "discovered", opening hours are notoriously fickle, restaurants and rooms raise prices or lower standards. If you feel we've got it wrong or left something out, we'd like to know, and if you can remember the address, the price, the hours, the phone number, so much the better.

Please send your comments with the subject line "**Rough Guide California Update**" to ℮mail@roughguides.com, or by post to the address above. We'll credit all contributions and send a copy of the next edition (or any other Rough Guide if you prefer) for the very best emails.

Have your questions answered and tell others about your trip at
ⓦcommunity.roughguides.com

SMALL PRINT

Acknowledgements

J.D. would foremost like to thank his editor Seph Petta, who contributed much energy and determination to this book, not to mention panache. Thanks also are due to grand editor Andrew Rosenberg, J.D.'s wife and family, his travel contacts and coordinators in California, Rough Guides cartographers in both Delhi and London, including Rajesh Mishra and Katie Lloyd-Jones, Ajay Verma for setting the guide, and Nicole Newman for taking care of the photos.

Nick would like to thank the many folk at the various CVBs and tourist organizations for their invaluable help: Adele, Berkeley; Sharon Hunt, Lake Tahoe; Suzi Brakken, Plumas Co; Joanne Steele, Siskiyou Co; Richard, Humboldt Co; Sharon Rooney, Mendocino Co; Nina Laramore, Russian River; Jenny Franklin, Truckee; Bob Warren & Karen Whitaker, Shasta Cascades. Many thanks to the East Bay contingent of Anandamayi, Clint, Laramie, Wendi, Hillary, Panos, Simon, Carol et al for various acts of hospitality and fine company. Here's to Alexandra for the Santa Barbara break and Carol and Eric for the South SF feast. For relief from driving duties, gratitude to Simon for the East Bay and Marin tours and Nikki and Eric for taking me round the southern mines. Finally, back east, well done to Seph in NYC for the smooth editing, and love as ever to Maria for holding Fort Pitt.

Paul would like to thank: Chris Kapka for backroad explorations and cold beers at the hot springs in Death Valley; Lydia Smith and Dan for wheels, meals, and a sympathetic ear or two; and everyone who shared a hike, suggested a great place to eat, or offered a smile to cheer a weary day on the road.

Jeff would like to thank his editor, Seph, for endless patience, guidance, and deft use of the red pen; J.D., Nick, and Paul for having him on board this edition; Iron Dukes "Andrew" Rosenberg; and, most of all, his wife, Susie. He would also like to extend his gratitude to everyone who shared their insights into San Francisco and beyond, including Greg Dicum (for a wonderfully sudsy tour of the Mission), Jodi Goldstein, Charles Hodgkins of burritoeater.com, Scott Jordan, Christopher Keenan, Craig "Stu" Stuart, Bret Thorn, Walter Yang, and Winnie and Michael.

The **editor** would like to thank Andrew Rosenberg, AnneLise Sorensen, Steve Horak, and everyone else in the Rough Guides New York office; Paul Whitfield, Nick Edwards, J.D. Dickey, Jeff Cranmer, and Mark Ellwood; Ajay Verma, Rajesh Mishra, and the rest of the Delhi crew; Nicole Newman, Katie Lloyd-Jones, Maxine Repath, Diana Jarvis, and their London colleagues; and, finally, his family and Christina and Elise Markel.

Readers' letters

Thanks to all the readers who took the trouble to write in with their comments and suggestions (and apologies to anyone whose name we've misspelt or omitted):

Jens Aerts, Helen Bashforth, Anouk Doove, Sean Ferris, Britta Geisenhainer, David and Nicky Grace, Astrid Heystee, Thomas Hine, Heidi Kinsey, Edward Knowles, Matthijs Moeken, Clive Morgan, Ed Shaw, William Solesbury, Matthew Sunderland, Lieneke Tchüss, Lieneke van Schaardenburg, Mary Walmsley, Charlotte Wilson, Martin York

Photo credits

All photos © Rough Guides except the following:

Introduction

Black bear cub © Nigel Bean/naturepl.com
Mount Shasta © Anthony Dunn/Alamy
San Andreas Fault © Baron Wolman/Getty

Things not to miss

03 Balboa Park © Richard Cummins/Robert Harding
06 La Jolla Cove, San Diego © Richard Cummins/Robert Harding
09 Gay pride, SF © Justin Sullivan/Getty
13 The Neptune Pool at Hearst Castle © Corbis/Phil Klein
14 Snow geese, Klamath Basin National Wildlife Refuge © FLPA
15 Mount Whitney © Darrell Gulin/Corbis
16 Mission La Purisima © Chuck Pefley/Alamy
17 Sunset Blvd © Jon Hicks/Corbis
19 Conservatory of Flowers, Golden Gate Park © Nicole Newman
23 Amtrak Coast Starlight © Phil Schermeister/Corbis
24 The Big Sur Coast © Getty/National Geographic
25 Grey whale © Minden Pictures/FLPA
27 Santa Monica Mountains © Wendy Connett/Alamy
28 Giant redwood © Grant Faint/Getty
29 Rafting the Kern River © Jonathan G. Walker/Hydro-Graphics

Color section: Exploring the outdoors

Cross-country skiing © Getty/Aurora Creative
Surfing at Mavericks © Jim Goldstein/Alamy

Color section: West Coast sounds

Sly Stone, 1974 © Hulton Archive/Getty
Janis Joplin © RB/Redferns
Hollywood Bowl © Visions of America, LLC/Alamy
Green Day © Martin Philbey/Redferns
Snoop Dogg © Matthew Simmons/Getty
The Eagles, 1974 © Henry Diltz/Corbis
The Doors © Henry Diltz/Corbis

Color section: Epicurean California

Sterling Vineyards, Napa Valley © Photolibrary
Organic farm, Bolinas © Nicole Newman

California cuisine © Bartley, Mary Ellen/StockFood UK
In-N-Out sign © Bohemian Nomad Picturemakers/Corbis
Quesadillas with salmon © Conrad & Company Photography/StockFood UK
Wine tasting, Robert Mondavi Winery © Photolibrary
Napa Valley vineyard © Nick Edwards

Black and whites

p.184 The Botanical Building, Balboa Park © Ron Niebrugge/Alamy
p.202 Star of India under sail © Michel Boutefeu/Getty
p.214 Pacific Beach ice cream parlor © Richard Cummins/Corbis
p.234 Queen Califia's Magical Circle, Escondido © LHB Photo/Alamy
p.252 Gay Pride Parade, Palm Springs © LHB Photo/Alamy
p.319 Bristlecone pines © Danita Delimont/Alamy
p.424 Mission Santa Barbara © Jon Arnold Images/Alamy
p.623 State Capitol, Sacramento © William Manning/Corbis
p.634 Nevada City © John Elk III/Alamy
p.646 Jumping frog © Robert Holmes/Corbis
p.655 Emerald Bay, Lake Tahoe © Danita Delimont/Alamy
p.665 Neon arch sign, Reno © Owaki-Kulla/Corbis
p.672 Elk, Redwood National Park © Ron Watts/Corbis
p.687 Gloria Ferrer vineyard, Sonoma © Nicole Newman
p.695 Bodega Bay, Sonoma Coast © Lee Foster/Alamy
p.706 Mendocino © Dennis Frates/Alamy
p.718 Eureka harbor, Humboldt County © Gary Crabbe/Alamy
p.725 Redwood National Park © Greg Probst/Corbis
p.737 Lassen Volcanic National Park © Craig Lovell/Corbis
p.751 Snow-covered Mount Shasta © Baron Wolman/Getty
p.790 Pulp Fiction (1994) poster © Moviestore collection

Index

Map entries are in color.

INDEX

I

821

Map symbols

maps are listed in the full index using colored text

------	International border	🏛	Stately home/Palace
--·--·	Province/US state border	🔱	Viewpoint
---	Chapter division boundary	⚓	Lighthouse
(80)	US Interstate	⚲	Church (regional maps)
(30)	US highway	✈	Airport
(1)	Highway	★	Bus stop
	Secondary highway	◆	Point of interest
	Local road	●	Museum
	Pedestrianized road	ⓘ	Tourist information
⊞⊞⊞	Steps	⊠	Post office
	Railway	⊞	Hospital/medical center
	River	⊠	Gate/Park entrance
-- --	Ferry route	◉	Accommodation
	Muni/Bart	■	Restaurant
-- -·	Tramline	Å	Campsite
	Light rail	◉	Swimming pool
-----	Footpath	✂	Battlefield
▪▪▪▪▪	Wall	⚡	Ski area
◠	Cave	)(	Bridge
⩕	Mountain range	⚑	Golf course
▲	Mountain peak	⊙	Statue
❋	Crater	⬯	Stadium
⚘	Waterfall	■	Building
⚘	Marshland/swamp	⊞	Church (town maps)
⌁	Dam	⊹	Cemetery
⌁	Rocks	▨	Park/Forest
♣	Sequoia grove	⬚	Beach
⌘	Oasis	⬛	Marine base
⋎	Spring	◩	Restricted zone
†	Wind farm		

I

MAP SYMBOLS